Gale Encyclopedia of
MULTICULTURAL AMERICA

THIRD EDITION

Edited by Thomas Riggs

GALE ENCYCLOPEDIA OF
MULTICULTURAL AMERICA

VOLUME 3

KENYAN AMERICANS–PUERTO RICAN AMERICANS

EDITED BY THOMAS RIGGS

GALE
CENGAGE Learning·

Detroit • New York • San Francisco • New Haven, Conn • Waterville, Maine • London

© 2014 Gale, Cengage Learning
WCN: 01-100-101

Gale Encyclopedia of Multicultural America

Thomas Riggs, Editor

Project Editor: Marie Toft

Editorial: Jeff Hunter, Carol Schwartz

Technical Assistance: Luann Brennan, Grant Eldridge, Jeffrey Muhr, Rebecca Parks

Rights Acquisition and Management: Sheila Spencer

Composition: Evi Abou-El-Seoud

Manufacturing: Wendy Blurton

Imaging: John Watkins

Product Design: Kristine Julien

Index: Shana Milkie

For product information and technology assistance, contact us at
Gale Customer Support, 1-800-877-4253.
For permission to use material from this text or product,
submit all requests online at **www.cengage.com/permissions.**
Further permissions questions can be emailed to
permissionrequest@cengage.com.

Cover photographs and art reproduced with the following permission:
For Asian business man, © aslysun/Shutterstock.com; for Indian businessman, © Kenneth Man/Shutterstock.com; for young Sephardic Jewish man, © Howard Sandler/Shutterstock.com; for African American female, © Flashon Studio/Shutterstock.com; for Rastafarian male, © Alan Bailey/Shutterstock.com; for Muslim woman (side view), © szefei/Shutterstock.com; for young woman in white t-shirt and jeans, © Vlasov Volodymyr/Shutterstock.com; for Hispanic woman in white blouse, © Warren Goldswaini/Shutterstock.com; for puzzle vector illustration, © VikaSuh/Shutterstock.com.

While every effort has been made to ensure the reliability of the information presented in this publication, Gale, a part of Cengage Learning, does not guarantee the accuracy of the data contained herein. Gale accepts no payment for listing; and inclusion in the publication of any organization, agency, institution, publication, service, or individual does not imply endorsement of the editors or publisher. Errors brought to the attention of the publisher and verified to the satisfaction of the publisher will be corrected in future editions.

Library of Congress Cataloging-in-Publication Data

Gale Encyclopedia of Multicultural America / Thomas Riggs, editor. — 3rd edition.
    pages cm
  Includes bibliographical references and index.
  ISBN 978-0-7876-7550-9 (set : hardcover) — ISBN 978-0-7876-7551-6 (vol. 1 : hardcover) — ISBN 978-0-7876-7552-3 (vol. 2 : hardcover) — ISBN 978-0-7876-7553-0 (vol. 3 : hardcover) — ISBN 978-1-4144-3279-3 (vol. 4 : hardcover)
  1. Cultural pluralism—United States—Encyclopedias. 2. Ethnology—United States—Encyclopedias. 3. Minorities—United States—Encyclopedias. 4. United States—Ethnic relations—Encyclopedias. 5. United States—Race relations—Encyclopedias. I. Riggs, Thomas.
  E184.A1G14 2014
  305.800973—dc23
                                                                                    2013049273

Gale
27500 Drake Rd.
Farmington Hills, MI, 48331-3535

ISBN-13: 978-0-7876-7550-9 (set)
ISBN-13: 978-0-7876-7551-6 (vol. 1)
ISBN-13: 978-0-7876-7552-3 (vol. 2)
ISBN-13: 978-0-7876-7553-0 (vol. 3)
ISBN-13: 978-1-4144-3279-3 (vol. 4)

This title is also available as an e-book.
ISBN-13: 978-1-4144-3806-1
Contact your Gale, a part of Cengage Learning sales representative for ordering information.

Printed in the United States of America
1 2 3 4 5 6 7 18 17 16 15 14

TABLE OF CONTENTS

CONTENTS OF ALL VOLUMES

EDITOR'S NOTE

The third edition of the *Gale Encyclopedia of Multicultural America*—a major revision to the previous editions published in 1995 and 2000—includes 175 entries, each focusing on an immigrant or indigenous group in the United States. Some entries provide historical and cultural overviews of commonly recognized groups, such as Mexican Americans and Japanese Americans, while others discuss much smaller groups—for example, Cape Verdean Americans, Jordanian Americans, and the Ojibwe. The third edition has 23 new entries; the 152 entries from the second edition were thoroughly revised and reorganized, creating up-to-date coverage and a more consistent approach throughout the book. The writing or revision of each entry was reviewed by a scholar with extensive research background in the group.

The structure and content of the *Gale Encyclopedia of Multicultural America* was planned with the help of the project's advisory board. Joe Feagin—professor of sociology at Texas A&M University and a member of the advisory board—revised and updated the encyclopedia's introduction, originally written by Rudolph Vecoli. The introduction provides a broad historical overview of race and ethnicity in the United States, explaining how cultural and legal influences, especially racism, helped shape the experience of indigenous and immigrant groups.

ORGANIZATION

The 175 entries are arranged alphabetically across three volumes. The length of the entries varies from about 4,000 to 20,000 words. All entries share a common structure, providing consistent coverage of the groups and a simple way of comparing basic elements of one entry with another. Birth and death dates are provided for people mentioned in the entries except when dates could not be found or verified. The encyclopedia has more than 400 color images.

Each entry has 14 sections:

Overview: Basic information about the group's origins, homeland, immigration to or migration within the United States, and population and principal areas of settlement.

History of the People: Significant historical events of the group in its original region or country.

Settlement in the United States: For immigrant groups, waves of immigration and notable settlement patterns; for indigenous groups, original area of settlement, as well as migration within North America after the group's contact with Europeans.

Language: Native languages and their influence on the present-day group. Some entries have a section on greetings and popular expressions.

Religion: Religions and religious practices of the group, both in the original country or region and in the United States.

Culture and Assimilation: Traditional beliefs and customs, as well as the status of these traditions in the present-day group; topics include cuisine, dress, dances and songs, holidays, and health care issues and practices. Some entries have a sidebar on proverbs.

Family and Community Life: Topics include family structure and traditions; gender roles; education; dating practices, marriage, and divorce; and relations with other Americans.

Employment and Economic Conditions: Types of jobs commonly done by early immigrants or by indigenous people as they came into contact with European settlers, as well as notable employment trends among later generations of the group.

Politics and Government: Topics include the group's involvement in American politics and government (including voting patterns, significant events, and legislation) and contemporary interest in the parent country.

Notable Individuals: Examples of accomplished members of the group in various fields, with brief summaries.

Media: List of television and radio stations, as well as newspapers and periodicals, that are directed toward the group or provide significant coverage of it.

Organizations and Associations: List of organizations and associations related to the group.

Museums and Research Centers: List of museums and research centers related to the group.

Sources for Additional Study: A bibliography of books and articles about the group, including recent sources.

ACKNOWLEDGMENTS

Many people contributed time, effort, and ideas to the third edition of the *Gale Encyclopedia of Multicultural America*. Marie Toft, senior content project editor at Cengage Gale, served as in-house manager for the project. The quality of the book owes much to her ideas and feedback, as well as to her oversight of the book's production.

We would like to express our appreciation to the advisors, who, in addition to creating the list of new entry topics, helped evaluate the second edition and proposed ideas for producing an improved third edition. We would also like to thank the contributors for their carefully prepared essays and for their efforts to summarize the cultural life of ethnic groups without stereotyping. We are grateful to the many scholars who reviewed entries for accuracy and coverage.

The long process of reorganizing and revising the second-edition entries, as well as preparing the new ones, was overseen by Joseph Campana, project editor, who also helped identify and correspond with the advisors. Anne Healey, senior editor, managed the editing process and was helped by Mary Beth Curran, David Hayes, and Lee Esbenshade, all associate editors. Hannah Soukup, assistant editor, identified and corresponded with the academic reviewers. Other important assistance came from Mariko Fujinaka, managing editor, and Jake Schmitt and Theodore McDermott, assistant editors. The line editors were Robert Anderson, Cheryl Collins, Tony Craine, Gerilee Hunt, Amy Mortensen, Jill Oldham, Kathy Peacock, Donna Polydoros, Natalie Ruppert, and Will Wagner.

Thomas Riggs

ADVISORY BOARD

CHAIR

David R. M. Beck
Professor, Department of Native American Studies, University of Montana, Missoula.

ADVISORS

Joe Feagin
Ella C. McFadden Professor, Department of Sociology, Texas A&M University.

Patricia Fernandez-Kelly
Professor, Department of Sociology, Office of Population Research, Princeton University.

David Gerber
University at Buffalo Distinguished Professor Emeritus, Department of History, University at Buffalo, The State University of New York.

Rebecca Stuhr
Coordinator for Humanities Collections, Librarian for Classical Studies and History, University of Pennsylvania Libraries, Member, Ethnic & Multicultural Information Exchange Round Table, American Library Association.

Vladimir F. Wertsman
Retired Chair, Publishing and Multicultural Materials Committee, Ethnic and Multicultural Information Exchange Round Table, American Library Association.

 # LIST OF ACADEMIC REVIEWERS

HOLLY ACKERMAN

Ph. D. Librarian for Latin American, Iberian, & Latino Studies, Duke University, Durham, North Carolina

DEIRDRE ALMEIDA

Director of the American Indian Studies Program, Eastern Washington University, Cheney

BARBARA WATSON ANDAYA

Professor of Asian Studies, University of Hawai'i, Manoa

BARBARA A. ANDERSON

Ronald Freedman Collegiate Professor of Sociology and Population Studies, University of Michigan, Ann Arbor

JOSEPH ARBENA

Professor Emeritus of History, Clemson University, South Carolina

LAURIE ARNOLD

Director of Native American Studies, Gonzaga University, Spokane, Washington

CHRISTOPHER P. ATWOOD

Associate Professor of Central Eurasian Studies, Indiana University, Bloomington

ANNY BAKALIAN

Associate Director of the Graduate Center, City University of New York

CARINA BANDHAUER

Professor of Sociology, Western Connecticut State University, Danbury, Connecticut

CARL L. BANKSTON III

Professor of Sociology, Tulane University, New Orleans, Louisiana

LAURA BARBAS-RHODEN

Associate Professor of Foreign Languages, Wofford College, Spartanburg, South Carolina

DAVID BECK

Department Chair of the Native American Studies Department and Professor of Native American Studies, University of Montana, Missoula

JOHN BIETER

Associate Professor of History, Boise State University, Idaho

ADRIAN VILIAMI BELL

Visiting Assistant Professor of Anthropology, University of Utah, Salt Lake City

BRIAN BELTON

Ph.D., as well as Senior Lecturer, YMCA George Williams College, London, United Kingdom

SAMIR BITAR

Lecturer of Arabic Language and Cultures, Department of Anthropology, and Assistant Director of Outreach-Central and Southwest Asian Studies Center, University of Montana, Missoula

LASZLO BORHI

Senior Research Fellow, Institute of History Hungarian Academy of Sciences, Budapest, Hungary

GREGORY CAMPBELL

Professor of Anthropology, University of Montana, Missoula

MAURICE CARNEY

Independent scholar, Friends of the Congo, Washington D.C

JUAN MANUEL CASAL

Professor and Chair, Department of History, Universidad de Montevideo, Uruguay

ELIZABETH CHACKO

Associate Professor of Geography and International Affairs and Chair of the Department of Geography, George Washington University, Washington, D.C.

ALLAN CHRISTELOW

Professor of History, Idaho State University, Pocatello

STEPHEN CRISWELL

Associate Professor of English and Native American Studies, University of South Carolina, Lancaster

JAMSHEED CHOKSY

Professor of Iranian and Islamic Studies, Indiana University, Bloomington

RICHMOND CLOW

Professor of Native American Studies, University of Montana, Missoula

STEPHANIE COX

Visiting Assistant Professor of French, Carleton College, Northfield, Minnesota

SHAHYAR DANESHGAR

Senior Lecturer of Central Eurasian Studies, Indiana University, Bloomington

JEAN DENNISON

Assistant Professor of Anthropology, University of North Carolina, Chapel Hill

JOSE R. DEUSTUA

Associate Professor of History, Eastern Illinois University, Charleston, Illinois

MUNROE EAGLES

Program Director of Canadian Studies and Professor of Political Science, State University of New York, Buffalo

SARAH ENGLAND

Associate Professor of Anthropology and Director of Social and Behavioral Sciences, Soka University of America, Alisa Viejo, California

PHYLLIS FAST

Professor of Anthropology, University of Alaska, Anchorage

SUJATHA FERNANDES

Associate Professor of Sociology, Queens College and the Graduate Center of the City University of New York

ANN FIENUP-RIORDAN

Independent scholar, Calista Elders Council, Bethel, Alaska

SEAN FOLEY

Associate Professor of History, Middle Tennessee State University, Murfreesboro

JAMES GIGANTINO

Assistant Professor of History, University of Arkansas, Fayetteville

EDWARD GOBETZ

Professor Emeritus of Sociology, Kent State University, Ohio

STEVEN J. GOLD

Professor of Sociology and Associate Chair in the Department of Sociology, Michigan State University, East Lansing

ANGELA A. GONZALES

Associate Professor of Development Sociology and American Indian Studies, Cornell University, Ithaca, New York

JONATHAN GOSNELL

Associate Professor of French Studies, Smith College, Northampton, Massachusetts

ISHTAR GOVIA

Lecturer of Psychology, University of the West Indies, Mona, Jamaica

YVONNE HADDAD

Professor of the History of Islam and Christian-Muslim Relations, Georgetown University, Washington, D.C.

JEFFREY HADLER

Associate Professor of South and Southeast Asian Studies, University of California, Berkeley

MARILYN HALTER

Professor of History, Institute on Culture, Religion, and World Affairs, Boston University, Brookline, Massachusetts

ANNE PEREZ HATTORI

Professor of History and Chamorro Studies, University of Guam, Mangilao

MICHAEL HITTMAN

Professor of Anthropology, Long Island University, Brooklyn, New York

INEZ HOLLANDER

Lecturer of Dutch Studies, University of California, Berkeley

JON D. HOLTZMAN

Associate Professor of Anthropology, Western Michigan University, Kalamazoo

KATHLEEN HOOD

Publications Director and Events Coordinator, The UCLA Herb Alpert School of Music, Department of Ethnomusicology, University of California, Los Angeles

MAREN HOPKINS

Director of Research, Anthropological Research, LLC, Tucson, Arizona

GUITA HOURANI

Director of the Lebanese Emigration Research Center, Notre Dame University, Kesrwan, Lebanon

SALLY HOWELL

Assistant Professor of History, University of Michigan, Dearborn

TARA INNISS

Lecturer in History, University of the West Indies, Cave Hill Campus, Barbados

ALPHINE JEFFERSON

Professor of History, Randolph-Macon College, Ashland, Virginia

PETER KIVISTO

Richard A. Swanson Professor of Social Thought, Augustana College, Rock Island, Illinois

MICHAEL KOPANIC, JR.

Adjunct Full Professor of History, University of Maryland University College, Adelphi, and Adjunct Associate Professor of History, St. Francis University, Loretto, Pennsylvania

DONALD B. KRAYBILL

Distinguished College Professor and Senior Fellow, Young Center for Anabaptist and

Pietist Studies, Elizabethtown College, Pennsylvania

GARY KUNKELMAN

Senior Lecturer, Professional Writing, Penn State Berks, Wyomissing, Pennsylvania

AL KUSLIKIS

Senior Program Associate for Strategic Initiatives, American Indian Higher Education Consortium, Alexandria, Virginia

WILLIAM LAATSCH

Emeritus Professor of Urban and Regional Studies, University of Wisconsin, Green Bay

BRUCE LA BRACK

Professor Emeritus of Anthropology, University of the Pacific, Stockton, California

SARAH LAMB

Professor of Anthropology, Brandeis University, Waltham, Massachusetts

LAURIE RHONDA LAMBERT

Doctoral candidate in English and American Literature, New York University

JOHN LIE

C. K. Cho Professor, University of California, Berkeley

HUPING LING

Changjiang Scholar Chair Professor and Professor of History, Truman State University, Kirksville, Missouri

JOSEPH LUBIG

Associate Dean for Education, Leadership and Public Service, Northern Michigan University, Marquette

ALEXANDER LUSHNYCKY

President of the Shevchenko Scientific Society Study Center, Elkins Park, Pennsylvania

NEDA MAGHBOULEH

Assistant Professor, Department of Sociology, University of Toronto, Ontario

WILLIAM MEADOWS

Professor of Anthropology, Missouri State University, Springfield

MARIANNE MILLIGAN

Visiting Assistant Professor of Linguistics, Macalester College, Saint Paul, Minnesota

NAEEM MOHAIEMEN
*Doctoral student in Anthropology at
Columbia University, New York*

ALEXANDER MURZAKU
*Professor and Chair of World Cultures and
Languages, College of Saint Elizabeth,
Morristown, New Jersey*

GEORGE MUSAMBIRA
*Associate Professor of Communication,
University of Central Florida, Orlando*

GHIRMAI NEGASH
*Professor of English & African Literature,
Ohio University, Athens*

JENNY NELSON
*Associate Professor of Media Studies, Ohio
University, Athens*

RAFAEL NÚÑEZ-CEDEÑO
*Coeditor of Probus: International Journal
of Latin and Romance Linguistics and
Professor Emeritus of Hispanic Studies,
University of Illinois, Chicago*

GREG O'BRIEN
*Associate Professor of History, University of
North Carolina, Greensboro*

GRANT OLSON
*Coordinator of Foreign Language
Multimedia Learning Center, Northern
Illinois University, DeKalb*

THOMAS OWUSU
*Professor and Chair of Geography, William
Paterson University, Wayne, New Jersey*

JODY PAVILACK
*Associate Professor of History, University of
Montana, Missoula*

BARBARA POSADAS
*College of Liberal Arts and Sciences
Distinguished Professor of History,
Northern Illinois University, DeKalb*

JASON PRIBILSKY
*Associate Professor of Anthropology,
Whitman College, Walla Walla,
Washington*

LAVERN J. RIPPLEY
*Professor of German, St. Olaf College,
Northfield, Minnesota*

MIKA ROINILA
*Ph.D., as well as International Baccalaureate
Program Coordinator and Fulbright*

*Specialist, John Adams High School, South
Bend, Indiana*

WILL ROSCOE
*Ph.D., Independent scholar, San Francisco,
California*

LEONID RUDNYTZKY
*Professor and Director of Central and
Eastern European Studies Program, La
Salle University, Philadelphia*

NICHOLAS RUDNYTZKY
*Independent scholar and Board member of the
St. Sophia Religious Association of Ukrainian
Catholics, Elkins Park, Pennsylvania*

YONA SABAR
*Professor of Hebrew, University of California,
Los Angeles*

LOUKIA K. SARROUB
*Associate Professor of Education, University
of Nebraska, Lincoln*

RICHARD SATTLER
*Adjunct Assistant Professor, University of
Montana, Missoula*

RICHARD SCAGLION
*UCIS Research Professor, University of
Pittsburgh, Pennsylvania*

HELGA SCHRECKENBERGER
*Chair of the Department of German
and Russian and Professor of German,
University of Vermont, Burlington*

BRENDAN SHANAHAN
*Doctoral student in North American history,
University of California, Berkeley*

KEMAL SILAY
*Professor of Central Eurasian Studies and
Director of the Turkish Studies Program,
Indiana University, Bloomington*

JEANNE SIMONELLI
*Professor of Cultural and Applied
Anthropology, Wake Forest University,
Winston-Salem, North Carolina*

GUNTIS ŠMIDCHENS
*Kazickas Family Endowed Professor in
Baltic Studies, Associate Professor of
Baltic Studies, and Head of Baltic Studies
Program, University of Washington, Seattle*

MATTHEW SMITH
*Senior Lecturer in History, University of the
West Indies, Mona, Jamaica*

MARY S. SPRUNGER
*Professor of History, Eastern Mennonite
University, Harrisonburg, Virginia*

THOMAS THORNTON
*Director for the MSc in Environmental
Change and Management, University of
Oxford, United Kingdom*

ELAISA VAHNIE
*Executive Director at the Burmese American
Community Institute, Indianapolis, Indiana*

DOUGLAS VELTRE
*Professor Emeritus of Anthropology,
University of Alaska, Anchorage*

MILTON VICKERMAN
*Associate Professor of Sociology, University of
Virginia, Charlottesville*

KRINKA VIDAKOVIC-PETROV
*Principal Research Fellow, Institute for
Literature and Arts, Belgrade, Serbia*

BETH VIRTANEN
*President, Finnish North American
Literature Association*

MARTIN VOTRUBA
*Director of the Slovak Studies Program,
University of Pittsburgh, Pennsylvania*

MARY WATERS
*M. E. Zukerman Professor of Sociology, Harvard
University, Cambridge, Massachusetts*

MARVIN WEINBAUM
*Professor Emeritus of Political Science,
University of Illinois, Urbana-Champaign*

BRENT WEISMAN
*Professor of Anthropology, University of
South Florida, Tampa*

THOMAS L. WHIGHAM
*Professor of History, University of Georgia,
Athens*

BRADLEY WOODWORTH
*Assistant Professor of History, University of
New Haven, West Haven, Connecticut*

KRISTIN ELIZABETH YARRIS
*Assistant Professor of International Studies
and Women's & Gender Studies,
University of Oregon, Eugene*

XIAOJIAN ZHAO
*Professor of Asian American Studies,
University of California, Santa Barbara*

List of Contributors

NABEEL ABRAHAM

Abraham holds a PhD in anthropology and is a university professor.

JUNE GRANATIR ALEXANDER

Alexander holds a PhD and has been a university professor.

DONALD ALTSCHILLER

Altschiller holds a PhD in library science and works as a university librarian.

DIANE ANDREASSI

Andreassi is a journalist and freelance writer

GREG BACH

Bach holds an MA in classics and is a freelance writer.

CARL L. BANKSTON III

Bankston holds a PhD in sociology and is a university professor.

CRAIG BEEBE

Beebe holds an MA in geography and works in nonprofit communications.

DIANE E. BENSON ("LXEIS")

Benson holds an MFA in creative writing and is a playwright, actor, and director.

BARBARA C. BIGELOW

Bigelow is an author of young adult books and a freelance writer and editor.

D. L. BIRCHFIELD

Birchfield was a university professor and novelist.

BENJAMIN BLOCH

Bloch holds an MFA in creative writing and an MFA in painting.

ELIZABETH BOEHEIM

Boeheim holds an MA in English literature and has been a university instructor.

CAROL BRENNAN

Brennan is a freelance writer with a background in history.

HERBERT J. BRINKS

Brinks was an author and editor and served as a curator at a university library.

K. MARIANNE WARGELIN BROWN

Wargelin Brown holds a PhD in history and is an independent scholar.

SEAN T. BUFFINGTON

Buffington holds an MA and is the president of The University of the Arts.

PHYLLIS J. BURSON

Burson holds a PhD in psychology and works as an independent consultant.

HELEN BUSH CAVER

Caver held a PhD and worked as a university librarian.

CIDA S. CHASE

Chase holds a PhD and is a university professor.

CLARK COLAHAN

Colahan holds a PhD and is a university professor.

ROBERT J. CONLEY

Conley holds an MA in English, is an award-winning novelist, and has served as a university professor.

JANE STEWART COOK

Cook is a freelance writer.

CHRISTINA COOKE

Cooke holds an MFA in creative nonfiction and works as a university instructor and freelance writer.

AMY COOPER

Cooper holds a PhD in anthropology and is a university professor.

PAUL ALAN COX

Cox holds a PhD in biology and is the director of the Institute of Ethnomedicine.

GIANO CROMLEY

Cromley holds an MFA in creative writing and is a university instructor.

KEN CUTHBERTSON

Cuthbertson is a writer, editor, and freelance broadcaster.

ROSETTA SHARP DEAN

Dean is a former school counselor and president of the Sharp-Dean School of Continuing Studies, Inc.

CHAD DUNDAS

Dundas holds an MFA in creative writing and has been a university instructor and freelance writer.

STANLEY E. EASTON

Easton holds a PhD and is a university professor.

TIM EIGO

Eigo holds a law degree and is writer and editor.

LUCIEN ELLINGTON

Ellington holds an EdD and is a university professor.

JESSIE L. EMBRY

Embry holds a PhD in history and is a research professor.

ALLAN ENGLEKIRK

Englekirk holds a PhD in Spanish and is a university professor.

RICHARD ESBENSHADE

Esbenshade holds a PhD in history and has been a university professor and freelance writer.

MARIANNE P. FEDUNKIW

Fedunkiw holds a PhD in strategic communications and is a university instructor and consultant.

DENNIS FEHR

Fehr holds a PhD in art education and is a university professor.

DAISY GARD

Gard is a freelance writer with a background in English literature.

CLINT GARNER

Garner holds an MFA in creative writing and is a freelance writer.

CHRISTOPHER GILES

Giles holds an MA in classics and an MA in history and is a college instructor and administrator.

MARY GILLIS

Gillis holds an MA has worked as a freelance writer and is a painter and sculptor.

EDWARD GOBETZ

Gobetz holds a PhD in sociology and is a retired university professor and former executive director of the Slovenian Research Center of America.

MARK A. GRANQUIST

Granquist holds a PhD and is a university professor.

DEREK GREEN

Green is a freelance writer and editor.

PAULA HAJAR

Hajar holds an EdD and has worked as a university professor and high school teacher.

LORETTA HALL

Hall is a freelance writer and the author of five works of nonfiction.

FRANCESCA HAMPTON

Hampton is a freelance writer and university instructor.

RICHARD C. HANES

Hanes holds a PhD and has served as the Division Chief of Cultural, Paleontological Resources, and Tribal Consultation for the Bureau of Land Management.

SHELDON HANFT

Hanft holds a PhD in history and is a university professor.

RODNEY HARRIS

Harris is a PhD candidate in history.

JOSH HARTEIS

Harteis holds an MA in English literature and is a freelance writer.

KARL HEIL

Heil is a freelance writer.

EVAN HEIMLICH

Heimlich is a freelance writer and university instructor.

ANGELA WASHBURN HEISEY

Heisey is a freelance writer.

MARY A. HESS

Hess is a freelance writer.

LAURIE COLLIER HILLSTROM

Hillstrom is a freelance writer and editor. She has published more than twenty works of history and biography.

MARIA HONG

Hong is a freelance writer and poet and was a Bunting Fellow at Harvard University in 2010-2011.

RON HORTON

Horton holds an MFA in creative writing and has been a high school English instructor and freelance writer.

EDWARD IFKOVIĆ

Ifković is a professor of creative writing and the author of four novels.

ALPHINE W. JEFFERSON

Jefferson holds a PhD in history and is a university professor.

CHARLIE JONES

Jones is a high school librarian.

J. SYDNEY JONES

Jones has worked as a freelance writer and correspondent and has published twelve works of fiction and nonfiction.

JANE JURGENS

Jurgens has been a university instructor.

JIM KAMP

Kamp is a freelance writer and editor.

OSCAR KAWAGLEY

Kawagley held a PhD in social and educational studies and was a university professor.

CLARE KINBERG

Kinberg holds a masters in library and information science and has been a literary journal editor.

KRISTIN KING-RIES

King-Ries holds an MFA in creative writing and has been a university instructor.

VITAUT KIPEL

Kipel held a PhD in mineralogy and an MLS and worked in the Slavic and Baltic Division of the New York Public Library.

JUDSON KNIGHT

Knight holds BIS in international studies, works as a freelance writer, and is co-owner of The Knight Agency, a literary sales and marketing firm.

PAUL S. KOBEL

Kobel is a freelance writer.

DONALD B. KRAYBILL

Kraybill holds a PhD in sociology and is a university professor.

LISA KROGER

Kroger holds a PhD in English literature and has been a university instructor.

KEN KURSON

Kurson is the editor-in-chief of the New York Observer.

ODD S. LOVOLL

Lovoll holds a PhD in U.S. history and is a university professor.

LORNA MABUNDA

Mabunda is a freelance writer.

PAUL ROBERT MAGOCSI

Magocsi holds a PhD in history and is the chair of Ukrainian Studies at the University of Toronto.

MARGUERITE MARÍN

Marín holds a PhD in sociology and is a university professor.

WILLIAM MAXWELL

Maxwell is a freelance writer who has worked as an editor at A Gathering of the Tribes magazine.

THEODORE McDERMOTT

McDermott holds an MFA in creative writing and has been a university instructor and freelance writer.

JAQUELINE A. McLEOD

McLeod holds a JD and PhD and is a university professor.

H. BRETT MELENDY

Melendy held a PhD in history and served as university professor and administrator.

MONA MIKHAIL

Mikhail holds a PhD in comparative literature and is a writer, translator, and university professor.

OLIVIA MILLER

Miller is a freelance writer, consultant, and university instructor.

CHRISTINE MOLINARI

Molinari is a freelance writer and editor and an independent researcher.

AARON MOULTON

Moulton holds an MA in Latin American studies. He is a PhD candidate in history and a university instructor.

LLOYD E. MULRAINE

Mulraine holds a DA in English and is a university professor.

JEREMY MUMFORD

Mumford holds a PhD in history and has worked as a university professor.

N. SAMUEL MURRELL

Murrell holds a PhD in biblical and theological studies and is a university professor.

AMY NASH

Nash is a published poet and has worked as a freelance writer and communications manager for Meyer, Scherer, & Rockcastle, Ltd., an architecture firm.

JOHN MARK NIELSEN

Nielsen is the executive director at the Danish Immigrant Museum.

ERNEST E. NORDEN

Norden holds a PhD and is a retired university professor.

SONYA SCHRYER NORRIS

Norris has worked as a freelance writer and website developer.

LOLLY OCKERSTROM

Ockerstrom holds a PhD in English and is a university professor.

KATRINA OKO-ODOI

Oko-Odoi is a PhD candidate in Spanish language literature and a university instructor.

JOHN PACKEL

Packel has worked as a freelance writer and is an associate director at American Express.

TINAZ PAVRI

Pavri holds a PhD in political science and is a university professor.

RICHARD E. PERRIN

Perrin was a university reference librarian.

PETER L. PETERSEN

Petersen holds a PhD in history and is a university professor.

MATTHEW T. PIFER

Pifer holds a PhD in composition and is a university professor.

GEORGE POZETTA

Pozetta held a PhD in history and was a university professor.

NORMAN PRADY

Prady is a freelance writer.

ELIZABETH RHOLETTER PURDY

Purdy is an independent scholar and has published numerous articles on political science and women's issues.

BRENDAN A. RAPPLE

Rapple holds an MBA and PhD and is a university librarian.

MEGAN RATNER

Ratner is a film critic and an associate editor at Bright Lights Film Journal.

WYLENE RHOLETTER

Rholetter holds a PhD in English literature and is a university professor.

LaVERN J. RIPPLEY

Rippley holds a PhD in German studies and is a university professor.

JULIO RODRIGUEZ

Rodriguez is a freelance writer.

PAM ROHLAND

Rohland is a freelance writer.

LORIENE ROY

Roy holds a PhD and MLS and is a university professor.

LAURA C. RUDOLPH

Rudolph is a freelance writer.

ANTHONY RUZICKA

Ruzicka is pursuing an MFA in poetry and has worked as a university instructor.

KWASI SARKODIE-MENSAH

Sarkodie-Mensah holds a PhD, is an author of research guides, and works as a university librarian.

LEO SCHELBERT

Schelbert holds a PhD in history and is a retired university professor.

JACOB SCHMITT

Schmitt holds an MA in English literature and has been a freelance writer.

MARY C. SENGSTOCK

Sengstock holds a PhD in sociology and is a university professor.

ELIZABETH SHOSTAK

Shostak is a freelance writer and editor.

STEFAN SMAGULA

Smagula has written for The Austin Chronicle and Zymurgy magazine and has designed software for Google, Bloomberg L.P., and The Economist. He works as software product designer in Austin, Texas.

HANNAH SOUKUP

Soukup holds an MFA in creative writing.

JANE E. SPEAR

Spear holds an MD and is a freelance writer and copyeditor.

TOVA STABIN

Stabin holds a Masters of Library and Information Science and works as a writer, editor, researcher, and diversity trainer.

BOSILJKA STEVANOVIĆ

Stevanović holds an MS in Library Science and is an independent translator.

SARAH STOECKL

Stoeckl holds a PhD in English literature and is a university instructor and freelance writer.

ANDRIS STRAUMANIS

Straumanis is a freelance writer and editor, as well as a university instructor.

PAMELA STURNER

Sturner is the executive director of the Leopold Leadership Program.

LIZ SWAIN

Swain has worked as a freelance writer and crime reporter and is a staff writer for the San Diego Reader.

MARK SWARTZ

Swartz holds an MA in art history, has served as writer for numerous nonprofits (including the American Hospital Association), and has published two novels.

THOMAS SZENDREY

Szendrey is a freelance writer.

HAROLD TAKOOSHIAN

Takooshian holds a PhD in psychology and is a university professor.

BAATAR TSEND

Tsend is an independent scholar and writer.

FELIX UME UNAEZE

Unaeze is a university librarian.

STEVEN BÉLA VÁRDY

Várdy holds a PhD in history and is a university professor.

GRACE WAITMAN

Waitman is pursuing a PhD in educational psychology. She holds an MA in English literature and has been a university instructor.

DREW WALKER

Walker is a freelance writer.

LING-CHI WANG

Wang holds a PhD and is a social activist and retired university professor.

KEN R. WELLS

Wells is a freelance writer and editor and has published works of young adult science fiction and nonfiction.

VLADIMIR F. WERTSMAN

Wertsman is a member of the American Library Association and the retired chair of the Publishing and Multicultural Materials Committee.

MARY T. WILLIAMS

Williams has worked as a university professor.

ELAINE WINTERS

Winters is a freelance writer, editor, and program facilitator. She has provided professional training for a number of Fortune 500 companies, including Apple, Nokia, and Nortel.

EVELINE YANG

Yang holds an MA in international and public affairs and is a PhD candidate in the Department of Central Eurasian Studies at Indiana University.

ELEANOR YU

Yu is the Supervising Producer at Monumental Mysteries at Optomen Productions.

INTRODUCTION

The term multiculturalism is used to describe a society characterized by a diversity of cultures. Religion, language, customs, traditions, and values are some components of culture, and culture also includes the perspectives through which people perceive and interpret society. A shared culture and common historical experience form the basis for a sense of peoplehood.

Over the course of U.S. history two divergent paths have led to this sense of peoplehood. All groups except indigenous Americans (Native Americans), have entered North America as voluntary or involuntary immigrants. Some of these immigrant groups and their descendants have been oppressed by the dominant group—white Americans that have been for centuries primarily of northern European descent—and were defined as inferior racial groups. A *racial group* is a societal group that people inside or outside that group distinguish as racially inferior or superior, usually on the basis of arbitrarily selected physical characteristics (for example, skin color). Historically whites have rationalized the subordination of other racial groups, viewing them as biologically and culturally inferior, uncivilized, foreign, and less than virtuous. To the present day Asian, African, Native, and Mexican Americans have been regularly "racialized" by the dominant white group. Even some non-British European immigrant groups (for example, Italian Americans) were for a short period of time defined as inferior racial groups, but within a generation or two they were defined as white.

Another term often used for certain distinctive social groups is *ethnic group*. While some social scientists have used it broadly to include racial groups, the more accurate use of the term is a group that is distinguished or set apart, by others or its own members, primarily on the basis of national-origin characteristics and cultural characteristics that are subjectively selected. "Ethnic" is an English word derived from the Greek word *ethnos* (for "nation") and was originally used for European immigrants entering in the early twentieth century. Examples are Polish Americans and Italian Americans, groups with a distinctive national origin and cultural heritage. Both racial groups and ethnic groups are socially constructed under particular historical circumstances and typically have a distinctive sense of peoplehood and cultural history. However, the lengthy historical and contemporary experiences of racial discrimination and subordination differentiate certain groups, such as African Americans and Native Americans, from the experiences and societal status of the ethnic groups of European origin that are now part of the white umbrella racial group.

"Multicultural America," the subject of this encyclopedia, is the product of the interaction of many different indigenous and immigrant peoples over the course of four centuries in what is now the United States. Cultural diversity was characteristic of the continent prior to the coming of European colonists and the Africans they enslaved. The indigenous inhabitants of North America numbered at least 7 million, and perhaps as many as 18 million, in the sixteenth century and were divided into hundreds of indigenous societies with distinctive cultures. Although the numbers of "Indians," as they were named by European colonizers, declined precipitously over the centuries as a result of European genocidal killings and diseases, their population has rebounded over the last century. As members of particular indigenous groups (such as Navajo, Ojibwa, and Choctaw) and as Native Americans, they are very much a part of today's cultural pluralism.

Most North Americans, in contrast, are the descendants of immigrants from other continents. Since the sixteenth century, from the early Spanish settlement at St. Augustine, Florida, the process of repopulating the continent has gone on apace. Several hundred thousand Europeans and Africans were recruited or enslaved and transported across the Atlantic Ocean during the colonial period to what eventually became the United States. The first census of 1790 revealed the racial and national origin diversity that marked the U.S. population. Almost a fifth of Americans were of African ancestry. (The census did not include Native Americans.) A surname analysis of the white population revealed that about 14 percent were Scottish and Scotch-Irish Americans and about 9 percent were German Americans—with smaller percentages of French, Irish, Dutch, Swedish, and Welsh Americans. English Americans comprised about 60 percent of the white population. At the time of its birth in 1776, the United States was already a complex racial and ethnic mosaic, with a wide variety of communities differentiated by the extent of racial oppression and by their national ancestry, culture, language, and religion.

The present United States includes not only the original 13 colonies but lands that were subsequently purchased or conquered by an often imperialistic U.S. government. Through this territorial expansion, other peoples and their lands were brought within the boundaries of the country. These included, in addition to many Native American societies, French, Hawaiian, Inuit, Mexican, and Puerto Rican groups, among others. Since 1790 great population growth, other than by natural increase, has come primarily through three eras of large-scale immigration. Arriving in the first major era of immigration (1841–1890) were almost 15 million newcomers: more than 4 million Germans, 3 million each of Irish and British (English, Scottish, and Welsh), and 1 million Scandinavians. A second major era of immigration (1891–1920) brought an additional 18 million immigrants: almost 4 million from Italy, 3.6 million from Austria-Hungary, and 3 million from Russia. In addition, more than 2 million Canadians immigrated prior to 1920. The following decades, from 1920 to 1945, marked a hiatus in immigration because of restrictive and discriminatory immigration policies, economic depression, and World War II. A modest postwar influx of European refugees was followed by a new era of major immigration resulting from the U.S. government abandoning in 1965 its openly discriminatory immigration policy favoring northern European immigrants. Totaling more than 40 million immigrants from 1965 to 2013—and still in progress—this third major era of immigration has encompassed about 20 million newcomers from Mexico and other parts of Central and South America and the Caribbean, as well as roughly 10 million newcomers from Asia. The rest have come from Canada, Europe, the Middle East, and Africa. While almost all the immigrants in the first two eras originated in Europe, a substantial majority since 1965 have come from Latin America, the Caribbean, Asia, Africa, and the Middle East.

Immigration has introduced a great diversity of racial-ethnic groups and cultures into the United States. The 2000 U.S. Census, the latest national census to report on ancestry, provides an interesting portrait of the complex origins of the people of the United States. Responses to the question "What is your ancestry or ethnic origin?" were tabulated for many groups. The largest ancestry groups reported were, in order of magnitude, German, Irish, African American, and English, all with more than 24 million individuals. Other groups reporting more than 4 million were Mexican, Italian, Polish, French, Native American, Scottish, Dutch, Norwegian, Scotch-Irish, and Swedish, with many other groups reporting more than 1 million each. There is also an array of smaller groups: Hmong, Maltese, Honduran, and Nigerian, among scores of others. Only 7 percent identified themselves simply as "American"—and less than one percent only as "white."

Immigration has contributed to the transformation of the religious character of the United States. The dominant Anglo-Protestantism (itself divided among numerous denominations and sects) of early English colonists was over time reinforced by the arrival of millions of Lutherans, Methodists, and Presbyterians and diluted by the heavy influx of Roman Catholics—first by the Irish and Germans, then by eastern Europeans and Italians, and more recently by Latin Americans. These immigrants have made Roman Catholicism the largest U.S. denomination. Meanwhile, Slavic Christian and Jewish immigrants from central and eastern Europe established Orthodox Christianity and Judaism as major religious bodies. As a consequence of Middle Eastern immigration—and the conversion of many African Americans to Islam—there are currently several million Muslims in the United States. Smaller numbers of Buddhists, Hindus, and followers of other religions have also arrived. In many U.S. cities houses of worship now include mosques and temples, as well as churches and synagogues. Religious pluralism is an important source of U.S. multiculturalism.

The immigration and naturalization policies pursued by a country's central government are revealing about the dominant group's public conception of the country. By determining who to admit to residence and citizenship, the dominant group defines the future racial and ethnic composition of the population. Each of the three great eras of immigration inspired much soul-searching and intense debate, especially in the dominant European American group, over the consequences of immigration for the U.S. future. If the capacity of this society to absorb tens of millions of immigrants over the course of more than 17 decades is impressive, it is also true that U.S. history has been punctuated by major episodes of vicious and violent nativism and xenophobia. With the exception of the British, it is difficult to find an immigrant group that has not been subject to significant racial or ethnic prejudice and discrimination. From early violent conflicts with Native Americans to the enslavement of Africans, Americans of northern European ancestry sought to establish "whiteness" as an essential marker of racial difference and superiority. They crafted a racial framing of society in order to legitimate and rationalize their subordination of numerous racial and ethnic groups. For example, the Naturalization Act (1790), one of the first passed in the new U.S. Congress, specified that citizenship in the United States was available only to an immigrant who was "a free white person." By this dramatic provision not only were African Americans ineligible for naturalization but also future immigrants who were deemed not to be "white." From that time to the present, the greater the likeness of immigrants to the northern European Protestants, the more readily they were welcomed by the dominant group.

There were, however, opposing, liberty-and-justice views held by racially and ethnically oppressed groups, as well as a version of this outlook supported by a minority of the dominant European American group. For example, in the nineteenth century, citing democratic ideals and universal brotherhood, many African Americans and some white Americans advocated the abolition of slavery and the human rights of those freed from slavery.

Since at least the 1880s debates over immigration policy have periodically brought contrasting views of the United States into collision. The ideal of the United States as a shelter and asylum for the oppressed of the world has exerted a powerful influence for a liberal reception of diverse newcomers. Early support for this liberal framing of immigration came from the descendants of early immigrants who were racially or ethnically different from the then dominant British American group. Poet Emma Lazarus's sonnet, which began "Give me your tired, your poor, your huddled masses yearning to breathe free, the wretched refuse of your teeming shore," struck a responsive chord among many Americans and was placed on the Statue of Liberty, a gift to the United States by the people of France. Emma Lazarus (1849-87) herself was the daughter of early Sephardic (Portuguese) Jewish immigrants to the colonies.

Over the centuries many U.S. businesses have depended upon the immigrant workers of Europe, Latin America, and Asia to develop the country's factories, mines, and railroads. Periodically, nonetheless, many white Americans have framed this immigration in negative terms—as posing a threat to societal stability, to their jobs, or U.S. cultural and biological integrity. Historically the strength of organized anti-immigrant movements has waxed and waned with the volume of immigration, as well as with fluctuations in the condition of the U.S. economy. Although the immigrant targets of nativistic attacks have changed over time, a constant theme in the framing of them by the dominant group has been the "danger" posed by "foreigners" to the core U.S. values and institutions.

For example, coming in large numbers from the 1830s to the 1850s, Irish Catholics were viewed as the dependent minions of the Catholic pope and thus as enemies of the Protestant character of the United States. A Protestant crusade against these immigrants culminated in the formation of the "Know-Nothing" Party in the 1850s, whose political battle cry was "America for the Americans!" This anti-Catholicism continued to be a powerful strain of nativism well into the middle of the twentieth century, including during the election and presidency of John F. Kennedy, an Irish Catholic American, in the early 1960s.

Despite frequent episodes of xenophobia, during its first decades of existence, the U.S. government generally welcomed newcomers with minimal regulation. In the 1880s, however, two important laws passed by a Congress controlled by (northern) European American politicians initiated a significant tightening of restrictions on some immigration. The first law established certain health and "moral" standards by excluding criminals, prostitutes, lunatics, idiots, and paupers. The second, the openly racist Chinese Exclusion Act, was the culmination of an anti-Chinese movement among European Americans centered on the West Coast. It denied admission to new Chinese laborers and barred Chinese workers already here from acquiring citizenship. Following the law's enactment, agitation for exclusion of Asian immigrants continued as the new Japanese and other Asian immigrant workers arrived. This European American nativism soon resulted in the blatantly racist provisions of the 1924 Immigration Law, which denied entry to "aliens ineligible for citizenship" (that is, those who were not "white"). It was not until 1950s and 1960s that a combination of international politics and civil rights movements, with their democratic ideals, resulted in the elimination of the more overtly racial restrictions from U.S. immigration and naturalization policies.

In the mid- to late-nineteenth century "scientific racism," which reiterated the superiority of whites of northern European origin, was embraced by many scientists and political leaders as justification for immigration restrictions and growing U.S. imperialism on the continent and overseas. By the late-nineteenth century the second immigration era was quite evident, as large numbers of immigrants from southern and eastern Europe entered the country. Nativists of northern European ancestry campaigned for a literacy test and other measures to restrict the entry of what they termed "inferior" European nationalities (sometimes termed "inferior races"). World War I created a xenophobic climate that prepared the way for the immigration acts of 1921 and 1924. Inspired by nativistic ideas, these laws established a national quota system designed to greatly reduce the number of southern and eastern Europeans entering the United States and to bar Asians. The statutes intentionally sought to maintain the northern European racial-ethnic identity of the country by protecting it from "contamination" from abroad.

Until 1965 the U.S. government pursued a very restrictive immigration policy that kept the country from becoming more diverse racially, ethnically, and religiously. The 1965 Immigration Act finally did away with the discriminatory national origins quotas and opened the country to immigration from throughout the world, establishing preferences for family members of citizens, skilled workers, entrepreneurs, and refugees. One consequence was the third wave of immigration. Since then, the annual volume of authorized immigration has increased steadily to about 1 million arrivals each year, and the majority of these new residents have come from Asia and Latin America.

The cumulative impact of the immigration of tens of millions of non-European immigrants since 1965 has aroused intense concerns, mostly in the dominant white group, regarding the demographic, cultural, and racial future of the United States. The skin color, as well as the languages and cultures, of most of the newcomers and their descendants have again been viewed negatively by many whites. Nativistic white advocates of tighter immigration restriction have warned that if current rates of immigration continue, white Americans will likely be a minority of the U.S. population by 2050.

One particular cause of white anxiety is the number of undocumented immigrants from Mexico (down to about 140,000 per year by 2013). Contrary to popular belief, the majority of undocumented immigrants do not cross the border from Mexico but enter the country with student or tourist visas and stay. Indeed, many are Europeans and Asians. The 1986 Immigration Reform and Control Act (IRCA) sought to solve the problem by extending amnesty for undocumented immigrants under certain conditions, imposing penalties on employers who hired them, and making provision for temporary agricultural migrant workers. Although more than 3 million people qualified for consideration for amnesty, employer sanctions failed for lack of enforcement, and for a time the number of undocumented immigrants did not decrease. Congress subsequently enacted the Immigration Act of 1990, which established a cap on immigrants per year, maintained preferences based on family reunification, and expanded the number of skilled workers admitted. The Illegal Immigration Reform and Immigrant Responsibility Act (IIRIRA), passed in 1996, established yet more regulations restricting legal and undocumented immigration and increased border control agents.

In 2006 Congress passed yet more restrictive legislation, the Secure Fence Act. It mandated the building of a billion-dollar border fence and other expensive surveillance technology and increased border enforcement personnel. Over recent decades the extensive border surveillance procedures have played a role in many of the estimated 5,100 lives lost as undocumented men, women, and children have tried to cross an ever more difficult U.S.-Mexico border—with its intensively policed and often extremely hot and waterless conditions--to improve their dire economic situations. Latin American immigration has continued to be a hotly debated U.S. political issue. Responding to the nativist mood of the country, politicians have advocated yet more restrictive measures to reduce immigration, as well as limiting access to government programs by legal and undocumented immigrants.

Forebodings about an "unprecedented immigrant invasion," however, have been greatly exaggerated. In the early 1900s the rate of immigration (the number of immigrants measured against the total population) was higher than in recent decades. While the number of foreign-born individuals in the United States reached nearly 40 million in 2010, an all-time high, they accounted for only 12.9 percent of the population, compared with 14.7 percent in 1910, giving the United States a smaller percentage of foreign-born individuals than some other contemporary nations. Moreover, in the early twenty-first century, Mexican immigration to the United States has been decreasing significantly, to the point that in 2005-10 there was a net zero migration to United States—that is, as many Mexicans were leaving the United States as were coming in. A persuasive argument has also been made that immigrants contribute much more than they take from the U.S. economy and pay more in taxes than they receive in social services. As in the past, new immigrants are often made the scapegoats for the country's broader economic and political problems.

Difficult questions face analysts of U.S. history. How have these millions of immigrants with such differing backgrounds and cultures been incorporated into the society? What changes have they wrought in the character of United States? The problematical concept of "assimilation" has traditionally been used to try to understand the process through which immigrants have adapted to U.S. society. Assimilation theorists view cultural assimilation (acculturation) as the one-way process whereby newcomers assume U.S. cultural attributes, such as the English language and political values, and social-group assimilation as the process of immigrant incorporation into important social networks (work, residence, and families) of the dominant group. In many cases such adaptation has not come easily. Many immigrants of color have culturally adapted to a significant degree but have experienced only limited incorporation into many mainstream networks and institutions because of persisting white racial bias and discrimination.

Indeed, since they have always wielded great social and political power, white Americans as a group have been able to decide who to include and exclude in the country. "Race" (especially skin color) has been the major barrier to full acceptance into historically white-controlled institutions. Asian and Latino Americans, as well as African Americans and Native Americans, have long been excluded from full integration into major white-dominated institutions. Race, language, religion, and national origin have been impediments to access. Social class has also strongly affected interactions among U.S. racial and ethnic groups. Historically, U.S. society has been highly stratified, with a close congruence between social class and racial or ethnic group. Thus, a high degree of employment and residential segregation has been central to maintaining the United States as a racially segregated society, with white Americans very disproportionately in the powerful upper and upper-middle classes.

The status of women within American society, as well as within particular racial and ethnic groups, has affected the ability of female immigrants to adapt to their new country. Historically, to a greater or lesser extent depending on their group, women have been restricted to traditional gender roles or have had limited freedom to pursue opportunities in the larger society. The density and location of immigrant settlements have also influenced the incorporation of immigrants into the dominant culture and institutions. Concentrated urban settlements and isolated rural settlements, by limiting contacts between immigrants and native-born Americans, tend to inhibit the processes of assimilation.

Historically one important variable is the determination of immigrants themselves whether or not to shed important aspects of their cultures. Through chain migrations, relatives and friends have often regrouped in cities, towns, and the countryside for mutual assistance and to maintain their customary ways in a sometimes hostile and difficult U.S. society. Establishing churches, newspapers, and other institutions, they have built communities and have developed an enlarged sense of peoplehood. Thus, national origin and home cultures have been important in many immigrants' attempts to cope with life in the United States. Theirs is often a selective adaptation, in which they have taken from the dominant U.S. culture what they needed and have kept significant aspects of their home culture that they value. The children and grandchildren of immigrants usually retain less of their ancestral cultures (languages are first to go) and have assumed more attributes of the dominant culture. Still, many have retained, to a greater or lesser degree, a sense of identity with a particular nationality or racial group. These patterns of societal adaptation vary greatly for different groups, historically and in the present. Immigrant groups of color and their descendants have been racialized by the dominant white group and have thus had quite different experiences from immigrants who are part of distinctive national origin groups within a white America. Racialized immigrant groups often use their home culture and its values and perspectives for resources in fighting against the racism and discrimination they face in their everyday lives.

For centuries the core culture of the colonies and early United States was essentially British American in most important aspects, and the immigrants (almost all European until the 1850s) and their offspring had to adapt to that dominant culture. Over time a few aspects of that core culture—such as music, food, and literature—have experienced some significant changes. These aspects of the core culture are today products of syncretism—the melding of different, sometimes discordant elements of the cultures of European and non-European immigrants and their descendants. Multiculturalism today is not a museum of immigrant cultures but rather a complex of the living, multitudinous cultures of the contemporary United States interacting with each other. Nonetheless, most of the central social, political, and economic realities of the U.S. core culture are still very much European American (especially British American) in their institutional structures, normative operation, and folkways. These include the major economic, legal, political, and educational institutions.

The country's ideological heritage includes the ideals of freedom and equality from the American Revolution. Such ideals have often been just abstract principles, especially for the dominant white group, that have been handed down from the eighteenth century to the present. However, subordinated racial and ethnic groups, taking these ideals very seriously, have employed them as weapons to combat economic exploitation and racial and ethnic discrimination. If the United States has been the "promised land" for many immigrants, that promise has been realized, if only in part, after prolonged and collective societal struggles. Through civil rights and labor movements, they have contributed greatly to keeping alive and enlarging the ideals of freedom, equality, and justice. If the

United States has transformed the numerous immigrant and indigenous groups in significant ways, these groups have on occasion significantly transformed the United States.

How has the dominant white American group historically conceived of this polyglot, kaleidoscopic society? Over the centuries two major models of a society comprised of various racial and ethnic groups have competed with each other. The dominant white model long envisioned a society based on racial "caste"— a society constitutionally and legally divided into those who were free and those who were not. Such a societal order existed for about 85 percent of this country's history (until the late 1960s). While the Civil War destroyed slavery, the Jim Crow system of segregation maintained extreme white oppression of black Americans for another hundred years. This model of intensive racial-ethnic oppression was not limited to black-white relationships. The industrial economy created a caste-like structure in much of the North. For a century prior to the progressive "New Deal" era of the 1930s, U.S. power, wealth, and status in the North were concentrated in the hands of a British-American elite, while U.S. workers there, made up largely of European immigrants and their children, were the low-paid serfs of factories, railroads, and farms. In subsequent decades this pattern has shifted as immigrants of color and their children have often filled many of these jobs on farms and in factories in the North and the South. By the 1960s official Jim Crow segregation ended in Southern and border states, and African Americans continued their movement out of the South to the North, which had begun in earnest in the 1930s and 1940s.

Over the centuries, since at least the 1700s, immigrants to this country have been expected by the dominant group to adapt and conform to the British-American ("Anglo-Saxon") core culture. Convinced of their cultural and biological superiority, Americans of British and other northern European descent have pressured Native Americans, African Americans, Latinos, and Asian Americans to modify or abandon their distinctive linguistic and cultural patterns and conform in a more or less one-way adaptive pattern to the dominant culture and folkways. However, even as they have demanded this conformity, European Americans have erected racial barriers that have severely limited egalitarian social intercourse and integration with those they have framed as racially inferior. Indeed, a prime objective of the U.S. public school system has been the one-way "assimilation" of "alien" children to the dominant cultural values and behaviors. The intensity of this pressure can be seen in the successful attacks, mostly white-led, on various programs of bilingual education, especially those involving the Spanish language of many Latin American immigrants and their descendants.

Nonetheless, over the course of U.S. history, and especially since the early 1900s, this intense one-way adaptation model has been countered by variations on a melting pot perspective. The "melting pot" symbolizes the process in which diverse immigrant groups are assimilated into a new "American blend." There have been many variants of this ideology of the melting pot, including the prevailing one in which the European American is still the cook stirring and determining the immigrant ingredients. In all versions the United States is viewed as becoming a distinctive amalgam of varied cultures and peoples emerging from the racial-ethnic crucible. Expressing confidence in the capacity of the country to incorporate diverse newcomers, the melting pot ideology has also provided the rationale for a more liberal approach to immigrants and immigration policy. Even so, this liberal melting pot ideology has periodically come under increasing attacks from anti-immigrant and other nativist groups, even after the progressive changes in U.S. immigration laws in the 1960s.

A third model of immigrant adaptation emerged during World War I in opposition to intensive pressures on immigrants for one-way "Americanization," a model often termed "cultural pluralism." In this model, while sharing a common U.S. citizenship and loyalty, racial and ethnic groups should be able to maintain and foster their particular languages and distinctive cultures. The metaphors employed for the cultural pluralism model have included a symphony orchestra, a flower garden, and a mosaic. All suggest a reconciliation of group diversity with an encompassing harmony and coherence of racial and ethnic groups. During the 1930s, when cultural democracy was more in vogue, pluralist ideas were more popular. Again during the social movements of the

1960s and the 1970s, cultural pluralism attracted a considerable following. By the early twenty-first century, heightened fears, especially among white Americans, that U.S. society is fragmenting and moving away from the dominance of the English language and Euro-American culture have caused many people to reject any type of significant cultural pluralism.

Questions about racial and ethnic matters loom large as the United States moves ever more deeply into the twenty-first century. Its future as a racially and ethnically plural society and socially just society is vigorously debated. Is the United States more diverse today than in the past? Can discriminatory racial and ethnic barriers be finally removed? Can this multiracial society really be made more just and democratic? The old model of one-way conformity to the white-controlled core culture has lost its ideological and symbolic value for a great many Americans who believe we need to implement a more egalitarian societal model. These Americans see the United States as a respectfully multicultural and truly democratic people in the context of a multicultural world.

Suggested Reading On issues of systemic racism and the creation of U.S. racial groups, see Joe R. Feagin, *Systemic Racism: A Theory of Oppression* (2006) and *The White Racial Frame* (2nd edition, 2013). On conventional assimilation theory, see Milton Gordon's *Assimilation in American Life: The Role of Race, Religion, and National Origins* (1964). On recent assimilation theory and applicable data, see Richard Alba, *Blurring the Color Line: The New Chance for a More Integrated America* (2009). For discussion of racial and ethnic group definitions, see Joe R. Feagin and Clairece B. Feagin, *Racial and Ethnic Relations (2011). Harvard Encyclopedia of American Ethnic Groups* (1980), edited by Stephan Thernstrom, is a standard reference work with articles on racial-ethnic themes and specific groups. Roger Daniels's *Coming to America: A History of Immigration and Ethnicity in American Life* (1991) is a comprehensive history. For a comparative history of racial-ethnic groups, see Ronald Takaki's *A Different Mirror: A History of Multicultural America* (1993). A classic work on nativism is John Higham's *Strangers in the Land: Patterns of American Nativism: 1860-1925* (1963). On the British American elite's history, see E. Digby Baltzell's *The Protestant Establishment: Aristocracy and Caste in America* (1964). On contemporary ancestry groups, see Angela Brittingham and G. Patricia de la Cruz, *Ancestry: 2000* (2004).

Rudolph Vecoli
Updated and revised by Joe Feagin

KENYAN AMERICANS

Laura C. Rudolph

OVERVIEW

Kenyan Americans are immigrants or descendants of people from Kenya, a country in eastern Africa. It is bordered to the north by Ethiopia and South Sudan, to the east by the Indian Ocean, to the northeast by Somalia, to the south by Tanzania, and to the west by Uganda. Kenya's total land area is 224,960 square miles (582,650 square kilometers), about a third larger than the state of California.

According to the 2009 Kenyan census, the country had a population of more than 43 million people. The country's official languages are Kiswahili and English. About 28 percent of Kenyans are Roman Catholic, 38 percent Protestant, and 7 percent Muslim; much of the remaining population holds indigenous religious beliefs, and there are a small number of Hindus, Sikhs, and Baha'is. Kenya has three major cultural and linguistic groups: the Bantu, Nilotic, and Cushitic. A poor country with a predominantly agricultural economy, Kenya nevertheless has a small but important industrial sector, and the country serves as an economic hub in eastern Africa. The tourism industry is also economically important in Kenya; in 2006, for example, tourism brought in $803 million to the national economy. Tourism ranks second to agriculture in revenue, attracting people from all over the world to see the game parks and reserves, the Indian Ocean beaches, and other natural wonders of Kenya.

The earliest Kenyans in the United States were most likely slaves and would have arrived between 1620 and 1808, when the U.S. Constitution called for an end to the importation of slaves. Voluntary settlement remained negligible until the last decades of the twentieth century. Recently Kenyans have been motivated to immigrate to the United States by educational opportunities, as well as by poor economic conditions and political unrest in their native country. Kenyans possess a distinct advantage over many other U.S. immigrants in that they are already fluent in English. This is one of the factors that has allowed them join the American workforce quickly and also achieve high levels of education.

According to the Migration Policy Institute in Washington, D.C., about 87,000 Kenyan immigrants were living in the United States in 2011 (approximately 6 percent of all African immigrants), not including Kenyans with student visas. Kenyan Americans have migrated most notably to Texas, California, parts of the Midwest, and Washington, D.C. Two states with important technological centers, Georgia and North Carolina, have also been attractive destinations for Kenyan immigrants.

HISTORY OF THE PEOPLE

Early History Throughout the first few centuries CE, Kenya was the destination of numerous migrating tribes that established themselves in various areas. The Kalenjin settled around the western part of what became Kenya, while the Kikuyu covered the fertile ground of the Highlands and the Rift Valley. Each group was a self-contained community with its own language, customs, and beliefs.

Arabs settled on the Kenyan coast as early as the tenth century, and the Portuguese contested for the coast during the fifteenth and sixteenth centuries. The Arabs regained control during the eighteenth century, and by the early to mid-nineteenth centuries, Sayyid Said of Oman loosely controlled the coast. By this time Africa's largely untapped wealth attracted scores of Europeans, and in 1885 Africa was partitioned into several sectors controlled by various European nations.

Modern Era The British government established Kenya as a British protectorate in 1895 and a crown colony in 1920. The British quickly built a railroad that promoted economic development by linking the regions together; the rights of Africans were restricted, while white settlement was encouraged. The Africans were overtaxed undereducated, and lacked political representation. In addition, they were not allowed to grow certain exportable crops and could not settle in the Highlands and the Rift Valley, regarded as the richest farmland in the country. In many instances tribal peoples were forced to relocate to designated areas in Kenya.

During World War I a large number of Kenyan soldiers were recruited to fight for the British. Following the war many Africans, particularly the Kikuyus, who had lost much of their land, began organizing to lobby for reform. One such group, the East African Association (EAA), encouraged protests and demonstrations. Although the EAA dissolved shortly thereafter, the Kikuyu Central Association (KCA) quickly took its place and continued the fight against white supremacy. The KCA lobbied for political representation, lower taxes, and the right to inhabit restricted lands. Although the organization enjoyed some success, it was unable to achieve its goals before it was banned in 1940, shortly after World War II began. However, the KCA helped pave the way for future organizations, which would ultimately achieve independence for Kenya.

World War II provided the impetus Kenya needed to achieve independence. Many Kenyans fought in the war, and they learned both organizational and military skills. In 1944 the Kenyan African Union (largely comprised of Kikuyus) was formed to continue the fight against white supremacy. In 1947 Jomo Kenyatta was elected the president of the KAU. Although most members were Kikuyus, they encouraged all ethnic groups to join together to achieve independence.

Other Kenyans, frustrated with the slow response to their demands, turned to more violent means. The Mau Mau uprising of 1952–1956 was characterized by numerous acts of violence and terrorism against the colonial government and settlers. Brutally suppressed, the uprising left thousands of Africans dead, while only a handful of British were killed.

The Mau Mau uprising was not wholly unsuccessful. In response to changes occurring throughout European-dominated countries across Africa, the colonial government was ready to capitulate in Kenya. Africans were allowed representation in the government, and they continued to lobby to gain autonomy. In 1960 they formed the Kenya African National Union (KANU). However, political infighting between the dominant Kikuyus and other groups led to the formation of a rival party, the Kenya African Democratic Union (KADU).

In 1962 the two parties laid aside their differences and united to form a coalition government. Jomo Kenyatta was elected the first prime minister. Kenya was officially declared independent on December 12, 1963, and became a republic in 1964. Shortly thereafter the KADU dissolved, and Kenya was ruled chiefly by the KANU until 1966, when the Kenya People's Union (KPU) was formed.

From the start, the KPU was at odds with the KANU and did not gain much support beyond the Luo peoples. The group was ordered to disband after an important member of government personnel was assassinated, a crime that was attributed to the KPU. The Kenyan government, largely under Kikuyu control, turned its attention to ongoing social and economic problems. In an effort to boost their flagging economy, they welcomed foreign investors, and Kenya rapidly became the most prosperous country in East Africa.

Although Kenya was fearful that its political stability would be shaken by the death of Jomo Kenyatta in 1978, Daniel Arap Moi succeeded without challenge. In 1982 the Royal Air Force staged a coup attempt, but Moi remained in office. In 1991, largely at the urging of foreign investors, Moi pledged to further address social and economic problems and encouraged the formation of a multiparty system, which prevailed through the end of the twentieth century.

In 2002, following defeats in 1992 and 1997, opposition leader Mwai Kibaki became Kenya's third president. His defeat of Uhura Kenyatta, the son of Kenya's first president, represented a historic change in modern Kenya, encouraging expectations of significant reform. For many, however, Kibaki was a disappointment. Corruption and dysfunction continued, leading to the formation of the Orange Democratic Movement. After a contentious presidential election in 2007, protest and violence erupted. A power-sharing agreement ended the tension, and in 2010 a new national constitution was created.

SETTLEMENT IN THE UNITED STATES

Prior to the 1970s very few Kenyans immigrated to the United States. Since then, however, the number of Kenyan immigrants has grown considerably. In 1988 about 800 Kenyans immigrated to the United States; by 1998 that number had doubled, to 1,688. In 2011 the number of Kenyans admitted to the United States was 7,762.

The increase in Kenyan immigration to the United States was partly a result of the changes that took place in Kenya in the decades following its independence from Britain in 1963. The country's growing modernization and liberalization made it more possible for Kenyans to pursue educational and economic aspirations that had been restricted under colonial rule and the one-party political system that succeeded it. At the same time that opportunity increased within Kenya, however, rapid population growth and political unrest made it difficult for many to attend school or find work. As a result, more Kenyans began to look outside the country to pursue their educational and professional aims. In the United States a majority of Kenyan immigrants came to pursue schooling, especially at universities, and many others were technical experts as well as executives, administrators, and managers.

Of Kenyans who immigrated to the United States, a majority (74 percent) arrived in the northeast and initially settled in the region, especially New York City, Massachusetts, and Newark, New Jersey. Soon after their arrival, however, 83 percent of Kenyan immigrants moved to another part of the United States, most commonly to the south, in particular Texas and North Carolina. Minnesota was another common destination for Kenyan Americans. This movement was largely motivated by the search for employment and affordable housing. In the South and Midwest, Kenyans have been able to find lower-cost

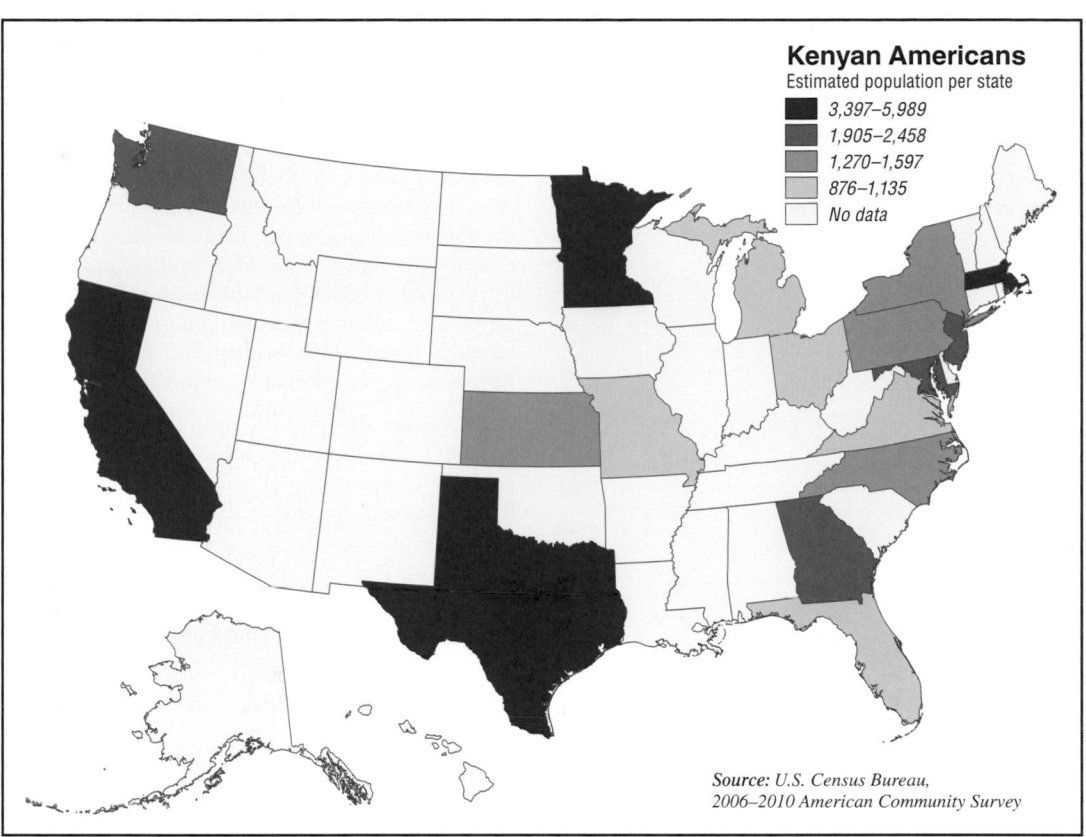

Kenyan Americans
Estimated population per state

- 3,397–5,989
- 1,905–2,458
- 1,270–1,597
- 876–1,135
- No data

Source: U.S. Census Bureau, 2006–2010 American Community Survey

housing (according to the 2010 U.S. Census, 18,234 Kenyan Americans owned their homes, while 25,586 occupied rental units), as well as jobs in growing sectors of the economy such as technology.

LANGUAGE

Kiswahili and English are the official languages of Kenya, and most Kenyans are multilingual. Typically Kenyans speak at least three languages, as each indigenous group has a fully developed language of their own. Kiswahili, a Bantu language that gradually incorporated Arabic words over the centuries, serves as a common language for the various regions in Kenya. Although everyday activities are conducted in Kiswahili, government and court business continue to use English. Other ethnic languages include Luo, Kikuyu, Kamba, Luyia, Gusii, and Kalenjin. In addition, English words have become incorporated into Kiswahili, which has led to a hybrid language composed of Kiswahili and English called *Sheng*. According to the 2010 U.S. Census, more than 30,000 Kenyan Americans speak a language other than English at home.

Because most Kenyans speak English, immigrants in the United States generally do not face linguistic obstacles and are comfortable switching to English as their principal language. As a result, Kenyan immigrants have traditionally adapted quickly to American educational and occupational environments. The 2010 U.S. Census indicates that 49 percent of Kenyan Americans work in the educational and health care industries.

RELIGION

More than 75 percent of Kenyans are Christian (45 percent Protestant, 23 percent Roman Catholic), while about 10 percent are Muslim, according to 2012 estimates in the *CIA World Factbook*. Various tribal religions are also prominent in Kenya. Of these, most are founded on a belief in witchcraft and spirit matter. Witch doctors are commonly called upon during times of distress from illness, drought, and other disruptive events. The latter part of the twentieth century saw a decline in the practice of traditional faith and a rise in Islam and Christianity.

The vast majority of Kenyans who immigrate to the United States are Christian, and many join a church, finding it helps ease the adjustment process to their new country, particularly if other Kenyan immigrants are members. Various organizations, such as Kenya Christian Fellowship in America, have been organized within the Kenyan American community to promote religious and ethnic unity. However, definitive religious statistics are difficult to come by because U.S. law bars the Census Bureau from asking faith-related questions.

KENYAN PROVERBS

- Even when the shield covering wears out, the frame survives.

- When a drum has a drumhead, one does not beat the wooden sides.

- When a scorpion stings without mercy, you kill it without mercy.

- A man does not rub backs with porcupines.

- Rooster, do not be so proud.

- Your mother was only an eggshell.

- The canoe must be paddled on both sides.

CULTURE AND ASSIMILATION

Kenyan Americans often assimilate easily into American culture, partially because English is widely spoken in Kenya and, thus, they do not face a language barrier upon arriving in the United States. In addition, many are well educated and have specialized job skills, allowing them to find careers in fields such as technology and health care.

Although Kenyan Americans are often successful educationally and in their work, most do not become U.S. citizens. In 2000, for example, only about 25 percent of U.S. residents claiming Kenyan ancestry were citizens. Furthermore, according to 2010 U.S. Census data, 27,579 of the 45,177 Kenyans in the United States were not naturalized citizens. Many Kenyan Americans are reluctant to abandon their ties to Kenya by becoming American citizens. In fact, it is not uncommon for Kenyan Americans to eventually return to their native country after completing their education or achieving their financial goals. Many of those who do become U.S. citizens maintain ties to their home country and return there for visits.

Traditions and Customs Kenyan culture is a rich mixture of indigenous traditions and various influences from its long history of Islamic, Portuguese, and British colonization. Many Kenyan customs and beliefs originate from an agricultural lifestyle and contain special prayers, dances, and rituals to encourage different natural events. During droughts, for instance, the Masai strip the bark off of tree, bury a skin around the root of the tree, and pour water over it, in addition to placing sacred objects on it and praying for rain. Other traditions stem from hunting and warring practices, where prayers and rituals would be performed before and after the hunt or raid. The Masai sacrifice a sheep before a raid. Reverence of various animals plays a role in other customs. The Suk revere snakes, and if a snake were to enter a hut, the animal could not be killed but was to be fed milk. Traditions also centered on life events, particularly the initiation of a child into adulthood or the birth of a baby.

In the nineteenth and twentieth centuries, many traditional Kenyan customs and beliefs began to fade away and change under the colonial dominance of the country by the British. The colonial administration brought missionaries, white settlers, and railways to the country. Over time this led to an infusion of European traditions and customs, which were not accepted into Kenyan society without alternation. Rather, new, hybrid forms of culture were created.

Cuisine Traditional Kenyan cuisine reflects the agricultural products of the region. Kenyan recipes are generally inexpensive and nourishing, relying heavily on potatoes, rice, and maize. Maize is found in a variety of recipes, especially a porridge called *ugali*, which is cooked with meat (chicken, goat, or beef) or greens and is eaten nearly every day. Other dishes include *karanga*, a stew cooked with goat meat, carrots, onions, and potatoes; *pillau*, a spiced rice dish that sometimes includes meat; *sukima wiki*, a fried dish with chopped spinach, onions, tomatoes, or other vegetables; *kienyeji*, a dish with mashed corn, beans, potatoes, and greens; and *mchicha*, which contains spinach, onions, and tomatoes.

Among Kenyan Americans, many of these traditional dishes remain popular. In cities such as Baltimore and Atlanta, which have significant Kenyan American populations, traditional Kenyan cuisine is served in ethnic restaurants.

Traditional Dress The traditional clothing of Kenyans varies from region to region. For example, the traditional clothing of the Masai men, who were known for their fierce warrior status, includes headdresses of lion's mane and ostrich feathers. In addition, they put white and red paint on their faces. The Suk men wear elaborate shoulder-length chignons, jewelry from animals' horns, capes made of skins, lip plugs, and pierced nose discs. Turkana women shave their hair at the sides, twist the top of their hair into strands, and wear oval-shaped plate earrings. Their shoulders are covered with disc-shaped ornamentation made from ostrich eggs. Married Turkana women also wear an apron decorated with beads, which is held with a beaded belt.

During events, particularly those related to the life cycle, clothing serves a special purpose. When girls and boys undergo initiation via circumcision or clitoridectomies, they wear certain clothing that reveals their status. Njemps boys undergoing circumcision wear a dyed black skin, held in place by a belt of cowry shells, and two ostrich feathers in their ears. Njemps girls don metal beads around their neck or face as a symbol of their on-going clitoridectomy process. Other life-cycle events require particular costumes as well. Women who have just given birth often paint the area around their eyes. Most Kenyans, as well as

Kenyan Americans, do not wear traditional garments except on special occasions.

Dances and Songs *Ngoma*, the traditional form of Kenyan music, is generally used to describe both music and dance centered on the drum. Many Kenyan dances and songs serve specific purposes and have a variety of themes, such as agricultural (for example, harvest, rain, or fire), mourning, jubilation, fertility, war, and peace. Most of the dances include stamps, hops, squats, slides, and hip swivels, reflecting the occasion for which it is intended. For instance, the battle dance of the Samburu contains fierce jumping motions, which simulate actions of a raid. In addition to continuing to celebrate traditional Kenyan holidays, many Kenyan Americans incorporate traditional Kenyan dances into traditional American holiday celebrations.

Contemporary Kenyan music is a blend of folk and modern forms. There are numerous traditional Kenyan instruments, including the drum; bow harp; lute; lyre; instruments made from animals' horns; wood trumpet; flute; rattle; bell; gong; and the pit xylophone. In Kenyan folk music, these instruments are combined with various forms of singing, including call-and-response vocals that entail one person shouting a line and the other people responding. In the early twentieth century, a genre of music known as *taraab* was introduced in Kenya. A blend of Arabic, Indian, and African melodies and instrumentation, *taraab* remains popular in the Kenyan diaspora. For many Kenyans and Kenyan Americans, however, the most popular musical forms are hip hop and reggae, as well as a Congolese style of dance music known as *soukous* and a French Caribbean style of dance music called *zouk*.

Holidays Kenyan holidays include the anniversary of the country's independence (December 12) and Kenyatta Day (October 20), which honors Kenya's first prime minister, Jomo Kenyatta. The small number of Kenyan immigrants in the United States prohibits lavish celebrations in honor of these events, but Kenyan American organizations sometimes hold special events for them. Kenyan American Christians celebrate traditional holidays of their faith, such as Good Friday, Easter, and Christmas Day. These days are typically celebrated with large meals and family gatherings. Kwanza is a harvest celebration (*kwanza* is a Swahili word that means "first harvest") that begins on December 26 and lasts until January 1. In recent years Kwanza has become more widely celebrated in the United States by both Kenyan Americans and African Americans in general.

Health Care Issues and Practices Despite recent efforts to address health issues, Kenyans have a fairly low life expectancy (62 years for males and 65 years for females in 2012) and a high percentage of infant deaths (43.61 per 1,000 births). Poor living conditions increase the risk of disease, and several diseases are particularly common in Kenya: poliomyelitis, schistosomiasis, intestinal parasites, malaria, respiratory ailments, and, increasingly, HIV infection.

Because most Kenyans speak English, immigrants in the United States generally do not face linguistic obstacles and are comfortable switching to English as their principal language. As a result, Kenyan immigrants have traditionally adapted quickly to American educational and occupational environments.

Most Kenyan Americans, however, are in good health when they enter the United States, and many have health insurance through their employers.

FAMILY AND COMMUNITY LIFE
Kenyans place a high value on family relationships and the importance of kinship. Close attention is paid to ancestry and lineage, particularly along paternal lines. In general, the individual is considered less important than his or her community, which centers on the extended family. Households normally contain at least one extended family member. Often several generations are present. Children sometimes refer to their cousins as "brother" or "sister" and call their aunts and uncles "mother" and "father." Grandparents and great-grandparents are revered for their wisdom.

Because of the emphasis placed on lineage, marriage is a sacred duty. Men are often allowed to marry more than one woman in order to ensure the survival of the patriarchal line. Women are expected to raise large families. Women who do not have many children often face public derision. Large families are rewarded in many instances, both financially and through the elevation of their status. Kenyan homes are traditionally conservative and strictly patriarchal. Husbands work outside the home while the women are expected to stay within the boundaries of the household.

For many years, because of strict immigration laws, Kenyans usually immigrated alone. This meant that many Kenyan Americans were separated from their families for a long period of time. In the mid-1990s, however, the United States reformed its immigrations laws to allow more people, including Kenyans, to immigrate with their families. This altered the makeup of Kenyan American communities and increased their diversity.

Kenyans often have a difficult time adjusting to American values, which they perceive as antithetical to their own, especially the emphasis on individualism, competitiveness, and materialism. Most Kenyan immigrants are accustomed to a close-knit community and being surrounded by family members, and they sometimes feel isolated when they first arrive.

A great concern among Kenyan immigrants is their inability to foster a sense of Kenyan identity in

Kenyan Americans William and Alice Mukabane are owners of the restaurant Safari DC in Washington, D.C. KEVIN CLARK / THE WASHINGTON POST / GETTY IMAGES

their children. Children often have a more difficult time understanding the importance of ancestry and lineage. While Kenyans usually marry within their own ethnic group, the children of Kenyan immigrants are much more likely to marry outside of it. Many Kenyan American parents are involved in Kenyan American organizations that sponsor events to help expose their children to Kenyan culture.

Gender Roles Through the end of the twentieth century, Kenyan households maintained rigid rules concerning women's roles within the patriarchal household. Wives and daughters were expected to stay strictly within the domestic sphere, except for designated agricultural tasks. The importance of these responsibilities was attested by the custom of paying bride price, which compensated the parents for the loss of their daughters. Women faced an enormous amount of social pressure to marry from the moment they were considered ready. Married women were under the protection of their husbands and forced to obtain permission from them to open a bank account or acquire a driver's license.

Families were always traced from the father's line, and all children from a marriage "belonged" to the father. The frequent pregnancies of Kenyan women further reduced their opportunities to break out of traditional domestic-related roles. Contraception remained difficult to obtain and was regarded with suspicion by communities. During the last two decades of the twentieth century, an emerging women's movement has brought about changes in women's educational opportunities, health care, and other matters.

Kenyan American women have embraced the educational and occupational opportunities available in the United States. Unlike many women in Kenya, Kenyan American women are able to obtain contraception, driver's licenses, and bank accounts without permission from their husbands. Since Kenyan American women are usually well educated, they do not have difficulties finding employment and are able to take advantage of the freedom of pursuing a career outside the home. Despite this, Kenyan American women typically earn substantially less than their male counterparts and are expected to perform more of the household chores.

Courtship and Weddings Since much emphasis is placed on family relationships, Kenyan marriages are taken very seriously and must be met with approval by both families. After it has been granted, there is an engagement period before the marriage ceremony takes place. The majority of Kenyans are Christians, and their weddings usually conform to the dictates of their religion.

There are also traditional indigenous customs that vary from group to group. For instance, the Kikuyu men choose their wives after carefully examining their personalities, integrity, and sociability. It is customary, however, for women not to accept a marriage offer immediately and to hesitate and refer the question to her father. After she does accept, the bridegroom presents his bride with gifts, which are termed "bridewealth." In addition to more practical items such as cattle or livestock, the gifts sometimes include a *mukwar* (leather strap), *neguo ya maribe* (woman's dress made out of skins and beads, presented to the mother of the bride), a *ruhiu* (sword), and an *itimu ria nduthu* (a man's coat made out of skins, presented to the father of the bride).

Other indigenous groups practice similar marriage customs, which are sometimes performed in addition to Christian ceremonies. While some close-knit Kenyan immigrant groups maintain traditional customs in the United States, most Kenyan Americans abandon such customs once they immigrate.

Circumcisions An important life-cycle event that takes place in Kenyan culture concerns the initiation of boys and girls into adulthood. This event is traditionally marked with male circumcision and female clitoridectomy (female circumcision) rituals. Although male circumcision is regularly practiced among many different groups, the practice of clitoridectomy is less common. These initiations are an important event for those involved as well as the entire community. Although the customs vary from tribe to tribe, circumcision usually occurs between the twelfth and sixteenth birthday of a boy or girl.

Before undergoing the ceremony, the initiates spend up to a year in preparation, undergoing a series of rituals. For instance, Nandi boys are circumcised around their thirteenth birthday. Their preparation includes learning their groups' folklore, shaving their heads, passing courage tests, and wearing certain garments. After the event, they are placed in seclusion and not allowed to eat with their hands for the first week. After undergoing another series of rituals, they take an oath of secrecy about what they have learned. They are then considered part of Nandi manhood and wear certain clothing to indicate their new status.

Nandi girls undergo a similar process. During their preparation, they wear certain garments and enter into seclusion. They are generally not allowed to see men during this time. At the end of the initiation period, following the clitoridectomy, the girls can wear different clothing to display their new status. They are then eligible for marriage. Both girls and boys are expected to undergo the experience without complaining.

Toward the end of the twentieth century, these customs were gradually abandoned. Clitoridectomies, in particular, were heavily criticized, in part because of the unhygienic conditions under which they were performed. Kenyan immigrants in the United States generally no longer observe the practice of traditional male or female circumcision as an initiation into adulthood.

Funerals The majority of Kenyans practice Christian burials and funeral services. Their reverence of ancestry dictates proper respect for the dead, and funerals are carefully performed.

There are also many indigenous beliefs regarding the afterlife and the spirit world, which are reflected in older customs of burial and funeral services. The Suk traditionally buried their dead so that their stomachs were tilted toward the Seker, the sacred mountain of the Suk. The Maragoli gave a widow her husband's spear and shield. During the funeral she carried them before handing them to his eldest brother immediately afterward. The Taveta buried their dead in a sitting position. Men were buried with their left arm positioned on the knee to support the head, while the women were buried near the door of their hut in a sitting position with their right arm positioned on their knee.

Kenyan American funerals usually do not vary greatly from the funerals of other Americans of their same religion.

EMPLOYMENT AND ECONOMIC CONDITIONS

The high value that Kenyan Americans place on education has allowed them to find skilled positions. Even during the initial adjustment period, Kenyans are less likely to need assistance than other immigrants, and they tend to have a high employment rate. Because most Kenyans are already fluent in English, they often have an advantage over other immigrant groups.

POLITICS AND GOVERNMENT

Kenya and the United States have maintained good relations since Kenya declared its independence in 1963. The United States has provided both political and financial support to Kenya. Kenyans and Americans alike were shocked when the U.S. Embassy was bombed in Nairobi in 1998. Both Americans and Kenyans lost their lives.

Relations with Kenya are important to Kenyan American immigrants. Most Kenyan Americans have left family and friends behind and thus have a personal connection to conditions in their home country. Kenyan Americans actively lobby to increase aid to Kenya. There are a number of organizations designed to provide such support. One is the Kenyan-American Chamber of Commerce (KACC), which was formed in 1999 from the existing Kenyan American

Association. KACC is an influential private investment company that strives to increase development of Kenyan communities through investments in technology, education, and other sectors and to promote trade and cultural relations between Kenya and the United States. The Kenya American Association is primarily financially focused. In addition to taking an aggressive investment stance to help Kenyans in the diaspora, it has a credit union for its members. The Kenyan American Philanthropic Association (KAPA) is a nonprofit organization dedicated to issues and challenges facing Kenya. KAPA works to provide adequate health care, potable drinking water, proper education, and job creation for the people of Kenya.

A similar organization is the American-Kenyan Educational Corporation. The corporation raises money to purchase textbooks and other items for primary school children and to help secondary school students pay their tuition. The corporation has also established a sponsor program in which individuals or businesses provide for the needs of an entire classroom.

NOTABLE INDIVIDUALS

Academia Ali Mazrui, political scientist, is a renowned expert on African politics. He was born in Kenya in 1933 and moved to the United States in 1974 to teach at the University of Michigan. In 1989 he was appointed the Albert Schweitzer Professor in the Humanities at the State University of New York, Binghamton.

Business Mwende Window Snyder (1975–) is a computer software engineer and senior security project manager at Apple Inc. She previously worked for Mozilla Corporation and coauthored *Threat Modeling*, a manual on application security. Her mother, Wayua Muasa, is from Kenya, and her father is an American.

Government U.S. president Barack Obama (1961–) was born to a Kenyan father (Barack Obama Sr.). Obama attended Harvard Law School, taught at the University of Chicago Law School, and served in the Illinois Senate and the U.S. Senate. In 2008 he was elected president, becoming the first African American in the country's history to hold that position.

Music Tom Morello, guitarist in the rock band Rage Against the Machine, is of Kikuyu, Irish, and Italian descent. He was born in Harlem, New York, in 1964. His father is Ngethe Njoroge, the nephew of Jomo Kenyatta, who took part in the Mau Mau rebellion and served as Kenya's first ambassador to the United Nations.

Sports Bernard Lagat (1974–), a middle- and long-distance athlete, was born in Kenya and had an athletic career their prior to his immigration to the United States. He is of Nandi Kalenjin descent. An Olympic gold medal winner, he has represented both Kenya and the United States in the Olympics.

Geoffrey Mutai (1981–), a Kenyan runner, was a record-holder in the marathon. He set his record in the 2001 Boston Marathon with a time of 2:03:02, and that same year he ran the New York City Marathon in 2:05:06. In general, Kenyans have come to dominate the marathon.

Stage and Screen Edi Gathegi (1979–), an actor, was born in Kenya and grew up in California. He is known for his recurring character, Dr. Jeffrey Cole, in the television series *House* and for his role as Laurent in the films *Twilight* and its sequel *The Twilight Saga: New Moon*.

ORGANIZATIONS AND ASSOCIATIONS

American Chamber of Commerce Kenya

A nonprofit organization founded by American investors in Kenya that promotes American investment there. An affiliate of the U.S. Chamber of Commerce, the organization seeks to coordinate business activity in order to promote the growth of not only companies but also the Kenyan economy.

P.O. Box 9746-00100
Nairobi, Kenya
Email: info@acck.org
URL: www.acck.org

Kenyan-American Chamber of Commerce (KACC)

An organization established in 1999 that is devoted to the development of communities in Kenya through investments in technology, education, and other sectors. It promotes trade and cultural relations between Kenya and the United States.

1875 I Street NW
5th Floor
Washington, D.C. 20006
Phone: (202) 591-9182
Email: together@kenya-uscc.org
URL: www.kenya-uscc.org

Kenyan American Philanthropic Association, Inc.

A nonprofit formed to work on issues and challenges facing Kenya.

Thairu Machua, President
Phone: (770) 771-4753
Email: info@kapainc.org
URL: www.kapainc.org

MUSEUMS AND RESEARCH CENTERS

Art Institute of Chicago

In addition to a substantial collection of traditional Kenyan art, the museum includes contemporary Kenyan art by Magdalene Odundo and others.

111 South Michigan Avenue
Chicago, Illinois 60603
Phone: (312) 443-3600
URL: www.artic.edu

National Museum of African Art

The collection includes a number of traditional Kenyan works of art, including jewelry, painted gourds, and sculpture.

950 Independence Avenue SW
Washington, D.C. 20560
Phone: (202) 633-4600
Fax: (202) 357-4879
Email: nmafaweb@si.edu
URL: africa.si.edu

Syracuse University Library

Contains a microfilm copy of the Kenyan National Archives, a collection of government documents.

222 Waverly Avenue
Syracuse University
Syracuse, New York 13244
Phone: (315) 443-2093
Fax: (315) 443-2060
Email: libref@syr.edu
URL: library.syr.edu

SOURCES FOR ADDITIONAL STUDY

Adam, Christopher, Paul Collier, and Njuguna Ndung'u. *Kenya: Policies for Prosperity*. New York: Oxford University Press, 2010.

Adamson, Joy. *The Peoples of Kenya*. New York: Harcourt, Brace & World, 1967.

Azevedo, Mario. *Kenya: The Land, The People, and the Nation*. Durham, NC: Carolina Academic Press, 1993.

Branch, Daniel. *Kenya: Between Hope and Despair, 1963–2011*. New Haven, CT: Yale University Press, 2011.

Kibua, Thomas N., and Germano M. Mwabu, eds. *Decentralization and Devolution in Kenya: New Approaches*. Nairobi: University of Nairobi Press, 2008.

Matua, Makau. *Kenya's Quest for Democracy: Taming Leviathan*. Boulder, CO: Lynne Rienner Publishers, 2008.

Maxon, Robert M., and Thomas P. Ofcansky. *Historical Dictionary of Kenya*, 2nd ed. Lanham, MD: Scarecrow Press, 2000.

Ochieng, William R., ed. *Themes in Kenyan History*. Athens: Ohio University Press, 1990.

Whiteley, W. H., ed. *Language in Kenya*. London: Oxford University Press, 1974.

KLAMATHS

Judson Knight

OVERVIEW

The Klamath Tribes, which include the Klamath, Modoc, and Yahuskin peoples, first occupied what is now southern Oregon and northern California. The Klamath tribe itself held a large area bounded by the headwaters of the Williamson River to the north and the Sprague River to the east and south, Crater Lake to the northwest, and Upper Klamath Lake to the southwest. Downstream were the Modocs, who lived near Lower Klamath Lake in an area whose general parameters included Lost River, Clear Lake, and Tule Lake to the west, Upper Klamath Lake to the north, Goose Lake to the east, and the Modoc Plateau to the south. Even less clearly defined was the homeland of the Yahuskin, farther to the south and east, near the Goose, Silver, Warner, and Harney lakes. The region consists of forests as well as wetlands and marshes. Running through much of the area is the Klamath River, which in one part is subject to such strong winds that it appears to flow upstream. The term *Klamath* comes from the language of the Chinook peoples to the north, but its meaning is unknown. The Klamath called themselves *maqlaqs* or "people" and referred to a neighboring tribe (who spoke a related language) as *moadokkni maklaks* or "southern people"—hence the term *Modoc*. The name of the Yahuskin is said to mean "crayfish-eaters," though the specific linguistic origin is unclear.

The number of people in the Klamath, Modoc, and Yahuskin tribes prior to contact with whites is not known, but according to mid-twentieth century estimates by anthropologists Leslie Spier and Theodore Stern, as well as tribal elders, the pre-contact population for all three groups would have been somewhere between 1,000 and 2,000. Though closely linked ethnically, the Klamaths and Modocs did not intermarry, and their relationship was cordial but not friendly, according to anthropologist Verne F. Ray. The Yahuskin, on the other hand, are a Shoshone tribe with a distinct cultural and linguistic heritage. The Yahuskin became a federally recognized Klamath tribe in 1864 when U.S. government established a reservation for the three groups. A key element of the Klamaths' traditional economy was the slave trade, which involved raids on tribes in the Pit River region of what is now California. The Klamaths were involved in an extensive trading network that put them in indirect contact with tribes throughout the Pacific Northwest. The Modoc and Yahuskin people subsisted by fishing, hunting, and gathering food.

In the twenty-first century, the Klamath Reservation consisted of twelve small, non-contiguous parcels of land in southern Oregon's Klamath County. Few of the tribe members lived on the reservation proper, but rather were scattered throughout the Klamath County and adjoining counties in southern Oregon and northern California. They remained close to the land where their ancestors lived, but their territories were greatly diminished from the 1.1 million acre (1,719 square miles; 4,452 square kilometers) Klamath Reservation established in an 1864 treaty with the federal government that brought the Klamath, Modoc, and Yahuskin together as the "Kamath Tribes." After the revocation of the treaty in 1954, the tribes went through a period of social and economic hardship, but began to revitalize in the 1970s and regained federal recognition as a tribal group in 1986.

Extrapolating from 2010 U.S. Census figures, there were roughly 5,000 persons in the Klamath, Modoc, and Yahuskin tribes. The Census reported 4,413 persons belonging to the "Klamath Indian Tribe of Oregon tribal grouping alone or in any combination"—a group that would include full-blooded Klamaths, persons of Klamath ancestry mixed with other ethnicities, Yahuskin, and most Modocs. The total population of the "Modoc tribal grouping alone or in any combination" was 1,732. However, there is some overlap between the numbers due to the fact that many Modocs were forced to relocate to Oklahoma in the aftermath of the 1872–1873 Modoc War. Aside from this group in Oklahoma, estimated at about 200, the vast majority of persons belonging to the Klamath Tribes in the early twenty-first century (including some 600 Modocs) live in southern Oregon.

HISTORY OF THE PEOPLE

Early History Archeological evidence indicates that the Klamath (pronounced "kluh-MATH") tribe settled along the headwaters of what became known as the Klamath, Williamson, and Sprague rivers in present-day southern Oregon between seven and ten thousand years ago. Farther south were the Modoc, who occupied the area between Lower Klamath Lake,

Tule Lake, and Lost River in what is now southeastern Oregon and northeastern California. Although the two groups were rivals, they were in fact close relatives: both spoke the Klamath-Modoc language, part of the Plateau Penutian family of Native American languages. The Yahuskin, on the other hand, spoke a Shoshonean language, which belongs to an entirely different linguistic family, the Uto-Aztecan. They were part of the group later dubbed "Snake Indians" by whites on the Oregon Trail, and their homeland lay to the south and east of the Klamath and Modoc, near the Goose, Silver, Warner, and Harney lakes.

These groups did not live in isolation from other peoples. Modoc lands adjoined those of the Shasta on the Klamath River, as well as the Karuk and Yurok downstream among others. The Yahuskin sometimes hunted with the Walpapi people, while the Klamath often launched raids against the Achomawi, sometimes taking them as slaves. They also conducted trade with the Chinookan peoples of what is now Oregon and Washington State. The Klamaths' first encounter with whites occurred in 1826, when Hudson's Bay Company (HBC) trapper Peter Skene Ogden traveled southward from the HBC regional outpost at Fort Vancouver along the Siskiyou Trail.

Nearly two decades passed before the next recorded interaction between whites and the Indians of the region. This occurred in 1843, when soldier and explorer John C. Frémont, along with his legendary guide Kit Carson, first entered Modoc lands. Forging the east-west route known as the Oregon Trail, they managed to pass through the area without major incident until the night of May 9, 1846, when a Modoc raiding party attacked their encampment on the shores of Klamath Lake, killing one member of their group. Frémont misidentified his antagonists, and in retaliation he and his men attacked a Klamath fishing village, killing men, women, and children.

Frémont's expedition was only the beginning of a massive migration into the region. During the late 1840s some 400,000 settlers arrived from the east via the Oregon Trail, even as the discovery of gold in California brought in thousands of prospectors to the south. In 1850 a Modoc attack on a group of whites near Tule Lake to the southeast of Klamath lands killed some eighty people and earned their tribe a reputation for violence such that they were blamed for incidents with which they had nothing to do. Thus, they became the target of a group of miners, led by Ben Wright, in a September 1852 attack that claimed forty-one Modoc lives.

The outbreak of the Civil War in 1860 had little direct impact on most tribes in Oregon, which had become a state the previous year. From the perspective of the indigenous people living in the Northwest, the most important collateral effect of the hostilities in the East was the removal of federal troops from the region and their replacement by local militias. Near the end of the war, however, the region experienced the Snake War (1864–1868), a series of battles between the U.S. Army and Indian groups that included the Yahuskin. Though overshadowed by events in the East and therefore largely forgotten, its 1,762 deaths made this conflict the bloodiest of the Indian Wars in the American West.

Modern Era In 1864 the U.S. government negotiated a treaty with the Klamath, Modoc, and Yahuskin peoples that put the three groups together on the newly established Klamath Reservation. The reservation was created out of Klamath lands to the northeast of Upper Klamath Lake, while the federal government took title to a much larger area surrounding the reservation. In return, the tribes were to receive cash payments, various supplies, and a number of guarantees. Signed on October 14, the treaty sparked a bloody war between the Modoc tribe and the U.S. Army, after which the treaty remained in force for ninety years.

Although the Modocs signed the treaty, a faction that included the Modoc chief Kintpuash (whose name is translated "Strikes the Water Brashly," and who was known to whites as Captain Jack) rejected its terms. The Modocs returned to their ancestral lands, but after much persuasion they agreed to take their place on the Klamath Reservation at the end of 1869. They made an attempt to establish a settlement on Modoc Point, the area of the reservation that had been assigned to them. However, the Modocs found themselves in continual conflict with the Klamath, and after several attempts to relocate within the reservation, Kintpuash and his band headed south again in April 1870. The federal government demanded that the Modocs take their place on the reservation. On November 29, 1872, a military force, along with a small militia unit and civilians, engaged the Modocs at Lost River. Only two Modocs died in the encounter, and the Battle of Lost River was to be the first in a string of Modoc victories.

The Modocs subsequently took up a position in the Lava Beds near Tule Lake—the entire conflict is sometimes called the Lava Beds War—and the army began preparing to attack Kintpuash's hideout, known as "Captain Jack's Stronghold." The Modocs surprised a militia raiding party in December, killing all 23. Shortly after, in the First Battle of the Stronghold on January 17, 1873, a group of 52 Modoc warriors held off a cavalry force of 400, killing 35 and suffering no deaths of their own.

In the weeks that followed, the federal government organized a peace commission that included General Edward Canby, Reverend Eleazer Thomas, and interpreters Toby Riddle and her husband, Frank Riddle. Toby Riddle, known as Winema (meaning "woman chief"), was a Modoc; Frank Riddle was a white settler. Meanwhile, Kintpuash, under pressure from other Modoc leaders, made plans for a surprise attack on the peace commission, and when Toby Riddle got word of it, she informed the commissioners. Nevertheless, Thomas insisted on holding the meeting, which occurred on April 11, 1873. In the middle of an argument between the Indians and the whites, two Modoc warriors rushed in and opened fire, killing both Thomas and Canby.

Some 675 troops attacked the Modocs in the Second Battle of the Stronghold (April 15–17), but the main body of warriors managed to escape. The Modocs' string of victories ended with the loss of five warriors at the Battle of Dry Lake on May 10. Morale plunged. A warrior known as Hooker Jim surrendered and, in exchange for amnesty, helped the army capture Kintpuash. By early summer they had rounded up the entire Modoc force, along with their women and children, and transported them to Fort Klamath between Crater Lake and Upper Klamath Lake.

After a trial, Kintpuash and three other warriors were hanged on October 3, 1873, and two others were sentenced to life imprisonment at Alcatraz in San Francisco. The remaining Modocs, a group of 163 men, women, and children, were transported to Indian Territory (present-day Oklahoma), where they remained until 1909. At that time, they received the option of returning to Oregon, but only twenty-nine of them did. (In fact, some had already made their way back to their homeland without federal permission.)

Although the Modocs and the U.S. Army both suffered heavy losses in the Modoc War, the Klamath and Yahuskin peoples prospered in the latter part of the nineteenth century. Their land was rich in timber, and the tribe and its members enjoyed lucrative earnings. Yet they too saw their way of life erode as more whites moved into Klamath lands, not as invaders but as workers in the lumber mills. Other threats were to come in the early twentieth century, with the building of six dams that hindered the flow of the Klamath River and gradually reduced its fish population. Federal measures such as dam building violated the treaty the government had signed with the Klamath in 1864, in which the government had promised to protect the deer population and the fisheries on the 2.2 million acres allotted to the tribes.

Outside business interests aggressively lobbied the government to capitalize on the vast natural resources on the Klamath Reservation, and in 1954 Congress rescinded the 1864 treaty with the Klamath Termination Act, which brought the Klamath Reservation to an end. The legislation allowed tribe members to take a monthly payment in exchange for their tribal lands, and more than 1,600 people— about 75 percent of the Klamath Tribes' population at the time—chose to do so. The termination process spanned 1954 to 1961, and in the aftermath of this devastating procedure the once-wealthy Klamath Tribes fell into poverty. According to the Klamath Tribes website, in 1953 the average individual income

A Klamath woman sitting on rush mats in front of her home, c. 1923. BUYENLARGE / GETTY IMAGES

among tribe members was 93 percent of the average income in the United States, and in 1957 there were only four people on the reservation receiving any kind of federally funded assistance. However, within a few years after they had been cut off from the resources on their lands, many tribal members were left destitute. Culturally, the concept of the tribes began to lose meaning as individuals went their separate ways into mainstream American culture, where they encountered racial prejudice and fell prey to dishonest businessmen. Having been raised on the Klamath Reservation, tribal members were ill prepared for American consumer culture and often found themselves burdened with debt and overwhelmed by contemporary technology.

The tide began to turn in the Klamaths' favor during the mid-1970s, however, as a U.S. district court upheld their right to continue hunting and fishing on former tribal lands. For years Klamath activists relentlessly petitioned local, state, and national politicians for the restoration of tribal status. In 1986 Congress passed the Klamath Restoration Act, which reversed the Termination Act of 1954 and once again conferred tribal status upon the Klamath. The Klamath Tribes estimated that they lost $148 million during the twenty-five year period of termination. During the same period, the Modoc Tribe of Oklahoma received official recognition (1978), and the federal government approved its constitution (1991).

At the turn of the twentieth century, as the Klamath Tribes sought to resume control of areas controlled by their ancestors, they faced a number of challenges. One was the fact that the properties of the former Klamath Reservation had been splintered into about a dozen noncontiguous pieces that together constituted a fraction of the vast tract they had once claimed—just over 309 acres, or about 1.25 square kilometers. Another issue was the damming of the

Klamath River, which diverted water to agricultural use and caused its population of salmon and other fish to plummet. A lengthy legal battle ensued, with the Klamath and environmentalists and fishermen on one side, and on the other side a coalition of farmers and others who supported the use of hydroelectric dams on the river. In February 2010 the various groups reached an agreement to remove four dams, pending a full study regarding the costs and benefits. At the end of 2012 they agreed to continue the study before taking action.

SETTLEMENT IN THE UNITED STATES

The Klamath, Modoc, and Yahuskin peoples are among the many tribes known as Plateau Indians. The latter were indigenous to an intermontane (that is, between mountains) region within what is now northeastern California, eastern Oregon and Washington, western Montana, northern Idaho, and central and southeastern British Columbia. The defining geographic features of this region are the inland basins of the Columbia and Fraser rivers as well as the eastern flank of the Cascade Mountains.

The homeland of the Klamath, Modoc, and Yahuskin peoples—the three groups that would later make up the Klamath Tribes—is located in southern Oregon and northern California. According to the Klamath Tribes website, the three tribes occupied an area of 22 million acres prior to contact with Europeans. Other groups in the region included the Takelma, the Upper Umpqua, and the Molala, all of whom lived on the western side of Crater Lake in south-central Oregon and were eventually exterminated by whites. Although they were not destroyed, the Klamath lost a great deal of their land to the outsiders who began entering the area at the beginning of the nineteenth century. The federal government regarded the tribes as violent and dangerous due to numerous hostile encounters between the native people and the white settlers coming via the Oregon Trail over the first half of the nineteenth century.

In 1864 the Klamath, Modoc, and Yahuskin tribes were combined, and their collective holdings were reduced to a 2.2-million-acre reservation in south-central Oregon near the Upper Klamath Lake, east of the Cascade Mountains. During the termination of the Klamath Tribes and the dispersal of the people, which lasted from 1954 to 1961, the U.S. government claimed 866,000 acres of land rich with ponderosa pine and declared the area to be national forest land. The remaining lands were to be administered by a private trustee appointed by the government. Many Klamath now believe that these lands were managed in a way that deliberately confused the Klamath people and led them to be defrauded of their property.

During the termination process, the U.S. government allowed the Klamath people to choose one of two courses of action. They could either declare themselves to be "withdrawing members" and accept a cash payment, or they could maintain an interest in the tribal estate, which was to be overseen by the government-appointed trustee. The tribal estate, in turn, was to be subdivided into two parcels, one of which would be sold to private investors to raise the cash to pay withdrawing members, and another that would be managed by the trustee. The government stipulated that plots of the tribal estate to be put on the market could be no smaller than 5,000 acres, which made it unlikely that any withdrawing Klamath could afford to buy any land. As a result, 78 percent of the Klamath chose to be "withdrawing members" and accepted the cash payout. Part of the confusion, according to some in the Klamath tribe, was that many of those who opted to withdraw and accept cash were not aware of the government provision that no plot of resold land would be less than 5,000 acres. In 1986 Congress rescinded the Termination Act, recognized the Klamath Tribes, and returned some of their lands in the form of twelve noncontiguous plots consisting of 309 acres. As of 2011 most Klamath tribal members still lived in southern Oregon.

In 1872, eight years after signing the 1864 treaty, the Modocs entered into a conflict with the federal government known both as the Modoc War and the Lava Beds War. In 1873, after the uprising had been quelled, 163 Modocs, including 39 men, 64 women, and 60 children, were transported on cattle cars to Oklahoma, where the government placed them on a 4,000-acre (6.25 square miles; 16.2 square kilometers) reservation purchased from the Eastern Shawnee in northeastern Oklahoma's Ottawa County. Their neighbors included the Cherokee Nation, who had been forcibly relocated from Georgia in 1836. In an effort to reduce corruption in Indian affairs, the government placed Modoc administration in the hands of such religious groups as the Society of Friends, or Quakers. Despite some negative experiences with Quaker leadership, the Modocs became active in the Society of Friends, and by 1881 most members of the group had converted. In 1909, two years after Oklahoma became a state, the federal government allowed the Modocs to return to Oregon. Records showed that twenty-nine people did so, though a few had already returned prior to that time. All Modocs, both in Oklahoma and Oregon, remained under the Klamath Tribes until the 1954 Termination Act. In May 1978 the federal government formally recognized the Modoc tribe in Oklahoma, and in 1991 the government approved their constitution. By 2011 an estimated 200 Modocs lived in Oklahoma, and about 600 lived in Oregon.

LANGUAGE

The Klamaths and Modocs traditionally spoke two different dialects of the same language, variously referred to as Klamath-Modoc, Lutuamian, or Klamath. The language belongs to the Plateau Penutian branch of the Penutian language family. The latter comprises

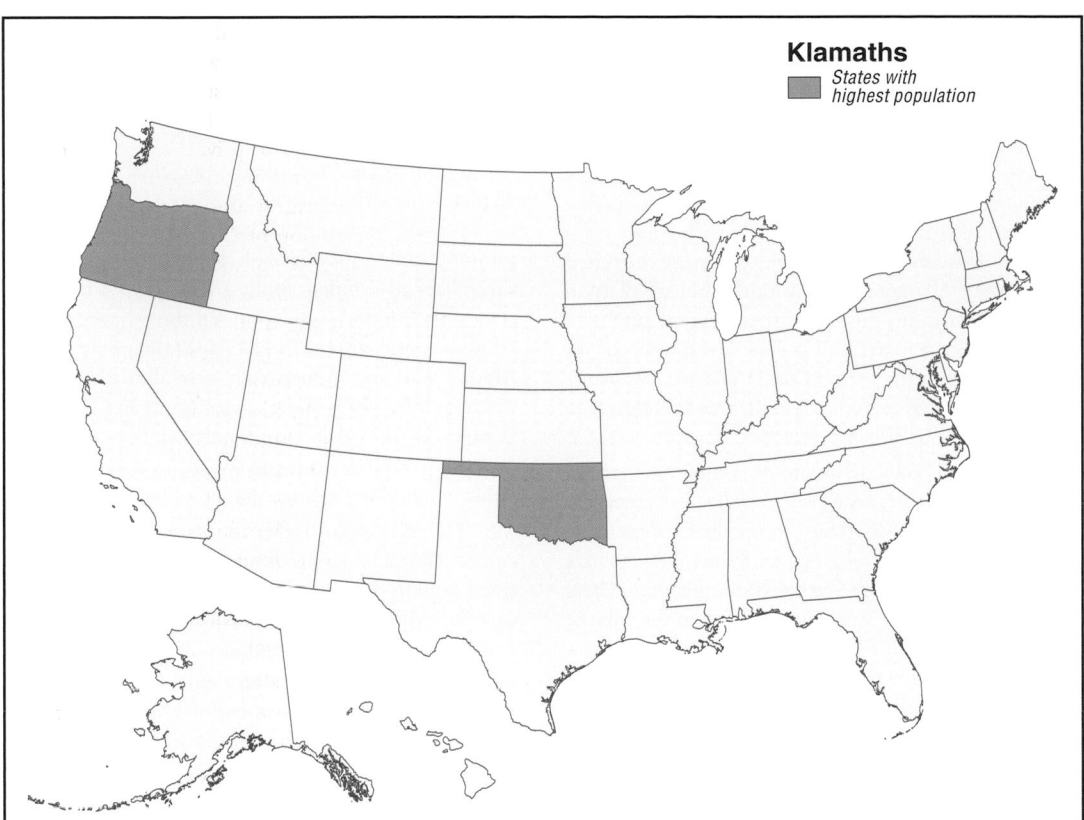

Klamaths
States with
highest population

numerous languages spoken by indigenous peoples along the Pacific coast of North America, primarily in what is now northern British Columbia, southern Washington State, Oregon, and central and southern California.

Because they were a small group to begin with and were later absorbed by the Klamath Tribes, little data is available regarding the Yahuskins' language. They were a Shoshonean people, part of a vast group of tribes who occupied much of what is now the northwestern United States. The Shoshone language belonged to the Numic sub-branch of the Uto-Aztecan family, which comprised more than thirty languages spoken by people across a wide area of what is now the western United States and northern Mexico. In modern times, the Klamath Tribes have made an effort to preserve their native language. In 2013 their tribal website had a page on the language, with information and a guide to available resources, including online lessons, a booklet, and a CD.

RELIGION

Little is known about the traditional religion of the Modocs or the Yahuskin, though that of the Klamaths may provide some clues, especially inasmuch as the Klamaths and Modocs were related peoples. Even in the case of the Klamaths, however, the information available is sketchy and primarily the result of anthropological study because the tribe did not pass down a codified set of beliefs. Moreover, theirs was a faith that was more concerned with objects and experiences than with specific deities.

Anthropologist Verne F. Ray has noted that in both Klamath and Modoc cultures, there was considerable emphasis on "making artificial rock piles for religious or commemorative purposes and for attributing mythological significance to rock piles of unknown origin." As with many indigenous peoples, the spiritual life of the Klamath involved the quest for spirit power through association with specific creatures or other natural phenomena. These included, according to ethnographer Leslie Spier, "predominantly birds and animals, winds, lightning and the like, and a handful of anthropomorphic beings." They also believed that a spiritual seeker could receive wisdom through songs heard in dreams.

The Klamaths employed the ritual of the vision quest common to a number of Native American religious systems. Vision quests took two basic forms. There was first and foremost the vision quest as a rite of passage upon reaching puberty, but people or families might also make such a journey at a time of crisis. The choice of the locale for the quest was not arbitrary, but rather involved consideration with regard to the spirits believed to inhabit a particular area. Vision quests typically involved separating oneself from the group and seeking spirits in nature: "Power is sought in lonely spots in the mountains," wrote Spier, "in mountain pools, in eddies in the rivers, in all places where spirits are known to dwell."

The Klamath practiced a shamanistic religion, or one involving revelations delivered by a shaman or holy man who was believed to communicate directly with the spirit world. Called *qyoqs* or specialists, these "medicine men" were usually but not always males. They served a medical function, but they also led a number of rituals and ceremonies and were consulted on a variety of matters. They might be called upon to interpret dreams, give a weather forecast, or advise tribal leaders on matters of policy. *Qyoqs* often delivered messages in the form of songs and were not only respected but also feared, since they were believed to possess enormous power to do good or evil.

With the encroachment of white civilization, Klamath religion began to evolve. This was especially the case after the 1864 treaty, as members of the tribe became involved in religious movements that were then gaining popularity among Native peoples. These included the Ghost Dance, which reached the tribe in 1871, and the Earth Lodge Cult in 1874. Such movements had a distinctly millenarian quality, meaning that they pointed toward cataclysmic future events and provided adherents with a doctrine that called for revolution both in spiritual and earthly terms.

The Ghost Dance movement, which originated among the Northern Paiutes (to whom the Yahuskin were closely linked), taught that if adherents practiced certain mystical dances properly, they would bring the dead to life. Similarly, the Earth Lodge movement

In order to properly benefit from their timber assets, the Klamaths had to allow the outside world to intrude on their lands. This meant not only the introduction of railroad lines but also the establishment of mill towns on Klamath lands, such that by the early twentieth century whites outnumbered Indians on the Klamath Reservation.

involved the idea that believers' ancestors would come back to life at the end of the world. Implicit in these belief systems was the promise that a coming spiritual transformation of the world would remove the white presence from Indians' lives. By contrast, the Dream Dance, which arose among the Klamath in the early twentieth century, was much more personal and less apocalyptic. Dream interpretation and visions of the dead were central aspects of this movement.

In 1914 the Indian Shaker Church, a movement that combined Christian and traditional elements, reached the Klamath. It would remain an influential force in Klamath religious life for several decades. By the mid-twentieth century, many Klamaths had embraced Christianity. An example was Ramona Soto Rank, who was briefly a national celebrity when she

won the Miss Indian America pageant in 1962. Rank later became a Lutheran minister and incorporated traditional Indian elements into the liturgy.

CULTURE AND ASSIMILATION

Much more is known about the traditional ways of the Klamath than those of the Modoc or the Yahuskin, in large part because the Klamath held the dominant position among the Klamath Tribes group created by the federal government in the 1864 treaty. A large portion of the Modoc population, on the other hand, was removed to Oklahoma in 1873 after their defeat in the Modoc War, and though they were allowed to return to Oregon in 1909, many chose to stay in Oklahoma. Separation from their homeland, combined with the traumas of removal and adjustment to a new environment, resulted in a loss of contact with their traditions.

The Klamaths followed an entirely different course. With its thousands of acres rich in timber, the Klamath Reservation became a source of great wealth in the mid-twentieth century, and its residents enjoyed prosperity unusual among indigenous peoples. Yet they too lost contact with traditional ways, though in their case it was not hardship but good fortune that dissipated their connection to the past. In order to properly benefit from their timber assets, the Klamaths had to allow the outside world to intrude on their lands. This meant not only the introduction of railroad lines but also the establishment of mill towns on Klamath lands, such that by the early twentieth century whites outnumbered Indians on the Klamath Reservation.

Traditions and Customs On one level, Klamath culture was shaped by its specific environment, which included marsh, lake, and river. This gave rise to such aspects as the importance of fish and pond-lily seeds or *wokas* in their diet. Yet their territory lay in an area where several indigenous cultures—Plateau, Great Basin, Northwest Coast, and California—intersected, and their culture reflected these disparate influences. For example, like the peoples of what became California, their society tended to be loosely organized around small hamlets, whereas their shamanistic religion was more reflective of traditions among the Plateau peoples.

Myth played a central role in Klamath spiritual and social life. The principal time for relating these tales was winter, when families gathered indoors. "The usual setting for Klamath myth-narration," wrote anthropologist Theodore Stern, "was the dark interior of a lodge, on a cold winter night when the earth lay snowbound. This was the season of social gatherings, the period when shamanistic performances drew many spectators of all ages together." The Modocs had their own mythology, whose central figure was a creator god known as Kumush. Among the myths handed down among the Modoc people were stories of creation and how old age and death came into the world. The Modocs told tales about the origin of snowstorm spirits known as Witsduks, and about a time when grizzly bears walked upright and a woman married a bear.

Cuisine Prior to contact with whites, the Klamaths survived by hunting, fishing, and gathering, with the last of these having the greatest importance. They migrated throughout the region in search of edible vegetables and fruits such as camas or camassia (*Camassia quamash*), *ipos* or *epos* (*Perideridia oregana*), bitterroot, kouse root, chokecherry, huckleberry, and wild strawberry.

Most important of all was *wokas*, the seed of the yellow water lily (*Nuphar polysepala*), which has remained a delicacy in modern times. The lily grows abundantly in marshes, from whence the Klamaths gathered *wokas* by canoe in late August and throughout September. Sticky when raw, the seeds were placed in a pit about two feet deep and two feet across and covered with a mat. More seeds were added throughout the season, such that they fermented together. At the end of the season the pits were emptied and the seeds mixed with water so as to separate them from the sticky substance. They were then dried and partially cooked, after which the kernels were cracked and separated from the hulls. A more thorough drying process followed, and the seeds were stored for some time before being cooked to the point where they burst. Roasted wokas could be eaten dry or ground and used to prepare porridge or bread. Seeds could be stored and eaten throughout the year, which was important for people living in subsistence conditions.

The rivers of the area provided abundant salmon, rainbow trout, and suckers. The last of these—known to the Klamath as *c'waam* or *qapdo* and to outsiders as Lost River suckers, shortnose suckers, or mullet—have been such an important part of tribal life that the group still holds an annual Return of the C'waam ceremony in spring. Spring was the principal season for fishing, just as late summer and early fall were concerned with the gathering of wokas.

The arrival of whites in the early nineteenth century introduced the Klamath to the horse, which expanded their diet not so much because of its use in hunting (at least at first) but because it made possible expanded travel and hence trade. Through contact with native peoples on the plains beyond the Rocky Mountains to the east, the Klamath obtained bison. As time went on, Klamath hunters began riding great distances to hunt for bison, deer, and elk themselves.

Traditional Dress Prior to contact with whites, the people of the Klamath, Modoc, and Yahuskin tribes dressed in a fashion similar to that of other indigenous peoples of the region or North America in general. In the cold, damp climate of the Pacific Northwest, men would have worn leather leggings or perhaps fur trousers. Woman would have worn skirts or leggings, as well as tunics or mantles for shirts. Men

KMUKAMPSH, THE TRICKSTER

Klamath mythology features many stories about Kmukampsh, a trickster figure who serves the functions, according to anthropologist Theodore Stern, of "culture hero, creator, ordainer of the present order." Stories about Kmukampsh relate his mischievous and lecherous nature. A number of these mention his impressive penis, and one of the more popular myths involves his attempt to seduce his foster son's wife. Having magically transported the son, Aisis, into the sky, Kmukampsh impersonates him in the bedroom. Aisis finally gets back to earth, where he tricks and destroys Kmukampsh, but it is clear that the trickster will simply return to life and cause more trouble.

Another myth tells about how the playful activities of Kmukampsh and his friend Gopher created the physical world of the Klamath. Others describe how Kmukampsh had assigned specific natural objects to particular groups of people: for example, the Klamaths themselves are associated with tules or bulrushes, which grow in swamplands. Other animal figures in the myths of the early Klamaths include Mink and his older brother Weasel as well as Coyote, Skunk, Bear, and Owl.

did not wear shirts, though they might wrap themselves in cloaks during cold weather. As with most native peoples, both sexes wore moccasins and *mukluks*, or heavy boots.

With the arrival of whites, styles of clothing changed for the Klamath as they did for most indigenous peoples. Not only did they adopt European garments in many cases, modifying them with native touches such as beadwork and embroidery, but contact with other tribes also led to the borrowing of fashions such as fringed buckskin, which spread beyond the peoples among whom they had originated.

In modern times, members of the Klamath Tribes, like most Native Americans, dress in typical apparel worn by other Americans except on special occasions, when they might don tribal regalia. The term "regalia" is preferred to "clothing" or especially "costume," with its suggestion of an outfit worn simply to elicit a reaction from others. Regalia, on the other hand, conveys the idea of traditional clothing with a ceremonial purpose.

Dances and Songs As with their clothing, many of the Klamaths' dances come from other regions of the United States and are not specifically Klamath. An example is the jingle dress dance for women, which originated among the woodland tribes of Minnesota and Wisconsin, where dancers used the lids of snoose (chewing tobacco) cans to make the jingling sound.

In the 1950s ethnomusicologist Bruno Nettl studied the music of the Great Basin, which includes the homelands of the Modoc, Klamath, and Yahuskin. He described the music of these peoples as being "extremely simple," with songs built around single repeated phrases. In many cases a range smaller than an octave was used, while some songs of the Modoc or Klamath used just two or three notes.

Holidays After New Year's Day, the first holiday of the year on the Klamath Tribes' calendar is the Annual Return of the C'waam Ceremony, which occurs after the first big snow in March in the town of Chiloquin, Oregon. Every year the fish known as suckers or *c'waam* swim up the Sprague River to spawn, and around the same time the "fish constellation" (Orion's Belt) begins appearing in the southwestern sky. According to Klamath tradition, spirit watchmen, or *swaso.llalalYampgis*, stood on the riverbanks waiting to see exactly when the fish returned, and the head shaman of the tribe would give thanks for their return. The celebration includes traditional dancing and drumming, the release of a pair of c'waam into the river, a feast, and other ceremonial events. In the twenty-first century, members chosen by the tribal leadership join tribal elders in performing the ceremony.

Also in March, the tribe holds its annual Peak-to-Peak World Championship basketball tournament. This has gone on since 1963 in Chiloquin, where every year sixteen men's and women's teams from throughout the United States and Canada gather for friendly competition. In the fourth weekend of August is the Restoration Celebration, which commemorates the official restoration of the Klamath Tribes on August 27, 1986. Events at the Twenty-sixth Annual Restoration Celebration in 2012 included a parade, powwow, youth rodeo, fun run/walk, and performances by Indian drummers from around the United States.

Health Care Issues and Practices In traditional Klamath society, health (as well as a number of other functions) fell within the purview of the shaman or medicine man (who was not always a man). These *qyoqs*, as they were called, treated the sick and presided over "doctor-dances" held in the communal dance house as a way of protecting the health of the community. Other functions peripheral to health care included consultation on dreams, weather forecasting, and providing advice during the pond-lily harvesting season.

Health care concerns among the Klamath in modern times include issues that plague much of American society, including overeating and its attendant risks, as well as the effects of tobacco and alcohol. The Klamath Tribes are particularly concerned about tobacco and alcohol dependency, and they use public events and platforms as a means of driving home a message of abstinence and sobriety. The official tribal commemoration of New Year's Eve includes a "sobriety celebration" in which the tribe crowns its "sobriety queen."

FAMILY AND COMMUNITY LIFE

A Klamath village typically centered around one or more families extended bilaterally—that is, with relatives on both sides. The leader was the wealthiest or most influential male head of household, or *laqi*. Membership in the household did not follow rigid rules; rather, households could include the nuclear family of the senior male as well as his wife or wives' relatives, elderly parents, grown children and grandchildren of the senior male, and even friends.

Gender Roles As in most societies, males had a dominant position among the Klamath: for instance, they could take multiple wives, and leadership in traditional Klamath society was almost exclusively male. However, there were many exceptions to this pattern. Shamans, though usually male, could be female. Females held specific roles: for instance, the picking of wokas in the late summer and early fall—an important function, given the significance of those seeds as a staple of the Klamath diet—was performed exclusively by females. Likewise, myth-telling, when not performed by the shaman, seems to have been within the purview of females.

Education The American Community Survey (ACS) estimates for 2006–2010 showed that, among Klamath people twenty-five years of age and over, almost 83 percent were at least high school graduates (a figure only slightly lower than the national rate of 85 percent during the same period). However, only about 13 percent held bachelor's degrees or higher (less than half the national rate of 27.9 percent), and only 3 percent had graduate or professional degrees (while the national rate was 10.3 percent).

Courtship and Weddings In traditional Klamath society, polygyny—the marriage of one man to multiple wives—was permitted. Sororal polygyny, or marriage of one man to two or more sisters, was not uncommon. The same was true of the levirate, or the marriage of a widow to her late husband's younger brother; though not considered obligatory, it was viewed as appropriate in Klamath society.

Marriage involved the exchange of gifts between families, with the bride's family expected to provide more than that of the groom. Girls usually married within a year of reaching puberty. A couple might have already been betrothed prior to adolescence, and in some cases the husband-to-be might be significantly older than the bride. It was not necessary to obtain the consent of the female. Young women were not likely to have received much sexual education, though puberty rituals might involve introduction to songs known as *pilpil* that contained lyrics describing the particulars of courting, desire, and romantic ecstasy and frustration.

In the wedding ceremony, brides wore dresses of various colors, each with symbolic significance. White represented the east, blue the south, yellow or orange the west, and black the north. Both bride and groom wore turquoise and silver jewelry, which the Klamath considered to be protection against bad luck, hunger, and poverty. Upon marrying, residence was typically uxorilocal, or with the wife's parents. This typically became virilocal (with the parents of the husband) after the birth of children or the acquisition of significant wealth.

EMPLOYMENT AND ECONOMIC CONDITIONS

With the signing of the 1864 treaty that established the Klamath Reservation, the timber industry became an important source of income for the Klamath, but it was not the only one. The Klamath had engaged in ranching even before the reservation was created, and afterward they began to expand their ranching activities with large numbers of horses and cattle. Members of the tribe also received vocational training on the reservation and held jobs in the town of Linkville (as Klamath Falls was then known) as well as at Fort Klamath.

Taking advantage of their precontact trading experience, the Klamath of the late nineteenth century became involved in shipping and trade throughout the local area. According to the tribe's website, by the 1950s the Klamath Tribes were among the wealthiest in the United States and were entirely self-sufficient, paying for all government services used by tribe members. The termination of the reservation in 1954 proved devastating to the Klamath in a number of ways, not least of which was its economic impact. In 1970 a team of economists studied the allocation of funds paid to the tribe and concluded that, despite the cash payouts, the Klamath received no long-term benefits from termination.

In the late twentieth and early twenty-first centuries, however, a number of economic developments benefitted the Klamath Tribes. The reinstatement of the tribes in 1986 brought with it an influx of federal aid money. In 2002 the Klamath received a grant from the Indian Land Tenure Foundation, established by the heirs of the nineteenth-century railroad tycoon James J. Hill, whose Great Northern Railroad and other lines often ran through native lands. The $115,000 from the foundation helped the Klamath Tribes begin negotiating to reclaim another 692,000 acres. Also in the early twenty-first century, support from the Trust for Public Land, a nonprofit land-conservation group, enabled the Klamath Tribes to enter into negotiations to buy back the 90,000-acre (139 square miles; 360 square kilometers) Mazama Forest. Additionally, the Tribes opened the Kla-Mo-Ya Casino, whose name is a portmanteau of Klamath-Modoc-Yahuskin, in 1997.

Nevertheless, statistics showed that, in the early twenty-first century, the Klamath were significantly less wealthy than the U.S. population as a whole. According to the U.S. Census Bureau's American Community Survey (ACS) estimates for 2006–2010, the median income for Klamath households was $31,333—only about 60 percent of the nationwide median household income, which was $52,762 during the period 2007–2011. The per capita income among Klamaths was $14,149, or about half the national figure of $27,915. More than 40 percent of Klamath households received food stamps or other forms of public assistance.

POLITICS AND GOVERNMENT

After the passage of the Termination Act, some Klamath tried to assert their hunting and fishing rights, but a U.S. district court ruled against them. They appealed this in *Kimball v. Callahan* (1974), and the U.S. District Court of Appeals of the Ninth Circuit ruled in their favor, finding that the Klamath Termination Act did not explicitly remove their hunting and fishing rights. In the last quarter of the twentieth century, the Klamath, spurred on by other examples of Native American activism, reorganized their government. Thanks in part to their efforts, in 1986 Congress rescinded the Termination Act, reestablishing the Klamath as a tribe with federal recognition and making them eligible for a number of economic, educational, and medical programs.

In the twenty-first century, the peoples of the Klamath, Modoc, and Yahuskin tribes have two separate tribal governments. The larger of these, serving those who live in the tribes' traditional homeland in Oregon, is known simply as the Klamath Tribes. Its annual budget is about $12 million. Tribal administration includes some thirty different departments and services involved in matters ranging from education and employment to preservation of the tribes' native culture. A general manager directs day-to-day operations, with oversight from an elected Tribal Council that in 2013 consisted of ten members. Economic self-sufficiency is a principal aim of tribal government.

The single most important political issue for the Klamath Tribes of Oregon in the early twenty-first century is the damming of the Klamath River and its effect on the fish population and the water supply. It is a problem that goes back more than a century, to 1906 and the beginnings of the federal government's Klamath Reclamation Project. The latter involved the construction of dams—a total of six between 1908 and 1962—on the river and its tributaries, as well as the draining of Lower Klamath and Tule lakes, in an effort to provide more water for irrigation.

By the turn of the century the river, once the third-largest producer of salmon on the West Coast, as well as an abundant source of trout, had been so tamed by dams that its coho salmon had been listed as threatened under the Endangered Species Act. The Klamath and other native peoples, along with a number of conservationists and fishermen, began lobbying for removal of the dams. In January 2007 the federal government ruled that PacifiCorp, which operated the dams, had to equip four dams with fish ladders to allow the salmon to move upstream.

A separate but clearly related controversy involved the use of waters from the Upper Klamath Basin for irrigated agriculture. This practice had been halted during a drought in 2001 so as to protect endangered salmon and lake fish, but U.S. vice president Dick Cheney intervened personally on behalf of local farmers. Although Klamath leaders argued that their treaty rights predated those of the farmers, the secretary of the Interior, Gale Norton, upheld the rights of the farmers. The Klamath River experienced its biggest die-off of fish that year. Meanwhile, local farmers petitioned the courts in a series of cases, but in 2002 a federal judge ruled that the Klamath Tribes' right to the use of the waters had precedent over that of the farmers.

Disputes over water rights continued over the next decade, and eventually the issue of the dams seemed close to resolution. After two years of negotiations, all sides reached an agreement on February 18, 2010, for removal of four dams, which would open up some 300 miles (480 kilometers) of river, by 2020. PacifiCorp would pay part of the estimated $800 million cost, with the State of California covering the rest.

NOTABLE INDIVIDUALS

Government Toby "Winema" Riddle (1848–1920) was an interpreter for the U.S. government. Born Nannookdoowah ("Strange Child"), a name given to her because of her unusual red-tinted hair, she earned the nickname Winema ("Woman Chief") after saving some playmates from drowning. She married white settler Frank Riddle, and together they served as interpreters before and during the negotiations that resulted in the October 1864 treaty that created the Klamath Reservation. Later, the Riddles interpreted for the peace commission that was attempting to bring an end to the Modoc War in 1873. In 1891 she became one of a very few Indian women awarded a military pension by U.S. Congress in recognition of her heroism during the 1873 attack.

Bogus Charley (c. 1852–1881) was a Modoc warrior and, later, chief of the Modocs in Oklahoma. His Indian name is not known, and it is believed that his nickname came from his penchant for playing practical jokes. Highly fluent in English, he often served as interpreter for Kintpuash.

Old Schonchin (1797–1892) was the head chief of the Modocs at the time of the Modoc War. Called Old Schonchin to distinguish himself from his brother, Schonchin John, he was born at Tule Lake long before contact with whites. Schonchin eventually emerged as a Modoc leader, but because his leadership was not hereditary, he faced challenges to his authority. By 1846 he was in command of some 600 warriors and led aggressive attacks against whites.

Scarfaced Charley (c. 1851–1896) was a Modoc chief who took leadership of the tribe after their removal to Oklahoma. His Indian name was Chic-chack-am or Lul-al-kuel-atko. Believed to have fired the opening shot of the Modoc War at the Battle of Lost River on November 29, 1872, Charley led an attack on a patrol of sixty-three soldiers on April 26, 1873, killing all five officers and twenty others. Then, however, he is said to have told the remaining whites, "We've killed enough of you, now go home." A skilled artisan, Charley designed the typeface for the phonetic transliteration of the Modoc language and developed a lucrative line of furniture in a traditional style.

Military Boston Charley (1854–1873) was a Modoc warrior. Reportedly, white miners gave him his nickname due to his light complexion, which made him look like a white person. Boston Charley fought in Kintpuash's band of warriors during the Modoc War, and on April 11, 1873, he participated in the surprise attack on the peace commission.

Kintpuash, also known as Captain Jack (1837–1873), was a Modoc chief and leader during the Modoc War. Dissatisfied with the 1864 treaty that created the Klamath Tribes, Kintpuash led a contingent of Modocs who returned to their traditional lands. After much persuasion, he brought the group to the Klamath Reservation in 1869, but relations with the Klamath were so bad that Kintpuash and his followers left once more, never to return. Kintpuash was ultimately betrayed by fellow Modoc leaders. Captured on June 1, he was taken to Fort Klamath, tried, and hanged along with three others on October 3.

Schonchin John (c. 1828–1873) was one of the leaders in the Modoc War. He played a key role by influencing the others to continue fighting and reject Kintpuash's efforts to make peace. A major instigator of the April 11, 1873, attack on the peace commission, he was later captured, tried, and executed along with Kintpuash and others at Fort Klamath.

Religion Curley Headed Doctor (1828–1890) was a Modoc spiritual leader who learned the Ghost Dance from a Paiute Indian and was instrumental in the spread of that movement to the Modoc. He was believed to have, through spiritual means, raised the fog that shrouded the Modoc warriors during the First Battle of the Stronghold in January 1873.

Ramona Soto Rank (1945–2007) was a Lutheran pastor and community leader born on the Klamath Reservation to a Mexican father and an Indian mother. Her Klamath name was Olsambunwas, meaning "flower that the bird drinks from in the morning." A talented ballet dancer, she won the Miss Indian America pageant in 1962 and went on a national tour that included a visit to the White House, where she met President John F. Kennedy.

Steamboat Frank, also known as Frank Modoc (d. 1886), was the first full-blooded Native American to become a Quaker (Society of Friends) minister.

Born Slat-us-locks, he gained his nickname from whites because of his mother's loud voice. While living with the tribe in Oklahoma, he requested and received permission to go to Oak Grove Seminary in Vassalboro, Maine. He died on June 12, 1886, and is buried in the Quaker cemetery in Portland, Maine.

Sports Jackson "Action" Bussell (1978–2007) was a professional boxer raised on the Klamath Reservation. Bussell won the Oregon Golden Gloves Championship as well as those for Washington State and Wyoming. Twice the Native National Champion (2004 and 2005), he was a gold medalist at the Native American Indigenous Games in 2006. Bussell died of injuries sustained in a six-round professional bout with Javier García Calderón in Calabasas, California, on September 20, 2007.

ORGANIZATIONS AND ASSOCIATIONS

Klamath Bucket Brigade

Formed in 2001, the Klamath Bucket Brigade is an organization opposed to the damming of the Klamath River and Basin. Though not directly associated with the Klamath Indians, its position is aligned with theirs where the use of Klamath waters is concerned.

Dan Nielsen, President
9350 Highway 66
Klamath Falls, Oregon 97603
Phone: (541) 884-9594
Email: Buckets@klamathbucketbrigade.org
URL: www.klamathbucketbrigade.org

Klamath Tribes

The official political organization of the Klamath, Modoc, and Yahuskin peoples living in southern Oregon, the Klamath Tribes was established in 1986 and directs some thirty departments and programs to assist members.

Taylor David, Public Relations Manager
P.O. Box 436
501 Chiloquin Boulevard
Chiloquin, Oregon 97624
Phone: (800) 524-9787
Fax: (541) 783-2029
Email: taylor.david@klamathtribes.org
URL: www.klamathtribes.org

Modoc Tribe of Oklahoma

The official political organization of the Modocs in Oklahoma, to which their ancestors were transported in 1873, the Modoc Tribe of Oklahoma began operation in 1990 and oversees a number of tribe-related programs, services, and business interests.

Jack Shadwick, Tribal Registrar & Historian
418 G Street SE
Miami, Oklahoma 74354
Phone: (918)542-1190
Email: modoctribe@cableone.net
URL: www.modoctribe.net

Klamath boy, 1923 ALINARI ARCHIVES / THE IMAGE WORKS

MUSEUMS AND RESEARCH CENTERS

Favell Museum of Western Art and Native American Artifacts

Established in 1972 from the private collection of native Oregonian Gene Favell, who dedicated it "to the Indians who roamed and loved this land before the coming of the white man and to those artists who truly portray the inherited beauty which surrounds us," the museum is home to some 100,000 Indian artifacts, including many items from the Klamath Tribes.

125 West Main Street
Klamath Falls, Oregon 97601
Phone: (541) 882-9996
Email: favellmuseum@gmail.com
URL: www.favellmuseum.org

Klamath County Museums

Combining three different facilities, including one at Fort Klamath, the Klamath County Museums offer extensive collections on the natural history of the area, the Modoc War, and other matters related to the Klamath Tribes.

Lynn Jeche, Curator
1451 Main Street
Klamath Falls, Oregon 97601
Phone: (541) 883-4208
Fax: (541) 883-5170
Email: ljeche@co.klamath.or.us
URL: www.co.klamath.or.us/museum/index.htm

Oregon Historical Society

Houses books, photographs, maps, documents, letters, and other archival items—including extensive materials relating to the Klamath Tribes.

Eliza E. Canty-Jones, Public Outreach Manager
1200 SW Park Avenue
Portland, Oregon 97205
Phone: (503) 222-1741
Fax: (503) 221-2035
Email: orhist@ohs.org
URL: www.ohs.org

Southern Oregon Historical Society

Founded in 1946, the Southern Oregon Historical Society houses an extensive collection of historical writings, data, and other items relating to the history of the region, including its indigenous peoples.

Amy Drake, Curator of Special Projects
106 N. Central Avenue
Medford, Oregon 97501

Phone: (541) 773-6536
Fax: (541) 858-1095
Email: amy@sohs.org
URL: https://sites.google.com/a/sohs.org/sohs/

SOURCES FOR ADDITIONAL STUDY

Barker, Muhammad Abd-al-Rahman. *Klamath Texts*. Berkeley: University of California Press, 1963.

Gatschet, Albert S. *The Klamath Indians of Southwestern Oregon*. Washington, D.C.: U.S. Government Printing Office, 1890.

Hood, Susan. "Termination of the Klamath Tribe in Oregon." *Ethnohistory* 19 (Fall 1972): 379–92.

Quinn, Arthur. *Hell with the Fire Out: A History of the Modoc War*. Boston: Faber & Faber, 1997.

Ray, Verne Frederick. *Primitive Pragmatists: The Modoc Indians of Northern California*. Seattle: University of Washington Press, 1963.

Riddle, Jeff C. *The Indian History of the Modoc War, and the Causes That Led to It*. San Francisco: Marnell, 1914.

Spier, Leslie. *Klamath Ethnography*. Berkeley: University of California Press, 1930.

Stern, Theodore. *The Klamath Tribe: A People and Their Reservation*. Seattle: University of Washington Press, 1965.

KOREAN AMERICANS

Amy Nash

OVERVIEW

Korean Americans are immigrants or descendants of people from North Korea or South Korea, the two countries that make up the Korean Peninsula in East Asia. The peninsula is connected to China in the north and is bordered by the Yellow Sea to the west and the Sea of Japan to the east. Mountains and rugged hills constitute more than 70 percent of the Korean landscape. North Korea occupies over 46,000 square miles (120,000 square kilometers), approximately the size of the state of Mississippi. South Korea is 38,000 square miles (99,000 square kilometers), slightly larger than the state of Indiana.

According to the *CIA World Factbook*, an estimated 73 million people lived on the Korean Peninsula in July 2012. Approximately 48.8 million lived in South Korea and 24.6 million lived in North Korea. Nearly half of South Koreans do not claim any religious affiliation, while 31 percent are Christian and 24 percent identify as Buddhist. Historically, North Koreans were Buddhist or Confucian, although during the seventeenth, eighteenth, and nineteenth centuries, missionaries converted a small number to Christianity. Today the majority of North Koreans have no religion. North Korea consistently struggles with a poor economy, while South Korea's economy has flourished as one of the twenty largest economies of the world, earning the country a prominent position in the global Organisation for Economic Co-operation and Development.

Korean immigrants began arriving in the United States after Korea established diplomatic relations with the United States in 1882. The first major wave of Korean immigration occurred between 1903 and 1905, when thousands of Koreans moved to Hawaii seeking work on sugar plantations or education in Christian mission schools. These workers intended to return to Korea with their newly gained fortunes, but few actually made the journey home. The next major wave of immigration occurred after World War II when Korean students, military brides, and adopted children entered the country. With the Immigration and Naturalization Act of 1965, more professional men and women, mainly South Korean doctors and nurses, arrived in the United States. However, in the 1980s the rate of Korean immigration began to decline as the South Korean economy improved.

According to the 2010 U.S. Census, there were 1,706,822 Americans of Korean descent living in the United States. California was the state with the highest number of Korean Americans (505,225), while New York and New Jersey also had significant numbers—153,809 and 100,334, respectively. Illinois, Texas, Washington, Georgia, and Virginia also have a large number of Korean Americans.

HISTORY OF THE PEOPLE

Early History Historians commonly refer to the first period of recorded Korean history (53 BCE–668 CE) as the Three Kingdoms period. These kingdoms were Koguryo, Paekche, and Silla. Toward the end of the seventh century, Silla conquered Koguryo and Paekche, uniting the peninsula under the Silla dynasty. This period saw many advancements in literature, art, and science. Buddhism, which had reached Korea by way of China, was practiced by virtually all of Silla society. By the mid-eighth century the Silla people had begun using woodblock printing to reproduce Buddhist sutras and Confucian writings.

In 900 the three kingdoms divided, and within thirty-six years the Koguryo kingdom took control. Its leader, general Wang Kon, established the Koryo dynasty, from which the name *Korea* is derived. During Koryo's 400-year history, there were many advances in the arts, science, and literature. Improving upon earlier Chinese printing methods, Korea in 1234 became the first country to use movable cast metal type. Medical knowledge also developed during the thirteenth century and was recorded in books such as *Emergency Remedies of Folk Medicine* and *Folk Remedies of Samhwaja*.

Mongolian forces invaded Koryo in 1231 and occupied the kingdom until 1368. The Chinese Ming dynasty forced the Mongols back into the far north. This struggle eventually led to the fall of Koryo in 1392, when general Yi Song Gye revolted against the king and founded the Yi dynasty. It remained in power until the early twentieth century and proved to be one of the world's longest-enduring regimes. The kingdom was ruled by civilians who devotedly followed Confucianism, a philosophy of life and ethics that stresses an individual's sense of duty to family members and society as a whole. The Yi regime emphasized hierarchical relationships, bestowing the highest respect on family elders, the monarch, and China as the older, more established country.

In 1592 Japan invaded the peninsula, and Chinese soldiers helped Korea regain control of the land from the Japanese armies. Japan attacked again in 1597, but Korea was able to force the withdrawal of the Japanese by the end of the year. However, Korea was left in tatters and suffered more attacks in 1627 and 1636 at the hands of the Manchus, who later conquered China. During this period, Western scientific, technological, and religious influences entered Korea by way of China. However, as France, Great Britain, and the United States began to dominate areas of China and other Asian countries in the eighteenth and nineteenth centuries, Korea, dubbed The Hermit Kingdom, maintained a closed-door policy toward non-Chinese foreigners.

In 1832 an English merchant ship landed off the coast of Chungcheong Province, and in 1846 three French warships landed in the same area. Eight years later two armed Russian ships sailed along the Hamgyong coast and killed a few Korean civilians before leaving the region. In 1866 the U.S.S. *General Sherman* sailed up the Taedong River to Pyongyang. The crew's goal of drawing up a trade agreement was thwarted by an enraged mob of Koreans who set fire to the ship, killing everyone aboard. The following year five U.S. warships appeared near the Korean island of Ganghwa and also were fought off. Korean animosity toward Western countries stemmed largely from awareness of China's troubles with these nations, particularly Great Britain, which had devastated China during the First Opium War of 1839–1842. Despite Korean resistance, Japan forced the country to open to trade in 1876, and in 1882 Korea reluctantly agreed to trade with the United States.

For two centuries China and Japan fought for control over Asia. China's defeat in the Sino-Japanese War (1894–1895) greatly weakened Chinese dominance. After this victory Japan invaded the Korean Peninsula, which infuriated Korean students from American-founded schools that served as a place to learn about democracy and national liberation. The Japanese army despised the American missionaries who had established these schools but knew better than to confront citizens of the powerful U.S. government. Instead they took control over Korean citizens and outlawed Korean customs. As Korea turned to Russia for financial support and protection, a ten-year struggle ensued between Russia and Japan for control over the Korean Peninsula. The Russo-Japanese War of 1904–1905 ended in another Japanese victory. U.S. president Theodore Roosevelt mediated the peace agreement and won a Nobel Peace Prize for his role in creating the Treaty of Portsmouth, under which Korea became a protectorate of Japan. Japan officially annexed Korea in 1910.

Modern Era During its thirty-five years as a Japanese colony, Korea experienced major economic and social developments, such as soil improvement, updated methods of farming, and industrialization in the north. However, Koreans also suffered under the policies of a highly repressive military state. Japan appropriated half of the Korean rice crop for its own industry and forced most Korean farmers off their land. It also seized control of Korean schools and temples, and by the 1930s, Koreans were forced to worship at Shinto shrines, speak Japanese in schools, and adopt Japanese names. Japan also prevented Koreans from publishing newspapers and organizing intellectual and political groups.

In response to Japanese government policies, thousands of Koreans participated in demonstrations. Most of the protests were peaceful, but some led to violence. On March 1, 1919, a group of thirty-three prominent Koreans in Seoul issued a proclamation of independence, prompting close to 500,000 Koreans, including students, teachers, and members of religious groups, to organize demonstrations in the streets. This mass demonstration, which became known as the March First Movement, lasted two months until the Japanese government suppressed it and expanded the size of its police force in Korea by 10,000. According to conservative estimates from Japanese reports, the Japanese police killed 7,509 Koreans, wounded 15,961, and imprisoned another 46,948 in the process of quelling the movement.

During World War II Japan sided with Nazi Germany, and the Japanese government put Koreans to work in Japanese munitions plants, airplane factories, and coal mines. Before the war, Korean nationalists living in Siberia, Manchuria, China, and the United States—many of whom were communists—organized independence efforts, often using guerrilla tactics against the Japanese. One of these nationalists residing in the United States, Syngman Rhee (1875–1965), went on to become the first president of South Korea. Another Korean who was making a name for himself as a rebel was Kim Song Je. Born in 1912 near Pyongyang, Kim spent most of his childhood in Manchuria and took the pseudonym Kim Il-Sung in 1930. He organized one of the first anti-Japanese guerrilla units in Antu, Manchuria, on April 25, 1932. North Koreans still celebrate April 25 as the founding date of the Korean People's Army.

When Japan attacked Pearl Harbor, Hawaii, on December 7, 1941, prompting the United States to enter World War II, the Korean provisional government created by nationalists such as Rhee finally had an opportunity to take a stand against Japan. On December 8 the provisional government declared war on Japan and formed the Restoration Army to fight alongside the Allies in the Pacific theater. When Japan surrendered to the Allies on August 15, 1945, ending the Japanese occupation of Korea, Koreans took to the streets to celebrate the end of thirty-six years of oppressive rule. But the freedom they expected did not follow. The Soviet Union immediately occupied Pyongyang, Hamhung, and other major northern cities. The United States followed by stationing troops in southern Korea. This division of north and south was supposed to have been a temporary measure.

In the months that followed the end of World War II, international decisions about the administration of Korea were made without the consent of the Korean people. The Soviet Union set up a provisional communist government in northern Korea, and the United States created a provisional republican government in the south. In 1948 the Republic of Korea was founded south of the 38th parallel, and the Democratic People's Republic of Korea was founded in the north, with Kim Il-Sung as prime minister. Both governments claimed authority over the entire peninsula and tempted fate by crossing the border at various points along the 38th parallel.

On June 25, 1950, North Korea launched a surprise attack on South Korea, beginning a costly, bloody three-year struggle known as the Korean War. This was perhaps the most tragic period in modern history for the Korean people. Neither side achieved victory, and on July 27, 1953, in the town of Panmunjom, the two sides signed an armistice designating a cease-fire line along the 38th parallel and establishing a surrounding a demilitarized zone 2.5 miles (4 kilometers) wide. Today the zone remains the boundary between the two Koreas.

The war left the peninsula a wasteland. An estimated four million soldiers had been killed or wounded, and approximately one million civilians had died. Nevertheless, both Koreas moved swiftly to rebuild after the war and emerged into modern, industrialized nations. North Korea, which was more industrialized than South Korea before the war, restored the production of goods to prewar levels within three years. However, its economy and industry suffered as a result of the breakup of the Soviet Union, one of its major trading partners. Since the 1960s South Korea has evolved from a rural to a postindustrial society, becoming an important exporter of products such as Hyundai cars, LG televisions, and Samsung cell phones. In the late 1980s the United States was the second-largest exporter to South Korea after Japan, and in 1989 South Korea was the seventh-largest exporter country to the United States.

Kim Il-Sung ruled as a communist dictator in North Korea for more than four decades, until his death in July 1994. Meanwhile South Korea underwent several political changes, including a military dictatorship that took power between 1961 and 1963. Corruption in the government and lack of free elections caused many student uprisings. The most notable was the April 19 student revolution, which was prompted by the shooting of a student who was protesting what the public believed was an unfair election. Tens of thousands of students protested his death,

culminating in the president stepping down from office. The revolution proved to be one of many steps toward democracy in South Korea. In the 1990s president Kim Young-Sam (1927–) instituted economic reforms and an aggressive anticorruption campaign.

All measures introduced to reunify the Korean Peninsula have ended in a stalemate. U.S. concern over North Korea's nuclear weapons program threatened to increase tensions between the two Koreas. The country's refusal to allow full international inspection of its nuclear facilities brought the United States close to proposing a resolution for a United Nations economic embargo against North Korea in June 1994. Before sanctions were implemented, however, former U.S. president Jimmy Carter met with the North Korean government and reported that the country would be willing to freeze all production of fuel for nuclear weapons if it could resume high-level talks with Washington. Although officials were hopeful that planned meetings between the two Korean governments would not break down as in the past, Kim Il-Sung's death once again put negotiations on hold. Reunification remains the most pressing issue on the minds of Koreans even in the twenty-first century.

After Kim Il-Sung died, his son Kim Jong Il (1941–2011) succeeded as the leader of North Korea. Under his leadership, North Korea experienced an economic decline that he did little to rectify, and North Korea became dependent on international aid to feed its people. Tensions between North and South Korea continued to rise, reaching a boiling point in 2005 when North Korea announced it had nuclear weapons. In 2011 Kim Jong Il died and was succeeded by his son Kim Jong-un (1983?–). South Korea, under the leadership of Kim Dae Jung (1924?–2009), pursued reunification with North Korea until 2002, when Roh Moo Hyun (1946–2009) took over as president. Roh worked to improve South Korea's relations with North Korea and the United States. His successor, Lee Myung-Bak (1941–), helped to rebuild the South Korean economy. In 2013 Park Geun-Hye (1952–) became South Korea's first female president.

SETTLEMENT IN THE UNITED STATES

Although emigration was illegal in Korea in the nineteenth century, natural disasters, poverty, high taxes, and government oppression drove many Koreans to leave the country. By 1900 the United States had become a refuge for a small number of Koreans, including three Korean political refugees who immigrated in 1885. Five more arrived in 1899 but were mistaken for Chinese. Between 1890 and 1905, sixty-four Koreans traveled to Hawaii to attend Christian mission schools. (Most returned to Korea after completing their studies.)

The first major wave of Korean immigrants to the United States began in 1903, when Hawaiian sugar plantation owners offered Koreans jobs. Initially, the sugar planters had hired native Hawaiians to work as contract laborers on the plantations, but by 1850 the native population had declined and the laborers became increasingly dissatisfied with the hard work. As demand for sugar continued to grow, the labor shortage prompted the planters to form the Royal Hawaiian Agricultural Society to recruit outside sources of labor. The first immigrant laborers entered Hawaii from China in 1852. By the time the United States annexed Hawaii in 1898, 50,000 Chinese immigrants lived in the territory. Low wages, long workdays, and poor treatment led many Chinese laborers to leave the plantations to find work in the cities, causing the sugar planters to recruit Japanese immigrants to supplement the plantation workforce.

In 1900 Hawaii became an official U.S. territory, making it legal for the Chinese and Japanese workers to go on strike, which many did. Moreover, the U.S. Chinese Exclusion Act of 1882 had prohibited further immigration of Chinese people to the United States. To offset another labor shortage and weaken the unions, Hawaiian sugar planters turned to Korea. In 1902 growers sent a representative to San Francisco to meet with Horace Allen, the U.S. ambassador to Korea, who began recruiting Koreans to work on the plantations with the help of David William Deshler, an American businessman living in Korea. Deshler owned a steamship service that operated between Korea and Japan. The Hawaiian Sugar Planters Association paid Deshler $55 for each Korean recruited. The Deshler Bank, set up in the Korean seaside town of Inchon, provided loans of $100 to each immigrant for transportation.

With conditions worsening in Korea, the offer appealed to a great number of laborers, who were promised a monthly wage of $16; free housing, health care, and English lessons; and a warmer climate. Newspaper advertisements and posters promoted Hawaii as a paradise and the United States as a land of gold and dreams. Recruiters used the slogan *Kaeguk chinch wi* (the country is open, go forward) to encourage potential recruits. American missionaries such as reverend George Heber Jones of the Methodist Episcopal Church in Inchon helped persuade Koreans with stories of how life in the West would make them better Christians.

In December 1902, 121 Koreans left their homeland aboard the U.S.S. *Gaelic*; all but 19 of the recruits who had failed their medical examinations in Japan arrived in Honolulu on January 13, 1903. This original group included 56 men, 21 women, and 25 children. More than 7,000 Korean immigrants joined them on the Hawaiian sugar plantations within two years. Most were bachelors or had left their families behind, hoping to save their wages and return to Korea to share the wealth with their families. Despite promises of fortune, they found only low-paying jobs, and most did not make enough money to return home. In fact, because of the higher cost of living in Hawaii, only about 2,000 were able to return to Korea. By 1905 the Japanese government banned emigration from the peninsula because so many Koreans were leaving to avoid Japanese oppression.

The next wave of Korean immigration to the United States occurred when Japan issued the Gentlemen's Agreement of 1907. This pact forbade further immigration of Japanese and Korean workers but included a clause that allowed wives to rejoin their husbands already in the United States, initiating the "picture bride" system. Korean village matchmakers and the groom's family would select women in Korea to exchange photographs with men in the United States. When a match was agreed upon, the groom's family would write the bride's name into the family register to legalize the union, and she would travel to the United States to meet her new husband. Marriage ceremonies were often performed on the boat ride to North America so that the women could touch American soil as legal wives of the immigrants. Between 1910 and 1924, more than 1,000 Korean picture brides came to the United States, mostly to Hawaii. These women were motivated by the opportunities for education and wealth they had heard were available in the United States. Education, travel, and careers were not open to women at home because traditional Korean society placed many restrictions on women.

> I arose at four o'clock in the morning, and we took a truck to the sugar cane fields, eating breakfast on the way. Work in the sugar plantations was back breaking. It involved cutting canes, watering, and pulling out weeds. … The sugar cane fields were endless and twice the height of myself. Now that I look back, I *thank goodness* for the height for if I had seen how far the fields stretched I probably would have fainted from knowing how much work was ahead.

However, these brides met with a harsh reality in the United States. Many discovered that their husbands were much older than they looked in the pictures, and a large number became widows at a young age. Moreover, these women faced hard work and long hours, leaving little free time to learn English. In the introduction to *Making Waves: An Anthology of Writings by and about Asian American Women* (1989), Sucheta Mazumdar recounts immigrant Anna Choi's description of her life in Hawaii as a picture bride:

Virtually all of the first Koreans immigrants to the United States settled in Hawaii and on the West Coast. Those working on the Hawaiian sugar plantations became increasingly frustrated by the harsh conditions and moved to cities to open restaurants, vegetable stands, and small stores, or to work as carpenters or tailors. Others returned to Korea. By 1907 approximately 1,000 Korean plantation workers had migrated to the U.S. mainland, settling in San Francisco or moving farther inland to Utah to work in the copper mines, to Colorado and Wyoming to work in the coal mines, or to Arizona to work on the railroads. Some moved as far north as Alaska and

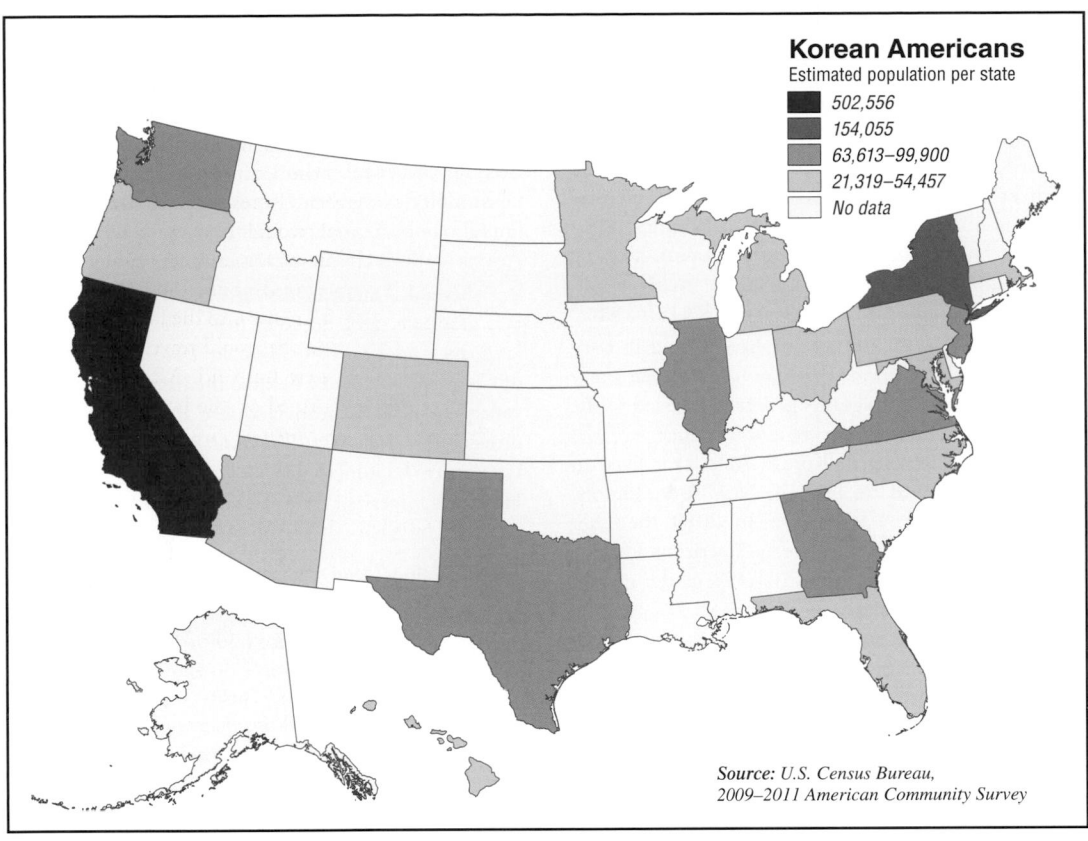

Korean Americans
Estimated population per state

- 502,556
- 154,055
- 63,613–99,900
- 21,319–54,457
- No data

*Source: U.S. Census Bureau,
2009–2011 American Community Survey*

found jobs in the salmon fisheries there. However, the majority settled in California.

In the years between 1907 and World War II, a few Korean political refugees and students came to the United States. Some were members of a secret Korean patriotic society called Sinminhoe (the New People's Society). To escape persecution by the Japanese government, they crossed the Yalu River and took trains to Shanghai. From there, they made their way to the United States. By 1924, 541 Koreans living in the United States had claimed to be political refugees. Among these political activists were Ahn Chang Ho, Pak Yong Man, and Syngman Rhee, the future first president of South Korea.

After World War II, the South Korean government discouraged emigration, while North Korea forbade emigration of any kind. Most of the Koreans who immigrated to the United States after the war were women. The quota system created by the U.S. Office of Immigration in the 1940s allowed between 105 and 150 immigrants from each of the Asian nations. This law favored immigrants with postsecondary education, technical training, and specialized skills. Most of the Koreans allowed to immigrate were women with nursing training. In particular the War Brides Act of 1945 helped women and children obtain papers to immigrate.

After the Korean War (1950–1953), more women who had married American soldiers were allowed into the United States. By this time, Koreans and all Asians in the United States were able to acquire citizenship through naturalization as a result of the McCarran-Walter Act of 1952. Foreign adoption of Korean babies also began at the end of the Korean War, which had left thousands of children orphaned in Korea. More than 100,000 South Korean children have been adopted abroad since the war, and roughly two-thirds of these have been adopted by American families. An estimated 10,000 Korean children have been adopted by Minnesota families alone. Criticized by other countries for running a "baby mill," the South Korean government began to phase out foreign adoptions in the 1990s. Although adopting children is traditionally frowned upon in Korean society, social workers are attempting to encourage domestic adoption.

In 1965 the U.S. Congress passed the Immigration and Naturalization Act, replacing the quota system with a preference system that gave priority to immigration applications from relatives of U.S. citizens and from professionals with skills needed by the United States. Thousands of South Korean doctors and nurses took advantage of the law, finding jobs in understaffed inner-city hospitals. Koreans with science and technological backgrounds also were encouraged to immigrate. Unlike earlier immigrants, these new immigrants came from middle- and upper-class families. The portion of the law informally known as the Brothers and Sisters

Act also was a factor in the dramatic increase in the Korean American population. In 1960, 10,000 Koreans were living in the United States, but by 1985 the number had increased to 500,000. This number continues to grow in the twenty-first century. By 2000 the population of Korean Americans was more than one million. Much of this immigration was prompted by political and economic motivations. With political unrest still a reality in South Korea and college education growing increasingly expensive and competitive, many immigrants moved to the United States to seek a better life.

Recent Korean immigrants have settled in concentrated areas around the country. Unlike early immigrants, later immigrants generally traveled to the United States to take up permanent residence. In 1970 the highest percentage of Korean Americans lived in California, followed by Hawaii, New York, Illinois, Pennsylvania, and Washington. In 2010 the U.S. Census reported 300,047 Korean Americans lived in the greater Los Angeles area, 201,393 in the greater New York metropolitan area, and 93,787 in the Baltimore–Washington metropolitan area. Every state has at least a small population of Korean Americans, though California, Illinois, New Jersey, New York, Texas, and Virginia have some of the largest populations of Korean Americans. Georgia and Washington also boast significant numbers of Americans of Korean descent. Most Koreans who settle in the United States reside in large cities where jobs are available and Korean communities have been established, though Korean American professionals who can afford it have moved to the suburbs. Korea towns have developed in areas such as the Olympic Boulevard neighborhood west of downtown Los Angeles. The Flushing, Woodside, and Jackson Heights neighborhoods within the New York City borough of Queens also have substantial Korean American populations.

Coming from a traditional society greatly influenced by the Confucian principle of placing elders, family, and community before the individual, Korean immigrants struggle to make sense of the American concept of individual freedom.

LANGUAGE

Virtually every citizen in North and South Korea is an ethnic Korean and speaks Korean. The Korean language was first written in the mid-fifteenth century when King Sejong invented the phonetically based alphabet known as *hangul* so that all Korean people, not just the aristocracy who knew Chinese characters, could learn to read and write. Today North and South Korea's literacy rates are among the highest in the world.

While most second- and third-generation Korean Americans exclusively speak English, new immigrants often know little or no English. The earliest Korean immigrants in Hawaii learned a form of English known as pidgin English, which incorporated phrases in English, Chinese, Japanese, Korean, Filipino, and Portuguese—all languages spoken by the different ethnic groups working on the plantations. Learning English is crucial for new immigrants who hope to become successful members of the larger American community. Nevertheless, most Korean American parents also hope to preserve their heritage by sending their American-born children to Korean language schools.

Several American universities offer undergraduate, graduate, and doctoral programs in the Korean language and Korean studies. In 1943 the University of California–Berkeley became the first American university to offer Korean language instruction. Other universities followed, including Brigham Young University, Columbia University, Cornell University, Harvard University, the University of Hawaii–Manoa, and the University of Washington–Seattle.

Greetings and Popular Expressions The following greetings are translated phonetically from the hangul alphabet according to the McCune-Reischauer system of romanization: *Annyonghasipnigga*—"hello" (formal greeting); *Yoboseyo*—"hello" (informal greeting); *Annyonghi kasipsio*—"good-bye" (staying); *Annyonghi kyeshipsio*—"good-bye" (leaving); *Put'akhamnida*—"please"; *Komapsumnida*—"thank you"; *Ch'onmaneyo*—"you're welcome"; *Sillyehamnida*—"excuse me"; *Ye*—"yes"; *Aniyo*—"no"; *Sehae e pok mani padu sipsiyo!*—"Happy New Year!"; *Man sei!*—"Hurrah! Long live our country! Ten thousand years!"; and *Kuh reh!*—"That is so! True!"

RELIGION

Throughout Korea's history, religion has played a prominent role in the lives of its citizens. A variety of faiths have been practiced on the peninsula, the most common being shamanism, Buddhism, and Christianity. Shamanism is the country's oldest religion and involves the worship of nature. The sun, mountains, rocks, and trees each hold sacred positions. Based on a belief in good and evil spirits that can only be appeased by priests or medicine men called shamans, early shamanism incorporated pottery making and dances such as the *muchon*, which was performed as part of a ceremony to worship the heavens.

China brought Buddhism to Korea sometime between the fourth and seventh centuries. This religion, based on the teachings of the ancient Indian philosopher Siddhartha Gautama (Buddha), holds that suffering in life is inherent and that one can be freed from it by mental and moral self-purification.

Christianity first reached Korea in the seventeenth century by way of China, where Portuguese missionaries came to promote Catholicism. American Protestant missionaries arrived in Korea in the nineteenth century but were persecuted by the Korean government because the laws of Christianity went against Confucian social order. By the mid-1990s, the majority of South Koreans were still Buddhists, but an estimated 30 percent of the population practiced some type of Christianity. However, by the twenty-first century, most South Koreans did not claim a religion, with 31 percent identifying as Christian and 24 percent identifying as Buddhist.

Of the 7,000 Korean immigrants who arrived in the United States between 1903 and 1905, only 400 were Christian. These Christians immediately formed congregations in Hawaii, and by 1918 close to 40 percent of Korean immigrants had converted to Christianity. Korean immigrants relied heavily on their churches as community centers. After Sunday service, immigrants spoke Korean, socialized, discussed problems of immigrant life, and organized political rallies for Korean independence. The churches also served as educational centers and provided classes in writing and reading Korean. Today they remain an integral part of the Korean immigrant community.

The majority of Korean Christians in the United States practice Protestantism, and there are more than 3,000 Korean Protestant churches across the country. Most Korean Protestants are evangelical Christians, who extensively study the Bible and closely follow the word of the gospel. In large cities like Los Angeles, New York, and Chicago, Korean Protestants have their own buildings and hold several services a week. The Oriental Mission Church and Young Nak Presbyterian Church in Los Angeles are two of the largest Korean Protestant churches in the United States, with 5,000 members each. A small segment of the Korean American population, about 7 to 8 percent, practices Catholicism, compared to about 30 percent who practice Protestantism. Korean Catholics established the Korean American Catholic Community in the 1960s, and the first Korean Catholic center opened in Orange County, California, in 1977.

Korean Buddhism was founded in the United States by a Buddhist monk named Soh Kyong Bo in 1964. Most Korean American Buddhists belong to the Chogye sect. Prominent Buddhist organizations in the United States include the Zen Lotus Society in Ann Arbor, Michigan; the Korean Buddhist Temple Association; the Young Buddhist Union in Los Angeles; the Buddhists Concerned with Social Justice and World Peace; the Western Buddhist Monk's Association; the Southern California Buddhist Temples Association, and several Son and Dharma centers across the country.

CULTURE AND ASSIMILATION

Like all immigrants arriving in the United States, Koreans have had to make major adjustments to live in a country that is vastly different from their homeland. Coming from a traditional society greatly influenced by the Confucian principle of placing elders, family, and community before the individual, Korean immigrants struggle to make sense of the American concept of individual freedom. Since the first immigrants arrived in Hawaii, Korean Americans have preserved their identity by creating organizations such as Korean Christian churches and Korean schools. The Korean word *han*, used to describe an anguished feeling of being far from what you want, accurately conveys the longing that accompanies most Koreans to the United States. Korean American organizations provide a sense of community for new immigrants and a way to alleviate this longing.

Traditions and Customs Korean immigrants bring with them a culture that incorporates aspects of Chinese, Japanese, and Western cultures. Yet Koreans also have maintained native elements of their literature, art, music, and way of life. The result is a wonderful collage of elements, both foreign and indigenous to the peninsula. Korean Americans tend to maintain aspects of their culture while also adopting elements of mainstream America.

Korean culture is often maintained through church organizations, schools, and culture camps. Korean Protestant churches offer classes in Korean culture and language. In addition, according to an estimate by the Korean Language Center of New York, in 2012 there were 1,000 Korean language schools in the United States catering mainly to children. Korean American parents often send their children to Korean culture camps during the summer. Located predominantly in California, Minnesota, New Jersey, and New York, these camps offer Korean American children, usually adoptees, an opportunity to learn about their heritage with other Korean American children.

Cuisine Korean cuisine is an important part of maintaining Korean culture among immigrant families and is commonly featured at family gatherings and holiday celebrations. Korean restaurants are often popular in areas with large Korean American populations. Like other East Asian groups, Koreans eat with chopsticks and frequently use tofu, soy sauce, rice, and a wide variety of vegetables. However, Korean food is distinct for its strong seasoning, including combinations of garlic, ginger, red or black pepper, scallions, sesame seeds, and sesame oil. Blander grain dishes, such as rice, barley, or noodles, are used to offset the heat of the spices. Red meat is scarce in both North and South Korea and typically is reserved for special occasions.

Koreans do not usually designate certain foods as breakfast, lunch, or dinner dishes. A standard meal consists of rice, soup, *kimchi* (a spicy Korean pickle), vegetables, and broiled or grilled meat or fish. Fresh fruit is usually served at the end of a meal. Kimchi is considered the national dish and is served at virtually every meal. Made from cabbage, turnips, radishes, or cucumber, kimchi can be prepared many ways, from mild to very spicy. Korean cuisine also includes many different kinds of *namul* (salads). A common type of namul is *sukju namul*, or a bean sprout salad made with soy sauce, vinegar, sesame oil, black pepper, and other ingredients. A common soup served at breakfast is *kamja guk* (potato soup), which is often spiced with

KKAKDUGI (RADISH KIMCHEE)

Ingredients

4 pound daikon radish

2 tablespoons salt

2 tablespoons sugar

¼ cup fish sauce

⅓ cup hot pepper flakes

4 green onions, chopped

2 tablespoons garlic, minced

1 teaspoon ginger, minced

Preparation

Peel radish. Rinse in cold water and pat dry. Cut it into ¾–1 inch cubes. Put into a large bowl. Add salt and sugar, mix well. Set aside for 30 minutes. Drain the juice from the radish into a small bowl.

To the radish, add garlic, ginger, green onions, fish sauce, hot pepper flakes, and 1 cup of the juice from the radish. Mix it up well until the seasonings coat the radish cubes evenly.

Put mixture in a glass jar and press down on the top of it to remove any air from between the radish cubes. Close jar and allow to sit outside refrigerator for 2–3 days, to allow for fermenting. It should smell strong and sour. Place in refrigerator.

Note: Kkakdugi can be eaten immediately as well.

chopped onion and chunks of tofu. At winter celebrations Koreans serve *mandu*, deep-fried wonton skins usually filled with beef, cabbage, bean sprouts, onions, and other ingredients. Another common Korean dish is *chap ch'ae*, a popular stir-fry dish that features cellophane noodles made from mung beans and is prepared with vegetables in a wok.

Traditional Dress Traditional Korean clothing is rarely worn on a daily basis in the United States or Korea. Modern Western-style clothes are standard attire in most of South Korea, with the exception of some rural areas. However, during holidays Koreans in the United States and Korea often wear traditional costumes. Women may wear a *chi-ma* (a long skirt, usually pleated and full) and *cho-gori* (a short jacket top worn over a skirt) during New Year's celebrations. Traditional attire for men includes long, white overcoats; horsehair hats; and colorful silk baggy trousers known as *paji*.

Dances and Songs Korean music incorporates Confucian rituals, court music, Buddhist chants, and folk music. Ancient instruments used for court music include zithers, flutes, reed instruments, and percussion. Folk music, which usually includes dancing, is

played with a *chango* (a drum shaped like an hourglass) and a loud trumpet-like oboe. *P'ansori*, stories, first sung by wandering bards in the late Choson dynasty, are an early form of Korean folk music. Modern Korean composers often draw from Western classical music. Korean American musicians such as Jin Hi Kim (1957–) use traditional Korean elements in their compositions. Kim is a *komungo* harpist who came to the United States in her twenties. She incorporates traditional Korean musical styles with other non-Western styles and is one of the leaders in the No World Improvisations movement, which promotes the performance and composition of new improvisational music.

Holidays Koreans in both the United States and Korea celebrate several important days throughout the year. Following Buddhist and Confucian traditions, Koreans begin the new year with an elaborate three-day celebration called Sol. Family members dress in traditional clothing and pay homage to the oldest members of the family. The festivities include several feasts, kite flying, board games, and various rituals intended to ward off evil spirits. In addition the first full moon is an ancient day of worship. Torches are kept burning all night, and often people set off firecrackers to scare away evil spirits.

Yadu Nal (Shampoo Day) is celebrated on June 15. Families bathe in streams or waterfalls to protect them from fevers. Chusok (Thanksgiving Harvest) is celebrated in autumn to give thanks for the harvest. Kimchi is prepared for the winter at this time. Other traditional holidays observed in many Korean American households include the Buddha's birthday on April 8, Korean Memorial Day on June 6, Father's Day on June 15, Constitution Day in South Korea on July 17, and Korean National Foundation Day on October 3. Korean American Christians also observe major religious holidays such as Easter and Christmas.

Health Care Issues and Practices Korean Americans hold prominent positions in the field of medical science. The proportionally large number of Korean American doctors and nurses attests to this fact. Data on the status of the health of Korean Americans is limited. Asian Americans in general have a longer life expectancy than Americans as a whole. However, job-related stress and other factors have contributed to mental health problems within the Korean American community. Most Korean Americans receive health insurance through their employers, but new immigrants and the elderly often do not have access to medical care because of language barriers. Organizations such as the Korean Health Education Information and Referral in Los Angeles work to address this problem.

Recreational Activities Several sports native to Korea have become popular around the world. For instance, tae kwon do, a method of self-defense that originated in Korea more than 2,000 years ago, has now become a commonly taught form of karate in the

United States. Involving sharper, quicker kicking than the Japanese style of karate, tae kwon do was a demonstration sport in the 1988 Summer Olympics in Seoul.

FAMILY AND COMMUNITY LIFE

Historically the family system was an integral part of Korean society. The male head of household played a dominant role, as did the oldest members of the family. Parents exerted control over much of their children's lives, arranging their marriages and choosing their careers. The eldest son, who received the family inheritance, was responsible for taking care of parents in their old age. These systems have changed in modern Korea, particularly in cities, though the family remains very important to Koreans in their homeland and in the United States. It is common for Korean American parents to pressure their children to marry someone who has a good relationship with the family.

Today Korean children—both male and female— usually are responsible for the care of elderly parents, although in South Korea the government has begun to carry some of the financial burden. Tight family bonds persist among Korean Americans. Current U.S. immigration laws encourage these bonds by favoring family reunions. Korean Americans who invite relatives to come to the United States have a responsibility to help the new immigrants adjust to their new home. Korean American families often include extended family members. The family ties also extend to strong networks of support within Korean American communities.

Gender Roles Korean husbands traditionally work outside the home, while their wives take full-time responsibility for the children and household. Living in a modern industrialized nation, many South Korean women have full-time jobs, especially in urban areas. Still, the majority of full-time female employees in South Korea are unmarried. In the United States economic needs often require both parents to work, but running the household remains solely the responsibility of the woman. Second-, third-, and fourth-generation Korean American women face conflicts between traditional familial values and mainstream American culture. These women have more opportunities than their mothers and grandmothers, and some have careers as lawyers, doctors, teachers, and businesswomen. However, most have behind-the-scenes positions as clerks, typists, and cashiers. Korean American women, like American women in general, are still discriminated against in the job market. Although many Korean women immigrate to the United States with professional skills, they are often forced to work in garment factories or as store clerks because of the language barrier.

The view that Korean American women are passive also persists. Contrary to popular perceptions, Korean American women have a long history of political activism. Unfortunately their work has gone largely unrecorded. Korean female immigrants played a significant role in organizing protests against

A boy performs in the Korean Day parade in New York City. DAVID GROSSMAN / ALAMY

Japanese occupation, establishing organizations such as the Korean Women's Patriotic League and writing for Korean newspapers. They also participated in labor strikes on Hawaiian plantations. Korean American women of the late twentieth and early twenty-first centuries joined other Asian American women in fighting unfair work practices in the hotel, garment, and food-packaging industries. Korean American women also have participated in efforts to reunify Korea and have begun entering into the political realm.

Education Koreans have always valued education, and Korean Americans place a strong emphasis on academic achievement. Traditionally, employment in the Korean civil service, which required passing extremely difficult qualifying examinations, was considered to be the most successful career path to take. Recent immigrants to the United States are strongly motivated to perform well in school and are often better educated than the general population in Korea.

Korean American parents pressure their children to perform well in school. In 2010, according to U.S. Census data, 91.7 percent of Korean Americans over the age of twenty-five had at least a high school education, compared with 85.6 percent of Americans overall. In addition 52 percent of Korean Americans had four or more years of college education, compared to only 28.5 percent of the general U.S. population. It is a common stereotype that Korean Americans excel in math and science. Although this is often true, they tend to perform well in all subjects.

Courtship and Weddings The importance placed on family in Korean society is apparent from the way special events in family members' lives are celebrated. Traditionally parents—with the help of a marriage broker or go-between—choose their children's marriage partners and plan and prepare the wedding ceremony. Female relatives spend days preparing special dishes for the wedding feast and making the wedding clothes. The picture bride system used to increase the population of Korean American women in Hawaii is one example of how these traditions were maintained in the United States.

While common in rural areas of Korea, these customs are no longer standard practice in cities. Korean Americans, who generally come from urban areas, usually allow their children to choose their own spouses. As members of Christian churches, most modern Korean Americans have Western-style wedding ceremonies and wear Western-style bridal gowns and suits. Another event that Koreans traditionally celebrate with great flourish is a baby's first birthday.

The child is dressed in a traditional costume and seated amidst rice cakes, cookies, and fruits. Friends and relatives offer the child objects, each one symbolizing a different career. A pen represents a writing career, and a coin signifies a career in finance. The first object the child picks up is said to indicate his or her future profession.

In Korean American communities, the marriage bond has in some ways become stronger than filial piety. While honoring one's parents remains important, physical distance and cultural barriers between Korean Americans and their parents have shifted priorities. Korean Americans are less likely than their ancestors to have arranged marriages, and marrying outside of the Korean community has become increasingly common. Recent surveys show that Korean American women in college are expressing a preference for mates from other ethnic groups.

Traditionally Koreans have frowned upon divorce. Of the marriages arranged through the picture bride system in Hawaii, few ended in divorce. However, recent statistics suggest that the stigma against divorce no longer exists. The divorce rate among Korean Americans has reached, and is possibly surpassing, the national average. Exhaustion due to working extremely long hours contributes to failed marriages. Women in particular suffer from stress, working long shifts in garment factories or managing small businesses while also running the household. Korean American community organizations have attempted to address these problems in order to make life in the United States more fulfilling.

At the Asian American Festival in New York City, Korean American boys practice Tae Kwon Do. RUDI VON BRIEL / PHOTOEDIT

Relations with Other Americans Anti-Asian prejudice first erupted in the United States when Chinese and Japanese immigrants began arriving in the nineteenth century. Early Korean immigrants suffered discrimination but were not specifically targeted until they became a significant percentage of the population. Americans generally knew nothing about Korea when Koreans first came to the United States. What little information they could find was written by non-Asians and claimed Western superiority over Asian cultures. William Griffis's *Corea: The Hermit Nation* (1882), Alexis Krausse's *The Far East* (1900), and Isabella Bird Bishop's *Korea and Her Neighbours* (1898) are examples of books that perpetuated the myth of Western superiority. American writer Jack London was also responsible for giving Americans an unfavorable view of Korea. As a war correspondent covering the Russo-Japanese conflict in 1904, he voiced his opinions in dispatches that appeared on the front pages of newspapers across the country. In an article titled "The Yellow Peril," which appeared in the *San Francisco Examiner* on September 25, 1904, London wrote that "the Korean is the perfect type of inefficiency—of utter worthlessness."

Anti-Asian sentiments grew during the early twentieth century when San Francisco workers accused Koreans, along with Japanese and Chinese immigrants, of stealing jobs by working for lower wages. Restaurants refused to serve Asian customers, and Asians were often forced to sit in segregated corners of movie theaters. Violent white gangs harassed Korean Americans in California, and the government did nothing to help the victims. In fact, California laws in the first few decades of the twentieth century supported anti-Asian attitudes. Asian students were banned from attending public schools in white districts in 1906. The 1913 Webb-Heney Land Law prohibited Asians from owning property, and the Oriental Exclusion Act of 1924 banned all Asian immigration to the United States for close to thirty years.

Korean Americans have been discriminated against in the job market, often receiving lower pay and having fewer opportunities for promotion than their non-Asian coworkers. The view of Korean Americans as "super immigrants" has also caused discord. Korean American success stories in business and education, which are often exaggerated, have led to resentment from other groups, generating false rumors that the U.S. government gives Korean immigrants money when they arrive. (Only refugees receive aid from the U.S. government, and very few Korean immigrants qualify as refugees.) Statistics showing that the mean income of Korean American families is higher than that of the general public are misleading because most Korean Americans live in large cities where the cost of living is much higher.

Nevertheless, such stereotypes have led to boycotts of Korean greengrocers in Brooklyn, Chicago, and elsewhere. In the April 1992 Los Angeles uprising that followed the Rodney King verdict, black rioters targeted Korean grocers, destroying countless Korean American businesses. Korean immigrants refer to this tragic episode as the Sa-i-kup'ok-dong (the April 28 riots). Because they started businesses in inner-city neighborhoods that had been abandoned by corporations, Korean immigrants had come to represent wealth, greed, materialism, and arrogance to some Americans. People living in low-income neighborhoods often used the Korean small businessperson as a scapegoat for their anger against corporate America. Organizations such as the Korea Society in New York and the Korean Youth and Community Center in Los Angeles have begun to address these issues.

In the twenty-first century, relations between Korean Americans and other Americans have improved. Korean Americans have become more involved in city and state governments. In addition, public opinion has changed with the rising popularity of Asian pop culture, particularly the K-pop music trend, and the majority of Americans now view Koreans in a positive and fair light.

EMPLOYMENT AND ECONOMIC CONDITIONS

Early Korean immigrants living on the West Coast were restricted from many types of employment. Discriminatory laws prohibited Asian immigrants from applying for citizenship, which meant that they were ineligible for positions in most professional fields. They took jobs with low pay and little potential for advancement, working as busboys, waiters, gardeners, janitors, and domestic help in cities. Outside the cities, they worked on farms and in railroad gangs. Many Korean immigrants opened restaurants, laundries, barbershops, grocery stores, tobacco shops, bakeries, and other retail shops. With the changes in immigration

KOREAN LITERARY TRADITIONS

Korean literature draws from Chinese and Japanese roots but has its own distinctive features. Poems, romances, and short stories represent only a portion of the breadth of the Korean literary tradition. This tradition includes both folk and highly advanced literary writings and works written in Chinese as well as Korean. Korean poems called *hyangga*, dating back to the sixth century, were written in Chinese characters. Hyangga were sung by Buddhist monks for religious purposes. Korean myths and legends were first recorded in Chinese in the thirteenth century. The first literary work written in the Korean alphabet, *hangul*, was the *Songs of Flying Dragons*, a multivolume account written between 1445 and 1447 by King Sejong's father during the Yi dynasty. Novels began to appear in the seventeenth century. Among the best known are Ho Kyun's *Life of Hong Kiltong* and *Spring Fragrance*, written anonymously in the eighteenth century.

laws after World War II, Korean immigrants moved into more professional fields such as medicine, dentistry, architecture, and science. Recent immigrants (those who have come to the United States since 1965) are mostly college educated and have professional skills. The language barrier, however, often prevents them from finding jobs within their fields. Korean doctors often work as orderlies and nurse's assistants. In 1978 only 35 percent of Korean teachers, administrators, and other professionals were working in their respective fields in Los Angeles.

According to the 2010 U.S. Census, the median Korean American household income was $64,401, which was higher than the average household income for Americans overall ($50,406). The same report indicates that 11.6 percent of Korean American families had incomes below the poverty level, which is about the same as the 11.3 percent reported for the total U.S. population. Asian American adults have lower unemployment rates than the U.S. adult population overall. In 2010 the U.S. Census Bureau also reported that 46 percent of Korean Americans age sixteen or older held managerial or professional positions; 27.7 percent had sales or administrative jobs; 14.5 percent held service jobs; 8.2 percent held precision production or transportation jobs; and 6.3 percent were unemployed.

Out of economic need, large numbers of recent Korean immigrants have started their own businesses, although most did not run small businesses in Korea.

A Korean American voter registration table during an event in New York City. ROBERT BRENNER / PHOTOEDIT

In 1977, 33 percent of Korean American families owned small businesses, such as vegetable stands, grocery stores, service stations, and liquor stores. As a whole, they have had a high success rate. In the 1980s an estimated 95 percent of all dry cleaning stores in Chicago were owned by Korean immigrants. By 1990, 15,500 Korean-owned stores were in operation in New York City alone. Since then the recession and internal competition have slowed growth. New Korean immigrants have begun opening businesses in cities where competition is less fierce than in New York, Los Angeles, and Chicago.

Support within Korean communities has contributed to the success of these small businesses. Recent immigrants still use the ancient Korean loan system based on the *kye*, a sum of money shared by a group of business owners. A new grocer, for instance, will be allowed to use the money for one year and keep the profits. The kye is then passed to the next person who needs it. Organizations like the Korean Produce Association in New York and the Koryo Village Center in Oakland, California, are another source of support for new immigrants hoping to set up their own businesses.

POLITICS AND GOVERNMENT

Koreans have a general distrust of central governments. Historically, individual citizens have had little power in Korea and have suffered through scores of tragic episodes at the hands of other governments controlling the peninsula. As a result, most Korean immigrants come to the United States unaccustomed to participation in the democratic process. Discriminatory laws against Asian Americans on the West Coast contributed to distrust of the government. Therefore, Korean American communities traditionally isolated themselves, relying on family and neighborhood networks for support. Today, Korean American participation in grassroots organizations and U.S. politics is growing and evolving.

From the church meetings on Hawaiian plantations in the early 1900s to the efforts of the Black–Korean Alliance in the 1990s, Korean immigrants have created settings to voice their opinions. Racial tensions within Korean American communities have led to the establishment of several grassroots organizations. The Black–Korean Alliance in Los Angeles and the Korea Society in New York have set up programs to educate the two ethnic groups about each other's culture. In 1993 the Korea Society launched its Kids to Korea program. Designed to improve the strained relationship between the Korean and African American communities, the program enabled sixteen African American high school students from New York City and Los Angeles to travel to South Korea in order to learn about its people, culture, and history. This successful program has been expanded to include students from other cities. The Korea Society also sponsors a program called Project Bridge in Washington, D.C., which offers classes in both Korean and African American cultures.

While research experts have extensively studied the economic development and work patterns of Korean American professionals and entrepreneurs, the general American public knows little about Korean immigrant laborers. Yet since the beginning of the twentieth century, American industries have employed Koreans. By the 1990s Korean Americans had begun to join forces with other Asian Americans to educate themselves about labor unions and their rights. The Asian Immigrant Women Advocates, founded in 1983, organizes Chinese and Vietnamese garment workers and Korean hotel maids and electronics assemblers in the Oakland, California, area, staging demonstrations and rallies to draw attention to unfair labor practices. Another labor group, the Korean Immigrant Worker Advocates, is unique among Asian American organizations in Los Angeles because most of the members of its board of directors are workers.

Studies have shown that voter participation among Korean Americans is low. Historically Korean immigrants have rarely been active in election campaigns and have seldom made financial contributions to individual candidates. Groups such as the Coalition for Korean American Voters in New York are working hard to address this problem. In just three years the coalition registered 3,000 voters and sponsored programs that educate Korean immigrants about local and national government. Its efforts include airing public service announcements on Korean American television channels, establishing a college internship program to foster community service and leadership skills in students, and joining forces with other Asian American organizations to increase Asian American involvement in government.

In *Strangers from a Different Shore: A History of Asian Americans* (1989), Ronald Takaki describes the plight of a Korean immigrant named Easurk Emsen Charr, who was drafted and served in the U.S. Army during World War I. After he argued in court that as a U.S. military veteran he should be entitled to citizenship and the right to own land in California, the court ruled that the military should not have drafted him because he was Asian and therefore ineligible for U.S. citizenship. Despite such discriminatory treatment, Korean Americans were eager to volunteer for military service during World War II. Doing so gave them a chance to support the American effort to curtail Japanese imperialism. Some Korean Americans served as language teachers and translators, and 100 Korean immigrants joined the California Home Guard in Los Angeles. They also participated in Red Cross relief operations. However, the U.S. government remained somewhat suspicious of Korean immigrants, as Koreans were technically still part of the Japanese empire. In Hawaii, Korean immigrants were referred to as enemy aliens and banned from working on military bases. Today many Korean American men and women hold positions in the military.

Since Koreans first began immigrating to the United States, they have remained active in the politics of their homeland. Studies have shown that Korean Americans are generally more actively involved in the politics of Korea than in that of their new home. The lives of early Korean immigrants revolved around the Korean independence movement. In the 1960s Korean Americans staged mass demonstrations and relief efforts in response to the massacre of civilians by the South Korean dictatorship in Kwangju, the capital of South Cholla province. Today virtually every Korean American organization supports reunification of the peninsula. Groups such as the Korea Church Coalition for Peace, Justice, and Reunification were formed specifically for this purpose. Other U.S.-based organizations, including the Council for Democracy in Korea, seek to educate the public about the political affairs of Korea.

NOTABLE INDIVIDUALS

Business Kim Hyung Soon (1884–1968) immigrated to the United States in 1914 and started a small produce and nursery wholesale business in California with his friend Kim Ho. The Kim Brothers Company developed into a huge orchard, nursery, and fruit-packing shed business. Kim Hyung Soon is credited with developing new varieties of peaches known as fuzzless peaches, including Le Grand and Sun Grand. He also crossed the peach with the plum and developed the nectarine and helped establish the Korean Community Center in Los Angeles and the Korean Foundation, a fund that offers scholarships to students of Korean ancestry.

Education Margaret K. Pai (1914–) taught English at Kailua, Roosevelt, and Farrington high schools on the Hawaiian island of Oahu for many years. Her father, Do In Kwon, immigrated to Hawaii to work on the sugar plantations in the early 1900s. Her mother, Hee Kyung Lee, was a picture bride and met and married her husband in Hawaii at age eighteen. After retiring, Pai wrote short Hawaiian legends, poems, and personal reminiscences including *The Dreams of Two Yi-Men* (1989), a vivid account of her parents' experiences as early Korean immigrants in the United States.

Elaine H. Kim (1943–) is a professor of Asian American studies and faculty assistant on the status of women at the University of California–Berkeley. Kim also served as president of the Association for Asian American Studies and founded the organizations Asian Immigrant Women Advocates and Asian Women United of California. Her publications include *Asian American Literature: An Introduction to the Writings and their Social Context* (2006).

Government Herbert Y. C. Choy (1916–2004) became the first Asian American to be appointed to the U.S. federal bench in 1971. Educated at the University of Hawaii and Harvard University, he practiced law in Honolulu for twenty-five years. He served as attorney general of the Territory of Hawaii in 1957 and 1958 and continued his law practice until

President Richard Nixon appointed him to the U.S. Court of Appeals.

Activist Grace Lyu-Volckhausen established an outreach center for women at a YWCA in Queens in the 1960s. The program offered sewing classes, after-school recreation for children, counseling for battered women, and discussion groups. She also served on the New York City Commission on the Status of Women, the Mayor's Ethnic Council, and governor Mario Cuomo's Garment Advisory Council, and was a founding board member of the Korean American League for Civil Action.

Literature Younghill Kang (1903–1972) was one of the first Korean American writers to offer a firsthand, English-language account of growing up in occupied Korea. He wrote his first novel, *The Grass Roof* (1931), after spending many years struggling to survive as an immigrant in San Francisco and New York. He later taught comparative literature at New York University and devoted the rest of his life to fighting racism in the United States and political oppression in his homeland.

Kim Young Ik (1920–1995) was the author of several novels and stories for children and adults. His books have won numerous awards and have been translated into many languages. They include *The Happy Days* (1960), *The Divine Gourd* (1962), *Love in Winter* (1962), *Blue in the Seed* (1964), and *The Wedding Shoes* (1984).

Marie G. Lee (1964–) has been at the forefront of the movement to create children's literature by and about Korean Americans. Raised in Hibbing, Minnesota, she graduated from Brown University and lived in New York City. Her young-adult novel *Finding My Voice* (1992) won the 1993 Friends of American Writers Award. Lee's other young-adult novels include *If It Hadn't Been for Yoon Jun* (1993), *Saying Goodbye* (1994), and *Necessary Roughness* (1998). Her work has appeared in many publications, including the *New York Times* and the *Asian/Pacific American Journal*, as well as several anthologies. She was president of the board of directors of the Asian American Writers' Workshop and a member of PEN and the Asian American Arts Alliance.

Music Nam June Paik (1932–2006) built a worldwide reputation as a composer of electronic music and producer of avant-garde "action concerts." He grew up in Seoul and earned a degree in aesthetics at the University of Tokyo before meeting American composer John Cage in Germany. Paik's interest in American electronic music brought him to the United States, where his work was exhibited at the Museum of Modern Art, the Whitney Museum, and the Kitchen Museum in New York City. His work also appeared at the Metropolitan Museum in Tokyo and the Museum of Contemporary Art in Chicago. Among his video credits are *TV Buddha* (1974) and *Video Fish* (1975). He also produced a program called *Good Morning, Mr. Orwell*, which was broadcast live simultaneously in San Francisco, New York, and Paris on New Year's Day 1984 as a tribute to George Orwell's novel *1984*.

Myung-Whun Chung (1953–) was born in Seoul into a family of talented musicians. He made his piano debut at age seven with the Seoul Philharmonic Orchestra and moved with his family to the United States five years later. He studied piano at the Mannes School of Music and conducting at the Juilliard School of Music in New York City. He served as assistant conductor of the Los Angeles Philharmonic Orchestra; music director and principal conductor for the Radio Symphony Orchestra in Saarbrucken, Germany; principal guest conductor of the Teatro Comunale in Florence, Italy; and music director and conductor for the Opera de la Bastille, located in the legendary French prison. In 2011 he made headlines when he visited North Korea with the Seoul Philharmonic and formed an orchestra of musicians from North and South Korea.

Sports Physician and diver Sammy Lee (1920–) made a name for himself in both sports and medicine. He won the gold medal for ten-meter platform diving in the 1948 Olympic Games in London, one year after earning a medical degree from the University of Southern California School of Medicine. Lee won another gold medal in the 1952 Olympic Games in Helsinki, along with a bronze medal in three-meter springboard diving. During that time he practiced medicine in Korea as part of the U.S. Army Medical Corps. He was named Outstanding American Athlete in 1953 by the Amateur Athletic Union and inducted into the International Swimming Hall of Fame in 1968. He served on the President's Council on Physical Fitness and Sports from 1971 to 1980 and coached the U.S. diving team for the 1960 and 1964 Olympics. He also was named Outstanding American of Korean Ancestry twice—by the American Korean Society in 1967 and the League of Korean Americans in 1986. After retiring from sports, he ran a private medical practice in Orange, California.

Stage and Screen Peter Hyun (1906–1993) worked in the American theater for many years as a stage manager for Eva LeGallienne's Civic Repertory Theatre in New York, director of the New York Federal Theater Children's Theater, and organizer and director of the Studio Players in Cambridge, Massachusetts. During World War II, he served as a language specialist in the U.S. Army. After settling in Oxnard, California, he taught English to immigrant students from Asia. In 1986 he published *Man Sei!: The Making of a Korean American*, a personal account of growing up as the son of a leader in the Korean independence movement.

Margaret Cho (1968–), a second-generation Korean American comedian, broke numerous barriers and stereotypes with her television and film appearances. In 1994 she became the first Asian American to star in her own television show, the ABC sitcom *All-American*

Girl, which centered on a Korean American family. After the show was canceled in 1995, she went on to have a successful film and television career, appearing in the popular Lifetime series *Drop Dead Diva*. She also authored the books *I'm the One That I Want* (1999) and *I Have Chosen to Stay and Fight* (2005).

MEDIA

PRINT

Korean Quarterly

This newspaper discusses the Korean American communities in the Twin Cities and other parts of the Midwest. It offers features on events in the Korean community, highlights people from first- and second-generation Korean American families, and provides Korean American–run businesses a place to advertise.

Martha Vickery, Managing Editor
P.O. Box 6789
St. Paul, Minnesota 55106
Phone: (651) 398-2325
Email: koreanquarterly@gmail.com
URL: www.koreanquarterly.org

Korean Studies

This journal addresses a broad range of topics through interdisciplinary and multicultural articles, book reviews, and scholarly essays.

Kim Min-sun, Editor
Korean Studies
Center for Korean Studies
1881 East-West Road
University of Hawaii
Honolulu, Hawaii 96822
Phone: (808) 956-7041
Fax: (808) 956-2213
Email: korstudy@hawaii.edu
URL: www.hawaii.edu/korea/pages/Publications/ks.html

RADIO

KBLA (1540 AM)

Radio Korea broadcasts around the clock, seven days a week.

David Choi
3700 Wilshire Boulevard #600
Los Angeles, California 90010
Phone: (213) 487-1300
Fax: (213) 487-7455
Email: info@radiokorea.com
URL: www.radiokorea.com

KFOX/Radio Seoul (1650 AM)

Affiliated with *Korean Times* and KTAN-TV, this Los Angeles-area radio station broadcasts entirely in Korean.

4525 Wilshire Boulevard
Los Angeles, California 90010
Phone: (323) 936-0606
Fax: (323) 945-8885
URL: www.radioseoul1650.com

Korean American Radio (1400 AM)

The first and only Korean-language radio station to serve northern California and the Bay Area.

Peter Kim
1290 Kifer Road
Suite 309
Sunnyvale, California 94086
Phone: (408) 735-1400
Fax: (408) 329-6648
Email: webmaster@hanmiradio.com
URL: www.hanmiradio.com

KRB (1660 AM)

Korean Radio Broadcasting serves the New York metropolitan area.

Kristine Chang
136-56 39 Avenue
Suite 400
Flushing, New York 11354
Phone: (718) 358-9300
URL: www.nyradiokorea.com

TELEVISION

KBS America

The Korean Broadcasting System provides programming aimed at promoting the culture of South Korea within the United States.

Ken Lee, News, Programming, and Production Team Director
625 South Kingsley Drive
Los Angeles, California 90005
Phone: (213) 739-1111
Fax: (213) 739-2729
Email: info@kbs-america.com
URL: www.kbs-america.com

MKTV

Media Korea TV ranks as the largest Korean American station in the United States.

Benjamin Yoo, President
140 Sylvan Avenue
Suite 304
Englewood, New Jersey 07632
Phone: (201) 363-0707
Fax: (201) 363-0404
URL: www.mediakoreatv.com

ORGANIZATIONS AND ASSOCIATIONS

Korean American Coalition

Founded in 1983, this organization seeks to bring together Korean communities within the United States through fundraising and educational programs. It also sponsors programs designed to educate non-Koreans about Korean culture.

Duncan Lee, Chairman
3540 Wilshire Boulevard
#911
Los Angeles, California 90010
Phone: (213) 365-5999

Fax: (213) 380-7990
Email: info@kacnational.com
URL: www.kacnational.com

Korean American League for Civil Action

This nonprofit organization promotes civic participation among Korean Americans and Asian Pacific Americans.

149 West 24th Street
6th Floor
New York, New York 10011
Phone: (212) 633-2000
Email: info@kalca.org
URL: www.kalca.org

Korea Society (U.S.-Korea Society)

The Korea Society is the result of a 1993 merger of the New York–based Korea Society and the U.S.-Korea Foundation in Washington, D.C. This nonprofit organization is dedicated to strengthening the bonds of awareness, understanding, and cooperation between the United States and Korea, and among Koreans, Korean Americans, and all other Americans. The society's efforts extend to education, public policy, business, the arts, and media.

Mark C. Minton, President
950 Third Avenue
Eighth Floor
New York, New York 10022
Phone: (212) 759-7525
Fax: (212) 759-7530
Email: korea.ny@koreasociety.org
URL: www.koreasociety.org

National Association of Korean Americans

This organization of individuals of Korean descent living in the United States seeks to safeguard the human and civil rights of Korean Americans and promote friendly relations between Korean Americans and other racial and ethnic groups.

H. K. Suh, General Secretary
3883 Plaza Drive
Fairfax ,Virginia 22030
Phone: (703) 267-2388
Fax: (703) 267-2396
Email: nakausa@naka.org
URL: www.naka.org

National Korean American Service and Education Consortium

Founded in 1994, NAKASEC seeks to promote immigrant rights and to bring together Korean Americans with a common goal of social change. Based in Los Angeles, NAKASEC also has an office in Washington, D.C.

Morna Ha, Executive Director
1701 K Street NW
Suite 650
Washington, D.C. 20006
Phone: (202) 299-9540
Fax: (202) 299-9729
Email: nakasec@nakasec.org
URL: www.nakasec.org

MUSEUMS AND RESEARCH CENTERS

Many major universities have a Center for Korean Studies, including Columbia University, State University of New York–Stony Brook, University of California–Berkeley, University of Michigan, and University of Hawaii–Manoa.

Korean American Resource and Cultural Center

The goal of this center is to empower Korean Americans through promotion of education and culture.

Sik Son, Executive Director
6146 North Lincoln Avenue
Chicago, Illinois 60569
Phone: (773) 588-9158
Fax: (773) 588-9159
Email: krcc@chicagokrcc.org
URL: www.chicagokrcc.org

Korean Cultural Center

Founded in 1980, the Korean Cultural Center offers programs that introduce Korean culture, society, history, and arts to the American public. It organizes exhibitions, lectures, symposiums, and multicultural festivals, and houses a 26,000-volume library, an art museum and gallery, and film archives and screening room. It also publishes *Korean Culture Magazine*.

Youngsan Kim, Director
5505 Wilshire Boulevard
Los Angeles, California 90036
Phone: (213) 936-7141
Fax: (213) 936-5172
Email: exhibition@kccla.org
URL: www.kccla.org

Korea Economic Institute of America

Founded in 1982, this educational group includes politicians, academics, trade organizations, banks, and other Americans concerned with the Korean economy. The Institute publishes updates on economic issues in Korea.

Abraham Kim, Interim President
1800 K Street
NW
Suite 1010
Washington, D.C 20006
Phone: (202) 464-1982
Fax: (202) 464-1987
Email: info@keia.com
URL: www.keia.com

Korean Institute of Minnesota

Founded in 1973, this nonprofit organization is dedicated to preserving Korean language and culture. It brings together Korean American and adoptive families with a variety of classes and social opportunities for all ages.

Yoonju Park
Korean Presbyterian Church of Minnesota
5840 Humboldt Avenue
Brooklyn Center, Minnesota 55430

Phone: (651) 324-0208
Email: kampark1@hotmail.com
URL: www.koreaninstitute.org

Korean Resource Center

The KRC was founded in 1983 with the goal of bringing together the Korean American community through education, social services, and cultural activities.

Dae Joong Yoon, Executive Director
900 South Crenshaw Boulevard
Los Angeles, California 90019
Phone: (323) 937-3718
Fax: (323) 937-3526
Email: krcla@krcla.org
URL: www.krcla.org

SOURCES FOR ADDITIONAL STUDY

Abelmann, Nancy. *The Intimate University: Korean American Students and the Problems of Segregation.* Durham, NC: Duke University Press, 2009.

Aguilar-San Juan, Karin, eds. *The State of Asian America: Activism and Resistance in the 1990s.* Boston: South End Press, 1994.

Kim, Ilpyong J. *Korean-Americans: Past, Present, and Future.* Elizabeth, NJ: Hollym International, 2004.

Kwak, Tae-Hwan, and Seong Hyong Lee, eds. *The Korean American Community: Present and Future.* Seoul: Kyungnam University Press, 1991.

Lehrer, Brian. *The Korean Americans.* New York: Chelsea House, 1988.

Mangiafico, Luciano. *Contemporary American Immigrants: Patterns of Filipino, Korean, and Chinese Settlement in the United States.* New York: Praeger, 1988.

Patterson, Wayne. *The Korean Frontier in America: Immigration to Hawaii, 1896–1910.* Honolulu: University of Hawaii Press, 1988.

Patterson, Wayne, and Hyung-Chan Kim. *Koreans in America.* Minneapolis: Lerner Publications, 1992.

Takaki, Ronald. *From the Land of Morning Calm: The Koreans in America.* Adapted by Rebecca Stefoff. New York: Chelsea House Publishers, 1994.

———*Strangers from a Different Shore: A History of Asian Americans.* Boston: Little, Brown, 1989.

Won Moo Hurh. *The Korean Americans.* Westport, CT: Greenwood Press, 1998.

KURDISH AMERICANS

Chad Dundas

OVERVIEW

Kurdish Americans are immigrants or descendants of people who are Kurds, an ethnic group indigenous to multiple countries throughout Southwest Asia. The bulk of the worldwide Kurdish population lives in Kurdistan, a roughly defined region of arid mountains and high plateaus that includes portions of eastern Turkey, northern Syria, northern Iraq, and western Iran. Kurdistan is typified by rugged terrain, high elevations, and extreme temperature swings between summer and winter seasons. It also boasts significant deposits of natural resources and is suitable in many areas for intensive agriculture. Estimates of the total size of the region range widely, from 74,000 square miles (190,000 square kilometers) to 151,000 square miles (390,000 square kilometers), the latter of which is roughly the size of the state of Montana.

The total population of Kurdish people is between 30 and 38 million, according to 2012 estimates from the *CIA World Factbook*. Although political and nationalistic factors make it difficult to accurately gauge the size of the Kurdish population, this estimate includes approximately 14.35 million in Turkey, 7.9 million in Iran, 6.2 million in Iraq, and an undefined population of several more million in Syria. The majority of Kurdish people practice Islam, though some adhere to indigenous religions and a small number practice Christianity or Judaism. Many Kurds subsist by farming and herding animals as part of the region's pastoralist economy. Since the 1990s they have had partial autonomy in the area of Iraqi Kurdistan, a district rich in oil and minerals such as coal, copper, gold, and iron. This has provided an economic boost for the Kurdistan Regional Government but has further worsened long-standing discord with the Iraqi government.

Kurdish people first began immigrating to the United States after World War I, though the most notable numbers arrived in three distinct migration waves during the late twentieth century. The largest population of Kurds in North America is in Nashville, Tennessee, where since the late 1970s Kurdish refugees have settled in a neighborhood affectionately known as Little Kurdistan. Early on, Kurds in the United States worked entry-level jobs, but in cities such as Nashville, where large populations have gathered, they now own an array of businesses that support their neighborhood communities. The vast majority of Kurdish immigrants are from Iraq, and the largest influx occurred during the 1990s, when Kurds fled that country in great numbers to escape a genocidal campaign waged against them by dictator Saddam Hussein.

Estimates of the Kurdish population in the United States vary greatly. In 2010 the U.S. Census Bureau's American Community Survey estimated that there were 15,300 people of Kurdish descent in the United States, but other informal estimates put the number closer to 40,000 or 60,000. Kurds often migrate secondarily to the United States, which makes it difficult to calculate accurate population numbers. In addition, many Kurdish Americans self-identify as being from the country from which they migrated, such as Iraq or Turkey. According to the American Community Survey as well as unofficial estimates from groups such as the Kurdish Achievers and the Kurdish American Youth Organization (KAYO), the largest populations of Kurdish people in the United States live in Davidson County, Tennessee (which includes Nashville and surrounding communities); Virginia; and San Diego, California. KAYO also reports that Kurdish Americans live in smaller but notable numbers in the states of Massachusetts, New Jersey, and New York.

HISTORY OF THE PEOPLE

Early History Historians still debate the exact origins of Kurdish people, and there remains some disagreement over the etymology of the term *Kurd*. Although Kurdish people were not recognized as a single, distinct ethnic group until the Middle Ages, archeological evidence suggests humans were inhabiting the mountains of Kurdistan as early as 8,000 to 12,000 years ago. The people of these early civilizations (such as the Guti, Subari, Lullu, Kassite, Mitanni, Mani, Urartu, Nairi, and Mede) are believed to have been of Indo-European decent or to have migrated south from lands in what would become the countries of Azerbaijan, Armenia, Georgia, and Russia. Modern Kurdish people are likely the descendants of these early tribes and their culture the result of centuries of assimilating the beliefs and customs of many disparate migratory groups.

By the rise of the Muslim Conquests of the region during the early seventh century, indigenous people were living a partially sedentary lifestyle, practicing basic agriculture and herding livestock in the rugged terrain of Kurdistan. In 641 CE, forces of the Muslim caliphate pushed north from the Arabian Peninsula, conquering lands claimed by the Sassanid and Byzantine empires, including Kurdish outposts in what is now northern Iraq. This period likely signaled not only the Kurdish civilization's first exposure to Islam but also the beginning of centuries of rule by outsiders, punctuated by countless Kurdish uprisings against various foreign invaders.

While under the rule of the caliphate, tribes in the empire's most remote, isolated areas began establishing their own independent states, and during the Middle Ages many Kurdish dynasties arose in the region. Of these dynasties, the Ayyubid dynasty (c. 1173–1250) was the largest, ruling over Egypt and what is now Syria, northern Iraq, and Yemen. Kurdish dynasties would rise and fall with the changing tides of invasions and conquests, though Kurds managed to maintain some autonomy over their homeland.

In 1514 Ottoman armies captured and annexed Kurdistan and Armenia as two separate lands. For a time Ottoman leaders allowed local chiefs to govern Kurdish domains, but by the nineteenth century the empire had begun centralizing its power around the capital city of Constantinople. In 1847 Kurdish leaders staged an unsuccessful revolt against the Ottomans; and despite its failure, by 1880 the first real Kurdish nationalist movement had taken root, with leaders demanding the recognition of an independent Kurdistan.

Modern Era Kurdish history during the twentieth century was largely defined by oppression and persecution at the hands of political leaders in Iraq, Iran, Turkey, and Syria as well as by a desire among Kurds to establish sovereign home rule over Kurdistan. When the Ottoman Empire was dissolved at the end of World War I, many Kurds resisted assimilation into the new Turkish Republic. During the war, the Young Turks, members of Turkey's secularist, nationalist reform party, had waged a widespread campaign of ethnic cleansing and forced deportation against Kurdish people, displacing as many as 700,000 Kurds from their homelands. It is estimated that perhaps half that number were killed.

From the 1920s until the 1940s, several short-lived independent Kurdish states blossomed and folded as the world's most powerful nations vied for control of the Middle East's oil-rich lands. These failed efforts included the Kingdom of Kurdistan in Iraq, the Republic of Ararat in Turkey, and the Republic of Mahabad in Iran. Each of these, as well as numerous other Kurdish uprisings, were suppressed by the ruling parties of their respective nations, resulting in the forced displacement of more Kurdish people and sporadic periods of martial law.

By the dawn of the Cold War, much of the Middle East was divided between countries welcoming support and influence from the United States and countries allying themselves with the Soviet Union. Kurds were caught in the middle, and their attempts at independence were often actively thwarted by the world's superpowers. In Turkey during the 1950s, Kurds enjoyed some increased freedoms and began working within the country's political system to improve their living conditions. In 1960, however, these efforts were halted when a military coup d'état ousted the country's democratically elected government.

At the same time in Iraq, war between a succession of governmental regimes and Kurdish people raged for nearly fifteen years, resulting in widespread atrocities. In 1970 Kurdish leadership negotiated an agreement with then–vice president Saddam Hussein that would allow Kurds to become members of the Iraqi government. After the attempted assassination of Kurdish leader Mustafa Barzani in 1971, however, Kurds began a new offensive against the Iraqi government and were supported in their efforts by the United States. When Hussein signed a surprise peace agreement with Iran in 1975, the United States abruptly withdrew its support of the Kurdish independence movement, and the Iraqi power structure renewed its attacks against Kurds. The sudden lack of aid from the United States also caused Kurdish groups to regress into factionalism and infighting, which further hampered efforts aimed at liberation.

Hussein's worst attacks against the Kurds took place during the Al-Anfal campaign from 1986 to 1989. During this offensive, thousands of Kurdish people were killed in ground attacks, chemical-weapons strikes, and the systematic destruction of 4,500 Kurdish settlements. It is estimated that as much as one third of Iraq's 3.5 million Kurdish citizens were displaced and more than 180,000 non-Arab minorities killed. The most high-profile attack against the Kurds was Hussein's 1988 chemical-weapons assault on the village of Halabja, during which thousands of men, women, and children died.

In 1990 Saddam Hussein's military invaded the country of Kuwait, and during the build up to the ensuing Gulf War, the U.S. government began aiding rebel groups in Iraq for the first time in fifteen years. The following year, in response to Saddam Hussein's defeat by the United States, Kurds joined Shias from southern Iraq in an armed revolt. Although the uprising met with initial success, Saddam Hussein's armies moved in and destroyed the guerilla forces once it was clear that U.S. troops had left the region and were no longer supporting the freedom fighters. Thousands of Kurdish people were again forced to flee into the mountains, and perhaps 1.5 million crossed the borders into Turkey and Iran. The United States, the United Kingdom, and France intervened to establish a "safe haven" for the Kurds in Iraq. Shortly thereafter Kurds in northern Iraq held parliamentary elections and established the semi-autonomous Kurdistan Regional Government (KRG).

The next decade was typified by internal strife in the Kurdish movement and widespread skepticism about the trustworthiness of aid and military support from the United States. After the United States' successful invasion of Iraq in 2003, however, Kurdish people gained control over expanded territory, and a new constitution was established recognizing KRG rule in parts of the country. Following the 2003 war, Iraq's governmental system (where traditional political identity often went hand-in-hand with religious beliefs) underwent a significant shift as Shi'a Muslims and Iraqi Kurds gained more power. Across Kurdistan, this coincided with a rise of religious pluralism and today many Kurds abroad and in the United States emphasize interfaith relations and religious tolerance.

In Turkey, however, the government has historically refused to acknowledge the existence of a Kurdish minority population altogether. In March 2013 the Kurdistan Workers' Party offered the Turkish government a cease-fire to long-standing guerrilla warfare in that country. In Syria, Kurdish rebels joined other insurgent groups in an ongoing civil war, hoping the outcome would result in added rights and land holdings for Kurds.

SETTLEMENT IN THE UNITED STATES

The first Kurds to arrive in the United States, in the 1910s and 1920s, likely were not specifically identified as Kurdish by immigration officials. Because of this, and because they left few historical accounts of their lives, little is known about their numbers or about their early experiences with American culture. The majority probably settled in traditional immigrant neighborhoods of major cities like Chicago, Detroit, and New York and in the farmlands of Southern California. Some Kurdish residents in those areas today can trace their ancestry back to these initial arrivals. Most Kurds of that era departed their homeland due to the political upheaval brought on by the end of the World War I, including the fall of the Ottoman Empire, widespread forced deportations from the new Turkish Republic, and the repercussions of several large-scale Kurdish rebellions during the next two decades. Additional armed conflicts during the mid-twentieth century, such as the Fourth of July Revolution in Iraq in 1958, also increased Kurdish immigration to the United States.

The next notable and well-documented influx of Kurdish immigrants to the United States did not occur until 1975, when a fifteen-year revolution against a string of Iraqi regimes ended in failure and the deportation of massive numbers of Kurds. Between 1975 and 1978 the Iraqi government forcibly dispossessed 200,000 Kurdish people, some of whom immigrated to the United States. By 1976 many were being processed at Kentucky's Fort Campbell near the Tennessee border, just 60 miles north of Nashville. At the time, the city's booming economy, strong network of charitable organizations, and availability of entry-level jobs made it a natural landing place for the majority of these Iraqi Kurds. By 1978 they were joined by Kurds from Iran, who escaped that nation following their own unsuccessful bid for autonomy.

According to the leaders of local charity organizations, the Kurds who settled in Nashville during the 1970s established the first real Kurdish American community. They also constituted the first of three modern waves of Kurdish immigration to this country. The second wave came during the late 1980s and early 1990s as many Kurds left Iraq

A Kurdish immigrant holds a baby during a Kurdish New Year celebration in 2005 in Lake Dallas, Texas. The area is home to several thousand Kurds who gathered together to celebrate the holiday with dancing and food. KARL STOLLEIS / GETTY IMAGES

to escape the genocidal attacks launched against their people by Saddam Hussein's regime. Many of these Kurds spent years languishing in Turkish and Iranian refugee camps before the end of the Gulf War in 1991, when a few thousand were accepted into the United States.

The final major wave of Kurdish immigration took place during the late 1990s, when Saddam Hussein's regime began threatening the families of nongovernmental organization staff members who had partnered with or received support from Western entities. In 1996 nearly 2,000 Kurdish people, mostly intellectuals and members of Kurdish leadership, crossed into Turkey and were quickly relocated to the United States by U.S. forces. Many of these immigrants—sometimes called the Guam Kurds due to the six months they spent there before being resettled in the United States—also found permanent homes in the Nashville area.

The Kurdish population in Tennessee has been estimated by groups such as the Kurdish American Youth Organization to be 11,000. Another estimated 10,000 live in San Diego County, which is home to up to a quarter of all Iraqi refugees in the United States. Many Kurdish people in Southern California work in agriculture, but the population also includes professionals, intellectuals, and activists. In Nashville the neighborhood known as Little Kurdistan features

restaurants, grocery stores, car dealerships, and other local businesses owned by Kurdish people. A Kurdish community of around 4,000 people lives in the area of Dallas, Texas, while similar numbers live in suburban Virginia outside Washington, D.C. The Kurdish American Youth Organization also reported small, but significant, populations of Kurdish Americans living in New Jersey and New York. In 2010 the American Community Survey listed much lower estimates for Tennessee (2,980), California (2,853), and Virginia (1,192). The discrepancy between the unofficial estimates and the U.S. Census numbers can be explained by the fact that Kurds migrate to the United States from various countries and may self-identify as being from that country rather than being of Kurdish descent.

LANGUAGE

The Kurdish language is less a single, unified language than a collection of related dialects spoken by Kurds throughout western Asia. As a whole these dialects are frequently referred to by the umbrella term "Kurdish" and are considered part of the Indo-European language family. Typically, Kurdish languages are organized into three major dialects, called Kurmanjî, Soranî, and Pehlewanî. Within these there are numerous subdialects, which are spoken by smaller but significant numbers of

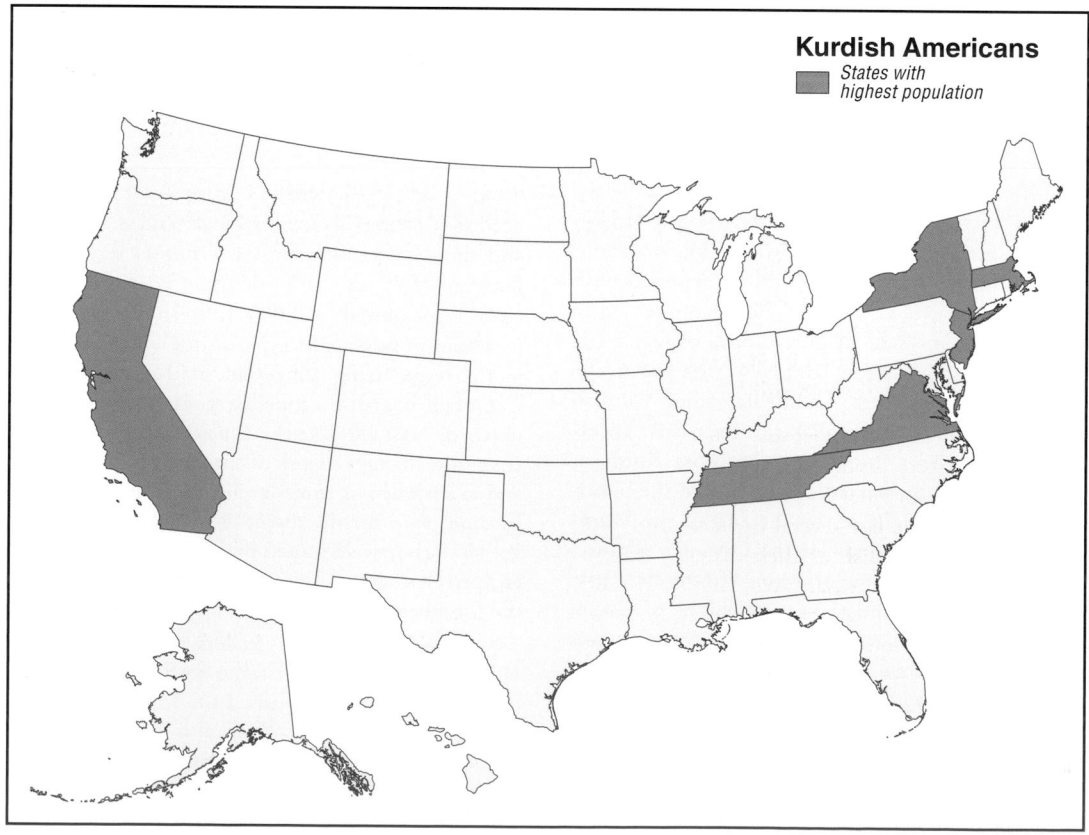

Kurdish Americans
States with highest population

Kurdish people. According to the Kurdish Academy of Language, there is "no standard nomenclature for the divisions of Kurdish dialects, not just in the works of Western scholars but among the Kurds themselves," so the organization and names of various dialects and subdialects vary from source to source.

Kurmanjî (sometimes referred to as Northern Kurdish) is the dialect spoken by the largest number of Kurds, with an estimated 21 million native speakers. It is the language of the majority of Kurdish people living in Turkey, Syria, and the northern areas of Iran and Iraq, as well as in many of the former Soviet republics.

Soranî (or Central Kurdish) is the dialect spoken by the majority of Kurds in Iran and Iraq, with an estimated 10 million native speakers. Unlike Kurmanjî, which is written using the Latin alphabet, Soranî is written in a modified Perso-Arabic script.

Pehlewaní (also called Southern Kurdish or Kermānšāni) is spoken by an estimated 6 million Kurds in western Iran and eastern Iraq. Likely once a more prevalent dialect, Pehlewaní is believed to have been diluted and partially assimilated into Central Kurdish by large numbers of Soranî-speaking refugees who have moved into areas traditionally dominated by Pehlewaní.

In some countries, the Kurdish language has been a subject of controversy, and Kurdish speakers have faced discrimination. In Syria it is forbidden to publish materials written in Kurdish. Prior to 2002 it was illegal in Turkey to speak or write in Kurdish, but the country has since granted some reforms regarding the language. In 2009 the Turkish government began operating a twenty-four-hour Kurdish-language television station. As of 2012 it announced plans to begin teaching Kurdish in schools and to allow the language to be used in courts. Kurdish was recognized as the second official language of Iraq after the fall of Saddam Hussein, and Soranî is now regarded as the dominant form of written Kurdish.

The 2010 U.S. Census counted 12,982 Kurdish speakers living in the United States. Because the majority of Kurdish American families arrived during the last several decades, many continue to speak Kurdish as their primary language at home. This is particularly true of older Kurdish Americans, some of whom never attended school in their home countries and may find it difficult to learn English—or may have no desire to learn it. In cities where Kurdish neighborhoods have been established, older immigrants sometimes isolate themselves inside Kurdish-speaking communities. In navigating English-speaking society, older Kurdish Americans sometimes rely on bilingual

A KURDISH LANGUAGE SUMMIT

In November 2010 the University of California–Los Angles hosted North America's first summit on the Kurdish language. The summit was sponsored by the Kurdish American Education Society and UCLA's Center for Near Eastern Studies. It drew twenty experts on the Kurdish language from all over the world for a day of lectures and panel discussions. Topics included language policy, Kurdish identity, literature, music, and the dilemmas faced when trying to standardize the language.

children or grandchildren who have attended school in the United States.

Greetings and Popular Expressions Common greetings and expressions in Kurdish include the following:

Bi xêr bî, Bi xêr hatî—Welcome; *Silaw*—Hello; *Demêke tum nebîniwe*—Long time no see; *Xoşhalim bi nasînit*—Pleased to meet you; *Beyanî baş*—Good morning; *Roj baş*—Good afternoon; *Êware baş*—Good evening; *Shaw Khosh/Shaw hash*—Good night; *Xoşbext bî*—Good luck; *Noş*—Cheers; *Rojêkî xoş*—Have a nice day; and *Sipas dekem*—Thank you.

RELIGION

The dominant religion among Kurdish people, including those living in the United States, is Islam. Most Kurds are Sunni Muslims who adhere to the mainstream Shafi'i school of religious law. Smaller numbers of Kurdish people are Shi'a Muslims, and others engage in mysticism as part of Sufi orders. An even smaller minority of Kurdish people continue to adhere to indigenous religions, some of which are believed to predate the culture's exposure to Islam.

Conversion to Christianity and Judaism never gained widespread popularity in Kurdish communities, though there are Kurds who identify as Christian or Jewish. In the United States many Kurdish families observe popular Christian holidays. A small number of Kurds adhere to Zoroastrianism, which was once the state religion of ancient Iran and is based on the teachings of the ancient philosopher Zoroaster. It is believed by some scholars to be the world's first monotheistic religion and focuses on the opposing forces of good and evil, embodied by two conflicting deities.

Notable indigenous religions among the Kurds include Yârsânism and Yazidi. Yârsânism (also known as Ahl-e Haqq, which is Arabic for "people of truth") features distinct holy scriptures written in Persian and the Kurdish Gorani dialect. Major themes include reincarnation, the presence of distinct but related internal and external worlds, and the existence of a divine entity that manifests itself in human form. Many similar beliefs appear in the Yazidi faith; its adherents believe in the intermittent reincarnation of seven holy beings left behind by the creator to look after the world. Its holy books are written in the Kurdish Kurmanjî dialect, and its teachings contain elements of Zoroastrianism and Islamic Sufi doctrine.

Initial waves of Kurdish Muslim arrivals to the United States likely found few opportunities to worship in public and a lack of religious centers in which to assemble. Even in large cities where mosques were available, few if any services were conducted in the Kurdish language. This posed considerable difficulty, because Muslim prayer is often conducted in congregation, and communal services are considered a focal point of many Kurdish communities. In 1997 Kurdish people in Nashville opened the Salahadeen Center, believed to be the first Kurdish mosque in North America. There, local imams frequently hold services in Kurdish and multiple daily prayer times are available to congregants. San Diego also features a Kurdish Community Islamic Center, which offers religious prayer services to Kurdish speakers.

In modern times, and especially in the wake of the overthrow of Saddam Hussein in 2003, Kurdish people have begun to emphasize a spirit of religious pluralism and interfaith cooperation both in Kurdistan and the United States. The new constitution of Iraqi Kurdistan "endorses and respects the Islamic identity of the majority of the people" but also guarantees individual religious freedoms, mandating that other groups have "the freedom to practice their religious rites and rituals." In 2012 the regional government of Iraqi Kurdistan declared that schools there would be religiously neutral, teaching all the great religions of the world without favor or discrimination. Additionally, in recent years more Kurds have begun to convert to Christianity, though their numbers remain comparatively small.

Maintaining a distinct cultural identity is important to Kurdish people, and they have worked to preserve their customs by establishing their own neighborhoods, religious centers, social clubs, and in some cases by continuing to wear traditional dress. Enclaves such as Nashville's Little Kurdistan have become vibrant Kurdish communities where Kurdish refugees from different geographic locations bring together their tribal heritage, religious beliefs, and social bonds.

CULTURE AND ASSIMILATION

The majority of Kurdish immigrants have been eager to adopt the trappings of mainstream life in the United States. However, maintaining a distinct cultural identity is important to Kurdish people, and they have worked to preserve their customs by establishing their own neighborhoods, religious centers, social clubs, and in some cases by continuing to wear traditional dress. Enclaves such as Nashville's Little Kurdistan have become vibrant Kurdish communities where Kurdish refugees from different geographic locations bring together their tribal heritage, religious beliefs, and social bonds.

Adapting to life in the United States also posed some problems, particularly for older Kurdish people. Many were used to the tribalism of traditional Kurdish culture and felt alienated from the mainstream values of the United States, which they often saw as overemphasizing the individual at the expense of the family and spirituality. Some harbored a distrust of government and police after negative experiences in their home countries. Many struggled to find or adjust to new careers and in general to navigate American society, leading to a feeling of cultural isolation. Some older Kurds began to depend on younger people who more easily learned the language and more deftly assimilated into the culture of the United States.

As a result, Kurdish American youths sometimes reported feeling caught between two worlds, charged with maintaining the customs and traditions of their parents and grandparents while simultaneously fitting into the mainstream culture they encountered at school and in the workforce. This could lead to its own form of isolation; for instance, some Kurdish youths felt they could not turn to their parents when they encountered trouble in school or with friends. They often identified with a mixed cultural identity, feeling both American and Kurdish. Some Kurdish American young people in Nashville have joked about being a generation of "Ameri-Kurds."

A turning point in Kurdish American culture may have occurred when educated Kurdish civic leaders with pronounced organizational skills began arriving in the United States during the late 1990s. These were professionals and intellectuals who left Iraq after being targeted by Saddam Hussein's regime. After settling in the United States, they began organizing the Kurdish American communities, helping earlier arrivals who had attained enough financial stability to start their own businesses and advocating for political engagement and activism in modern Kurdish American communities.

Traditions and Customs Kurdish immigrants have often forged close-knit communities upon their arrival in the United States, and many of these communities maintain decidedly traditional customs and beliefs. Although they often come from different regions and disparate backgrounds, Kurds typically share similar family and community values. The leaders of charitable organizations who helped settle Kurdish refugees in Nashville from the 1970s through the 1990s theorized that one reason the city seemed attractive to Kurds was that its relatively conservative morals and strong religious fundamentals were compatible with their own traditions.

Family and community are central themes in the lives of Kurdish Americans, and gatherings at the homes of extended family members are frequent, important events. Traditional Kurdish culture places considerable emphasis on the concept of hospitality, and it is considered an honor for Kurdish people to host other family members, friends, and even strangers in their homes. Guests are considered as important as family and no rooms in a host's home are closed to them. Hosts are commonly prepared to entertain at any time, frequently rescheduling other plans and organizing impromptu feasts or social gatherings when visitors arrive unannounced.

Cuisine Traditional Kurdish foods are as diverse and eclectic as the people themselves. Common staples of the Kurdish diet include meats such as chicken and lamb as well as a wide variety of fruits, vegetables, herbs, and grains. Traditional dishes include meat dumplings called *kofta* or *kibbe*; dishes of rice, meats, and egg known as *biryani*; meat and vegetable pies called *kuki*; stuffed-vegetable dishes called *dolma*; an eggplant, pepper, potato, and tomato dish called *tapsi*; as well as a variety of soups, stews, salads, and sweets. Meals are often accompanied by rice or flatbread. Kurdish beverages include sweet black tea or strong, bitter coffee, as well as a mixture of yogurt, water, and salt known as *mastow*.

For Kurdish Americans, preparing traditional foods provides an important link to the culture of their homelands. Family dinners are common, and food typically fulfills a central role in community gathering or while entertaining guests. Even small, simple gatherings often begin with servings of Kurdish tea or coffee, followed by offerings of sweets, nuts, meats, and cheeses. The presentation of fruits typically comes last and can often signal the end of a gathering. Religious families view food as a gift from God, meant to be shared with others. Refusing food in the home of traditional Kurdish American families can be considered an insult or a sign that some slight or offense has been perceived.

In cities with larger Kurdish populations, traditional breads and pastries are sometimes available from Kurdish-owned bakeries. Restaurants offering Kurdish foods can also be found in cities such as Nashville; New York City; Washington, D.C.; and Minneapolis, Minnesota.

Traditional Dress Many Kurdish Americans, especially younger, second-generation members of the community, opt to wear Western or Americanized attire when in the workplace, at school, or attending mainstream social activities. At cultural gatherings, at home, or at religious services, however, some still opt to wear traditional clothing. This is especially true of older Kurdish Americans, who often hold onto traditional styles of dress in their everyday lives.

For Kurdish men, traditional dress usually consists of baggy trousers and loose-fitting shirts. Head wraps or turbans (called *jamadanis* in Kurdish) are typically only worn by very traditional older men and in some rural areas. They are rarely worn in the United States. Women's traditional dress generally consists of long, colorful dresses and headscarves. Kurdish women do not wear veils. Some younger Kurdish American women continue to wear headscarves in everyday life, many for religious reasons and to show that they adhere to the traditional customs of the culture.

Dances and Songs Music plays an important role in Kurdish culture, and traditional Kurdish music and dance are often performed during cultural gatherings among Kurdish Americans. Various regions throughout Kurdistan are known for producing different musical styles, and classical Kurdish musicians typically come in the form of storytellers, bards, and minstrels. They perform a wide gamut of styles, including songs of epic stories, love ballads, work songs, religious hymns, and songs used to mark special occasions such as wedding and holidays. Traditional Kurdish instruments include long-necked stringed lutes called the *tembÛr* and the *saz*, reed pipes known as the *qernête* and the *bilÛr*, and numerous percussion instruments.

Kurdish dances are often traditional round dances, where groups of participants join hands and perform choreographed steps while moving in a circle. In the Kurdish folk dance known as *halparke*, a single dancer comes to the head of the circle and performs a variety of intricate solo steps. Unlike some neighboring Muslim peoples, Kurdish dances are also often performed by men and women dancing together. Variations of Kurdish dances include the *dilan*, *sepe*, and *chapi*. Kurdish people also have a belly dancing tradition that dates back to their inclusion in the Ottoman Empire.

Holidays Kurdish Americans who practice Islam generally observe the major holy days of the Muslim calendar, and many Kurdish families in the United States also recognize popular Christian holidays. In addition to that, the largest Kurdish holiday of the year is Newroz (sometimes spelled Nawroz, NÛroj, or Nowruz), the Iranian new year. The celebration coincides with the spring equinox on March 21, though the Kurdish festival typically lasts several days, when community members gather for dances, games, special feasts, and the reading of Kurdish poetry. According to Kurdish lore, Newroz commemorates the deliverance of the Kurds from a terrible tyrant and celebrating it demonstrates solidarity with the cause of Kurdish independence.

In the United States, Kurdish communities typically hold gatherings to celebrate Newroz with music, dancing, and food. Sizable Newroz festivals are held each year by the Kurdish community in places such New York City, Southern California, Nashville, and Chicago.

Health Care Issues and Practices The bulk of Kurdish people who have immigrated to the United States have come as refugees escaping oppression and war-torn environs in their homelands. Before arriving in the United States, some first-generation Kurdish Americans experienced the kind of significant psychological trauma, physical injuries, and substandard treatment

KURDISH PROVERBS

Haka ta nazani, chava da jeerani.

If you don't know, look to your neighbor.

Yek ziman her bes niye.

One language is never enough.

Berxwedan jîyane Û jîyan berxwedane.

To struggle is life, and life is struggle.

Çi dil hizir deket, dev xeber dedet.

Whatever the heart thinks, the mouth will speak.

Derdî xencer asane, derdî dil pir girane.

The pain of a dagger is easy, the pain of a heart is heavy.

Destê betal ser zikê birçî.

A hand that does not work will rest on a stomach that is hungry.

Tenha çiyakan dostmanin.

We have no friends but the mountains.

Tîrek mehawe ke le xot bigerêtewe.

Don't throw the arrow that will return against you.

that can cause lasting medical problems. Some suffered through genocidal campaigns and chemical-weapons attacks. Early on, language barriers and economic conditions may have prevented some Kurdish immigrants from seeking medical treatment, but access to health care has likely increased for most, particularly among the younger generation and Kurdish American professionals.

Literature from the U.S.-based Kurdish Human Rights Watch encourages refugees to seek medical care upon arriving in the United States, including reassurances that there is "no stigma attached to mental health or psychosocial services in the U.S." It also warns that "public health care coverage is limited. … It may take weeks to see a doctor for a routine appointment, although critical health needs will be met in a timely manner. Once you become employed and can purchase private medical insurance, your health care options will increase."

FAMILY AND COMMUNITY LIFE

Traditional Kurdish families are patrilineal, and communal living is common, with extended families often living together under the same roof or as part of a larger, shared family compound called a *mal*. Several nuclear-family units typically live together in a mal, sharing the responsibilities of household duties as well as providing economically for the family. According to Kurdish customs, a family's eldest son, his wife,

and their children continue to reside with parents and grandparents. If a family's economic status permits it, younger brothers and their families may eventually begin their own mals, over time enlarging the size and clout of the family compound.

Many first- and second-generation Kurdish Americans adhere to some of these familial customs, though life in the United States has altered some practices. It is still common for Kurdish American children to live with their parents well into adulthood, but most move out and start their own families after marriage. It is typical for Kurdish American extended families to stay in close contact, often living in the same neighborhoods, and to regularly gather for weekly or nightly communal family meals.

Gender Roles Kurdish families typically have both a male and a female leader (called the *malxî* for males and the *kabanî* for females), and although males are regarded as the traditional heads of patriarchal households, gender roles have often been defined by a family's living conditions. Generally, men are tasked with most agricultural duties and make most social and political contact with the outside world. Women are the primary caregivers for children and are charged with preparing family meals, but they are also expected to contribute to the social, economic, and political affairs of Kurdish society.

The lifestyle of seminomadic clans in Kurdistan often allow women and men to be nominal equals, while in sedentary rural families, and with the exception of the kabanî, women historically take a subordinate role in family units. Among more urbanized families, the entry of women into the workforce has weakened patriarchal traditions and allowed women to exercise more power in their households.

Kurdish American women, especially younger, second-generation family members, sometimes express mixed feelings regarding the expanded opportunities available to them in the United States. While largely enthusiastic about taking advantage of the economic, educational, and social freedoms offered by mainstream society, many also wish to honor and stay connected with their Kurdish heritage. In the United States, Kurdish wives often equally share with their husbands the responsibility of financially supporting their family. Many also accept traditional roles inside the household, saying they consider it an honor to be able to cook meals and complete housework to better the family's life.

Courtship and Weddings Kurdish marriage arrangements often occur according to tribal traditions and can be a method of establishing alliances and creating hierarchies. Historically, marriages were arranged, with parents sometimes making marriage plans before children were even born. Arranged marriage partners were typically from the same tribe and the marriage ceremony itself seen as the passage to adulthood for boys and girls. After marriage, a wife traditionally left her family to move into the mal of her husband's family. In the past, this did not cause a woman to be geographically separated from her family, since tribes typically lived or traveled together. During modern times, however, the large-scale forced deportations and considerable Kurdish diaspora have often required women to leave their own relatives behind and travel great distances with their new families.

During the twentieth century, urbanization, separation from traditional clans, and modern economic factors have all weakened Kurdish tribal influence. This can be seen among Kurdish Americans, for whom arranged marriages are rare and tribal associations are less influential, though still present in their lives. Although some more traditional Kurdish elders still expect women to marry within their own tribes, younger Kurdish American women are exercising more agency in choosing their own partners, marrying outside of tribal traditions or marrying outside of the Kurdish community entirely. As a result of this modernization, Kurdish American wedding ceremonies often blend Western traditions with Kurdish customs.

Relations with Other Americans Kurdish Americans work to foster close relationships within the Kurdish immigrant community, but they are also typically welcoming to outsiders. By and large, they have positive relations with other Americans. As an immigrant group whose greatest numbers have arrived within the last three decades, many Kurds feel they are still building their reputation in the United States and express excitement at the prospect of sharing their own culture with their new neighbors here. In this way, Kurds stay in touch with their traditional culture while also welcoming members of outside groups into the fold.

However, Kurds have also experienced some high-profile difficulties in relating socially to other Americans. According to a 2007 article in the *New York Times*, a Kurdish street gang called Kurdish Pride had emerged on the south side of Nashville; it was believed to have "formed to present Kurdish bravado to this city's mix of Latino, Asian and black gangs." After a string of crimes and criminal indictments, the gang was denounced by Kurdish community leaders and by the Kurdish American Youth Organization.

EMPLOYMENT AND ECONOMIC CONDITIONS

A strong work ethic is a point of pride for many Kurdish Americans, a growing number of whom have worked their way up from the hardships they initially faced as refugees and are now sending their children to college, starting their own businesses, and enjoying the fruits of life in the United States. The obstacles faced by Kurdish refugees coming to this country are formidable. Although charitable humanitarian organizations often provide some support in finding homes and entry-level jobs, some Kurdish people

enter the U.S. workforce at positions far below the status they had in their home countries. Most Kurdish immigrants must navigate the working world initially knowing very little English and with a limited understanding of American culture.

Despite these difficulties, many Kurds have found success in the United States. In cities with large Kurdish populations, many immigrants have been able to rely on the support and patronage of other Kurds. In Nashville, for example, Kurdish people own businesses that are largely geared to serving Kurds, such as bakeries, restaurants, grocery stores, and car dealerships. It is not uncommon for Kurds from other areas of the country to relocate to Nashville in order to start businesses they know will be supported by the Kurdish community. Kurdish Americans also own businesses that cater to the public at large.

Kurdish neighborhoods in other locations may be slightly less organized and less visible. In a 2009 interview with the *Kurdish Herald* online newspaper, Luqman Barwari, president of the California-based Kurdish National Congress of North America, said first-generation Kurdish immigrants in Southern California had historically not been economic climbers. Barwari said that unemployment and dependence on government-funded social assistance programs remained high in his community and that the population of professional Kurds in the San Diego area was small enough to be considered "insignificant." Second-generation Kurdish Americans are working to change these realities, Barwari said, as more young Kurdish Americans are pursuing higher educations aimed at starting professional careers. He credited the organizational efforts of youth groups such as the Kurdish American Youth Organization with mobilizing young Kurds and helping them work to better the community.

POLITICS AND GOVERNMENT

In many instances, Kurds were forcibly disenfranchised from the political process in their home countries, and, perhaps as a result. Kurdish Americans have largely been keen to partake in the process after relocating to the United States. As in many diaspora communities, this includes not only an interest in their new country's political landscape but also attempts to organize and support political causes in their homeland. In March 2010, Nashville was selected as one of nine voting centers in the United States to participate in Iraqi parliamentary elections. As many as 12,000 Iraqi expatriates (many of them Kurds) from Tennessee, Georgia, Kentucky, and Missouri traveled to the city to take part in a three-day voting process to elect candidates to represent them in the provincial council in Iraq. American wings of the Kurdish Democratic Party and the Patriotic Union of Kurdistan were both active in the elections.

In 2008 the Tennessee Immigrant and Refugee Rights Coalition honored the Nashville chapter of the

An American Kurd demonstrates in front of the White House. B CHRISTOPHER / ALAMY

Kurdish American Youth Organization for its efforts to motivate the Kurdish community to participate in the U.S. presidential election. Kurds in Nashville also organized a movement around supporting the candidacy of Barack Obama.

NOTABLE INDIVIDUALS

Academia Azad Bonni (1963–) is a noted professor of neurobiology at Washington University in St. Louis, Missouri, where he serves as chair of the Department of Anatomy and Neurobiology. In 1976 his family left Kurdistan and settled in Canada, where he completed college and began his career in science and academics. In 1995 he received a PhD from Harvard University, where his laboratory made seminal contributions to the study of neurobiology, with an emphasis on neuronal connectivity, mental disorders, autism, and the developing brain. He has dual Canadian and American citizenship.

Activism Reza Jalali (1949–) has been a national director for Amnesty International as well as the multicultural director for the Department of Health in the state of Maine. Born in a Kurdish town in Iran, Jalali

as a child witnessed family members jailed and forced into hiding for opposing the policies of the Iranian government. In 1981 he fled to India, and in 1985 he was granted admission to the United States. He settled in Portland, Maine, and became a U.S. citizen in 1991. Jalali continues to work organizing humanitarian relief efforts for Kurds throughout the world and has established numerous organizations, such as the Maine Kurdish Relief Fund and the Ethnic Minority Coalition.

Religion Edip Yuksel (1957–) is a leading intellectual and author in the modern Islamic reform movement. He has published more than twenty books on religion, politics, philosophy, and law while working against negative stereotypes of Muslim people and espousing a progressive view of Islam. Many of his texts were originally published in Turkish and have been translated into English. Born in Turkey, he has dual citizenship in Turkey and the United States and works as a professor of philosophy at Pima Community College in Tucson, Arizona.

Stage and Screen Alia Shawkat (1989–) is an actress who has appeared in numerous films and television series, mostly in comedic roles. She is best known for her work in the role of Maeby Fünke on the television sitcom *Arrested Development*. Born in Riverside, California, Shawkat is of Kurdish decent on her father's side and of Irish and Norwegian descent on her mother's side. Her filmography also includes the comedies *Deck the Halls* (2006), *Whip It* (2009), and *Cedar Rapids* (2011), as well as the war satire *Three Kings* (1999).

MEDIA

PRINT

The Kurdish Review

Billed as the only nationwide newspaper for Kurdish Americans, the *Review* is a monthly publication based in Washington, D.C., that seeks to "inform, educate, and promote awareness of Kurdish news, topics, and ideas that are relevant to today's vibrant Kurdish American community." Archived issues are available online.

Behar Godani, Editor in Chief
Email: KurdishReview@gmail.com
URL: www.kurdishreview.com

BROADCAST

Voice of America: Kurdish

An international news and information service that offers a news broadcast as well as a website in the Kurdish language.

David Ensor, Director
330 Independence Avenue SW
Washington, D.C. 20237
Phone: (202) 203-4959
Fax: (202) 203-4960
Email: askvoa@voanews.com
URL: www.dengeamerika.com

ONLINE

Rudaw

An online newspaper published in both English and Kurdish providing coverage on Kurdish news and issues.

Ayub Nuri, Editor in Chief
Email: ayub@rudaw.net
URL: http://rudaw.net/english

ORGANIZATIONS AND ASSOCIATIONS

Chicago Kurdish Cultural Center

A nonprofit group dedicated to bringing Kurdish people together and to educating people about Kurdish culture.

4803 North Milwaukee Avenue
Unit A
Chicago, Illinois 60630
Email: info@kurdishcenter.org
URL: www.kurdishcenter.org

Kurdish American Society

A Kurdish cultural organization headquartered in New York City.

Phone: (718) 635-0064
Email: info@usakurds.org
URL: www.usakurds.org

Kurdish Human Rights Watch

An organization providing refugee assistance to Kurdish people in the United States and around the world. Includes offices in California, Maryland, Michigan, Oregon, Tennessee, Virginia, and Washington State as well as in Iraq.

2805 Foster Avenue
Suite 207
Nashville, Tennessee 37210
Phone: (703) 385-3806
Fax: (703) 385-3643
Email: admin@khrw.org
URL: www.khrw.org

Kurdish National Congress of North America

A nonprofit benefiting Kurdish people in the United States and Canada.

Luqman Barwari, President
P.O. Box 50216
Irvine, California 92619
Email: kncna@kncna.net
URL: www.kncna.net

Washington Kurdish Institute

A nonprofit research and educational organization dedicated to Kurdish issues around the globe.

Najmaldin O. Karim, President
1612 5th Street NW #2
Washington, D.C. 20001
Phone: (202) 484-0140
Email: wki@kurd.org
URL: www.kurd.org

MUSEUMS AND RESEARCH CENTERS

Center for Near Eastern Studies

A department at the University of California–Los Angeles dedicated to the study of Near Eastern peoples. Sponsored the first Kurdish language summit in North America.

Sondra Hale, Interim Co-Director
10286 Bunche Hall
Los Angeles, California 90095-1480
Phone: (310) 825-1181
Fax: (310) 206-2406
Email: cnes@international.ucla.edu
URL: www.international.ucla.edu

Kurdish Political Studies Initiative

A research center that seeks to "develop knowledge and understanding about the Kurds and Kurdistan" as part of the University of Central Florida's Global Perspectives program.

John C. Bersia, Co-Director
University of Central Florida
Howard Phillips Hall 202
4000 Central Florida Boulevard
P.O. Box 160003
Orlando, Florida 32816
Phone: (407) 823-0688
Email: John.Bersia@ucf.edu
URL: http://ucfglobalperspectives.org/

**Vera Beaudin Saeedpour Kurdish Library &
Museum Collection**

An exhibit among the special collections archive of
Binghamton University that includes items from the
collection of Vera Beaudin Saeedpour, the former
director of the now-defunct Kurdish Heritage
Foundation of America.

Jean L. Root Green, Head of Preservation
Binghamton University Libraries
P.O. Box 6012
Vestal Parkway East
Binghamton, New York 13902-6012
Phone: (607) 777-4844
Email: jgreen@binghamton.edu
URL: http://library.binghamton.edu/specialcollections/
saeedpour.html

SOURCES FOR ADDITIONAL STUDY

Emery, Thero. "In Nashville, a Street Gang Emerges in a
Kurdish Enclave." *New York Times*, July 15, 2007.

Gibney, Matthew J., and Randall Hansen. *Immigration
and Asylum: From 1900 to the Present.* Santa Barbara,
CA: ABC-CLIO, 2005.

Lawrence, Quil. *Invisible Nation: How the Kurds' Quest
for Statehood Is Shaping Iraq and the Middle East.* New
York: Walker and Co. Books, 2008.

Mansfield, Stephen. "Religious Neutrality in 94%;
Muslim Iraqi Kurdistan." *Huffington Post*, June 18,
2012. http://www.huffingtonpost.com/stephen-mans-
field/religious-neutrality-iraqi-kurdistan_b_1587042.
html

Meho, Lokman I. *The Kurdish Question in U.S. Foreign
Policy: A Documentary Sourcebook.* Westport, CT:
Praeger, 2004.

O'Connor, Karen. *A Kurdish Family: Journey Between Two
Worlds.* Minneapolis: Lerner Publishing Group, 1996.

Power, Samantha. *A Problem from Hell: America in the Age
of Genocide.* New York: Harper Perennial, 2007.

Winders, Jamie. *Nashville in the New Millennium:
Immigrant Settlement, Urban Transformation, and Social
Belonging.* New York: Russell Sage Foundation, 2013.

LAOTIAN AMERICANS

Carl L. Bankston III

OVERVIEW

Laotian Americans are immigrants or descendants of people from the Southeast Asian nation of Laos. The term *Laotian* is sometimes distinguished from the term *Lao*, with *Laotian* referring to anyone from Laos (including the Hmong) and *Lao* referring to the ethnic Lao. In this entry *Laotian American* is used for ethnic Lao in the United States. (See the entry on Hmong Americans for information about the other major American group from Laos.) Laos is bordered by Thailand to the southwest, Cambodia to the south, Myanmar to the west, China to the north, and Vietnam to the east. Laos has a tropical climate, with a rainy season that lasts from May to November and a dry season that lasts from December to April. The ethnic Lao make up a majority of the lowland population. The minority groups, including the Khmou and the Hmong, mostly live on the mountainsides and in the highlands. Laos measures approximately 91,400 square miles (236,800 square kilometers), making it slightly larger than the state of Utah.

According to the *CIA World Factbook*, Laos had an estimated population of 6,586,266 in 2012. About 67 percent were Buddhist, 1.5 percent were Christian, and 31.5 percent adhered to religions unspecified in any official estimates. Shamanism, ancestor worship, and animism, or spirit worship, are common, and many Laotian Buddhists also hold animistic beliefs. The overwhelming majority of the ethnic Lao are Buddhists. The ethnic Lao made up a slight majority (55 percent) of the country's population. The minority group known as the Khmou made up 11 percent, the Hmong constituted 8 percent, and 26 percent was divided among more than one hundred small ethnic groups. Although Laos has experienced economic growth in recent years, lowering its official poverty rate from 46 percent of the population in 1992 to 26 percent in 2012, it continues to be one of the poorest countries in Southeast Asia, despite a wealth of natural resources, such as minerals, timber, and rubber. Three-quarters of the country's labor force works in agriculture.

Refugees from Laos began arriving in the United States as refugees in late 1975, after Communist forces came to power in their native country, and their numbers increased greatly during the 1980s. By 2010, according to U.S. Census data, Laotian Americans lived in every state, but they were concentrated in California, which was home to one-third of the Laotian Americans. They tended to work in blue-collar occupations such as machine operators, cashiers, and cooks.

The 2010 U.S. Census reported 209,640 Laotians (not including Hmong), plus 22,484 individuals who identified themselves as Laotian in addition to another racial or ethnic category. The ten metropolitan areas with the largest Laotian populations in 2010 were Sacramento, California; San Francisco–Oakland-Vallejo, California; Minneapolis–St. Paul, Minnesota; Seattle-Everett, Washington; Fresno, California; Dallas–Fort Worth, Texas; San Diego, California; Los Angeles–Long Beach, California; Nashville, Tennessee; and Stockton, California.

HISTORY OF THE PEOPLE

Early History Laotians trace their ancestry to the T'ai people, an ethnolinguistic group that migrated south from China beginning in the sixth century CE. Originally part of the Khmer (Cambodian) Empire, Laos achieved independence in 1353 when Fa Ngum, a prince from the city of Luang Prabang, claimed a large section of the declining empire and declared himself king, calling the newly established state Lan Xang, or "The Kingdom of a Million Elephants." Luang Prabang was the nation's capital for more than two hundred years until, in 1563, King Setthalhiralh moved the capital to Vientiane, which is still the capital of Laos today.

The Lao kingdom reached its height in the late 1600s, under King Souligna Vongsa. After his death in 1694, three claimants to the throne broke the kingdom into three distinct principalities—the kingdoms of Vientiane, Luang Prabang, and Champassak. Each kingdom struggled for hegemony, causing the weakened Lao states to become vulnerable to the more powerful neighboring nations of Siam (now called Thailand) and Vietnam. While the Siamese took Vientiane, the Vietnamese took other parts of Laos. By the mid-1800s almost all of northern Laos was controlled by Vietnam, and almost all the southern and central parts of the country were controlled by Siam. Only Luang Prabang and its environs remained independent.

Modern Era In 1897 Luang Prabang also fell to foreign powers, this time to France's growing

Indochinese empire, and Laos became a protectorate, or colony, of France. By 1899 Vientiane had become the administrative capital of French Laos, with French commissioners holding administrative power in all the provinces.

Although there were some local rebellions against French rule—mainly by the tribes of the hills and mountains—widespread Laotian resistance to the French did not begin until after World War II, when Japan, which had taken control of Indochina during the war, was defeated. In 1945 the Laotian prime minister, Prince Phetsarath, declared Laos an independent kingdom and formed a group known as the *Lao Issara*, or "Free Lao." Some Laotians supported a return to French colonization, feeling that their country was not ready for immediate independence. The Lao Issara, however, was strongly opposed to French rule in Laos. The prime minister's half-brother, Prince Souphanuvong, called for armed resistance and sought support from the anti-French movement in neighboring Vietnam, the Viet Minh, led by Ho Chi Minh. This Laotian political group became known as the *Pathet Lao* ("Lao Nation").

The Viet Minh defeated French troops at Dien Bien Phu in 1954. Afterward, an international conference held in Geneva separated Vietnam at the seventeenth parallel into North and South Vietnam to prevent Ho Chi Minh's Communist government from gaining control over the entire nation. Many Laotians supported the Viet Minh and, when North Vietnam invaded South Vietnam in 1959, Laos was drawn into the war.

The United States also became involved in the war to block the spread of communism in Southeast Asia. In Laos, American forces provided tactical and economic support to the royal government but were unsuccessful in their efforts. U.S. troops withdrew from the area in 1973, and South Vietnam fell to the North in April 1975. Later that same year, Pathet Lao forces overthrew the Laotian government, renaming the country the Lao People's Democratic Republic. Thousands of Laotians fled to Thailand, where they were placed in refugee camps.

After 1975 Laos remained under the control of the Lao People's Revolutionary Party (LPRP), a communist political organization. The new constitution adopted by Laos in 1991 recognized a leading role in government for the LPRP. During the 1990s the LPRP liberalized its economic policies, moving away from previous efforts to centralize economic activities in order to achieve socialism, but the party retained control of the government. Seeking economic improvement, Laos also began to open up to tourism in the 1990s.

The United States and Laos established full diplomatic relations in 1992, despite continued accusations by the United States and others against Laos of human rights violations, especially against the Hmong

minority, during the 2000s. The movement of Laotian refugees to the United States became negligible after the mid-1990s. Although several thousand refugees with origins in Laos did enter the United States in 2004 and 2005, these were almost entirely Hmong who had been living in refugee camps in Thailand.

SETTLEMENT IN THE UNITED STATES

While there was some migration from Laos to the United States prior to 1975, the immigrants were so few that there is no official record of them. Available records do suggest, however, that they were highly professional and technically proficient. After 1975 thousands of Laotian people fled their homeland for the United States; the passage of the Indochina Migration and Refugee Assistance Act of 1975 by Congress aided them in this effort. Early Laotian immigrants included former government administrators, soldiers from the royal army, and shopkeepers. Later immigrants from Laos included farmers and villagers who were not as educated as their predecessors.

While large numbers of Vietnamese and Cambodians began to settle in the United States almost immediately after socialist governments came to power in the spring of 1975, Laotian refugees did not begin to arrive in the United States in great numbers until the following year. In contrast to the 126,000 Vietnamese and 4,600 Cambodians who arrived in 1975, only 800 refugees from Laos were admitted into the United States. This is partially due to the fact that the new Laotian government obtained power in a relatively peaceful manner, despite fighting between the Hmong and the Pathet Lao. Moreover, the U.S. government was reluctant to accept refugees who had fled Laos for bordering Thailand, many of whom were viewed by U.S. officials as economic migrants rather than refugees from political oppression.

Statistics provided by the Department of Homeland Security on refugees do not distinguish between the ethnic Lao and the Hmong, so records state only that 10,200 refugees from Laos who had fled across the border into Thailand were admitted to the United States in 1976. The number of Laotian refugees dipped to only 400 in 1977 and then climbed to 8,000 in 1978. In the years between 1979 and 1981, the number of Laotians entering the United States increased dramatically because of international attention given to the plight of Indochinese refugees in the late 1970s and to the family unification program, which allowed refugees already in the United States to sponsor their relatives' immigration. During these three years, about 105,000 people from Laos resettled in the United States: 30,200 in 1979, 55,500 in 1980, and 19,300 in 1981. After 1988, when 14,597 refugees from Laos entered the United States, numbers began to steadily decline, except for 2004–2005, when thousands of Hmong were allowed to settle in the United States from refugee camps in Thailand. In 2010 only 36 refugees who had been

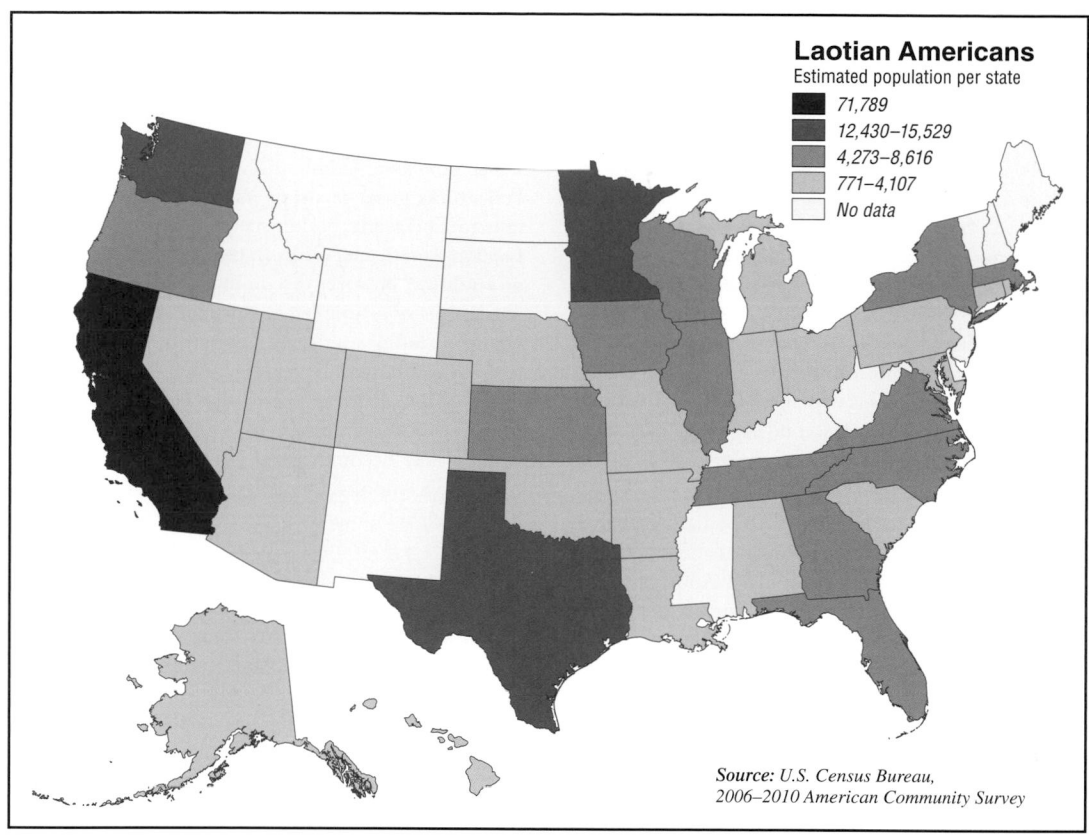

Laotian Americans
Estimated population per state

- 71,789
- 12,430–15,529
- 4,273–8,616
- 771–4,107
- No data

*Source: U.S. Census Bureau,
2006–2010 American Community Survey*

born in Laos arrived in the United States, according to the Department of Homeland Security's *Yearbook of Immigration Statistics.*

The large wave of Laotian immigrants in the 1980s and early 1990s meant that by the early twenty-first century most adult Laotian Americans were immigrants and most children had been born in the United States. In 2010, according to U.S. Census estimates, 60 percent of all Laotian Americans were immigrants; however, more than two-thirds of Laotian Americans over eighteen years of age were immigrants, whereas only about 3 percent of those aged eighteen or under had been born outside the United States. Thus, Laotian Americans were moving very quickly from being an immigrant group to being a new native-born American minority.

According to the U.S. Census, in 1990 there were about 150,000 Laotian Americans living in the United States (not including the Hmong and other minority groups from Laos.) This increased to 179,103 by 2000 and reached an estimated 209,646 in 2010, counting only those who did not report being of another ethnicity in addition to Lao. Most of the growth during the 1990s and 2000s was the result of Lao Americans born in the United States. The largest number of Laotian Americans (61,384) lived in California, according to 2010 U.S. Census estimates, primarily in Sacramento (11,350), Fresno (8,030), Oakland (7,255), and San Diego (6,382). Texas had the second-largest Laotian American

population (12,966), residing mainly in the Dallas–Fort Worth (7,717) and Houston-Brazoria (3,405) areas. Minnesota, which was a center for the Hmong from Laos, was also a center for Laotian Americans defined as ethnic Lao. Minnesota was home to an estimated 12,170 of these Laotian Americans, most of whom (9,314) lived in Minneapolis–St. Paul. Washington State had a reported 12,430 Laotian American residents, many of whom lived in Seattle. There were 8,616 people of Laotian descent living in Tennessee, especially Nashville.

LANGUAGE

Lao is a tonal language; that is, the meaning of a word is determined by the tone or pitch at which it is spoken. Although the tones vary somewhat from one part of the country to another, the dialect of the capital, Vientiane, is considered standard Lao. In Vientiane there are six tones: low, mid, high, rising, high falling, and low falling. Changing the tone of a word makes it a different word. For example, the sound "kow," pronounced much like the English word *cow*, spoken with a high tone means "an occasion, a time," spoken with a rising tone means "white," and spoken with a mid-tone means "news." These tones give the Lao language a musical quality, so that its speakers often sound like they are singing or reciting melodic poetry.

The Lao alphabet is phonetic, meaning that each letter stands for a sound. Lao writing has twenty-seven consonant symbols that are used for twenty-one consonant sounds. There are more symbols than sounds because different consonants are used to begin words of different tones. The Lao alphabet also has thirty-eight vowel symbols, representing twenty-four vowel sounds. These sounds are made up of nine simple vowels and three diphthongs (vowel sounds made up of two vowels together), each of which has a short form and a long form. The sounds are written with more than twenty-four symbols because some of them are written differently at the end of a word than they are in the middle of a word. All Lao words end in a vowel or in a consonant sound similar to the English sounds *k, p, t, m, n,* or *ng.* This is why some Laotian Americans who learned English as a second language may occasionally pronounce "fish" as "fit" or "stiff" as "stip."

The graceful, curving letters of the Laotian alphabet are based on the Khmer (Cambodian) alphabet, which, in turn, was developed from an ancient writing system in India. Although the Lao writing system is not the same as the Thai writing system, the two are very similar, and anyone who can read one language can read the other with only a little instruction.

Because Laotian Americans are almost all either immigrants or children of immigrants, the Lao language is still widely spoken. Only 14 percent of Laotian Americans reported speaking English at home in estimates from 2010 U.S. Census data. Another 14 percent of those who described themselves as Laotian in the census spoke various minority languages from Laos, and 71 percent spoke Lao at home. Nevertheless, many young Laotian Americans speak Lao primarily with their parents and use English with their friends. Young people will often speak English with a few Lao phrases even with other young Laotian Americans. Some cultural centers, set up around Buddhist temples or elsewhere, have attempted to teach Lao language classes to young people. The ability to read Lao is rapidly becoming rare in the American-born generation, though.

Greetings and Popular Expressions Common Laotian American greetings and expressions include the following: *Sabai dee baw*—How are you? (literally, are you well?); *Koy sabai dee*—I'm well; *Jao day*—And how are you? (used when responding to *Sabai dee*); *Pai sai*—Where are you going? (used as a greeting); *Kawp jai*—Thank you; *Kaw toht*—Excuse me; *Baw pen nyang*—You're welcome, never mind (literally, it's nothing); *Ma gin khao*—Come eat! (literally, come eat rice); *Sab baw*—Is the food good?; and *Sab eelee*—It's delicious.

RELIGION

In Laos almost all lowland Laotians are Buddhists, and the temple, known as a *wat,* is the center of village life. Most Laotian Americans are Buddhists as well, although many have converted to Protestant Christianity, especially in areas where there are no large Laotian populations to sustain traditional religious practices. Despite such conversions, Laotian Buddhism is flourishing in the United States.

Buddhism is divided into two major types. The Northern School, known as Mahayana Buddhism, is most often found in China, Japan, Tibet, Korea, and Vietnam. The Southern School, or Theravada (also called Vinayana) Buddhism, is predominant in Laos, Thailand, Cambodia, Burma, and Sri Lanka. Performing good deeds, or "creating merit," is important to Theravada Buddhists, including Laotians and Laotian Americans. One can create merit through acts of kindness; however, becoming a monk or supporting monks or a temple are considered the best methods for creating merit. All Laotian men are expected to become monks for a time, usually in early manhood, before marriage. It is also common for older men, especially widowers, to become monks. Laotian women may become nuns, although nuns are not as respected as monks. In Laos, some men are not able to fulfill their religious duty of entering the temple for a time. This is even more difficult for Laotian American men because of demands in the workplace and the scarcity of temples in the United States. Laotian American monks sometimes share temples with Thai American or Cambodian American monks, since they also adhere to Theravada Buddhism, but the number of purely Laotian temples in the United States has grown rapidly over the past thirty years.

The history of Laotian Buddhist temples in America can be dated from 1980, when the first Lao Buddhist monk in the New York metropolitan area, Satu Khampoui Sinnolai, found housing with Thai Buddhist monks in the Bronx. At that time, according to newspaper accounts, he was one of only five Lao Buddhist monks in the United States. Two others were in Washington, D.C., one was in Oregon, and one was in Illinois. Lao families in the New York area raised money to build a temple around Satu Khampoui. In the years that followed, other Laotian American communities around the country established their own temples in a wide variety of locations, including Tucson, Arizona; Denver, Colorado; Saint Petersburg, Florida; Atlanta, Georgia; Salt Lake City, Utah; New Iberia, Louisiana; and the California metropolitan areas with large Laotian American populations. These temples frequently function as community centers and places for the maintenance and transmission of culture, as well as religious institutions.

A belief in spirits, or *phi* (pronounced like the English word *pea*), dates back to the time before the Lao were introduced to Buddhism. Since then, the spirit cult has become a part of popular Buddhist practice in Laos. Some of these spirits are "ghosts," the spirits of human beings following death. Other *phi* are benevolent guardians of people and places or malevolent beings who cause harm and suffering. Spirit cults continue in the United States, but their influence is diminishing among younger Laotian Americans.

Many Laotian Americans retain ritual practices of their culture connected to the spirit cult. The most common of all Laotian rituals is the *baci* (pronounced "bah-see") or *sookhwan*, which is performed at important occasions. The word *sookhwan* may be interpreted as "the invitation of the *khwan*" or "the calling of the *khwan*." The *khwan* are thirty-two spirits that are believed to watch over the thirty-two organs of the human body (in Lao anatomy). Together, the *khwan* are thought to constitute the spiritual essence of a person. The *baci* is a ritual binding of the spirits to their possessor. Even Laotians who do not believe in the existence of the *khwan* will usually participate in the *baci* as a means of expressing goodwill and good luck to others.

In the *baci* ceremony, a respected person, usually an older man who has been a monk, invokes the *khwan* in a loud, song-like voice. He calls on the spirits of all present to cease wandering and to return to the bodies of those present. He then asks the *khwan* to bring well-being and happiness with them and to share in the feast that will follow. After the invocation of the *khwan* is finished, the celebrants take pieces of cotton thread from silver platters covered with food and tie them around each other's wrists to bind the *khwan* in place. While tying the thread, they will wish one another health and prosperity. Often an egg is placed in the palm of someone whose wrist is being bound as a symbol of new life. Some of the threads must be left on for three days, and when they are removed, they must be broken or untied, not cut. Non-Laotians are not only welcomed to this ceremony, they are frequently treated as guests of honor.

CULTURE AND ASSIMILATION

As a group, Laotian Americans are substantially younger than the national average. According to 2010 U.S. Census estimates, the median age for Laotian Americans was 30 years, while the median age for other Americans was 37.2 years. This meant that half of all Laotian Americans were younger than 30. Because so many Laotian Americans are young and were either born in the United States or have spent most of their lives here, adapting to American culture is mainly an issue for older people.

Traditions and Customs Over the years, immigrant Laotian Americans have had to adjust to a culture that is markedly different from the culture of their country of origin. According to interviews given by Laotian Americans, it is apparent that many individuals have had to alter their worldviews considerably to better adapt to American society. For example, such common American interactions as touching, kissing, slapping someone on the back, waving at another person, and looking directly into someone's eyes are considered rude in Laotian culture. As Saelle Sio Lai has explained in John Tenhula's *Voices from Southeast Asia*, "Some of the Laotian customs I can use in my own way and some I must forget."

Cuisine Laotian cuisine is spicy. Most meals contain either rice (*khao*) or rice noodles (*khao poon*).

The rice may be glutinous (*khao nyao*) or nonglutinous (*khao chao*), but glutinous, or "sticky," rice is the food most often associated with Laotian cuisine. The rice is accompanied by meat, fish, and vegetables. Meats are often chopped, pounded, and spiced to make a dish known as *lap*, and fish is usually eaten with a special sauce called *nam ba*. The sticky rice is usually taken in the thumb and first three fingers and used to scoop up other foods. A papaya salad spiced with hot peppers, which is known as *tam mak hoong* to Laotians and *som tam* to Thais, is a popular snack food.

Many Laotian Americans still eat Lao-style foods at home. These dishes are also available at most Thai restaurants, since the cooking of northeastern Thailand is almost identical to that of Laos. Sticky rice and other ingredients for Lao foods are likewise available at most stores that specialize in Asian foods. In areas that have large Laotian American communities, there are also a number of Lao markets where these ingredients may be purchased.

Traditional Dress On special occasions marked by the *sookhwan* ceremony, some Laotian American women wear traditional costumes. The staple of their attire is the *sinh*, a skirt made from a piece of silk brocade about two yards long that is wrapped around the waist. It is often held in place by a belt made of silver buckles or rings. Accompanying the *sinh* is a shawl, or a

> My children will surely be influenced by their scholastic environment and be Americanized very fast. I can't and don't intend to stop this natural process. I just want them not to forget their own culture. The ideal is the combination of the positive traits of the two cultures.
>
> A Laotian refugee, cited in *Voices from Southeast Asia: The Refugee Experience in the United States*, edited by John Tenhula (New York: Holmes & Meier, 1991)

strip of material, which is draped over the left shoulder and under the right arm. Some Laotian American men wear ethnic costumes at weddings, especially during the *sookhwan* ritual, and onstage during a *maw lam* performance, when actors sometimes don the *sampot*, or baggy trousers worn in Laos before the French occupation.

Traditional Arts and Crafts The Lao people are best known for their woven and embroidered textiles. Women do most of the weaving, especially of cloths for everyday use, but male Lao craftspersons also work in textiles. The weaving of silk for *sinh*, and other articles of clothing is one of the valued traditional Lao crafts. Traditional Lao crafts also include working with silver, often to make jewelry; wood carving; and painting murals on temple walls.

Many Laotian American women are skilled at sewing, but weaving with traditional looms is rarer among Laotian Americans than among people in Laos.

Nonetheless, the older Laotian arts and crafts still survive in the United States. A number of organizations, such as the Lao Heritage Foundation in Washington, D.C., are dedicated to preserving traditional Laotian arts and crafts.

Dances and Songs Laotian Americans brought a variety of folk dances, or *lam*, with them, but the most popular is the *lam vong*, or "circle dance." The *lam vong* and most other dances involve graceful swaying movements of the legs and hips, accompanied by intricate gestures of the hands. Traditional dances are common at ceremonial events, most notably the New Year festival, in Laotian American communities.

Most Laotian poetry is sung or chanted to the accompaniment of a handheld bamboo pipe organ called the *khene* (pronounced like the word *can* in American English). The *khene* is frequently accompanied by the music of a *saw*, a stringed instrument played with a bow.

Lao singing is often used in popular theater, or opera, known as *maw lam* or *lam lao*. The term *maw lam* may also be used to refer specifically to the singer or singers in such a performance. The *lam leuang*, or "story *lam*," is similar to European opera; a cast of actors in costume sing and act out a story, often drawn from historical or religious legend. *Maw lam khoo*, or "*maw lam* of couples," involves a young man and a young woman. The man flirts with the woman through inventive methods, and she refuses him with witty verse responses. *Maw lam chote*, or "*maw lam* competition," is a contest in verse sung between two people of the same gender, in which each challenges the other by asking questions or beginning a story that the other must finish. In *maw lam dio*, or "*maw lam* alone," a single narrator sings about almost any topic.

The music of the *khene* and *maw lam* operas may be heard at gatherings in cities with large Laotian American communities, especially in cultural activities organized around Buddhist temples. Younger, American-born Laotian Americans, though, often prefer American pop music to the traditional music of their elders

Holidays Many Laotian holidays and festivals have religious origins. The Lao word for "festival," *boon*, literally means "merit" or "good deed." Scheduled according to the lunar calendar, festivals usually take place at Buddhist temples, making it difficult for Laotian Americans to participate due to the limited availability of monks and temples in the United States. Two of the most important festivals are the *Pha Vet*, in the fourth lunar month, which commemorates the life of the Buddha, and the *Boon Bang Fay*, or "rocket festival." Held in the sixth month to celebrate the Buddha, it is marked by fireworks displays.

The most important holiday in Laos and among Laotian Americans is the lunar New Year festival, known as *Pi Mai Lao* (literally, "Lao New Year") or *Songkan*. This takes place in the spring (usually around mid-April), and the date varies because it is based on the lunar calendar. Some Laotian American communities will celebrate this holiday on Easter because of work schedules. Water is a prominent part of this holiday, and celebrants will frequently throw water on each other. The New Year involves an abundance of flowers as well. Most Laotian American communities will hold beauty pageants at the New Year, usually with the contestants dressed in traditional costumes. Laotian Americans welcome non-Lao visitors as participants in the New Year festivities.

Health Care Issues and Practices Traditional Laotian medicine involves massages and herbal cures. Practitioners of traditional medicine may be laypeople or monks. Since sickness is often seen as a problem of spiritual essence (i.e., of the *khwan*), chants and healing rituals are often used to cure illnesses. Although some traditional Lao medicine may be found in the United States, particularly in places that have large Laotian American communities, the practice of mainstream Western medicine by Laotian Americans appears to be much more common.

Laotian Americans are more likely to visit a community clinic than any other type of medical establishment. When they were new arrivals, their mental health generally followed a pattern common among refugees. The first year in the United States tends to be a period of euphoria at having reached their destination. The second year tended to be a time of psychological shock, producing feelings of helplessness as the strangeness of the new environment becomes apparent. New Laotian Americans usually began to adjust during their third or fourth year in the United States.

Laotian Americans show some specific health challenges. The Laotian American National Alliance (LANA) reported in 2011 that diabetes was on the rise in this population. The organization has also stated that Laotian Americans are plagued by Hepatitis B, lung cancer, liver cancer, and obesity. Some of these ailments may be related to the diets adopted by Laotians in the United States.

Death and Burial Rituals Laotians and other Theravada Buddhists normally cremate their dead. In a traditional Laotian funeral, the body of the deceased is washed, dressed, and then displayed in a coffin, usually surrounded by flowers. A photograph of the deceased accompanies the body. White, not black, is the Buddhist color of mourning, and family members dress in white for funeral ceremonies, and white flags are placed outside the house.

Buddhist monks are essential to performing the rituals for moving the dead from the present life to the next. The monks form part of a procession to bring the body to the place of cremation. In the United States, the rituals are somewhat modified. Some Laotian Americans have adopted the practice of wearing black as the color of mourning. Since American law does not permit bodies to be kept at home, the bodies are displayed at funeral homes, which take charge of cremations. Buddhist monks will often recite prayers by bodies at the funeral homes in the evenings or immediately before the body is taken to the crematorium or burial place.

Recreational Activities In addition to the dances and music described above, Laotian Americans also enjoy sports of all varieties. International football, known in the United States as soccer, is popular with people in Laos and with Laotian Americans. Most Laotian American communities have soccer clubs and teams. A related sport that Lao Americans brought with them from the ancestral country is a version of hacky sack. Known as *thuck thay* in Lao, this is played with a rattan ball that players must keep in the air using their feet, knees, chest, and head without touching it with their hands.

FAMILY AND COMMUNITY LIFE

In Laos, where the majority of people work in agriculture, members of families often work together to produce what they need. This situation is not the same in the United States for Laotian Americans since the majority work outside the home in urban or suburban communities. Laotian Americans sometimes do live near their extended families and such family values as respect for one's parents continue to be important. Laotian American children, upon becoming adults, are expected to respect and care for their parents. Intergenerational tensions between a mainly immigrant generation of parents and a mainly American-born generation of children sometimes do arise, however.

In the first decades of Laotian settlement in the United States, former military men often became the community's leaders. By the 2000s, however, these former military men were getting old, and newer community leaders tended to be persons with substantial experience in the United States. People in highly educated professions and business leaders have become important figures in Laotian American communities across the nation.

Gender Roles In Laos men represent their family in village affairs, while women are responsible for running the household and controlling the financial affairs of the family. Among Laotian Americans, however, female employment is an important source of family income, and it is common for Laotian American women to work outside the home. According to U.S. Census estimates, 72 percent of Laotian American women and 81 percent of Laotian American men of at least twenty-five years of age and less than sixty-five years of age participated in the American labor force in 2010. Because of the relative equality between men and women in Laotian American society, many Laotian American men share responsibility for household tasks. While Laotian American men most often hold the official positions of leadership in community

LAOTIAN PROVERBS

Ai koo baw mi kahm hoo; Ai koo baw mi nawn nam.

If you're shy with your teacher, you'll have no knowledge; if you're shy with your lover, you'll have no bedmate.

Rak ngeua hai pook.

If you love your cow, tie it up.

Rak look hai dtee.

If you love your children, spank them.

Kawng gin baw gin man nao.

Food that is uneaten spoils.

Kawng gao baw lao man leum.

Old tales untold are forgotten.

Wehlah mi ngun, kon bpen nai ngun.
Wehlahj jon, ngun bpen nai kon.

When you have money, you control the money. When you're poor, money controls you.

Yang nam hang poo yai mah baw gat.

Follow the old people to avoid the bite of a dog.

Yah sawn kalae wai nam.

Don't teach a crocodile how to swim.

Peuan gin ha ngai; peuan dtai ha yaak.

It's easy to find friends who'll eat with you; it's hard to find one who'll die for you.

Sang di you nga.

A good elephant is one you hold by the tusk.

Bpla di yo meua.

A good fish is one you have in the hand.

Jai rai bpen pi.

An angry heart is an evil spirit.

Jai dib pen pa-jao.

A kind heart is a holy lord.

organizations, women are also quite active in their communities and are often important (though frequently unacknowledged) decision makers.

The most common family arrangement in Laos is that of a nuclear family that lives close to their extended family. In the United States, extended families have, in many cases, become even more important to Laotian Americans for social and financial support.

A Laotian American woman with an infant. NEVADA WIER / CORBIS / AGE FOTOSTOCK

This interdependence may account for the lower divorce rate among Laotian Americans. In the 2010 U.S. Census, 11 percent of Laotian Americans over the age of fifteen who had been married were divorced, while 15 percent of the general American population over fifteen years of age who had been married were divorced. It should be noted, however, that the percentage of formerly married Laotian Americans had risen markedly over the twenty-year period since 1990, when only 4 percent of Laotian Americans were divorced. This is one of the ways in which the families of Laotian Americans have become more like those of other Americans over time.

Education Because Laotian Americans come from a primarily agricultural homeland, they have fewer educational credentials than other Americans. In 2010, 67 percent of Laotian Americans aged twenty-five and over had completed high school, compared with 85 percent of all Americans in that age group. Only 13 percent

of Laotian Americans who were at least twenty-five years old were college graduates in 2010, compared with 28 percent among Americans in general.

Although many Laotian American adult immigrants arrived with relatively little formal education, many have recognized education as being extremely important for their children. Often the family's future is dependent upon their children's success in school. "My husband and I always remind [our children] to study first, study hard, not play, not go out without permission from us," explained one Laotian American woman in *Voices from Southeast Asia*. "We tell them that we want to go to school, too, but we have to work to feed them. We sacrifice for them, and the only thing they can pay back is to study well."

Because of their long-standing commitment to education, Laotian Americans' educational levels have risen. Among members of the twenty-five to thirty age group, 85 percent were high school graduates and 18 percent were college graduates, rates that were still below the general American educational levels but increasing. Among traditionally college-aged Laotian Americans (eighteen to twenty-four), 37 percent were enrolled in institutions of higher education in 2010, approximately the same percentage as Americans in that age group in the general population.

Courtships and Weddings The practice of dating was new to early Laotian American immigrants, as it simply was not done in their homeland. In Laos couples usually come to know one another in the course of village life. In the United States, however, many young Laotian American people date in order to get to know each other better. This custom is not always embraced by their parents, but it has become fairly widely accepted.

The *khwan* ceremony is significant to traditional Laotian wedding ceremonies. When a couple adheres to Laotian traditions strictly, the groom goes to the bride's house the day before the wedding feast, where monks await with bowls of water. The bride's and groom's wrists are tied together with a long cotton thread, which is looped around the bowls of water and then connected to the monks. The celebrants return home after this, and the next morning, friends and relatives of the couple sprinkle them with the water and then hold a *baci* ceremony. Afterward, the couple is seated together in front of all the guests and the monks chant prayers to bless the marriage. Laotian Americans still celebrate marriages in this fashion. However, civil weddings and weddings that follow wider American fashions are becoming more common.

Relations with Other Americans Lao culture emphasizes hospitality and friendliness, so Laotian Americans generally have excellent relations with other Americans. They warmly welcome outsiders to community events and holiday celebrations. Some Laotian Americans do have prejudices against the Vietnamese, resulting from a complicated history between Laos and

Vietnam. However, many Laotian Americans live in or near Vietnamese communities and get along well with their neighbors.

High rates of intermarriage reflect the ease with which Laotian Americans interact with members of other groups. In 2010, according to U.S. Census estimates, about 25 percent of married Laotian American women and 17 percent of Laotian American men were married to non-Laotians. White Americans, the majority population of the United States, constituted most of the non-Laotian spouses. About 12 percent of married Laotian American women and 6 percent of married Laotian American men had white spouses. Most of the other non-Laotian spouses were members of various Asian groups. The frequency of such mixed marriages indicates that there will be many more people of partly Laotian ancestry in the United States in the future.

Most intergroup conflicts occur between young Laotians and young people in other groups. Laotian youth gangs first arose in the United States during the 1980s, as young Laotian Americans came into contact with ethnically and racially based youth gangs of other groups. By the 2000s, youth gangs had become an established problem in many Laotian American communities around the country.

Philanthropy Laotian Americans have organized a number of philanthropic groups that raise funds to address the medical and social problems of members of their ethnic group. The Laotian American National Alliance, Inc. (LANA) began at the 1997 meeting of the National Association for the Education and Advancement of Cambodians, Laotians, and Vietnamese. Some of the attendees at that meeting decided that Laotian Americans needed an organization of their own, and LANA took shape in 1999, after two years of planning. It raises funds to meet community needs and promotes civic participation and public policy advocacy. The Lao American Women Association (LAWA) was organized in 1995 in the Washington, D.C., area. Among its other activities, LAWA has an educational scholarship fund for Laotian American women. Numerous local philanthropic Laotian American organizations operate around the country as well.

EMPLOYMENT AND ECONOMIC CONDITIONS

During the early years of Laotian American settlement, Laotian immigrants were among the most disadvantaged in their new country. In 1990, while one out of every ten Americans lived below the poverty line, about one out of every three Laotian Americans lived below the poverty line. By 2010, however, only about 15 percent of Laotian Americans were below the poverty line, according to U.S. Census estimates, and this was not significantly different from the poverty rate for all Americans. Unemployment among Laotian Americans was high in 1990 (9.3 percent), but by

A Laotian American groom and bride participate in a traditional Laotian wedding in a private home in Providence, Rhode Island. DAVID H. WELLS / PICADE LLC / ALAMY

LAOTIAN SURNAMES

The use of surnames is relatively recent in Laos. During the French colonial period, toward the end of World War II, the government mandated the adoption of family names. These names are usually long by Western standards and consist of Lao, Sanskrit, and Pali (classical Indian languages) words strung together. For example, one of the most common elements of Lao last names is the Sanskrit word *Vongsa* or *Vong*, which means "of royal family." This is the basis of fairly common names such as Sayavong, Sayavongsa, Manivong, Lattanvong, and Khantavong. Other common surnames are Phetsavanh, Chantalangsy, and Xayansy. People in Laos often use given names even in formal situations, so that, for example, Khamsook Manivong will be addressed or referred to as "Mr. Khamsook," rather than "Mr. Manivong." Laotian Americans usually follow the general American practice of identifying themselves and others by their family names when they interact with non-Laotians but will most often use only given names when addressing each other.

2010 the Laotian American unemployment rate was just below 6 percent, compared with more than 9 percent for all Americans.

Despite the educational disadvantages of many Laotian Americans, their participation in the American labor market has been largely successful because of their focus on skilled, semiskilled, and service occupations. Although these are generally lower-paying jobs than most white-collar professions, the willingness of Laotian Americans to work hard at them have yielded higher rates of employment and incomes. Beginning in the 1980s Laotian Americans became a large percentage of the welders in oil-related construction. The 2010 U.S. Census data shows that the most common occupation for Laotian Americans was as assemblers of electrical equipment, which was the occupational category of more than 8 percent of Laotian Americans in the labor force. Other common occupations included unclassified machine operators (4 percent), cashiers, wood lathe and planing machine operators (3 percent), cooks (3 percent), graders and sorters in manufacturing (2 percent), waiters and waitresses (2 percent), janitors (2 percent), and nursing aides and orderlies (2 percent). Because Thai food is popular in the United States and Lao food and Thai food are similar, Laotian Americans often work in Thai restaurants. Although Laotian Americans were affected by the recession that began in 2008, their concentration in necessary blue-collar occupations has helped them weather the difficulties of the recession.

POLITICS AND GOVERNMENT

According to information from the U.S. Census, 40 percent of Laotian Americans were U.S. citizens by birth in 2010, slightly more than 37 percent were naturalized

citizens, and 22 percent were not citizens. Among Laotian Americans old enough to vote, 29 percent were not citizens. The relatively high rate of noncitizenship reflects the fact that Laotian Americans as a group have not yet become very active in American politics. A number of local Laotian American organizations have held voting drives and programs to encourage civic engagement. The Laotian American National Alliance (LANA) has urged members of the group to register and vote.

NOTABLE INDIVIDUALS

Academia and Education Boonsang Khamkeo was born in Vientiane, Laos, in 1942. He received his education in France, where he completed a doctorate in political science. He returned to Laos in 1973. In 1981 Communist officials arrested him and sent him to a so-called re-education camp, where he remained until 1988. His book, *I Little Slave: A Prison Memoir from Communist Laos* (2006), tells of these years. After reaching the United States, he received training in addiction therapy at the Oregon Health & Science University, where he subsequently became a behavioral health counselor.

Banlang Phommasouvanh (1946–), a respected Laotian American educator, was the founder and executive director of the Lao Parent and Teacher Association. Educated in Laos and France before settling in the United States, Phommasouvanh went on to teach English as a Second Language at Hiawatha Elementary School in Minneapolis. She was one of three teachers honored at the Hiawatha Elementary Celebration in 2011 and was the recipient of the Minnesota Governor's Commendation in 1990.

Literature Bryan Thao Worra is a writer and cultural activist. Born Thao Somnouk Silosuth in Vientiane, Laos, in 1973, Worra was adopted as an infant by John Worra, an American pilot working for Royal Air Lao. Worra lived in various parts of the United States while growing up. He began writing seriously in 1991 while attending Oberlin College. His works include plays, short stories, and poetry. These have been published in several books, as well as in literary journals. In 2009 Worra became the first Laotian American writer to receive a fellowship in literature from the National Endowment for the Arts.

Sports Khan "Bob" Malaythong (1981–) is a badminton player who competed for the United States at the 2008 Summer Olympics. He is a coach at the Royal Badminton Academy in Menlo Park, California.

Stage and Screen Ova Saopeng is an actor and playwright. Born in Savannakhet, Laos, and raised in Honolulu, he has acted in numerous plays and films, including *Pirates of the Caribbean*. He is married to the actress Leilani Chan.

Nitaya Panemalaythong was born in a refugee camp in Thailand in 1985 and moved with her family to the United States in 1986. While working in an office to help support her family and attending college at Normandale Community College in Minneapolis, she was named Miss Minnesota 2012, the first Asian American to hold that title.

MEDIA

LaoAmericans

An online magazine in English based in Northern California. It publishes stories and reports by and about Laotian Americans.

Siamphone Luankang, Editor
URL: www.laoamericanmagazine.com

Lao Broadcasting Channel

A television channel offering Lao programming throughout North America.

Email: info@laobc.com
URL: www.laobc.com

ORGANIZATIONS AND ASSOCIATIONS

Lao Advancement Organization of America (LAO)

The LAO builds on the traditions of Lao culture to enable Laotian Americans in Minnesota to succeed. It acts as an advocate in education, employment, and economic opportunity as well.

Khamchanh Phanthavong, Executive Director
2648 West Broadway Avenue
Minneapolis, Minnesota 55411
Phone: (612) 302-9154
Fax: (612) 522-2431
Email: kphanthavong@laoamerica.org
URL: www.laoamerica.org

Lao American Women Association (LAWA)

Bounchanh Senthavong, President
c/o NCSC
1628 Sixteenth Street NW
Washington, D.C. 20009
Phone: (301) 941-5378
Email: info@lawadc.org
URL: www.lawadc.org

Lao Heritage Foundation

A Washington, D.C.-based organization devoted to preserving and promoting Lao culture through traditional Lao arts.

Niphasone Souphom, President
Phone: (202) 607-7466
Email: info@laoheritagefoundation.org
URL: www.laoheritagefoundation.org

Laotian American National Alliance, Inc. (LANA)

Sourichanh Chantyasack, CEO
1628 Sixteenth Street NW
Washington, D.C. 20009
Phone: (202) 370-7841
Fax: (202) 462-2774
Email: sourichanh@lana-usa.org
URL: http://lana-usa.org

Laotian American women in traditional dress gather near the Vietnam Veterans Memorial in Washington, D.C. REUTERS PHOTOGRAPHER / REUTERS

Laotian American Society

An organization for promoting cultural awareness and communication and providing social resources to Laotian people in Georgia.

Noy Lounnarath Bozarth, President
P.O. Box 48432
Atlanta, Georgia 30362
Email: info@lasg.org
URL: www.lasg.org

MUSEUMS AND RESEARCH CENTERS

Center for Lao Studies

An organization to pursue Lao studies that serves the needs of scholars, the general public, and people of Lao heritage around the world. In addition to study-abroad programs, it also has conferences, an oral history archive, and a variety of publications. Although concerned primarily with the nation of Laos, it also provides publications and other resources on Laotian Americans.

Vinya Sisamouth, Executive Director
65 Ninth Street
San Francisco, California 94103
Phone: (415) 874-5578
Fax: (415) 565-0204
URL: www.laostudies.org

Lao Community Cultural Center of San Diego

An organization to preserve and promote Lao cultural heritage in San Diego and to promote cross-cultural communication.

Khampeng S. Phabmixay, President
5520 Wellesley Street
Suite 109
La Mesa, California 91942
URL: www.lcccsd.com

Southeast Asian Resource Action Center

A national organization that advances the interests of Cambodian, Laotian, and Vietnamese Americans. The organization's resource center is one of the best sources of information on these groups.

1626 Sixteenth Street NW
Washington, D.C. 20009
Phone: (202) 667-4690
Email: searac@searac.org
URL: www.searac.org/content/publications-and-materials

SOURCES FOR ADDITIONAL STUDY

Bankston, Carl L., III, and Danielle Antoinette Hidalgo. "Southeast Asia: Laos, Cambodia, Thailand." In *The New Americans: A Guide to Immigration since 1965*, edited by Mary Waters and Reed Ueda. Cambridge, MA: Harvard University Press, 2007.

———. "The Waves of War: Immigrants, Refugees, and New Americans from Southeast Asia." In *Contemporary Asian America: A Multidisciplinary Reader*, edited by Min Zhou and James V. Gatwood. 2nd ed. New York: New York University Press, 2007.

———. "Temple and Society in the New World: Theravada Buddhism in North America." In *North American Buddhism: Social Scientific Perspectives*, edited by Paul Numrich. Leiden: Brill, 2008.

Dorais, Louis-Jacques. "Between Necessity and Choice: Rhode Island Lao American Women." In *Displacements and Diasporas: Asians in the Americas*, edited by Wanni W. Anderson and Robert G. Lee. New Brunswick: Rutgers University Press, 2005.

Lee, Jonathan H. X. *Laotians in the San Francisco Bay Area*. Mount Pleasant, SC: Arcadia, 2012.

Proudfoot, Robert. *Even the Birds Don't Sound the Same Here: The Laotian Refugees' Search for Heart in American Culture*. New York: Peter Lang, 1990.

Rumbaut, Ruben. "Vietnamese, Laotian, and Cambodian Americans." In *Asian Americans, Contemporary Trends and Issues*, edited by Pyong Gap Min. 2nd ed. Thousand Oaks, CA: Pine Forge Press, 2006.

Shah, Bindi V. *Laotian Daughters: Working Toward Community, Belonging and Environmental Justice*. Philadelphia: Temple University Press, 2012.

Tenhula, John. *Voices from Southeast Asia: The Refugee Experience in the United States*. New York: Holmes & Meier, 1991.

Zhou, Min, Carl L. Bankston III, and Rebecca Kim. "Rebuilding Spiritual Lives in the New Land: Religious Practices among Southeast Asian Refugees in the United States." In *Asian Immigration and Transplanting and Transforming Religions*, edited by Pyong Gap Min and Jung Ha Kim. Walnut Creek, CA: Altamira Press, 2001.

LATVIAN AMERICANS

Andris Straumanis

OVERVIEW

Latvian Americans are immigrants or descendants of immigrants from Latvia, a Baltic country in northeastern Europe. It is bordered by Estonia to the north, Lithuania to the south, Russia to the east, Belarus to the southeast, and the Baltic Sea to the west. The country has more than 12,000 rivers and 3,000 small lakes but only two major waterways: the Daugava (Dvina) River, which flows north across the center of the country, through the capital, Riga, and into the Baltic Sea; and the Gauja River, which begins in the hills southeast of the northern town of Cesis and also flows into the Baltic. Latvia's total land area measures 24,034.5 square miles (62,249 square kilometers), making it slightly larger than the state of West Virginia.

According the *CIA World Factbook*, Latvia had a population of 2,191,580 in July 2012. The *Factbook* notes that in 2006 more than 60 percent of Latvians failed to specify a religious preference, but among those affiliated with a particular faith, 36 percent were Christians, with nearly 20 percent of those identifying as Lutherans and another 15 percent as Orthodox. The per capita income in 2011 was equivalent to $15,900, placing Latvia among the world's upper-middle-income nations. Corruption and a population that declined by about 10 percent between 2000 and 2012 have impeded Latvia's economic development.

The largest wave of Latvian immigrants came to the United States after World War II under the 1948 Displaced Persons Act, which helped victims of Nazi persecution. More than 37,000 Latvians, many of them educated political refugees who had held professional and managerial positions, settled primarily in cities such as New York, Boston, Chicago, and Philadelphia, where they worked as low-skill laborers. Immigrants who arrived in the United States after Latvia was reestablished as an independent nation in 1991 were motivated to emigrate by economic concerns and personal reasons, such as professional advancement and family reunification, rather than by political issues. Latvians who have entered the United States since 2000 have been a more heterogeneous group than were earlier waves of Latvian immigrants.

According to the U.S. Census Bureau's American Community Survey estimates for 2009–2011, an estimated 88,508 people in the United States claim some degree of Latvian ancestry (approximately the population of Trenton, New Jersey). The greatest number of Latvian Americans lives in California, although the highest regional concentration of those of Latvian descent continues to be in the Northeast and upper Midwest, a pattern that has remained consistent for decades.

HISTORY OF THE PEOPLE

Early History Latvia's experience as an independent nation has been limited. Inhabited as early as 9000 BCE, the area was by 1500 BCE peopled by the Latvians' ancestors—early tribes of Couronians, Latgallians, Livs, Selonians, and Semigallians. Through the centuries these pagan groups developed societies and cultures. Beginning in the late twelfth and early thirteenth centuries, however, they were subjugated by German invaders. In particular, the Teutonic Knights of the Holy Roman Empire forcibly Christianized the tribes and built an economic and political system that continued in power until the twentieth century. The Germans were responsible for the growth of Riga, established in 1201, as an important Baltic Sea port that continues today to serve as a transportation link between Western Europe and Russia.

As Sweden, Poland, and Russia sought territories in the Baltic region in the 1600s, German military control weakened. Beginning in the 1620s and continuing into the 1700s, the northern part of Latvia was subject to Swedish rule, while the south and the east came under Polish-Lithuanian domination. Only the Duchy of Courland, located in western Latvia by the Baltic Sea, maintained some independence. The Duchy even managed to briefly extend its influence beyond its boundaries, establishing colonies in Gambia in Africa (1651) and on the Caribbean Sea island of Tobago (1654).

The 1721 Treaty of Nystad, which settled the Great Northern War between Russia and Sweden, placed the region that would later become Latvia under the political and military rule of the Russian tsar. Its economy, however, continued to be controlled by German barons who lived off the labor of Latvian peasants. Latvians began to gain some economic power after 1819, when Russians emancipated serfs in the Baltic provinces.

Modern Era A so-called National Awakening movement began in the mid-nineteenth century with the study of Latvian folk customs and the publication of the first Latvian-language newspapers. By the late nineteenth century it had produced a generation of Latvian nationalists. This political development and industrialization gave rise to new hopes for a specific Latvian identity but also to discontent among Latvians about their social and political subjugation to the Russians and Germans. Radicalism was increasing among the working class, and their dissatisfaction was intensified by the spread of Marxism. Their frustration led to the 1905 Revolution in Latvia. In January seventy peaceful demonstrators were shot in Riga, the capital. In response, workers mounted large strikes and peasants burned feudal manor houses. Authorities responded to the uprising with brutal force, shooting 3,000 and sending many others into exile in Siberia. Although the revolution failed, it served to bring together the Latvian working class and intelligentsia and to heighten aspirations for independence.

Amid the confusion resulting from the Russian Revolution of 1917 and the German capture of Riga that same year, Latvian nationalists pushed for sovereignty. The country declared its independence on November 18, 1918, but the fight for control continued until January 1920, when all foreign forces were expelled from Latvian soil. Soviet Russia signed a peace treaty with Latvia in August 1920, recognizing the country as a sovereign nation. Independent for the first time in seven hundred years, Latvia became a member of the League of Nations in 1921. Lacking a dominant political party, it was governed by various democratic coalitions until 1934, when Prime Minister Kărlis Ulmanis, a centrist and one of the founders of Latvian independence, took control in a bloodless coup. The country flourished economically, and the twenty-year period of self-rule came to be viewed as a golden age of Latvian history, with Ulmanis as a symbol of Latvian patriotism.

Ulmanis's efforts to maintain a neutral position between the Soviet Union and Nazi Germany proved futile in the long run. The Red Army occupied Latvia from June 1940 to June 1941, when the Germans drove them out. In what is now known among Latvians as the *Baigais gads* (The Year of Terror), more than 40,000 people were executed or deported, most in the final three days before the country fell to the Germans, when an estimated 30,000 Latvians were shepherded onto boxcars bound for Siberia. Under Nazi domination, up to 100,000 more Latvian citizens were murdered; the majority were Jews.

As the Allies began to gain the upper hand, the Red Army marched back into Latvia, occupying about two-thirds of the country by 1944. As many as 100,000 Latvians fled the country in advance of Soviet troops, some to Sweden and more to Germany. Many of these ended up as displaced persons in refugee camps, where they strove to maintain the Latvian language and culture. Within the next decade thousands of these displaced Latvians immigrated

to the United Kingdom, the United States, Canada, and Australia. In the brief period between October 1948 and March 1952, more Latvians arrived in the United States than had in the previous sixty years. Many saw themselves as political exiles who would one day return to their homeland.

Meanwhile, Latvia itself, reinstated as a republic of the Soviet Union when Latvian territory again came under Soviet control, was becoming less Latvian as large-scale immigration to Latvia from other parts of the Soviet Union accelerated. Within four decades nearly half of the country's population was non-Latvian. In the late 1980s, as Soviet policy adopted *glasnost* ("openness") and *perestroika* ("restructuring"), opposition to Communist rule grew in Latvia. Mass demonstrations in 1987 gave rise to the 1988 establishment of the Latvian Popular Front. In December 1989 the Latvian Supreme Soviet ended the Communist Party's monopoly on political power in Latvia, a decision that led to the Latvian Popular Front's victory in the free and open elections of 1990. On May 4, 1990, the Latvian legislature declared a renewal of independence. With the collapse of the Soviet Union in 1991, Latvia again became a fully independent nation.

In September 1991 Latvia became a member of the United Nations and within the next few years moved to privatize the national economy. By 2004, the year Latvia entered the European Union, the country had become a successful post-Soviet society. Latvia's economy grew by 50 percent between 2004 and 2007, but the global financial crisis of 2008 to 2009 pushed the nation into one of the worst recessions among European Union countries. Social turmoil followed the financial crisis, but the austerity measures that evoked anger within Latvia persuaded international leaders to agree to a $10 billion (in U.S. dollars) bailout in 2009. Despite the aid, unemployment had reached 20 percent by January 2010. Ongoing economic woes and political corruption have proven to be major obstacles to continued progress.

SETTLEMENT IN THE UNITED STATES

Some historical evidence suggests that the first Latvians in North America may have settled with Swedish and Finnish migrants in present-day Delaware and Pennsylvania in around 1640. A group of Latvians from the island of Tobago migrated to Massachusetts in the late 1600s. Latvians were also among the thousands of fortune seekers who headed to California during the 1849 Gold Rush. Two histories of Latvians in the United States claim that Mārtiņš Būčiņš, believed to be a Latvian sailor, was among the first to die during the American Civil War.

Latvian American immigrants since that time have comprised two distinct groups: the *Veclatviešu*, or Old Latvians (those who settled in the United States before World War II), and those who came after the war. The Old Latvians immigrated in three waves, the first beginning in 1888 with the arrival of several young men in Boston. Among them was Jēkabs Zībergs (1863–1963), who became one of the most important Latvian American community leaders in the pre-World War II era. These young men journeyed to the United States to escape being drafted into the Russian tsar's army and, like other Latvian immigrants who followed in the early years of the twentieth century, to find their fortunes. Politically, these early immigrants were divided into two groups, mirroring the politics of their homeland: one was nationalist, devoted to the creation of an independent Latvia; the other was socialist and more focused on freeing Latvian workers from the oppression of imperial Russia.

Typically young, single men (although some were single women or families), the early immigrants settled primarily in east coast and Midwestern cities, such as Boston, New York, Philadelphia, Cleveland, and Chicago, as well as in some cities on the west coast, including Seattle, Portland, and San Francisco. Some Latvians also settled in rural areas, although usually not in great enough numbers to form long-lasting communities.

In this first wave of immigrants were several hundred Baptists who settled in various east coast locations. Perhaps the best-known Latvian Baptist settlement was in Bucks County, Pennsylvania, not far from Philadelphia, where, beginning in 1906, a community was formed that eventually grew to about one hundred individuals.

The next wave of Old Latvians arrived in around 1906, after the failed 1905 revolution against the Russian empire. Political leaders and rank-and-file revolutionaries alike faced certain death if caught by Russian soldiers. Many chose to emigrate and continue their revolutionary activities from abroad. Generally possessing more radical political views than the earlier Latvian immigrants, they caused splits not only between conservative and leftist Latvian groups but also within the Latvian leftist movement.

With the advent of World War I, Latvia became a battleground for German and Russian forces. Migration stopped until, in the aftermath of the 1917 Russian Revolution, many revolutionary Latvian Americans returned to their homeland to help create a Bolshevik government (a forerunner to the Communist Party) in Latvia and Moscow. Among these reverse migrants was Fricis Roziņš (1870–1919), a radical Marxist philosopher who had arrived in the United States in 1913. He returned home in 1917 to head a short-lived Latvian Soviet government. A few nationalist Latvian Americans returned to Latvia after the country declared independence in 1918.

The final wave—more of a trickle—of Old Latvians immigrated after the U.S. government put quotas in place in 1924. A limited number still settled in the United States, but the promise of better economic times in the newly independent Latvia—coupled with the Great Depression in the United States—generally inhibited immigration.

In *Our Racial and National Minorities* (1937), Francis J. Brown and Joseph Slabey Roucek published figures they had compiled on Latvian immigration through 1936. According to their data, 4,309 Latvians came to the United States before 1900; 8,544 from 1901 to 1910; 2,776 from 1911 to 1914; 730 from 1915 to 1919; 3,399 from 1921 to 1930; and 519 from 1930 to 1936. Until the 1930 Census the U.S. government lumped Latvians with Lithuanians and Russians. Ten years later the Census counted 34,656 people of Latvian origin, about 54 percent of them born outside of the United States.

The ravages of World War II turned many Latvians into refugees. Fearing the Soviet communists, they headed to Western Europe. By the end of the war, an estimated 240,000 Latvians were camped in displaced person (DP) facilities in Germany, Austria, and other countries. Some were eventually repatriated to Soviet Latvia, but the rest resettled in Germany, England, Sweden, Australia, Canada, and the United States, among other countries. As documented by Andris Skreija in his unpublished thesis on Latvian refugees, an estimated 40,000 Latvians immigrated to the United States from 1949 to 1951 with the help of the U.S. government and various social service and religious organizations. These displaced persons constituted a new category in the history of Latvian immigration. Many had been members of the professional class in their homeland, but in the United States they often had to take jobs as farmhands, custodians, or builders until they managed to find better-paying positions.

Most Latvian DPs settled in larger cities, such as New York, Boston, Philadelphia, and Chicago. Unlike the Old Latvians, many of whom considered themselves immigrants, the Latvian DPs saw themselves as living in *trimda*, or exile, and dreamed of the day they could return to a free Latvia. Since the reestablishment of an independent Latvia, however, few have returned (many of them elderly), although about 9,000 have declared dual citizenship as a way to offer political support to the reemerging nation. Many travel to their homeland frequently and provide financial and material support for relatives and various organizations. A number of Latvian Americans have been elected to the Saeima, or Parliament, in Latvia.

The Department of Homeland Security reported in 2010 that from 1991 to 2009, nearly 11,000 Latvians obtained legal permanent resident status in the United States. These immigrants entered the country as immediate relatives of U.S. citizens, under family- or employee-sponsored preferences, as refugees or asylees, or under the diversity programs established in U.S. immigration laws. Unlike the substantial immigration of displaced persons after World War II,

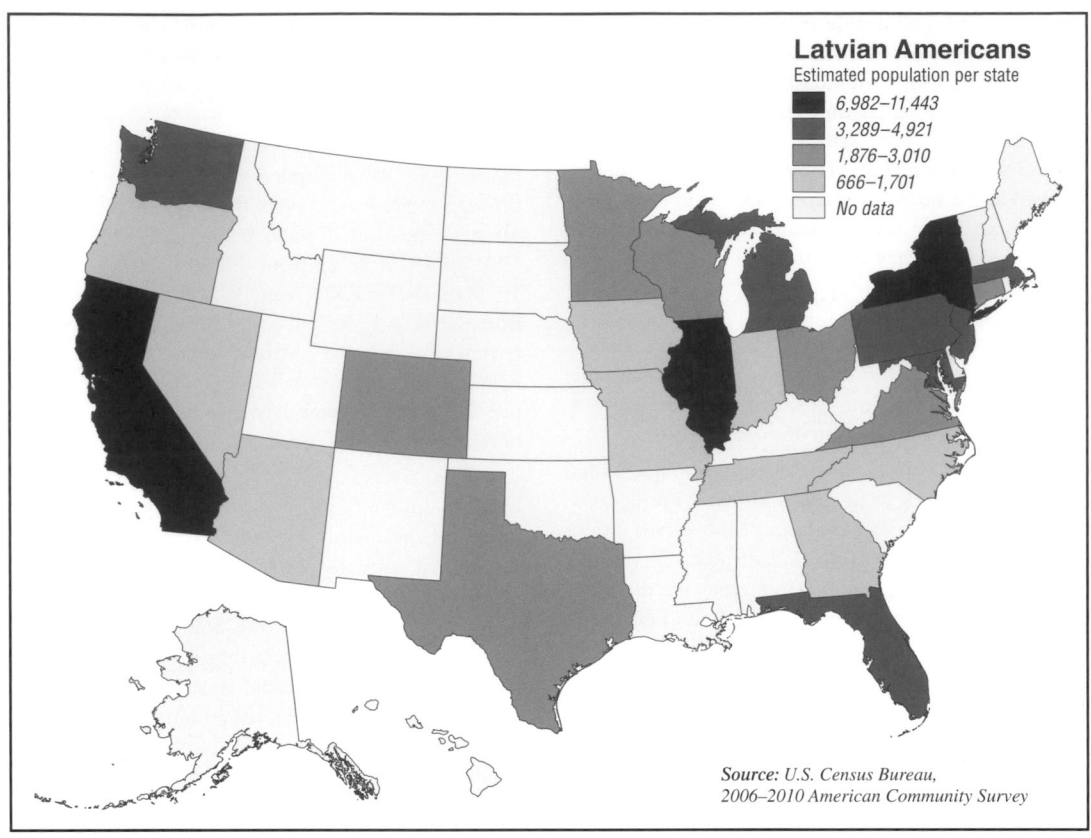

Latvian Americans
Estimated population per state

- 6,982–11,443
- 3,289–4,921
- 1,876–3,010
- 666–1,701
- No data

Source: U.S. Census Bureau,
2006–2010 American Community Survey

post-Latvian independence migration averaged 572 people annually from 1990 to 2009, ranging from a low of 86 in 1991 to a high of 892 in 2006. Politically and economically, this more recent group of Latvian immigrants exhibits greater heterogeneity than did the post-World War II group.

Newly arriving Latvian Americans also demonstrate greater diversity in their choice of destination, although the largest numbers have replicated the settlement pattern of earlier Latvian immigrants. California and New York are home to the most Latvian Americans. About 10 percent of the total population lives in the area that includes New York City, Long Island, and northern New Jersey. According to the U.S. Census Bureau's American Community Survey estimates released in 2010, Chicago (6,560) and Los Angeles (4,176) have sizable Latvian American communities, and Illinois, Florida, Massachusetts, and Michigan also have groups in the 4,000 to 7,000 range. Smaller but still significant concentrations can be found in Boston (3,971), Philadelphia (2,904), Washington, D.C. (2,684), and Minneapolis–St. Paul (2,643).

LANGUAGE

Latvian and Lithuanian are the only living languages remaining in the small Baltic language group of the Indo-European family. Latvian uses the Latin alphabet, excluding the letters *q*, *w*, *x*, and *y*, and employs diacritical marks on some letters (*ā*, *č*, *ē*,

g', *ī*, *ķ*, *ļ*, *ņ*, *ŗ*, *š*, and *ž*) to differentiate long or soft sounds from short or hard sounds. Latvian words are stressed on the first syllable, and written Latvian is largely phonetic.

Latvia's location and history have exposed its language to the influence of German, Russian, and Swedish. During the fifty-year occupation of Latvia by the former Soviet Union, the impact of Russian became particularly strong. Some feared that Russian would displace Latvian entirely, a concern that motivated Latvian Americans to work hard to preserve their language. According to Latvia's 2000 census, slightly more than 50 percent of the population of Latvia speaks Latvian; another one-third identifies Russian as its primary language. Since the country regained independence, declaring Latvian its official language, however, more and more English words have crept into the vocabulary, thanks to the growing global influence of English.

In the United States, Latvian is spoken most widely among the first generation of post-World War II immigrants. The 1990 U.S. Census reported that about 13 percent of people who claim Latvian ancestry—most of them aged 65 and older—said they do not speak English very well. American Community Survey data from 2009 to 2011 reports a decrease of more than 50 percent among those who are not proficient in English. Although usage has dropped significantly among second and third generation Latvian

Americans, 50,000 people in the United States, the largest group outside Latvia, still speak the language. Many churches continue to offer services in Latvian, although some have begun to use English as a way to attract and serve non-Latvian speakers. The United States has only one Latvian-language newspaper (the semiweekly *Laiks* of Brooklyn, New York), but there are several small Latvian-language magazines and numerous church newsletters.

Greetings and Popular Expressions Perhaps the most widespread salutation in Latvian is *veiks*! (svayks)—"greetings!" It is commonly used when addressing friends but also appears on bumper stickers in the United States. Other terms include: *apsveicu* (ap-svaytsu)—"congratulations"; *Atā* (a-tah)—"goodbye"; *daudz laimes dzimšanas dienā* (daudz laimes dzim-shan-as dien-ah)—"happy birthday"; *labdien* (labdien)—"good day"; *labrīt* (labreet)—"good morning"; *labvakar* (labvakar)—"good evening"; *lūdzu* (loodz-u)—"please"; *paldies* (pal-dies)—"thank you"; *priecīgus svētkus* (prie-tsee-gus svehtkus)—"happy holidays," used at Christmastime; and *uz redzēšanos* (uz redz-eh-shan-os)—"until we meet again."

RELIGION

Although exact figures are difficult to obtain, the majority of Latvians in the United States are Lutherans. There are also sizable communities of Catholics and Baptists, as well as a small group of *dievturi*, followers of Latvian folk religion.

The first Latvian Lutheran church service in the United States was organized by the Boston Latvian Society in 1891. The earliest-known congregation, St. John's Latvian Evangelical Lutheran Church, was formed in 1893 in Philadelphia and continued to operate for more than a century. The Reverend Hans Rebane (1862–1911) was the first Latvian Lutheran minister ordained in the United States. Of both Estonian and Latvian heritage, Rebane also served Estonian and German congregations. With Jēkabs Zībergs, he began publishing *Amerikas Vēstnesis* (*America's Herald*, 1896–1920), a nationalist and religiously oriented newspaper based in Boston. Zībergs also published an almanac and other religious materials. In a few short years, additional Latvian congregations were established in New York, Philadelphia, Baltimore, Cleveland, Chicago, northern Wisconsin, San Francisco, and other locations. Radical Latvians in the United States criticized these early churchgoers; to them, the church in Latvia—largely controlled by German-appointed pastors—contributed to the oppression of Latvian peasants. By World War II only a few congregations remained, but the arrival of Latvian displaced persons beginning in 1949 gave new life to the Latvian church movement. Latvian Lutheran displaced persons saw theirs as a church in exile. Although a Lutheran church still existed in Latvia, its activities were suppressed by the Soviet regime.

The Latvian Lutheran church in the United States remains conservative. In many cities congregations have become a focus of community activity. Many have organized Saturday or Sunday schools that offer language and cultural heritage lessons in addition to religious instruction. In locations where Latvians have acquired their own church buildings, the facilities often double as cultural centers that present concerts and other programs.

A key question for Lutheran clergy has been whether they can continue to spread Christianity while still conserving Latvian culture. Attempts by some pastors to introduce English into religious instruction have in the past been met with resistance. Like other Latvian social and cultural institutions in the United States, however, the Lutheran church is concerned about its decreasing membership, which erodes both the vitality of congregations and the church's financial base. In 2007 there were sixty Latvian Evangelical Lutheran churches in the United States with a collective membership of 10,950.

Latvian Baptists were also active in the United States by the late 1880s. The first Latvian Baptist congregation was founded in Philadelphia in 1900. By 1908, congregations were also meeting in Boston, Chicago, and New York, as well as in Bucks County, Pennsylvania. The Bucks County Latvian Baptist Church in Quakertown is one of a handful of Latvian Baptist churches that were still active in 2012. Latvian Baptists published a number of magazines and newsletters before World War II, including the monthly *Amerikas Latvietis* (*America's Latvian*, 1902–1905) and *Jaunā Tēvija* (*New Fatherland*, 1913–1917). *Kristīga Balss* (*Christian Voice*), which began as a Baptist publication in Latvia, was reestablished as a monthly Latvian-language publication for Latvian Baptists in the United States in the post–World War II period. In 2012, despite declining subscriptions, it continued to publish quarterly, claiming readers in South America, Europe, and Australia as well as in the United States.

Latvian American Catholic groups sprang up after World War II, but they were not large enough in any city to have their own church. Latvian Catholics are represented by the American Latvian Catholic Association (Amerikas latviešu katoļu apvienība), formed in 1954.

Also active in the United States are the *dievturi*, followers of a folk religion registered as the Latvian Church Dievturi, Inc., which developed in the 1920s in Latvia. *Dievturība* is neopagan in origin, claiming roots in the pre-Christian, pantheistic religion of Latvia. Followers in the United States gather at Dievseta, a property in rural Wisconsin, to celebrate seasonal holidays. In 2012 Dievseta was the only property in the world devoted specifically to the practice of *dievturība*.

CULTURE AND ASSIMILATION

Except for the political radicals among them, the Latvians who immigrated to the United States before World War II are generally thought to have assimilated quickly into the American mainstream. By contrast, the exiles of the post-World War II period maintained their ethnic distinctiveness. Now, however, these Latvian Americans face deepening concerns about their future, as new generations become more assimilated and postindependence immigrants arrive with a different experience of what it means to be Latvian.

Although most of the early Latvian immigrants, like those from other countries, started out in low-paying, unskilled jobs, they were usually well educated. Their superior knowledge and skills allowed them to move to more lucrative positions in a relatively brief span of time and to assimilate quickly. They did not experience much of the stereotyping that plagued southern, central, and eastern European immigrants during the early twentieth century. This immunity most likely occurred because the Latvians were a little-known group; their smaller numbers and the scarcity of well-defined Latvian communities ensured them a low profile.

The arrival of thousands of Latvian displaced persons after World War II sparked an era of heightened ethnic conservation efforts. Fiercely anticommunist, the immigrants saw the Soviet occupation of their homeland not only as an infringement on their right to autonomy but also as an effort to eradicate their ethnic group altogether. The migration of Russians and other non-Latvian groups into Latvia, part of a Soviet effort at "Russification," became a threat to Latvian culture. Latvian displaced persons in the United States had often spent years in refugee camps where ethnic group identity intensified their nationalism and anti-Communism. Once resettled in their new home, they launched a number of political and cultural movements to fight assimilation and help make Americans aware of Latvia's plight. Weekend Latvian schools were organized in several cities, while summer camps offered children and adults cultural immersion. *Runāsim latviski* ("Let's speak Latvian") was both a political statement and an expression of cultural preservation. Marriage outside of the Latvian community was often discouraged, because children of mixed couples might not learn the language.

Although post-World War II Latvian immigrants frequently viewed their stay in the United States as temporary, they established their own churches, welfare organizations, Boy and Girl Scout troops, sports and literary groups, and so on. In 1990 around five hundred of these organizations continued in existence, all committed to the defense of Latvia against Communism and to preserving Latvian culture for the day the Latvians would return home. When Latvia regained independence, however, few of them actually returned. In 2010 the American Latvian Association reported a sharp decline in membership from 1990, and the number of Latvian organizations in the United States had shrunk to 160. Although a substantial majority of Latvian Americans were descendants of the displaced persons who arrived after World War II, the aging of the émigré community and the transfer of power to a younger generation more assimilated into mainstream American culture left many of the remaining organizations struggling for survival.

As in the case of the Old Latvians, few cultural prejudices exist against post-World War II Latvian immigrants. Indeed, the Latvians faced a lack of identity because of their small numbers and the erasure, before 1991, of Latvia from many world maps. As a result, few Americans know anything about Latvians, and they often confuse Europe's Balkan states with the Baltic countries, of which Latvia is one.

The Latvian immigrants who arrived in the United States after 1991 were markedly different from those who had arrived in the years following World War II. They emigrated from their homeland for economic reasons or to seek adventure rather than for political reasons. Having grown up in a Latvia that was part of the Soviet Union, they lacked the ardent nationalism of the earlier generation. The differences sometimes created conflict between the two groups in the United States. Many Latvians who had spent decades fighting for Latvian independence and preserving Latvian culture thought the new immigrants should not have come, but instead should have remained at home and contributed their youth and energy to building a democratic Latvia and an emerging market economy. Some saw the personal goals that inspired the new immigrants as selfish. The younger immigrants found the established Latvian American community frozen in Latvian traditions that no longer existed in contemporary Latvia. They often spoke of feeling unwelcome in Latvian groups, and even when friendly relationships existed, they felt that the differences were greater that the commonalities.

Traditions and Customs Like many other ethnic groups in the United States, Latvians have adopted some American ways, but they also maintain a cultural heritage from their homeland. Until the late nineteenth century, when industrialization created a demand for workers in several Latvian cities, Latvians remained a largely rural people. As a result, many of the traditions, customs, and beliefs still recognized by Latvian Americans are based in agricultural life. For example, the wreaths of flowers (for women) and oak leaves (for men) that are worn during the celebration of *Jāņi* (summer solstice) are remnants of an ancient fertility festival. Some scholars believe that the oldest knitting tradition in Europe may be Latvian: a Latvian bride-to-be proved her worthiness by knitting many intricately designed wool mittens, as well as linen handkerchiefs and wool socks. The more she had in her dowry, the more valuable she might appear to her suitor. Hand-knitted mittens were then used to decorate the home of the newly married couple as a symbol of a productive future. In the United States wool mittens and socks are sometimes used as adornments in wedding ceremonies. The gauntlet-shaped mittens and the designs particular to different regions of Latvia link the custom to practices dating to the fourteenth and fifteenth centuries.

Cuisine Traditional Latvian foods include *pīrāgi*, pastry stuffed with bacon or ham; *Jāņu siers*, a cheese usually made for the Midsummer Eve's holiday; various soups; sauerkraut; potato salad; smoked fish and eel; and beer. At major celebrations, such as holidays and birthdays, Latvians serve a popular sweetbread—*kliņģeris*—flavored with raisins and cardamom and shaped like a large pretzel. Because of the work involved in preparing many of these dishes, as well as the difficulty of obtaining some of the ingredients, Latvians in the United States now save them for special occasions. The foods tend to be rich, although Latvian Americans have been known to modify recipes by using lower-fat ingredients and less salt.

Traditional Costumes Latvian Americans wear folk costumes primarily when performing in song groups or dance troupes. The men wear monotone (white, gray, or black) wool trousers and coats, white shirts, and black boots. Women's costumes usually include an embroidered white linen blouse and a colorful ankle-length wool skirt. Both men and women wear wide, brightly colored belts and silver jewelry. Unmarried women wear a *vaiņags* (crown) on their heads, while married women wear a cap or kerchief. The designs of costumes are characteristic of specific locales in Latvia.

Dances and Songs Among the Latvian people's strongest traditions are their songs, called *dainas*, and their interest in folk culture. The *dainas*—simple verses that tell old stories and reveal the wisdom of centuries of Latvian culture—were handed down orally over generations. Beginning in the nineteenth century, as interest in Latvian nationalism grew, folk lorists transcribed about 900,000 of these songs, culminating in a multivolume collection compiled by Krišjānis Barons (1835–1923). Even by the end of the twentieth century, dozens of Latvian ensembles still maintained the musical tradition in the United States, often performing at community events and ethnic festivals. On a grander scale Latvians in the United States and in Latvia have organized song festivals that feature performances of traditional folk songs and dances, choral music, and even musicals and plays. These song festivals serve as a ritual, reminding Latvians of their common ideals. The first such festival was held in Latvia in 1873; the tradition has since been carried on in the United States, beginning in Chicago in 1953.

Holidays Latvian Christians observe Easter and Christmas, attending church services and gathering with relatives and friends. At Easter, they color eggs using onion skins rather than paint. The skins are wrapped around uncooked eggs, which are then boiled. One Easter dinner custom is to play a game

SWEET SAUERKRAUT

Ingredients

2 12-inch kielbasa

½ cup apple cider, apple juice, or beer

1 32-ounces bag sauerkraut (or equivalent jar)

2 medium-sized carrots, shredded

1 apple or pear, chopped

1 medium white onion, chopped

3 tablespoons brown sugar

1 tablespoon paprika

1½ teaspoons caraway seeds

Preparation

Turn on the broiler and begin to warm a saucepot on the stovetop, medium heat.

Put the kielbasa on a pan with juice or beer. Slice down the center. Broil about 10 minutes or until the top opens, juices bubble, and the skin darkens. Remove from oven.

While kielbasa is cooking, add 1 tablespoon butter to the saucepot. Add onions and sauté; 5 minutes. Add carrots and apple. Sauté; 10 minutes. Add sauerkraut, brown sugar, and paprika. Stir well.

Cut kielbasa into bite-sized pieces. Add to pot, stir. Turn heat to medium-low, leave slightly uncovered, allow to cook at least 2 hours. The longer the sauerkraut cooks, the better, but refresh with more juice if kraut gets too dry. Stir periodically. Serve with a hearty and flavorful rye or pumperknickle bread, preferably from Latvia, buttered and toasted.

Serves 4

to determine whose egg is strongest: two people each hold a boiled egg; they knock the ends of their eggs together, and the person whose egg does not break goes on to challenge someone else. At Christmas Latvians bring an evergreen tree into the home and decorate it. Before they open their Christmas gifts, they recite a line of poetry or words from a song. At New Year's celebrations some Latvians still observe a custom of "pouring one's fortune": each person pours a spoonful of molten lead into a bucket of cold water. The shape of the hardened lead is then examined to determine the future.

Perhaps the favorite Latvian holiday, however, comes in June on the summer solstice—the longest day of the year. Called *Jāņi* (also known as St. John's Eve or Midsummer's Eve), the day features a traditional celebration of nature's fertility. Those who still observe the old practices prepare an elaborate feast—including the symbolic *Jāņu siers*, a rich cheese—and decorate their home with oak leaves and flowers. The celebration, featuring bonfires and sing-alongs, lasts through the night and well into the following morning. In the United States many of these customs survive. In modern-day Latvia, *Jāņi* is an official holiday.

Health Issues Latvians in the United States have largely accepted modern medical treatments, although some families still use certain folk cures. A number of Latvians have entered the medical profession. In addition to taking advantage of health insurance offered through their place of employment or through government programs, many Latvians have also joined the Latvian Relief Fund of America (*Amerikas latviešu palīdzības fonds*), founded in 1952. No illnesses specific to Latvian Americans are known.

The majority of Latvians who came to the United States after World War II had received at least some higher education in their homeland. Many were already academic or cultural leaders, and they placed a high value on education for their children.

FAMILY AND COMMUNITY LIFE

Latvians in the United States tend to have small nuclear families, usually not exceeding two adults and two children. The 2009 to 2011 American Community Survey reported a total of 41,219 households of Latvian ancestry. Nearly 60 percent of Latvian Americans lived in family households in this period, but only 20.7 percent of those households included children under eighteen, a statistic that reflects the aging of the Latvian American population. Those over sixty-five years of age make up 22.4 percent of the community. Most families are middle class; the median household income for 2009 to 2011 was $71,820. Less than 3 percent of Latvian American families lived below the poverty line in 2011.

Within the post-World War II Latvian émigré population, young men and women were encouraged to seek each other out in the hope that new Latvian families would result. For some youth, however, the close-knit nature of Latvian community life made it difficult to transform longtime acquaintances into romantic involvements. Others, perhaps thinking that their participation in the Latvian community would make a relationship outside the ethnic group difficult, seem to have deliberately chosen Latvian mates. The rate of marriage to non-Latvians has continued to increase over the years, however, and older members of the population have become concerned that Latvian culture in the United States might be threatened. At one point in the early 1970s, it was even suggested that Latvian newspapers should not carry announcements of marriages involving non-Latvians.

Gender Roles With its late-twentieth-century achievement of independence, Latvia extended broad democracy to its inhabitants and guaranteed equal rights to women. Equality remained more goal than reality, however. In 2006 women's salaries were 82 percent of men's. Men were more likely to be employed in construction and transport, which offered relatively higher salaries, and women more often worked in lower-paying fields such as education, health care, and hospitality. In the United States Latvian women have often been placed in such traditional roles as homemaker and cook. About 4 percent fewer women than men of Latvian ancestry were employed between 2009 and 2011, and employed women earned, on average, $41,220 less per year. The high degree of assimilation among Latvian Americans beyond the first generation of immigrants makes it difficult to observe discernible differences in gender roles from other Americans.

Education While recognizing the value of education, the Old Latvians did not appear to want or to be able to afford college degrees. By 1911—more than twenty years after the first Latvian immigrants had arrived in the United States—only two individuals had obtained American university degrees, the first one being a woman, Anna Enke, who studied at the University of Chicago.

The majority of Latvians who came to the United States after World War II had received at least some higher education in their homeland. Many were already academic or cultural leaders who placed a high value on the education of their children. Between 1940 and 1982, according to a 1984 study, 28 percent of Latvian men outside the Soviet Union who had earned bachelor's degrees studied in the engineering sciences, while another 15.6 percent studied in the humanities. Among women, 22.5 percent studied humanities and 16.9 percent studied medicine. According to data from the 2009–2011 American Community Survey estimates, 97.6 percent of Latvian Americans were high school graduates and 59.5 percent held college degrees, higher figures than the national average in both cases.

EMPLOYMENT AND ECONOMIC CONDITIONS

Many of the Old Latvians had been either farmers or factory workers at home. Upon arriving in the United States, they first took jobs as unskilled laborers; later, however, some moved into management and professional positions. Many of the displaced persons, on the other hand, had held professional positions in Latvia before immigrating to the United States. Most were unable to immediately resume their professional careers—at least until they had mastered English and proven their qualifications.

The 2009 to 2011 American Community Survey counted 56,114 persons of Latvian ancestry in the nation's civilian labor force, of which 5.1 percent were

Philippe Halsman (center) was a U.S. photographer of Latvian descent. Here he stands with Robert Kennedy in front of his 1947 portrait of Albert Einstein. AKG-IMAGES / JEAN DIEUZAIDE / NEWSCOM

unemployed. Almost 60 percent of Latvians in the labor force had positions in management, business, and science; 11.8 percent were employed in service occupations; and 20.8 percent had sales and office occupations. About three-fourths of the Latvians in the labor force worked in the private sector, about 15 percent had jobs in government, and slightly more than 10 percent were self-employed.

Latvian Americans were among those affected by the economic recession of the late 1980s and early 1990s. The relocation of families in search of employment sometimes had a dramatic effect on Latvian social and cultural life in U.S. communities. When two young but large families had to leave Minneapolis in the mid-1980s, for example, their departure resulted in the loss of about one-third of the enrollment in the small Latvian Saturday school. The global economic crisis of the 2000s, which was particularly severe in Latvia, led to increased emigration, with as many as 30,000 more Latvians leaving their homeland annually, by some estimates. Immigrants from Latvia to the United Kingdom, Ireland, and Russia significantly exceeded those immigrating to the United States, however. The number of Latvians attaining legal permanent residence in the United States per year has declined steadily since 2006, dropping to 426 in 2011.

POLITICS AND GOVERNMENT

Latvian Americans have always been politically active. Before Latvia declared its independence, radical Old Latvians were particularly vigorous in working for the creation of a socialist government in their homeland as well as in the United States. The first Latvian American socialist organization, the Lettish Workingmen's Society, was founded in Boston in 1893. By World

War I, almost every U.S. city with a Latvian population had at least one socialist club. With the arrival of revolutionary Latvians after the failed 1905 Revolution, Latvian radicalism moved further to the left. During the 1917 Russian Revolution, Bolshevik rhetoric supporting peoples' right to self-determination was a key factor in attracting some Latvians to radical Marxism. Latvians were among those immigrants who helped form the American communist movement in 1919. Radicals produced a number of newspapers and other publications; the most important was the Boston-based weekly *Strādnieks* (*Worker*; 1906–1919). The failure to establish a permanent socialist government in Latvia following the 1917 Russian Revolution—compounded by U.S. government repression of radical activities in the States during the Red Scare of the 1920s—largely put an end to Latvian radical activity in the United States.

The radicals, who had been at the forefront of isolationist and antiwar activism in the United States, were opposed by nationalist Latvians, who focused on independence for their homeland. Under the leadership of Zībergs, Christopher Roos (1887–1963), and other Latvian immigrants, the nationalists organized in 1917 to support the U.S. World War I military effort by selling Liberty bonds. Despite such differences, Latvian Americans were united on the issue of Latvian independence. The American National Latvian League (Amerikas latviešu tautiskā savienība [ALTS]) was formed the next year in Boston to represent Latvian interests in the United States. When their homeland declared independence later in 1918, ALTS representatives urged the U.S. government to recognize the new nation of Latvia; de jure recognition came in 1922.

The Soviet occupation of Latvia during World War II was criticized by nationalist Latvians in the United States, who sought to inform the American public about atrocities committed by the Russians. The arrival of Latvian displaced persons after the war heightened political activity among Latvian Americans. A number of Latvian civic and political organizations were founded, including the American Latvian Association in 1951 and the American Latvian Republican National Federation in 1961. Latvians also joined with Estonians and Lithuanians to form groups such as the Baltic Appeal to the United Nations (BATUN), organized to press world governments to oppose Soviet power in their homelands, and the Association for the Advancement of Baltic Studies, founded in 1968.

Officially, the U.S. government never recognized the incorporation of the Baltic countries into the Soviet Union, but U.S. efforts to use negotiation rather than forceful opposition to combat communism was viewed as naïve by Latvian immigrants. Attempts by U.S. diplomats to ease tensions with the Soviets usually drew swift criticism from the Baltic groups. At election time Latvians tended to support Republican candidates over Democrats—particularly

the first generation of postwar Latvian immigrants, who felt the Republicans had a stronger anticommunist foreign-policy platform. Within the Latvian community, efforts during the 1970s and 1980s by some Latvian Americans to establish cultural exchanges with Soviet Latvia were viewed with suspicion and criticism by nationalists.

Latvian independence opened the door for direct political involvement in the homeland. Latvian immigrants and their descendants were allowed to reclaim their pre-World War II citizenship and voting rights; by May 1993 more than 8,700 Latvian Americans held dual U.S. and Latvian citizenship, according to American Latvian Association statistics. In June 1993, during the first free democratic elections after the end of Soviet rule, a number of Latvian Americans were elected to the Latvian Parliament, or *Saeima*. Among them were twin brothers Olġerts Pavlovskis (1934–) and Valdis Pavlovskis (1934–), both of whom returned to Latvia to take government posts. Without the key issue of Latvian independence to unite them, Latvian Americans have become less homogenous as a political group. Comments by Latvian Americans in online discussion groups during the 2012 presidential campaign suggested that they are as divided in political allegiance as other Americans.

NOTABLE INDIVIDUALS

Art and Architecture Florida's famed Coral Castle, a sculpture garden carved from coral, was created over a thirty-year period by Edward Leedskalnin (1887–1951), a Latvian immigrant. Jilted by the girl he wanted to marry, Leedskalnin journeyed to the United States and built the sculpture garden as a testament to his love for her. The garden, located in Homestead, Florida, was completed in 1940 and was placed on the National Register of Historical Places in 1984. Latvian-born Gunnar Birkerts (1925–) is an internationally acclaimed architect who became an American citizen in 1955. His designs include the Corning Museum of Glass in Corning, New York; the U.S. Embassy in Caracas, Venezuela; and the National Library in Riga, Latvia. Vija Celmins (1938–), who immigrated to the United States when she was ten, established an international reputation for creating photorealistic paintings, prints, and drawings, particularly of nature, and drawings and sculptures of common objects.

Education Edgars Andersons (1920–1989) was a prolific historian who taught at San Jose State University in California. A specialist in European and early American history, he received a Distinguished Academic Achievement Award in 1978. Oswald Tippo (1911–1999), a botanist by training, held several top academic posts during his career, including as chancellor of the University of Massachusetts at Amherst.

Film, Television, and Theater Actress Rutanya Alda (1942–) has appeared in numerous film, stage,

Latvian American Edward Leedskalnin (1887–1951) created this set of stone structures called Coral Castle in Homestead, Florida. Leedskalnin spent twenty-eight years building Coral Castle. It is now a privately run tourist attraction. MATT PROPERT / NATIONAL GEOGRAPHIC SOCIETY / CORBIS

and television productions, including the films *The Long Goodbye* (1973), *Pat Garrett and Billy the Kid* (1973), *The Deer Hunter* (1978), and *Prancer* (1989). Actor Buddy Ebsen (1908–2003), best known for his television roles as Jed Clampett in *The Beverly Hillbillies* and as the title character in *Barnaby Jones*, was of Latvian and Danish parentage. Chicagoan Mārīte Ozere (1944–) was crowned Miss U.S.A. in 1965.

Industry Augusts Krastiņš (1859–1942) began building gasoline-powered automobiles in 1896, several years before Henry Ford. The Cleveland, Ohio-based Krastin Automobile Company operated until 1904. Leon "Jake" Swirbul (1898–1960) was a cofounder of the Grumman Aircraft Company and helped lead the company's production of fighter planes for the U.S. Navy during World War II. In 1946 Swirbul became president of the company, which is now part of Northrop Grumman Corporation.

Literature and Journalism Anšlevs Eglītis (1906–1993), a novelist and movie critic, wrote many popular Latvian books and was a frequent contributor to the Latvian American newspaper *Laiks*. Jānis

Freivalds (1944–) has worked as a journalist, consultant, and entrepreneur. In 1978 he published a novel, *The Famine Plot*. Peter Kihss (1912–1984) spent nearly fifty years working as a journalist, including thirty years for the *New York Times*. Agate Nesaule (1938–) won critical and popular acclaim for her memoir *A Woman in Amber: Healing the Trauma of War and Exile* (1995), which tells how she and her family fled the Soviets after World War II. In the book she discusses the effects of being exposed to the atrocities of war as a seven-year-old. *A Woman in Amber* won the American Book Award in 1996. Nesaule's first novel, *In Love with Jerzy Kosinski* (2009), explores the same themes.

Music Several Latvian Americans have made significant contributions to symphonic music and opera, including concert pianist Artūrs Ozoliņš (1946–), who has recorded with the Toronto Symphony Orchestra, and composer Gundaris Pone (1932–1993), whose work received international recognition but whose radical politics did not endear him to Latvian Americans. Alternative pop singer-songwriter Ingrid Karklins (1957–) of Austin, Texas, has released two albums, *A Darker*

Passion (1992) and *Anima Mundi* (1994). Some of her songs draw inspiration from traditional Latvian instruments and songs. Leors Dimants (1972–), known as DJ Lethal, is a turntablist and producer who earned fame as a DJ, first in the Irish American hip-hop group House of Pain and later in the new metal band Limp Bizkit.

Science John D. Akerman (1897–1972), a professor of aeronautics, had a long career teaching and researching at the University of Minnesota. Akerman Hall on the Minneapolis campus is named in his honor. Lectures about the Star of Bethlehem by retired astronomy professor Kārlis Kaufmanis (1910–2003) were a popular Christmas attraction in Minnesota. Mārtiņš Straumanis (1898–1973) was a professor of metallurgy at the University of Missouri at Rolla. Esther Sans Takeuchi (1953–), daughter of Latvian political refugees, is a SUNY Distinguished Professor with a joint appointment in the Department of Chemistry and the Department of Materials Science and Engineering at Stony Brook University. She is also chief scientist of Brookhaven National Laboratory's Global and Regional Solutions Directorate. The holder of more patents than any other female scientist, Takeuchi received the National Medal of Technology and Innovation in 2009 for her invention of the battery that powers many of the world's implanted medical devices. She was also named as the 2013 recipient of the E. V. Murphree Award in Industrial and Engineering Chemistry from the American Chemical Society.

Sports Latvians in the United States and in Latvia became ardent fans of the National Hockey League's San Jose Sharks in 1991, when the team acquired two Latvians, goalie Arturs Irbe (1967–) and defenseman Sandis Ozolinsh (1972–).

Latvian American children gather flowers. AP PHOTOS

Ozolinsh played for four other NHL teams before returning to Latvia to play with Dinamo Riga in 2009. Irbe played with three other teams before returning play in Europe in 2004. Gundars Vetra (ca. 1967–) was the first Latvian to play for a National Basketball Association team. He was recruited by the Minnesota Timberwolves after playing for the Russian-led Unified Team in the 1992 Olympics.

MEDIA

PRINT

Laiks (*Time*)

A semiweekly Latvian-language newspaper published in Brooklyn, New York.

Ilavars Spilners, Editor
7307 Third Avenue
Brooklyn, New York 11209-2466
Phone: (718) 836-6382
Fax: (718) 748-1426
URL: www.laiks.us

ORGANIZATIONS AND ASSOCIATIONS

American Latvian Association (Amerikas latviešu apvienība, ALA)

Founded in 1951, the ALA is the largest Latvian association in the United States; it has about 6,000 members and represents approximately 160 organizations. In the past it served as an umbrella organization, coordinating the political, cultural, and educational activities of Latvian communities and lobbying the U.S. government for legislation and policies supporting independence for Latvia. Since independence, the ALA has given increased attention to welfare and education efforts in Latvia.

Anita Bataraga, President
400 Hurley Avenue
Rockville, Maryland 20850-3121
Phone: (301) 340-1914
Fax: (301) 340-8732
Email: alainfo@alausa.org
URL: www.alausa.org

American Latvian Youth Association (Amerikas latviešu jaunatnes apvienība, ALJA)

Founded in 1952 and incorporated in 1964, the ALJA is a national organization for Latvian youth (generally those under age thirty). It has served as a voice for its members in the exile community. During the 1970s and 1980s, it was especially active on the political front, organizing demonstrations at the Soviet embassy in Washington, D.C., and in other locations. Some former officers of the association have gone on to other leadership posts in the Latvian American community as well as in newly independent Latvia.

Karlis Lenss, President
Email: klenss@gmail.com
URL: www.alja.org

Grand Rapids Latvian Association

There are dozens of local Latvian American Associations in the United States. The Grand Rapids organization is typical. It runs a community center and a credit union and coordinates the activities and events of the center, the Latvian Lutheran and Catholic churches, and the Latvian Welfare Association.

Liga Gonzalez
504 Grand Ave NE
Grand Rapids, Michigan 49503
Phone: (616) 774-8609
URL: www.saites.org/grpage-3.htm

Latvian Evangelical Lutheran Church in America (Latvieš evaŋ'eliski luteriskā baznīca Amerikā, LELBA)

Founded in 1975, LELBA carries on the work of a Latvian American church association formed in 1957. Before 1975 local Latvian Lutheran congregations belonged to one of the U.S. churches, such as the American Lutheran Church. Since then many have dropped their ties to U.S. churches and are now members only of LELBA. As of 2012 LELBA included fifty-nine congregations in the United States; not all congregations, however, have their own churches or ministers.

Dean Lauma Zusevics, President
1853 North 75th Street
Milwaukee, Wisconsin 53213
Phone: (414) 258-8070
Email: pastorlauma@gmail.com
URL: www.lelba.org

Latvian Welfare Association (Daugavas Vanagi)

Founded in 1945 in Belgium, this is a global organization of war veterans—primarily those who fought in the two Latvian divisions organized during the German occupation of Latvia in World War II. In addition to offering support for disabled Latvian veterans, Daugavas Vanagi supports cultural and educational efforts and works to preserve the history of the Latvian military. The organization has national and local chapters in several countries and in eighteen states.

Zigurds Riders, Chairman of the Board
Email: zigurds.riders@daugavasvanagi.us
URL: www.daugavasvanagi.us

MUSEUMS AND RESEARCH CENTERS

Association for the Advancement of Baltic Studies, Inc.

This independent, nonprofit research association focuses on the Baltic area, including the people of Estonia, Latvia, and Lithuania, and on Baltic literature, history, and economics.

Irena Blekys, Administrative Executive Director
University of Washington
Box 353420
Seattle, Washington 98195-3420
Email: aabs@uw.edu
URL: depts.washington.edu/aabs

Balch Institute for Ethnic Studies

Houses Latvian material in its archives, including some records of St. John's Latvian Evangelical Lutheran Church. The institute was integrated into the Historical Society of Pennsylvania in 2004.

Kim Sajet, President
Historical Society of Pennsylvania
1300 Locust Street
Philadelphia, Pennsylvania 19107-5699
Phone: (215) 732-6200
Fax: (215) 732-2680
Email: ksajet@hsp.org
URL: http://hsp.org/about-us/the-balch-institute

Immigration History Research Center (IHRC)

Devoted to collecting archival materials concerning eastern, central, and southern European immigrants, as well as immigrants from the Middle East, the IHRC continues to expand its collection of Latvian books, newspapers, serials, and manuscripts. In 1993 the center embarked on a two-year project to organize materials pertaining to displaced persons from Latvia and Ukraine.

Haven Hawley, Program Director
Elmer L. Andersen Library
222 21st Street South
Suite 311
Minneapolis, Minnesota 55455
Phone: (612) 625-4800
Fax: (612) 626-0018
Email: ihrc@umn.edu
URL: www.ihrc.umn.edu

Latvian Museum

Housed in the Latvian Lutheran Church in Rockville, Maryland, the museum opened in 1980. It provides an overview of Latvian life in the homeland and in exile.

400 Hurley Avenue
Rockville, Maryland 20850
Phone: (301) 340-1914
Email: alainfo@alausa.org
URL: www.alausa.org/en/what-we-do/museums

SOURCES FOR ADDITIONAL STUDY

Andersons, Edgars, and M. G. Slavenas. "The Latvian and Lithuanian Press." In *The Ethnic Press in the United States: A Historical Analysis and Handbook*, edited by Sally M. Miller. Westport, CT: Greenwood Press, 1987.

Dreifelds, Juris. *Latvia in Transition*. New York: Cambridge University Press, 1996.

Kārklis, Maruta, Līga Streips, and Laimonis Streips. *The Latvians in America, 1640–1973: A Chronology and Fact Book*. Dobbs Ferry, NY: Oceana Publications, 1974.

Lieven, Anatoly. *The Baltic Revolution: Estonia, Latvia, Lithuania and the Path to Independence*. New Haven, CT: Yale University Press, 1993.

Misiunas, Romuald J., and Rein Taagepera. *The Baltic States: Years of Dependence, 1940–1980*. Berkeley: University of California Press, 1983.

Plakans, Andrejs. *The Latvians: A Short History*. Stanford, CA: Hoover Institution Press, 1995.

Šimanis, Vito Vitauts. *Latvia*. St. Charles, IL: Book Latvia, 1984.

Straumanis, Alfreds. "Latvian American Theatre." In *Ethnic Theatre in the United States*, edited by Maxine Schwartz Seller. Westport, CT: Greenwood Press, 1983.

Veidemanis, Juris. *Social Change: Major Value Systems of Latvians at Home, as Refugees, and as Immigrants.*

Greeley: Museum of Anthropology, University of Northern Colorado, 1982.

Zake, Ieva. *American Latvians: Politics of a Refugee Community.* New Brunswick, NJ: Transaction Publishers, 2010.

LEBANESE AMERICANS

J. Sydney Jones and Paula Hajar

OVERVIEW

Lebanese Americans are immigrants or descendants of people from Lebanon, a nation located at the extreme eastern end of the Mediterranean Sea. Syria forms Lebanon's northern and eastern borders, while the Mediterranean Sea composes the western border; Israel lies directly to the south. The country is famous for its Cedars of God forest, which is mentioned over ninety times in the Old and New Testaments of the Bible, and the capital, Beirut, has often been referred to as the Paris of the Middle East. Lebanon's land mass is 4,015 square miles (10,400 square kilometers), roughly the size of Jamaica and smaller than the state of Connecticut.

According to the World Bank in 2011, the population of Lebanon is estimated to be around 4.26 million. In Lebanon, Muslims account for a slight majority, with 59.7 percent of the population belonging to one of the seventeen sectarian groups of Shia, Sunni, Druze, Ismaili, Alawite, and Nusairi. Christians make up 39 percent of the population and include the subpopulations of Maronite Catholics, Greek Orthodox, Melkite Catholics, Armenian Orthodox, Armenian Catholics, Syrian Orthodox, Syrian Catholics, Roman Catholics, Chaldeans, Assyrians, Copts, and Protestants. The other 1.3 percent of the population has alternative religious beliefs, such as Baha'i. Lebanon's cost of living is high, and its inflation rate in 2012 was approximately 10.3 percent. Of the total Lebanese population, 28 percent lives below the poverty line, and the unemployment rate for youths below age twenty-four is around 22 percent.

Lebanese immigrants first came to the United States during the late 1870s. Many were peddlers who traveled to New England and upstate New York. Others opened general stores in the Midwest and West. Subsequent Lebanese immigration occurred in waves. One of the most notable occurred in response to the 1975–1991 civil war in Lebanon. Lebanese Americans worked with governmental officials to establish the Arab Anti-Discrimination Committee in 1980, and by the twenty-first century, this group was the largest Arab American organization in the United States.

According to the U.S. Census Bureau's American Community Survey, an estimated 494,639 Lebanese Americans—roughly the population of Albuquerque, New Mexico—lived in the United States in 2011. There are clusters of Lebanese in many cities throughout the Northeast, as well as in Jacksonville, Florida. Some of the most densely populated areas of Lebanese Americans are located in Chicago; Cleveland and Toledo, Ohio; and Detroit and Dearborn, Michigan. Toward the end of the twentieth century, new Lebanese American communities began springing up in Los Angeles and Houston. The states with the highest total population of Lebanese Americans are Michigan, California, Massachusetts, Texas, New York, Florida, and Ohio.

HISTORY OF THE PEOPLE

Early History As a witness to the rise and fall of the Mesopotamian, Hittite, Egyptian, Assyrian, Babylonian, Persian, and Greek empires, Lebanon has a distinct history. In the second and early first millennia BCE, the Canaanites, who became known as Phoenicians, were the first inhabitants of Lebanon. Famous as sailors and traders, the Phoenicians lived along the Lebanese coast in the port cities of Tyre, Sidon, and Byblos. They also founded colonies in North Africa, Europe, and the Mediterranean. Phoenician seafarers invented the alphabet and disseminated it to the Greeks, built the Temple of David from the Cedars of Lebanon, and became known for their commercial ingenious. A succession of peoples, including Persians, Greeks, and Romans, challenged Phoenician power. With the rise of Islam in the East, the population adopted the Arabic language but also maintained its multireligious character as the mountains of Lebanon became a haven for various religious sects.

From 1516 to 1916 Lebanon, like the rest of the Near East, was under the dominion of the Ottoman Empire. During this period the Ottomans established the province of geographic Syria, which covered the present-day states of Syria, Lebanon, and Jordan, and parts of southeastern Turkey. Under Ottoman rule, Lebanon maintained a feudal system of rule by local chieftains. Because of measures imposed by the Ottomans, early immigrants from present-day Lebanon identified with their religious sect rather than any nationality. After 1860, when the Druze massacred thousands of Christians in Lebanon and Damascus, the French—who had held economic and strategic interests in Lebanon since the Crusades—intervened.

The result was the establishment of autonomous rule for the Mount Lebanon region in 1861.

During the next fifty years, the people of Lebanon cultivated their openness toward the West and were instrumental in preserving the Arabic language and the revival of Arabic culture in the late nineteenth and early twentieth centuries. However, with the outbreak of World War I, Mount Lebanon was stripped of its autonomous status, and in 1916 the Turkish/Ottoman authorities executed Lebanese leaders in Beirut for allegedly engaging in anti-Turkish endeavors. With the conclusion of the war in 1918, British general Edmund Allenby came to the rescue of the Lebanese, and the victors of World War I dismembered the Turkish Empire. Thus, a sense of national identity did not begin to form among the Lebanese until the after 1920, when France established the present boundaries of present-day Lebanon.

Modern Era With the fall of the Ottoman Empire during World War I, England and France divided Lebanon into English and French protectorates. England assumed control of what became Palestine and Jordan, and France took over what became Syria and Lebanon. France combined Mount Lebanon with several other geographical areas and created an entity called the State of Greater Lebanon. In 1926 the Republics of Lebanon and Syria were created under the French mandate, but it was not until 1943 that each gained full independence. The last French troops did not depart until 1946.

After gaining independence from the French in 1943, Lebanon became known as the Switzerland of the Middle East. However, its delicate political and demographic equilibrium was shattered in 1975 when civil war erupted. The Cold War, the Arab–Israeli conflict, and international interference exacerbated the political inequities that had existed within Lebanon for decades, fueling the civil war between Christians and Muslims for more than a decade and a half. Although a tentative peace agreement in 1991 ended the war, many problems remained. Several thousand Syrian troops, which had entered Lebanon during the civil war as peacekeepers, remained in the country and became an occupation power. In 1982 Hezbollah (the Party of God) was born, initially supported by the Syrian and Iranian regimes to fight Israel; however, the party also had a political plan to control Lebanon and transform it into a country ruled by Shiite Sharia law. Lebanon's relations with Israel have long been contentious, and the two nations periodically fight wars and border skirmishes.

Following the conclusion of the civil war, as Lebanon was striving to reconstruct itself physically, economically, and politically, the country was occupied by Syria from 1976 to 2005. In addition, portions of its southern villages were occupied by Israel until 2000. The Syrian occupation was legitimated by the Taif agreement, which was administered by the Arab League. During this period, Syria occupied almost 90 percent of Lebanon, and most militia groups, except for organizations like Hezbollah, were not allowed to remain armed. The Lebanese Army's movements were mostly restricted to situations related to national security. A puppet parliament was elected in 1992 after 90 percent of eligible Lebanese voters boycotted an election organized by Syria.

Living conditions for native Lebanese in their home country during this time deteriorated because of Syria's acts of naturalizing Syrians as Lebanese citizens. This situation was further exacerbated through Syria's support of its 1.5 million citizens working illegally in Lebanon. These policies and high insecurity forced many native Lebanese to leave the nation to find work or a new country abroad. To combat these conditions, native Lebanese began a peaceful movement to initiate United Nations Resolutions 425 and 520 for the withdrawal of Israel and Syria in 2000 and 2005, respectively.

During the early twenty-first century, Syria persisted in its occupation of Lebanon, and native Lebanese suffered heavily. They were subject to imprisonment, kidnapping, torture, and murder. Although a brief reconciliation was negotiated in 2001, this was short-lived, and hundreds of Lebanese protestors were arrested. On August 7, Syrian troops attacked Lebanese students in an infamous incident later called the Events of August 7. This event catalyzed the support of people of Lebanese descent on a global scale. The terrorist attacks in the United States on September 11, 2001, further raised consciousness of the potential for terrorism to cause devastation such as that wreaked by Hezbollah in Lebanon.

In 2002 the Syrian government made attempts to purify its reputation by holding a by-election of the Syrian-controlled Lebanese parliament. Despite measures to rig the election, however, the anti-Syrian candidate won. In response the pro-Syrian Lebanese government threw out the results and selected its own appointee, eradicating the television and radio stations in the process. In 2003 advocacy groups of Lebanese Americans succeeded in drafting and passing the Syria Accountability and Lebanese Sovereignty Restoration Act of 2003. The U.S. Congress passed the bill, and other nations, including France, followed suit in issuing support for an independent Lebanon. In September 2004 the UN drafted Resolution 1559, which stated that a corruption-free and just election should be held in Lebanon to elect a president.

When former premier Rafik Hariri was assassinated by car bomb on February 14, 2005, the Lebanese opposition launched an independent peaceful uprising, coined the Cedar Revolution, to catalyze the liberation of Lebanon. Following these actions, the Lebanese president, a Syrian sympathizer, announced a two-step process to eliminate Syrian occupation. By April 30, 2005, after intervention by the UN, the

Syrian government had evacuated Lebanon, and a special international tribunal investigating the Hariri assassination and the assassination of Syrian opposition leaders had been formed. With international support, a Christian–Muslim front enacted the general elections in May 2005 despite fears of violent reaction from Syria.

In 2006 Hezbollah instigated a war with Israel; the latter retaliated, devastating the country. Prominent Lebanese American groups denounced Israel's response, while other groups blamed Hezbollah for its actions, dividing the country. By 2008 Hezbollah leaders came to dominate the Lebanese government, locking the country into a struggle between prodemocratic and fundamentalist political forces.

SETTLEMENT IN THE UNITED STATES

The earliest immigrants from the eastern Mediterranean were generally lumped together under the common rubric of Syrian Lebanese. Consequently, it is difficult to separate the number of Lebanese ethnic immigrants from the number of Syrian ethnic immigrants. Neither of these countries came into being as nation-states until the mid-twentieth century; thus records and statistics for both groups are generally combined in the data on early immigration patterns.

Immigrants from the region of the former Ottoman Empire account for close to two-thirds of the estimated 3.5 million people in the United States who are of Middle Eastern descent. Christian Lebanese were the first Arabic-speaking people to come to the Americas in large numbers. Their immigration to the United States began in the late 1870s, peaked in 1914 at 9,023, dropped to a few hundred a year during World War I, and rose again during the early 1920s, fluctuating between 1,600 and 5,000 per year. Later, with the passage of the Immigration Quota Act (1929–1965), the number of Lebanese immigrants dropped to a few hundred per year. When the second wave of Middle Eastern immigration to the United States began in the late 1960s, the third-generation descendants of early Lebanese immigrants had almost completely acculturated to mainstream America. In the 1970s and 1980s the Arabic-speaking population of the United States began to grow again, and Lebanese Americans assumed a higher ethnic profile. Today the majority of Arab Americans hail from Lebanon.

Many factors spurred large-scale Lebanese immigration to the United States in the late nineteenth century. For instance, many immigrants were inspired by tales of American freedom and equality told by American missionaries, doctors, and teachers. In addition, the world's fairs that took place in Philadelphia (1876), Chicago (1893), and St. Louis (1904) exposed participating Middle Easterners to Americans and American society. For the majority of Lebanese immigrants, the decision to move to the United States was based on economic ambition and family competition.

For many Lebanese families, having a son or daughter in the United States became a visible mark of status. Young men were the first to emigrate, followed by young women and later wives and entire families. Some villages lost their most talented young people to the United States. Between the late 1870s and World War I (1914–1918), Lebanon lost over one-quarter of its population to emigration. During World War I it lost about another fifth to famine. Nevertheless, immigrants abroad played a major role in the country's postwar reconstruction and subsequent independence.

The 1975–1991 civil war sparked a new wave of emigration from Lebanon. Many Lebanese went to Europe; those who came to the United States reinvigorated Lebanese American ethnic life. Most were better educated and more conscious of their ethnic identity than their predecessors. Many Lebanese Americans who are Muslims devoutly maintain their Islamic traditions and are cautious about fully assimilating into American culture. By contrast, Lebanese Christians built their own ethnic churches, intermarried with Americans, and were very active in the political and cultural life of the United States.

In general, Lebanese Americans have settled across the United States. Among the early immigrants, those who became peddlers settled in New England and cultivated communities in upstate New York. Others migrated to the Midwest and the West, often opening general stores as a livelihood. Lebanese Americans developed important communities in Utica, New York; Boston, Lawrence, Lowell, and Springfield, Massachusetts; Fall River, Rhode Island; and Danbury, Connecticut. They also settled in Jacksonville, Florida; Detroit and Dearborn, Michigan; and Cleveland and Toledo, Ohio. Detroit has one of the largest Lebanese American communities in the country, and there are new communities in Los Angeles and Houston. Michigan, California, Texas, Massachusetts, Ohio, Florida, and New York are the states with the highest concentration of people of Lebanese descent.

LANGUAGE

Arabic is the official language of Lebanon and is even spoken by the minority population of Lebanese Jews. Whereas the Armenian population speaks mostly Armenian, Assyrians, Syriacs, and Chaldeans speak a dialect of Aramaic. Kurdish communities speak Kurmanji, and Turkmens speak Turkish. French and English are also widely spoken.

However, in their desire to embrace American culture, many Lebanese Americans did little to teach their U.S.-born children to read Arabic. Immigration quota restrictions accelerated the problem. Without a continuous influx of new readership, once-flourishing Arab American newspapers and journals experienced a steep decline. Christian churches streamlined their Arabic services and changed many of them to English to accommodate non-Arabic-speaking youths. Newly arrived Lebanese immigrants to the United States,

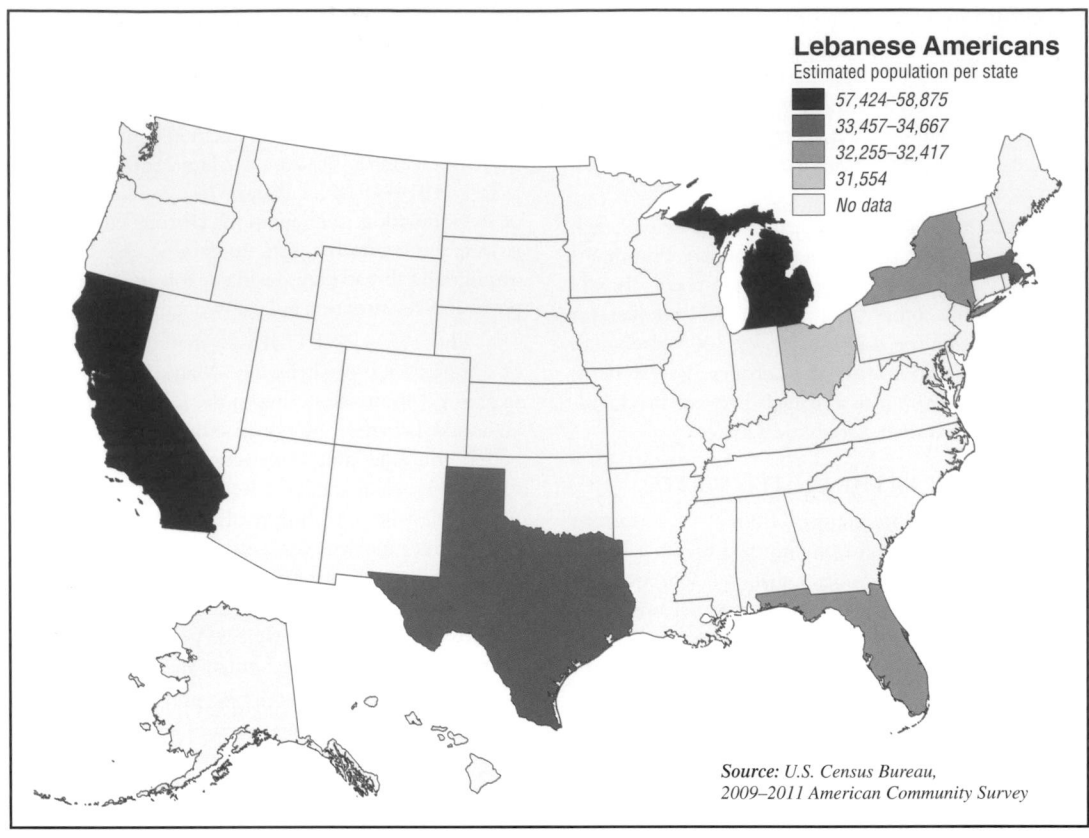

Lebanese Americans
Estimated population per state

- 57,424–58,875
- 33,457–34,667
- 32,255–32,417
- 31,554
- No data

*Source: U.S. Census Bureau,
2009–2011 American Community Survey*

however, have reinvigorated Arabic language usage within the community. The numbers of Lebanese Americans who speak a language other than English attest to their acquisition of the Arabic language as a result of efforts to increase educational opportunities to learn the Arabic language. Many Middle Eastern churches now have bilingual announcements, bulletins, and sermons, and the business signs in Middle Eastern commercial neighborhoods are often painted prominently in Arabic. In particular, Lebanese Muslim and Christian immigrants have contributed to the increase in Arabic usage and have developed Arabic language classes for children. According to the American Community Survey, 69 percent of the Lebanese American population over the age of five speaks only English, whereas 31 percent speaks a language other than English. Of this population, only 8.3 percent reports speaking English at less than a very high proficiency.

Greetings and Popular Expressions Greetings in Arabic are elaborate, and each usually has a response and counterresponse. *Ahlein* (welcome) or the longer *Ahlan wa Sahlan* (You are with your people and in a level place) is a greeting appropriate at the door or when being introduced to someone for the first time. The more casual *Marhaba* (hello) is responded to with *Marhabteen* (two hellos), to which the response is *Maraahib* (a bunch of hellos).

Similarly, the response to the morning greeting *Sabaah al-kheir* (The morning is good.) is *Sabaah an-noor* (The morning is light.). The evening greeting and response are *Masa al-kheir* and *Masa n-noor*. Leave-takings are extremely elaborate: the person leaving says *Bkhatrak* (to a woman *Khatrik* and to a group *Khatirkum*), which translates as "by your leave." The response is *Ma'a salaame* ("with safety" or "Go in peace"), to which the counterresponse is *Allay salmak* (*Allay salmik* to a woman and *Allay salimkum* to a group), meaning "May God keep you safe." The holiday greetings are *'Eid Mubarak* (Holiday blessings) and *Kull sane w'inte saalim* (Every year and you are safe.). *Sahteen* is the Arabic toast (May your good health be twofold.). Arabic is filled with references to God. For example, the most common response to *Keif haalak?* (How are you?) is *Nushkar Allah* ([We] Thank God.). Often heard after a statement of intention are the words *In sha Allah* (If God wills it.). Such phrases imply the belief that humans are impotent to control the affairs of the world.

RELIGION

For centuries religious affiliation in the Near East was tantamount to membership in a small nation. The millet system, which the Ottomans used to institutionalize governing relations between the Ottoman state and its large and varied non-Muslim population, had religious, social, and political meaning. The system served to create a sense of boundaries beyond doctrinal disputes among differing sects. Because brides often converted to the faith of their husbands, especially in Islam, all of the major religions within Lebanon considered interfaith marriage taboo.

Although Lebanese Americans include Christians and Muslims, Christians are in the majority due to the number of Lebanese Christians who immigrated in the late nineteenth and early twentieth centuries and the large number that migrated during and following the civil war of 1975. The Lebanese American population is about 90 percent Christian and 10 percent Muslim (or other). Many Lebanese Jews and a smaller number of Druze are part of the Lebanese American community. The vast majority of Lebanese Christians in the United States belong to one of three Eastern rite churches: Maronite, Eastern Orthodox, or Melkite Greek Catholic. Orthodox and Melkite liturgies are in Arabic and Greek; Maronite liturgy is in Arabic and Aramaic. In the United States all three denominations also celebrate their liturgical rituals in English.

The differences among these churches are jurisdictional rather than dogmatic. In particular, the churches differ on the question of the infallibility of the pope in matters of faith. Since its beginnings in the fourth century, the Maronite Church, which is of Syriac tradition, has been steadfast in its allegiance to Rome and the West and resistant to the Arabic identity embraced by the Eastern Orthodox and Melkite Greek Catholic churches. All three churches administer confirmation at baptism and use bread soaked in wine for the Eucharist. The marriage ceremony in each rite contains similar components: the blessing of the rings, the crowning of the bride and groom as queen and king, and the sharing of bread and wine—the couple's first meal together. In the Orthodox and Melkite churches, the bride and groom walk around the altar as a symbol of their first journey together as a couple. Orthodox priests can marry, but those who do cannot climb the clerical hierarchy. While Eastern canon law encourages Melkite and Maronite Catholic priests in the Middle East to marry, Western canon law forbids it. Unlike the Roman Catholic Church, Eastern rite churches have icons rather than statuaries.

Most Lebanese American Muslims arrived in the United States after 1965. Generally Muslims pray five times a day and attend Friday prayers. When no mosque is available, they rent rooms in commercial and business districts where they can go for midday prayers. These small prayer places are called *masjids*. Muslims are supposed to fast during the daylight hours for the month of Ramadan, and many, including young schoolchildren, keep the fast.

Lebanese Americans who have been in the country longer, or who are more acculturated, have found the influence of mainstream American culture and practices has affected their religious practices and personal identities. For example, although the Muslim religion traditionally requires a woman to obtain permission from her husband for a divorce, some women have drawn from American civil laws to find ways around this tradition. For Lebanese American Christians, the church has long served as a place that solidifies the bonds of a community. Events held at churches, in addition to worship-based ceremonies and meetings, not only have served as a venue through which Lebanese Americans can interact but also have provided immigrants solace and consolation. This trend has proven especially true when Lebanon itself was immersed in political turmoil, such as during the years of the civil war and in the period of occupation following it. Religious faiths of both Christian and Muslim sects have served as channels through which Lebanese Americans can connect with family members in Lebanon and maintain such ties and a sense of association with the home country.

CULTURE AND ASSIMILATION

The first Lebanese who came to the United States were considered exotic. Their baggy pants (*shirwal*) and fezzes made them stand out even among other immigrants. As time passed, the growth of Lebanese immigrant communities and the ubiquity of peddlers from the Near East caused Lebanese Americans to become a visible presence and face increased prejudice. From 1914 to 1915 Lebanese and Syrians fought and won legal battles in the Supreme Court to gain status as whites in order to acquire American citizenship and other related privileges such as education and property ownership. Thus the Lebanese acculturated quickly to mainstream American culture.

Working as peddlers allowed Lebanese immigrants to meet regularly with other Americans and helped them to quickly absorb the English language and American culture. Service in the U.S. armed forces during World Wars I and II also hastened the further integration of Lebanese Americans into U.S. culture. Many Lebanese American women worked in war-related industries during World War II, which hastened their assimilation into American culture. By the end of World War II, it was not uncommon for Lebanese American women to work outside the home or family business. Lebanese Americans worked hard to integrate rapidly into mainstream American society. Many Anglicized their names, joined Western churches, and focused their energies on becoming financially successful.

In the late 1990s and early twenty-first century Lebanese Americans faced many of the same problems as other Arab Americans. They have often been the victims of negative stereotyping, especially in films, theater, books, and cartoons. This type of prejudicial treatment increased after September 11, 2001. Lebanese Americans have also experienced anti-Arab sentiments in American politics. Because the United States has strong ties with Israel, Middle Eastern Americans have often felt that American politicians have little interest in understanding Arab hostility toward Israel. During the 1980s some political candidates rejected financial support from Arab Americans in order not to appear unsympathetic toward Israel. This problem was addressed by a number of U.S. presidents during the twilight of the twentieth century and the dawning of the twenty-first century; nevertheless U.S. ties to Israel remain controversial, especially from the viewpoint of some Arab Americans.

Traditions and Customs Lebanese Americans' practices and habits are impacted by the culture and customs of their home country. In addition, the contrast between these traditions and the characteristics of mainstream U.S. culture have affected the way that Lebanese Americans conduct their lives. In Lebanese culture, age is greatly respected, and respect for parents is highly valued. Family is at the core of Lebanese social identity, and loyalty to family has traditionally superseded all other allegiances. Each person is expected to protect the family's honor. In Lebanese culture, roles are often defined by gender, and this social definition anchors both men and women in their respective roles. Women are to be protected by other family members. Men are the undisputed heads of families and take the concerns of other members into consideration. In Lebanese American families, the welfare of the group is considered more important than the needs of the individual. Lebanese Americans are known for their elaborate and warm hospitality, and it is considered rude not to offer food and drink to a guest. Religious affiliation also plays a strong role in the Lebanese people's sense of identity.

American culture, with its emphasis on youth, personal achievement, individualism, and independence, has eroded some of these traditional beliefs and practices. The Middle Eastern respect for age has decreased in the United States, though it is still stronger among Lebanese Americans than in the dominant culture. Although the family is highly valued among Lebanese Americans, the belief in family honor has lessened in part because families are no longer living together in close circles. Family roles are less defined by gender in the United States. Hospitality has also changed: doors are locked, schedules are tight, and people are preoccupied with personal concerns. New immigrants who come expecting the kind of help from settled relatives that they would receive in Lebanon are often sorely disappointed; they soon discover that they are expected, like everyone else in the United States, to make it on their own. This does not mean that Lebanese Americans do not offer help to family and friends; rather they offer it in a different way than it is offered in the home country. Chain migration is a type of assistance Lebanese Americans provide to their kith and kin. In addition, as a deeply religious people, Lebanese Americans still find religion a strong source of bonding.

Cuisine In general the seasoning used in Lebanese cuisine is subtle. *Kibbee* is ground lamb meat mixed with bulgur wheat and served baked or raw. Yellow and green squash, called *koosa*, are hollowed out, stuffed with rice and ground lamb meat, and cooked in a tomato sauce. The insides of the squash are often fried in olive oil as a separate dish. The ground lamb and rice stuffing mixture (*mahshee*) is sometimes wrapped in grape leaves (*wara' 'anab*) and served with yogurt, or wrapped in cabbage leaves (*malfoof*) and served with lemon juice. *Sfeeha* are small, open square pies of ground lamb meat and pine nuts sometimes made with a thin tomato sauce.

Lebanese food is widely available in gourmet food shops and health food restaurants. Pita bread, hummus (chickpea dip), baba ghanoush (eggplant dip), and tabbouleh (a salad of parsley and bulgur or cracked wheat) have become mainstays of health food menus. Lebanese Americans also eat fresh fruits and vegetables, cheese, yogurt, yogurt cheese (*labnee*), pickles, hot peppers, olives, and pistachio nuts. One of the most popular Lebanese desserts is baklava, which is filo dough laced with sugar syrup and wrapped around finely chopped walnuts. The national alcoholic beverage of Lebanon is '*arak*, which is a liqueur flavored with aniseed.

Other popular dishes include stuffed grape leaves, meat kabobs, falafel, lentil soup, and other dishes that utilize eggplant. In addition to preparing these dishes in their homes, many Lebanese Americans frequent the wide selection of Lebanese American restaurants that exists in various cities across the United States. Some of these restaurants include locations like Labasha Lebanese American Cuisine in Southfield, Michigan, and the Sylvania Diner, which serves both Lebanese and American food, in Sylvania, Ohio. Along the same lines, many Lebanese American festivals feature cuisine popular in Lebanon. These festivals may be organized by communities or religious organizations and offer a wide array of food options.

Traditional Dress Western dress is the norm in Lebanon and among most Lebanese Americans. Religiously observant Muslim women wear the hijab, a long-sleeved coat or dress and a scarf that completely covers the hair. Young girls and married women can decide whether or not to wear the hijab. Traditional Lebanese clothing is worn only by performers at ethnic dance festivals. Men wear the *shirwal* (baggy black pants that fit at the shin); high black boots; a white, blousy shirt; a dark vest; and a fez. Women wear long dresses with embroidered bodices and side panels, and tall hats with long, white veils.

Holidays Different sects within Lebanon celebrate various religious holidays. Christians celebrate the feast days of saints, Easter, and Christmas. Easter is celebrated on the Sunday after the first full moon following the vernal equinox. Orthodox Easter must come after Passover; thus Western Easter often falls on a different Sunday than Orthodox Easter. Muslims celebrate three major holidays: Ramadan (the thirty-day period of daytime fasting); 'Eid al Fitr, a five-day holiday that marks the end of Ramadan; and 'Eid al-Adha, the Feast of the Sacrifice, which commemorates Abraham's agreement with God that he would sacrifice his son Ishmael. In the past, Lebanon's National Independence Day, which is celebrated on November 22, has received little attention from Lebanese Americans. However, during the first decade of the twenty-first century, Lebanese Americans increasingly celebrated it. Students at the University of Michigan at Ann Arbor and Oakland University hold popular Independence Day celebrations, as do various cultural organizations, such as the Lebanese American Heritage Club of Dearborn.

Health Care Issues and Practices Except for higher-than-average incidences of anemia and lactose intolerance, Lebanese do not exhibit a higher incidence of any disease. As a rule they support the conventional medical establishment. The psychological health of Lebanese Americans is sometimes affected by the dual cultural identities they experience as a result of their combined ethnic backgrounds. For example, recent research has investigated the ways that Lebanese Americans—especially female adolescents—report experiencing this sense of a dual cultural identity.

FAMILY AND COMMUNITY LIFE

In traditional Lebanese culture, families operate as a unit with members of their extended relations. They implicitly rely on each other in social, financial, and business affairs. The father is the decision maker, and the mother serves as his close advisor. Her domain is the daily life of the children and all the happenings within the domestic sphere. By contrast, the man's domain is strictly outside the home. The firstborn son plays a special role in the family, in large part because tradition states he must bring his bride to live with his parents. The couple also raises their family in the household of the paternal grandparents, and they care for the husband's parents as they grow older.

These traditions have gradually deteriorated, especially as Lebanese American families become more assimilated to American culture and adopt the American pattern of nuclear families. In particular, the dividing line between gender roles has blurred. Fathers spend more time with their small children, and mothers frequently represent the families in public—for example at school meetings. Mothers also work outside the home in increasing numbers. Independent households are now the norm, and it is no longer customary for a married woman to move into the households of her husband's family. Consequently, sisters share responsibility with their brothers for their aging parents. According to the American Community Survey, 60.9 percent of women aged sixteen or older participate in the labor force. Of the total Lebanese American population, 67.8 percent participates in the labor force, meaning that a considerable number of women are employed outside the home.

LEBANESE PROVERBS

- The last resort is the hot iron.
- The son of a son is dear, the son of a daughter a stranger.
- When your son is young, discipline him; when he grows older, be a brother to him.
- A man with one plan goes out to execute it; a man with two plans becomes perplexed.
- Exert effort and you shall be rewarded.
- Tire your body but not your mind.
- An intelligent deaf–mute is better than an ignorant person who can speak.
- If you conduct yourself properly, fear no one.

Gender Roles The traditional roles of women are more demarcated in Lebanon than they are among Lebanese Americans. In Lebanon women have always been the heart of the family. Although men traditionally have had the final say in family decisions, the opinions of women are also valued. Now that women are pursuing higher education and are becoming doctors, engineers, architects, and other professionals, they are becoming more involved in the family decision-making process. Many women are heads of households while their husbands, fathers, or brothers are working abroad. Husbands depend on their wives to maintain the household and raise the children.

Many Lebanese American women are employed outside the home and frequently play key roles in running family businesses. They often take over the family business if their husband dies or becomes incapacitated. Moreover, as Lebanese American men have become more active in public life, women have begun to follow suit. Donna Shalala, a Lebanese American woman, was the chancellor of the University of Wisconsin and president of Hunter College in New York before becoming President Bill Clinton's secretary of health, education, and welfare. According to the American Community Survey, 50.5 percent of Lebanese American women aged sixteen or older work in management, business, science, or the arts; 15.5 percent work in service occupations; 31.3 percent are employed in sales or office positions; 2.4 percent are part of the production and transportation industry; and 0.3 percent serve as part of the natural resources, construction, and maintenance workforce.

Education By the time Lebanese immigrants began arriving in the United States, they had already attended private school. British, French, Russian, and

American schools had been established in Lebanon since the eighteenth century. These local and foreign schools had also stimulated the establishment of local government schools, and many of these schools encouraged the education of girls. In fact the Synod of Mount Lebanon of 1736 mandated the education of Maronite girls, a pioneering effort. When Lebanese immigrants arrived in the United States, they adapted to the American school system and culture. Their attitudes paralleled the evolution of the attitudes of other Americans toward education. By the third generation of immigrants, the education of girls was considered equal in importance to that of boys. The generation of Lebanese Americans born after World War II attended college at the same rate as the rest of the nation's youth, studying business, medicine, law, pharmacy, computer science, and engineering. Because the vast majority of third-generation Lebanese Americans are middle class, they enjoy a higher educational level than Americans on average. People of Lebanese descent typically place a high value on education, and first-generation Lebanese Americans have enjoyed upward mobility and success in politics, medicine, business, entertainment, and other fields.

The Middle Eastern respect for age has decreased in the United States, though it is still stronger among Lebanese Americans than in the dominant culture. Although the family is highly valued among Lebanese Americans, the belief in family honor has lessened in part because families are no longer living together in close circles.

Many Catholic Lebanese children receive their education at Catholic schools. Muslim Lebanese immigrants to the United States even occasionally send their children to Catholic schools, where there is discipline and emphasis on respect for authority. Many Muslim immigrants have set up Islamic schools, some as supplements to their children's education and a few as full-day parochial schools that teach Arabic language, history, and culture in addition to basic subjects. The American Community Survey showed that only 7.3 percent of Lebanese Americans aged twenty-five or older did not graduate from high school. In fact 28 percent have completed some college or have earned an associate's degree, and 27.4 percent have graduated with a bachelor's degree. One-fifth of Lebanese Americans hold a graduate or professional degree. Lebanese American boys and girls matriculate at about the same rates: 93.4 percent of men aged twenty-five or older graduated from high school, as did 92.1 percent of women. Similarly 49.5 percent of men have earned a bachelor's degree or higher, and 44.4 percent of women have the same educational attainment.

Courtship and Weddings Because marriage was traditionally an opportunity for a family to strengthen its prestige and economic situation, marriages in Lebanon were often arranged. Some conservative Lebanese Americans still practice this custom. To arrange a marriage, parents and other relatives seek out mates for their children. They set up a chaperoned meeting, which allows the prospective couple to get acquainted. Courtship is conducted under the watchful eye of family members and always carries with it a sense of responsibility and purpose. In the twenty-first century this practice is more prominent among lower-income Lebanese American families. However, even if young adults in this situation acquiesce to such an arrangement, many young women insist they delay marriage until after they have finished their education and can be viably employed. Casual dating is frowned upon by more conservative Lebanese Americans because it can jeopardize the reputations of the couple and families involved. Among acculturated Lebanese Americans, however, dating takes place in accordance with more mainstream U.S. cultural practices and norms.

Lebanese Americans have married, and continue to marry, Americans of various ethnic groups. The majority of early Lebanese American immigrants married within their ethnic and religious groups or with Irish and Italian immigrants. Many early immigrant men returned to Lebanon to find a bride, particularly in the years when single men outnumbered single women in the immigrant community. Most of the first American-born generation of Lebanese Americans married within the community.

Divorce among Lebanese Americans is less common in arranged marriages than in other marriages. The basis of the arranged marriage is a contract of shared responsibility and self-sacrifice. There is no expectation that the needs of the individual will be satisfied in the marriage. The purpose of such marriages is to build a family. In fact, many Lebanese frown upon divorce on the grounds of personal unhappiness. Since divorce has traditionally been viewed as a source of family shame, families often become involved in solving marital problems.

According to the American Community Survey, 50.5 percent of Lebanese Americans are married; only 9 percent are divorced and 1.4 percent are separated. Because many delay marriage until they are older, 34.6 percent of the population aged fifteen or older has never been married. This percentage is higher among men (36.8 percent) than women (32.4 percent). By comparison, 52.7 percent of Lebanese American men fifteen or older are married, while 48.3 percent of Lebanese American women are married. The divorce rate is somewhat higher among women, at 10.3 percent (1.5 percent are separated); by comparison only 7.6 percent of men are divorced (1.2 percent are separated).

EMPLOYMENT AND ECONOMIC CONDITIONS

During the early waves of immigration to the United States, Lebanese Americans engaged in a variety of occupations. Upon their arrival, many were engaged in peddling because the occupation did not require a large amount of capital or a high level of education. Peddlers carved out routes from New England to the west, developing a regular clientele and eventually opening their own general stores, frequently in the Midwest. Some immigrants who stayed in the city developed their small dry goods businesses and transformed them into import/export empires. By 1910 a handful of Lebanese American millionaires had emerged. Other early immigrants were factory workers, who often settled in Detroit or Dearborn, where they worked in the auto industry.

The occupational profile of Lebanese Americans is very broad. Lebanese Americans tend to be self-employed, and they enter managerial and professional positions at a higher rate than Americans as a whole. Lebanese Americans are well represented in medicine, law, banking, engineering, and computer science. According to the American Community Survey, Lebanese Americans work primarily in management, business, science, and the arts (49.1 percent), although many are employed in sales or office positions (27.2 percent). The remaining Lebanese Americans workers are in the service industry (12.7 percent), production and transportation (6.2 percent), or natural resources and construction (4.8 percent). The economic crisis of the early twenty-first century have not strongly affected Lebanese Americans; however, those who work in the auto industry in Michigan have not been immune. Because Lebanese banks are subjected to stringent economic regulations and were not allowed to participate in much subprime lending, they did not delve too deeply into credit or borrowing from foreign sources. As a result, the stability of Lebanon in uncertain economic times has had a positive impact on the sensibilities of Lebanon Americans.

POLITICS AND GOVERNMENT

Lebanese American political involvement has revolved around American policies in the Middle East, particularly those relating to Israel. Through the Eastern Federation of Syrian Lebanese Organizations, which was established in 1932, Lebanese Americans quietly protested the 1948 partitioning of Palestine. Following the 1967 war between Israel and its Arab neighbors, Lebanese Americans began to work with other Arabs to form organizations that promoted their common interests.

Members of the Association of Arab American University Graduates, which was established in 1967, educated the American public about the Arab-Israeli conflict. Five years later the National Association of Arab Americans was created to lobby Congress and the White House on Middle Eastern issues. In

PRESIDENT KENNEDY'S LEBANESE AMERICAN INSPIRATION

The Arabic language is known for its poetic quality, and poets are highly valued in the Middle East. In the early twentieth century the Lebanese American community enjoyed a golden age of letters. Although living in the United States, New York experimental poets of Lebanese descent, such as Khalil Gibran, Ameen Rihani, and Elia Abu Madi, cast their influence on literary circles of the Middle East.

Khalil Gibran (1883–1931) was the author of *The Prophet* (1923), one of the best-selling books of all time. But Gibran's exhortation, "Are you a politician asking what your country can do for you or a zealous one asking what you can do for your country?" from his "Letter to Syrian Youth" proved just as influential. It inspired President John F. Kennedy's most famous line, delivered in his inaugural address: "Ask not what your country can do for you. Ask what you can do for your country."

1980 former senator James Abourezk established the American Arab Anti-Discrimination Committee to combat defamation of Arab Americans in the media. As conditions in the Middle East continued to worsen during the 1980s, Lebanese Americans, along with other Arab Americans, became the targets of government surveillance and civil rights infringements. When the United States bombed Libya in 1986, for example, Immigration and Naturalization Services had a list of thousands of Arab (including Lebanese) and Iranian students, permanent residents, and even U.S. citizens for possible detention in internment camps in the United States.

Between 1995 and 1997, it was illegal for Americans to visit Lebanon. The travel ban expired in 1997 with assurances from the Lebanese government of cooperation on antiterrorism measures and security. Among the Arab American organizations that lobbied for lifting the travel ban was the American Task Force for Lebanon. This group of prominent Lebanese Americans meets regularly with congressmen and administration officials to advise them on American support for the reconstruction of Lebanon and the normalization of diplomatic relations between Lebanon and the United States.

Lebanese Americans have traditionally supported the Republican Party due in part to its support for business interests. Lebanese Americans have also been influenced by the Arab American Institute (AAI), which was founded in 1985 to foster Arab American participation in American politics, support candidates who champion Arab American causes, and encourage Arab Americans to run for public office. During the 1988 presidential election, the AAI gathered more than three hundred Arab Americans to serve as delegates

Lebanese American designer Reem Acra poses backstage at the Reem Acra 2014 Bridal Spring/Summer Collection show in New York City. JP YIM / GETTY IMAGES

international audiences. Research has revealed that individuals who are associated with these associations tend to be highly educated members of the upper classes. Political organizations typically fall along sectarian lines and can be linked with a political party in the home country of Lebanon. However, these organizations tend to represent the Lebanese American population as a whole in terms of fiscal policies and economic initiatives, and they serve important advocacy functions for Lebanese Americans' involvement in politics. Moreover, Lebanese political parties, along with hundreds of Lebanese American associations, organizations, and clubs, have branches and supporters among Lebanese Americans and play an important role in homeland politics and American public diplomacy.

NOTABLE INDIVIDUALS

Academia Joseph Aoun (1953–) was the seventh president of Northeastern University in Boston.

Business Najeeb Halaby (1915–2003) was the head of the Federal Aviation Agency and Pan American Airways. Paul Orfalea (1947–) founded Kinko's, an international chain of copying and business service stores.

Fashion Norma Kamali (1945–) and Joseph Abboud (1950–) are prominent New York fashion designers. Mansour Farah (1895–1937) established Farah Brothers, a large competitive pants manufacturer.

Government Career diplomat Philip Habib (1920–1992) helped negotiate an end to the Vietnam War and the Israeli war in Lebanon in 1982. Senator James Abourezk (1931–) from South Dakota was the first Lebanese American to serve in the U.S. Senate (1974–1980). He also founded the American Arab Anti-Discrimination Committee. Nick Rahal (1949–) served as a U.S. congressman from West Virginia for more than thirty years. Donna Shalala (1941–) was the president of New York City's Hunter College and served as the secretary of health, education, and welfare in the Clinton administration. George Mitchell (1933–) was a senator from Maine who served as Senate majority leader from 1989 to 1995. Ralph Nader (1934–) was one of America's most prominent consumer advocates. He was the author of *Unsafe at Any Speed* (1965) and founder and head of Public Citizen, an organization that spawned a number of other citizen action groups such as Congress Watch and the Tax Reform Research Group.

Journalism Helen Thomas (1920–2013) was the United Press International White House correspondent for half a century and was known for opening and closing every White House press conference.

Literature William Blatty (1928–) authored of the book and screenplay *The Exorcist* (1971). Vance Bourjaily (1922–2010) was the author of

to the National Democratic Convention, where they successfully introduced platforms that supported Palestinian statehood and the restoration of Lebanon as a sovereign state. The convention marked the first time that an Arab American served as cochairperson of the Democratic National Committee. After the turn of the twenty-first century, other Lebanese Americans occupied important political positions, including James Abdnor and James Abourezk, two U.S. Senators from South Dakota in the 1970s and 1980s, respectively. Other positions that Lebanese Americans have filled include mayors of major cities, such as St. Paul, Minnesota; U.S. ambassadors; and governors.

In the twenty-first century, groups like the Lebanese American Coalition continue to issue statements of support and advocacy concerning the Lebanese–Israeli conflict. Of particular concern are the actions of Hezbollah, which professes to represent the "vast majority of Americans of Lebanese descent" and which exists as a coalition to represent the four largest associations of Lebanese Americans. These four organizations are the American Lebanese Alliance, located in St. Louis, Missouri; the American Lebanese Coordination Council, based in Miami, Florida; the Assembly for Lebanon, based in Redford, Michigan; and the Lebanese Information Center, based in Alexandria, Virginia. The spokespersons for these organizations interact with a wide variety of sectors related to Lebanese American concerns, and they frequently provide council and perspectives to

Confessions of a Spent Youth (1960) and *The Man Who Knew Kennedy* (1967). Poet and artist Khalil Gibran (1883–1931) was the author of *The Prophet* (1923), one of the best-selling books of all time. Steven Naifeh (1952–) won the 1991 Pulitzer Prize for his biography *Jackson Pollock: An American Saga.*

Music Paul Anka (1941–) wrote and recorded popular hit songs beginning in the 1950s, including "Diana," "She's a Lady," and "My Way." Rosalind Elias (1929–) was a mezzo-soprano with the New York City Metropolitan Opera. Guitarist and musician Frank Zappa (1940–1993) is a legend in the rock world. Casey Kasem (1932–) is America's most famous disc jockey, originator of the radio show *American Top 40*, and host of *American Top 10*. He also provided the principal voice-over for the NBC network.

Science and Medicine Heart surgeon Michael DeBakey (1908–2008) invented the heart pump and pioneered the bypass operation in the United States. Harvard University professor Elias J. Corey (1928–) won the Nobel Prize in Chemistry in 1990. Danny Thomas (1912–1991) founded St. Jude Children's Research Hospital in Memphis, Tennessee, which is the leader in the field of research and treatment of childhood leukemia. (Thomas was also an actor-singer-comedian who starred in the popular 1950s television situation comedy *Make Room for Daddy*.)

Sports Racecar driver Bobby Rahal (1953–) won the Indianapolis 500 in 1986. Joe Robbie (1916–1990) was owner of the Miami Dolphins.

Stage and Screen Jamie Farr (1934–) played Corporal Klinger for eleven years on the popular television series *M*A*S*H*. Marlo Thomas (1937–), daughter of actor Danny Thomas, is an Emmy Award-winning actress who starred in the 1960s television situation comedy *That Girl*. Danny's son Tony Thomas (1948–), a television and film producer, has won many Emmys for his work on the *Golden Girls* and other television series. Actor Tony Shalhoub (1953–) starred in the television shows *Wings* and *Monk*. Kathy Najimy (1957–) was a costar of the film *Sister Act* with Whoopi Goldberg. Callie Khouri (1957–) was the first woman to receive an Oscar for Best Original Screenplay (for *Thelma and Louise*).

MEDIA

TAC (The Arabic Channel)

Serving the New York City metropolitan area, this station offers satellite feeds from twenty-two stations in the Middle East. Its programming includes children's and adult programs focused on entertainment, news, music, film, drama, sports, and other genres.

648 Live Oak Drive
McLean, Virginia 22101
Phone: (703) 333-2008
Fax: (888) 747-0957

Email: tac-tv@allied-media.com
URL: www.allied-media.com/ARABTV/
the_arabic_channel_NY.html

ORGANIZATIONS AND ASSOCIATIONS

American Arab Anti-Discrimination Committee

The largest grassroots Arab American organization, the ADC combats stereotyping and defamation in the media and in other venues of public life, including politics.

Warren David, President
1990M Street
Suite 610
Washington, D.C. 200036
Phone: (202) 244-2990
Fax: (202) 333-3980
Email: adc@adc.org
URL: www.adc.org

American Lebanese Alliance

Headquartered in St. Louis, this group is affiliated with the American Lebanese Coalition, a partnership to advocate for the interests of Lebanese Americans.

Elie Semaan, Executive Director
8025 Bonhomme Avenue
Suite 1403
Clayton, Missouri 63104
Phone: (314) 727-7494
Fax: (314) 721-8588
Email: ala@alcoalition.org

American Lebanese Coordination Council

The American Lebanese Coordination Council is a think tank that delivers research and information about issues associated with Lebanon and its people to American scholars and officials to spread understanding and acceptance of Lebanese culture.

Joseph Hage, President
19300 West Dixie Highway
#12-20
Miami, Florida 33180
Phone: (305) 542-6322
Fax: (305) 402-0364
Email: josephhage@all-research.com
URL: www.alcc-research.com

American Task Force for Lebanon

The ATFL lobbies Congress and various administrations on issues related to Lebanon and its reconstruction.

Peter J. Tanous, President
1100 Connecticut Avenue NW
Suite 1250
Washington, D.C. 20036
Phone: (202) 223-9333
Fax: (202) 223-1399
Email: atfl@atfl.org
URL: www.atfl.org

Arab American Institute

The AAI fosters participation of Arab Americans in the political process at all levels.

James Zogby, Executive Director
1600 K Street NW
Suite 601
Washington, D.C. 20006
Phone: (202) 429-9210
Fax: (202) 429-9214
Email: webmaster@aaiusa.org
URL: www.aaiusa.org

Lebanese Information Center

This nonprofit research center is committed to raising awareness of and support for Lebanon and its people.

Joseph Gebeily, President
4900 Leesburg Pike
Suite 203
Alexandria, Virginia 22302
Phone: (703) 578-4214
Fax: (703) 578-4615
Email: ic@licus.org
URL: www.licus.org

MUSEUMS AND RESEARCH CENTERS

Faris and Yamna Naff Family Arab American Collection Archives Center

This collection at the Smithsonian Institution National Museum of American History contains artifacts, books, personal documents, photographs, oral histories, and doctoral dissertations pertaining to the Arab American immigrant experience, beginning with the earliest wave of immigrants.

14th Street & Constitution Avenue NW
Washington, D.C. 20560
Phone: (202) 633-3270
Fax: (202) 312-1990
Email: archivescenter@si.edu

Khayrallah Program for Lebanese-American Studies

This program at North Carolina State University was established in 2010 to explore the traditions, customs, culture, and history of the Lebanese American community in North Carolina and more generally in the South.

Akram Khater, Director
Department of History
Box 8108
North Carolina State University

Raleigh, North Carolina 27695
Email: akram_khater@ncsu.edu
URL: www.nclebanese.org

University of Minnesota Immigration History Research Center Near Eastern American Collection

This collection contains the archives of the Muslim scholar Philip Hitti, a collection of research focusing on materials related to Syrian, Lebanese, and Turkish Americans.

311 Elmer L. Andersen Library
222 21st Avenue S
Minneapolis, Minnesota 55455
Phone: (612) 625-4800
Fax: (612) 626-0018
Email: ihrc@umn.edu
URL: www.ihrc.umn.edu

SOURCES FOR ADDITIONAL STUDY

Abdelhady, Dalia. *The Lebanese Diaspora: The Arab Immigrant Experience in Montreal, New York, and Paris.* New York: New York University Press, 2011.

Abu-Laban, Baha, and Michael Suleiman, eds. *Arab Americans: Continuity and Change.* Normal, IL: Association of Arab American University Graduates, 1989.

Kayal, Philip, and Joseph Kayal. *The Syrian Lebanese in America: A Study in Religion and Assimilation.* Boston: Twayne, 1975.

Khater, Akram. *Inventing Home: Emigration, Gender, and the Middle Class in Lebanon, 1870–1920.* Berkeley: University of California Press, 2001.

Labaki, George. *The Maronites of the USA.* Notre Dame, IN: Notre Dame University Press, 1993.

Shakir, Evelyn. *Remember Me to Lebanon: Stories of Lebanese Women in America.* Syracuse, NY: Syracuse University Press, 2007.

Shehadi, Nadim, and Albert Hourani, eds. *The Lebanese in the World: A Century of Immigration.* London: Centre for Lebanese Studies, 1992.

Sherman, William C. *Prairie Peddlers: The Syrian-Lebanese in North Dakota.* Bismarck, ND: University of Mary Press, 2002.

Wakin, Edward. *The Syrians and the Lebanese in America.* Chicago: Claretian, 1974.

Walbridge, Linda S. *Without Forgetting the Imam: Lebanese Shi'ism in an American Community.* Detroit: Wayne State University Press, 1997.

LIBERIAN AMERICANS

Ken R. Wells

OVERVIEW

Liberian Americans are immigrants or descendants of people from Liberia, a country located on the western coast of Africa. Liberia lies north of the Equator and is bordered by Sierra Leone to the northwest, Guinea to the north, Ivory Coast (Cote D'Ivoire) to the east, and the Atlantic Ocean to the west and south. Liberian summers, which run from May to October, consist of frequent, heavy showers, whereas the slightly drier winters are characterized by dust-laden winds (called *harmattan*) blowing in from the Sahara Desert during December. The nation is approximately 44,548 square miles (111,370 square kilometers), an area slightly larger than the state of Tennessee.

According to the *CIA World Factbook*, Liberia's population was 3,989,703 as of 2013. The *Factbook* also reports that, according to a 2008 census, 85.6 percent of Liberians were Christian, 12.2 percent were Muslim, and approximately 0.6 percent followed traditional African religions. Of the remaining population, 1.4 percent claimed to follow no religion and about 0.2 percent could not be accounted for. Approximately 95 percent of the population are made up of ethnic tribes, with the largest tribes being Kpelle (20 percent), Bassa (13 percent), Grebo (10 percent), Gio (8 percent), Mano (7.9 percent), Kru (6 percent), and Lorma (5.1 percent). Descendants of immigrants from former slaves in the United States, called Americo-Liberians, make up 2.5 percent of the population. Despite having an unemployment rate of just 3.7 percent, according to a Liberian Institute of Statistics report from 2010, Liberia is among the poorest countries in the world, with an estimated 80 percent of its population living under the poverty line.

The first Liberians to come to the United States arrived as part of the slave trade between 1600 and 1800 and were settled in South Carolina and Georgia. According to the Department of Homeland Security's *Yearbook of Immigration Statistics: 2011*, Liberians first began immigrating voluntarily to the United States in very sparse numbers in the early nineteenth century. Beginning in the 1980s the number of Liberians immigrating to the United States increased exponentially, as thousands fled the civil war. The Department of Homeland Security reports that 6,420 Liberians obtained Legal Permanent Resident Status between 1980 and 1989. This number more than doubled in the 1990s and climbed to 23,316 between 2000 and 2010.

According to the 2010 U.S. Census Bureau's American Community Survey estimates for 2006–2010, the official number of Liberian Americans residing in the United States was 52,299. However, Liberian American organizations estimate the actual number of persons of Liberian descent in the United States to be between 245,000 and 498,000. Liberian Americans have tended to settle on the East Coast of the United States, with many populations residing in New York; New Jersey; Maryland; Washington, D.C.; Pennsylvania; and Rhode Island; in addition, the state with the largest population of Liberian Americans is Minnesota. Many Liberian Americans have acquired positions in the health care, hospitality, and service fields; some have opened their own businesses. Others have become security guards, hair braiders, or janitors.

HISTORY OF THE PEOPLE

Early History Anthropologists believe that people from northern and western areas of Africa began settling in what is now Liberia in around 3000 BCE. Most came because the fertile soil of the coastal areas was conducive to agriculture and the tropical rain forests of the interior held an abundance of game. Over a few centuries, these people dispersed to other areas of Africa. It is believed that present-day Liberians are descendants from several African tribes that migrated into the area between the eleventh and seventeenth centuries from the belt of Sudan, which stretches from the North African Atlantic coast to the Red Sea. Scientists speculate that these people came to Liberia for two reasons. First, they were seeking new land to farm since the Sahara Desert was slowly expanding into their existing homelands. Second, the invasion of Ghana in 1076 by a Muslim sect called the Almoravids forced thousands to flee south and west. By the eleventh century, more than a dozen ethnic groups had settled in Liberia. Over time, these groups formed tribal territories, each with its own culture and oral language.

The first known outsiders to visit Liberia were a group of Portuguese explorers, led by Pedro de Sintra, in 1461. De Sintra named the region the Malagueta

Coast, after a spicy green pepper grown in the area. From this first contact, trade routes developed between Europe and coastal Liberia.

The name *Liberia* is Latin for "place of freedom." It was given to the country, formerly known as Cape Mesurado or Cape Montserrado, by the American Colonization Society, which acquired the land from local tribal chiefs in 1821. Liberia was conceived by American political and religious leaders of the time as a place to relocate African Americans who had been freed from slavery. The first African American settlers, known as Americo-Liberians, landed in 1822. By 1864 approximately 15,000 African Americans had settled there. The colony declared itself an independent nation in 1847. The flow of immigrants dwindled to nearly zero following the end of the American Civil War and the emancipation of slaves in the United States. Despite making up only about one percent of the population, Americo-Liberians became the intellectual and ruling class, modeling the government after that of the United States. Rising economic problems, including a large foreign department, led to the overthrow of the government in 1871. Instability, fueled by a sour economy, continued into the early twentieth century. The first major economic development came in 1926, when the Firestone Rubber Company leased large areas of Liberia for rubber production.

Modern Era In 1930 the government of president Charles D. B. King resigned after an investigation by the League of Nations (now the United Nations) revealed that the government was involved in the slave trading of Liberia's native people. With the election of William V. S. Tubman in 1944, Liberia began a period of sustained economic growth and democracy. Under Tubman, Liberia's native tribes were given a greater voice in the political process. They were able to vote in presidential and legislative elections, a privilege previously reserved only for Americo-Liberians. Liberia remained a close ally of the United States, siding with the Allies during World War II. After a visit to Liberia by U.S. president Franklin D. Roosevelt in 1943, the United States agreed to develop a modern port in Monrovia. Liberia was a founding member of the United Nations (UN), and Liberians helped write the UN Charter. Under Tubman's benevolent rule, Liberia prospered. A road system was developed, a major port was built in Monrovia, and investment by foreign corporations was encouraged. A strong economy and expanded rights for all ethnic groups proved popular, and Tubman was reelected president six times.

After Tubman died from prostate cancer in 1971, the vice president, W. R. Tolbert, became president. He was formally elected to that position in 1972. Soon afterward, an organized opposition to Tolbert began to rise, including support from some Liberian college students in the United States. It reached its peak in 1979, when increases in the price of rice, the Liberian staple, led to widespread civil unrest and riots. Tolbert was

assassinated in a bloody 1980 military coup led by Master Sergeant Samuel K. Doe. Democracy collapsed and a prolonged period of dictatorship, corruption, and human rights abuses followed. Civil war broke out in 1989 and was followed in 1990 by Doe's assassination by a rebel group led by Prince Yormie Johnson. Another rebel force opposed to Doe, led by Charles Taylor, took over the government, and Taylor proclaimed himself president. After Taylor threatened to take foreign residents hostage in late 1990, the United States sent a naval unit with 2,500 Marines to Liberia to evacuate U.S. and other foreign citizens. The Economic Community of West African States (ECOWAS) brokered a peace between the warring factions, but the peace agreement soon fell apart.

The civil war raged on between Taylor's forces (the National Patriotic Front of Liberia) and rebel factions. According to the United Nations High Commission on Refugees, nearly one-third of the population, 755,000 Liberians, fled into neighboring countries and several hundred thousand were killed. The scope of the problem could be seen in the capital city, Monrovia, which went from nearly one million residents in 1990 to about 350,000 by 1996. In 1990 a peacekeeping force of 10,000 troops from the sixteen ECOWAS nations led by Nigeria entered Liberia and installed an interim government headed by Amos Sawyer. Despite several peace agreements, the civil war continued until 1997, when citizens elected a new government, again headed by Charles Taylor. Opposition parties charged that Taylor had rigged the election and that many opposition voters did not turn out at the polls because they feared violence.

Despite sporadic fighting throughout 1998, the country began the slow and difficult task of rebuilding its economic, social, and political structures. Thousands of refugees who had fled into neighboring countries began returning to Liberia. However, the situation remained unstable and uncertain, and hundreds of thousands of refugees remained outside Liberia. Opposition parties and the U.S. State Department accused the Taylor regime of various human rights violations, including murder, rape, torture, and arbitrary arrest and detention. Freedom of speech and of the press continued to be restricted by the government. It was also suspected that Taylor funded civil wars in neighboring Sierra Leone and Guinea.

Violence escalated again in Liberia in 2000, when a rebel party called Liberians United for Reconciliation and Democracy (LURD) invaded northern Liberia with the backing of Sierra Leone and Guinea and quickly became a threat to the Taylor regime. By 2003 fighting had also broken out in southern Liberia as another group, the Movement for Democracy in Liberia, rose up against Taylor. Meanwhile, the women of Liberia had begun in 2002 what would be a successful nationwide campaign for peace. Initiated by Leymah Gbowee, the group held sit-ins and other nonviolent protests and eventually forced Taylor to attend peace talks in Ghana in 2003. International pressure in the form of UN-sanctioned embargos on timber and diamonds began to mount against Liberia, and the rebel forces in the north and south made serious advances against Taylor, who finally resigned shortly after UN peacekeeping forces arrived in August 2003. Fighting continued under the rule of newly appointed chairman of the transitional government, Charles Gyude Bryant. In 2005 Ellen Johnson Sirleaf was elected president from a field of twenty-three candidates; she was re-elected in 2011.

SETTLEMENT IN THE UNITED STATES

Liberia is unique among nations because it was settled by former slaves from the United States. Nearly all immigration between the two countries was from the United States to Liberia. Voluntary Liberian immigration to the United States began in the early nineteenth century, but prior to 1980, a very small number of Liberians came to the United States. For example, the *Yearbook of Immigration Statistics* reports that, between 1820 and 1860, fewer than ten Liberians per decade obtained Legal Permanent Resident Status in the United States. The numbers fluctuated somewhat but remained small until the turn of the twentieth century, when immigration halted before resuming again in small numbers from 1930 to 1950. Immigration growing steadily up until the 1970s, when the number jumped to 2,391; it then more than doubled in the 1980s.

The civil war, which started in 1989 and continued through 1997, sent a wave of immigrants from Liberia to the United States. The Department of Homeland Security reported that 13,587 Liberians obtained Legal Permanent Immigration Status from 1990 through 1999, while the Immigration and Naturalization Service (INS) reported that 13,458 Liberians fled to the United States between 1990 and 1997. This does not include the tens of thousands who sought temporary refuge in the United States. In 1991 alone, the INS granted Temporary Protective Status (TPS) to approximately 9,000 Liberians.

Between 1998 and 2003, over 12,000 Liberians with permanent non-refugee status arrived legally in the United States, and by 2002, Liberian immigrants were the largest groups to arrive in the United States. In 2004 the United Nations High Commissioner for Refugees (UNHCR) began assisting some Liberians with settlement in the United States as well as in Europe and Canada. The United States maintained a practice of granting Temporary Protected Status (TPS) to Liberian immigrants due to the chronic violence in Liberia.

By 2006 conditions in Liberia had begun to stabilize, and Liberian immigrants' TPS status was set to expire in 2007. The impending change created widespread strife among Liberian Americans. Some of them even lost their jobs in the face of potentially expiring visas. The anxiety became so intense that the Liberian government itself requested an extension of

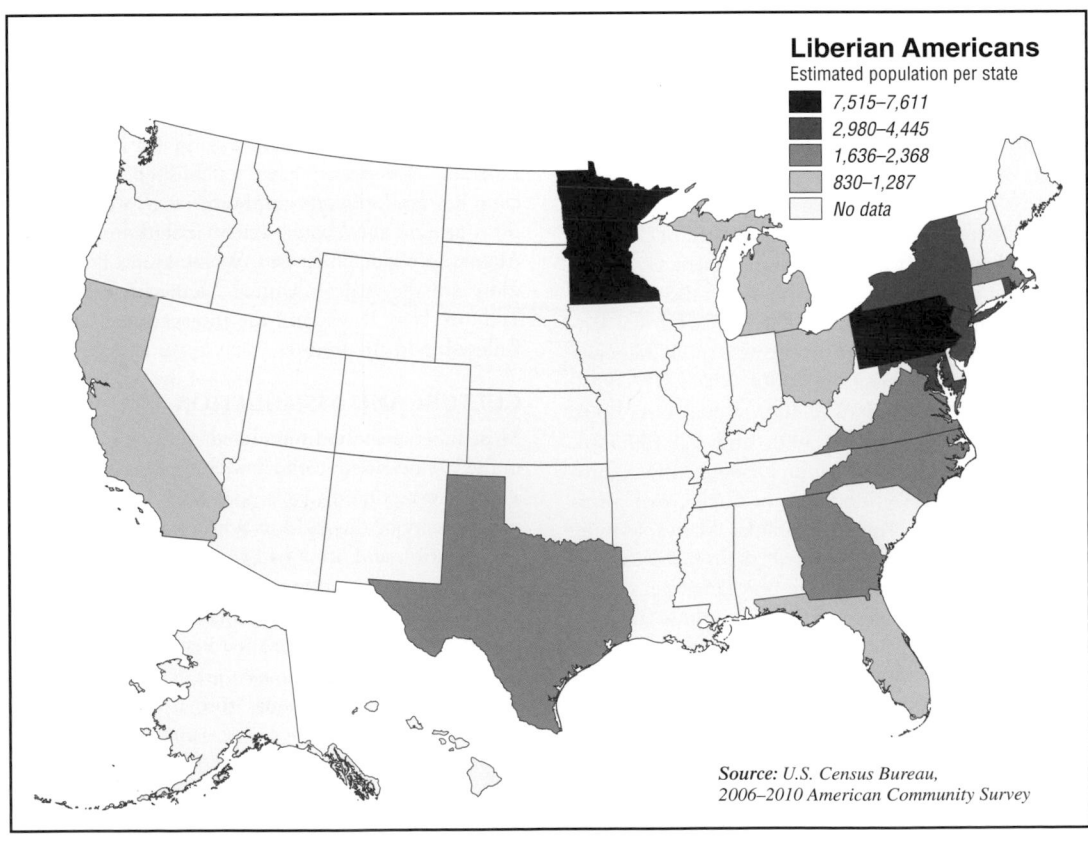

Liberian Americans
Estimated population per state

- 7,515–7,611
- 2,980–4,445
- 1,636–2,368
- 830–1,287
- No data

Source: U.S. Census Bureau, 2006–2010 American Community Survey

the TPS status, as they were concerned a return of so many Liberians who had been displaced for such an extended period of time could overwhelm the country's fragile and potentially still volatile infrastructure. As a result, the U.S. government under the Bush Administration allowed Liberian refugees to stay with a similar status, Deferred Enforced Departure (DED). As of 2013 the Obama administration had maintained DED status of temporary Liberian immigrants.

A majority of Liberian Americans have settled on the East Coast; in particular, large communities can be found in New York, Maryland, New Jersey, and Rhode Island. The two states with the highest overall population of Liberian Americans are Pennsylvania and Minnesota. While many the Liberian immigrants who arrived prior to 1980 were well-educated and aspired to continue their educations in the United States, many of those that came after 1980 were from impoverished rural areas where they had received little schooling. Many Liberian Americans have found positions in a variety of sectors, including hospitality, health care, and the service industry. Those with more skills and education have often opened their own businesses or attained professional positions. Other Liberian Americans have capitalized on their unique talents, like hair braiding, to find employment. Female Liberian immigrants on the East Coast and in San Francisco have especially found this type of work. Still others work in the agricultural sector, based on their experiences living in rural areas of Liberia. This trend is especially true of Liberian men living in California.

LANGUAGE

English is the official language of Liberia, but it is the primary language of only about 20 percent (69,000) of the population. There are thirty-four ethnic languages spoken in Liberia and within each are multiple dialects, most of which are oral and cannot be written. Because of this, there is a dearth of recorded historical and other information on Liberians prior to the arrival of European and American missionaries in the mid-nineteenth century. The primary tribal languages and the number of people who speak them are: Kpelle (487,400), Bassa (347,600), Mano (185,000), Klao (184,000), Dan (150,800), Loma (141,000), Kisi (115,000), Gola (99,300), and Vai (89,500). Other languages include Bandi, Dewoin, Gbii, Glaro-Twabo, Glio-Oubi, nine forms of Grebo, two forms of Krahn, Krumen, Kuwaa, Maninka, Manya, Mende, Sapo, and Tajuasohn. About half the population (1.5 million) speaks English as a second language, mainly for communication between different ethnic language groups. In the mid-nineteenth century, a member of the Vai invented an alphabet for his tribe. Later that century, European missionaries created a system for writing two other tribal languages, Bassa and Grebo. The ethnic languages are very tonal in quality and are often spoken with musical characteristics. They usually contain two or three distinct tones, based on pitch,

which indicate semantic or grammatical differences. The Liberian "talking drum" can imitate these sounds. Proverbs, songs, and prose narratives are the primary forms of verbal expression within many Liberian ethnic groups. In many of the ethnic languages, there are up to twenty classes of nouns, compared to three (masculine, feminine, and neutral) in English. For example, one set of nouns designates human beings, another is for animals, and a third is for liquids.

Among Liberians in the United States, English is almost universally spoken, and the most widely spoken ethnic language is Kru. Another language spoken by some Liberian Americans is Gullah, a Creole language with influences from the Gola ethnic group of Liberia. It is limited mainly to a small group of people in the Carolina Sea Islands and middle Atlantic coast of the United States. Several Gullah words have become common in American English, including *goober* (peanut), *gumbo* (okra), and *voodoo* (witchcraft). According to the 2006–2010 estimates by the American Community Survey, 69 percent of Liberian Americans reported speaking only English in their homes, and 86 percent reported being fluent in English.

RELIGION

In Liberia approximately 85 percent of the population is Christian and about 12 percent practices the Islamic faith. The remaining residents either follow traditional African religions or do not practice religion. Many individuals blend elements of Christianity, Islam, and indigenous religions in their practices. Most Liberian Americans are Christians.

Christian Liberians are spread among a wide range of denominations, including Lutheran, Episcopal, Methodist, Baptist, and Catholic. Many Liberian Americans have established their own churches and religious communities in various locations around the United States, including in Dallas, Atlanta, Philadelphia, and Washington, D.C. Two more are the African United Methodist Church in Trenton, New Jersey, and the International Christian Fellowship in Atlanta.

CULTURE AND ASSIMILATION

Most Liberians who immigrated to the United States in the late twentieth century were fleeing civil war and a social and economic collapse in their homeland. As a result, many of the children who immigrated had little education and often had trouble catching up with their American counterparts. Newer immigrants are also unfamiliar with American culture and sometimes have difficulty adapting to their new environment.

However, one advantage for Liberian immigrants entering the United States is that many Liberian customs, as well as social and economic traditions, originally came from the United States with the freed African American slaves who immigrated to Liberia in the nineteenth century. Social gatherings, such as weddings, birthdays, and funerals, are similar in nature to those of Americans in general and more specifically to African Americans. Liberians also celebrate many of the same holidays as Americans, including Christmas, Easter, New Year's Day, and Thanksgiving. These holidays are generally celebrated according to American custom, although occasionally some Liberian and African traditions are incorporated.

Traditions and Customs Many occasions are cause for celebration among Liberians, in both Liberia and the United States. Ethnic Liberians will sing and dance, sometimes for days, during weddings, funerals, the birth of a child, circumcision ceremonies, and initiation into the traditional ethnic societies (usually around puberty). A group of dancers, singers, and musicians may perform in one location, or they may move from one neighborhood house to another. It is customary for the neighbors to provide drinks and sometimes money to the musicians and dancers.

A unique custom among Liberians is the "snapshake" greeting. When shaking hands, you grasp the middle finger of the other person's right hand between your thumb and ring (third) finger, and bring it up quickly with a snap. The custom is derived from the days of slavery in the United States when a slave owner often would break the middle finger of a slave's hand to indicate bondage. The "snapshake" greeting began in the nineteenth century as a sign of freedom among former slaves. It is sometimes used by Liberian Americans to greet dinner guests.

The ethnic groups of Liberia are known for their collective rather than individual artwork. Members of the secret Poro men's society, for example, make ceremonial masks used in various rituals. The Dan group is noted for their carved wooden masks representing spirits of the forest, and for large spoons carved with the features of humans and animals. Another form of Liberian art is drums and other musical instruments, usually made from wood, animal skins, raffia, and gourds. Because nearly all of the ethnic languages of Liberia are oral rather than written, there is very little traditional Liberian literature.

Cuisine Traditionally, Liberians eat a healthy diet consisting mainly of fish, rice, greens, and vegetables. Rice is often served with breakfast, lunch, and dinner. Liberians like their food hot and typically spice their dishes with cayenne and other peppers. Another staple of Liberian cuisine is *cassava*, a tropical plant with starchy roots from which tapioca is obtained. *Dumboy* are fresh cassava roots, which are boiled, beaten with a mortar and pestle, and then cut into small pieces. It is usually served with a soup made of peanuts and okra. *Fufu* is made from granulated cassava that is fermented, then the liquid is boiled until it thickens. It is served with soup. The cassava leaves are also used in Liberian cooking. They are washed and beaten, mashed, or finely chopped with pepper and onion. They are then boiled with beef or chicken until

LIBERIAN FAMILIES ADJUST TO LIFE IN AMERICA

Lanla Labi came to the United States from Liberia in 1977, when she was seven years old. She went to live with her mother, already in this country, in Los Angeles. In a January 1999 article in *Essence* magazine, Labi recalled her difficulty in adjusting to a new culture. "My initial excitement about attending an American school quickly faded. My thick accent and sudden shyness alienated me from my classmates, who taunted me with names like 'Cheetah,' Tarzan's chimpanzee companion. After school, I rode the bus home and entered the solitary world of a latchkey child." Another account of Liberian immigrants' experience of adjusting to American life is author Stephen Chicoine's book *A Liberian Family*, in which he writes about a Liberian family who fled to the United States in 1990 to escape the civil war. Chicoine details their new life in Houston, Texas, including problems adjusting to living in a small apartment, low-wage jobs for the adults, and isolation from their culture.

well done and most of the liquid has evaporated. Palm oil is added and, after simmering a few minutes, the dish is served with rice.

Potato greens, which often called potato "grains," are popular among Liberians and Liberian American alike. This dish is served fried with onions and hot peppers. Water is then added to the dish, and it is boiled until done. The resulting taste and texture is similar to spinach. Liberians and Liberian Americans also enjoy stews and soups. Goat soup, considered the national soup, is more of a thick, meat stew than a soup and is usually heavily spiced with peppers. Other favorites are pigs' feet with bacon and cabbage, fish with sweet-potato leaves, shrimp and palm nuts in fish or chicken stock, and a combination of rice and okra called check rice. Liberians and Liberian Americans enjoy sweet desserts, such as sweet potato, coconut, and pumpkin pie. Peanuts are commonly used in cookies and other desserts. Another delicacy is a sweet bread made from rice and bananas. The preferred drinks are ginger beer (usually homemade), palm wine, and Liberian coffee.

Traditional Dress Traditional Liberian dress tends to be very colorful. Both men's and women's clothing is loose fitting and flowing. Among women, the most traditional garment is the *lappa*, a skirt made from handwoven material called country cloth, which comes in an assortment of bright colors, sometimes with intricate designs woven into it. The women also wear a headband or bandana that often matches the *lappa*. The style and design varies according to ethnic group. Traditionally, the clothing is woven into cloth from cotton picked and twined into thread on a spool. Gowns for men are made by cutting a hole in the center of a piece of cloth for the head to go through.

LIBERIAN PROVERBS

Liberian folklore is filled with proverbs and parables, most of which are specific to particular tribal groups. Animals are a common theme in the sayings. A general proverb is "He who knows the way must conduct others."

Two proverbs from the Kpelle tribe are "When pointing an evil finger at a man, three fingers are also pointed at yourself"; and "The stones that you throw into the well to kill frogs are the same stones that will cause you to suffer when you drink the dirty water."

A common saying from the Bassa tribe is "He who steps in (a river) first shows the depth of the current."

Proverbs from the Krahn tribe include "To cure a bad sore, you must use bad medicine"; and "The leaf that is very sweet in a goat's mouth sometimes hurts his stomach."

From the Gola tribe, sayings include "A man cannot be taller than his head"; and "Washing with dirty water does not clean a dirty object."

Two sayings from the Vai tribe are "Do not look where you fell, but where you slipped"; and "A curled snake never gets fat."

The entire process of making a garment usually takes weeks or months.

Liberian Americans have generally adopted Western styles of dress, and traditional clothing is usually reserved for special events, such as holidays, weddings, and Liberian Independence Day celebrations.

Dances and Songs Traditional Liberians dance according to the sounds of various musical instruments. The heart of Liberian music is the drum, ranging from large drums three or four feet tall and placed on the ground, to smaller ones that fit between the legs or under the arms. At the center is the "talking drum" player, who tells a proverb or story through musical tones that imitate the native languages. The *tardegai* is the traditional Liberian drum, which is played with a stick shaped like a hammer. Another instrument is the *saa-saa*, usually played by women. It is made from a dried gourd enclosed in a net tied into a knot at the top and decorated with shells. By shaking the gourd, the basic rhythm is established, accompanied by the sound made by pulling on the netting.

Among the Kpelle ethnic group, a popular instrument is a foot-long drum made of hollow wood and shaped like an hourglass. The top and bottom drumming surfaces are made from monkey skin. A set of raffia strings connect the skins on either end. It is held under the arm, and by pressing these strings between the arm and body, the player changes the drum's pitch. Another musical instrument of Liberia is the *gowd*, the dried round shell of a gourd that is fitted between a string of beads. When the gourd is moved around between the beads, it creates a rhythmic rattling sound. Liberians also play a trumpet-like instrument made out of logs, animal horns, or elephant tusks. Because each instrument has its own sound quality, several are usually played together, creating a unique melody.

Liberia has a vibrant popular-music scene. Highlife and hipco are two of the most popular contemporary genres. Originally developed in Ghana in the 1920s, highlife is a jazzy, up-tempo form of music that became popular throughout West Africa in the 1950s. Contemporary highlife music is especially fast-paced and often features synthesizers. Among Liberians, the Kru people, who make up 6 percent of the population, are known to be fond of Highlife. The most famous Liberian Highlife singer is Fatu Gayflor, who is of Lorma origin and fled the country in the late 1980s to escape the civil war. Gayflor lived for a time in the Ivory Coast and Guinea before immigrating to the United States and continuing her career in Philadelphia.

Hipco is a uniquely Liberian form of music that was developed in the 1980s and 1990s in response to the political turmoil in the country. Sometimes written "Hip-Co," the term is a combination of the words "hip" (trendy) and "colloquial," and Hipco songs, which are highly politicized, attempt to convey a sense of outrage in vernacular speech. The most popular Hipco performer is Takun J, who was arrested and beaten for his 2007 song "Police Man." Liberian Americans tend to prefer reggae, hip-hop, and R&B music, all of which are popular in Liberia as well.

Holidays In Liberia, Christmas Day is traditionally celebrated with a large feast but without a Christmas tree or the exchange of presents. However, more Liberian Americans are adopting the Western traditions of the holiday. Liberians celebrate Thanksgiving on the first Thursday in November; Liberian Americans are more likely to celebrate the holiday at the end of the month, like other Americans. Liberians celebrate New Year's Day in much the same way as Americans. Although Easter is celebrated among some Christian Liberian Americans, a more traditional holiday is Fast and Prayer Day on the second Friday in April.

July 26 is National Independence Day; Liberian Americans celebrate it with communal picnics and other outdoor gatherings. As with all Liberian celebrations, there is plenty of music, song, and dance. The birthdays of Liberia's presidents are also formal holidays, but few Liberians in the United States commemorate the dates. The only exception is former president William V. S. Tubman's birthday on November 29. Much like the birthdays of George Washington and Abraham Lincoln are to Americans, Tubman's birthday is more a matter of remembrance than celebration for Liberian Americans.

Health Care Issues and Practices In Liberia the major health issue is infectious diseases, including yellow fever, cholera, typhoid, polio, and malaria. These problems are almost nonexistent in Liberian Americans because of improved health care, housing, and sanitation conditions. Instead, the major health concerns are hypertension (high blood pressure), diabetes mellitus type 2 (adult onset or non-insulin dependent diabetes), high cholesterol levels, stroke, and heart disease. These conditions are not widespread in Liberia, and physicians suggest the increased risk among Liberians in the United States is due to a less healthy diet and less exercise. Specifically, a Liberian American's diet generally has less fiber and more fat and cholesterol than the typical diet in Liberia.

Many Liberians and Liberian Americans who experienced trauma during the civil war suffer from post-traumatic stress disorder.

FAMILY AND COMMUNITY LIFE

Extended families are the cornerstone of the Liberian American community. Each member is held in high esteem and treated with deep respect by the others. The elderly in particular command veneration, and younger family members respect their elders' opinions and thoughts. Family elders are considered sources of wisdom and knowledge, and therefore are often asked to make important decisions. It is rare to find an elderly Liberian American in a nursing home because families take care of their elders. A household is often composed of a husband and wife, their children, and the parents of the couple. The typical Liberia American household is an extended family, which can also include brothers, sisters, nieces, nephews and cousins. Children are very important, and their parents endeavor to make sure they receive an education. Financial sacrifices are commonly made by the family to pay for schooling.

Although the bulk of Liberians in the United States have only been here since 1989, the community has sought to develop strong ties with other West African immigrants, particularly those from the Ivory Coast and Sierra Leone. They also have close ties with African Americans in general. Several U.S. civil rights groups have embraced the Liberian community and have supported granting permanent residency to the tens of thousands of Liberian immigrants with temporary status in the United States. There are also efforts by groups such as civil rights leader Jesse Jackson's PUSH/Rainbow Coalition and the National Association for the Advancement of Colored People (NAACP) to bring Liberian Americans into the mainstream of African American society and culture.

Gender Roles The role of Liberian women in the United States is somewhat different from the traditional role of women among Liberia's ethnic groups. In Liberia the main responsibility for women is child rearing, although women are responsible for some agricultural work. In the United States, women are still the center of the Liberian American family, but many also have jobs, are more educated than their counterparts in Liberia, and are more involved in community dynamics. One significant difference is the practice of female circumcision, also called female genital cutting or mutilation. While at least half of females in Liberia undergo the experience, the practice is largely nonexistent among Liberian American females born or raised in the United States.

One of the major ramifications of the civil war in Liberia is the fact that many households were broken up by death, and consequently many Liberian American households are run by females.

Extended families are the cornerstone of the Liberian American community. Each member is held in high esteem and treated with deep respect by the others. The elderly in particular command veneration, and younger family members respect their elders' opinions and thoughts. Family elders are considered sources of wisdom and knowledge, and therefore are often asked to make important decisions.

Education Education is extremely important to Liberian Americans, with adults often taking general education and self-improvement classes. A number of Liberian American organizations in the United States fund college scholarships for students. Graduates remain very loyal to their high schools and universities and often sponsor students from Liberia who want to attend school in the United States.

However, school-age children who have recently immigrated to the United States often have difficulty in American schools, mainly because the educational system in Liberia was severely damaged during the civil war. Many schools were destroyed and teachers were killed or forced to flee the country. Also, when children arrive in the United States, their English may be limited. Likewise, many Liberian Americans find the accent, tone, and idioms of American English challenging to understand and learn. But education is so valued in the Liberian community, they are motivated to overcome these difficulties. Many Liberian Americans go on to colleges and universities, receive degrees, and find employment in a wide range of professional fields, such as teaching, medicine, science, engineering, and technology.

Courtship and Weddings A traditional Liberian wedding is a verbal contract between the groom and the bride's family. The prospective groom must give

A business owner in St. Paul, Minnesota, is a Liberian refugee who lost his house and two brothers to the war. His business assists Liberians looking for blueprints for new buildings back home in Liberia. ZUMA PRESS, INC. / ALAMY

the bride's family a dowry to compensate for the loss of a daughter. The dowry usually consists of any combination of money, animals, and household goods. The wedding itself is a festive affair, with singing, dancing, drumming, and a lavish feast. At the conclusion, the guests lead the bride and groom to the home they will live in together.

A Liberian American wedding is deeply rooted in American customs and slightly influenced by Liberian tradition. A dowry is rarely involved. Because most Liberians in the United States belong to a Christian denomination, the ceremony follows along the lines of what is prescribed by the particular church, such as Catholic, Mormon, Lutheran, or Methodist. Marriage vows are exchanged and the ceremony is conducted by a priest or minister. The bride and other women in the entourage wear dresses that are flowing and brightly colored. They also wear their hair tied up with a piece of cloth. Women wear a lot of jewelry, including multiple necklaces, bracelets, and earrings. The groom usually wears a long, baggy ceremonial gown that is brightly decorated with traditional African colors: red, yellow, green, and black. The groom also wears a traditional hat that is as colorful as the wedding gown.

A popular saying in the Liberian American community is that a prospective couple need only send out a dozen wedding invitations; the word will get around so quickly that ten times that number will show up for the ceremony. Like traditional American weddings, the Liberian ceremony is followed by a reception with a lot of food, song, and dance. In the

United States, as in Liberia, one or several traditional drummers are usually on hand to provide the underlying beat of the festivities.

EMPLOYMENT AND ECONOMIC CONDITIONS

Liberian Americans have sought employment in a variety of fields, including health care, law, education, service, and hospitality. A few have started their own businesses. Their professions often depend on where they live. For example, Liberian Americans in the Central Valley of California tend to find agricultural jobs. In Washington, D.C., Maryland, and Virginia, many work for the federal government. In the San Francisco Bay Area, Liberian American women lean toward the health care professions, such as nursing, nursing assistant, and even physician. Many newer immigrants start with low-paying jobs, such as kitchen workers, janitors, or in-home health care, because of limited education, a lack of English proficiency, and unfamiliarity with the American work culture.

POLITICS AND GOVERNMENT

Politics plays an important role in the life of Liberian Americans, especially when it involves their homeland. Liberia is divided into thirteen local government subdivisions called counties. A fierce identification with these counties has caused dozens of county organizations to spring up in areas of the United States with large numbers of Liberian immigrants. These include the Sinoe County Association of Georgia, the United

Nimba (County) Citizens' Council, and the Grand Cape Mount County Association of Georgia.

Liberian Americans have taken an active role in lobbying the U.S. government to support freedom and democracy efforts in Liberia. They also have organized in support of various issues affecting Liberia, including humanitarian assistance, wildlife and nature preservation, and women's rights. Liberian American organizations played a crucial role, for example, in maintaining temporary protected status (TPS) for the thousands of Liberian immigrants and refugees who arrived in the United States in the 1980s, 1990s, and 2000s. When the federal government wanted to revoke TPS in 1997 and 2006, the efforts of Liberian American organizations helped extend this status for Liberian American immigrants and refugees.

Although Liberian Americans still maintain close ties with family, friends, and organizations in Liberia, there is widespread dissatisfaction with the current economic and political situation. Many Liberian Americans are working to help rebuild the political, social, educational, and commerce institutions of their homeland. Yet that does not mean all Liberian Americans speak with a unified voice. The Liberian community in the United States is divided between several political parties in Liberia, including the ruling National Patriotic Party and the opposition Liberian National Union, National Democratic Party, and the United People's Party, all of which have organizations in the United States. Despite the political differences, the Liberian American community is united in the goal of helping the people of Liberia recover from its years of civil war and armed conflict. Of particular interest is rebuilding schools and restoring the freedom Liberians enjoyed under the leadership of former president William V. S. Tubman's administration.

NOTABLE INDIVIDUALS

Academia Benjamin G. Dennis (1929–2009) was born in Monrovia, Liberia, and immigrated to the United States, where he received his doctorate in 1964 from Michigan State University. A professor of sociology and anthropology at the University of Michigan at Flint, Dennis published *The Gbandes: A People of the Liberian Hinterland* in 1972 and *Slaves to Racism: An Unbroken Chain from America to Liberia* (with Anita K. Dennis) in 2008.

Music E. G. Bailey, a Liberian American spoken-word artist and filmmaker, received accolades for his album *AMERICAN AFRIKAN*, which was nominated for an Independent Music Award in 2011.

In 1996 Jacob M. Daynuah, a Liberian immigrant, started an independent record production company and label in Minneapolis, Minnesota, called Zoto Records, specializing in Liberian music and artists. *Zoto* means "lizard ears" in the Dan language of Liberia. Daynuah released three albums under the pseudonym Jake D: *African Lady* in 1990, *Unity* in

1992, and *Banjay* in 1996. His musical style is known as *korlor*, an infectious and happy sound from Nimba County in northeastern Liberia. His wife, Naser Daynuah, is a drummer from Nimba County, Liberia, who immigrated to the United States and settled in Minneapolis. Her traditional *sokay* sound comes from the harmonica and a conga drum known as a *balah*. Her first album, *Sokay*, was released in 1998.

Politics Paye Flomo, an immigrant from Liberia, served as the mayor of Hampton, Minnesota, from 2008 to 2012, making him reportedly the first elected Liberian American mayor in the United States.

Sports George Weah (1966–), a Liberian American soccer player, was the first player to simultaneously hold the titles of World Player of the Year, European Football Player of the Year, and African Football Player of the Year, all in 1995. He has played for national championship teams in Liberia, Cameroon, France, Monaco, and Italy.

Liberian Americans also represented their homeland in the 1996 Summer Olympics in Atlanta, Georgia. Of particular note are four members of the Liberian national men's track and field 100-meter relay team. They are Sayon Cooper (1974–) and Robert H. Dennis III (1975–) of Maryland, Kouty Mawenh (1971–) of Indiana, and Eddie Neufville (1976–) of South Carolina. Liberian American Grace Dinkins (1966–) competed for the Liberian women's track and field team in the 1996 and 2000 Olympics.

MEDIA

PRINT

Liberian Studies Journal

Publishes articles on scholarly research in a wide range of disciplines, including social sciences, arts, humanities, science, and technology.

Dr. Mary Moran, Secretary Treasurer
Department of Sociology and Anthropology
Colgate University
Hamilton, New York 13346
Phone: (315) 228-7548
Email: mmoran@mail.colgate.edu
URL: www.onliberia.org/lsa_journal.htm

ORGANIZATIONS AND ASSOCIATIONS

Coalition of Progressive Liberians in the Americas (COPLA)

COPLA, based in Maryland, describes itself as "a watchdog of vice and virtue" in the Liberian community.

2803 Diamond Ridge Road
Suite 204
Baltimore, Maryland 21244
Phone: (410) 944-8699
URL: www.copla.org

Liberia First, Inc.

Established in 1998, Liberia First is a nonprofit organization serving the metropolitan Triangle Area of Raleigh, Durham, and Chapel Hill, North Carolina. It promotes cultural and social values among Liberians in the Triangle Area. It also seeks to help with rebuilding the social, economic and education structures in Liberia.

Siaka Kromah, President
P.O. Box 5655
Raleigh, North Carolina 27650-5655
Phone: (919) 286-5774
URL: www.liberiafirst.com/membership.htm

Liberian Association of Southern California

The Liberian Association of Southern California is a social and economic support group for the estimated 2,000 Liberians living in the Los Angeles area. Services include helping newly arrived immigrants adjust to life in the United States and providing community outreach, especially to the young and elderly. It was founded in the early 1960s to serve the needs of Liberian American students. It later broadened its scope to include all Liberians in Southern California.

David Beyan, President
P.O. Box 44941
Los Angeles, California 90007
Phone: (310) 254-5783
URL: http://lacosc.org/

Liberian Community Association of Washington, D.C.

The association has 400 members and serves the social and economic needs of Liberians in Washington, D.C., Maryland, and Virginia. It holds quarterly general assembly meetings.

10169 New Hampshire Avenue
P.O. Box 174
Silver Spring, Maryland 20903
URL: www.lcadcmetro.org

Liberian Community Foundation (LCF)

A nonprofit organization founded in 1995, the LCF has an office and warehouse where it dispenses information, food, clothing and small appliances to needy Liberians in the San Francisco Bay Area. It also provides relief supplies, including food and medical equipment, to Liberia. It is staffed by unpaid volunteers and is run solely on private contributions.

3050 66th Avenue
Sacramento, California 95822
Phone: (916) 393-1974

MUSEUMS AND RESEARCH CENTERS

American Colonization Society–Liberia Collection

Prints and Photographs Division, Maryland Historical Society

The society provides collections related to the colonization of the United States. It is affiliated with the Maryland Historical Society, and it has a collection specifically related to Liberia.

201 W. Monument Street
Baltimore, Maryland 21201
URL: www.mdhs.org/findingaid/
american-colonization-society/
liberia-collection-pp161

James E. Lewis Museum of Art

Located in the Carl Murphy Arts Center, the university art museum has a large collection of art works from Africa, including several dozen from Liberia. The Liberian collection includes Dan masks, drums, wood statues, clay bowls, and carved figurines.

Morgan State University
2200 Argonne Drive
Baltimore, Maryland 21251
Phone: (443) 885-3030
Fax: (443) 885-8258
Email: jelmamuseum@morgan.edu
URL: www.jelmamuseum.org

Liberian Museum of City College

The collection of Liberian art and handcrafted artifacts includes eating and cooking utensils, musical instruments, and traditional clothing donated by citizens in Monrovia, Liberia, Baltimore's sister city in Africa. The museum is in the library of Baltimore City College, a college preparatory high school in Baltimore.

Joette Chance, Librarian
Baltimore City College
3320 The Alameda
Baltimore, Maryland 21218
Phone: (410) 396-7423

SOURCES FOR ADDITIONAL STUDY

Chicoine, Stephen. *A Liberian Family*. Minneapolis: Lerner Publications Co., 1997.

Cooper, Helene. *The House at Sugar Beach: In Search of a Lost African Childhood*. New York: Simon and Schuster, 2009.

Henries, A. Doris Banks. *Liberian Folklore*. London: Macmillan and Co. Ltd., 1966.

Hope, Constance Morris. *Liberia*. Broomall, PA: Chelsea House Publishers, 1987.

Kulah, Arthur. *Liberia Will Rise Again: Reflections on the Liberian Civil Crisis*. Nashville, TN: Abingdon Press, 1999.

Moses, Wilson Jeremiah, ed. *Liberian Dreams: Back-to-Africa Narratives from the 1850s*. University Park: The Pennsylvania State University Press, 1998.

Owen, Harrison. *When the Devil Dances…* Los Angeles: Mara Books. 1970.

LIBYAN AMERICANS

Tova Stabin

OVERVIEW

Libyan Americans are immigrants or descendants of people from Libya, a country in Northern Africa. Libya is bordered by the Mediterranean Sea to the north; Egypt to the east; Chad, Niger, and Sudan to the south; Algeria to the west; and Tunisia to the northwest. Libya is a member of both the Arab League and the African Union, and in modern usage it is included in discussions of the Middle East. The Sahara Desert covers 90 percent of the country. Libya has an average rainfall of only one inch per year, and summer temperatures can reach 120 degrees Fahrenheit. Aside from the desert, the country has a rocky coastline, and less than 1 percent of its land is arable; this land is mostly in the Jabal al Akhdar region near the city of Benghazi and the Jifarah Plain near the capital, Tripoli. Libya is the seventeenth-largest country in the world, with a total land area of 679,362 square miles (1.76 million square kilometers)—as a basis for comparison, it is somewhat larger than the state of Alaska.

According to the *CIA World Factbook*, the population of Libya was 5.6 million in 2012. The cities with the greatest population are Tripoli and Benghazi. The official religion is Sunni Muslim, which 97 percent of the people claim as their religious affiliation. Other Muslim sects represented in Libya include Sanusis, Ibadhis, Sufis, and Sharifs. The vast majority of the population, 97 percent, is Berber, Arab, or a combination of these ethnicities. The remaining people represent ethnic groups that include Greeks, Maltese, Italians, Egyptians, Pakistanis, Turks, Indians, and Tunisians. The economy is centered primarily on oil and gas exports, which accounts for about 80 percent of its gross domestic product (GDP); the other 20 percent of the GDP arises primarily from the service and construction industries. As a result of its arid climate and poor soil, Libya imports about 80 percent of its food. Libya's high overall national income from natural resources and its small population give it one of the highest per capita GDPs in Africa, but many years of inequitable government distribution of wealth and poor infrastructure have left the majority of citizens impoverished.

The first people from Middle Eastern and North African Arabic-speaking countries to immigrate to the United States arrived in the 1880s. This wave of Arab immigrants likely included Libyans. From the 1880s to World War II, national borders and imperialistic rule over various areas in the Middle East changed frequently, and the U.S. government did not always accurately differentiate between Middle Eastern national identities. Specific waves of Libyan immigration were first noted in the late 1970s, when people began fleeing the oppressive dictatorship of Muammar Gaddafi that had begun in 1969. A significant number came to the United States ostensibly for educational reasons and stayed. When the Iraq War was launched in 2003, the U.S. Immigration and Naturalization Service (INS) began to require special registration and added other conditions for the entry of Libyans, Iraqis, Iranians, Syrians, and Sudanese into the country.

The 2010 U.S. Census estimated the Arab American population to be 1,967,219; this number included immigrants from Libya and their descendants. Libya was just one of the nations "collapsed" into the category "Other Arabs," which also included people from Algeria, Bahrain, Djibouti, Kuwait, Libya, Oman, Qatar, Saudi Arabia, Tunisia, the United Arab Emirates, and Yemen. Libyan Americans reside in significant numbers in the states of New York, Texas, Michigan, California, Illinois, Virginia, and Kentucky.

HISTORY OF THE PEOPLE

Early History Libya has a long and complex history. Archeological evidence shows a continuous presence of Berber tribes—the population indigenous to the area—for approximately 100,000 years. The name *Libya* was derived from the ancient Egyptians' name for one of the Berber tribes, the Lebu people. The Greeks used the name for most North Africans, including all Berbers from all the tribes who lived there.

The area that is now Libya was under control of various ancient empires, each of whom wanted to control the trade routes of the Mediterranean. From about 1000 BCE, the Phoenicians, who inhabited the region of present-day Lebanon and Israel, established a colony in the ancient Libyan city of Carthage (now in Tunisia). In 632 BCE the Greeks founded the city of Cyrene in the modern-day Libyan area of Jabal al Akhdar. Cyrene later became a province of the Roman Empire (in 67 BCE). During the Punic Wars (264–146 BCE), the Romans won control of Carthage, but the wars had virtually destroyed the city, and the victors had to rebuild it. The Romans also established cities in the western Libyan area called (until 1963) Tripolitania. After the decline of the Roman Empire in about 429 CE, a German tribe, the Vandals, took possession of the area but surrendered it in 533 to the Byzantine Empire. The Byzantines, in turn, were conquered by peoples from the Arabian Peninsula in 642. The Arabs brought the Islamic religion to Libya, and most Berbers converted to Islam from their indigenous religions.

Various Muslim dynasties from Egypt and Baghdad, including the Umayyad Dynasty (661–750) and the Abbasid Empire (750–1258), both Sunni Islamic groups, ruled during the next few hundred years, with different caliphs (successors of the Prophet Muhammad) controlling the region. The Shiite Fatimid caliphate, based in modern-day Tunisia, conquered Egypt in 972 and then moved into Libya. The Fatimids had a significant impact on the area. They sent as many as 200,000 families from the Bani Salim and Bani Hilal tribes to settle in and around Cyrene and Tripoli in the eleventh century. The Berbers were effectively displaced from their traditional lands; Arab culture and language spread rapidly and has remained the predominant culture since that time.

In 1551 Muslims from the Ottoman Empire invaded Libya, capturing Tripoli and launching the first period of Turkish rule. In 1711 an Ottoman soldier, Ahmed Karamanli (the son of a Turkish officer and a Libyan woman), murdered the governor of Tripolitania and seized power. When he died, his successors had difficulty maintaining control. Large debts to France and England put great stress on the economy, and a civil war broke out, creating chaos and allowing the Ottoman Empire to regain dominance in 1835. During this second period of Ottoman rule, strict Islamists established a religious brotherhood called the Sanusiyah that became a significant political and cultural force in Libya. The group built their first *zawiya* (monastery) in 1843 in Cyrene.

Modern Era The Ottomans tolerated the Sanusiyah at first, believing that they would help fight against French colonizers intent on expanding from present-day Chad into Libya. Before long, however, power struggles developed between the government and the Sanusiyah, ending only when Italy declared war on the Ottoman Empire and invaded Libya. Preferring the Islamic Turks to Christian European rulers, the Libyans united to resist the Italians, forming the *mujahideen* (freedom fighters). By the end of 1911, however, Italy had captured Libya. Libyan resistance continued after the occupation, but Italian military forces and settlers prevailed.

In 1934 Italy adopted the name *Libya* for its colony, which consisted of the provinces of Cyrenaica, Tripolitania, and Fezzan. Having found ruins of Roman culture in Libya, the Italians thought of the area as part of their ancient homeland. During the three

decades of their rule, they killed one-quarter of the Libyan population, using hangings, forced starvation, concentration camps, and heavy settlement to destroy the culture. Libya became one of the poorest regions in the world.

When World War II arrived, the Allied and Axis powers fought many battles in Libya, as well as in Egypt and Tunisia. The Sanusi leader Muhammad Idris sided with the Allies. After its defeat Italy surrendered Libya to French and British occupation. At the end of the war, some 11 million unexploded mines were estimated to be on or under Libyan soil; some of them are still there. The British formally took charge of Tripolitania and Cyrenaica in 1943; the French were given Fezzan. In 1949 the United Nations assembly approved the formation of an independent state that would include all three provinces. The United Kingdom of Libya declared independence in 1951 as a constitutional and hereditary monarchy with Idris as king. (Later, in 1999, the Italian government formally apologized to Libya for their cruel colonization.)

After a contentious election in 1952 during which riots broke out, King Idris banned all political parties and deported the leaders of the main opposition party, the Congress Party. Libya had remained poor after the occupiers left, and King Idris made treaties with the United Kingdom and the United States that allowed them to operate military bases in Libya in exchange for economic and technical help. In 1959, after the American corporation Esso (now Exxon) discovered an oil field in Cyrenaica, oil companies from all over the world began explorations in Libya, which resulted in an economic boom during the 1960s. The government initiated major infrastructure improvements, building roads, schools, and hospitals. Nonetheless, much of the money went to either foreign interests or a small elite group in Libya.

As a member of the conservative traditionalist bloc in the League of Arab States (or Arab League), King Idris was dependent on and aligned with Western powers. Meanwhile, Arab nationalism was growing in other parts of the Arab world. Autocratic rule, political corruption, and poor economic conditions led to widespread unrest in Libya. Tensions increased after Israel defeated the Arab states of Egypt, Jordan, and Syria in the 1967 Six-Day War; Libyans felt their government was not committed enough to Arab causes.

In September 1969 army captain Muammar Gaddafi led a successful coup in Benghazi, seizing control of the government while King Idris was in Turkey for medical treatment. The Free Officers Movement claimed credit for the coup, and its Revolutionary Command Council became the Libyan government, declaring the country a "free and sovereign state" called the Libyan Arab Republic. Gaddafi was named chairperson of the council as well as head of the armed forces.

The new government embraced strict Islamic law (prohibiting gambling and drinking, for instance), socialism, and Arab nationalism and was fervently anti-Western. In 1970 Gaddafi removed U.S. and British military bases; expelled Jewish and Italian Libyans; shut down newspapers, banks, and political parties that had been affiliated with the monarchy; replaced Sanusi clerics; and arrested so many political opponents that Libya had the world's highest prison population per capita. He also instituted the death penalty for antig-overnment activities. Libya cut off relations with Egypt after Anwar Sadat made peace with Israel in 1979. The Gaddafi government instituted some positive changes, investing large amounts of money in agriculture and other development plans, raising the standard of living for many Libyans, and committing to gender equality.

During the 1970s and 1980s, Gaddafi supported insurgent groups around the world, including those in Northern Ireland, Palestine, the Basque Country (a separatist movement in Spain), and South Africa; in 1979 he sent troops to back Ugandan dictator Idi Amin. Citing Gaddafi's "support of international terrorism," the United States severed ties with Libya in 1981; Great Britain followed suit in 1984. In 1989 Libya reconciled with Egypt and formed an economic alliance called the Arab Maghreb Union that included Tunisia, Algeria, Morocco, and Mauritania.

In 1991 the U.S. and British governments accused two Libyans of organizing the 1988 bombing of Pan Am Flight 103 over Scotland that killed 270 people. The following year the United Nations Security Council ordered the men to be extradited; when Libya refused, the international body enacted sanctions. Gaddafi ultimately allowed the Pam Am bombing suspects to be tried in 1999; one suspect was found guilty, and the other was acquitted. In 2003, after Libya agreed to compensate the victims of the plane crash, the United Nations lifted its sanctions. In December 2003 Gaddafi pledged to stop developing weapons of mass destruction, and the United States resumed diplomatic relations with Libya. In 2006 the U.S. government lifted its remaining sanctions.

The first mass demonstrations of the Arab Spring began in 2010; in Libya antigovernment protests started in February 2011 with demands for Gaddafi's resignation. Gaddafi ordered the army to quell the protests, and many were killed in what became a civil war between the military and rebels. The United Nations adopted a resolution to try to protect civilians. Through a NATO mission, France, the United States, and the United Kingdom began bombing Gaddafi's forces and were ultimately joined by other European and Middle Eastern countries. The International Criminal Court issued a warrant to arrest Gaddafi on charges of crimes against humanity in March. In July foreign governments began recognizing the anti-Gaddafi forces, the National Transitional Council. By August most government officials, including Gaddafi, had taken flight or gone into hiding. Fighting continued until October, when Gaddafi was killed. In July 2012 the first democratic elections were held, and Mahmoud

Jibril's National Forces Alliance won a majority over the religious conservative Muslim Brotherhood Party.

In September 2012 Islamist militants killed American ambassador, J. Christopher Stevens, and three of his staff people who were on a diplomatic mission in Benghazi. Many Libyans and Libyan Americans grieved for Stevens, who had supported the 2011 revolution.

SETTLEMENT IN THE UNITED STATES

Generally, the early waves of immigrants (those who arrived between the 1880s and World War II) from Arabic-speaking countries were Lebanese Christians designated by the U.S. government as Syrians. A more varied group of Arabic-speaking immigrants, including Libyans, arrived after World War II, in part because the Immigration Act of 1965 made it easier for non-Europeans to come to the United States. The act abolished the national origins quota system put in place by the 1921 Emergency Quota Act (which had attempted to preserve the ethnic ratios of the U.S. population by accepting new immigrants based on those proportions). The 1965 law instead allowed new immigration according to skills and relationships with U.S. citizens or residents; it allowed more immigrants from developing countries and had a separate quota for refugees. In Libya the economic impact of the oil boom resulted in greater economic freedom for certain populations, particularly a newly created middle class, who were able to travel and study abroad. Libyans began to settle in higher numbers in the United States starting the 1970s, primarily to escape Gaddafi's oppressive regime. Some young men immigrated to avoid forced conscription into the pro-Gaddafi military.

The Libyan American community is among the smallest of the Middle Eastern and North African immigrant populations. In 1990, according to the U.S. Census, there were 2,172 Americans of Libyan ancestry, making up 0.25 percent of the total Arab American population (which was 860,354); by 2000 the number of Libyan Americans had risen to 2,979 and remained at 0.25 percent of the total Arab American population (1,189,731). The State Department's Office of Refugee Resettlement tallied 354 Libyan refugees who had arrived in the United States between 1990 and 2002. According to the report *Middle Eastern and North African Immigrants in the United States* (2011), by Aaron Terrazas of the Migration Policy Institute, "One-third of the foreign born from the Middle East and North Africa in the United States arrived in 2000 or later." Because the newer censuses have counted Libyans as part of the grouping "Other Arabs" for statistical purposes, the number of Libyan Americans is difficult to ascertain. Even though the 2000 Census specifically mentioned that Berbers may not consider themselves Arabs, it counted them as Arab in order to remain consistent with the 1990 Census.

In 2002 the U.S. government began requiring men over the age of sixteen from Libya, Iraq, Sudan, and Syria to be interviewed, fingerprinted, and photographed by an INS agent. With the second Gulf War in 2003, new rules came into effect for asylum seekers from those countries (as well as those from Iran), obliging them to remain in detention while their asylum requests were processed and to complete special registration and comply with other specified conditions. Some of the restrictions—having to do with travel and financial transfers, for example—also applied to American citizens from these countries. The new requirements sparked protests from the Muslim community and civil-liberties groups.

According to a 2010 report by the Arab American Institute, 94 percent of Arab Americans live in metropolitan areas. During the late twentieth century, a number of Libyans settled in Lexington, Kentucky, including former members of the National Front for the Salvation of Libya, a group opposed to Gaddafi.

While Arab Americans may have dissimilar countries of origin, they often join together across nationalities because they may share cultural, linguistic, or religious identities. They also come together because they experience similar discrimination, profiling, and hostility for being Arab or, if they are Muslim, for religious reasons—particularly since the terrorist attacks in the United States in September 2011. Libyan Americans, especially because they are such a small group, may, for instance,

join a mosque community with Muslims from a variety of backgrounds.

During the 2011 Libyan uprising against Gaddafi, some Libyan Americans went back to Libya either to join in the struggle or to help with humanitarian efforts. One Libyan American was reported killed in the fighting.

LANGUAGE

Arabic is the official language of Libya and is spoken by the vast majority of the population. The written language is called Modern Standard Arabic. A modern Libyan dialect that is used for everyday conversation can be understood by other Arabic-speaking peoples. Sometimes school texts (including the Quran) and official documents are written in Classical (or Quranic) Arabic. Other languages spoken include Berber, tribal languages such as Tamasheq and Toubou, Italian, English, and French.

Libyan Americans who are active Muslims—who read and pray from the Quran—speak and read Classical Arabic. Full-time Islamic schools exist around the United States, including the Lexington Universal Academy, which offers prekindergarten through eighth-grade classes in Lexington, Kentucky, where there is a notable Libyan American presence. The Islamic Society of Central Kentucky supports the Al-Bayan Weekend School, whose goal is in part to teach students Arabic terms and phrases and to read the Quran.

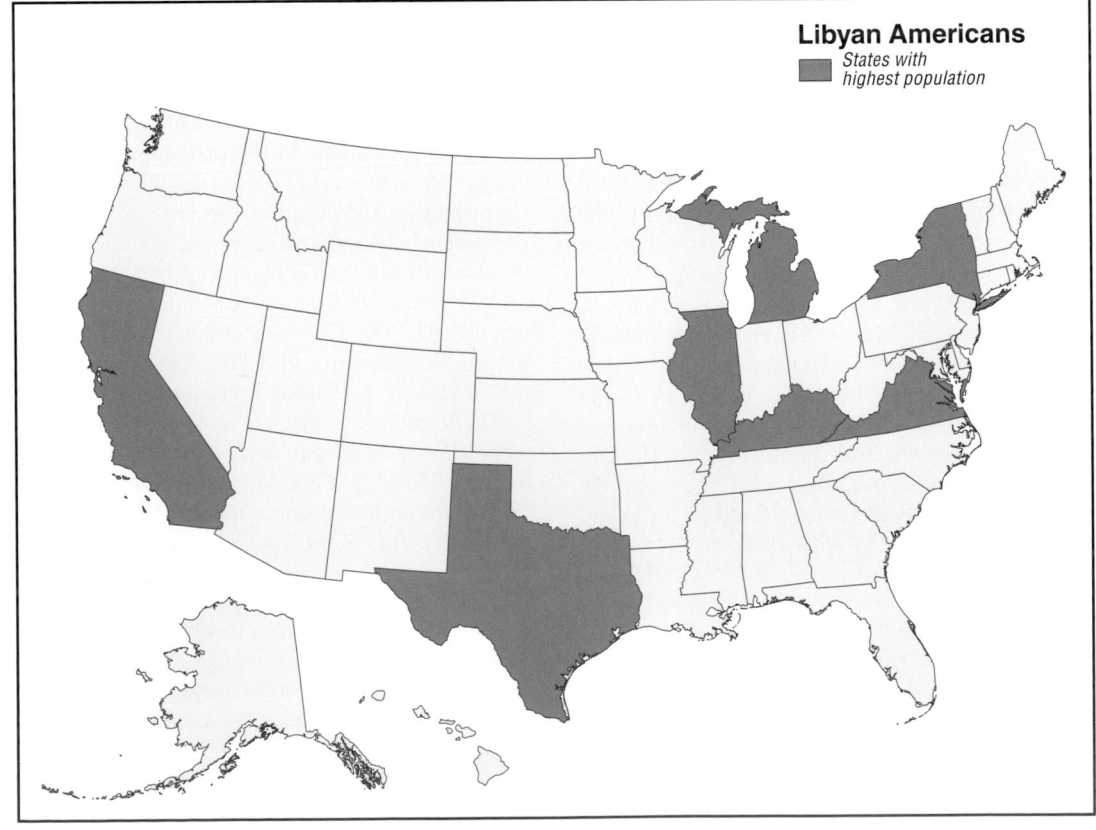

Libyan Americans
States with highest population

RELIGION

Islam is the official religion of Libya. More than 97 percent of the population identifies as Sunni Muslim. Other Muslims include Sufis, Ibadhis, and Sanusis. Coptic Orthodox Christianity (the Christian Church of Egypt) is one of Libya's other religions.

To varying degrees, Libyan Americans join with other Muslims to practice their faith, studying the Quran, praying, worshipping on Fridays, and fasting during the month of Ramadan. Those who are more religious make a variety of accommodations and compromises to adjust to Western school or job schedules, in order, for instance, to perform the five-times-daily prayers. A small number of American public schools allow Muslim students the freedom to gather and pray during the school day.

CULTURE AND ASSIMILATION

Like other Middle Eastern Arabic speakers in the United States, Libyan Americans have preserved their culture in various ways while assimilating in the areas of work, school, and other public functions. In *The New Americans: A Guide to Immigration since 1965*, Mary C. Waters and Reed Ueda posit that, across Middle Eastern Arab American communities, individual immigrants sometimes emphasize their ethnic identity, religious identity, or national identity, as well as multiple identities, depending on the particular situation. Waters and Uedo also point out that Middle Eastern Americans often intermarry, "creating hyphenated identities in the second generation."

Cuisine Traditional Libyan food is influenced by a blend of traditions from African cuisine (often Tunisian), Mediterranean cuisine (often Egyptian), and Italian cuisine. Olives and olive oil, dates, grains, milk, couscous, garlic, and lamb are all common ingredients. Eating and drinking tea provide important gathering times for family and friends.

The most typical Libyan dish is *sharba libiya* (Libyan soup), usually made with lamb, onion, tomatoes, orzo (or other soup pasta), tomato paste, spices such as cayenne and saffron, chickpeas, and lemon. It is often eaten every evening during Ramadan. Other common dishes include *hassa*, a gravy usually made from lamb or beef, garlic, tomatoes, flour, hot peppers, turmeric, cilantro, basil, and mint; and *m'batten*, fried potatoes stuffed with meat and herbs. *Bazin* is a dome made from barley and wheat flour placed in the middle of a plate and covered with a sauce made from such ingredients as fried onions, garlic, lamb, turmeric, and other spices, served with boiled eggs around the outside of the dish, *amsayar* (pickled chilies), and lemon. Among popular Libyan desserts are *asidah*, a boiled dough served with date syrup or honey; *magrood*, date-filled cookies; *ghreyba*, butter cookies; and *mhalbiya*, rice pudding.

Libyan tea is usually very strong, almost syrup-like, and is served with sugar and sometimes mint. Mint tea is also common. Tea is often served with peanuts.

SHARBA (LAMB SOUP WITH MINT)

Ingredients

7 ounces lamb meat, chopped into small cubes

1 onion, chopped

1 tomato, finely chopped

¼ cup olive oil

2 tablespoons tomato paste

1 tablespoon dried mint

4 tablespoons parsley, finely chopped

½ cup orzo

½ cup canned chickpeas

6½ cups boiling water

1 heaped teaspoon each of: turmeric, black pepper, red paprika

1 cinnamon stick

5 cardamom pods, crushed

A few shaiba leaves (known as dagad phool in Indian cuisine, optional)

3 bay leaves

Preparation

Pour the oil in a pot, add the chopped lamb and chopped onion, drop in any whole spices you are using, and stir on medium heat for a few minutes until the oil is infused and spices are aromatic. Add the ground spices, chickpeas, chopped tomato, and tomato paste and cook for few minutes on medium heat, stirring occasionally. Add 2 cups water and 2 tablespoons of parsley, then cover and cook on low heat for 45 minutes.

Once the lamb is cooked, remove the whole spices. Add 4 cups of boiling water, then add the rest of the parsley and orzo. Continue cooking for 15 more minutes, then turn off heat.

After turning off the heat, rub a handful of dried mint between the palms of your hands straight into the pot, then give the soup a final stir.

Serve with lemon wedges and tanoor bread.

Serves 4

Muslim Libyan Americans also follow Islamic standards for what foods and drinks are and are not permissible (pork and alcohol are *haram*, or forbidden), as well as for specific religious preparations for food.

Traditional Dress Male traditional dress usually includes drawstring pants, a long, loose gown, a vest (*faramla*), and a tasseled cap (*tagevaor*). Women who dress traditionally wear long dresses (*farashia*) and hair coverings or scarves and are covered from head to toe. A profusion of gold jewelry is customary. In Libyan cities, especially among the younger

LIBYAN PROVERBS

The absentee has his own justification.

Others have reasons for their actions.

Stretch your legs according to your coverlet.

Do not live beyond your means.

They sell the monkey and laugh at the buyer.

Describes a person known for deceiving other people.

The flute player dies with his finger shaking.

Habits are lifelong.

If the sun starts to move west, find a shady tree.

Problems are constant, and you need to continuously solve them.

Who would tell the lion that his breath stinks?

Be careful who you criticize because of how they could retaliate.

The needle will be lost if the thread is too long.

Use what you need and not more; do not talk too much.

Only you can scratch your itch.

Look after your own interests.

generation, Western clothing (such as business suits or jeans) or a mix of styles is more common than full traditional dress, except on holidays or other special occasions. Libyan Americans commonly follow Western styles, although religious Muslims wear more traditional dress, especially head coverings for women.

Dances and Songs Dance and music often accompany Libyan celebrations such as weddings. According to custom, men and women dance separately. Typical traditional instruments include the *'oud* (similar to a lute), *zokra* (similar to bagpipes), *darbuka* (a type of drum), and *al-nayy* (a bamboo pipe).

An important contemporary musical figure amongst some in the Libyan American community is hip-hop artist Khaled M. At the start of the revolution against Gaddafi, Khaled and a network of resistance groups created a protest song to raise awareness about the atrocities in Libya. The song and video, "Can't Take Our Freedom," features Khaled, Iraqi-British rapper LowKey, and graphic footage from Libya and was uploaded to YouTube.

Holidays Most Libyan Americans are Muslims and celebrate Islamic holidays. Ramadan is a month-long fast during which Muslims refrain from eating, drinking, and other physical needs during daylight hours. It is a time for spiritual renewal, focusing on what is important in life, and for practicing self-sacrifice. Eid al-Fitr (sometimes spelled Id al-Fitr or Eid ul-Fitr), the feast of breaking the fast at the end of Ramadan, is one of the two major Muslim holidays. It starts on the first day of the Islamic calendar month of Shawwal (the Islamic calendar is a lunar calendar, so the time of the holiday varies in the Gregorian calendar). The feast can last up to three days. Eid al-Fitr is a joyful holiday spent praising and giving thanks to God. People eat special foods with family and friends, sometimes dress in their best (often traditional) clothes, decorate their homes with lights, give presents to children, forgive wrongdoings, give charity, and participate in early daily prayers.

The second major Muslim holiday is Eid al-Adha, the feast of sacrifice, which commemorates the willingness of the biblical figure Ibraham (Abraham) to sacrifice his son Isaac to God. It occurs at the end of the time of the Hajj (a set date on the Islamic calendar, it varies from year to year on the Gregorian calendar), an important pillar of Islam that requires Muslims to undertake a pilgrimage to Mecca at least once in their life, provided they have the financial means and are healthy enough to do so. In the United States, Muslims celebrate Eid al-Adha for up to four days with praying and social gatherings, wearing traditional clothing, sharing special foods, giving gifts, and offering blessings to others.

FAMILY AND COMMUNITY LIFE

Family life is very important in Libyan culture. Children are taught to respect and obey adults, especially the elderly. The Libyan-American Scholarship Fund conducted a survey of Libyan American youths of high school and college age in 2008. They reported that a high percentage of survey participants came from large households, with an average of 4.7 people per household, compared to a median of 2.6 for the overall American population. The survey also found that community life was of great importance to young Libyan Americans—60 percent of those surveyed said they were involved in some type of community or volunteer work. Additionally, the survey found that education was greatly valued and pursued.

Gender Roles Islam has traditionally been enacted as a patriarchal religion that generally mandates different roles for males and females in family and community. However, for Libyan Americans the concepts of gender roles, particularly in the public sphere, have been influenced by their time living under the Gaddafi regime. At that time the government emphasized working toward gender equality in the political and public spheres, especially in the arenas of legal status, education, and "public presence." For instance, in 1979 women were required to have military training before marriage. Various laws were enacted to give women equal pay, control of their income and assets, rights in marriage and divorce, equal access to education, and rights to participate in the General People's Committees. However, the laws were often ignored, avoided through loopholes, and applied unequally (particularly family laws and those contradicting Islamic law and tradition). Despite opposition to Gaddafi's regime, Libyan Americans' ideas about the need for gender equality may be stronger than those of Arab immigrants from countries where the topic was not addressed as openly.

Libyan women played prominent roles in the fight against Gaddafi, helping smuggle arms, among other activities. As in other nations that have experienced the Arab Spring, however, women have been underrepresented in high-level decision making. In 2011 the first international women's rights conference was held in Libya. Debates about the importance of gender equality and women's participation in the new government continue. Many Libyans living in the diaspora, including Libyan Americans, have been actively involved and connected with the Libyan revolution and have informed these debates.

Education The Libyan-American Scholarship Fund's 2009 Community Survey canvassed fifty-four Libyan Americans ranging in age from fifteen to thirty (the average age was twenty-one). It reported that 13 percent were high school students, 53.7 percent were undergraduates, and 16.7 percent were pursuing graduate or professional degrees. The vast majority of their families were highly educated, with 92.7 percent of fathers and 47.2 percent of mothers having earned bachelor's degrees. Of the college students, 87 percent wanted to pursue postgraduate studies. Business and biological sciences were the most common fields of study.

Young Libyan American Muslims may attend after-school or immersion programs that teach Arabic, Islam, Arab cultural topics, and sometimes traditional academic subjects.

Courtship and Weddings For Sunni Muslims (the predominant religion of Libyans), marriage is a legal agreement with a contract that can be drawn up in a mosque or in someone's home; the agreement is called a *nikaahnamah*. Traditional weddings in Libya can last as long as four days. Immersion in Western traditions, scheduling, and costs usually limit Libyan American weddings to one day. There is often music, dancing, and a feast with special foods. A common tradition is for the bride and other females to decorate their hands and feet with elaborate designs using henna dye.

Relations with Other Americans Aside from generalized misconceptions about Islam and anti-Arab sentiments in the United States, Libyan Americans also experienced a certain amount of fear of discrimination after their countrymen's 1988 bombing of the Pan Am flight over Scotland and again after the terrorist attacks in the United States on September 11, 2001.

Islam has traditionally been enacted as a patriarchal religion that generally mandates different roles for males and females in family and community. However, for Libyan Americans the concepts of gender roles, particularly in the public sphere, have been influenced by their time living under the Gaddafi regime. At that time the government emphasized working toward gender equality in the political and public spheres.

EMPLOYMENT AND ECONOMIC CONDITIONS

U.S. Census statistics for those in the "Other Arabs" category suggest that Libyan Americans have a higher than average income (for both men and women) and tend to be in professional or managerial positions more often than in blue-collar jobs.

The 2009 Libyan-American Scholarship Fund survey reported on the earnings of the survey participants' (aged fifteen to thirty) parents: 11.7 percent earned less than $30,000 annually, 57.6 percent earned more than $50,000, and over 40 percent earned more than $70,000. While these figures seem to reflect relative affluence amongst a majority of participants, the report also points out that participants came from larger-than-average households that, accordingly, had greater financial need; 35.3 percent of participants, for instance, qualified for federal government Pell Grants for higher education, which are given only to those with serious financial need.

Like other Arab Americans, Libyan Americans have experienced employment discrimination. It became so frequent after 9/11 that the U.S. Equal Employment Opportunity Commission published a document for employers about the workplace rights of Muslims, Arabs, South Asians, and Sikhs.

As a result of the civil unrest in Libya in 2011, Libyan students who were enrolled as members of a Student and Exchange Visitor Program in an institution certified by U.S. Immigration and Customs Enforcement (ICE) were allowed to increase the number of hours they could legally work because of "the worry of financial burdens due to the armed conflict."

POLITICS AND GOVERNMENT

In 2011 and 2012, Libyan Americans became very involved on a number of levels with the anti-Gaddafi uprising and Libya's new provisional government. Many were young second-generation Libyan Americans who had not previously been politically active. Some Libyan Americans returned to Libya to fight in the struggle or provide humanitarian assistance.

Libyan Americans continued to be highly involved with their home country after the uprising. When democratic Libyan elections were held in July 2012, Libyan Americans were able to vote in Washington, D.C. Many traveled from around the country to do so, the majority of whom were voting for the first time and, not infrequently, hoping to elect relatives or friends to the parliament. In "Libya Hurra: Hope Runs High for Libyan American Voters" (July 13, 2012), an article published by the Arab American Institute, Sara Jawhari explained their pride, quoting the words of Abdulrahman Aduib, a Libyan American from Chicago:

> Getting on the airplane with my parents this morning [to vote in Washington, D.C.], we were discussing who we were going to vote for and we were talking about people who we actually know. These are people I've broken bread with, have had conversations with and in some cases I'm related to, people [on the ballot]. To think I could vote for someone I actually know, that in and of itself, is tremendous. I cannot explain how proud I am of my people, my generation, my cousins and the people that made the ultimate sacrifice throughout it all.

NOTABLE INDIVIDUALS

Academics Khaled Mattawa (1964–) was born in Benghazi and immigrated to the United States in 1979. He is a poet, literary translator (mostly translating Arabic poetry into English), and professor of creative writing at the University of Michigan, Ann Arbor. His books include *Ismailia Eclipse: Poems* (1995), *Zodiac of Echoes* (2003), *Amorisco* (2008), and *Tocqueville* (2010).

Journalism Fadel Lamen is a Libyan journalist, writer, and Middle East/North Africa expert and cultural advisor based in Washington, D.C. His work has been published in Arabic and English newspapers and magazines. He has been interviewed by major media outlets in English and Arabic on issues related to the Middle East, Islam, and American foreign policy. He is the president of the American-Libyan Council in Washington, D.C.

Music Khaled M is a Libyan American hip-hop artist. His father was a Libyan revolutionary who was tortured in a Libyan prison for protesting against the Gaddafi regime. Most of Khaled's younger years were spent moving frequently across North Africa, Europe, and the United States to escape detainment by the Libyan government. He and his family settled in Lexington, Kentucky, with other anti-Gaddafi activists and refugees. Now based in Chicago, Khaled has been featured on CNN, ABC World News, Yahoo! News, the BBC, and

NPR and in *Complex* and *Mother Jones* magazines. CNN placed him on its list of Most Interesting People.

ORGANIZATIONS AND ASSOCIATIONS

Libyan American Organization

The association originated in a 2011 meeting of Libyan Americans called to celebrate the end of the Gaddafi regime and discuss their role in Libya's future. The official founding and election of a board of directors occurred during the 2012 Libyan Community Conference in Washington, D.C. The association states that its mission is "to provide a platform for the Libyan American community to network, advance mutual interests, and organize at a national level."

Email: info@libyanamericanorganization.org
URL: www.libyanamericanorganization.org

Libyan-American Scholarship Fund (LASF)

The LASF is a grassroots nonprofit organization helping to support the educational needs of Libyan Americans by providing need- and merit-based scholarships and enrichment programs for students and parents.

P.O. Box 36-20220 PACC
New York, New York 10129
Email: info@libyanscholar.org
URL: http://libyanscholar.org

MUSEUMS AND RESEARCH CENTERS

The Center for Libyan American Strategic Studies (CLASS)

CLASS's stated aim is "fostering strategic economic, political, and cultural relationships between the United States and Libya." The center works on information exchange, critical analysis, and research, providing policy recommendations to United States and Libyan government officials and to scholars and civic leaders.

Asma Rekik, Executive Director
3133 Barkley Drive
Fairfax, Virginia 22031
Phone: (888) 998-0618
Email: info@libyanamericanstudies.org
URL: www.libyanamericanstudies.org

SOURCES FOR ADDITIONAL STUDY

Abdalla, Saleh E., and Janice T. Gibson. "The Relationship of Exposure to American Culture on the Attitude of Libyan Nationals toward the Role of Women in the Workforce." *Contemporary Educational Psychology* 9, no. 3 (July 1984).

Kramer, Sarah Kate. "Young Libyan Americans Driving Diaspora Opposition Movement." *Feet in Two Worlds*, March 3, 2011. http://fi2w.org/2011/03/03/

LIBYAN AMERICANS AND THE ARAB SPRING

Sarah Kate Kramer interviewed Libyan Americans for the article "Young Libyan Americans Driving Diaspora Opposition Movement," published in 2011 on the website *Feet in Two Worlds*. Kramer stated, "The uprising against Colonel Muammar el-Qaddafi in Libya has sparked fire in the Libyan Diaspora, particularly among second-generation youth who have never touched Libyan soil." One interviewee was Yasmeen Ar-Rayani, a twenty-year-old Libyan American student at Columbia University. She organized a 2011 protest in front of the United Nations and helped network with Libyan Americans around the country to support anti-Gaddafi forces. Yuseff Assed, a second-generation twenty-seven-year-old Columbia University student, said he always had an interest in Libya, but until the uprising it was academic rather than political. After the uprising, he began working on writings on the Libyan political situation that he hoped would correct how it was "erroneously depicted in Western media." He also helped organize events at the Middle East Institute in Washington, D.C., to inform people of a more realistic view of what is happening in Libya.

Other Libyan Americans became even more involved by returning to Libya to fight or work in humanitarian efforts. The MSNBC report "Libyan-Americans Rush Off to Join Fight Against Gadhafi," by Miranda Leitsinger (March 31, 2011), discussed Libyan American Ibrahim Elifirijani, a sixty-year-old auto repair shop owner from Illinois, and his son, Sanad, an operations manager for an oil company who had fled Libya with his mother and sister in 2003. Both returned to Libya during the uprising. Ibrahim helped with communications equipment on the front lines, while Sanad worked on humanitarian and communication efforts.

young-libyan-americans-driving-diaspora-opposition-movement/.

Kumeh, Titania. "Rebel Music, Libyan Edition." *Mother Jones*, April 11, 2011. http://www.motherjones.com/mixed-media/2011/04/libya-interview-khaled-m-lowkey-hip-hop.

Mills, Gregory J. "Beyond the Backlash: Muslim and Middle Eastern Immigrants' Experiences in America, Ten Years Post-9/11." PhD diss., University of South Florida, Scholars Commons, 2012.

Reimers, David. *Other Immigrants: The Global Origins of the American People*. New York: NYU Press, 2005.

Waters, Mary C.; Reed Ueda; and Helen B. Marrow, eds. *The New Americans: A Guide to Immigration since 1965*. Boston: Harvard University Press Reference Library, 2007.

LITHUANIAN AMERICANS

Mark A. Granquist

OVERVIEW

Lithuanian Americans are immigrants or descendants of people from Lithuania, a country in northeastern Europe. Lithuania is the most southern of the Baltic states, bordered by the Baltic Sea on the east, by Poland and Kaliningrad (Russian Federation) in the southwest, Belarus in the east, and Latvia in the north. The country has four main regions: Dzūkija, the southeast; Suvalkija, the southwest; Žemaitija, the northwest; and Aukštaitija, the center/northeastern lakes. Lithuania has 750 rivers and 4,000 lakes. It measures 25,174 square miles (64,445 square kilometers), making it slightly larger than West Virginia.

According to the *CIA World Factbook*, the population of Lithuania in 2012 was 3,525,761. The majority, 79 percent, are Roman Catholic; other significant religious affiliations are Russian Orthodox at 4.1 percent and Protestant, including Lutheran and Evangelical Christian Baptist, at 1.9 percent of the population. While small in population, Lithuanian Muslims and Jews also have active communities. A quarter of a million Lithuanian Jews perished during the Holocaust. According to 2009 figures, 84 percent of the population is ethnically Lithuanian, 6.1 percent are Poles, 4.9 percent are Russians, and 3.9 are percent Belarusians. Lithuania and the other Baltic republics formerly under Soviet rule were hit hard in the 2008–2009 European financial crisis; the country's gross domestic product (GDP) fell 15 percent in 2009 alone. However, economic reforms by the government have helped Lithuania recover quickly. The GDP rose 1.3 percent in 2010 and 5.8 percent in 2011, making Lithuania's economy one of the fastest growing in the European Union.

The first significant wave of Lithuanian immigration to the United States began in the late 1860s. Many settled in Pennsylvania, where they worked in the coal mines; others made their way to urban areas, such as Boston and Chicago, where the majority worked in industry, stockyards, and slaughterhouses. The number of immigrants who arrived before 1899 is unknown, however, because until that year the U.S. Immigration Bureau recorded Lithuanian immigrants as Polish or Russian. The second wave of immigration had a greater impact on U.S. Census figures. Following World War II, a flood of displaced refugees fled west to escape the Russian reoccupation of Lithuania. Eventually 30,000 *dipukai* (war refugees or displaced persons), including educated leaders and professionals who hoped to return someday to Lithuania, settled in the United States. Many of these post-World War II Lithuanian immigrants settled in Southern California. The third wave of immigration to the United States began after the dissolution of the Soviet Union in 1990; this wave ebbed with the decline of the dollar and the entry of Lithuania into the European Union in 2004.

The U.S. Census Bureau's 2011 American Community Survey reported an estimated 654,004 people of Lithuanian descent in the United States, which is around 0.2 percent of the U.S. population. The states with the largest populations of Lithuanian Americans are Pennsylvania, Illinois, California, Massachusetts, New York, and Connecticut.

HISTORY OF THE PEOPLE

Early History The Lithuanians are ethnically part of the Baltic group of Indo-European peoples, most closely related to the Latvians. While Lithuanians started to form a distinct group in the early second century, it was not until Duke Mindaugas united several groups in 1236 to form the Grand Duchy of Lithuania that a Lithuanian state was established. During the fourteenth century the state grew in importance by maintaining a strong monarchy and annexing neighboring lands. Vilnius became the capital in 1323.

Lithuania became one of the largest kingdoms in medieval Europe and remained pagan for many years despite attempts by the Catholics and the Orthodox Church to Christianize it. In 1386 the region forged a close alliance with Poland and the two crowns united, and the following year Lithuania accepted Roman Catholicism as its official religion. The combined forces of Lithuania and Poland defeated the German (Teutonic) invaders of 1410. By 1569, Polish language and culture had begun to dominate the Lithuanian upper classes, although the peasantry remained culturally and linguistically Lithuanian.

In the eighteenth century, the rise of Russia, combined with the weakness of the Polish-Lithuanian state, led to increasing Russian domination of Lithuania. In 1772, 1793, and 1795 Poland was partitioned. By the second partition, whatever remained of Lithuanian Belorussia was transferred to Russian rule, and in the third partition, Russia incorporated Lithuanian territory east of the Nieman River. Throughout the nineteenth century, Russia attempted a program of "Russification" of Lithuanian lands, which included the prohibition of Lithuanian language and literature, the imposition of Russian legal codes, and the forcible integration of Uniate (or Byzantine Rite) Catholicism into the Orthodox Church. Beginning in the 1880s, a nationalistic movement emerged, challenging Polish cultural domination and Russian governmental controls. Following the Russian Revolution of 1905 and the organization of the *Lietuvi Socialista Partija Amerikoje* (Lithuanian Socialist Party of America), a Lithuanian assembly convened and demanded a greater degree of territorial and cultural autonomy.

Russian rule of Lithuania came to an end with the German invasion and occupation of the territory during World War I, and the Lithuanian Republic was born in 1918. Achieving actual independence proved more complicated, with opposing forces of Germany, Poland, and the Soviet Union involved in the new country's dealings, but within two years the region attained self-rule. From 1920 to 1940, Lithuania was an independent nation with a free-market economy that traded agricultural products with European and Scandinavian countries.

Modern Era With the outbreak of World War II, political upheaval returned to Lithuania. In 1940 the Soviet Union took over control of the country only to lose it to the Germans from 1941 to 1944. Soviet forces then retook Lithuania at the conclusion of the war, and many thousands of Lithuanian refugees fled westward along with the retreating German army. Between 1940 and 1954, armed guerrilla fighters, called "Forest Brothers," fought for Lithuanian independence. The Soviet Union responded harshly to these challenges to its authority, enacting mass deportations and other cruelties.

In 1990 the freely elected Lithuanian legislature declared independence, and the Soviet Union, itself very weakened during this time, was not able to force Lithuania back under its power. After the collapse of the Soviet Union in 1991, Russia recognized Lithuania's autonomy. Independence hero Vytautas Landsbergis led the new Lithuanian government with members of his Sajudis political party/movement. They enacted strong economic and social reforms concerning, for instance, land reform and restitution of property, health care, and citizenship. One of their first pieces of legislation restored Lithuanian citizenship to those who requested it. Their policy of full employment and payments for illness, disability, maternity leave, and old age were extremely ambitious. Many of their economic policies proved to be slow and ineffective, largely due to the overwhelming impact of the global economy and rising energy costs.

A new constitution was needed, but Sajudis members disputed what should be in it, and passage of the constitution was delayed. Failed policies and infighting were major reasons why voters rejected Sajudis leadership in 1992 and voted in those who had been members of the former Communist Party. In this 1992 referendum, a majority of the electorate voted to approve a new constitution based on earlier Lithuanian constitutions, as well as those from France, Germany, and the United States. The new constitution addressed human rights, defense, and minority status; laid out a structure for the legislative and executive branches; enumerated democratic principles such as freedom of speech and religion; and instituted social rights, including free education and health care. While the policies of the Communist Party differed from those of Sajudis, economic hardships continued due to high energy costs and price deregulation. A banking crisis erupted in 1995 after the country's two largest banks were charged with embezzlement, leading the government to suspend their operations. This ultimately led to the dismissal of Prime Minister Adolfas Šleževičius in 1996.

The Russian financial crisis of 1998 and other global economic crises greatly impacted both economic and political reforms in Lithuania. However, by 2004 the country was stable enough to gain membership in the North Atlantic Treaty Organization (NATO) and the European Union (EU). Its 2007 application to join the eurozone was rejected because of its high inflation rate. In 2009 the country's first female president, Dalia Grybauskaitė, was elected with nearly 70 percent of the vote. Lithuanian leaders hoped to meet all the requirements for joining the Eurozone by 2014 or 2015.

SETTLEMENT IN THE UNITED STATES

The first Lithuanians immigrated to the New World long before the American Revolution. As early as 1660, Aleksandras Kursius, a Lithuanian physician and Latin teacher, is believed to have lived in New York, then known as New Amsterdam. During the U.S. Civil War, people with Lithuanian surnames fought in the armies of both the North and the South. It is difficult to know exactly how many Lithuanians came to the United States before 1900 because they were recorded as Poles or Russians in census data. The best estimate is that during that time nearly 400,000 Lithuanians immigrated to the United States.

Lithuanians had many reasons to emigrate. The abolition of serfdom in the Russian Empire allowed peasants more personal freedom, including the freedom to leave; the "Russification" of Lithuania after the failed 1863 uprising led to a compulsory and oppressive Russian tsarist military draft; and Lithuania experienced a famine in 1867 and 1868. Emigration was also motivated by an economic crisis in which many farms failed as industrialization took hold. Many immigrants who arrived during these

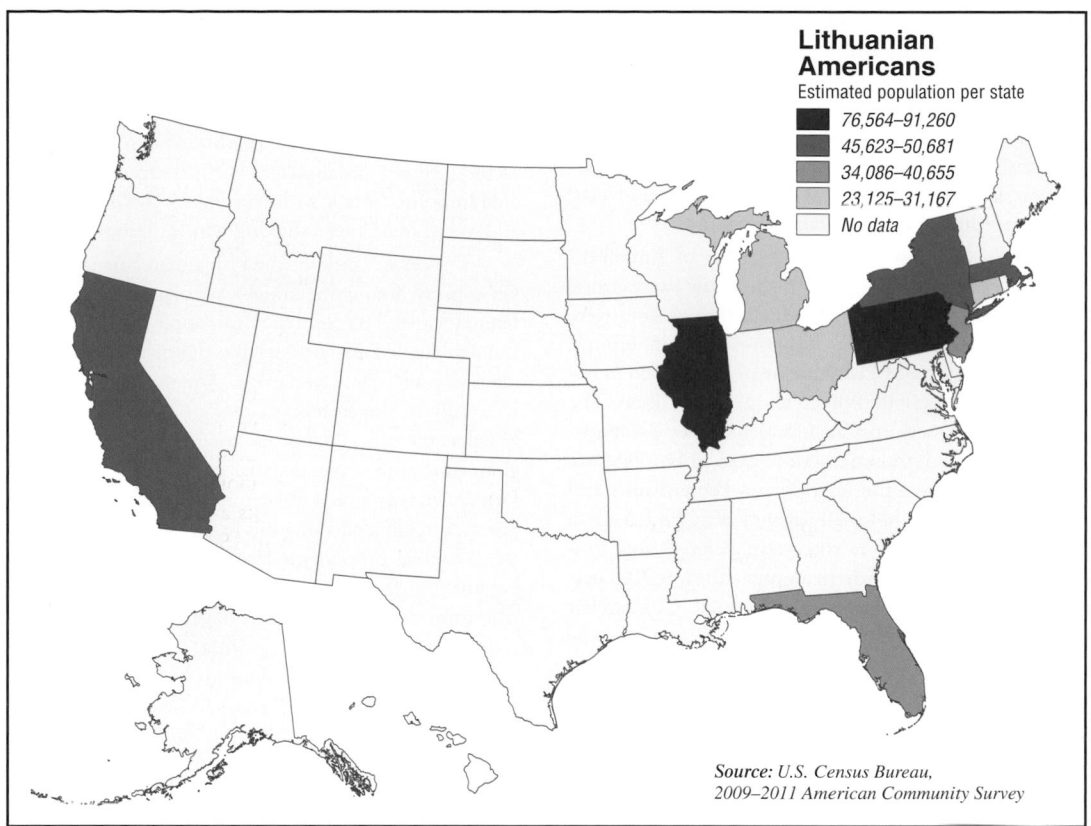

Lithuanian Americans

Estimated population per state

- 76,564–91,260
- 45,623–50,681
- 34,086–40,655
- 23,125–31,167
- No data

Source: U.S. Census Bureau, 2009–2011 American Community Survey

years were peasants and workers with little economic cushion. They lived and worked on farms in the New York area, helped build railroads, and worked in coal mines in Pennsylvania. Many moved to Chicago after the Great Chicago Fire of 1871, working in the city's factories and its vast slaughterhouses and stockyards. Some became tailors in New York and Baltimore.

A larger wave of immigration occurred between 1880 and 1914, which included political dissidents who emigrated illegally and Jews who were forced to emigrate. In 1930 the U.S. Census Bureau listed 193,600 Lithuanians in the United States, with almost 50 percent of Lithuanian Americans living in just ten metropolitan areas. Chicago, Cleveland, Detroit, Pittsburgh, New York, and Boston had the largest Lithuanian American population. Nearly 20 percent of all Lithuanian immigrants at this time settled in Chicago. The Johnson-Reed Act of 1924, which instituted a national origins quota for immigration, virtually stopped all Lithuanian immigration to the United States until after World War II.

Settled Anglo Americans viewed Lithuanian immigrants as part of the "immigration problem" of the late nineteenth century. The poverty and illiteracy of many of the new arrivals, their Eastern European language and culture, and their devotion to Roman Catholicism put them at a distinct disadvantage in a country where scores of immigrants from a multitude of countries were competing for jobs, housing, and a better life. Because Lithuanians often took low-paying, unskilled labor positions, they were considered less desirable than other immigrant groups. In addition, their involvement in the U.S. labor movement at the turn of the twentieth century led to even more discrimination and resentment from a suspicious American public. Lithuanians played an important role in the growth of the United Mine Workers Union and the United Garment Workers Union and were involved in labor unrest in the meat packing and steel industries. Throughout the twentieth century, however, Lithuanian Americans began to climb the economic ladder.

During the second wave of immigration, U.S. Census figures listed the nationality of those from Lithuania as Lithuanian. In World War II, Lithuania was invaded first by the Soviet Union in 1940, then by Nazi Germany in 1941, and again by the Soviet Union in 1944. Lithuanian refugees fled from the Soviets at the end of the war, many under the Displaced Persons Act of 1948. Many of these immigrants were middle and upper class, including doctors, professors, lawyers, and civil servants who hoped to return to Lithuania someday, but the ensuing Cold War made this difficult.

A smaller third wave of immigration began after the dissolution of the Soviet Union in 1991. With Lithuania's independence, the borders were opened, but decades of Soviet rule had resulted in a weak economy. Many of those who emigrated during this wave were younger people seeking better economic opportunities outside the country. Lithuanian immigration has slowed with the decline of the dollar and the entry of Lithuania into the EU in 2004, making countries such as Ireland and the United Kingdom better economic options for Lithuanian immigrants.

Accurately estimating the number of Americans of Lithuanian ethnic origin is difficult, in part because of the long period during which Lithuanians were considered part of other Eastern European groups. Modern estimates of Lithuanians in the United States have ranged from 500,000 to about two million. The 2009–2011 American Community Survey estimated the number of Lithuanian Americans to be 680,066. Many Lithuanian Americans live in Pennsylvania and Chicago. In 2011 the small town of New Philadelphia in the coal region of northeastern Pennsylvania estimated its Lithuanian American population at 20.8 percent, the largest percentage in the country. Chicago has been called "the American capital of Lithuania" because of its large Lithuanian population. The only sizable immigrant community in Grand County, Colorado, a predominantly homogenous rural community in the mountains, is that of the Lithuanians.

LANGUAGE

Lithuanian, the official language of the country, is a part of the Baltic branch of the Indo-European language family, closely related to Latvian and the now-extinct language known as Old Prussian. Wider relationships, whether to German or the Slavic languages, are difficult to establish. Lithuanian maintains many early features that other Indo-European languages have lost. The first attempts at creating a written version of the language date from the sixteenth century, when the first book in Lithuanian was printed. Strong Polish cultural influences and Russian imperial policies combined to stymie development of the Lithuanian language for hundreds of years; thus, modern literary Lithuanian is essentially a product of the twentieth century. During the many periods of history when Russia and the Soviet Union ruled over Lithuania, Russia forcefully encouraged the population to speak Russian, and as a result most Lithuanians today also speak Russian.

Lithuanian is divided into Low and High dialects, with numerous subdialects. The language uses eleven vowels (*a*, *ą*, *e*, *ę*, *ė*, *i*, *į*, *y*, *o*, *u*, *ų*, and *ū*) along with six diphthongs (*ai*, *au*, *ei*, *ui*, *ie*, and *uo*). In addition to most of the standard consonants of the English language, Lithuanian makes use of *č*, *š*, and *ž*; however, the consonants *f* and *h* and the combination *ch* are used only in foreign words.

Lithuanian "curses" or "oaths" are also informative of the culture. They are a mix of folk beliefs from different times, containing pagan and Christian elements, with references to mythological characters and magic, such as *Suk tave devynios!*, which literally translates as Twist yourself in nine," meaning leave me alone, and *O tu rupuzgalvi!*, which means ("Oh, you toad head").

Gestures are also an important accompaniment to the Lithuanian language. For instance, it is considered impolite to talk with your hands in your pockets, and one should avoid shaking hands in doorways.

The preservation of the Lithuanian language was a key concern among the initial wave of immigrants to the United States. The cultural domination of the Polinified Lithuanians led to considerable dissension among the members of the Lithuanian American community. Especially in the Roman Catholic Church, Polish prevailed as the official language used in worship and religious education, a practice that came under attack from Lithuanian Americans. Religious organizations and their priests were divided along this issue; eventually, however, the Polophile proponents lost and modern Lithuanian became the language of the community. Immigrants who came after World War II have worked to keep the Lithuanian language alive within the community by developing a network of schools to encourage its preservation. The U.S. Census Bureau's American Community survey reported in 2010 that 42,300 Americans spoke Lithuanian at home (about 6 percent of the Lithuanian American population). Of those who did, 66 percent also stated that they spoke English fluently.

A number of Lithuanian American newspapers are published in Lithuanian, including the *Vakarai*, published in Chicago and online and distributed internationally. Several universities and colleges offer Lithuanian language courses, such as the University of Illinois at Chicago, the University of Washington (Seattle), and the University of California in Los Angeles.

Greetings and Popular Expressions Common Lithuanian greetings and other expressions include the following: *labą rytą* (lahba reehta)—good morning; *labą* vakara (lahba vahkahra)—good evening; *labanaktis* (lahba-nahktees)—good night; *sudievu* (sood-yeeh-voo)—goodbye; *kaip tamsta gyvuoji* (kaip tahmstah geeh-vu-oyee)—how are you?; *labai gerai* (lahbai gar-ai)—quite well; *dėkui* (deh-kooy)—thanks; *atsiprašau* (aht-see-prah-show)—excuse me; *sveikas* (say-kahs)—welcome; *taip* (taip)—yes; *ne* (nah)—no; *turiu eiti* (toor-i-oo ay-tee)—I must go.

RELIGION

The large majority of Lithuanian immigrants were Roman Catholic. The first Lithuanian Roman Catholic parish in the United States was the St. George parish in Shenandoah, Pennsylvania, founded March 30, 1891. Small numbers of Lithuanian immigrants were Lutherans, Jews, and Orthodox Christians. The dominance of Roman Catholicism in the Lithuanian American community is pronounced due to the religion's influence in a number of Lithuanian institutions. However, the Roman Catholic presence was not universal.

Lithuania adopted Christianity in the late fourteenth century when Lithuanian Grand Duke Jogailo married the heiress to the throne of Poland, converted to Christianity, and was crowned King of Poland as Władysław II Jagiełło. For many centuries Lithuanian Catholicism was Polish in language and orientation. Because Lithuanian was considered to be a barbaric language, Polish was used for all religious business. This language dominance extended to the immigrant communities in the United States as well; early Lithuanian immigrants tended to join Polish-language Roman Catholic parishes, and Polish-leaning priests dominated many of the early institutions of the Lithuanian American community.

The rising tide of Lithuanian nationalism toward the end of the nineteenth century sparked profound changes in the Lithuanian American religious community. Under the leadership of Aleksandras Burba, a priest from Lithuania, some Lithuanian Americans began to pull away from Polish parishes and Polish-dominated institutions and establish their own Lithuanian parishes. More than 100 Lithuanian parishes were formed by 1920. This movement created considerable tension within the immigrant community but also helped define a sense of ethnic consciousness among Lithuanian Americans. Not all Lithuanians wanted to distance themselves from Polish Roman Catholicism, however, and divisiveness soon clouded the ranks of many Lithuanian American organizations.

An immigrant priest, Father Antanas Staniukynas, formed the Lithuanian American Roman Catholic Priests' League in 1909 and was instrumental in the establishment of many Lithuanian American parishes. Staniukynas also contributed to the establishment of religious orders in the immigrant community, including the Sisters of St. Casimir and an American branch of the Lithuanian Marian Fathers. Around the same time, many lay Roman Catholic organizations were also founded; fraternal and social organizations were formed for men, women, workers, students, and other lay groups. Probably the most lasting and impressive achievement was the formation of a large parochial school system in affiliation with the Lithuanian American Roman Catholic parishes, a system run largely by the immigrant religious orders. By 1941 there were 124 parishes. Most of them had a grammar school headed by Lithuanian priests and nuns and taught Lithuanian language classes.

Religious life in the United States was not without conflict for the Lithuanian Roman Catholics. The old style of autocratic priestly leadership soon gave way to the realities of a democratic and pluralistic America, and the laity demanded an increased role in parish government. After 1945 the influx of war refugees brought new members to Lithuanian American Roman

Catholicism. New religious orders were established, including the Sisters of the Immaculate Conception and the Lithuanian Franciscan and Jesuit priestly orders.

In 1914 the Lithuanian National Catholic Church was formed in Scranton, Pennsylvania. This movement, which broke away from the Roman Catholic hierarchy in the United States, stressed the Lithuanian dimension of Catholicism. Lithuanian National Catholic parishes flourished in areas of heavy Lithuanian settlements early in the twentieth century.

In the late twentieth and early twenty-first century, a religious divide has often separated immigrants of different waves and generations. Saulius Kuprys, president of the Lithuanian American Council in 2013, said that recent Lithuanian immigrants who lived under the Soviet occupation of Lithuania are less likely to follow the Catholic religion. In Soviet-occupied Lithuania, atheism was strongly encouraged by the state and many Lithuanians never learned

A grotto depicting Jesus in the garden of Gethsemane at the Holy Cross Church, a Lithuanian parish in Chicago. AKG-IMAGES / JAMES MORRIS / NEWSCOM

of their country's pre-Soviet religion. For many Lithuanian Americans, however, religion still plays a crucial role in maintaining a national and ethnic identity, providing community centers and other institutions. Newer immigrants participate in the church to embrace the community, but often with less understanding of and commitment to church practice, creating a divide between newer immigrants and the more established communities.

Lithuanian Lutherans hailed mainly from the northern and western regions of Lithuania, areas that had been influenced by Baltic German and Latvian Lutheranism. The Protestant Reformation of the sixteenth century took hold in Lithuania until it was largely eliminated by the Counter-Reformation, yet over the centuries a small Lutheran minority remained. When these immigrants came to the United States during the initial surge of Lithuanian immigration, they tended to develop separate Lutheran congregations apart from the mainstream Lithuanian American community. The German-speaking Lutheran Missouri Synod sponsored several pastors who reached out to this community. After 1945 a second wave of Lithuanian Lutherans formed the Lithuanian Evangelical Lutheran Church in Exile, headquartered near Chicago. In 2000 the Evangelical Lutheran Church in Lithuania declared itself in full fellowship with the Lutheran Church–Missouri Synod, aligning with a conservative confessional Lutheran stance. In 2006 the ELCL had 21,000 active members, 52 congregations, and 15 pastors.

Passing on religious and cultural traditions to the next generation is of continued importance to the Lithuanian American community. In the 2000s the Lithuanian-American Community Council, for instance, produced two children's workbooks for Christmas and Easter outlining the connection between the cultural and religious traditions of Lithuanians.

Before World War II, Jewish Lithuanians made up about 7 percent of the total Lithuanian population; by 1941, Jewish refugees from German-occupied Poland had increased the number of Jews to 10 percent of the total population. Lithuanian Jews were well educated and contributed greatly to many Jewish philosophies, including the Jewish workers' movement, Zionism, and "rational religious thought." They also had their own dialect of Yiddish. Nonetheless, the Jews of Lithuania were forced to assimilate somewhat into Roman Catholic culture, and many experienced some degree of anti-Semitism. Many Lithuanian Jews immigrated to the United States during the latter part of the nineteenth century and formed their own communities, mainly in the cities of the Northeast and the Midwest. During the assimilation process, these communities became affiliated with larger Jewish communities throughout the country. At the same time in Europe, the rise of anti-Semitism and the Nazi regime had a devastating effect on the Lithuanian Jewish

LITHUANIAN PROVERBS

The following are some common Lithuanian figures of speech:

badyti akis

> to be highly visible, to put to shame, to stick out like a sore thumb; literally "to poke the eyes."

lyja kirviais

> a downpour, a heavy rain; literally "it's raining axes."

man šakės

> to be in a very bad situation; literally, "it's the pitchfork for me."

nėra to blogo, kas neišeitų įgera

> every cloud has a silver lining; literally "there is no evil that doesn't turn into good."

panosė šlapia

> to be inexperienced; literally "to be wet under the nose."

community. Immediately before the German invasion of 1941, violent anti-Jewish riots erupted. After the German invasion, Jews were either murdered or sent to concentration camps. By 1944 about 90 percent of Lithuania's Jews had been killed.

CULTURE AND ASSIMILATION

Two important developments in Lithuania led to the growth of a strong Lithuanian American ethnic identity: the late-nineteenth-century rise of Lithuanian national consciousness and the achievement of Lithuanian independence in the early twentieth century. Lithuanian Americans were staunch supporters of their newly independent homeland during the 1920s and 1930s, and some even returned to assist in establishing the country's economy and government.

In 1930 only about 47 percent of Lithuanian immigrants to the United States had become citizens, despite the formation of many Lithuanian citizens' clubs to promote naturalization. However, with their rise toward economic and social success throughout the twentieth century, Lithuanian Americans began to adapt to life in the United States. The U.S.-born second generation, which by 1930 made up the majority of the immigrant community, assimilated much more quickly than their parents. Generally, Lithuanian Americans were discriminated against or stereotyped as being Slavs or Poles, rather than for being Lithuanians. Also, Catholic Lithuanians experienced discrimination targeted at Catholics in general, and Jewish Lithuanians experienced anti-Semitism.

Lithuanian immigrants who came to the United States before 1990 were able to have dual citizenship, becoming U.S. citizens while maintaining their Lithuanian citizenship, including Lithuanian voting rights. Because of this, many immigrants were interested in maintaining a connection to Lithuanian politics. However, the 1992 Lithuanian constitution did not allow for dual citizenship, and those who became naturalized U.S. citizens after that time had to renounce their Lithuanian citizenship. One of the best-known Lithuanian immigrants who gave up dual citizenship was Valdas Adamkus, president of Lithuania from 1998 to 2003 and 2004 to 2009. He immigrated to the United States in 1949 and became a U.S. citizen. After a significant career in the Environmental Protection Agency (EPA), Adamkus retired in 1997 and returned to Lithuania. He renounced his U.S. citizenship before being sworn into office for his first term as president.

Along with assimilation came the development of an extensive network of immigrant institutions that sought to preserve the community's traditions. Foremost among these were the Lithuanian parishes of the Roman Catholic Church, which were joined together by various religious orders and lay and clerical organizations. In addition, each immigrant community also boasted numerous social and fraternal organizations, newspapers, and workers' societies, all of which helped to buttress a Lithuanian identity.

The post-World War II wave of Lithuanian immigrants—the *dipukai*—also experienced a surge of Lithuanian pride. These immigrants saw themselves as an exiled community and clung to their memory of two decades of freedom in Lithuania. They developed an extensive network of schools, churches, and cultural institutions to maintain their Lithuanian identity in the United States. Ironically, they felt more able to express their national and religious identity in the United States than they did in their homeland, which was under Soviet occupation, although they also felt pressure to assimilate into American culture. By the second and third generations, however, assimilation and acculturation took a deeper hold, and ethnic identity, though still important, was no longer central to the community's existence.

Patterns of assimilation are different for different waves of Lithuanian immigrants. For instance, in Soviet-occupied Lithuania, new slang and the incorporation of more Russian into the Lithuanian language was common. This style of language is common to immigrants of the third and most recent wave. Earlier immigrants use more traditional Lithuanian. Recent immigrants find themselves feeling pressured not only into assimilating into American society, but also in choosing to adhere to "modern" or "traditional" Lithuanian, if they are so inclined. Because of the differences between pre-Soviet and Soviet-era Lithuanian, Lithuanian American gatherings are now more often conducted in English. While English may be a more common thread between different waves of immigrants, not using Lithuanian potentially furthers the loss of ethnic identification.

In the Chicago area, home to a large Lithuanian community, the two major Lithuanian schools—*Čikagos Lituanistinė Mokykla* in Chicago and *Maironio Lituanistinė Mokykla* in Lemont—each cater to a different wave of immigrants. The more recent immigrants tend to have a higher interest in activities that help them to assimilate. These newer immigrants are more readily drawn to organizations such as the Lithuanian Student Association of North America (LSANA) that helps them prepare for American college or university and make connections both within and outside the Lithuanian American community. Families whose ancestors arrived during earlier waves of immigration tend to be more involved with keeping the culture of Lithuania alive. They are drawn to preserving Lithuanian traditions because they or their children did not grow up in Lithuania or it has being many years since immigration.

Cuisine Lithuanian cuisine is influenced by the foods of the land itself and by the various cuisines of its neighbors. More than the other Baltic nations, Lithuanian cooking looks to the east and the south, having much in common with the cuisine of Russia, Belarus, Germany, and the Ukraine, as well as with traditional Ashkenazi Jewish foods. Lithuanian recipes rely heavily on pork, potatoes, and dairy products. One specialty is *suris*, which resembles cottage cheese. Dark, flavorful mushrooms, herring, eels, sausages, and dark rye breads are also central to the Lithuanian diet. Popular drinks include *gira*, a fermented non-alcoholic beverage made from black or regular rye bread, and *kompotas*, a cold fruit tea. Holiday foods include jellied pig's feet, goose stuffed with prunes, and roasted suckling pig. A long table filled with food is considered an important aspect of hospitality and a symbol of affluence. Leaving food on a plate is considered impolite and an indication that the diner did not enjoy the meal.

In some Lithuanian American communities, such as in the Chicago area, one can find Lithuanian restaurants, some that serve only Lithuanian cuisine and others that serve Polish, Russian, and standard American food as well. The menu at Grand Duke's Restaurant in Chicago, for instance, includes such items as sauerkraut soup, beet soup, and cooked peas with smoked pig ears. Mabenka's in Chicago serves dishes such as *kugelis babka ziemnieczana*, a baked potato pudding, and *cepelinai-pyzy*, dumplings made from grated potatoes stuffed with meat, as well as grilled cheese sandwiches and Yankee pot roast.

Traditional Dress The colorful regional dress of Lithuania was worn in the old country at times of festivals, market days, and special events. Costumes are based on nineteenth-century peasant costumes from different regions of the country. They are mainly handmade and are sometimes passed down from generation to generation. Embroidery on women's and girls' costumes often depicts flowers or other nature-inspired designs. The outfits are made up of multiple layers—a skirt, blouse, vest, sash, and scarf or hat. Immigrants in the United States sometimes wear traditional clothing for festivals and for folk dancing. Children who learn folk dancing in Lithuanian American schools, churches, or community centers dress in traditional costumes for performances. Contemporary dress in Lithuania is similar to that in Western Europe and the United States. The daily working clothes of Lithuanian immigrants have never significantly differed from that of other Americans in similar positions.

Dances and Songs Traditional Lithuanian dances encapsulate the stories and the morals of the people, and different steps signify different meanings. Lithuanian dance styles include the *rateliai*, which is done in the round and was originally danced without musical accompaniment, but is now generally accompanied by instruments such as fiddles; *basetles*, a bass string instrument played with a bow; *lamzdeliai*, a woodwind whistling instrument; and *kankles*, a plucked string instrument. Another dance is the *šokiai*, which consists of consecutively repeated movements, steps, and figures. Other Lithuanian instruments still played today include *ragai*, or horns, and *skuduciai*, the pan pipes. Lithuanian folk songs, called *calleddainos*, are mainly concerned with the agricultural themes of planting, reaping, and cultivating, or with praising or reproaching animals such as grasshoppers, mosquitoes, or goats. Other folk songs may be about weddings, rituals, or holidays such as Christmas and Advent.

Lithuanian Americans continue to perform folk dances to celebrate their ethnic heritage. Children often take lessons and perform these dances at recitals and festivals. Large folk dance festivals bring together different Lithuanian dance groups. In 2012, for instance, the Boston Lithuanian American Community hosted the 14th Lithuanian Folk Dance Festival, which included 47 Lithuanian folk dance groups made up of 1,800 dancers from around the world, all dressed in traditional costumes.

Holidays Along with the traditional Catholic and American holidays, there are several festival days of special significance to the Lithuanian American community. February 16 is Lithuanian Independence Day, marking the country's formal declaration of independence in 1918. September 8 is known as Lithuanian Kingdom Day. This celebrates the day in 1514 when the combined Lithuanian and Polish armies defeated 80,000 Russian soldiers at the Battle of Orsha. The Russians lost over 30,000 men while the Lithuanian and Polish armies, comprising 30,000 troops, lost only

500. It is considered one of the greatest victories in Lithuanian history.

Kučios is a symbolic Christmas Eve meal, shared by other Eastern European Catholics, such as Poles. Honoring the twelve apostles, twelve meatless dishes are served, including herring, porridge, and pickled mushrooms. Hay is sometimes put under the tablecloth to represent Jesus' manger. *Kučiukai* (bite-sized biscuit-like cakes) with poppy milk (poppy seeds boiled with water and sugar) is often served for dessert. *Dievo pyragai*, symbolic Christmas wafers, are broken while family members announce their wishes for the coming year. A chair, plate, and candle are placed at the table for any family member who died during the year to allow his or her spirit to participate in one last family gathering.

Lent is an important time, and the three days before Easter—Holy Thursday (*Didysis Ketvirtadienis*), Good Friday (*Didysis Penktadienis*), and Holy Saturday (*Didysis Šeštadienis*)—are associated with many legends and traditions. For instance, during these days people avoid lending anything or they will be unlucky, having lent their luck away. Bugs and other pests can be eliminated on Good Friday by bringing sand or dirt from the cemetery and putting it where bugs breed. Easter itself is a time of celebration, family gatherings, and games. Easter eggs are decorated by using hot wax and etching designs, a tradition amongst Baltic cultures.

The Feast of St. Casimir on March 4 is both a Roman Catholic and a national holiday, with celebrations often led by the Knights of Lithuania fraternal organization. St. Casimir, being the only Lithuanian saint, is a very popular figure and hero of many tales and legends. Often *muginukas*, heart-shaped cookies with colored sugar designs, are made for the holiday.

Health Care Issues and Practices With the formation of a solid Lithuanian American community at the end of the nineteenth century, the need for health care among immigrants became a key issue. Immigrant fraternal and benefit societies provided help for sick or injured Lithuanians, as did social and charitable organizations. Roman Catholics organized Holy Cross Hospital in Chicago, as well as homes for the aged and infirm. Many of these activities came under the control of Lithuanian Roman Catholic orders, especially the Sisters of St. Casimir. Few Lithuanian medical professionals set up practice in the United States until after 1945, following the postwar influx of Lithuanian doctors from the European refugee community.

More recent immigrants who retain strong ties to Lithuanian culture often use homeopathic and herbal remedies that are popular in Lithuania and elsewhere in Europe. Some Lithuanian American general stores, such as *Lietuvele*, a store in an area of Chicago known as Little Lithuania, sell some of these imported products, which include *kalio permanganatas* (potassium permanganate, used as an antiseptic to treat wounds and abscesses) and *karsil* (a milk thistle formula used for liver health). Immigrants also obtain these remedies by having them sent directly from Lithuania. They also do this sometimes with prescription drugs that are less expensive in Lithuania than the United States. Issues can arise as these prescription and nonprescription formulas are unregulated and sometimes out of date.

FAMILY AND COMMUNITY LIFE

Many Lithuanian American families maintain strong social ties. The term "friend" is usually reserved for people who are very close and like a member of the family, while others are designated "acquaintances." Families and communities support each other socially and economically. Many families in the United States continue to send money and goods to those still living in Lithuania, and established Lithuanian American communities help newer immigrants. Traditional gender roles, with women taking care of the children and household and men working in the public sphere, are still somewhat in place, but many women have important positions in religious and community organizations. Higher education for both young men and women is considered important, and organizations such as Lithuanian Student Association of North America (LSANA) help Lithuanian Americans who are applying to and attending college or university. Many communities with large Lithuanian populations, such as Chicago, Boston, Pittsburgh, Kansas City, and Washington, D.C., have Lithuanian day schools and "Saturday schools" that provide classes in language, dance, music, and the cultural traditions of Lithuania. Religious and social organizations, such as the family club, *Krantas*, or artists' or musicians' organizations, fulfill immigrants' needs for social and emotional support and help them maintain their ethnic identities.

During the first wave of Lithuanian immigration to the United States, the immigrant community developed slowly because most of the new arrivals were young males seeking temporary employment. This made it difficult for immigrants to establish a Lithuanian American identity. Long hours, poverty, and isolation fragmented the community. Slowly, as more families began to settle permanently in the United States, religious, social, and cultural institutions were formed. Then, as now, churches were the cornerstone of the community. A growing sense of nationalism within the community allowed the Lithuanians in the United States to see themselves as a people separate from the Poles and the Russians.

During the wave of immigration after World War II, a significant relationship developed between Lithuanian Americans and the other Baltic immigrants, the Estonians and the Latvians. These groups banded together in the interest of freeing the Baltic Republics from Soviet rule. Their solidarity is especially evident in the creation of groups such as the Joint Baltic-American National Committee (1961) and the Association for the Advancement of Baltic Studies (1968).

A Lithuanian American family of twelve is reunited in the United States in the late 1930s. UPI / CORBIS-BETTMANN. REPRODUCED BY PERMISSION.

The third wave of immigrants that came after independence from the Soviet Union are generally less attached to their native culture than the previous waves, as well as less attached to religious life. They have not supported Lithuanian churches with the same enthusiasm as earlier immigrants. Additionally, some of the older generation of Lithuanians who were heavily invested in Lithuanian culture have died, which has negatively impacted the ethnic identity of some families and communities. Other cultural organizations remain strong: the Springfield Lithuanian-American Club, for instance, publishes a quarterly newsletter promoting community events and informing members of important milestones within families. Technology is being used to create new ties and virtual communities, with blogs such as *Lithuanians in Springfield* devoted to sharing stories and photos about the histories of Lithuanian American families.

Gender Roles Coming from a traditional agricultural society, the first wave of Lithuanian immigrants brought with them rigid beliefs about gender roles. The husband was the head of the family, and women took care of child-rearing, home, and family. This social system was hard for immigrants to maintain in the United States, especially in the urban areas where the majority of the immigrants settled and where more flexibility in gender roles was needed to combat poverty. As the immigrants became assimilated into the mainstream of American life and as gender roles changed in the United States, women's roles began to change and grow. One new independent role for women came through the formation of Lithuanian American religious orders, which afforded Lithuanian women a leading role in their religious community. They headed parochial schools and established institutions of mercy, such as hospitals, orphanages, and nursing homes. The Catholic Women's Alliance was founded in 1914, the Chicago Lithuanian Women's Club in 1923, and the Omaha Lithuanian Club in 1974. Traditional gender roles are still evident in the songs and dances performed in association with these and other Lithuanian cultural organizations.

While gender roles are not as strict as they once were in the community, those that remain serve as reminders of how things used to be with regard to one's economic and immigrant status. For instance, middle- and upper-class Lithuanian Americans who are well established in the United States primarily hire recent female immigrants who speak Lithuanian for domestic work. Often, these are the only jobs available for these women. But these positions can make assimilation more difficult and may keep women in low-paying jobs, because they may hinder the women's opportunity to learn English. Lithuanian men who are newer immigrants also receive support from the established community in terms of being informed of job opportunities. More frequently than women, however, they seek ties outside the local ethnic community for assistance, allowing them to assimilate more quickly and gain economic power.

Education Like many other immigrant groups, Lithuanians have seen that the road to success in the United States lies with education. Many immigrants from Lithuania, especially before 1920, arrived as illiterate peasants. But the community soon established a system of parochial schools among the Lithuanian Roman Catholic parishes in the United States, many of which were run by the Sisters of St. Casimir. A smaller network of Lithuanian American Roman Catholic high schools and academies appeared later, numbering approximately ten by 1940. Parochial schools still exist, such as *Čikagos Lituanistinė Mokykla* in Chicago and *Maironio Lituanistinė Mokykla* in Lemont, Illinois.

Responding to a plea from the immigrant community, the Marian Fathers opened a high school and college in Hinsdale, Illinois, in 1926. Later the college was relocated to Thompson, Connecticut, and renamed Marianapolis Preparatory School. Another early center of Lithuanian education was Indiana's Valparaiso University. Though not strictly a Lithuanian institution, the school attracted a number of Lithuanian students early in the twentieth century; between 1902 and 1915 the school graduated doctors, fifteen lawyers, and fourteen engineers of Lithuanian heritage. Lithuanian refugees of World War II—many of whom were highly educated, skilled professionals—exhibited an intense interest in education. Their main educational contribution to the community was the formation of a series of Lithuanian schools to transmit Lithuanian language and culture to succeeding generations of Lithuanian Americans.

As the educational level of the third and fourth generation immigrants increased, so did their social and physical mobility. With the community more dispersed geographically and more assimilated socially, there were fewer teachers for and students to attend Lithuanian day schools or "Saturday schools" that taught language and culture. Assimilation also meant more marriages between those of Lithuanian heritage and other heritages, resulting in less commitment to learning the Lithuanian language and culture and attending Lithuanian schools. Saturday schools now teach Lithuanian more as a second language than as a language of instruction.

The majority of third wave immigrants, arriving since the restoration of Lithuania's independence, have graduated from college by the time they arrive in the United States. They often immigrate for economic reasons, and economic stability for their family is important. This often translates into a strong emphasis on public, mainstream education (not Lithuanian schools) and higher education at public or private colleges and universities.

EMPLOYMENT AND ECONOMIC CONDITIONS

The first wave of Lithuanian immigration, which ended around 1920, included mostly unskilled and often illiterate immigrants who settled in the cities and coal fields of the East and the Midwest and provided the raw muscle power of urban factories. They were especially drawn to the garment trade in the east, the steel mills and forges of the Midwest, and the meatpacking houses of Chicago and stockyards of Omaha. Other immigrants opened businesses within their communities to provide goods and services for the Lithuanian American community, thus reinforcing cultural ties.

To assist their people in the economic transition to life in the United States, the immigrants established many institutions, including fraternal and benefit societies and building and loan associations. The fraternal societies assisted needy immigrants and provided inexpensive insurance and death benefit protection. The building and loan associations met the immigrants' banking needs and helped them purchase their own homes. By 1920 there were at least thirty such associations within the Lithuanian immigrant community.

The war refugees who came to the United States after 1945 tended to be more educated and professional. Although many had been leaders in independent Lithuania from 1918 to 1940, as immigrants some had difficulty finding suitable employment in the United States. The language barrier and other factors resulted in many of them taking positions that were beneath their level of training and education. These refugees were an enterprising group, however, and quickly attained economic success.

The third wave of immigrants who during the Soviet era or post-Soviet years; this group was primarily from the middle or upper-middle class. Uncertainty about Lithuania's economy in the new era prompted them to make the move. At first, they did not always fare well economically. A 2000 study of recent Lithuanian immigrants to Chicago, for instance, found that many lost their social status upon arriving in the United States. They first found hourly wage positions as domestics, waitresses, cooks, teachers, and musicians and as workers for Lithuanian-language radio stations in the United States or as reporters for Lithuanian-language newspapers. Many of these immigrants, often with support and connections from the Lithuanian communities, eventually climbed the economic ladder and re-established their social standing. Even those who did not participate in the established Lithuanian American community would seek career and educational connections, support, and counseling from the Lithuanian community. Organizations such as Lithuanian International Student Services (LISS) help provide educational and professional support to those with Lithuanian heritage. The American Community Survey estimates for 2009–2011 indicated that the median household income for Lithuanian Americans was $67,179 (compared with $51,484 for the general U.S. population). In addition, 46.6 percent of Lithuanian Americans over the age of 24 held a bachelor's degree or higher (compared with 28.2 percent of the general U.S. population).

POLITICS AND GOVERNMENT

Much of the Lithuanian Americans' initial political activity was confined to the immigrant community itself, as immigrants sought to define themselves, especially in terms of the rising tide of Lithuanian nationalism that dominated the latter part of the nineteenth century. Slowly, the immigrant community's interests broadened. The first examples of immigrant political activity came in areas that directly affected the new immigrants, namely labor issues and U.S. relations with the new Lithuanian state.

Lithuanians were active in the formation of some of the first U.S. labor unions, especially in coal mining and the garment trade. The Lithuanian coal miners of Pennsylvania and Illinois became members of the United Mine Workers unions, and local unions of Lithuanian garment workers soon merged with either the Amalgamated Clothing Workers Union or the United Garment Workers Union. In other industries, such as steel or meat packing, union organization was slower, but Lithuanian workers were a formidable force in labor agitation. A number of nationalist, Roman Catholic, and socialist immigrant organizations were developed to provide support to laborers. Socialist and radical workers groups, such as the Industrial Workers of the World (IWW), succeeded in recruiting Lithuanian workers in the first part of the twentieth century, but these groups declined rapidly after 1920. The Lithuanian community was generally sympathetic to the union cause and supported their fellow immigrants during labor unrest. One of the most well-known characters in the classic 1906 novel *The Jungle* by Upton Sinclair is Jurgis Rudkus, who Sinclair based on a real-life Lithuanian immigrant worker. The book portrayed the poor working condition in the meat packing industry in the early twentieth century and led to the government forming the Food and Drug Administration (FDA).

For some, union activity grew into a wider push for socialism, a political and economic doctrine espousing collective rather than private ownership of property. This sentiment was behind the formation of the Lithuanian Socialist Party of America in 1905. This prewar socialism declined after 1918 as the so-called Red Scare deemed all socialist groups a threat to the American way of life. The first major political push among Lithuanian Americans came after 1918, when they tried to influence U.S. foreign policy to recognize and support Lithuanian independence.

Relations with their native country have always been important to the Lithuanian American community. Tensions ran high among Lithuanians in the United States during those periods when the Soviets controlled Lithuania. Immigrant communities in the United States were fertile ground for nationalistic sentiment, and during the last decades of the nineteenth century many radical Lithuanian nationalists sought refuge in the United States from political oppression in Russia. Most Lithuanian Americans supported the nationalist cause, although a small group of radical communists backed Soviet attempts to forcibly annex Lithuania to the Soviet Union.

When Lithuania was declared a republic in 1918, the immigrant community supported independence with financial, military, and political help. A number of the leaders of independent Lithuania had even lived and studied for a time in the United States. Lithuanian Americans pressured the U.S. government to recognize Lithuanian independence and support Lithuanian border claims in the dispute with Poland. In 1919 Lithuanian Americans collected a million signatures on a petition and 25,000 protested in Chicago to support Lithuanian independence. Joining together for these actions for their home country strengthened ties in the Lithuanian American community.

With the Soviet invasion of Lithuania in 1940, the Lithuanian American community again exerted pressure on the U.S. government for Lithuanian rights. A Lithuanian American delegation, for instance, met with President Roosevelt in 1940 to protest the Soviet takeover of Lithuania. War refugees from Lithuania flooded the United States after 1945, and many new groups and organizations were formed to rally for an independent Lithuania—and to support this cause with money and publicity. Lithuanian Americans worked to keep the dream of an independent Lithuania alive with publicity, lobbying efforts, and various political and cultural activities. These actions moved Lithuanian Americans into the wider sphere of the Lithuanian exile community worldwide, uniting American organizations with others in Europe and elsewhere. Agitation efforts also brought Lithuanian Americans into closer contact with other Baltic Americans, with whom they shared the dream of independence for the Baltic states.

Political involvement has continued in the twenty-first century, though it has diminished. During the German and Russian occupations of Lithuania throughout the twentieth century, Lithuanian immigrants feared for the future of their language and culture. To preserve cultural heritage, it was imperative to hold onto traditions through activities like Saturday schools and youth associations. The threat of losing Lithuanian language and culture eased when Lithuania became independent. For instance, multiple generations of Lithuanian Americans in 1989 and 1990 demonstrated for Lithuanian independence from the Soviet Union. For some of the youth of the time, the social and cultural connections to the community became a political one, often encouraged by their parents, many of whom were first generation immigrants. This motivation and involvement is less common with more assimilated second and third generations. Political and cultural involvement in the Lithuanian American community has decreased because of the older generation dying out and the third wave of immigrants feeling less of a need for involvement.

While political activity has waned, national organizations such as the Lithuanian American Council (LAC) are still involved in the politics of Lithuania and the Baltic countries. Their initiatives have included promoting the expansion of NATO and the European Union into the Baltic countries; supporting Voice of America and Radio Free Europe/Radio Liberty broadcasts; promoting a visa waiver program for Lithuanian citizens entering United States; and supporting U.S. economic and military cooperation with Lithuania.

Another issue impacting Lithuanian Americans' political involvement is that of dual citizenship. Immigrants before 1990 can have dual citizenship, but the constitution of the newly independent Lithuania (approved in 1992) states that any Lithuanian who has citizenship in another country must denounce their Lithuanian citizenship. This means that third wave immigrants are unable to vote in Lithuanian elections or to be directly involved in Lithuanian politics if they become U.S. citizens. First and second wave immigrants, who are usually older, retain their voice in Lithuanian policy and thus may feel more of a need to remain involvement in such matters. This divide reflects the differing mindsets between first and second wave immigrants and third wave immigrants. First and second wave immigrants fled foreign occupations of Lithuania and initially believed they would return there, while third wave immigrants came primarily for economic reasons from a state that was already independent.

Initially, the Lithuanian immigrant community was mostly working class, and many aligned themselves with the Democratic Party during the twentieth century. Although they were not a real force in national politics, Lithuanian Americans used their numbers to dominate local politics, electing local officials, state legislators, judges, and occasionally members of the U.S. House of Representatives. In turn they became loyal supporters of the local Democratic political machines in areas such as Chicago, Cleveland, and Detroit. In many communities Lithuanians formed their own Democratic clubs for the support of political and ethnic priorities. A smaller number of Lithuanians were attracted to the Republican Party, especially after 1945. Along with some members of other Baltic groups, these Lithuanians blamed the Democrats for the betrayal of Lithuanian independence in the Yalta agreement of 1945, which extended Soviet territories to the west of Russia. Post-World War II immigrants, because of their strong anti-communist feelings, often favored the Republicans. As the community has grown and diversified, Lithuanians of the early twenty-first century continue to be strongly involved and active in both major political parties; some have even become important political figures. Most notable are Senator Dick Durbin of Illinois, who began serving as the Senate Majority Whip in 2007, and Representative John Mondy, a Republican from Illinois.

Lithuanians have long been active in the U.S. military. Soldiers with Lithuanian names served under George Washington. In the American Civil War, 373 Lithuanians fought for the Union, and 44 fought for the Confedcracy. Lithuanian Americans were especially interested in both World Wars, since they directly influenced the fate of Lithuanian independence. In 1918 a group of 200 Lithuanian Americans who had served in the U.S. military went to Lithuania to help in the fight for freedom. Lithuanian Americans had a strong military presence in World War II and have continued to serve in the military.

NOTABLE INDIVIDUALS

Activism Father Jonas Zilinskas (1870–1932) was instrumental in developing the Lithuanian Alliance of America and served as its president.

Emma Goldman (1869–1940) was a radical political activist. She was born in present-day Kaunas, Lithuania, which at the time was part of the Russian Empire. She immigrated to the United States in 1886 and became a political leader in the anarchist and communist movements. She wrote and lectured extensively in support of atheism, revolution, birth control, and "free love," and she wrote a famed autobiography, *Living My Life*. She founded the anarchist journal *Mother Earth* in 1906. In 1917 she was arrested, and the FBI had her deported to Russia in 1919. While she supported the ideals of communism, she later became disillusioned with it and left Russia to live in Europe and Canada; she was eventually allowed to return to the United States to lecture. She died in 1940 in Toronto, Canada, but was buried in Forest Park, Illinois, a suburb of Chicago, among the graves of other like political activists.

Art Victor David Brenner (1871–1924) was a Jewish Lithuanian who designed the Lincoln penny. He was an artist, sculptor, engraver, and metalsmith. He immigrated to the United States in 1890 and changed his name from Viktoras Barnauskas.

Vytas Valaitis (1931–1965) was a Lithuanian photographer and journalist who worked for several major publications, including *Newsweek*, the *Saturday Evening Post*, and *U.S. News and World Report*. He won numerous prizes for his work.

Business Lane Bryant (1879–1951) was the creator and manufacturer of the Lane Bryant clothing company for larger women, as well as the first clothing maker to introduce maternity clothes. She began working in the garment industry when she immigrated to New York from Lithuania in 1895. Her second husband, Albert Maslin, who was also Lithuanian, helped with her business. She was born in Lithuania as Lena Himmelstein and was raised there by her grandparents. In 2002 her great-grandsons started the company Fashion to Figure, which also designs clothes for plus-sized women.

Juozas (Joseph) P. Kazickas (1918–) was a businessman, entrepreneur, venture capitalist, and philanthropist. He was born in Lithuania and was part of the resistance movement during World War II. He became a refugee in Germany and later immigrated to the United States. He received a doctorate degree from Yale University and an honorary doctorate from Lithuania's Kaunas University of Technology. He has worked throughout his life to help free Lithuania and help the Lithuanian people. He founded the Kazickas Family Foundation in 1998. He recounted his story in his memoir, *Odyssey of Hope* (2006).

Film Jonas Mekas (1922–) is a filmmaker, writer, and curator. He has been called "the godfather of American avant-garde cinema." He was born in the farming village of Semeniškiai, Lithuania, and was sent to a forced labor camp in Germany by the Nazis in 1944. After the war, in 1949, he and his brother were brought to the United States by the UN's International Refugee Organization. Together the brothers started *Film Culture* magazine. Jonas Mekas wrote the movie column for the *Village Voice* and in 1970 cofounded the Anthology Film Archives, a repository of avant-garde cinema. He has published numerous books of poetry and prose. Mekas has also produced a number of award-winning films, including *The Brig*, which won the Grand Prize at the Venice Film Festival in 1963, *Reminiscences of a Journey to Lithuania* (1972), and *Sleepless Nights Stories* (2011). In 2007 he created a short film each day for a year (365 films) and posted them online. He has won numerous awards and honors, including the Los Angeles Film Critics Association Award (2007) and the Baltic Cultural Achievement Award

for Outstanding Contributions to the Field of Arts and Science (2008). The Jonas Mekas Center for the Visual Arts opened in Vilnius, Lithuania, in 2007.

Robert Zemeckis (1951–) is a film director, producer, and screenwriter. He was born in Chicago to a Lithuanian American father and an Italian American mother. He is particularly known for his special effects in comedy and drama. His films include *Romancing the Stone* (1984), *Who Framed Roger Rabbit?* (1988), *Back to the Future* (1985), *Forest Gump* (1994), *Contact* (1997), *Castaway* (2000), and *The Polar Express* (2004).

Journalism Ellen Cassedy is a Jewish Lithuanian writer and journalist. She is the author of *We Are Here: Memories of the Lithuanian Holocaust* (2012), which explores how Lithuanian Jews and non-Jews are dealing with their Nazi and Soviet past and its impact on their lives today. She is also the author of the play and short film *Beautiful Hills of Brooklyn*, which was nominated for an Academy Award. Previously a columnist for the *Philadelphia Daily News*, she is a regular contributor to *VilNews*, the international web magazine based in Vilnius, Lithuania. She is a frequent speaker on Jewish and Lithuanian issues. She translates work from Yiddish, and with her colleague, Yermiyahu Ahron Taub, she won the National Yiddish Book Center 2012 Translation Prize for translation of fiction by Blume Lempel. Her articles have appeared in numerous newspapers and journals, including the *Huffington Post*, *Ha'aretz*, *Jewish Telegraphic Bridges*, and the *Utne Reader*.

Liūtas Mockūnas (1934–2007) was an important figure in Lithuanian journalism and literature. He was a writer, editor, cultural critic, and activist, whose works included social commentaries such as *Pavargęs herojus* (*Tired Hero*), published in 1997, about the Lithuanian resistance to the Soviet Union, and *Laisvės horizontai* (*Horizons of Freedom*), published in 2001. He was an active member of Santara-Šviesa, a Lithuanian American organization that supported Lithuanian independence, and edited its publication *Akiračiai: Atviro Žodžio Ménraštis* (Viewpoints: A Monthly for the Free Word). He was born in Lithuania, then moved to Germany with his family in World War II and to the United States in 1949; in 2005 he moved back to Lithuania.

Music Pink (1979–), born Alecia Beth Moore, is a pop singer, songwriter, musician, and actress. She is of Lithuanian-Jewish, German and Irish ancestry. In 2000 she released her first solo album, *Can't Take Me Home*, a double platinum hit. In 2002 she collaborated with Christina Aguilera on the soundtrack for the film *Moulin Rouge*. Her second album, *M!ssundaztood*, was a rock-infused recording that sold more than 10 million copies worldwide. Her third album, *Try This*, was even more rock based and earned her a Grammy for Best Female Rock Vocal Performance. Pink is also an animal rights activist.

Politics Alexander Bruce Bielaski (1883–1954), an American of Lithuanian descent, was a lawyer and the first director of the Bureau of Investigation (now the FBI), from 1912 to 1919. He was later the head of the National Board of Fire Underwriters team of arson investigators and president of the Society of Former Special Agents.

Richard Joseph "Dick" Durbin (1944–) is a Lithuanian American who has been the senior U.S. Senator from Illinois since 1997. Since 2007, he has been the Senate Majority Whip, the second highest position in the Democratic Party leadership in the Senate. He was formerly U.S. Representative for the Springfield, Illinois–based Twentieth congressional district.

Sidney Hillman (1887–1946) was a Lithuanian Jewish immigrant who led the Amalgamated Clothing Workers Union for over thirty years. After decades of leading the union, in 1941 he became director of the United States Office of Production Management. He also helped get President Franklin D. Roosevelt elected by rallying support from labor. The Sidney Hillman Foundation bestows its annual award to journalists and writers whose work supports social justice and progressive politics.

John Mondy Shimkus (1958–) has been the U.S. Representative for the 19th congressional district of Illinois since 1997. He is a member of the Republican Party.

Science and Medicine Marija Alseikaite Gimbutas (1921–1994) was a renowned archeologist born in Vilnius, Lithuania. She fled Lithuania during World War II while it was occupied by the Soviets and immigrated to the United States in 1949. She is known for developing the Kurgan hypothesis. *Kurgan*

is the Russian term for graves built by Proto-Indo-Europeans. Her hypothesis was the result of studying Kurgan burial mounds and linguistics in order to understand the origins and migrations of the Proto-Indo-Europeans. She taught at Harvard University, where she was made a fellow of Harvard's Peabody Museum, and the University of California at Los Angles (UCLA), where she was the Chair of European Archeology, created the Institute of Archeology, and was the curator of Old World Archeology at the Cultural History Museum. She cofounded the *Journal of Indo-European Studies* and wrote *The Goddesses and Gods of Old Europe* (1974), *The Language of the Goddess* (1989), and *The Civilization of the Goddess* (1991). She was awarded an honorary PhD from Vytautas Magnus University in Kaunas, Lithuania, in 1993.

Sports Richard Marvin "Dick" Butkus (1942–) was a Lithuanian American who was a linebacker for the Chicago Bears in the 1960s and 1970s. He was named first-team All-NFL for six years and played in eight Pro Bowl games. A serious knee injury that did not respond to surgery ended his career. He was inducted in the Pro Football Hall of Fame in 1979. His jersey number was retired in 1994, considered a high honor. In 2000 he was named to the NFL All-Time team. He has also done a number of commercials, including for Miller beer and Fedex.

Vitas Gerulaitis (1954–1994), a Lithuanian American born Vytautas Kevin Gerulaitis, was a professional tennis player in the 1970s and 1980s. In 1975 he won the men's double title at Wimbledon and in 1977 he won the Grand Slam singles title in the Australian Open. From 1977 to 1983 he was in the top ten ranking of international players. He was also known for having a wild life and was treated for substance abuse and accused of cocaine dealing. His father was a Lithuanian and Baltic States tennis champion and taught tennis in the United States for many decades.

Joseph Michael Jurevicius (1974–), who is of Lithuanian descent, was a football wide receiver. He was originally drafted to the New York Giants and played for them for four seasons from 1998 to 2002. He then played for the Tampa Bay Buccaneers until 2005, when he signed up with the Seattle Seahawks and then the Cleveland Browns. He played in two Super Bowl games. He has a tattoo of a Vytis, a swordsman on a horse which is the national symbol of Lithuania, on his right bicep.

Jack Sharkey (1902–1994) was born Joseph Paul Zukauskas to Lithuanian parents. He was a world heavyweight champion boxer in the 1920s and 1930s and the only person to fight both Jack Dempsey and Joe Louis.

Johnny Unitas (1933–2002) is considered a legendary hero of the football world. Nicknamed "the Golden Arm," he was named the National Football League's

Portrait of Lithuanian-born American singer and actor Al Jolson standing beside an NBC radio microphone, November 1932. HULTON ARCHIVE / GETTY IMAGES

all-time greatest quarterback at events marking the league's fiftieth anniversary. His parents were Lithuanian immigrants and his surname was a phonetic transliteration of the common Lithuanian name *Jonaitis*. He holds the record for most touchdown passes with at least one touchdown pass in forty-seven consecutive games. He was the first quarterback to pass more than 40,000 yards. He played in ten Pro Bowls, was named Most Valuable Player three times, and was inducted into the Pro Football Hall of Fame in 1979.

Stage and Screen Charles Bronson (1920–2003) was born Charles Dennis Buchinsky. A popular movie actor of Polish-Lithuanian heritage, Bronson is known for his action roles in such movies as *The Great Escape, Once Upon a Time in the West, Death Wish*, and *Hard Times*.

Ruta Lee (1936–), an actor, was born Ruta Kilmonis to a Lithuanian tailor. Although born in Montreal, she has made significant contributions to American film and lives in the United States. She has appeared in films, theater, and television since the 1950s. Some of her most notable films include *Seven Brides for Seven Brothers, Funny Face*, and *Witness for the Prosecution*. She has had leading roles in many theater productions, including *Annie, Peter Pan, Mame, Irene, Woman of the Year*, and *The Best Little Whorehouse in Texas*. She has made over 2,000 appearances on television in shows such as *Perry Mason, Power Rangers, Twilight Zone, Murder She Wrote, Roseanne*, and HBO's *1st & Ten*.

John C. Reilly (1965–) is an American film and theater actor, singer, and comedian. He was born and in Chicago to a Lithuanian American mother and an Irish American father. He has been in over fifty films and was nominated for an Academy Award for Best Supporting Actor for his role in *Chicago* (2002). He was nominated for a Grammy Award for the song "Walk Hard," which he performed in *Walk Hard: The Dewey Cox Story* (2007). He has also appeared in the comedies *Step-Brothers* (2008), *Cyrus* (2010), and *Wreck-It Ralph* (2012) and the critically acclaimed films *Boogie Nights* (1997), *Gangs of New York* (2002) and *Magnolia* (1999).

Jason Sudeikis (1975–) is an actor, comedian and writer of Lithuanian descent. In the 1990s he performed with the improv troupe ComedySportz and was a member of Second City in Las Vegas. He was hired as a sketch writer for *Saturday Night Live* in 2003 and then a cast member in 2006. His film roles include *Horrible Bosses* (2011) and *The Campaign* (2012).

Elizabeth Swados (1951–) is an award-winning composer, writer, and director whose works include the Broadway musicals *Runaways* (1978), *Doonesbury* (1983), and *Kaspar Hauser* (2009). *Runaways* received Tony Award nominations for Best Musical, Best Direction of a Musical, Best Book of a Musical, Best Original Score, and Best Choreography. She has written music for many classical dramatic productions and television specials as well as books such as *My Depression*

(2005) and *At Play: Teaching Teenagers Theater* (2006). She is the recipient of numerous awards including a Guggenheim Fellowship, a Ford Foundation Fellowship, and a special International PEN citation.

Members of the Lithuanian American Hall on 46th Ave. in Chicago chat while cooking. ST PETERSBURG TIMES / ZUMAPRESS / NEWSCOM

MEDIA

PRINT

Bridges

The official publication of Lithuanian-American Community, Inc. It is published ten times a year in English and geared toward the general public. It is available via subscription and on the publications page of the Lithuanian-American Community website.

Teresé Vekteris, Editor
6125 McCallum Street
Philadelphia, Pennsylvania 19144
Phone: (800) 625-1170
Fax: (856) 428-6014
Email: bridges.terese@gmail.com
URL: www.lithuanian-american.org/main/explore-lac/publications

Čikagos Aidas (Echo of Chicago)

One of the largest Lithuanian-language weekly newspapers published in the United States, it was established in 2003. It is distributed free of charge in the Chicago area to over 1,000 locations. The full newspaper is available online and it also has its own music radio station.

Leonid Khodos, Editor in Chief
704 South Milwaukee Avenue
Wheeling, Illinois 60090
Phone: (847) 272-9222
Fax: (847) 215-8455
Email: aidas@aidas.us
URL: www.aidas.us

Dirva (The Field)

Lithuanian-language weekly newspaper that contains items of interest to the Lithuanian community of Cleveland, published since 1916.

19807 Cherokee Avenue
Cleveland, Ohio 44119
Phone: (216) 531-8150

Draugas (Friend)

A Lithuanian-language newspaper published in Chicago by the Lithuanian Catholic Press Society, published three days a week. It is the oldest continuously published Lithuanian language newspaper in the world, celebrating its one hundredth anniversary in 2009. It includes a weekly supplement called *Kultūra: Menas Literatūra Mokslas* (Culture: Art Literature Science).

Dalia Cidzikaitė, Editor
4545 West 63rd Street
Chicago, Illinois 60629-5589
Phone: (773) 585-9500
Fax: (773) 585-8284
Email: redakcija@draugas.org
URL: www.draugas.org

Lituanus, The Lithuanian Quarterly

A multidisciplinary peer-reviewed academic journal that covers Lithuania and the Baltic region. It publishes research articles in English as well as essays on literature and art. It is published by the nonprofit Lituanus Foundation, Inc., and has 2,000 subscribers.

Elizabeth Novickas, Editor in Chief
47 West Polk Street
Suite 100-300
Chicago, Illinois 60605
Email: editor@lituanus.org
URL: www.lituanus.org

Vytis (The Knight)

The official publication of the Knights of Lithuania. The magazine, published seven times annually, contains articles in Lithuanian and English about Lithuanian culture, activities, and organizational matters.

URL: www.ourladyofsiluva.com/knights/vytis/

RADIO

KTYM-AM (1460)

Offers thirty minutes of Lithuanian information and thirty minutes of music programming weekly.

Bobby A. Howe
6803 West Boulevard
Inglewood, California 90302-1895
Phone: (310) 672-3700
Fax: (310) 673-2259
URL: www.ktym.com

WCEV-AM (1450)

WCEV offers programs in various languages directed toward several ethnic groups: Poles, Lithuanians, Czechs, Slovaks, Moravians, Montenegrins, Irish, Arabs, and Bosnians.

Lucyna Migala, Program Director
5356 West Belmont Avenue
Chicago, Illinois 60641-4192
Phone: (773) 282-6700
URL: www.wcev1450.com/index.htm

Lithuanian online radio stations for streaming can be found at www.multilingualbooks.com/online-radio-lithuanian.html and www.worldtvradio.com/internet-radio-online-tv-lithuania. Both include news, music, and variety shows from Lithuania.

ORGANIZATIONS AND ASSOCIATIONS

Lithuanian American Community (LAC)

The LAC works to preserve Lithuanian cultural identity for future generations and to foster the growth of the democratic institutions of Lithuania. In 2012 the LAC had sixty local chapters in twenty-seven states and the District of Columbia. LAC organizes educational, cultural, religious, community, social, and sports activities; works with Lithuanian institutions, businesses, and organizations; promotes Lithuanian culture in the United States and provides information to Americans about Lithuania; and works for human and civil rights and economic reform in Lithuania.

2715 East Allegheny Avenue
Philadelphia, Pennsylvania 19134
Phone: (800) 625-1170
Fax: (815) 327-8881
Email: admin@lithuanian-american.org
URL: www.lithuanian-american.org

The Knights of Lithuania

The Knights of Lithuania is an organization of Roman Catholics of Lithuanian descent that fosters an appreciation of the Lithuanian language, customs, and culture while also stressing Roman Catholic beliefs and traditions. They organize cultural presentations, lectures, trips, choral and dance groups and have a national scholarship fund. Many chapters have junior councils for youth participation.

Andrew Berczelly, National 2nd Vice President
1445 Bernwald Lane
Dayton, Ohio 45432
URL: www.knightsoflithuania.com

The Lithuanian Foundation, Inc.

The Lithuanian Foundation, Inc., is a nonprofit dedicated to preserving and fostering Lithuanian culture and traditions in the United States, Lithuania, and Lithuanian communities worldwide. It awards grants and scholarships.

14911 127th Street
Lemont, Illinois 60439
Phone: (630) 257-1616
Fax: (630) 257-1647
Email: admin@lithfund.org
URL: www.lithuanianfoundation.org

Lithuanian Roman Catholic Federation of America

Founded in 1906, the Lithuanian Roman Catholic Federation of America is composed of Lithuanian American Catholic organizations, parishes, religious orders, and publications; agencies and institutions; and individuals. It seeks to unite Lithuanian American Catholics, promote Catholic action, and uphold Lithuanian culture. It hosts the one-week Lithuanian Heritage Summer Camp at Camp Dainava in Michigan (www.lithuanianheritagecamp.org) each year.

12690 Archer Avenue
Lemont, Illinois 60439-6732
Phone: (630) 243-0416

The Lithuanian Student Association of North America, Inc.

The Lithuanian Student Association of North America, Inc., is a national nonprofit representing students of Lithuanian descent. It helps students maintain their heritage and educates them about Lithuanian culture and history through events, annual conferences, and collaboration with other international student organizations and assists in educational and professional networking.

6500 South Pulaski Road
Chicago, Illinois 60629
Email: info@lsana.org
URL: www.lsana.org

The Lithuanian World Center (LWC)

The LWC is a nonprofit organization established in 1988 whose mission is to attend to the needs of ethnic Lithuanians, care for the preservation of ethnic identity and heritage, and advance the integration of Lithuanians into local communities. It operates a community center that includes banquet halls and sports facilities.

14911 127th Street, Lemont
Illinois 60439
Phone: (630) 257-8787
Fax: (630) 257-6887
URL: www.lcenter.org

MUSEUMS AND RESEARCH CENTERS

Balzekas Museum of Lithuanian Culture

Founded in 1966 in Chicago, the Balzekas Museum is dedicated to the preservation and perpetuation of Lithuanian culture. The museum celebrates the notable achievements of Lithuanian Americans, the Lithuanian nation, and Lithuanian communities worldwide, and has the largest collection of Lithuanian memorabilia outside of Lithuania.

6500 South Pulaski Road
Chicago, Illinois 60629
Phone: (773) 582-6500
Fax: (773) 582-5133
Email: info@balzekasmuseum.org
URL: www.balzekasmuseum.org

Institute of Lithuanian Studies (ILS)

Founded in the United States in 1951 to research Lithuanian culture, the ILS consists of the following divisions: Lithuanian language, literature, ethnography, Lithuanian pre-history, history, geography, and Lithuanian American history. It organizes college level courses on Lithuania,

symposiums and conferences, and publishes books such as the series *Lithuanian Studies*.

5600 South Claremont Avenue
Chicago, Illinois 60636-1039
Phone: (773) 434-4545
Fax: (773) 434-9363
URL: www.lithuanianresearch.org/eng

Lithuanian American Cultural Archives

Run by the Lithuanian Marian Fathers, the Lithuanian American Cultural Archives focuses on Lithuanians in America. It has an extensive collection of early materials on the immigrant community, especially on Lithuanians in the Northeast and Middle Atlantic states and includes a library of over 60,000 books and a museum.

J. Rigel, Director
37 Mary Crest Drive
Putnam, Connecticut 06260
Phone: (860) 928-5197 or (860) 923-3043
URL: www.plbe.org/English/Archives.htm or www.litua.com/lt/zinynas/alka

Van Pelt Library, University of Pennsylvania

The library houses one of the largest collections of materials about Lithuania and Lithuanian Americans in the United States.

3420 Walnut Street
Philadelphia, Pennsylvania 19104
Phone: (215) 898-7088
URL: www.library.upenn.edu/collections/policies/russian.html

SOURCES FOR ADDITIONAL STUDY

Budreckis, Algirdas. *The Lithuanians in America, 1651–1975: A Chronology and Factbook*. Dobbs Ferry, New York: Oceana Publications, Inc., 1975.

Eitdintas, Alfondas. *Lithuanian Emigration to the United States, 1868–1950*. Vilnius: Išleido Mokslo ir enciklopedijų leidybos institutas, 2003.

Fainhauz, David. *Lithuanians in the U.S.A.: Aspects of Ethnic Identity*. Chicago: Lithuanian Library Press, Inc., 1991.

Gedmintas, Aleksandras. "Lithuanians." In *American Immigrant Cultures: Builders of a Nation*, Vol. 2, edited by David Levinson and Melvin Ember, 588–96. New York: Macmillan, 1997.

Grazulis, Marius K. *Lithuanians in Michigan (Discovering the Peoples of Michigan)*. Detroit: Michigan State University Press, 2009.

Kuzmickaitė, Daiva Kristina. *Between Two Worlds: Recent Lithuanian Immigrants in Chicago (1998–2000)*. Vilnius: Versus Aureus, 2003.

Markelis, Daiva. *White Field, Black Sheep: A Lithuanian-American Life*. Chicago: University of Chicago Press, 2010.

LUXEMBOURGER AMERICANS

Drew Walker

OVERVIEW

Luxembourger Americans are immigrants or descendants of people from the small country of Luxembourg, officially the Grand Duchy of Luxembourg. Luxembourg is surrounded by Belgium to its north and west, France to its south, and Germany to its east. The history and culture of Luxembourg have been significantly affected by its proximity to the great European centers of power and culture. Because of its location and history, Luxembourg is referred to as one of Europe's most important crossroads. Along its border with Belgium are the Ardennes Mountains, forming a plateau between 1,300 and 1,600 feet (400 to 490 meters) in height. This area is known as the Oesling. To the south of the Ardennes is an area known as Gutland or Bon Pays (literally, "good land"), which contains various contours of fertile farmland. Luxembourg is contained within some 998 square miles (2,586 square kilometers), about two-thirds the size of Rhode Island.

The estimated 2012 population of Luxembourg was 509,074 according to the *CIA World Factbook*. Luxembourgers are overwhelmingly Catholic, 87 percent, with small numbers of Jews, Protestants, and Muslims. Sixty-five percent of the population identify as native Luxembourger, while over 13 percent are Portuguese, with smaller numbers of French, German, and other Europeans. Luxembourg has a relatively stable economy and, since the late twentieth century, has enjoyed the highest standard of living in Europe. Nearly one-third of Luxembourg's economic activity is in financial services such as banking. It is a data and telecommunications center, housing the regional headquarters for both Skype and Amazon. It also has a diverse industrial sector, although about 60 percent of its workers are foreign born or live in one of the neighboring countries.

The greatest influx of Luxembourgers into the United States was during the mid- and late nineteenth century. Between 1841 and 1891, an estimated 45,000 Luxembourgers immigrated to the United States. In the 1830s and 1840s the Luxembourgers arrived primarily in Maryland, New York, and Louisiana. The largest portion of Luxembourger immigrants traveled up the Mississippi from Louisiana and settled in Minnesota, Iowa, Illinois, and Wisconsin. The greatest attraction of the Midwest, where most of them eventually settled, was the availability of fertile and inexpensive farmland. By the 1880s community networks among the settled Luxembourger Americans made further Luxembourger immigration easier and less costly. During this time many came on board ships of the Red Star Line, which sailed from Antwerp, Belgium. A small number of Luxembourger Jews fleeing Nazi persecution arrived in the United States in the late 1930s and early 1940s.

According to the U.S. Census, in 2009 there were 45,597 descendants of Luxembourgers in the United States, though it is likely this is an undercount because many Luxembourgers publicly identify with more recognizable European nationalities such as German, Belgian, or French. According to Jean-Claude Muller's book *De l'État à la Nation: 1839, 1989* (State of the Nation 1839–1989), in 1940 there were 100,000 Luxembourgers in the United States. The majority, 64 percent, still live in the Midwest—primarily Illinois, Wisconsin, and Minnesota—with most of the rest in the western states.

HISTORY OF THE PEOPLE

Early History Prior to the fifth century CE, Luxembourg was inhabited by two Belgic tribes, the Medioatrici and the Teveri. In the fifth century the Franks began to occupy the area. In the following centuries, the people began to convert to Christianity. Under the domination of the Holy Roman Empire of Charlemagne, the area was first a section of the Kingdom of Austrasia and then the Kingdom of Lotharinga. From an exchange of land in 963 by Siegfried, the Count of Ardennes, the Kingdom of Luxembourg became an independent land. Involved in this exchange was Siegfried's acquisition of a Roman castle on the Alzette River. The name Luxembourg derived from the name of the castle: *Lucilinburhuc*, or "Little Fortress." Siegfried was succeeded by a long line of his descendants. Around 1060 one of these descendants, Conrad, became the first Luxembourger ruler to take the title "Count of Luxembourg." In 1354 Luxembourg was made a duchy (a sovereign area ruled by a hereditary monarch) by Charles IV, who was one of the three members of the House of Luxembourg to rule as Holy Roman Emperor in the fourteenth and fifteenth centuries.

In 1443 the Duchess of Luxembourg, Elizabeth of Görlitz, gave up the throne to the Duke of

Burgundy, Philip the Good (Philip III). Therefore, when all of Burgundy and its lands passed into the hands of the Hapsburg rulers in 1477, so did the Duchy of Luxembourg. In 1556, through a series of changes brought about by the abdication of Habsburg emperor Charles V, Luxembourg became a property of Spain and part of what were known as the Spanish Netherlands. Through the two turbulent centuries that followed, Luxembourg often found itself at the geographic and political center of wars and disputes; when these conflicts ended, Luxembourg, along with Belgium, passed from the Spanish into the hands of the Austrian Habsburgs.

Modern Era Austrian rule continued until 1795, when the French under Napoleon took over the duchy. Following this occupation by French revolutionary forces, a modern state bureaucracy was installed in Luxembourg that resembled the French system at the time. In their zeal to institute these reforms, along with their disempowerment of the clergy and the call for mandatory military service by the Luxembourgers, the French created dissent. This dissent eventually led to a rebellion against French rule in 1798, which was brutally put down.

With the fall of Napoleon in 1814 and the end of French rule came the decision of the Allied powers in 1815 to cede parts of the duchy to Prussia and to give the rest to William I, king of the Netherlands, while also elevating the duchy to the status of a grand duchy. This resulted in confusion over Luxembourg's identity. While owned by William I of the Netherlands, it was also a member of the German Confederation and had close ties with Prussia. In addition it was, technically, an independent state. What ensued in the decades immediately following the possession of Luxembourg by the Netherlands was a struggle against this rule, which was undertaken in cooperation with Belgium. In a revolution against Dutch rule, the Belgians also declared Luxembourg to be a part of Belgium against the claim of the Netherlands. The series of international reactions that followed led in 1831 to a decision by the "Great Powers" of France, Prussia, Russia, and Britain. Despite Belgium's claim, Luxembourg remained the possession, albeit in altered form, of William I and was also to remain a part of the German Confederation. Dividing Luxembourg once again, the French-speaking part of Luxembourg was given to Belgium while the Netherlands retained the parts that spoke the native Luxembourger language. After a series of disputes on this decision between the Netherlands and Belgium, it eventually came to be accepted, and the Netherlands ruled this area alone from 1839 until 1867.

William I and his successor William II made several moves on behalf of the Luxembourg-Netherlands union, including making Luxembourg part of the Customs Union directed by Prussia. When the German Confederation was dissolved in 1866, Luxembourg became a sovereign nation. In the years that followed, however, a series of disputes among the Great Powers regarding the status of Luxembourgian independence led to the decision in 1867 that Luxembourg be deemed an independent nation with perpetual neutrality. While still a part of the Dutch house of Nassau, which had been ruled by the royal family of the Netherlands for generations, Luxembourg at that time was controlled by William III, who remained ruler until his death in 1890. At that time the grand duchy passed into the hands of Adolf, Duke of Nassau.

Following Adolf's death in 1905, his son William ruled for seven years until he died in 1912. Led by William's daughter, Grand Duchess Marie Adélaïde, the grand duchy, with its small army, put up little resistance to the German invasion and occupation of Luxembourg in 1914, and in return for political independence, it cooperated with the German military during World War I (1914–1918). Disliked by her people and severely criticized by the victorious Allied powers in 1919, Marie Adélaïde was forced to abdicate in favor of her sister Charlotte. Shortly afterward the people of Luxembourg voted to retain Charlotte as grand duchess and not to turn Luxembourg into a republic.

In the following decades Luxembourg established and pursued an economic union with Belgium with mixed results. When the German army invaded and again occupied Luxembourg in May 1940, Grand Duchess Charlotte went into exile with her family. When Luxembourg was liberated in the summer of 1944, Charlotte returned, and the country formed an economic union with both Belgium and the Netherlands. In 1948 Luxembourg abandoned its perpetual neutrality by taking part in forming the North Atlantic Treaty Organization (NATO). Upon the death of Grand Duchess Charlotte in 1964, her son Prince Jean assumed the throne as the Grand Duke of Luxembourg. Grand Duke Jean ruled until 2000, when his son Grand Duke Henri, born in 1955, became the head of state of Luxembourg.

In 1957 Luxembourg became one of the six founding countries of the European Economic Community (later the European Union), and in 1999 it joined the euro currency area. The Court of Justice of the European Union, the European Court of Auditors, and the General Secretariat of the European Union are all located in Luxembourg.

SETTLEMENT IN THE UNITED STATES

The earliest Luxembourgers to immigrate to the United States came in 1630 with the Dutch to New York City (then New Amsterdam). The first Luxembourger American is thought to be Philip de la Noye (or de Lannoy), who arrived on the ship *Fortune*, the sister-ship of the *Mayflower*. Another notable figure from the early years of Luxembourgers in North America was Father Raphael de Luxembourg, who arrived in Louisiana in 1723. Chosen by the king of France to

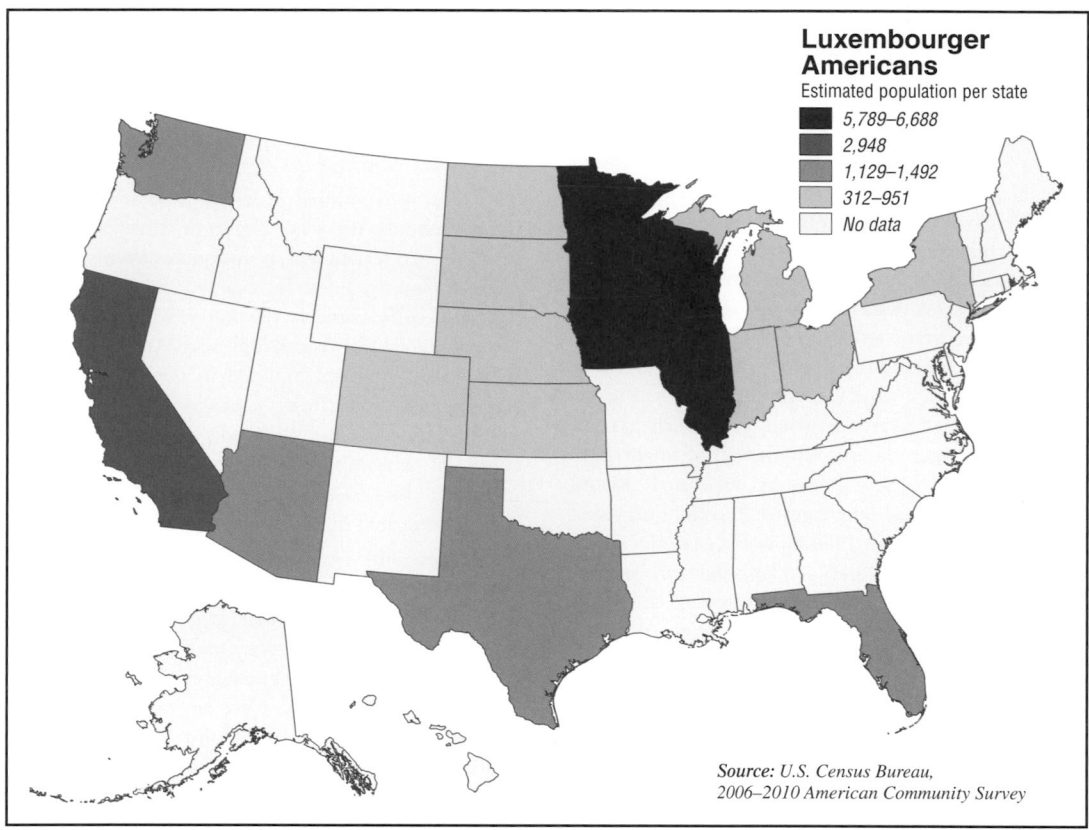

Luxembourger Americans

Estimated population per state

- 5,789–6,688
- 2,948
- 1,129–1,492
- 312–951
- No data

Source: U.S. Census Bureau, *2006–2010 American Community Survey*

represent the king's interests in the then-French colony of Louisiana, Father Raphael also became a leading figure in the Christianization of Native Americans, and he facilitated further Luxembourgish immigration.

The reasons Luxembourgers left their homeland to come to America have been described as a "push-pull." In the mid-nineteenth century, Luxembourg experienced an increase in population and uncertain harvests, which led to a gradual but debilitating decrease in the standard of living of the largely agrarian villages. Political unrest and conscription into the Dutch, Belgian, and Prussian military also added to the "push." At the same time increased accessibility of rail and ship transportation, and the promise of plentiful, fertile farmland pulled the Luxembourgers toward the midwestern settlements founded by their friends and relatives. The farmers and laborers who came to the United States were generally not the poorest of the poor, but rather lower-middle-class families, who with the proceeds of sales of their small farms were able to purchase passage and much more land than they had owned at home.

The first significant wave of immigration took place between 1830 and the mid-1840s. These immigrants settled in western New York State's Wyoming County and Erie County. Significant numbers of settlers also settled in Ohio in Seneca County and Wyandot County.

The second important wave, between 1846 and 1860, led to a great expansion in the population of Luxembourger Americans. Moving westward, they settled in Illinois. A large number settled in Chicago while smaller yet significant numbers settled in Rogers Park, Rosehill, Evanston, Aurora, and what is now Skokie. Further settlements formed across Wisconsin and Iowa and in the Mississippi Valley. Luxembourgers formed settlements in Winona County, Minnesota, and in Jackson County, Iowa.

The third major wave of immigration took place between 1860 and 1900. During the American Civil War (1861–1865) this movement slowed but then gradually rose to an all-time high in the 1880s. Following the general trend of earlier settlement patterns, many of these people made their homes in the Midwestern states and moved west into South Dakota and Nebraska. Throughout the nineteenth century, contacts between the Luxembourgers in the United States and in Luxembourg were maintained in various ways. It was not uncommon for visitors from either land to stay awhile with extended family and work, often to return with news from either side of the Atlantic. A smaller influx of Luxembourgers took place between 1937 and 1940, when 200 to 300 Luxembourger Jews fleeing Nazi persecution settled in the United States.

LANGUAGE

The native language of the majority of Luxembourgers is called *Letzebuergesch* (variant spellings include *Letzebuergisch*, *Luxembourgois*, *Luxembourgish*, and

Luxembourgian). Until the late twentieth century, Letzebuergesch was primarily a spoken language, used at home. Its orthography was standardized in 1975, long after most Luxembourgers had already immigrated to the United States. This language descends from a Frankish dialect spoken by people who moved into the area between the fourth and sixth centuries CE. The closest relatives to this language are Flemish, Dutch, and the Plattdeutsch dialects still spoken in Germany's Rhineland. Only a few words derived from Celtic tongues exist in Letzebuergesch today. Perhaps the most important retention of Celtic influences are in the very name of the country and language. The presence of French words and phrases is evident in the modern usage of Letzebuergesch, yet French has not had the influence on this language that might have been expected over so many years. Between 1930 and 1984, the two legal languages of Luxembourg were German and French. In 1984, however, Letzebuergesch was named the official national language and became, together with German and French, one of the country's three official administrative languages. Although German has been a more popular language within the media, a great many Luxembourgers are wholly conversant in French as well. In the twenty-first century few Luxembourger Americans speak Letzebuergesch, though there are many familiar words and a growing interest via Internet language instruction.

Greetings and Popular Expressions Following are a few Letzebuergesch expressions used in daily life: "Good morning/hello" is *Moien*; "Good-bye" is *Äddi* or *a'voir*; "Thank you (very much)" is *Merci (villmols)*; "Sorry" is "*Pardon*"; "Excuse me" is *Entschëllegt*; and "Please" is *Wannechglift*. The national motto, found everywhere in Luxembourg, is *Mir Wöelle Bleiwe Wat Mir Sin*, or "We want to remain what we are."

RELIGION

Throughout their history, the vast majority of Luxembourgers and Luxembourger Americans have been Catholic. The region along the lower Rhine, including Luxembourg, southeast Belgium, and the adjacent areas of Germany, was a Catholic stronghold throughout the seventeenth and eighteenth centuries. The country of Luxembourg is covered by one diocese that contains thirteen deaneries and 265 parishes. Luxembourg has also traditionally been the home of a great number of convents and religious orders, though that number dwindled at the end of the twentieth century. A small number of Protestants and Jews have also been active for centuries in Luxembourg.

Among Luxembourger Americans, Catholic churches have served important roles in preserving their heritage. As is common with many immigrant groups, religious practices maintain certain continuities and ties to the homeland. In the beginning of their settlement in the Midwestern states, there were very few, if any, established churches or assigned priests to minister to the settlers. The building of a church or the establishment of membership to one nearby was often a top priority. Typically much of a community's resources went into establishing local religious institutions. In the year 1877, ninety-two priests of Luxembourg extraction were ministering to communities in the Midwest.

A great of number of saints popularly venerated in Luxembourg also serve as patron saints of churches in those areas settled by Luxembourger immigrants. In Jackson County, Iowa, for example, there is a parish dedicated to St. Donatas, the martyr who is thought to protect against storms and lightning. Another example is St. Henry's parish, founded in the Luxembourger settlement area north of Chicago and named after a saint who was closely related to Siegfried, the first count of Luxembourg. Symbols of Luxembourg, including the Luxembourg crest, are often found in shrines dedicated to Luxembourger saints.

Among the many traditions that center on the church, perhaps the most prominent is the one called the *Kirmes*. This term, which is a contraction of the words *kirch* (church) and *messe* (mass), signifies the mass that is performed when a church is consecrated. This celebration traditionally took place on the Sunday following the feast day of the patron saint of the consecrated church. The more secular aspects of this event and celebration in Luxembourger culture involved the gathering of families during the anniversaries of such church consecration masses. At such times very special meals were prepared, and the celebration would last for days.

In the United States Kirmes took a different form. It was not the consecration of their churches that was celebrated but rather the day in which Kirmes had been celebrated in the village in Luxembourg from which they came. Kirmes was, then, an occasion for reunions of families and family friends from the old country. This being the case, as those born in Luxembourg grew older and died, this tradition faded.

The importation and circulation of religious objects and figures have helped to maintain contacts between Catholic Luxembourgers in the homeland and the United States. For example, a church in St. Donatus, Iowa, received a pietà sculpture by Luxembourg artist Victor Thibeau for its pietal chapel. Another of Thibeau's creations was also donated to a church in Schewebsange, Luxembourg.

In 1942 sixty-one Luxembourger Jews led by Rabbi Robert Serebrenik founded Congregation Ramath Orah—named after their synagogue in Luxembourg—on Manhattan's upper west side. Rabbi Serebrenik had negotiated with Nazi leader Adolf Eichmann for the transport of Luxembourg's Jews but was only able to arrange convoys for about 250 in 1941.

CULTURE AND ASSIMILATION

Traditions and Customs Like many long-settled groups in the United States, very few Luxembourger Americans can speak the language of their ancestors.

Despite this, however, a considerable number still practice traditions handed down through the generations. Even though they have been culturally mixing for over a century with German Americans, many retain a strong Luxembourger identity of independent, hard-working Catholic farmers and gardeners. Whether in the suburbs of Chicago or the smaller towns of Illinois, Ohio, Wisconsin, or Minnesota, the descendants of Luxembourgers are proud of their heritage. The connection between Luxembourger Americans and Luxembourg have been strengthened in the twenty-first century by the rising fortunes of Luxembourg, which had the highest standard of living in Europe, and the fact that there are more people of Luxembourger descent in the United States than in Luxembourg itself. The architecture of the Luxembourg American Cultural Center in Belgium, Wisconsin, exhibits the fusion of culture then and now. The entrance to the center is a rebuilt stone barn, moved from its original location near Port Washington, Wisconsin, where it was built in 1872. The rest of the building is all modern glass, reflecting the present and future.

Cuisine There are two especially notable indigenous Luxembourger foods found in Luxembourger American settlement areas. The first is *traïpen* (*moustraipen* or *mustripen*), a sausage consisting of hog's head, pork blood, cabbage, and spices. It is similar to black pudding. Included in a tradition in which a large meal with *traïpen* would be served after Midnight Mass on Christmas Day, *traïpen* was a winter food, produced at a time when pigs would be butchered to be made into smoked ham and other pork products. A second popular food is known as *stärzelen* (*sterchelen*), buckwheat dumplings with lard greaves. These foods are still served at Luxembourg heritage festivals, but not so often cooked at home.

Music, Dances, and Songs A number of traditional forms of music and dance were a part of holiday celebrations. In Luxembourg, people would travel to towns such as Echternach to take part in well-known national festivals. The International Music Festival in Echternach, held every year since 1975 in a town in eastern Luxembourg near the border with Germany, has become an event where renowned classical performers play alongside younger musicians in styles ranging from medieval and classical through jazz and world music. Although there is little information on the exact forms of dance and music carried through the generations of Luxembourger Americans, bands with horns and tubas were likely included. In places such as New York and Chicago, military bands were made up of Luxembourger Americans whose repertoire included tunes from the homeland. Among the variety of songs brought to the United States by Luxembourgers, perhaps the most well known would have been the national song called the *Wilhelmus*. Other well-known Luxembourger songs included

De Feierwon [Chariot of Fire], D'Fëscher an d'Jëer, De Kueb an de Fuuss, Den Éim Steffen, De Schmatt, D'Pierle vum Da, Léiwer Härgottsblieschen, Marsch vun der Iechternacher Sprangprëssessioun, Ons Hemecht (Our Homeland, the national hymn), *Rommelpott, Schuebermëss, Tass Fréijor,* and *Wéi meng Mamm nach huet gesponnen.* Luxembourg American heritage festivals are likely to include a performance by Buffalo C. Wayne. Known as the "European Texan," Wayne combines American rock and roll and country music with songs from his Luxembourg homeland.

> *The connection between Luxembourger Americans and Luxembourg have been strengthened in the twenty-first century by the rising fortunes of Luxembourg, which had the highest standard of living in Europe, and the fact that there are more people of Luxembourger descent in the United States than in Luxembourg itself.*

Holidays In Luxembourg, around sunset on the first Sunday of Lent, bonfires are lit in every community. This tradition, called *Burgbrennen*, is one of four times of the year when such fires are lit. The other times are Easter, the summer solstice, and in the late fall. According to the popular "solar theory" of such festivals found throughout Europe and elsewhere, the fires are in some sense a magical imitation of the sun. A great sacrifice to the spirits of the dead, ancestors, and nature is symbolized in the massive destruction such bonfires represent. Often accompanied by feasting and carnivalesque behavior, these bonfires are important elements in communal sentiment and the preservation of tradition.

Burgbrennen begins with a form of trick-or-treat. Village youngsters go from house to house begging for wood and kindling for the fire. Carrying these materials up the hill to the site of the fire, the boys hold the stack of wood and kindling while a large pole with a wooden cross is hoisted and planted into the ground. As the cross is secured, the youngsters heap the combustible material around the pole, and it is set ablaze by the last man to marry in the village. Other variations of this ritual involved affixing a large wheel and streamers to the top of the pole, which would in turn be set ablaze and spun.

Burgbrennen has not remained a strong custom among Luxembourger Americans. While many communities in the United States have retained bonfire-like festivals usually in the late fall, the tradition of fires at Lent seems to have greatly faded. In Vermillion, Minnesota, however, memories remain of its existence earlier in this century. One account was told by a village elder:

> *Bjork Sonntag* was the First Sunday of Lent and the last day of drinking alcohol during Lent. They had a very unusual custom in this area during the evening of *Bjork Sonntag.*

LUXEMBOURGER PROVERBS

Luxembourgers are fond of sayings that mark important moments in their history and the formation of national identity. One such saying is *Et get fir de glaf* or "Here goes for faith," a saying that was used in the Kloppelkrieg rebellion against the French during the reign of Napoleon. This motto was used by peasants when they rose up and by their captured leaders before they were executed

Many of the farmers would erect a pole on the highest point of the farm, put rags on top of the pole or put a wheel on top of the pole and cover that with old rags, pour oil on the rags and start them rags/wheel and pole on fire.

In late August and early September of every year there is a festival called the Schueberfouer (also called Schobermesse) or "Shepherd's Fair." This festival was founded by John the Blind in 1340. Lasting eighteen days (except every fifth year, when it lasts twenty-five days), the Schueberfouer began as a livestock fair. In addition to livestock and pottery, cloth and woolen articles were also displayed and sold. Craftsmen and weavers were originally the organizers and directors of the fair, giving way to a broader sponsorship and direction in the late eighteenth century. Traditionally, each Schueberfouer began with the marching of a flock of sheep called the *Hämmelsmarsch*. A shepherd and his sheep were followed by a band playing the *Hämmelsmarsch* tune. During this procession a door-to-door collection was made. The origin of the tune for the *Hämmelsmarsch* is unknown. It is known, however, that the carillon of the cathedral was said to have played it in the eighteenth century. The Schueberfouer was brought to the United States by Luxembourgers in the nineteenth century.

There was a noted observance of the Schueberfouer near the end of the American Civil War. An immigrant publication named the *Luxemburger Gazette* reported on September 20, 1917, that a northern army military unit had been founded in 1865 in the Williamsburg area of Brooklyn, New York, which was referred to as the *Lëtzebörger Gard*. When the eighty members of this unit met for a reunion after the war, they decided to organize a yearly gathering on the first Monday of September and to organize this event as a Schueberfouer as they had known it in Luxembourg. This event, like the festival in the old country, included a parade, games, dance, and target shooting.

As a result of this reunion and annual Schueberfouer, a united group of Luxembourger Americans was formed. By 1871 this veterans' group had grown and changed into a new organization called the Luxembourger Mutual Aid Society. The growth of this organization was not, however, unique among Luxembourger Americans across the country. Several organizations grew out of an organized *Schueberfouer* in this way, including Chicago's Luxembourger Brotherhood of America, which was founded on the occasion of its annual *Schueberfouer* in 1904.

The twentieth century saw a gradual decline in traditionally Luxembourger communities. However, in Belgium, Wisconsin, the Luxembourger community hosts an annual Luxembourg Heritage Weekend and Fest in early August featuring musical performances and other activities. In 2001 the Luxembourg Brotherhood of America rekindled the *Schueberfouer*. About 100 people attended and in 2011 the Brotherhood celebrated seventy-five years of *Schueberfouer* in Chicago. The June 23 Luxembourg National Day (*Nationalfeierdag*) continues to be commemorated in Luxembourger American settlements throughout the Midwestern United States. The Luxembourg Society of Wisconsin hosts a community fair and bazaar, *Kirmes*, at the end of each summer. St. Donatus, Iowa, hosts an annual Schueberfouer in October. Remsen, Iowa's Luxembourg Oktoberfest continued well into the twenty-first century. Rollingstone, Minnesota, hosts an annual Treipenfest in January. "While it seems just about everyone in Rollingstone, Minnesota, a small community about 45 miles east of Rochester, can claim some relation to the European country, during Treipenfest it seems everyone is a Luxembourger," reported the *Rochester Post-Bulletin* in 2012.

Among Luxembourger Americans, Santa Claus is not a Christmas figure. Rather, a special day was marked early in December to celebrate a "St. Nicholas Day." It is the custom one week before this day for children to put their slippers in front of their bedroom doors so that they might be filled with a small gift by St. Nicholas while they slept. On the eve of December 6, children place plates on dining room or kitchen tables to be filled overnight with sweets and gifts from St. Nicholas.

Many Luxembourger Americans continue to follow Christmas traditions handed down from the old country. Many celebrate Christmas Eve with family and friends after attending Midnight Mass. It is not uncommon for local clubs and association to organize nativity plays with children as actors and to arrange concerts to be given later on Christmas Day. Many families of Luxembourger descent today also include traditions from the more mainstream Anglo and German American cultures.

FAMILY AND COMMUNITY LIFE

In Luxembourger communities of the Midwest, people interacted with one another in several ways. The first was the sharing of farm work. Luxembourger immigrants who were farmers often came to possess farms in the United States ten times larger or more than the farms of their forebears in the old country. So much land created a great need to organize labor at crucial times of the planting, growing, and harvesting seasons. In these crucial times farmers of an area would band together to share in the labor. To offer aid and participate in such communal work was thought of as a responsibility not only to one's neighbor but also to one's family. These activities would provide opportunities for people to come together and share their lives, often holding feasts, dances, and other events once the seasonal work was finished. The second important factor in family and community dynamics was the church. Whether providing a time for meeting or holding religious services, the local parish was the focus of community pride.

Gender Roles The roles of women among Luxembourger immigrants were varied. In towns, women worked in shops and other businesses, raised families, and did the great share of domestic chores. They also took part in church activities involving education, community awareness, and minor fund-raising for projects. In the country, women were responsible for much of the overall work of the business of the farms, often relying on one another for mutual support in the tasks of child-raising, health care, education, and household economizing. Luxembourger American farm families were characterized by large families, self-reliance, and connection to community through church. Suzanne L. Bunkers' book *In Search of Susanna* (1996) details the lives of several generations of the women of her Luxembourger family. Her father's mother, Lillian Bunkers, was born in Iowa to Luxembourger immigrants. The particulars of her life were hers alone but were typical of many northern Midwest farm-family women.

> Grandma Bunkers' married life was not easy. Her first child, Larry, was born two years after her marriage to Frank Bunkers. During the next fifteen years, Lillian gave birth to seven more children, two of whom (Cletus and Vincent) died as babies. At the age of thirty-eight, Lillian found herself a widow with six children to support. A dog-eared photograph from that era shows a weathered Lillian, in housedress and work shoes, posing in the farmyard with her children—her five-year-old son, Tony, who would grow up to be my father, standing with his stomach thrust forward and a quizzical expression, like his mother's, on his face, as if both mother and son were trying to figure out how life had gotten them into that predicament.

Education In many settlement towns, Luxembourger American education went hand-in-hand with religion. Many of the schools were Catholic and largely staffed by priests, nuns, and lay persons of the Catholic faith. Thus religious and academic instruction were given together, with moral education having great priority. Lessons related to the Catholic rite of catechism were always a part of the school curricula. In the country far from towns, Luxembourger American immigrants often were educated in a one-room schoolhouse not affiliated with the Catholic Church. Despite their isolation from Catholic school instruction in towns, many children were sent to towns to receive weeks of religious education to prepare them for the rite of confirmation or to receive first communion. In some towns there also were literary societies that aided in the advancement of education within their communities by raising funds and establishing libraries.

The 2010 U.S. Census reported that over 95 percent of Luxembourger Americans graduate from high school and nearly 50 percent of adults have at least a bachelor's degree, with women obtaining slightly more advanced degrees than men.

Courtship and Weddings In Luxembourger American communities, there were many opportunities for courtship between persons of all ages. Going to church, dances, and school and community events provided a means for socializing. Most persons were allowed to choose whom they wished to court or be courted by, although issues of class, ethnicity, and faith often acted as barriers to courting outside one's own group as defined by parents or other family members.

For Catholic Luxembourgers, marriages are traditionally performed along with a Catholic mass. After the marriage a great feast is held, sometimes lasting days, during which gifts are given, traditional dishes are served, songs are sung, and games are played.

Relations with Other Americans In Luxembourger American communities, there has traditionally been a close alliance and kinship of custom with German Americans. However, their distinct heritage is very important to Luxembourgers. In 2011, Keven Wester, the executive director of the Luxembourg American Cultural Society (LACS), was quoted as saying, "If you want to upset a Luxembourger, call him a German." Many Luxembourgers spoke German and shared many customs, songs, cuisine, and morals with Germans. Although this helped forge a bond between the two groups, religious differences between many Protestant Germans and Catholic Luxembourgers could still result in friction. Politics from the homeland also came to influence relations between older Luxembourgers and Germans as seen in the many anti-Prussian sentiments expressed by this group around the turn of the twentieth century in Chicago, Milwaukee, New York City, and elsewhere. Luxembourgers living in towns were often taken for Germans and were sometimes embroiled in anti-German sentiments that arose during World War I. In time, however, German Americans and Luxembouger Americans overcame most of their differences in opinion.

EMPLOYMENT AND ECONOMIC CONDITIONS

Among the many farmers who emigrated from Luxembourg, a significant number moved to the Chicago area and began cultivating vegetables, finding a specialized niche in growing celery. After 1880 they erected greenhouses for year-round industrial production of vegetables and flowers. Perhaps a hundred greenhouses dotted the Luxembourger areas of North Chicago, and their growers' association numbered some 1,200 families. By 2000 most of the farms were gone, but surviving greenhouses had relocated to northern and northwestern Chicago suburbs such as Niles and Des Plaines. Many of the small farms settled by Luxembourgers in the 1800s were still owned and worked by their descendants into the twenty-first century. Others have become quite large businesses, such as the Oberweiss Dairy. When Peter Oberweiss of Aurora, Illinois, began selling milk to his neighbors in 1915, it was the beginning of a family business that has grown to include retail stores in Illinois, Michigan, Indiana, and Missouri. The dairy still offers home delivery.

POLITICS AND GOVERNMENT

Luxembourger Americans did not shy away from politics or government in their new home. Many were active proponents of political causes and several held elected and nonelected positions in public service. Among their group's notable political sentiments was anti-Prussianism, a position that reflected concerns both with the government of Luxembourg and Luxembourgers' place in relation to German Americans in many parts of the United States. Another notable moment in Luxembourger American political history occurred when the United States entered the war against Germany in 1914. At this time Luxembourger Americans came out in numbers strongly for the United States effort against Germany.

Military One example of a Luxembourger who found success through the military was Dominik Welter. At the age of eleven, Welter came from Luxembourg to settle with his family in Ohio. As a young man Welter struck out and traveled west to seek a fortune in the Gold Rush but eventually returned to his family in Ohio without having had success. In 1861, at the advent of the American Civil War, Welter joined the Fourth Ohio Cavalry and worked his way up the ranks to become a captain. Captured at the battle of Chickamunga, he was detained in a prisoner of war camp until the war's end in 1865. After the war in 1877, still a member of the army, he traveled to Chicago, where he was given the command of a cavalry unit. After resigning from the army Welter was hired as Secretary of Police for the city of Chicago and given the rank of inspector. In the following years he and fellow Luxembourger Michael Schaack, were the leaders of a political and social organization named the Luxembourg Independent Club of Chicago.

Many native Luxembourgers feel a bond with the United States because of the role the U.S. Army played in liberating the country from Nazi control in September 1944. At the beginning of the twenty-first century, Henri Bourbon, the grand duke of Luxembourg, made a significant effort to maintain ties with Luxembourger Americans. "There are more people in the United States that have Luxembourgish blood than in the country of Luxembourg," Keven Wester of the Luxembourg American Cultural Society (LACS) said in an article that appeared in Chicago's *Daily Herald* on April 20, 2011. Headquartered in Belgium, Wisconsin, the LACS was founded in 2004 with the support of the Grand Duchy.

NOTABLE INDIVIDUALS

While Luxembourger Americans have been a relatively small group in population, with only some 50,000 total descendants of immigrants, they have made a great many contributions to American society.

Academia One of a few internationally known diaries scholars, Suzanne L. Bunkers joined the English department at Minnesota State University, Mankato, in 1980 and retired in 2011 as a distinguished professor. She taught and wrote particularly about women's literature and life writing and is the author or coauthor of eight books and dozens of scholarly articles and reviews. Her creative nonfiction book, *In Search of Susanna*, traces her families' roots in Luxembourg and their immigration to the Midwest.

Eduard Conzemius (1892–1931) gained acclaim in the early twentieth century as one of the foremost ethnographers of Central American peoples. Emigrating from Luxembourg to the United States to join his brother, Conzemius moved to Chicago and was first employed by the Sherman House hotel. In the following years he studied English and Spanish while making money as an accountant in Chicago and New Orleans. In 1916 he decided to pursue his dream to study Central American Indians. He spent time in Honduras and Nicaragua living with the Miskito, Sumu, and Rama Indians. In 1932 the Smithsonian Institution published the results of his work on the native languages of these people in a monograph entitled *Ethnological Survey of the Miskito and Sumu Indians of Honduras and Nicaragua*.

Arno Joseph Mayer was born in 1926 into a Jewish family in Luxembourg. The Mayers fled to the United States in 1940, shortly after the German army invaded Luxembourg. Mayer became the Stockton professor emeritus of history at Princeton University. His areas of scholarship include modern Europe, diplomatic history, and the Holocaust.

Activism Richard J. Witry, born in 1950, was a Chicago attorney, author, and activist. He was the longtime president/director of the *Luxembourg News of America*.

Art Jean Noerdinger (1895–1963), a prominent modernist artist and proponent of modernism, emigrated from Diekirch, Luxembourg, to the Chicago area in 1925. While in Luxembourg, Noerdinger had been an outspoken critic of the Luxemburg Artists Union, whose power in support of conservative art he opposed, along with a group of artists he led. While in the United States he continued to exhibit his art and paint portraits.

Edward Steichen, one of the most prominent American figures in the art of photography, was born in Luxembourg on March 27, 1879. In 1882 his parents moved from Luxembourg to settle in Hancock, Michigan. By the age of twenty-one, Steichen had achieved a moderate degree of success as a photographer, having had his work exhibited in Chicago and Philadelphia. His photographs portrayed a distinctive soft and fuzzy quality. In his day these photographs were considered highly innovative. In the following decades, Steichen became one of the most sought after and lauded photographers in the United States, showing his photos in many of the major shows of this era. During his service in World War I Steichen's artistic philosophy and direction changed profoundly. Returning home after the war, he loudly proclaimed his rejection of impressionism and the other elements of style he had made famous and strongly supported a stark form of realism. Steichen then burned all his paintings in a bonfire and took up commercial photography in a studio that he operated from 1923 to 1938. During this time he photographed literary and artistic personalities as well as members of the elite of New York City, and he became the chief photographer for *Vanity Fair* and *Vogue* magazines. With the outbreak of World War II, Steichen, then sixty-two years old, was commissioned by the U.S. Navy to photograph the war at sea. During and after the war Steichen continued to have major shows and became the director of photography at the Museum of Modern Art in 1947, a post that he held until 1962. He worked until his death on March 25, 1973.

Journalism Nicholas Gonner (1935–1982) is chiefly known as the author of an authoritative study of the emigration of Luxembourgers into the New World entitled *Die Luxemburger in der neuen Welt: Beiträge zur Geschichte der Luxemburger* (Luxembourgers in the New World: Contributions to the History of the Luxembourgers). This work was written for and published by the *Luxembourger Gazette*, published in Dubuque, Iowa, in 1889 and was meant not only to be a chronicle of Luxembourger success in the New World but also to be read in Europe as a testament to the success in "the land of opportunity," as the United States imagined itself.

Politics The longest-serving Republican Speaker of the U.S. House of Representatives (1999–2007), Dennis Hastert, was a Luxembourger American from Aurora, Illinois. Hastert was first elected to congress in 1987, and was re-elected to Congress ten times. His family owned a restaurant in Plainfield, Illinois. Hastert was a high-school teacher before being elected to the Illinois House of Representatives in 1980.

The first Luxembourger American to serve in the U.S. Congress was Nicholas Muller. Born in Luxembourg on November 15, 1836, he attended common schools in the city of Metz and thereafter attended the Luxembourg Athenaeum. Upon

Former Speaker of the House Dennis Hastert is of Luxembourgian descent. JIM SPELLMAN / WIREIMAGE / GETTY IMAGES

immigrating to the United States, the family settled in New York City. Muller was employed as a railroad ticket agent for over twenty years, during which time he was one of the promoters and directors of the Germania Bank in New York. From 1875 to 1876 Muller served as a member of the State Assembly of New York and was also a member of the State Central Committee. In 1876 Muller was elected as a Democrat to Congress, serving from March 4, 1877, to March 3, 1881. Losing his seat after an unsuccessful re-election bid in late 1880, Muller regained it in 1882, serving another five years until 1887. In 1888 Muller was appointed president of the New York City Police Board and to one other minor office until he was again elected to the U.S. Congress, where he served until his resignation on December 1, 1902. After holding and attempting to hold other minor offices, Muller died in New York City on December 12, 1917.

Another addition to the history of Luxembourger Americans was the thirty-second president of the United States, Franklin Delano Roosevelt. Roosevelt is said to be a descendant of Philip de la Noye (or de Lannoy), who arrived on the ship *Fortune*. De la Noye is thought to be the first Luxembourger to immigrate to North America. Roosevelt was born on January 30, 1882, in Hyde Park, New York, and served as president from 1933 until his death on April 12, 1945.

Science Among prominent scientists of Luxembourger descent are Johann and Joseph Druecker, two brothers from Ozaukee County, Wisconsin. In 1884 the Drueckers invented a gas-fired lime kiln that greatly improved their own business and the lime industry overall. Also notable is biologist Francois Mergen (1925–1989), dean of the Yale school of forestry from 1965 to 1975. Born in Luxembourg, Mergen fought the Nazis during the occupation of Luxembourg and was interned in a concentration camp.

Sports Perhaps the most famous athlete of Luxembourger American descent is tennis star Chris Evert. Born in Fort Lauderdale, Florida, on December 21, 1954, Evert came to dominate the sport of tennis throughout the late 1970s and early 1980s and continued to win many important matches into the late 1980s. In 1970, at the age of fifteen, Evert made her first mark in an important match, beating top-ranked Margaret Court in a small tournament. Evert become a professional on her eighteenth birthday in 1972, and by the time of her retirement in the late 1980s she had earned nearly $9,000,000. Evert won the U.S. Open women's singles title from 1975 to 1978 and in 1980 and 1982. She won the Wimbledon singles title in 1974, 1976, and 1981, the French Open singles title in 1974, 1975, 1979, 1980, 1983, 1985, and 1986, and the Australian Open singles title in 1982 and 1984. Her World Tennis Association singles titles number 157. In 1995 Evert was inducted into the International Tennis Hall of Fame. In 1985 she was named Greatest Woman Athlete of the last twenty-five years by the Women's Sports Foundation.

Stage and Screen Perhaps the greatest star of Luxembourger American descent was the actress Loretta Young. Born in Salt Lake City, Utah, in 1913, Young received her first part when she was four years old through her uncle, who was working as an assistant director in Hollywood. In 1927 she had another small part in the film *Naughty But Nice*. From this point into the early 1930s, Young was acting in six to nine films each year. In the mid-1930s Young joined the Fox studios; by then she had become one of Hollywood's most prominent leading ladies. In 1947 she was awarded the Academy Award for best actress in *The Farmer's Daughter*, a film about a girl from a rural area who works her way into the U.S. House of Representatives as a congresswoman. In 1949 she was nominated again for an Academy Award. In 1953 Young began her television career with her series *The Loretta Young Show*. This show gained Young Emmy Awards in 1954, 1956, and 1958. After 1962 Young did not appear before the camera until 1986, when she starred in a made-for-television film called *Lady in the Corner*. Young died on August 12, 2000.

MEDIA

Luxembourg News of America

Serves as a medium of communication for Luxembourgers living in the United States and also for their descendants and friends. Contains news of Luxembourg societies and anything of interest in the Grand Duchy of Luxembourg.

Maryann Hughes, Luxembourg News Editor
5204 Brown Street
Skokie, Illinois 60077
Email: maryann.hughes@att.net

ORGANIZATIONS AND ASSOCIATIONS

Luxembourg-American Descendants Society of La Crosse

Jim Birnbaum, President
P.O. Box 2182
La Crosse, Wisconsin 54602-2182
Phone: (608) 785-2740

Luxembourg American Social Club

Karen Winandy, President
39690 N. Cambridge Boulevard
Beach Park, Illinois 60083
Phone: (847) 599-9655

Luxembourg Brotherhood of America

Founded in 1887 in Chicago, this is the oldest Luxembourger association in the United States. It consists of four sections located in the Chicago area and is dedicated to maintaining the strong ties between the Grand Duchy and Luxembourger Americans.

Richard Witry
Email: witry@msn.com
URL: www.luxam.info

Luxembourg Heritage Society of Northwest Iowa

Rick Roder, President
44565 110th Street
Remsen, Iowa 51050
Email: rick@rulesofbaseball.com
URL: http://genealogynwia.homestead.com/luxembourg.html

MUSEUMS AND RESEARCH CENTERS

The Henry J. Leir Luxembourg Program, Clark University

LLP-CU was founded to honor Dr. H. C. Leir's wish that Clark students and faculty deepen contacts with Luxembourg, the country that gave him safe haven at the outset of World War II.

Clark University
950 Main Street
Worcester, Massachusetts 01610
Phone: (508) 793-7711

Luxembourg American Cultural Society & Center

The LACS was founded in 2004 by individuals of
Luxembourg descent in the United States as well
as citizens of the Grand Duchy of Luxembourg.
Its mission is symbolized as "roots and leaves":
Preserve the roots of Luxembourg heritage/culture
in America and nurture the leaves of ongoing
relationships of family, friendship, commerce,
and tourism between Luxembourg and the
United States.

100 Peter Thein Avenue
P.O. Box 157
Belgium, Wisconsin 53004-0157
URL: www.luxamculturalsociety.org

Luxembourg-American Families Genealogy Pages

URL: www.luxembourgamericanfamilies.org

Luxembourgiana Bach-Dunn Collection

Built from a core collection of the Luxembourg Heritage
Society of 270 books, periodicals, and maps related
to the history and civilization of Luxembourg, this
collection is located in the O'Shaughnessy-Frey

Library Center at the University of St. Thomas in St.
Paul, Minnesota.

2115 Summit Avenue
St. Paul, Minnesota 55105
Phone: (651) 962-5014
Fax: (651) 962-5406
Email: libweb@stthomas.edu

SOURCES FOR ADDITIONAL STUDY

American Luxembourg Society 1882–1982. Luxembourg:
Imprimerie Saint-Paul, 1991.

Bunkers, Suzanne L. *In Search of Susanna*. Iowa City:
University of Iowa Press, 1996.

Dibble, Susan. "Proud to Be a Luxembourger." *Arlington
Heights (IL) Daily Herald*, June 21, 2011.

Gardini, Fausto. *Luxembourg on My Mind*. Jacksonville,
FL: Fausto Gardini, 2011.

Klein, Frank W., and Suzanne L. Bunkers. *Good Earth, Black
Soil*. Winona, MN: Saint Mary's College Press, 1981.

Lies, Joseph J. *Luxemburger Immigrants to Aurora*. Aurora,
IL: Aurora Historical Society, 1976.

Nilles, Mary E. *A Legacy from Luxembourg: A Historical
Guide to the Early Settlement of Rollingstone, Minnesota*.
Winona, MN: W & C Printing Co., 1986.

Story, Lonnie D. *The Meeting of Anni Adams: The Butterfly
of Luxembourg*. Eugene, OR: ACW Press, 2004.

MACEDONIAN AMERICANS

Elizabeth Shostak

OVERVIEW

Macedonian Americans are immigrants or descendants of people from the Republic of Macedonia or from several other Balkan countries where Macedonians are an ethnic minority. Located on the Balkan Peninsula in southeastern Europe, Macedonia is bordered on the north by Serbia and the disputed territory of Kosovo, on the south by Greece, on the west by Bulgaria, and on the east by Albania. It is a landlocked and mountainous country, and only about 4 percent of its land is suitable for crops. The region experiences a high rate of seismic activity, making it susceptible to earthquake damage. It has few natural resources other than mineral deposits. Macedonians have traditionally made their living from farming, herding, and mining. The Republic of Macedonia's total land area is 9,781 square miles (25,333 square kilometers), slightly larger than the state of Vermont.

According to the *CIA World Factbook*, Macedonia's population was an estimated 2,082,370 in July 2012. The majority of citizens, 64 percent, are identified as ethnic Macedonians. Albanians make up the largest minority, at 25.1 percent of the population; small Turkish, Roma, and Serbian populations are also represented. The Municipality of Suto Orizari, within the capital Skopje, is the only municipality in the country where the majority of the population is Roma. The majority of Macedonians, 64.7 percent, belong to the Eastern Orthodox Church. The other 33.3 percent of the population consists of Muslims. Small Catholic, Protestant, and Jewish communities are also present. Of the almost 12,000 Jews living in Macedonia at the beginning of World War II, only several hundred survived. Eight languages are spoken in Macedonia. The official language, Macedonian, is spoken by 66.5 percent of the population. Other languages include Albanian (25 percent), Turkish (3 percent), and Serbo-Croatian (3 percent). Adyghe, Romanian, Romani, and Balkan Gagauz Turkish are also spoken. Macedonia was the least developed of the Yugoslav republics before its independence in 1991; the official rate of unemployment was listed at almost 30 percent in 2012.

Early in the twentieth century about 50,000 impoverished Macedonian men came to the United States seeking to make their fortune before returning home to their families. After World War I ended in 1919, most of them did return to the Balkans. Strict limitations on immigration kept the number of new immigrants low; however, a steady trickle of Macedonians who had immigrated to Canada came to the United States through Detroit and settled in Michigan and other states in the upper Midwest. They worked on building the railroads and in other heavy industrial trades; they also started small businesses. Immigration during and after World War II slowed even more. With the breakup of Yugoslavia in the 1990s, which led to a high level of ongoing regional conflict in the Balkans, Macedonian immigration to the United States increased slightly.

The U.S. Census Bureau's American Community Survey estimated in 2011 that there were 59,638 American residents of Macedonian descent. Of these, 60 percent, or 35,808, were born in the United States. Of the Macedonian Americans born outside the United States, about 10,400 entered the United States before 1990; 6,982 entered between 1990 and 2000; and 6,400 entered after the year 2000. Most Macedonians have settled in large urban areas in the East (including several cities in New Jersey and New York state) and in the northern Midwest (including Detroit and Chicago).

HISTORY OF THE PEOPLE

Early History The Republic of Macedonia was created in 1991 when the country obtained independence from Yugoslavia. But Macedonian history is long and complex. The Macedonians are a Slavic people, with close ethnic and linguistic ties to Bulgaria, as well as political and religious ties to Greece. The earliest civilizations in the Macedonian region have been traced back to at least 3500 BCE, and by about 1000 BCE several population groups, including Dacians, Thracians, Illyrians, Celts, and Greeks, coexisted in the area. Macedonia had perhaps its greatest period of political power during the fourth century BCE, when King Philip of Macedon and his son, Alexander the Great, strengthened and expanded the Macedonian empire. By 29 CE, however, Rome had subdued the region, and it ruled it for several centuries thereafter. The Romans incorporated Macedonia into the Eastern Roman Empire. Beginning in the third century CE, tribes of Goths, Huns, and Avars invaded the region.

By about the middle of the sixth century, Slavic peoples had begun to settle in Macedonia. A century later, Bulgars, a Turco-Ugrian people of remote Mongolian origin, invaded; they were eventually assimilated by the Slavs. The Bulgars established the First Bulgarian Kingdom, which included much of Macedonia's territory.

During the ninth century, future saints Cyril and Methodius brought Christianity to the region. Their disciples devised a Slavic alphabet (the Cyrillic alphabet that is also used in Russian) in order to promote literacy in the vernacular. In the tenth century, the Bulgarian Kingdom split into two. The western kingdom, with its capital in Ohrid, is considered the first Slavic Macedonian state. It was ruled by Tsar Samuil (997–1014) but was conquered by the Byzantine Empire in 1018. Except for a brief period of Serbian control under Stefan Dusan (1331–1355), Macedonia remained under Ottoman rule until 1912. This long period of Turkish control was considered the most stable in Macedonian history and deeply influenced language and social traditions throughout the Balkan region. At the same time, however, Ottoman rule was harsh and authoritarian, and it fueled increasing dissent from the subjected population. In 1876 the Bulgarians staged an armed revolt against the Turks, which was brutally subdued and resulted in an indiscriminate massacre of civilians. From that time, intense anti-Turkish sentiment continued, and the region became increasingly destabilized.

Modern Era The early twentieth century was a period of intense conflict and volatility throughout the Balkans as various states competed for power. When the Ottoman Empire began to dissolve at the end of the nineteenth century, Serbia, Greece, and Bulgaria all sought cultural and territorial claims over Macedonia. In response to these threats, Macedonians organized the Internal Macedonian Revolutionary Organization (IMRO) in 1893. IMRO's aim was to preserve "Macedonia for the Macedonians," and on August 2, 1903, it proclaimed independence from the Turks. Though this rebellion was harshly suppressed, it made the "Macedonian Question" an international concern for several years. In 1912 Serbia, Montenegro, Greece, and Bulgaria successfully united in the First Balkan War to eject the Turks from Europe, after which the competing states sought to strengthen their claims to Macedonia. The Serbian army occupied Skopje and claimed "Vardar Macedonia" as a Serbian colony. The Greek army occupied Salonika, which it deemed part of "Aegean Macedonia," virtually excluding Bulgaria from the region. The occupying forces instituted harsh campaigns to force the population to renounce its Macedonian identity. They encouraged Serbian and Greek colonists to move to these regions, suppressed the Macedonian language, and forced priests to convert to the Greek or Serbian Orthodox religions.

Bulgaria's loss of Macedonia in 1912 at the end of the First Balkan War precipitated decades of conflict and violence, which arguably contributed to the ethnic hostilities that resurfaced in the Balkans during the 1990s. After a surprise attack on Serbian forces in Macedonia in 1913, which initiated the Second Balkan War, Bulgaria was again defeated and stripped of its claims to Macedonian territory. Despite alliances with Germany in both the First and Second World Wars, during which Macedonia suffered brutal invasions and "Bulgarization" campaigns, Bulgaria was unable to reestablish its hold on Macedonia. In 1945 the new Federal Socialist Republic of Yugoslavia, controlled by a Communist party actively sympathetic to the Macedonian cause, created a People's Republic of Macedonia. This region, which incorporated the boundaries of the later independent republic, was a semiautonomous constituent republic within the Yugoslav federation. The Communist party encouraged the renewal of Macedonian cultural life, promoting the Macedonian language and restoring the Macedonian Orthodox Church.

The Yugoslav federation broke up in 1989, and Macedonia declared independence on November 20, 1991. A new constitution went into effect that day, and Kiro Gligorov was elected president. Ethnic and political discord, however, remained. There was sporadic discord between the majority ethnic Macedonians and the 25 percent minority ethnic Albanians. In 2001, ethnic Albanians, concentrated in the northwest regions that border Kosovo and Albania, waged an eight-month insurgency seeking greater autonomy. The internationally brokered peace agreement expanded minority rights in Macedonia, but distrust and incidents of violence continued. Greece, which had a province called Macedonia in its northern region, objected to the country's use of that name and blocked international acceptance of Macedonia. Bulgaria, which had a significant Macedonian minority population, also historically objected to the idea of an independent Macedonian nation.

By 2012 the United States and 133 other countries had recognized the Republic of Macedonia by its constitutional name, yet the dispute with Greece continued to be an obstacle to Macedonia's admittance in the European Union, which was seen by the Macedonian government as a very high priority for the country's economic future. As the dispute with Greece dragged on, economic growth was slow, unemployment was relatively high, and modernization did not keep up with other parts of Europe.

SETTLEMENT IN THE UNITED STATES

Although Macedonian immigration to the United States did not truly begin until the early twentieth century, there is evidence to suggest that the first Macedonian to arrive in America, Dragan of Ohrid, sailed with Christopher Columbus. There are different accounts of Dragan. One story claims he was a religious heretic who escaped persecution in Macedonia by fleeing to Spain. He was later discovered, however, and condemned to death. Columbus saved Dragan from burning at the stake by recruiting him for his first trip to America. Another account claims that Dragan was expelled from Ohrid with his family when he was a child, after the city fell to the Turks. The family moved to Spain, where Dragan advanced in the military, became a favorite of the crown, and sailed with Columbus on his second voyage. According to this story, after Dragan returned to Europe he formed his own expedition and sailed with this crew to Venezuela. Seeing that the native people there lived along the water in marshy areas, as in Venice, he bestowed the name "Venezia" on the land. He then went to Panama, allegedly becoming the first white man to set foot in that country.

Macedonian immigration to the United States began in the early twentieth century, as poverty forced many peasants to seek economic opportunities abroad. Most of these early immigrants considered themselves Bulgarians from Macedonia, and entry records from the period usually listed them as Bulgarian, Turkish, Serbian, Albanian, or Greek nationals. For this reason, it is difficult to determine precise numbers of Macedonian immigrants. It is estimated, however, that between 1903 and 1906, approximately 50,000 Macedonian Bulgarians entered the United States. From 1906 to the outbreak of the Balkan Wars and World War I, a few thousand more arrived. The first Macedonian immigrants came primarily from the western parts of Macedonia, near the towns of Kastoria, Florina, and Bitola. About 80 percent of these immigrants were peasants, with small craftsmen such as carpenters, workers, and intellectuals making up the remainder. The vast majority of early Macedonian immigrants were *gurbetchii* or *pechalbari*, single men driven by poverty to seek their fortunes in the United States, but who expected to return to their homeland after a few years.

American Protestant churches played a notable role in Macedonian immigration. In the 1860s and 1870s, Congregational and Methodist churches began missionary activities in the Balkans and sent many Bulgarians and Macedonians to the United States to attend college. When these individuals returned to their homeland, they spoke highly of their experiences in the United States. In addition, the churches established numerous schools in Balkan cities and towns. These activities created a positive image of the United States and prompted interest in immigration.

After World War I many Macedonians living in the United States returned to Europe, with only about 20,000 Macedonians remaining. Further immigration was seriously affected by passage of the Immigration Act of 1924 (the Johnson-Reed Act), which established quotas for each national group based on their numbers in the U.S. population in 1920. Because Macedonian immigration had begun so late, and because many immigrants had returned to their homeland after the war, the basis for the Macedonian quota was extremely low. Nevertheless, though new immigration was much slower during the period between the world wars, Macedonians continued to enter the United States. Many arrived via Canada, crossing the border into Detroit to evade quota restrictions. During this period, increasing numbers of Macedonians also arrived from Greece. By 1945 the number of Macedonians in the United States had reached an estimated 50,000 to 60,000 people.

When the Yugoslav federation was created after World War II, however, Macedonian immigration slowed significantly. Yugoslavia's support of Macedonian autonomy, as well as economic improvements in Macedonia, encouraged Macedonians to remain there. From 1945 to 1960, only about 2,000 Macedonians arrived in the United States from Yugoslavia. During the 1960s and 1970s, however, after emigration policies were liberalized, as many as 40,000 Macedonians left Yugoslavia for Canada, Australia, and the United States. Few from Bulgaria, however, were allowed to leave. As many as 70,000 Macedonians living in Greece left that country after World War II, when Slavs were expelled from the area. Many settled in Canada, where the Macedonian community in Toronto grew to more than 100,000. Smaller numbers moved to Australia and the United States.

Though a small proportion of Macedonians who came to the United States from Yugoslavia in the 1950s and 1960s were political dissidents, the majority of Macedonian immigrants were compelled by economic motives. Early Macedonian immigrants from Bulgaria settled in the northern and eastern industrial centers of the United States, especially in the Midwest, where they were able to find unskilled jobs in heavy industry. A large community sprang up in Detroit, which by the 1980s numbered from as many as 15,000 to 20,000 Macedonian Americans. Macedonians also settled in large numbers in Gary, Indiana; Chicago, Illinois; and the Ohio cities of Columbus, Akron, Lorain, Cincinnati, Canton, and Massilon. Other communities were established in Passaic, New Jersey, and in New York City, Lackawanna, Buffalo, Rochester, and Syracuse, New York.

Adjusting to industrial jobs and a competitive economic setting was often difficult for Macedonian immigrants, who had come from relatively poor rural areas dominated by an authoritative political regime. Upon their arrival in the United States, they often took hazardous jobs in mines, steel mills and foundries, and railroad construction. Because most immigrants were single men, residents from the same village or region tended to stay together in the United States for social support. Coffeehouses and boardinghouses became important places where immigrants could socialize and share job prospects, read newspapers and discuss politics, and participate in their associations. Where Macedonians were few in number, they often associated with other Slavic or Orthodox communities.

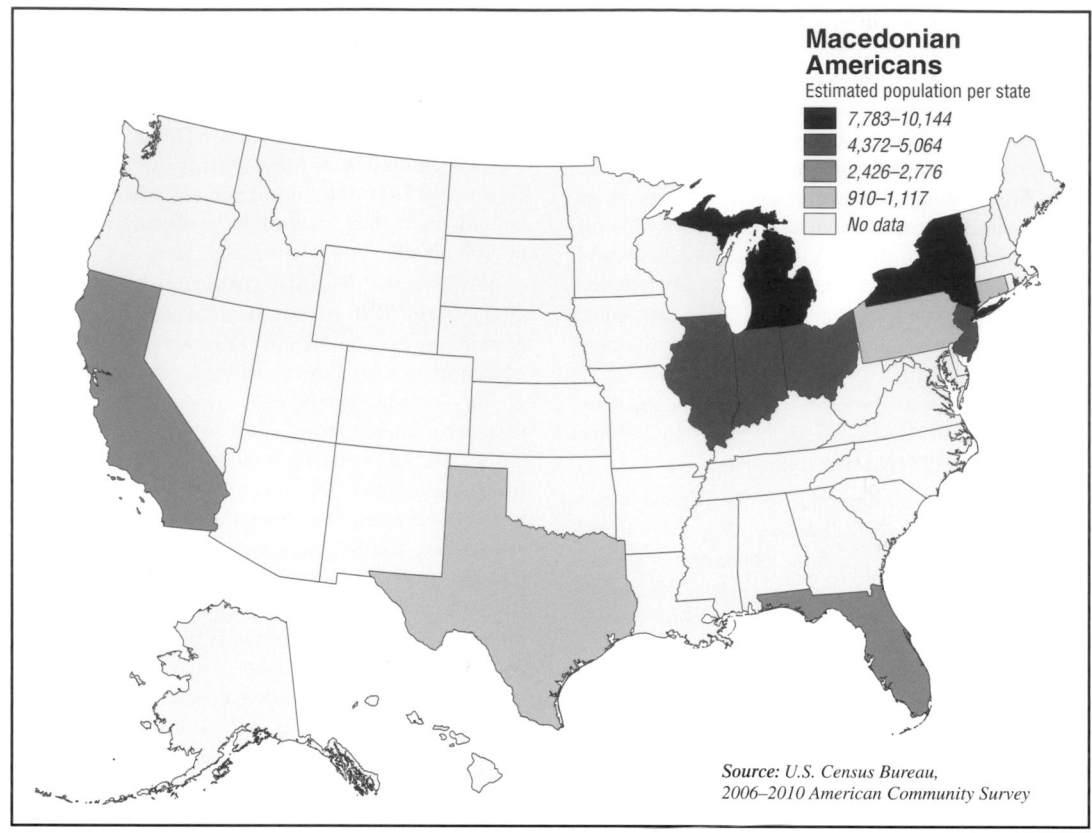

Macedonian Americans

Estimated population per state

- 7,783–10,144
- 4,372–5,064
- 2,426–2,776
- 910–1,117
- No data

Source: U.S. Census Bureau, 2006–2010 American Community Survey

Macedonian immigrants established fraternal, mutual aid, and cultural societies in the United States that offered assistance when members lost their jobs or became ill. These societies were organized according to place of origin and often sent material aid back to their respective villages in Macedonia. Some of these societies still exist, though their significance has declined as native-born Macedonian Americans have replaced immigrants as the norm. The Orthodox Church also serves as an important cohesive presence.

During the 1990s, Macedonian immigration again increased. Between 1990 and 1999, about 6,300 Macedonians came to the United States, and between 2000 and 2010, almost 5,000 arrived. Newcomers followed the same settlement patterns of earlier immigrants, settling in large urban centers in the Midwest. The American Community Survey reported that in 2009 there were 57,200 Americans of Macedonian descent, with 47 percent living in the Midwest, 32 percent living in the Northeast, 10 percent living in the South, and 10 percent living in the West. Like earlier generations, most came to take advantage of economic opportunities. Others entered the United States to enroll in colleges and universities.

LANGUAGE

Macedonian is a South Slavic language closely related to Bulgarian. Like Russian, it is written in the Cyrillic alphabet. Unlike Russian, however, modern Macedonian does not change the endings of nouns according to their grammatical case. Standard Macedonian is based on the country's western dialects, which are the most distinct from the Bulgarian and Serbo-Croatian languages. Northern dialects are similar to Serbian dialects, and eastern dialects are closest to Bulgarian. Macedonian has thirty-one sounds and a letter for each sound, making it a completely phonetic language that is easy to learn to read and write. Even into the twenty-first century, more than half of Macedonian Americans reported speaking more than one language. Meto Koloski, born in Garfield, New Jersey, in 1983, reported in an interview in 2012, "Our first language was Macedonian, or more like Maklish, a combination of Macedonian and English. It was not until I was twelve that I started to learn to read and write in Macedonian."

Greetings and Popular Expressions The usual Macedonian greeting is *zdravo* (ZDRA-vuh), or "hi." More formal greetings are *dobro utro* (DOE-bruh OO-troh)—"good morning"—or *dobar den* (DOE-bar DAIN)—"good day." "Good night" is *dobra nok* (DOE-bruh NOK-yih). *Kako cte*? (KAK-uh STAI) means "How are you?" and *dobrodojdovte* (DOE-bruh DOY-duv-tai) means "welcome."

RELIGION

The vast majority of Macedonians who immigrated to the United States were members of the Eastern Orthodox Church, and religious affiliation played a central role in maintaining ethnic identity, language, and native traditions. Early immigrants established parishes under the jurisdiction of the patriarch (head of the church) in Sofia, Bulgaria. The first Bulgarian Orthodox church in the United States was Sts. Cyril and Methodius, established in Granite City, Illinois, in 1909. Others included St. Stephen in Indianapolis, founded in 1915; St. Clement Ohridsky in Detroit, founded in 1929; and St. Trinity in Madison, Illinois, founded in 1929. The Bulgarian Orthodox Mission for the entire United States and Canada (which in 1937 was renamed the Bulgarian Eastern Orthodox Church, Diocese of the United States and Canada) was centered in Indianapolis. In 1962 a group of Macedonian Americans in Gary, Indiana, founded a separate Macedonian Orthodox Church, which was recognized by the Holy Synod of the Macedonian Orthodox Church in Skopje. Within twenty years, eleven Macedonian Orthodox parishes had been established. By the late 1990s, nineteen parishes were listed in the United States. However, Bishop Kyril, head of the Bulgarian Church in the United States and Canada, refused to recognize the Macedonian Orthodox Church; this rift caused bitter feelings between Macedonian and Bulgarian immigrant communities.

Macedonian Orthodox churches are organized under the guidance of a metropolitan (a bishop who is head of an ecclesiastical province) for the United States, Canada, and Australia. Parishes offer liturgical services in both Macedonian and English and provide a variety of social and cultural activities such as festivals, dinners, and holiday bazaars. Women's groups contribute a great deal to the church's social functions. Sunday schools, which teach the Macedonian language, are also important cultural institutions.

Like other Eastern Orthodox churches, the Macedonian Orthodox Church follows the Julian calendar. Orthodox sacraments and liturgy closely resemble those of the Roman Catholic Church, but in the Orthodox Church, great reverence is attached to icons of Christ, the Virgin Mary, and the saints. Homes as well as churches often have icons in a place of honor. Unlike the Roman Catholic Church, the Orthodox Church allows married men to become priests. Orthodox churches adhere to the Nicene Creed and follow the liturgy of St. John Chrysostom (circa 347–407 CE). They observe seven sacraments: the Eucharist, Baptism, Confirmation, Penance, Matrimony, Holy Orders, and the Anointing of the Sick. The Macedonian Orthodox Church also observes the ritual of *Agiasmos*, or Holy Water, as a means of bestowing grace upon the congregation. There are Greater and Lesser Blessings of Water. The Lesser Blessing can be performed on any day of the year, either in the church or within a home or designated space. The Greater Blessing of Water is performed on the Feast of the Epiphany (in the Julian calendar, January 19). On this day, churchgoers often take a bottle of holy water to their homes, where it is kept until the following year. Macedonian

Americans retain strong ties to Orthodoxy, even when Macedonian Orthodox churches are not accessible. In these instances, they will attend Greek, Syrian, Russian, or pan-Orthodox churches.

CULTURE AND ASSIMILATION

The first Macedonian immigrants endured poverty and harsh working conditions when they arrived in the United States. Many lived in crowded and unhealthy conditions in large cities. It was customary for several men from the same village in Macedonia to share a small flat or house, often without running water and electricity. Space was so limited that the men had to sleep in shifts, sharing the same bedding. Most lived extremely frugally, reluctant to spend their hard-earned money on anything except the most basic necessities so that they could more quickly save enough to return to their homeland. Though many did eventually return, a large number embraced Americanization. Some Anglicized their surnames and severed all ties with Macedonia. Others, however, developed identities tied to both their new American homes and their native traditions.

Much about American life was exciting or even shocking to early Macedonian immigrants, who had come from a very isolated and impoverished area. Electricity, telephones, and other modern inventions amazed them. However, the large buildings, crowded conditions, pollution, and frantic pace of industrialized cities often demoralized them. In his 1976 memoir, *The Eagle and the Stork: An American Memoir*, Macedonian immigrant Stoyan Christowe describes the profound disappointment and alienation his uncle and his father found in the factory work and anonymity of the city:

> My uncle was here only with his body. His mind, his heart, his whole being were back in the homeland where life had meaning for him, where life was rooted in decency and dignity. The man he worked for there was his host and not his boss. That was because he was building him a house to live in, or a barrel to keep his wine in, or a wedding chest for his daughter. He could sit down with him for a glass of brandy or a cup of Turkish coffee. This America was boring into his life like a worm into the core of an apple, hollowing out the soundness, the meaning.

For other immigrants, however, the United States offered opportunities they were eager to exploit. Christowe himself avidly learned English and sought an education, and other immigrants were able to establish themselves in better-paying jobs as they increased their job skills and experience. Younger generations of Macedonian Americans have become fully integrated into mainstream American culture.

Traditions and Customs Many Macedonian customs and traditions were associated with religious

STUFFED PEPPERS

Ingredients

3 red peppers

2 green or yellow peppers

1 cup minced beef

3 green onions, chopped

1 clove garlic, minced

170 grams cream cheese, softened

1 egg

3 tablespoons heavy whipping cream

1 teaspoon cumin

Dash salt and Pepper

water

Preparation

Preheat oven to 350°F

Slice the tops off the peppers. Remove seeds and cores. Dice 1 red pepper. Set aside. Save the tops. Combine the diced red pepper and beef in a mixing bowl. Add the green onions and garlic. Stir in softened cream cheese and blend with a wooden spoon. Stir in the egg and cream. Season with cumin, salt, and pepper.

Place the pepper shells in a baking dish that will hold them snugly together. Spoon the filling into the peppers. Replace the tops. Pour 3 tablespoons of water around the peppers.

Bake at 350°F until the filling is cooked and the peppers are soft, about 40 minutes. Serve immediately.

Serves 2

holidays, pre-Christian beliefs, or the agricultural cycle. Making and jumping over bonfires, a practice that probably originated in pagan times, was often incorporated into the celebration of Christian holidays. On festive occasions throughout the year, villagers would visit their neighbors to wish them good luck, health, and prosperity. On the Eve of St. John (Midsummer's Day), it was customary to tell omens. Bulgarian and Macedonian housewives observed several customs to ensure prosperity and to keep their homes free of dangers. For example, they used cakes to rid their homes of evil spirits. On Mice Day, October 27, they would spread mud over the threshold and hearth to "muddle over" the mice's eyes, preventing them from seeing food stored in the house. During Wolf Days in November, women would tie their scissors shut to keep wolves from opening their mouths and would refuse to sew any clothes for their husbands to keep them from turning into werewolves. On November 30, St. Andrew's Day, women cooked wheat, lentils, and beans to keep bears away. However, among successive generations born in the United States,

as well as among more recent immigrants, these mostly rural traditions are regarded as relics of an earlier time and have typically fallen by the wayside.

Cuisine Traditional Macedonian foods reflect both the region's indigenous crops and its ethnically mixed history. Ingredients such as feta cheese, yogurt, peppers, cucumbers, tomatoes, and eggplant are commonly used. Food is often flavored with paprika, lemon juice, garlic, or vinegar. When meat is served, it is usually lamb or mutton. Seasonal fruits such as sour cherries, plums, quinces, and grapes are made into thick jam (*slatko*), which is traditionally served to visitors and eaten from a glass jar with a spoon. Milk is used to make a rich cheeselike appetizer, *kajmak*, or is fermented into yogurt. There are several versions of *pindzhur*, a traditional Macedonian spicy relish made from tomatoes, green peppers, and eggplant. *Tarator* is a cucumber salad seasoned with yogurt, vinegar, and garlic, and sometimes garnished with walnuts.

Other traditional dishes include stuffed peppers (*polneti piperki*), stuffed grape leaves (*sarma od lozov list*), and mousaka (*musaka*), a casserole of meat, eggplant, and rice bound with a custard sauce. A popular item at barbecues is *kjebapchinja*, a seasoned mixture of beef or veal and lamb that is grilled and served with scallions, tomatoes, and hot peppers. Also served is *muchkalica*, seasoned mutton grilled on skewers. Festive occasions call for special baked goods such as *baklava*, a honey-dipped layered pastry often filled with ground walnuts, and *burek*, a yeast pastry filled with feta cheese. Macedonians also enjoy Turkish coffee (*tursko kafe*), a legacy from centuries of Turkish rule. Such food traditions are kept alive at Macedonian Orthodox churches such as St. Nikola's in Totowa, New Jersey, where annual food festivals feature Macedonian specialties such as *kebapi* (a minced-meat kebab), shish-kebab, goulash, stuffed peppers, and baklava. Although many aspects of native Macedonian life and tradition have been left behind by those with North American roots, traditional food remains popular among all generations.

Dances and Songs Macedonian folk music combines influences from several ethnic traditions. Centuries of Ottoman rule brought to Macedonian music a distinctly Eastern tone and style, which was further enhanced by the significant contributions of Roma (Gypsy) musicians. A notable legacy from the Turks was the nineteenth-century introduction of brass bands, which Macedonian and Roma musicians adapted to their own musical traditions. The popularity of brass bands waned in the late twentieth century, however, as Macedonian nationalism gained momentum.

Macedonian folk songs were to be played or sung by shepherds in their fields, and they are distinguished by very slow introductory parts and sections of intricate improvisations known as *trepaza*. These variations are thought to resemble the several courses of a grand feast, in which many flavors are mingled in one meal.

Their melodies show an Eastern influence, which ethnic musicologists have linked to the ancient oboe technique of circular, continuous breathing. Instruments commonly used in Macedonian music include the *zurla*, an ancient folk oboe similar to those used in Turkey, Central Asia, and Northern Africa, and the *kaval*, a vertical flute. One of the region's most characteristic instruments is the *gaida*, or Bulgarian bagpipe, which is often used as a solo instrument but is also sometimes accompanied by the *dumbek*, a handheld drum. The *tambura*, a pear-shaped stringed instrument, is similar to the Bulgarian *gadulka* and has been compared in tone to the American banjo. The clarinet and the accordion are also popular instruments.

Many Macedonian folk songs were influenced by Roma music, which was in turn affected by Macedonian traditions. A humorous song popular among Roma musicians but sung in Macedonian is "*Da Me Molat Ne Se Zhenam*" ("I Won't Get Married"). The singer laments that if he married a young girl she would never stay home, but if he married an older one she would quarrel with him. If he married a village girl, she would call him Daddy, and if he took a widow for his wife she would already have children. He decides a divorcée would leave him, and a town girl would drive him away. So he will marry no one at all. "*Pesna I Devojka*" ("The Song and the Girl") is also performed in Macedonian. A haunting Macedonian pastoral melody is "*Aj Zajdi Zajdi Jasno Sonce*," sung to kaval accompaniment. Other traditional Macedonian songs include "*Makedonsko Kevojce*" ("Macedonian Girl"), "*Majko Mila Moja Makedonijo*," and "*Katerino*."

Balkan dances are colorful and festive. As with music and songs, they show some borrowing from Roma traditions. Many Macedonian dances are based on the *horo*, or circle dance.

Beginning in 1996, Seattle, Washington, became a center of revival of Macedonian music in the United States when David Bilides founded Izvor Music, which has published several books of Macedonian folk songs in addition to selling recordings, books, and instruments. Izvor Music has also produced many performances of Macedonian musicians, including the 2011 U.S. tour of Makedonski Biseri ("Macedonian Pearls"), a group of master musicians from the Republic of Macedonia. Dozens of groups across the United States, such as the Balkan Babes in Pittsburgh, perform Macedonian music and dance, often as part of a Balkan, Slavic, or Eastern European repertoire.

Weddings, bazaars, and community celebrations in Macedonian American communities typically feature ethnic music. Recent immigrants have been known to observe that traditional songs, dance, and costume are more prevalent in North America than in the homeland. As with other Eastern European immigrant groups, Macedonian Americans often cling not to contemporary music from "home," but rather to traditional music that represents an older, rural way of life that is increasingly rare.

Traditional Dress Costumes worn for ceremonial occasions in Macedonia are often heavily embroidered and very colorful. The Valley bridal dress worn in the Prilep region is dominated by red and bright yellow, whereas the Bitola Valley dress is mostly yellow and black. According to an article in James Nicoloff's *Macedonia*, the Prilep dress is heavily ornamented with embroidery and metal and bead ornaments. It consists of a smock (*golema*), which is almost completely covered with embroidered circles on the sleeves and with stylized blossom and horseshoe patterns on the front and the border of the skirt. Knitted multicolored cuffs are worn on the lower arms. An embroidered cotton upper garment, the *valanka*, is embellished with tufted fringes and braid along the seams. The *chulter*, an intricately woven apron, is worn below the black wool girdle or belt. In back, the *potkolchelniche*, trimmed with beads and old silver coins, is worn beneath the girdle. Scarves and a necklace, both trimmed with old coins, are also worn. On the head is placed a *fes*, a headdress ornamented with rows of silver coins that hang down beside the face. A garland of spruce is placed above the fes. A hair decoration, the *kocelj*, is made from twisted woolen yarn and hangs down from the shoulders. Flame-colored stockings and homemade slippers complete the costume.

The corresponding men's dress consists of the *aba*, an undershirt made of handwoven wool; a long linen smock with embroidered sleeves, front, and skirt; knitted cuffs worn on the arms below the elbow; and white broadcloth breeches. A brightly colored girdle (*kemer*) is worn beneath a black broadcloth waistcoat, which is embellished with multicolored embroidery, buttons, and flame-colored trimmings. A distinctive black astrakhan (lamb's pelt) and velvet cap is worn on the head, and white stockings, decorated garters, and cowhide slippers with straps complete the costume. Men also wear a knife (*zhrenche*) with a chain and a horn sheath as part of this traditional garb. Although it is relatively uncommon for adults to appear costumed, children and teenagers will typically wear traditional dress for such functions as bazaars, dance exhibitions, and holiday celebrations. In 2005 the Macedonian Arts Council initiated an outstanding collection of Macedonian folk costume at the Museum of International Folk Art in Santa Fe, New Mexico.

Holidays Easter is the most significant holiday in the Eastern Orthodox Church, and Macedonians in the United States continue to observe it seriously. The Macedonian Orthodox Church, like most Eastern Orthodox Churches, celebrates Easter according to a calculation based on the ancient Roman Julian calendar. The dates are usually at least a week after those used by the Roman Catholic Church but can sometimes be more than a month later. In 2013, for example, Easter was commonly celebrated on March 31, but the Eastern Orthodox celebrated it on May 5. Macedonian American families continue the tradition of dying eggs a deep red to symbolize the blood of Christ. They also enjoy the custom of tapping an egg against another person's to try to crack it without cracking one's own; the egg that remains intact represents good luck. Christmas Day (*Bozhik*) is also important. Though the traditions of Santa Claus and Christmas trees did not exist in Macedonia, they have become a part of holiday celebrations for many Macedonian American families.

FAMILY AND COMMUNITY LIFE

Macedonian immigrants who chose to remain in the United States in the early 1900s often returned to their native land when it was time to marry and then brought their new brides back with them to the United States. Those who chose their wives in the United States often favored women of Macedonian or Bulgarian ancestry. Though marriage outside the ethnic group was tolerated, Macedonians practiced a high rate of endogamy (same-group marriage), which strengthened family and community bonds. It was not unusual for several generations of Macedonian American families to remain in the same geographic area and to maintain close personal and professional contacts. The family remains at the center of Macedonian American life. Everyday rituals such as family meals are sacrosanct, and there is strong adherence to traditional values.

One of the first customs to be lost in this country, and indeed, a custom which lost favor some years ago in Macedonia, is the arranged marriage. Match-makers (Macedonia: *posturnitsi*; Bulgarian: *svatovnitsi*), usually older women, were contacted by one of the sets of parents and it was she and she alone who completed the necessary negotiations. The bride and groom-to-be were simply not consulted.

Philip R. Tilney, "The Immigrant Macedonian Wedding," *Indiana Folklore* 3, no. 1 (1970).

Perhaps because the Macedonian American population is relatively small, the community has organized associations and festivities, such as folk dancing, concerts, and picnics, to foster group solidarity. Virtually every Orthodox Church has a community center where these activities take place. In many areas, the community center is the locus of meals or coffee hours after church services and on holidays. Church-supported Sunday schools, language schools, and dance troupes help preserve Macedonian culture and language. The church community serves as a meeting place for teenagers and young adults, and marriages often result from these interactions. Although children are no longer subjected to arranged marriages, parents will often work to promote "good matches" within the community—subject to the approval of the couple.

Gender Roles When Macedonian women followed their husbands to the United States, they often took jobs outside the home, a departure from their customary role in Europe. Female immigrants often worked with their husbands in family businesses. In addition, they played a central role in maintaining Macedonian culture in the United States. They preserved culinary traditions in their homes and were active in church groups, Sunday schools, and social organizations. This trend continues among Macedonian Americans. Regardless of what a woman's professional or other obligations may be, she remains responsible for transmitting Macedonian culture by ensuring that children are exposed to traditional religion, values, and language.

Education Though the earliest Macedonian immigrants arrived in the United States with little or no formal education, they quickly availed themselves of new opportunities to improve their literacy skills. Political organizations such as the American Socialists were an important means of spreading literacy. They published several newspapers and magazines in Macedonian and other Slavic languages and found an interested readership. Many immigrants eagerly studied English and went to school to learn the skills that would enable them to take full advantage of opportunities in the United States. Within a few generations, Macedonian Americans were attending college and universities and entering the professions. By the twenty-first century, Macedonian Americans' educational attainment and participation in the professions was higher than the U.S. average. The American Community Survey in 2011 reported that 35 percent of Macedonian American men and 33 percent of women had a bachelor's degree or higher.

Birth and Birthdays It is a Macedonian custom to prepare a special type of fritter, called *pituli*, to celebrate the birth of a baby. Babies are ceremonially baptized according to the rites of the Eastern Orthodox Church.

Courtship and Weddings Macedonian Americans have maintained many wedding traditions from earlier generations. The night before the wedding (*kolak* or *kvas*) is spent feasting and dancing. The next morning, friends and family of the groom gather at his home for the groom-shaving ritual. The godparents, known as *kym* and *kyma*, ceremoniously give the groom his last shave as a single man as the guests sing, dance, and feast. During the wedding ceremony or at the reception, the bride and groom, sometimes joined by their fathers, participate in a dance/game, "breaking of the bread," to see who will "wear the pants" in the new household. A special sweetened round bread decorated with white flowers, called a *koluk*, is held above the head of the newly married couple while guests perform a circle dance. After the dance, the bride and groom vie for the bigger piece of the bread to decide who will be the "breadwinner." The bread may then be served, along with cake, at the reception dinner. The male members of the wedding party often perform the Macedonian Pig Dance at the reception. Holding bottles of wine as well as forks and knives, they dance into the reception area carrying a roasted pig. They dance, shout, and whistle in front of the *kym* and *kyma*, demanding "payment" for the feast, and continue until the pig bearer is satisfied with the amount paid.

Relations with Other Americans The first groups of Macedonian Americans tended to congregate in areas where there were other Southern Slavic populations. They lived among their fellow Macedonians and Bulgarians, as well as Croats and other immigrants from the Balkan region. In areas with only small numbers of Macedonians, they tended to be most comfortable with other Orthodox Slavs. Their pan-Slavic attitudes often brought them into contact with Poles, Ukrainians, and Russians, with whom they frequently associated in left-wing political groups.

After the creation of the Republic of Macedonia in 1991, tensions escalated between Slavic and Greek Macedonians in the United States and Canada. When a Macedonian group organized a pavilion at the Toronto International Caravan (a celebration of the city's multiculturalism) in 1991, the Greek pavilion boycotted the festival, claiming that the Republic of Macedonia had stolen territory from Greece. Macedonians coined the derogatory term "Gerkoman" to refer to ethnic Macedonians who considered themselves Greek instead of Slavic.

EMPLOYMENT AND ECONOMIC CONDITIONS

Macedonian immigrants were known to be hard workers in their new country. Because they often arrived with little education and limited job skills, they frequently took the most hazardous and poorly paid industrial jobs. According to George Prpic in *South Slavic Immigration in America*, immigrants from the Macedonian region were drawn to railroad work, which—though demanding—at least allowed them to labor under the open sky and escape the crowded conditions that beset them in the cities. For several months at a time, these workers lived together in railroad cars and ate meals prepared by their own cooks. Data from 1909 estimated that as many as 10,000 immigrants from Bulgaria and Macedonia were then working on the railroads in North and South Dakota, Montana, Iowa, and Minnesota. Among the Macedonians who sought railroad work was the future writer Stoyan Christowe, who described his living conditions as very harsh. Railroad work, however, paid a little better than some of the industrial jobs available in the cities.

By 1910 almost 15,000 Bulgarian and Macedonian immigrants worked in the steel mills near Chicago, Illinois. Living and working conditions there were, according to Prpic, extremely primitive and unsanitary.

Similar communities of Balkan immigrant workers existed throughout the industrial belt. Though they did not have the skills to move immediately into more prestigious jobs, Macedonian immigrants developed a reputation as hardworking, strong, sober, intelligent, and eager workers. Often a Macedonian immigrant dreamed of saving up enough money to open a store or to buy a small farm. Although many immigrants were illiterate in their native land, they acquired reading and writing skills in the United States, which enabled them to move into more highly paid jobs over time. By the 1940s, many Macedonian Americans had opened small businesses such as stores or bakeries. In the city of Pittsburgh alone, thirty-three Bulgarian and Macedonian bakeries were in business during this period.

Macedonian Americans supported Macedonia's declaration of independence in 1991 and have organized for international acceptance of the new republic. Over the years, this has led to increased friction with supporters of Greece in the United States, as Greece has not recognized the Republic of Macedonia on its northern border and has attempted to block international recognition.

With access to education, subsequent generations of Macedonian Americans have made careers in medicine, law, academia, broadcasting, and other professions, as well as in business. By the end of the 1900s, new immigrants brought more specialized skills to their adopted country, and individuals trained in the sciences, technology, and business have established themselves in those fields. One of the most prominent business leaders in the United States, Frank Popoff, who is president and CEO of Dow Chemical, is of Bulgarian-Macedonian descent. Another business mogul, Mike Ilitch (originally Iliev), began his career in the United States with a single pizza shop, which he built into the successful Little Caesar's franchise. Each succeeding generation has achieved increased economic success. As with Greeks and Italians, Macedonians broadly follow the pattern of manual-labor jobs among first-generation immigrants, small-business ownership among the second, and professions and skilled occupations among third and later generations.

At the beginning of the twenty-first century, there was again an increase in newly arrived individuals with limited skills and education. Some have immigrated because of political and civil unrest in Macedonia, but more have done so because of the economic downturn. The Macedonian economy is fragile, and unemployment has historically topped 30 percent. City dwellers have been hardest hit. Although these new immigrants have sometimes generated friction in established, well-to-do American communities, it is also common for communities to create a welcoming and supportive structure and to aid in finding work and gaining English competency.

POLITICS AND GOVERNMENT

The long struggle of Macedonians to free themselves from Ottoman rule and to maintain autonomy amid the political turmoil of the Balkan region prepared Macedonian immigrants for active political engagement in the United States. As early as 1908, for example, a group of 600 unemployed and starving immigrants from Bulgaria and Macedonia marched on Chicago's city hall to demand work. Such an action was shocking at the time, and the incident had little effect, but it demonstrated the determination of these immigrants to stand up for their rights. Like other Slavic groups, Macedonians tended to support leftist causes more than the general U.S. population, but few were outright radicals.

A commitment to pan-Slavic solidarity also contributed to Macedonian Americans' interest in socialism. Macedonians had been traditionally friendly toward Russia, with whom they shared ethnic, linguistic, and church ties, and the American Communist Party was very active in enlisting their support for the Soviet cause. Official Soviet support for Macedonian independence further strengthened the bond between Macedonian Americans and Russia. The Socialist Labor Party of America, too, worked to gain Bulgarian and Macedonian membership, and it published many newspapers and periodicals to promote their political education. George Pirinsky (born George Zaikoff), a Bulgarian communist leader in the United States, was the most active leader in this cause.

During World War II, pro-socialist activity among Macedonian Americans and other Slavic groups intensified. On April 25 and 26, 1942, an All-Slavic Congress was held in Detroit, out of which was created the American Slav Congress. The Macedonian-American People's League was a member organization. Macedonian Americans attended the Michigan Slav Congress held in Detroit in 1943 and were involved in the creation of the United Committee of South Slavic Americans. Macedonian Americans also were attracted to the International Workers Order, a communist front organization that included special sections for individual South Slavic groups. Throughout the war years, these groups criticized U.S. foreign policy toward the Soviet Union, arousing the suspicion of the conservative political establishment. In 1948 the House Un-American Activities Committee and the U.S. attorney general accused the American Slav Congress and its affiliate groups of being communist organizations under the influence of Moscow. For the next several years, congressional investigations conducted a witch hunt against left-wing radicals, among them some leaders of the South Slavic groups. During this difficult period, many either chose to leave the country or were deported. Despite the leftist orientation of many Macedonian Americans, the vast majority of them, according to Prpic, were loyal to the U.S. government and found such political hostility troubling.

They supported U.S. involvement in World War II, served in the military, and worked on the home front to help the war effort.

Macedonians in the United States generally maintained great interest in events in their homeland. Political strife in the Balkans and the Macedonian struggle for autonomy were frequent subjects of discussion when Macedonians gathered to socialize. They organized material relief for Macedonian villages, sending parcels of clothing and financial assistance to areas in need. They were also very active politically. During the 1920s and 1930s, increased violence in Serbian and Greek-occupied Macedonia caused intense concern among Macedonians in the United States. Dedicated to the "liberation and unification of Macedonia," Macedonian Americans in Fort Wayne, Indiana, founded the Macedonian Patriotic Organization (MPO) in October 1922. Anastas Stephanoff became president of its Central Committee and Atanas Lebanoff was elected secretary. In 2012 the PMO held its ninetieth annual convention in Fort Wayne and made plans for its 2013 convention in Pittsburgh. The MPO began publishing the *Makedonska Tribuna* (*Macedonian Tribune*) on February 10, 1927. This weekly newspaper was still in publication as of 2012. Another political organization, United Macedonian Diaspora, was cofounded by Meto Koloski in 2008 to have a full-time presence in Washington, D.C. When Koloski's father, a veteran of the anti-fascist and anti-communist movements, moved to the United States from Macedonia in 1979, "he helped form the Macedonian Human Rights Movement of New Jersey, which advocated for civil rights of Macedonians living in Albania, Bulgaria, Greece, and Yugoslavia."

Macedonian Americans supported Macedonia's declaration of independence in 1991 and have organized for international acceptance of the new republic. Over the years, this has led to increased friction with supporters of Greece in the United States, as Greece has not recognized the Republic of Macedonia on its northern border and has attempted to block international recognition. In early 2011, Michigan Republican Congresswoman Candice Miller launched the first ever congressional caucus on Macedonia and Macedonian Americans. In 2012, with primary support from representatives from Ohio, Michigan, and Illinois (which have significant Macedonian constituencies), the Macedonian Caucus succeeded in getting fifty-four members of Congress to sign a letter urging President Obama to support Macedonia's entrance into NATO, something that Greece has opposed. Conservative on social issues, yet strong supporters of organized labor, Macedonian Americans were activists in and donors to both the Republican and Democratic parties. For instance, the Ilitch family, prominent Detroit business owners, have often been involved with Democratic Party fundraisers. The 2007 speaker at the Macedonian Patriotic Organization's annual convention was George W. Bush's assistant Tim Geoglein, who spoke about his connections to the faith-based communities.

NOTABLE INDIVIDUALS

Academia Professor George Mitrevski of Auburn University was born in the village of Podmochani, in the Prespa region of Macedonia. He received his BA in Russian from SUNY Stony Brook and his MA and PhD in Russian/Slavic Ohio State University. In the spring of 1997, he was a Fulbright Teaching Fellow in Skopje, Macedonia. He gave the 2007 Mary Choncoff Endowed Lecture, "The Macedonian Immigration Narrative; from There to Here—and Back," at Arizona State University in Tempe.

Business Businessman Mike Ilitch (1929–), who was born in Detroit to Macedonian immigrant parents, founded the international pizza chain Little Caesars. He purchased the Detroit Red Wings, a professional hockey team, in 1982, and the Detroit Tigers, a professional baseball team, in 1992.

Activism Metodija A. Koloski is cofounder and president of the United Macedonian Diaspora (UMD), headquartered in Washington, D.C. Koloski's family immigrated to the United States from Macedonia in the early 1950s, and he was born and raised in Garfield, New Jersey.

A Columbus, Ohio, lawyer, Thomas Taneff is called Macedonia's Honorary Consul General in Columbus. He was born in Canton, Ohio, and when he was seven, his family moved to his mother's village, Gaveto—between Bitola and Resen—to try to make a life in Macedonia. He attended the same school as his mother, and Macedonian was his first language. Less than two years later, the family moved back to Ohio.

Journalism The first editor of the *Macedonian Tribune* was Boris Zografoff, who came to the United States from Bitola to accept the position. He wrote and edited the paper's first issue, published on February 10, 1927, and served as editor for three years. Zografoff was admired as a talented editor with a sophisticated understanding of the Macedonian independence movement. His most renowned successor, Christo N. Nizamoff (1902–1989), worked for the *Macedonian Tribune* for more than forty years. In the early 1920s, Nizamoff was a member of the Macedonian Press Bureau in New York City. He was the first foreign-born writer to be invited to join the Indianapolis Literary Club. Nizamoff was a founding member of the Indianapolis Press Club and was elected its Man of the Year in 1974. He was also elected to the Indiana Journalism Hall of Fame in 1974.

Literature The most esteemed Macedonian American writer, Stoyan Christowe, was born in Konomlady, Macedonia, in 1898. He came to the United States as a child and attended Valparaiso University in Indiana. Christowe published six books, including *This Is My Country* (1938), *My American*

Macedonia American director Milcho Manchevski is known for his moving full-length feature film *Before the Rain*. KURT KRIEGER / CORBIS

Pilgrimage (1947), and *The Eagle and the Stork: An American Memoir* (1976). As a young man, Christowe identified himself so wholeheartedly as an American that when he returned to the Balkans to visit, he found it easier to converse with the Bulgarian king in English than in Bulgarian. In his books, Christowe explored both the process of assimilation and the strong ties that he continued to feel for his native land. In the late 1930s, Christowe moved to Vermont, where he served for twelve years in the state legislature. He died in Brattleboro, Vermont, on December 28, 1995.

Dean Dimitrieski's family moved from Macedonia to Detroit when he was five years old. His 2011 book *Tears for My City: An Autobiography of a Detroit White Boy* is an immigrant's story of moving to a neighborhood plagued by gang violence. In it he tells of befriending two of Detroit's most wanted drug lords and witnessing a horrific crime that shatters his American dream and the life he loved in Detroit.

An immigrant from Macedonia in 2006. NAJLAH FEANNY / CORBIS

Sports Macedonian Americans have participated actively in both amateur and professional sports. National Basketball Association (NBA) hall-of-famer Pete Maravich (1947–1988), born in Pennsylvania to parents of Serbian and Macedonian backgrounds, scored more points during his college career than any other player and was named a three-time All American as well as the 1970 College Player of the Year. He went on to a professional career with the Atlanta Hawks, the New Orleans Jazz, the Utah Jazz, and the Boston Celtics.

Peter T. George, born in Akron, Ohio, in 1929 to Tony and Para George (Tryan and Paraskeva Taleff), won three Olympic medals for the United States in weightlifting. He won a gold medal in 1952 in Helsinki and silver medals in London in 1948 and in Melbourne in 1956. Beginning his athletic career in his teens, George won five world championships from 1947 to 1952, and he was middleweight champion at the Pan-American Games in 1951 and 1955. George was named coach of the 1980 Olympic team but did not attend the games in Moscow because of the U.S. boycott.

Since the early 1990s, soccer in the United States has been greatly enhanced by the presence of foreign-born players, among them Jovan Kirovski (1976–), a U.S. citizen of Macedonian descent. Kirovski scored the winning goal in the British 1992–1993 Youth Cup semifinal for Manchester United before joining the U.S. national team.

Stage and Screen Filmmaker Milcho Manchevski, born in Skopje in 1959, immigrated to the United States in 1982 to study film and photography at the University of Southern Illinois. After directing dozens of commercials and music videos, for which he became well known, he made his feature film debut in 1994 with *Before the Rain*. A three-part story set in contemporary Macedonia and London, the film explores love and fate within the context of ancient Macedonian traditions and conflicts. The film won the Golden Lion award at the Venice Film Festival.

Nick Vanoff (1929–1991), born in Vevey, near the Greek port of Salonika, had a highly successful career as a Hollywood television and film producer. Vanoff was associate producer for such programs as *The Perry Como Show* and *The Tonight Show*. He originated several others, including the *Bing Crosby Specials*, the *Perry Como Specials*, the *Phil Silvers Specials*, *Hollywood Palace*, the *Andy Williams Specials*, the *Sonny and Cher Show*, and the *Kennedy Center Honors Sho*w. Vanoff was the creator of the comedy series *Hee-Haw*, which he later syndicated. He served as coproducer for the acclaimed film *Eleni* (1985), based on the memoir of his close friend Nicholas Gage, who grew up near Vanoff.

MEDIA

PRINT

The Macedonian Tribune

A weekly newspaper published since 1927 by the Macedonian Patriotic Organization. It is printed in Macedonian and English.

124 West Wayne Street
Fort Wayne, Indiana 46802
Phone: (219) 422-5900
Fax: (219) 422-1348
URL: www.macedonian.org

UMD Voice

UMD Voice Magazine/OMD Glas Spisanie, published by the organization United Macedonian Diaspora, is a magazine about all things Macedonian, including news, analysis, history, and culture, as well as interviews that celebrate the achievements of notable Macedonians and friends of Macedonia.

1510 H Street NW
Suite 900
Washington, D.C. 20005
Phone: (202) 756-2244
Email: editor@umdiaspora.org
URL: www.umdiaspora.org

ORGANIZATIONS AND ASSOCIATIONS

Macedonian Arts Council

The Macedonian Arts Council, founded in 1991 by Macedonian native Pavlina Proevska, is dedicated to the promotion and affirmation of Macedonian cultural heritage.

Pavlina Proevska, Executive Director
380 Rector Place
Suite 21 E
New York, New York 10280
Phone: (212) 799-0009
Fax: (815) 301-3893
Email: info@macedonianarts.org
URL: www.macedonianarts.org

Macedonian Patriotic Organization (MPO)

MPO was established in 1922 in Fort Wayne, Indiana. Its purpose was to advocate for the liberation of Macedonia, and it began publishing the *Macedonian Tribune* in 1927. Since 1991 the MPO has focused on increasing awareness of Macedonian history and culture.

Chris Evanoff, President
124 West Wayne Street
Fort Wayne, Indiana 46802

Phone: (219) 422-5900
Fax: (219) 422-1348
Email: info@macedonian.org
URL: www.macedonian.org

United Macedonian Diaspora (UMD)

United Macedonian Diaspora (UMD) is a leading international nongovernmental organization addressing the interests and needs of Macedonian people and communities throughout the world outside of Macedonia. UMD's main goals are to foster unity among Macedonian people and to advance their cause. UMD works to promote Macedonian historical, spiritual, and cultural heritage while preserving and promoting the Macedonian tradition within the framework of various advocacy, educational, and charitable programs. With headquarters in Washington, D.C., UMD has representatives serving Macedonian communities around the world, including in Australia, Austria, Canada, France, Germany, Greece, Russia, the United Kingdom, and throughout the United States.

1510 H Street NW
Suite 900
Washington, D.C. 20005
Phone: (202) 350-9798
Email: info@umdiaspora.org
URL: www.umdiaspora.org

MUSEUMS AND RESEARCH CENTERS

Allen County Public Library

The Fred J. Reynolds Historical Genealogy Department, the second largest genealogical repository in North America, includes federal and state census and mortality records, state indexes, Soundex, and Michigan state census data for selected years. It also contains passenger lists, naturalization records, city and town histories, military records and regimental histories, cemetery and church records, land and probate records, city directories, and so forth. It maintains the largest English-language genealogy and local history periodical collection in the world.

900 Library Plaza
Fort Wayne, Indiana 46802
P.O. Box 2270
Fort Wayne, Indiana 46801-2270
Phone: (219) 421-1200
Fax: (219) 422-9688
Email: genealogy@acpl.info
URL: www.genealogycenter.org

ASU Melikian Center: Russian, Eurasian and East European Studies

As a research unit, the Melikian Center capitalizes on its partnerships with more than a dozen East European and Eurasian universities to build programs of academic exchange, international development, and collaborative research.

Coor Hall 4451
P.O. Box 874
975 S. Myrtle Avenue

Tempe, Arizona 85287-4202
Phone: (480) 965-4188
Fax: (480) 965-1700
Email: melikiancenter@asu.edu
URL: http://melikian.asu.edu/

Bulgarian Macedonian National Educational and Cultural Center (BMNECC)

BMNECC was formed in 1980 from the Bulgaro-Macedonian Beneficial Association, which had originally been established in 1930. The BMNECC offers exhibits, displays, and educational programs; maintains an archive of folk artifacts; runs a museum and library; and has done research on the contributions of individual Macedonians and Bulgarians in the United States.

Patricia Penka French, President
449-451 West 8th Avenue
West Homestead, Pennsylvania 15122
Phone: (412) 461-6188
Email: bmnecc@gmail.com
URL: www.bmnecc.org

SOURCES FOR ADDITIONAL STUDY

Christowe, Stoyan. *The Eagle and the Stork: An American Memoir*. New York: Harper's Magazine Press, 1976.

Dimitrieski, Dean. *Tears for My City: An Autobiography of a Detroit White Boy*. Morgan Hill, CA: Bookstand Pub, 2011.

Evanoff, Michael W. *St. John St: A Remembrance; An Ethnic Feature of the St. John St. Community, Flint, Michigan, 1874–1974*. Flint, MI: Edelweiss Press, 1986.

Groves, Susanna. "Macedonian-American Advocates for Homeland; Interview with Metodija Koloski." International Diaspora Engagement Alliance website, July 24, 2012. http://diasporaalliance.org/macedonian-american-advocates-for-homeland-interview-with-metodija-koloski/.

Kaplan, Robert D. *Balkan Ghosts: A Journey through History*. New York: St. Martin's Press, 1993.

Nicoloff, James. *Macedonia: A Collection of Articles about the History and Culture of Macedonia*. Toronto: Selyani Macedonian Folklore Group, 1982.

Prpic, George J. *South Slavic Immigration in America*. Boston: Twayne Publishers, 1978.

MALAYSIAN AMERICANS

Karl Heil

OVERVIEW

Malaysian Americans are immigrants or descendants of immigrants from Malaysia, a country located in Southeast Asia. The nation is roughly equally divided between the Malay Peninsula, which lies between the Indian Ocean and South China Sea, and the northern and western parts of the island of Borneo, which is also occupied by Indonesia and Brunei. Malaysia is unique in that its two parts are separated by 400 miles (644 kilometers) of ocean. Malaysia has a combined area of 127,320 square miles (329,758 square kilometers), which is slightly larger than the state of New Mexico.

According to a 2011 World Bank estimate, Malaysia has a population of about 29 million. Islam is the religion of 60 percent of the population; other major religions include Buddhism (19 percent), Christianity (9 percent), and Hinduism (6 percent). Roughly one-half the population is Malay, while ethnic Chinese (24 percent), indigenous groups (11 percent), and ethnic Indians (7 percent) make up the country's largest minorities. The Malaysian economy, considered one of the strongest in Southeast Asia, was once based mostly on the extraction of raw materials such as rubber and tin but has shifted to manufacturing, tourism, and technology. Malaysia is one of the world's leaders in palm-oil production and an exporter of petroleum.

Because Malaysia did not become an independent country until 1957, the period of Malaysian immigration to the United States has been relatively brief. Unlike many other groups, Malaysians have not been driven to migrate by severe economic distress, natural disasters, or serious violent conflict. Instead, many of the Malaysians who have immigrated to the United States have been people of Chinese or Indian descent who have left Malaysia because of ethnic or linguistic discrimination. Their status in the United States is complicated because they are often mistaken for, or they themselves may consider themselves to be, Chinese Americans or Indian Americans. Yet they maintain distinctly Malaysian customs that set them apart. In recent years, Malaysian immigration to the United States has been dominated by Malaysians of educated and professional classes, many of whom retain strong ties to their home country.

According to the American Community Survey, in 2011 there were about 25,000 people of Malaysian ancestry living in the United States, making them one of the smallest Asian American groups. Metropolitan areas with a significant number of Malaysian Americans included Houston, Los Angeles, New York City, San Francisco, San Jose, and Washington.

HISTORY OF THE PEOPLE

Early History Archaeological evidence indicates that the ancestors of Malay people migrated to the Malay Peninsula from southern China about 35,000 years ago. At that time the peninsula was occupied by small groups of aboriginal peoples, who gradually retreated into the rain forests. Chinese, Indian, and Arab documents from before 1400 CE contain references to the area that is now Malaysia and show that the Malay Peninsula, with its valuable forest products such as timber and resins, had already become part of a global trading network. Trade connections between the Malay Peninsula and India, dating to as early as the beginning of the Common Era, were particularly strong. Indians set up trade centers along the East Coast of Sumatra and the Malay Peninsula, and these areas were influenced by Indian scripts, laws, literature, Hinduism, and Buddhism. From the thirteenth century, China also began to expand its trade substantially in the region.

In about 1400 a major trading port developed in Melaka on the western coast of the Malay Peninsula. A prince from Palembang in Sumatra became its first ruler, and he received recognition as such by the Chinese around 1405. The port became a nexus for trade, the spread of Islam, and the dissemination of the Malay language to other islands of Southeast Asia, including what is now Indonesia, the Philippines, and Singapore. During this period there were several significant developments that helped to shape aspects of contemporary Malaysia. First, the rulers of Melaka accepted Islam around 1430, and as a result Islam supplanted a localized form of Hindu-Buddhist beliefs as the dominant religion. Second, the country's sultanate structure consisting of various states ruled by a Muslim leader and a court elite evolved, and the notion that "to be a Malay is to be a Muslim" took root. Third, Melaka became one of the greatest powers in the region because of its ideal location on the Straits of Melaka, serving as a meeting place where traders exchanged local products and spices from eastern

Indonesia for cloth from India and ceramics and other goods from China. The burgeoning wealth of Melaka piqued the interest of Europeans. The Portuguese attacked and seized the town in 1511. Despite this victory, the Portuguese faced frequent attacks from the refugee rulers as well as from Java and Aceh. The Portuguese retained control of Melaka until 1641, when the Dutch East India Company conquered it and subsequently became the region's dominant European trader.

Under Dutch rule Melaka's importance and size diminished. The Dutch tried to exploit trade in gold, tin, and pepper. To do so, they exacted high duties from merchant vessels passing through Melaka. Although many ships navigated around Dutch-controlled territories to avoid paying these duties, Dutch efforts proved successful overall. Melaka remained under Dutch rule for more than two centuries, but Great Britain eventually came to control sizable interests in the region. In 1786 the British East India Company established a port to the north, on the island of Penang, which competed with Dutch-held Melaka, and in 1819 Britain claimed the island of Singapore. The British took temporary control of Melaka in 1795, and in 1824 the Anglo-Dutch Treaty brought the city under British control.

To facilitate governing Penang, Melaka, and Singapore, Great Britain combined them to form the Straits Settlements in 1867. Because the British were interested exclusively in trade, they initially followed a policy of noninterference in the Malay states. Social upheaval in the region, however, eventually forced Britain to play a greater role in the affairs of the Peninsula Malay states. In 1874 an agreement with the ruler of the state of Perak allowed for the appointment of a British adviser. This was followed by agreements with four other states, which were brought together in 1896 as the Federated Malay States. Subsequently, the remaining states also accepted a British advisor. By World War I the British controlled all of the Malay Peninsula, through direct rule in the Straits Settlements and indirect rule in the nine Malay states. Also by this time, the Borneo state of Sarawak was under the control of the Brookes (an English family) and Northern Borneo was under the control of a chartered company.

The economy of British Malaya was radically changed during the colonial period. Many Chinese arrived to work in tin mines while the British brought in Indians to work on rubber plantations. Malays generally continued as farmers and fishermen and were vastly outnumbered in urban areas. The economic tensions that resulted, however, did not surface until after Malaysia's independence. British rule became increasingly centralized, but when World War II broke out Britain was unprepared for the Japanese invasion of early 1941. Japan seized Malaya, Sarawak, and North Borneo, and it occupied them until the war ended in 1945. Race relations deteriorated during the war because the Malays were generally favored by the Japanese and the Malayan Chinese Communist Party was helping lead anti-Japanese activities.

Modern Era After the war, Britain administered the Malay states and the Straits Settlements of Penang and Meleka as the Malayan Union, which was superseded in 1948 by the Federation of Malaya. A movement to gain independence from Britain took root, but it had to overcome the differences among the various ethnic groups in the peninsula, especially those between the Malays, the Chinese, and the Indians. Around 1950 the Alliance Party, representing the country's three major ethnic groups, emerged as a voice for independence, and the federation became independent of British rule in 1957. In 1963 the federation was joined by the Borneo states Sabah and Sarawak, and it changed its name to the Federation of Malaysia. Singapore entered the federation in 1963, too, but defected in 1965 because of disputes with the Malaysian leadership.

During its infancy, Malaysia faced opposition from Indonesia, which attacked Malaysian states in an effort to break up the fledgling country. Indonesia saw Malaysia as a throwback to the colonial era with its dependence on British military assistance. Malaysia also saw growing conflict between its Malay and ethnic-Chinese citizens. Race riots in May 1969 resulted in as many as 2,000 dead, and they prompted the New Economic Policy of 1970, an affirmative-action policy designed to reduce the economic inequality between the rural ethnic Malays and urban Chinese Malaysians. It also played a major role in transitioning the nation's economy from one based on raw-material exports to one based on manufacturing. Yet some criticized it for ineffectiveness and for unfairly favoring Malays, and it played a role in driving the "brain drain" of educated Indian and Chinese Malaysians to other countries, including the United States, Great Britain, and India. Nevertheless, economic changes ultimately proved successful to a large extent in expanding the overall economy and helping rural Malays move into urban areas and reap a greater share of the country's economic benefits. As a result the country enjoyed relative prosperity and stability in the late twentieth century. It expanded its manufacturing capacity and embarking on a wide range of major infrastructure projects, including the construction of the Petronas Towers, which were the world's tallest buildings from 1998 to 2004.

The Asian economic crisis of the late 1990s caused significant damage to the country's economy, undermining its currency and property markets. Although the country recovered in the next decade, profiting from higher prices for its petroleum exports and new investments in biotechnology and other high-tech industries, some observers warned that Malaysia remained vulnerable to global economic shifts because of its export-dependent economy. In addition, concerns over the country's ability to retain its educated citizens continued. The World Bank reported in 2011 that as many as 20 percent of Malaysians with college degrees were opting to live elsewhere, drawn by better career prospects and compensation elsewhere. Because of discriminatory policies in Malaysia, emigrating Chinese and Indian Malaysians constituted a relatively high percentage of educated Malaysians leaving the country.

SETTLEMENT IN THE UNITED STATES

Many Malaysian Americans live in U.S. metropolitan areas, particularly in financial centers such as New York and San Francisco. They are a relatively young, educated Asian American group. According to the American Community Survey, the average age of a Malaysian American was thirty-three in 2009. Consistent with concerns about a "brain drain," Malaysian Americans have above-average educational attainment among Asian American groups, with 93 percent possessing a high school degree or higher, and 57 percent possessing at least a bachelor's degree—well above the averages for most American ethnic groups.

LANGUAGE

Bahasa Malaysia, a standardized version of Malay, is the official language of the country and is spoken by more than half of the population. Ethnic Chinese, Indians, and indigenous groups tend to speak the languages of their respective peoples. Because the use of Malay as the national language of Malaysia is viewed as a sensitive topic by Chinese and Indian ethnic minorities, tensions can arise among different Malaysian American groups regarding language use.

English is the second language of Malaysia and is commonly spoken by Malaysian Americans, even recent immigrants. Roughly 30 percent of Malaysian Americans speak only English at home. However, about 20 percent have only limited English proficiency—a relatively low rate among Asian American populations. In 2010 about 20 percent of Malaysian American households were considered "linguistically isolated," meaning that no resident of the home over sixteen years of age spoke English proficiently. Malaysian Americans who do not speak English mostly speak Malay, though some speak Chinese. There are about 13,000 Malay speakers in the United States.

RELIGION

Like other aspects of Malaysian American culture, religion depends on ethnic background. In Malaysia nearly all Malays and some Chinese and Indian Malaysians are Muslims. The Malaysian government ensures freedom of religion, and many Chinese Malaysians are Christian, while others practice Buddhism, Daoism, and Confucianism. The majority of Indian Malaysians are Hindus or Sikhs, although some are Christians. The indigenous Malay-Polynesian religion has influenced to some extent the other religions practiced in Malaysia.

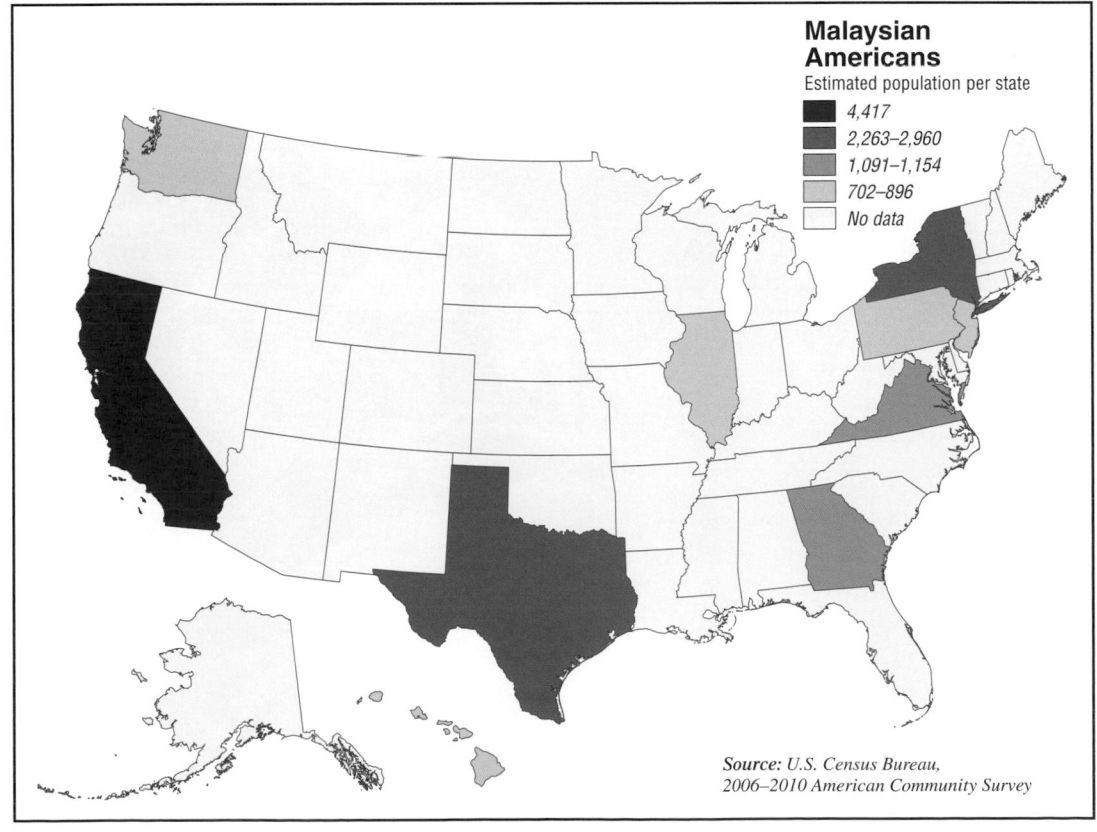

Malaysian Americans
Estimated population per state
- 4,417
- 2,263–2,960
- 1,091–1,154
- 702–896
- No data

Source: U.S. Census Bureau, 2006–2010 American Community Survey

Given the diversity of religions in Malaysia, there is considerable variation in the religions practiced by Malaysian Americans, and some conflict exists between adherents to different religious groups. Most Malaysian Americans practice their faith in houses of worship alongside people of different origin or ethnicity. Yet there is also a desire among Malaysians in the United States to band together to maintain a rooted national identity.

Malaysian Sunni Muslims believe that the prayers and language of Islam came from Allah through Muhammad. They therefore consider the words powerful in and of themselves, and their religious practices include chants and readings of the holy words and prayers of Islam. In the United States, most Muslim Malaysian Americans worship in mosques with people of a variety of ethnicities.

Chinese Malaysians tend to believe or follow one of the three main religions of China—Confucianism, Daoism, and Buddhism—though many are Christians. The doctrines of Confucianism call for strong family ties; Daoist beliefs emphasize spiritual and mystical life over materialism; and Buddhism holds that there is salvation and reincarnation and that people must venerate their ancestors. Outside of California and New York, there are few organized Buddhist temples in the United States and very few Daoist monasteries. Therefore, Malaysians who live elsewhere who wish to maintain their faith typically need to do so in private practice.

Most Indian Malaysian Americans are Hindus, and most venerate a major Hindu deity such Shiva. They also try to live up to a variety of ideals and practice a range of rituals. The beliefs of the Hindus emphasize family welfare, land cultivation, and veneration of the family home. Hindu temples are designed as homes for the gods rather than for communal worship, and Hindus go to temples to give offerings and receive blessings. Hindu priests tend to the temples, maintaining shrines, accepting offerings, and serving as intermediaries between humans and gods. In the United States, most Hindu temples are clustered in metropolitan areas in California, Illinois, Texas, and New York. Hindu Malaysian Americans living in other areas may find it necessary to practice their religion more informally or at home.

CULTURE AND ASSIMILATION

According to the American Community Survey, in 2009 about 70 percent of Malaysian Americans were foreign born. Most maintain overt cultural, familial, and economic ties with their home country. This is particularly true among ethnic Malays, who are more likely to view their stay in the United States as short-term. Just over one-quarter of Malaysian Americans were citizens in 2011, well below the average for Asian American populations.

Because Malaysia has long had a very global society and has been open to Western entertainment, music, and dress, assimilation is relatively smooth for most Malaysian Americans. Recently, however, many Malaysian Americans have begun to celebrate and assert their national identity—even beyond differences in ethnic origins—through festivals of Malaysian food, art, and culture.

A vendor preparing food at the Malaysia Noodle Market in New York City's Meatpacking District. RICHARD LEVINE / ALAMY

Cuisine The cuisine of Malaysian Americans depends on the particulars of ethnicity, although rice and noodles are common across all groups. Muslim Malays do not eat pork and Indian Malays do not eat beef. Nevertheless, the mélange of cultures in Malaysia has led to interesting crossover between different ethnic groups' signature dishes.

Among the more popular Malaysian dishes of Malay origin eaten in the United States are *satay* (grilled chicken and beef skewers), *kari ayam* (a chicken curry dish), and *nasi lemak* (coconut rice accompanied by chili paste, anchovies, vegetables, and other foods).

Ethnic Chinese Malaysians developed their own brand of Chinese cuisine, which varies from the food of mainland China, and Chinese-influenced dishes eaten in Malaysian American restaurants are different from dishes seen in Chinese American restaurants. Popular dishes include prawn noodle soup and *char kway teow*, a stir-fried rice noodle dish. Chinese Malaysian Americans have also adopted Indian-style curries, though they are generally prepared to be less spicy.

Malaysian American dishes of Indian origin tend to reflect the cuisine of southern India and include curries and *roti canai* (a crispy pancake). Indian Malaysians also enjoy *teh tarik*, a sweet milk tea that is more like Thai tea than Indian *chai*.

Because Muslims do not eat pork and Hindus do not eat beef, in Malaysia Muslims and Hindus tend to eat at separate restaurants to maintain their dietary rules. In the United States, however, they often set aside these strict rules and eat at a restaurant that may also be serving food they do not eat. In addition, to satisfy American tastes, some Malaysian dishes are modified when they are served in the United States. For instance, most spicy dishes are less spicy, and the foods that accompany many dishes may be different.

In 2010 Susheela Rhagavan, an Indian Malaysian American, published a cookbook called *Flavors of Malaysia*, featuring dishes from across Malaysia's ethnic groups and regions. The book received high praise from chefs and other culinary experts and sparked considerable interest in Malaysian cuisine.

Traditional Costumes Because Malaysia is a largely Islamic country, the traditional clothing of Malaysian Muslims reflects Islamic beliefs in modesty—that is, keeping the body covered, especially among women. Nevertheless, Malaysian Muslim clothing tends to be colorful with abstract and floral patterns and embroidery, much of it influenced heavily by Indian design. Some Muslim Malaysian Americans continue this modest dress in the United States, but others do not. Chinese Malaysian Americans are generally very Westernized and do not retain traditional clothing in the United States. Indian Malaysian Americans are more likely to alternate between traditional clothing, including colorful saris for women and the Punjabi suit for men, and Western-style clothing.

Holidays Some Malaysian Americans celebrate Malaysia's Independence Day, August 31, and the birthday of the Agong (Malaysia's king), which is celebrated on the first Saturday in June. In addition, Malaysian Americans may observe a number of other holidays, depending on their ethnicity. Because Islamic, Chinese, and Hindu calendars are all lunar calendars, these holidays do not have set dates and change from year to year.

Islamic Malaysian Americans may observe *Hari Raya Puasa* (or *Hari Raya*), which comes at the end of Ramadan (*Puasa* in Malay). This holiday involves special prayers at the mosque and gatherings of families and friends. For the occasion, people dress formally and houses are usually decorated with lights.

Ethnic Chinese Malaysian Americans may celebrate China's three important holidays: the Chinese New Year, the Feast of the Hungry Ghosts, and the Moon Cake Festival. The Chinese New Year usually falls in January or February, and its traditional Malaysian celebration involves the closing of businesses for two days, parades, and dances. In addition, the holiday brings families and friends together, usually for dinner and celebration. The Hungry Ghosts Festival usually is held between July and August when it is believed that the spirits of the dead circulate on earth and need to be fed. When celebrating this holiday, Malaysian Americans may offer food to the spirits and hold feasts for themselves. Finally, the Moon Cake Festival, which is held in September around the autumn moon, commemorates the defeat of the Mongols in ancient China. The celebration includes the preparation and eating of pastries that typically contain an egg yolk in the center representing the full moon.

Hindu Malaysian Americans may celebrate the major Hindu holidays. The most popular of these holidays is Deepavali, the Festival of Lights, which usually takes place in October or November. For the holiday, family and friends gather to celebrate stories in which good overcomes evil. Families usually have open houses for the holiday and decorate their homes with colored lights, lamps, fruit, flowers, and other kinds of decorations. Another important Hindu holiday is

Because Malaysia is a largely Islamic country, the traditional clothing of Malaysian Muslims reflects Islamic beliefs in modesty—that is, keeping the body covered, especially among women. Nevertheless, Malaysian Muslim clothing tends to be colorful with abstract and floral patterns and embroidery, much of it influenced heavily by Indian design.

Thaipusam, which usually takes place in January or February. The holiday honors Lord Subramaniam, and it is day of giving thanks for courage and answered

A Malaysian parade float in Pasadena, California, c. 1990.

of ethnic Malay origin place a high value on shared responsibility between men and women within the family, sometimes including older generations that live in the household. The families of Chinese Malaysian Americans often have a greater resemblance to a traditional nuclear family, in which the father works and the mother bears heavier responsibility for managing the household and caring for children. These roles may be more flexible for Chinese Malaysian Americans than they would be for Chinese families in Malaysia.

Education As a relatively well-educated and professional immigrant group, Malaysian Americans generally place a very high value on education for their children. In many Malaysian American families, both boys and girls are expected to attend college and pursue professional careers. This is particularly true for secular Chinese Malaysian Americans and Indian Malaysian Americans. Most Malaysian American children attend secular schools, which may be either public and private, depending on the means of the family. At least 90 percent of the children graduate from high school, a higher percentage than the U.S. national average. As with many Asian Americans, college attendance is relatively high. According to American Community Survey estimates, 54 percent of Malaysian Americans over age twenty-five have at least a bachelor's degree, and 22 percent have more advanced degrees. These levels of academic achievement are nearly has high for Malaysian American women as they are for Malaysian American men. Many Malaysian Americans study business, finance, or science, and many incorporate study abroad into their education.

Weddings and Courtship Malaysian American weddings are often colorful ceremonies, traditionally held in the home of the bride. Many Malaysian Americans return to Malaysia for their wedding ceremony. In a traditional Malay wedding, the groom and his entourage enter the bride's home in procession, accompanied by musicians and singers and bringing gifts. While customs may vary depending on which region and ethnic group Malaysian Americans come from, the bride and the groom both typically wear profusely decorated garments. The bride's costume is decorated with the traditional Malay colors of gold and silver. The ceremony features a lavish feast for the guests as well as the *bersanding*, in which the bride and groom sit together on ornate chairs while the guests come forth individually to offer their congratulations and blessings. The ceremony also may involve the *tepong tawar*, a ritual performed by guests of honor who anoint the groom's forehead rice flour or sandalwood and dapple the groom's head and hands with flowers or rice grains.

prayers. Traditionally, the holiday includes more elaborate celebrations such as parades and processions.

FAMILY AND COMMUNITY LIFE

As with so many other aspects of the Malaysian American community, many details of family and community life depend on ethnic and religious backgrounds. However, all of the major Malaysian American groups place a high value on family, which often includes the extended family and older generations in the household. Many Malaysian Americans move in with other Malaysian Americans soon after arriving in the United States and remain nearby after settling. They also maintain ties to each other and their home country.

Gender Roles In Malaysian American life, gender roles and attitudes vary depending on such factors as ethnicity, religion, and how long a family has been in the United States. Generally, Malaysian Americans

EMPLOYMENT AND ECONOMIC CONDITIONS

Malaysian Americans are a relatively prosperous immigrant group. Their per capita income of roughly $33,000 exceeded that of non-Hispanic whites in 2009, and it exceeded that of other Asian Americans except Taiwanese Americans and Indian Americans. Median household income was more than $60,000, which was above the U.S. average overall. Poverty rates stood at 13 percent, while 2009 unemployment was well below that of the United States as a whole, at just 4 percent even amid the Great Recession.

According to the 2011 American Community Survey three-year estimates, about three-quarters of Malaysian Americans work in management, business, science, and sales. Most of the remainder work in service positions. These patterns were true for both male and female Malaysian American workers. The largest proportion of Malaysian Americans—about one-quarter—worked in education or health care. Other significant industries included the arts, professional services, and manufacturing. Very few Malaysian Americans worked in agriculture or construction, reflecting their above-average education and income.

Unlike many ethnic groups, Malaysian Americans largely do not have a story of working their way up from menial industries to professional industries. Many Malaysian Americans came to the United States to do professional work, and they remain relatively affluent among immigrant groups to the United States.

Children of Malaysian Americans are likely expected to attend college and pursue professional careers like those of their parents. Many attend American colleges and plan to live in the United States permanently. In college, many join associations of Malaysian American and Malaysian students.

POLITICS AND GOVERNMENT

Because Malaysian Americans are a relatively small, dispersed group, and only one-quarter of them are U.S. citizens, they do not exert a major influence on politics in the United States at any level. Although they have been mentioned in federal legislation pertaining to Asian Americans generally, they have not been the subject of any specific legislation. Overall, their political impact is small.

Malaysian Americans may continue to be active politically in Malaysia, however, since many travel back and forth between the two countries. In addition, because of the "brain drain" issue, Malaysian expatriates have indirectly influenced Malaysian politics as Malaysian leaders attempt to find strategies to keep educated, prosperous Malaysians at home to further the country's development.

NOTABLE INDIVIDUALS

Fashion Yeohlee Teng is considered one of the most important Asian American fashion designers. Of Chinese ethnic heritage, she was born in Penang in 1955. She came to the United States in the 1970s and studied fashion at the Parsons School of Fashion, New York. She founded her own fashion house, YEOHLEE, Inc., in 1981. Her work, known for being very minimalist, has been displayed in the New York Metropolitan

MALAYSIAN AMERICAN MEMOIR

Shirley Geok-lin Lim, the daughter of a Chinese father and Malaysian Chinese mother, published *Among the White Moon Faces: An Asian-American Memoir of Homelands* in 1997. She describes her childhood in Malaysia and her life after age eight when her mother abandoned her family. Unconventionally for Malaysian society, her father was left to raise her and her siblings. She later rejected the role of demure wife in Malaysia, leaving a potential marriage to immigrate to the United States, where she pursued a career as professor, writer, and mother. Her journey is a particularly rich exploration of gender roles in her native and adopted countries. The memoir won a 1997 American Book Award.

Museum of Art and London's Victoria & Albert Museum. In 2004 she received the prestigious Cooper-Hewitt National Design Award for fashion design from the Smithsonian Institution. Teng also been active in discussions concerning zoning and planning for New York's Garment District, and she joined the Board of the Municipal Art Society of New York in 2010.

Literature Shirley Geok-lin Lim is a renowned novelist, poet, and literary critic who has sought to embody the Malaysian cultural experience. She was born in Malacca, Malaysia, in 1944 and is of Chinese ethnic heritage, although her parents lived a very Westernized lifestyle. Confronting the challenges of cultural identity and language has guided much of her work. She attended the University of Malaya, where she studied English and earned a BA in 1969. After winning a prestigious fellowship, she went on to earn a PhD in English and American Literature at Brandeis University (Massachusetts) in 1973. Her first book of poems, *Crossing the Peninsula and Other Poems*, won a Commonwealth Prize in 1980. In addition to four other poetry collections, she has published many essays, and stories. *Among the White Moon Faces* is a memoir concerning her life in Malaysia and the United States. In 2012 she was Professor of English at the University of California, Santa Barbara.

Music Nicolette Louisa Palikat, better known by the stage name "Nikki," was born in Michigan in 1985. She is a descendant of the Dusun, an indigenous group from northern Malaysia. She became well known among Malaysians and Malaysian Americans after appearing in 2004 on the *Malaysian Idol* television program and performing pop hits by a variety of stars, including Mariah Carey, the Jackson 5, and Phil Collins. Though Nikki's performances consisted mostly of songs in English, she is fluent in Malay and the Dusun language. In 2005 she released the album titled *Maharani*. Her second album, *Hawa*, was released in 2008.

Stage and Screen Irene Ng, born Sze Ng in 1974, is a Malaysian American actress of Chinese descent. She is best known for the 1990s Nickelodeon series *The Mystery Files of Shelby Woo*. She also appeared in the *Joy Luck Club* and several episodes of *Law and Order*. Ng is a Harvard graduate and has worked as a financial adviser at Merrill Lynch.

MEDIA

Because the Malaysian American population is small, relatively dispersed, and of diverse linguistic and ethnic backgrounds, there are no significant media sources in the United States for Malaysian Americans. For Malaysian news, many read Malaysian newspapers online and watch Malaysian television channels via satellite.

ORGANIZATIONS AND ASSOCIATIONS

Malaysian Americans of Michigan (MAM)

Seeks to create a sense of identity among Malaysian Americans living in Michigan and to contribute to members' business success.

Geck Bud, President
Email: geck.budd@malaysianassociationofmi.org
URL: www.malaysianassociationofmi.org

Malaysian Association of Southern California (MASC)

Builds business and social ties among Malaysians of southern California to help build a sense of community in the region.

Mimi Lioe, President
P.O. Box 81105
San Marino, California 91118-1105
URL: www.mascusa.com

Malaysian Club of Chicago (MCC)

Promotes personal and professional development for Malaysian Americans and cultural activities to enhance awareness of Malaysian Americans in Illinois.

Stanley Thai, President
601 West 31st Street
Chicago, Illinois 60616
Email: info@malaysianclubchicago.com
URL: www.malaysianclubchicago.com

Malaysian Professional Business Association (MPBA)

Helps provide contacts for Malaysians living in the United States or anyone with a Malaysian connection for business and professional opportunities.

Belinda Gong, President
226 Airport Parkway
Suite 480
San Jose, California 95110
URL: www.mpba.org

Malaysian Students Association at the University of Michigan (U.M.I.M.S.A.)

Strives to unite Malaysian Americans or Malaysians studying in the United States and serves to foster friendships and camaraderie among Malaysian students.

Duo-Ren Cheng, President
Malaysian Students Association at the University of Michigan
Ann Arbor, Michigan 48107-7054
URL: www.umimsa.com

MUSEUMS AND RESEARCH CENTERS

Asian American Justice Center

Member of the Asian American Center for Advancing Justice coalition and dedicated to research, education, and advocacy on behalf of the civil rights of Asian American groups.

Maria Etcubañez
1140 Connecticut Avenue NW
#1200
Washington, D.C. 20036-4003
Phone: (202) 296-2300
Email: information@advancingequality.org
URL: www.advancingequality.org

SOURCES FOR ADDITIONAL STUDY

Andaya, Barbara Watson, and Leonard Y. Andaya. *A History of Malaysia*. 2nd ed. Honolulu: University of Hawaii Press, 2001.

Hopkins, Julian, and Julian C. H. Lee, eds. *Thinking Through Malaysia: Culture and Identity in the 21st Century*. Selangor, Malaysia: Strategic Information and Research Development Center, 2012.

Lim, Shirley Geok-lin. *Among the White Moon Faces: An Asian American Memoir of Homelands*. New York: Feminist Press, 1996.

Rhagavan, Susheela. *Flavors of Malaysia: A Journey through Time, Tastes, and Traditions*. New York: Hippocrene Books, 2010.

Tham, Hilary. *Lane with No Name: Memoirs and Poems of a Malaysian-Chinese Childhood*. Boulder, CO: Lynne Rienner, 1997.

MALTESE AMERICANS

Diane Andreassi

OVERVIEW

Maltese Americans are immigrants or descendants of people from Malta, a European country of several islands with a total area of 122 square miles. Slightly smaller than twice the size of Washington, D.C., the country is sometimes referred to as "the mouse that roars." It is located 58 miles south of Sicily and 180 miles north of Africa and has three inhabited islands: Malta, Gozo, and Comino. Malta, 17 miles long and about 9 miles across, is the largest of the three islands. Its topography is characterized by a series of low hills with terraced fields. Gozo, the northernmost island, has an area of 35 square miles and is known for its grottoes, copper beaches, and the third-largest church dome in the world. Comino, which is located between Malta and Gozo, has an area of only 1 square mile and its population is small.

According to the *CIA World Factbook*, Malta's population in July 2012 was 409,836, making it one of the most densely populated countries in the world. The vast majority, 96 percent, of the population is of Maltese descent, 2 percent are British, and the remaining 2 percent are of various other heritages. The chief languages are Maltese, English, and Italian. The population is predominantly Roman Catholic. Malta's main industries are tourism and the manufacture and export of electronics. It never snows in Malta, and the total average annual rainfall is 20 inches. The summers are warm and breezy and the winters are mild, with an average winter temperature of 54 degrees Fahrenheit. Taking advantage of the climate and Malta's scenic terrain and coastline, a number of movies and television programs have been filmed on Malta, including the movies *Popeye*, *Gladiator*, and *Alexander*. MTV hosts a televised, one-day music festival on Malta called Isle of MTV, which in 2012 had more than 50,000 attendees.

Large groups of Maltese began emigrating from Malta to the United States in the late 1800s and early 1900s, settling first in New York and later Detroit, where they took jobs as automotive workers. In her book *Maltese in Detroit*, Diane Gale Andreassi explains that

> unemployment, poverty, and political frustration were some of the main factors that prompted people to leave their island homes. Detroit was building cars, and people around

the world learned of jobs that were available. Detroit became the largest Maltese colony outside the islands.

According to the U.S. Census Bureau, the Maltese population in the United States as of 2011 was 39,457, which is roughly twice the capacity of New York City's Madison Square Garden arena. Immigrants of Maltese descent live in all fifty states, and cities with large Maltese American populations include Chicago, Detroit, New York, and San Francisco. Although working-class Maltese Americans tend to live in tight-knit, ethnic communities, emigrants in professional fields tend to be more dispersed, with settlement patterns related to their respective businesses.

HISTORY OF THE PEOPLE

Early History During the late Stone Age, before 4000 BCE, farmers immigrated to Malta from Sicily. Remains of these early people have been found in the ruins of large structures believed to have been temples, and at least one underground temple catacomb has been associated with the cult of a Mother Goddess. By the year 2000 BCE these early people were replaced by bronze-using warrior-farmers who likely arrived from southern Italy.

Phoenicians followed during the Iron Age period around 800 BCE, and they were succeeded by Carthaginians. During the Punic Wars, Malta became part of the Roman Empire, and its inhabitants were treated well by their Roman conquerors. During this time, the Maltese enjoyed peace and prosperity based on a well-developed agricultural economy. In 870 CE Aghlabite Arabs invaded Malta by way of Sicily, followed by the Norman invasion by Count Roger who brought Malta back into the European Christian fold.

In 1530 Malta became the new home of the Knights of Rhodes, who then became known as the Knights of Malta. They fortified the island stronghold and defended it against a siege by the Ottomans in 1565. They also undertook the building of grand churches and palaces, especially in the city of Valletta, Malta's capital.

Modern Era In 1798 the Knights of Malta were forced from Malta when Napoleon landed with his Republican Army. The Maltese revolted against the French, and with the help of British troops they brought French rule to an end in 1800. In 1814 Great

Britain was officially granted possession of Malta, and the British later built a first-class dockyard there. Malta has limited natural resources, and as a result of economic pressures during the nineteenth century the government sought to reduce the population by encouraging emigration. Many immigrated to other British possessions in the Mediterranean and to the West Indies and Australia. Others immigrated to northern Africa.

Malta's position in the Mediterranean Sea made the islands strategically important to the Allies during World War II, especially for fighting on the African front. This key location also made Malta a primary target for massive bombing by Germany and Italy during the war. For their fortitude and dogged determination in the face of the enemy, English prime minister Winston Churchill awarded the Maltese people a George Cross, Great Britain's highest civilian honor for bravery.

Malta became an independent country and a member of the Commonwealth in 1964. Ten years later Malta became a republic, and in 2004 it joined the European Union. In 2008 Malta adopted the euro, which made the country more dependent on the global economy. Malta suffered financial problems during the worldwide economic downturn of the early twenty-first century, but it experienced lower unemployment than other European countries.

A large influx of Maltese immigration to the United States followed the discharge of skilled workers from Malta's Royal British Dockyard in 1919. More than 1,300 Maltese immigrated to the United States in the first quarter of 1920, and most found work in automobile manufacturing.

SETTLEMENT IN THE UNITED STATES

The earliest Maltese settlers in the United States came in the mid-eighteenth century, mostly to New Orleans. These settlers were often regarded as Italians, and tombstones sometimes mistakenly noted the deceased as "natives of Malta, Italy." The burial grounds were inscribed with such common Maltese names as Ferruggia (Farrugia), Pace, and Grima. By 1855 there were 116 Maltese living in the United States, and in the 1860s it was estimated that five to ten Maltese came to the United States every year. The majority of the migrants were agricultural workers, and in New Orleans the majority worked as market gardeners and vegetable dealers.

A large influx of Maltese immigration to the United States followed the discharge of skilled workers from Malta's Royal British Dockyard in 1919. More than 1,300 Maltese immigrated to the United States in the first quarter of 1920, and most found work in automobile manufacturing. The *Detroit Free Press*

reported in October 1920 that Detroit had the largest Maltese population in the United States, with 5,000 residents. It is estimated that over the next several years more than 15,000 Maltese settled in the United States. Many of these immigrants intended to stay for a short time and return home, but opportunities in America seemed more plentiful and stable than the uncertainties at home, and many Maltese remained in the United States. By the late 1920s Detroit, New York, and San Francisco all had large Maltese populations. These groups often stayed in tight-knit communities, forming social clubs in their respective cities to maintain their unique cultural heritage.

After World War II the Maltese government launched a program to pay passage costs to Maltese willing to emigrate and remain abroad for at least two years. A surge of Maltese left their homeland, and a reported 11,447 Maltese left the country in 1954 alone. The program resulted in about 8,000 Maltese coming to the United States between 1947 and 1977. In 2000 the U.S. Census reported the number of Maltese Americans as 40,000, and this number grew through 2009 to almost 48,000. By 2011, however, the number of Maltese Americans had decreased to fewer than 40,000, possibly a result of the major economic downturn in cities with large Maltese populations such as Detroit.

LANGUAGE

Like its people and history, the Maltese language is varied. It is Semitic, chiefly Arabic, written in the Roman alphabet, with words and phrases taken from the Italian, Spanish, English, Greek, and some French. The official languages in Malta are Maltese and English. With Malta's proximity to Italy, many people also speak Italian. Spoken English typically reveals a British influence. Although the main language spoken by Maltese Americans is English, Malta's mix of languages is often reflected in speech at home and at Maltese social clubs and other venues where Maltese immigrants gather in larger groups.

Greetings and Popular Expressions Typical Maltese greetings and other expressions include: *bongu* (bon-ju)—good morning; *bonswa* (bon-swar)—good night; *grazzi* (grats-ee)—thank you; *taf titkellem bl-Ingliz?* (tarf tit-kell-lem bilin-gleez)—do you speak English?; *kemm?* (kem)—how much? The word *sahha* (sa-ha) can be used as a greeting, as a farewell, or as a toast—it is the Maltese equivalent of "good health."

RELIGION

Christianity has a long history in Malta, dating to the Apostle Paul, who was shipwrecked on the island in 60 CE. The hospitality shown to him by the locals was well documented in the Acts of the Apostles in the New Testament of the Bible. Legend has it that when he was shipwrecked with his crew, the people made a

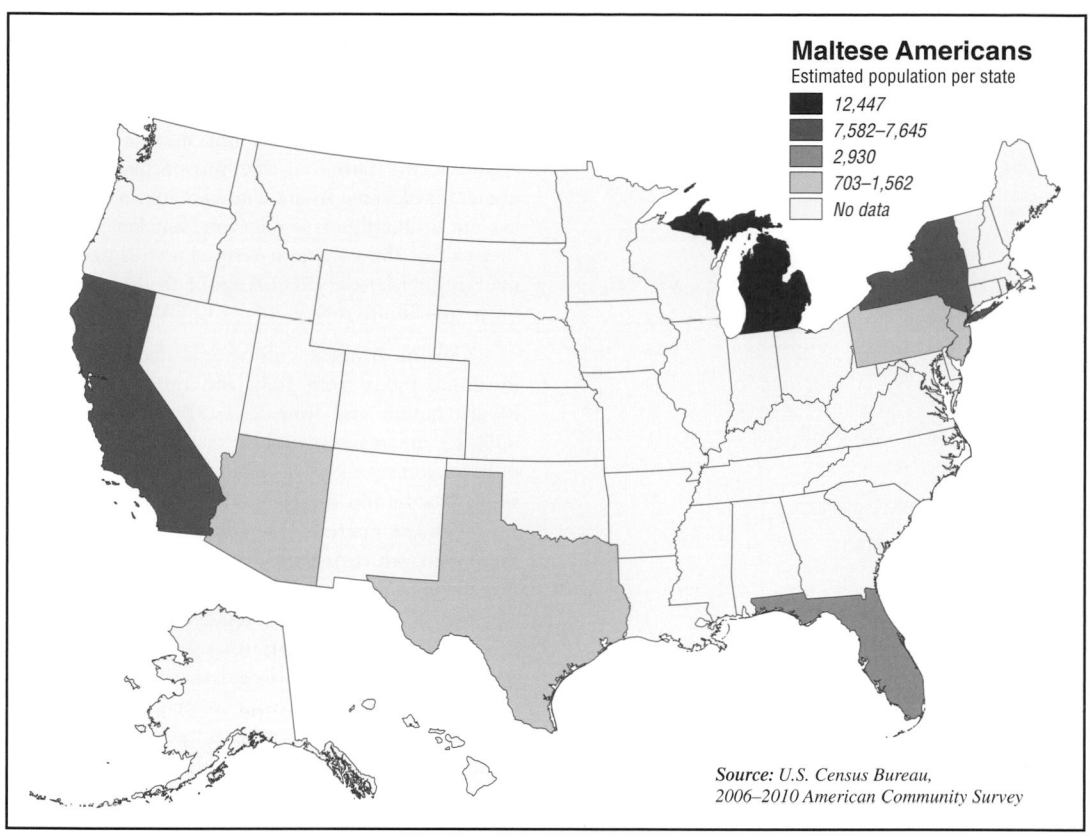

Maltese Americans
Estimated population per state

- 12,447
- 7,582–7,645
- 2,930
- 703–1,562
- No data

*Source: U.S. Census Bureau,
2006–2010 American Community Survey*

bonfire to make them warm, and a viper snake came out of the wood and went toward St. Paul. According to the legend, because he was not bitten the people thought Paul was a god, but he told them that "I am not a God, but I came to talk to you about God."

An important part of Malta's religious history was the period from 1530 to 1798 when it was under the control of the Knights of Malta, a religious and military order of the Roman Catholic church. The Knights of Malta traced their origins to the Order of St. John, which was established in the eleventh century to build a church, convent, and hospital for pilgrims in Jerusalem.

The official religion of Malta is Roman Catholicism and today more than 95 percent of the population is nominally Roman Catholic. Maltese Americans maintain a strong devotion to the Roman Catholic church, typically attending Mass weekly and staying active in their local parishes. One American parish notable for having a large number of Maltese Americans is that of the church of St. Paul of the Shipwreck in San Francisco.

CULTURE AND ASSIMILATION

In part because of their country's small size, Maltese are often confused with other nationalities, specifically Italians. Although the people of the Maltese islands are not particularly well known, there are a number

of Maltese influences on United States culture. For instance, many people are familiar with the Maltese, a tiny fluffy white dog, which originated in Malta. The movie *The Maltese Falcon*, a drama about a detective trying to find a priceless statue, is a classic part of American cinema (the falcon was a symbol of honor for the Knights of Malta). In most U.S. towns and cities, the badge worn by firefighters to identify their company is in the shape of the Maltese Cross, an eight-sided emblem of protection and courage. The history of the cross goes back to the knights of the Order of St. John, who would courageously come to the aid of other knights whose clothing had been set on fire by their enemy. (A military tactic of the time consisted of hurling containers spewing flammable liquid onto enemy fighters and then igniting it with a thrown torch.)

Traditions and Customs Maltese have traditions and folklore dating back centuries. One popular belief was that if someone gave you "the bad eye," you would have bad luck. To rid the house a bad spirit, some Maltese would undergo an elaborate ritual involving old dried olive branches, which were blessed on Palm Sunday. The Maltese would burn the olive branches in a pan and spread the incense through every room of the house while saying a special prayer to chase away the spirit. Another belief was that women who were menstruating could taint new wine,

IMQARRUN IL-FORN (BAKED MACARONI)

Ingredients

7 tablespoons onions, finely diced

4 cloves garlic, crushed

2 tablespoons olive oil

⅓ pound bacon, finely diced

⅓ pound ground pork

⅓ pound ground beef

⅓ pound chicken livers, diced (optional)

2¼ cups dried macaroni

4 tablespoons parmesan cheese, grated

4 tablespoons Edam cheese, grated

4 eggs, beaten

7 tablespoons tomato paste

1 cup tomato purée

2¼ cups chicken or beef stock

3 tablespoons butter

salt and pepper

Preparation

Preheat oven to 350°F.

Fry onions and garlic in olive oil for 5 minutes, add the bacon and pork. Stir well to separate from each other. Add the beef and cook for another 10 minutes. If using, add the chicken liver and cook for 5 more minutes. Add the stock, mix well and bring to boil. Simmer for 20 minutes, then add the tomato paste and tomato purée.

In the meantime, cook the pasta until soft, but not fully cooked. Don't let it cook completely as it will continue cooking in the oven. A bit before al dente is good enough. Drain the pasta and mix with sauce, add the parmesan and the Edam cheeses. Stir the eggs in.

Butter a baking dish and pour in the macaroni. Add salt and pepper to taste. Bake for 1–1½ hours.

so they were banned from the cellar while wine was made. Other beliefs were that bad luck would follow a person who dropped a knife or sighted a black moth. Good luck, however, would come when a white moth was seen, and some people therefore believed that you should never kill a moth.

In the United States, as Maltese assimilated into American society, traditional Maltese beliefs have been gradually forgotten or are related only through family stories.

Matchmaking in Malta traditionally involved an elaborate sequence of events. When a young woman was ready for marriage her parents would place a flower pot on the front porch. A matchmaker would take note and alert the single men about her availability. Interested suitors would then tell the matchmaker they wanted to marry. Next the matchmaker would approach the father of the prospective bride and obtain his blessing. In the United States matchmaking has not ordinarily involved a matchmaker, but in the first half of the twentieth century men interested in marrying a Maltese girl still spoke to the girl's father for permission to marry.

Cuisine Maltese cuisine has many influences, including foods from Italy and other areas of the Mediterranean and from Great Britain. Garlic and olive oil are mainstays. The most popular Maltese dish is *pastitsi*, which is made from a flaky dough similar to the filo dough used in Greece. A meat or ricotta-cheese mixture is wrapped inside a pocket of the dough, which is then cooked. The meat mixture is made with ground beef, onion, tomato paste, peas, salt, pepper, and curry powder, and the ricotta-cheese mixture is made with ricotta cheese, egg, salt, and pepper. *Imquarrun fil forn* (baked macaroni) is another popular dish. The macaroni is served with a sauce containing ground beef, tomato paste, garlic powder, eggs, grated cheese, and a dash of curry powder. This dish can be served without baking, in which case it is called *mostoccoli*.

A mainstay of Maltese cuisine both in Malta and in the United States is rabbit, which can be served in stews, meat pies, or other dishes. Other common dishes include pastas with ricotta and tomato sauce; fish and seafood dishes such as fried cod, octopus stew, and tuna; and stuffed artichoke and eggplant.

For dessert or treats, a deep-fried pastry called *imqaret* is common in Maltese homes in Malta and the United States. It is made with dates, orange and lemon extract, anisette, chopped nuts, orange rind, and lemon rind. Cream-filled or ricotta-filled cannoli shells are also common. These Maltese sweets are often served at functions such as showers, weddings, and baptisms.

Traditional Dress The traditional attire of Maltese women was the *ghonella*, or *faldetta*, a black dress with a black cape and a black veil shaped by a hard board. It was worn by some women in Maltese villages as late as the 1950s. In the United States, Maltese Americans typically wear the same fashions as other Americans.

Dances and Songs The traditional Maltese dance is an interpretive routine called *miltija*, which describes the victory of the Maltese over the Turks in 1565. Old-time singing was called *ghana* and involved bantering similar to "call and response" songs of Africa. It was commonly sung between two people who good-heartedly tease each other, using rhyme and jokes in a relay of comments about each other. The singer Joe Grech, often referred to as the "voice of Malta," won the first Malta Song Festival in 1960, and he has toured worldwide, including in the United States and Canada.

Holidays The Maltese love festivals, and between May and October almost every town and village in Malta celebrates the feast day of its patron saint. The *festa* is the most important day in each village, where the church is the focal point of the event. The churches are elaborately decorated with flowers. Gold, silver, and crystal chandeliers are placed on display as a backdrop for the statue of the patron saint. After three days of preparation, the statue is carried shoulder high along the streets of the city or village in a paradelike procession, including bands and church bells. Since the Maltese specialize in making elaborate fireworks, colorful displays are part of the party. Cities and villages compete with one another to put on the best show. Maltese in the United States, especially in large communities such as Detroit and San Francisco, privately commemorate and remember the patron saint of their town, but gone are the big festivals and fireworks. Roman Catholic celebrations dominate in Maltese culture among Maltese Americans. Holy days include Christmas, Easter, and an annual observance of February 10, which is the day St. Paul, Malta's patron saint, was shipwrecked on the island.

Health Care Issues and Practices Many people from Malta have been stricken with thalassemia, which is sometimes called Mediterranean anemia. It is an inherited blood disorder in which the body has a reduced level of normal hemoglobin, which carries oxygen in the blood. In the United States most cases occur in persons of Maltese, Italian, Greek, Portuguese, or Levantine descent. There are several forms of the disease. The form that occurs most commonly among persons of Maltese descent is beta-thalassemia, which involves the two genes that produce a component of hemoglobin called beta globin protein. A person inherits one of the genes from one parent and the other from the other parent. When one of the two genes that a child inherits is a mutated gene, a mild anemia usually results; however, when both are mutated, the results can be severe. Beta-thalassemia is usually discovered during infancy.

Death and Burial Rituals The Maltese in the United States have adopted the tradition of holding a wake when someon dies. In Malta when a person died they were usually buried within twenty-four hours, and very few people were embalmed. In the villages during the early part of the twentieth century, a local person would visit the home, clean and dress the deceased. This person usually was on the lowest rung of the social ladder. Superstition prevailed, and some people were afraid of the undertaker to the point that when village people saw him walking down the street they would walk on the other side of the road. As time passed, however, these traditions faded in Malta and were not followed in the United States.

Maltese Americans girls march in a Maltese parade in New York City. © ROBERT BRENNER / PHOTO EDIT. REPRODUCED BY PERMISSION.

FAMILY AND COMMUNITY LIFE

Family Life There were many changes in the family structure when the first Maltese immigrants came to the United States. Married men typically arrived without their families. Their plan was to bring their entire family after becoming financially stable and establishing themselves their new country. Frequently, years lapsed before the entire family was reunited. Single men who came to the United States from Malta typically lived with relatives or close family friends who had come to the country earlier. They lived in communities that were heavily populated by other Maltese and often married Maltese women who had come to the United States with their parents and siblings. Downtown Detroit and neighboring Highland Park were once heavily populated by Maltese. However, by the 1970s many the Maltese in this area began moving to Detroit suburbs, a testament to the mass assimilation of Maltese Americans.

Maltese family members were usually very close, and aunts, uncles, and cousins were often regarded as immediate family. Before 1980 most Maltese American families were large, with four or more children as the norm. In later years, however, Maltese Americans, like most other ethnic groups in the United States, began to have smaller families, with two or three children commonly found in each household.

Immigrants and first-generation Maltese could find camaraderie in groups such as the Maltese American Benevolent Society and the Maltese American Community Club in Michigan and the Maltese American Social Club in San Francisco. New immigrants also turned to the Maltese clubs and organizations for information and direction on life in their new country and for meeting other Maltese who could help in the assimilation process.

Gender Roles The constitution of Malta, like that of the United States, holds equal rights for men and women, and the Ministry of Social Development in

MALTESE PROVERBS

- Unless the baby cries, he or she will not be put to the mother's breast.

- Build your reputation and go to sleep.

- Who I see you with is who I see you as.

- Little by little the jar will fill.

- Essence comes in small bottles.

- Cut off the tail of a donkey and it's still a donkey.

- If you want it to be, it never will be.

- I'll be there if I'm not dead.

- A friend in the market is better than your money in the hope chest.

- God does not pay every Saturday.

- He who waits will sooner or later be happy.

- Only God knows when death and rain will happen.

- Always hold onto the words of the elderly to show respect and to gain from their wisdom.

Malta has an official department for the "Equal Status for Women." Among Maltese American immigrants, however, married women tend to take a back seat to their husbands as the main breadwinners for the family. Within traditional Maltese American households, women perform most of the domestic duties including cleaning, cooking, child-rearing, and other household chores. While many of these traditional family units have become more Americanized with life in the United States, Maltese immigrants tend to follow the standard gender roles of traditional Roman Catholic families.

Baptisms The Roman Catholic religion dictates much of what happens at baptisms. A *parrina*, or godmother, and a *parrinu*, or godfather, are chosen. Usually, these people are brothers or sisters or other close relatives of the baby's parents. In Malta a party celebration with tables of cookies, ice cream, and drinks will follow the religious ceremony. However, as the customs changed in their new country, Maltese Americans adopted new traditions, such as having a full meal at the party after the baptism.

Education In Malta a high priority is placed on education, bringing the literacy rate to nearly 93 percent. Education is mandatory for Maltese children from age five to sixteen, and by age four there is already almost 100 percent enrollment. Instruction is available in state as well as private schools, with the private sector catering to about 27 percent of the total population. The literacy rate for females and males in Malta is relatively equal, with many women going on to higher education and jobs in the public sector.

Courtship and Weddings A Maltese bridal shower is usually very elaborate, with a multicourse meal and a sweets table, and it is typically held in a hall or banquet room to accommodate the large number of family and friends who are invited. In Malta the typical wedding is based on the Roman Catholic mass. The bride would be accompanied by several bridesmaids and the groom had one male, the best man, at his side. Maltese weddings in the United States, however, are usually dictated by the typical traditions followed in American culture.

EMPLOYMENT AND ECONOMIC CONDITIONS

Many of the Maltese who came to the Detroit area in the twentieth century worked on the assembly line at one of the three automakers, Ford Motor Company, General Motors, and Chrysler Corporation. Other Maltese immigrants worked at various jobs on ships, in restaurants and hotels, selling real estate, and in religious orders as priests and nuns. While the auto industry has suffered greatly with the Great Recession of the early twenty-first century, many Maltese Americans still find work in manufacturing, shipbuilding, and other blue-collar jobs in major cities such as Chicago, New York, and San Francisco. Other Maltese immigrants are employed in academia, entertainment, finance, law, and politics.

POLITICS AND GOVERNMENT

The Maltese government is a republic with a president and prime minister. As of 2013 the president of Malta was George Abela and the prime minister was Joseph Muscat. The major political parties are the Malta Labor Party and the Nationalist Party. In Malta the first American consul was nominated in 1796, which made Malta among the first countries to have a consular office of the United States.

Relations with Malta During the first decade of the nineteenth century American ships brought a variety of goods to Malta, including flour, rice, pepper, salted meat, rum, tobacco, and mahogany wood from Boston and Baltimore, as well as dried fruits, cotton, wax, pearls, goat hides, coffee, potatoes, drugs, and sponges from Smyrne and the Greek archipelago. Trade would rise and fall cyclically. Malta's biggest boon of American shipping was during the Crimean War, between 1854 and 1856, when Great Britain and France were fighting Russia. Malta also emerged as a stepping stone in the wool trade between Barbary and the United States because it received wool from different ports in North Africa for shipment to the United States. Later, American tobacco was shipped to Barbary and Sicily through Malta. About 1,500 Maltese were employed in making cigars, which were exported to Italy, Barbary, Turkey, and the Greek Islands. Malta also imported petroleum, rum, pepper, flour, logwood, pitch, resin, turpentine, coffee, sugar, cloves, codfish, wheat, cheese, butter, and lard. Meanwhile, the island nation exported to the United States goods such as olive oil, lemons, sulfur, ivory, salt, rags, goat skins, stoneware, soap, sponges, and donkeys.

NOTABLE INDIVIDUALS

Academia Paul Vassallo, formerly of Marsa, Malta, headed the Washington Research Library Consortium, a group of eight universities in the Washington, D.C., area that have served as a national model to demonstrate how university libraries can keep up with vast amounts of new material. Vassallo, born in 1932, immigrated to the United States when he was fifteen years old, and his mother and siblings lived in the Detroit area.

Joseph P. Borg, born in 1951, has worked as an American financial regulator and as president of the North American Securities Administration Association. In 2011 Borg was listed as one of the top financial players in the United States by *Smart Money* magazine.

Art The Liberty Bell was made in England in 1751 for use in the State House of the City of Philadelphia. However, when it was being tested the bell cracked. It was recast in Philadelphia by John Pass, a Maltese immigrant, and John Stow; their last names appear on the bell, which is on display at Liberty Bell Center in Philadelphia.

Joe Sacco, born in 1960, is a Maltese American cartoonist and journalist known for his book *Palestine* (1993), a nonfiction graphic novel. He has since published several other works of journalistic comics, including the graphic novels *Safe Area Gorazde: The War in Eastern Bosnia 1992–95* (2000) and *Footnotes in Gaza* (2010).

Military Joseph Borg went to the United States at the time of the American Revolution. He was described as having been a sea captain who fought in many battles for American independence.

Patrick P. Caruana achieved the rank of lieutenant general in the U.S. Air Force before he retired in 1997. Caruana, a St. Louis resident, was a KC-135 tanker pilot during the Vietnamese War and commanded the 17th Air Division and its fleet of bombers, refueling tankers, and spy planes. During the 1990–91 Persian Gulf War, Caruana commanded the fifty B-52 bombers flying out of Saudi Arabia, England, Spain, and the Indian Ocean.

Music Oreste Kirkop (1923–1998), an opera singer, appeared in *Student Prince*. Legend had it that he was encouraged to change his name to increase his fame, but he refused to take the suggestion and instead returned to Malta. World-renowned pop icon Britney Spears (1981–) is also of Maltese descent.

Maltese American Joseph Calleja is a tenor for the Metropolitan Opera in New York City. AP PHOTO / STEPHEN CHERNIN

Science and Medicine John Schembri, with degrees in electronics, engineering, mathematics, and industrial relations, and became a recognized expert in the design and application of optical-fiber transmissions systems. While working at Pacific Bell he was granted several patents for the designs and applications he developed.

Stage and Screen Joseph Calleia, a Maltese native and actor, appeared in a number of Hollywood movies, including *Wild Is the Wind* in 1957. More recently Danielle Fishel (1981–) portrayed Topanga Lawrence on the popular 1990s sitcom *Boy Meets World* and went on to become a host of Style Network's talk show *The Dish*.

ORGANIZATIONS AND ASSOCIATIONS

American Association, Sovereign Military Order of Malta

1011 First Avenue
Suite 1350
New York, New York 10022-4112
Phone: (212) 371-1522
Fax: (212) 486-9427
Email: info@maltausa.org
URL: https://orderofmaltaamerican.org/

The Malta Emigrants Commission

Edwin Borg-Manche, Website Editor
Dar l-Emigrant, Castille Place
Valletta, VLT 01 Malta
Phone: (356) 222644, 232545, 240255
Fax: (356) 240022
Email: mec@maltamigration.com
URL: http://www.maltamigration.com

Maltese American Benevolent Society

Serves social and patriotic needs of Detroit's Maltese population, which is believed to be the largest in the United States. Supports children's services. Offers activities for members and their families.

1832 Michigan Avenue
Detroit, Michigan 48216-1332
Phone: (313) 961-8393
Fax: (313) 961-2050
URL: facebook.com/pages/Maltese-American-
Benevolent-Society/116085168413257

Maltese American Community Club

Phone: (313) 846-7077
URL: www.malteseamericanclub.org
John Caruana, President
5221 Oakman Boulevard
Dearborn, Michigan 48126

Maltese Center

Frank Borg, President
Malta Square
27-20 Hoyt Avenue South
Astoria, New York 11102
Phone: (718) 728-9883
URL: www.webspawner.com/users/maltesecenter

Permanent Observer Mission of the Order of Malta to the United Nations in New York

Chancellerie
216 East 47th Street
New York, New York 10017
Phone: 212 355 6213
Fax: 212 355 4014
Email: orderofmalta@un.int
URL: www.un.int/orderofmalta

MUSEUMS AND RESEARCH CENTERS

Maltese American Benevolent Society

Contains a library covering Maltese issues, concerns, and related information.

John Caruana, President
1832 Michigan Avenue
Detroit, Michigan 48216
Phone: (313) 961-8393
Fax: (313) 961-2050

SOURCES FOR ADDITIONAL STUDY

Andreassi, Diane Gale. *Maltese in Detroit*. Charleston, SC: Arcadia, 2011.

Balm, Roger. *Malta*. Blacksburg, VA: McDonald & Woodard, 1995.

Cassar, Paul. *Early Relations between Malta and the United States of America*. Valletta, Malta: Midsea Books, 1976.

Dobie, Edith. *Malta's Road to Independence*. Norman: University of Oklahoma Press, 1967.

Lubig, Joseph M. *Maltese in Michigan*. East Lansing: Michigan State University Press, 2011.

Luke, Harry. *Malta: An Account and an Appreciation*. 2nd ed. London: Corgi, 1968.

Price, Charles A. *Malta and the Maltese: A Study in Nineteenth Century Migration*. Melbourne: Georgian House, 1954.

MENNONITES

Clare Kinberg

OVERVIEW

The Mennonites in the United States are a religious and cultural group who trace their roots to the Protestant Reformation and the subsequent development of a religious movement called Anabaptism in the early sixteenth century. Anabaptism began in Switzerland and spread quickly to Austria, the Netherlands, Alsace in eastern France, and the southwest area of Germany called the Palatinate. The term *Mennonite* derives from name of Menno Simons, a Dutch Catholic priest who became a leader in the reformist Anabaptist movement after disagreements arose among the Anabaptists over issues of polygamy and the use of violence against nonbelievers. The region of northern Holland where Menno Simons was born and eventually became an Anabaptist leader is the Fryslân (or Friesland), a coastal region that includes four islands in the North Sea. It is one of Holland's larger provinces, about 1,293 square miles (3,350 square kilometers), about the size of Rhode Island.

The population of Fryslân in 2010 was 646,000, according to Statistics Netherlands. Friesians have always maintained a level of independence, and Fryslân is the only Dutch province to have its own language, recognized by the government since 1956. In the twenty-first century, 85 percent of Friesians were Protestant, most either Dutch Reformed or Reformed Church; 5 percent were Mennonites. Fryslân is primarily an agricultural region, known for cattle and horses, but tourism is also an important part of the economy. This includes Mennonite pilgrimages to monuments at Menno Simon's birthplace and old Mennonite churches.

Mennonite immigration to the United States came in four major waves. In each case they were spurred by economic motives as well as the desire to practice their religion free from persecution. The first group of Mennonites to successfully establish a community in the United States came in the 1680s, with early immigration continuing through the mid-1700s. They settled on land north of Philadelphia, in what would become Germantown, and in other areas of eastern Pennsylvania. The second wave, which included Amish Mennonites, was in the mid-1800s. The third wave consisted of Mennonites who had first settled in Russia but found it inhospitable there

after 1870 and came to the United States. A fourth smaller wave came after 1920 from Russia, which had become the Soviet Union. Due to Mennonite missionary activity in many regions of the world, there are also significant numbers of African Americans, Native Americans, Hispanics, and Asians who have formed Mennonite congregations in the United States.

In his *Concise Encyclopedia of Amish, Brethren, Hutterites, and Mennonites* (2010), Donald Kraybill estimated the number of Mennonites in the United States to be 305,000, and the number of Amish to be close to 280,000. Pennsylvania remains the state with the highest concentration of Mennonites, with more than 300 congregations and more than 40,000 members. There are also large numbers of members in Ohio, Indiana, Kansas, Illinois, and California. Other states with significant populations of Mennonites include Florida, Michigan, Texas, Colorado, and Washington. The U.S. Conference of Mennonite Brethren Churches has a membership of 35,400 in 196 congregations, the Brethren in Christ Conference has 22,120 members, and there are many smaller conferences.

HISTORY OF THE PEOPLE

Early History A history of Mennonites in the United States needs to begin with the rise of Anabaptism, meaning "re-baptism," in the early 1500s during the Protestant Reformation (1517–1648). Anabaptists objected to the baptism of children, believing that only adults who understood and were committed to their faith could become baptized. Since the beginning of Christianity, the rite of baptism, a ceremony of washing with water, has indicated membership in the church and been a prerequisite for salvation. Until the 1500s Christians practiced universal infant baptism. When required by civil law, as was often the case, baptism became an effective means for unifying church and state and creating social cohesion in a nation. Thus the Anabaptist view of baptism as the voluntary act of an adult challenged the reigning authorities of the European world.

The founding of the Anabaptists arose out of a dispute between Swiss reform leader Ulrich Zwingli (1484–1531) and his disciple Conrad Grebel (ca. 1498–1596), who was frustrated by Zwingli's unwillingness to hasten reform in the Catholic Church. In 1525, shortly after a council of reform-minded though moderate church leaders voted to support the Catholic Church's position on infant baptism, Grebel and fellow radical reformer George Blaurock (ca. 1491–1529) held a secret meeting at which Grebel baptized Blaurock, which was the first recorded adult baptism in the Anabaptist movement. Anabaptists soon began gathering elsewhere in Switzerland as well as the Netherlands, Austria, and the Palatinate region of southwest Germany, whose authorities exhibited relative, and intermittent, tolerance for religious dissidents.

The Anabaptists viewed the church as a voluntary fellowship, free from coercion and necessarily independent of the state. At first, Anabaptists did not have an organized movement or set of dictates, but as the persecution against them increased, and people within the movement were increasingly drawn to violence, other Anabaptists searched for more solid, sober-minded leadership. Amid the atmosphere of the Protestant Reformation, as various reform movements were springing up in many different places, Menno Simons (1496–1561), a Dutch Catholic priest, emerged as a cerebral, even-handed reform leader. In the late 1520s Simons began to question a tenet of Roman Catholic doctrine called transubstantiation, the claim that God, working through the Catholic priest, transforms the bread and wine to be offered to churchgoers at the end of a Catholic Mass, into the body and blood of Jesus Christ. According to Catholic doctrine, this transformation is actual and not symbolic. While conducting an in-depth analysis of the Bible in the hope of resolving his questions about transubstantiation, Simons instead found nothing in the text that justified the church's position on this issue. He also discovered numerous other points on which Roman Catholic doctrine conflicted with his reading of the Bible.

Simons did not begin to consider the issue of adult baptism until 1530, when the church executed some men who were baptized in Leeuwarden, Friesland, near his home. When he consulted the Bible, Simons found nothing that justified the Roman Catholic Church's position on infant baptism. He also found nothing that justified the gruesome murders, which repulsed him. Despite his misgivings, Simons remained loyal to the church until 1535, when his brother Pieter, who had joined the Anabaptists, was killed for his beliefs. Simons joined the Anabaptists the following year; however, he did so with considerable reservations, as he was aware that many Anabaptists were not averse to violence.

In the mid-1530s, just prior to Simons's conversion, factions within the Anabaptist movement had become attracted by radicals who were actively trying to bring about the Second Coming. This slide toward extremism culminated with the Münster Rebellion of 1534–1535, in which a group of militant Anabaptists invaded a German city, expelled the presiding bishop, Franz von Waldeck, proclaimed the town a "New Jerusalem," and instituted the practices of adult baptism and polygamy. The movement's leaders were executed the following year when von Waldeck reclaimed the city, and thereafter the Anabaptists had great difficulty winning converts because the population at large regarded them as fanatics.

Upon his conversion in 1536, Simons followed the teachings of brothers Obbe and Dirk Philips, fellow Anabaptists who advocated nonviolence. In a climate that was unwelcoming of Anabaptists, Simons lived as an underground fugitive for the rest of his life, writing pamphlets and preaching nonviolence while moving quickly from one location to another throughout the Netherlands, coastal Poland, and Germany. By 1540 Simons was recognized as a leader among the Anabaptists, and by 1544 the term *Mennonite* was used to describe Dutch Anabaptists. Simons died in 1561, a quarter-century after his conversion.

Over the next 100 years, Anabaptists, including Mennonites, went through cycles of persecution, migration, tolerance, and acceptance. Although many had been city dwellers and craftspeople, some, particularly those people outside of the Netherlands, Northern Germany, and Poland, became rural farmers when it was necessary to escape persecution. Their beliefs kept them from serving in any military, and often the threat of conscription would prompt them to move. The period of the Thirty Years' War (1618–1648) between Catholic and Protestant forces greatly affected the Mennonites even though they were not directly involved. The treaty that ended the Thirty Years' War established legal status for Catholics and Protestants, but Mennonites were not recognized, which left them vulnerable to the policies of individual rulers. For example, the Mennonites were expelled from Switzerland but were welcomed in the Palatinate in southwestern Germany, which became a center of settlement.

Modern Era As the Mennonite movement grew, it experienced many schisms, or divisions based on different understandings of practice or belief. Mennonite communities were especially prone to schism primarily because membership in the church was voluntary and there was no coherent, centralized doctrine. Furthermore, there was no connection between the movement and major government leaders. With neither the authority of the state, nor of a leader such as the pope to answer to, each local Mennonite was responsible for insuring adherence to communal practice. However, communal practice varied from community to community, as did methods of disciplining those who did not adhere to accepted communal practice. Mennonites most frequently disputed the required strictness of practice and how to deal with members who deviated from the accepted level of observance. While some leading Anabaptists argued that dissenters should be coerced back into the group, others said they should be avoided or shunned.

The most pronounced of these schisms occurred in 1693, when followers of the Swiss Mennonite Jakob Ammann (ca. 1644–ca. 1730) adopted different practices regarding communion and stricter doctrinal purity and spiritual discipline. His followers became the Amish. Another subgroup of the Mennonites developed in the mid-1700s, when the rulers of Russia began encouraging immigration by western Europeans into its vast underpopulated areas. In 1786 a specific invitation to German Mennonites was issued, and over the next few years, at least 750 Mennonite families formed communities in the Ukraine.

In the early and mid-1800s more streams of Mennonites immigrated to Russia, and by 1870, when the immigration stopped, there were some sixty Mennonite villages with approximately 2,300 families, according to the *Global Anabaptist Mennonite Encyclopedia Online*. In the 1860s and 1870s, some of the Mennonites living in Russia developed an off-shoot religious practice that became the Mennonite Brethren Church.

Another schism occurred in North America in the mid-1800s. Differences among Mennonites in North America regarding missions, education, and publications led to a separation between what would be called "Old Mennonites" and what would become the General Conference Mennonite Church. In 1847 John H. Oberholtzer and other Mennonite ministers in Pennsylvania introduced the ideas of a written constitution, Sunday schools, and missionary work. The new movement was less concerned with details of dress and separation from the developments of mainstream America. In the 1860s Mennonites of the new General Conference began training missionaries and sending them to work among Native Americans. The new conferences established schools and colleges and also became more involved in relief work and peace education.

Large numbers of the Mennonites who had settled in Russia started immigrating to the United States in 1874; they felt that their protection from conscription was threatened when Russia began demanding universal military service. Even though Emperor Alexander II granted the Mennonites an "alternate service" provision, immigration to North America had become more appealing. Mennonites continued emigrating from Russia in steady numbers throughout the twentieth century due to a series of massive upheavals, including World War I, the Russian Revolution, World War II. Furthermore, the pervasive oppression of the Soviet regime during the Cold War made the Mennonites' position in the communist society precarious. Some who immigrated to the United States joined the General Conference, and others, members of the Mennonite Brethren Church, formed a third stream of Mennonites in the United States, the Mennonite Brethren.

By the end of the twentieth century, the Mennonite Brethren was the largest group of Mennonites in North America. In 2001, however, the Old Mennonites and the General Conference merged into the Mennonite Church USA, making it the largest Mennonite denomination and the Mennonite Brethren the second largest. By 2012 there were 1.7 million Mennonites worldwide, with only 3.6 percent of these in Europe. About one-third of Mennonites live in North America, 38 percent in Africa, 10.5 percent in Latin America and the Caribbean, and 18 percent in India and Southeast Asia.

SETTLEMENT IN THE UNITED STATES

Before significant waves of Mennonites arrived in the United States, a small group of Mennonite traders came to New Amsterdam (now New York) in 1663 and tried to establish a communal settlement on the Delaware River under the leadership of Dutch utopian Pieter Corneliszoon Plockhoy. Within a year, however, the English destroyed the colony.

The four major waves of Mennonite settlement in the United States can be divided into two ethnic-cultural groups, the Swiss-German group and the Russian group. The first wave, which spanned from 1683 to 1756, consisted of Swiss and German immigrants and included a small subset of Amish people. The second wave, which spanned from 1815 to 1860, was primarily Amish. Both of these groups settled in Pennsylvania. The first of the two waves of Russian Mennonites came in 1874, and the second arrived after 1930. Russian Mennonites settled mostly in the prairie and Pacific states.

The earliest permanent U.S. settlement that included Mennonites was established in Germantown, Pennsylvania, and started with a mix of thirteen Quaker and Mennonite families that arrived aboard the *Concord* on October 6, 1683. Led by Francis D. Pastorius, who had purchased the land they would settle in Pennsylvania, these Dutch-speaking families were mostly poor weavers from the city of Krefeld in Germany. Between 1683 and 1708, approximately forty more Mennonite families settled in Germantown, making up about 15 percent of this early settlement. The next group of Mennonite immigrants during this period consisted mostly of German-speaking farmers from the Palatinate region of southwest Germany, who settled in the rural areas of Franconia and Lancaster, Pennsylvania. This first wave included the beginning of the Amish immigration. By 1756 about 4,000 Mennonite and 200 Amish families had immigrated to eastern Pennsylvania.

The second wave, 1815–1860, included many Amish who settled further west in Pennsylvania, and even further west into Ohio, Illinois, Indiana, and Iowa. Mennonites from these first two waves also spread west, as well as southward into Virginia and Maryland. Only a small percentage went west of the Mississippi.

The largest numbers of Mennonite immigrants, over 10,000, came in the third wave (1874–1880)

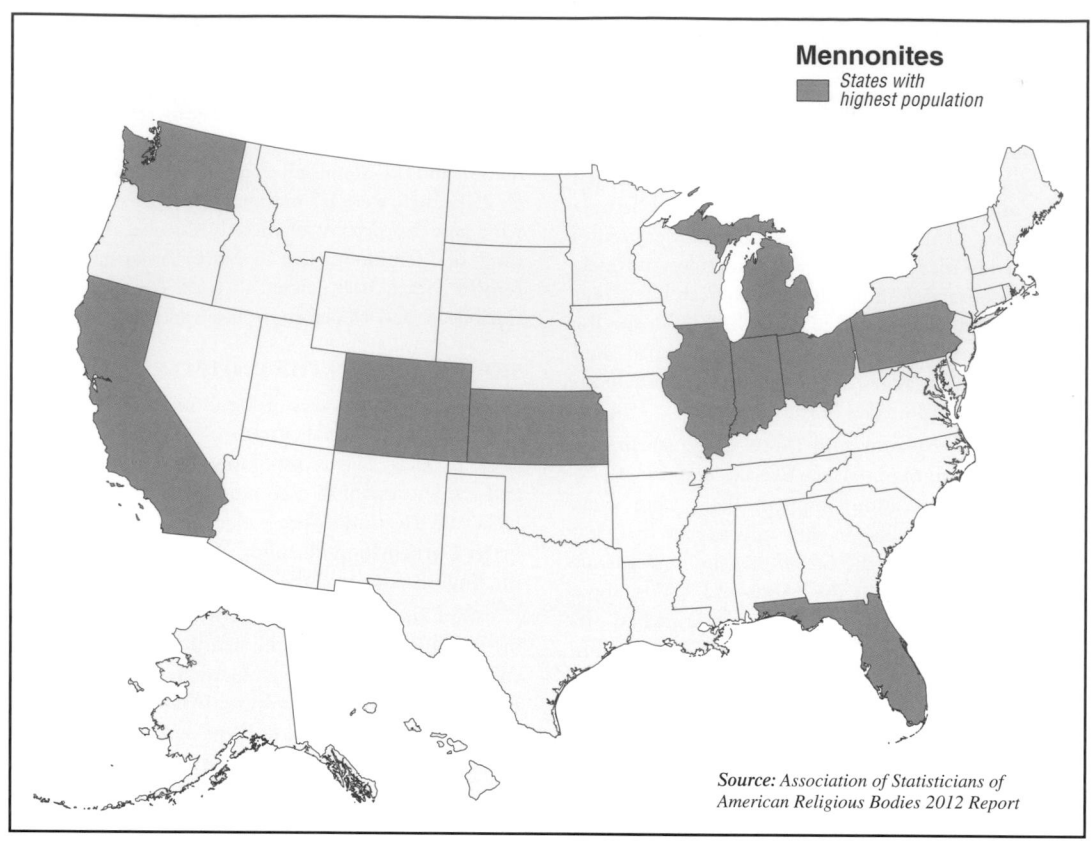

Mennonites
States with highest population

Source: Association of Statisticians of American Religious Bodies 2012 Report

from the Ukraine in Russia and settled in the prairie states, primarily in Nebraska and Kansas, but also in South Dakota and Minnesota. These Mennonite families had settled in Russia less than eighty years prior and had flourished there, growing to number over 100,000. During the latter half of the nineteenth century, however, the Russian government introduced a universal military conscription law and other laws that threatened the Mennonite way of life. At the time, Russia had lost the Crimean War (1853–1856) and was preparing for what would become the Russo-Turkish War (1877–1878). During this period, a third of all Russian Mennonites left for North America even though the Russian government allowed them to fulfill their military service by serving in the forestry. By 1879 Mennonites from Kansas, South Dakota, Minnesota, and Nebraska had met and formed the first Mennonite Brethren Conference in the United States.

After 1930 another small wave of Russian Mennonites immigrated from what had become the Soviet Union and settled primarily in Reedley, California. The Mennonites have converted a substantial number of Americans since arriving in the United States. In 2006, 26 percent of Mennonites in the United States had become Mennonite even though neither of their parents were Mennonite. According to the Association of Statisticians of American Religious Bodies estimates for 2012, many members of the

Mennonite Church USA reside in Pennsylvania, Ohio, Indiana, Illinois, Kansas, and California. Other states with significant numbers include Florida, Michigan, Colorado, and Washington.

LANGUAGE

The first Mennonite immigrants were Dutch speakers, but the vast majority of Mennonite immigrants to the United States spoke German, including the immigrants from Russia. While it can be said that German is the mother tongue of the Mennonites, immigrants spoke different dialects, depending on the time they migrated and the place they came from. For example, the Russian Mennonites brought with them their everyday language, the Low German dialect, Plattdeutsch or Plautdietsch, in addition to the more formal High German. Mennonite texts were written in German, and for the first generation of Mennonites, sermons and religious discussions were carried on in German. Prayer books, catechisms, and devotional books were also written in German, with only a few in English throughout the nineteenth century. One of the most important Mennonite books, *Martyrs Mirror* (1660) by Tieleman Jansz van Braght, was first translated into German from the original Dutch by American Mennonites in Pennsylvania in 1749. The book details the sixteenth-century persecution of the group and celebrates their courage through stories of steadfastness even when faced with imprisonment and execution.

Although the American Mennonites' transition to English was well on its way by World War I, the anti-German sentiment in the United States during the war hastened the process so that by 1925, almost all Mennonite services (except among the Amish) were conducted in English. The German dialect spoken by Amish, referred to as Pennsylvania Dutch, is still spoken in Amish communities. For other Mennonites in the United States, by the late twentieth century spoken German was not common but was preserved in folklore, art, and the use of German hymnals and sermons by some Old Order Mennonites (principally the Groffdale Conference).

RELIGION

Mennonites are a Christian denomination that emphasizes the separation of church and state and regards the Bible as the ultimate authority on matters of faith and theology. For Mennonites, if there is a conflict between the kingdom of the "world" (the state) and the kingdom of God (the church), their loyalty must be to God. Although they support governing authorities for instituting order among humans, they believe that, as violence is not the will of God, they witness against all violence, including war among nations. Mennonite doctrine requires members to offer a voluntary confession of faith, practice pacifism, and serve the church. According to the "Shared Convictions" from the Mennonite World Conference of 2006, it is incumbent upon all Mennonites to "become peacemakers who renounce violence, love our enemies, seek justice, and share our possessions with those in need."

Mennonites practice their faith and foster virtue through daily prayer, Bible study, sermon-centered worship in plain church buildings, and singing hymns in four-part harmony, with or without musical instruments. Mennonite religious rituals are referred to as "ordinances," practices or symbols that demonstrate faith, rather than "sacraments," or sacred mysteries in which God is directly involved. For instance, among Mennonites the Lord's Supper (practiced two to four times a year) is an ordinance in which the sharing of bread and wine is a symbol or a sign to remind believers of Christ's sacrifice. It takes on the additional meaning of perfect togetherness, in which the individual fuses with the group as a whole, foregoing self-will of any kind. Among some groups foot-washing is another ordinance that may be part of the Lord's Supper.

The Mennonites have an impressive record of helping those afflicted by poverty and natural disasters. For them, such assistance is a manifestation of their conviction that word and deed must be one and that love must be visible. The large and active Mennonite Central Committee (MCC), whose byline is "relief, development and peace in the name of Christ," was founded in 1920 to coordinate Mennonite relief activities in response to famine in the Ukraine. In 2012 the MCC employed over a thousand people in dozens of countries in Africa, Asia, and Europe, providing disaster relief, sustainable community development, and justice and peace-building services. Another Mennonite organization, Ten Thousand Villages, was founded shortly after World War II by Mennonite Edna Ruth Byler, who purchased needlework from poor women in Puerto Rico that she marketed directly to people in Central Pennsylvania. Her work grew into one of the leading fair-trade organizations; in 2012 Ten Thousand Villages worked in nearly forty countries and sold over 20 million dollars of crafts. Mennonite Disaster Service is another organization that serves people in need, primarily the victims of natural disasters in the United States and Canada.

Over time Mennonites have developed a highly nuanced relationship with mainstream America that involves both a noticeable separation from popular culture and a willingness to incorporate aspects of American life into their daily routines.

CULTURE AND ASSIMILATION

Over time Mennonites have developed a highly nuanced relationship with mainstream America that involves both a noticeable separation from popular culture and a willingness to incorporate aspects of American life into their daily routines. In order to maintain this complex relationship with the culture at large, Mennonites must acculturate (adopt aspects of the host culture such as dress, tools, and housing) without assimilating (being absorbed and fully integrated into the majority group). The adoption of English is an example of something Mennonites have accepted as necessary and proper acculturation. Because the early Mennonites did not speak English when they arrived and lived almost exclusively in communities with other German speakers, they did not need to learn English. However, the acquisition of English became necessary when the group decided that they wanted to be able to speak about their faith to others (they are evangelical). In addition, the older generation wanted to communicate with their children and grandchildren who were learning English and abandoning German. Thus, Mennonites consciously decided that the adoption of English was not a threat to their faith but a necessary component to the cohesion and growth of the group. Similar reasoning went into decisions regarding the use of electricity, farm equipment, cars, and other technology. Since the latter part of the twentieth century, many Mennonites have used technology that was available to them. However, Old Order Mennonites and some others have been very cautious about adopting technology because they find it a threat to their way of life.

The Mennonite doctrine of nonconformity holds that obedience to the teachings and example of Jesus Christ includes separation from mainstream society in everyday areas such as dress, social activities, and schooling. Thus, for Mennonites, the adoption of any aspect of mainstream culture is potentially controversial and could be considered wrongful assimilation. This includes not only secular culture such as radio, television, and movies but also many of the practices of other Christian denominations, such as Sunday schools and religious revivals. Even missionary activity was at first, in the mid-nineteenth century, seen as borrowing from the mainstream. By the late twentieth century the outward characteristics of "plain" people, simple dress and non-technological lifestyle, were primarily practiced by Amish and Old Order Mennonites and a few other groups. Among other Mennonites there was increasing conformity with mainstream America in dress, use of new technology, and other external expressions of mainstream lifestyles. It is notable that into the twenty-first century those groups that have maintained the higher levels of nonconformity continued to grow fairly rapidly, with high retention and high birthrates, while the number of Mennonites who are less distinguishable by outward appearances had lower birth rates and declining numbers or grew slowly, mostly through gaining new members.

Traditional Dress Traditional Mennonite dress has been influenced by several Mennonite values, including simplicity, humility, and separation from the mainstream. Although dress requirements and prohibitions have been common throughout Mennonite history and have varied by region, they are often adhered to by custom and tradition rather than written rule. In keeping with the ideal of simplicity, there have been Mennonite traditions or regulations concerning, for example, head coverings for men and women (wide-brimmed hats for men, white bonnets for women), dresses (the "cape dress" with an extra layer of fabric to cover the bosom), pants (knee-breaches), coats (no lapels), fasteners (no buttons, only hooks and eyes or pins), shoes and stockings (silk stockings forbidden), color and type of fabric (sometimes bright colors forbidden), and wedding dresses (not floor length) and shrouds (white required). There was traditionally a general prohibition against wearing jewelry or other outward signs of wealth.

However, since the mid-twentieth century, regulation among different Mennonite groups has been highly diverse. While Old Order Mennonites and several other smaller conservative groups adhere to plain dress (and became more uniformly strict in the early twentieth century), the clothing of General Conference Mennonites is indistinguishable from that of the general U.S. population.

Cuisine Mennonite food traditions are an expression of the values of hospitality and simplicity. Traditional Mennonite cooking in the United States consists of German/Dutch and Ukrainian/Russian recipes. Two favorites in the German/Dutch tradition are *Paska* (Easter Bread)—a sweet, yeasted bread made with flour, cream, sugar, eggs, and butter—and cabbage *borscht* (soup). Other foods in the German/Dutch Mennonite heritage include *kartoffelpuffer* (potato pancakes), farmer's sausage, *kotletten* (meatballs), and *spaetzle* (German dumplings). The most recognizable foods from the Russian Mennonite heritage include *verenyky* (cheese-filled dumplings), *zwieback* (distinctive yeast rolls with two unequally sized parts), and peppernuts (tiny spiced cookies). In Mennonite communities where women are responsible for the cooking, sharing recipes is a cherished tradition. Many widely distributed cookbooks emerged from the Mennonite tradition, such as Doris Janzen Longacre's *The More with Less Cookbook* (1976), an early expression of concern with world hunger and overconsumption of the world's resources. *More with Less* not only introduced Mennonite families to different ways of cooking and eating but also helped bring new people into the Mennonite church.

Music and Song Throughout their history Mennonites have adapted contemporary musical forms when composing hymns for their church. At times, American culture at large has, in turn, borrowed from those hymns and incorporated aspects of Mennonite song into popular music. The earliest Mennonites in America brought with them a sixteenth-century German/Swiss hymnal, the *Ausbund*, written partially by martyrs in prison using tunes of then-well-known folk songs. The *Ausbund* was still in use in the twenty-first century by the Amish in the United States. Throughout the nineteenth century, numerous Mennonite hymnbooks, in German and without notation, were edited and published in the United States, beginning in 1803 in eastern Pennsylvania. *The Harmonia Sacra*, originally published in 1832 by Joseph Funk in Mountain Valley, Virginia, as *A Compilation of Genuine Church Music*, is a shape-note hymnbook in the Mennonite tradition that is still used; its twenty-sixth edition was published in 2008. Mennonites began publishing English-language hymnals in the mid-nineteenth century. Mennonite singing of hymns was known for being a cappella, four-part harmony. In fact, in 1913 the institution that would become Eastern Mennonite University in Harrisonburg, Virginia, wrote into its constitution a rule that vocal music could be taught, but musical instruments were not permitted. This restriction had given way to a full music-education program by the 1960s, however.

The American folk music revival and protest-song movement of the 1960s were influenced by Mennonite musical traditions, and they were reflected in hymnbook supplements such as *Sing and Rejoice!* (1979). Since that time, guitar and other folk instruments have become more acceptable in the Mennonite church, especially in less formal contexts such as school or community events. Mennonite hymnals published in 1992, 2005, and 2007 increasingly included contemporary music and songs from around the world.

Traditional Arts and Crafts Folk arts, including quilting, glass painting, paper cutting, weaving, and woodworking, are widely associated in the United States with Amish and Mennonite communities. Mennonites have commonly used the popularity of their crafts to raise money for their large relief programs. In 2012 the Mennonite Central Committee raised over $5 million for victims of natural disasters around the world from the sale of quilts, homemade food, woodwork, and other items. At the Mennonite Quilt Center in Reedley, California, volunteer quilters and weavers gather to make quilts and weave rugs; their motto is "friends quilting for global relief."

Health Care Issues and Practices Care for the needy is a central tenet of Mennonite practice, and Mennonites have a long tradition of providing health care both within their own community and to the population at large. Early Mennonite communities in the United States made efforts to care for their own with local midwives, bone-setters, good deeds among neighbors, and even mutual aid (insurance) groups. In the early twentieth century Mennonites began building hospitals for the general public in Kansas, Nebraska, Minnesota, and Colorado. It also became common for Mennonites to enter health care professions. A Mennonite Nurses Association was founded in 1942, and a Mennonite Medical Association was founded in 1946.

Mennonites have made significant contributions to other areas of the medical field, including psychiatric and geriatric care. For example, in the 1940s many young Mennonite conscientious objectors in Civilian Public Service, an alternative to service in World War II, were assigned to work in mental hospitals. The appalling conditions in those facilities motivated them to develop a more compassionate system for treating mental illness. Many consider this to be the Mennonites' most meaningful contribution to society, and through early part of the twenty-first century, Mennonites have continued to operate a number of psychiatric facilities. Mennonites also run a number of reputable nursing homes and retirement communities. However, since the latter part of the twentieth century, as health care became more expensive and technological and the profession has been complicated by ethical issues such as abortion, end-of-life decisions, and government regulation of procedures, Mennonites have reduced their direct involvement in hospitals, while still supporting their peers who enter into the healing professions.

As is the case throughout the United States, for Mennonites, access to health care depends on socioeconomic factors, and the poorest members of the church are less likely to get proper medical attention than those of better means. A 2003 study revealed that 43 percent of the migrant farmworkers in Kansas were German-speaking Mexican Mennonites who had migrated from Russia, through Canada and

MENNONITES AND THE FOLK MUSIC REVIVAL

In 1974 a Mennonite, Connie Wiebe Isaac, recorded the folk album *Sing Alleluia*, a celebration of the centennial of the Russian Mennonite migration to Central Kansas. The album's folk style, ballads, and translations of German Mennonite hymns both interpreted the Mennonite story for the wider public and served as a bridge to mainstream culture for Mennonites. Another American who grew up in the Mennonite community and had a significant impact on American music was Gordon Friesen, longtime editor of the protest music magazine *Broadside*, which he and his wife, Sis Cunningham, began publishing in 1962 in New York. *Broadside* promoted the use of folk music to challenge traditional values and express compassion for the oppressed. Over its twenty-six-year history, the magazine published some of the most popular songs of socially conscious folk singers such as Bob Dylan, Rev. Frederick Douglass Kirkpatrick, Malvina Reynolds, and Pete Seeger.

Mexico, before coming to Kansas. As a linguistically and culturally isolated group, their access to health care was limited and targeted for improvement. In 2007 Mennonite Church USA issued a statement of "Healthcare Policy Principles" that both reflected their community values and shaped their involvement in public policy. The principles emphasized shared responsibility and access to health care by all, with special concern for the weakest and most vulnerable members of society.

FAMILY AND COMMUNITY LIFE

Human relationships expressed through family and community life are extremely important to Mennonites, who understand "family" to include not only relationships of blood, marriage, or adoption, but also the family of the church, where all members are brothers and sisters. More liberal Mennonites' family structure may not be distinguishable from other mainstream American families. The more conservative Mennonites, such as Old Order Mennonites, have a distinct family life, however; they live on farms, with the father working the fields and the mother taking care of the home and the children.

Gender Roles Typical of conservative rural Mennonite community and family life in the early twenty-first century were the thirteen families who lived near Plainview in the Texas Panhandle area and attend the Plainview Bible Fellowship church. The families in this area came from Pennsylvania, Canada, Mexico, Iowa, and Ohio; they had settled in Texas because of inexpensive land, low population, and unregulated private schools. In these families, the women and girls sew their clothes and do the

shopping and gardening, while the father—the head of the home—and sons do the farming.

In the early Anabaptist movement women had a significant role, as the Anabaptist belief in voluntary church membership demanded individual responses from men and women. Both women and men were taught scripture and were respected leaders, and about one-third of the Anabaptist martyrs were women. The first record of a woman ordained in a Mennonite church in North America was in 1911, when Ann Jemima Allebach (1874–1918) was ordained a minister in the First Mennonite Church of Philadelphia. The Mennonite Church and General Conference Mennonite Church began ordaining women as pastors in 1973 and 1975, respectively, though in 2013 some churches still rejected the idea of women in pastoral ministry.

Education The first Mennonites in the United States established a system of private schools, often on church property. By the latter half of the nineteenth century, however, Mennonites increasingly used the public school system. The more conservative Mennonite Church (Old Order Mennonites) and Amish Mennonites each built a system of private schools beginning in the early twentieth century, even as the more liberal General Conference Mennonites abandoned their system of private schools. However, secular public schools and the Mennonite value of nonconformity to worldly society continued to be matters of concern in all Mennonite communities. In 1972 the U.S. Supreme Court ruled in a Wisconsin case (*Wisconsin v. Yoder et al.*) that Old Order Amish

could not be compelled to send their children to school beyond eighth grade. This led to a resurgence of private, parochial Amish and Mennonite schools in which each sect could teach their children their own traditions and ways of relating to the world.

In 2001, when the General Conference Mennonites and the Mennonite Church (Old Order Mennonites) merged into the Mennonite Church USA, the Mennonite Education Agency was formed. By 2012 this education arm of the Mennonite Church USA ran a system of over twenty-five schools (kindergarten through twelfth grade), more than half of which were in Pennsylvania. Several colleges and universities were also part of this network, including Bethel College (North Newton, Kansas; founded 1887), Bluffton University (Bluffton, Ohio; founded 1900), Eastern Mennonite University (Harrisonburg, Virginia; founded 1916), Anabaptist Mennonite Biblical Seminary (merger of Goshen Biblical Seminary and Mennonite Biblical Seminary in Elkhart, Indiana), Goshen College (Goshen, Indiana; founded 1903), and Hesston College (Hesston, Kansas; founded 1909). Other universities founded by Mennonites include Fresno Pacific University, founded in 1944 by the Mennonite Brethren Churches; Rosedale Bible College (1952), owned by the Conservative Mennonite Conference; and Tabor College (1908) in Hillsboro, Kansas, owned by the Mennonite Brethren Church.

Early Anabaptists had a suspicion of elite scholarship, believing it weakened the simplicity of faith, and led to pride and unprincipled compromise for the sake of financial gain. Over time, Mennonites have seen the benefits of professional training in science, medicine, teaching, engineering, and business, and decided that these did not lead to a loss of faith. In 1972, 19 percent of Mennonites held college degrees, and by 2006 the figure had doubled to 38 percent.

Courtship and Weddings Like the other areas of life, traditions regarding courtship and weddings vary across Mennonite denominations and congregations. Mennonites do not arrange marriages, but parental approval and sometimes permission from the local bishop are sought. In the twenty-first century, many Mennonite weddings do not differ from other Protestant church weddings. However, in keeping with Mennonite value of simplicity, the bride may have made her own dress, which is often white and sometimes blue or purple. The ceremony, often like a regular church service, will likely be in the bride's home church; it may have no flowers or other decorations but is likely to have a considerable amount of singing. A long sermon or a short meditation given by the pastor before the standing wedding party may be part of the service, followed by a celebration with home-cooked foods.

EMPLOYMENT AND ECONOMIC CONDITIONS

During the latter half of the twentieth century, Mennonites became less likely to live on a farm and were much more likely to live in small towns of under 50,000 people. In 1972, 36 percent of Mennonites lived on a farm; by 2006 this had declined to 12 percent. Still, in 2006 the vast majority of Mennonites in the United States (80 percent) lived in small towns, only 10 percent living in urban cities of 250,000 or more people.

Before World War II, most Mennonites were discouraged from participating in industry and commerce, particularly outside of their own community, but Mennonites did establish colleges and seminaries, hospitals, and mutual aid societies. As the post–World War II economy of the United States expanded, Mennonites began exploring opportunities in the business world, and by 2006, 41 percent of Mennonites in the United States held business or professional jobs.

POLITICS AND GOVERNMENT

Mennonite political activity runs the gamut from total noninvolvement in partisan politics to active participation at the party level. Of the early immigrants, those of Swiss background and those who became Old Order Amish and Old Order Mennonites remained much more separate from worldly politics, while the Dutch-Russian immigrants became somewhat more active in local and national politics. A study in 1972 indicated that 76 percent of Mennonites believed that church members should vote in public elections; at that time, 37 percent of respondents did not have a party preference, and around 75 percent of the respondents who did have a party preference were Republican. By 2006

only 11 percent of Mennonites did not have a party preference, with 50 percent identifying as Republicans and 22 percent identifying as Democrats. Data from the 2012 U.S. presidential election indicates that Mennonites may have moved further to the right. For example, Holmes County, Pennsylvania, voted 73 percent for the losing Republican (Romney/Ryan) ticket.

Many historical factors led to the strong Republican leaning of the Mennonite electorate. Leading up to the Civil War and World War II, Democrats were more associated with war, leading Mennonites to vote Republican. In addition, Mennonites have long favored Republican land policies in the frontier states because they benefited Mennonite farmers. Mennonites in rural Pennsylvania and in Kansas and Nebraska vote much like their non-Mennonite neighbors. However, one of the only Mennonites to be elected to public office, South Dakota governor Harvey L. Wollman, was a Democrat. Wollman was elected lieutenant governor in 1975 and became governor for six months in 1978 to complete the term of Richard Kneip, who had resigned. Governor Wollman and his brother, U.S. Eighth Court of Appeals judge Roger Wollman (who was nominated for the court by President Ronald Reagan in 1985), were educated in Mennonite Brethren Church schools, and had both served in the U.S. Army.

NOTABLE INDIVIDUALS

Academia Shirley Hershey Showalter, president of Goshen College from 1997 to 2004, is a writer and teacher who graduated from Eastern Mennonite University in 1970.

John D. Roth is the editor of the *Mennonite Quarterly Review*, director of the Mennonite Historical Library, and director of the Institute for the Study of Global Anabaptism at Goshen College. He is the author of a number of books, including *Teaching That Transforms: Why Anabaptist-Mennonite Education Matters* (2011); *Practices: Mennonite Worship and Witness* (2009); *Stories: How Mennonites Came to Be* (2006); and *Beliefs: Mennonite Faith and Practice* (2005). He is a member of the Berkey Avenue Mennonite Fellowship in Goshen.

Harold Stauffer Bender (1897–1962), a professor at Goshen College, was born in Elkhart, Indiana. He helped found the Mennonite Historical Library in 1906 and founded the *Mennonite Quarterly Review* in 1927.

Activism Edna Ruth Byler (1904–1976) was born in Hesston, Kansas, where she attended Mennonite church. She founded the nonprofit Ten Thousand Villages, a forerunner of the global fair-trade movement.

Author and activist Doris Janzen Longacre (1940–1979) was born in Newton, Kansas. She was the author of two books, *More with Less Cookbook* (1976) and *Living More with Less* (published posthumously in 1980). With her husband, Paul Longacre, and two daughters, Cara Sue and Marta Joy, she worked with the Mennonite Central Committee in Vietnam (1964–1967) and Indonesia (1971–1972). She served as chairperson of the Akron Mennonite Church, as a member of the Board of Overseers of Goshen Biblical Seminary, and as a frequent speaker on world hunger.

Business Erie J. Sauder (1904–1997) was a furniture maker from Archbold, Ohio, whose woodworking was the foundation for the ready-to-assemble furniture business in the United States. By 1999 the family company he founded had $545 million in sales and employed 3,400 people. His company's success, which was supported in crucial ways by his Mennonite community, was an early example of successful Mennonite involvement in commerce.

Literature Julia Spicher Kasdorf is a writer born in Lewistown, Pennsylvania, in 1962. Her poetry collections include *Sleeping Preacher* (1992), which won the Agnes Lynch Starrett Poetry Prize and the Great Lakes Colleges Association Award for New Writing; *Eve's Striptease* (1998); and *Poetry in America* (2011). She is also the author of the essay collection *The Body and the Book: Writing from a Mennonite Life* (2001) and the biography *Fixing Tradition: Joseph W. Yoder, Amish American* (2002).

Jeff Gundy, professor of English at Goshen College, was born in 1952 on a farm in Illinois. His numerous books of poetry and essays include *Rhapsody with Dark Matter* (2000), *Scattering Point: The World in a Mennonite Eye* (2003), *Deerflies* (2004), *Walker in the Fog: On Mennonite Writing* (2005), and *Spoken among the Trees* (2007).

Ann Hostetler is a poet who teaches English and creative writing at Goshen College in Goshen, Indiana, and is the editor for their online site Center for Mennonite Writing. She was born in Mt. Pleasant, Pennsylvania, and graduated from the University of Pennsylvania. Her first book of poems, *Empty Room with Light*, was published in 2002. Her poems have appeared in the *American Scholar*, *Cream City Review*, *Mid-America Poetry Review*, and other journals.

Music Professor and musician Mary Oyer (1923–) began her career teaching cello in 1940 at Goshen College, Goshen, Indiana. She was a major contributor to Mennonite hymnals, and through her study of African musical traditions in twenty-two countries on a series of Fulbright grants, she greatly expanded the musical idiom of Mennonite music. She taught music in Africa as well in Taiwan.

MEDIA

Christian Leader Magazine

Christian Leader was founded in 1937 as an English-language youth publication and became the official publication of the Mennonite Brethren in 1951. Connie Faber became editor in 2004.

Box 155
Hillsboro, Kansas 67063
Phone: (620) 947-5543

Shortly after the September 11, 2001 terrorist attack, a group of Mennonites visit Ground Zero at the former site of the World Trade Center. ANDY LEVIN / ALAMY

Email: editor@usmb.org
URL: www.usmb.org/cl-magazine
URL: www.christianleadermagazine.org

MennoMedia

MennoMedia is the multimedia arm of the Mennonite Church USA and Mennonite Church Canada. It includes the book-publishing imprint Herald Press; the Third Way, a Café; a website for Mennonite information; periodicals; and other church resources.

1251 Virginia Avenue
Harrisonburg, Virginia 22802-2434
Phone: (800) 245-7894
Email: info@MennoMedia.org
URL: www.mennomedia.org

The Mennonite

A monthly magazine published by the Mennonite Church USA, the *Mennonite* began publication in 1998 as a merger of *Gospel Herald* (1908–1998) of the Mennonite Church and the former publication the *Mennonite* (1885–1998) of the General Conference Mennonite Church.

3145 Benham Avenue
Suite 4
Elkhart, Indiana 46517
Phone: (800) 790-2498
Fax: (316) 283-0454
Email: editor@themennonite.org
URL: www.themennonite.org

The Mennonite Quarterly Review

A quarterly journal devoted to Anabaptist-Mennonite history, thought, life, and affairs, published at Goshen College since 1927.

1700 South Main Street
Goshen, Indiana 46526
Phone: (574) 535-7433
Fax: (574) 535-7438
Email: mqr@goshen.edu
URL: www.goshen.edu/mqr/index.html

Mennonite World Review

This publication, formerly called the *Mennonite Weekly Review*, is an independent journalistic ministry that has published a newspaper since 1923.

129 West Sixth Street
P.O. Box 568
Newton, Kansas 67114
Phone: (316) 283-3670
Fax: (316) 283-6502
Email: editor@mennoworld.org
URL: www.mennoworld.org

ORGANIZATIONS AND ASSOCIATIONS

Mennonite Central Committee

A relief and development worldwide ministry of Anabaptist churches.

21 South 12th Street
P.O. Box 500
Akron, Pennsylvania 17501-0500

Phone: (717) 859-1151
Email: mailbox@mcc.org
URL: www.mcc.org

Mennonite Church USA

Mennonite Church USA was formed in 2002 by the merger of the General Conference Mennonite Church and the Mennonite Church. It has more than 100,000 adult members in about 900 congregations and 21 area conferences. It is the largest of numerous Mennonite groups in the United States.

1251 Virginia Avenue
Harrisonburg, Virginia 22802
Phone: (540) 434-6701
Fax: (316) 283-0454
URL: www.mennoniteusa.org

U.S. Conference of Mennonite Brethren Churches (USMB)

The USMB is the umbrella association of the U.S. Mennonite Brethren family of churches, which consists of five districts.

11000 River Run Boulevard
Suite 215
Bakersfield, California 93311
Phone: (661) 412-4939
Fax: (661) 412-4938
URL: www.usmb.org

MUSEUMS AND RESEARCH CENTERS

Lancaster Mennonite Historical Society

Established in 1958, this is a research facility specializing in Mennonite as well as Amish history. There are over 60,000 volumes of material covering theology, history, and genealogy.

2215 Millstream Road
Lancaster, Pennsylvania 17602
Phone: (717) 393-9745
Fax: (717) 393-8751
Email: lmhs@lmhs.org
URL: www.lmhs.org

Menno Simons Historical Library

The Menno Simons Historical Library (MSHL), located at Eastern Mennonite University, collects, preserves, and provides access to the recorded history, life, and arts of Anabaptists, and especially Mennonites in eastern North America. The library also actively maintains a large collection of materials on Shenandoah Valley history, culture, and genealogy.

1200 Park Road
Harrisonburg, Virginia
Phone: (540) 432-4177
URL: www.emu.edu/library/historical-library/

Mennonite Church USA Archives

This collection is the official repository of the Mennonite Church and the General Conference Mennonite Church. It has two locations, in Goshen, Indiana, and North Newton, Kansas.

1700 South Main Street
Goshen, Indiana 46526
Phone: (574) 523-3080 (Goshen location)
Phone: (316) 284-5304 (North Newton location)
Email: History@MennoniteUSA.org
URL: www.mennoniteusa.org/executive-board/archives/
300 East 27th Street
North Newton, Kansas 67117

Mennonite Heritage Museum

This museum, opened in 1974, has a complex of eight buildings that visitors can see on a self-guided tour.

P.O. Box 231
200 North Poplar
Goessel, Kansas 67053
Phone: (620) 367-8200
Email: mhmuseum@mtelco.net
URL: http://skyways.lib.ks.us/museums/goessel/

Mennonite Historical Library

A special collection within Goshen College's main library, this is one of the most comprehensive Anabaptist collections in the world.

Harold and Wilma Good Library
Goshen College
1700 South Main Street

Goshen, Indiana 46526
Phone: (574) 535-7418
Fax: (574) 535-7438
Email: mhl@goshen.edu
URL: www.goshen.edu/mhl/

SOURCES FOR ADDITIONAL STUDY

Epp, Maureen. *Sound in the Lands: Mennonite Music Across Borders*. Kitchener, ON: Pandora Press, 2011.

Janzen, Rhoda. *Mennonite in a Little Black Dress: A Memoir of Going Home*. New York: Henry Holt, 2009.

Kanagy, Conrad L. "A Landscape of Change: A Look at Members of Mennonite Church USA." *Mennonite*, February 6, 2007.

Kraybill, D. B. *Concise Encyclopedia of Amish, Brethren, Hutterites, and Mennonites*. Baltimore, MD: Johns Hopkins University Press, 2010.

Loewen, Royden; Steven M. Nolt; John A. Lapp; and C A. Snyder. *Seeking Places of Peace*. Intercourse, PA: Good Books, 2012.

Roth, John D. *Stories: How Mennonites Came to Be*. Scottdale, PA: Herald Press, 2006.

Roth, John D., and James M. Stayer. *A Companion to Anabaptism and Spiritualism, 1521–1700*. Leiden: Brill, 2007.

MENOMINEE

Kristin King-Ries

OVERVIEW

The Menominee are an indigenous, or native, people whose ancestors lived until the 1800s in a territory that covered millions of acres in present-day Wisconsin and Michigan, stretching from the Escabana River in Michigan's Upper Peninsula south to what is now the city of Milwaukee, east to Wisconsin's Door Peninsula, and west to the Mississippi River. Estimates of acreage in the early 1800s vary from 9 to 14.5 million. The Menominee had occupied these lands for at least five thousand years—lands that were home to a variety of wildlife, including bobcats, beavers, and bears; old-growth forests of pine, hemlock, and yew; and hundreds of lakes as well as hundreds of miles of rivers. Tribal members call themselves *Mamãceqtaw*, which means "Indian" or "human being." The name *Menominee* is thought to be an adaptation of the Algonquian word *Manoominii*, which meant, literally, "Wild Rice People" (though a Chippewa phrase, *mano mini*, meaning the same thing, may also be a source). Neighboring Algonquian tribes such as the Ojibwa called them this because of the Menominee's reliance on wild rice as a dietary staple.

French explorer Jean Nicolette and his party were the first Europeans to record a visit to Menominee territory when they passed through in 1634 in search of the Orient. Because the tribal population records for that time were pieced together decades if not centuries after the fact, no one knows the exact size of the Menominee tribe before the Europeans arrived. Scholarly and tribal estimates vary. According to prominent scholars George and Louise Spitzer (in their entry on the Menominee in *The Encyclopedia of World Cultures*, 1996), the first population count of 3,900 was taken in 1820, after a decline resulting from exposure to European diseases. The tribe divided themselves into thirty-four clans, each of which fell into one of five larger groups based on social function and named after sacred animals: bear (civil administration), eagle (war), wolf (hunting), crane (construction), and moose (maintenance). The Menominee did not live together during most of the year. Rather, they functioned as autonomous bands made up of extended families who spread across the Menominee ancestral lands and migrated on a seasonal basis. They subsisted on hunting in the winter, fishing in the spring, and trade with other tribes. The only time the entire tribe gathered was for religious ceremonies and during the rice harvest in the fall.

The present-day Menominee Indian Reservation is in northeastern Wisconsin, approximately 45 miles northwest of Green Bay. It covers 235,523 acres (358 square miles) that supports 187 rivers and streams, 53 lakes, and, blanketing most of the land, 219,000 acres of diverse forests. Persistent European encroachment successively reduced the area of the tribe's original lands to its current size, which was determined by the 1854 Wolf River Treaty between the Menominee and the U.S. government. The tribe resisted the federal policy that encouraged them to farm the land and instead achieved success through the area's more traditional occupations of logging and forest industries. The Menominee created one of the world's first sustainable harvest programs and have become international leaders in sustainable forestry. The College of Menominee Nation's Sustainable Development Institute trains people from around the world.

In 2012, according to Menominee tribal statistics, the tribe had 8,551 enrolled members, of whom 46 percent lived on the reservation, which has five main communities: Keshena, Neopit, Middle Village, Zoar, and South Branch. Another 9.5 percent lived in Shawano, Wisconsin, which borders the reservation, and 20 percent lived within 90 miles of the reservation. Approximately 25 percent of tribal members lived in urban areas of Wisconsin (with high concentrations in Green Bay and Milwaukee) and Illinois. The largest number of tribal members outside of Wisconsin lived in Chicago, and small numbers lived scattered throughout the rest of the country.

HISTORY OF THE PEOPLE

Early History The Menominee are an Algonquin-speaking nation whose culture and history have survived for over five thousand years in the Midwest. Their ancestral villages were located near the mouth of the Menominee River, which today forms the border between Wisconsin and the Upper Peninsula of Michigan. The tribe's main staple was wild rice, which they supplemented with corn, squash, and beans grown on small plots, and they made tools out of copper. Prior to European contact the bands spent the winter at their inland hunting grounds, moving to fishing grounds on Lake Michigan, Lake Winnebago, and rivers such as the Wolf and the Menominee in the spring. They lived in semipermanent villages set up in each location. Carved dugouts and birch-bark canoes served for water travel and fishing. Menominee hunters used bows and arrows to take down large game such as deer and bison. Tribal governance was fairly informal.

The Menominee first encountered Europeans in 1634. Soon the tribe became involved in the fur trade with the French, and the more permanent village lifestyle was replaced by a nomadic existence. In the mid-1600s Iroquois tribes from New York began sending war parties into the Midwest, displacing many tribes in an effort to control the fur-producing lands that sustained the Iroquois Nation's trade with the French. Besieged by the French presence and Iroquois aggression, many Menominee succumbed to starvation and disease or were killed in battle. The remaining Menominee were forced to leave the Upper Peninsula and seek refuge further south in Wisconsin. By 1667 they had started their own trade with the French, exchanging pelts for rifles, cooking utensils, cloth, and knives. As fur traders the Menominee found it advantageous to adopt a more nomadic lifestyle. French Jesuit missionaries established their first mission with the tribe in 1669.

Through their connections with French fur traders, the Menominee developed ties to the French authorities, aiding the French in battles against neighboring tribes in the 1720s and again during the French and Indian War (1754–1763). When the British defeated the French in 1763, Britain claimed control over the rich lands of the Midwest, including Menominee territory. The Menominee retained ties to those French traders who stayed, but during the American Revolution they allied themselves with the British colonial authorities. After the colonists defeated the British and later evicted them from the territories during the War of 1812, a newly formed U.S. government turned its attention to consolidating its holdings and seeking expansion. The Menominee lost the bargaining power that their military alliance with the British had afforded them. By 1800 the federal government had begun to encroach on tribal lands in the Midwest. Although the roughly one hundred years of European presence on Menominee lands had created a host of problems, among them disease and increased competition for resources, neither the French nor the British colonial authorities had attempted to control the tribe's way of life or its use of the land. The United States occupation presented the Native Americans with problems of a different order.

Modern Era During the nineteenth century, the increasing strength of the U.S. Army forced the Menominee to negotiate one unfavorable treaty after another until their land base had been whittled down to a fraction of its former size. The 1854 Wolf River Treaty created the current 235,523-acre reservation in northeastern Wisconsin. The government opened some of the former Menominee lands to white settlers and used other sections in negotiations with tribes such as the Oneida and Stockbridge-Munsee, who had been pushed west by an ever-expanding number of U.S. citizens.

Federal Indian policy in the late nineteenth century promoted the assimilation of Native Americans into mainstream culture and worked to eradicate traditional tribal culture and language. To this end, Menominee children were taken from their families at an early age and forced to attend a government-sponsored boarding school, St. Joseph's Indian Industrial School, which was on tribal land in Keshena, Wisconsin. Nevertheless, the Menominee remained a cohesive group, rejecting the federal government's insistence on tribal farming, thwarting efforts of outside groups to log tribal land, and establishing their own viable forest-related industries in the 1870s. With the proceeds from tribal logging, the Menominee were able to provide tribal members with a number of services. By 1890 the tribe had a hospital, a trade school, law enforcement, and a legal system. Any profit not needed to operate those services was divided equally among tribal members in the form of a small per capita payment. At the turn of the century, Menominee was one of the country's most financially viable tribes.

The success of the logging industry invited corporate and federal meddling almost from the beginning, however. In the 1870s large lumber companies, informally organized into a cartel known as the "Pine Ring," attempted to force the Menominee to sell their timber below market value. For a time, the Menominee were able to hold out and obtain fair prices. The pressure continued with the 1887 passage of the Dawes Act, in which the government claimed the right to divide communally owned reservation lands into allotments for individual members of the tribe. The Menominee successfully resisted allotment. (They and the Chippewa of the Red Lake Reservation in Minnesota were the only tribes in the Great Lakes area to achieve this goal.) Nevertheless, by the turn of the century, the government finally obtained a foothold in the Menominee logging business, and a thirty-year period of corruption followed.

The business was still prosperous in the 1920s, but by that time representatives from the Bureau of Indian Affairs (BIA) had more control over daily operations and long-term planning than the Menominee Advisory Council and tribal managers. The Menominee tribe sued the federal government for mismanagement in 1934 and was awarded an $8.5 million settlement in 1951.

Government interference continued shortly after the case was settled. The tribe experienced another twenty-year period of hardship after the federal government passed the Menominee Termination Act in 1954, revoking the tribe's status as a sovereign nation and ending government services. Although the tribe had achieved international renown for creating one of the world's first sustainable harvest programs and developing some of the world's largest and most productive sugar maple stands, the new law wreaked havoc on tribal economy and culture. The tribal council was disbanded, the tribal constitution was abrogated, tribal assets were lost, and treaty rights were threatened. The reservation hospital was closed because it lacked funds, and a number of other reservation services disappeared. The forestry program was shut down, and the federal government failed to preserve $10 million in forestry revenues it held in trust for the tribe. The Menominee tribal land was turned into Menominee County, the seventy-second county in Wisconsin.

The tribe fought back. In lieu of a tribal government, tribal leaders incorporated as a nonprofit organization called DRUMS (Determination of Rights and Unity of Menominee Shareholders), which protested sales of tribal land and worked for the return of federal status. Tribal members held rallies, circulated petitions, and eventually sued the federal government for failing in their fiduciary and trust duties. In 1973 tribal members and their supporters succeeded in convincing Congress to approve the Menominee Restoration Act, which reinstated sovereign immunity, treaty rights, and trust status. Over the next decade the tribe drafted a new constitution and bylaws and formed a new tribal government, rebuilding tribal services. The tribe has worked toward cultural renewal through the establishment of the Menominee Department of Historic Preservation and promotion of language classes, powwows, and drumming circles. The forestry program resumed operations and the Menominee once again became international leaders in sustainable forestry. The Menominee Nation College's Sustainable Development Institute is involved in research, education, and policy recommendations.

The tribe's economy continued to grow in the late 1980s, when the Menominee began running casinos and hotels on the reservation. Their overall financial stability has yet to translate into material well-being for all of its members, however. A 2008 study conducted by the University of Wisconsin's La Follette School of Public Affairs reported that during the 2006–2007 fiscal year, the tribe relied on the federal government to provide 56 percent of its operating costs. The Wisconsin Department of Workforce Development recorded Menominee County's unemployment rate in 2008 as 10 percent, more than twice as high as that year's rates for Wisconsin (4.4 percent) and the United States overall (4.8 percent). A 2010 University of Wisconsin School of Medicine and Public Health study showed that 51 percent of children in Menominee County were living in poverty.

Through Menominee Tribal Enterprises (MTE; the tribe's business arm), the tribe owns a sustainable logging operation, a sawmill, and a forest products industry. Its first gaming operation opened in 1982 and expanded in 1987. The tribe also owns a gas station and a grocery store. Along with these industries, the reservation is home to tourist industry offerings such as dining, hotel, entertainment, golf, a museum, and river rafting. By 2013 the Menominee Tribe once again owned 95 percent of the land set aside for the Menominee Indian Reservation.

SETTLEMENT IN THE UNITED STATES

Before the Menominee encountered Europeans, the tribe lived in a cluster of permanent villages located near the mouth of the river in present-day Michigan. Hunting and gathering activities involved travel within a 100-mile radius of the villages. When the tribe fled to Wisconsin to escape the encroachment and war parties of the fur-trading New York Iroquois, the Menominee, too, joined the fur trade and began migrating to different homes on a seasonal basis. In summer they lived in larger villages of longhouses built near streams and rivers, where they fished and planted gardens. In winter they lived in wigwams close to their hunting and trapping grounds or to French trading posts. The five bands became more dispersed.

The treaties the Menominee were coerced into signing with the government, beginning in the 1820s reduced the tribe's holdings to the size of the present-day Menominee Reservation located on the Wolf River in Wisconsin. Unlike many other tribes who were ordered to relocate to reservations far from home, the Menominee managed to remain on their ancestral lands. In 1854 two thousand Menominee tribal members lived on the newly created reservation. There, the dispersed bands once again lived in close proximity. Epidemics of foreign diseases such as smallpox, along with malnutrition, caused hundreds of deaths. Clan distinctions became less important and were replaced by a division between tribal members who kept the traditional ways of the Medicine Lodge and those who had converted to Christianity. The traditionalists preferred to log and engage in industries related to the forests, whereas the newly converted Christians chose to fish and farm.

The first significant wave of migration away from the reservation occurred during World War II, when sixty-eight Menominee men left to serve in the war. Another ninety saw action in the Korean War. In 1951 the BIA created a Branch of Placement and Relocation, which dovetailed with the then-current federal policy of terminating tribal recognition, moving people off reservations, and encouraging them to assimilate into mainstream culture. The BIA provided limited financial incentives and some vocational training for Native Americans who agreed to move to an urban center. Menominee tribal members relocated to places such as Green Bay and Milwaukee, Wisconsin,

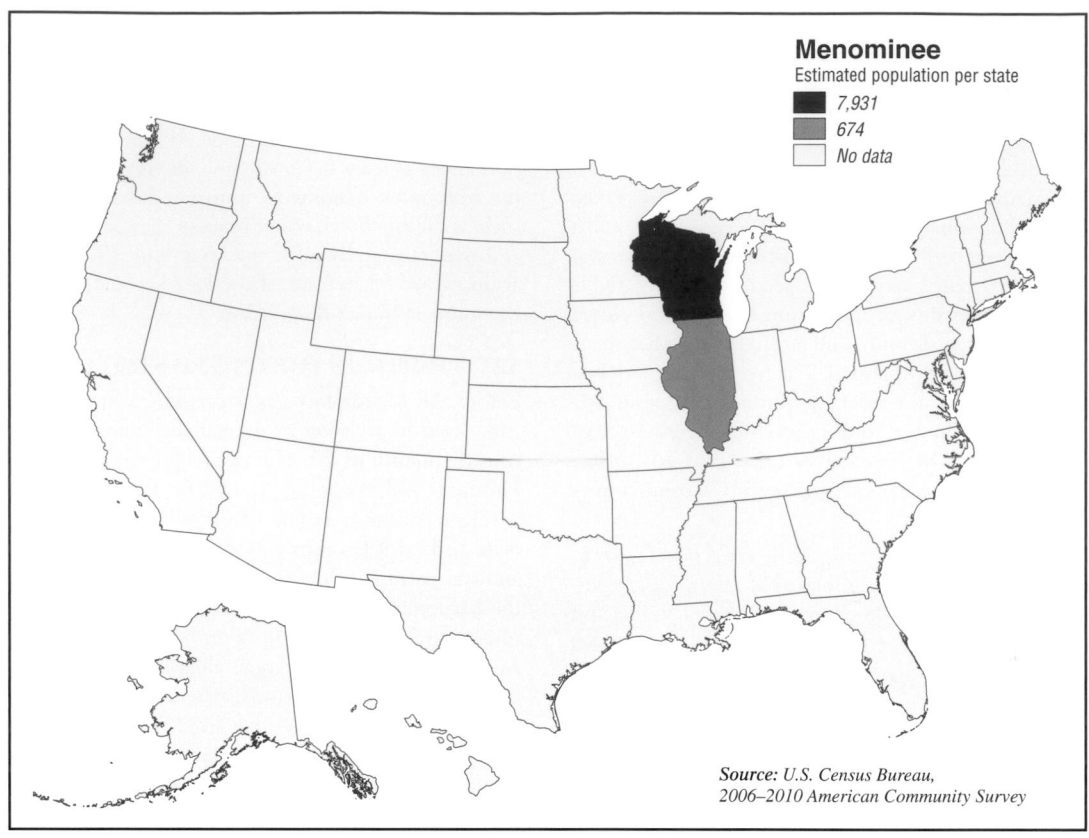

Menominee
Estimated population per state

- 7,931
- 674
- No data

Source: U.S. Census Bureau, 2006–2010 American Community Survey

and Chicago, Illinois, where they tended to live in poor neighborhoods near other Native Americans. Between 1950 and 1960 the population on the Menominee Reservation dropped 11.2 percent. The program, staffed by non-Indians, had a high rate of failure. The so-called migrants experienced discrimination in every facet of life, especially employment and housing; poverty; a lack of access to medical care and other services; and tremendous culture shock in their new and foreign environment. The relocation program peaked between 1952 and 1957 but sputtered on until 1970, when it was renamed Employment Assistance.

According to the Menominee tribe's Facts and Figures Reference Book (2008), there was virtually no change in the tribal population between 1960 and 1970. Since 1970 the population on the reservation has steadily increased, growing at a rate of 25 percent between 1990 and 2000 and nearly doubling between 2000 and 2010. In 2012, with a population of 8,551, slightly fewer than half of all enrolled members lived in towns on the reservation. The two largest towns were Keshena and Neopit. Keshena houses the tribal government, the tribal college, the Menominee casino complex, and all schools in the Menominee Public School District; Neopit is the site of the tribal sawmill, the tribal K-8 school, a church, and some privately owned businesses, including several grocery and convenience stores. As of 2012 the tribe was the largest employer on the reservation, providing jobs in public administration, government, education, health care, and social services. Private businesses owned by tribal members also provided employment.

LANGUAGE

The Menominee language belongs to the Algonquian family of languages. One of the things that distinguishes Menominee from other Algonquian languages is the frequent use of vowel sounds at the beginning of words. Typically, words do not end in vowels. Stress is complex in the Menominee language. Long vowels and every other short vowel in a series receive some degree of stress, whereas final syllables usually are not stressed. Verb inflections indicate the difference between animate and inanimate subjects. This is different than English, in which inflection remains constant regardless of who or what is being described.

The Menominee traditionally believed that their language was given to them by their Creator; thus, it was their sacred duty to speak it. They believed that if they did not speak it, the world would cease to exist. Federal Indian policies that strove to obliterate native languages were extremely distressing for the tribe and succeeded in nearly wiping them out. In 1991 the tribe created the Menominee Historic Preservation Department with the primary objective of preserving their language. The department reported in 1997 that only thirty-nine people spoke Menominee as their first language and twenty-six spoke it as their second language. Since that time at least six tribal members have received Menominee Language and Culture teaching certificates. Menominee language classes are offered at all schools on the reservation, including the college. The tribe began offering a Menominee language immersion camp 2005.

Greetings and Popular Expressions Common Menominee greetings include: *Pōsōh*—"Hello!"; *Āneq nap*—"How are you?"; and *Nemāēnīnehtan 's kew-nian*—"I am happy to see you!"

RELIGION

According to Menominee religion, Mecawetok Māēc-awāētok (pronounced "ma-jen-a-WAY-tuck match-a-waah-took"), or Great Spirit, created the universe. The universe was divided into eight levels, four above the earth and four below. The levels above the earth were inhabited by good spirits and those below by evil spirits, and the two forces were always in conflict with each other. Spirits inhabited the sun, moon, stars, plants, animals, and water. Of all the spirits, the Menominee considered the Great Bear to be their true ancestor.

The creation myth states that each tribal clan is descended from one of five animal spirits (Bear, Eagle, Wolf, Moose, and Crane) representing five brothers who must divide tasks between them in order to sustain tribal culture and achieve a balance with nature The powerful spirits could help or harm the people, so the tribe developed a tradition of prayers, ceremonies, and gift giving to please them and enlist their help. All aspects of life involved rituals that sought assistance from the spirits, from major events such as births and deaths to daily occurrences of growing food and hunting.

The tribal priests were shamans, individuals who were deemed to possess special powers in connection to the spirits. There were shamans who were healers (called medicine men and women), shamans who used their visions to tell the future, and shamans who appealed to the spirits on behalf of the tribe during rituals and ceremonies. When children reached young adulthood, they went on a vision quest, during which they painted their faces and spent many days alone in a wigwam, fasting. Other religious elements of Menominee life included sweat lodges, singing, dancing, and the ceremonial use of tobacco. Tribal members could only become initiates to the Medicine Lodge through a period of instruction in supernatural and traditional medicines and cures followed by a formal ceremony. The Lodge's primary religious ceremony, the Medicine Dance, was held once or twice a year and involved a complex series of rituals, the details of which were known only to the initiated.

French missionaries sought converts among the Menominee as early as the mid-1600s. Later, religious indoctrination was an integral part of the Catholic Indian boarding school education at St. Joseph's. Pressure to convert was intense. By the late twentieth and early twenty-first centuries, many tribal members were Christian, most often Catholic; some had returned to the traditional religion, however, while others practiced a combination of the two.

CULTURE AND ASSIMILATION

Since the beginning of the reservation era, the Menominee have been subject to persistent pressure from outside forces, particularly the federal government, to assimilate on a cultural level. On the spiritual front various Christian churches sought converts among tribal members and demonized traditional Menominee religious practices. The Medicine Lodge, once a widely practiced faith, was nearly defunct by the end of the twentieth century. A culture of ceremonial drumming, by contrast, remained strong on the reservation into the twenty-first century. As drumming gained popularity, it increasingly served some of the same functions as the Medicine Lodge.

On the political level the Menominee consistently resisted attempts to assimilate into mainstream culture. The tribe refused to relocate, to divide the reservation into allotments, or to sell off their ancestral land. When they regained tribal sovereignty in 1973, it was through a series of organized campaigns. Loss of tribal language and traditional culture has proven more difficult to avoid.

To combat the erosion of tribal traditions, the tribe began sponsoring an annual summer language and culture camp in 1994. Young Menominee youth and counselors spend a week in the forest immersed in tribal culture. Elders tell stories in the evening. The campers speak Menominee, play drums, play lacrosse, make ceremonial offerings of tobacco, practice identifying trees, make traditional medicines, and create traditional craft items such as birch baskets. In 2005 the tribe introduced a Menominee language immersion camp that is held annually at the Menominee Logging Museum.

Cuisine Wild rice was the staple of the Menominee diet. This was supplemented with fish, especially sturgeon, as well as venison and bison. Sturgeon featured so prominently in the early Menominee economy and culture that many tribal myths and creation stories contain numerous references to the fish. Depending on the season, the tribe also ate corn, beans, and squash that they cultivated and mushrooms, wild berries, and herbs that they gathered. In the spring the Menominee made syrup and sugar from tree sap. They sun-dried food to eat during the winter. Food was prepared using pottery jars and holes dug in the ground for steaming, boiling, or roasting.

The herds of bison in the Midwest began to disappear during the 1800s. As of 1883 the last of them had been exterminated. Historians disagree about what caused the eradication of the bison but not about the

fact that this loss resulted in hunger for many of tribes, including the Menominee. After relocation the tribe's diet underwent further changes. Confined to the reservation and no longer allowed to hunt, the Menominee had very limited access to what fresh game remained, supplemented with wild rice. They were forced to rely on the BIA agent to supply them with U.S. government rations consisting primarily of white flour, salt, sugar, bacon, and lard. Certain foods that could be made with these rations, such as Indian fry bread, became popular on reservations across the United States.

In the twenty-first century, members of the Menominee Nation ate a wide variety of foods, including typical American food.

Traditional Dress Traditionally, Menominee men and women wore clothes made of deerskin. Deerskin robes were worn as outer layers in winter. The men wore buckskin pants in the cooler months and a breechclout (loincloth) in warmer weather. During ceremonies the men wore feathered headdresses and skins decorated with quills in addition to armbands and leg bands. The leg bands were tied over pants below the knee. The women wore sleeveless fringed leather dresses and leggings with moccasins. For ceremonial events the women wore decorated headbands and necklaces and had their hair in two braids. After contact with Europeans, leather and quills were increasingly replaced by beads and cloth.

Toward the end of the nineteenth century, tribal members began dressing like mainstream Americans.

Traditional Arts and Crafts Traditional crafts included basket making using strips of black ash, beading, wood carving, and decorating leather and fabric with quillwork.

Dances and Songs The Menominee Tribe has numerous, centuries-old traditional dances that are performed at tribal ceremonies, celebrating everything from military exploits to a good harvest. For instance, the women's Scalp Dance commemorates a military victory, the men's Grass Dance evokes earlier times, and the Owl Dance honors the tribe's creation story. Two traditional ceremonies that included the entire tribe were the Drum Dance and the Brave Dance.

The Drum or Dream Dance was its own religion, introduced to the Menominee by the Sioux Tribe during the nineteenth century. All drummers were men, and specific drums were played by specific groups. Speeches, singing, and dancing were also part of the festivities. The large ceremony typically lasted four days and was held twice a year. Throughout the rest of the year, smaller ceremonies took place in people's homes. In the early twenty-first century, Drum Dances were still held, but they had taken on a more social, less spiritual quality.

The Brave Dance was performed as an appeal for assistance from tribal members' spirit guardians, either for a specific person or for the whole tribe. The person holding the Brave Dance sent invitations with a messenger who carried a gift of tobacco. In the early days it was performed before battle. Warriors told stories of their experiences in combat, the tribe offered food and tobacco to the spirits, and everyone feasted, sang, and danced. In the early twenty-first century Brave Dances were held for a variety of reasons—for example, to seek help for a sick person, to ask protection for someone joining the army, or to pray for favorable weather.

Some Menominee traditional songs were played on a special kind of flute. In the 1920s Frances Densmore, an ethnomusicologist affiliated with the Smithsonian Institute, recorded Menominee elders singing traditional love songs and lullabies. Densmore wrote down and published the scores, and in 2004 the professional flute player and Oneida tribal member Robert Messner played and recorded the songs using a traditional flute. Some traditional Menominee music was played on drums accompanied by singing. In 2007 a group of Menominee musicians released an album called *Wild Rice—Songs from the Menominee Nation.* The album is a mix of traditional and contemporary singing and drum music.

Recreational Activities Traditional Menominee activities included storytelling, berry picking, games, and spending time in the forests. Children and adults played the moccasin game. Accompanied by drumming and singing, the game involved four sticks or tokens (one marked and three unmarked) and four moccasins, with two teams of four or five people sitting facing each other across a blanket. Players took turns hiding the tokens in or under the moccasins and guessing where the marked token was hidden. Each player on a team was allowed four attempts. The team with the most correct guesses won. Sometimes a team of Menominee players would challenge a team from a neighboring tribe to the moccasin game. People enjoyed placing bets on the outcome.

Menominee men also traditionally played games of chance involving betting and competed at wrestling, archery, and running. During the winter women played a game involving six circular dice; these were made of bison rib bone and were painted on one side, with the other side left white. One was carved to resemble a turtle and another to resemble a horse's head. Two teams faced off across a blanket, and players from each team took turns shaking the dice in a bowl before turning the bowl upside down. Points were assigned to different combinations: if four dice in a roll were the same color and two were other colors, the player was awarded one point; if all of the dice were the same color except the turtle, the player earned five points, and so forth. In warmer weather the women played Double Ball, a game similar to lacrosse. Each player on a team had a three- to four-foot-long stick, and the object was to hit a deerskin ball through the opposing team's goal. After contact with Europeans the tribe incorporated card games into their recreational time. Men, women, and children all played cards, but men and women rarely played together.

Holidays The Sturgeon Feast is an important Menominee celebration that occurs in the spring, during the running of the sturgeon. Sturgeon played a central role in the tribe's traditional culture. In addition to providing sustenance, the fish has symbolic meaning. It figures prominently in Menominee creation stories; one of the clans is named for it; and, according to myth, it served as the keeper of the wild rice. Sturgeon is also used in making traditional medicines. The Sturgeon Feast has both ceremonial and celebratory aspects. Rituals, prayers, and offerings give thanks to the sturgeon for maintaining life. Prior to the feast dancers perform an ancient sturgeon dance, accompanied by drumming and singing.

Few continued to celebrate the holiday after sturgeon disappeared from tribal waters in the late 1800s, after dams built on the Wolf River prevented the migration of sturgeon from Lake Winnebago to their spawning grounds at Keshena Falls. The ceremony and celebration experienced a revival in popularity in 1973, when the tribe entered into talks with the Wisconsin Department of Natural Resources (DNR) to restore sturgeon to the traditional Menominee fishing sites. From 1973 to 2012 the tribe observed this ritual on an annual basis. The ceremony held special significance both in 1993, when the tribe and the DNR introduced sturgeon into the Wolf River, and again in 2012, when sturgeon began to spawn at Keshena Falls for the first time in 125 years.

Ghost Feasts were held on the anniversary of a loved one's death. The family feasted, prayed, and made food offerings to the spirit of the deceased. During the early reservation years, when traditional Menominee religious practices were forbidden by the reservation agents, ceremonies such as the Ghost Feast took place in secret. Tribal members now celebrate all the national holidays.

Health Care Issues and Practices A 2010 study by the University of Wisconsin's School of Medicine and Public Health revealed that residents of Menominee County had the lowest overall level of health of any county in the state, with the highest rates of obesity (38 percent) and mortality. Also in 2010 the Menominee Environmental Health Department released a report naming alcohol as a contributing factor in 46 percent of all reported injuries that year on the reservation. Most of these injuries were sustained in automobile crashes and assaults, while others were suicides. Other leading causes of death included cancer (primarily lung and breast), heart disease, and diabetes.

As of 2011 the tribe had introduced a number of health programs and initiatives to improve the well-being of tribal members. The Indian Health Services

MENOMINEE PROVERBS

The following are two examples of Menominee proverbs:

When the tribe leaves an area, the wild rice follows them.

Start with the rising sun and work toward the setting sun, but take only the mature trees, the sick trees, and the tress that have fallen. When you reach the end of the reservation, turn and cut from the setting sun to the rising sun and the trees will last forever.

clinic on the reservation provided health care to all Menominee and offered exercise classes, a diabetes-prevention program, a smoking-cessation program, and nutrition classes and information. Schools and youth programs on the reservation had joined a national fitness campaign called "Let's Move!" to encourage children and teens to exercise more. The community had organized running, walking, and biking events. The reservation grocery store offered fresh fruits, meats, and vegetables, including some locally grown produce.

Death and Burial Rituals The Menominee traditionally believed that a person's ghost remained at the site of burial. The dead and a selection of their favorite possessions were placed on free-standing burial platforms made of logs. A shaman performed the burial ritual, and family members returned to the site to leave gifts, including food, and to play games in order to make the ghost happy.

Today Menominee are usually given a Christian funeral and are buried in caskets underground, but family members may build a small house on top of the grave and put food and other traditional offerings inside.

FAMILY AND COMMUNITY LIFE

Family relationships had great significance in the tribe, including politically. The bands consisted of extended family, and one member was picked to represent the family on the tribal council. In the domestic arena young couples often lived with the husband's family for a year before establishing their own home nearby. Grandparents, siblings, aunts, uncles, and cousins played important roles in a person's life.

During the reservation era, Menominee family structure was broken down. Compulsory boarding-school attendance was particularly damaging because it removed children from home at the age of six and taught them to speak a different language from their parents and other relatives still living on the reservation. Federal relocation and assimilation policies also had a detrimental impact on Menominee family structure; tribal members who moved to urban areas were separated from their extended families and their tribe and experienced tremendous culture shock.

Forced boarding-school attendance ended in the 1950s, and relocation programs had petered out by 1970, allowing families on the reservation to live together without external pressures to disperse. Since the 1970s the tribe has made concerted efforts to counter antifamily federal policies by celebrating traditional culture and language. In the twentieth and early twenty-first centuries, family was politically important to the Menominee for other reasons. As of 2004, in order to be entered onto the tribal rolls, a person had to be at least one-quarter Menominee by blood.

Gender Roles Men were traditionally the tribal leaders, serving as priests, chiefs, warriors, and hunters. Women gathered plants and herbs, cooked, gardened, and preserved food. They also wove mats, bags, and clothes, and sometimes they decorated these with quills or natural dyes. Over the years, however, Menominee women have become active in tribal politics and have often been the most vocal advocates of tribal interests in disputes with the federal government. Women have served in the Menominee legislature since its inception and on the boards of tribal entities since the early twentieth century. Menominee women's first forays into national politics were sparked by external threats to tribal survival. Beginning in 1925 the Menominee chapter of the League of Women Voters organized against outside efforts to divide the reservation into allotments. By 1943 their efforts met with success, and allotment was avoided.

When the federal government began the process of terminating the tribe's sovereign status in 1954, a group made up primarily of women led the resistance. The economic situation on the reservation had deteriorated, and, according to the Menominee activist Shirley Daly, the men had to struggle to find ways to support their families. They had little time for anything else, including political activism. The Menominee scholar and activist Ada Deer and her peers formed an organization called Determination of Rights and Unity for Menominee Stockholders (DRUMS) that launched a multipronged attack, which included lobbying Congress on the tribe's behalf. The passage of the Menominee Restoration Act in 1973 set a precedent for tribal restoration that paved the way for other tribes nationwide. Deer continued to serve in positions of authority for her tribe, at national universities, and in the federal government. Between 1993 and 1997 she was assistant secretary for the U.S. Department of the Interior.

In the late twentieth and early twenty-first centuries, Menominee women have followed the example of their mothers and grandmothers and taken on leadership roles in increasing numbers. Women have served as chair and vice chair of the tribal council. In 2013 five of the nine top tribal government officials were women. The tribe awarded its highest honor, an eagle feather, to Jamie Awonohopay in 2011 in recognition of her positive impact on tribe. She was commended for setting an example of excellence during her career with the U.S. military and later with the U.S. Secret Service. She was also honored for being a mentor to the younger generation of her tribal community, primarily in her role as bailiff of the tribal court and as the head veteran dancer at Menominee powwows.

Education From roughly 1880 through the mid-1950s, the federal office of the Bureau of Indian Affairs (BIA) opened Indian boarding schools across the United States. In a number of instances, including on the Menominee Reservation, the Indian Office contracted with groups such as the Bureau of Catholic Indian Missions to run the schools.

The Menominee Reservation has a private school and a public school district. The Menominee Tribal School for grades K-8, located in the town of Neopit, is a tribally operated private school that requires students to study Menominee language and culture for four to five hours of their class time each week. Attendance is free to enrolled members of any federally recognized tribe. Nontribal members may attend if admitted, but they must pay tuition. The public Menominee Indian School District was established by the state of Wisconsin in 1976. The district operates in cooperation with the tribe but is run by a separate entity and is subject to state laws and regulations. The public grade school, middle school, high school, and alternative school are all located in Keshena, almost entirely on Menominee tribal lands. Classes in Menominee language and culture are offered but not required.

The Menominee Tribe chartered the College of Menominee Nation in 1993. The school became fully accredited in 1998. Located on a 52.6-acre campus in Keshena, the college provides tribal members with access to higher education that is close to home and that promotes the interests of the Menominee Nation, the reservation, and its people. The college also has a small urban campus in Green Bay. Students can earn an associate's degree or a bachelor's degree. Of the 697 students attending the college in 2011, 41 percent were Menominee tribal members, and 80 percent belonged to one of the federally recognized tribes. Of the 165 staff members, 72 belonged to the Menominee Tribe. According to the U.S. Census Bureau's American Community Survey estimates (2006–2010), 84 percent of Menominee over the age of twenty-five had a high school degree or higher (comparable to the overall U.S. rate of 85 percent), and 9.9 percent had a bachelor's degree or higher (notably lower than the national rate of 27.9 percent).

ST. JOSEPH'S INDIAN INDUSTRIAL SCHOOL

One of the Indian boarding schools opened by the U.S. government was St. Joseph's Indian Industrial School, which operated from 1883 to 1980. Especially during its early decades, the school stressed acculturation and religious training along with academics. Menominee children were forced to live away from their families for nine months of the year (in some cases longer) for years at a time. Upon entry students were subjected to a complete transformation in lifestyle. Directives from the Bureau of Indian Affairs required St. Joseph's to follow a strict military-style regimen with an English-only policy, an emphasis on learning how to farm, and a dress code. Overcrowding, malnutrition, substandard teaching, excessive labor, and poor medical care resulted in much suffering. Teachers were known to use severe corporal punishment to enforce discipline. In one recorded incident in 1939, a nun struck a twelve-year-old Menominee girl with hemophilia and left her to bleed to death. In the St. Joseph's graveyard, there are 189 gravestones of children who died while attending the school between 1883 and the 1950s. St. Joseph's closed its doors in 1980.

EMPLOYMENT AND ECONOMIC CONDITIONS

Menominee County has a notably higher poverty rate than Wisconsin as a whole. According to the American Community Survey estimates for 2011, 32 percent of families in Menominee County were living below the poverty line; in comparison, the rate for families in all of Wisconsin was 8.8 percent.

In 2013 the Menominee Tribe was the largest employer in the county. According to the state's Department of Workforce Development, the top three employment sectors in the county were government, education, and social and medical services. Menominee Tribal Enterprises owns and operates a tourist complex that includes a casino, hotel, conference center, gift shop, and restaurant. The tribe also owns a supermarket and an auto repair shop. Approximately fifty private-sector businesses operate on the reservation. In 2012 two new businesses opened there: Subway and Family Dollar. The tribe also received their own CITES (Convention on International Trade in Endangered Species of Wild Fauna and Flora) permit to carry out sustainable harvest of wild ginseng grown on their lands.

The reservation's longest-running tribal enterprises are in timber harvesting and forest management. These operations began in the 1870s. About one quarter of the tribe's workforce is employed in tribal forest-based industries. Tribal policy on logging practices, established by Chief Oshkosh (1795–1858) in the 1860s and 1870s, mandates sustainability in that no more resources may be harvested than are produced during natural cycles. As a result the tribal forests, while very productive, were still thriving 150 years later. The reservation's first sawmill was built at Keshena Falls in 1854. Later that site was used for the tribe's first hydroelectric power plant. The present sawmill at Neopit, built in the early 1900s, continued in operation in the early twenty-first century.

The tribe has worked toward cultural renewal through the establishment of the Menominee Department of Historic Preservation and promotion of language classes, powwows, and drumming circles. The forestry program resumed operations and the Menominee once again became international leaders in sustainable forestry.

POLITICS AND GOVERNMENT

The Menominee's early tribal government operated at the village level, with each village run by a council, and each council made up of a group of chiefs, one from each extended family. These chiefs served under a head chief. Shamans and military leaders also held positions of authority within the tribe.

The present tribal constitution and bylaws were passed in 1977, after the 1973 restoration of tribal status. The first legislature under this constitution was convened in 1979. The constitution mandates government by legislative, judicial, and executive branches. Nine representatives are elected by enrolled tribal members to form the legislature, and these representatives choose a chair, vice chair, and secretary annually. The tribal judicial system consists of a lower court and a supreme court. These courts have jurisdiction over all Native Americans acting within the Menominee Indian Reservation.

The Menominee Tribe has participated in state and national politics through lobbying and campaign donations. According to the Sunlight Foundation's website *Influence Explorer*, between 1999 and 2012, the Menominee tribal government paid $166,330 to lobbyists to represent the tribe's interests in Indian/Native American affairs, gaming, and health care. During that same time period, the tribal government and individual tribal members donated a total of $39,000 to political campaigns. Of those funds, 69 percent went to Democrats and 31 percent to Republicans.

In spite of sometimes troubled relations between the tribe and the federal government, many tribal members have served in the armed forces. Citing a U.S. Census Bureau report, the Tribe's Facts and Figures Reference Book, updated in 2008, stated that 500 Menominee Tribal members served in the U.S. Army from World War II through 2008.

NOTABLE INDIVIDUALS

Activism Scholar and activist Ada Deer (1935–) was born in Keshena on the Menominee Reservation. She earned an MA from the University of Wisconsin (UW)–Madison and a master's in social work from New York University. After finishing graduate school, she moved to Minneapolis and began working on improving social services for urban Native Americans. She was also a founding member of DRUMS, a nonprofit group that was dedicated to promoting the restoration of Menominee's status as a federally recognized tribe in the 1960s and early 1970s. She has served on the board for the Native American Rights Federation and in 1993 was appointed the Department of the Interior's assistant secretary for Indian affairs. Deer ran the BIA from 1993 to 1997. She has taught social work at her alma mater in Madison and is a fellow at the Harvard Institute for Policy Studies and the John F. Kennedy School of Government. In 1999 she was appointed the chair of the American Indian Studies Department at the University of Wisconsin.

Chief Oshkosh (1795–1858) served as Menominee tribal chief from 1927 until he died in 1858. In that role he negotiated many treaties with the U.S. government, including the Wolf River Treaty that established the Menominee Reservation. The town of Oshkosh, Wisconsin, was named after him.

Ingrid Washinawatok (1957–1999), born in Keshena, became an internationally renowned activist on behalf of indigenous people around the world through her involvement with the United Nations (UN); she was a delegate to the UN Commission on Human Rights, a representative to the UN for two nongovernmental organizations (the United Nations International Decade of the World's Indigenous Peoples and the International Indian Treaty Council), and a member of the UN's Working Group on Indigenous Populations. She produced the documentary film *Warrior: The Life of Leonard Peltier* (1992) and was an award-winning speaker. In 1999 Washinawatok traveled to Columbia, South America, at the behest of the indigenous U'wa people to set up a school for preserving their language and culture and to help prevent the Occidental Petroleum Company from drilling on their land. While there she was murdered by the Revolutionary Armed Forces of Columbia (FARC).

Art James Frechette (1930–2006) was born on the reservation and grew up learning the traditional arts and crafts from his elders. He served in the U.S. military for many years and later in the civil service. After retirement he returned to the reservation, where he created several large wooden sculptures of clan animals. These are on permanent display at the Menominee Tribal College in Kenosha. His works have been purchased by museums and private collectors.

Literature Chrystos (1946–) is a Menominee lesbian poet born in San Francisco. She worked with famous Native American activist Leonard Peltier and was an activist for the Chippewa Tribe's Turtle Mountain Band. Her poetry appeared in *This Bridge Called My Back*, an anthology published by Kitchen Table: Women of Color Press in 1981. She has since published a number of well-received books of poetry, including *Not Vanishing* (1988), *In Her I Am* (1993), and *Firepower* (1995), and her work appeared in the anthology *Poems by Some People I Like* (1997).

Stage and Screen Sheila Tousey (1960–), actress, is the daughter of Menominee and Stockbridge-Munsee parents. Born in Keshena and raised between the two reservations, she became interested in dance as a young child. She studied theater and dance at the University of New Mexico in Albuquerque and later as a graduate student at the Tisch School of Arts, New York University's prestigious performing arts program. Between 1992 and 2001 she played roles in thirteen movies. She has acted in movie adaptations of Tony Hillerman's novels, including *Skin Walkers* (2002) and *Coyote Waits* (2003).

MEDIA

Menominee Nation News

The leading news source for the tribe, the *Menominee Nation News* is published bimonthly and covers issues connected to tribal membership, culture, the local economy, and community events. The paper has been in publication since 1976 and is also available on the Menominee tribal website.

Devan Erdman, Editor
W2908 Tribal Office Loop Road
Keshena, Wisconsin 54135
Phone: (877) 209-5866
URL: www.menominee-nsn.gov

Shawano Leader

An online newspaper, the *Shawano Leader* covers local and Menominee tribal news, events, sports, obituaries, and more for the town of Shawano, Wisconsin (located 9 miles south of the Menominee tribal headquarters in Keshena Falls), and surrounding areas.

Greg Mellis, Publisher
1464 East Green Bay Street
Shawano, Wisconsin 54166
Phone: (715) 526-2121
Email: editor@shawanoleader.com
URL: www.shawanoleader.com

ORGANIZATIONS AND ASSOCIATIONS

Menominee Casino Resort

A Vegas-style casino with 850 slot machines and dozens of gaming tables, the hotel, conference center, and entertainment venue hosts weddings, business meetings, and more. The hotel has a swimming pool, spa, and fitness center. The conference center can seat up to 1,000.

James Reiter, General Manager
N277 Highway 47/55
Keshena, Wisconsin 54135
Phone: (800) 343-7778
URL: www.menomineecasinoresort.com

Menominee Chamber of Commerce

A nonprofit organization founded in 2005, the chamber serves Indian and non-Indian local business owners who want to promote the economic vibrancy of the community and to diversify Indian-owned businesses through education, resources, and networking.

Judy Newton, President
N559 Library Road
Keshena, Wisconsin 54135
Phone: (715) 799-6000
Fax: (715) 799-5721
Email: www.jcsclean_n_one@hotmail.com
URL: www.menomineechamber@frontiernet.net

Menominee Tribal Government

Denise Palmer, Director
W2908 Tribal Office Loop Road
Keshena, Wisconsin 54135
Phone: (877) 209-5866
Email: dpommer@mitw.org
URL: www.menominee-nsn.gov

MUSEUMS AND RESEARCH CENTERS

Center for the Study of Upper Midwestern Cultures

The center fosters research about and preservation of regional languages and cultures. It creates educational materials and offers outreach programs for the general public in addition to assisting community groups, tribal schools, and linguistic scholars with projects. The center has a program dedicated to assisting the Menominee Tribe with the revitalization of its traditional language.

James Leary, Director
432 East Campus Mall, Room 332
Madison, Wisconsin 53706
Phone: (608) 262-8180
Email: jpleary@wisc.edu
URL: www.csumc.wisc.edu

Menominee Indian Tribe Cultural Museum

The museum contains artifacts that document the tribe's cultural heritage, such as headdresses (war bonnets), other headgear, a Menominee bible, wooden ladles, and moccasins.

David Grignon, Director
PO Box 910
Keshena, Wisconsin 54135
Phone: (715) 799-5258
Email: dgrignon@mitw.org

Museum of Natural History, University of Wisconsin-Stevens Point

The museum has a collection of wood carvings by Menominee artist James Frechette (1930–2006) and a permanent exhibit on Menominee Clans that includes historic maps and research.

Ray Reser, Director, Central Wisconsin Archeology Center
College of Letters and Sciences
University of Wisconsin-Stevens Point
Room D314A Science Building
Stevens Point
Wisconsin 54481
Phone: (715) 346-2858
Email: rreser@uwsp.edu
URL: www4.uwsp.edu/museum/menomineeClans/collection

SOURCES FOR ADDITIONAL STUDY

Beck, David R. M. *Siege and Survival: History of the Menominee Indians, 1634–1856.* Lincoln: University of Nebraska Press, 2002.

———. *The Struggle for Self-Determination: History of the Menominee Indians since 1854.* Lincoln: University of Nebraska Press, 2007.

Campbell, Lyle. *American Indian Languages: The Historical Linguistics of Native America.* Oxford: Oxford University Press, 1997.

Carlson, Leonard A. *Indians, Bureaucrats, and Land: The Dawes Act and the Decline of Indian Farming.* Westport, CT: Greenwood Press, 1981.

Fixico, Donald Lee. *Termination and Relocation: Federal Indian Policy, 1945–1960.* Albuquerque: University of New Mexico Press, 1986.

———. *The Urban Indian Experience in America.* Albuquerque: University of New Mexico Press, 2000.

Hoffman, Walter James. *The Menomini Indians.* 1896. New York: Johnson Reprint Corp., 1970.

Jenks, Albert Ernest. *The Wild Rice Gatherers of the Upper Lakes: A Study in American Primitive Economics.* Washington: Government Printing Office, 1901.

Keesing, Felix Maxwell. *The Menomini Indians of Wisconsin; A Study of Three Centuries of Cultural Contact and Change.* Philadelphia: American Philosophical Society, 1939.

Loew, Patty. *Indian Nations of Wisconsin: Histories of Endurance and Renewal.* Madison: Wisconsin Historical Society Press, 2001.

MEXICAN AMERICANS

Allan Englekirk and Marguerite Marín

OVERVIEW

Mexican Americans are immigrants or descendants of immigrants from Mexico, which is bordered by the United States to the north; the Gulf of Mexico to the east; Guatemala, Belize, and the Caribbean Sea to the southeast; and the Pacific Ocean to the south and west. The northwestern portion of Mexico, called Baja California, is partially separated from the rest of the nation by the Gulf of California. The central highlands, where the majority of Mexico's population lives, lies between the Oriental range and Occidental range of the Sierra Madre Mountains. Overall, Mexico occupies 758,449 square miles (1,964,375 square kilometers), an area approximately three times the size of the state of Texas.

In 2013, according to the *CIA World Factbook*, the population of Mexico was estimated to be 116,220,947. More than 80 percent of Mexicans identify as Roman Catholic, and about 5 percent are Evangelical. There were also small groups of Protestants and Jehovah's Witnesses. While Mexico is not a poor country in gross economic terms—in 2013 it ranked twelfth in the world in gross domestic product (GDP)—income distribution is highly unequal, and according to the *CIA World Factbook*, about half the population lives below the poverty line. Among Mexico's most important industries are petroleum, mining, automobile manufacture, food and beverages, clothing, chemicals, and iron and steel.

There was significant migration between Mexico and the United States even before Mexico gained its independence from Spain in 1821. Moreover, the majority of what is now the southwestern United States belonged to Mexico prior to the 1848 Treaty of Guadalupe. Most early Mexican immigrants worked as miners, railroad workers, or field hands. Under the Bracero Program, in effect from 1942 to 1964, millions of Mexicans arrived in the United States with temporary work contracts primarily in the agriculture and cattle industries. Between 1995 and 2010 Mexican immigration to the United States decreased by more than half.

According to the U.S. Census Bureau, there were more than 31 million Mexican Americans in the United States in 2010, making up roughly 63 percent of the total U.S. Hispanic population. Because Mexicans have a long history in the United States, many Mexican Americans have fully integrated into the broader population and do not live in immigrant communities. Nevertheless, there are large Mexican American communities in such cities as Los Angeles, Chicago, San Antonio, El Paso, and Phoenix. According to the U.S. Census Bureau's American Community Survey estimates for 2009–2011, about 11.7 million Mexican Americans reside in California, making it the state with the largest population of Americans of Mexican descent. Other states with large numbers of Mexican Americans include Arizona (1.7 million), Illinois (1.6 million), and Texas (8.3 million), as well as Colorado (more than 800,000), Washington (600,000), and Florida (600,000).

HISTORY OF THE PEOPLE

Early History The earliest inhabitants of Mexico are believed to have been hunters who migrated from Asia approximately 18,000 years ago. Over time these early peoples built highly organized civilizations, such as the Olmec, Teotihuacan, Mayan, Toltec, Zapotec, Mixtec, and Aztec (also known as Mexica) societies, the majority of which were accomplished in art, architecture, mathematics, astronomy, and agriculture. In 1517 Spanish explorer Francisco Fernández de Córdoba discovered the Yucatán, a peninsula located in the southeast of Mexico, and by 1521 the Spanish conquistador Hernando Cortés had managed to conquer the Aztec Empire, the most powerful indigenous nation in Mexico at the time. Spain's conquest of Mexico was a bloody and cruel process during which the conquistadors murdered thousands of indigenous men, women, and children. The conquest also entailed the destruction of the Aztec Empire and culture. This period is referred to by many as the biggest genocide in the Americas. The Spanish alone did not carry out the massacres, however; large bands of Indian allies participated in the killing of their tribal enemies. Many more indigenous people died from the new diseases introduced by the Europeans, including smallpox, which reached epidemic proportions and led to the death of more Indians than those who died at the hands of the conquerors.

For the next 300 years Mexico, or New Spain, would remain under colonial rule. During this period approximately 60 percent of the indigenous population

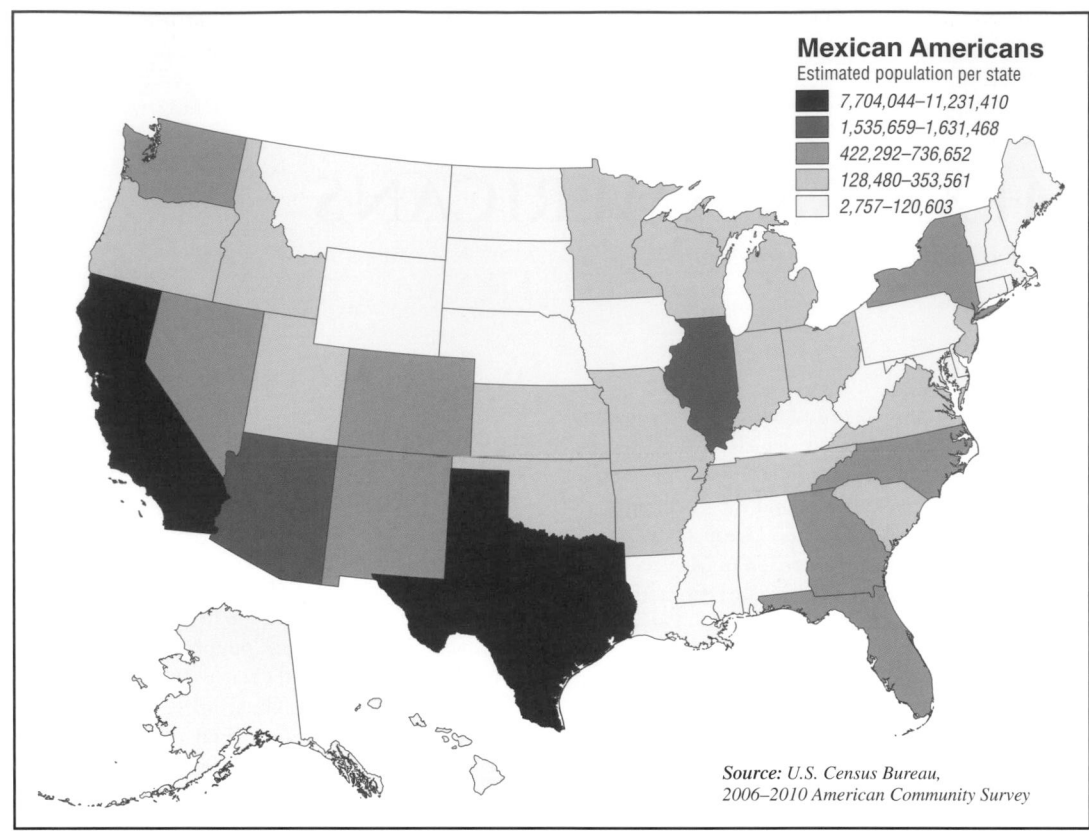

Mexican Americans
Estimated population per state

- 7,704,044–11,231,410
- 1,535,659–1,631,468
- 422,292–736,652
- 128,480–353,561
- 2,757–120,603

Source: U.S. Census Bureau,
2006–2010 American Community Survey

in the region died. Spain's generally repressive colonial regime limited access to the highest-ranking political positions almost exclusively to native-born Spaniards, although both creoles and mestizos did earn midlevel military and civil appointments. An unequal distribution of land and wealth developed and, as the nation grew in numbers, the disproportion between the rich and poor continued to increase, as did a sense of social unrest among the most neglected of its populace. Their discontent resulted in a successful revolt against Spain in 1821.

The Mexican American War began a little more than two decades later, as skirmishes over land holdings turned into an official war over territory between Mexico and the United States. The war ended with the Treaty of Guadalupe Hidalgo in 1848 in which Mexico surrendered 890,000 square miles, close to one-half of its territory, although the United States did later compensate Mexico for their lost land. Six years later, in order to finish construction of a transcontinental railway, the United States purchased an additional 30,000 square miles of Mexican land for $10 million in modern-day Arizona. This acquisition was made final through the Gadsden Treaty of 1854.

In the latter part of the nineteenth century, under the thirty-year authoritarian rule of Porfirio Díaz, noticeable industrialization occurred in Mexico, financed in large part by foreigners. Mining was

revitalized, and foreign trade increased. Dynamic growth brought relative prosperity to many economic sectors in various regions of the country, complemented by increased levels of employment. As the century ended, however, a vast majority of the nation's inhabitants had realized little if any improvement in their standard of living. Those residing in rural areas struggled to produce enough to survive from their own small parcels of land or, much more likely, worked under a debt-peonage system—farming lands owned by someone infinitely wealthier than they were. Most residents of urban areas, if they were lucky enough to have full employment, worked long hours under poor conditions for extremely low wages and lived in housing and neighborhoods that fostered diseases. The economic depression of 1907 soured the aspirations of the small but growing middle class and brought financial disaster to the newest members of the upper class.

Although Díaz was able to manipulate his reelection in 1910, opposition to his regime was strong. In 1911, when small rebellions led by other revolutionary leaders, including Emiliano Zapata, Francisco Madero, Pancho Villa, General Victoriano Huerta, and Pascual Orozco Vazquez, began to proliferate in the northern states of the nation, Diaz resigned his post and left the country. The same year, Zapata issued his famous "Plan de Ayala," a document that called for land reform and freedom for the disenfranchised

Mexican peasants, which became the manifesto of the Zapatista movement until Zapata's death in 1919. After Francisco Madero, the newly elected president following Díaz, failed to define an agenda that satisfied the several disparate groups in Mexico, he likewise agreed to self-exile but was assassinated in 1913 by supporters of General Huerta, the man who next assumed national leadership. Violence escalated into a bloody and prolonged civil war known as the Revolution of 1910. The majority of the conflict during the period from 1914 to 1919 was between supporters of the liberal Zapata and proponents of the Constitutionalist Venustiano Carranza, who led the government beginning in 1914 and faced the continual opposition of the Zapatistas. The turmoil and bloodshed motivated Mexican people from all levels of society to flee the country, most often northward to the United States. The United States, in turn, made several attempts to take advantage of Mexico's weakened borders in order to expand its territory further. A notable example of this interventionist maneuvering by the United States is the Vera Cruz incident, when the United States invaded and held the city of Veracruz for a six-month period in 1914.

Following the assassination of Zapata in 1919, Alvaro Obregon successfully overthrew Carranza's government with the support of Zapatistas, Villistas, and other revolutionaries. Obregon assumed the presidency in 1920, bringing the majority of the fighting to an end. By the early 1920s, though relative peace had been restored, the social and economic reforms that had become associated with the revolution were still unrealized, chief among them the redistribution of land to a greater percentage of the populace. A nonviolent revolution was to continue until the goals related to social and economic justice were attained. National presidents focused on promoting growth in the industrial sector, but the opening of new jobs did not keep pace with the employment needs of the rapidly expanding population.

Modern Era Since the 1950s economic conditions in Mexico have improved at a gradual pace. Expanding industrialization has provided additional jobs for greater numbers of workers, and increased oil production has brought in needed foreign currencies. Nevertheless, high levels of unemployment, low wages, and the many social problems related to a prolonged period of intense urbanization remain as sources of concern for the government and as causes of unrest for a significant segment of the population. Between the late 1970s and the turn of the twenty-first century, those people unable to earn subsistence wages in Mexico moved in increasing proportion to the northern borderlands and crossed into the United States, where the economic prospects were more promising.

During the 1980s and 1990s Mexico faced a number of challenges, the most notable of which were an economic crisis and the Mexico City earthquake of 1985. The nationalization of all financial institutions in 1982 attempted to address the country's economic instability and the enormous devaluation of the peso. The decade of the 1980s is now referred to as "The Lost Decade" in Mexico in reference to the severe economic uncertainty of that period. During the same decade a powerful earthquake shook Michoacán, leading to widespread destruction in Mexico City. The estimates of lives lost from the earthquake range from 6,500 to 30,000. The government faced severe criticism for its mishandling of relief efforts following the earthquake, which threatened to disrupt the monopoly of the Institutional Revolutionary Party (Partido Revolucionario Institucional; PRI) in Mexican politics; the PRI had been in power since 1929. The ongoing economic crisis and the devastation following the earthquake worked as push factors that prompted more Mexican nationals to migrate to the United States in search of better economic opportunities.

In 1994 Mexico joined the North American Free Trade Agreement (NAFTA), along with the United States and Canada, facilitating trade between the three countries. The commercial benefits of this accord, combined with the continued growth of international trade with other Latin American nations, have invigorated areas of economic investment and production in the Mexican economy. On the same day that NAFTA went into effect, however, the Zapatista Army of National Liberation (Ejército Zapatista de Liberación Nacional; EZLN) declared war on the Mexican government in opposition of its neoliberal economic ideology and encouragement of globalization. The EZLN also called for increased indigenous control over land and other local resources in Chiapas—the headquarters of the Zapatistas. While the rise of the EZLN brought about a constant military presence in the southern state of Chiapas and gained international attention, their actions since 1994 have been mostly defensive and nonviolent in nature and have not interfered greatly with the growth of Mexico's economy.

The one-party rule of the PRI in Mexico lasted for seven decades, finally ending with the presidential election of National Action Party (Partido Acción Nacional; PAN) candidate Vicente Fox in 2000. Mexico's economy surpassed $1 trillion in the early 2000s, and its GDP continued to grow in spite of the global economic crisis. However, the country still suffered from drastically unequal income distribution, an issue that Mexican presidents failed to address with any success. In addition, the rampant violence as a result of the so-called Mexican Drug War, which increased exponentially after 2006, threatened the security of the nation's residents, as well as Mexico's large tourist industry. Violence related to drug cartels began to rise drastically following President Fox's Operation Michoacán, carried out in December 2006, which is generally regarded as the first major operation against organized crime in Mexico. The operation initiated a war between the government and the

TERMS OF IDENTITY

In the 1990s two terms were widely used to identify Spanish-speaking people: Hispanic and Latino. The latter has grown in acceptance, especially by younger people who reject the term "Hispanic." The popular use of "Hispanic" grew out of the federal government's efforts, beginning with the 1980 census, to identify and count all people of Spanish-speaking backgrounds with origins from the Western hemisphere. Since the term was employed in most federal government reports, the media soon appropriated it and popularized its use. Some members of the Hispanic community have employed the term to create political alliances among all ethnic groups with ties to the Spanish language. However, according to the Latino National Political Survey, the majority of respondents indicated that they defined their identities in terms of place of origin.

Terms of identity vary greatly from region to region and from generation to generation. Traditionally residents of northern New Mexico have referred to themselves as Spanish Americans or *Hispanos*, terms which are essentially a reflection of their early ancestors from New Spain who settled the region. People from Texas, in the recent past, referred to themselves as Latin Americans, although there is growing use of the term "Tejano" by Texas residents of Mexican ancestry. "Mexican" is more commonly used in the Los Angeles area. More recently "Mexican American" has gained popularity.

In general, varying group identities are a reflection of the changing self-definitions of an ethnic group. The term "Chicano" is perhaps the best example of this social process. Chicano appeared in the mid-1960s as a political term of choice primarily among the young. The term identified an individual actively promoting social change within the context of the social movements of the 1960s and 1970s. To the older generation and the more affluent, to be identified as a Chicano was an insult. In the past the term specifically referred to the unsophisticated immigrant. However, to the generation of political activists, their term of ethnic identity came to signify a sense of pride in one's community and heritage.

drug cartels, which only further escalated in 2008 with allegations of cartel-related corruption in the Baja California police force. The toll of drug-related deaths rose by 11 percent in one year, from 9,616 in 2009 to 15,273 in 2010, according to a Mexican government report issued in January 2012. As of 2013 the violence continued to rise, and the Mexican government was unable to make any concrete steps toward bringing the situation under control.

SETTLEMENT IN THE UNITED STATES

Approximately 80,000 Mexicans resided in the territory transferred to the United States at the conclusion of the Mexican American War in 1848, the greatest numbers of whom were located in present-day New Mexico and California. Only a small proportion of the total, slightly more than 2,000, decided to leave their homes after the signing of the treaty. Those who

remained north of the border were required to decide between retaining Mexican citizenship or becoming an American citizen within one year of the treaty. Those who did not formally choose to maintain Mexican citizenship became American citizens by default after one year. Many Mexican families were ultimately stripped of their property, which was then often granted to American settlers instead.

When compared with various periods of the twentieth century, Mexican immigration to the United States between 1850 and 1900 was relatively low. The discovery of gold in the Sierra Nevada of California in 1849 was an initial stimulus for migration, as was the increase in fruit production in California in the 1850s and 1860s and the expansion of copper mining in Arizona beginning in the 1860s. During this same period and into the twentieth century, ranching and agriculture lured many inhabitants of the northern and central states of Mexico to Texas. By 1900 approximately 500,000 people of Mexican ancestry lived in the United States, principally in the areas originally populated by Spaniards and Mexicans prior to 1848. Roughly 100,000 of these residents were born in Mexico; the remainder were second-generation inhabitants of these regions and their offspring.

Only about 31,000 Mexicans migrated to the United States in the first decade of the twentieth century, but numbers increased significantly over the next two decades, especially from 1920 to 1929, when almost 500,000 people of Mexican ancestry entered the country. However, since the frontier was virtually open to anyone wishing to cross it until the creation of the Border Patrol in 1924, immigration figures for years prior to this date are questionable. The actual number may have been appreciably higher. Rural areas of California, Arizona, New Mexico, Colorado, and Texas attracted a vast majority of these migrants, but during the years of World War I, mounting numbers of newcomers moved to the upper Midwestern states, mainly to the region around Chicago. They were attracted by jobs in industry, railroads, steel mills, and meat packing.

In these initial periods of heavy immigration, it was most common for Mexican males to cross the border for work and return to Mexico periodically with whatever profits they were able to accumulate over several months. Alternatively, they remained in the United States for a longer duration and sent money southward to family members; between 1917 and 1929, Mexican migrants in the United States sent over $10 million to relatives in their home country. During these same decades, some men also established residency in the United States and returned for their families, though still quite often with the ultimate objective of returning to Mexico permanently in a not-too-distant future. It is estimated that half the immigrants who entered the United States from 1900 to 1930 returned to Mexico.

Mexican immigration to the United States decreased considerably in the 1930s because of the Great Depression. Though approximately 30,000

Mexicans entered the United States during these years, more than 500,000 left the country, most of them forced to do so because of the Repatriation Program, which sought to extradite Mexicans without proper documentation. In the 1930s jobs or land were promised to those who would return, but when this commitment was not fulfilled, many families or individuals moved back to the border towns of the north and often attempted again to return to the United States.

After the 1940s legal immigration from Mexico to the United States remained at or above the high levels of 1910 to 1930. There was a rise in immigration as a result of the Bracero Program, which offered temporary work contracts to Mexican migrants for work in the U.S. agriculture and railroad industries from 1942 until 1964. Originally intended for wartime labor relief, the program extended well past the end of World War II. More than 4.5 million temporary work contracts were signed during this period, which represented around 2 million *bracero*s (workers) employed by U.S. businesses as part of the program. Although canceled in 1948, the program was renewed shortly thereafter and continued in force until 1964, when the program was becoming obsolete because of immigration reform.

Despite federal legislation limiting the number of immigrants from most countries in the 1960s and 1970s, Mexican migrants crossing the border totaled 453,937 and 640,294 for the two decades. It is estimated that approximately one million entered the United States legally between 1981 and 1990. The number of undocumented workers increased consistently from the 1960s through the 1990s; approximately one million undocumented workers were deported annually to Mexico in the late 1980s and early 1990s (this figure includes individuals deported more than once). The availability of jobs in the United States, coupled with high rates of unemployment and periodic slowdowns in the Mexican economy, served to encourage this continued migration northward. Several factors in the early twenty-first century, however, caused a sharp decline in the rate of Mexican migration to the United States, including the global economic crisis sparked by the recession in the United States in 2007 and 2008 and the increasing vigilance and implementation of advanced security technology along the border between the United States and Mexico.

In 2012 the Pew Research Hispanic Center documented that the number of Mexicans who legally immigrated to the United States between 2005 and 2010 was half the number who legally immigrated from 1995 to 2000, when a total of 3 million Mexicans arrived in the country. Even more significant was the rise in the number of Mexicans in the United States who returned to Mexico—1.4 million between 2005 and 2010, nearly double the number who had returned a decade earlier.

In the early twenty-first century increased advocacy for children of undocumented immigrants in the United States led to significant developments in immigration reform. Most notable was Deferred Action for Childhood Arrivals (DACA), a memorandum signed by President Obama in June 2012, which defers legal action by immigration officials against currently enrolled undocumented students, allowing them to remain enrolled in school until they graduate high school.

According to the U.S. Census Bureau, approximately 31.8 million people of Mexican ancestry lived in the United States in 2010, a figure that represented 10 percent of the total national population and 63 percent of the total Hispanic population in the country. More than 65 percent of people of Mexican ancestry were born in the United States, while approximately 8 percent were naturalized citizens. In 2010 East Los Angeles had the highest concentration of Hispanics outside of Puerto Rico, at 97 percent. According to the U.S. Census Bureau's American Community Survey estimates for 2009 to 2011, the states with the highest populations of Mexican Americans were, in descending order, California, Texas, Arizona, Illinois, Colorado, Washington, and Florida.

LANGUAGE

Spanish remained the principal, if not sole, language of almost all Mexicans in the southwestern United States after the signing of the Treaty of Guadalupe Hidalgo in 1848. Because most early Mexican immigrants moved to areas already populated predominantly by people of their background, and because they worked side-by-side with them in the same jobs, learning more than rudimentary English was of minor importance. The proximity to Mexico, as well as the continued entry of additional immigrants, constantly revitalized the culture and native language of those who chose to become permanent residents of the United States.

In the twentieth century, as second- and third-generation Mexican Americans began to move into professions in which many of their coworkers were non-Hispanic, proficiency in English became practical and necessary. Young Mexican Americans entered American schools in which English was a fundamental part of their curriculum. The use of Spanish was strongly discouraged and sometimes even prohibited in many school systems. Equally important, English was introduced to ever-greater numbers of Hispanic households through television. Although few low-income Mexican American families could afford televisions in the 1950s, it had entered most living rooms by the end of the next decade and brought the language (as well as other aspects) of the broader American culture nightly to the ears of a growing Mexican American audience.

In part because Mexicans continued to immigrate to the United States, Spanish remained a dominant language in the Mexican American community. In the state of New Mexico, for example, Spanish was a governmental language until the mid-1990s. In

Our Lady of Guadalupe (also called the Virgin of Guadalupe) is so revered in Mexico that she has been referred to as the "Queen of Mexico." Mexican Americans retain the same devotion to this religious icon. DAVID MCNEW / GETTY IMAGES

the use of *caló*, a variation of Mexican Spanish that employs slang from Mexican Spanish, American English, and African American English. It was used extensively in urban settings in the Southwest during the 1940s and 1950s by young Mexican Americans who wished to set themselves apart from their parents.

Mexican Americans who have been exposed extensively to English and Spanish and employ both languages actively in speaking or writing may move from one language to another within a given sentence, a linguistic phenomenon referred to as "code-switching." The alternation may occur because of a momentary memory lapse by the speaker, with use of proper nouns, or when a specific word has no exact equivalent in the other language. This tendency was once perceived in a negative light, as it sometimes occurs because of the lexical deficiencies of a speaker. But it also practiced by many Mexican Americans who are bilingual and who are able to separate English from Spanish completely and use either language effectively and persuasively depending upon the situation; code-switching for these speakers is sometimes an attempt to use the most appropriate phrase to convey a certain idea.

RELIGION

In the early twenty-first century more than three-fourths of Mexican Americans were Roman Catholic. Others faiths among Mexican Americans included Protestant, Pentecostal, Southern Baptist, Mormon, Seventh-Day Adventist, and Jehovah's Witnesses. The American settlers who immigrated in the early nineteenth century to the area of present-day Texas were predominantly Protestant, as were those who in later decades traveled to California and most other regions north of the Rio Grande. Over time they converted a small number of Mexican Americans to Protestantism.

After the Treaty of Guadalupe Hidalgo in 1848, Mexican Americans had the freedom to maintain their religious faith, but throughout the nineteenth century Mexican American Catholics had no institutional voice at any level in the American Catholic Church. It was not until the mid-1940s that the Catholic Church in the United States began to devise strategies and programs to meet the pastoral and social needs of Mexican Americans and other Hispanics. In 1944 meetings and seminars were organized for delegates of Western and Southwestern dioceses at the request of Robert E. Lucey and Urban J. Vehr, the archbishops of San Antonio and Denver, respectively, to analyze the scope and effectiveness of the church's efforts in these areas. In 1945 the Bishop's Committee for the Spanish-speaking was formed, the objectives of which were to construct clinics, improve housing and educational and employment opportunities, and eliminate discrimination.

2010 there were 832 Spanish-language newspapers in the United States and approximately 1,323 Spanish-language radio stations, and Spanish-language television programming was also on the rise.

Mexican American Spanish has qualities that distinguished it from standard Spanish. For example, while the standard Spanish words for "soldier" and "you" are respectively *soldado* and *usted*, the corresponding words in Mexican American Spanish for many speakers have altered to *soldau* and *usté* through the elimination of the consonant of the last syllable. There have also been changes in certain verb conjugations, such as the shift from *decía* ("I/she/he/you were saying") to *dijía*. English words have been incorporated into Mexican American Spanish, with appropriate orthographic changes to make the words more similar in sound to Spanish—for example, *troca* for "truck," *parquear* for "park," and *lonche* for "lunch." Still prevalent among young Mexican Americans is

A dynamic force for change between Mexican Americans and the Catholic Church and its clergy in the United States was the Chicano movement of the 1960s and early 1970s. In seeking to define their unique identity within North American society by affirming a strong sense of pride in their Spanish and indigenous American heritage, leaders of this movement also condemned U.S. institutions that they believed had fostered or condoned the oppression of Mexican Americans in the past and present. In the early 1970s the activist group *Católicos por la Raza* dramatized their discontent over lingering evidence of segregation in the church and its failure to bring about reforms to correct inequities in society by organizing a Christmas Eve demonstration. Many of the participants were arrested, but their sentiments were publicized. By the 1990s an increasing number of Mexican Americans were mainstream Catholics, and through the 1990s and into the twenty-first century, Catholic churches were increasingly offering Mass in Spanish.

Despite the numerical importance of Mexican Americans in the U.S. Catholic church, the first Mexican American bishop was not ordained until 1970. As of 2007, according to the United States Conference of Catholic Bishops, only 6 percent of Catholic bishops in the country were of Hispanic origin.

CULTURE AND ASSIMILATION

Most immigrant groups in the United States have, to a lesser or greater extent, attempted to maintain their distinctive cultural ways. However, the general pattern has been that with each successive generation the use of the mother tongue and other cultural practices diminishes. Mexican Americans do not fit this pattern for a number of reasons.

Some Mexican Americans can trace their ancestry back ten generations. The ancestors of many Mexican Americans living in rural Colorado and northern New Mexico, for example, predate the presence of other American in that region. Some members of these older generations are still not completely acculturated; some (although few) speak English with difficulty and appear to be more traditionally oriented than the newly arrived Mexican immigrants. In addition, because Mexican immigration has been a constant pattern throughout the twentieth century, each successive wave of Mexican immigration has served to reinforce certain aspects of Mexican culture and maintain the use of the Spanish language within the United States. Intermarriage between immigrant

During the 34th Annual Three Kings Day Parade, which celebrates the Feast of Epiphany, giant puppets make their way down East 106 Street in the Spanish Harlem section of New York. STAN HONDA / AFP / GETTY IMAGES / NEWSCOM

CHILAQUILES

Ingredients

For sauce:

2 tablespoons vegetable oil

2 ancho chiles, seeds and veins removed

1 cascabel chile (optional for a bit more spice)

8 roma tomatoes, roughly chopped

½ onion, roughly chopped

3 garlic cloves

salt to taste

1 cup chicken broth

For tortillas:

vegetable oil for frying

24 stale tortillas, cut into pieces

For toppings:

crema

½ red onion, thinly sliced

3 sprigs of cilantro

⅓ cup queso fresco, crumbled

Preparation

Heat the oil in a skillet. Fry the chiles for about 1 minute on each side. Remove the chiles, cover them with hot water, and soak for 5–10 minutes.

Add tomatoes, onions and garlic to the same pan and grill until they are softened. Transfer the drained chile, tomatoes, onions and garlic to a blender and blend until smooth.

Reheat the oil and add the sauce. Season with salt and cook over moderate heat, stirring occasionally, about 4 minutes. Add the broth and cook for 1 minute more. Remove from the heat and keep warm.

Heat the oil and fry the tortilla pieces, about ⅓ at a time so they cook evenly, until they just stiffen but do not brown, about 3–4 minutes a batch. Transfer the fried tortillas to paper towels to drain while you fry the rest; add a bit more oil to the skillet and lower the heat if necessary.

Stir the tortillas into the sauce and cook over medium heat for 5–8 minutes, or until most of the sauce has been absorbed. Allow just enough time for tortillas to absorb the salsa. Stir constantly; the tortilla pieces should be soft yet crunchy.

Serve immediately and top with crema, cilantro, and red onion.

Serves 6

males and Mexican American women has encouraged the use of Spanish. Immigrants have also encouraged the continuous growth of Spanish-language enterprises, such as the Spanish-language media, print as

well as electronic, and small businesses that cater to the Spanish-speaking community.

The close proximity of Mexico is another factor resulting in their slower rate of assimilation. Since the United States shares an almost 2,000-mile-long border with Mexico, Mexican Americans have been able to maintain close ties with the "old country." Many have the opportunity to visit Mexico frequently. The millions of undocumented Mexican immigrants, however, generally do not return to Mexico out of fear of getting caught by the border patrol and not being able to regain entry into the United States.

Cuisine The basic diet of the inhabitants of Mexico has changed little from the pre-Colombian era to the present period. Corn, beans, squash, and tomatoes were staples until the arrival of the Spaniards in the early 1500s. The culinary preferences of these Europeans, plus the addition of some items from trade, brought pork, beef, rice, and various spices, among other foods, to the diet of this region. Pork and beef, in steaks or stews, along with chicken, were the meats eaten in areas from which migration to the United States was highest in 1848 and subsequent decades. This same cuisine forms the day-to-day food of most contemporary Mexican Americans: prepared with tomato-based sauces flavored by a variety of chilies, spices, or herbs, such as cumin and cilantro, these meats are generally served with rice, beans, and corn tortillas.

On festive occasions, such as religious holidays or family reunions, one or more of the following traditional meals consumed in Mexico are prepared by most Mexican American families: *tamales* (shredded and spiced pork or beef caked within cornmeal and wrapped in a corn husk before steaming); *enchiladas* (corn tortillas lightly fried in oil then wrapped around sliced chicken, shredded beef, cheese, or ground beef and various spices and coated with a tomato and chili sauce before baking); *mole* (most often chicken, but sometimes pork, combined with a sauce of chilies, chocolate, ground sesame or pumpkin seeds, garlic, and various other spices, slow-cooked under a low flame on the stove); *chilaquiles* (dried tortilla chips complemented by cheeses, chili, and perhaps *chorizo* [spiced sausage] or chicken and a tomato-based sauce of green or red chili stirred into a hash-like dish on the stove); *chiles rellenos* (green chilis stuffed with a white cheese and fried in an egg batter that adheres to the chilis); and *posole* (a soup-like stew which contains hominy as its essential ingredient, as well as stew meat and various spices).

Traditional Clothing The clothing identified as most traditional by Mexicans and Mexican Americans and, according to scholar Olga Nájera-Ramírez, recognized as "official national symbols of Mexico," is now worn most frequently at festivals of historic importance to the community. Men dress as *charros*, or Mexican cowboys, and wear wide-brimmed *sombreros* along with tailored jackets and pants lined with silver or shining metal buttons. Women dress in *china poblana* outfits, which include a white peasant blouse and a flaring red skirt adorned with sequins of different colors. This apparel is linked most closely to people of more humble origin in Mexico.

Holidays Two secular holidays of national importance in Mexico are celebrated by a significant number of Mexican Americans. Mexican Independence Day, celebrated on September 16, commemorates the date when the priest Miguel Hidalgo y Costilla initiated the war for liberation from Spain with the *grito*, or call to battle, "*Viva Mexico y mueran los gachupines*" ("Long live Mexico and death to all *gachupines*," a derogatory term for Spaniards used during the colonial period and afterward). Part of the festivities may include the pronouncement of the *grito* or a Mass with *mariachis* (Mexican street bands), followed possibly by a speech or parade. Since the central idea related to this date is ethnic solidarity, many of the participants wear the *charro* and *china poblana* outfits. Along with traditional dishes such as *mole*, other food served on this date traditionally stress the colors of the Mexican flag: white, red, and green. These items may include rice, limes, avocados, chopped tomatoes, peppers, and onions.

Perhaps the most widely recognized Mexican holiday celebrated by Mexicans and Mexican Americans residing in the United States, as well as by other Hispanics nationwide, commemorates the victory of Mexican troops in the Battle of Puebla over the invading French army on May 5, 1862. The Cinco de Mayo celebration may include parades or other festivities and, as with Independence Day, reinforces for many Mexican Americans a sense of ethnic pride. Many other Americans join in commemorating this date, though its historic importance is known by few of revelers. Over the years the holiday has been highly commercialized.

In addition, various rituals and festivals of Spanish or Mexican Catholic origin continue to have an important spiritual role in the lives of many Mexican Americans. In some instances these public manifestations of faith have remained virtually unchanged since 1848, but the number of believers who practice them is decreasing with each new generation. The degree to which a family participates in these activities depends on the nature of their religious convictions and the level of contact they maintain with more tradition-oriented members of churches of the Mexican American Catholic community.

An important celebration for many Mexican Americans is the Feast of Our Lady of Guadalupe on December 12. The festivity commemorates the apparitions of the Virgin Mary to a converted Christian Indian, Juan Diego, in Mexico on the hill of Tepeyac (located within the boundaries of present-day Mexico City) on this date in 1521. Although she had identified herself as the Virgin Mary to Diego, in appearing before him she spoke his language, Nahuatl, related herself to indigenous deities, and, most importantly, was of a skin color similar to his. In the years immediately after her apparition, Indians who had previously sought to maintain their native religions converted to the Catholic faith, seeing the coming of the Virgin in a new identity as a symbolic act of supreme consequence.

To commemorate the day of the Virgin's final apparition to Juan Diego on December 12, some Mexican Americans may rise early and unite at some high point in the area (symbolic of the hill at Tepeyac) and sing "Las Mañanitas," a traditional

Young girls in a Cinco de Mayo parade, c. 1997, New York. CORBIS / CATHERINE KARNOW.

The Feast of Our Lady of Guadalupe, named for the patron saint of Mexico and the Americas, is celebrated among Latino immigrants in Southern California on December 12. In Los Angeles, believers touch the image of the Virgin Mary during a procession at the Cathedral of Nuestra Senora de Los Angeles prior to a Mass in 2003. HECTOR MATA / AFP / GETTY IMAGES

song that in this festivity, according to scholar Virgilio Elizondo, who noted in *Galilean Journey: The Mexican American Promise* that represents the Mexican Americans' "proclamation of new life". A special Mass is said, and roses are an important part of the celebration; most families take these flowers to the service and place them at the altar of the Virgin. Some Mexican Americans may make a pilgrimage to the Basilica of Our Lady of Guadalupe in Mexico City.

Ceremonies and rituals related to the birth and death of Jesus Christ are an essential part of the religious calendar of many Mexican Americans. During the nine days prior to Christmas, Masses are held at dawn, and the festivities of "Las Posadas" honor the arrival of Mary and Joseph to Bethlehem and their search for lodging at an inn (*posada*). Dressed in clothes similar to that likely worn by these personages, a couple visits designated houses of friends or family members on consecutive nights. It is common for the participants to read dialogues that re-create the conversation between the Holy Family and the innkeepers. Although the contemporary Mary and

Joseph, like those whom they represent, are denied entry each night, after the dialogues and other ritual acts are completed, they may return to the house and unite with friends and family for fellowship. On the ninth night, which is Christmas Eve, Mary and Joseph visit a house that accepts their request for a night's lodging. All those who participated in the events of prior evenings generally attend the *Misa de Gallo* (Midnight Mass), which usually starts with a procession down the main aisle during which two godparents carry a statue of the Christ Child to a manger near the front altar. During the evening, in most instances, children break a *piñata* (a paper maché figure often in the shape of a farm animal filled with candy and hung from a high spot in the house). Christmas Day is spent at home with members of the extended family, and traditional Mexican dishes are principal elements of the menu.

Another significant event of the Christmas season is *El Día de los Reyes Magos* (Three Kings' Day) on January 6, when children receive gifts to mark the arrival of the Magi and their offerings for the Christ Child. The night before this special date, children leave a note in one of their shoes explaining their behavior during the past year, followed by a list of requests for specific gifts. The shoes often are filled with straw and left under the bed or on a windowsill, along with water, symbolically to provide sustenance to the camels of the kings. On the evening of January 6, families and close friends unite to cut and share a special round bread with the figure of the infant Jesus in the center.

Activities throughout the Hispanic world occur to recall the last days of Christ's life on earth. *El Miércoles de Ceniza* (Ash Wednesday) is of particular importance to Mexican Americans. On Good Friday in many parishes *La Procesión de las Tres Caídas* (The Procession of the Three Falls), in conjunction with religious services, brings to the memory the agony associated with Christ's journey to Calvary. Families may visit a statue or altar of Our Lady of Sorrows, a Virgin Mary with tears of anguish for her son in his last moments on earth. The Mexican American mother, in visiting the statue, demonstrates her pity for the Virgin on this anniversary day. On Easter Sunday another procession commemorates the reunion of the resurrected Christ and His mother. The burning of an effigy of Judas may also form part of the religious activities.

Funerals Rituals practiced in Spain and colonial Mexico associated with the death of family members are still observed by some Mexican American families. The body of the deceased may be dressed in special clothing (*la mortaja*) and remain in the family home overnight, making it possible for relatives and friends to pay respects to the departing soul. Food is generally served at the *velorio* (wake). On this same date in subsequent years, people who attended the *velorio* may reunite to affirm once again their bonds to the deceased person. On the day of burial, the family accompanies the body to the grave, frequently singing songs of a religious theme. Flowers are thrown into the grave, and the entire family generally stays at the site until the casket is completely covered. Mexican American families whose deceased members were born in Mexico may sometimes arrange for the body to be transported back to the person's town of origin. It was once customary for the spouse and certain family members to wear black clothing for varying periods and make *promesas* (vows) to honor the dead. This is now practiced by fewer families, and the length of time of mourning differs considerably from group to group.

Health Care Issues and Practices A majority of Mexican immigrants and Mexican Americans relied on traditional medical practices to resolve health problems through the early twentieth century. Physical ailments were treated by herbs or other natural medicines or remedies. These cures, prescribed most often by mothers or grandmothers, represented the accumulated knowledge gained from personal experience or observation of others passed down from generation to generation. When relief from a specific affliction was not achieved through home remedies, individuals or families sometimes solicited the assistance of a *curandero* (folk curer) or other type of folk healer. In general, folk healers possessed a certain *don*, or God-given gift or ability, that provided them the power to restore the health of others. They might accomplish this through the use of herbs, massages, or oils, and some used cards to divine an illness or to prescribe a remedy.

Mexican Americans relied more on folk healers than on practitioners of the U.S. medical community in part because of their geographic isolation in rural areas and segregated neighborhoods, as well as because of their limited financial resources. Even those with ready access to conventional medical assistance, however, were often more confident in relying on a local *curandero* because of the faith their parents and grandparents had placed in these traditional curers and because of the more personal approach they employed.

As more Mexican Americans moved to large cities and integrated neighborhoods, a higher percentage of them came to depend on conventional doctors. Many had easier access to conventional facilities, medical insurance through their employers, and decreasing contact with families maintaining ties to traditional health practices. By the 1950s the majority of Mexican Americans relied on doctors and clinics of the modern medical establishment. Surveys in the 1970s and 1980s in various urban areas of California suggested that as low as 5 percent of Mexican Americans had consulted a folk healer to resolve a health problem.

Even so, the underutilization of medical services has been a pressing health problem among Mexican Americans. Causes include low disposable income, inadequate language skills, and lack of transportation. A significant deterrent for nonresidents is the fear of being identified as undocumented and facing the possibility of detainment or deportation. There are fewer public health facilities in some urban areas with a large Hispanic population. In rural areas where many Mexican Americans live, medical centers are sometimes poorly staffed and lack medical services needed to detect or cure complex ailments. For Mexican Americans whose income is at survival level, preventative health measures are a privilege too expensive to consider.

In 2010 more than a third of Mexican Americans were obese, raising their risk for certain health problems, including diabetes. According to data in 2009 from the National Institute of Health, the risk of diabetes for Mexican Americans was 87 percent higher than for non-Hispanic white adults. Among Mexican American adults twenty years of age or older, 13.3 percent had been diagnosed with diabetes in 2009. Poor eating habits contributed to this problem.

In Langley Park, Maryland, young women wait to make their grand entrance into their quinceanera party. Thirteen young women participated in the Miss Quince Anos Celebration 2012 at the Langley Park Community Center. The program features a variety of self improvement workshops and culminates with a big quinceanera celebration. SARAH L. VOISIN / THE WASHINGTON POST VIA GETTY IMAGES

Hispanic Americans, including Mexican Americans, were much more likely than the average person in the United States to be diagnosed with the HIV virus. Since the 1990s higher HIV rates were also found within the migrant farm community (a considerable proportion of which is Mexican and Mexican American). Farmworkers were at higher risk of exposure to tuberculosis; in 2009 farmworkers were six times more likely to have tuberculosis the overall population of the United States.

FAMILY AND COMMUNITY LIFE

In the mid-nineteenth century *la familia*, or the extended family, of Mexican Americans included aunts and uncles, as well as grandparents and even great grandparents. Beyond these direct familial ties between generations, *compadres* (co-parents) were most often an integral part of the family, as were adopted children and intimate friends. As close personal friends of the mother or father of a child, the *padrinos* (godfathers) or *madrinas* (godmothers) developed a special relationship with their *ahijados*

(godchildren), a relationship that started at the child's baptism. From this point forward, in most instances, they provided emotional, financial, and other forms of assistance or advice, especially in times of family crisis. They were essential participants in events of social or religious importance to the godchild, and as much as any immediate family member, godparents contributed to strong family unity.

This system of mutual dependence and respect for elders created a close-knit family unit. Family honor and unity were of paramount significance. If problems arose for individual members, the immediate or extended family could be relied upon to resolve the issue. Important decisions were always made with consideration to the needs of the group rather than the individual. Traditional social and religious practices passed from one generation to the next virtually unchanged because they were perceived as intrinsic values to the family's cultural heritage.

While extended family households are less common today, the importance of the family as a unit and the ties between extended family members remains strong. Newly arrived immigrants generally continue to seek out relatives in the United States (as did the initial generations in the nineteenth century) and sometimes rely upon them for temporary residence and assistance in arranging employment, especially in rural regions.

Gender Roles In Mexican American families the husband was traditionally the principal, if not the sole, breadwinner. He made the important social and economic decisions and was the protector of the family's integrity. Wives had general control over household matters but were expected to be obedient and submissive to their husbands. Although the wife might perform work outside the household, this was usually an acceptable alternative only in cases of extreme economic duress. In such cases, her efforts were limited to a restricted number of options, almost always of a part-time nature, and did not change her subservient status within the household. This division of authority established between husband and wife was passed on to their offspring. Beginning at an early age, girls were taught distinct behavior patterns and were encouraged to adopt aspirations quite different from their brothers. Motherhood was the ideal objective of all young girls and the primary virtue of all those who achieved it.

By the turn of the twentieth century, there was a gradual shift in the pattern of male dominance and division of work by gender within Mexican American families. Economic necessity provided the initial impulse toward a more egalitarian relationship between husband and wife. In the late nineteenth century Mexican American husbands in the Southwest were frequently absent from the household for long periods of time; drovers, miners, farmworkers, and other laborers often strayed considerable distances from their families in pursuit of work, and their wives were left as authority figures. Although men almost always assumed control upon returning home, the structure of power within the family altered somewhat, and it was not uncommon for women to continue to exert a more pronounced role in decision making. As more Mexican American women moved into the full-time labor force in the early decades of the twentieth century, this trend continued, and the family became less male dominant.

Today Mexican American families exhibit a wide range of decision-making patterns, including male authoritarianism. Many studies in the 1990s and the early twenty-first century reported that both parents generally shared in the day-to-day management of the family. The mother, as before, was generally seen as the person most responsible for the domestic needs of the husband and children, but in families in which the mother had become the disciplinarian, she frequently found this role is in conflict with her traditional identity as nurturer. As in other American families, though women have taken on new roles, men still had low levels of participation in household chores, and the father often remained the ultimate authority.

Education In the late 1800s and early 1900s, the desire of low-income migrant families from Mexico to provide their children with educational opportunities was counterbalanced by more fundamental needs: the wages earned by these immigrants for their work in fields, mines, factories, or railways were often so low that families needed the additional income provided by their children to meet the basic necessities required for survival. Attendance at the primary level of instruction was high when schools were available in the predominantly rural areas where Mexican immigrants resided. But attendance in secondary schools was less common. It was often hard for parents to maintain a positive attitude about their children's education, as they would need to pull their children out of classes or at least reduce the amount of time spent in school so the children could begin working. In addition, low-income immigrant families, as well as those with greater financial stability whose children consequently had a better chance of staying in school, were dissuaded from adopting a more positive attitude toward the U.S. educational system because of the tendency of teachers and administrators to deny the existence or importance of Catholic or Hispanic traditions. In the late nineteenth century significant numbers of Mexican Americans were attracted to Catholic schools because of their religious orientation.

As more Mexican Americans moved to urban areas in the early twentieth century, the opportunities for public school education increased measurably. Segregated educational facilities were the rule, however, until the mid-twentieth century. The suits brought by *Menendez v. Westminster School District* in Southern California and *Delgado v. Bastrop Independent School District* in Texas represented important steps in the 1940s toward outlawing segregation, but some school systems practiced "integration" by joining Mexican American and African American students rather than combining these minorities with other American students. The separate educational facilities provided to minority students were often poorly maintained, staffed by undertrained instructors, and provided with inadequate supplies.

As segregated facilities slowly diminished over time, Mexican Americans who entered integrated schools were often classified as learning disabled because of linguistic deficiencies or inadequate academic preparation afforded by their previous learning institutions. This factor caused many of these students to be channeled into "developmentally appropriate" classes or curricular tracks. It was only in the late 1960s that the judicial system took steps to mandate the establishment of bilingual programs in education, but many groups at national and local levels have challenged funding for these programs. The pedagogical approach adopted by the vast majority of bilingual programs has stressed rapid conversion to the use of English without regard for the maintenance of skills in the native languages of first- and second-generation immigrants.

According to U.S. Census Bureau estimates for 2011, 57.8 percent of the "Mexican-origin" population twenty-five years of age and over was a high school graduate or higher, and 9.6 percent of this same age category had a bachelor's degree or more advanced degree. In 2011, 59.1 percent of women in the United States of "Mexican-origin" were high school graduates or higher, whereas 10.6 percent had continued on to complete their bachelor's or graduate degree. A UCLA study released in 2008 entitled "Generations of Exclusion: Mexican Americans, Assimilation, and Race" documented that "the educational levels of second-generation Mexican Americans improved dramatically. But the third and fourth generations failed to surpass, and to some extent fell behind, the educational level of the second generation." The study also recognized that the educational levels of the entire Mexican American population remain below the national average. The number of Hispanics with advanced degrees remained extremely low and continued to lag behind both African Americans and non-Hispanic whites in 2010. The National Center for Education Statistics documented that in 2010, 12.9 percent of all Hispanics in the United States held master's or doctoral degrees, with well over half of them conferred to women.

By 2007 approximately 2.3 million Hispanic-owned businesses existed in the United States, the majority of them in New Mexico, Florida, and Texas, with Mexican Americans representing 45.8 percent of the industry.

Courtship and Weddings Teen marriages were most prevalent in Mexican American families in the first decades of the twentieth century. The premarital procedures involved in joining a couple in matrimony varied depending on the social background of the families. Until the 1920s and perhaps later in rural areas, a *portador* (go-between) would deliver a written proposal of marriage to the father of the would-be bride. Fathers decided on the acceptability of the suitor based on the apparent moral respectability of the young man and his family, and though the opinions of his spouse and daughter were important in the final decision about marriage, the father might often overrule the wishes of either or both of these individuals.

Except among the most traditional Mexican American families, courtship practices have changed substantially over the past few generations. Parents have far-reduced and sometimes incidental influence on the selection of marriage partners for their offspring, except in the most traditional families, but their sentiments on the issue are most always considered of significance.

EMPLOYMENT AND ECONOMIC CONDITIONS

Mining, agriculture, transportation, and ranching attracted the highest numbers of Mexican immigrants and Mexican Americans in search of work in the United States from shortly after the mid-nineteenth century through the first decades of the twentieth century. As these sectors of the economy grew in importance, their demand for low-wage laborers multiplied, and the completion of local and transcontinental rail lines expanded the markets for ranchers and farmers in this region, prompting further demand for additional workers. Laws limiting or excluding Chinese and Japanese immigration made jobs even more abundant for others in certain regions of the western United States. For Mexican immigrants, repeated downturns in the Mexican economy and the sociopolitical turbulence from the Revolution of 1910 made "the North" an attractive location for at least temporary residence.

Although mining, ranching, and transportation employed many new immigrants, the highest percentage of foreign workers were drawn to agriculture, mostly in Texas and California but also in parts of New Mexico, Arizona, and Colorado. By 1930, 41 percent of the agricultural laborers in the Southwest were Mexican or Mexican American. Eight-, ten-, or twelve-hour workdays, with few if any days of rest, combined with generally high temperatures to make this work in fields or orchards extremely demanding and physically draining. Housing made available to laborers by their employers was of inferior quality. Unsanitary and confined living quarters facilitated the spread of disease. Clean drinking water was not easily accessible, and indoor plumbing was uncommon. In areas of colder climate, inadequate heating was the norm. The transitory nature of this work was difficult on immigrant families, whose children seldom had the opportunity to attend anything but makeshift schools on a temporary basis and were most often forced, for economic reasons, to begin work in the fields at a young age.

The 1930s brought severe cutbacks in hiring in agriculture and other industries because of the worldwide economic depression. High levels of unemployment nationwide made immigrant labor less needed. Those workers not of U.S. origin were deported in large numbers; more than 500,000 were forced to return to Mexico during this ten-year period. Frequently, families were separated: parents of foreign citizenship were returned to their home countries, whereas their children, if born in the United States and, thus, American citizens, sometimes remained in their country of birth with relatives or family friends, hoping for the prompt return of their parents.

Less than ten years after the first of these deportations, however, labor shortages caused by World War II—principally in agriculture—stimulated a renewed need for immigrant labor. To resolve this matter, the governments of the United States and Mexico signed an agreement in 1942 that initiated the Bracero Program, which allocated temporary work visas to Mexican immigrants seeking farm work in the Southwest. Farmworkers, however, accused their employers of providing substandard housing and work conditions (documented in studies conducted by the Labor Department in the 1950s); agencies such as the National Council of Churches of Christ in America, the National Catholic Welfare Council, and the National Consumers League spoke out against these conditions, helping Americans become more aware of the problems.

In the decades following the 1960s, wages for Mexican and Mexican American farmworkers continued at inequitable, low levels, and living and work conditions failed to improve by any marked degree. Strikes and boycotts organized by labor leader César Chávez (1927–1993) further publicized the injustices perpetrated by many employers in this rural industry. The formation of the United Farm Workers union gave somewhat greater strength to migrant labor demands, but unfair practices by employers continued to be a source of grievance in the fields.

Beginning in the 1920s and becoming increasingly noticeable in the years after World War II, job opportunities, especially for second- and third-generation Mexican Americans, shifted away from their initial sources of employment into a wider range of occupations in other regions of the country. The Midwestern states, particularly Illinois, offered jobs in meat packing and manufacturing to Mexican Americans seeking alternatives to the transient life of field work. By 2011 only 5.1 percent of Mexican Americans were employed in agriculture, forestry, and mining. Professional and health and education services employed approximately 25 percent of Mexican Americans, while 14 percent were in accommodation and food services, and 11 percent were in manufacturing. More than 10 percent held construction and retail jobs.

The small Mexican American entrepreneurial sector—evident beginning in the second decade of the 1900s—expanded considerably after World War II. By 2007 approximately 2.3 million Hispanic-owned businesses existed in the United States, the majority of them in New Mexico, Florida, and Texas, with Mexican Americans representing 45.8 percent of the industry (according to a U.S. Census Bureau news release dated September 21, 2010). These businesses earned more than $345 billion annually and contributed to the growth of the Mexican American middle class.

Mexican American women entered the labor market as farmworkers, laundresses, and domestics starting in the first decades of the twentieth century. By 1930, 15 percent were employed, and of these, 45 percent worked in domestic and personal service,

A paletero sells ice cream in Los Angeles. MARMADUKE ST. JOHN / ALAMY

with smaller percentages in textile and food processing industries, agriculture, and sales. The proportion of Mexican American women in the labor force increased substantially in the decades that followed, reaching 21 percent by 1950 and over 57 percent by 2011. In 2011 the sectors with the highest levels of employment for Mexican American women were sales, service, and administrative support (including management and business positions) at 22 percent, followed by production and transportation jobs at 10.9 percent. Although Mexican American women were employed at approximately the same percentage as white women in 2011, their earnings were only 68 percent of this other group, reflecting an income gap that had widened by more than 10 percent since 1990.

Despite their diversification into other sectors of the economy, wages for most Mexican Americans have remained low. In 2011 more than 60 percent of Mexican American families had two wage earners, but the median family income was $39,528, considerably lower than the national average for all Americans. The median incomes for Mexican American males and females were $29,879 and $26,508, respectively.

A Mexican migrant worker drives a tractor on a farm in Florida. JAMES QUINE / ALAMY

According to the U.S. Department of Labor, the unemployment rate for Mexican Americans peaked in 2010 at slightly more than 12 percent and had decreased to approximately 11.5 percent by 2011.

The U.S. recession beginning in 2007 had a negative economic impact on the Latino population in the United States, as it did on the American population in general. One of the most notable effects of the recession was the growth in the wealth gap between white households and Latino and African American households. According to a report by the Pew Research Center, in 2009 the estimated median wealth of white households was fifteen times higher than in Hispanic households—compared with seven times in 2004. In contrast, the estimated median wealth of Hispanic households was four times higher than in the African American population—a rate that remained static from 2004 to 2009. Furthermore, the reported median net worth among Hispanic households fell 66 percent from 2005 to 2009. Much of the job loss within the Hispanic community during the recession was in the construction, domestic service, and public service sectors. As President Obama indicated in a speech given to the National Council of La Raza in July 2011, hundreds of thousands of construction workers, many of whom were Latinos and Mexican Americans, lost their jobs after the housing bubble burst.

POLITICS AND GOVERNMENT

Political participation by Mexican Americans has historically been limited by discrimination. In the Southwest before 1910, small numbers of Mexican Americans held offices in territorial and state legislatures in California, Colorado, and New Mexico. However, they were usually handpicked by the white American community of these regions. In other cases, American businessmen who controlled the railroads, mines, and large ranches dominated the state and local politics of the Southwest. During the first decades of the twentieth century—to insure white American political control—various discriminatory policies were used to keep voting by Mexican Americans to a minimum. These policies included the poll tax, literacy tests, all-white primaries, and coercion. In

this atmosphere it is not surprising that few Mexican Americans voted.

During the early part of the twentieth century, while political participation of Mexican Americans was limited, they formed protective organizations—*mutualistas* (mutual aid societies)—which were quite similar to those that developed among European immigrant groups. Members of these organizations found that by pooling their resources they could provide each other with funeral and insurance benefits, as well as other forms of assistance. For example, the Lázaro Cardenas Society was formed in Los Angeles soon after World War I to improve municipal facilities available to Mexican Americans. By the 1920s it became evident to Mexican Americans that if their interests were to be protected, political power was essential.

However, even as Mexican Americans began to adapt to the political and social traditions of the United States, they were still viewed as "foreigners" by the larger society. Thus, they set out to demonstrate that they were true Americans, which was reflected in the goals of organizations formed in the early twentieth century. The *Orden Hijos de América* (Order of the Sons of America; OSA), established in 1921 in San Antonio by members of a small emerging middle class, restricted its goals to that of "training members for citizenship." Membership was consequently limited to "citizens of the United States of Mexican or Spanish extraction." Thus, as an organization consisting of upwardly mobile individuals, OSA attempted to demonstrate to the larger community that they were people to be respected.

World War II would prove to be a turning point in the bid by Mexican Americans for expanded political participation. Mexican Americans who served in the armed services faced discriminatory treatment by other servicemen, but the needs of the industrial wartime economy drew many Mexican Americans into the nation's urban centers seeking employment, thus fostering a greater participation in larger society. In essence, their participation in the war effort at home and abroad served as a unifying force, setting the stage for political activism.

The discriminatory treatment frequently experienced by Mexican American veterans of World War II during and after the war led to the creation of the American G.I. Forum (AGIF), a Congressionally chartered Hispanic veterans and civil rights organization. Founded in 1948 by Dr. Hector P. Garcia in Corpus Christi, Texas, AGIF advocated for World War II veterans of Mexican origin who were denied medical services and veteran's benefits by the United States Department of Veterans Affairs. The organization gained national recognition in 1948 when it advocated for Mexican American serviceman Felix Longoria, whose family was denied funeral services for him after he was killed in action during

World War II. At that time, AGIF was the only veterans group to which Mexican American veterans had access, since they were excluded from other organizations on the basis of race. AGIF is generally regarded as one of the early political groups that initiated the struggle for Chicano civil rights, laying the foundation for the emergence of the Chicano movement in the late 1960s. Soon after AGIF was founded, it expanded its scope to address wider issues within the Mexican American community, including jury selection, voting rights, and educational segregation. In the early twenty-first century the organization continued to advocate strongly for veterans, having expanded its representation to include all Hispanics.

The political activism of this period is also exemplified by the actions of the Community Service Organization (CSO). It was founded in 1947 to promote social change within the Mexican American communities of Los Angeles. The founding members set out to improve social conditions by promoting participation in the political process. The CSO was determined to elect people responsive to the needs of the Mexican American community. Through the efforts of the CSO, Edward Roybal, one of the founders of the CSO, was elected to the Los Angeles City Council in 1949, the first Latino to do so since the nineteenth century. Other important early political groups in the community included the Mexican American Political Association (MAPA) and the Political Association of Spanish-Speaking Organizations (PASSO).

Created in 1960, MAPA was one of the first organizations to clearly articulate ethnic political goals. According to the MAPA Fourth Annual Convention program, "An organization was needed that would be proudly Mexican American, openly political, and necessarily bipartisan." MAPA helped elect several Mexican Americans to office. PASSO, created a few years earlier in Texas, also organized to lobby for Mexican American interests. Both organizations carried out voter education and registration drives; however, they were primarily oriented toward winning concessions for Mexican Americans at the party level.

In the 1970s, unhappy with both the Democratic and Republican parties, some Mexican Americans opted for an entirely different political strategy. They set out to create an alternative political party—La Raza Unida (LRU). Established in Texas in 1970, the LRU had remarkable successes. Most notable were the party's achievements in Crystal City, Texas, a community of approximately 10,000 where LRU candidates won control of the city council and the school board. These newly elected officials, in turn, hired more Mexican American teachers, staff, and administrators. They also instituted bilingual programs and added Mexican American history to the school curriculum. The newly elected officials made changes throughout the city government, including the police department, to rectify years of neglect by city officials.

The LRU then sent organizers throughout the Southwest in efforts to duplicate their success. LRU candidates were placed on many local and statewide ballots, but they were unable to generate the type of support that led to the victories in Crystal City. After the mid-1970s the LRU rapidly declined; internal ideological splintering and personality conflicts played a part, but harassment and repression of the party was the most significant force.

National attention during this period was focused on the actions of *La Alianza Federal de Mercedes* (Federal Alliance of Land Grants) and the United Farmworkers of America (UFW). Reies López Tijerina and the members of La Alianza demanded the return of stolen lands to the indigenous peoples of northern New Mexico. In 1966 La Alianza occupied a part of the Kit Carson National Forest in New Mexico. Arrested for trespassing, Tijerina spent the next few years awaiting trial. In 1975 the land dispute was partially resolved when about a thousand acres of the forest were transferred to 75 Mexican American families.

The organizing efforts of César Chávez, Dolores Huerta, and the UFW brought the plight of the farmworker to national attention and served as a mobilizing force for many Americans of all walks of life. The UFW's first success was the grape boycott beginning in 1965, which carried the struggle of the farmworkers into the households of many Americans. With the refusal to buy table grapes by many Americans, the UFW was able to negotiate its first union contract with California growers (the first union contract in the history of California farm labor). During the late 1980s the UFW began addressing the issue of pesticide use in agricultural production.

From the Mexican American communities of Denver, Colorado, emerged the Crusade for Justice, founded by Rodolfo "Corky" Gonzales in 1966. This organization was primarily concerned with civil rights issues of urban Mexican Americans; however, it was also one of the first groups to advocate and promote issues of cultural diversity. In 1969 and 1970 the Crusade for Justice was instrumental in organizing a series of Chicano youth liberation conferences, bringing together hundreds of young Chicanos from throughout the nation and generating a series of discussions concerning the question of ethnic identity.

By the late 1960s high school and college students were calling for social change within the educational system. The high school "blowouts" of East Los Angeles in 1968 galvanized student discontent. Chicano high school students walked out of their classes in mass, demanding quality education and local community control of their schools. In several other communities students staged similar events. High school students abandoned their classes in Riverside, California; Denver; Crystal City; San Antonio;

Mariachi musicians go from house to house to encourage people to vote on election day at the Sun Valley's Latino district, Los Angeles County, on November 6, 2012 in California. JOE KLAMAR / AFP / GETTY IMAGES

and several other cities with high concentrations of Mexican Americans. College students also mobilized. In the Los Angeles area, college students came together to support high school walkouts and the students' demands for a quality education. Throughout the Southwest, college students were instrumental in establishing the first Chicano studies programs and educational opportunities programs on many college campuses.

Mexican Americans have traditionally voted Democratic, especially at the presidential level. According to the 2006 Latino National Survey, 46 percent of Hispanics identified themselves as Democrats, 16 percent as Republican, and 38 percent as belonging to independent parties or having no political affiliation. Mexican American voters have followed the voting patterns of the general Latino population. In 2012, for example, 78 percent of Mexican Americans and 75 percent of all Hispanics voted democratic in the presidential election. Mexican Americans have played a significant role in several historic elections. In 1960 John F. Kennedy won an estimated 85 percent of the Mexican American vote, which allowed him to win the states of New Mexico and Texas. To insure Kennedy's victory, "Viva Kennedy" clubs were formed throughout the Southwest, promoting voter education and registration drives. In 1964 Lyndon B. Johnson won an estimated 90 percent of the Mexican American vote, and in 1968 Herbert Humphrey won 87 percent.

Several factors have worked against the political participation of Mexican Americans. A large segment of the population is ineligible to vote because they are not citizens. Even among those eligible to vote, the turnout of 47.6 percent (for all Hispanics) in the 2008 elections was nearly 20 percent lower than for non-Hispanics. Lower socioeconomic status also serves as an obstacle for many Mexican Americans. The educational attainment of Mexican Americans is still far below the general population, and the poverty rate is much higher for Mexican Americans than for the general population. Thus, many Mexican Americans have not had the opportunity to develop the skills necessary to participate fully in the voting process.

While the percentage of Mexican American elected officials is not representative of their total U.S. population, significant changes have taken place since the mid-1960s. The number of state legislators in 1950 with Spanish surnames totaled 20. By the late 1980s the number had increased to 90. The 2011 Directory of Latino Elected Officials listed 5,850 Latino elected officials nationwide; the states with the largest number of elected Hispanic officials (the majority of Mexican origin) were Texas, California, New Mexico, and Arizona. The increase in Mexican American officials is due in part to the Twenty-fourth Amendment (1964) to the U.S. Constitution, which banned the poll tax (a fee for voting); also notable was the elimination of the English-only literacy requirements for voting in some states. A change in political districts following the 1980 census (creating districts with a higher percentage of Hispanics), as well as a substantial growth in the Mexican American population, have also contributed to the rise in the number of Mexican American elected officials.

NOTABLE INDIVIDUALS

Mexican Americans have made significant and lasting contributions to virtually every element of American culture and society. The following individuals represent merely a sample of this growing community's achievements.

Business Born to undocumented Mexican parents in Miami, Arizona, Romana Acosta Bañuelos (1925–) was deported at the age six during the Repatriation Program of the 1930s. After returning to the United States at age nineteen, she converted a small tortilla factory into Romana's Mexican Food Products, a multimillion-dollar firm. In 1971 she became the first Mexican American to serve as treasurer of the United States. Hector V. Barreto (1961–) became the twenty-first administrator of the U.S. Small Business Administration in 2001 after George W. Bush nominated him to the post. He served in this position until 2006.

Education Born in Albuquerque, New Mexico, George I. Sánchez (1906–1972) directed his energies toward improving the quality of education available to Mexican Americans, as well as defending their civil rights. *Forgotten People: A Study of New Mexico* (1940), one of his many publications, revealed the inadequacies of the educational system for Mexican Americans in his home state. Sánchez served as president of LULAC (League of United Latin American Citizens) and, in 1956, founded the American Council of Spanish-Speaking People, a civil rights organization. Alicia Gaspar de Alba (1958–), a Chicana scholar, writer, and cultural critic, is a prominent figure in the study of Chicano culture, art, and sexuality (*Desert Blood: The Juarez Murders*, 2005, among others). In 1991 Gaspar de Alba became one of six faculty members who founded the César Chávez Center for Interdisciplinary Instruction in Chicana and Chicano Studies at the University of California, Los Angeles. David Gutierrez is professor of Chicano history at the University of California, San Diego, beginning in 2004 and the author of the acclaimed book *Walls and Mirrors: Mexican Americans, Mexican Immigrants and the Politics of Ethnicity* (1995).

Film, Television, and Theater Mexican American dancer and choreographer José Arcadia Limón (1908–1972) was a pioneer of modern dance and choreography. Edward James Olmos (1947–) received critical acclaim for his portrayal of the *pachuco* in the stage and film version of Luis Valdez's *Zoot Suit* (1981) and for his role as Jaime Escalante in the film *Stand and Deliver* (1988). In addition to his appearances in other movies of merit, Olmos starred in *Miami Vice*, a popular television series of the 1980s. Paul Rodríguez (1955–), who has worked on a number of television series and movies, is perhaps the most popular and widely recognized comedian of Mexican descent in the United States. The head of his own company, Paul Rodríguez Productions, he released his first comedy album in 1986 entitled *You're in America Now, Speak Spanish*. The son of Mexican migrant farmworkers, Luis Valdez (1940–) is the founding director of the Teatro Campesino, an acting troupe that was originally organized to dramatize the oppressive existence of the migrant worker. In addition to directing the stage and film version of *Zoot Suit*, he wrote and directed the 1987 film *La Bamba*, about the Mexican American rock star Ritchie Valens. Guadalupe "Lupe" Ontiveros (1942–2012) was a film, television, and theater actress recognized for her roles in *Selena, Desperate Housewives*, and *Real Women Have Curves*. She also played Dolores in Luis Valdez's historic play *Zoot Suit* in 1978 and went on to perform the role in the Broadway and film versions. Salma Hayek (1966–), a Mexican American film actress, director, and producer, was born in Veracruz, Mexico, and began her career in Mexico as a *telenovela* actress. She received a Golden Globe, an Academy Award, and a Screen Actor's Guild Award for her performance as artist Frida Kahlo in the 2002 film *Frida Kahlo*. Eva Longoria, (1975–), a celebrated American television and film actress of Mexican descent, earned numerous accolades for her performance as Gabrielle Soulis in the long-running television series *Desperate Housewives*. Longoria was recognized several times by *People* magazine as one of the most beautiful people, and she made the top spot on *Forbes* magazine's list of the highest-paid television actresses for 2011.

Folklore Born in Brownsville, Texas, Americo Paredes (1915–1999) achieved national and international recognition for his research and scholarship in the area of folklore and Mexican American popular culture and served as president of the American Folklore Society. Among his many noteworthy publications are *With His Pistol in His Hand* (1958), *Folktales in Mexico* (1970), and *A Texas Mexican Cancionero* (1976).

Labor César Chávez (1927–1993) was born in Yuma, Arizona, to a family of farmworkers. Chávez attended more than thirty schools as a youth because of the mobile pattern of existence of migrant agriculture. In 1962, after working as a community organizer in the CSO, he moved to Delano, California, and soon cofounded and became the head of the United Farm Workers. From the mid-1960s until his death, Chavez dedicated his life to improving the living conditions, wages, and bargaining power of Mexican and Mexican American farmworkers by means of organized work stoppages, demonstrations, hunger strikes, and boycotts. Dolores Clara Fernandez Huerta (1930–) was a civil rights activist and labor leader who cofounded the United Farm Workers alongside Chávez. Huerta received many awards recognizing her advocacy on behalf of women, workers, and immigrants, including the Presidential Medal of Freedom, the United States Presidential Eleanor Roosevelt Award for Human Rights, and the Eugene V. Debs Foundation Outstanding American Award.

Literature Lucha Corpi (1945–) was a notable poet and novelist whose works often address the struggles of women in contemporary society. She gained popularity among readers with her Gloria Damasco series of mystery novels but also published lesser-known works, including the 1989 *Delia's Song*. Rolando Hinojosa (1929–) was one of the first Chicano writers to achieve national as well as international fame. His *Estampas del valle y otras obras: Sketches of the Valley and Other Works*, a series of "sketches" that portray Mexican American life in a fictional town in Texas, won the Premio Quinto Sol for Chicano literature. Another of his works on the same theme, *Klail City y sus alrededores*, won the prestigious international award, Premio Casa de las Americas, in 1976. Born in Linares, Mexico, literary critic Luis Leal (1907–2010) was a highly esteemed, productive scholar of Latin American and Chicano literature. In addition to teaching at numerous universities, he wrote and edited more than sixteen books. Leal was honored by the National Association for Chicano Studies in 1988, as well as a recipient of the National Humanities Medal. Chicana novelist, poet, and essayist Ana Castillo (1953–) is the author of the acclaimed novels *So Far From God* (1993) and *The Guardian* (2007), as well as her collection of poetry *I Ask the Impossible* (2000). Sandra Cisneros (1954–), one of the most widely read Chicana authors in the late twentieth and early twenty-first centuries, was nationally recognized for her novel *House on Mango Street* (1984)—which became required reading in schools nationwide—and her later short story collection *Woman Hollering Creek and Other Stories* (1991). Lorna Dee Cervantes (1954–) was one of the most prominent Chicana poets in the late twentieth century. Of Mexican and Native American (Chumash) origin, Dee Cervantes authored the award-winning poetry collection *Emplumada* (1981; American Book Award) and her more recent *Ciento: 100 100-Word Love Poems* (2011). Jimmy Santiago Baca (1952–), a celebrated Chicano poet from New Mexico, earned numerous awards for his poetry, including the American Book Award, the International Award, and the International Hispanic Heritage Award. Baca's best-known works are *Immigrants in Our Own Land* (1990)—a semiautobiographical epic poem—and *Martin and Meditations on the South Valley* (1987). In 2004 Baca founded a nonprofit organization, Cedar Tree, Inc., to fund the numerous writing workshops with children and adults that he organizes across the country, primarily among marginalized communities, including prisoners and at-risk youth.

Music Ritchie Valens (1941–1959) was a celebrated Mexican American singer, guitarist, and songwriter whose career was tragically cut short when he died in a small-plane crash in Iowa only eight months after his recording career had begun. Upon his untimely death, Valens was already a recognized pioneer in rock and roll and was regarded as one of the forefathers of Chicano rock. Valens' most famous hit was "La Bamba," which topped the record charts in

1958. Eduardo Mata (1942–1995) is among the most respected conductors in the world. The former director and conductor emeritus of the Dallas Symphony Orchestra, he was awarded the White House Hispanic Heritage Award in 1991. Singer and musician Lydia Mendoza (1916–2007), through her many recordings, was the first interpreter of rural popular Tejano and border music to acquire star status. Grammy award-winning Tejano singer and entertainer Selena Quintanilla Perez (1971–1995), best known as Selena, had achieved international fame at the time of her murder in April 1995. Dolores Janney Rivera (1969–2012), a.k.a. Jenni Rivera, was a singer-songwriter of banda and norteña music, as well as an actress, television producer, and entrepreneur who was dearly loved by the Mexican American community. Carlos Augusto Alves Santana (1947–) is an award-winning guitarist and singer who gained fame in the late 1960s and early 1970s with his band Santana. Known for his fusion of rock and Latin American music, Santana has won ten Grammy Awards and three Latin Grammy Awards.

Politics After her election as a state assemblywoman in California in 1982, Gloria Molina (1948–) was voted into the Los Angeles City Council in 1987. In 1991 she was elected to the Los Angeles County Board of Supervisors, thus becoming the first Hispanic in California to be selected by voters to serve at these three levels of government. Hilda Lucia Solis (1957–) served as the twenty-fifth United States Secretary of Labor during President Barack Obama's first presidential term. A member of the Democratic Party, Solis served in the United States House of Representatives from 2001 to 2009, and in 2000 she became the first female recipient of the John F. Kennedy Profile in Courage Award. Born in Mexico City, Republican politician Rosario Marin (1958–) served as Treasury Secretary from 2001 to 2003 under George W. Bush, becoming the highest-ranking Latina in his administration. In 2005 Alberto R. Gonzales (1955–) became the first Hispanic United States Attorney General after his appointment by President George W. Bush, making him the highest-ranking Hispanic to work in the executive branch.

Religion The first Mexican American to be named as a bishop of the Catholic Church in the United States, Patrick F. Flores (1929–) worked in the diocese of Galveston-Houston and became the director of the Bishop's Committee for the Spanish-Speaking. He was a strong defender of the civil rights of Hispanics in the United States for more than four decades and won many honors for these efforts, including the Ellis Island Medal of Honor in 1986. Virgilio Elizondo was a Roman Catholic priest and theologian who taught Pastoral and Hispanic theology at the University of Notre Dame in South Bend, Indiana. He is a major theologian in liberation theology and Hispanic theology. In 2007 Elizondo was named the co-recipient of the 2007 Community of Christ International Peace Award along with Dolores Huerta.

Science A renowned physicist and educator, Mexican American Alberto Vinicio Baez (1912–2007) and his co-researcher, Paul Kirkpatrick, developed the Kirkpatrick-Baez Lamar x-ray telescope, which was later approved for flight on the Freedom Space Station. A pioneer in x-ray radiation, optics, and microscopy, Baez also made noteworthy achievements in the field of environmental education; he served as chairman of the Committee on Teaching Sciences of the International Council of Science Unions and as chairman emeritus of Community Education, International Union for the Conservation of Nature and Natural Resources, in Glantz, Switzerland. Chemist Mario Molina (1943–) earned national prominence by theorizing, with fellow chemist F. Sherwood Rowland, that chlorofluorocarbons deplete the Earth's ozone layer. Elsa Salazar Cade (1952–) was an award-winning Mexican American science teacher and entomologist.

MEDIA

PRINT

El Chicano

William Harrison, Publisher
P.O. Box 110
Colton, California 92324
Phone: (909) 381-9898
Fax: (909) 384-0406
Email: iecn1@mac.com
URL: www.elchicano.com

El Mundo

Subsidiary of the *Oakland Post* newspaper.

William Fonsea, Editor
P.O. Box 405
Oakland, California 94612
Phone: (510) 287-8200
Fax: (510) 287-8247
Email: info@postnewsgroup.com
URL: http://content.postnewsgroup.com

Mexican American Sun

Dolores Sanchez, Editor-in-Chief
111 S. Avenue 59
Los Angeles, California 90042
Phone: (323) 341-7970
Fax: (323) 341-7976
Email: publisher@egpnews.com
URL: http://egpnews.com/category/editions/mexican-american-sun

Saludos Hispanos Magazine

Rosemarie Garcia-Solomon, Managing Editor
31938 Temecula Parkway
#A324
Temecula, California 92592
Phone: (323) 726-2188
Email: info@saludos.com
URL: www.saludos.com/newslette/index.html

RADIO

Radio Latina (104.5 FM)

Southern California radio station that broadcasts in Spanish across San Diego and Tijuana.

2403 Hoover Avenue
National City, California 91950
Phone: (619) 336-7800
Email: comentarios@1045radiolatina.com
URL: http://1045radiolatina.com

TELEVISION

Telemundo Media

National Spanish-language cable network with nationwide and local programming across the country.

Emilio Romano, President
2340 West 8th Avenue
Hialeah, Florida 33010
Phone: (305) 884-8200
Email: Te.Escuchamos@telemundo.com
URL: http://msnlatino.telemundo.com

Univision Communications, Inc.

National media company that owns and operates the Spanish-language broadcast networks Univision Network and UniMás, as well as the Spanish-language cable network Galavisión.

Randy Falco, President and Chief Executive Officer
605 Third Avenue
New York, New York 10158-0180
Phone: (212) 455-5331
Fax: (212) 867-6710
Email: info@univsion.net
URL: http:///univsion.net

ORGANIZATIONS AND ASSOCIATIONS

Mexican American Legal Defense and Education Fund

Founded in San Antonio in 1968 in response to a historical pattern of discrimination against Mexican Americans. Through litigation and community education, it protects and promotes the rights of Latinos in the United States in the areas of employment, education, immigration, political access, and language.

Thomas A. Saenz, President and General Counsel
634 South Spring Street
11th Floor
Los Angeles, California 90014
Phone: (213) 629-2512
Fax: (213) 629-0266
Email: info@maldef.org
URL: www.maldef.org

National Association for Chicano and Chicana Studies

Founded in 1971, with membership consisting of college professors, graduate and undergraduate students, and others whose professional or personal interests center on sociological, historical, political, or literary themes or concerns pertaining to Mexican Americans. It sponsors an annual conference and publishes selected proceedings.

Julia E. Curry Rodriguez, Executive Director
P.O. Box 720052
San Jose, California 95972-0052
Phone: (408) 924-5310
Fax: (408) 920-0711
Email: naccs@naccs.org
URL: www.naccs.org

National Council of La Raza

The nation's largest constituency-based Hispanic organization. Its goal is to reduce poverty and discrimination and improve life opportunities for all Hispanics nationally. Nearly 200 formal affiliates serve 37 states, Puerto Rico, and the District of Columbia.

Janet Murguía, President and CEO
1126 16th Street NW
Suite 600
Washington, D.C. 20036-4845
Phone: (202) 785-1670
Fax: (202) 776-1792
Email: comments@nclr.org
URL: http://www.nclr.org

Southwest Voter Registration Education Project

Founded in 1975. Conducts nonpartisan voter registration drives, compiles research on Hispanic and Native American voting patterns, and works to eliminate gerrymandered voting districts. It publishes *National Hispanic Voter Registration Campaign*.

Antonio Gonzalez, President
1426 El Paso Street
Suite B
San Antonio, Texas 78207
Phone: (800) 404-VOTE; or (210) 223-2918
Fax: (210) 922-7095
Email: agonzalez@svrep.org
URL: http://svrep.org

MUSEUMS AND RESEARCH CENTERS

Chicano Studies Institute

Part of the University of California, Santa Barbara, the institute supports and conducts research on historical and contemporary issues related to the Mexican-origin population of the United States. It also encourages and facilitates academic investigations and training of minority students and sponsors events that increase public awareness and appreciation of Mexican and Mexican American culture.

Laura Romero, Director
Room 4518
South Hall
UC Santa Barbara
Santa Barbara, California 93106-6040
Phone: (805) 893-3895
Fax: (805) 893-4446
Email: lromo@education.ucsb.edu
URL: www.research.ucsb.edu/ccs

Center for Mexican American Studies (CMAS)

Part of the University of Texas at Austin. The center provides financial and technical support for research by faculty and graduate students and offers courses as part of the Ethnic Studies curriculum of the College of Liberal Arts.

Domino Renee Perez, Director
F 9200
Austin, Texas 78712
Phone: (512) 471-4557
Fax: (512) 471-9639
Email: cmas@austin.utexas.edu
URL: www.utexas.edu/cola/centers/cmas/

Chicano Studies Research Center (CSRC)

Part of the University of California, Los Angeles. The center promotes the study of people of Mexican descent and other Latinos in the United States. It publishes *Aztlán: A Journal of Chicano Studies*.

Chon A. Noriega, Director
193 Haines Hall
Los Angeles, California 90095-1544
Phone: (310) 825-2363
Fax: (310) 206-1784
Email: crscinfo@chicano.ucla.edu
URL: www.chicano.ucla.edu

Guadalupe Cultural Arts Center

Latino arts and cultural institution sponsoring instructional programming and presentations.

Patty Ortiz, Executive Director
1300 Guadalupe Street
San Antonio, Texas 78207
Phone: (210) 271-3151
Email: dam@guadalupeculturalarts.org
URL: www.guadalupeculturalarts.org

Mexic-Arte Museum

An arts museum founded by Sylvia Orozco in 1983. It exhibits include work of Mexican artists, pre-Cortez artifacts, and photographs of the Mexican Revolution.

Sylvia Orozco, Executive Director
419 Congress Avenue
Austin, Texas 78701
Phone: (512) 480-9373
Email: info@mexic-artemuseum.org
URL: www.mexic-artemuseum.org

Mexican Museum

Pre-Hispanic, colonial, folk, Mexican, and Mexican American fine arts. The museum includes a permanent collection as well as temporary exhibits.

David J. de la Torre, Director
Fort Mason Center
Building D
Laguna and Marina Boulevard,
San Francisco, California 94123
Phone: (415) 202-9700
Email: themexicanmuseum@gmail.com
URL: www.mexicanmuseum.org

National Museum of Mexican Art

Founded in 1987, it houses one of the country's largest Mexican art collections, including more than 7,000 works of art from Mexico. It is the only Latino museum in the United States that is accredited by the American Alliance of Museums. The museum also hosts presentations of current and past Mexican literary works.

Carlos Tortelero, President
1852 West 19th Street
Chicago, Illinois 60608
Phone: (312) 738-1503
Email: info@nationalmuseumofmexicanart.org
URL: www.nationalmuseumofmexicanart.org

Plaza de La Raza

Offers instruction in theater, dance, music, and visual and communication arts. Its exhibits include Mexican American folk art of the surrounding region.

Maria Jimenez-Torres, Interim Executive Director
3540 North Mission Road
Los Angeles, California 90031
Phone: (323) 223-2475
Fax: (323) 223-1804
Email: info@plazadelaraza.org
URL: www.plazadelaraza.org

Southwest Hispanic Research Institute/ Chicano Studies

Part of University of New Mexico. Established in 1980, the institute coordinates and conducts investigations of interdisciplinary scope. The Visiting Scholars Program, funded by Rockefeller Foundation, provides economic support to scholarly research of regional focus. The institute also sponsors a colloquium series that allows faculty to present findings of research to the academic and local community.

Christine M. Sierra, Director
1829 Sigma Chi Road NE

Albuquerque, New Mexico 87131
Phone: (505) 277-2965
Fax: (505) 212-0342
Email: shri@unm.edu
URL: http://shri.unm.edu/

SOURCES FOR ADDITIONAL STUDY

Chambram-Dernersesian, Angie, ed. *The Chicano/a Cultural Studies Reader*. New York: Routledge, 2006.

Gutiérrez, David G., ed. *Between Two Worlds: Mexican Immigrants in the United States*. Wilmington, DE: Scholarly Resources, 1996.

———. *Walls and Mirrors: Mexican Americans, Mexican Immigrants, and the Politics of Ethnicity*. Berkeley: University of California Press, 1995.

Jimenez, Tomas. *Replenished Ethnicity: Mexican Americans, Immigration, and Identity*. Berkeley: University of California Press, 2010.

Limon, Jose. *American Encounters: Greater Mexico, the United States, and the Erotics of Culture*. Boston: Beacon Press, 1998.

Meier, Matt S., and Feliciano Rivera. *Mexican Americans/ American Mexicans*. New York: Hill and Wang, 1993.

Orozco, Cynthia. *No Mexicans, Women, or Dogs Allowed: The Rise of the Mexican American Civil Rights Movement*. Austin: University of Texas Press, 2009.

Saldívar-Hull, Sonia. *Feminism on the Border: Chicana Gender Politics and Literature*. Berkeley: University of California Press, 2000.

Vargas, Zaragoza. *Crucible of Struggle: A History of Mexican Americans from Colonial Times to the Present Era*. New York: Oxford University Press, 2011.

Vento, Arnoldo Carlos. *Mestizo: The History, Culture, and Politics of the Mexican and the Chicano: The Emerging Mestizo-Americans*. Lanham, MD: University Press of America, 1997.

MONGOLIAN AMERICANS

Baatar Tsend

OVERVIEW

Mongolian Americans are immigrants or descendants of people from the Mongolian Plateau in central Asia who speak dialects of the Mongol language and share a traditionally nomadic culture. Mongols are mainly from Mongolia (a large landlocked country in east-central Asia that shares a border with Russia to the north and China to the south) and the Inner Mongolia Autonomous Region in northern China. The term *Mongol* may also be used to describe Kalmyks (western Mongolians living in Russia on the shores of the Caspian Sea in the republic of Kalmykia) and Buryats (an indigenous nomadic people located mainly in the Buryat Republic, a federal state of Russia in south-central Siberia). Former home of the famous warrior-king Genghis Khan, Mongolia is a land of extremes that range from the mountains of the west and southwest to the vast Gobi Desert in the south-central portion of the country. Mongolia is so far inland that no sea moderates the climate, there is very little humidity, and the sunshine on most days is intense. The country of Mongolia measures 604,100 square miles (1,564,616 square kilometers), making it slightly smaller than the state of Alaska. The Inner Mongolia Autonomous Region (often referred to as Inner Mongolia) measures 454,600 square miles (1,177,500 square kilometers).

According to the *CIA World Factbook*, Mongolia had an estimated population of 3,179,997 in July 2012; over 95 percent of the population are Mongols. More Mongols live outside of the country than within, including approximately 4 million in the Inner Mongolia Autonomous Region of China and some 600,000 in Russia. Within Mongolia, about half of the population identifies itself as Buddhist Lamaist, another 6 percent is either Shamanist or Christian, and 40 percent declare no religion. The economy of Mongolia has undergone great changes since the Soviet Union ceased giving military and economic aid to the country in the early 1990s, plunging the country into deep recession. However, in the early twenty-first century a mining boom was setting off an economic transformation. Per capita income rose from $1,089 in 2000 to $4,800 in 2011, when Mongolia was ranked 154th out of 228 countries on this significant social indicator. Despite major improvements in the standard of living, more than 39 percent of the population continued to live in poverty in 2010.

A small number of Mongolians immigrated to the United States from China's Inner Mongolia before the mid-twentieth century, but it was not until 1950 that the first wave of Mongolians fled to the United States to escape the harsh realities of communism. With assistance from the U.S. government, many settled in Howell Township, New Jersey, followed by settlement during the 1970s in New York City and the surrounding area. The next wave of emigration from Mongolia began during the 1990s as the country began the transition from a state to a private economy. By 1991 the number of Mongolian Americans had risen to about 2,000, with the majority continuing to reside in New Jersey and Pennsylvania. In 2000 a major winter storm hit Mongolia, wiping out more than a million head of livestock and setting off a new wave of emigration. By that time about 5,000 Mongolian Americans were living in New York, New Jersey, Pennsylvania, and Illinois. Additionally, Northern California had become home to 3,000 Mongolian Americans.

Since 2002 the number of Mongolian Americans has grown significantly. According to the U.S. Census Bureau's American Community Survey, there were 16,856 Mongolian Americans living in the United States in 2010. That figure represented a 300 percent increase over the 2000 Census. The largest number of Mongolian Americans in 2010 were residing in California (4,500), particularly in the Los Angeles and San Francisco areas, and Illinois (2,600), especially in Chicago. Responding to educational and employment opportunities, large numbers have also settled in Virginia (1,800) and New Jersey (750). Wherever they have settled, Mongolian Americans have established tight-knit communities and have frequently formed alliances with groups from similar regional or religious backgrounds, such as Tibetan Buddhists. While most Mongolian Americans educated in the United States have settled into the American mainstream, many who immigrated after being educated in their homeland have had to settle for low-paying, low-status jobs in the service field. For this reason, a number of Mongolian Americans have begun to consider returning to Mongolia to take advantage of the current mining boom and economic upswing.

HISTORY OF THE PEOPLE

Early History Mongolia is one of the world's oldest nomadic civilizations. Archaeologists have uncovered human remains in the Gobi and other regions dating back nearly 500,000 years. Agriculture seems to have preceded nomadic herding of animals, and despite Mongolia's short summers, wheat cultivation has coexisted with nomadic life for thousands of years. It was only after the Mongolians began raising horses, sheep, cattle (including some yaks), goats, and camels that they took to a nomadic herding lifestyle.

Early Chinese manuscripts refer to nomadic peoples living in what is now Mongolia as early as the fourth or fifth century BCE. The name *Mongol* was first recorded by the Chinese during the Tang dynasty (618–907 CE). At that time Mongolia was dominated by the Turkic-speaking Uighurs, who would control most of Mongolia until 840 CE. The defeat of the Uighurs created a vacuum, which was filled by the Khitans, a Mongolic-speaking ethnic group from what is now northeastern China. By the tenth century the Khitans ruled most of Manchuria, eastern Mongolia, and much of China north of the Yellow River. The Khitans continued warring with other Mongol tribes, most significantly with the western Xi, during the eleventh and twelfth centuries. The Khitan empire was finally defeated in 1122 CE.

Until the end of the twelfth century, the Mongolians were little more than a loose confederation of rival clans. In 1182 a twenty-year-old Mongolian named Temujin rose to power to become the leader of the Borjigin Mongol clan. He later managed to unite all the Mongol tribes and founded a united Mongol state. In 1206 he was given the honorary name of Genghis Khan, sometimes thought to mean "universal (or oceanic) king." He subsequently conquered adjacent lands and later set up a vast empire that covered most of Asia and Europe. By the time of Genghis's death in 1227, the Mongol Empire extended from Beijing to the Caspian Sea. Power passed into the hands of Genghis's favorite son, Ogedei, who continued this program of military conquest. His generals pushed as far west as Hungary and were planning to invade western Europe when Ogedei died.

Mongol custom dictated that all noble defendants of Genghis had to return to Mongolia to democratically elect a new khan (king). Genghis's grandson, Kublai Khan (circa 1216–1294), completed the subjugation of China, effectively ending the Song dynasty (960–1269). He became the emperor of China's Yuan dynasty (1271–1368; also called the Mongol dynasty) and established his winter capital in Daidu, today's Beijing.

After Kublai died in 1294, Mongol control steadily disintegrated until they were finally expelled from Beijing by the first emperor of the Ming dynasty (1368–1644). A major civil war occurred from 1400 to 1450 between the main group of Mongolians in the east and the Oirats in the west. A revival of sorts occurred under Dayan Khan (1480–1517), who united the eastern Mongolians, defeated the Oirats, and brought most of Mongolia under his control. After his death Altan Khan (1507–1583) initiated the conversion of Mongolians to Buddhism. With the death of Altan, Mongolia reverted to a collection of aristocratic fiefs. Meanwhile, the Manchus established the Qing dynasty (1644–1911), to which most of the Mongolians sooner or later surrendered.

In 1911 China's last dynasty, the Qing dynasty, crumbled. Mongolian independence from China was declared on December 1, 1911. On May 25, 1915, the Treaty of Kyakhta, granting Mongolia limited autonomy, was signed by Mongolia, China, and Russia. After a confused period from 1919 to 1921, when Chinese control was briefly restored, a new People's Government of Mongolia was declared in July 1921, under the guidance of the Soviet Union. Within three years Mongolia became a People's Republic.

Modern Era The years following the World Wars were filled with upheaval in Mongolia. Between 1930 and 1940, the Soviets waged a campaign to entrench communism in Mongolia, slaughtering scores of men, including nobles, lamas (Buddhist clergy), and even party leaders and secular intellectuals. Many who survived were exiled to Siberia. By 1940 Mongolia was a communist satellite of the Soviet Union. Once control was firmly established, the communists began rebuilding Mongolia's infrastructure and improving education and health care. As a satellite state of the Soviet Union, Mongolia had Soviet-style political and economic institutions.

Beginning in 1989 the country underwent a peaceful revolution that established it as a free and democratic state with a multiparty parliamentarian system under a president. In 1990, as the Soviet regime began to break apart, the Mongolian People's Revolutionary Party (MPRP), formerly communist, reinvented itself as a democratic party and won the elections of 1992. However, the Democratic Union Coalition (DUC) won a majority in the next elections, in 1996. The MPRP returned to power in 2004 but chose to form a coalition government with the DUC until 2008. In 2010 the MPRP renamed itself the Mongolian People's Party and continued to coexist with the DUC and other minor political parties. The discovery of approximately $1 trillion of unexploited minerals and metals has spurred international investment in Mongolia and has revitalized the economy, which boasted a real growth rate of 17.5 percent in 2011.

The Mongolian government, with support from the United States, has been involved in an intense effort to incorporate English into Mongolian life as a means of ensuring a profitable future. This was precipitated in large part by access to the Internet and the pervasiveness of American culture. Many government websites in Mongolia are now available in both English and Mongolian, and bilingual signs have become the norm in Mongolian cities. The country also has two English-language newspapers.

SETTLEMENT IN THE UNITED STATES

The first Mongolians to come to the United States were from Inner Mongolia: Gombojob Hangin, a native of Chakhar, and Urgunge Onon, a Daur. They arrived with their families in 1948 to join American author and educator Owen Lattimore's program in East Asian Affairs at Johns Hopkins University. Early Mongolian immigration to the United States was also indirectly spurred by the arrests of high-ranking lamas during the antireligious campaigns that began in 1930. At that time some lamas left Mongolia for China and India. The first Mongolian lama to immigrate to the United States was the "Living Buddha," Diluv Khutagt (also spelled Dilowa Khutugtu). A Khalkha Mongol, he headed a ministry in Mongolia before coming to the United States in 1949 as a political refugee, also joining Lattimore's program.

In 1951 Mongolians from Europe began to immigrate to the United States. The first large group to arrive was made up of Kalmyk Mongols. These Kalmyks were a branch of the Oirats (western Mongolians), who had migrated to the Don-Volga region of eastern Europe and had maintained their customs and political autonomy within Russia since the beginning of the seventeenth century. During the Russian Revolution in 1917, close to 2,000 Kalmyks fled from Russia by way of the Black Sea ports. After landing in Turkey, they traveled to Yugoslavia, Bulgaria, Czechoslovakia, and France. As World War II came to a close and Germany retreated from Russia, many Kalmyks were conscripted into the German army and forced to serve as laborers aiding the retreat. The thousands of Kalmyks displaced throughout Europe—both as a result of the Russian Revolution and the German retreat out of Russia during World War II—were then detained in refugee camps, where they languished until the early 1950s. An organization called Kalmyk Representation in Western Europe was able to negotiate the release of some of the detained Kalmyks and find them homes in the United States. Then, on August 31, 1951, the U.S. Congress passed a law granting Kalmyks immigration rights as Europeans, which resulted in the arrival of more than 550 Kalmyks between December 1951 and March 1952. By the 1990s there were approximately 1,000 Kalmyks in the United States. Most were of the Dörböd (Dervet) sub-ethnic group, supplemented by Torghuds and Buzavas (Kalmyk Cossacks).

The third wave of Mongolian immigration to the United States was small (between 150 and 200 people). In 1965 the United States accorded an equal quota to Asian immigrants via the Immigration and Naturalization Act Amendments. Small numbers of Mongols from Inner Mongolia, as well as western Mongols from Xinjiang and Kökenuur (Qinghai) and those in exile in India and Taiwan, arrived between 1965 and 1975.

Another wave of Mongolian immigrants, mostly from independent Mongolia, the Republic of Kalmykia, and Buryat, arrived after Mongolia's democratic transition in 1990. The majority came to the United States for academic and economic reasons. Most Mongolian immigrants initially came to the United States on student or tourist visas, and many of them stayed. Although the large number of illegal immigrants has made it difficult to obtain accurate numbers, statistics from the Immigration and Naturalization Service show that more than 5,000 people from Mongolia became permanent residents of the United States between 1991 and 2011.

The first Mongolian immigrants settled around Baltimore and New York City before moving to other cities. Kalmyk Mongol immigrants moved to Lakewood and Freewood Acres, New Jersey. The International Refugee Organization provided a special grant to several social service groups, notably the Tolstoy Foundation and the Church World Service, on behalf of the Kalmyk Mongols, to jointly sponsor efforts to help them find homes. A smaller group of Kalmyks settled in an older section of north-central Philadelphia, where successive waves of first-generation immigrants have settled since colonial times. There are also several Mongolian immigrant families living in New Brunswick and Paterson, New Jersey, and in Valley Forge, Pennsylvania. The Kalmyk Mongol community has not expanded significantly. By the late 1990s there were still only about 1,000 Kalmyks living in the United States. Some continued to live in New Jersey and Pennsylvania, while others, beginning in the 1970s, moved to New York; Washington, D.C.; West Virginia; Florida; Arizona; Texas; New Mexico; and California. Mongolian American communities of recent immigrants are settled in San Francisco; Los Angeles; Chicago; New York City; Washington, D.C.; Philadelphia; and the Howell-Jackson area of central New Jersey.

These settlement patterns continued into twenty-first century, with the majority of Mongolian Americans residing in New York, New Jersey, Illinois, and California, with substantial numbers in Virginia and New Jersey as well.

LANGUAGE

The Mongolian language is the most widely spoken and written language in the Mongolic language family, a group of numerous closely related languages used by people living throughout Mongolia, Russia, China, and the Inner Mongolia Autonomous Region of China. It is the official language of Mongolia, where most people speak the Khalkha dialect, whose name is derived from the Khalkha tribe (the largest ethnic subgroup in Mongolia since the fifteenth century) and the Khalkha River in eastern Mongolia. Though

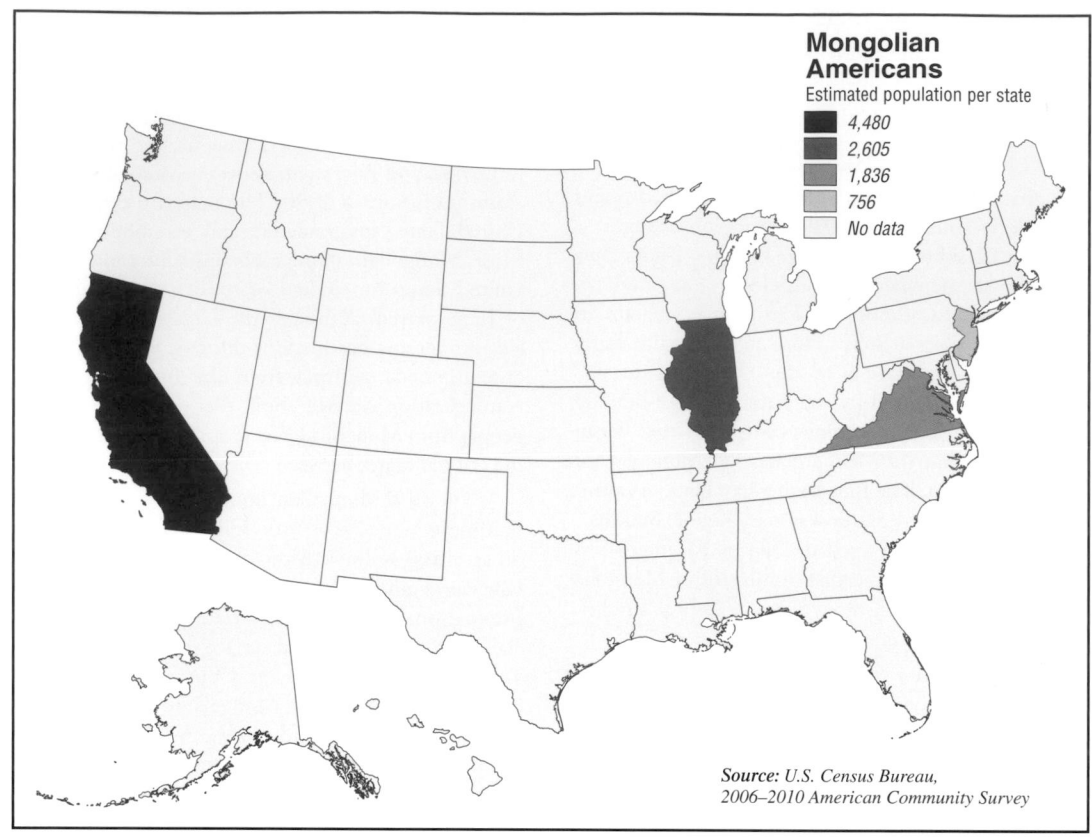

Mongolian Americans
Estimated population per state

- 4,480
- 2,605
- 1,836
- 756
- No data

Source: U.S. Census Bureau, 2006–2010 American Community Survey

the source of the word has confounded scholars for years, there is general agreement among linguists that the term *khalkha* means "shield." Linguists have subdivided the Khalkan dialect into eastern, western, and central subcategories, and the Cyrillic script used to write Mongolian since 1941 is based on the central Khalkha sub-dialect.

The Mongolic languages belong to the Altaic language family, named for the Altai Mountains of western Mongolia. Spread by ancient migrations of Inner Asian peoples, and the conquests of the Mongol Empire itself, the Altaic language family also includes Turkish, Uzbek, Kazakh, and Manchu. All of these languages are characterized by agglutinative grammar and vowel harmony. In languages structured according to the logic of agglutinative grammar, words are formed and acquire their meaning by adding, or "gluing," suffixes to a stem. As they are added in sequence to the stem, these suffixes indicate aspects of language such as possession, tense, voice, point of view, and plurality. The rules of agglutinative languages tend to be more consistent across the group than the rules of Romance languages. For example, there are few irregular verbs in Mongolian. Mongolian languages also exhibit vowel harmony, which means the sound indicated by a vowel depends on which vowels come after it, both immediately after it and later in the word. There are also rules indicating which vowels can be used in succession and which can be used in the same word.

Other Mongolic languages include Inner Mongolian, which has dialects such as Ordos and Chakhar; Buriat, spoken in Siberia by the Buryat Mongols, as well by Buryats and Barga Mongols in Mongolia and Inner Mongolia; Oirat, used by the Oirat Mongols of Xinjiang; and Kalmyk, spoken by the Kalmyk Oirats of Eastern Europe. In eastern Inner Mongolia, dialects include Baarin, Kharachin, and Khorchin, which are very different from the standard language. In Qinghai (Kökenuur) the Mongols of the Haixi district and Henan County also speak dialects related to Oirat. The language of the Daurs of northeastern Inner Mongolia contains many ancient features and cannot be understood by other Mongolians.

Following independence and the withdrawal of the Soviet Union from Mongolia in 1990, the influence of the Russian language declined, although Russian is still spoken widely by those of the older generation in Mongolia.

With funding from the United States–Mongolian Council on Trade and Investment and Jalsa and David Urubshurow, leaders in the New Jersey Kalmyk community, the first Internet connection was established in Mongolia in January 1996. Internet access opened up a range of opportunities for Mongolia, and officials began to promote the adoption of English as a strategy for Mongolia's future prosperity. After becoming prime minister in 2005, Tsakhiagiin Elbegdorj announced that Mongolia would aim to become a bilingual nation, with English as the second language. English-language schools have become commonplace in Mongolia, as have schools teaching Korean, Japanese, and Chinese, as well as European languages.

The prevalence of the English language in Mongolia has made it somewhat easier for recent immigrants to the United States to adapt to American culture. According to the American Community Survey's estimates for 2006–2010, 61 percent of Mongolian Americans reported being proficient in English, and 27 percent spoke only English at home. Many Mongolian Americans have become concerned about the continuation of their language and culture. They continue to keep their native language alive through events that celebrate Mongolian culture. In both the Denver and the Washington, D.C., areas, parents have established a Mongolian-language school to teach their children about their heritage.

Greetings and Popular Expressions Some common expressions in the Mongolian language include the following: *Tiim*; *Ugui*; *Bayarlaa/Gyalailaa* (Thanks); *Uuchlaarai* (I'm sorry/Excuse me); *Yuu genee?* ("Sorry?" or "What did you say?"); *Khun guai!* (Excuse me, sir/madam!); *Sain baina uu?* (literally, "How are you?"); *Sain ta sain baina uu?* (Fine); *Bayartai* (Goodbye); and *Za* (Okay).

RELIGION

The majority of Mongolian Americans practice Buddhism of the Tibetan (lama) variety. Religion was suppressed in communist Mongolia for most of the twentieth century. Shortly after their arrival in the United States in the 1950s, the Kalmyk Mongol immigrants began reconstructing their religious system. Only twenty priests, a few less than the total number who had emigrated from Russia during the first and second waves of immigration, settled in the United States. All were over sixty years of age and represented primarily the higher ranks in the traditional ecclesiastical hierarchy. Until his death in 1965, the highest-ranking cleric in Mongolian Buddhism was not a Kalmyk but a Khalkha Mongol—the "Living Buddha," Diluv Khutagt, who was the final authority in religious decisions. He lived in Baltimore and also participated frequently in rituals and ceremonies in New Jersey and Pennsylvania, maintaining residences in religious establishments in Freewood Acres and New York City. Several priests were also sent from India by the Dalai Lama to augment the dwindling number of Tibetan Buddhist priests.

The physical architecture and layout of the religious establishments erected in the United States usually include a place of worship that is furnished with a multitude of *thangkas*, or Tibetan religious pictures, as well as flowers, satin banners, prayer flags, and several small tables opposite the door that serve as the altar. Incense and offerings are placed around the altar. Along the left side, facing the altar, are the low seats, or

MONGOLIAN SCRIPT

Alterations in the Mongolian script are a relatively recent phenomenon, having occurred twice in the twentieth century. In the early thirteenth century the Mongols adopted a vertical alphabetic script from the Turkic-speaking Uyghurs, which is still used officially in Inner Mongolia and unofficially by many in independent Mongolia even today. In 1931 the Mongolian government adopted the Latin script. Ten years later, due to pressure from the Soviet Union, the Mongolian government switched to a phonetic alphabet derived from Cyrillic script, variations of which are the norm in countries where Slavic languages are spoken. Mongolian script is rendered vertically, left to right, and as of 2013, this modified Cyrillic script remained the official script in Mongolia. Kalmyks and Buryat Mongols in Russia have adopted distinct versions of the Cyrillic script, while the Oirats of Xinjiang use the Todo script, which is based on the traditional Mongolian alphabet, but with reforms to make it more precise.

divans, and tables of the clergy, arranged in the order of their hierarchical standing—the highest being closest to the altar. The religious precinct also includes a place of residence for its priests. In effect, the complex is a reconstruction of the traditional monastic establishment. The whole is referred to by Mongolians in English as the temple and in Mongolian as *Khurul* (assembly of monks) or *Olna Gazur* (holy ground).

Three temples have been serving the Mongolian Buddhist community since the 1950s: Rashi Gempil Ling and Gaden Chopel Ling in Howell, New Jersey, and the Tibetan Literary Center in Washington, D.C. Other temples were subsequently established in Philadelphia and New York City, and a temple was built in the Chicago area in 2004 by Lama Tsedendamba Chilkhaasuren. By 2012 there were Buddhist temples in twenty-nine of the fifty states. At the various temples lamas prepare *thangkas*, forge idols, and build *stupas* (religious monuments).

The number of Christians in Mongolia has grown since the withdrawal of the Soviet Union in 1990, and both American and South Korean missionaries have been working to convert Mongolians. As a result many recent Mongolian immigrants to the United States have been Christian. They are often absorbed into existing Asian American communities. In Los Angeles, for instance, the Christian Mongolian community has forged strong ties with churches in Koreatown.

CULTURE AND ASSIMILATION

The Mongolian American community still retains its heritage. Most Mongolian American families strive to preserve traditional Mongolian values and transmit these to their children. The social interaction that occurs with the host culture is primarily a result of the necessary participation of Mongolian Americans in economic and politico-administrative institutions. In essence, these communities mitigate the shock of transition into a foreign culture, and they also prolong the period of acculturation. While Mongolian American communities tend to be insular, the younger generation of Mongolian Americans has generally been educated in U.S. schools and has been exposed to American culture through the media and other means. As a result, younger Mongolian Americans interact more frequently than their parents and grandparents with other Americans. Such acculturation is more common among the descendants of Kalmyk immigrants than among the descendants of Mongolian immigrants. Young Kalmyk Americans have gradually adopted American standards of beauty and fashion and are more likely to marry outside of their communities than other Mongolian immigrants. Second- and third-generation Kalmyks often have prestigious jobs that allow them to build American-style homes and fill them with a contemporary suite of American furnishings. However, Kalmyks typically enlist the support of people in their communities to construct this lifestyle, using Kalmyk contractors to construct and maintain their homes. Thus, acculturation is not a simple process of exchanging one heritage for another, nor is it a process that is common to all second- and third-generation Mongolians.

As a community, Mongolian Americans have been combatting the loss of heritage through organized efforts to teach the younger generation and the American public about Mongolia through festivals and other events regularly held in areas with large Mongolian American populations. The community worked with the Mongolian mission to the United Nations to host the first Festival of Mongolia ever held in the United States. Opening in New York City on May 19, 2000, the festival consisted of twenty-one separate events held over a period of several weeks. Events included exhibits of Mongolian sports and arts, such as archery, wrestling, and felt making, as well as native songs and dances. Examples of *gers*, 22-foot-wide circular tents used by Mongolian nomads, were on display. In addition, the American Museum of Natural History in New York City held an exhibiting for the first time in North America the famed Fighting Dinosaurs—a Velociraptor and Protoceratops that were uncovered in Mongolia in 1971 after being buried in the Gobi Desert for eighty million years.

As a result of reclaiming Genghis Khan as a national Mongolian hero, in 1999 Mongolian Americans in North Brunswick, New Jersey, began hosting an annual memorial service. In 2006 San Francisco hosted a celebration at Golden Gate Park to honor the 800th anniversary of Genghis's exploits. An annual children's festival is held in Virginia, where Mongolian has become the third most spoken language in the state. Each July Mongolian Americans in Chicago recognize Naadam, a major Mongolian holiday, with a large waterfront party. A similar event was initiated in 2012 in Los Angeles.

MONGOLIAN PROVERBS

Hunii erkheer zovokhoor ööriin erkheer jarga.

> Better to suffer in liberty than delight under captivity.

Takhiatai ch üür tsaina, takhiagui ch üür tsaina.

> Dawn will come with or without the rooster.

Ner khugarakhaar yas khugar.

> Better to break a bone than blemish your name.

Urag törliin khol baij us tülshiin oir ni deer.

> Kin and relatives are better far away, while water and fuel are better nearby.

Sanaa sokhor bol nüd sokhor.

> The eye cannot see when the mind is oblivious.

Traditions and Customs Assimilation for Mongolian American immigrants has been difficult, often causing them to become more attached to the traditions of their homeland. For instance, Mongolian Americans' sense of art is closely related to their mystic sense of identity with nature. Humanity, nature, and art constitute an unbroken continuity. Artistic expression in Mongolian art is particularly evident in native dress. Traditionally, Mongolian Americans believe in astrology and consider certain days in the year more conducive to closing business deals, purchasing new houses or cars, and embarking on marriage. They turn to astrology on important days such as the beginning of a new job, the commencement of college, or the birth of a child. Mongolians use a lunar calendar and have adopted the Chinese zodiac with its twelve animal signs, and those customs play a significant role in Mongolian Americans' daily lives.

Mongolian Americans have brought a love of art and literature with them to their adopted country. The beautiful Mongolian landscape abounds with an ecological wonder that is expressed in song and dance and represents the varied lives on the Mongolian steppes. Many Mongolians practice Western arts, from oil painting to metal sculpture, the subjects of which are often inspired by Mongolian life and traditions. The literary arts are also popular. Early Mongolian literature consisted largely of local folk tales and traditional religious stories. *The Secret History of the Mongols*, Mongolia's most famous book, has no known author. This saga of the Mongols—which contains tales of war and feuding, myths of origin, administrative manuals

of empire, and biographies of great khans and commanders—was first compiled in 1252. Francis W. Cleaves, who published a translation of the book in 1982, states in his introduction, "*The Secret History of Mongols* is not only the capital monument of thirteenth century Mongolian literature, but it is one of the great literary monuments of the world."

Mongolians' most famous heroic epic, *Jangar*, is one of the longest known and is told among the Kalmyks. Also, the majority of people in Mongolia, and many Mongolians outside the country, know and admire the writings of the modern Mongolian authors Dashdorjiin Natsagdorj (1906–1937) and Choijil Chimid (1927–1980), especially their famous poems *Minii Nutag* (My native land) and *Bi Mongol Khun* (I am Mongolian), respectively.

Cuisine Most traditional dishes in Mongolia continue to be part of Mongolian Americans' cuisine today, although in many instances they are served only on ceremonial occasions. The most popular beverage is Mongolian tea, which is made from an infusion of tea, milk, salt, and butter. The tea is used as a ceremonial drink as well and is served at most rites. Fermented mare's milk is also a Mongolian staple, as are vodka and beer.

Mongolian and Kalmyk cuisine are very similar, but the names of the dishes vary in each culture.

A Mongolian-inspired gown is modeled. AP PHOTO / MITCH JACOBSON

Boortsog (Mongolian) or *borts'k* (Kalmyk), small cakes made of flour, water, and yeast and fried in oil, are still made in the United States but are used primarily at ceremonies and rites. *Guriltai shöl* (Mongolian) or *budan* (Kalmyk)—a stew of lamb meat or beef, water, and flour—and *bulmuk*, a gravy-like dish of broth and flour, are also still prepared. Another popular dish among Mongolian Americans is *buuz* (Mongolian) or *varenk* (Kalmyk). These are small pockets of dough, filled with meat, onion, and garlic, and steamed. Most Mongolians prefer mutton to meat in these dumplings. Similar to Buuz, *khuusuur* are dumplings filled with meat (preferably mutton), onion, and garlic but fried in oil instead of steamed. *Tarag* (Mongolian) or *chign* (Kalmyk)—fermented cow's milk—is made and drunk primarily by older people. Many believe it has therapeutic value and ensures a long life. These dietary customs are usually observed by Mongolian Americans during holidays and special events. For everyday meals, Mongols in the United States have readily adapted American food and drink.

Traditional Dress Mongolian Americans wear Western-style clothes, but on some special celebration days they wear traditional Mongolian attire. The main garment is the *deel*, a long, one-piece gown made from wool. The deel has a high collar, is often brightly colored, and comes with a multipurpose sash. Mongolians, but not untrained Westerners, can differentiate ethnic groups by the color, design, and shape of their deel. The *gutal* is a high boot made from thin leather. They are easy to fit, as both the left and right boot are the same shape. The traditional Mongolian hats are the *toortsog* and the *loovuz*. The loovuz is made from fox skins.

Dances and Songs Traditional Mongolian music involves a wide range of instruments and uses the human voice in a unique way. The *khöömii* singing of Mongolia, in which a carefully trained male voice produces a whole harmonic from deep in the throat, gives the impression of several notes coming at once from one singer. It is often performed solo but can also be combined with fiddles, lutes, zithers, drums, and other instruments made from python-skin, bamboo, metal, stone, and clay. The instrument most identified with Mongolia is arguably the horse-head fiddle, known as the *morin khuur*. It has two strings, made from horse hair, and a distinctive and decorative carving of a horse's head on top. Traditionally, the morin khuur accompanies the unique "long songs" that regale the beauty of the countryside and relive tales of nomadism. The name refers not to the length of the song itself but rather to the way that the singer draws out each syllable of the lyrics for the maximum amount of time. For example, a three-minute long song might have only six words.

Some Mongolian music, particularly instrumental music, is intended to accompany dancing. Mongolian dance includes *bujig*, which are a number of group folk dances similar to round dancing and square dancing; these might be performed by groups of men, women, or mixed couples. The most typical Mongolian dance form, however, is the *bii* or *biyelgee* (upper-body dance), which is normally performed by women. Accordingly, leg movements are restricted or entirely absent; some forms of biyelgee are performed in a sitting or kneeling position. The dance consists of intricate, rhythmic movements of the head, shoulders, arms, and upper torso; some dancers display their skill by dancing with bowls of tea or a rag balanced on their wrists, elbows, and heads. The Kalmyk American Dance Ensemble performs these traditional Mongolian dances in Howell, New Jersey.

Holidays Despite their ethnic diversity, Mongolian Americans observe several of the same major holidays. Mongolians have been celebrating *Tsagaan Sar* (White Month) for thousands of years. Now held over three days at the start of the lunar new year (at the end of January or start of February), Tsagaan Sar marks the end of winter and the start of spring. Mongolian Americans continue the tradition of gathering with family and friends for a feast and gift exchange. During this holiday people greet each other with the traditional *Zolgokh*, in which the younger person places his or her forearms under those of the elder person.

The other major Mongolian national holiday is Naadam, which is celebrated in mid-July. It is also known as Eriin Gurban Naadam, after the three "manly" sports of wrestling, archery, and horse racing. The appellation is misleading, however, as women participate in the horse racing and archery contests. After 1921 the holiday also became a celebration of Mongolian national independence. Mongolian Americans do not host a similar event in the United States, but the wealthier among them sometimes return to Mongolia to witness the competition firsthand.

Kalmyks have traditionally participated in two religious festivals. The first is Urus-Ova, which is now held for convenience on the first weekend after the start of the first month of summer to permit greater lay participation. The ceremony, which takes place at an *oboo*, or shrine, honors Shagja-muni, or the Buddha, and is celebrated annually to placate malicious spirits. The second festival is the ritual of *Zul* or *Zula* (lamp). Held during the middle of winter on the twenty-fifth day of the month of *Ukher* (cow), it marks the passing on to the next world of Tsong-kha-Pa, the great Tibetan religious reformer. Each year Mongolians gather in a public space to light sky lanterns, which resemble miniature hot air balloons, and release them into the night sky.

The Kalmyk Mongols in the United States recently have established Kalmyk Day to recognize Kalmyk Mongolian culture and history. All are invited to an exhibit with artifacts, literature, movies, and

Kalmyk song and dance performances. The inaugural Kalmyk Day festivities were held in August 2012 in Howell, New Jersey.

A Mongolian khoomii singer and musician. AP PHOTO / MICKEY KRAKOWSKI

Health Care Issues and Practices Most Mongolian Americans accept the role of modern medicine and pay careful attention to health matters. Nevertheless, the services of medical practitioners trained in traditional Tibetan medicine are often utilized in concert with Western medical science, or sometimes as a last resort. Traditional herbal remedies are still employed by some Mongolian Americans, primarily the elderly. The dietary advice, blessed water, and special prayers of Buddhist clerics are also sought. Diagnosis and treatment in traditional Mongolian medicine is based on the five vital elements of earth, water, fire, air, and space. Medicines are often made from herbs, plants, mineral water, and animal organs and are administered according to the weather, the season, and the individual's metabolism. Acupuncture, massage, and blood-letting, as well as prayers, are also important factors.

FAMILY AND COMMUNITY LIFE

Mongolian Americans' family ties are typically very strong, and more prosperous members tend to look after their less well-to-do relatives. The traditional Mongolian American household is a patriarchy, in which the head of the household is the eldest male. Mongolian women are expected to hold jobs as well as keep house and raise children, an expectation that reflects the communist influence of the Soviet Union. The children have a duty to honor their parents and respect their wishes. There are some important differences between Kalmyk and Mongolian Americans. For example, most Kalmyk parents do not approve of American dating practices, but some have started to yield to their children's demands to be allowed to date. Parents still prefer that potential mates come from within the Kalmyk American community, however. In fact, family and community members are often involved in the selection of a suitable partner, and the family and educational backgrounds of a potential suitor are thoroughly examined before introductions are made. On the other hand, Mongolian immigrants who arrived after 1990 came from a Mongolian culture that took a more liberal view of premarital relations between the sexes. Arranged marriages and scrupulously monitored courtship is not common among these immigrants.

English-language schools have become commonplace in Mongolia, as have schools teaching Korean, Japanese, and Chinese, as well as European languages. The prevalence of the English language in Mongolia has made it somewhat easier for recent immigrants to the United States to adapt to American culture.

Gender Roles Traditionally, Mongolian American women have the responsibility of preserving the memories, customs, and traditions of the Mongolian homeland. A women's first obligation is to be a good wife and to raise a family. In Kalmyk American communities girls traditionally have not been allowed as much freedom as boys and have not been encouraged to pursue their interests outside the home. Instead, they have been kept at home and taught domestic skills. Mongolian American adolescent girls, however, enjoy many of the freedoms common to most American girls. After graduating from high school young women are encouraged to pursue higher education and a career. Once they complete college and before starting a career, many Mongolian American females help with the family business. Mongolian American women typically marry between the ages of twenty-two and twenty-six. Today many Mongolian American women feel caught between worlds. They often feel obligated to conform to the standards and mores of their community, but at the same time, are pressured to "Americanize." However, many Mongolian American women still manage to pursue higher education and have careers outside the home.

Education According to the U.S. Census Bureau's 2006–2010 American Community Survey (ACS) estimates, 95 percent of Mongolian Americans had achieved a high school degree or higher and 60 percent had achieved a bachelor's degree or higher. In recent years young Mongolians have immigrated to the United States to attend American colleges or graduate schools. Afterward, many choose to apply for permanent residency or for citizenship. Young people from Kalmykia, Buryatia (southern Siberia), and Inner Mongolia have also immigrated to the United States to attend college and graduate school. Mongolian students pursue careers in medicine, business, computer sciences, biotechnology, engineering, administration, law, and social sciences, among other areas.

The successful personal adjustments and academic achievements of these students are decided by mainly two factors: language efficiency and the ability to adjust to American society. The U.S. government, the Mongol American Cultural Association, and family already settled in the United States help Mongolian students obtain scholarships and adjust to their new country.

Courtship and Weddings Accounts of Mongolians from their earliest period to the recent past contain a great deal of information regarding the institution of marriage. Even the medieval *Tsaajiin Bichig*, or "Great Code of Nomads," which has been passed down from the period of the first Oirat federation in 1640, contains, of its eight provisions, four provisions relating to the fines to be exacted when adultery is committed. Marriage, with its rites and ceremonies, provides a focal point for social interaction among Mongolians in the United States today. It involves a complex series of formal visits and gift exchanges extending over a period of time and leading up to the marriage rite and beyond. Marriage also provides a continuing focus of activity not only for the two families directly involved but also for close and distant relations, and certain events may involve an entire Mongolian American community.

In traditional Mongolian society, a man seeking a woman's hand would ask a matchmaker to send simple gifts, such as sugar or tea leaves, wrapped in a handkerchief on his behalf. In addition to these gifts, the suitor was expected to send wine three times to his intended's home. The bride's family and friends would then welcome the suitor and his family and play well-recognized tricks on the young man. They might, for example, test his strength by asking him to break a dead sheep's neck. One of the intended's friends would put an iron rod in the sheep's throat; however, the groom would typically be tipped off and make a show of removing the iron from the sheep before snapping its neck.

Although such traditions were not maintained in modern Mongol society, variations on them were. For example, through the first half of the twentieth century, the groom and his family visited and brought gifts to the intended's home after her family had accepted his proposal. Also, in older as well as modern times, the engaged couple visited a lama to seek his blessing. At the ceremony two candles were placed side-by-side, the union of the flickering flames representing the bond uniting the couple. Such Buddhists traditions disappeared from the 1950s until the fall of the Soviet Union in 1991 but gradually returned in the 1990s. Many Mongolian Americans have Western-style weddings, but they may preserve some of the Buddhist traditions, such as taking vows in the presence of lit candles that symbolize the wedding bond.

EMPLOYMENT AND ECONOMIC CONDITIONS

The vast majority of Mongols who came to the United States in the first wave of immigration were from rural backgrounds and found work as farmers, while others procured skilled and semiskilled factory jobs in various soft-goods industries and mechanical trades. Later, many found employment in the house-building trades, and it was common for Mongolian American women to work as seamstresses.

Some Mongolian Americans have opened their own businesses. The most successful Kalmyk Mongolian enterprises are in the house-building trade or are small businesses. Today Mongolian Americans are employed in a variety of professions, including about 46 percent in nonservice or nonlabor positions, according to the American Community Survey's 2006–2010 estimates. The inability of many Mongolian Americans to find jobs commensurate with their education and training has had an ongoing negative impact on all aspects of life within the Mongolian American community.

POLITICS AND GOVERNMENT

Mongolian Americans have always felt a strong attachment to Mongolia and have supported events that occur in their homeland. During the deportation period of the Kalmyk people to Siberia after World War II, the Kalmyk Committee in the United States played an important historical role. One of the leaders of this committee is the well-known Kalmyk human rights activist Djab Naminov Burchinov, who helped many Russian Kalmyks return to their native land. In 1960 and 1961 Burchinov sent several memoranda requesting Mongolia's admission to the United Nations (UN). After a fifteen-year struggle, Mongolia was finally accepted to the UN on October 27, 1961. While Burchinov's efforts proved helpful, Mongolia's admission was largely due to pressure exerted by the Soviet Union. Burchinov fought not only for the human rights of Kalmyk Mongols but also for the rights of the Tibetans and Inner Mongols. During the time of the AIDS epidemic in Kalmykia, he obtained donations from a number of large U.S. companies.

The Mongol American Cultural Association, founded in 1988 by John Gombojab Hangin (1921–1989) of Indiana University, has played an important role in Mongolian nationalism in the United States. Since 1990 Mongolian Americans have shown an increasing interest in U.S. government policy decisions concerning Mongolia. Before founding the association, Hangin published a Mongolian-language dictionary and numerous textbooks on the country. He also was among those who lobbied for Mongolia's admission to the UN.

Since the fall of the Soviet Union, the United States has supported Mongolia's democratic reforms and provides technical and humanitarian assistance. The United States views Mongolia as important because it has abundant mineral resources, has educated and motivated people, and is located between two large, emerging markets with millions of consumers. People of both countries are interested in developing trade, economic, cultural, and personal relations. Bilateral trade in 1997 reached $51 million, and both countries have granted each other most favored nation (MFN) status. The United States and Mongolia believe that there is enormous potential for developing trade and economic relations. Because the history of Mongolian Americans is so brief, there is no documentation of their participation in U.S. politics or in the voting process.

NOTABLE INDIVIDUALS

Academics John Gombojab Hangin (1921–1989) was a professor of Mongolian studies at Indiana University at the time of his death. He was a principal founder of both the Mongolia Society and the Mongol American Cultural Association. He authored *A Mongol Reader* (1956), *A Concise English-Mongolian Dictionary* (1970), and *A Modern Mongolian-English Dictionary* (1986). Jagchid Sechin (1914–2009), born in Mongolia, was a professor at Brigham Young University. He wrote *Essays in Mongolian Studies* (1988); *Mongolian Living Buddha: Biography of the Kanjurwa Khutukhtu* (1983); *Mongolian Cultural and Society* (1979); and *Peace, War, and Trade along the Great Wall: Nomadic Chinese Interaction through Two Millennia* (1989). Arash Bormanshinov (1922–2011) was the author of *Kalmyk Manual* (1961), which is considered to be the first work in English on Kalmyk Mongol written by an Kalmyk Mongolian.

Activism Djab Naminov Burchinov (1921–2010) was a well-known Kalmyk Mongol human rights activist and the author of *The Struggle for Civil Rights of the Kalmyk People* (1997). Sanj Altan (1947–) is a Mongolian American cultural activist. Lee Urubshurow is a Kalmyk Mongolian cultural activist; she was a principal founder of the Kalmyk American Cultural Association and the Kalmyk American Dance Ensemble.

Sports Vyambajav Ulambayar (1984–) may be the best-known Mongolian American athlete in the world. He won the Sumo World Championship in 2006 and again in 2007. He appeared in the blockbuster movie *Ocean's 13* in 2007 and was featured in a commercial for Subaru automobiles.

MEDIA

The popularity of the Internet and online access to newspapers, radio, television programming, and Mongolian-language websites has provided Mongolian Americans with 24/7 access to all forms of Mongolian and Mongolian American media.

ORGANIZATIONS AND ASSOCIATIONS

The Mongol Tolbo Newsletter

In 1993 the Mongol American Cultural Association began publishing its quarterly newsletter, *Mongol Tolbo*. It provides commentary and analysis on the subject of the Mongol culture and offers news of the economic, political, and social development of northern and southern Mongolia, Tuva, Xinjiang, Buryatia, and Kalmykia. The printed version has been replaced with an electronic version, *eTolbo*.

Chinggeltu Borjiged, Editor
Mongol American Cultural Association
50 Louis Street
New Brunswick, New Jersey 08901
Phone: (732) 297-1140
Email: maca@maca-usa.org
URL: www.maca-usa.org/eTolbo.html

Asian American Heritage Council of New Jersey

An organization that works to assist and integrate Asian culture in the state of New Jersey.

Shashi K. Agarwal, President
290 Central Avenue
Orange, New Jersey 07050-3414
Phone: (973) 676-1234
Fax: (973) 676-5858

Kalmyk American Cultural Association

This organization was formed for the purpose of planning the celebration of the fiftieth anniversary of the first Kalmyks' arrival in the United States.

P.O. Box 24272
Philadelphia, Pennsylvania 19120
Phone: (732) 364-4304
Fax: (215) 924-2201
URL: www.kalmykamericansociety.org

Mongol American Cultural Association

Serves as the central point of networking for all Mongolian tribes residing in the United States. The goal of the association is to promote cultural exchange between all of the Mongolian ethnic groups, Khalkha, Buryats, Kalmyks, and Inner Mongols. It also provides support to Mongolian youth; scholarships to students; and aid to the poor, homeless, and handicapped.

Dr. Sanj Atlan, President
50 Louis Street
New Brunswick, New Jersey 08901
Phone: (732) 297-1140
Email: maca@maca-usa.org
URL: www.maca-usa.org

Mongolia Society

The Mongolia Society has several hundred members and is concerned with presenting information dealing with the history and culture of this area of Inner Asia. The society issues four publications devoted to Mongolian topics: *Mongolian Studies: Journal of the Mongolia Society* and *Mongol Survey*, which appear every year, and *Occasional Papers* and *Special Papers*, which consist, respectively, of scholarly articles and reproductions of rare works in Mongolian and are published sporadically. The society is the only importer of Mongolian books in the United States. It also sells Mongolian dictionaries and a wide variety of items that pertain to Mongolia.

Alicia Campi, President
322 Goodbody Hall
Indiana University
Bloomington, Indiana 47405
Phone: (812) 855-4078
Fax: (812) 855-4078
Email: monsoc@indiana.edu
URL: www.mongoliasociety.org

North America–Mongolia Business Council

An international trade association founded in 1990 that supports bilateral trade and investment between American and Canadian businesses and Mongolia.

Edward T. Story, Chairman of the Board
1015 Duke Street
Alexandria, Virginia 22314-3551
Phone: (703) 549-8444
Fax: (703) 549-6526
Email: HQinfo@nambc.org
URL: www.nambc.org

SOURCES FOR ADDITIONAL STUDY

Burchinov, Djab Naminov. *The Struggle for Civil Rights of the Kalmyk People*. Moscow: Elista Press, 1997.

Guchinova, Elza-Bair. *The Kalmyks*. Translated by David C. Lewis. Abingdon: Routledge, 2006.

Keevak, Michael. *Becoming Yellow: A Short History of Racial Thinking*. Princeton, NJ: Princeton University Press, 2011.

Kotkin, Stephen, and Bruce A. Elleman, eds. *Mongolia in the Twentieth Century: Landlocked Cosmopolitan*. New York: M. E. Sharpe, 2000.

Major, John S. *The Land and People of Mongolia*. New York: J. B. Lippincott Press, 1990.

Rossabi, Morris. *Modern Mongolia: From Khans to Commissars to Capitalists*. Berkeley: University of California Press, 2005.

Trinh, Linda Võ. *Mobilizing an Asian American Community*. Philadelphia: Temple University Press, 2004.

Tweed, Thomas A., and Stephen R. Prothero, eds. *Asian Religions in America: A Documentary History*. New York: Oxford University Press, 1999.

Woo, Deborah. *Glass Ceilings and Asian Americans: The New Face of Workplace Barriers*. Walnut Creek: AltaMira Press, 2000.

MORMONS

Jessie L. Embry

OVERVIEW

Mormons are members of the Church of Jesus Christ of Latter-day Saints (LDS Church), based in Salt Lake City, Utah, and smaller, related groups. Unlike members of other Protestant churches, they view their founder, Joseph Smith, who established the LDS Church in 1830 in upstate New York, and his successors as prophets. They also accept the Book of Mormon, which Smith produced, as a sacred text along with the Bible. In the early twenty-first century about half of all Mormons lived in the United States, mostly in Utah and elsewhere in the West. The church also had a large number of followers in Latin America.

Scholars disagree about whether Mormons can be considered an ethnic group. For example, using survey results from the late twentieth century, sociologist Armand Mauss argues that Mormons are typical Americans. Anthropologist Keith Parry, however, contends that Mormons have a distinctive lifestyle and language that set them apart from the rest of American culture. Much of the group's identity comes from church doctrine as recorded in the Book of Mormon, which presents the United States as a land of promise where Christ's church can be restored before his second coming. As historian Dean May explains, "The Mormons have been influenced subsequently by ritual tales of privation, wandering, and delivery under God's hand, precisely as the Jews have been influenced by their stories of the Exodus. A significant consequence of this tradition has been the development of an enduring sense of territoriality that has given a distinctive cast to Mormon group consciousness."

When the LDS Church was founded in 1830, the culture of upstate New York resembled the frontier life of the American West. The area came to be known as the "burned-over district," as it was a popular site for fiery religious revivals, which helped increase membership in many Christian churches. Because of the Mormons' unorthodox views, including their support of polygamy, the church faced hostility and violence from its critics. Smith and his followers moved to Kirkland, Ohio, and then to Missouri and Illinois. After Smith was killed by a mob in 1844, most Mormons followed Smith's successor, Brigham Young, to the Great Basin of Nevada and Utah. Since 1848 the headquarters have been in Salt Lake City.

During the nineteenth century, church leaders encouraged converts from the United States and other countries, mainly the British Isles and Northern Europe, to immigrate to Utah and the surrounding areas. Initially most of the immigrants were farmers, although some worked as miners and merchants. Mormons gained greater acceptance in American life in the late nineteenth century, after the church renounced the practice of polygamy.

In 2013 the LDS Church claimed to have a worldwide membership of fifteen million, with approximately seven million living in the United States. Since the mid-nineteenth century the church has dominated the economic, social, and religious life of Utah. Over 60 percent of the state's population is Mormon, and in Utah County, which includes the city of Provo and church run Brigham Young University (BYU), over 80 percent of the residents are Mormon.

HISTORY OF THE PEOPLE

Early History The founder of the Mormon church in the United States, Joseph Smith Jr., was the third son of a New England farming family. When he was a teenager he attended a religious revival where his family lived in upstate New York. Confused by the different religions, Smith prayed for direction in 1820, and over the next few years he recorded several personal revelations. He organized his first church on April 6, 1830. Members accepted him as a prophet who could speak the will of the Lord. As the church grew and developed, he received additional revelations that are recorded in a Mormon book of scripture, the Doctrine and Covenants.

From his New York base, Smith sent his followers out to seek converts. After a number of people joined in Ohio, the church in 1831 moved its headquarters to Kirtland, a town located south of Cleveland, Ohio. The church built its first temple there. Smith later received a revelation that the Mormons were to move to Jackson County, Missouri, to establish "Zion," a "New Jerusalem" to prepare for the millennium—the return of the Savior who would usher in a thousand-year reign of peace. Mormons started to gather there—but tension arose between the Mormons, who opposed slavery, and slaveholding immigrants from Tennessee and Kentucky. Then the Mormons moved

Mormons travel in a caravan of covered wagons, c.1879. NATIONAL ARCHIVES AND RECORDS ADMINISTRATION

to Illinois and settled on undeveloped land along the Mississippi River, where they built a city they named Nauvoo. The Mormons received a liberal charter from the state that allowed them to have their own militia and courts. From there Smith continued to send out missionaries. Those dispatched to England were very successful, and soon immigrants from that country and Canada, as well as converts from other areas of the United States, arrived and helped establish what became the second-largest city in Illinois. The Saints again started to build a temple.

One of Smith's revelations, plural marriage, caused special problems for the Mormons. Historians do not know when Smith received this revelation; there is some evidence that he married his first plural wife, Fanny Alger, in 1831. He did not write down the revelation until 1843, when he attempted to convince his first wife, Emma Hales Smith, of the principle. Although Smith and some of his closest followers practiced polygamy in Nauvoo, the church did not publicly announce the doctrine until 1852, after the Mormons moved to Utah. Some Mormons who knew of the doctrine opposed the practice, and in June 1844 they published a newspaper expressing their views of Smith as a fallen prophet. Using the powers granted by Nauvoo's charter, Smith destroyed not only the newspaper but also the press. The state then arrested him for treason. As Smith, his brother Hyrum, and other church leaders were held in jail awaiting trial, a mob broke into the jail and killed Joseph and Hyrum Smith on June 27, 1844.

Following Smith's death, most of his followers placed their trust in Brigham Young (1801–1877), the president of the Quorum of Twelve Apostles. Some Mormons reported that when Young spoke to them, he sounded like Smith. These people saw this as a heavenly manifestation that Young was to be the next leader, and he eventually became church president. Young led the work to complete the temple in Nauvoo and continued to give the members the ordinances he learned from Smith.

Problems between the Mormons and the local residents continued, and by February 1846 the Mormons had begun to leave Illinois, heading first for Nebraska and then to Salt Lake Valley. Isolated from the rest of the nation, Young and the Mormons set out to establish "Zion in the tops of the mountains," following Smith's visions. He planned Salt Lake City and other communities using Smith's Plat of Zion, a grid system. Young encouraged the Mormons to be self-sufficient, created an independent commonwealth, and sent settlers to southern Utah, where they attempted to raise cotton and manufacture iron so they would not have to depend on outsiders for these goods. He asked communities to live the "United Order," wherein people shared resources. Communities had varying success for several years, but eventually most communal attempts failed because the majority of Mormons supported the American ideal of free enterprise. The Mormons completed the first temple in the area in St. George, Utah, in 1877. The Salt Lake Temple, which has become a symbol of Mormonism, took forty years—from ground-breaking to dedication—to complete. It was dedicated on April 6, 1893.

Young also announced for the first time publicly that the church endorsed plural marriage. In 1852 Apostle Orson Pratt delivered a discourse on the virtues of plural marriage. While church members now knew the church sanctioned polygamy, most of the Latter-day Saints did not practice it. The practice of polygamy varied by community, apparently based on how strongly local leaders encouraged it. Current research suggests that around 20 percent of the Mormons belonged to plural families.

Because of the Mormons' practice of polygamy and their political and economic isolation, many Americans questioned their loyalty to the nation. In 1857 the U.S. government sent an army to Utah with a federal appointee, Alfred Cumming of Georgia, to replace Young as governor of the territory. In 1862 and in the 1880s, Congress passed legislation outlawing polygamy and giving the government control of territorial courts and policies. In 1890 church president Wilford Woodruff issued a manifesto (now referred to as the 1890 Manifesto) stating that the church would no longer practice polygamy. In 1904 church president Joseph F. Smith presented a second manifesto that rebuked those who continued to practice polygamy or perform plural marriages.

Modern Era With the ending of polygamy and the establishment in 1896 of Utah as a state, the Mormon church began its modern era. Besides abandoning plural marriage, which was required for statehood, the church put less focus on communalism and switched to a capitalist economy. Mormons no longer belonged to a church political party and became members of the Democratic and Republican parties.

Throughout the twentieth century, Mormons gradually fit into the American mainstream. Utahans volunteered to fight in the Spanish American War and World War I. They experienced an economic depression before the rest of the nation did in the 1930s because their economy was based on agricultural and mining industries, which did very well during World War I, when some worldwide markets were not available, but dried up after the war. While Mormons supported Republicans prior to the 1930s, they favored Franklin D. Roosevelt's New Deal even when church leaders questioned its socialist leanings. Mormons supported the United States during the Korean and Vietnam wars as well as other conflicts in the late twentieth and early twenty-first centuries. Historian Jan Shipps has described Mormonism of the latter half of the twentieth century as "the *Reader's Digest* church" because members seemed to fit the American ideal.

Scholars have referred to the early twenty-first century as the "Mormon moment." It started with a focus on the church during the Salt Lake City Winter Olympics in 2002, which led reporters and visitors to learn more about the religion's beliefs and practices. The moment continued when a Mormon, Mitt Romney—head of the Salt Lake City Olympics and governor of Massachusetts from 2003 through 2006—tried unsuccessfully for the Republican presidential nomination in 2008 but earned it in his next bid in 2012 before losing to Barack Obama in the general election. Additionally, Mormons have used social media to introduce people to the church through the "I am a Mormon" campaign.

The Mormon moment has also made a difference in the study of the church. In the 1980s Mormon leaders discouraged students from writing the church's history except from the vantage point of the faithful. The Church History Division was transferred to Brigham Young University in 1982 and became the Joseph Fielding Smith Institute for Church History. One possible reason was to avoid having scholars' work seen as the official church history. In 1993 several scholars were excommunicated because their research and writing were not approved by church leaders. In the early twentieth century, however, the Smith Institute started a Joseph Smith Papers project. That project was transferred back to the Church History Library, and with a change of church historians, the Mormon leadership now seemed more interested in history. In addition, non-Mormon universities have encouraged students to write on LDS history, and Utah State University, Claremont Graduate School, and the University of Virginia have added Mormon studies to their curriculum and created endowed chairs and centers.

Evangelical and other churches have often raised the question of whether Mormons are a sect rather than a Christian religion. During the twenty-first century, however, the beliefs of Mormons have aligned with those of conservative Christians, and the two groups have sometimes found common ground.

A Mormon family in Utah, 1875. © BETTMANN / CORBIS

SETTLEMENT IN THE UNITED STATES

As Mormons arrived in Utah's Great Basin in the mid-1800s, Brigham Young sent them throughout the West. Although some colonies were short-lived, Mormon communities extended from southern Idaho to San Bernardino, California. During the years when the federal government arrested polygamists, Mormons also moved into northern Mexico and southern Alberta, Canada. Young and the presidents who followed him also sent missionaries throughout the United States and northern Europe. The church encouraged the new converts to "gather to Zion." Church-sponsored ships carried immigrants across the Atlantic Ocean. Once in the United States, converts traveled by rail as far as possible and then continued by wagon. Some groups that could not afford wagons pulled two-wheeled handcarts. The church established an endowment, the Perpetual Emigrating Fund, to help the new arrivals.

Those already in Utah understood the desire of the newcomers to be in Zion and felt a religious obligation to accept and love their brothers and sisters in the gospel. With all groups working together, European immigrants often married out of their cultural groups. So while Salt Lake City's foreign-born population during the 1880s ran as high as 80 percent, there were very few conflicts. Mormon immigrants assimilated into the mainstream of Mormonism's unique culture in one generation.

Since the 1920s, Mormon leaders have encouraged members worldwide to practice the religion in their own countries rather than immigrate to the United States. However, immigrants continue to come from throughout the world to the church headquarters. During the late twentieth and early twenty-first centuries, many came from Latin America and Mexico. While the northern European immigrants assimilated in one generation, these new members have maintained their language and much of their cultural identity. The Mormon church has tried various approaches to help these members, including establishing separate congregations, integrating them into existing congregations without translation support, and facilitating partial integration to allow them to "fuse" their culture with the Mormon lifestyle. In the 1960s, for example, church president Spencer W. Kimball (1895–1985) actively organized Indian congregations (generally called Lamanite branches), and congregations of other ethnic groups, including a Chinese branch and a German-speaking ward in Salt Lake City, were also formed. In the early 1970s, church leaders again questioned the utility of sponsoring separate branches and urged the integration of ethnic members into the church. However, before the end of the decade, the church's Basic Unit Program encouraged ethnic branches again. In practice the church's policy has vacillated because neither ethnic branches nor integrated wards have met the needs of all church members. Language and cultural barriers often weaken the ties of religion, and questions about how to resolve these issues still face the Mormon leadership.

One major problem facing the Mormon church is the growing diversity of its membership, both worldwide and in American ethnic communities. Church leaders must contend with the dilemma of separating gospel values from the American secular traditions that have been interwoven into Mormon culture. Before the priesthood revelation, a policy prior to 1978 that blacks could not be ordained to the lay priesthood, there was an informal rule in many missions that they should not recruit African Americans. As a result, only a limited number of African Americans joined. After 1978, however, missionaries actively ministered among blacks, and increasing numbers of African Americans continue to become part of the religion. Hispanic Americans and Asian Americans are also becoming members. In addition, Polynesian Americans who joined the church in the islands have been immigrating to the United States and bringing extended family members with them; not all are Mormons, but some have joined after arriving. The church has also continued its efforts, although on a lesser scale, to convert Native Americans.

LANGUAGE

Traditionally, the church encouraged immigrant church members to assimilate as quickly as possible. They learned English and the Mormon way of life. Brigham Young proposed an alphabet that spelled English phonetically. Although it was never adopted, the alphabet demonstrated the church's attempt to help newcomers. European immigrants were allowed at first to attend congregations speaking their native languages but were encouraged also to attend the congregation in which they lived, which usually spoke English. In 1903, when a disagreement developed over the celebration of a Swedish holiday, a group of church leaders known as the First Presidency emphasized,

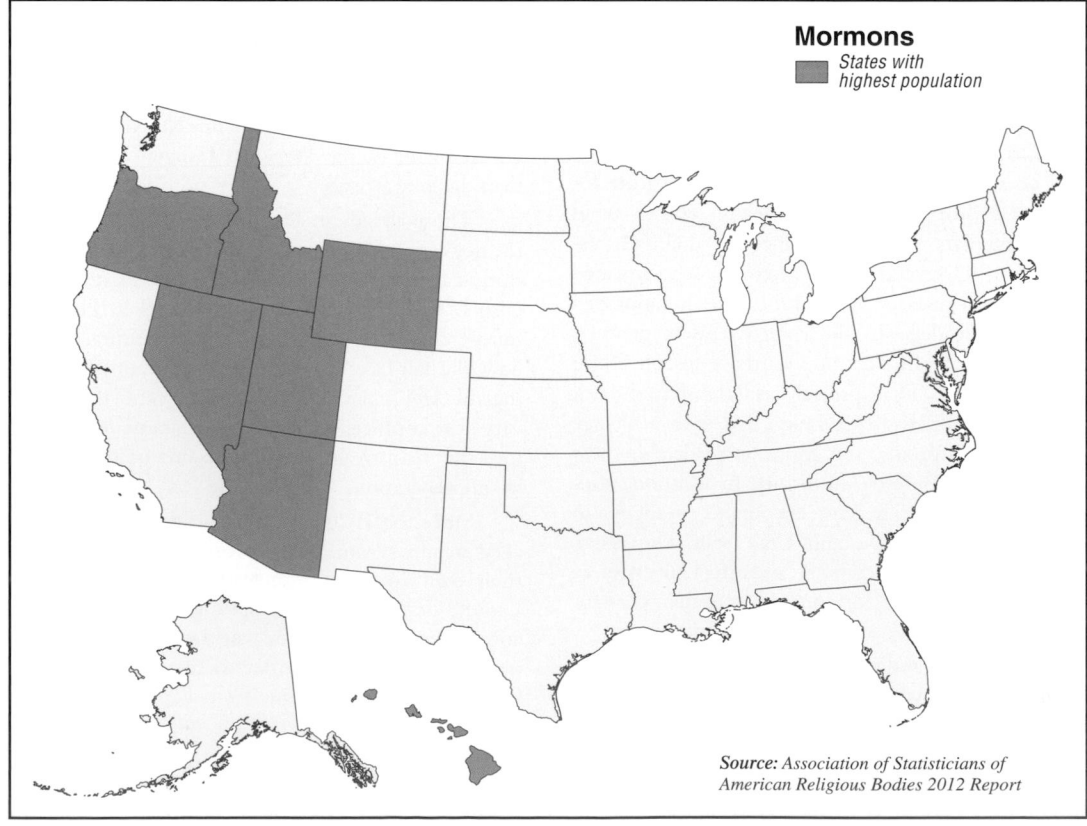

Mormons
States with highest population

Source: Association of Statisticians of American Religious Bodies 2012 Report

The counsel of the church to all Saints of foreign birth who come here is that they should learn to speak English when possible, adopt the manners and customs of the American people, fit themselves to become good and loyal citizens of this country, and by their good works show that they are true and faithful Latter-day Saints.

RELIGION

Although Mormons are found throughout the world, the church is thoroughly American. This is true especially of its leadership. While the church has appointed local leaders to represent its worldwide membership, the most influential, the First Presidency and the Quorum of Twelve, have always been white males. In 2013 these leaders were not American-born, however. Members of the Quorums of Seventy are also General Authorities in the church and are presided over by the Seven Presidents of the Seventy. Initially the First Quorum's members were considered lifetime appointments, but they now become emeritus at a designated age. More of the Seventies are being called from the international membership as the church has grown and more leaders have been trained. Most Apostles have come up through the ranks of other church leadership, and the president of the Church is always the Apostle who has been a member of the Quorum the longest. There is no possibility that a woman can be ordained to the priesthood or become a church leader.

Mormons attend geographically structured congregations known as wards. In Utah a ward might include only a few blocks; in other areas it might encompass an entire middle-sized or metropolitan city. In Utah boundaries frequently split neighborhoods, and there is very little contact among Mormons outside assigned wards. Wards support religious and social life by sponsoring athletic events, parties, and other activities for all age groups. Five to six wards form a unit known as a stake, which is similar to a diocese.

As the Mormons gave up such distinctive practices as polygamy and the United Orders, the responsibility of "boundary maintenance" shifted from the church to the individual. According to historian Jan Shipps, "The LDS dietary, behavior, and dress codes" are now important boundary markers, while correspondingly, "worship activity … seems almost mandatory" (*Mormonism: The Story of a New Religious Tradition*, 1985).

The importance of attending worship services is reflected in contemporary Mormon church statistics. While the general trend among Christians in the United States is toward less frequent church attendance, Mormon figures have remained the same. More educated Mormons attend church with greater frequency, which is the reverse of the national trend. On Sundays Mormons attend a three-hour block of meetings that includes a general worship service—known as the sacrament meeting—for everyone. Adults and teenagers attend Sunday school classes, and males and females then split. Women attend Relief Society (a

In this 2013 photo, Mormon missionaries walk through the halls at the Missionary Training Center in Provo, Utah. RICK BOWMER / AP IMAGES

Mormon charitable program), and men go to a priesthood meeting; teenage girls attend Young Women (a program devoted to the spiritual development of females), and teenage boys take part in priesthood classes. Children between the ages of three and twelve go to Primary (religious instruction). A nursery serves children between eighteen months and three years of age. The church used to scatter these meetings throughout the week, but starting in 1981, they were consolidated into a Sunday block. Church leaders hoped this would not only cut down travel times—thereby providing relief from the gasoline shortage that had hit in the late 1970s—but also allow families more of a chance to be together.

Mormons develop a sense of community by working together in the wards. The only paid full-time clergy in the church are the General Authorities. Ward and stake leaders accept positions to serve as bishop (similar to a pastor or priest), stake president (similar to a bishop in the Catholic church), and staff for other church organizations. In his extensive study *The Mormons* (1957), Catholic sociologist Thomas F. O'Dea observes that the church's lay ministry means "the church has provided a job for everyone to do and, perhaps more important, has provided a formal context in which it is to be done. The result is a wide distribution of activity, responsibility, and prestige." O'Dea explains that the lay structure has historical roots. Mormonism, he writes, came into being

> when lay responsibility in church government was widespread and developed in circumstances that demanded lay participation for the survival of the group and the carrying-out of the program. … If western conditions caused … established churches to make use of laymen, a new and struggling religious movement had all the more reason to do so, and no inhibiting traditions.

For decades the church has emphasized family worship, including family scripture reading and weekly family meetings (now called family home evenings). The practice of family gatherings started in the Granite Stake in the Salt Lake Valley in 1909. Church leaders instructed families to set aside time to learn the gospel, participate in activities, sing songs, read the scriptures together, play games, and enjoy refreshments. Six years later, in 1915, the First Presidency of the church announced its official endorsement of the church program. It asked "presidents of stakes and bishops throughout the church [to] set aside one evening each month for a 'Home Evening'" during which "fathers and mothers may gather their boys and girls about them in the home and teach them the word of the Lord." The church formalized the program in 1965 as the "family home evening" program. General church leaders encouraged local leaders to set aside Monday for the weekly meeting, prohibiting ward or stake meetings that night, and they provided lesson and activity manuals to assist families in their time together.

Mormons are more involved in personal religious practices than most Americans. Sociologists Tim Heaton, Stephen Bahr, and Cardell Jacobson conducted a study in 2005 in which 75 percent of Mormons surveyed said they attended church at least once a week, while only 39 percent of Americans surveyed nationwide reported attending religious services weekly. According to the work of these sociologists, most Mormons pray several times per day (66 percent versus 39 percent of Americans in general), and they frequently do so in groups, often as families (64 percent compared to 23 percent of Americans in general). In addition, more Mormons read scripture outside of church than the rest of Americans (76 percent versus 35 percent).

CULTURE AND ASSIMILATION

During the nineteenth century, Mormons were often viewed as the "other" by most Americans, particularly because of their practice of polygamy. After the 1890 Manifesto disavowing plural marriage and the establishment of Utah as a state in 1896, Mormons focused on meshing with the American model. When converts came to the United States from other areas of the world, they were encouraged to adapt to the American culture and to assimilate with fellow church members. While there are some beliefs and practices that are unique to Mormons, they are, for the most part, indistinguishable from other Americans.

Traditions and Customs Mormons have largely adapted to American society and share many of the same traditions and customs. One unique gathering, however, is the semi-annual General Conference, usually held in April and October, when members from all over the world gather in Salt Lake City to hear the church leaders speak. The conference used to be a three-day event and always started on April 6, the date of the church's founding. Now the meetings are

on Saturday and Sunday, with a two-hour session in the morning and another in the afternoon each day and a special priesthood session on Saturday night for men. (The church-owned bookstore Deseret Book sponsors a "girls' night out" during the priesthood session.) In Utah members have been able to gather around their televisions to watch the conference if they do not attend it in person; in other areas the church used to depend on public-service TV time, but later the conference became available on the Internet and over church-owned stations such as BYU-TV.

Cuisine Mormons joke about having unique cuisine, but their foods are often the same as those that are eaten throughout the United States. Green Jell-O is often cited as a Mormon favorite. In recent years "funeral potatoes," a cheesy potato casserole, have been served at not only funerals but also at ward parties.

Traditional Dress Most Mormons dress like other Americans. There is, however, a focus on modesty; for example, women who have been to the temple and received their endowment do not wear sleeveless tops and dresses or shorts above the knees. Men and women traditionally wear their best clothes to church. Women always wear dresses or skirts, and men are clad in suits or at least ties. For some men, it is important to wear a white shirt. Some breakoff groups, such as the Fundamentalist Church of Jesus Christ of Latter-day Saints, wear pioneer-style dress. Some Americans mistake them for members of the LDS Church.

Traditional Arts and Crafts In the past, Mormon women frequently sewed their own clothes, but with the increased costs of patterns and materials, this is now less the case. Women still, however, often quilt. In the 1960s and 1970s, many Utah and other Mormon women made glass grape decorations.

Dances and Songs Mormons have always enjoyed dancing. Church leader Brigham Young grew up in a non-dancing tradition, but he believed that dancing was a good form of recreation. In the nineteenth century, Latter-day Saints frequently held dances. During a beehive period from the 1930s to 1960s when the church sponsored many social events, local congregations held balls each year. As part of a training program for adults who work with teenagers, known as June Conference, an all-church dance festival took place until 1971.

Singing and music are important parts of the Mormon worship service, which always features an opening hymn, a sacrament hymn to prepare for communion, and a closing hymn. Often between speakers (members asked to prepare a talk for the meeting), there is a song (referred to as a rest hymn) or a special musical number.

Holidays Generally, American Mormons observe national holidays. They also celebrate July 24, Pioneer Day, in honor of the day Brigham Young entered the Salt Lake Valley in 1847. This is a state holiday in Utah,

Mormon cast members gather for the 75th annual Hill Cumurah Pageant. ZUMA PRESS, INC. / ALAMY

and residents celebrate with parades and fireworks. Mormons in other areas of the United States celebrate Pioneer Day on a smaller scale.

There are no special celebrations during Lent or holy week, but a special program takes place on Easter Sunday, as Mormons emphasize the resurrected Christ but not the cross. Christmas is usually a family celebration. While Halloween is not a religious holiday, local congregations might have a Halloween party; members often decorate the trunks of their cars, and children go from car to car for treats (referred to as "trunk or treat").

Death and Burial Rituals Mormon families plan funerals with the assistance of church leaders. Occasionally in funeral-service sermons, leaders ask members to focus on the purpose of life, but there is not set format. Mormons often have a viewing before the funeral during which people can meet and comfort the family. The coffin is usually open to allow friends and family to say a last goodbye. Before the funeral, the family has a prayer together that is usually given by a senior priesthood member. After the funeral, the family goes to the grave site, where a priesthood holder will dedicate the grave. Members who have been through the temple are buried in special temple robes.

Health Care Issues and Practices Mormons consider the Word of Wisdom, a revelation received by Joseph Smith, to be a commandment from God. According to Mormon tradition, in 1833 Emma Smith questioned male church leaders who were using chewing tobacco and spitting in her home. As a result, Joseph Smith asked the Lord for guidance and received Section 89 of the Doctrine and Covenants. It cautions against "wine and strong drinks," tobacco, and "hot drinks." It also says meat should be "used sparingly" and urges the use of grains, especially "wheat for man," and herbs. When the revelation was first received, the church considered it only advice; violation did not restrict church membership. During the 1890s, however, church leaders started placing more emphasis on the Word of Wisdom, leading the prohibition fight in Utah. In 1921 church president Heber J. Grant made obeying the Word of Wisdom a requirement to enter the temple. The church interprets the revelation to forbid coffee, tea, tobacco, and alcohol, but it does not stress other elements of the teaching, including guidelines about the use of meat and grains.

Strict adherence to the Word of Wisdom has led to greater health among Mormons. Studies have found that Mormons in Utah have fewer cases of diseases, especially cancers, most likely because they do not use tobacco or alcohol. One study declared that Mormons showed that one-third of the cancers in the United States could be prevented by avoiding these substances. Mormons have also aided cancer research through their high birth rates and the keeping of genealogical records. University of Utah professors have encoded this information and identified high-risk cancer patients. In addition, information provided by the Mormons helped lead to the identification of a gene that frequently occurs in colon cancer patients.

Nineteenth-century Mormon health practices and problems were similar to those of other Americans at the time. Mormons suffered a high rate of infant mortality and death from infectious diseases. A mistrust of the medical profession was common among Mormons. Some early Mormons believed in herbal treatments, and many practiced faith healing. Leaders encouraged members to depend more on the power of God than on doctors. In the church's early days, men and women gave blessings as a way of healing. Usually women blessed other women at the time of childbirth; now, though, the church only authorizes men holding the priesthood to give blessings.

Mormons believe all people existed as spirits before they were born and that to progress they needed to come to this earth to receive a body and to be tested. Many believe that the spirits on the other side need to be provided with bodies. For that reason, the church discourages birth control and suggests that Mormons have large families; Latter-day Saints have families larger than the U.S. average. Mormon church leaders also speak against abortion, as ending a pregnancy is viewed as "one of the most … sinful practices of this day." The only allowable exceptions are where "incest or rape was involved, or where competent medical authorities certify that the life of the mother is in jeopardy, or that a severely defective fetus cannot survive birth."

Mormon health practices have been modified over the years, partially in response to changes in American views. After the Mormons moved to Utah, Brigham Young encouraged members to go to doctors for medical treatment, a suggestion that slightly preceded the general American shift to greater support of the medical profession. Young asked second-generation Mormons to return to the East Coast to study medicine, and men and women responded. While leaders still stressed faith healing, they also encouraged members to seek the assistance of secular medicine.

Around the turn of the twentieth century, Mormons participated in public health programs that were popular throughout the United States. Church leaders encouraged voluntary vaccination programs and supported quarantines. The women's organization the Relief Society sponsored maternal and child health programs, and it also held milk clinics and organized "Swat the Fly" campaigns. Women worked closely with the state government to implement the services

Congress provided through the 1921 Sheppherd-Towner Maternity and Infancy Protection Act. Under this law, the stake Relief Society in Cottonwood, Utah, opened a maternity hospital, and other church groups provided layettes and promoted pregnancy and well-baby care.

The Mormon church also sponsored hospitals in Utah to provide assistance to the sick. The Relief Society started the Deseret Hospital in 1882, and when that hospital closed ten years later, members worked to raise money for the W. H. Grover Latter-day Saint Hospital, which opened in 1905. The Mormon church owned and operated hospitals in Utah and Idaho until the 1980s, when its leaders turned them over to a newly created private institution, the Intermountain Health Corporation.

While blessings at the time of illness continue to this day, Mormon leaders recommend that members seek medical advice. Physician and historian Lester Bush concludes in *Health and Medicine Among the Mormons: Science, Sense, and Scripture* (1993), "With regard to most aspects of medical practice, Mormons are indeed no longer a 'peculiar people.'"

FAMILY AND COMMUNITY LIFE

Mormons believe strongly in a traditional family structure. The 1995 book *The Family: A Proclamation to the World* describes men as the breadwinners and women as the nurturers. Mormons believe that family units will continue for eternity, and they stress improving those relationships. The church's role is to be a source of support to the family. At the same time, church leaders encourage members to be involved in neighborhoods, cities and towns, the nation, and the world. Mormons see all people as children of God and feel a need to assist them whenever possible.

Gender Roles Traditional Mormon gender roles have changed along with overall American values. Nevertheless, there are differences in the training of boys and girls among Mormons. Boys receive the priesthood when they are twelve years old and progress through priesthood offices, and church leaders ask all males to serve a two-year mission when they turn eighteen. They receive the "temple endowment" before leaving on their missions. Females, who had always been allowed but not encouraged to go on missions, can embark on this service when they turn nineteen, and they, too, receive the temple ordinances before they leave. Most women attend the temple for the first time just before their marriages. In marriage, a woman is sealed to her husband, and the church teaches that the man, the priesthood holder, is the head of the home. The church discourages women from working outside the home; while many do work, studies show that they are likely to have part-time jobs.

Despite this relatively conservative stance toward women, Utah was the second state (after Wyoming) to give them the right to vote, in 1896.

Some Mormon women were active in the national suffrage movements. Women, especially those involved in suffrage, were also known to become active in political parties. Historically, Mormon women have been involved mostly in community health, social welfare, and adoption programs, most notably the Relief Society.

In the late twentieth century, women were afforded more opportunities to participate in church meetings. Before the 1970s, men who were priesthood holders gave the prayers in worship services, but that policy was changed so that women could pray. Women auxiliary leaders also began to speak at the church's semiannual General Conference and served on boards. In the twenty-first century, local congregations are encouraged to include women in decision making as part of a congregational (ward) council.

Education Mormons place a high value on education. Joseph Smith founded the School of the Prophets and stressed the importance of learning, and Mormon scripture encourages members to "seek learning even by study and also by faith." Once the Mormons arrived in Utah, they established and sponsored the first schools on all levels in the state. Formal statehood brought public education, and gradually the church closed or transferred to the state most of its high schools (or academies). Weber State University in Ogden, Snow College in Ephraim, and Dixie College in St. George are examples of state-sponsored institutions that were first established as Mormon academies. The church did not abandon all of its educational facilities, however. It still sponsors Brigham Young University, a four-year college with a large campus in Provo, Utah, as well as a smaller campus in Laie, Hawaii. In 2001 church leaders announced that a two-year junior college in Rexburg, Idaho, would become a four-year university known as BYU-Idaho. The church continues to operate LDS Business College in Salt Lake City, as well as high schools and smaller colleges throughout the world in areas with limited public education.

With the closing of its academies, the church feared the loss of religious instruction. To provide the spiritual training other than that provided at Sunday activities, it established seminaries at high schools and institutes at universities. The first seminary was established at Granite High School in Salt Lake City in 1912; the first institute was created at the University of Idaho in Moscow in 1926.

The Mormons' emphasis on education has led to a learned Mormon populace in the United States. Using general religious surveys, sociologists Tim B. Heaton and Cardell Jacobson found that Mormons have more education, by about year, than the U.S. population as a whole. This has been true since the 1970s.

Courtship and Weddings Church policy discourages anyone from dating until the age of sixteen

SPORTS AND MORMONISM

Brigham Young once explained there should be eight hours for work, eight hours for play, and eight hours for sleep each day. In keeping with this notion, he had a gym in his home. During the progressive era from 1890 to 1920, Mormons enticed young men to remain in church through what some historians have called "muscular Christianity." Mormons started playing basketball soon after the game was invented in the late 1800s, and their cultural halls often have basketball hoops. From 1923 to 1971, a church-sponsored basketball tournament took place. For a number of years after World War II, the church also staged volleyball and softball tournaments. Mormons continue to focus on recreational activity as a means for promoting health and family togetherness.

and no serious dating for males until after they serve their two-year mission. Leaders also stress that young people should marry other Mormons within their own racial group. An issue of *Church News* announcing the change in policy toward blacks holding the priesthood in 1978 includes an article restating the church's opposition to interracial marriages. The article points out that marriage, which is difficult in the first place, becomes more of a challenge when the partners come from different backgrounds.

Mormon women marry at a slightly younger average age (twenty-three) than other American women, while men marry at about the national average (twenty-six). The church teaches that sexual intercourse outside marriage is a sin. Thus, most Mormons marry rather than cohabit. According to studies by Mormon sociologists Tim Heaton, Stephen Bahr, and Cardell Jacobson using the Mormons listed on general religious surveys, Mormons are 1.77 times more likely to be married than other Americans. In one survey, 71 percent of LDS members sampled were married (the second-highest percentage of any religious group in the United States). As divorce has become more acceptable in the United States, more Mormons are separating. However, the sample showed only 9 percent were divorced or separated. The number of divorced Mormons has remained lower than the national average and has leveled off in the last decade. Divorce is even less likely among educated Mormons and frequent church attendees.

Mormons believe that through marriages performed in the temple, families are sealed for eternity. While most American Mormon families reside with just a nuclear family, they value extended family members, both living and dead. They feel that the temple "saving ordinances," such as baptism, a special "endowment" session, and marriages, are also essential for family members who have died. Since these ordinances can only be performed on earth, living Mormons perform them as proxies for deceased relatives. To facilitate this, church leaders encourage Mormons to research their genealogies and collect the names of their deceased relatives.

Relations with Other Americans During the nineteenth century, most Americans saw the Mormon church as an eccentric religion that practiced polygamy, voted as a bloc, and lived together. Following the issuing of the Manifesto, though, Mormons not only abandoned polygamy but also gave up many of their unique economic and political practices. In order for Utah to become a state, the federal government required the church to dissolve its political arm, the People's Party. Most Mormons became Republicans and Democrats like the rest of the nation. The church gave up its communal and cooperative efforts and embraced the capitalist economy.

Despite the previously described "Mormon moment" in the early twenty-first century, the Pew Forum found in 2012 that many Americans still do not know much about Mormons. Of the Americans surveyed, 82 percent said they learned little or nothing about the Mormon religion during Mitt Romney's 2012 presidential campaign. Less than half of Americans felt they knew much about the church and could give factual information about it; 61 percent of non-Mormons felt that Mormons were very different than them; and only 25 percent said the two groups had a lot in common.

Philanthropy Mormons tithe 10 percent of their income to the church, and the funds are used to support its activities. In addition, members are asked to fast two meals the first Sunday of the month and to donate the money that would have been spent on food to help those in need. Historically, members also paid a budget to fund local church programs and were asked to contribute to a local building fund. Those expenses are now covered by the general church funds. The church as a whole has focused on providing financial assistance and volunteers, especially at times of natural disasters. Members wearing yellow "helping hands" T-shirts have provided aid following earthquakes, tornados, and floods. The church has a humanitarian center that ships good around the world.

EMPLOYMENT AND ECONOMIC CONDITIONS

Early Mormons were often from the working class. Joseph Smith Jr.'s family farmed and struggled to survive. Other early converts, such as Brigham Young (a carpenter) and Heber C. Kimball (a potter), were craftsmen. The first converts in England were miners, potters, and factory employees. When the Mormons arrived in Utah, they attempted to be as self-sufficient as possible. Church leaders encouraged an agricultural lifestyle and discouraged mining, though some early members worked in mines. As late as World War I, Utah's economy was based on farming and natural resources.

Over the years, Mormons have come to have a wider variety of occupations. Sociologist Wade Dewey Roof and theologian William McKinney examined religious "streams" in the "circulation of the saints." The "upward movement" from one social and economic class to another is one of these streams. They concluded that the Mormon church moved from the bottom of the lowest scale in the 1940s, based on education, family income, occupational prestige, and perceived social class, to the highest in the middle category by the 1980s. Because Mormons accept the Victorian ideal that women should raise children at home, fewer women work out of the home, especially women who attend church.

Church leaders have continued to encourage Mormons to be self-sufficient. Since 1930 the church has operated its own welfare system to help members in need. However, members are urged to use their own resources and seek their extended families' assistance before coming to the church for aid. To help in times of emergency, leaders ask members to maintain a year's supply of food and other necessities. During the 1930s the church claimed that it could support its own members, but studies showed that members depended on the federal programs to a greater extent than other Americans did.

POLITICS AND GOVERNMENT

Since the breakup of the People's Party, church leaders have claimed to speak out only on political issues that they consider to be of moral concern. In 1968 the church opposed the sale of liquor by the drink, supported Sunday closing laws, and favored right-to-work laws. The Mormon church also took a stand opposing the Equal Rights Amendment (ERA) in the 1970s. While LDS women were split, the church's Relief Society came out against the amendment, and in October 1976 a First Presidency statement opposed the ERA. The church's stand influenced the vote in Utah, Florida, Virginia, and Illinois and affected states such as Idaho that attempted to reverse their ratification of the amendment. The Mormon church made national news when an outspoken supporter of the ERA, Sonia Johnson, was excommunicated. Johnson, however, has not been the only Mormon female to go against the grain. The Mormon Women's Forum, a group of Mormon feminists seeking to reform the church, examines what it views as the suppressive influence of the church on its female members and focuses on such issues as the ordination of women to the priesthood.

The First Presidency also spoke out against the location of the MX missile system in Utah and Nevada in 1981. The church issued a statement declaring, "Our fathers came to this western area to establish a base from which to carry the gospel of peace to the peoples of the earth." It continued, "It is ironic, and a denial of the very essentials of that gospel, that in this same general area there should be a mammoth weapons system potentially capable of destroying much of civilization." The federal government then considered moving the project to Wyoming before abandoning it altogether.

The Mormon church has taken a stand on other issues, too. Leaders came out strongly against abortion, and Utah passed one of the most pro-life legislation packages in the United States in 1991. In 1992 the LDS Church opposed a pari-mutuel betting proposal in the state of Utah; several general authorities mentioned this subject in the October General Conference just before the election. The measure was defeated.

In the 1990s, the First Presidency and the Quorum of the Twelve issued a proclamation about the church's stand supporting the traditional nuclear family. It states that God ordains marriage between a man and a woman. Within a family the husband is to provide the economic support, while the wife is to nurture and raise the children. The proclamation supports the notion that a father and mother should work together. With that view, the LDS Church has come out strongly against gay marriage. Its leaders have encouraged members to campaign against same-sex marriage. In 2012 the church created a webpage to counsel members with homosexual feelings. Those who are attracted to people of the same sex are expected to remain celibate, just like other unmarried Mormon men and women. While the church did not directly campaign for California Proposition 8, a 2008 proposal to reverse the previously established legality of same-sex marriages in that state, its leaders did ask Mormons as individuals to contribute time and money to support the measure and, where applicable, to vote for it.

Other than speaking out on issues and encouraging members to vote and be involved in the political process, Mormon leaders do not officially support any political party. Nearly half of American Mormons are Republicans, and the rest are independents, Democrats, or members of small political parties. Regardless of their political affiliation, Mormons tend to be conservative.

NOTABLE INDIVIDUALS

Academia Leonard J. Arrington (1917–1999) was an economics professor at Utah State University when he was appointed LDS Church historian in 1972. He also became the director of the Charles Redd Center for Western Studies at Brigham Young University (BYU). Arrington promoted the study of Mormon history at the LDS Church and BYU. He wrote many books on church history and mentored two generations of historians.

Laurel Thatcher Ulrich (1938–) won the Pulitzer Prize for History for her book *A Midwife's Tale: The Life of Martha Ballard, Based on Her Diary, 1785–1812* (1990). Her other publications include *Well-Behaved Women Seldom Make History* (2007). She has held an endowed chair at Harvard University and served as president of the American Historical Association.

Terryl Lynn Givens (1957–) is a professor of literature and religion at the University of Richmond. His book *By the Hand of Mormon* (2003) is a study of the Book of Mormon.

Richard L. Bushman (1931–), a professor emeritus at Columbia University, has written extensively on Joseph Smith and the early history of Mormonism. His publications include *Joseph Smith: Rough Stone Rolling* (2005). He was the first holder of the Howard W. Hunter Chair in Mormon Studies at Claremont College, and in 2012 a new chair was named after him at the University of Virginia in recognition of his work in establishing Mormon studies as an academic discipline.

> *Mormons believe that through marriages performed in the temple, families are sealed for eternity. While most American Mormon families live with just the nuclear family, they value the extended family, living and dead.*

Art Minerva Bernetta Kohlhepp Teichert (1888–1976) was known for her paintings of Mormon and Western scenes.

Arnold Friberg (1913–2010) earned acclaim for his painting *The Prayer at Valley Forge of George Washington* (1975). Among Mormons, he is best known for his paintings used to illustrate the Book of Mormon, which portray strong, muscular characters.

Music Donny Osmond (1957–) and Marie Osmond (1959–) were the most famous members of the Osmond entertainment family. They had their own TV variety show, *Donny and Marie* (1976–1979), and continued to perform together in the following decades.

Literature Vardis Fisher (1895–1968) was a Mormon writer whose works include the historical novel *Children of God* (1939), a fictionalized account of the history of the Mormon church. Others with a Latter-day Saint background who wrote about Mormon themes include Samuel W. Taylor (1907–1997), Virginia Sorsensen (1912–1992), and Maurine Whipple (1904–1993).

Another contemporary Mormon author is Levi S. Peterson (1933–), whose books include *Backslider* (1986), the short story collection *Canyons of Grace* (1982), and *A Rascal by Nature, A Christian by Yearning: A Mormon Autobiography*. Orson Scott Card (1951–), an award-winning science fiction author, has written novels about the Mormon past.

Politics and Government Terrell H. Bell (1921–) served as Secretary of Education in the early 1980s under President Ronald Reagan.

Ezra Taft Benson (1899–1994) served as president of the LDS Church. Benson also served as Secretary of Agriculture under President Dwight D. Eisenhower and was active in farm organizations.

David M. Kennedy (1925–), a banker, was Secretary of the Treasury under President Richard Nixon from 1969 to 1971, an ambassador-at-large from 1971 to 1973, and the ambassador to NATO in 1972 and 1973. He later became an ambassador-at-large for the LDS Church.

Rex Lee (1935–1996) was U.S. Solicitor General under President Ronald Reagan and served as president of BYU from 1989 to 1995.

George Romney (1912–1995) was president and general manager of American Motors (1954–1962), governor of the state of Michigan (1963–1967), and a candidate for the Republican presidential nomination in 1968.

Mitt Romney (1947–), the son of George Romney, served as the governor of Massachusetts from 2003 through 2006. He was the Republican presidential nominee in 2012, losing to Barack Obama in the general election. He also ran for president in 2008 but did not receive the nomination. Previously, he was a successful businessman who helped save the imperiled 2002 Salt Lake City Olympics when he became its chief executive officer.

Stewart L. Udall (1920–2010) served as Secretary of the Interior in the 1960s under president John F. Kennedy.

Science and Medicine John A. Widstoe (1872–1952) was among the first Mormons who went east in the 1890s to study science at secular universities. Widstoe directed the Utah Agricultural Experiment Station and was a professor of chemistry at the Utah State Agricultural College. He developed dry farming and irrigation methods.

Henry Eyring (1901–1981), a chemist, developed the absolute rate theory of chemical reactions and received the National Medal of Science. He served as president of several leading scientific organizations.

Harvey Fletcher (1884–1981), a physicist, worked for Bell Labs and helped develop stereophonic reproduction.

James Chipman Fletcher (1919–1992) was the director of NASA from 1971 to 1977. He was asked to return to that position after the Space Shuttle *Challenger* disaster in 1986 and remained until 1989.

A BYU professor and a Mormon, Alan Ashton (1942–) developed WordPerfect, one of the most successful word processing systems before Microsoft Word.

Sports Larry H. Miller (1944–2009) was the owner of the Utah Jazz and other sports teams in Utah. He made his money as a car dealer. Besides owning sports teams, he was well known for his donations to sports and charities. His donation to the LDS Church made the Joseph Smith Papers project possible.

MEDIA

PRINT

Church News

A weekly publication that includes the activities of Mormons worldwide. It is published as an insert in the Mormon-owned newspaper the *Deseret News*.

40 East South Temple
P.O. Box 30178
Salt Lake City, Utah 84130
Phone: (800) 453-3876
Fax: (801) 578-3338
URL: www.deseretnews.com

Dialogue: A Journal of Mormon Thought

A quarterly scholarly journal examining the relevance of religion to secular life and expressing Mormon culture.

Kristine L. Haglund, Editor
P.O. Box 381209
Cambridge, Massachusetts 02238
Phone: (857) 600-1620
URL: www.dialoguejournal.com

Ensign

A monthly magazine published by the Mormon church for its adult English-speaking members. It includes a message from the First Presidency and articles concerning LDS life and members, as well as a section called "News of the Church."

R. Val Johnson, Managing Editor
50 East North Temple
23rd Floor
Salt Lake City, Utah 84150
Phone: (800) 453-3860
or

Phone: (801) 240-2950
Fax: (801) 240-5997
Email: majones@chg.byu.edu

Exponent II

A quarterly newspaper for Mormon women.

Aimee Evans Hickman, Editor
and

Emily Clyde Curtis, Editor
Email: president@exponentii.org
URL: www.exponentii.org

Friend

An LDS Church magazine for children. Its stories and articles provide information for youth ages three to twelve.

Jan Pinbourgh, Managing Editor
50 East North Temple
23rd Floor
Salt Lake City, Utah 84150

New Era

A Mormon publication for teenagers and young adults.

> Brittany Beattle, Managing Editor
> 50 East North Temple
> 23rd Floor
> Salt Lake City, Utah 84150

Sunstone: Mormon Experience, Scholarship, Issues, and Art

Magazine published by Sunstone Foundation, which also sponsors symposiums in the United States.

> Stephen Carter, Editor
> 343 North 300 West
> Salt Lake City, Utah 84103-1215
> Phone: (801) 355-5926
> URL: www.sunstonemagazine.com

RADIO

BYU Radio

Bonneville International, which operates radio stations throughout the United States, started a radio service in 1992 providing a 24-hour radio service that is sent by satellite to church members who own satellite receivers. It is also repeated by a few stations across the nation as an FM sideband service. In 2002 the network became part of BYU Broadcasting and became BYU Radio in connection with BYU TV

> Richard Linford, Manager
> P.O. Box 1160
> Salt Lake City, Utah 84110-1160
> Phone: (801) 575-7505

ORGANIZATIONS AND ASSOCIATIONS

Affirmation/Gay and Lesbian Mormons

The purpose of this organization is to promote understanding, tolerance, and acceptance of gay men and lesbians as full, equal, and worthy members of the Mormon church and society. It studies ways of reconciling sexual orientation with traditional Mormon beliefs.

> Tianna Owens, Executive Director
> P.O. Box 46022
> Los Angeles, California 90046
> Phone: (213) 255-7251
> URL: www.affirmation.org

Mormon History Association

This association promotes the study of the Mormon past. It publishes the *Journal of Mormon History*, a biannual scholarly publication.

> Ronald Barney, Executive Director
> Crandall Building
> 10 West 100 South
> Suite 610
> Salt Lake City, Utah 84101
> Phone: (888) 642-3678
> or
> Phone: (801) 521-6565
> Fax: (801) 521–8686
> URL: www.mormonhistoryassociation.org

Mormon Social Science Association

This association encourages the study of Mormon life.

> URL: www.mormonsocialscience.org

Young Women of the Church of Jesus Christ of Latter-day Saints (YW)

Founded in 1869, YW seeks to strengthen the spiritual life of females ages twelve to eighteen through Christian values and experiences. YW reinforces the values of faith, divine nature, individual worth, knowledge, choice and accountability, good works, and integrity, and it works to develop leadership attributes in young women through service in the community.

> Elaine S. Dalton, President
> 76 North Main Street
> Salt Lake City, Utah 84150
> Phone: (801) 240-2141
> Fax: (801) 240-5458

MUSEUMS AND RESEARCH CENTERS

Church History Library

Chronicling the history of the Church of Jesus Christ of Latter-day Saints from its beginning in 1830, the library's collection contains manuscripts, books, church records, photographs, oral histories, architectural drawings, pamphlets, newspapers, periodicals, maps, microforms, and audiovisual materials. The Church completed the new library in 2009.

> Steven E. Snow, Church Historian
> 15 East North Temple
> Salt Lake City, Utah 84150
> Phone: (801) 240-2272
> URL: churchhistorylibrary.lds.org

Church History Museum

The Church History Museum opened in 1984 and includes exhibits that tell the history of the LDS Church through artifacts and art. The museum sponsors an art competition every three years to encourage LDS artists. It has an exhibit about presidents of the church and rotates other exhibits.

> 45 North West Temple
> Salt Lake City, Utah 84150
> Phone: (801) 240-3310
> URL: www.lds.org

SOURCES FOR ADDITIONAL STUDY

Allen, James B., and Glen M. Leonard. *The Story of the Latter-day Saints*. 2nd ed. Salt Lake City, UT: Deseret Books, 1992.

Arrington, Leonard J., and Davis Bitton. *The Mormon Experience*. New York: Alfred A. Knopf, 1979.

Bowman, Matthew. *The Mormon People: The Making of an American Faith*. New York: Random House, 2012.

Bushman, Claudia L. *Contemporary Mormonism: Latter-day Saints in Modern America*. Westport, CT: Praeger, 2006.

Bush, Lester E. *Health and Medicine Among the Mormons: Science, Sense, and Scripture*. New York: Crossroads, 1993.

Heaton, Tim B.; Stephen J. Bahr; and Cardell Jacobson. *A Statistical Profile of Mormons: Health, Wealth, and Social Life*. Lewiston, NY: The Edwin Mellen Press, 2004.

Ludlow, Daniel H. *Encyclopedia of Mormonism*. New York: Macmillan, 1992.

Mauss, Armand L. *The Angel and the Beehive: The Mormon Struggle with Assimilation*. Urbana: University of Illinois Press, 1994.

Shipps, Jan. *Mormonism: The Story of a New Religious Tradition*. Urbana: University of Illinois Press, 1985.

Moroccan Americans

Elizabeth Shostak

OVERVIEW

Moroccan Americans are immigrants or descendants of people from Morocco, the African nation closest in location to Europe. Located to the far northwest of the continent, it is bordered on the east by Algeria and to the south by Western Sahara. To its north is the Mediterranean Sea, and to its west is the Atlantic Ocean. Morocco's two coasts are separated by the Strait of Gibraltar, a strategic point that provides entry to the Mediterranean from the west. Only ten miles across the Strait to the north lies Spain. Two northeast-southwest mountain ranges, the Rif and the Atlas Mountains, bisect the country and occupy more than a third of its total area. The country's highest point is Jbel Toubkal (13,671 feet, or 4167 meters) in the southwestern Atlas Mountains, and its lowest elevation is Sebkha Tah (-55 meters) in the far southwest, near the Western Sahara and Atlantic coast. Its capital city is Rabat, on the Atlantic coast, and its principal economic and cultural center is Casablanca, also on the Atlantic coast. Morocco's total land area is roughly 172.5 square miles (446,775 square kilometers), of which only 21 percent is arable land. The entire country of Morocco is slightly larger than the state of California.

According to the *CIA World Factbook*, Morocco's population in July 2012 was estimated at 32,309,239. Approximately 75 percent of the population is of Berber ancestry, and almost 99 percent is Muslim. Christians make up about 1 percent of the population, and Jews number around 6,000, or less than 1 percent. Morocco has relatively high birth and population growth rates, which exacerbates housing shortages and produces a high level of unemployment. As of 2011 the unemployment rate in the country was at 8.9 percent. Morocco's main exports include fruits, vegetables, clothing, textiles, crude minerals, phosphates, and petroleum products. As of 2013 Morocco was the only African country to have a bilateral Free Trade Agreement with the United States, which began in 2006.

The Moroccan American community is relatively new, with significant waves of immigration occurring in the wake of World War II through the 1980s and another major influx from 1990 to 2000. According to the 2000 U.S. Census, nearly 13,000 Moroccan Americans reported having entered the United States during that decade. However, America's relationship with Morocco dates from the very beginning of U.S. history. Morocco was the first country to grant official recognition to the newly formed United States of America after the country obtained independence from Great Britain. While Moroccans who migrated to European countries were typically unskilled workers hoping to escape their country's high unemployment rate, those who came to the United States tended to have more education and better job skills. By the late 1990s a large proportion of Moroccans in the United States were students or recent university graduates. In general, the number of Moroccan immigrants remains relatively low.

According to the U.S. Census Bureau's American Community Survey, the estimated population of Moroccan Americans in 2010 was 74,908, which is roughly the same size as the population of Gary, Indiana. Many Americans of Moroccan descent have settled in urban areas, especially in New York, New Jersey, Massachusetts, Virginia, California, and Florida, where they have often established small businesses or entered professional fields. With this trend in mind, the assimilation of Moroccan immigrants into American culture remains mixed. While many early entrants to the country established small businesses in tight-knit ethnic communities, business professionals and a younger generation of students assimilated more into American society, thus adapting or disbanding altogether their traditional cultural rituals.

HISTORY OF THE PEOPLE

Early History The early history of Morocco includes Amazigh (also known as Berber), Arabic, and Jewish influences, a legacy that serves as the foundation for modern Morocco's multiculturalism. The Amazigh, a group of non-Arabic tribes scattered throughout North Africa, inhabited Morocco by the end of the second millennium BCE. Early Amazigh were a mix of nomadic herders and agricultural settlers. Because much of the land is arid and infertile, they raised crops and pastured their flocks in Morocco's coastal regions and inland mountains. Phoenician merchants established trading ports along Morocco's Mediterranean coast in the twelfth century BCE. Their presence brought increased commerce to the region and introduced new skills to the Amazigh, including weaving, masonry, and iron and metal work. By the fifth century BCE, the Phoenicians had expanded their ports along Morocco's Atlantic coast as well. After the Roman Empire defeated Carthage, Morocco's Amazigh King Juba (25 BCE–24 CE) encouraged his country to ally itself with Rome. In 46 CE Morocco was annexed as part of the province of Mauretania to the Roman Empire. Although Moroccans are today predominantly Muslim, it is believed that during the period of Roman rule the province was almost entirely converted to Christianity.

Even prior to Roman colonization, Jewish people lived in Morocco. Small groups of Jews entered the area in the first century CE after they were forced out of their ancestral land. Sephardic Jews of Spanish and Portuguese descent fled to Morocco and other North African countries to escape the Inquisition from 1391 through the last decades of the fifteenth century. There they engaged in small crafts or trades, such as silversmithing, and often moved from town to town. By 1438 the Jews in the city of Fez were forced to live in special quarters called *mellahs*, a derivation of the Arabic word for salt. *Mellah* referred to the fact that Jews were given the job of salting the heads of executed prisoners to prepare them for public exhibition.

The Arab conquest of Morocco brought Islam to the country in the late seventh century. The Amazigh fiercely resisted Arab control, staging a successful revolt in 740. Nevertheless, Arab religious, social, and linguistic traditions became a central part of Moroccan culture After regaining their independence from the Arabs, various Amazigh factions vied for control in the area, leading to a series of local wars spanning almost 300 years. Finally, in the mid-eleventh century, a confederation of tribes called the Almoravids conquered all of Morocco, as well as much of Spain, and in 1070 they established the city of Marrakesh, which remained a center of Islamic knowledge and military might for several decades.

Early in the twelfth century the Almohads, another clan, overthrew the Almoravid dynasty and assumed rule. During the Almohads' reign, a number of Moroccan scholars, including al-Murrakushi (1237–1303) and Ibn al-Banna (1256–1321), made major contributions to the fields of science, mathematics, and astronomy that are credited with helping to bring Europe out of the Dark Ages. By the thirteenth century the Almohads had been expelled from Spain; in 1269 they were defeated in Morocco by the Marinids, under whom the explorer Ibn Battuta (1304–1369) traveled throughout the Islamic world, mapping a region spanning from northern Africa to eastern China. Marinid rule lasted until the mid-fifteenth century, after which the country was partitioned into small independent states. In around 1550 the Sa'dis took control, remaining in power for the next century. These North African tribes who conquered Spain were commonly known as Moors.

Modern Era European interest in North Africa increased during the 1800s, as France and Spain vied for power in the region. After invading Algeria in 1830, France became the dominant colonial power in North Africa. The Treaty of Fez, signed in 1912, made Morocco a French protectorate, which resulted in improved conditions, equal rights, and religious autonomy for Moroccan Jews. During World War II these equal conditions changed, however, when the occupied French Vichy government cooperated with the Nazis. Morocco's King Mohammed V, who remains a beloved figure in Morocco for his resistance to French involvement in the region, prevented the deportation of Jews from Morocco during the Holocaust, thereby saving them from almost certain death in Nazi concentration camps. However, with the establishment of the Jewish state of Israel in 1948, most of the estimated 270,000 Jews in Morocco left for new opportunities. Most immigrated to Israel, but many also traveled to France, Canada, and the United States.

In the decade following World War II, anticolonial sentiments increased throughout Africa. Morocco negotiated its independence from France in 1956, when King Mohammed V formed a constitutional government. Upon his death in 1961, his son Hassan II ascended to the throne. King Hassan II's rule was tumultuous, with opposition from rival political parties leading to successive attempted military coups in 1971 and 1972, which, Hassan claimed, he survived due to his *baraka*, or divine powers. Over the following twenty years, Hassan established strong relationships with the United States and Israel, though he faced criticism for his harsh treatment of political dissidents. Morocco's constitution, signed by Hassan in 1972 and later revised in 1980, 1992, and 2011, gives supreme executive power to the hereditary king, who appoints a prime minister. The constitution also created a House of Representatives and an independent judiciary.

Hassan's son Mohammed VI succeeded his father in 1999, a period in which Morocco was experiencing problems typical of developing nations: high government spending and inflation, a huge external debt, limited access to health care, poor housing and living conditions, and high unemployment. Mohammed VI made several efforts at addressing the issues he inherited, releasing thousands of political prisoners, instituting land reforms and economic-modernization initiatives, and strengthening a highly developed tourism industry. Nevertheless, Moroccans still faced inhospitable living conditions within their country. According to the World Bank Report (2012), the estimated birth rate reached an all-time high of 50.4 births per 1,000 people in 1960, resulting chiefly from Muslim opposition to family-planning measures. This level decreased to 19.5 out of 1,000 by 2010 (compared to 13 out of 1,000 in the United States during the same period). This consistently high birth rate has led to Morocco's relatively high rate of population growth, estimated at 1.2 percent from 2010 to 2015 by the United Nations Statistics Division. Moreover, as of 2010 approximately 28 percent of the country's population was younger than fifteen years old. Morocco's high unemployment rate, estimated at 9.4 percent but reaching as high as 30 percent among those between the ages of fifteen to twenty-nine, particularly affects this segment of the population.

In the late twentieth century, with average wages in nearby Europe about twenty times higher than those in North Africa, Moroccan migrants in search of jobs frequently attempted to enter the continent through Spain, which lies a mere 14 kilometers across the Strait of Gibraltar from Morocco's coast. According to the Migration Information Source website,

> In many respects, the Strait of Gibraltar is the European Union's equivalent of the Rio Grande between the United States and Mexico. Despite intensified border controls, tens of thousands of Moroccans managed to enter Europe each year. This makes Spain the main entrance to an internally borderless Europe for African immigrants.

By the end of the 1990s, the European Union had begun limiting visas for North Africans and barring illegal migrants from entering Europe. The elimination of access to European jobs caused significant problems in Morocco. Some Moroccan workers sought illegal entry to Spain—a practice fraught with dangers: the *Economist* reported in 1999 that, during the preceding five years alone, 3,000 Moroccans had drowned in illegal attempts to cross the Strait of Gibraltar to enter Spain. This situation affected mostly unskilled workers; Moroccans with higher levels of education and job skills were able to consider immigration to the United States.

The global economic downturn that began in 2007, however, severely affected the economies of many European nations, leading to a considerable slowing of Moroccan immigration to Spain and a slight increase in immigration to the United States. In the 2010s the unemployment levels among Moroccans living in Spain easily surpassed unemployment in Morocco, reaching as high as 60 percent. This trend served to discourage further immigration by Moroccans into Spain and even led to a net loss of 22,000 Moroccans from Spain in 2011. Furthermore, the Spanish population in Morocco quadrupled between the years 2003 and 2011, indicating that Morocco had become something of a destination for Spanish job seekers.

In the twenty-first century, citizens of Morocco and the other North African nations (Algeria, Egypt, Tunisia, and Libya) began to demand government reforms, social programs aimed at alleviating unemployment, and democratic representation. On February 20, 2011, tens of thousands of Moroccans—the majority of whom were students and other youths particularly affected by Morocco's high unemployment rate—took

ESTEVANICO: THE FIRST MOROCCAN IN AMERICA

Although Moroccans did not begin to arrive in the United States in large numbers until the mid-twentieth century, there are records of their presence in North America as early as the sixteenth century. The first documented African explorer of the New World, and perhaps the first Muslim to step foot in America, was a man named Mustafa Zemmouri from the North African coastal city of Azemmour in present-day Morocco. Although little is known of his early life before he was sold into slavery by Spanish slave traders in the 1520s and given the name Estevanico by his owner, a Castilian named Andrés Dorantes, Estevanico would eventually travel across the New World, exploring areas that now constitute the American Southwest.

Dorantes and Estevanico originally set sail in 1527 as part of an ill-fated expedition by Spanish *conquistador* Pánfilo de Naváez. After most of the expedition was lost while crossing the Gulf of Mexico, Dorantes and Estevanico made landfall on Galveston Island off the southeastern shore of Texas and eventually made their way into mainland North America, where they were captured by a group of Native Americans. Estevanico's dark skin color and ability as a translator made him an object of fascination, and he was assumed to have magical healing powers. After six years Estevanico and Dorantes escaped and made their way back to Spain, though Estevanico returned to North America again in 1539, leading a trek into present-day New Mexico. There, he became the first non-native person to step foot in a Zuni pueblo. Estevanico was eventually captured and killed for unknown reasons in the Zuni pueblo of Hawikuh, but his legacy as one of the first explorers of the American Southwest remains a source of pride to Moroccans and North African Muslims to this day.

to the streets in protest, staging largely peaceful protests in public spaces and in front of government buildings. The so-called February 20 Movement continued to challenge King Mohammed VI's policies throughout 2011, prompting an official response from the king on March 9, 2011, in which he proposed granting the prime minister greater authority, initiating parliamentary elections, and granting recognition of Berber as an official language of Morocco. The proposed reforms were ratified in a July referendum, though some dissenters argued that the reforms did not go far enough and continued to protest into 2013.

SETTLEMENT IN THE UNITED STATES

Although it is believed that Moroccans may have been present in America from the earliest years of European exploration, Moroccan migration to the United States was not widespread until the mid-twentieth century. Evidence indicates that one of the earliest explorers of America was a Moroccan man named Estevanico, from the town of Azemmour, who landed in America in 1528. There are also accounts of Sephardic Jews from Morocco making their way to the United

States early in the twentieth century by way of South America. A century earlier, large numbers of young Moroccan Jewish men went to the Amazon region in South America and achieved substantial business success by developing the Amazon's rubber trade. While some returned to Morocco after making their fortunes, many others remained in South America. When the South American rubber industry collapsed in 1910, most Moroccan Jews left the area, either returning to North Africa or moving on going to other opportunities in the Western Hemisphere. Although little documentation exists to trace their various routes, it is entirely possible that some of them entered the United States, either by boat or through Mexico.

The end of World War II and Morocco's subsequent independence from France in 1956 spurred a significant wave of Moroccan immigration to the United States. Prior to this time most Moroccans who emigrated went to Europe via Spain due to the close proximity of the two country's borders; this was true regardless of whether they were of Jewish or Arabic descent. After World War II, the vast majority of Sephardic Jews who left Morocco went to Israel. Some of these Jewish immigrants entered the United States, however. While the Moroccan government did not deport Jews from the country during the Holocaust, the political, social, and economic climate during and after the war was difficult for Moroccan Jews. Those who subsequently immigrated to the United States tended to settle in areas where earlier Sephardic immigrants from Spain, Turkey, or the Balkans had established communities.

Arabized Moroccans, however, did not begin to enter the United States in significant numbers until much later in the century, after the 1965 Immigration and Naturalization Act abolished the use of quotas, based on data from the 1920 Census, that had favored the entry of immigrants from northern and western Europe.

In general, less educated, unskilled laborers immigrated to Europe while educated professionals immigrated to the United States. The reason for this socioeconomic breakdown lies in the nature of immigration laws, as Spain and France welcomed unskilled migrants from Morocco and other North African countries until the late 1990s. It was easy, inexpensive, and quick to go back and forth across the Strait of Gibraltar, making this option attractive for workers who hoped to improve their earnings and then return to their homes and families. Furthermore, Spain's Moorish heritage and France's colonial dominance of the Maghreb—a geographical term describing the region of northwestern Africa that includes Morocco, Algeria, and Tunisia—had established strong cultural and linguistic connections between these countries and Morocco. This undoubtedly eased the transition for migrants who sought opportunities there.

Since the first major wave of Moroccan immigrants to reach the United States in the wake of World War II, the number has grown steadily. Each decade witnessed an increase in Moroccans entering the United States in both the small business and corporate sector and predominantly in the academic environment with student visas. Many Moroccan Americans who have founded retail establishments maintain close business ties with Morocco, from which they obtain many goods for sale in the United States, including rugs and other textiles and crafts. Such trade is favorable to Morocco, and organizations in both Morocco and the United States facilitate increased reciprocal business between the two countries. In addition, many Moroccan Americans have close family members in Morocco and maintain frequent contact with them. While some immigrants have chosen to return to their homeland after finishing their educations, many have stayed in the United States as citizens. According to the U.S. Census Bureau, the number of Moroccan Americans in the United States almost doubled in the decade between 2000 and 2010, from roughly 38,000 to 75,000, as rising unemployment in northern Africa and western Europe led job seekers and students to seek opportunities in more distant locations. The American Community Survey estimated in 2010 that the states with the largest population of Moroccan Americans were California (8,147), Florida (8,858), New York (12,364), Massachusetts (6,471), New Jersey (4,481), and Virginia (4,839).

LANGUAGE

The official language of Morocco is Arabic, although French is still widely used in business, because Morocco was a French colony up until 1956. Spanish is also frequently spoken, particularly in the northern regions of the country. Standard Arabic, used in newspapers and broadcasts, speeches, and correspondence, is the language of the Quran (or Koran, the sacred book of Islam) and is understood throughout the contemporary Arab world. There are, however, many different dialects of the language spoken in the Arabian Peninsula, Iraq, Syria, Egypt, and North Africa. Moroccan Arabic, known as *Derija*, is recognized by its shortened vowel sounds.

While Arabic remains the main language spoken in Morocco as well as by Moroccan Americans in their homes, many immigrants speak English at their jobs and during the course of their daily lives in the United States. According to the 2011 American Community Survey estimates, one-third of Moroccan Americans speak only English in their homes. The traditional Moroccan language is spoken among friends in informal settings and when conducting business among people of their own nationality, although Moroccan Americans make a point of using English in mixed groups or when attempting to include Americans in conversations.

Greetings and Popular Expressions In Moroccan Arabic, the word for "hello" is *ahlan*. "Goodbye" is *beslama*. "How are you?" is *"Labass alaik?"* "Please" and "thank you" are *affak* and *shoukran*, respectively.

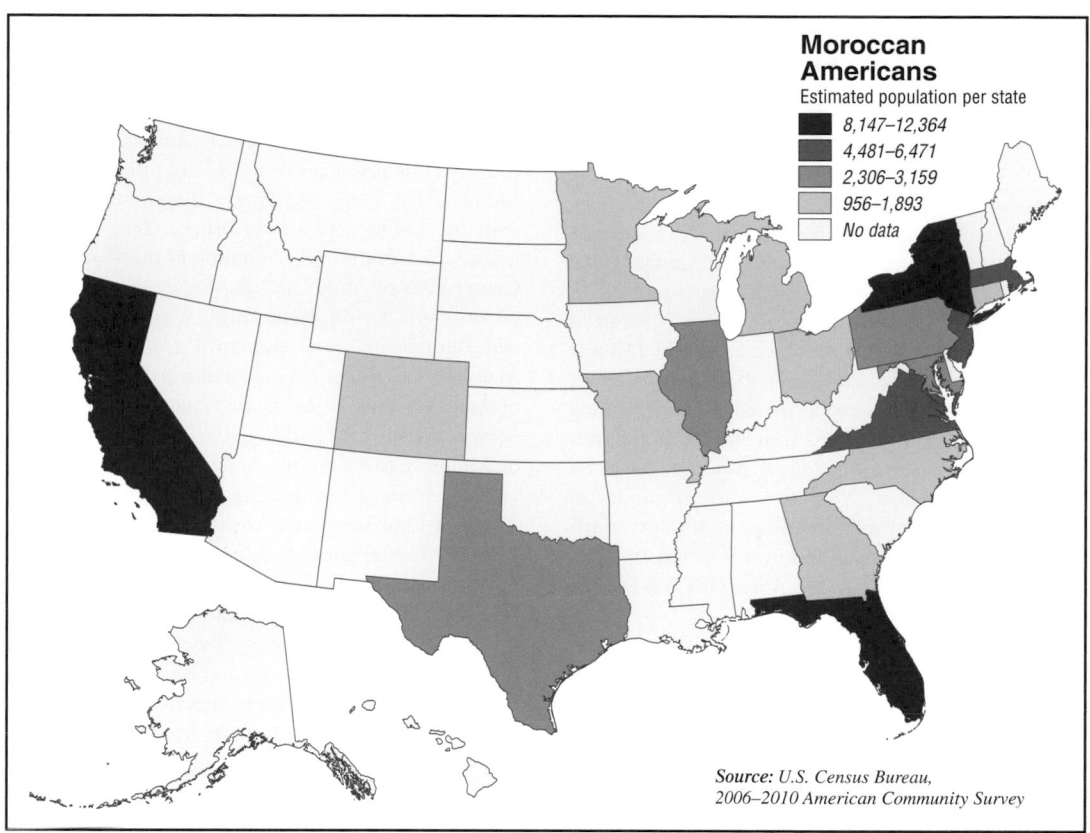

Moroccan Americans
Estimated population per state

- 8,147–12,364
- 4,481–6,471
- 2,306–3,159
- 956–1,893
- No data

Source: U.S. Census Bureau, 2006–2010 American Community Survey

RELIGION

Although there are a small number of Christian and Jewish Moroccan American immigrants, the majority of Moroccans and Moroccan Americans practice Islam, which was founded in the seventh century CE by the Arabian prophet Muhammad. The faith quickly spread throughout the Middle East and North Africa and was established in Afghanistan, Pakistan, the Balkan Peninsula, Turkey, and Malaysia. By the late twentieth century, Islam was the second-largest religion in the world (after Christianity); in 2012 there were an estimated 1.6 billion followers worldwide. The principal sects of Islam include the Sunni, Shi'ah, Sufi, and Ismaili Muslims. Most Moroccans are Sunni Muslims of the Malakite order, which differs from other schools of Sunni Islam in that it relies heavily upon the teachings of Malik ibn Anas (c. 715–795) of Medina, Saudi Arabia—where the prophet Muhammad is said to have lived and died—in its interpretation of the Quran.

The word *Islam* means "submission to the will of God" in Arabic. The Muslim faith is based on the Quran, the holy book considered God's revelation to humankind. Muslims believe that the Quran confirms and replaces earlier books of revelation, such as the Bible, and that the Prophet Muhammad is the last and most perfect of several prophets sent by God, including Adam, Abraham, Moses, and Jesus. Although Muslims consider Jesus a prophet, they reject the Christian belief that he is the Messiah, or the son of God sent from heaven to forgive humans their sins and thereby save the world. Muslims believe in one omnipotent God (Allah), angels, revealed books (sacred texts handed down to people from Allah), the prophets, and the Day of Judgment. Muslims also believe strongly in predetermination—sometimes interpreted as fatalism.

Muslims are expected to practice the Five Pillars of Islam: to recite the profession of faith ("There is no God but God, and Muhammad is the prophet of God"); to observe public and collective prayers five times a day; to pay a purification tax (*zakat*) to help support the poor; to abstain from food from sunup to sundown every day during the holy month of Ramadan; and to perform the *hajj*, or pilgrimage to the holy city of Mecca. The most important religious concept of Islam is the *Shari'ah*, or the Law. The Shari'ah was formulated by Muslim theologians during the eighth and ninth centuries, and it encompasses teachings that address the entire way of life as commanded by God. These include such things as dietary restrictions, sexual mores, and other matters of conduct.

While most Moroccan Americans are Muslims, many "old world" Muslim traditions and strict interpretations of the Quran have become more lax as Moroccan Americans adapt to life in the United

States. Some traditional Islamic laws, from the commonplace, such as requiring women to cover and veil themselves in public, to the extreme, as in punishing adultery by death, have been widely dismissed in Morocco for some time and have little to no presence in Moroccan Americans' lives in the United States.

Moroccan Muslims have long played an active role in American religious life. In the 1930s a Moroccan Sunni Muslim named Sheikh Daoud Ahmad Faisal established plans to build the second-ever mosque in the New York area, founding the Islamic Mission of America for the Propagation of Islam and the Defense of the Faith and the Faithful in Brooklyn in 1938. Sheikh Daoud's proselytizing is credited with helping to introduce Islam to the African American community, and the Islamic Mission of America's Dawood Mosque in Brooklyn, New York City, continues to play a major role in the New York community, hosting interfaith conferences and events meant to foster relationships between Muslim Americans and the rest of American society.

CULTURE AND ASSIMILATION

Both Sephardic Jews and Sunni Muslims who migrated from Morocco to the United States were generally attracted to areas where other people of their respective faiths lived. The Sephardic Jews settled in religious communities with which they shared linguistic and cultural traditions. This practice united them with the country's larger Jewish community in some ways, but it also set them apart, as the vast majority of American Jews are of Ashkenazi descent, meaning that their ancestors had settled in Germany and eastern Europe. Ashkenazi Jews living in the United States developed cultural traditions that differed from those observed by the Sephardim. Sephardic Jews, for example, spoke Ladino and Arabic rather than Yiddish or German, pronounced Hebrew words differently from the Ashkenazim, used different melodies in religious services, and served North African or Iberian versions of kosher foods during holidays. Some Sephardic Jews in the United States have felt that their culture is little appreciated and resent the fact that Ashkenazi traditions have largely determined American conceptions of Jewishness. In addition, some have felt that their relatively dark skin has caused them to be treated with prejudice. Yet their shared Jewish identity still connected Sephardic immigrants with those of Ashkenazi descent and helped them adapt to life in the United States, where the Jewish community has worked hard to combat anti-Semitic attitudes and to achieve social and economic success.

Arab people in the United States, including Moroccans of Arab descent, have also had to deal with prejudice. From the earliest days of Arabic Moroccans' post—World War II immigration to the United States, Americans have sometimes been suspicious of Arabs, due largely to the fact that Americans have been less exposed to Islam, the predominant religion of the

Arab world, than to Judaism and Christianity. In addition, the United States' strong political ties to Israel have fostered mistrust of Arabic groups—in particular the Palestinian Liberation Organization, which has been locked in a violent conflict with Israel since the country's establishment in 1948—despite the fact that Morocco has long maintained diplomatic relations with Israel. The activities of other extremist Islamic groups, such as the 1993 bombing of the World Trade Center in New York City, the September 11, 2001, terrorist attacks on New York, Washington, D.C., and Pennsylvania, and the April 15, 2013, Boston Marathon bombings have created negative stereotypes of Arab Muslims in the United States. Although the Moroccans' history has differed dramatically from that of Middle Eastern Arabs, Americans have tended to view all Arabs as a monolithic group, and Moroccan Americans are sometimes treated with undue suspicion. In the aftermath of the Boston Marathon bombing, for example, a Moroccan American teenager, Salah Eddin Barhoum, and his friend were falsely accused on the front page of the *New York Post* of committing the attacks, forcing Barhoum and his family to go into hiding until the true culprits were apprehended several days later. However, because Moroccans typically enter the United States as students or with high levels of education and job skills, they tend to assimilate into American culture rather than live in smaller, isolated communities. By blending in with American society, the Moroccan American community has generally encountered a more positive environment than that of less educated or more traditional Arab immigrants.

Traditions and Customs Moroccan culture is traditionally centered around the *souk*, an open-air market where artisans peddle goods, musicians and dancers perform, and people gather for shopping, conversations over a cup of tea, and meals. Handshakes are common greetings in public places, though close friends or family may be greeted with kisses on the cheeks.

Moroccans are known for being quite generous, and it is very common for them to extend invitations to friends and new acquaintances to visit their homes for lunch or dinner. These events often last for many hours, and guests typically bring small gifts such as flowers, figs, or dates to share with their hosts. The meal is usually shared at a low, round table, with guests seated on carpets or cushions on the floor and food served in a large bowl at the center of the table, which is eaten from using the thumb and first two fingers of the right hand, as the left hand is considered unclean. Guests' hands are washed with rose or orange-infused water before the meal, and the food is blessed by saying "*Bismillah*," ("in the name of God"). The meal concludes with the pronouncement "*Al Hamdu Lillah*," ("thanks be to God").

Other traditions in Morocco include visiting public bath houses, or *hammams*. Hammams cater to both men and women, though with separate areas for each gender. The bath house experience typically includes a steam room and a bathing room, where paid attendants or companions will scrub customers' skin with an olive oil–based soap known as *sabon beldi* and sometimes offer massages with scented oils. Sporting events, such as football (soccer) matches, are also popular meeting places, though mostly for men.

Although the United States has no direct equivalents to Moroccan cultural centers such as souks, hammams, or tea houses, Moroccan Americans are largely able to uphold their traditional dining practices and methods of greeting and socializing with their neighbors in the United States at home or in farmer's markets, mosques, and the increasingly common Moroccan restaurants found in urban areas. Organizations such as the Moroccan American Cultural Center in Washington, D.C., the Moroccan American House Association in New York, and the Moroccan Association of Chicago also offer opportunities for Moroccan Americans to gather and share their culture and customs with other Americans, including feasts, speeches, celebrations during Ramadan and other Islamic holidays, and soccer tournaments. Because Morocco is a very diverse country, Moroccan Americans rarely have trouble integrating with other American ethnic groups.

Cuisine Situated on the route of the Arabia–North Africa spice trade, Morocco developed traditional foods enhanced by such exotic flavorings as cinnamon, ginger, turmeric, saffron, cumin, cayenne, anise, and sesame seed. Native crops of mint, olives, oranges, lemons, prickly pear, pomegranates, almonds, dates, walnuts, chestnuts, barley, melons, and cherries further increased available ingredients. Fish was plentiful along the Atlantic coast, whereas inland areas produced lamb and poultry as well as honey.

In Morocco the main meal is eaten at mid-day (except during the holy month of Ramadan, in which the Muslim faithful fast until sundown). A typical main meal begins with hot and cold salads. Some popular salads are made with mixed herbs, with eggplant, or with greens and oranges. During Ramadan, Moroccans typically break their fast with *harira*, a soup made with milk, dates, and boiled eggs.

After the salad course, Moroccan cooks typically serve main dishes that include meat and vegetables, followed by *couscous*. One of the most familiar Moroccan foods in American supermarkets, couscous is made from grains of very fine semolina (wheat) steamed until barely soft. It has a delicate, rather bland taste that sets off the spicier flavors in the dishes that accompany it. Traditional couscous takes a significant amount of preparation time, as the grains are soaked and washed multiple times before the 45-minute cooking process begins. While mass-produced couscous that is similar to grits or Italian pasta in that it takes only minutes to prepare is available in most grocery stores across the United States, Moroccan Americans usually prefer to cook with authentic couscous.

Other dishes include chicken with lemon and olives, a traditional Moroccan favorite. Another popular dish is chicken *tagine*, which includes butter, onions, pepper, saffron, chickpeas, almonds, and lemon. The dish is named *tagine* after the terra-cotta pot it in which it is prepared. Other tagines include lamb, beef, and fish. Chicken is also stuffed with raisins, almonds, rice, or eggs. Moroccans often use fish in stews, but they also serve it fried or stuffed. A popular recipe that suggests a strong Spanish influence combines fish with tomatoes, green peppers, and potatoes. Lamb, which has been called the "king of the Moroccan table," is served in a variety of ways. *Mechoui* is a holiday dish in which lamb is seasoned with paprika, cumin, butter, and salt and then roasted. Lamb is also roasted on skewers as *shish kebab* or can be braised, browned, or steamed. *Kefta* is a mixture of spicy lamb or beef that is rolled into a sausage shape and then cooked on a skewer or broiled. It is also rolled into meatballs that are used in tagines.

Other traditional Moroccan dishes include *bisteeya*, a savory pastry with possible Persian or Chinese origins. In this dish, layers of shredded chicken, eggs curdled in lemon-onion sauce, and sweetened almonds are wrapped in a paper-thin pastry called *warka*, then sprinkled with cinnamon and sugar. Moroccans also enjoy both Arab-style bread and pita bread. Desserts are not frequently served, but sweetened green tea flavored with fresh mint traditionally ends the meal on a sweet note. A flat, round bread called *khubz* is commonly served with most Moroccan dishes and serves as a point of pride for Moroccan cooks, who often bake a fresh loaf every morning to serve with the day's meals.

Variations on Moroccan cuisine are served in some of the finest restaurants across the United States, some prepared in the traditional form and others a mix or fusion of French, Spanish, and American elements. Moroccan Americans do not always eat the food of their homeland, however. Many newly immigrated Moroccans tend to explore the vast array of American and European inspired foods available in the states. The fast-paced work environment mixed with the fact that both men and women often work in the United States makes it inconvenient to spend a great deal of time preparing meals. While traditional cuisine is often served in the homes of Moroccan Americans, the food often includes different, substituted ingredients and takes less time to prepare.

Traditional Dress Because Morocco is a multicultural country, there is a great diversity of dress among Moroccans. More conservative Moroccans may wear traditional clothing, while those who identify as "continental" wear clothing more closely aligned with Western European fashion.

The *kaftan*, a long, loose-fitting robe, is still worn throughout much of Morocco, in both rural and urban areas, though most often during special occasions. It is a garment well suited to Morocco's climate, protecting wearers from the harsh sun and allowing for ventilation, but also providing warmth for chilly nights. A more common garment for Moroccan women is called a *djellaba*, which is a long, hooded, loose-fitting robe that is often accompanied by intricately designed scarves. Men also wear djellabas, though without the matching scarf. The traditional headgear for Moroccan men is the *fez*, named after the Moroccan city of the same name. It is a close-fitting red felt hat with a flattened top and a tassel worn to the side. The fez became common throughout much of the Islamic world but is thought to have originated in Morocco. Today, the fez has becoming something of a relic and is typically only worn in the company of tourists. In earlier years, Moroccan women, like those in other Islamic countries, wore veils to cover their faces in public. Although this custom has largely disappeared in urban parts of the country, women in rural areas sometimes still wear full or partial veils.

In the United States traditional dress is often abandoned, as the majority of adult Moroccan Americans work at professional jobs that often require suits or uniforms specific to their trade, and younger generations begin to adopt a typical Western style of dress. The traditional kaftan, which is well suited to the warm North African environment, is not always appropriate for certain regions of the United States or seasons in this hemisphere. Many Moroccan American women hold jobs equal to those of their male counterparts, so the traditional full or partial veil is not as common as it once was, though some women do wear headscarves by choice, as a symbol of their religious convictions. Moroccan Americans will also wear traditional outfits on holidays or for religious purposes as they see fit.

Dances and Songs A Moroccan dance tradition that has become familiar to many Americans is *Shikat*, or belly dancing. The term refers to the closely controlled abdominal movements the female dancers make to achieve a rapid rhythmic swaying of the belly and hips. Belly dancers wear a tight garment similar to a brassiere and wide, flowing trousers gathered at the ankle. They use coordinating long scarves or shawls to accentuate their graceful arm and hand movements, and they often ornament their brows with headbands decorated with jewels or old coins. Belly dancing is often offered as entertainment at Moroccan and Middle Eastern restaurants in the United States. During the 1970s and 1980s, many American women became interested in learning how to belly dance, and in the twenty-first century American dance organizations have organized classes, tournaments, and events such as Wiggles of the West and Rakkasah West that have served to maintain American interest in the dance style. Some of the earliest Moroccan American immigrants may have come to the states through

this tradition as well, when several Moroccan dancers known as "whirling dervishes" refused to return to their homeland in 1904. They renounced their allegiance to the Sultan of Morocco and sought asylum in the St. Louis, although they were later deported by the U.S. Department of Immigration.

Other traditional Moroccan dances include the *Guedra*, a circle dance performed by veiled women that is common among the Amazigh, and the *Tissint*, a folk dance performed by both men and women, in which a male holding a dagger slowly advances upon a female dancer until the blade is at the female's throat and the male falls suddenly to his knees. The Tissint is often performed during marriage ceremonies.

Moroccan music reflects the country's hybrid culture, blending Arabic, African, and European influences. *Gnaoua* music, a product of African slaves from Mali being brought to Morocco in the sixteenth and seventeenth centuries, combines religious Arabic songs with African rhythms. Every year the city of Essaouira, Morocco, holds a popular Gnaoua music festival that has been called "Morocco's answer to Woodstock." One of the most prominent Gnaoua bands, Nass El Ghiwane, has found an international audience; it was featured on the soundtrack to the 1988 film *The Last Temptation of Christ*. In May 2011 Hassan Hakmoun, a Moroccan American musician, organized a concert by several renowned Gnaoua groups at Florence Gould Hall in New York that was favorably received by a culturally diverse audience.

Andaloussi music is traced to Abu Hassan Ali Ben Nafi, who fled Baghdad in the ninth century to settle in Cordoba, in the part of Spain then ruled by Morocco. More popular, or folk, music is called *Chaabi*. Many contemporary Moroccan singers record in this style. Instruments used in traditional Moroccan music include the *tbal*, a double-headed drum, and the *querqbat*, or metal castanets. Others are the *tambour* (tambourine); the *oudh*, or lute; the *buzuq*, a larger and deep-toned stringed instrument; the *rebab*, a stringed instrument something like a dulcimer and played with a bow; the *tablah*, a small hand drum; and the *qanun*, similar to a zither. Two reed instruments are also used: the *ney*, a single-reed pipe; and the *maqrum*, a double-reed clarinet.

In recent decades, hip-hop has become an increasingly popular musical style in Morocco. Groups such as Fnaire, DJ Key, and H-Kayne are particularly well-liked by Moroccan youth, who share music from with second- and third-generation Moroccan Americans who visit the country during the summer months. In 2006 American filmmaker Joshua Asen received a Fulbright grant from the U.S. State Department to film a documentary on Moroccan hip-hop culture titled *I Love Hip Hop in Morocco*, which was later screened at venues throughout the United States.

Moroccan music has been studied and appreciated in the United States since the earliest Moroccan immigrants arrived in the mid-twentieth century. In 1959 the U.S. Library of Congress sponsored a tour of Morocco by author and composer Paul Bowles, who recorded samples of Moroccan music that were later issued in the United States as a two LP set titled *Music of Morocco* (1972). Moroccan music is still celebrated in the United States as it is played in the homes of Moroccan Americans and at cultural as well as religious functions. In 2007 the Kennedy Center in Washington, D.C., hosted the Genesis World Music Ensemble, in which musicians from Israel and across the Arab world—including acclaimed Moroccan singer and lute player Haj Youness—performed together in a symbol of unity. In 2011 Moroccan singer and human rights activist Saida Fikri organized the Magical Morocco festival in Stamford, Connecticut, complete with musical performances, food, dance, and art. The Moroccan American center in Washington, D.C., along with the Foundation for Middle East Peace and the Moroccan Embassy, hold a series of mixers known as "Talk Souk" for students and young professionals in the area to embrace their Moroccan heritage through dance, food, and music.

Arts and Crafts Moroccans are recognized as strong artisans, skilled in jewelry making, sculpture, and textiles, among other arts. In 2011 the Metropolitan Museum of Art in New York staged a Moroccan Courtyard exhibit as a centerpiece for its Islamic Art Galleries, complete with sculpted archways hand-crafted by several Moroccan and Moroccan American artists. Beautiful woven tapestries, ornate carpets, and stylish clothing are just some of the fiber arts produced by Moroccans and Moroccan Americans. The ancient art of henna, in which designs are drawn on the skin with a temporary, plant-based dye, provides an alternative to body art for those unwilling to commit to a permanent tattoo. Traditionally associated with Moroccan women's rituals surrounding mourning, procreation, and weddings, henna tattooing has become quite popular in the United States, with people of all generations, both male and female.

Holidays Moroccan Americans who are Muslims celebrate the Islamic holy month of Ramadan. Occurring late in the calendar year, Ramadan is a period of fasting and purification. During the thirty days of Ramadan, nothing—no food, drink, or cigarette smoke—is allowed to pass the lips from daybreak to sunset. This twelve-hour fast is then broken each night with the *iftar*, a celebratory family meal. During Ramadan, the faithful donate food and money to the needy, and spend time in prayer. Ramadan ends with the Eid al-Fitr, a special feast during which holiday foods are served and presents are given.

The most common celebrations of Moroccan holidays in the United States are religious in nature: the Moroccan Society of Houston, for example, hosts an annual Ramadan *Iftar*, as well as a celebration of Eid al-Adha, the feast in honor of the prophet Ibrahim's willingness to sacrifice his firstborn son. Likewise, the Moroccan American Community Organization of Chicago offers an annual Eid Festival to celebrate the end of Ramadan.

Other important Moroccan national holidays observed by both Muslims and Jews include the Presentation of Moroccan Independence Proclamation on January 11, Throne Day (commemorating King Mohammed VI's ascension to the throne) on July 30, and the Feast of Morocco's Independence from France on November 18. While not all of these holidays are observed by Moroccan Americans with as much fervor as they are in Morocco, they are still considered an important part of Moroccan heritage. In the United States these political holidays are sometimes commemorated with dinners, dances, or musical performances in community centers.

Health Care Issues and Practices Health issues among Moroccan Americans differ greatly from those in their homeland. Many medical issues in Morocco are directly related to malnutrition, poverty, and limited availability of health care. Many areas of Morocco have poor sanitation levels and lack access to clean water, and there is a shortage of hospitals, doctors, and nurses in the country. Major diseases, such as cholera, hepatitis, HIV, and internal parasites like giardia and hookworm, are all prevalent in Morocco. Health care in Morocco is mostly available for the upper-middle class and above. Because the majority of Moroccan Americans are from this well-educated, higher class, they generally fall into the category of Americans with health care. Medical studies suggest that some general health problems shared by people of Arab descent include sickle-cell anemia, malaria, type 2 diabetes, hypertension, and high cholesterol. Immigrants from Morocco often experience dental problems as well from their higher intake of processed foods upon arrival to the United States. Death rates in Morocco are generally higher than that of Moroccan Americans due to the lack of doctors and hospitals and unsanitary conditions among the lower class.

Death and Burial Rituals Jewish and Muslim Moroccans follow the death and burial rituals of their respective faiths. For instance, Muslims believe that the body of the deceased must be buried no later than twenty-four hours after death. Preparation of the body is done by the family at home with the help of a caregiver from the community. Moroccan Americans follow the practices of their faiths as well, but a more rigid sense of legality applies, with the issuance of a death certificate and other formalities in accordance with U.S. laws. Some Moroccan Americans choose to adhere to their cultural heritage surrounding the burial practices, while others conform to American standards of church services and funeral homes.

MOROCCAN PROVERBS

Moroccans use proverbs quite liberally in their speech in order to clarify situations or provide insight. Some proverbs are religious in nature, while others are related to everyday occurrences, bits of wisdom, or elements of culture like food or music.

- Believe what you see and lay aside what you hear.

- A wise woman has much to say and yet remains silent.

- He who follows the right path, thorns will not hurt him.

- He who wants honey should tolerate bee stings.

- Evening promises are like butter: morning comes, and it's all melted.

- A known mistake is better than an unknown truth.

Proverbs are often spoken in a call-and-response fashion; one speaker will deliver the first part, and the other will reply with second half as the sole means of discourse in passing.

FAMILY AND COMMUNITY LIFE

Moroccan Americans maintain many of the cultural norms and traditions surrounding the family unit in their native land. The family is still largely ruled as a patriarchy, with men taking the dominant role as breadwinners and women tending to the house and raising of the family. The Moroccan American community has adapted relatively easily to American's secular urban society, but their small numbers and their dispersal throughout cities across the country have presented challenges to the maintenance of ethnic unity. Moroccans in the United States, who are scattered across the country in many different urban areas or college towns, have increasingly used the Internet to share information about themselves and keep in touch with others who share their background.

Gender Roles In traditional Moroccan households, as with most Islamic cultures, family dynamics are strictly patriarchal, with the husband accorded power and the wife relegated to a subordinate status. Families tended to be large because of a 1939 law that made the advertisement or distribution of birth control illegal. However, with the repeal of the contraceptive ban by royal decree in 1967 and the subsequent modernization efforts in Morocco, family dynamics

also changed. In 2004, for example, the Moroccan parliament made a number of changes to the country's *Moudawana*, or Islamic family code, raising the minimum age of marriage from fifteen to eighteen, allowing women the right to divorce their husbands, and making it illegal for husbands to punish their wives with physical violence. Certainly, access to education has changed family relationships throughout much of the country as women have entered the workforce and gained more autonomy. Among Moroccan families in the United States, many women work outside the home and balance careers with family obligations.

Although Moroccan culture was heavily influenced by Arabic traditions, Amazigh customs generally accorded women more freedoms than they enjoyed in Middle Eastern Arab countries. Even in the modern era, though, males still dominate society and are given more opportunities to succeed and general freedoms than their female counterparts. Women are in charge of daily tasks around the household, and girls as young as five assist their mothers around the house with cleaning, cooking, babysitting, and other chores. Unlike many Muslim countries, where women are not allowed to receive an education or seek employment, women in higher-class Moroccan families are given opportunities to attend schools and work professional jobs in education, law, and medicine. Moroccan American women, who enjoy a relatively high level of education, are likely to work outside the home, with the 2011 American Community Survey indicating that over half of all Moroccan American women over the age of sixteen were in the labor force. Moroccan American women are provided with even more opportunities than their counterparts in the homeland. As citizens of the United States, they are given equal rights to men and the right to vote, although in the home they are still oftentimes seen as subservient to their male counterparts. In Morocco unmarried women experience relatively difficult lives both economically and socially; single Moroccan American women experience less hardship because their opportunity for success in the work environment is far greater.

Education Schooling in Morocco is compulsory for both girls and boys from ages seven through fifteen, but according to the *CIA World Factbook*, in 2012 the country's literacy rate was only 56.1 percent (68.9 percent for males and 43.9 percent for females). Moroccans who have settled in the United States, though, generally had higher levels of education and stronger job skills. Many arrived as students and furthered their education at American colleges and universities. The Moroccan American community values education as an important means of acquiring the knowledge and skills necessary to succeed in a commercial and high-tech economy. The American Community Survey estimated that in 2011 over one-third of all Moroccan Americans were enrolled in college or graduate school. Many Moroccan students return to their native country after graduating, as their likelihood of gaining employment there becomes far greater with an American education.

Courtship and Weddings Even in the modern world, Moroccan parents still exert some influence over their adult child's choice of a husband or wife, though this is becoming increasingly less common, particularly among Moroccan Americans. According to Islamic law, Muslim women must marry within their faith; however, Muslim men are allowed to marry non-Muslim women. In the United States especially, it is not uncommon for a Moroccan American man to marry a woman of different ethnic or religious background, while it is less common—though not unheard of—for a Moroccan American woman to marry outside of her religious and ethnic group. In traditional Moroccan courtship, the groom offers his future wife's family a bride price for the woman's hand in marriage, and the bride's family prepares a dowry and ensures that the girl is a virgin.

Weddings in Morocco are festive affairs, generally held during the summer months and often lasting for several days. Special garments are painstakingly woven and embroidered for the bride and groom. So important are these costumes that wedding garments from the city of Fez are exhibited on poles during parades on national holidays. Often, the bride orders several garments to be worn during the course of a long wedding. For the ceremony itself, the groom wears a long, loose fitting garment called a *jellaba*, and the bride wears the traditional long head shawl and kaftan. Special textiles are also used during the bride's henna ceremony, in which intricate patterns are traced on her hands with henna, a temporary red dye. Traditionally, a set of velvet accessories, embroidered with gold thread, is used for this custom. The *mendil*, a large rectangular cloth, is placed on the bride's lap while two pillows support her arms. Two special mitts protect her decorated hands. A special domed canopy, also decorated with gold thread, is used to cover the bride and groom while they are carried on trays above their guests. While divorce does occur in Morocco, it is looked upon as a disgrace, and statistics show that divorce is more common among Moroccan families of lower income than of higher income. Polygamy is also tolerated among Moroccan Muslims, although it is rare, and the practice is illegal in the United States.

Moroccan American weddings differ from traditional Moroccan weddings, with variations depending on the local community. In larger Moroccan American neighborhoods, cultural traditions hold more true, as there are a greater number of churches, cultural centers, and mosques available for such affairs, though events are usually limited to a single day rather than spanning several days. Moroccan American brides are typically adorned in henna and may change clothes between the ceremony and reception. Receptions include Moroccan music, dance, and foods such as tagine, though an American-style wedding cake is often served alongside more traditional Moroccan sweets and pastries. In more isolated areas, Moroccan Americans may keep their religious and marital practices in the home or attend less traditional churches or mosques that are not strictly related to Moroccan culture.

Although the United States has no direct equivalents to Moroccan cultural centers such as souks, hammams, or tea houses, Moroccan Americans are largely able to uphold their traditional dining practices and methods of greeting and socializing with their neighbors in the United States at home or in farmer's markets, mosques, and the increasingly common Moroccan restaurants found in urban areas.

Relations with Other Americans Arabized Berber immigrants from Morocco found only limited common ground with the existing Arab American community, which was overwhelmingly Christian until the influx of Palestinians and other Middle Eastern Arabs after the creation of Israel in 1948. These earliest groups of Arab Americans were the descendants of Syrian Christians, mostly merchants and traders, who had moved to the United States in the late 1800s. The newer Palestinian immigrants, however, were Muslim. Moroccans shared a linguistic tradition with both these groups and shared a religious affiliation with the Palestinians, but much in Moroccan history and culture differed from the Middle Eastern Arab experience. Moroccan Americans have not been excluded from the many Arab American associations that emerged to counteract prejudice and advocate for better access to jobs and social services in the United States. However, few Moroccan immigrants have allied themselves with such organizations because their focus is emphatically on the conditions that affect Arab immigrants from the Middle East.

In most large American cities, there are Moroccan organizations that seek to unify immigrants as well as share their country's culture with the greater community. Washington, D.C., home of the Moroccan Embassy, also has the Moroccan American Center, a nonprofit organization that shares Moroccan culture with the local community. Other organizations include the Moroccan Society of Houston, the Moroccan American House Association, and the Association of Moroccan Professionals in America. These organizations hold conventions, host message boards for members, share community concerns, raise awareness of issues affecting Moroccan Americans, and provide scholarships and aid to people in need, among other services. With the advent of the Internet, Moroccan American immigrants also connect via Facebook, Twitter, Tumblr, and other social media outlets to stay informed of issues within their respective communities and in their native country.

EMPLOYMENT AND ECONOMIC CONDITIONS

During the 1980s and 1990s many Moroccans entered the United States to attend colleges, universities, graduate schools, and medical schools. After completing their educations, some remained to begin careers in such professions as banking, engineering, computer science, medicine, architecture, journalism, research, and teaching. Other Moroccan immigrants have set up small businesses such as retail establishments or restaurants. Shops dealing in textiles (especially rugs), pottery, jewelry, and other handcrafts from Morocco have found a receptive clientele in the United States, as have restaurants featuring traditional Moroccan foods and entertainment. By the early twenty-first century, Moroccan Americans had branched out into all fields of business. While some immigrants live in tight-knit communities and run traditional businesses, many Moroccan Americans have assimilated into mainstream American culture as doctors, lawyers, and teachers as well as actors, athletes, and writers. According to the 2011 American Community Survey, the most common fields for Moroccan Americans were health care and education, followed by positions in the service industry, the arts, and retail.

POLITICS AND GOVERNMENT

The U.S. government has maintained strong diplomatic relations with the government of Morocco since Muhammed Ibn Abdullah, sultan of Morocco, first recognized the independent United States in 1777 and signed a friendship treaty along with Thomas Jefferson and John Adams in 1778. In 1957, the year after Morocco gained its independence, then–Vice President Richard Nixon visited Morocco to extend an official congratulation and reaffirm U.S.-Morocco ties. In 1999 President Bill Clinton visited Morocco to attend the funeral of King Hassan II, and in 2004 the United States and Morocco signed a landmark Free Trade Agreement, the first trade agreement signed between the United States and a country on the African continent. It eliminated tariffs on over 95 percent of goods exchanged between the two nations and paved the way for several American companies, including Dell and Fruit of the Loom, to open factories and offices in Morocco.

Because Moroccan immigrants to the United States are highly educated, they have been very quick to establish advocacy groups aimed at improving conditions in Morocco and strengthening opportunities for Moroccan Americans. The Moroccan American Center in Washington, D.C., operates both the Moroccan American Center for Policy and the Moroccan American Trade and Investment Council, which seek to influence public and private investment initiatives in Morocco. Other groups, such as the Morocco Foundation and Association of Moroccan Professionals in America, organize fundraisers and other events meant to provide relief for Moroccans living in poverty, particularly children.

NOTABLE INDIVIDUALS

Activism Hassan Samrhouni (1952–), a Moroccan-born activist who immigrated to the United States in 1982, is the CEO of Casablanca Travel and Tours and the founder of the Washington Morocco Club.

Government John Fritchey (1964–), a Louisiana-born second-generation Moroccan American, served in the Illinois House of Representatives from 1996 to 2010.

Literature Ruth Knafo Setton (1951–), a Sephardic Jew born in Said, Morocco, has established herself as a significant voice in American letters. Her short fiction and essays have appeared in numerous publications. Setton has received a National Endowment for the Arts fellowship and two Pennsylvania Council of Arts fellowships. She is the author of the novel *The Road to Fez* (2001) and teaches at Lafayette College.

Moroccan American author Laila Lalami (1968–) has written several books from the Moroccan perspective, including her second novel in English, *Secret Son* (2009), about belonging and identity.

Sports Khalid Khannouchi (1971–), born in Meknes, Morocco, immigrated to the United States in 1992. He holds world records in both the marathon and 20 km distance races.

A Moroccan American woman displays her new American citizenship certificate following a naturalization ceremony in Charleston, South Carolina, 2010. RICHARD ELLIS / GETTY IMAGES

Stage and Screen Danny Nucci (1968–) is a Moroccan American actor who has starred in such films as *Eraser* (1996), *The Rock* (1996), and *Titanic* (1997) as well as the TV shows *Criminal Minds*, *Twilight Zone, House M.D.*, and *The Mentalist*.

Khaleed Leon (Khleo) Thomas (1989–), is a musician and actor who has appeared in the films *Holes* (2003), *Walking Tall* (2004), and *Roll Bounce* (2005).

MEDIA

Morocco News Board

This news board is a source for Moroccan American affairs and contains news, local events, commentary, links, classifieds, and other sources for Moroccan immigrants and other interested parties. It encourages the Moroccan American community to become active participants in American business, society, and politics.

Mostapha Saout, Editor
Phone: (703) 623-8421
Fax: (888) 747-0957
Email: info@moroccoboard.com
URL: www.moroccoboard.com

Morocco World News

This news site is dedicated to reporting news of interest to Moroccans, Moroccan Americans, and other interested parties. It strives to bring people of different backgrounds together in a greater understanding of the needs of Morocco and the country's immigrant population in the United States.

30-23, 42nd Street
Apt 3L
Queens, New York 11103
Phone: (312) 282-6909
Email: info@moroccoworldnews.com
URL: www.moroccoworldnews.com

Wafin: Moroccan Connections in America

"Wafin" translates to "what's up" or "what's new." The site allows users to find Moroccan businesses, stay on top of Moroccan events, and discuss topics important to Moroccans and Moroccan Americans.

Gourad Media Group LLC
P.O. Box 874
Georgetown, Connecticut 06829-0874
Phone: (203) 340-6537
Fax: (203) 659-4791
Email: info@wafin.com
URL: www.wafin.com

ORGANIZATIONS AND ASSOCIATIONS

Association of Moroccan Professionals in America

This association promotes networking between Moroccan American business professionals as well as community service and education opportunities for Moroccan Americans.

P.O. Box 77254
San Francisco, California 94107
Fax: (801) 996-6334
URL: www.amp-usa.org

Friends of Morocco (FOM)

Established in 1988 with the intention of "promoting educational, cultural, charitable, social, literary and scientific exchange between Morocco and the United States of America," FOM maintains a "yellow pages" of organizations of interest to Moroccan Americans.

Tim Resch, President
P.O. Box 2579
Washington, D.C. 20013-2579
Phone: (703) 470-3166
Fax: (202) 219-0509
Email: timresch@gmail.com
URL: http://friendsofmorocco.org/

Moroccan American Business Council Ltd. (MABC)

The MABC was created to strengthen business ties and friendly relations between Morocco and the United States.

Ron Leavell, Executive Director
1085 Commonwealth Avenue
Boston, Massachusetts 02215
Phone: (508) 230-5985
Fax: (508) 230-9943
Email: Info@usa-morocco.org
URL: www.usa-morocco.org

The Moroccan American House Association

This association is involved with Moroccan American community building, religious teachings, and legal assistance for immigrants to New York specifically as well as the greater United States.

307 Bayridge Avenue
Brooklyn, New York 11220
Phone: (347) 513-1399
Email: info@moroccanamericanhouse.com
URL: http://moroccanamericanhouse.com/

Moroccan Association of Chicago (MAC)

The MAC is a nonprofit organization that promotes community involvement among Chicago-area Moroccan Americans. Events include religious celebrations, professional workshops, fundraisers, and an annual soccer tournament.

Email: MAC-US@hotmail.com
URL: http://mac-us.org

Morocco Foundation

Founded in 2004, the Morocco Foundation is a nonprofit group aimed at alleviating poverty in Morocco. Members organize fundraisers and events to promote schooling for underprivileged children and to provide material aid to rural communities in Morocco.

Nadia Serhani
6423 Richmond Hwy.
301
Alexandria, Virginia 22306

Phone: (703) 577-5317
Email: info@moroccofoundation.org
URL: www.morocco-foundation.org

MUSEUMS AND RESEARCH CENTERS

American Institute for Maghrib Studies (AIMS)

Established in 1984, this scholarly association focuses on North African history and culture. It sponsors the *Journal of North African Studies*, provides grants for scholarship on the region, and organizes an annual conference and workshop.

845 N. Park Avenue
Marshall Building
Room 470
P.O. Box 210158-B
Tucson, Arizona 85721-0158
Phone: (520) 626-6498
Fax: (520) 621-9257
Email: aims@aimsnorthafrica.org
URL: www.aimsnorthafrica.org

Moroccan American Center

This conglomeration consists of three centers: The Moroccan American Center for Policy, the Moroccan American Trade and Investment Center, and the Moroccan American Cultural Center. Based in Washington, D.C., these groups deal with all aspects of Moroccan immigrants' adjustment to life in the United States.

Fatima-Zohra Kurtz, Executive Director
1220 L Street NW
Suite 411
Washington, D.C. 20005
Phone: (202) 587-0855
Email: info@moroccanamericancenter.com
URL: http://moroccoonthemove.wordpress.com

Moroccan Studies Program at the Harvard University Center for Middle Eastern Studies

This Harvard University program is the only one of its kind in the United States; it is devoted to teaching about the history, politics, culture, and arts of Morocco.

William Granara, Director
38 Kirkland Street
Cambridge, Massachusetts 02138
Phone: (617) 495-4055
Fax: (617) 496-8584
Email: cmes@fas.harvard.edu
URL: http://cmes.hmdc.harvard.edu/research/msp

SOURCES FOR ADDITIONAL STUDY

Ben-Ur, Aviva. *Sephardic Jews in America: A Diasporic History*. New York: New York University Press, 2009.

Bibas, David. *Immigrants and the Formation of Community: A Case Study of Moroccan Jewish Immigration to America*. New York: AMS Press, 1998.

Dellal, Mohamed, and Amar Sellam, eds. *Moroccan Culture in the 21st Century: Globalization, Challenges and Prospects*. Hauppauge, NY: Nova Publishers, 2013.

Edwards, Brian T. *Morocco Bound: Disorienting America's Maghreb, from Casablanca to the Marrakech Express*. Durham, NC: Duke University Press, 2005.

Lahlou, Mourad. *Mourad: New Moroccan*. New York: Artisan, 2011.

Miller, Susan Gilson. "Kippur on the Amazon." *Sephardi and Middle Eastern Jewries: History and Culture*. Jewish Theological Seminary, 1996.

Pratt, Ruth Marcus. *The Sephardim of New Jersey*. Jewish Historical Society of Central New Jersey, 1992.

NAVAJOS

D. L. Birchfield

OVERVIEW

The Navajo are a Native American people whose traditional lands are the region of the American Southwest that is today known as the Four Corners (where the boundaries of Colorado, New Mexico, Arizona, and Utah meet). Navajos teach that their Creator set them in this region on the land between four mountains: Mount Blanca (Dawn or White Shell Mountain) near Alamosa in San Luis Valley, Colorado, the Sacred Mountain of the East; Mount Taylor (Blue Bead or Turquoise Mountain) north of Laguna, New Mexico, the Sacred Mountain of the South; the San Francisco Peak (Abalone Shell Mountain) near Flagstaff, Arizona, the Sacred Mountain of the West; and Mount Hesperus (Obsidian Mountain) in the La Plata Mountains of Colorado, the Sacred Mountain of the North. The land is mostly a plateau in which canyons plunge to a depth that almost equals the height of the mountains. The Spanish borrowed the word *Nabahu*, meaning "those with large cultivated fields," from the Tewa Pueblos and called this group "Apaches de Nabajo." The term eventually became *Navajo*, although Navajos refer to themselves as the Diné, meaning "the people."

The Navajo first came into contact with the Spanish in 1598, and a Spanish account from the early 1600s refers to 30,000 "Apaches de Navajo." However, most scholars distrust this number and believe a more accurate estimate to be considerably under 10,000. The largely nomadic Navajos were hunters and gatherers who lived in small, independent bands based on matrilineal kinship, migrating around the Southwest according to the seasons and the availability of food. They raided other groups of Native Americans, particularly Puebloan tribes, primarily for corn and women. They were known for their adaptability, integrating into their culture pieces of the cultures of their captives or of wanderers who joined them. From the Pueblos they borrowed many agricultural practices, and from the Utes, who were formidable warriors, they learned a variety of warfare techniques. By the time the Spanish arrived in the Southwest during the late sixteenth century, the Navajos had become a large and powerful tribe engaged extensively in agriculture.

The Navajo Nation, located on the southwestern Colorado Plateau where Arizona, New Mexico, Utah, and Colorado meet (although the reservation is not in Colorado), is the largest reservation in the United States, covering 27,673 square miles (71,673 square kilometers). A majority of Navajos have lived on the reservation since the Treaty of 1868. The treaty allowed surviving Navajos to return from the Bosque Redondo internment camp to a portion of their ancestral homeland, about one-fourth the size of the territory they inhabited before being displaced to Bosque Redondo. Executive orders and Congressional legislation gradually increased the size of the reservation to its current size of more than six million acres. Despite employment in the health and education sectors on the Navajo Reservation and the fact that the Navajo Nation is a large employer of the Navajo people, many Navajos live in poverty. There was some employment in the oil and gas industry, but in the twenty-first century that has become far less predictable. Also, much of the oil and gas mining is done by corporations, benefiting the Navajo treasury, which in turn supports programs that benefit the individual tribal members.

The United States Census Bureau's American Community Survey estimates for 2006–2010 reported that there were 346,017 people of Navajo ancestry in the United States (this number is roughly the same as the population of Honolulu, Hawaii). The Navajos are far more likely to live on the reservation than are other Native Americans: while 78 percent of Native Americans live outside the boundaries of their reservations, only half of Navajo people live off the Navajo Nation. Nevertheless, many young Navajos are leaving the reservation for cities such as Albuquerque, Los Angeles, and Phoenix, typically because of the lack of jobs on the reservation. According to the American Community Survey estimates for 2009–2011, the states with the largest number of Navajos were Arizona (149,113), New Mexico (118,974), and Utah (19,955)—the states where the Navajo Nation is located.

HISTORY OF THE PEOPLE

Early History The earliest Navajos were hunter-gatherers, but shortly after the arrival of the Spanish in the late sixteenth century, the Navajos exchanged their nomadic lifestyle for a pastoral one of sheep-herding and farming. Their transition to farming was greatly influenced by their relationship with the

Pueblo people. The Navajos alternately raided and traded with the Pueblo. Many female Pueblo captives became the wives of Navajo men, so their children were both Pueblo and Navajo. After the Spanish arrived, young Navajo males continued to raid other tribes as well as Spanish settlements to claim livestock. Predictably, those they raided responded. The Spanish were particularly brutal in their slave-raids and land grabs. During the seventeenth century, the Southwestern tribes organized uprisings against the Spanish, but those were quickly suppressed. When the Tewa leader, Popé, organized the successful Pueblo Revolt of 1680, the Navajos participated, and the movement ended Spanish rule in what is now New Mexico for twelve years.

By 1692 Spanish governor Diego de Vargas Zapata y Luján Ponce de León had begun a re-conquest of the territory, and the Navajo homeland became a refuge for various tribes fleeing Spanish forces. Aiding refugee tribes such as the Hopi, Apaches, and various Pueblo groups had a profound influence on Navajo culture. Archeologists have noted the Pueblo introduced weaving, painted pottery, and the *pueblito*— defensibly located stone structures—into Navajo culture. At Cañon de Chelly in 1804, a war begun by the Navajos led to a Spanish victory that meant the destruction of traditional Navajo homes (domed earth structures known as *hogans*), and crops as well as the capture of their animals and dozens of their women and children.

The pattern continued after Mexico gained independence from Spain in 1821. When the Southwest was annexed by the United States in 1848, conflict continued. The Office of Indian Affairs—later renamed the Bureau of Indian Affairs (BIA)—failed to end the slave-trading or destruction of Navajo crops. The U.S. government's inability to understand Navajo social structure exacerbated the problems, and a series of treaties failed because those representing the United States never understood that the Navajos had no chief with the authority to negotiate for the Diné.

In 1864 Cañon de Chelly was once again the setting for a devastating Navajo defeat. Famed Indian fighter Kit Carson, acting under the orders of Brigadier General James H. Carleton, commander of the Federal District of New Mexico, had instituted a scorched-earth policy against the Navajos; it culminated in January 1864 at Canyon de Chelly, the last Navajo stronghold, where the group was forced to choose to surrender or be killed. In an ordeal known as the "Long Walk," about eight thousand Navajos were forced to march about three hundred miles to Bosque Redondo, an internment camp located at Fort Sumner in New Mexico. The journey claimed the lives of three hundred, and as many as three thousand of those who completed the trip died of starvation or disease during the four years the Navajos were captive. Many Navajos avoided the Long Walk by hiding out in the Grand Canyon and Navajo Mountain; others were captured

and sold into slavery. With the signing of the Treaty of 1868, the Navajos were free to return to their homeland, albeit one that was less than one-fourth the size of the land that they had previously inhabited.

As the Navajos settled onto their land and reclaimed their way of life, they became more prosperous. As livestock increased, so did the demand for pasture land. At the same time, ranchers and homesteaders were moving deeper into public domain lands. Conflicts were inevitable. Navajo land was extended five times between 1878 and 1886. Trading posts where Navajo rugs were particularly popular brought other changes as a barter economy increased. Blanket weaving and silverwork for Navajo consumption evolved into a profitable trade as the Navajos began selling their art to tourists. The construction of railroads brought some wage-earning jobs and provided new markets for the sale of Navajo crafts and art. The railroad also allowed Navajos the chance to experience life off the reservation. The Treaty of 1868 also required all Navajo children to attend school. The first school, operated under the supervision of the Presbyterian Church, was opened in 1869 at Fort Defiance, but closed soon after due to poor attendance. In the 1900s additional boarding schools were erected on the reservation.

Modern Era By 1900 the Navajo Reservation had almost quadrupled in size, mostly through executive orders, and the population had reached 15,000. In 1901 Navajo territory was divided into six agency jurisdictions for more effective governance. In 1927 John Hunt, superintendent of Leupp Agency, introduced the first Chapter system, a system more culturally compatible with the Navajos, who were accustomed to discussing issues in face-to-face conversations. The Chapter system remained in effect in the early twenty-first century, when there were 110 chapters of the Navajo Nation.

The first legislative council of the Navajos was put in place in 1923 in response to outside interests in oil and mineral rights on reservation land. Because the treaty of 1868 required the consent of 75 percent of all Navajo adult males for legal decisions, an almost impossible number to attain, businesses interested in oil leases lobbied the U.S. government for the creation of a business council that would "represent" the views of Navajo men. The result was a tribal council of six members and six alternates that met for the first time in July 1923. Unfortunately the group lacked any real power because all tribal matters were under the supervision of the federal government and the BIA. The council could not even meet without the approval of the Special Commissioner to the Navajo Tribe. A larger, more representative group was established in 1938 under the U.S. government's "Rules of the Navajo Tribal Council," issued in 1936. This second council formed the basis for the Navajo Nation's government, which remains in effect in the early twenty-first century.

While the Navajos derived some benefit from the oil leases, the federal government did a poor job of protecting the tribe's interests. When the Navajos requested information on their oil royalties, they discovered that the government had not monitored production, obtained accurate royalty figures, or policed the protection of land from pipeline leaks. Even when it became evident that oil companies were defrauding the Navajos, little was done to correct the problem.

However, the losses from oil leases paled in comparison to those from uranium mining that began in the 1940s. Between 1944 and 1986, mine operators extracted nearly four million tons of uranium ore from mines on Navajo land. Dust from the waste blew into local communities, filling the air and settling on the water supplies. The Atomic Energy Commission assured worried local residents that the dust was harmless. It was not until thirty years after mining started that the Department of Energy released a report saying that people living near the tailings ran twice the risk of lung cancer of the general population. One Public Health Service study warned that one in six uranium miners had died, or would die prematurely, of lung cancer. The Navajos who worked in the uranium mines had been exposed to between 100 and 1,000 times the limit later considered safe for exposure to radon gas.

By 1978 more than 700,000 acres of Navajo land were under lease to companies exploring and developing uranium. The largest nuclear accident in the United States was not at Three Mile Island but at Church Rock, New Mexico, where on July 16, 1979, more than 1,100 tons of uranium-mining waste and more than 100 million gallons of radioactive wastewater gushed into the Puerco River, which carried it downstream to the Navajo Reservation. Press releases warning residents not to drink the water were of little benefit to the Navajos who could not read English or who lacked electricity to power televisions and radios. Congress apologized for failing to warn the Navajos about the dangers of uranium mining and eventually passed legislation guaranteeing compensation for miners in the Southwest who had developed lung cancer or other respiratory diseases as a result of their work for the nuclear-weapons industry from 1947 to 1971. However, twenty years after the tragedy, fewer than 30 percent of Navajo claims had been approved. In 2007 the United States Environmental Protection Agency, along with four other government organizations, developed a five-year plan to address the uranium contamination on the Navajo Reservation. By 2013 more than five hundred sites of contaminated land, water, air, and homes across the Navajo Nation remained to be cleaned up, a toxic legacy confronting a new generation.

Less costly in terms of human life and environmental damage, livestock reduction took a heavy cultural toll of the Navajos. Since their return to their

Navajo family, 1930s. EVERETT COLLECTION / NEWSCOM

land in 1868, the Navajos had worked hard to increase their herds, believing that doing so was the best way to sustain their way of life. With the increase in livestock, however, came concerns about overgrazing. Due to the 1930s Dust Bowl, soil erosion had become an issue, leaving most of the land on the Navajo Reservation unfarmable. The U.S. government, claiming that overgrazing had created these environmental problems, instituted a livestock-reduction policy without Navajo consent. This drastically reduced a large portion of Navajo sheep and produced devastating economic and psychological effects on the Navajos, who depended on their sheep for meat, clothing, textiles, and trade. The Navajos first rejected the Indian Reorganization Act (IRA) in 1935 because they feared it would increase livestock reduction, but their opposition was fruitless. The program continued throughout the 1930s. Due to the carrying capacity of the land, which could not support large herds, the number of sheep and goats has continued to decline, and young Navajos of the twenty-first century are more likely to be found seeking jobs in nearby towns to aid family and reservation economy than herding family livestock.

During the 1960s, as the civil rights movement gained momentum, Navajo leaders asserted more authority, and the power of the BIA waned. In 1965 the Navajo Tribal Council established the Office of Navajo Economic Opportunity, which supported programs that promoted community development. Two years later a legal services program bearing the name Dinebeeina Nahiilna be Agitahe (meaning "attorneys who contribute to the economic revitalization of the people"), better known as DNA, was inaugurated. In 1969 the Navajo Tribal Council formally declared the Navajo Reservation to be "the Navajo Nation," emphasizing the cultural unity and the sovereign status of the Navajos. In 1970 legislation established the Navajo Agricultural Products Industry, an agribusiness owned and operated by the Navajos that in 2006 became the first company in New Mexico to sign a trade deal with

Cuba. In 1972 the Navajo Environmental Protection Commission was established and charged with protecting the environment and developing, implementing, and enforcing environmental laws and regulations. In 1995 the commission became the Navajo Nation Environmental Protection Agency (NNEPA), a separate regulatory branch of the Navajo Nation government with the mission of protecting human health, welfare, and the environment of the Navajo Nation. In the early twenty-first century, the Navajos continue to adapt in order to survive and to commit to the preservation of Navajo culture.

SETTLEMENT IN THE UNITED STATES

Many anthropologists believe that the Navajos and Apaches, as members of the Athabaskan language family, were among the last peoples to have crossed the land bridge from Siberia to Alaska thousands of years ago during the last Ice Age. The Athabaskan language family is one of the most widely dispersed language families in North America, and most of its members still reside in the far north in Alaska and Canada.

It is not known, and will probably never be known, exactly when the Navajos and Apaches (Southwestern Athabaskans) began migrating from the far north to the Southwest or what route they took. Linguists who study changes in language and then estimate how long related languages have been separated have offered the year 1000 CE as an approximate date for the beginning of the migration. Excavations north of Farmington, New Mexico, uncovered a dozen sites with twenty-three radiocarbon dates that predate the 1500s, some as early as the 1300s.

What is now known as the Navajo homeland was inhabited by one of the most remarkable civilizations of ancient people in North America, the Ancestral Puebloans. Ancestral Puebloan ruins are among the most spectacular ruins in North America—especially their elaborate cliff dwellings, such as the ones at Mesa Verde National Park, and such communities as Chaco Canyon, where multistory stone masonry apartment buildings and large underground kivas (ceremonial rooms) can still be seen today.

Scholars originally thought that the arrival of the Southern Athabaskan in the Southwest was a factor in the collapse of the Ancestral Puebloan civilization. It is now generally accepted that the Ancestral Puebloans expanded to a point where they had stretched the delicate balance of existence in their fragile, arid environment to where it could not withstand the severe, prolonged droughts that occurred at the end of the fourteenth century. In all likelihood, the Ancestral Puebloans had moved close to the more dependable sources of water along the watershed of the upper Rio Grande River and had reestablished themselves as the Pueblo peoples by the time the Navajos entered the Southwest. The Navajos then claimed this empty land as their own. They first settled in what they call *Dinetah*, which means "homeland of the Diné," in what is now

the far northwestern corner of New Mexico. After they acquired sheep and horses from the Spanish—which revolutionized their lives—and acquired cultural and material attributes from the Pueblos—which further enhanced their ability to adjust to the environment of the Southwest—the Navajos then spread out into all of *Diné Bikeyah*, "the Navajo country."

Following the arrival of the Spanish in the late sixteenth century, the Navajos were forced to fight to maintain their sovereignty and native lands. Between constant conflicts with the Spanish and later with the American government, the Navajos lost much of their land to white settlers. After the Long Walk in 1864, the Navajos were granted a reservation one-fourth the size of their original territory. During the early 1900s, the Navajo population grew significantly, forcing the U.S. government to extend the size of the reservation. However, the lack of education, jobs, and economic opportunity, as well as a variety of environmental issues, plagued the tribe during much of the twentieth century. Uranium mining continues to be an issue that challenges the Navajos in the early twenty-first century. The Navajo tribal government has outlined their concerns about the gathering of energy resources, reminding the U.S. Congress that public land and tribal land are not the same thing.

In the early twenty-first century, many Navajos are leaving the reservation to live elsewhere. The Navajo tribal government cites the lack of jobs, especially for college graduates, as a reason why the majority of young Navajos are moving to urban areas such as Albuquerque, Los Angeles, and Phoenix.

As of 2011 almost half of Navajos still lived on the Navajo Reservation, and the American Community Survey reported that the states with the highest number of Navajos are Arizona, New Mexico, and Utah, the states where the Navajo Reservation is located.

LANGUAGE

The Athabaskan language family has four branches: Northern Athabaskan, Southwestern Athabaskan, Pacific Coast Athabaskan, and Eyak, a southeast Alaska isolate. The Athabaskan language family is one of three families within the Na-Dené language phylum. (The other two, the Tlingit family and the Haida family, are language isolates in the far north, Tlingit in southeast Alaska, and Haida in British Columbia.) Na-Dené is one of the most widely distributed language phyla in North America. The Southwestern Athabaskan language, sometimes called Apachean, has seven dialects: Navajo, Western Apache, Chiricahua, Mescalero, Jicarilla, Lipan, and Kiowa-Apache.

The Navajo language first appeared in writing in 1849 in the form of a Navajo word list published in James H. Simpson's *Journal of a Military Reconnaissance*. The earliest books in the Navajo language were the work of missionaries, who early

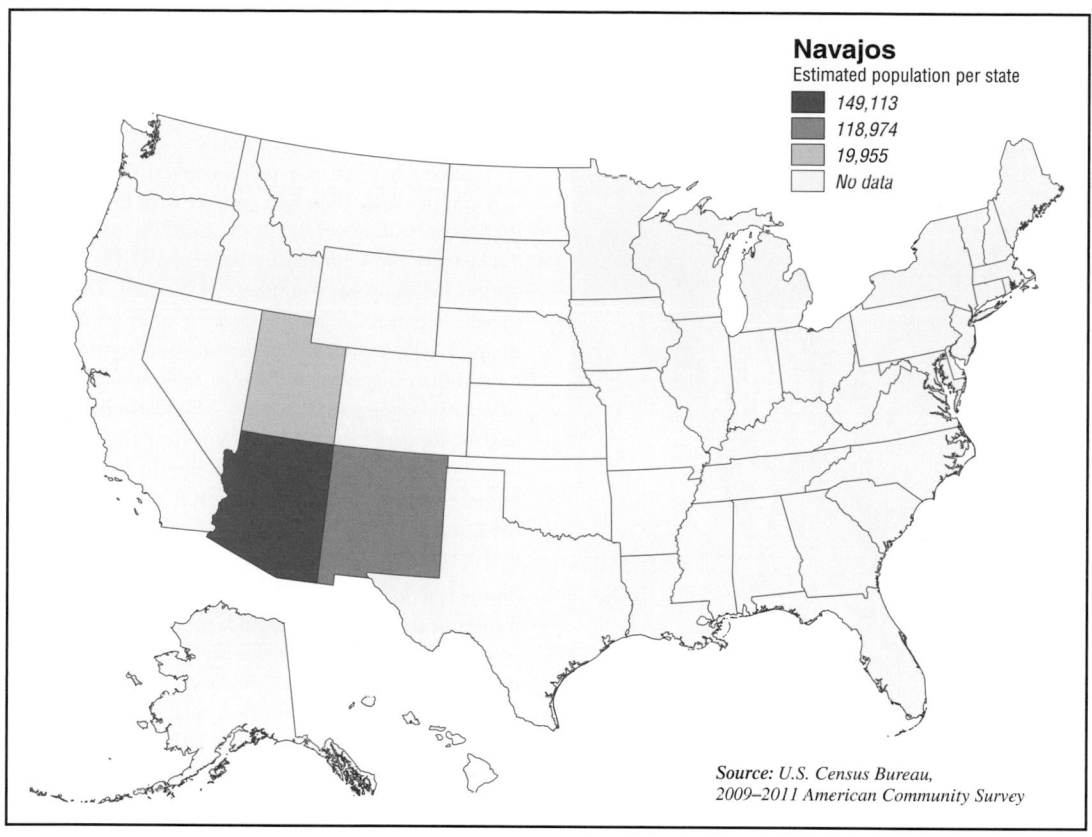

Navajos
Estimated population per state

- 149,113
- 118,974
- 19,955
- No data

*Source: U.S. Census Bureau,
2009–2011 American Community Survey*

in the twentieth century created religious texts, dictionaries, and grammars in the Navajo language, but they were handicapped by the lack of standardized spelling. It was not until the 1930s that John Collier, the head of Indian Affairs, and Willard Beatty, the head of Indian Education, gave John Harrington, Robert Young, William Morgan, and Oliver LaFarge the task of creating a standard Navajo alphabet. A decade later the first bilingual primers—Navajo-language children's books, a modern dictionary, and a monthly newsletter—were published using the alphabet. Anger over the federal government's livestock reduction program led the Navajos to distrust the written alphabet, a situation that seriously hampered literacy efforts.

Despite attempts by the federal government to eradicate the Navajo language through boarding schools and other assimilation efforts, beginning in the late nineteenth and continuing through much of the twentieth centuries, the Navajo language has survived. According to 2000 U.S. Census data, more than 120,000 of the Navajos residing on the Navajo Nation reservation spoke the Navajo language, but those under the age of eighteen were less likely to do so. Almost 25,000 Navajo children at that time spoke only English. The twenty-first century has seen a revival of interest in the Navajo language, and the development of Navajo computer fonts has made it considerably easier to write and

publish material in Navajo. Unfortunately, after the global economic recession that began in the early twenty-first century, schools' Navajo language immersion programs have been falling victim to budget cuts, and many Navajos worry that their children will not have the opportunity to learn the language.

RELIGION

Navajo religion is made up of a complex system of ceremonials. There are two different kinds of ceremonials: rites, in which a rattle is not used, and chantways, in which a rattle is used and singing accompanies the ritual. Each ceremonial is uniquely linked to a different group of powers, or supernatural beings, although there is much overlap. There are many personalized beings who are similar to humans or capable of assuming human properties. Even mountains contain an inner form. Some of these powers include Snake, Bear, Corn People, Ant, Cactus, Winds, Water Monster, and Endless Snake.

The chantways are known as *hataal* or "sings" and are performed by medicine men called *hataalii*. Hataalii singers train for a long time with older experts before performing in actual ceremonials. Because there are many chants, each of which requires accurate knowledge of prayers, plant medicines, ritual acts, and hundreds of songs, hataalii learn only one or two chants. A few singers have learned half a dozen chants. Chantways focus

A Navajo woman from Arizona. UNIVERSAL IMAGES GROUP LIMITED / ALAMY

are quite complex and exemplify the highly developed religious practices of Navajo society. Most of the ceremonial system is considered sacred, and non-Navajo are not allowed to view the procedures or the sand-painting imagery.

Efforts have been made to convert the Navajo to Christianity since their first contact with Europeans in the seventeenth century, but not until the mid-twentieth century did Christianity become a viable spiritual option for significant numbers of Navajos. In a 1976 survey, between 25 and 50 percent of Navajos called themselves Christians, the percentage varying widely by region and gender. Dozens of denominations have adherents among the Navajos. The Catholic Church has the longest history, but evangelical sects, particularly Southern Baptists, have a significant presence. Some estimates place the Mormon converts among the Diné as high as 20 percent.

The Native American Church is the most popular on the reservation. Over 25,000 Navajos participate in it to some degree, and thousands more attend its peyote ceremonies. (Peyote is a small cactus—with psychoactive properties and entheogenic uses—grown primarily in Texas and Mexico.) Some scholars have estimated the participation rate to be around 60 percent. The popularity is due in part to the blend of traditional Navajo beliefs with the peyote ritual. In the late 1960s the tribal council approved the religious use of peyote, ending twenty-seven years of persecution. The Native American Church had originally gained a stronghold on the Ute Mountain Reservation, which adjoins the Navajo Nation to the northeast. In 1936 the church began to spread to the south into the Navajo Nation, and it grew strong among the Navajos in the 1940s.

Many Navajos practice more than one religion, and most maintain a degree of loyalty to traditional Navajo beliefs regardless of any other religious beliefs they hold, including Catholicism and Mormonism.

CULTURE AND ASSIMILATION

Because they have remained relatively isolated from the centers of European population, because they have been able to hold onto a large part of their ancestral homeland, and because of the great distances and poor roads within the region, the Navajos have been more successful than most Native Americans in retaining their culture, language, and customs. Until early in the twentieth century Navajos were also able to carry out their traditional way of life and support themselves with their livestock, remaining relatively unnoticed by the dominant culture. Boarding schools, the proliferation of automobiles and roads, and federal land management policies—especially regarding traditional Navajo grazing practices—have all made the reservation a different place than what it was in the late nineteenth century. As late as 1950, paved roads ended at the fringes of the reservation at Shiprock, Cameron, and Window Rock. Even wagons were not widely used until the

on curing, and one of three rituals can be performed: Holyway, Evilway, or Lifeway. The Holyway rituals are sung over a sick person as a way to restore health, while Lifeway rituals treat injuries. Evilway rituals are sung to ward off evil, and both Evilway and Holyway rituals include sand-painting ceremonies.

Two of the major rites are Blessingway and Enemyway. The Blessingway rites are the core of Navajo traditional religion. Blessingway is employed for protection—for example, the departure or return of a soldier or for livestock safety. It is also used for blessing things such as a new hogan or consecrating a marriage or ceremonial tools. The Enemyway rite was performed to protect Navajo warriors from the ghosts of fallen enemies. Today it is used to cure sickness caused by the ghosts of non-Navajos.

The ceremonies, chantways, ceremonial procedures, equipment, and other aspects of Navajo religion early 1930s. By 1974, however, almost two-thirds of all Navajo households owned an automobile. The Navajos are finding ways to use some changes to support traditional culture. Bilingual education programs and broadcast and publishing programs in the Navajo language are also using the tools of change to preserve and strengthen traditional cultural values and language.

Traditions and Customs Navajo traditional life has remained strong. In 1941 an anthropologist interviewed an entire community of several hundred Navajos and could not find even one adult over the age of thirty-five who had not received traditional medical care from a "singer," a Navajo medicine man called a *hataalii*. Virtually all of the 3,600 Navajos who served in World War II underwent the cleansing of the Enemyway ceremony upon their return from the war. Today when a new health care facility is built on the reservation it includes a room for the traditional practice of medicine by members of the Navajo Medicine Man's Association. There are twenty-four chantway ceremonies performed by singers. Some last up to nine days and require the assistance of dozens of helpers, especially dancers. Twelve hundred different sand-painting designs are available to the medicine men for the chantways.

Cuisine Traditionally, the Navajos were hunter/gatherers, and their diet represented this lifestyle. Mutton was the main meat, since the Navajos were successful sheep farmers, although wild game, such as deer and antelope, was also hunted and consumed. Mutton was often boiled and served with corn, an important staple of the Navajo people. Corn was prepared a variety of ways: boiled, roasted, or dried and ground into cornmeal, which could be prepared as mush or cake (cornbread). The Navajos ate a variety of fruits and vegetables grown in their gardens or foraged such as chokecherries, melons, yucca, and potatoes. Squash and beans were also important crops. After forcing them to relocate to Bosque Redondo in 1864, the U.S. government gave the Navajos rations of lard, sugar, flour, and salt. It was likely that this was when the Navajos created their version of frybread, a deep-fried flatbread popular in many Native American cultures.

Today Navajos eat the same types of foods as other Americans. However, there are many restaurants on the Navajo reservation that serve traditional foods such as Navajo tacos, a traditional taco filling served on frybread instead of a tortilla, and mutton stew. The Choohostso Indian Market in Window Rock, Arizona, serves mutton stew, squash stew, mutton sandwiches, frybread, and Navajo tacos along with other Navajo fare.

Traditional Dress During precolonial times, the Navajos made many of their garments from deer skin, including shirts, leggings, moccasins, and skirts. Women's clothing evolved into the squaw dress, or *biil* dress, which consists of two woven blankets laced at the sides. The most famous biil belonged to Juanita, the wife of Chief Manuelito, the great Navajo leader. The dress,

part of the collection of the Autry National Center in Los Angeles, is seen by many Navajos, especially women and weavers, as an important symbol of Navajo culture. After the Long Walk, typical dress for men became a cotton or velvet shirt with deerskin leggings. Women donned a long-sleeved shirt with a pleated cotton or velvet skirt.

Today the Navajos wear typical Western clothing such as jeans and T-shirts. However, many weavers have begun to make the biil dress again for girls to wear on special occasions such as graduations and during ceremonies. Also, ceremonial clothing such as intricately woven sashes, moccasins, and painted masks are still worn for dances, festivals, and powwows.

Dances and Songs Dance in Navajo culture is a way for tribal members to honor themselves and their surroundings. Except for dance and singing competitions held at powwows, most Navajo traditional dances and songs are a part of healing ceremonies, at which visitors are allowed only with the permission of the family. Photography and video or tape recording of the ceremonies are not permitted without the express authorization of the healers. Charlotte Heth of the Department of Ethnomusicology at the University of California, Los Angeles, noted in a chapter of *Native America: Portrait of the Peoples*, that

> Apache and Navajo song style are similar: tense, nasal voices; rhythmic pulsation; clear articulation of words in alternating sections with vocables. Both Apache Crown Dancers and Navajo Yeibichei (Night Chant) dancers wear masks and sing partially in falsetto or in voices imitating the supernaturals.

The Dineh Tah' Navajo dance troupe from Albuquerque, New Mexico, performs a variety of traditional dances for both Navajo and non-Navajo audiences. They modify their performances for non-Navajo audiences in order to protect the sacred religious aspects. Some of the dances they showcase include the Enemyway ceremony; the Navajo Gourd Dance; and the Navajo Ribbon Dance. Traditionally, the Enemyway ceremony was performed in the summer to protect the Navajos from the ghosts of slain enemies. Today it is performed socially as a contest. The Gourd Dance is a performed as a blessing ceremony and is concerned with aspects of healing and restoring harmony. The Navajo Ribbon Dance is one of the most colorful performances, due to the different colored ribbons used to represent the different seasons and stages of life. The dance is part of the Mountain Way ceremony, which is held during the fall and winter. Any Navajo who performs the dance for a non-Navajo audience must greatly modify the performance to protect the sacred songs and dances that are part of the actual ceremony.

Traditional Crafts Navajo jewelry, especially work done in silver and turquoise, is internationally famous. Navajo silversmithing dates from 1853, when a Mexican silversmith arrived at Fort Defiance in what is now Arizona. A Navajo named 'Atsidi Sani learned the craft from him and taught it to others. By 1867 several Navajos were working with silver, and by 1880 they had begun to combine turquoise with their designs. At the turn of the century the Fred Harvey Company asked Navajo silversmiths to make lighter pieces for the tourist trade and guaranteed them a sales outlet. Today silversmithing is a craft practiced by many Navajos.

According to Navajo tradition, Spider Woman and Spider Man first introduced weaving to the Navajos. Spider Man built the first loom, and Spider Woman taught the people how to weave. Many Navajo scholars have found archeological evidence that the Navajos learned to weave from the Zuni Pueblos. In precolonial times, weaving was mainly a male activity, but since then has largely been considered a female occupation. Weaving is also an important economic activity throughout the nation. Navajo weaving has undergone many changes in designs. The Navajos are continually creating new ones, and various locations within the nation have become famous for particular types of rugs and patterns. Weaving underwent a revival in the 1920s, when Chinle, Arizona, weavers introduced the multicolored Wide Ruins, Crystal, and Pine Springs patterns.

Because they have remained relatively isolated from the centers of European population, because they have been able to hold onto a large part of their ancestral homeland, and because of the great distances and poor roads within the region, the Navajos have been more successful than most Native Americans in retaining their culture, language, and customs.

Today the Navajo Nation owns the Navajo Nation Arts and Crafts Enterprise at Window Rock, where customers can be assured of purchasing authentic Indian crafts made by Indian people. Many weavers have to sell their rugs wholesale to traders, but the Navajo Weavers Market is one way that weavers can sell to collectors at retail prices. The rug weavers' auction at Crownpoint is known worldwide. These events also offer weavers the chance to view other designs and styles, inspiring them to create new pieces. Weavers have also begun to establish cooperatives and auctions in order to gain more control over the market. Although the majority of weavers are women, more men are beginning to take up the art as a way to stay connected to their culture. In 2012 the Hood Museum of Art at Dartmouth College in New Hampshire displayed two Navajo rugs, one made by Helen Curley and another by her grandson, Jason Curley. This display represented the passing of the weaving tradition

from an older family member to a younger family member. Another weaving tradition that has become popular again is that of the biil, or the traditional woven dress. The biil used to be made only by weavers for family members, but an increasing number of weavers are now making and selling the dresses.

Holidays While the Navajos traditionally did not celebrate holidays, many of the most important dances and ceremonies were performed on a yearly basis. The Enemyway ceremony is performed in the summer and spring, while the Mountain Way ceremony is performed during the winter and fall. The Navajo Mountain Chant is held during the transition from winter to spring. This nine-day healing ceremony is performed for the sick and to restore balance and harmony. Today many Navajos still perform these ceremonies, and they also celebrate nationally recognized U.S. holidays such as Christmas, Easter, Memorial Day, and Thanksgiving.

Although not holidays, events such as fairs, All-Indian rodeos, and powwows are popular, yearly events for many Native American tribes, including the Navajos. The premier annual events open to visitors are the Navajo Fairs. One of the largest is the Northern Navajo Fair, ordinarily held on the first weekend in October at Shiprock, New Mexico. The dance competition powwow draws dancers from throughout the continent. Another large Navajo Fair is held annually at Window Rock, usually during the first week in July.

Health Care Issues and Practices Four full-service Indian hospitals are located in northwestern New Mexico. The one at Gallup is the largest in the region. The others are at Crownpoint, Shiprock, and Zuni. In northern Arizona, full-service Indian hospitals are located at Fort Defiance, Winslow, Tuba City, and Keams Canyon. Indian Health Centers (facilities staffed by health professionals, open at least forty hours per week, and catering to the general public) are located at Ft. Wingate and Tohatchi in northwestern New Mexico and at Greasewood, Toyei, Dilkon, Shonto, Kayenta, Many Farms, Teec Nos Pos, and Chinle in Arizona. Indian Health Stations (facilities staffed by health professionals and catering to the general public, but open only limited hours, often only one day per week) are located at Toadlena, Naschitti, Navajo, Pinedale, Pueblo Pintado, Ojo Encino, Torreon, Rincon, and Bacca in northwestern New Mexico and at Gray Mountain, Pinon, Dinnebito Dam, Red Lake, Page, Coppermine, Kaibito, Dinnehotso, Rock Point, Rough Rock, and Lukachukai in Arizona. Indian School Health Centers (facilities meeting the same criteria as Indian Health Centers, but catering primarily to school populations) are located at Crownpoint, Sanostee, and Shiprock in northwestern New Mexico and at Leupp, Tuba City, Holbrook, and Chinle in Arizona. Additionally, non-Indian hospitals are located in Flagstaff, Winslow, and Holbrook in Arizona; in

Gallup, Rehoboth, Grants, and Farmington in New Mexico; in Durango and Cortez in Colorado; and in Goulding, Utah. In keeping with the trend throughout the United States in the early twenty-first century, the Navajos are now administering many of their own health care facilities, taking over their operation from the U.S. Public Health Service.

Traditional Navajo healers are called *hataalii*, or "singers." Traditional Navajo medical practice treats the whole person, not just the illness, and is not conducted in isolation but in a ceremony that includes the patient's relatives. The ceremony can last from three to nine days, depending upon the illness being treated and the ceremony to be performed. For the Navajos, illness means that there is disharmony in the universe. Proper order is restored with sand paintings in a cleansing and healing ceremony. There are approximately 1,200 designs that can be used; most can be created within the size of the average hogan floor, about 6 feet by 6 feet, though some are as large as 12 feet in diameter and some as small as 1 foot in diameter. The hataalii may have several helpers in the creation of the intricate patterns. Dancers also assist them. In some ceremonies, such as the nine-day Yei-Bei-Chei, fifteen or sixteen teams of eleven members each dance throughout the night while the singer and his helpers chant prayers.

When the painting is ready, the patient sits in the middle of it. The singer then transmits the orderliness of the painting—symbolic of its cleanliness, goodness, and harmony—into the patient and puts the illness from the patient into the painting. The sand painting is then discarded. Many years of apprenticeship are required to learn the designs of the sand paintings and the songs that accompany them, skills that have been passed down through many generations. Most hataalii are able to perform only a few of the many ceremonies practiced by the Navajos, because each ceremony takes so long to learn. Sand painting is now also done for commercial purposes at public displays, but the paintings are not the same ones used in the healing rituals. The hataalii and the sand paintings are only one example of the numerous Navajo practices and specialists attending to health in the traditional system.

The Navajo Nation suffers from a suicide rate that is three times higher than the national average. They also have higher rates of substance abuse, diabetes, heart disease, and mental illness. Both suicide and alcohol abuse are exacerbated by poverty: more than half of all Navajos live below the poverty line. State governments and other agencies have begun to take notice and offer financial support in order to address these issues. On March 31, 2011, the governor of New Mexico, Susana Martinez, signed the Native American Suicide Prevention Law, which would provide prevention programs and a statewide clearinghouse for Native American suicide prevention. The clearinghouse would compile data that can then be used by Native American tribes in New Mexico to obtain resources

NAVAJO PROVERBS

- A man can't get rich if he takes proper care of his family.

- A rocky vineyard does not need a prayer, but a pick ax.

- Always assume your guest is tired, cold and hungry, and act accordingly.

- Be still and the earth will speak to you.

- Before me peaceful, behind me peaceful, under me peaceful, over me peaceful, all around me peaceful.

- Coyote is always out there waiting, and Coyote is always hungry.

- I have been to the end of the earth, I have been to the end of the waters, I have been to the end of the sky, I have been to the end of the mountains, I have found none that are not my friends.

- If you want to see what your body will look like tomorrow, look at your thoughts today.

- There is nothing as eloquent as a rattlesnake's tail.

for use in combatting suicide within their tribe. The Navajo Nation is working to create awareness about substance abuse, especially in grade schools. One outreach program, the Navajo Nation Fetal Alcohol Spectrum Disorders (FASD) Prevention Program, works to education the tribe, and women specifically, about the dangers of drinking while pregnant. As of 2011 the Navajo Nation was the only U.S. Native American tribe with an official FASD prevention program. In 2008 the Brigham and Women's Hospital, a teaching affiliate of Harvard Medical School, developed the Brigham and Woman's Outreach Program (BWOP) to assist the Indian Health Service hospitals in Gallup and Shiprock, New Mexico—both Navajo Reservation hospitals. The BWOP sent fifteen physician volunteers who assisted with rotations and clinical teaching.

FAMILY AND COMMUNITY LIFE

No tribe in North America has been more vigorously studied by anthropologists than the Navajos. The Navajo kinship system, or *k'e*, governs all aspects of the Navajo family and community life. When a man marries, he moves into the household of the wife's extended family. The Navajos joke that a Navajo family consists of a grandmother, her married daughters and their husbands, her daughters' children, and an anthropologist. A Navajo is "born to" the mother's clan and "born for" the father's clan. The clans are exogamous, meaning marriage is only allowed outside of the clan. According to Navajo tradition, four clans were created by Changing Woman, the being who personifies Earth. Due to marriage between tribal and non-tribal members, such as the marriage of Navajo men and Pueblo women, the number of clans grew. As of 2012 there were about 130 clans. Because of the large numbers of clans, it has become difficult for young Navajos to find other non-related, Navajo tribal members to marry. Navajo Nation president Ben Shelly has suggested that the Navajos consider marrying Native Americans from different tribes, especially small tribes who have few members and are in danger of extinction. Shelly recognizes that a plan of intertribal marriage would result in one tribe losing members, since Native Americans must choose membership in a single tribe. He argues that it is a good alternative to maintain the existence of Native peoples as a whole. However, many Navajos are reluctant to adopt this solution because it means abandoning the clan system, which is an important part of the Navajo culture. In traditional Navajo culture, divorce could be obtained by either the husband or the wife. Wives could leave their husbands if they proved unfaithful or irresponsible, while husbands could leave their wives if no children could be produced. Marriage was seen as an arrangement that should benefit both parties. Today Navajos settle divorce matters in court, as has become the norm in the United States.

The Navajos maintain strong ties with relatives, even when they leave the reservation. It is not uncommon for Navajos working in urban centers to send money home to relatives. On the reservation, an extended family may have only one wage-earning worker. Other family members busy themselves with traditional endeavors, from stock tending to weaving.

From the late 1860s until the 1960s, the local trading post was the preeminent financial and commercial institution for most Navajos, serving as a local bank (where silver and turquoise could be pawned), a post office, and a store. One of the most famous, the Hubbell Trading Post, has been declared a National Historic Site. Traders served the community as interpreters, business managers, funeral directors, grave diggers, and gossip columnists. Trading posts also offered Navajos an outside market for their crafts and art. Traditionally, items such as woven blankets, baskets, pottery, and silverwork had been made only for Navajo consumption, but with the arrival of the trading post, many Navajos were able to sell their crafts or trade them for supplies. By the late twentieth century the automobile and the proximity of big discount stores in the urban centers at the fringes of the nation had greatly diminished the role of the trading posts.

Gender Roles Because the principal Navajo deity, Changing Woman, established the matrilineal system within the first four clans, Navajo women have been the core of both the economic and the social structure of the society. Women were potters and weavers, and once trading posts became central to

Navajo women watch the events of the Pioneer Day Fair at Navajo Mountain in Utah. TOM BEAN / ALAMY

Navajo life in the late nineteenth and early twentieth centuries, these crafts made up a large portion of the Navajo economy. A wife could divorce her husband if he proved to be an unsuitable partner, an economic drain on the household, or unfaithful. Women owned, and still own, property and livestock and teach their daughters how to manage those resources. Daughters would later inherit their mother's possessions. The mother-child bond in Navajo culture is sacred, and mothers are seen as the source of life and care. Despite all of this, women were not allowed to participate in tribal government or in most of the ceremonial dances and songs.

The girl's puberty ceremony, her *kinaalda*, is one of the most important rituals in Navajo culture. The four-day ceremony marks each thirteen-year-old girl's journey into womanhood. During the four days, girls are forbidden to dress themselves, or even comb their hair, and must rely on family members to do these tasks for them. Each girl performs ceremonial duties of grinding corn and using the cornmeal to prepare *alkaan*, a cake that is eaten during the final day of the ceremony.

Even though the Navajo society is viewed as matrilineal, many women and scholars note the discrepancy between this aspect of Navajo culture and the lack of women in positions of power. Scholar AnCita Benally argues that the Navajo government is a patriarchal system that reflects Euro-American values about gender rather than Navajo values. Also, Navajo scholar Jennifer Nez Denetdale notes that the emphasis placed on the perceived value of Navajo women obscures important issues that many Navajo women face, such as gender and race discrimination, domestic violence, and sexual harassment. She notes that Navajo women meet with resistance when they attempt a political career, or even high-ranking positions in education or medicine. In 1998, when LeNora Fulton announced her intention to run for president of the Navajo Nation, she was met with sharp criticism from both women and men who felt that Navajo women in government would lead to a breakdown of traditional Navajo values and culture. Women form a majority of college graduates among the Navajo people, and they are still the primary (and often times only) caregivers at home. There are signs of progress. In 1979 Lori Arviso Alvord became the first Navajo woman surgeon, and Claudeen Bates Arthur served as the first woman attorney general of the Navajo Nation from 1983 to 1987. She was elected to the Navajo Nation Supreme Court as the first Navajo woman chief justice. Several Navajo women have served as delegates on the Navajo Nation Council, although as of 2013 Katherine Benally was the only woman serving.

Education An 1868 treaty provided for schools for Navajo children. The number of schools increased greatly after compulsory school attendance was mandated in 1887. In 1907 a Navajo headman in Utah was imprisoned without trial for a year and a half for speaking out against forced removal of local children to the Shiprock Boarding School. Others were strongly in favor of schools, especially after nineteen influential Navajo headmen were exposed to the outside world at the 1893 World's Columbian Exposition in Chicago.

Until 1896 Navajo schools were operated by missionaries, who were frequently more interested in attempting to eradicate the Navajo religion, culture, and language than in educating their charges. The establishment of boarding schools far from Navajo homes subjected Navajo children to the trauma of being removed from their families and their cultures for extended periods of time and also deprived them of strong parenting role models. Instruction was conducted only in English. With the secularization of the federally maintained Navajo public school system in 1896, civil servants replaced the missionaries, but lack of understanding and appreciation of Navajo culture—and instruction only in English—continued to be the norm. Some religiously affiliated schools continue to the present day, but they display a greater appreciation for Navajo culture and traditions than their nineteenth-century predecessors. By 1958, 93 percent of Navajo children were in school.

In the 1960s Navajos began to exercise much stronger management of their children's education with the establishment of community-controlled contract schools. The Rough Rock Demonstration School was the first of these schools. It introduced bilingual education for young children, the adult training of Navajo medicine men, and other innovative programs based on the perceived needs of the local community.

In 1969 the Navajos established Diné College, the first college operated by Indians. At first located at Many Farms High School, it moved to Tsaile, Arizona, with the opening of its new campus in 1974; there is a branch campus in Shiprock, New Mexico. In 1972 the College of Ganado, a junior college in Ganado, Arizona, was incorporated as a successor to the Ganado Mission School. Following the lead of the Navajos, there are now a total of twenty-nine Indian institutions of higher education in the United States, all members of an American Indian higher education consortium. Navajo Community College Press is a leading native-owned academic press. A number of state-supported baccalaureate institutions are located near the Navajo Nation. These include branch campuses of the University of New Mexico at Gallup and Farmington; Northern Arizona University at Flagstaff; Ft. Lewis College in Durango, Colorado; and the Navajo Technical College in Crownpoint, New Mexico.

Even with increased attention on education by the Navajo Nation Council, educational attainment among the Navajos remains substantially below the national average and the average for Native Americans and Alaskan Natives. The U.S. Census Bureau's American Community Survey estimates for

2006–2010 indicate that 73.6 percent of Navajos over the age of twenty-four had graduated from high school, and 9 percent of Navajo people over twenty-four had a bachelor's degree or higher.

Courtships and Weddings Because the Navajos are an exogamous society, both the man and woman must marry outside their respective clans. Traditionally, once a suitable, non-related partner was found, the man's family offered jewelry, livestock, and other gifts to the woman's family. A new hogan was constructed for the couple, and the wedding took place in it. During the wedding ceremony, the bride and groom ate corn mush from a basket, which signified their joining. After the wedding the couple could live with either the bride's family or the groom's, although the expectation was that they would live with the wife's family. In the twenty-first century, most Navajos have adopted the courtship and dating practices of mainstream U.S. culture.

EMPLOYMENT AND ECONOMIC CONDITIONS

Nearly every Navajo extended family has members who engage in silversmithing and weaving as a matter of occasional economic enterprise. Farming and stock raising are also still important in the economic life of the nation. The largest employers of Navajo people, however, are the federal and tribal governments. The Navajos have their own parks and recreation department, fish and wildlife department, police department, educational programs, and health service, as well as many other jobs in tribal government and administration. Many federal agencies have offices either on or near the reservation. Other Navajos are employed at the tribally operated electronics plant at Fort Defiance, Arizona, and at the Navajo Forest Products Industry, an $11 million sawmill also run by the tribe. It is located at Navajo, New Mexico, the only industrial town on the reservation, which was created and planned to serve the needs of its industry.

Until the early twentieth century Navajos were able to continue deriving their livelihood from their traditional practices of stock raising. Since the 1920s a decreasing number of Navajos have been able to maintain themselves in this manner. Chronic high rates of unemployment and dependency on governmental assistance have gradually replaced the traditional way of life. In 1941 the Navajos had earned only $150,000 from industry, but World War II was a boom time for the economy. By 1943 more than half the Navajos age nineteen and older had wartime jobs, and they earned a collective $5 million.

By 1973 a study released by the Navajo Office of Program Development found that only 20,000 people were employed on the reservation, and of these, only 71 percent were Navajos. Public-service jobs—such as those in health, education, and government—were found to account for nearly three-fourths of all

employment on the reservation. In 1975 the Navajo unemployment rate was 67 percent. In 1991 the unemployment rate was 36 percent and remained at about that level in 1999. According to the American Community Survey (ACS) estimates for 2006–2010, the median household income was $32,322, and 31.7 percent of the population lived below the poverty level.

Since the late 1960s, developing projects have diversified employment within the Navajo Nation. The Navajo Indian Irrigation Project (NIIP) was designed to irrigate 110,000 acres of cropland from water impounded in the upper San Juan River basin, using open canals, pipelines, lift stations, and overhead sprinkler systems. The Navajo Agricultural Products Industry (NAPI), a tribal enterprise, manages the program. It includes agribusiness plant sites, grazing lands and a feedlot for cattle production, and an experimental research station. A coal-gasification plant near Burnham and Navajo-Exxon uranium leases, along with the irrigation project, are making northwestern New Mexico and the eastern portion of the Navajo Reservation the focus of new economic activity. Uranium mining, however, has produced health risks, including alarmingly high rates of cancer.

Because of their legal status, Navajo business owners must deal with state and federal agencies as well as Navajo officials and must pay both state and Navajo Nation taxes. In addition, complicated paperwork requirements for obtaining business licenses and land leases for businesses hamper start-ups.

The Navajo people's biggest economic ventures have been coal leases. By 1970 the Navajo Nation had the largest coal mine in the world. The 1964 and 1966 Black Mesa coal leases to Peabody Coal Company have become a source of controversy within the nation, as an increasing number of Navajos decry the scouring of their land, the displacement of families for the sake of mining activity, and the threat to sacred places posed by mining operations.

In 2011, according to a *Business Week* report, approximately 600,000 visitors spent nearly $13 million on the Navajo Nation, an increase of 32 percent in tourism spending since 2002. Although the number of visitors from the United States has declined since 2002, an 11 percent increase from international visitors, most of them from France and Germany, accounted for the increase. The news was good for Navajos looking for work as well. Nearly 1,800 full-time jobs on the reservation were directly involved in the tourism industry. However, at over 27 percent, the highest number of employed Navajos were working in the education, health care, or social assistance fields.

Still, Navajos are the largest group of farmers among all Native American tribes. According to the U.S. Department of Agriculture's 2007 Census of Agriculture—the first census to count individual Indian farmers on all U.S. Indian reservations—there are almost

56,000 Native American farmers. One out of five is Navajo. Although the numbers also show that Navajo farmers counted in the survey were often financially unsuccessful and lost money, many Navajos attribute this to poor conservation practices. However, many Navajos, even the younger generation, continue to feel that farming is important for maintaining Navajo tradition.

POLITICS AND GOVERNMENT

The basic unit of local government in the Navajo Nation is the Chapter, each with its own Chapter House. The Chapter system was created in 1922 as a means of addressing agricultural problems at a local level. Before the 1920s, the nation had no centrally organized tribal government. Like many other Indian nations, the tribe was forced to create a central authority by the United States. For the Navajos, the seminal event was the discovery of oil on the reservation in 1921, after which the United States desired some centralized governmental authority for the Navajos for the purpose of executing oil leases, largely for the benefit of non-Navajos. At first the Bureau of Indian Affairs appointed three Navajos to execute mineral leases. In 1923 this arrangement gave way to a plan for each of several Navajo agencies to provide representatives for the Navajo government.

After World War II the Navajo Tribal Council became recognized as the Navajo government. During the 1970s and 1980s, Peter MacDonald, a former Navajo Code Talker, served four consecutive terms as the chairman of the council. During his administration, he fought for tribal self-sufficiency and new federal and private assistance programs that were not controlled by the BIA. When he began fighting for more water and mineral rights on Navajo Nation land, he ran afoul of Republican senator Barry Goldwater, who supported the Hopi tribe in the Navajo-Hopi land dispute. In 1988 a divided Navajo Tribal Council placed MacDonald on administrative leave. Although three grand juries refused to indict him, in 1990 a Navajo court ordered him to face three separate trials, which raised the issue of double jeopardy, for allegedly accepting kickbacks from corporations and illegal campaign contributions from non-Navajos. This issue caused turmoil within the Navajo tribe, culminating in a riot in Window Rock, Arizona, in which two MacDonald supporters were shot to death and two tribal police officers were murdered. MacDonald was convicted by the tribal court of defrauding the Navajo Nation and a few months later was convicted in a federal court on charges of conspiracy to commit burglary and kidnapping stemming from the events at Window Rock. He was sent to prison in Fort Worth, Texas. The Navajo Tribal Council issued a pardon in 1995, and in 2001 President Bill Clinton commuted his federal sentence. MacDonald and his supporters maintain that his conviction was politically motivated. While he acknowledges accepting campaign contributions from non-Navajos, which violates tribal law, he asserts that other charges against him were unfairly pursued.

On May 19, 1976 in Window Rock., Arizona, approximately 350 Navajo walked two miles to ask tribal officials for an investigation into the Navajo Nation's governmental operation. AP PHOTO

The Navajo Nation does not have a constitution. Instead it maintains a set of guidelines known as the Navajo Tribal Code, which consists of, among other things, old tribal resolutions, the Navajo Bill of Rights, federal laws, and tribal government structure. The tribal government has rejected a constitution three times. In 1935 they rejected the Indian Reorganization Act of 1934, which would have allowed them to officially organize as a tribe though along constitutional lines. Then in 1950 the Navajo-Hopi Rehabilitation Act included a provision that the Navajos adopt a constitution, but because the federal government would not allow the Navajos to develop their mineral resources, the idea of drafting a constitution was again rejected. In the 1960s then-chairman Raymond Nakai pushed for a constitution, and the Tribal Council approved a draft in 1968. However, it has never been put before the Navajo people for ratification. The Navajo Tribal Council has said that a constitution would severely limit the powers of the council, constitutional provisions would require some council actions be approved by the people, and involving the Navajo people in these tribal matters would be too time-consuming and costly.

Indians in Arizona and New Mexico were not allowed to vote in state and national elections until 1948. In 1957 Utah finally allowed Indians living on reservations to vote—the last remaining state to do so. It required a 1976 U.S. Supreme Court ruling to force Apache County, Arizona, where the population was 70 percent Navajo, to allow the Navajos to serve on its board of supervisors. As of 1984 no Native American had ever been elected to public office in Utah. In that year the U.S. Department of Justice ordered San Juan County, Utah, where the population was 50 percent Navajo, to redistrict. The next year a Navajo was elected county commissioner.

NAVAJO CODE TALKERS: "WALKING CODE"

Philip Johnson, born to missionaries and raised on the Navajo Reservation, is credited with a leading role in the formation of the Navajo Code Talkers. As a child he learned fluent Navajo as well as Navajo culture and traditions. At the age of nine he served as interpreter for a Navajo delegation that traveled to Washington, D.C., to present Navajo grievances to President Theodore Roosevelt. After serving in World War I, Johnson worked as a civil engineer in California. When war broke out with Japan in 1941, Johnson learned that the military hoped to develop a code using American Indians as signalmen. He met with Marine Corps and Army Signal Corps officers and arranged a demonstration of Navajo as a code language. The demonstration took place on February 28, 1942, at Camp Elliott with the cooperation of four Navajos from Los Angeles and one who was in the Navy in San Diego.

Within a year the Marine Corps authorized the program, which at first was classified as top-secret. Johnson, though over age, was allowed to enlist in the Corps and was assigned to help supervise the establishment of the program at Camp Pendleton in Oceanside, California. In May 1942 the Marine Corps, with the approval of the Navajo Tribal Council, began recruiting Navajo men at Window Rock, Arizona, for the program. The first group to receive training consisted of 29 Navajos who underwent basic boot-camp training at the San Diego Marine Corps Recruit Depot. They were then sent for four weeks to the Field Signal Battalion Training Center at Camp Pendleton, where they received 176 hours of instruction in basic communications procedures and equipment. They were later deployed to Guadalcanal, where their use of the Navajo language for radio communication in the field proved so effective that recruitment for the program was expanded. Eventually, approximately 400 Navajo Code Talkers saw duty in the Pacific in the Marine Corps. Their platoon members referred to them as "Walking Code." By the end of the war they had been assigned to all six Marine divisions in the Pacific and had taken part in every assault—from Guadalcanal in 1943 to Okinawa in 1945. Today the surviving Navajo Code Talkers maintain an active veterans' organization. In 1969, at the Fourth Marine Division Association reunion in Chicago, they were presented with a medallion specially minted in commemoration of their services.

The most divisive issue among the Navajos in recent years, and the cause of the greatest strain in relations with the United States, has been the so-called Navajo-Hopi Land Dispute, in which thousands of Navajos have been forced to relocate from lands that were jointly held by the two tribes since 1882. Many prominent Navajos and some prominent Hopis believe that the relocation of the Navajos and the division of the 1882 Joint Use Area has been undertaken by the U.S. government for the benefit of the American extraction industry, so that valuable mineral deposits within the area could be strip-mined. By 1999 most Navajos had relocated, and many who did so moved to the Pinon area of New Mexico because it is close to their former homeland.

The loss of their land, livestock, and way of life has made the readjustment difficult for many, because their physical and spiritual well-being as well as their identity is directly linked to land use. Relocatees did not like depending on the federal government for housing, and many of the houses, which were poorly built, did not have electricity or running water. In 1966 commissioner of Indian Affairs Robert Bennett had halted all development on the lands held by both tribes after 1882. This federal statute, commonly referred to as the Bennett-Freeze, was an attempt to hasten negotiations between the Navajos and the Hopis. Instead, it prevented members from both tribes from repairing their homes or getting electricity for over forty years. In 2000 the Navajos and Hopis agreed to a $29 million settlement as payment for use of Hopi land by Navajo residents and damages caused by overgrazing. President Barack Obama further resolved matters in 2009 when he repealed the Bennett-Freeze, making it possible for residents living in the impacted areas to make the necessary repairs to their homes and develop the land. Despite the money and aid promised to rehabilitate of the area, it has been slow to arrive, and in the early twenty-first century many Navajos were still living in the same conditions or only slightly better ones.

Military Service The Navajos have served with distinction in the armed forces of the United States in every war in the twentieth century, including World War I, even though they—and other reservation Indians—did not become citizens of the United States until citizenship was extended to them by an act of Congress in 1924. Their most heralded service, however, came during World War II in the U.S. Marine Corps, when they employed the Navajo language for military communication in the field as the Marines stormed Japanese-held islands in the Pacific. They have become known as the Navajo Code Talkers. The Code Talkers entered the military primarily to defend their own land and the Navajo Nation.

NOTABLE INDIVIDUALS

Academia Among the first Navajos to earn a PhD, Ned Hatathli (1923–1972) was the first president of the Navajo Community College—the first college owned and operated by the Navajo people. Annie Dodge Wauneka (1910–1997) was a public health educator responsible for largely eliminating tuberculosis among the Navajo Indians. Wauneka was later elected to the Navajo Tribal Council and in 1963 was the first Native American to receive the Presidential Medal of Freedom. Peterson Zah (1937–) is an educator and leader who has devoted his life to serving the Navajo people and retaining Navajo culture, especially among young people. In 1990 Zah was elected the first president of the Navajo people; he was later awarded the Humanitarian Award from the City of Albuquerque and an honorary doctorate from Santa Fe College. Jennifer Nez Denetdale is the first Navajo to earn a PhD in history. A strong advocate for Navajo rights, particularly Navajo women's rights, Denetdale has authored many books and papers on Navajo history and culture, including *Reclaiming Diné History: The Legacies of Navajo Chief Manuelito and Juanita*, and *The Long Walk: The Forced Exile of the Navajo*. Tiffany S. Lee is a sociologist and professor who focuses on indigenous education and language. She was awarded a postdoctoral fellowship from the American Educational Research Association in 2003 to study indigenous learning communities. Paul Platero is a Navajo linguist who studied under the famous Massachusetts Institute of Technology linguist Ken Hale. Platero has taught at Swarthmore College, the University of New Mexico, and the Navajo Language Academy. He has published numerous articles about Navajo grammar and syntax and coedited *The Athabaskan languages: Perspectives on a Native American Language Family* (2000).

Art Harrison Begay (1917–2012) is one of the most famous of all Navajo painters. Noted for their sinuous delicacy of line, meticulous detail, restrained palette, and elegance of composition, his watercolors and silkscreen prints have won a number of awards. Carl Nelson Gorman (1907–1998) is a prominent Navajo artist whose oil paintings and silk screening have won acclaim for their divergence from traditional Indian art forms. His contributions to Navajo and Native American art and culture inspired the dedication of the Carl Gorman Museum at Tecumseh Center at the University of California at Davis. Rudolph Carl Gorman (1931–2005) was one of the most prominent contemporary Native American artists of the twentieth century. His art combines the traditional with the nontraditional in style and form. Clara Nezbah Sherman (1914–2010) was a Navajo artist particularly known for her Navajo rugs. Yazzie Johnson (1946–) and Gail Bird (1949–) are known for their innovative jewelry. They have collaborated in designing and fabricating jewelry since 1972. Best known for their thematic belts, they have drawn inspiration from prehistoric pictograph and petroglyph sites. Emmi Whitehorse (1957–) is known primarily for her large, abstract, mixed-media panels, which often suggest water images.

Literature Navajo author Vee Browne (1956–) has achieved national recognition with her retellings of Navajo creation stories. Her books have included *Monster Slayer* and *Monster Birds*, a children's biography of Osage international ballet star Maria Tallchief, and a volume in a new series of Native American animal stories from Scholastic. Her honors include the prestigious Western Heritage Award from the Cowboy Hall of Fame and Western Heritage Center in 1990. A guidance counselor by training, Browne is active in helping emerging Native American writers hone their skills and find outlets for their work, serving as a mentor in the Wordcraft Circle of Native American Mentor and Apprentice Writers. She has also served on the 1994–1996 National Advisory Caucus for Wordcraft Circle.

Elizabeth Woody (1959–), born on the Navajo Nation but raised mostly in the Pacific Northwest, has been influenced by the Pacific Northwest tribes as well as her Navajo heritage. She returned to the Southwest to study poetry and art at the Institute of American Indian Arts in Santa Fe, New Mexico. Her first volume of poetry, *Hand Into Stone*, published in 1988, won the American Book Award. Her other books include *Luminaries of the Humble* and *Seven Hands, Seven Hearts*. Woody's poetry has been anthologized in *Returning the Gift* and *Durable Breath*; her short fiction, "Home Cooking," has been anthologized in *Talking Leaves*; her nonfiction, "Warm Springs," has been anthologized in *Native America*. Woody now teaches at the Institute of American Indian Arts. Her illustrations can be found in Sherman Alexie's *Old Shirts & New Skins*, and her art has been the subject of a five-week exhibit at the Tula Foundation Gallery in Atlanta, Georgia.

Actress and writer Geraldine Keams (1951–) has appeared in several films, including *The Outlaw Josey Wales*, and has been published in *Sun Tracks* and *The Remembered Earth*.

Rex Lee Jim (1962–), a highly regarded medicine man, is the first author to have published a volume of poetry in Navajo, with no translation, with a major university press (*Ahi'Ni'Nikisheegiizh*, Princeton University Press). Jim's fiction and nonfiction have also been published by Rock Point Community School in the Navajo Nation and include such works as "Naakaiiahgoo Tazhdiya" and "Living from Livestock." In 2010 Jim became vice-president of the Navajo Nation.

Laura Tohe's volume of poetry, *Making Friends with Water*, was published by Nosila Press, and her poetry and nonfiction have appeared in such publications as *Nebraska Humanities*, *Blue Mesa Review*, and *Platte Valley Review*. Tohe, daughter of a Navajo code talker, received her PhD in English literature from the University of Nebraska and teaches at the University of Arizona.

Luci Tapahonso (1953–) is the author of four books of poetry, including *Saanii Dahataa*. She has taught at the University of Kansas at Lawrence, the University of New Mexico, and the University of Arizona. Della Frank lives and works on the Navajo Nation. Her poetry has appeared in such publications as *Blue Mesa Review* and *Studies in American Indian Literature* and has been anthologized in *Neon Powwow* and *Returning the Gift*. She is coauthor of *Duststorms: Poems from Two Navajo Women*. Rachael Arviso (Navajo and Zuni) lives and works on the Navajo Reservation; her short fiction has been anthologized in *Neon Powwow*. Esther G. Belini's poetry also appeared

in *Neon Powwow*; she received her BA degree from the University of California at Berkeley.

Film Sierra Teller Ornelas was a writer and producer for the weekly college comedy show *Comedy Corner*. She has worked at the Smithsonian Institution's National Museum of the American Indian and helped to create entertaining programs about Native film and media. Ornelas is also an award-winning sixth-generation weaver. Billy Luther studied filmmaking at Hampshire College and has worked at the National Museum of the American Indian and Third World Newsreel. His 2007 film *Miss Navajo* explores the concept of Navajo womanhood in relation to the pageant, and the film was an official selection at the 2007 Sundance Film Festival. Ramona Emerson is a Navajo filmmaker who has worked as a videographer, writer, and editor for over thirteen years. She won the New Mexico Governor's Cup Short Documentary Competition in 2007, which provided production funds for her film *A Return Home*.

Science and Medicine Nuclear physicist and educator Fred Begay (1932–2013) served as a member of the technical staff at the Los Alamos National Laboratory for many years. His research was directed primarily toward the use of laser, electron, and ion beams to demonstrate the application of thermonuclear fusion. He provided science and technology expertise to the Navajo Nation's Environmental Protection Commission (1974–1976); Navajo Community College (1972–1976); the Board of Science and Technology for International Development, U.S. National Academy of Sciences (1979–1981); and the National Research Council (1979–present). His career was documented in many films, such as *Nation within a Nation* (1972) and *The Long Walk of Fred Young-Begay* (1978), as well as being featured in *National Geographic* magazine other published articles. Begay received numerous awards, including from the Department of Energy and the Navajo Tribe for his work in science, science education, and public service.

Weavers There are many accomplished contemporary Navajo weavers, but two of the most famous historical figures include Daisy Taugelchee (1909?–1990), considered by many to be the world's most famous weaver, and Hosteen Klah (1867–1937), a Navajo artist, medicine man, and master weaver. Taugelchee began weaving as a young girl and soon became a master weaver. She dyed and spun her own yarn, which was not common among weavers at that time. Her textiles were so finely woven that they were often mistaken as machine-made. Throughout her career, she won numerous prizes and competitions for her art. Her pieces now sell for tens of thousands of dollars, and in 2004 one of her pieces was featured on a U.S. postage stamp as part of the U.S. Postal Service's stamp series called Art of the American Indian. Klah learned to weave during the late nineteenth century from his mother and sister. Because of his participation in the ceremonial system, Klah incorporated imagery from Navajo religion into his weaving, including sand-painting imagery. This was, and is still, considered by many Navajo to be sacrilegious. In 1921 Klah collaborated with Mary Cabot Wheelwright in founding the Wheelwright Museum of the American Indian. He is buried on the museum's grounds.

MEDIA

PRINT

Navajo-Hopi Observer

This is a weekly newspaper in English, founded in 1981and serving the Navajo and Hopi Nations.

Ryan Williams, Managing Editor
2717 N. Fourth Street
Suite 110
Flagstaff, Arizona 86001
Phone: (800) 408-4726
Fax: (928) 635-4887
Email: rwilliams@williamsnews.com
URL: www.navajohopiobserver.com

Navajo Nation Enquiry

This is a monthly newspaper.

P.O. Box 490
Window Rock, Arizona 86515

The Navajo Post

This is a monthly newspaper that began in 2011 as an online publication and launched a print version in 2012. With a circulation of 5,000, its target audience is the Navajo Nation.

Alexander Chambers, CEO/Publisher
625 W. Southern Ave E-126
Mesa, Arizona 85210
Phone: (480) 809-4587
Fax: (480) 809-4646
URL: http://thenavajopost.com/

Navajo Times

The first daily newspaper owned and published by a Native American Indian Nation, the *Navajo Times* was established by the Navajo Tribal Council in 1959 as a newsletter. The first issue of the newspaper was published in 1960. Since 2004 it has been financially independent of the tribal council.

Candace Begody, Editor
P.O. Box 310
Window Rock, Arizona 86515-0310
Phone: (928) 871-1130
Fax: (928) 871-1159
Email: editor@navajotimes.com
URL: http://navajotimes.com/

RADIO

The following radio stations are owned by the Navajo Broadcasting Company: KDJI-AM (1270); KZUA-FM (92.1); KTNN-AM (660); KNMI-FM (88.9); KPCL-FM (95.7); KABR-AM (1500); and KTDB-FM (89.7).

ORGANIZATIONS AND ASSOCIATIONS

Arizona Commission for Indian Affairs

Consisting of twenty members, including seven Indian and four at-large commissioners appointed by the governor, and nine ex-officio members who serve by the virtue of their office, the Commission serves as a liaison agency between the state of Arizona and twenty-two Indian tribes and nations.

Kristine Fire Thunder, Executive Director
State Capitol Building—Executive Tower
1700 West Washington Street
Suite 430
Phoenix, Arizona 85007
Phone: (602) 542-4426
Fax: (602) 542-4428
Email: iaiinfo@az.gov
URL: http://azcia.gov/

Diné CARE (Citizens Against Ruining our Environment)

Diné CARE, located on the Navajo Nation, is a nonprofit organization that works with many Navajo communities affected by energy and environmental issues.

Anna Marie Frazier, Staff
63 Box 263
Winslow, Arizona 86047
Phone: (928) 380-7697
Email: frazierann1@hotmail.com
URL: www.creativegeckos.com/dinecare/

Navajo Code Talkers Association

Founded in 2009, the Navajo Code Talkers Foundation is a nonprofit organization dedicated to educating current and future generations about the history, ideals, and heroic accomplishments in World War II by the Navajo Code Talkers and to preserving the Navajo language.

Dr. Samuel Billison, President
P.O. Box 1266
Window Rock, Arizona 86515
Phone: (928) 688-5202
Fax: (928) 688-5204
Email: pr@navajocodetalkers.org
URL: www.navajocodetalkers.org

MUSEUMS AND RESEARCH CENTERS

Maxwell Museum of Anthropology

The museum offers exhibits and programs relating to culture around the world, with an emphasis on the cultural heritage of the Southwest. One permanent exhibit, "People of the Southwest," explores 11,000 years of the cultural heritage of the Southwest and includes a reconstruction of a room at Chaco Canyon, an outstanding collection of prehistoric pottery, and colorful panels showcasing the daily environment and subsistence of Southwestern peoples.

E. James Dixon, Museum Director
MSC01 1050
1 University of New Mexico
Albuquerque, New Mexico 87131-0001
Phone: (505) 277-4405
Email: maxwell@unm.edu
URL: www.unm.edu/maxwell/

The Navajo Nation Museum

The Navajo Tribal Museum first opened to the public in 1961. Permanent exhibits include one about the Navajo's forced march to Bosque Redondo in 1864.

Clarenda Begay, Museum Curator
P.O. Box 1840
Window Rock, Arizona 86515
Phone: (928) 871-7941
Fax: (928) 871-7942
Email: info@navajonationmuseum.org
URL: www.navajonationmuseum.org

The Wheelwright Museum of the American Indian

Founded in 1937 as the Navajo House of Prayer and House of Navajo Religion, the museum became the Museum of Navajo Ceremonial Art soon after it opened. In 1977 it became the Wheelwright Museum of the American Indian. No longer actively involved in the study of Navajo religion, the museum maintains growing, world-renowned collections that document Navajo art and culture from 1850 to the present. It also presents changing exhibitions on traditional and contemporary Navajo and other Native American arts.

704 Camino Lejo
Santa Fe, New Mexico 87505
Phone: (505) 982-4636
Fax: (505) 989-7386
Email: info@wheelwright.org
URL: www.wheelwright.org

SOURCES FOR ADDITIONAL STUDY

Benally, Malcolm D. *Bitter Water: Diné Oral Histories of the Navajo-Hopi Land Dispute.* Tucson: University of Arizona Press, 2011.

Denetdale, Jennifer Nez. *Reclaiming Diné History: The Legacies of Navajo Chief Manuelito and Juanita.* Tucson: University of Arizona Press, 2007.

Holiday, John, and Robert S. McPherson. *A Navajo Legacy: The Life and Teachings of John Holiday.* Norman: University of Oklahoma Press, 2011.

Iverson, Peter, and Monty Roessel. *Diné: A History of the Navajos.* Albuquerque: University of New Mexico Press, 2002.

Lamphere, Louise. *To Run After Them: The Social and Cultural Bases of Cooperation in a Navajo Community.* Tucson: University of Arizona Press, 1977.

Lee, Tiffany S. "'If They Want Navajo to Be Learned, Then They Should Require It in All Schools': Navajo Teenagers' Experiences Choices, and Demands Regarding Navajo Language." *Wicazo Sa Review* 22, no. 1 (2007): 7–33.

Schwarz, Maureen Trudelle. *Blood and Voice: Navajo Women Ceremonial Practitioners.* Tucson: University of Arizona Press, 2003.

———. *"I Choose Life": Contemporary Medical and Religious Practices in the Navajo World.* Norman: University of Oklahoma Press, 2008.

Wilkins, David Eugene. *The Navajo Political Experience.* Lanham, MD: Rowman and Littlefield, 2003.

Wilkins, Teresa J. *Patterns of Exchange: Navajo Weavers and Traders.* Norman: University of Oklahoma Press, 2008.

NEPALESE AMERICANS

Olivia Miller

OVERVIEW

Nepalese Americans are immigrants or descendants of people from Nepal, a landlocked country in southern Asia surrounded by India on the west, south and east, and by the Tibet Autonomous Region of the People's Republic of China on the north. Nepal is known for its majestic Himalayan Mountains and is the home of eight of the world's ten highest peaks, including Annapurna and Mount Everest, the world's highest mountain. Nepal has three broad geographic regions—the mountainous north, a central hill region, and a southern region called the Terai that features fertile and humid plains. Nepal occupies an area of 56,136 square miles, which is roughly the size of the state of Tennessee.

Population data for Nepal vary considerably, with the World Bank reporting nearly 30.5 million in 2011, the Nepal government reporting 26 million, and the *CIA World Factbook* stating that the population of Nepal in 2011 was 28.5 million. A country with a diverse ethnic population, Nepal has a complex mix of fifty-nine ethnic groups or indigenous nationalities, high and low Hindu caste groups, and almost one hundred distinct languages or dialects. Nepali is the official language and is spoken by about 58 percent of the population. Some of the more well-known ethnic groups include Newars, Indians, Tibetans, Gurungs, Magars, Tamangs, Bhotias, Rais, Limbus, and Sherpas. Although Nepal is said to be the birthplace of the Buddha, over 80 percent of Nepal's population is Hindu, with smaller numbers of Buddhists and also Muslims, Christians, Baha'is, Jains, and others. Nepal was the only officially Hindu kingdom in the world until 2007, when the Nepalese abolished the monarchy and began a transition to a secular republic. Nepal is unique in the way Hinduism and Buddhism peacefully coexist. The national capital is Kathmandu, which has an urban population of over one million people. Kathmandu is in one of the most earthquake-prone regions of the world. The lack of all-weather roads in much of the country is a major economic challenge. Over one-third of the people living in the hills are hours away from roads that can be traveled year-round. Although Nepal is one of the poorest and least developed countries in the world, with more than 25 percent of its population living below the poverty line, the proportion of poor people and levels of income inequality have significantly improved since 2000.

It is generally accepted that until the 1990s, less than one hundred Nepalis immigrated to the United States each year. (Until 1975, Nepalese immigrants to the United States were classified as "other Asians," and thus no specific official information exists.) In 1990 it was estimated that there were just over 2,500 Americans with Nepalese ancestry. Many Nepalese immigrants to the United States came in search of educational and employment opportunities; the earlier waves of immigration were from families of wealthy Nepalese who sent their children to the United States and other countries for higher education. After 1990 more Nepalese began immigrating for economic and social reasons, including low income (the annual per-capita income was less than $750 in 2012, according to a survey by the Nepalese government) and prolonged turmoil following a violent ten-year political conflict that lasted from 1996 through 2006.

By 2011 the number of Nepalese in the United States was estimated by the U.S Census to be over 86,000, 84 percent having entered after the year 2000. Nepalese communities have grown throughout the United States, with the highest concentrations in New York, Washington, D.C., Dallas, Boston, and San Francisco.

HISTORY OF THE PEOPLE

Early History Although archeologists have found evidence of settlement in Nepal as long as 9,000 years ago, what is known about prehistoric Nepal is a rich blend of legend and myth recounted in Nepali Buddhist and Hindu scriptures and festivals. Verifiable history of dynastic kingdoms in the Nepal Valley begins in the late fifth century CE, when rulers calling themselves Licchavis recorded details concerning the politics, society, and economics of Nepal. The Licchavis ruled from the fourth to the eighth centuries, and the Malla kings ruled from the twelfth to the eighteenth centuries. Both Licchavis and Malla dynasties were Hindu, though Hindu social and legal codes, including the caste system, were not imposed until the fourteenth century by the Malla ruler Jaya Sthiti.

In 563 BCE, Siddhartha Gautama, a prince who rejected the world to search for the meaning of existence and became known as the Buddha, or the Enlightened One, was born in Nepal. Since the fourth century, Nepalese civilization has been based on Buddhism and Hinduism. In the sixteenth century, there were dozens of kingdoms throughout the Himalayan region. Gorkha, a small kingdom, conquered and united the entire nation in the late eighteenth century. The armies of Nepal conquered territories far to the west and east and challenged the Chinese in Tibet and the British in India.

Modern Era The Anglo-Nepalese War (1814–1816) was disastrous for Nepal. According to the Treaty of Sagauli, which was signed in 1816, Nepal lost its territories west of the Kali River and most of its lands in the Terai, the lowland region south of the Himalayas. From 1846 to 1951 a dynasty of prime ministers known as the Rana controlled the government and reduced the kings to puppets. Rana rule lasted one hundred years, during which loyalty to family took precedence over the interests of the nation. By the 1950s only 2 percent of the adult population was literate, the infant mortality rate was more than 60 percent, and average life expectancy was only thirty-five years. Less than 1 percent of the population was engaged in modern industrial occupations, and 85 percent of employment and income came from agriculture. The entire nation had approximately 100 kilometers of railroad tracks and only a few kilometers of paved roads. Telephones, electricity, and postal services served only 1 percent of the population. Government expenditures were focused solely on salaries and benefits for the army, police, and civil servants. Health and education received less than 1 percent of the government's expenditures. The nation still contained autonomous principalities (*rajya*) based on deals with former local kings, and landlords acted as small dictators on their own lands. A revolt in 1950 overthrew the Rana, brought the king back from exile, and a constitutional monarchy was declared. Nepal began on a long road toward a democratic political system while struggling to overcome its long legacy of underdevelopment and to incorporate its varied ethnic populations into a single nation.

Between November 1951 and February 1959, a succession of short-lived governments ruled under an interim constitution or under the direct command of the king. In 1959 Nepal held the first national elections in its history, but free elections were not held again until 1990, when a prodemocracy movement forced the king to lift the ban on political parties. In 1996 a small but growing Maoist guerrilla movement, seeking to overthrow the constitutional monarchy and install a communist government, began operating in the countryside and initiated a protracted civil war that killed more than 15,000 people, severely affected the national economy (increasing the poverty rate from an already-high 42 percent), and led to a large increase in emigration from Nepal. Having declared a state of emergency and disbanded the national government in

2005, the monarchy survived until May 2006, when Nepal's parliament, newly reformed after a series of large-scale strikes and street protests, voted to declare a secular nation and strip the king of all control of the military. A few months later, the government and the Maoist rebels signed a peace agreement ending ten years of violence and beginning a many-year process of writing a new constitution. The country was declared a Federal Democratic Republic in May 2008, and Ram Baran Yadav was elected president July 2008. However, as of 2012, little progress had been made on enacting a new constitution because the competing political movements in the country—Maoists, Monarchists, and Democrats—have been unable to reach a consensus on a number of issues.

SETTLEMENT IN THE UNITED STATES

Until 1996, Nepalese people made up only a small number of the United States' immigrant population. For example, in 1995 only 55 Nepalese became American citizens and 312 received permanent-resident status. However, this number steadily increased after 1995 with implementation of the Diversity Immigrant Visa program, which annually made available fifty thousand permanent-resident visas to persons from countries with low rates of immigration to the United States. Between 2001 and 2010, over 33,000 Nepalese received legal permanent resident status. By 2012, Nepal ranked ninth among nations with the most diversity visa lottery winners: 4,259. To be eligible for the lottery, one must have at least twelve years of formal schooling or two years of work experience in a field desired in the United States. Many Nepalese immigrants found, however, that finding good jobs in the United States was very hard. A spokesperson for the New York-based Nepalese nonprofit Adhikaar explained that when educated Nepalese move to the United States "they become cheap labor for local businesses. They are desperate and willing to work very hard for very little money."

Although Nepalese Americans were more widely and thinly dispersed than some other Asian American groups, significant communities of Nepalese Americans existed in large metropolitan areas such as New York, especially in the "Little India" section in Jackson Heights, Queens; Boston; Chicago; Washington, D.C.; Denver, Colorado; Dallas; Portland, Oregon; Gainesville, Florida; and St. Paul, Minnesota. Sizable numbers also lived in various cities of California.

Between 2008 and 2012, 50,000 ethnic Nepali Bhutanese refugees who had been living for almost two decades in refugee camps in southeastern Nepal were resettled throughout the United States, with the largest concentrations in New York, Pennsylvania, and Texas. According to the U.S. Department of Homeland Security, in 2011, 10,266 Nepalis born in Nepal were granted permanent residence. Of these, about 2,000 were immediate relatives of U.S. citizens or family

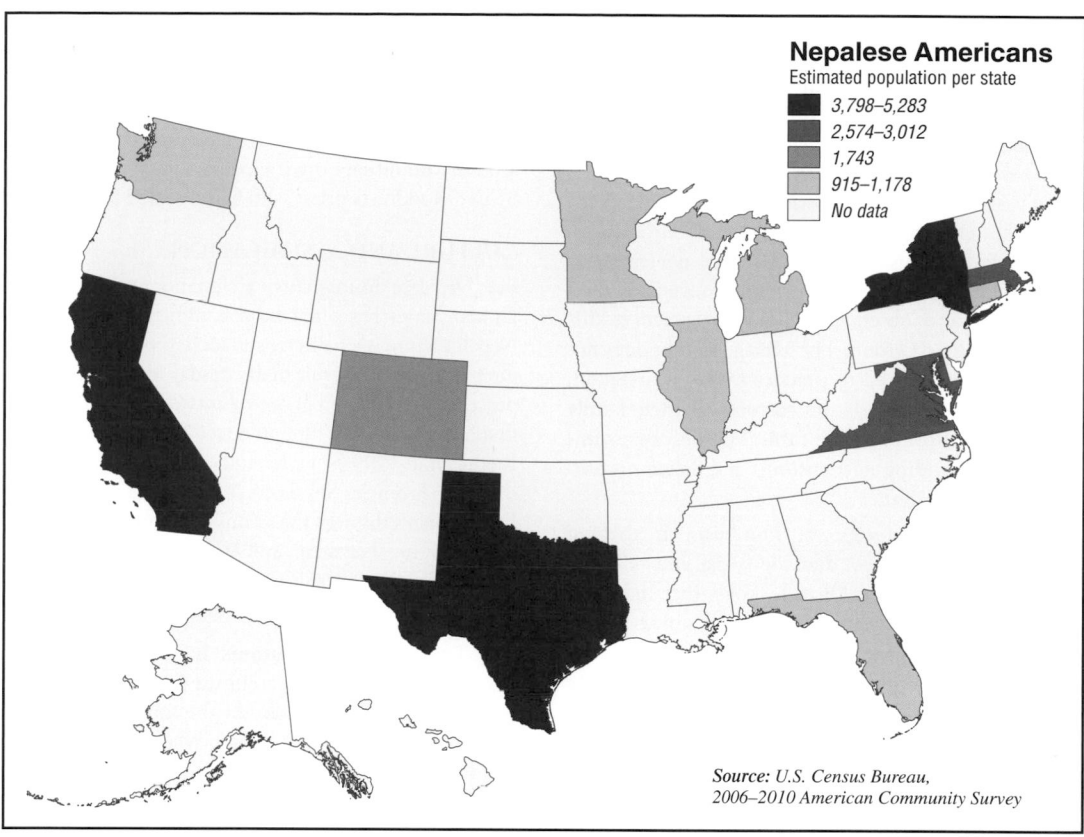

Nepalese Americans
Estimated population per state

- 3,798–5,283
- 2,574–3,012
- 1,743
- 915–1,178
- No data

*Source: U.S. Census Bureau,
2006–2010 American Community Survey*

sponsored, 1,148 had employment-based visas, 1,421 had diversity visas, and 5,299 were refugees or asylees. However, in the same year, twice as many people, 20,243, whose last country of residence was Nepal were granted permanent residence in the United States, and 15,486 of these were refugees, primarily from Bhutan.

LANGUAGE

Nepal's ethnic groups can be roughly divided between the Tibeto-Nepalese, who are related to the Chinese and Mongolians to the north and speak Tibet-Burman languages, and the Indo-Nepalese, who are related to the Indians of the south and use Indo-Aryan languages. The Newars, who are thought to be the original inhabitants of the Kathmandu Valley, speak a Tibeto-Burman language known as Newari.

Since the creation of a national educational program in Nepal during the 1950s, the majority of Nepalese, 58.3 percent, speak Nepali. Because the diversity visa program requires at least a high school diploma, most immigrants to the United States speak Nepali and perhaps another ethnic language. Nepalese Americans educated in Western schools also speak English fluently. Other languages include Maithili, Bhojpuri, Tharu, Tamang, Newari, and Abadhi. Non-Nepali languages and dialects are rarely spoken outside their ethnic enclaves.

Although about 90 percent of Nepalese Americans speak both English and at least one other language,

only 44 percent rated themselves as speaking English "very well" in a 2010 survey. The pre-1995 waves of Nepalese immigrants often spoke English at home and work and did not try to maintain the Nepali language. However, as the Nepalese American communities grew, organizations and cultural centers began using and teaching Nepali more often. Many Nepalese American websites are in both Nepali and English.

Greetings and Popular Expressions The word *namaste* is a common expression. It is used for greetings such as "hello," "good morning," and "good night." *Namaskaar* is another form of greeting and is mostly used on formal occasions. The fundamental role of rice in Nepalese culture is evident in the language. *Bhaat* is the word for rice, and a common Nepalese greeting is "*Bhaat khaayo?*" meaning literally, "Have you eaten rice?"

RELIGION

Hindu and Buddhist beliefs intermingle without conflict in Nepalese culture. More than 80 percent of the population is Hindu, 11 percent is Buddhist, 4 percent are Muslim, and about 2 percent embrace other religions, including Christianity.

Hinduism generally is regarded as the oldest formal religion in the world. The origins of Hinduism go back to the pastoral Aryan tribes from inner Asia. Unlike other world religions, Hinduism had no single founder and has never been missionary in orientation.

It is believed that about 1200 BCE, or even earlier by some accounts, the Vedas, a body of hymns originating in northern India, were produced. These texts form the theological and philosophical precepts of Hinduism. Hindus believe that the absolute (the totality of existence, including God, man, and the universe) is too vast to be contained within a single set of beliefs. Hinduism embraces six philosophical doctrines (*darshanas*). Individuals select one of these doctrines, or conduct their worship simply on a convenient level of morality and observance. Religious practices differ from group to group. The average Hindu does not need any formal creed to practice his or her religion, complying instead with the customs of their family and social groups. Because of this, Hindus can assimilate easily by adding new customs and beliefs according to personal needs.

One basic concept in Hinduism is that of dharma, or natural law, and the social and religious obligations it imposes. Dharma holds that individuals should play their proper and determined role in society. The caste system is an integral part of dharma. Each person is born into a particular caste, whose traditional occupation is graded according to the degree of purity and impurity inherent in it. Other fundamental ideas common to all Hindus concern the nature and destiny of the soul and the basic forces of the universe. Hinduism is polytheistic, incorporating many gods and goddesses with different functions and powers. The religion's three major gods are Brahma, Vishnu, and Shiva.

One part of karma (universal justice) is the belief that the consequence of every good or bad action must be fully realized. Another basic concept is that of samsara, the transmigration of souls. An individual's role throughout life is fixed by his or her good and evil deeds from a previous existence. Veneration for the cow has come to be intimately associated with all orthodox Hindu sects. Because the cow is regarded as the symbol of motherhood and fruitfulness, the killing of a cow, even accidentally, is regarded as one of the most serious of religious transgressions.

Buddhism is the common religion in the more sparsely populated northern mountainous region of Nepal and among some of the ethnicities in the middle hill region. Hinduism has influenced most Buddhist practice in Nepal, and often Buddhist and Hindu temples are shared places of worship.

While Hinduism and Buddhism are commonly practiced in the United States, where around 0.5 percent of the population is Hindu and 0.7 percent is Buddhist, distinctly Nepalese places of worship have only recently appeared in the United States, coinciding with the largest wave of Nepalese immigration. The first Nepalese Hindu temple in the United States, the Sanatan Temple in Denver Colorado, was established in 2006. Other Nepalese Hindu temples, such as the Sworg Dwari temple in Auburn, California, exist throughout the country. The first Nepalese Buddhist temple in North America was founded in Portland, Oregon, in 2009 by Kathmandu native Prajwal Ratna Vajracharya and U.S.-born Helen Appell. The opening ceremony featured ritual dances and a parade of around 100 different participants, and it was attended by two Buddhists priest who had traveled from Nepal.

CULTURE AND ASSIMILATION

For Nepalese immigrants, acclimation to life in the United States has often been a difficult process. The Nepali culture is a collectivistic society where group values play a dominant role in day-to-day functioning. This process was illustrated in *Ista-Mitra* (*Relative-Friends*) the first Nepalese feature film produced in the United States. Produced in 1999 by writer and director Hari Siwakoti, the film chronicles Siwakoti's life from his arrival in the United States through the assimilation process. Siwakoti described the Nepalese immigrant experience as difficult. "The Nepali culture helps each other," he said. "This is a different culture, a different life."

Traditions and Customs In Nepal social identity is tied to language, culture, and land, which may be seen as inseparable. At the same time, Nepali national identity is very strong. Many Nepalese customs and beliefs are heavily influenced by Buddhist or Hindu values. For example, many Nepalese American women continue to wear the *tika*, a red sandalwood dot pasted on the forehead, as an indication of marriage. Although most Nepalese eat with their right hand, Nepalese American diners have adopted silverware. In Nepal many people believe that metal spoons ruin the flavor of food and make a person thinner. Food may be served in a *thaali*, a metal plate divided into separate compartments.

Cuisine Like Indian food, Nepalese food is full of spice and flavor. The Nepalese use spices such as cumin, chili, turmeric, fennel, fenugreek, mustard seed, coriander, and the mixed-spice masala. *Besaar*, a bright orange spice, gives Nepalese curries their characteristic golden tint. Mustard oil is used for cooking as well as for oil lamps, temple offerings, and massage. Food is fried in mustard oil and liberally seasoned with garlic, onions, and fresh ginger. Authentic Nepalese food is not overwhelmingly spicy, but it does have a definite flavor of *koorsani*, or chili pepper.

The national dish of Nepal is *daal bhaat*, which consists of boiled rice (*bhaat* with a thin lentil sauce (*daal*), accompanied by curried vegetables (*tarkaari*) and a pungent pickle (*achaar*). *Daal bhaat* is eaten twice a day in the rice-growing regions of Nepal. The first meal is served around 10:30 a.m. and the second shortly after sunset.

Roasted flour, known as *sattu* or *tsampa*, is a staple food made from local grains: maize, wheat, millet, barley, or buckwheat. Sweet, milky tea, beaten or popped rice, flat bread, and curried potatoes are popular snack foods.

Regional foods within Nepal are distinct. The principal food of most hill families is *dhiro*, a cooked mush of maize or millet flour. It can be eaten alone, with fried vegetables, or with a thin soup. The staple food among the highland Bhotia people is Tibetan *tsampa*, which is ground roasted barley flour. In highland mountain regions such as the Sherpa homeland of Khumbu, the main dish is boiled potatoes, peeled and eaten with salt and a relish of pounded chilies and garlic. Sherpa women often make *rigi kur*, delicious crispy potato pancakes served with yak butter. *Chiura* is made by pounding soaked, uncooked rice. It is served with yogurt, vegetable curry, and fried meat (*chuela*) at Newar ritual feasts. *Bhuja*, or popped rice, resemble puffed rice crisps and are popped in a pan.

Other favorite snacks include curried potatoes (*alu daam*), dried peas in sauce (*kerau*), chewy dried meat (*sukuti*), and deep-fried triangular dumplings (*samosas*). Breads vary from fried rings of rice-flour (*sel roti*) to Gurung corn cakes, to the Indian flat, thin wheat-flour disks (*chapaati*) and the smaller fried *puri*.

Yogurt, called "curd," has a smoky taste from the wood fire it is cooked on. Bhaktapur's thick, creamy *juju dahu*, or "king of curd," is known as the best. *Chhurpi* is a cheese made from the solids of *mahi*, or buttermilk, which is dried in the sun and then cut into squares and strung on cords of yak hair. The *chhurpi* is very hard when first made but slowly softens when boiled in a soup or stew.

Most traditional Nepalese ingredients, such as potatoes, curry, rice, flatbread, and chilies, are available in U.S. grocery stores and various ethnic markets. There are also a number of Nepalese restaurants scattered throughout the country that cater to Nepalese American tastes, such as the Sherpa House and Cultural Center in Golden, Colorado, and Mustang Thakali Kitchen in Jackson Heights, Queens, New York, where at least five other Nepalese restaurants have appeared since 2004. An important project of the Association of Nepalis in America was the production of a cookbook that reflected the diverse cuisines of Nepal, which have been influenced by both India and Tibet.

Traditional Dress The clothing of Nepal varies according to tribes and regions. Nepal is known internationally for its wool garments, which are made from fur of the pashmina goat, a mountain goat that scales the snow-capped mountains. Pashmina shawls are usually bright red, green, muted beige, or oatmeal in color. Some pashmina garments are also embellished with embroidery. The intricate stitching on a pashmina can take five years to complete. Wealthy families are expected to include pashminas in a marriage dowry.

Nepalese women wear saris, which consist of unstitched cloth wrapped in a variety of ways. The saris are made of silk and cotton and can be either simple in design or brilliantly adorned. Buddhist monks wear

TARKARI

Ingredients

2 tablespoons cooking oil (eg. coconut or ghee)

1 onion, diced

½ teaspoon cumin powder

1 teaspoon coriander powder

2 cloves garlic, crushed

1 2-centimeter piece ginger, crushed

½ teaspoon turmeric powder

pinch chile powder

¼ tablespoon pepper

½ teaspoon salt

3 large potatoes, cubed

3 cups chopped mixed vegetables, eg. cauliflower, green beans, aubergines, zucchinis, carrots

3 tomatoes, quartered

Preparation

Heat oil in a heavy-bottomed saucepan and fry onion until golden brown. Stir in cumin, coriander, garlic, ginger, turmeric, chile powder, pepper, and salt. Add potatoes, chopped vegetables of your choice, and tomatoes. Turn vegetables over to coat with oil and spices. Cover and cook over low heat until all the vegetables are tender, turning gently from time to time.

Serve with *daah bhaat* and rice.

Serves 4

yak-hair boots and beautiful brocade robes in bright colors with wide sleeves. At the annual *Tiji* festival, celebrants wear traditional white silk *khatas* (scarves).

The nomadic Chepang do not have a distinct tribal costume. The men wear loincloths and vest-like clothes called *bhotos*, while the women wear saris and *cholos* (full-sleeved blouses). Bangles made of glass and plastic, along with various hair ornaments, are worn by women to show their marital status. In modern Nepal, all Nepalese officials are required to wear black caps, called *topi*, when formally dressed. The traditional Nepalese coat, which is often made from maroon velvet, overlaps at the front and is closed with four ties. The *chuba* is a long woolen coat worn by Sherpas.

While many Nepalese Americans have adapted to the typical American style of dress, a number of Nepalese clothing items have retained their popularity and have even become somewhat common throughout the general population. Brightly colored saris, for instance, are popular with women of all ethnic backgrounds, as are various kinds of

NEPALESE PROVERBS

Just as there are many different cultures and tribes within the Nepalese population, there are also various proverbs.

- The crow does not care for the cow's wound.

- You don't get smoke without a fire.

- A person with money has no wisdom and a person with wisdom has no money.

- The discontented are always unhappy and the contented are always happy.

- The person who works does not get credit.

- The country you hear about is always nice, and the country you live in is unhappy.

- You may talk about everything, but don't talk about your household.

- No one sees the cat stealing the milk, but everyone sees the cat get beaten.

- Even a monkey can dance if he is taught.

- A barking dog never bites.

- A dog can't fight with a group of monkeys.

Nepalese jewelry, and knit woolen ponchos, hats, and bags are popular with both men and women. There are numerous importers and manufacturers of Nepalese and Nepalese-style goods and clothing in the United States.

Traditional Arts and Crafts Nepalese arts and crafts, particularly metalwork, paintings, woodwork, stone sculpture, and weavings, reflect geographic locations and religious themes of Hinduism and Buddhism. Nepalese art is a national treasure that attracts tourists and art lovers to Nepal. Jewelry worn for everyday and ceremonial use is made of gold, silver, and beads of glass, coral, turquoise, amber and agate. Nepalese religious painters were widely known for the quality of their work, and their style influenced the art of Tibet and China. The Metropolitan Museum of Art in New York has displayed Nepalese illuminated manuscripts, paintings on cloth, and gilded metal sculptures.

Dances and Songs Nepalese music combines whimsical and rhythmical sounds of melodies with a characteristic sharp twang. Traditional folk tunes sung in the remote villages of Nepal celebrate religious and agricultural life. A music group popular with Nepalese Americans is Sur Sudha, a trio that performs Nepalese music on the flute, sitar, and tabla; they are known as Nepal's "Musical Ambassadors."

Three of the most popular traditional musical instruments in Nepal are the *bansuri*, the *madal*, and the *sarangi*. The *sarangi* is the most widely played musical instrument in Nepal. The *madal* is a double-headed drum made from a hollow tree trunk and animal skin. Both ends of this drum are played, with each end having its own distinct tone. The *madal* is traditionally played by hanging it over the shoulders or around the neck. It is an ancient folk instrument that is frequently played during festivals and celebrations in the Kathmandu Valley and surrounding areas. The *sarang*i is a violinlike four-stringed wooden instrument, the lower part of which is hollow and wrapped with thin leather. It is played vertically. The *bansuri* is a flute made of bamboo and is played horizontally. All of these instruments are handmade, and they are played in both traditional and modern Nepalese music.

Tharu, the indigenous people of Nepal, perform a stick dance known as the *phejaiti*. The dance has been an important part of Tharu culture and is popular among the Tharu communities in the districts of Chitwan, Bardiya, Dang, and Nawalparasi. A circle is created by more than a dozen dancers, each with a stick in hand, and in the center is the group leader with a *madal*. The group leader signals participants to dance, making a circular movement on the ground. As the group leader plays the *madal*, others dance swinging their sticks in the air while either standing or sitting. A combination of music and song accompanies the movement of the dancers.

A *jhilli* dance, a version of the stick dance, is also popular in the Tharu society. The *jhilli* is a musical instrument made of copper that produces an alarming sound. The *jhilli* dance originated when the cow herders went to the forest to look after their domestic animals and encountered wild animals. To protect themselves and their cows, the herdsmen used the *jhilli* to scare predators. Twelve to fifteen people participate in the dance and are accompanied by a group of four singers.

During the month of September, mask dancing is popular in Kathmandu. Papier-mâché masks are used in festivals to frighten evil spirits. Dances are rituals learned at an early age and performed in exact sequences.

From 2010 to 2012, many popular Nepalese singers, dancers, and other performers—including Anju Panta, Jagdish Samal, Kannaiya Singh, Manoj Sewa and Sarisma Amatya, Himgyap Tashi, and Bindu Tamang—toured the United States as part of a popular Namaste-America program.

Holidays Nepalese Americans celebrate Hindu and Buddhist holidays set by an ancient lunar calendar, the Nepal *Sambat*. The current official calendar is a solar calendar, the *Bikram* (or *Vikram*) *Sambat*, which is 56 years, 8 months, and 16 days ahead of the standard Western calendar. For example, the year 2012 in the Western (or Gregorian) calendar was the year 2069 in the Nepal calendar. In Nepal, calendars are printed each spring at the beginning of the Nepalese year showing dates from all three calendars—the lunar Nepal Sambat, the official Bikram Sambat, and the Gregorian.

Dashain, the celebration of victory of good over evil, is the longest and most celebrated festival in Nepal and among Nepalese Americans. It generally occurs in September and October. Dashain is also called Dasain, Vijaya Dashami, and Dahsera. The way of celebration and name differs, but most Nepalese celebrate it for about fifteen days with the same zeal and enthusiasm.

Another major holiday celebrated by Nepalese Americans is Navavarsha, the lunar New Year, usually falling in mid-April of the Gregorian calendar. Navavarsha is celebrated with street dances, parades, and reunions.

Other major holidays include Buddha Jayanti, a celebration of Buddha's birth, in May; Janai Purnima (also called Rakchshya Bandhan), a celebration of the changing of the protective yellow thread worn by Hindus in Nepal, India, and Mauritius as a sign of their commitment to the beliefs and practices of Hinduism, in August; Gai Jatra (the cow festival), in August; Krishnaastami, a Hindu celebration, in September; Teej, a festival for women, in September; Indra Jatra, a Hindu festival, in September; Tihar, a Hindu animal worship festival, in October and November; and Maha Shivaratri, a festival honoring the Hindu god Shiva, in February.

Health Care Issues and Practices Most health studies of Nepalese in the United States grouped them with other South Asians, including people from India, Pakistan, Bangladesh, and Sri Lanka. Ayurvedic medicine, a Hindu system of traditional medicine, and traditional Tibetan medicine based on ayurvedic and Buddhist literature, are widely practiced in Nepal. Health practitioners assumed that South Asians in the United States still held many beliefs based in these models, including a holistic mind-body relationship and the importance of food and digestion in health.

Domestic violence was identified as a particular issue for South Asian immigrants. The vulnerability of immigrants and reluctance to bring shame on the family may make South Asian women reluctant to report it.

Several studies showed that South Asian immigrants may be more likely to have diabetes or prediabetes than other ethnic groups in the United States. This may be due to both genetic and other cultural factors. Even though cancer was the leading cause of death among Asian Americans, Nepalese immigrants were perhaps less likely than other Americans to get screening tests for cancer, even if they had insurance.

FAMILY AND COMMUNITY LIFE

In Nepal, ethnic identity is distinguished primarily by language and dress, and it limits the selection of a spouse, friends, and career. This is evident in social organization, occupation, and religious observances. Nepalese Americans were not limited in this way because caste limitations are typically abandoned by Nepalese immigrants in the United States.

In most areas of Nepal, the basic social unit in a village is the family, or *paribar*. According to the 1990 Nepalese census, the typical *paribar* consisted of a patrilineally extended household made up of 5.8 persons. By the time of the 2011 census, this number had decreased to 4.7. This extended family system did not continue once Nepalese immigrate to the United States. Although Nepalese Americans might offer living assistance for a time to newly arrived relatives, they lived mostly in single-family units.

Gender Roles Nepal is a rigidly patriarchal society. In virtually every aspect of life, women are subordinate to men. However, a woman's status varies from one ethnic group to another. The status of women in Tibeto-Nepalese communities was generally better than that of Pahari and Newari women. Women from lower-caste groups also enjoyed relatively more autonomy and freedom than Pahari and Newari women.

The senior female within the family played an important role by controlling resources, making crucial planting and harvesting decisions, and determining the expenses and budget allocations. Nonetheless, women's lives remained centered on their traditional roles of household chores, including childrearing. Moreover, their standing in society depended on their husbands' and parents' social and economic positions.

Nepalese music combines whimsical and rhythmical sounds of melodies with a characteristic sharp twang. Traditional Nepalese folk tunes sung in the remote villages of Nepal celebrate religious and agricultural life.

Women had limited access to markets, reproductive services, education, health care, and local government. According to Nepal's 2010 census, 73 percent of the male population was literate, compared with only 48.3 percent of the female population. Women faced malnutrition and poverty. Female children usually were given less food than male children, especially when the family experienced food shortages. Women generally worked harder and longer than men. By contrast, women from high-class families had maids to take care of most household chores and other menial work and thus worked far less than men or women in lower socioeconomic groups. When women were employed, their wages normally were 25 percent less than those paid to men. In most rural areas, women's employment outside the household generally was limited to planting, weeding, and harvesting. In urban areas, they were employed in domestic and traditional jobs, as well as in the government sector, mostly in low-level positions.

Although the Nepalese constitution offers women equal educational opportunities, many social, economic, and cultural factors contribute to lower enrollment and higher dropout rates for girls. Although the female literacy rate had improved noticeably, increasing from 12 percent in 1985 to 48.3 percent in 2010, it was still far short of the level of male literacy (73 percent). The level of education among female children of wealthy and educated families was much higher than that of female children from poor families. A direct correlation exists between the level of education and status. Educated women have access to relatively high-profile positions in the government and private service sectors, and they have a much higher status than their uneducated counterparts. However, within the family, an educated woman does not necessarily hold a higher status than her uneducated counterpart. A woman's status, especially as a daughter-in-law, is more closely tied to her husband's authority and to her parental family's wealth and status than to any other factor.

Nepalese American women face many of the same difficulties in the United States that they did in Nepal. Researchers attribute this in part to U.S. Immigration laws, which encourage educated and skilled Nepalese (typically men) to immigrate first and establish themselves and to bring their wives and family over later. Such a process reinforces the traditional dependence of Nepalese women on their husbands for financial support and limits their ability to obtain education or employment once they arrive, as reported by Shamita Das DasGupta in *Body Evidence: Intimate Violence Against South Asian Women in America.*

One integral part of historical Nepalese society is the Hindu caste system. The fourfold caste divisions are the Brahman (priests and scholars), the Kshatriya (or Chhetri; rulers and warriors), the Vaishya (merchants and traders), and the Sudra or Dalits (farmers, artisans, and laborers). The only way to change caste status was to undergo "Sanskritization," which is achieved by migrating to a new area and changing one's caste status and/or marrying across the caste line. This can lead to the upgrading or downgrading of caste, depending on the spouse's caste. However, given the rigidity of the caste system, intercaste marriage carries a social stigma, especially when it takes place between members of castes from opposite ends of the social spectrum. In recent years, however, the has been a gradual abandonment of the caste system in Nepal, as Dalits have taken on prominent roles in society, even attaining government positions. In April 2011 the Nepalese parliament passed a bill outlawing caste discrimination, though many prejudices still remain. Nepalese Americans have almost completely given up the caste system, as no political or social infrastructure exists in the United States to facilitate such discrimination. In fact, the Nepalese American community is an active participant in the fight for equal civil rights in Nepal.

Education Nepal's educational system was dramatically revised after the revolution in 1951. In the early 1950s, while still under Rana rule, the average literacy rate in Nepal was 5 percent, with only the most privileged families educating their sons. In 1975 the government took responsibility for providing school facilities, teachers, and educational materials free of charge. Primary schooling was compulsory. It began at age six and lasted for five years. The curriculum was greatly influenced by American models, and it was developed with assistance from the United Nations Educational, Scientific, and Cultural Organization (UNESCO).

Since the transition to democracy, literacy has sharply improved. Nepal's literacy rate in 1998 was 27.5 percent, and by 2011 it had jumped to 60.3 percent, according to the Nepal census. However, there was still a very big difference between the literacy rates of males and females. Among males in Nepal, the literacy rate in 2010 was 73 percent, while for females it was 48.3 percent. This was changing, however, as evidenced by the fact that in 2010, according to estimates by the United Nations Educational, Scientific and Cultural Organization (UNESCO), 77 percent of young women between the ages of fifteen and twenty-four were literate.

Each year between 2008 and 2012, there were over ten thousand students from Nepal studying in American colleges and universities, mostly as undergraduates. This made Nepali students the eleventh-largest group of international students in the United States. The largest number of Nepali students were in Texas, primarily Houston and Dallas, with many also in California and Ohio. The top fields of study were business, physical and life sciences, and engineering.

By 2011, Nepalese Americans were twice as likely to hold a graduate or professional degree as the average American, with 47 percent having at least a bachelor's degree and 20.5 percent having a higher degree. However, they were also more likely to not have graduated high school; 86 percent of Americans have graduated high school in 2011, while only 75 percent of Nepalese Americans over the age of twenty-five had at least a high school diploma or equivalency.

Courtship and Weddings *Saipata* is the name given to both the official engagement announcement and the wedding day. Among Nepalese Americans, *saipata* is performed only for symbolic purposes. In this ceremony, the eldest family member from the groom's family, excluding his father and mother, formally requests the bride's hand in marriage while presenting the bride with food, gifts, and clothing. Traditional gifts include fruits, pastries, fish, and sweets. Other presents include clothing, makeup sets, shoes, and jewelry. *Saipata* is designed to showcase the groom's family wealth. The bride places the red *tika* on her forehead and is given a ceremonial blessing.

The *jaanti* is the procession to the bride's home for the *swaymber*, the main wedding ceremony. Traditionally, a marching band performs. In the United States, however, friends of the bride or groom improvise with a few drums and other instruments. The procession arrives at the bride's house. The groom's family circles the bride's car three times, symbolic in Hinduism, to welcome the bride, who wears red, and her family. The bride is welcomed with garlands, and the bride and groom exchange garlands. The families join hands to accept the couple. The bride and groom take turns feeding each other. They exchange rings and wedding vows, which is a Western adaptation of the traditional ceremony, in witness of the eternal *agni*, the ceremonial fire of existence. They circle the *agni* seven times. Then the groom applies red powder to the bride's head, which is symbolic of marriage. The husband is the first person to apply this powder to the bride. The groom also gives *pothey* (beads) and *toka* and *churi* (bangles), which are accessories worn by a married woman. The couple then receives a blessing from Suyra, the sun god, by standing together in the sun with their arms in front and their hands cupped to receive the sun.

Relations with Other Americans First-generation Nepalese Americans interacted peaceably with many ethnic groups in Nepal. Nepalese Americans who share Hindu and Buddhist beliefs form a ready bond with other Hindus and Buddhists of other nationalities. There were no major ethnic conflicts traditional to Nepalese that affected the way Nepalese Americans interacted with other groups.

EMPLOYMENT AND ECONOMIC CONDITIONS

The median family income for Nepalese Americans in 2011 was $49,535, just below the average in the United States. However, Nepalese families were almost twice as likely to be living below the poverty line, with a 20.5 percent poverty rate.

According to the U.S. Census Bureau, most Nepalese Americans worked in management, business, science, and arts occupations (35 percent); service occupations (28.4 percent); or sales (24.2 percent). 20 percent worked in the retail trades; 22.5 percent in education and health care or social services; 16.7 percent in entertainment and food services; and 13.4 percent in professional, scientific, and management administration. Many recent immigrants found low-wage work in restaurants and other service industries while either in school or intending to go to school or start a small business. In New York City alone, there were fifty Nepalese beauty salons that employed hundreds of Nepalese women. Nepal had thirteen medical schools, and many Nepalese doctors came to the United States to practice. For instance, in 2010 there

A Nepalese American works as a river-rafting guide in Colorado. H. MARK WEIDMAN PHOTOGRAPHY / ALAMY

were six Nepalese hospitalists (doctors who specialize in treating hospital patients) practicing in Rapid City, South Dakota.

POLITICS AND GOVERNMENT

Nepalese Americans who participated in lobbying efforts for Nepal were typically involved in medical and humanitarian assistance projects. Their political activity generally did not involve foreign policy or attempt to influence U.S. relations with Nepal in other arenas.

NOTABLE INDIVIDUALS

Art Sushma Joshi (1973–) is a writer, painter, and filmmaker born and raised in Kathmandu. She is a graduate of Brown University, the New School for Social Research, and the Breadloaf School of English at Middlebury College, Vermont. While based in Kathmandu, Joshi traveled around the world doing

Nepalese American designer Prabal Gurung takes a bow after one of his shows during fashion week in New York. 2010 AP IMAGES / STUART RAMSON

research and presentations on social change, politics, environment, and gender. Her first book of short stories, *The End of the World*, was published in 2009.

Fashion The Nepalese American fashion designer Prabal Gurung (1974–) was born in Singapore, raised in Kathmandu, and studied at Parsons the New School for Design in New York City. Before launching his own collection, he worked with Cynthia Rowley and Bill Blass design teams. By 2010 he was an award-winning designer whose fashions have been worn by First Lady Michelle Obama.

Journalism Kiran Carrie Chetry (1974–) is a Nepalese-American television broadcast journalist. She was an on-air reporter for Fox News from 2001 until 2011, the last four years as an anchor. Chetry was born in Kathmandu and grew up in Maryland.

Literature Samrat Upadhyay, director of graduate studies at Indiana University and professor of creative writing, was a short-story writer and novelist. Upadhyay, the first Nepal-born fiction writer writing in English to be published in the West, began winning awards with his first book, the short-story collection *Arresting God in Kathmandu* (2001). His 2010 novel *Buddha's Ghosts*, which takes place in Nepal over fifty years beginning in 1962, was favorably reviewed.

Science and Medicine Dr. Prativa Pandey (1953–) was born into a literary and activist Nepali family. Although she was an instructor of internal medicine at Harvard University and had a practice in Boston, she returned to Nepal in 1993 and worked as the medical director of CIWEC Clinic Travel Medicine

Center in Kathmandu. She was involved with America Nepal Medical Foundation, which raised money and support for rural medical services in Nepal.

MEDIA

The Nepali Times

Nepali Times is a world-class English-language weekly that provides in-depth reporting and expert commentary on Nepali politics, business, culture, travel, and society. It has a loyal readership among Nepalis at home and abroad, as well as the expatriate and diplomatic communities in Kathmandu.

Kunda Dixit, Publisher and Editor
Himalmedia Private Limited
G P O Box 7251
Kathmandu, Nepal
Phone: +977 1 5250333
Fax: +977 1 5251013
Email: letters@nepalitimes.com
URL: www.nepalitimes.com

TexasNepal.com

A community-oriented website for global Nepali-speaking communities. The website, based in Dallas, is intended to be informative and serve the needs of the community, with Nepal and Nepali community-related news, events, and happenings.

Avinash Shrestha
GPO Box 6312 House No. 11
Shrestha Colony Tahachal
Kathmandu, Nepal
Phone: (214) 519-8585
Email: avinash@texasnepal.com
URL: www.texasnepal.com

USNepalOnline.Com

New York-based community news portal dedicated to the Nepalese community in New York and around the world. It is published by the nonprofit American-Nepalese media organization US Nepal Media Center.

US Nepal Media Center
P.O. Box 13173
Jersey City, New Jersey 07303-4173
Phone: (917) 570-1098
Email: usnepalonline@gmail.com
URL: http://usnepalonline.com

ORGANIZATIONS AND ASSOCIATIONS

Adhikaar

A New York-based nonprofit organization working with Nepali communities to promote human rights and social justice.

7107 Woodside Avenue
Woodside, New York 11377-3939
Phone: (718) 937-1117
Email: info@adhikaar.org
URL: http://adhikaar.org

America-Nepal Society of California, Inc.

Formed in 1973 to promote harmonious relations between the United States and Nepal, and to promote educational opportunities for economically or otherwise disadvantaged persons.

Rabindra Pradhan, President
Email: rabimp@yahoo.com
URL: www.ansca.org

Association of Nepalese in Midwest America (ANMA)

Promotes Nepali culture and language. The association is concerned with keeping the Nepali cultural heritage alive in Nepal.

Mr. Gopendra Bhattarai, President
Email: gopendrarb@hotmail.com
URL: www.anmausa.org

Chicagoland Nepali Friendship Society (CNFS)

A nonprofit organization established in 2007 to support Nepalese immigrants and refugees in the Chicagoland area. Every year many Nepali immigrants and refugee are coming in Chicago continues to grow. It has become increasingly difficult for us to manage and coordinate our efforts in the Nepali community. As this trend continues, we are having great demand of supports and assistance for their survival and continuity of their journey in different walk of life. It is emerging need to have a better space (CHAUTARI) for all to share their pain and pleasure, and to mark their festivals and culture on their own environment.

Tek Bahadur KC, President
URL: http://cnfsusa.org

Florida-Nepal Association

Nonprofit organization of individuals of Nepali ethnicity promoting Nepalese culture in the Florida area, and relations with Nepal.

Dr. Archana Kattel, President
6320 NW 33rd Terrace
Gainesville, Florida 32606
Email: archana.kattel@gmail.com
URL: http://floridanepal.org

International Nepali Literary Society

International Nepali Literary Society, established in 1991, is an international organization of volunteer members who are interested in the languages, literature, art, and music of Nepal.

1727 Horner Road
Woodbridge, Virginia 22191
Phone: (703) 221-2656
Email: president@inls.org
URL: http://www.inls.org

Nepal Association of Northern California

Nonprofit organization of individuals of Nepali ethnicity promoting Nepalese culture in Northern California.

Gopal Khadgi, President
1812 Delaware St. Apt. 205
Berkeley, California 94703
URL: www.nanconline.org

Nepal Education and Cultural Center

A center to promote the historical, artistic, educational, cultural, linguistic, and religious heritage of Nepal.

9114 Margo Lane
Lanham, Maryland 20706
Phone: (301) 552-2299
Email: info@neccusa.org
URL: www.neccusa.org

MUSEUMS AND RESEARCH CENTERS

Association for Nepal and Himalayan Studies (ANHS)

Founded in 1971 as the Nepal Studies Association, ANHS is the oldest academic organization devoted to the study of Himalayan art, politics, and culture in the United States.

Mary Cameron, President
Macalester College
Department of Anthropology
1600 Grand Avenue
St. Paul, Minnesota 55105-1801
Phone: (651) 696-6362
Email: info@anhs-himalaya.org
URL: www.anhs-himalaya.org

The Lowe Art Museum at the University of Miami

A permanent collection of Indian, Nepalese, Tibetan, Chinese, and Japanese sculptures and paintings,

"Gods and Goddesses, Myths and Legends in Asian Art," examines the development of myth, legend, and religion in southern and eastern Asia.

1301 Stanford Drive
Coral Gables, Florida 33124-6310
Phone: (305) 284-3535
Fax: (305) 284-2024
URL: www.lowemuseum.org

Nepal Study Center, University of New Mexico

Organizes scholarly panels and conferences on Nepal and Himalayan studies.

Alok K. Bohara
MSC05 3060
1 University of New Mexico
Albuquerque, New Mexico 87131-0001
Phone: (505) 277-5903
Email: bohara@unm.edu
URL: http://nepalstudycenter.unm.edu

Rubin Museum of Art

The most prominent museum of Himalayan art and culture in the United States.

150 W. 17th Street
New York, New York 10011
Phone: (212) 620-5000
Email: info@rmanyc.org
URL: www.rmanyc.org

Virginia Museum of Fine Arts

The Nepalese galleries showcase collections of opaque watercolors on cloth or palm leaf.

200 N. Boulevard
Richmond, Virginia 23220-4007
Phone: (804) 340-1400
Email: visitorservices@vmfa.museum
URL: www.vmfa.state.va.us

SOURCES FOR ADDITIONAL STUDY

Dasgupta, Shamita D. *Body Evidence: Intimate Violence against South Asian Women in America.* New Brunswick, NJ: Rutgers University Press, 2007.

Hangen, S. *Creating a "New Nepal": The Ethnic Dimension.* Washington, D.C.: East-West Center Washington, 2007.

Mishra, P. B. "Nepalese Migrants in the United States of America: Perspectives on Their Exodus, Assimilation Pattern and Commitment to Nepal." *Journal of Ethnic and Migration Studies* 37, no. 9 (2011): 1527–37.

Narayan, Anjana, and Bandana Purkayastha. *Living Our Religions: Hindu and Muslim South Asian American Women Narrate Their Experiences.* Sterling, VA: Kumarian Press, 2009.

Upadhyay, S., and J. Schilb. "Writing Cross-Culturally: An Interview with Samrat Upadhyay." *College English* 74, no. 6 (2012): 554–66.

NEW ZEALANDER AMERICANS

Judson Knight

OVERVIEW

New Zealand Americans are immigrants or descendants of people from New Zealand, a country that lies about 900 miles (1,500 kilometers) southeast of Australia. New Zealand consists of the two large land masses called the North Island and the South Island, the self-governing Cook Island, and several dependencies, in addition to several small outlying islands. New Zealand's geographic features vary from the mountains and fjords of South Island to the volcanoes, hot springs, and geysers of North Island. Because the outlying islands are scattered widely, they vary in climate from tropical to nearly subantarctic. Excluding its dependencies, the country occupies an area of 103,483 square miles (268,021 square kilometers), about the size of Colorado.

According to Statistics New Zealand, the government statistics office, New Zealand had about 4.44 million residents in 2012. Although some 54 percent of New Zealanders identified themselves as Christian in the 2006 national census, the data indicated that New Zealand was to a great degree a secular society, with about 34 percent of the respondents indicating no religious affiliation at all. The remainder of the population included adherents of Hinduism, Buddhism, and other religions. Ethnically New Zealand was about 68 percent European, 15 percent Māori (the indigenous people of New Zealand), 9 percent Asian, 7 percent Pacific Islander other than Māori, and 1 percent other ethnicities. New Zealand has a highly advanced, industrialized economy, with the world's fifth-highest Human Development Index ranking for 2011, which placed it just below the United States in terms of income, education, and life expectancy. New Zealand's economy has long had a strong agricultural base, and for many years its principal agricultural export was wool, but as this became less profitable in the late twentieth century, New Zealand's farmers have turned to other sources of income, such as viniculture (cultivating grapes for winemaking). In 2007 wine overtook wool as the country's most exported commodity.

New Zealanders first came to the United States in the wake of the California gold rush that began in 1848, and they were likely to settle in the western United States, though many turned to farming once the prospect of riches through gold-mining proved elusive. Then and afterward, New Zealanders typically came to the United States not because they were fleeing something negative, but because they were pursuing opportunities. For instance, in the aftermath of World War II, some 1,500 "war brides"—women from New Zealand who had married U.S. servicemen stationed in their country during the war—moved to the United States. Likewise, in a trend that began during the late nineteenth century and continued into the early twenty-first, Māori individuals and families affiliated with the Church of Jesus Christ of Latter-day Saints relocated to the Mormon heartland in Utah.

The U.S. Census Bureau's American Community Survey estimates for 2009–2011 indicated that were over 18,000 people of New Zealander heritage living in the United States. Areas of the country with relatively large populations of New Zealander Americans included California, particularly San Francisco, Washington, Texas, Florida, and New York; while Utah was home to a relatively significant Māori population.

HISTORY OF THE PEOPLE

Early History Humans first appeared in New Zealand in around 1280, when settlers from eastern Polynesia began arriving. Their distant ancestors had migrated from the island of Taiwan in about 3000 BCE, moving through the Philippines and Melanesia and ultimately spreading to a large region of islands in the South Pacific. According to Māori legend the first Polynesian settlers came to New Zealand on canoes from a mythical island in the South Pacific called Hawaiki. Although anthropologists do not accept that Hawaiki is an actual place, they have recently accepted that the Polynesians sailed the Pacific in open canoes.

The first settlers of New Zealand called themselves *tangata whenua*, or "people of the land," but became known collectively as Māori (pronounced "MAH-aw-ree"). Because the Māori lacked a written language, and because their physical world was made up of materials highly susceptible to decay—especially in the humid Pacific climate—archaeologists studying their settlement patterns have had to rely on indirect evidence. Among these are signs of deforestation and the disappearance of native animal species, such as the flightless moa, that were overhunted into extinction by the Māori.

The resulting loss of food sources brought enormous changes to the Māori culture in about 1500. One group migrated over 400 miles southeast to the Chatham Islands, an archipelago of ten islands, where they became known as the Moriori. They would be destroyed in the mid-nineteenth century, not by Europeans but by the Māori, who attacked and enslaved them. As for those who remained on the main islands, their livelihood depended greatly on available resources. Some groups enjoyed better agricultural land than others, and the preservation and pursuit of sustenance helped spawn a strong warrior ethos within Māori culture.

Researchers divide the early history of New Zealand into the Archaic Period, which began at the time of Māori arrival and ended with the loss of abundant food resources in approximately 1500 CE, and the Classic Period, which came to an end on December 13, 1642, when Dutch navigator A. J. Tasman and his crew became the first *Pākehā* (people of European ancestry) to arrive on the islands. First landing on the South Island, they encountered a group of Māori and fought a skirmish in which four crew members and a least one Māori died. As he explored the North Island, Tasman mistakenly believed that the areas he had seen were part of a larger landmass connected to South America. He called the place Staten Landt, but three years later Dutch cartographers named it Nova Zeelandia or Nieuw Zeeland after the province of Zeeland in the Netherlands.

In the early twenty-first century there were some 300 Māori families living in Utah, most of them drawn there by opportunities for education and work within the Mormon community. The existence of this group has its roots in the efforts of nineteenth-century Mormon missionaries from the United States who traveled to the other side of the world at a time when theirs was still a persecuted fringe group within American society.

More than a century passed before the arrival of the next whites, a British crew under the command of Captain James Cook, who sailed into Poverty Bay on October 8, 1769. They were not the only Pākehā to arrive that year: a French crew led by Jean de Surville explored parts of the coastline and in Doubtless Bay on December 25 held a mass, the first Christian service in the islands. Cook himself surveyed most of the coastline on that first voyage, and he returned again in 1773. A skirmish in Queen Charlotte Sound on December 18 resulted in nine English and two Māori deaths. On his third voyage, Cook landed again at Queen Charlotte Sound on February 12, 1778, before sailing on. Cook, who died almost exactly a year later at the hands of natives in Hawaii on Valentine's Day 1779, anglicized the Dutch name for the islands, calling them New Zealand.

Modern Era On his first voyage, Cook had sighted a region of southeastern Australia that he named New South Wales, and in 1788 Great Britain identified that territory and New Zealand as one colony under the name New South Wales. Two years later, an outbreak of an illness believed to have been influenza killed more than half the Māori on the North Island. The Māori on the South Island had meanwhile adopted European firearms, which they used to fight one another and the British. About 20,000 Māori died in the Musket Wars, a series of some five hundred intertribal battles between 1807 and 1842. Diseases brought by the Europeans killed even more, and by the middle of the nineteenth century, the Māori population of New Zealand had fallen to 40 percent of precontact levels.

In the early nineteenth century New Zealand gradually became a settled colony, a process marked by milestones that included the arrival of the first European woman in 1806; the introduction of European livestock; the establishment of the first Christian (i.e., Anglican) mission, in 1814; and the birth of the first white child, Thomas Holloway King, in 1815. Eight years later, Philip Tapsell and Maria Ringa became the first English-Māori couple married in an Anglican service.

In 1837 the New Zealand Association, which would later be renamed the New Zealand Company, was established in London to promote and oversee the continued colonization of New Zealand. On January 22, 1840, a group of settlers arrived at the southern tip of the North Island and established a settlement called Wellington. More British followed, and on May 3, 1841, New Zealand became a colony separate from New South Wales. Okiato was named the first capital in 1840, but in 1841 the colonial government moved to Auckland, where in 1854 New Zealand's Parliament opened its first session. The colony became self-governing in 1856, and in 1865 it moved its capital to Wellington to better administer over all of the New Zealand territory. At the time, government officials worried that the South Island would separate from the North Island.

On December 26, 1907, New Zealand moved closer to becoming a sovereign nation when it was named a dominion of the British Empire. This designation meant that, for all intents and purposes, it was an independent nation, though officially it remained under British rule. Despite this high degree of autonomy, New Zealand was obliged to fight alongside the British at the onset of World War I in 1914. Its involvement began with a relatively limited action close to home, as troops seized the German colony of Samoa in 1914, but soon members of the New Zealand Expeditionary Force were serving in Europe and Egypt. In 1915 and 1916, forces from New Zealand, along with their Australian counterparts and other British and dominion troops, fought the Ottoman Turks in the disastrous campaign on the Gallipoli Peninsula. New Zealanders also saw action in the bloody battles of Passchendaele and the Somme, but the worldwide influenza outbreak in the waning days of the war claimed as many lives as the fighting. In 1919 New Zealand prime minister William Massey, along with other Allied heads of state, signed the Treaty of Versailles, officially ending the war with Germany.

In the interwar years, New Zealand became well known for its welfare state, which had its roots in progressive legislation such as the Old Age Pensions Act of 1898 and the Public Health Act of 1900. This socialist vision of society reached a new level in 1935, when New Zealanders elected a Labour Party government. In the following year the government took over the reserve bank, launched a state housing program, introduced guaranteed prices for dairy products, and reduced the working week from forty-four to forty hours.

When World War II broke out in Europe in the fall of 1939, New Zealand's government formed a Māori battalion as part of the newly created Second New Zealand Expeditionary Force (2NZEF). Despite New Zealand's location in the Pacific theater of war, its troops saw a great deal of action elsewhere, and even when the fighting came close to home, it did not necessarily involve the Japanese. The New Zealand ship *Achilles* took part in one of the war's earliest actions, the Battle of the River Plate in Argentina in December 1939, and in 1940 members of the 2NZEF began arriving in Egypt. Back home, German raiders attacked New Zealand civilian ships on a number of occasions, as on November 25, 1940, when they sank the steamer *Holmwood* near the Chatham Islands. New Zealand experienced heavy losses at the Battle of Crete in Greece in May and June 1941, and in December New Zealand declared war on Japan after the attack on Pearl Harbor. June 1942 saw the arrival of the first American troops from the 37th Division in Auckland, as well as Marines from the 1st Corps in Wellington.

After the war, in 1947, New Zealand's Parliament passed the Statute of Westminster Adoption Act, through which Parliament adopted or accepted the terms of Great Britain's 1931 Statute of Westminster, a law granting full legislative equality to dominion nations but retained a tie by including former dominions in the Commonwealth of Nations. New Zealand entered the Korean War in 1950. In 1954 New Zealand joined the Southeast Asia Treaty Organization (SEATO), which bound the country in a program of collective defense of the region and drew New Zealand into the Vietnam War, to which the country sent 3,500 military personnel and fought with the United States on the side of South Vietnam.

Although New Zealand remained on the fringes of world politics, outside events continued to pull the country onto the world stage in the 1970s and 1980s. In 1973 nuclear testing became a focal point of activism as the French government conducted activities in the South Pacific, and New Zealanders again rallied against nuclear forces when the U.S. Navy frigate *Texas* (which was simply nuclear-powered, rather than armed) visited their country in 1983. Two years later, the government refused entrance to a U.S. warship, the USS *Buchanan*, and French agents blew up the Greenpeace vessel *Rainbow Warrior* in Auckland Harbor. The government enacted antinuclear legislation in 1987.

The 1980s and 1990s saw New Zealand's government attempting to cut back some aspects of its extensive welfare system. Yet New Zealand continued to pursue socially liberal policies, as in 2003, when Parliament legalized prostitution. The year 2004 saw the formation of the Māori Party and the first broadcasts of Māori Television, established to help revitalize Māori language and culture. New Zealand sent troops to the War in Afghanistan that started in 2001, but not to Iraq. Its economy was adversely affected, though not devastated by the worldwide recession that began in 2008.

SETTLEMENT IN THE UNITED STATES

Throughout the years, the trickle of migrants from New Zealand has been slight, in part because there were not many New Zealanders to begin with. Only in 1908 did the national population reach 1 million, whereas that of the United States was nearing 89 million at the same time. When New Zealand's population reached 2 million in 1952, the United States' was over 157 million. Likewise, the population density of New Zealand is low compared to the United States: in 2013 New Zealand had less than half as many people per square mile as the United States. New Zealand, like the United States, was a country much more likely to receive immigrants than to send out emigrants—a fact that remained true even in the early twenty-first century, with record percentages of New Zealanders emigrating. Indeed, the period actually saw a much larger tide of emigration from the United States to New Zealand rather than vice versa. Furthermore, there was the fact that, for many decades, figures for immigrants from New Zealand were lumped with the much larger (though still minuscule) numbers of immigrants from neighboring Australia. Data compiled by the U.S. Immigration and Naturalization Service (INS) indicates that only about 64,000 Australians and New Zealanders came to the United States in the seventy-year period between 1820 to 1890—an average of slightly more than 900 per year.

From the beginning, New Zealanders typically entered the United States not as political or economic refugees but rather for their own personal reasons. The first notable migration occurred in the wake of the 1848 gold rush in California. Would-be prospectors in New Zealand and Australia greeted the news from California with enthusiasm and pooled their resources to charter ships that would take them on the month-long transpacific voyage. Of course the dream

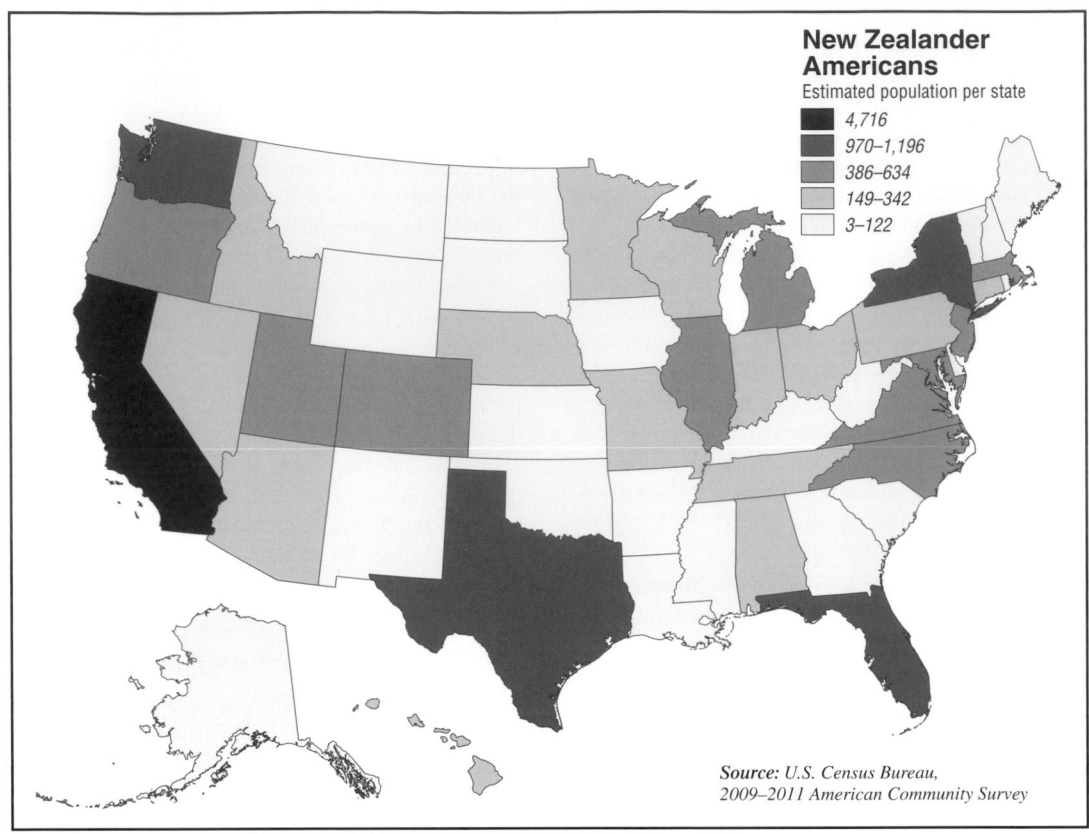

New Zealander Americans

Estimated population per state

- 4,716
- 970–1,196
- 386–634
- 149–342
- 3–122

*Source: U.S. Census Bureau,
2009–2011 American Community Survey*

of striking it rich in the goldfields eluded all but a very few, but gold was only the initial attraction: in the end, those who stayed were more likely to do so because of what they regarded as abundant economic opportunities in the United States.

During the period of the American Civil War (1861–1865) and its aftermath, immigration to the United States from Oceania (the islands in the Pacific Ocean, including New Zealand) virtually came to a standstill: statistics show that between January 1861 and June 1870, just thirty-six Australians and New Zealanders made the move across the Pacific. This situation changed in the 1870s, however, as the U.S. economy entered a postwar boom and Reconstruction came to an end. The same period saw the beginnings of regular steamship service between the United States and the Australian ports of Melbourne and Sydney—both on the continent's east coast, making them easily accessible to New Zealanders on their way across the Pacific.

In the years between 1871 and 1880, a total of 9,886 persons from Oceania immigrated to the United States, but in the next two decades, as the world economy faltered, those numbers fell by half.

During the 1930s, immigration numbers dwindled to about 2,400 persons from Oceania for the entire decade, but the aftermath of World War II brought new waves of migrants. Among these were approximately 1,500 New Zealand "war brides," or women who married U.S. servicemen they met while the latter were stationed in their country during the war. In total, over 100,000 war brides entered the United States in the aftermath of World War II, their entry made possible by the War Brides Act of 1945, which allowed the immigration of the non-Asian spouses and the children of U.S. military personnel into the United States.

U.S. Census Bureau figures show that in 1960, there were 5,826 people living in the United States who had been born in New Zealand. For the next thirty years, approximately 3,000 New Zealanders came to the United States per decade. However, many of these people were not immigrants but rather were New Zealand expatriates who came to the United States to work for a short time and then returned to New Zealand. In the 1990s, due to a strong U.S. economy, over 7,000 New Zealanders came to the United States, as the New Zealand–born population, which rose over the course of the decade from 15,415 in 1990 to 22,870 in 2000. The American Community Survey (ACS) estimates for 2009–2011 show that there were 18,000 people of New Zealander ancestry living in the United States. The ACS also reported that the states with the highest numbers of New Zealander Americans included California, New York, Texas, Washington, and Florida. Also, a significant population of person of Māori descent were residing in Utah.

LANGUAGE

According to Statistics New Zealand, the 2006 national census showed that about 96 percent of New Zealanders spoke English. Slightly more than 4 percent, or about 157,000, spoke Māori. The latter, an Eastern Polynesian language closely related to Tahitian and somewhat more distantly related to Hawaiian, is spoken fluently by only about 29,000 people, according to the New Zealand statistic bureau's 2001 "Survey on the Health of the Māori Language." The 2006 national census also showed more than 24,000 people with some degree of proficiency at the country's third official language, New Zealand Sign Language. More than 6,000 New Zealanders were able to communicate fluently in all three languages.

Native English speakers constituted the overwhelming majority of New Zealander Americans. The U.S. Census Bureau does not provide information indicating the number of Māori among the New Zealand–born population, and there have been no formal efforts to preserve the Māori language among New Zealander Americans. A number of Māori words have entered the vocabulary of New Zealander English. Among these is *Pākehā*, the name for New Zealand–born descendants of Europeans; *hui*, which can either be a noun ("assembly") or verb ("to assemble"); and *iwi*, which means tribe.

By far the most significant Māori word is the one given to a flightless bird that became a symbol of New Zealand and New Zealanders, especially overseas: *kiwi*. Much as Australians call themselves "Aussie," *Kiwi* is an affectionate term used at least as much by New Zealanders as by outsiders. Unlike many names for ethnic groups, this one carries no offensive connotation but is rather regarded with affection and pride by those who bear it. The term derives from the use of the kiwi symbol on regimental emblems sported by New Zealand troops in the Second Anglo-Boer War and later conflicts. The term came into widespread use during World War I, when large numbers of New Zealanders served in Europe and the Middle East and, due to the difficulties of transport back to their distant homeland, remained on in Great Britain for many months following the Armistice. By the end of World War II, the term had come to apply to all New Zealanders. It is rendered in uppercase and pluralized with an "s," whereas that of the bird is lowercase and—in keeping with its Māori origins—remains the same in singular and plural form. To avoid confusion, the fruit of the same name, formerly known as Chinese gooseberry, is called *kiwifruit* or *kiwi fruit*.

New Zealander and Australian Americans speak in a similar accent (though there are subtle differences) and share many expressions. Thus many terms that Americans associate with Australian English—"barbie" for barbecue, or the greeting "G'day"—are used in New Zealand as well. However, New Zealand English has its own terms and expressions for a number of situations. A person with "big bickies" (a great deal of money) might find him- or herself surrounded by "bludges," or people willing to live off of the generosity of others. Bludges might hope for easy money—"money for jam"—but might find that bludging is a "mission," or difficult undertaking. A bludge might simply wait for a rich relative to "cark it"—that is, die. A "bun-fight" (social gathering that involves food) might be just "bog-standard" (average), but if the fare were excellent, guests would be a "box of birds" (very happy). A "piss-up," or social gathering with alcohol, runs the danger that someone might get the "collywobbles" (an upset stomach) and perhaps even "chunder" (vomit). In the end, host and guests alike would hope to be "home and hosed"—that is, safe and sound.

RELIGION

The 2006 New Zealand census showed that about 54 percent of the population claimed Christianity as their religion, and slightly more than 4 percent identified as Hindus, Buddhists, or adherents of other religions. Of the remaining 42 percent, about 34 percent claimed no religion at all, while about 8 percent identified themselves as "undeclared." Extrapolating from this data, it may be assumed that New Zealander Americans tend to be almost evenly divided between Christians and persons who do not identify with any religion.

The only notable religious group among New Zealander Americans is that portion of the Māori population who belong to the Church of Jesus Christ of Latter-day Saints (the LDS Church or Mormon faith). According to the *Encyclopedia of New Zealand*, in the early twenty-first century there were some 300 Māori families living in Utah, most of them drawn there by opportunities for education and work within the Mormon community. The existence of this group has its roots in the efforts of nineteenth-century Mormon missionaries from the United States who traveled to the other side of the world at a time when theirs was still a persecuted fringe group within American society.

The first Mormon missionaries arrived in New Zealand in 1854, and by the mid-1880s they had begun making converts among the Māori people. According to a 1981 *New Era* article by Mormon scholar R. Lanier Britsch, "Māori Traditions and the Mormon Church", the Māori proved particularly receptive to the Mormon message because in the preceding decades five different *tohungas*, or priests, had delivered prophecies indicating that their people would soon be taught religious truths by visitors from far away.

CULTURE AND ASSIMILATION

Assimilation to American society has not been difficult for the majority of New Zealander Americans, as they are white and their native language is English. Their presence has thus made little visible impact in

MĀORI ROOTS DEEPEN IN UTAH

A June 2003 article in Utah's *Deseret Morning News* ("Polynesian Roots Grow Deeper in Utah") illustrates the difficulties experienced by Māoris attempting to assimilate to American society. Celeste Tonga, who had moved to Ogden, Utah, in 1986, told author Diane Urbani that "A lot of the time we feel like we're not OK. Over here, people are very practical. [Americans] think with their minds, not with their hearts." By contrast, "in the islands, away from the tourist areas, there are still people who are very poor. Yet they're so kind, so generous. We see ourselves in them, and it's a way to say, oh, we're OK." She went on to state, "Our people will never be rich. Because of how we were raised, we don't aspire to have things."

Tonga told Urbani that, when she first came to Utah, her children were mistreated in school because they looked different and had traditions that set them apart from their U.S.-born classmates. However, she was able to change the situation by taking action: "We contacted all the teachers and asked if we could go into the social studies classes and share something about our culture." According to Urbani, "At schools all over Utah, [Tonga] has taught children that Polynesian music and dance are not only entertainment; they are also a form of spiritual renewal, in which people reconnect with nature and their creator."

Tonga and others were involved in building a *marae*, or meeting house, in Lehi, Utah. In 2002 the group held a groundbreaking service, for which they invited members of the Northern Ute tribe to participate. Urbani writes, "The Māori, first people of New Zealand, wanted to honor the first people of Utah. A look into their histories turns up some parallels: Children were forbidden to speak their native language. Europeans brought diseases that ravaged the populations, and conflicts over land rights left native people with less than the newcomers."

a country where non-Hispanic whites constitute the majority. The same is not true for that portion of the New Zealander American population who have Māori heritage.

The 2006 New Zealand census indicated that the average Māori income in New Zealand was about 59 percent of the average non-Māori income, and Māori who immigrate to the United States for religious purposes are less affluent than other New Zealander immigrants. Many Māori immigrants do not seek wealth or have an affinity for consumerism and do not feel included in mainstream American culture. In addition, unlike New Zealanders of European descent, Māori immigrants, who have darker skin, have experienced racial prejudice in the United States. As a minority, Māori New Zealander Americans feel a much greater need to preserve the stories and practices handed down from their ancestors.

Traditions and Customs While New Zealanders of European descent certainly have their own traditions and customs, the most distinctive aspects of New Zealander culture come from the Māori. Like many peoples without a written language, the early Māori developed a rich oral tradition that included tribal genealogies, or *whakapapa*, going back centuries. In addition to oratory, or *whaikōrero*, Māori cultural traditions include *haka* and other dance forms, song composition, weaving, wood carving, and *tā moko* (tattoo).

Cuisine The diet of New Zealanders of European descent is similar to the British diet, with a considerable amount of red meat. New Zealanders especially enjoy barbecued meats such as lamb. One popular tradition among New Zealanders of both Māori and European heritage is the *hāngi*, a cookout using a Māori method of food preparation. When New Zealander Americans speak of "laying [or putting down] a *hāngi*," they are referring to a process that involves digging a pit and building a fire in it, heating stones in the fire, then placing tightly closed baskets of food atop the fire and covering all of it for several hours. The hangi, which dates back to the earliest days of Māori presence in New Zealand, has evolved over time: wire baskets, used in the nineteenth century, were replaced by gas-burning, stainless steel "hāngi machines" in the twenty-first.

A variant of the hāngi is the *umu*, used for cooking the roots, stems, and tops of the cabbage tree (*Cordyline australis*). Māori use of these and other plants dates back at least to 1500, when their ancestors faced a food crisis due to the rapid decline in available flora and fauna on the islands. In regions with good agricultural land, the starchy root vegetables like *taro* and *kumara* (sweet potato) became staples, while the southern part of the South Island offered abundant edible wild plants, such as fernroot and cabbage trees. In addition to these vegetables, potatoes are an integral part of the New Zealander diet: in fact, the slang term "spud" comes from New Zealand English. These foods have remained significant parts of the Māori diet both in New Zealand and in the United States.

Traditional Dress New Zealanders of European descent have long dressed in a fashion similar to their counterparts in other former British colonies, and the apparel of New Zealander Americans tends to make them largely indistinguishable from their neighbors in the United States. Inasmuch as there is a distinctive item of white New Zealanders' clothing, it would probably be gumboots, which are large rubber overshoes that may extend to the calves or even above the knees.

Traditional Māori clothing was similar to the attire worn throughout Polynesia, though with some adjustments due to the fact that New Zealand lies much farther south than Polynesia and therefore gets much colder. One significant item of clothing was the *puipui*, a kilt-like knee-length garment worn by both male and female Māori. Gender distinctions applied to the puipui, with men having ornately designed waistbands in contrast to the plain belt worn by women. Another item of clothing was a cloak, which went by different names depending on specific elements of its design: for instance, a *korowai* had tassels, while a *kahu huruhuru* included feathers, but the addition of dog fur as decoration constituted a *kahu huri*. The Māori used various dyes, including a black mud-like substance called *paru*, tan-colored tanekaha bark, and yellowish raurekau bark. Māori New Zealander Americans rarely wear traditional clothing, except on special festive occasions. One such instance would be when performing the *haka* war dance, one of the most widely known aspects of New Zealand culture in general, and Māori culture in particular.

Dances and Songs A widely recognized example of Māori performing arts is the haka, a dance that involves a group stamping their feet and shouting rhythmically. The haka, which resembles a war dance, has been adopted by sports teams as a means of intimidating opponents, but for Māori people the dance is not necessarily meant to signal aggression and is often performed for mere amusement. The dance can also serve as a greeting to people arriving at an event or can be used as a way of raising morale.

Holidays ANZAC or Anzac Day (April 25) commemorates the Australian and New Zealander troops killed during the disastrous campaign on Turkey's Gallipoli Peninsula that began April 25, 1915, and ended the following January 9 with 2,721 New Zealanders dead. Many New Zealanders as well as people of New Zealander heritage around world honor this day by attending events that feature music, dance, and speeches. Another holiday celebrated by New Zealander Americans is Waitangi Day. The date, February 6, commemorates the 1840 signing of the Treaty of Waitangi, which made New Zealand part of the British Empire. Among New Zealander Americans, especially the various Māori communities in the United States, autumn is known as the "hāngi" season and is a time for numerous barbecues, mostly featuring lamb and chicken.

FAMILY AND COMMUNITY LIFE

New Zealand families are similar in size and structure to most American families. The U.S. Census Bureau's American Community Survey (ACS) did not publish detailed data on Americans of New Zealander ancestry, but it did provide figures on New Zealand–born U.S. residents. According to the ACS estimates for 2009–2011, the average family size among New Zealand–born U.S. residents was 3.15, which was slightly smaller than the national average of 3.23.

Gender Roles New Zealand has long been known as a leading nation where gender equality and women's rights are concerned. New Zealand was first

MĀORI PROVERBS

The following are some Māori *whakatauki*, or proverbs:

Moe atu nga ringa raupo.

Marry a man with calloused hands.

Naku te rourou nau te rourou ka ora ai te iwi.

With your basket and my basket the people will live.

Kaore te kumara e whaakii ana tana reka.

The sweet potato does not say how sweet he is.

Ko te reo te tāhuhu o tēnei whare.

The language is the ridgepole of this house.

Māu anō e rapu he orange.

Your livelihood is in your own hands.

Whāia te iti kahurangi—ki te tūohu koe, me he maunga teitei.

Pursue excellence—should you stumble, let it be from a lofty mountain.

He aha te mea nui o te ao? He tangata! He tangata! He tangata!

What is the most important thing in the world? It is people! It is people! It is people!

He kotuku rerenga tahi.

A white heron flies once. (Meaning: "When something is special, it does not happen often.")

to grant female suffrage, as women earned the right to vote in 1893, though in some parts of the country they had been participating in elections even before this time. Women have long held important roles in New Zealand politics. Within traditional Māori society, long before contact with Westerners, women enjoyed a higher status than in many traditional cultures. As with many other societies faced with material scarcity, the need to acquire and maintain control of food and other resources spawned a strong warrior culture among the Māori, but this did not necessarily exclude women. Either males of females could become chieftain. In the United States, New Zealander Americans divide work and domestic duties as many other American families do, with both partners working jobs and sharing in domestic chores and child-rearing.

Education New Zealander Americans value education and have performed well in school. According to the 2011 ACS five-year estimates, of the 23,745

Body painter, makeup artist, and New Zealander American Joanne Gair transforms Heidi Klum into vintage, Hollywood-glamour style for the 2006 *Sports Illustrated* swimsuit issue. LOUD AND CLEAR MEDIA / PHOTOSHOT

expatriates and immigrants) was in management, business, science, or arts occupations, while nearly 12 percent was in service professions and 17.5 percent was in sales and office occupations. Another 7.5 percent held jobs related to natural resources, construction, or maintenance, and just under 6 percent worked in production, transportation, or material moving occupations. New Zealanders living in the United States tend to be significantly wealthier than the U.S. population as a whole. The ACS reported that for 2009–2011, the estimated median household income for New Zealand–born U.S. residents was $86,241 a year. By comparison, the median income for the nation's more than 114.7 million households during the period 2007–2011 was $52,762. Likewise the poverty rate of 7.7 percent for the New Zealand–born population was about half the national figure of 14.3 percent.

POLITICS AND GOVERNMENT

There is no significant data, either statistical or anecdotal, regarding the political views or voting habits of New Zealander Americans. Other than Leo T. McCarthy, California's longest-serving lieutenant governor (1983–1995) and a member of the Democratic Party, there have been few significant American political leaders of New Zealander descent. New Zealander Americans tend to hold liberal views on matters such as national defense, the economy, and social policy. New Zealander Americans in the Republican Party tend to be more moderate than most members of the party.

NOTABLE INDIVIDUALS

Academia David Teece (1948–) moved to the United States in the early 1970s. He earned his PhD in economics from the University of Pennsylvania and taught at the Stanford University Graduate School of Business from 1975 to 1982 before taking a position with the Walter A. Haas School of Business at the University of California, Berkeley. In 2001 Teece cofounded a global network of New Zealanders called the Kea Foundation. In 2013 he was awarded an Order of Merit by the New Zealand government for his efforts in developing U.S.–New Zealand relations.

Activism Donaldina Cameron (1869–1968) was a Presbyterian missionary noted for her work to stop human trafficking. She was credited with rescuing and educating some three thousand young women.

Architecture Mark Antony Wigley is a New Zealand American architect, author, and educator. Born in New Zealand, he earned his bachelor of architecture and PhD degrees from the University of Auckland in the late 1970s and early 1980s. In 2004 he became dean of the Graduate School of Architecture, Planning, and Preservation at Columbia University in New York, and in 2005 cofounded *Volume*, a quarterly devoted to avant-garde architecture.

New Zealand–born U.S. residents aged twenty-five or over, nearly 96 percent were at least high school graduates, as compared to about 85.5 percent for the nation as a whole during the period 2007–2011. Fully 20 percent had graduate or professional degrees, and more than 25 percent had bachelor's degrees, both above national averages.

EMPLOYMENT AND ECONOMIC CONDITIONS

New Zealander Americans have, on the whole, led successful, affluent lives in the United States. The U.S. Census Bureau's American Community Survey (ACS) did not release data on the economic characteristics of Americans of New Zealander ancestry, but it did provide such figures on New Zealand–born U.S. residents. According to the ACS estimates for 2009–2011, more than 58 percent of the New Zealand–born labor force (which consists of

Fashion Joanne Gair (1958–), a makeup artist and body painter, was born and raised in Auckland and moved to Los Angeles at the age of twenty-one. She achieved fame for a widely noted 1992 *Vanity Fair* magazine cover known as "Demi's Birthday Suit," for which actress Demi Moore wore a Gair body painting made to resemble a suit and tie. Gair's work has also appeared in the annual *Sports Illustrated* swimsuit issue 1999.

Rachel Hunter (1969–) is a model, actress, and reality-television host. Born in the Auckland suburb of Glenfield, Hunter began modeling at age seventeen. She went on to become a spokesperson for Cover Girl cosmetics and to appear in several *Sports Illustrated* swimsuit issues. Hunter, who became a naturalized U.S. citizen, was married to singer Rod Stewart since 1999.

Journalism Peter Arnett (1934–) is a journalist known for his war coverage, particularly in the Vietnam, Gulf, and Iraq wars. Born in Riverton, New Zealand, Arnett began his career in Southeast Asia. He earned the Pulitzer Prize in 1966 for his Vietnam reporting as an Associated Press correspondent, and he later worked for *National Geographic* and several television networks. His reporting for CNN during the Gulf War in 1991 and for NBC during the 2003 invasion of Iraq attracted both high praise and controversy for what many regarded as his sympathetic coverage of the Saddam Hussein regime.

George Silk (1916–2004) was a photojournalist most famous for his work during World War II. Born in Levin, New Zealand, he became an enthusiastic amateur photographer and took a job at a camera shop as a teenager. Hired by *Life* magazine in 1943, he covered the Allied invasions of Italy and France as well as the war in the Pacific. Silk became the first photographer to record the atomic devastation of Nagasaki, Japan, in 1945. Silk became a U.S. citizen in 1947.

Music Tosca Berger Kramer (1903–1976) was a violinist and violist who, along with her parents, helped bring classical musical instruction and performance to the American heartland in the early part of the twentieth century. Born in New Zealand, she traveled extensively with her parents, Kurt and Lucy Berger, themselves well-known musicians. While on a U.S. tour, her father fell ill in Tulsa, Oklahoma, and during his period of recovery the city fathers persuaded him to stay. The family established the Tulsa Philharmonic, and Tosca Kramer became widely known throughout the state as an instructor and performer on violin and viola.

Politics Leo T. McCarthy (1930–2007) was lieutenant governor of California from 1983 to 1995. Born in Auckland, McCarthy moved with his family to San Francisco at age four. After serving in the U.S. Air Force during the Korean War, he returned to California and soon became active in Democratic Party politics. He won a seat on the San Francisco Board of Supervisors in 1963, and five years later he went on to the California State Assembly, where he served as speaker from 1974 to 1980. After losing the speakership to fellow Democrat Willie Brown, McCarthy won the first of three elections to the lieutenant governorship in 1982. He lost his 1988 and 1992 bids for the U.S. Senate, but his twelve years in the state's number-two executive position (brought to an end by mandatory term limits) made him the longest-serving lieutenant governor in California history.

Religion Hirini Whaanga Christy (1883–1955) was a leader in the Mormon Church. Of Māori descent, Christy was born in Nuhaka, Hawke's Bay, and moved to Utah with his family at the age of eleven. He attended Latter-Day Saints' University in Salt Lake City, and became a member of the Mormon Tabernacle Choir. Christy married an American and later moved his family back to New Zealand, where he remained active in the Mormon Church.

Science and Technology Anton Anderson (1892 1960), nicknamed "Mr. Alaska Railroad," was an engineer involved in the building of railroads, dams, and other infrastructure in Alaska. Born in Moonlight, New Zealand, to a Swedish father and Irish mother, he moved to the United States in 1914 to work as a surveyor in Hoquiam, Washington. He subsequently moved to Anchorage, Alaska, then a recently founded city. He worked for the Alaskan Engineering Commission, and in the 1930s he became involved in a massive infrastructure project in the Matanuska Valley. During World War II, Andersen served with the U.S. Army Corps of Engineers, and he later participated in the building of the Eklutna River hydroelectric dam. Late in life, Andersen became an Anchorage city councilman and mayor.

Derek Ernest Denny-Brown (1901–1981) was a neurologist noted for his work involving electromyography, the physiology of micturition, and Wilson's disease. Born in New Zealand, he studied at the University of Otago in Dunedin, and in 1928 he took a clinical post in London. In 1941 he received an appointment to Harvard Medical School, along with a directorship of neurology at Boston City Hospital. Denny-Brown later served as president of the American Neurological Association.

William Hayward Pickering (1910–2004) was a rocket scientist and senior figure with the National Aeronautics and Space Administration (NASA). Born in Wellington, he attended Wellington College and Canterbury University College before moving to California, where he earned his PhD in physics at the California Institute of Technology in 1936. In 1954 he became director of NASA's Jet Propulsion Laboratory in Pasadena, a post in which he remained until his retirement in 1976.

New Zealand-born Scott Campbell warms up at Yankee Stadium in New York City 2008. CHRIS MCGRATH / GETTY IMAGES

Sports Scott Campbell (1984–) was a baseball player for the Toronto Blue Jays. Born and raised in Auckland, he went to the United States to play for Central Arizona Community College. His batting skills won him a spot on the Las Vegas 51s, a minor-league team in the Blue Jays organization, and in 2006 he went on to play for the Blue Jays themselves. Campbell retired in 2012 due to problems resulting from a hip injury.

Thomas "Tommy Gun" Heeney (1898–1984) was a professional boxer, nicknamed "the Hard Rock from Down Under" by journalist Damon Runyon. Born in Gisborne, New Zealand, Heeney became his country's national heavyweight champion after defeating Brian McCleary of Dunedin in 1920. He moved to the United States in 1926, and after defeating Jack Sharkey he won the right to fight the world heavyweight champion Gene Tunney at Yankee Stadium on July 26. Heeney, who entered the ring wearing a Māori cloak, lost in the eleventh round. He retired from boxing in 1934, married an American, and became a U.S. citizen. Heeney later opened a bar in Miami and often went fishing with his friend Ernest Hemingway, the renowned novelist.

Peter Snell (1938–), a runner, won three Olympic and two Commonwealth Games gold medals. Born in the town of Opunake, he attended Te Aroha College in Waikato. Snell, who showed athletic prowess from his earliest days, won gold medals in the 800-meter event at the 1960 Olympic Games in Rome and the 1964 Games in Tokyo, where he also won gold in the

1500 meters. He broke the world mile record in 1962, a year in which he also won gold and set records at the Commonwealth Games and received a Member of the British Empire (MBE) award. Snell moved to the United States in 1971, and after earning a PhD in exercise physiology, he took a position at the University of Texas Southwestern Medical Center in Dallas.

Stage and Screen Rupert Julian (1879–1943) was New Zealand's first notable film actor, director, writer, and producer, who went on to a career in Hollywood during the latter part of the silent-film era. Born in Whangaroa, New Zealand, he moved to the United States in 1912. He worked as an actor for a few years before taking up directing in 1915. His anti-German World War I film *The Kaiser, the Beast of Berlin* (1918) won him fame and fortune and led to a number of other important opportunities in Hollywood. After the advent of sound in 1927, his career fell into decline, but he continued to live in Hollywood until his death.

Lee Tamahori (1950–) is a film director whose works include *Once Were Warriors* (1994) and the James Bond film *Die Another Day* (2002). Born in Wellington, Tamahori is of Māori ancestry on his father's side and British on his mother's. He worked his way up through the New Zealand film industry and after the breakthrough success of *Once Were Warriors* relocated to Hollywood.

Charles Bennett (1889–1943) was a film actor whose career began in the silent era and continued well after the advent of film. Born in Dunedin, he appeared in more than a hundred films beginning in 1912. Among the most notable of these were *America* (1924), *The Adventures of Robin Hood* (1938), and *Citizen Kane* (1941).

ORGANIZATIONS AND ASSOCIATIONS

Australia New Zealand America Society (ANZAS)

ANZAS is a nonprofit organization representing the interests of expatriate Australians and New Zealanders living in the Pacific Northwest and the many Americans who have interest in Australian or New Zealand sports, art, culture, business, politics, or trade. ANZAS is affiliated with the Australia New Zealand American Chambers of Commerce (ANZACC).

Greg Pearce, President
18525 NW Village Park Drive
Issaquah, Washington 98027
Phone: (425) 865-0375
Email: ANZAS@Comcast.net
URL: www.anzas.org

Australian New Zealand American Association of Minnesota

Affiliated with the Australia New Zealand American Chambers of Commerce (ANZACC), the Australian New Zealand American Association of Minnesota hosts events and sponsors programs in the Twin Cities that bring Australians, New Zealanders, and Americans together.

Richard McCoy, President
P.O. Box 65010
Saint Paul, Minnesota 55165
Phone: (763) 442-1095
Email: rmccoy@ci.robbinsdale.mn.us
URL: www.anzaa.com

New Zealand American Association of Atlanta

Organized for the purpose of hosting athletes and visitors from New Zealand during the 1996 Summer Olympics, the New Zealand American Association in Atlanta describes itself as a group "determined to continue the joint Olympic and Kiwi ethic."

Marcus Van Ameringen, President
5605 Whitner Drive NW
Atlanta, Georgia 30327-4746
Phone: (770) 365-2197
Email: mvanameringen@gmail.com
URL: www.atlantanz.org

New Zealand American Association of San Francisco

The New Zealand American Association of San Francisco provides a social and networking forum for Kiwis and their American friends in the Bay Area and works to "promote New Zealand—the people, the culture, the food, the wine, the sport, the place (and the hobbits!)."

Lesley Tilley, President
Email: sfkiwis@gmail.com
URL: www.sfkiwis.com

MUSEUMS AND RESEARCH CENTERS

ANZSANA: Australian and New Zealand Studies Association of North America

Founded in 1993, ANZSANA is a multidisciplinary academic association whose purpose is to deepen understanding of Australia and New Zealand in North America.

Patty O'Brien, President
Email: pao4@georgetown.edu
URL: www.anzsana.net

Center for Australian and New Zealand Studies

Established in 1995 with funding from the governments of Australia and New Zealand, the Center for Australian and New Zealand Studies is part of the School of Foreign Service at Georgetown University.

Marie Champagne, Program Coordinator
Edmund A. Walsh School of Foreign Service
Georgetown University
37th and O Streets NW
Washington, D.C. 20057
Phone: (202) 687-7464
URL: http://canz.georgetown.edu/

Edward A. Clark Center for Australian & New Zealand Studies

Named after President Lyndon B. Johnson's ambassador to Australia during the Vietnam War, the Clark Center was established at the time of the Australian Bicentenary in 1988 and added New Zealand studies to its program a decade later.

Rhonda Evans Case, Director
Harry Ransom Humanities Center
Suite 3.362
The University of Texas at Austin
Austin, Texas 78713-7219
Phone: (512) 471-9607
Fax: (512) 471-8869
Email: ClarkCenter@austin.utexas.edu
URL: www.utexas.edu/cola/centers/cas/

SOURCES FOR ADDITIONAL STUDY

Gregory, Angela. "Many Expat Kiwis Unlikely to Return, Says Survey." *New Zealand Herald,* June 7, 2006.

McCall, Grant, and John Connell, eds. *A World Perspective on Pacific Islander Migration: Australia, New Zealand, and the USA.* Kensington, Australia: Centre for South Pacific Studies, University of New South Wales, 1993.

Robinson, Ruth. "Living in America, New Zealanders Get Together." *New York Times,* September 25, 1994.

Spickard, Paul; Joanne L. Rondilla; and Debbie Hippolite Wright, eds. *Pacific Diaspora: Island Peoples in the United States and Across the Pacific.* Honolulu: University of Hawai'i Press, 2002.

Tindall, Stephen. "The Power of Global Connections." *New Zealand Management* 58, no. 3 (April 2011): 20.

Urbani, Diane. "Māori Roots Deepen in Utah." *Deseret Morning News,* June 27, 2003.

NEZ PERCÉ

Laurie Collier Hillstrom and Richard C. Hanes

OVERVIEW

The Nez Percé (nez-PURSE or nay-per-SAY) are a group of indigenous people who reside primarily in the interior Pacific Northwest of the United States. The group's traditional homeland includes areas of north-central Idaho, northeastern Oregon, and southeastern Washington, along the interior of the Columbia River Plateau between the Cascade Range and the Rocky Mountains. The Nez Percé call themselves *Nimipu*, which means "our people." The name *Nez Percé* is French for "pierced nose" and was applied to the tribe by early French Canadian fur traders, who apparently observed a few individuals in the region with pendants in their noses. Nose piercing, however, is not a common Nez Percé custom.

According to Michael G. Johnson's *The Native Tribes of North America*, the Nez Percé civilization boasted more than seventy permanent villages and a population that exceeded 6,000 by 1805, when tribal scouts first encountered members of the Meriwether Lewis and William Clark expedition. The Nez Percé lifestyle was semisedentary: many of the Nimipu migrated from place to place with the seasons, subsisting as fishermen, hunters, and gatherers. Once among the most numerous and powerful tribes of the region, the Nez Percé were regarded as excellent horsemen and raised one of the largest domesticated herds in North America. By the early nineteenth century, however, their lack of access to guns and ammunition left them vulnerable to other tribes, who had already begun to acquire such weapons from Canadian traders.

The Nez Percé Indian Reservation is located in north-central Idaho near the Clearwater River. The tribe was forcibly relocated there in 1877 from lands in the Wallowa Valley of northeastern Oregon, but not before the Nez Percé attempted an unsuccessful escape to Canada, leading the U.S. military on a four-month, 1,600-mile chase through the difficult terrain. After suffering extreme hardships throughout the nineteenth and early twentieth centuries, the Nez Percé began to once again gain some economic power within the region during the later twentieth century. Today, through a number of business ventures, including casino ownership, the tribe employs about 1,100 people, annually brings more than $107 million in gross product to the region, and has become a driver in the economy of northern Idaho, according to tribal spokespersons.

The total population of Nez Percé in the United States is about 3,500, according to the 2010 U.S. Census. The vast majority of tribal members live throughout the Pacific Northwest in the states of Idaho, Montana, Oregon, California, and Washington. The seat of the Nez Percé government exists in Lapwai, Idaho, a town with a population of about 1,200 people that also boasts the highest percentage of Nez Percé people in the nation (84.6 percent). The Colville Indian Reservation in northern Washington also contains a population of Nez Percé.

HISTORY OF THE PEOPLE

Early History Before the Nez Percé acquired horses in the early 1700s, they lived in semisubterranean pit houses covered with branches and earth. They spent most of their time fishing, hunting, or gathering wild plants for food. The use of horses rapidly changed the lifestyle of the Nez Percé, allowing them to trade with neighboring tribes and to make annual trips to the Great Plains to hunt buffalo. The increased contact with tribes of the Great Plains and the Pacific Coast also led to the advent of more decorative Nez Percé clothing styles and new forms of housing, such as hide-covered tipis and pit tipis. The rich grasslands of the Nez Percé territory enabled the tribe to raise some of the largest horse herds of any Native American group. Skilled horse breeders and trainers, the Nez Percé became particularly well known for breeding the sturdy, spotted horses now called Appaloosas.

Typical of many native groups in the west, the Nez Percé lacked an overall tribal organization, living instead in bands composed of families and extended kinship groups. Each autonomous village or band had a headman who could speak only for his own followers. When a major decision needed to be made, the headmen of the various bands, along with respected *tooats* (spiritual leaders), elders, and hunting and war leaders, would meet in a combined council and attempt to reach a consensus.

The Nez Percé maintained friendly relations with most tribes of the Plateau area, including the Walla Walla, Yakama, Palouse, and Cayuse, as well as other tribes to their north. The Nez Percé were traditionally part of a large trading network, swapping directly with other Columbia River Basin tribes to the west and native groups to the east in western Montana, and even onto the Great Plains. A variety of raw materials and goods passed through this network. The main enemies of the Nez Percé were the Great Basin groups to the south (in what are now the states of Nevada and Utah), including the Shoshone, Northern Paiute, and Bannock. Raids motivated by revenge regularly occurred back and forth between the Nez Percé and these groups.

The first contact between the Nez Percé and nonnative people occurred in the fall of 1805, when the Lewis and Clark expedition wandered into what is now western Idaho. The American explorers were cold, tired, and running low on food when they encountered the Nez Percé. The tribe provided assistance that may have prevented members of the expedition from starving. They also helped the explorers build boats and guided them toward the Pacific Coast. Over the next few decades, the Nez Percé established friendly relations with French Canadian and American fur traders, missionaries, and settlers. At the request of the Nez Percé, a Methodist minister named Henry Spalding established a mission near Lapwai in 1836. Three years later Asa Smith established a mission at Kamiah. The Nez Percé consulted these ministers for the special powers they seemingly held.

As the number of white settlers in the Northwest increased through the mid-1800s, the Nez Percé avoided many of the conflicts that plagued other tribes. At the Walla Walla Council of 1855, the Nez Percé signed a treaty ceding most of their 13-million-acre ancestral territory to the government in exchange for money and a guarantee that 7.5 million acres of their lands would remain intact as a reservation. Immediately after signing treaties with the Nez Percé and several other Plateau tribes, the governor of Washington Territory, Isaac Ingalls Stevens, wrote a letter to an eastern newspaper proclaiming the Northwest open for settlement. Other area tribes reacted violently to his duplicity by attacking settlers arriving in the territory. This violence led to the Plateau Indian, or Yakama, War of 1855–1858. Although the Nez Percé remained neutral in the conflict, the treaty signing had split the tribe. The Christianized Nez Percé led by Hallalhotsoot (nicknamed "Lawyer"), who signed the treaty, supported the agreement, but many of the tribe's traditionalists balked at signing away their lands.

In the early 1860s gold was discovered on Nez Percé lands. In violation of the 1855 treaty, settlers rushed in and laid claim to the land. They soon began pressuring the U.S. government to open more tribal territory for mining and settlement. In 1863 Governor Stevens again approached the Nez Percé about relinquishing more tribal lands. Although many leaders, including Old Chief Joseph (Tu-ke-kas, 1790?–1871) and White Bird (?–1892), refused to negotiate,

Lawyer and several others signed a new treaty with Stevens. This treaty reduced the Nez Percé reservation to 780,000 acres. In what came to be known among tribal members as the Thief Treaty, the Nez Percé lost their claim to many important areas, including Joseph's home territory in the Wallowa Valley of northeastern Oregon. Upon hearing this news, Joseph, who had converted to Christianity some years earlier, destroyed his Bible. Despite the anger and resentment caused by this treaty, the Nez Percé remained peaceful in their relations with whites and expressed their discontent through passive noncompliance.

Upon the death of Old Chief Joseph in 1871, his son In-mut-too-yah-lat-lat (known as Chief Joseph) took over leadership of the Wallowa band. In 1873 the government tried to create a Wallowa reservation but abandoned the attempt two years later under pressure from the white settlers. Representing his people in a meeting with General Oliver Howard at the Lapwai Council of 1876, Chief Joseph firmly refused to honor the 1863 treaty and give up the tribe's ancestral valley. In 1877 the government gave the tribe thirty days to vacate Wallowa Valley and move to a reservation near Lapwai, Idaho. When it became clear that war would result if the Wallowa band continued to resist, Chief Joseph agreed to relocate. He stated, "I would give up everything rather than have the blood of my people on my hands."

Before the move could begin, young rebels within the tribe attacked a group of whites in retribution for previous mistreatment of the Nez Percé. Three men were killed and another wounded. Panic spread quickly on both sides, and the U.S. Cavalry was mobilized. When the Nez Percé did not leave the Wallowa Valley as ordered, the cavalry attacked Chief Joseph's village. Joseph and the rest of the Wallowa band, which consisted of 250 men and 500 women, children, and elderly people, fled into the surrounding mountains. About 2,000 U.S. Army troops under General Howard followed, marking the beginning of the Nez Percé War of 1877. Over the next four months, in a chase that came to be known as the Flight of the Nez Percé, Joseph's band traveled 1,600 miles through the rugged wilderness of Idaho, Wyoming, and Montana. During this time they fought fourteen battles against a larger and better-equipped enemy.

In one of the more embarrassing moments of the war, U.S. troops built a barricade across Lolo Pass in the Bitterroot Mountains to prevent the Nez Percé from entering Montana. After the tribe avoided the barricade by leading their horses along the face of a cliff, the ineffective structure came to be known as Fort Fizzle. The final battle between the U.S. Cavalry and the Nez Percé took place near Snake Creek in the Bear Paw Mountains of Montana, just thirty miles from the Canadian border. For six days the Nez Percé fought off troops led by Colonel Nelson Miles, who had been dispatched to prevent the Nez Percé from reaching Canada before General Howard's troops could catch up and surround them. After fighting for so long, the Nez Percé finally decided to surrender. An exhausted Chief Joseph delivered to his people his famous surrender speech, in which he stated: "Hear me, my chiefs, I am tired. My heart is sick and sad. From where the sun now stands, I will fight no more forever." Following their surrender, Joseph and his band were not allowed to go to the Nez Percé reservation. Instead, they were taken to Indian Territory, first in Kansas, then in Oklahoma. They eventually returned to the Northwest at the Colville reservation in north-central Washington, despite Joseph's repeated attempts to reclaim their home.

For the rest of the Nez Percé, the late nineteenth century was a period of great difficulty. Members of the tribe were forced to attend Christian churches and government schools, institutions used in an attempt to destroy the Nez Percé culture. Under the General Allotment Act of 1887, the U.S. government divided the reservation into relatively small allotments and assigned them to individual tribal members. By 1893 reservation lands not allotted were deemed excess and sold to non-Indians. In all, 90 percent of tribal lands within reservation boundaries were lost. Those retained amounted to 90,000 acres scattered in a checkerboard pattern of ownership. In spite of this, Nez Percé tribal traditions have persisted into the twenty-first century.

Modern Era In recent times the Nez Percé have been involved in several fishing rights cases affecting the entire Columbia River Basin. As active sponsors of the Columbia River Inter-Tribal Fish Commission, they have taken a number of steps to revitalize salmon and steelhead runs in the region. In 1996 the Nez Percé regained 10,000 acres of their homeland in northeastern Oregon from the U.S. Bonneville Power Administration. This land is managed as a wildlife preserve. In 2004 the tribe settled a decades-long dispute with the state of Idaho over water rights on the Snake River, giving the tribe access to ancestral fishing areas and allowing it to make some much needed improvements to the infrastructure in the region.

Today the Nez Percé remain very active culturally and economically within the Pacific Northwest region, continuing to honor their unique tribal history. During the 1990s the tribe began to reestablish its reputation for exquisite horsemanship, founding the Nez Percé Horse Registry to being to reacquaint tribal youths with the art. By the early 2000s the tribe was also operating the Clearwater River Casino near Lewiston, Idaho.

SETTLEMENT IN THE UNITED STATES

Anthropologists believe the Nez Percé descended from the Old Cordilleran Culture, which is thought to have migrated south from Alaska, through Canada and into

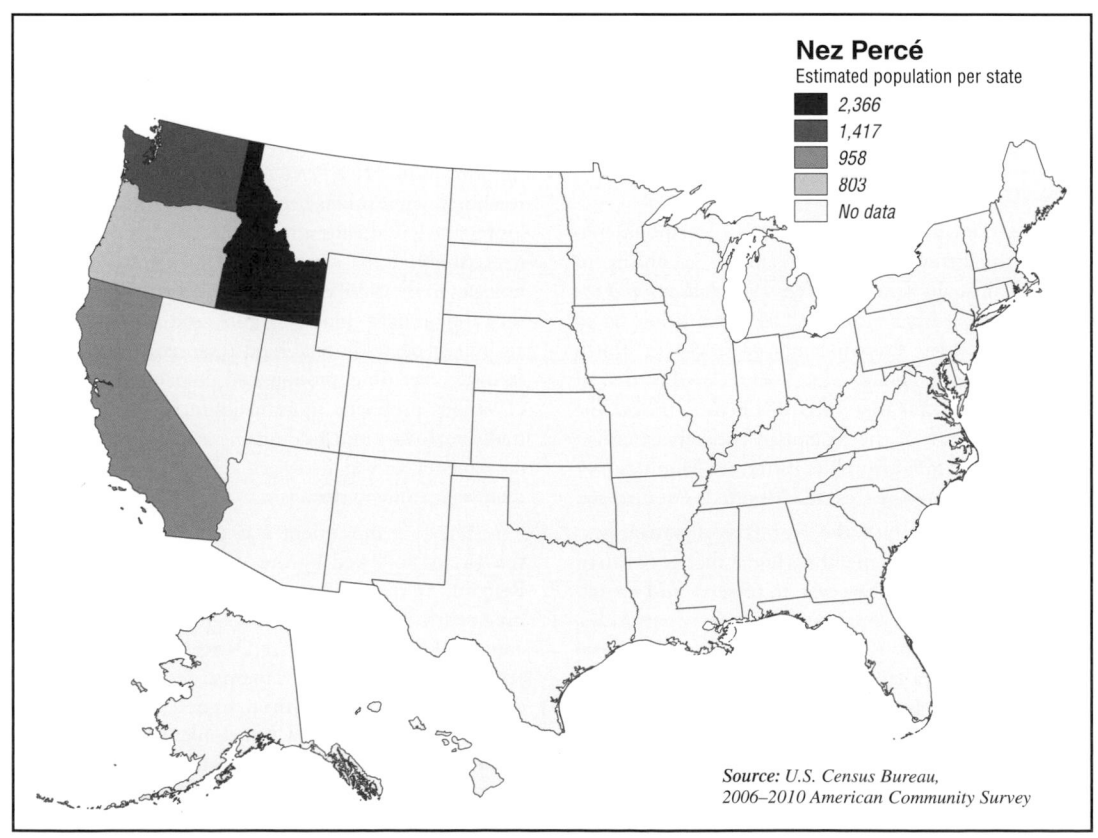

Nez Percé
Estimated population per state
- 2,366
- 1,417
- 958
- 803
- No data

Source: U.S. Census Bureau, 2006–2010 American Community Survey

the Pacific Northwest region between 10,000 BCE and about 5500 BCE. According to the Nez Percé's own traditional origin story, they were created when Coyote (a common hero character in Nez Percé stories) freed the people of the world from inside the body of a great monster. After cutting up the monster with a knife, Coyote used the pieces to create the indigenous tribes of the West. The monster's blood was used to create the Nez Percé in the Kamiah Valley of Idaho. The tribe eventually occupied more than 17 million acres of land in what would become the states of Idaho, Montana, Oregon, and Washington. By the time the Nez Percé encountered the Lewis and Clark expedition's Corps of Discovery in 1805, they were the largest tribe on the Columbia River Plateau.

Throughout their history, before and after making contact with Euro-Americans, the Nez Percé occupied the same general region, though their land holdings and migratory patterns were obviously greatly affected by the influx of white settlers. Following their surrender to the U.S. cavalry in 1877, Chief Joseph's Wallowa band of Nez Percé was sent to reservations in Oklahoma and Kansas before finally settling on the Colville reservation near Nespelem, Washington. The remainder of the Joseph band members and other Nez Percé live on the Nez Percé Reservation in north-central Idaho. Many also live in various urban areas where better employment opportunities exist. On the Idaho reservation, most of the Nez Percé live in the principal communities of Lapwai, Kamiah, Cottonwood, Nez Percé, Orofino, Culdesac, and Winchester. Some descendants of the Joseph band remained in Oklahoma, and others live in Canada. The 2010 U.S. Census reported that the largest populations of Nez Percé reside in Idaho, Washington, California, and Oregon.

LANGUAGE

The Nez Percé traditionally spoke a Sahaptian dialect of the Penutian language family. According to Alvin M. Josephy Jr. in *The Nez Percé Indians and the Opening of the Northwest*, the Nez Percé belonged to one of the oldest known language stocks in North America. Their language was closely related to that of the Walla Walla, Yakama, and other Plateau tribes. The original territory of the Sahaptian speakers extended for almost 400 miles from the Bitterroot Mountains of Idaho westward to the Cascade Mountains of Oregon.

By the late 1990s the Nez Percé language was rarely spoken by tribal members under the age of thirty. Efforts are underway, however, to preserve and revitalize the language. For example, for nearly twenty years, from the 1970s to 1990s, Japanese linguist Haruo Aoki worked with tribal elders to create a Nez Percé dictionary, published in 1994. The tribe also funds a revitalization program, and Nez Percé museum collections operated by the U.S. National Park Service now include exhibits on the Nez Percé language. A project based in Lapwai, Idaho, is ongoing, seeking not only to preserve the Nimipu language but also to create strategies for how teachers and parents can introduce it into classroom instruction and home life.

RELIGION

The Nez Percé feel a deep spiritual connection with the earth and seek to live in harmony with nature. They believe all living things and all features of the natural environment are closely related to each other and to people. Historically every member of the Nez Percé tribe had a personal link with nature in the form of a guardian spirit, or *wyakin*, that protected him or her from harm and provided assistance during his or her life. For example, a person might pray to his or her wyakin for success in war or for help in crossing a dangerous river. It was common to carry a small medicine bundle containing materials that represented one's wyakin.

Around the onset of puberty, a young Nez Percé would leave the village in hopes of acquiring a wyakin through a sacred experience. The youth traveled alone to an isolated place, often at a high mountain or along a river, without food or weapons, and sat upon a pile of stones and waited for the wyakin to reveal itself. The wyakin might appear as something material, such as an elk illuminated in a flash of lightning, or as a hallucination or dream. After returning to the village, the young person did not tell others of the experience but interpreted the power of the wyakin privately. From that point on there were certain rules to follow in order to avoid bad fortune, but one could also appeal to the wyakin in times of need.

Until the 1863 treaty, the Nez Percé were generally open to white settlement and Christian missions in the region. However, with the continued loss of tribal lands, Christianity became a major cause of factionalism within the tribe. Some Nez Percé remained open to Christian teachings, while others began to reject Christianity after losing much of their traditional homelands to white settlers. Although the white culture introduced new technologies to the Nez Percé during the nineteenth century, they also brought epidemics, guns, and whiskey and had an impact on traditional food resources and land possession. Over time, pronounced despair led to the rise of various prophetic movements focused on restoring traditional ways and ridding the area of whites. These movements arrived in cycles as interest would grow, then wane, only to rise again.

The first movement was the Prophet Dance in the 1820s, followed by the Washat, or Seven Drum Religion, in the 1850s; an Earth-lodge cult in the late nineteenth century; and the Columbia River Feather cult in 1905. The Prophet Dance, the oldest of the series of prophetic movements, generally involved dancing in a circle with a leader making vision-inspired prophecies in a trance-like state. The messages were deeply religious in tone and emphasized a renewal of life. The Seven Drum Religion, considered a direct descendant of the Prophet Dance, has long been a focal point in the revitalization of Nez Percé traditional religious practices. The religion is a blend of vision quests seeking personal spirit powers and some Christian elements in a native communal worship framework. It is also known as the Longhouse Religion, as it was performed in traditional longhouses throughout the Columbia Plateau region and led by highly charismatic individuals. The first roots feasts in spring, a first salmon feast slightly later, and a berry feast toward summer's end as well as funerals and memorials are commonly celebrated in the Washat format.

Today, some Nez Percé are practicing Christians, and among the Idaho Nez Percé Presbyterianism is popular. Each year in Talmaks, Idaho, a two-week-long gathering of Christian Nez Percé draws tribal members from all over the Pacific Northwest. They gather on Talmaks' 400-foot butte to pray, sing hymns, and enjoy social engagements such as cookouts and outdoor activities. Many members of the group mix traditional Nez Percé beliefs with the teachings of the gospel, the combination of which creates what some call an "Indian Bible."

CULTURE AND ASSIMILATION

In modern times most Nez Percé people have adopted the trappings of mainstream life in the United States while still finding ways to honor their traditional indigenous heritage. Beginning in the 1960s, the Nez Percé initiated an era of cultural revitalization during which they worked to preserve their traditional language, religion, dance, and arts and crafts. This effort is still ongoing today, with the Nez Percé boasting one of the most economically successful tribal structures and vibrant indigenous cultures in the northwestern United States.

Traditions and Customs Before acquiring horses, the Nez Percé lived in houses covered with plant material. In the summer they moved often in search of food, living in lean-tos consisting of a pole framework covered with woven mats of plant fibers. During the winter they built pole-framed structures over large pits and covered them with layers of cedar bark, sagebrush, packed grass, and earth. Each dwelling usually housed several families, and a village might consist of five or six such pit houses. As horses increased their mobility and contact with other tribes, Nez Percé buildings grew larger and more sophisticated. Their winter pit houses sometimes extended up to one hundred feet in length and housed many families. They also adopted the use of hide-covered tipis during summer fishing and hunting trips.

Cuisine In the dry, rugged high country where the Nez Percé lived, gathering food was a time-consuming prospect. They subsisted primarily by fishing, hunting, and gathering vegetables from spring through the fall. Surplus food was stored for winter use. During the spring, when large numbers of

A young Nez Percé woman prepares for the annual Chief Joseph Days parade in the small town of Joseph, Wallowa County, Oregon. NIK WHEELER / DANITA DELIMONT / ALAMY

salmon swam upstream to spawn, the Nez Percé used a variety of methods to catch them, including spears, handheld and weighted nets, small brush traps, and large enclosures. They also used bows and arrows to hunt elk, deer, and mountain sheep, although hunting was often difficult on the hot, open plateaus of their homeland. The Nez Percé sometimes disguised themselves in animal furs or worked together to surround a herd of animals so that they could be killed more easily.

In the spring Nez Percé women used sharp digging sticks to turn up *qaws* (the root of the *lomatium cous*, a plant in the carrot family) on the grassy hillsides. These roots were ground, then boiled to make soup or shaped into cakes and stored for later use. During the summer the Nez Percé gathered a wide variety of plants, including wild onions and carrots, bitterroots, blackberries, strawberries, huckleberries, and nuts. In late summer the various Nez Percé bands came together to gather sweet-tasting camas lily bulbs. These were steamed and made into a dough or gruel.

Today traditional foods are still key elements of celebrations and powwows. Nez Percé families often hold ceremonial dinners to mark important events such as the naming of a child or a child's first hunt or powwow dance. At these dinners traditional staples such as bison and deer meat are often served. Roots such as the bitterroot, camas root, carrots, and potatoes continue to be harvested and used in the preparation of traditional foods, as are regional berries such as the huckleberry and chokecherry. Guests at ceremonial meals also frequently receive small servings of water, which are consumed in unison at the beginning of the meal to signify the Nez Percé's strong cultural relationship with water. Salmon, deer, and bison are still considered among the Nez Perce's most sacred foods, and many Nez Percé people participate in the recreational hunting and fishing activities common in in the Pacific Northwest.

Traditional Dress Traditional Nez Percé clothing was made of shredded cedar bark, deerskin, or rabbit skin. Men wore breechcloths and capes in warm weather, adding fur robes and leggings when it turned cold. Nez Percé women were known for the large basket hats they wove out of dried leaves and plant fibers. By the early 1700s, when horses expanded the tribe's hunting range and brought them into contact with tribes of the Pacific Coast and Great Plains, the Nez

Nez Perce man in ceremonial dress, wearing a horsehair roach with feathers, a beaded breastplate and a beaded stole, c. 1996. C. 1996, IDAHO, PHOTOGRAPH BY DAVE G. HOUSER. CORBIS. REPRODUCED BY PERMISSION.

Percé began wearing tailored skin garments decorated with shells, elk teeth, and beads. As they prepared to make war, Nez Percé men wore only breechcloths and moccasins and applied brightly colored paint to their faces and bodies. Red paint was applied to the part in a warrior's hair and across his forehead, while other colors were applied to his body in special, individual patterns. The warriors also adorned themselves with animal feathers, fur, teeth, and claws representing their connection to their guardian spirits. Elaborate adornments for horses are characteristic of Nez Percé society, including brightly colored beaded collars and saddlebags, appliquéd with brass tacks and bells added for decorative purposes.

In modern times traditional dress is still often worn during musical performances, cultural celebrations, powwows, and other gatherings.

Dances and Songs Music among the Nez Percé was traditionally a dynamic medium of celebration and ritual, marked by improvisation. It involved not only musical instruments and verse but also improvised vocalizations of sounds, such as sighs, mimicked animal sounds, moans, and yelps. Flutes made from elderberry stems were one of the preferred musical instruments used by the Nez Percé. It usually had six finger holes. For protection in war, men played wing bone whistles to call guardian spirits. The rasp, which involved scraping a serrated stick with a bone, was standard for war dances prior to the nineteenth century. During the 1800s hand drums replaced the rasp. Larger drums associated with Washat ceremonies began to be used in the 1860s, and by the 1890s some drums were large enough to accommodate up to eight drummers. For traditional ceremonies a shaman used rattles composed of deer hooves on a stick. After the Nez Percé came into contact with white settlers, bells were used instead of hooves. A simple wooden rod beaten rhythmically on a plank was also used as an instrument.

Among the Nez Percé, song is considered essentially the same as prayer. Song accompanied most daily activities, from morning to night, and most life events. Individuals often had their own personal songs that others might sing to indicate support. Through special songs and dances, the Nez Percé honored the spirit of Hanyawat (the "Great Spirit") and Mother Earth in an effort to maintain a balance with nature and express thanks to fish, birds, plants, and animals.

Song and dance focused on guardian spirits, prophet visions, winter ceremonies, and shamanic rituals; seasonal food thanksgivings for first roots, first fruits, first salmon, and first game; and important rites of passage, including birth, naming, puberty, marriage, and death. For instance, each year during the winter the Nez Percé traditionally held the Guardian Spirit Dance, or *Wee'kwetset*. In this ceremony young people who had recently acquired a wyakin, or guardian spirit, would dance and sing in prescribed ways in order to become one with their wyakin. By watching and participating, other tribal members could often discover the identity of a young person's wyakin. The ceremony sometimes involved contests among older members to see who had received the greatest powers from his or her wyakin. This dance was meant to ensure a desirable life, with safety, health, wealth, skill, and strength.

The war-dance complex consisted of a set of dances focused on various aspects of war-related activities. A five-day Scalp Dance would conclude the sequence upon the return of warriors. After acquisition of horses in the mid-eighteenth century, the Nez Percé began journeying annually to the Northern Plains to hunt buffalo, some staying for years at a time. They brought back with them some of the Plains customs they had encountered, including certain war dance styles and drumming. New religions also brought new songs and dance. When Smohalla of the Wanapum tribe of central Washington introduced the Washat religion to his people in the 1850s, he also presented a new dance and song that sought restoration of traditional life and removal of white influence. Later, worship at the Indian Shaker Church consisted of stomp dances with loud vocalizations and bells. In addition, a number of Anglican hymns introduced by the Presbyterian Church were translated into Nez Percé language and printed in the later 1830s.

Holidays The Nez Percé regularly participate at the Celilo Wy-Am Salmon Feast at Celilo Village in Oregon each spring. Also in north-central Oregon is the All-Indian Rodeo held in spring at Tygh Valley, sponsored by the Western States Indian Rodeo Association. The event includes Western dances, a fun run, arts and crafts, and baseball tournament. Thanksgiving, Christmas, and New Year are also celebrated.

Death and Burial Rituals The death of a leader or highly respected elder is a major event in Nez Percé society. Traditional funerals were elaborate and consisted of many components. Close female relatives of the deceased immediately began wailing as criers announced the death in the area. The deceased's face was traditionally painted red, and the body was washed, dressed in new clothes, wrapped in a robe, and buried the following day. A number of the deceased's favorite valuables were placed in the grave. A favorite horse might even be killed and left in the vicinity. The grave was placed on a prominent hill overlooking a valley or in a rocky talus slope. A shaman would perform rituals to prevent the deceased ghost from returning, and individuals who had tended to the body ritually purified themselves. After the burial a feast was held and the remaining items of the deceased disbursed. For the following year the surviving spouse cut his or her hair short, wore old clothes, did not smile in public, and was prohibited from remarrying. At the end of the yearlong mourning period, relatives supplied a new set of clothes and a new spouse if a brother or sister of the deceased spouse was available.

A Nez Percé child dances at an All Indian Pow Wow. STEVE BLY / ALAMY

Today the Nez Percé and other natives in the region still practice various religions, including Washat, Feather, and Shaker sects. In some instances a modern-day funeral may include more than twenty Washat songs performed during a night-long wake. Graveside Washat songs may also be performed at the burial.

FAMILY AND COMMUNITY LIFE

The Nez Percé family tradition has stayed very much the same over the years. In the modern world, Nez Percé typically live in nuclear family units, but close relations with the larger tribe and individual bands as well as with family elders remain important. Many Nez Percé mothers and fathers speak of feeling a responsibility of passing on the tribe's traditional values and customs to their children. In this way, they believe Nez Percé people can continue to be contributing members of modern society while still preserving their essential heritage as indigenous peoples in the Pacific Northwest.

MAINTAINING DANCE AND SONG TRADITIONS

Dance and song are important to the modern Nez Percé community, instilling pride and conveying tribal heritage while also providing a forum for socialization. Annual festivals consist of celebrations and powwows such as the Four Nation Pow Wow at Nez Percé County Fair Grounds in Lewiston, Idaho, in the fall; the Chief Joseph and Warriors Memorial Pow Wow at the Nez Percé Reservation in Lapwai, Idaho, in June; the Pendleton Roundup at Pendleton, Oregon; the Nee-Mee-Poo Sapatqayn and Cultural Days at the Nez Percé Reservation in Spalding, Idaho, in late August; and the Chief Looking Glass Pow Wow at the Nez Percé Reservation in Kamiah, Idaho, the third weekend in August. These events commonly feature horse parades, cultural demonstrations, speakers, stick games, arts and crafts, and drumming and dancing, including war dances and social and contest dancing. Other celebrations include the Root Festival the first week of May and the Talmaks celebration, which consists of an early summer camp meeting sponsored by the Presbyterian Church. Many of the festivities are an integral part of the process of cultural rejuvenation still occurring. By observing these events, the Nez Percé maintain connections with the earth, their ancestors, and their historic symbols.

Some traditional family practices varied for boys and girls as they came of age. Historically, boys were introduced to activities such as hunting and fishing by the elder men of the tribe, while girls were steered by the elder women toward tasks such as the gathering of plants and roots. These practices remain the norm today, but it has become more common for the lines to be blurred; for example, some modern Nez Percé women enjoy activities such as hunting and fishing, while children of both genders help in the gathering of roots for ceremonial feasts.

Gender Roles As in many indigenous societies, Nez Percé women held a prominent role in food acquisition and preparation. Although men were mainly in charge of the fishing, women assisted in gutting, drying, and storing the large volumes of fish that were caught. Women assumed leadership in food and medicinal plant collecting, using digging sticks to collect various types of roots, or tubers. The bulb of the camas lily, which grows primarily in wet meadows, was a principal plant food. With the absence of a pottery tradition, baskets were used for numerous tasks, including food storage and even cooking, which was accomplished by placing heated stones in a basket full of water to boil foods.

Nez Percé women were given more respect within the tribe than women in other American Indian tribes. They were eligible to be shamans, who were believed to have miraculous powers that enabled them to cure the sick by singing sacred songs and prescribing herbal remedies.

During tribal council meetings the women could speak up, although they could not lead the meetings.

During pregnancy women were encouraged to exercise vigorously and take a number of medicinal herbs. Nez Percé custom dictated that deformed animals and humans should not be ridiculed for fear of causing similar deformities in the baby. The tying of knots was also avoided because they represented the obstruction of the umbilical cord. Babies were delivered in small separate houses with the help of midwives and female relatives. Shamans were called if major problems arose. The baby's head and feet were shaped immediately upon birth. For good luck the umbilical cord was sown into a small hide pouch and attached to the cradleboard. Feasts and gifts were given to the mother and baby, especially for firstborn children, and at adolescence a formal naming ceremony was held.

Today, as nearly all Nez Percé have been assimilated into mainstream culture, gender roles most often reflect those of the United States at large. Women still play an important role in governing Nez Percé life. As of 2013 eight of the nine officials to the tribe's general council were women, and two women served on the executive committee as well. Women's roles in powwows changed in the late twentieth century, with increased participation in drumming and war dancing, both prohibited to Nez Percé women several generations earlier.

Education Traditionally, the extended family raised the children, with grandparents teaching many of life's basic lessons. The first nonnative schools were introduced by the Presbyterian missionaries who settled in Nez Percé country at the tribe's invitation in 1836. Catholic missionaries followed later. In the late nineteenth century the Bureau of Indian Affairs (BIA) established on-reservation elementary schools operated by Indian agents, designed to "civilize" the Nez Percé. Students were discouraged from practicing long-standing tribal traditions and speaking the Nez Percé language. Reflecting the biases of white society, emphasis was placed on educating the boys. Although many of the basics of U.S. elementary schools were taught, including English, vocational training was emphasized. Older children were sent off-reservation, frequently long distances away from their families, to BIA-operated boarding schools such as Carlisle in Pennsylvania and Haskell in Oklahoma. These forced education policies posed dramatic changes to Nez Percé life.

An increasing number of Nez Percé tribal members earned college degrees in the late twentieth century. Today Nez Percé frequently attend the University of Idaho, Washington State University, the University of Washington, and Eastern Washington University, among others. It is not uncommon for graduates to return to the tribe to serve the reservation in various capacities, including wildlife management and administration. In 2008 the University of Idaho began an extension program on the Nez Percé Reservation. As a partnership between the university and the tribe, the program offers classes for youths and other community members taught by university faculty, guest lecturers, and other educations. It addresses "youth development, community development, agriculture and natural resources," and its largest program focuses on horsemanship.

Courtship and Weddings Heads of families often arranged marriages in traditional Nez Percé society, sometimes during childhood. The relative prestige of both families was weighed when making selections. Kin relationships, even distant ones, were avoided; on the other hand, it was common for several sons and daughters of two families to marry. For marriages that were not arranged, an older female relative of the male initiated negotiations with the female's family. The woman might be observed by the elder relative over a period of time to determine if she was acceptable. The couple might then live together for a while to determine compatibility. Once the couple decided to marry, a ceremony and somewhat competitive gift exchange was held. Relatives of the groom might give horses, equipment for hunting and fishing, and skins. The bride's relatives would give baskets, root bags, digging sticks, and beaded bags. When two prestigious families were involved in an exchange ceremony, many people participated. After a second exchange ceremony, the wedding was considered complete. Today, some Nez Percé find ways to incorporate their heritage and traditional customs into mainstream Euro-American wedding rituals. Weddings are also still sometimes conducted in traditional longhouses.

Relations with Other Tribes One of the Nez Percé's strongest present-day forums for interaction with other tribes is the Columbia River Inter-Tribal Fisheries Commission (CRITFC). The CRITFC was formed to facilitate the restoration of salmon and steelhead runs in the Snake River system, an issue of primary importance in the latter years of the twentieth century. The Nez Percé, Yakama, Warm Springs, and Umatilla tribes are CRITFC members. The commission developed its own comprehensive restoration plan for the region in the mid-1990s, and it continues to be a key player with various federal agencies and several states in the major restoration effort.

EMPLOYMENT AND ECONOMIC CONDITIONS

In the past, the Nez Percé economy was based on fishing, gathering, hunting, and, later, raising large herds of horses. The traditional territory contains a diversity of landscapes, including rugged mountains and numerous valleys and high prairies, primarily within the Snake River drainage system. Each area offered something different in terms of resources. Prior to incursions by white settlers, a number of major villages existed along the lower courses of the Snake, Salmon, and Clearwater rivers and their tributaries. With rich fisheries on these watercourses, including seasonal runs of a variety of salmon and steelhead trout, annual fish consumption in the traditional economy is estimated to have been more than 500 pounds per person.

The loss of a viable land base greatly undermined both the traditional Nez Percé economy and the ability to join the burgeoning market economy of the non-Indians. In the latter half of the twentieth century, the tribe won several Indian Claims Commission monetary awards in payment for lost lands. It received $3.5 million for lands ceded in the 1855 treaty and more than $5 million for territory lost in the 1863 treaty and 1893 allotments. Along with several other tribes, the Nez Percé also received compensation for a key fishery location on the Columbia River that was flooded for reservoir construction in the 1950s. The Nez Percé share was almost $3 million.

The Nez Percé tribe has occasionally leased approximately 80 percent of its lands to non-Indians. During modern times the tribal economy has been largely based on funding from these leases and a timber program. Reacquisition of tribal lands was a key goal of the tribe during the twentieth century. In the mid-1990s, as Wallowa Valley encountered difficult economic times with declines in the timber and cattle markets, residents began to invite the Nez Percé back to the area. Residents raised money and built an interpretive center and purchased 160 acres of land for the tribe to use for cultural events. Although valley residents viewed the return of the Nez Percé as an opportunity to promote tourism, most members of the tribe were pleased to recover some of their ancestral territory. "The whites may look at it as an economic plus, but we look at it as a homecoming," tribal member Soy Redthunder told journalist Timothy Egan in 1996. The Nee-Me-Poo National Historic Trail, the Nez Percé National Historical Park, and the burial site of Old Chief Joseph have become major tourist attractions. One tourism-related Nez Percé-owned business is Old West Enterprises in Lapwai, Idaho, which makes traditional tipis.

In 1992 the Nez Percé helped build the ambitious, $14 million Clearwater River fish hatchery facility, which aims to restore salmon and trout to the tribe's fishing sites scattered over 2 million acres of central Idaho. The hatchery's long-term goal is to restore salmon to 13 million acres of ceded lands in Oregon and Washington.

In 2004, after twenty years of litigation, Congress passed the Snake River Water Rights Act. Among other things, this allowed the Nez Percé to make major repairs and updates to tribal infrastructure, including a $9 million state-of-the-art waste-to-water treatment facility in Lapwai, Idaho. Tribal leaders cited this as a major step in their ability to grow, plan, and recruit new businesses to the reservation. Beginning in 2008 the Nez Percé's Tribal Enterprises organization began hosting annual economic summits in northern Idaho. The summits are open to other tribes and focus on the state of tribal economies and various ways to spur economic development. Today the Nez Percé operate a number of revenue projects, including Lewiston, Idaho's Clearwater River Casino, which began paying out per-capita shares of its profits to tribal members in 2011.

In modern times the Nez Percé have not been reluctant to enter mainstream American society. They are receptive to the U.S. educational system, and their members have thrived in academia. Nez Percé members are doctors, nurses, engineers, journalists, and teachers. The Nez Percé tribe operates a printing plant and a marina. Many tribal members work outside of tribe-affiliated businesses, as in communities such Lapwai and Kamiah, Idaho, where Nez Percé people own construction companies, logging enterprises, heating and air conditioning repair businesses, landscaping operations, design companies, and engineering firms, among others. The Nez Percé tribe maintains an online database of "certified Indian businesses" in its area.

POLITICS AND GOVERNMENT

In 1923 the nontraditionalists of the tribe, seeking an elective form of government, formed the Nez Percé Home and Farm Association, with James Stuart as its first president. The Nez Percé rejected the Indian Reorganization Act of 1934 and the Indian New Deal, instead establishing their own tribal constitution in 1948. The Nez Percé constitution was revised in 1999, laying out the modern bylaws and organizational systems that continue to govern the tribe as a sovereign entity.

Today the Nez Percé elect a nine-member executive committee that is responsible for representing the tribe in negotiations, administering tribal funds, and protecting "the health, education and general welfare of the tribal members," according to the tribe's website. Each member's term lasts three years, and the committee's highest-ranking official is the chairperson. The executive committee also includes five more specialized subcommittees, including human resources, law and order, natural resources, budget and finance, and land enterprise. Individual members of the executive committee serve as chairs of these subcommittees.

Any enrolled member of the Nez Percé Tribe who is eighteen or over is allowed to vote in tribal elections and at what the constitution calls "general council meetings." According to the constitution, the tribe holds two general council meetings each year, on the first Friday and Saturday in May and on the last Friday and Saturday in September. Although these meetings are open to any tribal member of voting age, the general council is governed by a number of elected officials, including a chairman, a secretary, three election judges, and a four-member resolutions committee.

NOTABLE INDIVIDUALS

Academics Nez Percé anthropologist and activist Archie Phinney (1903–1949) played a significant role in preserving the traditional language and folklore of the tribe. Phinney was born on the Nez Percé Reservation and raised in a traditional manner, including speaking the language. He attended the University of Kansas, where he became the first Native American to receive a degree from that school. Phinney then attended Columbia University and earned a graduate degree in anthropology. Returning to the Nez Percé Reservation, he began a project to preserve the Nez Percé language and folklore. Phinney authored two books and several journal articles. One book, *Nez Percé Texts* (1934), contains traditional stories of the tribe. Phinney demonstrated that folklore was a legitimate academic field of study. Promoting Native American causes nationwide, he held leadership positions with the Bureau of Indian Affairs, including that of superintendent of the Northern Idaho Agency, and in the National Congress of American Indians. Phinney lobbied the U.S. Congress regarding education issues and land claims. Internationally recognized, he received an honorary degree from the Russian Academy of Science in Leningrad as well as the Indian Council Fire Award in 1946.

Another Nez Percé academic, historian Allen P. Slickpoo Sr., coauthored (with the Nez Percé tribe) *Noon Nee-Me-Poo: We, the Nez Percés* (1973).

Literature The works of Phil George (1946–2012), a Wallowa Nez Percé poet, were published in several anthologies, including *The Remembered Earth: An Anthology of Contemporary Native American Literature* (1979) and *Dancing on the Rim of the World* (1990). His poetry has even been read on popular television shows such as *The Tonight Show* and *The Dick Cavett Show*. Born in Seattle, George attended Gonzaga University in Spokane, Washington, and the Institute of American Indian Arts in Santa Fe, New Mexico. He was also a champion Traditional Plateau dancer. George wrote, produced, and narrated the program *A Season of Grandmothers* for the Public Broadcasting Service in 1976. His work is showcased at Nez Percé National Historical Park in Spaulding, Idaho.

Politics The Nez Percé have been blessed with a number of influential leaders. These leaders are not only recognized by Native Americans but have also been an integral part of American history. Old Chief Joseph (1790?–1871), also known as Tu-ke-kas and Wellaamotkin, was the primary leader of the Wallowa band of Nez Percé in northeastern Oregon during the period of substantial encroachment of white settlers. Peacefully accepting non-Indians into Nez Percé territory, Joseph was one of the first Nez Percé baptized by the Presbyterian minister Henry Spalding. Joseph reluctantly signed the 1855 treaty with territorial governor Isaac Stevens, since it reserved the Wallowa

Valley lands for his band. However, the continued influx of non-Indians into the territory led him to angrily disavow Christianity and to align himself with the more militant, anti-treaty Nez Percé. In 1886, nine years after his death, whites opened his grave and displayed his skull in a dental office. In 1926 he was reinterred in his homeland valley.

Lawyer (1796–1876), also known as Hallalhotsoot or Aleiya, was the son of Twisted Hair, the Nez Percé leader who welcomed and aided Lewis and Clark in 1805. Following his father's tradition, Lawyer became leader of the band of Nez Percé living along the Clearwater River in north-central Idaho. He also sought friendship with the non-Indians entering the area, serving as guide and interpreter for early explorers and trappers in the region. In addition, Lawyer taught at the Presbyterian missionary established by Asa Smith at Kamiah. Lawyer was known for his oratorical skills and mastery of English. He became leader of the treaty faction of the Nez Percé, signing both the 1855 and 1863 treaties with Governor Stevens, and even protecting Stevens from attacks by natives. In his later years Lawyer traveled to Washington, D.C., to protest the breaking of treaty terms by the United States. He died the year before the Nez Percé War.

Looking Glass (c. 1823–1877) was born Allalimya Takanin. His father, also known as Looking Glass, was leader of the Asotin band of Nez Percé living in the Clearwater River basin of north-central Idaho. He was also recognized as leader of the non-treaty Nez Percé in general. Takanin inherited the band leadership and the name. Young Looking Glass was appointed a war leader for the Nez Percé in 1848. Like a number of his contemporary Nez Percé leaders, Looking Glass followed a path of passive resistance to white encroachment into Nez Percé territory. However, he was drawn into the 1877 war between the Joseph band and the United States when his own village was attacked by a combined volunteer militia and U.S. Army force. Looking Glass became the initial leader of the fleeing force of Nez Percé attempting to join Sitting Bull's Sioux, already exiled in Canada after the Battle of Little Bighorn the previous year. Looking Glass's consistent underestimation of the U.S. determination to track down the Nez Percé lost him his leadership role to others, including Chief Joseph. Looking Glass was killed as the Nez Percé fought their last battle just short of the Canadian border.

Chief Joseph (c. 1840–1904), also known as In-mut-too-yah-lat-lat, or Thunder-Traveling-Across-Lake-and-Fading-on-Mountainside, was the son of Old Chief Joseph. The younger Joseph led a large band of Nez Percé in the most successful, sustained resistance to the U.S. Cavalry ever achieved by Native American fighters. The Nez Percé War of 1877 broke out after the federal government's efforts to relocate the tribe to accommodate settlers' demands. In 1877, after several years of passive noncompliance with

A Nez Percé family in a three-seated car, 1916. THE LIBRARY OF CONGRESS

the 1863 treaty, he prepared to lead his band out of Wallowa Valley in Idaho in 1877 under the threat of war with the United States. When rebels from the band attacked and killed a group of white settlers, however, Chief Joseph and his whole band began a 1,600-mile trek through Idaho and Montana toward Canada with the army in pursuit. After outsmarting the American troops numerous times and engaging in fourteen separate battles, the Nez Percé were finally forced to surrender just 30 miles short of their goal. At that time Chief Joseph uttered the famous words, "I will fight no more forever." He continued to be a respected leader during the early reservation years, as he eloquently pleaded the tribe's case before government representatives. In 1879 he gave an interview that was published in the *North American Review* under the title "An Indian's View of Indian Affairs," which brought national attention to the Nez Percé. He died in 1904 on the Colville reservation in Washington. Other leaders of the period included Timothy, White Bird, Yellow Wolf, and Ollikut.

In 2007 Claudia Kauffman (1959–) became the first Native American woman to serve in the Washington State Senate after winning election as a Democratic candidate in the state's 47th District, an area serving southeastern King County, including the towns of Covington and Black Diamond. Kauffman served as assistant majority whip during her term. In 2010 she was defeated in a general election by Republican challenger Joe Fain.

Stage and Screen Broadcast journalist Hattie Kauffman, winner of four Emmy Awards, was a national correspondent for *CBS This Morning* (previously called *The Early Show*) from 2008 to 2011 and a feature reporter for ABC's *Good Morning America* from 1987 to 1990.

Elaine Miles (1960–) is a film and television actress best known for her role as Marilyn Whirlwind on the hit television series *Northern Exposure* during its run from 1990 to 1995. Miles has also appeared in feature films such as *Mad Love* (1995), *Smoke Signals* (1998), and *The Business of Fancydancing* (2002). She is a native of Pendleton, Oregon.

MEDIA

Ta'c Tito'oqan News

The official newspaper of the Nez Percé tribe, published monthly both in print form and online.

17500 Nez Perce Road
Lewiston, Idaho 83501
Phone: (208) 298-1122
Fax: (208) 743-7121
Email: yvettew@nezperce.org
URL: http://crcasino.com/Newspaper/newspaper.html

ORGANIZATIONS AND ASSOCIATIONS

Affiliated Tribes of Northwest Indians

A nonprofit organization dedicated to the tribal sovereignty and well-being of fifty-seven tribal governments in the Northwest.

6636 Northeast Sandy Boulevard
Portland, Oregon 97213
Phone: (503) 249-5770
Fax: (503) 249-5773
Email: atni@atnitribes.org
URL: www.atnitribes.org

Columbia River Inter-Tribal Fish Commission

A group with a mission "to ensure a unified voice in the overall management of the fishery resources" for the Yakama, Warm Springs, Umatilla, and Nez Percé tribes.

729 Northeast Oregon Street
Suite 200
Portland, Oregon 97232
Phone: (503) 238-0667
Fax: (503) 235-4228
Email: fdsk@critfc.org
URL: www.critfc.org

Confederated Tribes of the Colville Indian Reservation

An organization representing the peoples of the Colville Reservation in northern Washington.

P.O. Box 150
Nespelem, Washington 99155
Phone: (509) 634-2238
Fax: (509) 634-2276
Email: francis.Somday@colvilletribes.com
URL: www.colvilletribes.com

Nez Percé Education and Building Development Center

An organization seeking to increase the employability of people living on the Nez Percé Reservation as well as stimulate new business in reservation communities.

Phone: (208) 843-2253
Email: mccoyo@nezperce.org
URL: www.nezperceeducationcenter.org

Nez Percé Tribe

The official tribal organization of the Nez Percé.

P.O. Box 305
Lapwai, Idaho 83540
Phone: (208) 843-2253
Fax: (208) 843-7354
Email: nptec@nezperce.org
URL: www.nezperce.org

Pi-Nee-Waus Community Center

A center in Lapwai, Idaho, with wide-ranging goals for the overall well-being of the community.

99 Agency Road
Lapwai, Idaho 83540
Phone: (208) 843-7360
Fax: (208) 843-7354
URL: www.nezperce.org/Programs/pineewaus.htm

MUSEUMS AND RESEARCH CENTERS

Clearwater Historical Museum

Holds Nez Percé artifacts, photographs, and papers.

315 College Avenue
Orofino, Idaho 83544
Phone: (208) 476-5033
Email: chmuseum@frontier.com
URL: www.clearwatermuseum.org

Gonzaga University Special Collection and University Archives

A department of the private Jesuit university that works to preserve and promote the cultural heritage of the Pacific Northwest.

East 502 Boone Avenue
Spokane, Washington 99258
Phone: (509) 313-3847
Fax: (509) 313-5904
Email: spcoll@gonzaga.edu
URL: www.gonzaga.edu

Idaho State Historical Society Museum

A state-funded museum dedicated to the history of Idaho, including many items and exhibits related to the Nez Percé.

610 North Julia Davis Drive
Boise, Idaho 83702
Phone: (208) 334-2120
Fax: (208) 334-4059
Email: jody.ochoa@isha.idaho.gov
URL: http://history.idaho.gov

Nez Percé National Historic Park

Houses photo archives and exhibits relating to the Nez Percé cultural history.

39063 U.S. Highway 95
Spalding, Idaho 83540-9715

Phone: (208) 843-7001
Fax: (208) 843-7003
URL: www.nps.gov/nepe/index.htm

University of Idaho Library Archives and Pacific Northwest Anthropological Archives

Located on the campus of the University Idaho, these archives contain collections concerning the history and heritage of the state.

875 Perimeter Drive MS 4023
Moscow, Idaho 83844-4023
Phone: (208) 885-1771
Fax: (208) 885-8021
Email: leahe@uidaho.edu
URL: www.uidaho.edu/class/anthrolab/pnaa

Whitman College Library Archives

This private college, founded in 1859, houses a collection of unpublished documents on Nez Percé culture.

Penrose Library, Room 130
345 Boyer Avenue
Walla Walla, Washington 99362
Phone: (509) 527-5922
Email: archives@whitman.edu
URL: www.whitman.edu/archives

SOURCES FOR ADDITIONAL STUDY

Brown, Mark. *The Flight of the Nez Percé.* Lincoln: University of Nebraska Press, 1967.

Egan, Timothy. "Expelled in 1877, Indian Tribe Is Now Wanted as a Resource." *New York Times,* July 22, 1996.

Josephy, Alvin M., Jr. *The Nez Percé Indians and the Opening of the Northwest.* New Haven, CT: Yale University Press, 1965.

McNeel, Jack. "Nez Perce Hosts Tribal Economic Sovereignty Summit." *Indian Country Today,* September 13, 2011.

Pearson, J. Diane. *The Nez Perces in the Indian Territory: Nimiipuu Survival.* Norman: University of Oklahoma Press, 2008.

McWhorter, Lucullus Virgil. *Yellow Wolf: His Own Story.* Caldwell, ID: Caxton Printers, 1948.

Sherrow, Victoria. *The Nez Percé.* Brookfield, CT: Milbrook Press, 1994.

Slickpoo, Allen P., and Deward E. Walker Jr. *Noon Nee-Me-Poo: We, the Nez Percés.* Lapwai: Nez Percé Tribe of Idaho, 1973.

Trafzer, Clifford E. *The Nez Percé.* New York: Chelsea House, 1992.

Walker, Deward E., Jr. "Nez Percé." In *Native America in the Twentieth Century: An Encyclopedia,* edited by Mary B. Davis. New York: Garland Publishing, 1994.

NICARAGUAN AMERICANS

Stefan Smagula

OVERVIEW

Nicaraguan Americans are immigrants or descendants of people from the Republic of Nicaragua, the largest country in Central America. Nicaragua is bordered on the north by Honduras, on the south by Costa Rica, on the east by the Caribbean Sea, and on the west by the Pacific Ocean. The country contains three distinctive geographic zones: the Pacific lowlands, the central highlands, and the Caribbean lowlands. The Pacific lowlands is the most populous region, but it also houses forty volcanoes and contains the two largest freshwater lakes in Central America, Lake Nicaragua and Lake Managua. Nicaragua's total land area is 50,336 square miles (130,370 square kilometers), slightly smaller than the state of New York.

According to the Nicaraguan census, the country had a population of 5.1 million people in 2005, and the *CIA World Factbook* estimated the population to be 5.7 million in 2012. The majority of the population practices Catholicism (83 percent), and a sizable percentage practices Protestantism (16 percent). Approximately 69 percent of the population is mestizo (a mix of European and the native Amerindian), and 17 percent is white. Close to 9 percent of the population is of African descent, while the native Amerindian population makes up about 5 percent of the total population. In spite of the government's efforts to spark the economy, Nicaragua remains the second-poorest country in Central and South America. Agriculture accounts for close to 17 percent of the country's gross domestic product, while nearly 56 percent of the economy is based on tourism and the service industry.

Nicaraguans began immigrating to the United States near the turn of the twentieth century. The majority of Nicaraguan immigrants prior to the 1970s were women who found employment as domestics or in the textiles industry. After the Sandinista Revolution (1974–1979), which culminated with the exile of dictator Anastasio Somoza Debayle, many wealthy Nicaraguans, as well as army officers allied with Somoza, fled to the United States. The revolution was followed by an eleven-year civil war, as well as severe drought and damage from hurricanes in the 1980s and 1990s. All these factors forced many working-class and poor families to seek economic and political stability in the United States. In 1998 Nicaragua was once again devastated by a hurricane. Since 1998, Nicaraguans have continued to immigrate to the United States seeking refuge from the devastation and the slowly recovering economy.

According to the U.S. Census Bureau's American Community Survey, in 2011 an estimated 387,104 people of Nicaraguan descent were living in the United States, constituting approximately 2 percent of the total U.S. population. The majority of Nicaraguan Americans live in California (100,790) and Florida (135,143). Approximately 90 percent of Florida's Nicaraguan American population lives in the Miami area (118,768), and California's population of Nicaraguan Americans tend to live in Los Angeles (15,572) and San Francisco (7,604). Sizable numbers also reside in the states of New York (13,006), New Jersey (8,222), Maryland (8,196), and Virginia (7,388), which include the Washington, D.C., area. Other states with significant Nicaraguan communities include Houston (9,496) with a total population of 19,817 in Texas, while 83 percent of Nicaraguan Americans living in Louisiana (6,390) reside in New Orleans (5,310).

HISTORY OF THE PEOPLE

Early History Around 2000 BCE, thousands of years after the first people arrived in North America from Asia, the Mayan empire began to develop along the Caribbean coast of Central America, and eventually its influence spread through a network of city-states that stretched from present-day southern Mexico into Honduras, just north of Nicaragua. The ancient Maya are known for their many intellectual and artistic accomplishments. They invented the first system of writing in the New World, developed a sophisticated knowledge of astronomy and mathematics, worshipped at brightly painted temples of stone, lived in large city-like centers, and sustained a rigid and highly structured society. The many Mayan temples and stone-paved roads that remain are testimony to the beauty, ingenuity, and durability of ancient Mayan architecture and engineering. The Maya also waged the brutal civil wars that may have contributed to the sudden and mysterious downfall of the Mayan empire in around 900 CE. Today the descendants of the ancient Maya live in Guatemala and the Yucatán Peninsula in southern Mexico. The Mayan influence is ubiquitous throughout Central America, and many Mayan-language words are present in the everyday Spanish spoken in modern Nicaragua.

After the fall of the Maya, the Aztecs, a Nahuat-speaking group who originated in northern Mexico, came into full power. They eventually established a series of allegiances that spread from Mexico to El Salvador. The Nicarao and some of the other indigenous groups of Nicaragua may have originally fled south to Nicaragua in order to avoid subjugation by the aggressive Aztecs. These migrating groups of people brought with them the Aztec language and culture, both of which persist in various forms today in Nicaragua.

Before the Spanish conquest in the early 1520s, Nicaragua was inhabited by numerous competing indigenous groups who probably originally came from both the north and the south. Among them were the Niquiranos, the Nicarao (also known as the Nahual or Nagual), the Chorotega, the Chontales (or Mames), the Miskito, the Sumu (or Sumo), the Voto, the Suerre, and the Guetar. The invading Spaniards and the epidemics that followed the conquest all but eradicated the Nicarao, Chorotega, Chontales, Voto, Suerre, Guetar, and numerous other indigenous Nicaraguan peoples. Having been decimated by war and disease, their societies in shambles, the surviving indigenous people were often forced to learn Spanish, to convert to Catholicism, and to work under slave-like conditions for the benefit of the Spanish colonizers and missionary priests. Over the years, many of these indigenous people assimilated and intermarried into Spanish colonial society, forming the racial-cultural group called mestizo.

Although a few Nicarao persisted in Nicaragua until the mid-twentieth century, their culture has been subsumed by mestizo culture, and their descendants are now only vaguely aware of their ethnic identity. Some indigenous groups in Nicaragua have, however, maintained their language, culture, and ethnic identity. Through a combination of fierce resistance to Hispanic control and isolation in the Caribbean lowlands, the Miskito, the Sumu, and the Rama have managed to survive and maintain their ethnic identity into the present.

From the time of the conquest until 1821, Spain controlled most of Nicaragua, while British colonizers controlled some areas along the Caribbean coast. Nicaragua gained independence from Spain first in 1821 as part of the Mexican empire and later as part of the Central American Federation. By 1838 the federation had collapsed, and rival conservative and liberal factions had begun violent struggles for power in Nicaragua. The rivalry was as much based on political differences as it was on *localismo*—the provincial rivalry between Grenada and León, the two oldest colonial cities in Nicaragua. In the mid-1800s the United States and Britain aggravated the

liberal-conservative feud when the two nations competed for control over a potential transoceanic canal route that would have crossed Nicaragua via the San Juan River and Lake Nicaragua.

In 1855 liberal leader General Francisco de Castellón invited a well-known Tennessee-born adventurer named William Walker to come to Nicaragua as a peaceful "colonist" with the understanding that Walker was to be the defender of the liberals. However, when Walker arrived with a gang of mercenaries named the "American Phalanx of Immortals," he promptly ended the civil war and declared himself president of Nicaragua. The same day he took office, he issued four decrees: the first was an agreement to borrow money from abroad with the Nicaraguan territory as collateral; the second confiscated the property of the conservatives, for sale to U.S. citizens; the third made English the official language of the country; and the fourth reinstated slavery.

Walker next attempted to conquer the other four Central American republics, but a combined effort by the Central American armies eventually forced his retreat in May 1857. Fortunately for Walker, there was a U.S. ship waiting to take him back to New Orleans, where he was given a hero's welcome. Completely discredited by the Walker incident, the liberals lost control to the conservatives, who established the Nicaraguan capital in Managua. The conservative government was stable but not democratic. In November 1857, Walker led another failed invasion of Nicaragua and once again was shipped safely back to the United States. Three years later Walker made his third attempt to achieve "manifest destiny," but this time a British ship overcame him and turned him over to the Honduran government; a Honduran firing squad ended Walker's life. It was just the beginning of a long era of U.S. intervention in Nicaraguan politics.

Modern Era Throughout the twentieth century, the people of Nicaragua suffered many disasters, both natural and man-made. Hurricanes, severe earthquakes, dictatorships, revolution, counterrevolution, famines, epidemics, civil war, volcanic eruptions, and foreign machination have all besieged the country. In 1909 the U.S. government supported a revolution that ousted liberal General José Santos Zelaya and instated conservative rule. In 1912 popular revolt against the conservatives led to a U.S. Marine occupation of Nicaragua. From 1927 to 1933 General Augusto César Sandino led a sustained guerrilla war against the Marines, who left in 1933. The following year Sandino was assassinated by the U.S.-trained Nicaraguan National Guard at the request of their commander, General Anastasio Somoza.

Somoza seized control of Nicaragua in 1936 and was the country's dictatorial ruler until his assassination in 1956. Somoza's sons, Luis Somoza Debayle and Anastasio Somoza Debayle, who both spoke English and were educated in the United States, assumed control of the country. When Luis, better known as Tachito, died a natural death in 1967, Anastasio became leader.

Dissatisfaction with the Somoza family continued to escalate, and the resistance acquired a greater degree of organization throughout the 1960s and 1970s. In 1961 Carlos Fonseca organized a cadre of insurgent socialist groups into a larger left-leaning organization that began calling itself the Sandinista National Liberation Front (FSLN) in 1963. Named after General Sandino, the organization was commonly known, in both Spanish and English, as the Sandinistas. Popular dissatisfaction with the Somoza regime erupted into violence in 1978 when Pedro Joaquín Chamorro Cardenal, the editor of an anti-Somoza newspaper, was assassinated. The Sandinistas took power in 1979 and set up a broad-based coalition government. Somoza fled to Miami and then to Paraguay, where he was assassinated in 1980.

The coalition government faced constant challenges from the right—most notably the leadership of the Roman Catholic Church and the leaders of the international business community. The U.S. government, however, proved to be the greatest threat to the stability of the new regime in Nicaragua. In 1985 President Ronald Reagan imposed an economic embargo against Nicaragua, citing what he saw as the threat of Marxism and communism in the "backyard" of the United States. The U.S. government denied that it was supporting anti-Sandinistas, but it was secretly aiding anti-Sandinista guerrillas, or "Contras." Exiled Nicaraguan Contra leaders who lived in Miami worked together with high-ranking officials in the Marines, the Central Intelligence Agency (CIA), and the National Security Council (NSC) to supply weapons and money to the Contras, despite the fact that Congress had passed a law banning U.S. government support for the Contras. This affair was partially brought to light in 1986 when attorney general Edwin Meese discovered that much of the money for the Contras came from a secret arms-for-hostages deal between the United States and Iran. Marine Lieutenant Colonel Oliver North and other high-ranking officials in the CIA and NSC were later convicted of crimes ranging from perjury to conspiracy to defraud the U.S. government. Presidents Reagan and George H. W. Bush denied prior knowledge of the Iran-Contra affair, as the scandal came to be called. In 1992 President Bush pardoned all of the high-ranking officials who were involved with the scandal.

Violeta Barrios de Chamorro, wife of slain anti-Somoza leader Pedro Joaquín Chamorro, was elected president in 1990. A conservative moderately opposed to the Sandinistas, Chamorro may have won partly because war-weary Nicaraguan voters were tired of the U.S. embargo and the ongoing violence of the Contra War. After Chamorro's election the U.S. trade embargo was lifted, and in November 1993, in response to Chamorro's pledge to place the army under non-Sandinista control, President Bill Clinton approved $40 million in aid for Nicaragua. Chamorro attempted to achieve peace by giving amnesty to both sides for crimes committed during the civil wars.

Sixteen years after the Sandinista revolution, Nicaragua was still in a desperate situation. There were an estimated 1,500 "recontras," former right-wing rebels, fighting for land rights. The annual per capita income in 1994 was $540, lower than it had been in 1960, according to the University of Central America. Some 60 percent of Nicaraguans were unemployed, and 70 percent lived in extreme poverty, according to United Nations estimates. The infant mortality rate was the highest in Central America: 81 deaths per 1,000 live births. Nicaragua had an external debt of about $14 billion and suffered from inflation. In a mid-1990s poll in Nicaragua, 50 percent of respondents said that Nicaragua had been better off under the brutal Somoza regime, and only 7 percent said that the country was better off under Chamorro, according to Canadian magazine *Maclean's*. In 1996 a conservative, Arnoldo Alemán, was elected president.

In the early twenty-first century, the United States continued its attempts to influence electoral politics in Nicaragua. George W. Bush's administration repeatedly characterized the FSLN as a terrorist group. In 2001 Sandinista leader Daniel Ortega (who had been president from 1985 to 1990) lost the presidential election to Enrique Bolaños, the U.S.-backed vice-president to Alemán who ran for office after Alemán was barred from elections due to allegations of corruption. Ortega initially refused to concede amidst widespread charges of electoral fraud. When Bolaños took office he alienated many of his conservative supporters by attempting to purge the government of corruption and working with the World Bank to stabilize Nicaragua's economy. Leading up to the 2006 elections, the United States attempted to thwart Ortega's presidential bid by implying that the United States and its allies in Americas would impose a trade embargo if the Sandinistas ascended to power. In spite of the threats, Ortega won the election and prevailed again in his re-election bid in 2011.

SETTLEMENT IN THE UNITED STATES

Little is known about the first Nicaraguans to immigrate to the United States, because the U.S. Census Bureau did not keep separate statistics for individual Central American countries until 1960. Pre-1960 Census reports simply counted Nicaraguans together with all Spanish-surnamed people, and estimates of the number of undocumented early immigrants are not available. Data on migration among Central Americans from the late nineteenth and early twentieth centuries show a great deal of variation from decade to decade. Documented immigration to the United States from Central America rose from 500 individuals entering between 1890 and 1900, to 8,000 individuals between 1900 and 1910. During World

War I, and 17,000 Central Americans legally entered the United States between 1910 and 1920, largely to meet the increased U.S. demand for labor. Due to 1920s legislation that restricted the flow of immigrants from countries in the Western Hemisphere, the number of Central American immigrants dropped to 6,000 during the 1930s.

Some critics of U.S. foreign policy contend that migration from Nicaragua to the United States in the latter half of the twentieth century has been caused by Nicaragua's economic dependency upon the United States. Many Nicaraguans have come to the United States to escape poverty and political turmoil at home and have arrived thinking that they would live more comfortably in the United States. Nearly 7,500 Nicaraguans legally immigrated to the United States between 1967 and 1976. According to the U.S. Census Bureau, 28,620 Nicaraguans were living in the United States in 1970. Over 90 percent of Nicaraguan immigrants self-reported as "white" on the 1970 Census. Most Nicaraguan immigrants during the late 1960s were women: there were only 60 male Nicaraguan immigrants for every 100 female immigrants during this period. This male-to-female ratio may be explained by the large number of Central American women who came to the United States to work as domestic servants so that they could send money home to Nicaragua. Most immigrants during this period settled in urban areas, many in Los Angeles and San Francisco, California.

The 1979 revolution triggered three large waves of Nicaraguan immigrants. Documented immigration increased two to three times after the revolution, and undocumented immigration rose dramatically. The first wave took place during the time of the revolution, when the wealthy families closely associated with the Somoza regime fled to Miami. Perhaps as many as 20,000 Nicaraguans immigrated to Miami during this period. After the revolution there was a period of repatriation, when people who had left Nicaragua to avoid the conflicts returned home.

The second wave occurred during the early 1980s, when the Nicaraguan government was reorganized. Many non-Sandinista members of the coalition as well as industrialists whose companies had been seized by the state left the country—some ending up in the United States. In the mid-1980s, fighting between the Sandinistas and the U.S.-supported Contras became more severe, which caused the country's economic and civil rights conditions to worsen significantly. The real wage paid to workers, for example, declined by over 90 percent from 1981 to 1987, according Sandinista figures, and the opposition newspaper was heavily censored. This economic chaos and social repression prompted the third and largest wave of immigrants to date. The immigrants in the third wave tended to be young men of all classes fleeing the involuntary military draft and poorer families seeking to escape harsh economic conditions and violence.

Between 1982 and 1992, approximately 10 percent to 12 percent of the population of Nicaragua left their native country. The largest numbers of people went to Costa Rica, but hundreds of thousands went to the United States, Honduras, and Guatemala.

In 1997 Congress passed the Nicaraguan Adjustment and Central American Relief Act (NACARA) Amnesty. By 2007, NACARA estimated that 966,480 Nicaraguans would be naturalized as U.S. citizens. The Department of Homeland Security estimates that close to 6,000 undocumented people from Nicaragua arrive each year. According to the 2010 Census, California and Florida are the states with the largest numbers of Nicaraguan Americans. Other states with smaller, but significant, numbers include Louisiana, Maryland, New Jersey, New York, Texas, and Virginia.

Miami is the center of Nicaraguan American life. The ousted dictator Anastasio Somoza was the first of about 175,000 Nicaraguans who arrived in Miami in the 1980s. A small city called Sweetwater, about sixteen miles from Miami, has been dubbed "Little Managua" because of the large number of Nicaraguans who settled there. Nicaraguans have also created communities in other large urban centers, such as Los Angeles and San Francisco. Smaller numbers of Nicaraguans live in large cities in Texas. All these cities have significant Spanish-speaking populations, which facilitates networking and the sense of community among the recent immigrants.

The anti-immigration sentiment in California contrasted markedly with the welcome that Nicaraguan immigrants received in the early days of the first wave after the revolution in the early 1980s. At that time, President Reagan painted the Nicaraguan revolution in stark Cold War tones: the Sandinistas were Marxists and communists who were going to destabilize the Central American isthmus through their close alignment with communist Cuba and the Soviet Union. According to this Cold War scenario, Nicaraguan immigrants were refugees and exiles who had escaped the communist regime and therefore deserved political asylum and assistance, essentially because they were viewed by some American conservatives as the outcasts of a newly formed socialist regime. Even though the political affiliation of the parent country is not supposed to enter into questions of asylum, Nicaraguan applicants were granted political asylum about 50 percent of the time in 1987. Salvadorans fleeing similar conditions received asylum only three percent of the time in 1987.

During the mid- to late 1980s, when many Americans were less hospitable to Nicaraguan and other immigrants from Central American, other Americans banded together to support Central Americans and Central American refugees. Over eighty municipal governments created U.S.-Nicaraguan sister city agreements. The U.S. cities sent medical supplies, food, and farming materials to their

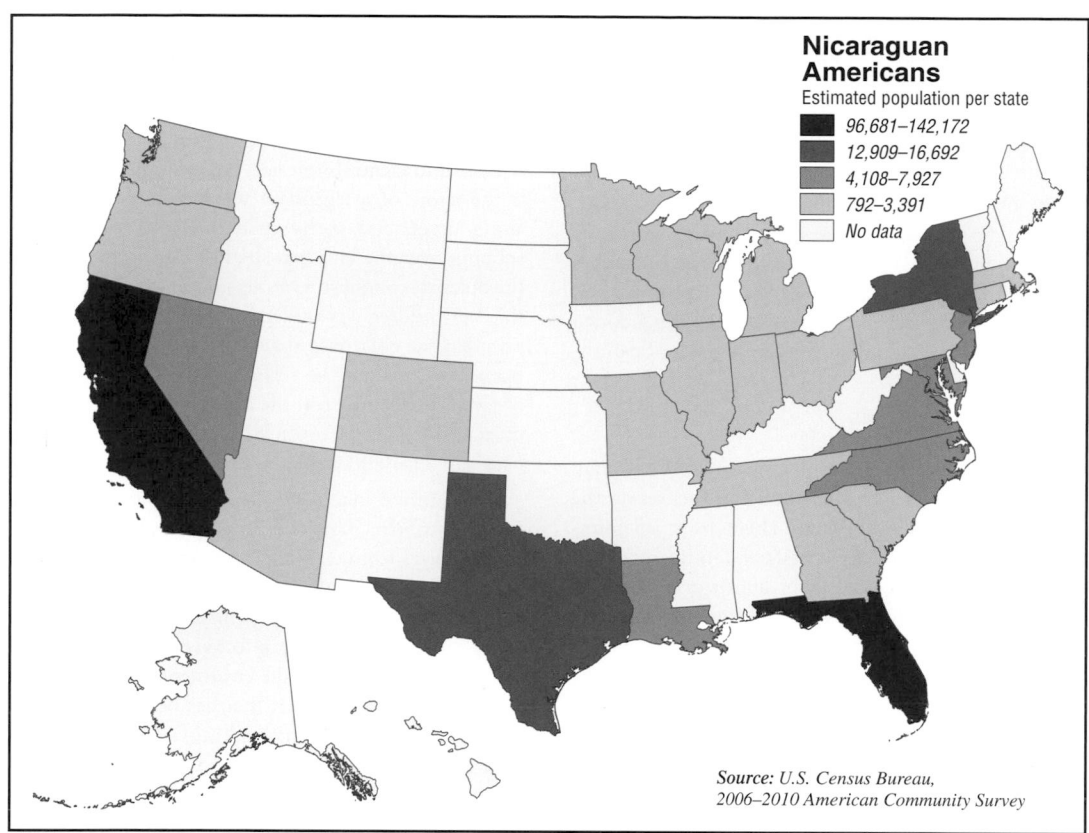

Nicaraguan Americans

Estimated population per state

- 96,681–142,172
- 12,909–16,692
- 4,108–7,927
- 792–3,391
- No data

Source: U.S. Census Bureau, 2006–2010 American Community Survey

counterpart cities in Nicaragua. Some churches created what were called "sanctuaries" for undocumented immigrants. The churches offered support and shelter to Central American immigrants. During this period Central American refugee centers appeared in nearly every large urban center in the United States.

Key issues facing Nicaraguans staying permanently in the United States are questions of identity. They wonder, for example, whether they are considered refugees or immigrants, or whether they are merely living in exile. CARECEN, which is located in Los Angeles and is one of the leading Central American assistance groups, reflected this shift in identity when it changed its name from Central American Refugee Center to Central American Resource Center. Another key issue is the return of millions of dollars' worth of property seized by the Sandinistas under a law that gave the government the right to seize property if the owner was absent from Nicaragua for more than sixty days. Many of the former owners of the seized property became citizens of the United States and attempted to regain their titles through U.S. law.

LANGUAGE

Spanish is the language spoken by most Nicaraguans, but several indigenous groups speak their own languages, sometimes in addition to Spanish or English. The Miskito, Sumu, and Rama on the Atlantic coast all speak related, but distinct, languages. Many

Garifuna also speak an Afro-Karib language of their own, sometimes in addition to Spanish and English.

Nicaraguan Spanish has several distinguishing characteristics. The Nicaraguan accent dates back to the sixteenth century in Andalusia, and the relative isolation of Nicaragua meant that the accent did not change in the same ways that the Andalusian accent has. For example Nicaraguans have a tendency to replace the "s" sound with an "h" sound when speaking. Nicaraguans also tend to use grammatical constructions that are now rare in most other Spanish-speaking countries. For example: *¡Y quien sos vos!* (And who are you!) uses *vos*, an antiquated form of "you." Some linguists have noted that onomatopoeic words are common in Nicaragua.

Nicaraguan Spanish also has many indigenous influences. Until the nineteenth century a hybrid form of Nahuat-Spanish was the common language of Nicaragua. Today Nahuat, Mangue, and Maya words and syntax can be found in everyday speech. As the words for two tropical fruits, *mamey* and *papaya*, testify, Nicaraguan Spanish has some Caribbean influences. *Béisbol* (baseball) and *daime* (dime) attest to Nicaragua's long association with the United States. However, the greatest number of Nicaraguanisms come from Aztec and Nahuat languages. An example of a Spanish-Aztec hybrid word is *chibola*, the Nicaraguan word for "bottled soda." It is formed from two words: *chi*, meaning "small" in Aztec, and *bola*, meaning "ball" in Spanish. Nicaraguan Americans and other Spanish-speaking newcomers in cities like Miami soon learn to speak "Spanglish"—a combination of Spanish and English. For example: "Have a nice day, *Señor*." This type of language usage is so common that it can be heard on Spanish-language radio shows and television.

In the United States, Nicaraguan Americans often modify their native language so that it matches the Spanish spoken by other Latin communities. Small turns of phrase or prepositions are abandoned so that they can assimilate within the larger Spanish-speaking community.

RELIGION

Nicaraguan Americans are overwhelmingly Roman Catholic, and Nicaragua's Catholicism focuses on the mysteries of the Virgin Mary. There are small numbers of evangelical, Pentecostal, and fundamentalist Protestants. Most, if not all, of Nicaragua's 60 or 70 Jewish families left the country during and after the Sandinista revolution. Many of the Jewish emigrants cited anti-Semitic harassment by FSLN soldiers as the main reason for leaving. One Managuan synagogue was firebombed, reportedly by people who identified themselves as members of the FSLN. Changes in worshiping practices since Nicaraguans have begun arriving in the United States are not well documented.

In addition to the Virgin Mary, Catholic Nicaraguan Americans venerate Nicaragua's patron saint, Santo Domingo. In Nicaragua, the celebration of the saint includes a procession of thousands of people; however, in the United States, worship of the saint is much more subdued, taking place inside the home and observed by placing small figurines around the house. Due to their Catholic heritage, many of the traditions and customs practiced by Nicaraguan Americans are colored with religious expressions.

CULTURE AND ASSIMILATION

Having arrived relatively recently in the United States, most Nicaraguan Americans have maintained their native traditions and beliefs and have, to some degree, merged their culture with the cultures of immigrants from other areas of Central and South America. Because the Nicaraguan American community in San Francisco, for instance, is relatively diffuse, Nicaraguan Americans there have been assimilating into a pan-Latino culture more rapidly than into non-Latino culture. In general, Nicaraguan Americans retain a large part of their culture due to their continued connection to the country and to the relationships they have forged with other members of Latino immigrant communities. Families typically visit Nicaragua at least once a year. Additionally, events like Hurricane Mitch in 1998 transcended political and social divisions, bringing the diasporic community together in a series of efforts to offer aid and support to the people who lost their homes and families.

Traditions and Customs Some of the Nicaraguan people's beliefs and traditions date back to pre-Columbian times, and others appeared during colonial times. Most are a mixture of both pre- and post-Columbian culture and are known throughout Mexico and Central America. For example, La Llorona is the name of a legendary woman-spirit who walks along streets and paths on dark nights sighing and sobbing over the children she lost during the time of the Spanish conquest. One version of the legend has it that her children were killed by an earthquake; another says that the children's Spanish father stole them away from her. This may be related to the Mexican legend of La Malinche, the real-life assistant and lover of conquistador Héman Cortés, who bore him a child that Mexican legend identifies as the first mestizo.

There are many folk beliefs in Nicaraguan culture. One belief says that if a person who has sun-irritated eyes from walking in the sun looks at a child, that child will be "infected with the sun" and will suffer from fever and diarrhea. The treatment is difficult unless the person who has infected the child is known. If the person is known, the treatment is simple: wrap the child in a sweaty shirt that has been worn by the person who originally infected him or her, and hours later the child will be healthy.

Cuisine The importance of corn to traditional Nicaraguan cuisine, religion, and folklore cannot be overstated. To a large extent, the traditional cuisine of Nicaragua consists of varied and imaginative ways of preparing corn, or *maíz*. Nearly every part of the plant is used—from the fungus that grows on the corn to the husk that covers the cob—and nearly every type of dish and beverage is made of corn. Breakfast cereals, breads, drinks that taste a bit like coffee, puddings, desserts, porridges, and even beer are made from corn. The *tamal* (pronounced "tahmahl") is a bit of corn dough with seasoned meat, sweet chocolate, or vegetables, wrapped inside of a corn husk or a banana leaf before it is steamed or boiled.

The small, round, unleavened tortilla, made of ground and processed corn, is the daily staple of Nicaraguans. The tortilla is bread, spoon, and plate for Central Americans. Traditionally made at home by hand in Nicaragua, tortillas are made by machines in the United States and sold in supermarkets all over California, the Southwest, and in southern Florida. In Nicaragua, the national tamal is called *nacatamal* (pronounced "naca-tahmahl") and consists of pork, chicken, or turkey, various vegetables, mint, and hot peppers, all combined with a corn dough made with sour orange juice. A small amount of this mixture is put inside of an individual corn husk or banana leaf and then folded or rolled and sealed before cooking. Restaurants in Miami have signs in their windows that say: "Nacatamales and other Nicaraguan foods."

Beans are also important. Unlike most of Central America, which prefers black beans, Nicaraguans tend to eat red beans. The most common national dish in Nicaragua is *gallo pinto* (fried white rice and red beans), and red bean soup is the most typical soup of Nicaragua. It is made from red beans boiled with garlic, onion, pork, and sweet red pepper. The soup is poured into a bowl, and then an egg is cracked into the hot soup. The heat of the soup partially cooks the egg.

While everyday cuisine is based upon abundant corn and beans, the *criollo* (pronounced "cree-o-yo"), or Creole, cuisine is based more on meats and sauces that are Nicaraguan adaptations of Spanish and European dishes. The scarcity and high cost of meats in Nicaragua has put meat normally out of reach of everyone but the upper classes. However, *baho vigorrón* is popular among a wide range of Nicaraguans. This dish is a combination of fried pork rinds and *yucca* (a shrub common in Nicaragua that has many edible parts) served with salad, or *ensalata*, consisting of shredded cabbage, onion, and carrots.

Desserts called *almibares* (pronounced "almee-barays") consist of honey- and syrup-coated fruits such as mango, mamey, jocote, papaya, and marañón. Almibares are eaten all over the country during *Semana Santa* (Holy Week). Many corn-based desserts also exist. For example, *motlatl atol* (pronounced "moetlahtel ahtol") is a yellow pudding-like dessert made from corn, milk, sugar, and a fruit, which is also eaten during Semana Santa. Chocolate, which is native to Central America, is used not only in sweet drinks and desserts but as a flavoring for meat dishes.

Holidays Until recently, La Purísima was a holiday celebrated only in Nicaragua. Now it is also celebrated in Los Angeles, Miami, and other Nicaraguan American communities. The holiday takes place from the last days in November until the night of the seventh of December, which is called the Noche de Gritería (Night of the Shouting). All through the week women make traditional sweets and drinks that will be exchanged during the last night. The centerpiece of the holiday is a small statue of the Virgin Mary covered with decorations of flowers, fruits, lights, and candles. Each night the family prays together in front of the statue. On the last night, neighbors, friends, and families from house to house in a secular-religious celebration that takes its name from the shouts raised in honor of the Virgin Mary: "Long live the Conception of Mary!" and "Who causes so much joy? The Conception of Maria!" are heard in the streets. Passersby receive candies, fruits, sugarcane, and even staples such as rice, beans, and cooking oils in honor of the assurances that Virgin Mary received from the archangel when she learned that she would that her child would be the son of God. Groups of people also sing traditional religious songs in front of the statue of the Virgin. Typically, the *gritería* culminates at midnight with elaborate fireworks display.

In Nicaragua, Semana Santa, or Holy Week, is a major spring holiday and a time for relaxing at the

GALLO PINTO

Ingredients

1 cup gallo pinto beans

1 bay leaf

1 small onion, peeled

1 whole clove

2 cloves garlic, peeled

salt

1½ cups long-grain white rice

¼ cup olive oil

1 onion, finely chopped

freshly ground black pepper

Preparation

Soak the beans in a pot in cold water covered by at least three inches at least four hours. Drain the beans and place in a large pot with two quarts of water. Pin the bay leaf to the onion with the clove, and add to the beans. Add the garlic. Gradually bring the beans to a boil, skimming off any foam. Reduce the heat and gently simmer the beans, uncovered, until tender, about 1–1½ hours, adding salt to taste during the last ten minutes. Drain the beans and refresh under cold water. Discard the onion.

Bring 2½ cups of water and 1 teaspoon salt to boil in a large heavy saucepan. Add the rice and return to a boil. Reduce the heat and gently simmer the rice until tender, about 18 minutes. Let the rice sit, covered, 5 minutes, and fluff with a fork.

Heat oil in a large skillet. Add the onion and thoroughly brown over medium heat, about 5 minutes. Add the beans and rice and cook over medium heat until the rice is lightly browned and the mixture is very aromatic, about 5 minutes. Correct the seasonings before serving.

beach or vacationing. On Easter Sunday villagers all over Nicaragua gather beneath bowers made of palm leaves decorated with fruits, vegetables, and flowers. Accompanied by a brass band, the villagers walk slowly around the town in a procession that commemorates the Stations of the Cross, a series of the most poignant events surrounding Jesus's arrest, interrogation, sentencing, and crucifixion. At the head of the parade are people dressed as symbolic characters: Hebrew elders and Apostles. The Apostles carry a life-size statue of Christ. The procession usually ends up in a public square in front of the town's church, where there is food for sale and carnival-like concessions. Nicaraguan American communities still observe this holiday, but the celebration is somewhat muted. In the Miami-Dade region, for example, masses are held on Sunday and during the week, but the level of celebration is not as grand as it is in Nicaragua. People often elect to celebrate at home with family and friends. Many churches in Florida, however, do offer dinners and processions leading up to the close of the week.

Attempts to rejuvenate Nicaraguan culture in the United States have led to celebrations like the *quinceañera*, a girl's fifteenth birthday, to become more prevalent in the United States than it is in Latin America. The celebration reflects the family's economic and social status. The ceremony resembles a ballroom dance, and its continued performance illustrates ways in which the Nicaraguan community navigates its identity within the larger culture of the United States. In her book *Once Upon a Quinceañera: Coming of Age in the USA* (2007), Julia Alvarez notes that the quinceañera marks a profound sense of social capital in the Latino community since families will spend large sums of money on the celebration, but it also provides a telling example of how Nicaraguan Americans reinvent their culture by merging the traditional ceremony with aspects of U.S. culture, such as cuisine, clothing, and music.

In the United States, Nicaraguan Americans often modify their native language so that it matches the Spanish spoken by other Latin communities. Small turns of phrase or prepositions are abandoned so that they can assimilate within the larger Spanish-speaking community.

Death and Funeral Rituals The observation of a *velorio*, or funeral party, after a person's death is an old tradition with Hispanic origins. During the velorio the family and friends of the deceased gather to share their grief. The relatives and close friends sit in the same room as the deceased and maintain a silent prayer vigil throughout the night until morning. Others at the velorio tell picaresque stories, drink liquor, eat large amounts of food, and even gamble. Following the velorio, the body is taken to the cemetery in a funeral procession with a brass band. The mourners follow the casket on foot to the cemetery.

The *velorios de los santos*, or velorios of the saints, are similar affairs in which small candles are lit on altars, festive decorations are hung, and prayers are made, accompanied by music and sometimes drunkenness. The most famous funeral procession of a saint is the procession of Managua's Saint Domingo. In this noisy and colorful parade, a tiny statue of the saint is carried to "sanctuary" in the hills of Managua. Marimbas, dancers, fireworks, and a carnival atmosphere mark the event.

Health Care Issues and Practices Nicaraguans, like all people native to the Americas and the Pacific Basin, are genetically prone to develop a small birthmark. The spot is a small, oval bluish mark found at the base of the spine on babies. Eventually this spot disappears, leaving no trace. In some cases a similar pigmentation, called Nevus of Ota, can appear on the cheeks or on the sclera of the eyes. Nevus of Ota is disfiguring, but usually not debilitating.

According to a study conducted in Los Angeles and published in 1992, post-traumatic stress disorder (PTSD) is common among Nicaraguan immigrant children who have witnessed or experienced violence. Fifteen of the thirty-one Central American children studied had witnessed violence. Of the children who both witnessed violence and lost contact with a caregiver, 100 percent suffered from some form of PTSD. The combined stress of living in guerrilla war conditions, forced emigration, and impoverished living conditions in the United States cause many Nicaraguan refugee children to suffer from the symptoms of PTSD, including nightmares, nervousness, insomnia, loss of appetite, and tearfulness.

When they arrived in the United States, Nicaraguan-educated doctors discovered that they could not practice medicine without a U.S. medical degree. Those who had studied in the United States were more fortunate and could more easily transfer their experience to a job in the United States. Frustrated by their situation, some Nicaraguan-educated doctors in Miami founded clandestine clinics to serve the uninsured Nicaraguan American population. These clinics do not appear in telephone books and do not advertise. During the time of the Contra war, some of the medical supplies that were headed for the fighting in Honduras ended up in some of these clandestine clinics. Other Nicaraguan-educated doctors found work in clinics that agreed to let them work at wages far below normal.

Health insurance remains an issue for immigrants from Nicaragua, as well as others from Central America. According to a 2007 report by the Centers for Disease Control, immigrants from Central America, including Nicaraguans, are twice as likely to not have a primary health-care provider, and 68 percent of the respondents indicated that they had not spoken with a health care provider within a year. In addition, many Hispanic immigrants do not have health insurance, but studies indicate that Hispanic Americans are in better health than people born in the United States.

The indigenous medicine of Nicaragua is one part magical and one part rational. Those who practice in this tradition maintain that, for every illness, there is a specific therapy, usually of vegetal origin. Many potent botanical medicines are part of the traditional medicine—some of them, like the leaves of the coca plant, which are the source of cocaine, have been recognized as potent pharmaceuticals by Western science and medicine. The various leaves, roots, and berries are usually made into a tea that the ill person drinks, or a poultice that is applied to the body. Certain foods, like *atol* made from corn, are also believed to have curative properties.

NICARAGUAN PROVERBS

Seemingly innocuous, the following Nicaraguan proverbs and sayings reveal quite a bit about Nicaragua and Nicaraguans:

Con eme-omo-de-odo, se consigue todo.

> With manners, everything can be obtained.

Cada uno tiene su modo de matar pulgas.

> Everyone has her or his manner of killing fleas.

El último mono se ahoga.

> The last monkey drowns. (Figuratively, the last in line will not receive her or his portion of food.)

No creer en santos que orinan.

> Don't believe in saints that urinate.

Voltearse la tortilla.

> The tortilla is flipped. (Refers to the way that tortillas are cooked. This is said when one party has fallen and another is ruling.)

Al mejor mono se le cae el zapote.

> Even the best monkey sometimes drops the sapote (a type of fruit).

A cada chancho le llega su sábado.

> For every pig his Saturday will come.

A donde te quieren mucho, no vengas a menudo.

> A constant guest is never welcome.

Amigo y vino, el mas antiguo.

> Old friends and old wine are best.

Con la honra no se pone la olla.

> Honor buys no meat in the market.

FAMILY AND COMMUNITY LIFE

Partly because of tradition, and partly because of the Catholic prohibition against birth control and abortion, Nicaraguan American families tend to be larger than is typical in the United States. The tradition of larger families may have its origin in Nicaragua's agricultural economy, where more children meant more help to plant and harvest. In the 1960s and early 1970s, few Nicaraguans immigrated as families—two-thirds of all Nicaraguan Americans during that period were women. As the reasons for immigration changed over the years, single women gave way to more families and widowed women with children. Sometimes families spanning three generations immigrated together.

When immigrants are fleeing from violence and economic problems, as Nicaraguans were in the 1980s, they want to take as many loved ones with them as they can. When the goal is to make money to send home, as it was in the late 1960s, immigrants tend to migrate alone.

Divisions are deep among some of the Nicaraguan American families that immigrated in the aftermath of the civil war. In many cases, the Sandinista revolution split sister from brother, mother from daughter, and friend from friend. Attitudes for or against the Sandinistas undermined efforts to create cohesive communities in cities like Los Angeles, where the headquarters of Casa Nicaragua, a Nicaraguan American social and political organization, was burned down in 1982, supposedly by Somocistas—the name given to those who sympathetic with Nicaragua's Somoza dynasty. However, as Nicaraguan Americans have become more assimilated, the political differences that have divided their communities are dissipating. Relatives of the deposed dictator Somoza own a chain of Nicaraguan restaurants in Miami, and these restaurants have become gathering places for a diverse group of Nicaraguans. Somocistas, Sandinistas, Cubans, and Americans come together, regardless of previous political divisions in Nicaragua. Pressing issues at home have also awakened national sentiment. Following the devastation of Hurricane Mitch in 1998, people put aside their lingering ideological differences in order to provide humanitarian support to the people who were injured or left homeless.

Gender Roles Traditional Nicaraguan culture is fairly conservative, with men overseeing the public sphere and women controlling the domestic sphere. Similar to other immigrant groups, however, subsequent generations of Nicaraguan Americans have transcended the traditional gender boundaries, with many women seeking employment outside the home. Children also resist aspects of the culture that they determine does not fit within the larger U.S. social structure. Teenagers, in particular, adopt aspects of American pop culture such as dress, slang, and music. Children choose which language they wish to speak with their peers and to what extent they evidence their heritage in the public sphere.

Education Many Nicaraguan families immigrate to the United States in order to improve their own or their children's education. It has been common for the wealthier families in Nicaragua to send their children to boarding schools and universities in the United States and Europe. Nicaraguan Americans' level of educational attainment tends to be lower than the national rates. According to the American Community Survey's estimates for 2006–2011, approximately 76.3 percent of Nicaraguan Americans had graduated high school (compared to a national rate of 85 percent) and 20.5 percent had earned a bachelor's degree or higher (compared to

BÉISBOL: A NICARAGUAN PASTIME

The national sport of Nicaragua is baseball. The first organized base-ball game in Nicaragua took place in 1892. For more than two decades in the early part of the twentieth century, U.S. Marines were stationed in Nicaragua. One result of the U.S. Marine occupation is Nicaragua's widespread fascination with baseball. In Nicaragua, the word for baseball is *béisbol* (pronounced "bays-bole"). Men and boys in small towns play baseball with whatever equipment they can muster—sometimes they use tough Nicaraguan grapefruits (for which the Nicaraguan word is *grapefruit*), or even an old sock rolled up around a rock, instead of a ball. There is also a professional league. At least five Nicaraguans who may have started by playing with rolled up socks later played for the major leagues in the United States.

28 percent for the overall U.S. population). Nicaraguan American men were slightly more likely (77 percent) to graduate from high school than women (76 percent), but women were more likely (23 percent) to graduate from college than men (18 percent).

EMPLOYMENT AND ECONOMIC CONDITIONS

Over the years, diverse groups of Nicaraguans have immigrated to the United States—some were doctors or bankers with university educations, and some were fifteen-year-old boys fleeing the draft. Upon arriving in the United States, many Nicaraguans, regardless of degrees, experience, and prior social standing, had to take low-paying jobs that did not offer benefits. Undocumented Nicaraguan immigrants often had to accept whatever employment they could find. They worked off the books and in many cases accepted wages that were below federally mandated standards.

The Nicaraguans who left Nicaragua between 1979 and 1988 tended to be of working age and were more likely to have been employed in a white-collar occupation before leaving Nicaragua, according to a statistical study published by Edward Funkhouser in 1992. They also tended to be from wealthier, larger, better-educated families compared to non-migrating Nicaraguans. According to Funkhouser, 64.2 percent of the immigrants had a secondary education, compared to 43.3 percent of all families surveyed in Managua. About 14 percent of the migrants had a university education, according to the same study.

Nicaraguan Americans typically find work through family or friends who have established themselves in the community, and they tend to work in specific niches that are related to these unofficial word-of-mouth networks. In San Francisco between 1984 and 1985, for example, it was common for

Nicaraguan American men to work as janitors. Nearly nineteen percent of Nicaraguan men worked as building cleaners, according to one San Francisco study that tallied the occupations of Nicaraguan-born men who listed their occupations on their children's birth certificates. Another 21.6 percent of Nicaraguan-born men worked in operations and fabrications, 10.8 percent worked at production and repair, and 1.1 percent worked as farmers, bringing the total percentage of Nicaraguan Americans who worked at blue-collar jobs to 33.5 percent. Nicaraguan Americans were also much less likely to work as food-service workers than were other Central Americans in the United States. Only 6.5 percent of the Nicaraguan Americans worked in food service, compared to 34.5 percent of Guatemalan Americans. Nicaraguan Americans were much more likely to work in white-collar jobs: 36.3 percent held administrative or other white-collar positions, compared to 6.9 percent of the Guatemalan Americans.

The American Community Survey (ACS) estimates for 2006–2010 indicated that the median household income among Nicaraguan Americans was $47,625, slightly less than the national average of $51,484. The ACS also reported that 15.6 percent of Nicaraguan American families were living below the poverty line (compared to a national rate of 11.1 percent).

Each year, Nicaraguan Americans send millions of dollars home to their families in Nicaragua. In 1988, Nicaraguan Americans sent somewhere between $50 million and $80 million to Nicaragua, making remittances nearly the second-largest source of foreign exchange in Nicaragua. Remittances remain a large source of income for Nicaragua. In 2011, Nicaraguans received over $1 billion from relatives living in the United States, El Salvador, Costa Rica, and various parts of Europe. In 2011 the average installment of a remittance was $152 per month, up from approximately $80 per month in the late 1980s.

POLITICS AND GOVERNMENT

Shortly after the revolution, Nicaraguan exiles living in the United States who were politically opposed to the Sandinistas organized an anti-Sandinista guerrilla army based in Miami and Honduras. Many of the guerrillas and guerrilla leaders were former National Guardsmen or were closely associated with the Somoza regime. The Somoza regime's long affiliation with the U.S. government meant that some Nicaraguan exiles already had well-placed U.S. government contacts and friends before they arrived in the United States. The U.S. government's support of the Contras—a blanket term that included all who took up arms against the Sandinistas—grew out of some of these relationships. Secret CIA involvement in the Contras' affairs dates back to at least 1981, according to Edgar Chamorro, former leader of the Contras, in his 1987 book *Packaging the Contras*. In a Senate subcommittee hearing in 1988, Octaviano Cesar, a Contra leader, admitted that the Contras had smuggled drugs into the United States for a profit, but he blamed it on the U.S. Congress, which cut off aid to the Contras in 1984. Notes taken by Marine Lieutenant Colonel Oliver North suggest that North knew about the drug running and that the profits may have been as high as $14 million.

In 1987 about two thousand Nicaraguan Americans protested publicly against the Immigration Reform and Control Act of 1986, which they said prevented the majority of Nicaraguans from remaining in the United States. About two months later, Attorney General Edwin Meese signed an order that permitted Nicaraguans to stay in the United States "for the present."

Since the 1990s, after the Sandinistas lost control of the government, Nicaraguan Americans have developed a richer interest in the Nicaragua's politics. The increased migration to the United States has built stronger ties to Nicaragua and created greater communication between the diasporic community and the nation. Nicaraguan Americans offered political and economic support to Alemán's Liberal Alliance and the Party of the Nicaraguan Resistance during the 1996 elections. Groups in Miami, consisting of former Contra fighters and exiled political leaders and businessmen, organized a series of political rallies. Leading up to Ortega's 2006 and 2011 campaigns, opposition forces and sympathizers continued to send money home in the hopes of electing their preferred candidate.

Nicaraguan Americans were thrust into a political struggle during the 2006 and 2011 elections. Pressure and intervention from the U.S. government on Nicaraguan politics led many Nicaraguan Americans to be suspicious of the relationship between the two countries. In 2008, when the United States cut off financial aid to Nicaragua, thousands of Nicaraguan Americans protested in Miami, San Francisco, and Washington, D.C. The 2009 military coup that removed Honduran President Manuel Zelaya from power reignited political and ideological divisions in Nicaraguan communities. The Nicaraguan American community has long protested against the School of the Americas, a facility in Fort Benning, Georgia, that trains Latin American government personnel. Leaders rejoiced in 2012 when President Ortega removed Nicaragua from the program. In the United States, Nicaraguans were among the growing group of Latin Americans who voted for President Barack Obama. Nearly 64 percent of the Latin American constituency voted to re-elect the president, indicating a significant shift in the Latin American community's political leanings. Although older generations of Nicaraguans are more socially conservative, issues such as immigration reform led to them supporting Obama's overall platform. Additionally, younger generations of Nicaraguan Americans are less likely to support measures concerning restrictions on abortion and cuts to education and social services.

A Nicaraguan American woman serves Cuban espresso in Miami, Florida. 2007 JOE RAEDLE / GETTY IMAGES

NOTABLE INDIVIDUALS

Academia Nicasio Urbina (1958–) is a Nicaraguan American writer and a professor of Latin American literature at the University of Cincinnati. He is the author of "El mito de paraiso perdido en la literature nicaragüense en los Estados Unidos" ("The Myth of Paradise Lost in Nicaraguan Literature in the United States"), published in *El Pez y la Serpiente* in 1989. Born in Buenos Aires, Argentina, to parents of Nicaraguan ancestry, Urbina was educated at Florida International University and at Georgetown University. He has been a member of the Modern Language Association since 1984 and has received numerous scholarships and fellowships throughout his academic career.

Eddy O. Rios Olivares (1942–) was educated in Minnesota and Puerto Rico. He has conducted microbiological research in Nicaragua and at the Universidad Central del Caribe in Puerto Rico, where he is professor and chairman of the department of microbiology. He has received various grants and research awards for his antitumor and HIV/AIDS research.

Medicine Norma F. Wilson (1940–) is an obstetrical/gynecological nurse practitioner who was born in Managua and lives in Kansas City. Wilson belongs to many professional associations and organizations relating to public health, family planning, and minority health. The Seward County Republican Women named her one of the women of the year in 1988.

Rolando Emilio Lacayo (1937–) is a physician and surgeon who specializes in gynecology, infertility, and obstetrics. Lacayo was born in Managua and educated in Nicaragua, the United States, and Mexico. From 1970 to 1971 he was an instructor in gynecology and obstetrics at Baylor College in Houston, Texas. He is a member of the American Medical Association, and a junior fellow of the American College of Obstetrics and Gynecology.

Literature Pancho Aguila (1945–) was born Roberto Ignacio Zelaya in Managua and immigrated to the United States in 1947. He wrote and read in

Nicaraguan American Roberto Aguirre Sacasa is a successful playwright, screenwriter, and comic book writer. ADAM NEMSER-PHOTOLINK.NET / PHOTOLINK / NEWSCOM

coffeehouses in San Francisco during the late 1960s until he was arrested and sentenced to life in prison in 1969 for a murder he committed during a robbery. He escaped from prison in 1972 and was arrested again five months later. While in prison, he wrote five books of poetry and contributed to several periodicals. He was paroled in 1992. One year later he and his girl-friend Heather Tallchief stole an armored vehicle containing $2.5 million dollars. Tallchief turned herself in in 2005, but Aguila remained on the run.

Horacio Aguirre is the publisher and editor of *Diario las Américas*, the leading conservative Spanish-language newspaper in Miami. In 1970 he was named man of the year by *Revista Conservadora del Pensamiento Centroamericano*. He holds honorary doctoral degrees from St. Thomas University (1976) and Barry University (1997) in Miami. He was awarded the Miami International Press Club's Good News Award in 1999, and the Great Floridian Award in 2001. Horacio's brother, Francisco Aguirre, has been called the godfather of the Contras. Francisco is a former National Guard colonel and has lived in exile in Washington, D.C., since 1947. He is well known in CIA and U.S. Department of State circles.

Roberto Aguirre-Sacasa (1973–) was born in Washington, D.C., the son of a Nicaraguan diplomat. He is best known for his work as a writer for Marvel Comics, including *Nightcrawler* and *The Stand*. He also worked as a writer for the Fox television series *Glee* and HBO's *Big Love*.

Politics and Business Roberto Arguello, president of the Nicaraguan American Banker's and Businessman's Association, educated at the University of Notre Dame, and a commercial banker in Miami, is one of the most visible Nicaraguan Americans. In 1990 Arguello took time off from banking to lobby in Washington, D.C., on behalf the Nicaraguan government. In the late 1980s he was a vocal opponent of the U.S. refugee policy for Nicaraguans.

Social Work Born in 1943 in Mexico to a Nicaraguan father and a Mexican mother, Carmela Gloria Lacayo has worked for many years to improve the lives of the poor and elderly. Lacayo established the National Association for Hispanic Elderly and founded Hispanas Organized for Political Equality. She has been appointed to a number of political positions, including vice-chair of the Democratic National Committee, member of the Census Bureau on Minority Populations, and an advisor on Social Security reform.

Sports Dennis Martinez (1955–) is a native of Grenada, Nicaragua. In 1976 Martinez became the first Nicaraguan ever to play in Major League Baseball. In 1990 he signed a three-year contract with the Montreal Expos that paid him more than $3 million per season. In an interview with *Sports Illustrated*, Martinez said that when he broke into the big leagues and told people that he was from Nicaragua, they did not know where it was. In 1991 he pitched a perfect game against the Los Angeles Dodgers. He has narrowly missed winning the Cy Young Award several times. During his off-seasons in Miami, Martinez put his celebrity among baseball-loving Nicaraguan Americans to good use by participating in drug-prevention programs for young Nicaraguan Americans in Miami. He retired following the 1998 season and shortly afterward began coaching. In 2012 he was named the bullpen coach for the Houston Astros.

William Robert Guerin (1970–) is the first Hispanic player to play in the National Hockey League. Guerin played for eighteen seasons on eight different teams. He won the Stanley Cup with the New Jersey Devils (1995) and the Pittsburgh Penguins (2009).

Eve Torres (1984–), a U.S.-born Nicaraguan American, is best known for her career as a professional wrestler in the WWE, winning the women's championship three times.

MEDIA

PRINT

La Estrella de Nicaragua

This newspaper is published in Spanish by and for Nicaraguan Americans in Miami, Florida.

Nora Caldera-Lopez, Administrator
P.O. Box 16-1094
Miami-Dade, Florida 33116-1094
Phone: (786) 472-1698
Email: nora@estrelladenicaragua.net
URL: www.estrelladenicaragua.net

NicaNet

This pro-Sandinista news and information service was founded in 1979 to support the revolution against the Somoza dynasty.

Alejandro J. Aguirre, Editor
225 E. 26th Street
Tucson, Arizona 85713
Phone: (202) 544-9355
Email: nicanet@afgj.org
URL: www.nicanet.org

ORGANIZATIONS AND ASSOCIATIONS

American Nicaraguan Foundation

This organization provides health care to Nicaraguan people.

81000 NW 57th Court
Suite 770
Miami, Florida 33126
Phone: (305) 374-3391
Fax: (305) 374-5993
Email: hvivas@anfnicaragua.org
URL: www.aidnicaragua.org

The Nicaragua Network

The Nicaragua Network was founded in 1979 to support the overthrow of the Somoza family and to support the Sandinista Revolution. The nonprofit network continues to produce publications and advocate for social and economic justice for Nicaragua.

1247 E Street SE
Washington, D.C. 20003
Phone: (202) 544-9355
Email: nicanet@afgj.org
URL: www.nicanet.org

MUSEUMS AND RESEARCH CENTERS

Dallas Museum of Art

The museum displays an extensive collection of pre-Columbian and eighteenth- to twentieth-century textiles, censers, and other art objects from the Nicaraguan area.

Karen Zelanka, Associate Registrar, Permanent Collection
1717 Harwood
Dallas, Texas 75201
Phone: (214) 922-1200
Fax: (214) 954-0174
URL: www.dm-art.org

Human Rights Documentation Exchange

Formerly known as the Central America Resource Center, the Human Rights Documentation Exchange maintains a library of information on human rights and social conditions in many countries, including Nicaragua. Also produces biweekly compilations of current news articles on Central America called NewsPaks.

Rebecca Hall, Executive Director
P.O. Box 2327
Austin, Texas 78768
Phone: (512) 476-9841
Fax: (512) 476-0130
Email: mail@hrde.org
URL: www.handplant.com

The Nattie Lee Benson Latin American Collection

Located at the University of Texas at Austin, this renowned collection consists of Nicaraguan books, books about Nicaragua, and resources relating to Nicaraguan Americans. Excellent electronic information resources.

Charles R. Hale, Director
Sid Richardson Hall 1.108
General Libraries
University of Texas
Austin, Texas 78713-7330
Phone: (512) 495-4520
Fax: (512) 495-4568
Email: blac@lib.utexas.edu
URL: www.lib.utexas.edu/benson/

SOURCES FOR ADDITIONAL STUDY

Cerar, K. Melissa, ed. *Teenage Refugees from Nicaragua Speak Out*. New York: Rosen Pub. Group, 1995.

Chamorro, Edgar. *Packaging the Contras. A Case of CIA Disinformation*. New York: Institute for Media Analysis, 1987.

Chavez, Leo Ralph. "Outside the Imagined Community: Undocumented Settlers and Experiences of Incorporation." *American Ethnologist*, May 1991, 257–78.

Crawley, Eduardo. *Nicaragua in Perspective*. New York: St. Martin's Press, 1979.

Funkhouser, Edward. "Migration from Nicaragua: Some Recent Evidence." *World Development* 20, no. 8 (1992): 1209–18.

Gobat, Michel. *Confronting the American Dream: Nicaragua under U.S. Imperial Rule*. Durham, NC: Duke University Press, 2005.

Hart, Dianne Walta. *Undocumented in L.A.: An Immigrant's Story*. Wilmington, DE: SR Books, 1997.

Lancaster, Roger N. *Life Is Hard: Machismo, Danger, and the Intimacy of Power in Nicaragua*. Berkeley: University of California Press, 1992.

Malone, Michael R. *A Nicaraguan Family*. Minneapolis: Lerner Publications Co., 1998.

Solaún, Mauricio. *U.S. Intervention and Regime Change in Nicaragua*. Lincoln: University of Nebraska Press, 2005.

NIGERIAN AMERICANS

Kwasi Sarkodie-Mensah

OVERVIEW

Nigerian Americans are immigrants or descendants of people from Nigeria, a West African state on the shores of the Gulf of Guinea. Nigeria is bordered by Niger to the north, Benin to the west, Cameroon to the east and southeast, and Chad to the northeast. The climate and the geography of Nigeria are diverse, with the arid Sahara desert in the north, a tropical rain forest in the south, mangrove swamps along the coast, and mountains in the southeastern part of the country. Nigeria's total land area is 356,669 square miles (923,768 kilometers), equaling the combined areas of New Mexico, Arizona, and California.

The 2010 Nigerian census put the country's population at 158,423,000. Nigeria's population is extremely diverse—more than 250 ethnic groups are identified, with 10 ethnic groups accounting for 80 percent of Nigeria's population. As in many other African countries, the distribution of religion can be broken down into three major areas: Christian, Muslim, and animist. In Nigeria 50 percent of the population are Muslims, the majority of whom reside in the northern part of the country; about 40 percent are Christians and mainly live in the southern part of the country; and 10 percent practice animism or traditional African religion. Nigeria is among the world's top oil-producing nations and is one of Africa's most powerful economies. However, political instability, corruption, and mismanagement continue to put Nigeria in the category of developing countries.

Over the course of the twentieth century, education has been the primary reason that Nigerians have immigrated to the United States. In its 1935 annual report, the New York–based Institute of International Education indicated that in 1926 there were three documented Nigerian students in U.S. universities. Almost two decades later, in 1944 the Institute of International Education reported that there were 44 Nigerian university students in the United States. The numbers began to increase dramatically in the 1970s when an oil boom made Nigeria one of the wealthiest countries in Africa. Most students were sponsored by their parents and relatives, both in Nigeria and in the United States, while others obtained financial assistance from American universities and colleges. In the late 1970s and 1980s Nigeria was among the top six countries in the number of students sent to study in the United States. In the 1980s, when Nigeria's economy began to decline precipitously, many Nigerians remained in the United States and obtained citizenship. After becoming citizens Nigerian Americans often brought their relatives into the United States. The Diversity Visa Program, also known as the Green Card Lottery, established through the Immigration Act of 1990, has been a source of migration to the United States. From 1990 through 2013, an average number of 6,000 Nigerians annually migrated to the United States through this program.

According to the U.S. Census Bureau's American Community Survey estimates, in 2011 there were approximately 271,098 people of Nigerian ancestry living in the United States. The largest numbers of Nigerian Americans are found in Texas, New York, Maryland, Georgia, and California.

HISTORY OF THE PEOPLE

Early History The name *Nigeria* was coined by the British colonial administrator Lord Lugard's wife in 1897 in honor of the 2,600-mile-long Niger River. The first Europeans to reach Nigeria were the Portuguese in the fifteenth century. In 1553 the first English ships landed at the Bight of Benin, then known as the "Slave Coast." Present-day Nigeria came into existence in 1914, when the Colony of Lagos, the protectorate of Southern Nigeria, and the protectorate of Northern Nigeria were amalgamated. Even before the arrival of Europeans, the many nationalities or ethnic groups were highly organized and had law and order. There were village groups, clans, emirates, states, kingdoms, and some empires. The Kanem-Bornu empire goes as far back as the tenth century. The Oyo empire, founded in the late fourteenth century by Oranmiyan, a prince of Ile-Ife, had a powerful army and maintained diplomatic contact with other kingdoms in the area. The Fulani empire was established in 1803 by a *jihad*, or holy war, against the rulers of the Hausa states by Usman Dan Fodio; it went on to become one of the most powerful kingdoms. Within two decades, parts of the Oyo empire, Bornu, and Nupe were added by conquest to the Fulani empire. Although there were no centralized governments, trade and commercial activities existed. Intermarriages flourished among the various groups.

One of the most prosperous trades even before the arrival of the Europeans was the slave trade. It was common practice in many African civilizations to sell war captives, delinquent children, and the handicapped; and Nigeria was no exception. With the arrival of the Europeans, slavery became more lucrative. Intertribal wars were encouraged by the Europeans so that more captured slaves could be sent to the New World. The British Parliament abolished slavery in 1807.

When the mouth of the Niger River was discovered in 1830, the British heightened their economic expansion into the interior of the country. Formal administration of any part of Nigeria goes back to 1861 when Lagos, a vital component of the lucrative palm oil trade, was ceded to the British Crown. At the Berlin Conference of 1884–1885, geographical units and artificial borders were created in Africa by European powers without any consideration for cultural or ethnic homogeneity. Britain acquired what is now Nigeria as a result of this contest between European powers known as the "scramble for Africa." In 1914 the various protectorates were consolidated into one colony, the Protectorate of Nigeria.

Modern Era After World War II, nationalism rose in Nigeria. Under the leadership of Nnamdi Azikiwe, Obafemi Awolowo, and Alhaji Sir Abubakar Tafawa Balewa, Nigerians began to demand self-determination and increased participation in the governmental process on a regional level. On October 1, 1960, Nigeria became an independent country, but this independence brought about a series of political crises. Nigeria enjoyed civilian rule for six years until January 15, 1966, when, in one of the bloodiest coups in Africa, the military took over the government of Prime Minister Tafawa Balewa, assassinated him, and replaced him with General J. Aguiyi-Ironsi. Later that month Ironsi was killed in a counter-coup and replaced by General Yakubu Gowon. In early 1967 the distribution of petroleum revenues between the government and the Eastern Region, where the majority of Igbos come from, sparked a conflict. Gowon abolished the four regions of Nigeria and replaced them with twelve states. Colonel C. Odumegwu Ojukwu, a soldier from the Igbo tribe, announced the secession of the Eastern Region and declared a Republic of Biafra. Events following this declaration resulted in the Nigerian Civil War, also referred to as the Biafran War (1967–1970). It was one of the most deadly civil wars in Africa, claiming the lives of over two million Nigerians.

Gowon was overthrown in a bloodless military coup on July 29, 1975, when he was attending a summit meeting of the Organization of African Unity. Brigadier General Murtala Ramat Muhammed became the leader of the government. He started a popular purging of the members of the previous government and announced a return of the country to civilian rule. On February 13, 1976, Muhammed was assassinated during a coup attempt. Lieutenant General Olusegun Obasanjo, chief of staff of the armed forces in Muhammed's government, became the new head of state. In 1978 Nigeria produced a new constitution similar to that of the United States.

The country returned to civilian rule in 1979 when Alhaji Shehu Shagari was sworn in as president. He was ousted in 1983 by a group of soldiers led by Major-General Muhammadu Buhari. Buhari introduced stringent measures to curb corruption, imprisoning many former government officials on corruption charges. Under Buhari's government, the death penalty was reintroduced in Nigeria and freedom of the press was rigorously restricted. Many newspapers were banned and journalists were imprisoned or tortured.

On August 27, 1985, Major General Ibrahim Babangida led a bloodless coup, deposing Buhari as the head of state. Babangida promised to restore human rights, establish a democratically elected government, and eradicate corruption, which has frequently been a part of Nigerian politics. Babangida not only violated his promises but also imprisoned journalists who stood up for the truth. After repeatedly postponing a return to a democratically elected government, Babangida annulled the results of the election held in June 1993, which was won by his opponent, Chief Moshood Abiola. Under pressure, Babangida resigned and left power in the hands of a handpicked and widely opposed interim government. Later in 1993, General Sani Abacha, a longtime ally of Babangida, became president; he ruled Nigeria until his death in 1998. The country returned to civilian rule in 1999, when Olusegun Obasanjo, the former military leader, won the presidential election; he was reelected in 2003. Umaru Yar'Adua won the 2007 election. After being hospitalized in 2009, he transferred power to his vice president, Goodluck Ebele Jonathan, in 2010. Jonathan subsequently won the presidential election held the following year.

SETTLEMENT IN THE UNITED STATES

Compared with other ethnic groups in the United States, the presence of Nigerian Americans in the United States does not date back very far. However, if the slave trade is considered, then Nigerians have been part of American society as far back as the eighteenth century. Even though Nigerian Americans of the modern era do not want to be associated with slavery or categorized as African Americans, history bears witness to the fact that the coastal regions of modern-day Nigeria were referred to as the Slave Coast. Nigeria provided a vast percentage of the Africans who were separated from their families and forced into slavery by European entrepreneurs.

World War I expanded the horizons of many Africans. Although European colonial masters wanted Africans in their territories to receive an

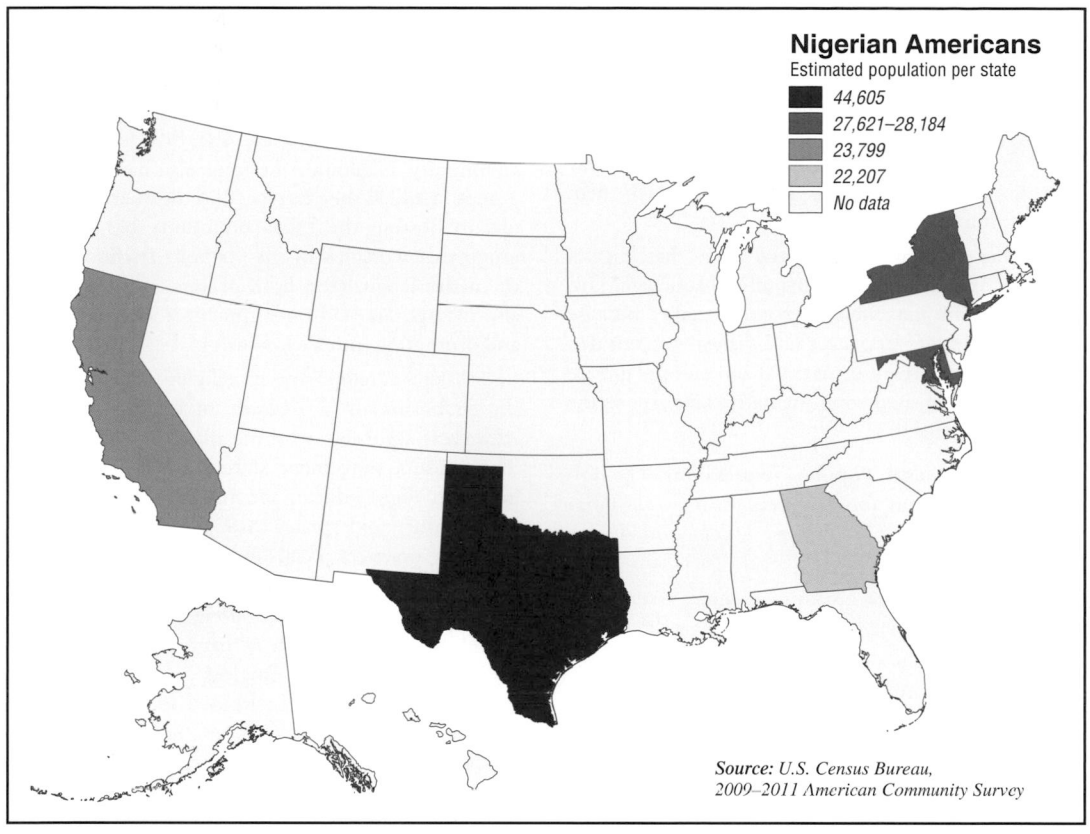

Nigerian Americans
Estimated population per state

- 44,605
- 27,621–28,184
- 23,799
- 22,207
- No data

Source: U.S. Census Bureau, 2009–2011 American Community Survey

African-based education with emphasis on rural development, many Africans wanted to go abroad to study. In the early parts of the twentieth century, it was traditional for Nigerians to travel to European countries such as the United Kingdom and Germany to receive an education and then return to their countries. Two dynamic ideological movements emerged after the war: Marcus Garvey's military platform of Africa for Africans, and W. E. B. Du Bois's Pan African movement. The colonial powers in Africa feared that the strong ideas of identity and freedom preached by both Garvey and Du Bois would turn the Africans against their colonial rulers.

Nigerian immigrants to the United States have typically settled near family relations or near colleges or universities previously attended by relatives and friends. They have tended to prefer areas where weather is similar to that of Nigeria. Most early Nigerians coming to the United States went to schools in the southern United States. Today large metropolitan areas attract Nigerian immigrants, many of whom hold prestigious professional jobs. Poor economic conditions have forced many highly educated Nigerian Americans to take up odd jobs. In many metropolitan areas, Nigerian Americans with one or several graduate degrees work as taxi drivers and security officers. According to the U.S. Census Bureau's American Community Survey estimates, in 2011 the states with the largest populations of Nigerian Americans included Texas, New York, Maryland, Georgia, and California.

LANGUAGE

English is the official language in Nigeria, but it is estimated that there are between 250 and 400 distinct dialects. There are three major ethnic languages in Nigeria: Yoruba, Igbo, and Hausa. Yoruba is spoken by more than 15 million people, primarily in southwestern Nigeria. Belonging to the Kwa group of languages, Yoruba is a tonal tongue. Depending on the tone used, the same combination of sounds may convey different meanings. Igbo is also spoken by more than 15 million people in Nigeria. Formerly considered a Kwa language, recent research has placed Igbo in the Benue-Congo family of languages. Hausa is spoken in the northern part of Nigeria and is considered to be the most widely spoken language in Africa. It is a member of the Chad group of languages frequently assigned to the Hamitic subfamily of the Hamito-Semitic family of languages.

Pidgin English has become the unofficial language in many African countries, and Nigeria is no exception. It can be loosely defined as a hybrid of exogenous and indigenous languages. It has become the most popular medium of intergroup communication in various heterogeneous communities in Nigeria. Nigerian Americans from different tribal entities who may not communicate in English can communicate with each other in Pidgin English.

First-generation Nigerian Americans speak their native languages at home and when interacting with people from the same tribal groups. English words have found their way into most of the traditional languages spoken by Nigerian Americans. Children born into Nigerian American homes speak English and may learn the native languages if their parents teach them or speak the languages at home.

It has been proposed several times that Nigeria needs an African language as its official language. This laudable desire may never become a reality because there are so many languages and dialects to consider. The existence of the diverse tribal and cultural groups makes it hard to single out one native language as the national language.

Greetings and Popular Expressions The following are common Yoruba greetings: *Bawo ni?* ("baa wo knee")—Hi, how are things?; *Daadaa ni* ("daadaa knee")—Fine.

Common Hausa greetings include: *Sannu* ("sa nu")—Hi; *Lafiya?* ("la fee ya")—Are you well?

Igbo greetings and expressions include: *Ezigbo ututu*—Good morning; *Kedu ka imere?*—How do you do?; *Gini bu aha gi?*—What is your name?

Popular greetings in Pidgin English are varied and may include: "How now?"—How are you? or How is it going?; "Which thing you want?"—What do you want?; and "How body?"—How's your health?

RELIGION

As in many African countries, Western religion was imposed on Nigeria. Traditionally, Nigerians believe that there are two types of divinities: the Supreme Being and the subordinate deities. The Supreme Being can be likened to God, and the subordinate deities to the saints and others through whom people can communicate with the Supreme Being. The Igbos, for instance, refer to the Supreme Being in powerful terms, such as *Chukwu* (the Great Providence) and *Chineke* (Creator and Providence). The traditional religion of the Yorubas focuses on different gods who represent aspects of one almighty, all-encompassing God, Olorun—owner of heaven and earth, who is too sacred to be directly approached or worshipped.

Through commercial contacts and colonization, Islamic and European religions were introduced in Nigeria. The majority of Nigerian Americans hailing from Nigeria's northern states are Muslims. Islamic groups in the northern part of Nigeria include the Hausa, Fulani, Kanuris, Kanemis, Bagirimis, and the Wadayans. About 40 percent of the Yoruba population also practices Islam. In 1973, Nigerian Muslims in the New York and Washington, D.C., area formed the Nigerian Muslim Association (NMA). Since then many Nigerian American communities in large cities in the United States have formed their own NMA. One reason Nigerian American Muslims have formed

their own worship communities is that, unlike many Muslim Americans, they do not speak Arabic.

The majority of Nigerian Americans from the Igbo tribe are Catholics. While many Nigerians worship in churches alongside the broader American community, Nigerian Americans also have their own groups in which they can worship together. For example, in Boston, the Igbo community has formed a group that worships in the Catholic tradition, using the native language in both prayers and songs. They also incorporate traditional practices such as dancing and drumming into their worship.

A key development in religion in Nigeria was the establishment of *Aladura*, or spiritual churches. *Aladura* is a Yoruba word meaning "one who prays." The Aladura movement started among the Yoruba people in Nigeria during the first decades of the twentieth century and spread throughout Africa. Among the many practices of this movement, all participants wear white robes when they worship. They may worship in a church building, along the beach, on top of hills, or by the mouth of rivers, praying, confessing their sins, healing, singing, and clapping. The Aladura movement can be likened to the charismatic movement in the United States. In many U.S. cities Nigerian Americans have established their own Aladura churches.

CULTURE AND ASSIMILATION

Nigerian culture defies easy generalization because the country's people and their traditions are so varied. Nigerian Americans come from diverse ethnic, religious, and financial backgrounds, and therefore they come to the United States with various levels of attachment to their native traditions.

There is no typical Nigeria American household decoration. Depending on which region in Nigeria they come from, Nigerian Americans decorate their houses with various art forms. Many of them bring such artifacts when they travel home to visit. Other Nigerian Americans become so Westernized that their households do not have any indication of their heritage. Nigerian Americans have always had the reputation of living comfortable lives and maintaining high standards of living.

Traditions and Customs Nigerians have a variety of traditions and lore dating back to antiquity. For example, peeking at the eggs on which a hen is sitting was believed to make you blind. Singing while bathing could result in a parent's death. A pregnant woman who ate pork could have a baby with a mouth like that of a pig. Among the Yoruba it was believed that there were spirits hidden in rivers and hills in various cities. Since these spirits were there to protect the people, they were not to be disturbed on certain days of the week. In almost all Nigerian societies, there is a strong belief that most disease and death is caused supernaturally, by witchcraft, curses, or charms. Witches are usually elderly women. For a long time the Igbos believed that twins were an abomination and killed them at birth. Among some of the Hausa people, it was believed that marrying a Yoruba woman could result in mystical dangers such as serious sickness or even death. As Nigerian immigrants became acculturated to mainstream American society, these beliefs and superstitions were forgotten.

In many Nigerian cultures elders are supposed to be served first during a meal but leave food in the bowl for the children to eat as leftovers. The proverb "the elder who consumes all his food will wash his own dishes" attests to this belief. However, in many Nigerian American homes children are served before adults, an indication of the Western influence whereby the needs of the child come first.

The younger generation of Nigerian Americans sometimes struggle with adhering to traditional cultural protocols. For example among Nigerian Americans of Yoruba origin, younger people are supposed to greet older people properly by prostrating to them, that is, by kneeling down or saluting them in some way. Many younger Nigerian Americans find it hard to keep this tradition alive, especially when their peers from other American groups are present. Outside of embarrassment, it makes them feel that they are breaking the common American right of all people to be treated equally. They ask in their minds, "Why should older people be treated as God, someone to be served?"

Cuisine Ask anyone who has tasted Nigerian cuisine, and one answer is almost guaranteed—it is hot. There is no typical Nigerian American dish. Among the Yoruba, a meal may consist of two dishes: a starch form of dough derived from corn or guinea corn, or mashed vegetables that may be served with stew. The stew is prepared in typical Yoruba way, using palm oil, meat, chicken, or other game cooked with many spices and vegetables, flavored with onions or a leaf vegetable called bitter-leaf. A common Yoruba food is *garri*, made from the roots of *cassava* (manioc).

Among the Igbo people, cassava, *cocoyam* (taro), potato, corn, okra, beans, peanuts, and pumpkins are common foods. In the northern part of Nigeria, grains constitute a good component of the diet. *Tuwo* ("tu-wo"), a porridge-like dish, is common in the north and is eaten with different types of soup and sauce made from onions, peppers, tomatoes, okra, meat, or fish.

For group functions, the most popular food item for both Yorubas and Igbos is pounded yam or its variant *fufu*, served with stew or soup. Both groups cook *ogbono* soup (so called because it is thickened with ogbono seeds) to go with the dishes. Jollof rice, which is usually yellow in color, is another popular and very common dish among both groups. The only reason why Nigerian Americans may abandon traditional cuisine is the difficulty in obtaining the right ingredients. Nigerian Americans living in major metropolitan areas

NIGERIAN PROVERBS

The following are some common Nigerian proverbs:

■ The voyager must necessarily return home.

■ Death does not recognize a king.

■ A foreign land knows no celebrity.

■ An elephant is a hare in another town.

■ The race of life is never tiresome.

■ The nocturnal toad does not run during the day in vain.

■ A child who does not know the mother does not run out to welcome her.

■ If birds do not seek a cause for quarrel, the sky is wide enough for them to fly without interference.

■ It is not a problem to offer a drink of wine to a monkey; the problem is to take the cup away from him.

■ Many words do not fill a basket.

■ Truth is better than money.

■ If the elephant does not have enough to eat in the forest, it puts the forest to shame.

There is a mine of proverbs in Pidgin English, including the following:

Man wey fool na him loss.

> It is the fool that loses.

Lion de sick no be say goat fit go salute am for house.

> Just because the lion is sick does not mean the goat can go to the lion's house to greet him.

Monkey no fine but im mamma like am so.

> The monkey may not look handsome, but his mother likes him as he is.

Cow wey no get tail na God dey drive him fly.

> God drives away the flies from the cow without a tail.

typically have easy access to shops selling the appropriate ingredients. Those living in smaller areas do not find it financially viable to drive several miles—sometimes fifty miles or more—to shop for authentic Nigerian ingredients.

Akara ("ah-ka-ra"), or Nigerian bean cakes, are fried patties made with uncooked, pulverized black-eyed peas ground into a batter with onion, tomatoes, eggs, and chili peppers. *Egusi* ("e-goo-she") soup is a fiery soup made from egusi seeds (these seeds come from certain kinds of gourds; pumpkin seeds are often substituted in the United States). Other ingredients required for a typical egusi soup include okra, hot peppers, onions, any type of meat, poultry, or fish, palm oil, leafy greens, tomato paste, and salt.

Chinchin ("chin-chin") are fried pastries made from flour mixed with baking powder, salt, nutmeg, butter, sugar, and eggs. *Kulikuli* ("cooley-cooley"), or peanut balls, are made from roasted peanuts (called groundnuts in Nigeria), peanut oil, onions, salt, and cayenne pepper. *Moi-moi* ("moy-moy") is a savory pate made from black-eyed peas, onions, vegetable oil, tomato paste, parsley or fresh vegetables, salt, and pepper. Okra soup is based on meat, smoked fish, seafood and vegetables, and okra. This dish is similar to New Orleans gumbo.

Traditional Dress Men from various Nigerian groups wear loose-fitting trousers called *sokoto* ("show-kowtow"), a *buba* ("boo-bah") or loose-fitting overshirt, and a cap. Yoruba men wear *agbada* ("ah-bah-dah"), which is flowing robe worn to the ankle. It covers an undervest with no sleeves and a pair of baggy pants. The women wear a wide piece of cloth that goes from below the neck to the ankles. A blouse hanging to the waist is worn over it. A head tie and a thin veil are also worn. Many Nigerian Americans wear their traditional costumes on special occasions such as National Day (October 1).

Dances and Songs Nigerian Americans boast of a wealth of traditional and modern music and dances because dancing and music are central to Nigerian life. At birth and death, on happy and sad occasions, and in worship, dancing and music are present. Traditionally in many Nigerian societies, men and women did not dance together. Western education and influence have changed this tradition, though Nigerian Americans who want to recreate their culture retain this separation.

Drums are an integral part of Nigerian dances and music. Juju music, a very popular form of music from Yorubaland, is a slow and relaxed guitar-based music. Highlife music is popular in all parts of West Africa, including Nigeria. It usually consists of brass, vocals, percussion, drums, double bass, and electric guitar. People from northern Nigeria who practice Islam enjoy music with origins in North Africa. Such music is varied, but the instruments commonly used include trumpets, flutes, long brass horns, cymbals, and kettle drums.

Today in Nigeria popular music includes hip-hop by young Nigerians, mostly sung in Pidgin and local languages—especially Yoruba and Igbo. Many Nigerian Americans listen to music by Nigerian musicians of the older generation as well as by Nigerian hip-hop artists such as P-Square, 2Face Idibia, Flavour N'abania, D'banj, Wizkid, and Aşa. Most of the music is accessible online. Nigerian Americans enjoy music from all over the world. In addition to American and British music, reggae, calypso, and Zairian music are popular.

Holidays The major public holidays in Nigeria are New Year's Day; Eid al-Fitr (end of Ramadan); Easter; Eid al-Kabir (Feast of the Sacrifice, known as Eid al-Adha in other parts of the world); Mouloud (birth of the Prophet Muhammad); National Day or Independence Day; and Christmas. Nigerian Americans also celebrate the major public holidays in the United States.

National Day (October 1), celebrating the independence of Nigeria from colonial rule, is one of the most important holidays for Nigerian Americans. A whole week of cultural, educational, and political events are scheduled in areas with Nigerian American communities. Activities include lectures on Nigeria, traditional Nigerian dances and music, fashion shows, and storytelling of myths and legends from various Nigerian communities. Many Nigerian Americans volunteer to talk to neighborhood schoolchildren about Nigeria and the African continent at large. When the holiday proper falls on a weekday, parties and other festive celebrations are held on the weekend. The parties and festivities culminating in the celebration of Nigerian's independence are open invitations to Nigerians, people of other African descents, and others associated in one way or the other with Nigerian living in the United States. In New York, for example, the staff of the Nigerian Consulate attend these festivities.

For Muslim Nigerian Americans, Eid al-Fitr, or the end of the Muslim fasting season, is the second most important holiday in the Islamic calendar. For the approximately thirty days of Ramadan, Muslims are expected to fast from dawn to sunset. They also abstain from sex, drink, tobacco, and other activities associated with physical pleasure. To celebrate Eid al-Fitr, Muslims say the special feast prayer in a community format and give special alms to the poor. Nigerian American Muslims also share food and gifts with relatives and friends, and children receive gifts of all kinds.

There are many other holidays and festivities observed by Nigerian Americans to preserve their cultural heritage. Igbos in large metropolitan areas make it a point to celebrate the New Yam Festival every year. Traditionally, the yam has been the symbol of the prowess of the Igbo man. Just before midnight, the *ezejis* or elders offer prayers of thanksgiving and break kola nuts. Drums are played while blessings are offered. Other participants perform libation using Scotch whiskey or other similar liquor by pouring from a ram's horn. During the ceremony, prayers are addressed to an almighty being and to the ancestral gods who control the soil, through whose constant kindness and guidance yams and other foods of the land bear fruit. The ceremony also includes dancing, eating, and exchange of greetings.

Even though Nigerian Americans take time to celebrate these holidays, Thanksgiving, Christmas, and Easter are moments for bigger family gatherings because it is easier for people to take time off from work.

Health Issues There are no documented health problems or medical conditions specific to Nigeria Americans. However, like all black people, Nigerian Americans are susceptible to sickle cell anemia, an abnormal hereditary variation in the structure of hemoglobin, a protein found in the red blood cell.

A 1994 deportation victory by a Nigerian immigrant brought the health issue of female circumcision to light. Lydia Oluroro won a deportation case in Portland, Oregon. If she had been sent home, her two daughters could have had their clitoris and part of their labia minora cut. Nigerian Americans reacted differently to this decision; some praised it, and others expressed concern that Americans might consider female circumcision a common practice in all of Nigeria. In a similar case in 2003, a federal appeals court upheld the deportation of Doris C. Oforji, a Nigerian illegal alien with two daughters born in the United States.

FAMILY AND COMMUNITY LIFE

Africans in general have strong family commitments. It is traditional in Nigeria to maintain extended families. Unannounced visits are always welcome, and meals are shared even if no prior knowledge of the visit was given. Nigerian Americans continue this tradition. However, as a result of hectic work schedules and economic realities, it is common for Nigerian Americans to make a phone call, e-mail, or text before paying visits to relatives or friends.

Children are required by tradition to be obedient to their parents and other adults. For example, a child can never contradict his or her parents; and the left hand cannot be used to accept money from parents, or as a gesture of respectful communication. Nigerian Americans try to maintain these traditional values, but as a result of peer pressure in American society, young Nigerian Americans resist this type of strict discipline from their parents. Even though children are treated equally in Nigerian American families, girls are usually the center of attention for several reasons. With teenage pregnancies on the rise in the United States, many parents seem to keep a closer eye on their female children. As part of sex education, many Nigerian American parents alert their children, both male and female, to the problem of teenage pregnancy and its ensuing responsibilities.

Gender Roles In a typical Nigerian American family, the man may still be regarded as the official head of household, but the role of women continues to be instrumental. While child care and other household chores may be expected to be equally divided between the husband and wife, there are usually areas

of tension. In his 2012 book, *Nigerian Immigrants in the United States*, Ezekiel Umo Ette relates the story of a Nigerian American couple's realization that in the United States, the husband needed to participate in household and child-rearing duties, since they no longer had help from extended family like they had in Nigeria. Equally important is the role of women not to draw attention of the police to domestic issues. One of Ette's Nigerian American interviewees recounts being "lectured" by her in-laws on the importance of not calling the police on her husband.

Years ago in Nigeria it was traditional for women to stay home and take care of children, but today, both in the United States and in Nigeria, educational opportunities are opened equally to men and women. The areas of specialization are not delineated between the sexes.

> Don't misunderstand me. I love America. The freedom, tolerance, and respect of differences that are a part of everyday public life are some of the first things a visitor to America notices. But I also saw a public school system disconnected from society's most important institution—the family. In Nigeria, with all its political and social problems, the family remains strong, and by doing so helps to define the social and economic expectations of the nation.
>
> Jide Nzelibe, a graduate of St. John's College in Annapolis and Woodrow Wilson School of Public and International Affairs at Princeton University (from "A Nigerian Immigrant Is Shocked by His U.S. High School," *Policy Review*, Fall 1993, p. 43).

Education Nigerian American families believe that education is the key to success in life. Both male and female children are encouraged to attain the highest level of education, whether the parents have a lower level of education or hold terminal degrees or are well established in various professions. The early immigrants were educated people and they instilled in their children the importance of education as a component of a successful life. A May 2008 article in the *Houston Chronicle* reported that Nigerian Americans—both women and men—were the most educated in the United States, with a notably high percentage of them holding at least a master's degree. Indeed, the American Community Survey's estimates for 2011 showed that 28.5 percent of Nigerian Americans over the age of twenty-four held a graduate or professional degree (whereas the rate for the total U.S. population was 10.5 percent). Nigerian Americans also had higher high school graduation rates (97.1 percent held a high school diploma or equivalent, compared to 85.6 percent for the total U.S. population), and a whopping 60.9 percent held a bachelor's degree or higher (compared to 28.2 percent for the total U.S. population).

CHILD-NAMING CEREMONIES

In many Nigerian American homes, the child-naming ceremony is even more important than the baptism.

Among the Igbos, when a child is born, the parents set a time for this ceremony to take place and invite friends, relatives, and well-wishers to the event. Grandmothers traditionally prepare the dish that will be served, but in modern times all the women in the household take part in the food preparation. At the ceremony, benches are arranged in a rectangular form with a lamp placed at the center, and guests are ushered in by the new mother. Kola nuts (the greatest symbol of Igbo hospitality) are served, followed by palm wine. When the guests have had enough to drink, the new mother asks her mother to serve the food, which is usually a combination of rice, *garri*, yams, or *fufu*, and soup and stew made with stock-fish, ordinary fish, meat, and other types of game meat. After the meal, more palm wine is served. The host, usually the most senior man in the household, then repeats one or more proverbs, orders the baby to be brought, and places the baby on his lap. The grandmother gives a name, followed by the child's father, and then the baby's mother. Guests can also suggest names. After more drinking and celebration, the guests depart and the household gathers to review the suggested names and to select one, which becomes the name of the child. Possible Igbo names include *Adachi* (the daughter of God), *Akachukwu* (God's hand), *Nwanyioma* (beautiful lady), and *Ndidikanma* (patience is the best).

The Yoruba naming ceremony takes place on the ninth day after birth for boys, and on the seventh day for girls. Twins are named on the eighth day. By tradition the mother and the child leave the house

Courtship and Weddings Traditionally, in many Nigerian communities, a man marries as many wives as possible. In the United States, where polygamy is illegal, Nigerian American men marry only one wife. While in their native country large families are common, Nigerian Americans have fewer children so that they will be able to give them the best education possible. Nigerian American parents encourage their children to marry people of Nigerian origins. They believe that such marriages can preserve Nigerian identity. They think it will be easier to build better family relationships with people familiar with their culture and traditions. Many want their male children to marry Nigerian women to reduce the chances of divorce. However, it is now common practice for young Nigerian Americans to court whomever they choose.

Different groups in Nigeria have different types of weddings, but usually they are a combination of the traditional and the modern. Among the Yoruba, for example, on the day of the traditional marriage, there is feasting, dancing, and merriment. At nightfall, the senior wives in the family of the groom go to the house of the bride's family to ask for the bride. At the door, the senior wives in the house of the bride ask for a door-opening fee before allowing the other women into the house. In addition to this initial fee, there are several others to be paid—the children's fee, the wives' fee, and the load-carrying fee. The family of the bride must be completely satisfied with the amount of monies given before the bride can be taken away. The senior members of the bride's family pray for and bless her and then release her to the head of the delegation.

A senior wife from the groom's family carries the bride on her back to the new husband's home. The feet of the new wife have to be cleaned before she can enter the house. This symbolizes that the new wife is prepared to start a completely new life.

In the United States, the traditional marriage ceremonies seem to be fading, but many Nigerian Americans continue to perform them at home and then hold a Western-type wedding in a church or a court of law. When there are no close relatives of the bride and the groom in the United States, friends take on the roles of the various participants in the traditional wedding. After the traditional wedding, if the couple practices Christianity, the ceremony is performed according to the tradition of the church. Friends, relatives, and well-wishers from the home country and across the United States are invited to the ceremony. Although many guests may stay in hotels, according to the African tradition of hospitality, friends and relatives of the couple living in the immediate surroundings will house and feed the visitors free of charge. The accompanying wedding reception is a stupendous feast of African cuisine, traditional and modern music and dancing, and an ostentatious display of both African and American costumes.

Funerals The African concept of death is that it is a transition, not an end. Igbo, Yoruba, and Hausa people, including those who practice Christianity and Islam, believe in reincarnation. Even though Western education and religion may have changed many traditional African beliefs, many Nigerian Americans hold on to those beliefs. Thus, if a person dies, he or she is for the first time on the day the naming ceremony takes place. Relatives, friends, and well-wishers join together to eat, drink, and make merry. Gifts are lavished on the newborn and the parents. An elder performs the naming ceremony using Kola nuts, a bowl of water, pepper, oil, salt, honey, and liquor. Each of these items stands for a special life symbol: Kola nuts are for good fortune; water symbolizes purity; oil symbolizes power and health; salt symbolizes intelligence and wisdom; honey symbolizes happiness, and liquor stands for wealth and prosperity. The baby tastes each of the above, as do all the people present. The name of the child is chosen before the ceremony. After dipping his hand in a bowl of water, the person officiating at the ceremony touches the forehead of the baby and whispers the name into the baby's ears, and then shouts it aloud for all around to hear. Some Yoruba names are *Jumoke* (loved by all), *Amonke* (to know her is to pet her), *Modupe* (thanks), *Foluke* (in the hands of God), and *Ajayi* (born face-down). Nigerian Americans preserve the traditional ceremonies, modifying as needed. For example, an older relative or friend plays the role of the grandmother when the real grandmother of the child is unable to be present.

After the traditional naming ceremony, if the family is Christian, another day is set aside for the child to be baptized in church. Hausa children born to Islamic parents are given personal names of Muslim origin. The Muslim name is often followed by the father's given name. Surnames have been adopted by a few Hausa people, especially those educated abroad. Some given Hausa names are *Tanko* (a boy born after successive girls), *Labaran* (a boy born in the month of the Ramadan), *Gagare* (unconquerable), and *Afere* (a girl born tiny).

born into another life completely different from the one he or she had. In addition to our visible world, there is believed to be another world where ancestors dwell and exert influence on the daily activities of the living. In many Nigerian societies, when a person dies, the entire community becomes aware of the death almost immediately. Wailing and crying from family members and unrelated people fill the town or village where the death occurs.

Funeral traditions vary in Nigeria according to group. For example, among the Kalabari people of eastern Nigeria, unless a person dies at childbirth or from what are considered abominable causes such as witchcraft or drowning, every adult receives an *Ede* funeral, which consists of laying the body in state and the chief female mourners donning a particular costume called *iria*. Traditionally the dead were buried the day after death. In the case of an older person, a whole week of ceremonial mourning was set aside. In modern times, the dead are kept in the mortuary up to eight weeks or more so that elaborate preparations can take place and relatives both local and abroad can come to the funeral. The initial wake is usually held on a Friday, and the burial takes places on a Saturday. After elaborate traditional burial ceremonies, those who practice Christianity are taken to the church for the established funeral rites before the corpses are taken to the cemetery. A week after that the final wake is held on a Friday, and the funeral dance and ceremonies on a Saturday. The day of the final funeral is filled with elaborate activities; relatives of the dead person dress up in expensive garments.

Many Nigerian Americans prefer to be buried in Nigeria when they die. For this reason they buy enough life insurance to cover the transportation of their bodies home. It is also common practice for Nigerian Americans to belong to societies within their communities where people, through monthly or annual dues, aid each other in times of hard economic expenditures, such as deaths and funerals. Bodies in the United States are usually kept in the funeral homes till the wake is done. When the body is flown home, in addition to the traditional burial ceremonies, Nigerian Americans who practice Christianity will be buried according to established rites. Nigerian American Muslims whose bodies are sent home are buried according to the Islamic tradition. Even though cremation is becoming a common and a more economical way of burial both within and outside of the United States, Nigerian Americans, like many of their counterparts in the African American community, have not embraced this funeral rite. The grandiosity of saying goodbye to a loved one has to be done while the deceased physical body can be seen by all. Most importantly, in the minds of Nigerian Americans, "burning" a loved one is very much against nature.

Interactions with Other Ethnic Groups
Nigerian Americans interact with other ethnic minorities and the community as a whole, though most Nigerian Americans will first seek out people from their own tribes. At one time, as a result of the Nigerian Civil War (or Biafran War), Nigerian Americans from the Yoruba tribe would not interact with others from the Igbo tribe and vice versa; but this situation has

improved in contemporary times. Interaction exists between Nigerian Americans and people from other African countries such as Ghana, Ethiopia, Kenya, and Uganda. Most Africans in the United States see themselves as brothers and sisters, since they all left their home countries to come here. There are some Nigerian Americans who prefer not to interact with people of their own heritage. There have been many cases of fraud, crime, and drug smuggling involving Nigerian Americans, and some Nigerian Americans want to avoid any implication in such criminal cases.

EMPLOYMENT AND ECONOMIC CONDITIONS

Early Nigerian Americans came to the United States to study, acquired terminal degrees, and returned home. Since then, many Nigerians have pursued studies in the United States and then settled here permanently. Through their status as U.S. citizens or permanent residents, some Nigerian Americans have been able to acquire prestigious jobs in academia and other professions. Nigerian Americans without such academic qualifications accept jobs in various sectors of society. It is also common for Nigerian immigrants to establish their own businesses in the United States. For many, trading in Nigerian and other African costumes has become a profitable business. This requires traveling between Nigeria and the United States to arrange importation of items. In large U.S. cities, it is not uncommon to find Nigerian and other African restaurants and grocery stores owned and operated by Nigerian Americans. Nigerian Americans have also

established small businesses such as travel agencies, parking lots, taxi stands, cultural exchange programs, and health and life insurance agencies. Even though they target the general population for their clientele, Nigerian American business owners also invest time in acquiring Nigerian and other African clientele.

In the United States, the medical, engineering, legal, and many other top professional areas are filled with people of Nigerian descent, both male and female. On their own initiative, or under pressure from their parents, young Nigerian Americans pursue higher degrees in these prestigious professions.

The U.S. Census Bureau's American Community Survey estimated in 2011 that, among employed Nigerian Americans ages sixteen and older, 48.7 percent had jobs in management, business, science, and arts occupations. This was higher than the rate of the overall U.S. population (35.9 percent). A significant proportion of Nigerian Americans, 43.2 percent, were employed in education, health care, and social assistance jobs (compared to 23.1 percent for the total U.S. population). Nigerian Americans' median household income stood at $54,546 (slightly higher than the total U.S. population's median of $51,484). The economic recession that began in 2008 did not affect well-educated Nigerian Americans in any significant manner.

POLITICS AND GOVERNMENT

Nigerian Americans as a group do not have political clout in the United States. They do work in small groups through established associations or where they

Guests dressed in the ceremonial robes of the Yoruba Tribe arrive at a wedding in Santa Ana, California. MARMADUKE ST. JOHN/ALAMY

reside to raise political consciousness when appropriate issues arise. When the press in the United States reports sensational stories that create stereotypical impressions about Nigeria, Nigerian Americans react by uniting to correct such impressions.

Nigerian Americans maintain a high sense of pride for their country. They remain attached to Nigeria no matter how long they stay away from it. Many go home to visit occasionally while others make a visit to the motherland an annual obligation.

When Nigerians first came to the United States, they would often gather with other African students to promote nationalism and protest against colonial domination in their homeland. In contemporary times, Nigerian Americans have been vociferous in protesting against injustice and despotic rule in Nigeria. In 1989, when Nigeria's military leader, Ibrahim Babaginda, summarily dissolved several groups that aspired to be registered as political parties to compete in elections, Nigerian Americans throughout the United States held demonstrations to protest against this act of despotism. In 1993, when Babangida refused to accept the June elections and proposed a second election in August, Nigerian Americans added their voice to the international protest. As the political situation in Nigeria remains in turmoil, Nigerian Americans have constantly expressed themselves and worked to ensure that justice prevails.

In 2011 there was a protest held in front of the Nigerian Consulate in New York in objection to the condemnation of homosexual marriage in Nigeria. In December 2012, the Christian Association of Nigerian-Americans (CANAN) mobilized thousands of Americans to sign a petition to ask President Barack Obama to declare Boko Haram, the jihadist group from northeastern Nigeria, as a terrorist organization.

Nigerian Americans forge strong ties with their motherland. Working with both private and governmental groups, Nigerian Americans have succeeded in organizing exchanges between businesspeople in the United States and Nigeria. Individual organizations also pool their resources to assist their motherland. A good example is the Network of Nigerian Engineers and Scientists, whose members sometimes offer free services to the government of Nigeria. As a result of these efforts, there has been a boost in trade between the United States and Nigeria as well as increased tourism in Nigeria. African American tourists visit Nigeria in huge numbers every year to explore their heritage.

NOTABLE INDIVIDUALS

Academia Bartholomew Nnaji (1957–) is known as one of the world's top scientists in the fields of robotics. He came to the United States on an athletic scholarship in 1977. After earning a PhD from Virginia Polytechnic Institute, he taught at the College of Engineering of the University of Massachusetts, Amherst, from 1983 to 1996. He was then appointed

A Nigerian store owner in Harlem, New York. AP PHOTO / BEBETO MATTHEWS

a professor at the University of Pittsburgh. Nnaji has won many awards, including the 1988 Young Manufacturing Engineering Award and the 2004 Nigerian Order of Merit, the nation's highest intellectual recognition.

Victor Ukpolo (1950–), born in Lagos, Nigeria, became the chancellor of the Southern University of New Orleans (SUNO) in 2006, shortly after Hurricane Katrina hit New Orleans in 2005. During the hurricane SUNO was severely damaged. Ukpolo led an aggressive and progressive campaign to restore all the damaged buildings and build two additional structures.

Toyin Falola (1953–) is a historian, writer, and professor of African studies. Falola became a professor at the University of Texas, Austin, in 1991. He has authored and edited numerous books, including *A History of Nigeria* (2008; with Matthew M. Heaton), *The Women's War of 1929: A History of Anti-colonial Resistance in Eastern Nigeria* (2011; with Adam Paddock), and a memoir, *A Mouth Sweeter than Salt* (2005). Falola has served on the Library of Congress' Scholars Council.

Art Toyin Odutola (1986–), artist, was born in Nigeria and studied art in the United States. Her intricate drawings have been exhibited in various places, including the Studio Museum in Harlem, and are included in the collections of museums such as the National Museum of African Art in Washington, D.C. In 2012 she was included in *Forbes* magazine's "30 Under 30," a feature highlighting accomplished young individuals in various fields.

Marcia Kure (1970–), born in Kano, Nigeria, is a painter and a performance artist who has had artist residencies in Atlanta; Bayreuth, Germany; Tampa, Florida, and other places. Her work has been exhibited all over the world. She began residing in the United States in 2000. The themes of her work include political violence, the plight of women, and motherhood. She has been commissioned by several agencies of the United Nations to design calendars for various occasions.

Film Femi Agbayewa (1966–), produced the film *God's Own Country* (2007), which depicts the plight of the immigrant in America. Based in New York, Agbayewa worked for a trucking company while he produced this impactful movie that combines American and traditional African themes.

Early Nigerian Americans came to the United States to study, acquired terminal degrees, and returned home. Since then, many Nigerians have pursued studies in the United States and then settled here permanently. Through their status as U.S. citizens or permanent residents, some Nigerian Americans have been able to acquire prestigious jobs in academia and other professions.

Government Bumi Awoniyi (1965–) is an expert in family and immigration law who practiced law in England before migrating to the United States. She was admitted to the California State Bar in 1991 and was appointed a judge by California governor Jerry Brown in 2012.

Journalism Folosade (Sade) Olayinka Baderinwa (1969–), an Emmy Award–winning television news anchor, is the daughter of a Nigerian father and a German mother. She has worked as a co-anchor at New York's WABC Channel 7.

Literature Michael Chikelu Mbabuike (1943–2006) authored many books and pieces of poetry, both in English and French. After completing his bachelor's degree at the University of Nsukka in Nigeria, he went to the University of Sorbonne, France, for his MA and PhD in literature. He migrated to the United States in the 1970s. Mbabuike was the director of the Center for Igbo Studies and chair of African studies at the City University of New York's Hostos Community College. He remained active in the African Studies Association in New York and around the world.

Music O. J. (Orlando Julius) Ekemode (1942–), born in Ijebu-Ijesha in Nigeria, started playing drums at age eight. His combination of traditional African music with contemporary jazz, religious, reggae, Afro-beat, and soul music in the fashion of James Brown has made him one of the living legends of real African music in the United States. Orlando Julius continues to entertain the Nigerian American community in the United States, as well as Nigerians elsewhere in the diaspora. His tours outside the United States have included performances in Germany and the United Kingdom.

Ralph Victor Folarin (1984–), a rapper better known as Wale, was raised in Washington, D.C., by Yoruba immigrant parents. He gained attention with his 2006 hit song "Dig Dug (Shake It)." His recognitions include BET's Best Collaboration Award in 2012, the Best New Artist Award (2010) at the Soul Train Awards, and a Grammy nomination in 2013 for his song "Lotus Flower Bomb."

Science and Medicine John O. Agwunobi (1954–) served as the secretary of Florida's State Health Department from 2001 to 2005. He was appointed by the Bush administration to be the assistant secretary for health in the U.S. Department of Health and Human Services and served as an admiral of the U.S. Public Health Service in 2005. He advocated for empowering the ordinary citizen to become familiar with over-the-counter medications as an asset to improving their health. In 2010 he was named director of the National Association of Chain Drug Stores.

Sports Hakeem Olajuwon (1963–), affectionately known as Akeem, led the University of Houston to three consecutive trips to the Final Four of the NCAA basketball tournament. Olajuwon subsequently led the Houston Rockets to NBA titles in 1994 and 1995. He was elected to the Naismith Memorial Basketball Hall of Fame as a member of the class of 2008. *SLAM* magazine ranked him thirteenth among the top fifty greatest basketball players of all time.

Donald Igwebuike (1961–) kicked five years for the Tampa Bay Buccaneers football team; when he was released in September 1990, he was picked up by the Minnesota Vikings for the 1990 football season. Soon afterward he was arrested and charged with being an accomplice to heroin trafficking, but he was later acquitted.

Christian Okoye (1961–), known as the "Nigerian Nightmare," was a running back for the Kansas City Chiefs from 1987 to 1992. His sports career in the United States started when he came from Nigeria on a track scholarship to Azusa Pacific University in 1982. Okoye was the NFL's leading rusher in 1989.

MEDIA

PRINT

The African Sun Times

Formerly the *Nigerian Times*, this newspaper bills itself as "America's only African weekly newspaper on newsstands. Now online."

Chika A. Onyeani, Editor
368 Broadway
Suite 307
New York, New York 10013
Phone: (212) 791-0777
URL: http://africansuntimes.com

ORGANIZATIONS AND ASSOCIATIONS

Christian Association of Nigerian-Americans (CANAN)

Formed in 2012 by a group of U.S.-based Nigerian Christian leaders and professionals, CANAN aims to represent Nigerian American Christians and their interests, views, and causes.

Pastor James Fadele
P.O. Box 1041
Bay Shore, New York 11706
Phone: (631) 647-3465
Email: contactus@cananusa.org
URL: www.cananusa.org

National Council of Nigerian Muslim Organizations in the USA

Initially founded in 1976, the NCNMO has six chapters. It strives to help strengthen Muslim communities through religious, social, educational, and charitable activities.

P.O. Box 91736
Washington, D.C. 20090
Phone: (832) 359-4202
Email: ncnmo@nmnationalcouncil.org
URL: www.nmnationalcouncil.org

Nigerian American Public Professionals Association

The NAPPA promotes social culture, economic, and professional development among members through various educational seminars, workshops, conferences, and publications.

Vitto Eneji-Okoye
28 East Jackson Boulevard
Chicago, Illinois 60604
Phone: (773) 933-0427
Email: vokoye@ameritech.net

Nigerian Healthcare Foundation

The Nigerian Healthcare Foundation was founded by a group of Nigerian Americans to provide medical services to people living in Nigeria and improve the country's health care conditions.

Ijeoma Obilo
P.O. Box 4070
Wayne, New Jersey 07470
Phone: (973) 831-0080
Email: info@nhfinc.org
URL: www.nhfinc.org

MUSEUMS AND RESEARCH CENTERS

African American Museum in Philadelphia

Maintains a vast collection of African sculpture and artifacts relating to Africa and the slave trade. Nigeria is well represented in the collection.

701 Arch Street
Philadelphia, Pennsylvania 19106-1557
Phone: (215) 574-0380
Fax: (215) 574-3110
Email: info@aampmuseum.org
URL: www.aampmuseum.org

National Museum of African Art

Part of the Smithsonian Institution, the museum has more than 6,000 objects of African art in wood, metal, ceramic, ivory, and fiber. Its collection of Nigerian art is extensive.

Johnnetta Betsch Cole, Director
950 Independence Avenue SW
Washington, D.C. 20560
Phone: (202) 357-4600
Fax: (202) 357-4879
Email: nmafaweb@si.edu
URL: http://africa.si.edu/

SOURCES FOR ADDITIONAL STUDY

Arthur, John A.; Joseph Takougang; and Thomas Y. Owusu. *Africans in Global Migration: Searching for Promised Lands.* Lanham, MD: Lexington Books, 2012.

Burns, Sir Alan. *History of Nigeria.* London: George Allen and Unwin Ltd.,1929; reprinted, 1976.

Casimir, Leslie. "Data Show Nigerians the Most Educated in the U.S." *Houston Chronicle,* May 20, 2008.

Ette, Ezekiel Umo. *Nigerian Immigrants in the United States: Race, Identity, and Acculturation.* Lanham, MD: Lexington Books, 2012.

Kalu, Ogbu, et al. *Religions in Africa: Conflicts, Politics and Social Ethics.* Trenton NJ: Africa World Press, 2010. Print.

Koepping, Elizabeth. *World Christianity.* London; New York: Routledge, 2011.

Obi, Samuel C. *Readings for Amerigerian Igbo: Culture, History, Language, and Legacy.* Bloomington, IN: Authorhouse, 2010.

Obiakor, Festus E., and Patrick A. Grant. *Foreign-Born African Americans: Silenced Voices in the Discourse on Race.* Huntington, NY: Nova Science Publishers, 2005.

Olupona, Jacob Obafemi Kehinde, and Regina Gemignani. *African Immigrant Religions in America.* New York: New York University Press, 2007.

NORWEGIAN AMERICANS

Odd S. Lovoll

OVERVIEW

Norwegian Americans are immigrants or the descendants of people from Norway, a country occupying the western part of the Scandinavian Peninsula in northwestern Europe, sharing borders with Sweden, Finland, and Russia. The country measures 1,095 miles from south to north, and one-third of its land mass lies north of the Arctic Circle, extending farther north than any other European country. Norway is slightly larger than the state of New Mexico, measuring 125,181 square miles (323,878 square kilometers).

According to Norway's Bureau of Statistics, in 2011 the country's population was 5,033,675, except for a minority of indigenous Sami (estimated at no more than 40,000) confined mainly to the northern half of the country. About 655,000 residents, or 13 percent of the total population, were either immigrants or children of two immigrants; about half had backgrounds from Europe, 34 percent from Asia, 12 percent from Africa, 3 percent from South and Central America, and nearly 2 percent from North America. In the early twenty-first century, Norway considered itself a multicultural society. Almost 80 percent of the inhabitants belonged to the Evangelical Lutheran Church, which in 2012 lost its distinction as a state church. Five percent were members of other Christian denominations and faiths, the largest of which was the Catholic Church, and 10 percent had no religious affiliation; among non-Christian religions, Islam was the largest. Norway's form of government is a hereditary constitutional monarchy. The capital city is Oslo. The national flag displayed a central blue cross with a white border on a red field. Norwegian is the official language, rendered in two different literary forms, the predominant *bokmål* (Dano-Norwegian) and the rural dialect-based *nynorsk* (New Norse). By the early twenty-first century, Norway was one of the world's most prosperous nations.

Norwegian overseas emigration began earlier than in the other Nordic lands, commencing dramatically on July 4, 1825, with the sailing of the tiny sloop *Restauration*, but annual immigration—during which large numbers of families set sail for the United States in the summer months—did not commence until 1836. Norwegian immigrants showed a strong bond to a rural way of life, and a commitment to farming was an idiosyncratic quality of Norwegians in America. They were in fact the most rural of any nineteenth-century immigrant group, and the rural attachment was passed to U.S.-born generations. The upper Midwest became the home of the majority of Norwegians. They also entered the professions and found employment in a variety of occupations in cities such as Chicago and Minneapolis, and also formed colonies in Brooklyn, New York, and Seattle, Washington. By the early twenty-first century, one could well conclude that a Norwegian tradition of immigrating to the United States belonged largely to the past.

By 2010, according to the U.S. Census, the number of Norwegian-born residents of the United States had fallen to 25,854, while 4,602,337 Americans claimed Norwegian ancestry. Emigration from its beginning in 1825 until the early twenty-first century totaled some 900,000 people. Of total emigration, 87 percent, or 780,000, Norwegians left in the period between 1865 and 1930, with the vast majority settling in the United States. By the early twenty-first century, there were no longer any Norwegian enclaves or neighborhoods in the United States' great cities.

HISTORY OF THE PEOPLE

Early History Norway (Old Norse: *Norvegr* or *Noregr*) designates the sea-lane as the "north way" along the country's extensive coastline as viewed from the south. Maritime connections west and south have, as a consequence of Norway's geography, characterized its history. During the Viking Age (800–1030), expansive forces moved the Norse Vikings to the historical stage of Europe; their westward expansion extended to Iceland, Greenland, and even to the continent of North America. Some time before 890, Harald Finehair consolidated Norway under the Yngling dynasty. The martyrdom of King Olav II of this royal line on July 29, 1030, at the Battle of Stiklestad made him Norway's patron saint, secured a national monarchy, and established the Christian church as a dominant institution.

Medieval Norway attained its political height under the reign of Haakon IV Haakonson (1217–1263), with territorial dominance to the western islands (the Orkneys, Shetlands, Hebrides, Isle of Man, and Faroe Islands), Iceland, and Greenland, and

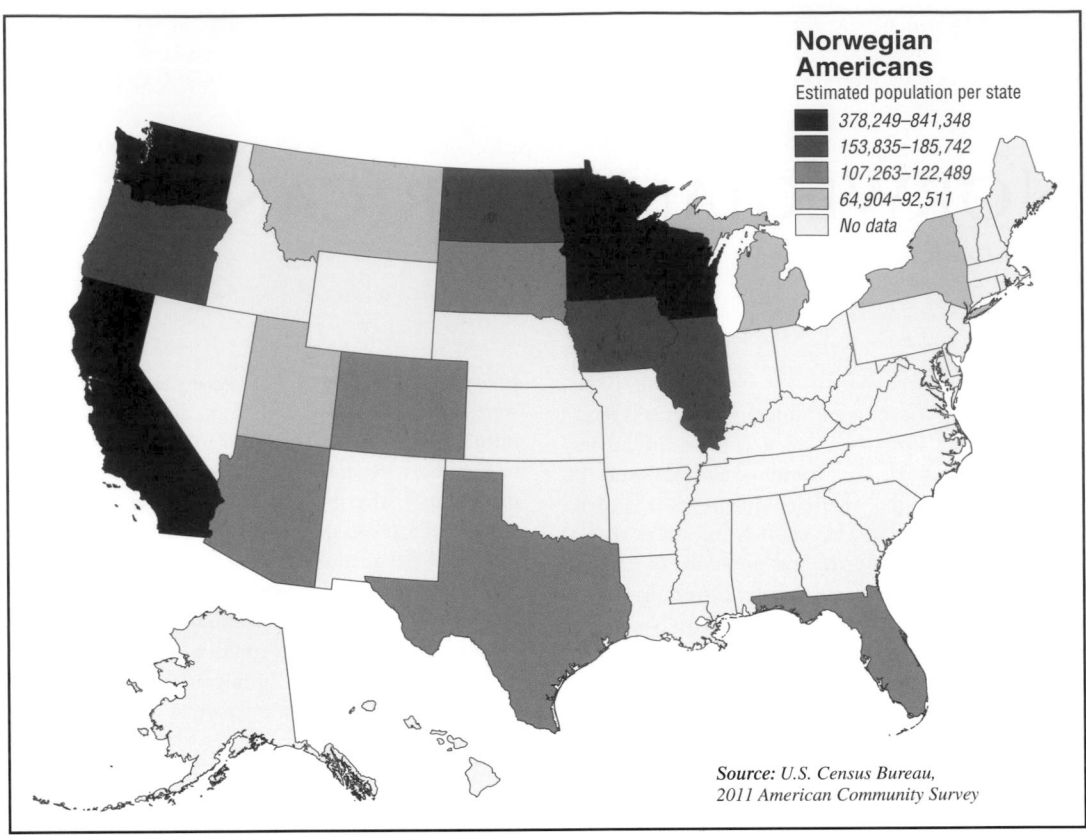

Norwegian Americans
Estimated population per state
378,249–841,348
153,835–185,742
107,263–122,489
64,904–92,511
No data

*Source: U.S. Census Bureau,
2011 American Community Survey*

three districts in present-day Sweden. It was then that Norway entered fully into close diplomatic and commercial relations with other European states.

Norwegian national decline manifested itself in dynastic unions with the two other Scandinavian nations, Sweden and Denmark. The bubonic plague that ravaged Europe in the mid-fourteenth century hit Norway, a country with greater poverty and fewer natural resources than the other Nordic lands, especially hard. Norway's population was devastated, resulting in a serious loss of income for the great landowners, the church, and the king. The last king of an independent and sovereign Norway died in 1380, and Norway then united with Denmark. In 1397 the three Scandinavian states were joined under one ruler in the Kalmar Union; in the case of Norway the union with Denmark lasted until 1814. The Lutheran Reformation in 1537 resulted in Norway's reduction in administrative arrangements to a province within the Danish state. The idea of Norway as an independent kingdom, however, remained alive throughout the union period and was evidenced in the term "the twin realms."

Modern Era The big power politics following the Napoleonic wars yielded a national rebirth. Rejecting the terms of the Treaty of Kiel, which transferred Norway to the king of Sweden, a constituent assembly meeting north of Oslo at Eidsvoll on May 17, 1814, signed a constitution establishing a limited and hereditary monarchy, and declared Norway's independence. Mindful of their pledge to the Swedish throne but also not wishing to quell Norwegian moves toward independence, the European powers endorsed a compromise that established a union under the Swedish king. The union preserved the Eidsvoll constitution and was based on the will of the Norwegian people rather than the Treaty of Kiel.

The Act of Union signed in 1815 declared, in principle, an equal partnership in the double monarchy of Sweden and Norway. In reality, however, Norway held an inferior position. Politically Norway feared Swedish encroachment and sought full equality in the union. Culturally the new nation struggled against Danish hegemony—a result of the four-hundred-year union—and engaged in a quest for national identity and cultural independence. There was a surge of nationalism, which was expressed in an idealized and romantic cultivation of the peasantry as the true carriers of the national spirit. Norway's ultimate goal was a separate and respected national status within the Nordic nations. In 1905 the union with Sweden ended after a dispute over foreign affairs, centering on Norway's demand for an independent consular service. The union was unnatural from the start with few, if any, positive elements linking the two countries.

Prince Carl of Denmark was elected King of Norway in 1905, taking the name Haakon VII, which linked him to the old Norwegian royal line. The first half-century of full independence witnessed a rapid transformation from a mainly agricultural society to an industrialized and commercial one. The laboring classes gained political influence, and from the mid-1930s the Norwegian Labor Party formed the government. German occupation from 1940 to 1945 suspended the party's political agenda, but in the postwar era it resumed power and transformed Norway into a prosperous social-democratic welfare state. The discovery of petroleum resources west of Norway in 1969 guaranteed substantial future prosperity. By the early twenty-first century, Norway was one of the world's most prosperous nations. In foreign affairs, the country abandoned its historically neutral stance and joined the western alliance in the North Atlantic Treaty Organization (NATO) in 1949. Norway was a founding member of the European Free Trade Association (EFTA) in 1960. Two referendums (in 1972 and 1994) on joining the European Union failed by narrow margins; however, Norway was part of EFTA' s successor, the European Economic Area, which included European Union countries

SETTLEMENT IN THE UNITED STATES

The first Norwegian immigrants to the United States numbered only fifty-three (with a baby born during the crossing), having set sail on the small sloop *Restauration* from Stavanger on the southwestern coast of Norway. The so-called Sloopers arrived in New York harbor on October 9, 1825; assisted by the kindly services of American Quakers, most went to Orleans County in western New York state and settled in what became Kendall Township. There was a strong religious motivation in the pioneer emigration, which was not significant in the later emigration: the Sloopers were Quakers, Quaker sympathizers, and dissenters in opposition to the religiously monopolistic position of the Norwegian Lutheran state church. In the mid-1830s the Kendall settlers gave impetus to the westward movement of Norwegians by founding a settlement in the Fox River area of Illinois. A small urban colony of Norwegians had its genesis in Chicago at about the same time.

Immigrant settlements were then ready to welcome Norwegian newcomers, who, beginning in 1836, arrived annually. The Norwegian exodus rose in the 1840s; by 1865, nearly 80,000 Norwegians had entered the United States. The "America fever" had moved from the southwestern coastal areas along the western coast and inland to the central highland region. Even though no part of Norway was entirely untouched by the overseas movement, the majority of emigrants in this founding phase came from the inner fjord districts in western Norway and the mountain valleys of eastern Norway. It was an emigration of rural folk mostly consisting of families. They were economic emigrants—people leaving the straitened circumstances in the homeland caused by rapid population growth and limited opportunities for a new and better life in America for themselves and their descendants. Land and the opportunity to reestablish themselves as farmers in a new rural setting held great appeal. As a result, the character of the immigrant community that evolved in the United States reflected traditions, mores, and religious as well as secular values of their districts in the old country and conveyed strong familial and communal bonds.

From the Fox River settlement in Illinois, Norwegian pioneers followed the general spread of population northwestward into Wisconsin. Wisconsin remained the center of Norwegian American activity until the Civil War. The end of the Civil War brought about a great increase in Atlantic crossings. The number of Norwegian emigrants leaped from 4,000 in 1865 to 15,726 in 1866, heralding the era of mass migration. This mass migration occurred until 1873; in the course of the previous eight years, some 110,000 Norwegians had left their homeland. The second, and also greatest, period of emigration lasted fourteen years, from 1880 to 1893, when an average of 18,290 emigrants left annually—ten for every one thousand Norwegians—for a total of about 264,600. During this period Norway's emigration intensity was the second greatest in Europe, surpassed only by that of Ireland. Norway experienced a final mass exodus in the first fourteen years of the twentieth century, when 214,985 Norwegians left the homeland. There was considerable emigration in the 1920s as well; 88,520 Norwegians emigrated in that decade. Emigration from its beginning totaled some 900,000 people. Of the total emigration, 87 percent, or about 780,000 Norwegians, left in the period between 1865 and 1930.

> A newcomer from Norway who arrives here will be surprised indeed to find in the heart of the country, more than a thousand miles from his landing place, a town where language and way of life so unmistakably remind him of his native land.
>
> Svein Nilsson, a Norwegian American journalist (in *Billed-Magazin*, May 14, 1870).

In the nineteenth century, Norwegian emigrants headed almost exclusively for the United States. Only after 1900 did other overseas areas, especially Canada, attract substantial number of Norwegians. However, the United States remained the most popular destination. Emigration dominated by families gradually changed in the last quarter of the nineteenth century to an emigration largely of individuals. Although young male laborers constituted the majority, single young women also moved overseas in large numbers; statistics show that between 1866 and 1940, women accounted for 41 percent of the total overseas movement. Emigrants came from the cities as well as the countryside, though the rural exodus was by far the larger. From the 1880s, young people with education and technical training joined the masses who traveled to the United States.

Improved transportation facilitated by steam passenger liners, allowed people to move back and forth across the Atlantic, yielding a two-way migration. The Norwegian Bureau of Statistics estimated that about 25 percent of the immigrants to North America between 1881 and 1930 resettled in Norway. The Great Depression and World War II impeded further emigration until 1945. The postwar emigration never attained great numbers, peaking in 1952, when close to three thousand emigrants departed for the United States. After that time there was a noticeable decline from decade to decade. From 1945 until the early twenty-first century, a total of about fifty thousand Norwegians had moved to the United States and around ten thousand to Canada. Still, as of 2010 there were 4,602,337 residents of Norwegian ancestry in the United States, nearly as many as in the home country.

The history of Norwegian settlement in America is a tale of dynamic change over time. In the 1850s Norwegian land seekers began moving into both Iowa and Minnesota, both directly from Norway and from older settlements in Wisconsin and Illinois, and noticeable migration to North and South Dakota was under way by the 1870s. The majority of Norwegian agrarian settlements developed in the northern region of the so-called Homestead Act Triangle, between the Mississippi and Missouri rivers. The Norwegians took up farming or settled in the many country towns that dotted the landscape. In 1900, according to the federal census, 49.8 percent of all Norwegian-born heads of household were engaged in agriculture as owners or renters of farms or as agricultural laborers. As many as 54.3 percent of the children of immigrants were farmers. No other nationality came close to this concentration on agriculture. As the composition of immigrants changed and their destination increasingly became urban areas and as people moved to the cities from farming communities, the percentage of Norwegians engaged in agriculture declined; however, as recently as 1990, when their occupational composition was not significantly different from other Americans of European ancestry, Norwegian Americans were still somewhat overrepresented in the industry group of "farming, forestry, and fishing."

The upper Midwest became the home for most Norwegian immigrants. In 1910 almost 80 percent of the one million or more Norwegian Americans—the immigrants and their children—lived in that part of the United States. By the early twenty-first century, about half of the Norwegian American population lived in the Midwest. In 2010 about 17 percent of the population in Minnesota, 30 percent in North Dakota, 15 percent in South Dakota, and 8 percent in Wisconsin were of Norwegian ancestry. Because of its location in the center of Norwegian settlement, from the 1890s Minneapolis functioned as a Norwegian American "capital" for secular and religious activities. It replaced Chicago, which actually housed a much larger colony of first- and second-generation Norwegians. The building trades employed urban Norwegian men; in Chicago specifically shipping on the Great Lakes also attracted Norwegian men. Young single women frequently entered domestic service. In addition, Norwegians entered business enterprises of many kinds and worked in industries created by compatriots, the latter much in evidence in Chicago.

The Pacific Northwest—especially the Puget Sound region and the cities of Tacoma and Seattle—became another center of immigrant life. Fishing, in addition to other common urban trades, became the livelihood of many Norwegians there. Norwegian Americans also developed the halibut industry in Alaska, where they also engaged in shipping. Enclaves of Norwegians emerged as well in greater Brooklyn, New York, and Texas. Bay Ridge in Brooklyn had the largest Norwegian colony on the eastern seaboard; its success depended on a high concentration of Norwegians.

By 2010 the largest concentration of Norwegian Americans was in Minnesota, followed by Wisconsin, then California, Washington, and North Dakota.

LANGUAGE

The Norwegian language, along with Danish and Swedish, belongs to the mutually comprehensible northern branch of the Germanic family of languages. During the centuries-long union with Denmark, Norwegians accepted Danish as their written language. Following independence in 1814, efforts to provide a national written standard created conflict between those who worked for a gradual "Norwegianization" of Danish orthographic forms and those who wished to create a totally new written language. The Norwegian government officially recognized the existence of the predominant *bokmål* (Dano-Norwegian), which continued the Danish written tradition greatly modified through a series of reforms under the influence of Norwegian speech habits, and *nynorsk* (New Norse), which was constructed on the basis of modern dialects and most faithfully preserved the forms of Old Norse. Because of the isolated nature of Norwegian rural communities, the local vernacular was distinct, with marked dialectal differences from one district to the next.

The cultural baggage of Norwegian immigrants included their specific local dialect and a Danish literary language. The latter played a significant role in the immigrant community, attaining a nearly sacred quality. It was the language of their secular and religious institutions and of sacred and profane literature. The immigrants had little appreciation for the linguistic reforms in the homeland; often such changers were viewed as a betrayal to a common cultural heritage. A series of official reforms of the written language in the early twentieth century in Norway made the older form even more difficult to retain in the United States. A newspaper such as *Decorah-Posten* in Decorah, Iowa, persisted in using a Dano-Norwegian orthographic tradition from the 1870s well into the 1950s. The situation created confusion among teachers of Norwegian at American high schools, colleges, and universities, who felt obligations to the language of the immigrant community; only just before World War II did they in principle agree to teach the written standard—generally the Dano-Norwegian *bokmål*, the official written language in Norway.

English was another threat to the maintenance of the Norwegian language in America. Rural settlement patterns protected spoken Norwegian, and it can still be heard in some Norwegian American communities. According to researcher Joshua A. Fishman, about half of second-generation Norwegians from 1940 to 1960 learned the language, and in 1960 there were as many as 40,000 of the third generation who had learned Norwegian. As of 1990, about 80,000 speakers of Norwegian remained in the United States, and in Minnesota, Norwegian was the second-most common European language, with 16,000 speakers, after German. Those number were thought to have dropped steeply by the early twenty-first century, and only one bilingual newspaper, the *Norwegian American Weekly*, of Seattle, remained. The *bygdelag* (Norwegian regional societies) promoted the use of rural vernaculars, and indeed, their annual reunions provided an environment where rural speech was honored and encouraged. It was, however, a mixed language, with English words and phrases integrated into it.

Greetings and Popular Expressions

Good afternoon/How do you do? *God dag* ("gooDAAG").

Good-bye. *Adjø* ("adyur").

How are you? *Hvordan står det til?* ("VOORdahn stawr deh til").

Just fine, thanks. *Bare bra, takk* ("BAArer braa tahk").

Thank you. *Takk* ("tahk").

Thank you very much. *Mange takk* ("MAHNger tahk").

Cheers. *Skål* ("skawl").

Merry Christmas. *God jul!* ("goo yewl").

Happy New Year *Godt nyttår* ("got newt awr").

Congratulations *Gratulerer!* ("grahtewLAYrerr").

RELIGION

The Norwegian Lutheran Church was a focal point and conservative force in rural settlements in the upper midwest well into the twentieth century. The congregation became an all-encompassing institution for its members, creating a tight social network that touched all aspects of immigrant life. The force of tradition in religious practice made the church a central institution

NORWEGIAN PROVERBS

Norwegians tend to integrate sayings and proverbs into daily conversations. Some common expressions include the following:

Det er ikke gull alt som glimrer, det kan også være diamanter.

> All is not gold that glitters; it can also be diamonds.

Brent barn skyr ilden.

> A burnt child avoids the fire.

Kjære barn gis mange navn.

> A dear child has many names.

I mørket er alle katter grå.

> All cats are gray in the dark.

Renslighet er en dyd, sa kjærringa, hun snudde serken sin julekvelden.

> "Cleanliness is a virtue," said the old woman, who turned her slip inside out every Christmas Eve.

Smuler er også brød.

> Crumbs are also bread.

Tomme tønner buldrer mest.

> Empty barrels make the most noise.

Mange bekker små gjør en stor å.

> Many small brooks make a big river.

in the urban environment, as well. The severe reality of urban life increased the social role of the church.

In the unbridled freedom of the vast United States, Norwegian Lutherans exhibited an extreme denominationalism and established a tradition of disharmony. The Evangelical Lutheran Church—the state church of Norway—largely abandoned the immigrants and provided no guidance. As a consequence, no fewer than fourteen Lutheran synods were founded by Norwegian immigrants between 1846 and 1900. In 1917 most of the warring Lutheran factions reconciled their doctrinal differences and organized the Norwegian Lutheran Church in America. It was one of the church bodies that in 1960 formed the American Lutheran Church, which in 1988 became a constituent part of the newly created Evangelical Lutheran Church in America.

Even though most might perceive that all Norwegian Americans were Lutheran, there were in fact substantial numbers of Methodists among Norwegian immigrants. They were especially concentrated in Chicago; a Norwegian Methodist theological seminary was established in Evanston, Illinois. Some

Hopperstadt Norwegian Stave Church, Moorhead, Minnesota. WALTER BIBIKOW / AGE FOTOSTOCK

the quintessential icon of a glorified Viking heritage. Norwegians found a second identifying quality by presenting themselves as an ethnic group with wholesome rural values and ideals. In fact, Norwegians were the most rural of any major nineteenth-century immigrant group. In 1900, for instance, only a little more than one-quarter of all Norwegian-born residents in the United States lived in towns with more than twenty-five thousand inhabitants. It was the lowest percentage for any European immigrant population. It has been claimed that the Norwegian farmer in the United States passed on a special rural bond from one generation to the next. Perhaps the greatest contribution was a dedication to farming as a way of life; in 1900, 54.3 percent of the children of Norwegian immigrants were farmers.

In their farming communities Norwegians exhibited a nationalistic solidarity that had no counterpart among other Scandinavian groups. The homeland's quest for a national cultural and political identity created a patriotic fervor that was transplanted as immigrant clannishness. Even in the early twenty-first century, Norwegian Americans appeared more focused on culture retention than their Nordic neighbors in the United States, as evidenced by the maintenance of their institutions. For example, a Norwegian-language Lutheran congregation continued to survive in Chicago, as well as in Minneapolis, whereas the Swedes, with a much larger population, had not maintained a Swedish-language church.

Norwegians' past in the United States was celebrated at the Norse American Centennial in the twin cities of Minneapolis and St. Paul, Minnesota, in June 1925. A century had passed since the landing of the *Restauration* in New York harbor. President Calvin Coolidge came to honor the Norwegians for being good Americans and validated their claim of sharing nationality with the original discoverer of America, as the Norwegian Americans reflected upon a successful one hundred years as an immigrant people. The festivities displayed an attachment to traditional rural values and a cultivation of ancient and heroic Norse roots but featured heroes from their American experience, as well. An impressive pageant centered on the life of Colonel Hans Christian Heg, a hero from the Civil War. The hostilities between the North and South gave Norwegian Americans a sense of a legitimate place in the United States, because Norwegian blood had been spilled in its defense.

Old-country traditions in food, festive dress, folk arts, and entertainment were given a powerful boost with the establishment of *bygdelag*, or old-home societies, around the turn of the twentieth century. These groups were rooted in Norwegian localities and loyalties to the home communities in Norway. The annual reunions of the fifty or so such societies, each bearing the name of a specific Norwegian home district, became grand celebrations of a regional and rural Norwegian cultural heritage.

Norwegians converted to the Baptist faith. There were also groups of Quakers, relating back to the "Sloopers"; Norwegian Mormons also joined the trek to the "New Jerusalem" in Salt Lake City, Utah, in 1846.

CULTURE AND ASSIMILATION

Norwegian history in the United States begins with pioneer immigrants in 1825. Viking ancestors had, however, established colonies in Greenland—outposts of European civilization—as early as 985. From there they found America, commonly associated with the voyages of the Norse adventurer Leif Eriksson, around the year 1000 and formed colonies on Newfoundland. These had no impact on the later European settlement in the New World, but they provided Norwegians and other Scandinavians with a claim to a birthright in the United States and gave them their most expressive identifying ethnic symbol.

The pioneers on the American frontier were the new Vikings of the West; Leif Eriksson became

The symbols and content of a Norwegian ethnic identity emerged among the more successful in such urban centers as Chicago and Minneapolis. They were the ones who most eagerly sought acceptable ethnic credentials and gathered their compatriots around the celebration of traditional Norwegian holidays.

Traditions and Customs In 1879 a Norwegian Unitarian minister and author was amazed after a visit to Wisconsin at "how Norwegians have managed to isolate themselves together in colonies and maintain their Norwegian memories and customs"; he had to ask himself if he was really in the United States. Adjustments were, however, made to American ways in clothing and food, although especially typical Norwegian dishes were retained. These became associated with Christmas celebrations, which in pioneer days were observed for the entire Twelfth Night period, as in Norway. Aaste Wilson of Wisconsin tells how transplanted Norwegians retained such old customs:

They invited one another for Christmas celebration and then they had home-brewed ale, made from malt or molasses or sugar cane. … Nearly everybody slaughtered for Christmas so that they could have meat and sausages. Then they had potatoes and *flatbrød* [flatbread] and *smultringer* [doughnuts] and sauce made from dried apples. And most of them had *rømmegrøt* [cream porridge]. We youngsters liked to stay and listen to the old folks and thought it good fun when they told about old things in Norway.

Aaste Wilson, "Live blant nybyggjarane."
Telesoga, September 1917

A gradual transition to American life weakened immigrant folkways. Some traditions and customs survived and were cultivated, others were reintroduced and given a heightened importance as part of an ethnic heritage. Toward the end of the nineteenth century, lutefisk, dried Norwegian cod soaked in a lye solution, assumed a role as a characteristic Norwegian American dish. It was served at lodge meetings, festive banquets, and church suppers, most regularly during the Christmas season. The dish was served with *lefse*, a thin buttered pancake made from rolled dough. Madison, Minnesota, erected a statue of a cod in its city park—Lou T. Fisk—and advertised itself as "Lutefisk Capital U.S.A." because it reportedly consumed more lutefisk per capita than any other American city.

The popularity of the peasant arts of wood carving and *rosemaling* (rose painting) also grew out of the *bygdelag* tradition. Vesterheim Norwegian-American Museum in Decorah, Iowa, has promoted the folk arts through instruction and exhibitions.

There are numerous folk festivals in Norwegian centers. Norsk Høstfest in Minot, North Dakota, and Nordic Fest in Decorah, Iowa, annually assemble thousands of Norwegian Americans from around the nation around

varied programs focusing on Norwegian American heritage, such as dancing, folk songs, and folk art.

At such events Norwegian stereotypes are regularly introduced to the amusement of those assembled. Invariably there are stories and jokes poking fun at the ignorance and foolishness of Norwegian types, such as the characters of Ole and Lena, who speak in broken English. New tales are constantly being created. A typical one might go as follows:

Ole and Lena invited a well-to-do uncle for dinner. Little Ole looked him over and finally approached the old uncle with a request. 'Uncle Knute … vill you make a noise like a frog for me?' said Little Ole. 'Vy in the world do you vant me to make a noise like a frog?' exclaimed the uncle. 'Because,' said Little Ole, 'Papa says ve are going to get a lot of money ven you croak!'

Red Stangeland, Ole & Lena Jokes, Book 4: Sioux
Falls, South Dakota: Norse Press, 1989,
p. 14.

Cuisine Traditional Norwegian cuisine is mainly limited to special occasions—family events such as weddings and anniversaries, and such holidays as Christmas, when other customs are revived as well. The *kransekake*, a cone-shaped cake of almond macaroon rings, is traditionally served at weddings and anniversaries. It is generally decorated with costumed figures and with flags, flowers, or medallions. The observance of the

A full size replica of a Stav church at the Scandinavian Heritage Center in Minot North Dakota. AMERICA / ALAMY

RØMMEGRØT (SOUR CREAM PORRIDGE)

Ingredients

1⅔ cups homemade, high-fat sour cream

1¼ cups flour

5 cups whole milk

¾ teaspoon salt

Preparation

For the sour cream:

Heat 1 cup whipping cream to 95°F, then whisk in 2 tablespoons buttermilk. Let stand at room temperature at least 8 hours, until thickened.

For porridge:

Simmer sour cream, covered, about 15 minutes. Sift ⅓ of the flour into the pot. Simmer until the butterfat begins to leach out. Skim off the fat. Sift the remaining flour into the pot and bring to a boil. Bring the milk to a boil in a separate saucepan and thin the porridge to desired consistency. Whisk until smooth. Simmer about 10 minutes more. Season with salt.

Serve with the sugar and cinnamon.

Christmas season begins on Christmas Eve, when a big meal is served, followed by the reading of the Christmas gospel and the opening of gifts. Hymns and carols are sung later, accompanied in some families by the tradition of holding hands and circling the Christmas tree.

A typical old-country Christmas meal consists of lutefisk; *rømmegrøt*, a sour cream and wheat flour porridge; pork or mutton spare ribs with pork sausages; as well as *fattigmann*, a deep-fried diamond-shaped cookie; *sandkake*, a cookie made of butter, flour, and almonds baked in small metal molds; *krumkake*, a wafer baked in a special iron and rolled into a cylindrical shape while still warm; *julekake*, a sweet bread containing raisins, citron, and cardamom; and the essential *lefse*, which appears in many regional variations.

The Norwegian *koldt bord*, or cold table, is basically the same as the better-known Swedish smorgasbord, with selected hot dishes. Some of the traditional dishes of the Norwegian cold table include herring in many forms; sardines; smoked salmon and other fish; sliced cold ham, lamb, and beef; cheeses such as Swiss, *geitost* (goat cheese), and *gammelost* (highly pungent sour milk cheese); *sylte* (pickled pork, pressed into loaf shape and sliced); pickles, cranberries, apple sauce, and spiced apples; and various types of bread, including flatbread. The meal is served with *akevitt* (a strong distilled alcoholic drink) and beer.

Traditional Dress Women especially revived the use of the festive rural dress, the *bunad*, wearing specific costumes of their old-country districts. A love for jewelry was demonstrated in the use of heavy silver brooches (*sølje*). The peasant costume of Hardanger, on Norway's western coast, a favored region for national romantics, inspired the official dress of the Daughters of Norway organization. These colorful outfits were worn at Norwegian American public events.

Dances and Songs There was renewed interest in the traditional Norwegian Hardanger fiddle and old rural dances. The Hardanger Violinist Association of America was founded in Mount Horeb, Wisconsin, in 1983 as a renewal of the Hardanger Violinist Association of America organized in Ellsworth, Wisconsin, in 1914, which grew out of the *bygdelag* movement. The association promoted traditional Norwegian folk music, dance, and the Hardanger fiddle, a traditional stringed instrument. Groups met to practice old folk dance steps and demonstrate their mastery. In the Seattle area, for example, the Skandia Folkdance Society, founded in 1949, was one of several popular folk dance groups in the area. Only about half the active members were of Scandinavian heritage.

Holidays The most important identifying ethnic symbol for Norwegian Americans is Norwegian Constitution Day on May 17. The day is still celebrated with a traditional parade featuring flags, banners, music, and speeches in Norwegian centers across the United States. The event, observed since the early days of settlement, communicates American patriotism as well as Norwegian memories; ethnic identities are firmly rooted in a positive view of the group's place in the United States, and images of the homeland's culture are equally prominent in the celebration.

Relations with other Americans In a letter from Chicago dated November 9, 1855, Elling Haaland from Stavanger, Norway, assured his relatives back home that "of all nations Norwegians are those who are most favored by Americans." This sentiment was expressed frequently as the immigrants attempted to seek acceptance and negotiate entrance into the new society. In their segregated farming communities, Norwegians were spared direct prejudice and might indeed have been viewed as a welcome ingredient in a region's development. Still, a sense of inferiority was inherent in their position. The immigrants were occasionally referred to as "guests" in the United States, and they were not immune to condescending and disparaging attitudes by old-stock Americans. Economic adaptation required a certain amount of interaction with a larger commercial environment—from working for an American farmer to doing business with the seed dealer, banker, and grain elevator operator—as products had to be grown and sold, all of which pulled Norwegian farmers into social contact with their American neighbors.

In places such as Brooklyn, Chicago, Minneapolis, and Seattle, Norwegians interacted with the multicultural environment of the city while constructing a complex ethnic community that met the needs of its members. It might be said that a Scandinavian melting pot existed in the urban setting among Norwegians, Swedes, and Danes, evidenced in residential and occupational patterns, political mobilization, and public commemoration. Intermarriage promoted interethnic assimilation. Beginning in the 1920s, Norwegians increasingly became suburban, and one might claim, more American. By the early twenty-first century, there were no longer any Norwegian enclaves or neighborhoods in the United States' great cities.

FAMILY AND COMMUNITY LIFE

Early Norwegian immigration exhibited a pronounced family character, in that nuclear families moved to the United States together. In a typical settlement, such as Spring Grove township in Minnesota, for example, in 1870 there was a near gender balance—107 men for each 100 women—as compared to 128 males to 100 females for all Minnesotans. An extended communal and familial network was encouraged by this circumstance. The regional composition of most rural settlements—in that immigrants from a specific Norwegian community were preponderant in different settlements—worked to the same end, recreating a familiar and comforting cultural and social environment.

Opportunities in America, where land was cheap and labor expensive, altered immigrant practices, however. The family farm, lacking the retinue of servants and landless agricultural workers common in Norway, encouraged greater marital fertility to produce needed labor. Immigrant families were large, and the sexual division of labor changed as women moved further into domestic roles. Men took over such farm chores as milking, which had been considered "women's work" in Norway.

Greater wealth allowed immigrants to imitate urban middle-class practices in housing, dress, household amenities (such as pianos), and leisure activities, yet the bourgeois lifestyle was colored both by the local Norwegian cultural background and by the dominant position of the immigrant Lutheran Church.

The male-dominated migration of single young people toward the end of the nineteenth century was also entrenched in kinship and community. Later immigrants traveled increasingly to urban centers to reunite with relatives in the United States. Carl G. O. Hansen, visiting an aunt in Minneapolis in the 1880s, described the Norwegian environment:

My aunt sent one of her children out to make some purchases. Some things were to be bought at Haugen's, some at Tharaldsen's, and some at Olsen & Bakke's. That surely sounded as if it were a Norwegian town.

Carl G. O. Hansen, My Minneapolis. Minneapolis, Minnesota: privately published, 1956, p. 52.

The many single men living as boarders in crowded quarters in the cities did foster marriage outside the Norwegian group. Yet there was a strikingly high percentage of in-marriage in both the immigrant generation and the U.S.-born first generation. In Chicago in 1910, 77 percent of married immigrant Norwegians had wed another Norwegian, and 46 percent of the married first generation had chosen a mate within their ethnic group. When most Norwegian Americans married outside their nationality, their spouse was Scandinavian or, if German, at least shared a Lutheran culture.

More current specific data on in-marriage and divorce were not available. With regard to the latter, Norwegian Americans did not seem to deviate much from the average for the American population as a whole. Anecdotal evidence also suggests a continued high degree of in-marriage, attributable to community and church relations, and even to loyalty to ethnic heritage. A persistent sense of family cohesion and values was evident in the common practice of arranging family reunions and the compilation of family histories. Such activities fortify ties to the past.

For most Norwegian families the "American dream" was the security of a middle-class existence. Only a few Norwegian Americans asserted themselves as financiers and captains of industry. Norwegians typically endorsed the American principle of equality and rejected American materialism. This attitude was reinforced by the Lutheran ethic of renouncing worldly pleasures. Most Norwegians did attain a middle-class status. According to 2011 estimates by the U.S. Census Bureau's American Community Survey, only 5.1 percent of Norwegian American families lived below the poverty level (compared to 11.1 percent for the general U.S. population), and the median household income was $61,310 (compared to $51,484 for the general U.S. population). In total, the 2010 U.S. Census defined Americans of Norwegian descent as a well-adjusted middle-class population.

Education Higher education in the United States is greatly indebted to religion. In the Norwegian immigrant community, the Lutheran Church recognized the salutary benefits of education in a Christian spirit. It emulated American denominations in establishing Lutheran Church academies and colleges.

Norwegians placed themselves in a singular position among Scandinavian groups in the United States to question the religionless "common" (public) school. The orthodox Lutheran clergy even dreamed of replacing the public schools with Lutheran parochial schools but lacked the means to do so. The ability to read and write was common among Norwegian immigrants, and it improved greatly after 1860, when Norway enacted new laws to improve public education. The Norwegian Lutheran Church in the United States did manage to operate congregational schools, some of which continued into the 1930s. During the summer months these schools offered lessons on Lutheran faith and rudimentary instruction in the Norwegian language.

The academy movement flourished for a while, and approximately seventy such schools were established; an academy was a parochial school roughly equivalent to a high school. They lasted until about World War I and assisted the immigrants in adjusting to American society. Inevitably they also strengthened a national Norwegian identity. Some academies were transformed into four-year liberal arts colleges. The college movement among Norwegians began in 1861 with the founding of Luther College, now located in Decorah, Iowa. The school was a facet of the church's effort to train Lutheran ministers, and as such it was a men's school, with nearly half the graduates entering the ministry. In the 1930s it began to admit women.

An additional five Norwegian Lutheran colleges were established later. All were founded before 1900, mainly as academies. Three were in Minnesota: St. Olaf College in Northfield, which admitted female students from its inception; Augsburg College, in Minneapolis; and Concordia College, in Moorhead. Augustana College is located in Sioux Falls, South Dakota, and Pacific Lutheran University is in Tacoma, Washington.

Norwegian women in the United States obtained higher education at a time when such studies were closed to women in the homeland. Some of these women were trained as physicians at the Women's Medical School, which opened in Chicago in 1870. As feminists and professionals, they became leaders in the Norwegian community.

According to the 1990 U.S. Census, of those who declared Norwegian as their primary ancestry, 21 percent of the women and 32 percent of the men twenty-five years or older had earned a bachelor's degree or higher. By 2011 that gender gap had closed, with an equal proportion of Norwegian American men (37 percent) and women (36.5 percent) earning a bachelor's degree or higher (American Community Survey estimates for 2009–2011). Also, by the end of the twentieth century, most attended public institutions rather than one of the "Norwegian" colleges.

EMPLOYMENT AND ECONOMIC CONDITIONS

In the nineteenth century, Norwegian Americans succeeded in commercial agriculture as wheat farmers—following frontier practice—but soon diversified into other products as dictated by topography, soil, climate, and market. In Wisconsin such considerations drew some Norwegians to tobacco farming. In Iowa they grew corn or raised cattle and hogs; in parts of Minnesota, dairy farming was prominent. In northwestern Minnesota, Norwegian farmers engaged heavily in spring wheat cultivation. The hard spring wheat region extended into South and North Dakota, where Norwegians adapted to the demands of grassland wheat production on the semiarid northern plains.

In the urban economy, Norwegian men, along with other Scandinavians, found a special niche in construction and building trades. It was a natural transfer of skills from home, as was their work as lumberjacks in the forests of northern Wisconsin and Minnesota. Norwegian men in Minneapolis earned a livelihood in the large flour mills. In the Pacific Northwest, logging and the sawmills engaged many. Another significant transplanted skill was shipping. On the Great Lakes, Norwegian sailors and boat owners dominated for as long as sailing vessels remained an important means of transportation. In 1870 approximately 65 percent of all sailors on Lake Michigan were Norwegian. Shipping was important on the Eastern Seaboard and the West Coast, as well. The coastal areas provided rich opportunity for fishing, also. Norwegians on the west coast and in Alaska began to develop the halibut industry at the turn of the twentieth century. By 1920 about 95 percent of all halibut fishermen and an even higher percentage of the owners of halibut schooners were of Norwegian birth or descent.

Traditional early employment for Norwegian women involved domestic and personal service. Accessibility to higher education gradually opened up new possibilities—especially for the American-born generations—in commerce, education, and in specialized professions. An examination of the occupational picture in 1950 of Norwegian Americans reveals striking social advances for both women and men. Still, Norwegians of the first and second generations revealed a preference for farming, and men born in Norway were overrepresented in construction work. By 2011 the U.S. Census Bureau's statistics indicated no such occupational concentration among Norwegian Americans. Of employed persons sixteen years old and over, only 2.9 percent were occupied in farming, forestry, and fishery, and 6.1 percent were in construction. Also by that time, a higher percentage of Norwegian Americans (42.7 percent) were employed in management, business, science, and arts occupations than the general U.S. population (35.9 percent).

POLITICS AND GOVERNMENT

Norwegians in the United States have participated the political culture and are to be found in conservative and liberal camps of both dominant political parties.

Norwegians had a certain passion for the political arena. Familiarity with democratic reform and local self-government in Norway, a dislike of officialdom, and a heightened assertion encouraged them to participate in local government in the United States. From the community, they made their way to state and even national politics. During the early decades of the twentieth century Norwegians in Minnesota and North Dakota, for example, were overrepresented in state administrations as well as in the legislatures and U.S. Congress.

Political affiliation, as expressed in a flourishing Norwegian immigrant press, was strongly influenced by the Free-Soil Party in the 1840s and early 1850s. In the late 1850s, this same press abandoned the Democratic Party for Abraham Lincoln's Republican Party, supporting its antislavery stance and the distribution of frontier land to serious settlers. The Homestead Act of 1862 and the heroic participation of Norwegian Americans in the Civil War assured a strong loyalty to the Republican Party and its ideals.

Toward the end of the nineteenth century, however, other issues came to the fore and weakened Republican loyalties. In regions suffering from agricultural depression and exploitation by outside financial interests, independent political thought led many Norwegians to the agricultural protest embodied in the Populist movement. This was especially the case in the wheat-growing regions of North Dakota and western Minnesota.

From about the turn of the twentieth century, the Progressive movement gained a broad Norwegian following, and Norwegians exhibited great faith in the benefits of legislative reform. The Nonpartisan League, organized in North Dakota in 1915, was further evidence of agrarian unrest. Norwegian farmers played a prominent role in its activities and advocacy, which included such socialist goals as public control and operation of grain silos and the sale of wheat. This radical policy was, however, less a consequence of ethnic predisposition toward social reform than of economic self-interest and the problematic local conditions faced by wheat farmers.

Norwegians were also attracted to the Socialist Party; many joined local socialist clubs, and some became members of the Scandinavian Socialist Union formed in Chicago in 1910. However, they did not do so in large numbers. Due to the high concentration of Norwegians in skilled occupations, especially in the building trades, many joined labor unions. The efforts of a Norwegian immigrant, Andrew Furuseth, to improve the working conditions for sailors, which resulted in the Seamen's Act of 1915, is one example of the significant contributions made by immigrants to the American union movement.

In the 1920s Norwegians joined a national trend toward the Democratic Party. The loyalty to the Republican Party was significantly frayed as working-class and reform-minded Norwegians took part in third-party movements, increasingly for Democrats, who seemed more committed to labor concerns and social justice than the Republicans. Republicanism remained common among middle- and upper-class Norwegian Americans, however.

Norwegian members of both parties were concerned with prohibition. Under the banner of temperance and local prohibition of the sale of intoxicating beverages, Norwegian politicians gained the support of their compatriots and were elected to public office. North Dakota, influenced by the agitation of the Norwegian American press, adopted a prohibition clause in its state constitution in 1889. National prohibition legislation, passed in 1919 as the Volstead Act, was named for Norwegian American Andrew J. Volstead, a Republican congressman from Minnesota. Opposition to prohibition and the corruption and crime it yielded, paradoxically, strengthened the move toward the Democratic Party, most especially among urban Norwegians.

Most Norwegians traditionally viewed military service as an affirmation of American patriotism. The first fallen hero was a private in the war with Mexico who had Americanized his name to George Pilson. He had immigrated to Chicago and then fell in 1847 in the bloody battle of Buena Vista, with Chicago newspapers claiming that "more patriotic blood does not enrich the field at Buena Vista than that of the Chicago Norwegian volunteer." Norwegian acts of heroism, valor, and sacrifice constituted a watershed experience during the Civil War; Norwegian men served in great numbers, suffered substantial casualties, and established themselves in America.

Norwegians supported the Spanish-American War and rallied around the American war objectives during World War I. In a patriotic spirit, Norwegian American societies and organizations published lists of "our boys" in the armed forces and memorialized the fallen of their nationality. Occupation of Norway by the Germans during World War II was a calamity that filled Norwegians in the United States with indignation and sorrow. During the summer of 1942 the U.S. Army established a Norwegian-speaking combat unit, the 99th Infantry Battalion, in the event of an invasion of Norway; it consisted of immigrants and Norwegians born in the United States.

Relations with Norway Norwegian Americans cultivated bonds with Norway, sending gifts home

Norwegian Americans in traditional dress stand in front of a large replica of a Valhalia Viking ship, Alaska. © JEFF GREENBERG / PHOTO EDIT. REPRODUCED BY PERMISSION.

often and offering aid during natural disasters and other hardships in Norway. Relief in the form of collected funds was forthcoming without delay. Only during conflicts within the Swedish-Norwegian union, however, did Norwegian Americans become involved directly in the political life of Norway. In the 1880s they formed societies to assist Norwegian liberals, collecting money to assist rifle clubs in Norway should the political conflict between liberals and conservatives call for arms. The ongoing tensions between Sweden and Norway and Norway's humiliating retreat in 1895 fueled nationalism and created anguish. Norwegians in America raised money to strengthen Norway's military defenses. The unilateral declaration by Norway on June 7, 1905, to dissolve its union with Sweden yielded a new holiday of patriotic celebration.

NOTABLE INDIVIDUALS

As in any large population, certain members of the Norwegian American community have excelled in many disciplines. A sample of group and individual achievements follows.

Academia Thorstein Veblen (1857–1929), a second-generation Norwegian, was a superb social critic. His best-known work is *The Theory of the Leisure Class* (1899), a savage attack on the wastefulness of American society. Einar Haugen (1906–1994) was a prominent linguist and professor emeritus at Harvard University. Marcus Lee Hansen (1892–1938), of Danish and Norwegian descent, was a pioneer historian of immigration. Theodore C. Blegen (1891–1969) was also a prominent historian of Norwegians in America, and his book *Norwegian Migration: The American Transition* was published in 1940. Agnes Mathilde Wergeland (1857–1914) was a professor of history at the state university in Laramie, Wyoming, and the first Norwegian woman to earn a doctoral degree.

Business Nelson Olson Nelson (1844–1922) founded the N. O. Nelson Manufacturing Company, which became one of the world's largest building and plumbing supply companies. Ole Evinrude (1877–1934), a self-taught mechanical engineer, developed the idea of the outboard motor; he formed the Evinrude Company in 1909. Arthur Andersen (1885–1947) was the founder of the world-famous accounting firm that bore his name. Conrad Hilton (1887–1979), Norwegian on his father's side, established one of the world's largest hotel chains and at the time of his death owned 260 first-class hotels worldwide. Fred Kavli (1927–) was raised in a small Norwegian village and immigrated to the United States soon after receiving his university degree; he founded Kavlico Corporation, a manufacturer of industrial sensors. Kavli later created the Kavli Foundation, a philanthropic organization dedicated to "advancing science for the benefit of humanity."

Government Knute Nelson (1843–1923) served as a Republican U.S. senator from Minnesota from 1895 to 1923. Andrew Furuseth (1854–1938)

organized American commercial sailors; he was considered their liberator and referred to as the "Abraham Lincoln of the sea." Earl Warren (1891–1974) served as chief justice of the U.S. Supreme Court from 1953 to 1969. Henry Jackson (1912–1983), Democratic U.S. senator from Washington, served from 1953 to 1983. Hubert Humphrey (1911–1978) served for two terms as U.S. vice president under President Lyndon Johnson and was the Democratic presidential nominee in 1968, losing to Richard Nixon in the national election. Walter Mondale (1928–) served as a U.S. senator from Minnesota (1964–1977), vice president under President Jimmy Carter (1977–1981), and was the Democratic presidential nominee in 1984; Mondale served as the U.S. ambassador to Japan under the administration of President Bill Clinton. Warren Christopher (1925–2011), whose great-grandparents emigrated from Norway in 1853, served as secretary of state from 1993 to 1997.

Journalism Victor F. Lawson (1850–1925) was editor and publisher of the *Chicago Daily News*, a philanthropist, and a community leader. William T. Evjue (1882–1970) gained great influence as the editor of the progressive and reform-minded Madison *Capital Times*. Eric Sevareid (1912–1992) enjoyed a distinguished career in journalism and as a radio and television reporter and commentator.

Literature Ole E. Rølvaag (1876–1931), the best-known Norwegian American author, wrote such books as *Giants in the Earth* (1927) that focused on the Norwegian immigrant experience. Hjalmar Hjorth Boyesen (1848–1895), a realistic novelist, literary critic, and social Darwinist, taught at Cornell and Columbia universities. Kathryn Forbes (1909–1966) authored the best-selling *Mama's Bank Account* (1943), a portrait of a Norwegian family in San Francisco. Adapted as *I Remember Mama*, Forbes's work became a hit Broadway play, motion picture, and television series.

Music Olive Fremstad (1868–1951) was an internationally renowned Wagnerian opera singer. Ole Bull (1810–1880) was a well-known concert violinist. F. Melius Christiansen (1871–1955) perfected a cappella singing as director of the St. Olaf College choir; he has been called the "Music Master of the Middle West."

Science and Medicine Ludvig Hektoen (1863–1951) made great progress in cancer research, and the Hektoen Institute of Medicine in Chicago continued his work. Ingeborg Rasmussen (1854–1938) graduated from the Women's Medical College in Evanston, Illinois, in 1892 and became a prominent physician, feminist, and cultural leader among the Norwegians in Chicago. Helga Ruud (1860–1956) graduated from the Women's Medical College in 1889 and enjoyed a distinguished medical career at the Norwegian American Hospital in Chicago. Ulrikka

Feldtman Bruun (1854–1940) was an influential temperance worker among Danes and Norwegians for the Women's Christian Temperance Union.

Ernest O. Lawrence (1901–1958), a professor of physics at Yale University, received the Nobel Prize in Physics in 1939. Ivar Giaever (1929–), a Norwegian-trained engineer and physicist, received the Nobel Prize in Physics in 1973. Lars Onsager (1903–1976) received the Nobel Prize in Chemistry in 1968. Norman E. Borlaug (1914–2009), an agricultural scientist, received the 1970 Nobel Peace Prize for his leadership in the "Green Revolution," which helped to dispel the fear of famine in underdeveloped countries. Ole Singstad (1882–1969) was chief engineer for the construction of the Holland Tunnel under the Hudson River, which connects New York City and New Jersey.

Sports Norwegian immigrants brought skiing to America in the mid-1800s by introducing cross-country racing and ski jumping and by organizing local clubs, including the National Ski Association. They dominated the sport into the 1930s. Beginning in 1856, John A. "Snowshoe" Thompson (1827–1876) delivered mail on skis across the Sierra Nevada mountains during the winter months for nearly twenty years, ensuring postal connection between the Utah Territory and California. Sonja Henie (1912–1969) was an Olympic and world figure skating champion, movie star, and pioneer of ice shows. Torger Tokle (1920–1945) arrived in the United States in 1939 and was unrivaled by any U.S. ski jumper. Tokle won forty-two of forty-eight competitions and in the process set twenty-four new hill records; he was killed in military action in the mountains of northern Italy while serving in the 86th Mountain Regiment, the "Ski Troops." Knute Rockne (1888–1931), head football coach at the University of Notre Dame from 1918 to 1931, revolutionized American collegiate football; his record consisted of 105 wins, 12 losses, and 5 ties. Mildred "Babe" Didrikson Zaharias (1913–1956), a daughter of Norwegian immigrants, was a champion in basketball, track, and golf. Tommy Moe (1970–) won a gold medal for skiing in the Olympic Games in 1994.

Stage and Screen Celeste Holm (1919–2012), a versatile actress of stage and screen, appeared on Broadway and in numerous motion pictures; in 1950 she was an Academy Award nominee for best supporting actress for her role in *All About Eve*. The grandfather of James Arness (1923–2011), who played the lead in the long-running Western television series *Gunsmoke*, and his brother, the screen and television actor Peter Graves, emigrated from Norway, and the two were raised in Minneapolis. The parents of screenwriter and director Brian Helgeland, who won an Academy Award for best screenplay for the film *L.A. Confidential*, were born in Norway. The mother of actress Renée Zellweger (1963–), who won an Academy Award for her performance in the film *Cold Mountain*, was born in Norway, and her heritage is Norwegian and Sami.

MEDIA

News of Norway

A magazine published by the Norwegian embassy in the United States, with news of Norway aimed at a general audience.

Kenneth Krattenmaker, Editor
Royal Norwegian Embassy
2720 34th Street NW
Washington, D.C. 20008-2714
Phone: (202) 333-6000
Fax: (202) 337-0870
Email: newsnor@interramp.com
URL: www.norway.org

Norwegian American Weekly

The only Norwegian American newspaper published in the United States.

Kelsey Larson, Editor
7301 Fifth Avenue NE, Suite A
Seattle, Washington 98115
Phone: (206) 784-4617
Fax: (206) 448-2033
Email: baw@norway.com
URL: http://noram.norway.com

The Scandinavian Hour

A program featuring Scandinavian music and news that has aired on Seattle radio since the 1920s. Doug Warne began hosting it in the 1960s. It airs every Saturday morning on KKNW-1150AM and can also be streamed on the station's website, http://1150kknw.com.

Doug Warne
2125 1st Avenue, Suite 2303
Seattle, Washington 98121
Phone: (206) 441 9490
Email: dwarne3400@aol.com
URL: www.thescandinavianhour.com

ORGANIZATIONS AND ASSOCIATIONS

American-Scandinavian Foundation

Promotes international understanding by means of educational and cultural exchange with Denmark, Finland, Iceland, Norway, and Sweden. It has an extensive program of fellowships and grants, and publishes the *Scandinavian Review*.

Edward P. Gallagher, President of the Board of Trustees
725 Park Avenue
New York, New York 10021
Phone: (212) 779-3587
Email: info@amscan.org
URL: www.amscan.org

Norwegians Worldwide (Nordmanns-Forbundet)

An international organization founded in Norway in 1907 to strengthen ties between men and women of Norwegian heritage in and outside Norway. It functions as a cultural and social organization and has chapters throughout the United States.

Hanne Aaberg, Secretary General
Rådhusgaten 23 B
Oslo, NO-0158
Phone: +47 23 35 71 70
Email: editor@nww.no
URL: www.nww.no
Norway

Norwegian-American Historical Association

Founded in 1925, the association is the primary research center for Norwegian American history. It possesses large documentary archives and extensive library holdings. The association publishes one to two volumes annually; more than ninety volumes of high scholarly merit on the Norwegian American experience have been released under its imprint.

Jackie Henry, Associate Director
St. Olaf College
1510 St. Olaf Avenue
Northfield, Minnesota 55057-1097
Phone: (507) 786-3221
Fax: (507) 786-3734
Email: naha@stolaf.edu
URL: www.naha.stolaf.edu

Sons of Norway

An international order founded in Minneapolis in 1895 as a fraternal society, with lodges throughout the United States as well as in Canada and Norway. It provides insurance benefits for its members and publishes a monthly magazine, *The Viking*.

Eivind Heiberg, CEO
1455 West Lake Street
Minneapolis, Minnesota 55408
Phone: (612) 827-3611
Fax: (612) 827-0658
Email: fraternal@sofn.com
URL: www.sofn.com

MUSEUMS AND RESEARCH CENTERS

Little Norway

Provides guided tours through a Norwegian pioneer homestead settled in 1856. It features the building patterned after a twelfth-century stave church built in Trondheim, Norway, for exhibition at the Chicago World's Columbian Exposition in 1893.

Scott Winner, Owner
3576 Highway JG North
Blue Mounds, Wisconsin 53517
Phone: (608) 437-8211
Fax: (608) 437-7827
Email: info@littlenorway.com
URL: www.littlenorway.com

Nordic Heritage Museum

Opened in 1980 in Seattle, its purpose is to collect, preserve, and present the Scandinavian heritage in the Pacific Northwest. It has an extensive collection of objects from Scandinavia and the Pacific Northwest.

Sandra Nestorovic, Director
3014 NW 67th Street
Seattle, Washington 98117
Phone: (206) 789-5707
Email: nordic@nordicmuseum.org
URL: www.nordicmuseum.org

Norskedalen Heritage and Nature Center

Features objects specific to Norwegian immigrants who settled in Vernon and LaCrosse counties, Wisconsin, before 1900, and two separate pioneer homesteads. It arranges an annual Midsummer Festival in late June.

Chris Hall, Executive Dirrector
P.O. Box 225
Coon Valley, Wisconsin 54623
Phone: (608) 452-3424
Fax: (608) 452-3157
Email: info@norskedalen.org
URL: http://norskedalen.org

Norwegian American Genealogical Center and Naeseth Library

Founded in 1974, the center is involved in a variety of activities related to Norwegian American genealogy.

415 West Main Street
Madison, Wisconsin 53703
Phone: (608) 255-2224
Fax: (608) 255-6842
Email: genealogy@nagcnl.org
URL: www.nagcnl.org

Scandinavian East Coast Museum

Founded in 1994, the museum documents and celebrates the Scandinavians who settled along the East Coast of the United States. It has begun a building fund campaign to create a permanent museum.

Victoria Hofmo
c/o Lutheran Elementary School
440 Ovington Avenue
Brooklyn, New York 11209
Phone: (718) 748-5950
Email: scandia36@optonline.net
URL: www.scandinavian-museum.org

Vesterheim Norwegian-American Museum

A major ethnic museum, it maintains high professional standards and supports an outdoor museum as well as a large collection of objects relating to the Norwegian homeland and life in the United States. It also features a museum store with Norwegian American crafts and books. The museum conducts workshops in Norwegian folk crafts.

Steven L. Johnson, Executive Director
502 West Water Street
P.O. Box 379
Decorah, Iowa 52101
Phone: (563) 382-9681
Fax: (563) 382-8828
Email: info@vesterheim.org
URL: www.vesterheim.org

SOURCES FOR ADDITIONAL STUDY

Anderson, Wilford Raymond. *Norse America, Tenth Century Onward.* Evanston, IL: Valhalla Press, 1996.

Bergland, Betty A., and Lori Ann Lahlum, eds. *Norwegian American Women: Migration, Communities, and Identities.* St. Paul: Minnesota Historical Society Press, 2011.

Gjerde, Jon. *From Peasants to Farmers: The Migration from Balestrand, Norway, to the Upper Middle West.* New York: Cambridge University Press, 1985.

Haugen, Einar. *The Norwegian Language in America: A Study in Bilingual Behavior.* 2 vols. Bloomington: Indiana University Press, 1969.

Lovoll, Odd S. *A Century of Urban Life: The Norwegians in Chicago before 1930.* Northfield, MN: Norwegian-American Historical Association, 1988.

————. *Norwegians on the Prairie: Ethnicity and the Development of the Country Town.* St. Paul: Minnesota Historical Society Press, 2006.

————. *Norwegian Newspapers in America: Connecting Norway and the New Land.* St. Paul: Minnesota Historical Society Press, 2010.

————. *The Promise Fulfilled: A Portrait of Norwegian Americans Today.* Minneapolis: University of Minnesota Press, 1998.

————. *The Promise of America: A History of the Norwegian American People.* Rev. edition. Minneapolis: University of Minnesota Press, 1999.

Schultz, April R. *Ethnicity on Parade: Inventing the Norwegian American through Celebration.* Amherst: University of Massachusetts Press, 1994.

OJIBWE

Loriene Roy

OVERVIEW

The Ojibwe ("oh-jib-way") are an indigenous people of North America. Ojibwe country is often associated with the Great Lakes region of the upper Midwest, particularly with the shores of Lake Superior; it extends over 1,400 miles from Ontario to Saskatchewan on the Canadian side of the border and from Michigan to eastern Montana on the U.S. side of the border. Known for its cold winters and hot, dry summers, this area includes the northern portions of five states (Michigan, Wisconsin, Minnesota, North Dakota, and Montana) and southern portions of three Canadian provinces (Ontario, Manitoba, and Saskatchewan). The Ojibwe call themselves the *Anishinabeg* (also spelled *Anishinaabeg* or, if singular, *Anishinabe*) for "first" or "original people."

According to Barry M. Pritzer's *A Native American Encyclopedia: History, Culture, and Peoples* (2000), there were at least 35,000 Ojibwe people at the time of first contact with Europeans, in this case the French. Precontact culture was heavily influenced by the natural terrain as the Ojibwe adapted their lifestyle to survive in a heavily forested land traversed by a network of lakes and rivers. The Ojibwe lived a seminomadic life, moving a number of times each year in order to be close to food sources. While distinct from the Potawatomi and Ottawa peoples, the Ojibwe migrated west with these groups and were referred to as the People of the Three Fires.

Today Ojibwe people live in cities, towns near reservations, and on reservation lands. Federally recognized Ojibwe reservations are located in Minnesota (Fond du Lac, Grand Portage, Leech Lake, Mille Lacs, Nett Lake [Bois Forte Band], Red Lake, and White Earth), Michigan (Bay Mills Indian Community, Grande Traverse, Keweenaw Bay Indian Community, Saginaw, and Sault Sainte Marie), Wisconsin (Bad River, Lac Courte Oreilles, Lac du Flambeau, Lac Vieux Desert, Mole Lake or Sokaogan Chippewa Community, Red Cliff, and St. Croix), Montana (Rocky Boy), and North Dakota (Turtle Mountain). There are also Ojibwe reserves in Canada, especially in Ontario and Saskatchewan. The Ojibwe are known for their political involvement in the Red Power movement of the 1970s and for their many writers. In the early twenty-first century they have made important contributions to the study and recovery of their indigenous language, Anishinabemowin.

According to the U.S. Census Bureau's American Community Survey estimates for 2009–2011, there were 187,410 people of Chippewa ancestry living in the United States. In addition to the states where Ojibwe reservations are located, other states where significant numbers of Ojibwe reside are California, Illinois, Oregon, and Washington. More recently, some Ojibwe have recognized reservation lands as homelands, and some members are working to preserve the reservations' natural resources while also recovering their traditional culture.

HISTORY OF THE PEOPLE

Early History The Anishinabeg acquired the names *Ojibwe* and *Chippewa* from French traders in the eighteenth century. The French called the Ojibwe living near the eastern shore of Lake Superior *Salteaux* or *Salteurs*, "People of the Falls," but these latter terms are now used only in Canada. The English preferred to use the names *Chippewa* or *Chippeway*, so these are the names typically employed on the treaties with the British government and later with the U.S. government. There is no standard spelling in English, and variations include *Ojibwe, Ojibwa, Ojibwey, Chippewa,* and *Chippeway*. There are several explanations for the derivation of the word *Ojibwe*. Some say it is related to the word for "puckered" and that it refers to a distinctive type of moccasin that has high cuffs and a puckered seam. Others say that the French used the word *o-jib-i-weg* or "pictograph" because the Anishinabeg employed a written language based on pictures or symbols. In 1951 Inez Hilger noted that more than seventy different names were used for the Ojibwe in written accounts. The term *Ojibwe* has become the common English language reference for encyclopedias and entries on this group of peoples. However, *Anishinabeg* is the preferred term, because it is the name the members of the group use.

Early legends indicate that many years ago, the Ojibwe lived in the Great Lakes area. At some point the moved east until they found themselves near the mouth of the Saint Lawrence River, close to the Atlantic Ocean shoreline. In about 1500 they migrated westward, guided by a series of prophecies that included a vision of a floating seashell referred to as the sacred *miigis*. At the Straits of Mackinac, the channel of water connecting Lake Huron and Lake Michigan, the vision ended, and the Anishinabeg divided into three groups. One group, the Potawatomi, moved south and settled in the area between Lake Michigan and Lake Huron. A second group, the Odawa or Ottawa, moved north of Lake Huron. A third group, the Ojibwe, settled along the eastern shore of Lake Superior, following the prophesy that they should stop their migration when they found food growing on water, or wild rice. Because of this early association, the Potawatomi, Odawa, and Ojibwe are known collectively as the Three Fires. The traditional stories do not date the specific times of these early events; the tradition just places that time in the past and prior to the arrival of Europeans. The Jesuits arrived in that area in the early 1600s, and in their reports they described the remnants of housing areas associated with the early Ojibwe. Ojibwe religious leaders recorded their beliefs and the migration stories in the form of pictographs on birch-bark scrolls, some of which have survived to this day.

The Ojibwe met Europeans in the 1600s, possibly hearing about them through the Huron people. The first written European accounts about the Ojibwe appeared in Jesuit diaries, published in collected form as the *Jesuit Relations and Allied Documents*. The Jesuits were followed by French explorers and fur traders, who were succeeded by British fur traders, explorers, and soldiers, and later by U.S. government officials and citizens. In the mid-seventeenth century there were approximately 35,000 Ojibwe on the continent.

By the 1700s the Ojibwe, aided with guns, had succeeded in pushing the Fox (Meskwaki) tribe south into present-day Wisconsin. Ojibwe and Dakota fighting extended over a 100-year period until separate reservations were established. Fur trading, especially the exchange of beaver pelts for European goods such as firearms, flourished until the 1800s. The Ojibwe traded with representatives of fur companies or indirectly through salaried or independent traders called *coureurs des bois*. In addition to furs, the land around the Great Lakes was rich in copper and iron ores, lumber, and waterpower, all natural resources that were coveted by non-Native peoples. Competition in trading led to intertribal conflict.

Until 1871 the Ojibwe tribes were viewed as sovereign nations. As such, the legal relationship between the Ojibwe and the U.S. government was largely defined by treaties. Treaties drew boundaries between Ojibwe lands and lands designated for other tribes or non-Native Americans, concentrated tribes on reservations, allowed the government to purchase Ojibwe land, and set regulations concerning commerce. Ojibwe and Dakota representatives signed a major treaty at Prairie du Chien in present-day Wisconsin in 1825 to stop fighting between the two nations and establish boundaries. In 1827 another treaty set the boundary between Ojibwe and Menominee land.

By the mid-nineteenth century the Ojibwe had enlarged their geographic boundaries and splintered into four main groups. The Southeastern Ojibwe lived southeast and north of Lake Huron, in present-day Michigan and southern Ontario. The Southwestern Ojibwe lived along the south and north shores of Lake Superior. The Northern Ojibwe lived in southern Ontario. The Plains Ojibwe or Bungi lived in the present-day states and provinces of Montana, North Dakota, Manitoba, and Saskatchewan. The Plains Ojibwe adopted a lifestyle resembling that of other Plains tribes, living in tepees, riding horses, and hunting buffalo for food and clothing. The Ojibwe ceded or sold land rights in Michigan, Minnesota, and Wisconsin to the federal government in a number of treaties, including one signed in 1854 that established permanent Ojibwe reservations in three states: Michigan, Minnesota, and Wisconsin. Bands were dispersed geographically, with members spread out in different reservations. In exchange for land or natural resources, the Ojibwe received annuities or annual payments of goods, livestock, food staples, clearance of debt with fur traders or fur company stores, and the services of blacksmiths, physicians, saw millers, and teachers.

The General Allotment Act of 1887, also known as the Dawes Act, adversely affected the Ojibwe, along with many other tribes. The act outlined a policy of encouraging assimilation to white culture, primarily through the adoption of agriculture as a means of subsistence and the allotment of land to individuals rather than to communities, bands, tribes, or nations. States also passed their own versions of the Dawes Act, such as Minnesota's Nelson Act of 1889. After Ojibwe families took their allotments, un-allotted land on reservations was then sold to the public. The Dawes Act not only severely restricted communal lands and traditional cultural patterns, it opened up huge tracts of native lands to white settlement and exploitation. Arguably, this was as much the reason for the act as the desired assimilation of native peoples. Members of the tribe gained U.S. citizenship when their allotments became fee patent lands. Initially, when individual tribal members received an allotment, usually 160 acres of land, the title to that property was still held by the U.S. government. This was trust land. When land was moved out of trust, a fee patent was given to the individual by the government. Fee patents allowed land to be taxed and also permitted individuals to sell the land. Prior to 1924, when all American Indians became U.S. citizens, taking title to allotted land through a fee patent was among the only ways for indigenous people to obtain citizenship.

Rather than converting the Ojibwe to self-sufficient living, the allotment system resulted in the loss of Native-held land and made the Ojibwe dependent on the government. The Ojibwe did not succeed as farmers, due to both environmental and cultural factors. In some reservation areas the land was sandy, rocky, swampy, or heavily wooded, and the weather limited the varieties of crops that could mature during the short growing season. The Ojibwe also resisted farming because they perceived gardening as women's work and disliked the permanency that farming required.

Modern Era In the 1930s Ojibwe men and women were employed in federal conservation, construction, and manufacturing projects organized under the Civil Works Administration and the Civilian Conservation Corps, Indian Division. Ojibwe also received vocational training through Works Progress Administration programs. This brought some economic relief to reservation areas hit hard by the Great Depression. In 1934 the passage of the Indian Reorganization Act reversed the allotment system, and tribes held elections to decide whether to reorganize their governments. In 1936 six of the seven Minnesota reservations incorporated as the Minnesota Chippewa Tribe. Red Lake, which elected not to join the Minnesota Chippewa Tribe, is still known for its adherence to traditional culture. (The Red Lake Reservation had been excluded from the Nelson Act of 1889, and, while it did sell some land to the United States, the original tribal areas remained the property of the entire tribe.)

Over time, Ojibwe people in other states have made various decisions about self-governance. The six reservations in Wisconsin are governed separately, as are the westernmost Ojibwe in North Dakota and Montana (including Rocky Boy Reservation, home of the Chippewa Cree tribe, and the Little Shell Chippewa Tribe, which has gained state recognition but is not yet federally recognized). There are four Ojibwe tribal groups in Michigan. The Sault Sainte Marie band is governed separately as the Bay Mills Indian Community; the Keweenaw Bay Indian Community includes the L'Anse and Ontonagon bands; the Lac Vieux Desert band was recognized as a separate tribe in 1988; and the Saginaw Chippewa Tribe comprises the Saginaw, Swan Creek, and Black River bands.

After World War II, federal policy toward Native Americans once again promoted assimilation and integration, a setback for the New Deal philosophy that had encouraged Native culture and autonomy. In the 1950s the BIA instituted the Indian Relocation Services campaign. Like the allotment system, relocation focused on individual Ojibwa rather than tribal group and Native culture. Ojibwa were encouraged to move off reservations to assimilate with non-Native culture in urban areas in order to reduce the need for federal support. Great Lakes Ojibwe moved to urban centers in Minnesota and Wisconsin, most notably Duluth, Milwaukee, and Minneapolis-St.Paul.

In the 1960s the movement for Native American self-determination (autonomy) gained strength and

produced a shift in U.S. policy. Under the Johnson administration (1963–1969), the Ojibwe qualified for Office of Economic Opportunity funds to open social programs, such as Head Start, and for Native businesses and housing. Federal legislation in the 1970s—most notably the Indian Education Act of 1972, the Indian Self-Determination Act of 1973, and the Education Assistance Act of 1975—provided funding for culturally based education and afforded tribes more direct control of programs once administered by the BIA.

Since the 1970s the Ojibwe have been involved in economic development (to reduce unemployment) and social services (to support community needs). Tribally operated commercial enterprises on the Rocky Boy Reservation include Bear Paw Energy and the Chippewa Cree Construction Corporation.

Portrait of Ka-Be-Nak-Gwey-Wence (Old Wrinkle Meat), an Ojibwe Indian. Cass Lake, Minnesota, early 1910s. UNDERWOOD ARCHIVES / ARCHIVE PHOTOS / GETTY IMAGES

Community service support includes elder and wellness centers as well as subsidized housing.

Ojibwe communities are investigating better management of natural resources and protection of treaty rights, both of which are affirmations of sovereignty. The White Earth Land Recovery Project helps defend the wild rice industry from commercial growers by harvesting wild rice and selling it through an online store. In 2013 all seven Wisconsin Ojibwe tribes participated in affirming their fishing rights by engaging in harvesting freshwater walleye using spearfishing methods. Through tribal colleges and financial aid they are increasing emphasis on higher education to train tribal members. Ojibwe tribes have also launched and expanded tourism and entertainment options.

Tribes have expanded their cultural heritage offerings to include new museums, cultural centers, and other heritage facilities and functions. The Sokaogon Chippewa Community of Wisconsin was recognized in 2003 for its efforts to restore the Dinesen House, a historic log cabin located on the Mole Lake Indian Reservation. In 2007 the Grand Portage National Monument Heritage Center opened a facility that is jointly operated between the tribe and the National Park Service. Tribes sponsor community celebrations such as powwows and the Grand Portage Rendezvous Days each August in northern Minnesota. Ojibwe tribes are also engaged in Anishinabemowin language recovery efforts. In 2009 the Sawyer Language Camp started offering an immersion experience about Ojibwe culture and language on the Fond du Lac Reservation in Minnesota.

SETTLEMENT IN THE UNITED STATES

Over time there have been several processes through which tribal groups were designated as tribal communities and through which reservation lands were established. These processes included treaties, executive orders, public acts, and, since 1978, an application process to the Bureau of Indian Affairs that awards federal recognition of the tribe. Four of the seven reservations in Wisconsin were created through the La Pointe Treaty signed with the U.S. government in 1854: Bad River, Lac Courte Oreilles, Lac du Flambeau, and Red Cliff. This treaty also established several reservations in Minnesota, including Fond du Lac and Grand Portage, and the Keweenaw Bay Indian Community in Michigan.

In the 1860s non-Native peoples put forward a plan to move all Minnesotan Ojibwe to a new reservation in the northwestern corner of the state. Members of the four bands living in Minnesota were eventually relocated to the White Earth Reservation, beginning in 1868. The history of White Earth is a particularly disruptive one, with much of the land initially designated for the Ojibwe lost through improper taxation and swindling. The history of the Ojibwe of Red Lake in Minnesota is unique, because the community refused to participate in allotment. The Red Lake land was reduced through treaties and agreements, but the people never sold their land or allotted it to individuals. They thus reside on land that has been their homeland since the 1700s.

Federal and state legislation replaced treaty making in 1871. The St. Croix Band of Wisconsin Ojibwe were federally recognized in 1934 through the Indian Reorganization Act; they received a small parcel of land for their reservation eight years later. Rocky Boy Indian Reservation in Montana was established in 1916 through an executive order. The Sault Sainte Marie Tribe of Michigan were federally recognized in 1972; Grande Traverse Ojibwe of Michigan were federally recognized in 1980. The Saginaw Chippewa Tribe of Michigan and the Turtle Mountain Band of North Dakota are also federally recognized.

It is also important to describe the movement of Ojibwe away from reservation lands during the relocation era. In the 1950s the Bureau of Indian Affairs (BIA) instituted the Indian Relocation Services campaign. Like the allotment system, relocation focused on individual Ojibwe rather than tribal group affiliation and Native cultural connections. Ojibwe were encouraged to move off reservations to assimilate with non-Native culture in urban areas in order to reduce the need for federal support. Great Lakes Ojibwe moved to urban centers in Minnesota and Wisconsin, most notably Duluth, Milwaukee, and Minneapolis-St. Paul.

Ojibwe continue to live both on and off reservation homeland areas. Those living away from their communities of origin may continue their cultural connections through tribal newspapers, through social networking sites, and through returning for community events such as powwows. The U.S. Census Bureau's American Community Survey estimates for 2010 indicate that states with large numbers of Ojibwe included California, Illinois, Michigan, Minnesota, Montana, North Dakota, Oregon, Washington, and Wisconsin.

LANGUAGE

Spoken Ojibwe or Ojibwemowin is an Algonquin language with regional dialectical differences. It is related linguistically to the languages not only of the Odawa and Potawatomi but also of the Fox, Cree, and Menominee. Because Ojibwe was a spoken rather than a written language, the spelling of Ojibwe words varies. According to the UCLA Language Materials Project, in 1992 the Ojibwe language was spoken by between 35,000 and 50,000 people. Once spoken only by elders, the Ojibwe language has seen a resurgence of interest and promotion in the early twenty-first century. Many Ojibwe demonstrate this interest in native identity by preferring to be called Anishinabe.

Instruction is available in both public and tribally directed educational settings. Classes and workshops offered at community colleges and state universities

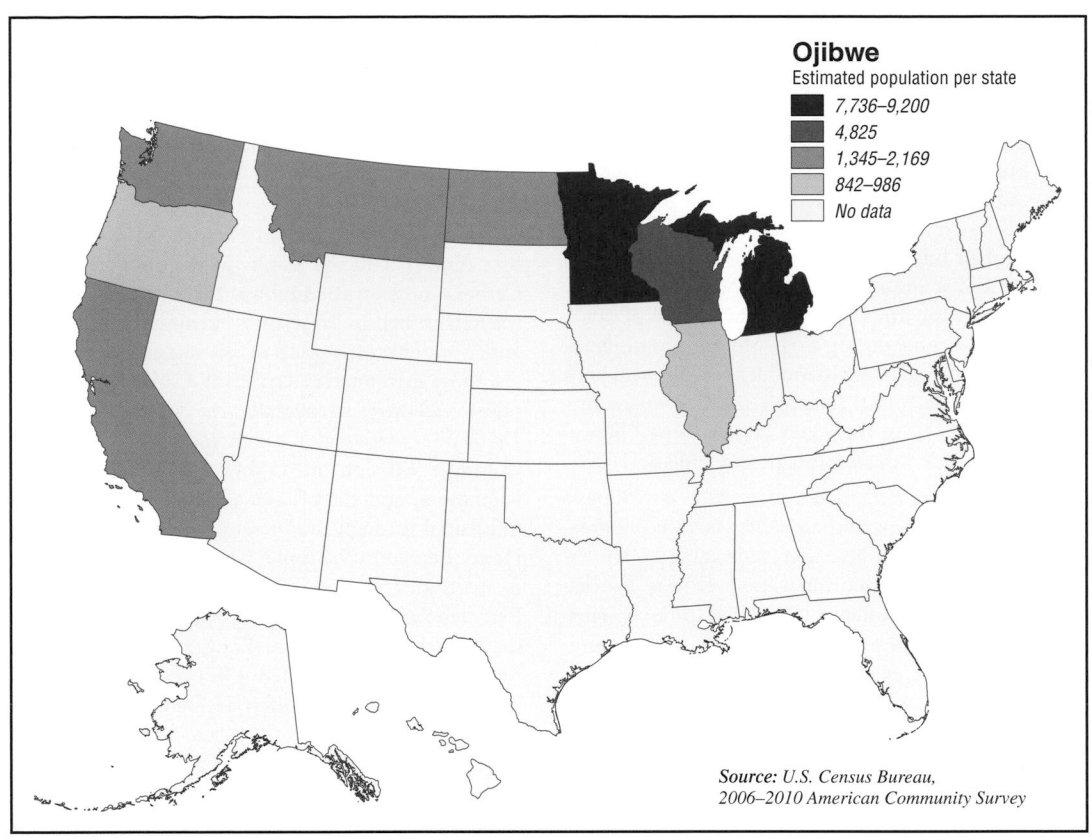

Ojibwe
Estimated population per state

- 7,736–9,200
- 4,825
- 1,345–2,169
- 842–986
- *No data*

Source: U.S. Census Bureau,
2006–2010 American Community Survey

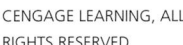

are sometimes broadcast to more distant locations. Language texts as well as instructional material in workbooks, bilingual texts, audio recordings, and multimedia formats have also been developed, including Ojibwe language instruction on YouTube and Facebook groups. Several immersion schools for young tribal members are available, such as the Wicoie Nandagikendan preschool in Minneapolis, the Niigaane Ojibwe Immersion School on the Leech Lake Reservation, and the Waadookodaading Language Immersion Charter School on the Lac Courte Oreilles Reservation. Tribal newspapers carry regular Ojibwe-language columns. The University of Minnesota–Duluth developed an online Ojibwe-English/English-Ojibwe dictionary with audio files. The Fond du Lac Reservation hosts a free Ojibwe cultural week that includes Ojibwe language study and is open to the public.

Greetings and Popular Expressions Common Ojibwe expressions include the following: *Boozhoo* (boo shoo)—Hello; *Miigwech* (mee gwitch)—Thank you; *Aaniin ezhi-ayaayan?* (a neen a shay i an)—How are you?; *Nimino-ayaa* (nay mi no a yah)—I am fine; *Mino-ayaag!* (minnow a yog)—All of you be well!

RELIGION

There is no single word in Ojibwe language that translates as "religion"; to Ojibwe today as in the past, religious observance and belief is practiced as a way of life. Most Ojibwe are spiritual people. Many practice a Christian religion and/or their traditional religion, Midewiwin.

While some aspects of religious observance are communal, traditional Ojibwe religious practice is focused on inward personal experience. There is a belief in spirits, called *manitou* or *manidoo*. The creator is referred to as Gitchie Manitou. *Manjimanidoo*, or evil spirits, exist; *windigos* are especially terrifying spirits associated with cannibalism. Animate and inanimate objects possess spiritual power, and the Ojibwe consider themselves one element of nature, no greater or less significant than any other living being. The cardinal directions are invested with sacred power and are associated with certain colors: white for the north, red for the south, yellow for the east, and black for the west. The Ojibwe recognize three additional directions: heaven, earth, and the position where an individual stands. Tobacco is considered one of four sacred plants, along with sage, sweetgrass, and cedar; it is smoked in pipes or scattered on lakes to bless a crossing, a harvest, or a herd, or to seal agreements or meetings with peoples.

Dreams carry great significance for Ojibwe people and have traditionally been sought through fasting or other purgative ceremonies. Dream catchers were once hung from the cradleboards of infants to capture good dreams and now continue to be displayed by

Ojibwe and others worldwide. The name "dreamer" was reserved for tribal visionaries who would dream of certain powerful objects—such as stones—that they would then seek on waking. Traditionally, youth were instructed in dreaming. Dreamers might also experience prophetic dreams that they would convey to others to forestall danger. At an early age young boys and girls fasted in order to obtain a vision of how to conduct their future. Some visions provided complete messages and songs; others were incomplete and were revealed in their entirety only with the fullness of time. Visions could come during sleep. Since it was difficult to adhere to the advice imparted by visions, men and women went on annual fasts or retreats to renew the vision and reflect on their lives. Today some Ojibwe still fast and seek visions through contemplation.

Sweat lodges were used to prevent or cure illness or to procure dreams and are still a feature of some Ojibwe gatherings. These were wigwams in which steam was created by pouring water over heated rocks and sealing the entrances. Bark and pine boughs might be added to the steam. Fasting was used to cure sickness and, like sweating, was thought to cleanse the body.

In the seventeenth century a religious movement emerged among the Ojibwe called the Grand Medicine Society or *Midewiwin* (also spelled *Mitewiwin*). Abbreviated *Mide*, the word *Midewiwin* most likely means "good-hearted" or "resonant," in reference to the belief that the Mide priest worked for the betterment of others and employed special sacred drums. The Mide culture is a hierarchical priesthood of four to eight degrees, or orders, with each level representing the attainment of certain skills or knowledge. Women and children as well as men could be priests (also referred to as medicine men or women). As many as twenty years of study might be required to progress to the highest degree. After one year of training, an apprentice was initiated as a first-level Mide priest and was allowed to perform certain duties. Initiations were held during an annual Grand Medicine Dance in the spring or early fall and lasted from one to five days. Conducted in large wigwams, the ceremonies incorporated the use of a sacred drum and sacred pipe, both of which were guarded by caretakers. Initiates offered gifts such as blankets, cooking utensils, and wild rice. Feasts featured wild rice, fresh or dried blueberries, maple sugar, and dog meat. Subsequent training required learning herbology for treating sickness or for acquiring personal power, a skill used in much the way that charms are used. Mide priests, therefore, acquired the role of healer.

Mide members were also reputed to use "bad medicine" to cause sickness or death. Mide priests carried personal medicine bundles, cloth squares, or cloth or yarn bags enclosing one or more decorated animal skins called medicine bags. Specific types of skins were associated with each of the Mide degrees. At the first level, the Mide priest would have a medicine bag made from the skin of an otter, marten, mink, or weasel. Objects found in medicine bags included shells, bear claws decorated with ribbons, glass beads, *kinikinik* (native tobacco), carved figures, dried roots, and herbs. Mide songs and instructions were recorded on birch-bark scrolls that were placed under the care of an appointed guardian priest.

Christianity was adopted slowly but started with first contact with the Jesuits in the 1660s. The first Catholic mission for Ojibwe, Saint Espirit Mission, was established in 1665 on Madeline Island in Lake Superior. The early part of the nineteenth century saw more missionaries, especially Catholic priests, in Ojibwe country, particularly in Wisconsin. In the 1850s the Episcopal Church established the Saint Columba Mission in Ojibwe country in central Minnesota, and the church teachings became more influential through the presence of Episcopal bishop Henry Benjamin Whipple, who played a crucial role in the urging the establishment of the White Earth Reservation. Episcopalian Ojibwe were among the first to relocate to White Earth in the late 1860s. At that site, full-blooded Ojibwe tended to follow a more traditional lifestyle focused on Mide or Episcopalian values, and the mixed-blood progressive Ojibwe, typically were Roman Catholic and followed a more acculturated lifestyle.

In the 1880s Franciscan nuns opened a Catholic mission school among the Bad River band of Chippewa in Wisconsin, increasing Catholic influence in the area over Episcopalian membership. By the early twentieth century, it was estimated that 65 percent of Ojibwe in Minnesota were Christian, with 55 percent of those Catholic; similar historical statistics are not available for Ojibwe in other geographic areas. Ojibwe were likely to have practiced a hybrid religious expression, blending aspects of Christian thought and expression, such as the singing of hymns, with Mide observance such as drumming and healing. Most modern Ojibwe are Roman Catholics or Protestant Episcopalians, though the Mide religion is also still practiced throughout Ojibwe land areas.

CULTURE AND ASSIMILATION

Traditional Ojibwe life was altered through contact with Europeans and, later, Americans. Fur trading with the French resulted in the Ojibwe becoming reliant on traded goods rather than the clothing, utensils, and weapons they had constructed. The establishment of reservations by the U.S. government restricted the Ojibwe's seasonal travel, the formalized educational system removed children from their families, and the government's relocation policies dispersed tribe members and altered the construction of their homes. Wigwam construction incorporated new materials: other forms of tree bark were more easily available than long strips of birch bark; wigwam doors were covered with blankets instead of animal skins; calico, cardboard, and tar paper replaced the rush matting.

By the late 1880s many Ojibwe lived in one-room log cabins, frame cabins, or tar-paper shacks rather than in wigwams. Birch-bark canoes were largely replaced by wooden and later aluminum boats.

Up until the mid-twentieth century, government policies such as the Dawes Act encouraged Ojibwe assimilation into majority culture through education, relocation, and general repression of Ojibwe cultural expressions. Although the rate of acculturation varied by reservation, by the mid-1940s only the elderly were bilingual, and most Ojibwe had adopted modern clothing. Few Ojibwe openly practiced their traditional religion except for the Red Lake Reservation, which did not follow incorporation into the Minnesota Chippewa Tribe when it was established in 1934.

With the Ojibwe's greater financial stability in the twenty-first century, Ojibwe culture has been experiencing a renaissance as natives and non-natives are studying Ojibwe botany, crafts, traditional stories, and language. Wild ricing by canoe is still a valued, even sacred, part of the culture, despite the facts that the once bountiful harvest is now regulated, that harvest time and volume have been reduced, and that the Ojibwe now compete with commercial growers. Making maple sugar is still popular as well, although the sap may be collected in plastic bags rather than in birch-bark baskets. Communal festivities such as the "Honor the Earth" powwows held every July at Lac Courte Oreilles have become a focal point of modern-day Ojibwe culture, and hundreds of dancers of all ages participate.

Many Ojibwe are concerned about the degradation of the environment by industry and mismanagement. Wild rice harvesting has suffered from changing water levels, housing construction, water pollution, boat traffic, and the incursions of alien species of plants and animals. Logging enterprises have destroyed traditional maple sugar camps, and fish caught in freshwater lakes are contaminated with mercury. State laws may change to allow mining operations to encroach on tribal lands. Yet in the midst of these challenges, contemporary Ojibwe continue to maintain their traditions. It is still common for Ojibwe to hunt, trap, and fish. The Midewiwin religion has been revived as well, and traditional importance is still afforded to visions and dreams. Ojibwe gatherings often begin with a prayer and a ritual offering of tobacco as an expression of gratitude and respect to the Heavenly Spirit. Powwows, the modern equivalent of multiband gatherings, are now elaborately staged competitions where costumed dancers perform to the accompaniment of vocalists who sing in Ojibwe while beating on bass drums with padded drumsticks. Clan and band affiliation still exists, and many Ojibwe seek to reclaim lands once tribally owned. If they are non-reservation dwellers, they often maintain ties to reservations, especially if they are enrolled or official members. Tribal newsletters are a means for members to stay abreast of local news, issues, and politics.

The Ojibwe have made a number of significant contributions to American life: they created maple sugar and harvested wild rice, designed hammocks, snowshoes, and canoeing, and developed lacrosse. The English language contains a number of Ojibwe words (moccasin, moose) and place-names (Mackinaw, Michigan, Mesabi).

Traditions and Customs Cultural values such as generosity, honesty, strength of character, endurance, and wisdom were traditionally instilled through education, religious practice, and by example within the tribe. The Ojibwe counted time by twenty-four-hour intervals (nights), months (moons), and years (winters). Each month had a name, denoting some natural feature or event. For example, the month of September, when tribes harvested wild rice along the lake shores, was called *manoominike-giizis*, or "ricing moon." October was "falling leaves moon." Time was sometimes reckoned by making notches on sticks.

Except for the Plains Ojibwe, who rode horses, the Ojibwe traveled on land by foot and wore snowshoes during the winter, transporting goods on dog sleds. The portability of Ojibwe lodging—the wigwam—enabled such moves to be made quickly and easily. Wigwams could be built in a day by bending peeled green ironwood saplings into arches; lashing the arches into a circular or oval shape with basswood fiber; and weaving birch-bark strips or rush, cedar bark, or cattail mats around the saplings. The dwelling had two openings, a door and a hole on top to emit smoke from the cooking fire located directly below. When they moved to another camp, the Ojibwe left the frame, taking the lightweight birch-bark strips and rush mats. During warm months the Ojibwe slept on cedar-bough mattresses, each person wrapped in a bearskin or deerskin robe.

Cuisine Native cuisine was closely influenced by the seasons, as the seminomadic Ojibwe changed camps to locate themselves closer to food sources. For example, because the Ojibwe used maple sugar or maple syrup as a seasoning, during the late spring they lived near maple trees. Each family or group of families returned to a traditional location where they had stored utensils and had marked with an axe-cut the trees they would tap. A typical sugar camp or sugar bush encompassed an area of some 900 taps or cuttings, with up to three taps made per tree. The Ojibwe collected maple sap in birch-bark containers and poured it into vats made of moose hide, wood, or bark, and later into brass kettles, where it was boiled until it became syrup. The syrup was strained, reheated, thickened, and stirred in shallow troughs until it formed granulated sugar. Birch-bark cones were packed with sugar, tied together, and hung from the ceiling of the wigwam or storage building. The Ojibwe also poured the sap into wooden molds or directly into snow to form maple sugar candy. Camps were moved in the summer to be close to gardens and

OJIBWE WILD RICING

Wild rice (in Ojibwe, *mahnomin, manomin,* or *manoomin*) is a grain that grows on long grasses in shallow lakes or along streams. In the summers the Ojibwe would settle nearby and harvest the rice by canoe. As the edible rice seeds began to mature, families marked the area they would harvest by tying the rice stalks together, using knots or dyed rope that would distinguish their claim. The rice harvest was a time of community celebration, starting with the announcement by an annually appointed rice chief or elder that the fields were ready. One team member stood in the canoe pushing a long forked pole to guide the canoe through the grasses. The other team member sat in the canoe, reaching to bend the grass over the canoe and hitting the grass with wooden stocks called knockers in order to shake the seeds from the grass without permanently injuring the plant. On shore, the rice was dried in the sun, and then parched in a kettle to loosen the hull. A person in clean moccasins then "danced the rice," carefully treading on it to remove the hull and then tossing it into the air to winnow the chaff. A medicine man blessed the first rice harvested, and each ricing pair donated rice to a communal fund to feed the poor. Rice was often boiled and sweetened with maple sugar or flavored with venison or duck broth. Up to one-third of the annual harvest was stored, usually in birch-bark baskets. The rice season lasted from ten days to three weeks. Ricers often poled through their sections every few days as the rice seeds matured at differing rates. They were also deliberately inefficient, leaving plenty of rice to seed the beds for the following year.

wild berry patches. The Ojibwe cultivated gardens of corn, pumpkins, and squash. Dried berries, vegetables, and seeds were stored in underground pits. They drank teas boiled from plants and herbs and sweetened with maple sugar. The Ojibwe fished throughout the year, using hooks, nets, spears, and traps. Fish and meat were dried and smoked so they could be stored. In late summer the Ojibwe moved again to be near fields of wild rice, which they harvested by canoe. Contemporary Ojibwe still engage in harvesting rice, and many families still hunt, fish, and gather berries while also eating foods that would be found in the common American diet.

Traditional Dress Before the Ojibwe began to trade with Europeans and Americans, they wore clothing made from animal hides, primarily from tanned deerskin. The women wore deerskin dresses, leggings, moccasins, and petticoats made of woven nettle or thistle fibers. The men wore leggings, breechcloths, and moccasins. Girls and women decorated the clothing in geometric designs with bones, feathers, dyed porcupine quills, shells, and stones, using bone or thorn needles and thread made from nettles or animal sinew. Jewelry was made from animal bones, claws, or teeth strung into necklaces. After European contact,

the Ojibwe began to wear woven clothing. Europeans introduced the Ojibwe to glass beads and Ojibwe women began to decorate their clothing and other items in floral designs, inspired by the patterns they saw in calico cloth. Both men and women wove and mended fish nets. Contemporary Ojibwe people wear clothing that would be worn commonly within the United States, although they might also wear a floral-beaded vest or beaded jewelry such as earrings.

Traditional Arts and Crafts Birch bark is a versatile natural product from which the Ojibwe created—and continue to create—many items, including canoes, toboggans, and storage containers. The Ojibwe built canoe frames from wood and covered the frame with sewn birch-bark strips, sealing the seams with pine or spruce gum. Each canoe weighed from 65 to 125 pounds and was typically 16 feet long, 18 inches deep, and 3 feet wide across the midpoint. Toboggans also had curved wooden frames covered with birch bark. The Ojibwe decorated birch-bark baskets with porcupine quills, sweet grass, birch-bark cutouts, or bitten designs that were created by folding thin pieces of birch bark in half and biting them. The dents made dark impressions on the light background. Birch-bark torches were fashioned by rolling the bark into tubes and covering the tube with pitch. The Ojibwe also carved wooden objects such as arrows, bowls, boxes, drums, paddles, rattles, spoons, shuttles for weaving fish nets, and war clubs.

Dances and Songs Before contact with non-Native Americans, the Ojibwe held annual spring and autumn celebrations at a central location, with singing, dancing, eating, sports competitions, and storytelling. In the early 1700s the celebrations took place in Bowating, near present-day Sault Sainte Marie, Michigan. In the late 1700s they were held near Lake Superior's Chequamegon Bay, and by the early 1800s they were held at Fort La Pointe on Madeline Island. These celebrations commemorated significant events in an individual's lifetime: the naming of a child, a boy's first hunt, a girl's first menstrual period, marriage, and death. Music played a central part in these events, as singers would perform to the accompaniment of drums, rattles, or flutes. At the gatherings, men showed off their skill at traditional, fancy, and grass dances, while women joined in the traditional dances and added shawl and jingle dances. Modern costumes for these dancing competitions, which still continue, have incorporated many novel elements; for example, jingle dancers may sew hundreds of snuff-can covers onto dresses in place of traditional seashells or bones.

Health Care Issues and Practices During their first contact with non-Native peoples, the Ojibwe were exposed to a number of diseases and suffered through epidemics of smallpox and other illnesses. The transition from traditional seminomadic living to permanent settlement in villages led to a high incidence of communicable diseases such as tuberculosis and trachoma (which causes blindness). When the Ojibwe ceded land, they sometimes did so in exchange for health care, such as the services of a physician, indicating an early concern for health issues. These rights are still in effect, and Ojibwe living on or maintaining social ties with reservations may have access to federally funded programs, including Indian Health Service clinics or hospitals. Today the Ojibwe use a blend of traditional and modern treatment methods to improve health. Traditional herbal cures include crushed sumac roots made into tea to stop bleeding, blackberry roots boiled and drunk to stop diarrhea or prevent miscarriage, wild onions cooked and sweetened with maple sugar to treat children's colds, yarrow roots mashed into creams for treating blemishes, strawberry roots boiled and eaten to treat stomach aches, and plantain leaves chopped and used as poultices for bruises, rheumatism, and snake bites.

The Ojibwe, along with other American Indian groups, continue to have concerns about poor health. There are high incidences of chemical dependency, diabetes, fetal alcohol effect or syndrome, obesity, suicide, and accidental death. Ojibwe community leaders actively discourage alcohol consumption and chemical dependency. Alcohol and drugs are banned from powwow sites, and some powwows are organized to celebrate sobriety. Mash-Ka-Wisen ("to be strong, accept help"), the oldest Native-owned and operated chemical-dependency treatment center, on the Fond du Lac Reservation, incorporates elements of Ojibwe culture into its services for its clients. The Minneapolis American Indian Center provides an array of social services, including programs on chemical dependency, developmental disabilities, and rehabilitation. It is difficult to measure alcoholism among Native peoples as a whole, and statistics are usually not available at the tribal community level.

Tribes are concerned with improving medical treatment. They offer general health support and information through locations such as the Red Cliff Community Health Center in Wisconsin and the prescription lock-box program launched in 2013 at the Bay Mills Indian Community in Michigan.

Death and Burial Rituals According to Ojibwe custom, if a person died inside a wigwam, the body was removed through a hole made in the west-facing side of the dwelling. The body was wrapped in birch bark and buried with food, cooking utensils, and items of special significance. During the next four days the individual's spirit or ghost was said to be walking westward to a place where the soul would dwell after death. Food and beverages were left at the grave site for the spirit's consumption during the walk. Grave sites were marked by erecting gabled bark-and-wood houses over the length of the grave. Placed at the head of the grave was a wooden marker painted with a pictograph illustrating the individual's achievements and clan affiliation; the totem animal was painted upside-down, denoting death. Community members often blackened their faces and the faces of their children with charcoal as protection against being the next to die. Families mourned for periods of up to one year. A Feast of the Dead service, scheduled each fall, was sponsored by families who had lost members over the previous year. Food continued to be left at the grave site at regular intervals over a period of many years.

Today, Ojibwe participate in a range of observances related to burials. For many, these observances are like those of any other family with a church service and grave-site ceremony. Some Ojibwe families may blend traditional and contemporary practice; for instance, portions of a Christian service may be spoken in Anishinabemowin. Others may incorporate traditional elements in the burial service, including a lengthy wake of several days marked by singing and a construction of the traditional burial house over the gravesite.

FAMILY AND COMMUNITY LIFE
In traditional Ojibwe culture, an individual lived in a band and was a member of a clan. Most people from the same clan shared a common ancestor on their father's side of the family. Some clans were matrilineal, and children were affiliated with their mother's clan. People of the same clan claim a common *dodaim* (*dodem*, *do dam*, or totem), the symbol of a living creature. The seven original clans were affiliated with the bear, bird, catfish, crane, deer, loon, and marten. Twenty or more clans with additional dodaims were added later. A dodaim could denote an attribute such as prowess, leadership, knowledge, healing power, spirituality, or sustenance. Bands consisted of groups of five to fifty families, up to 400 people, and lived within the same village. Examples are the five large bands of Minnesota: the Superior, Mississippi, Pillager, Red Lake, and Pembina. Bands were formed of people from a number of clans.

Traditionally, Ojibwe behavior was controlled by protocol or etiquette that governed actions during pregnancy, birth, illness, death, and mourning. Parents appointed an elder to give the baby its sacred, or dream, name. The parents would also give the child one or more nicknames. Ojibwe babies were wrapped in swaddling and kept in cradle boards—rectangular wooden frames with a backrest or curved headboard to protect the baby's head, as well as a footrest. Dream catchers—willow hoops encircling woven animal-sinew designs resembling spider webs—and toys of bone, birch bark, shells, or feathers hung from the headboard. Dried moss, cattail down, and rabbit skins served as diapers. Grandparents typically had living with them at least one grandchild, including at least one granddaughter. Childhood was divided into two periods: the time before the child walked, and the time from walking to puberty.

An Ojibwe mother walks with a papoose strapped to her back. THE LIBRARY OF CONGRESS

Family members enjoy teasing each other and sharing stories. Many traditional tales center on Nanabush, a half-human, half-spirit trickster, who was often entangled in humorous scrapes and brought innovations, such as medicine, to humankind from the spirits. Nanabush went by many other names: Naanabozho, Nanibush, Nenabozho, Manabozho, Minabozho, Waynaboozhoo, Wenabozho, Wenabozhoo, Wenebojo, Winabojo, or Winneboshoo. Gambling was another popular pastime. In the moccasin game, players on different teams guessed the location of a marked bullet or metal ball hidden under a moccasin. Gambling was a social event often accompanied by drumming and singing.

The Ojibwe culture has traditionally revered the warrior. The Ojibwe often engaged in battles with and against other Native peoples and joined non-Natives in their fighting. During the French and Indian Wars (1754–1763), the Ojibwe sided primarily with the French. Ojibwe also participated in Pontiac's Rebellion (1763–1764), most notably in the capture of the British-held Fort Michilimackinac (in present-day Michigan). During the War of 1812, Ojibwe living west of Lake Superior sided with the Americans, while those living in present-day Michigan sided with the British. During World War I, the Ojibwe responded to the war effort by buying war bonds and donating money to the Red Cross. Ojibwe men also served in active duty. Ojibwe men served during World War II (1941–1945), and both men and women moved to urban areas for employment in war industries. The grand entrance march at many powwows begins with an honor guard of Ojibwe war veterans. Ojibwe may still be awarded eagle feathers in recognition of extraordinary achievement.

Gender Roles In precontact times, Ojibwe girls became adult around twelve years of age, while boys became men around sixteen. Traditionally, women took care of the needs of the lodging, constructing the wigwams, tending gardens and gathering food, cooking, and preparing clothing. Women also organized the tasks associated with such activities as maple sugaring and wild ricing and helped with the fishing. Women could also hold leadership roles within their villages, and some might have hunted. Men, on the other hand, did the overwhelming majority (if not all) of the hunting and served as protectors of the family. Men also assumed most of the leadership roles within the community. Civil leaders who helped set policy for communities were often chosen on the basis of their rhetorical skill. Warrior leaders were more temporary, convincing a few others to join them in aggressive action against other tribes. Ojibwe men and women worked cooperatively and shared duties and supported each other in accomplishing the tasks they needed for everyday life. For example, men and women traveled in canoes to gather wild rice, with the men poling the canoe through the rice beds and the women knocking the rice from the stalks into the canoe. Ojibwe lived in hunting camps in late fall and winter, and families could become isolated during this time. In winter, men trapped and hunted, and women tanned hides and sewed.

After they encountered the French and began engaging in the fur trade, the Ojibwe's gender roles became more distinct and the labor more clearly divided. Men were responsible for hunting and trapping, and women prepared the animal hides for trade. While some Ojibwe women negotiated with traders, men did most of the negotiating, as this was the practice followed by the Europeans. Ojibwe women sometimes married French traders. Rhetorical skill was important as Ojibwe tribes entered into negotiations with the U.S. government and with other tribes, and men's roles as leaders became more prominent as the United States preferred to communicate with them. After reservations were established, gender roles were defined even more narrowly, with women overseeing homemaking and men taking on new jobs in logging, farming, and selling merchandise.

Today Ojibwe men and women follow lives that mirror those of the majority culture while also incorporating traditional cultural elements. Both men and women may work in varying careers such as education, health, construction, or tribal governance. They may be single heads of households and have connections with an extended family. They may still harvest wild rice together, and both may be involved in fishing and hunting. They may both be craftspeople, with women often creating beaded jewelry and men crafting birchbark baskets. If they participate in powwows, males and females often have distinct dance forms, and women are more likely to prepare the foods served at the gathering, such as fry bread.

Education Before their interactions with the U.S. government, Ojibwe children were tended to and taught by their mothers, aunts, and elders until they reached adolescence. After that age, boys were taught hunting and fishing skills by the men, while girls continued to learn domestic skills from the women and elders. Moral values were taught by example and through storytelling.

From the late nineteenth century through mid-twentieth century, federal policy toward Native education emphasized American Indian assimilation into U.S. society. Consequently, instruction in vocational skills was promoted over the teaching of Native traditions. In fact, Native traditions and languages were forbidden in the government and mission schools. From the 1870s until the 1950s, many Ojibwe children were sent to government day schools, mission schools, or boarding schools located as far away as Kansas and Pennsylvania. School attendance for Ojibwe became compulsory in 1893. A significant step toward Native American education occurred with the passage of the Johnson O'Malley Act in 1934, authorizing states and territories to contract with the Bureau of Indian Affairs (BIA) for services, including education. Public schools were encouraged to incorporate information on Native cultures into their curricula.

Contemporary Ojibwe children living off-reservation have the same educational options as all American students: they attend public or private schools or are homeschooled. Since 1989 public school curricula in Wisconsin have been required by law to incorporate lessons on American Indian cultures; Anishinabe and Dakota history, cultural, and contemporary issues are included in the K-12 social studies standards in Minnesota. Ojibwe living on or near reservations may also be taught in tribally run schools or Bureau of Indian Education contract schools. Some academic institutions offer degree programs specializing in Ojibwe culture. In addition, nine of the thirty-eight tribal colleges in the United States and Canada that are affiliated with the American Indian Higher Education Consortium (AIHEC) are located on Ojibwe reservations: Bay Mills Community College (Brimley, Michigan), Fond du Lac Tribal and Community College (Cloquet, Minnesota), Keweenaw Bay Ojibwa Community College (Baraga, Michigan), Lac Courte Oreilles Ojibwe Community College (Hayward, Wisconsin), Leech Lake Tribal College (Cass Lake, Minnesota), Red Lake Nation College (Red Lake, Minnesota), Saginaw Chippewa Tribal College (Mount Pleasant, Michigan), Turtle Mountain Community College (Belcourt, North Dakota), and White Earth Tribal and Community College (Mahnomen, Minnesota). These institutions offer certificates, associate's degrees, and, sometimes, bachelor's degrees, and, in their roles as community centers, serve as focal points of Ojibwe culture.

As with other Native peoples, Ojibwe have lower rates of postsecondary educational attainment than the rates for the overall U.S. population. According to the American Community Survey (ACS) estimates for 2009–2011, the Ojibwe (Chippewa) high school graduation rate was equivalent to the overall U.S. rate, with 85 percent of the people ages twenty-five and over holding a high school diploma (or equivalent) or higher. The ACS indicated that 15.6 percent of Ojibwe (Chippewa) had a bachelor's degree or higher (compared to the U.S. rate of 28.2 percent). The composition of Ojibwe students in higher education often differs significantly from that of non-Native students: they generally are older, drop out at higher rates, take longer to complete their degrees, and often are married with children. These students face many obstacles, including culturally rooted learning differences and homesickness if they relocate. Students requesting financial aid from their tribe may be channeled into certain fields of study, such as education, social work, or medicine.

Courtship and Weddings Traditionally, Ojibwe women were allowed to marry soon after puberty, at age fourteen or fifteen. Boys were allowed to marry as soon as they could demonstrate their ability to support a family through hunting. Parents sometimes selected the wives or husbands for their children. During courtship the couple's contact was supervised. If both young people were found acceptable to each other and to their families, the man moved in with the wife's family for a year. There was no formal wedding ceremony. If the marriage proved to be disharmonious or if the wife failed to conceive, then the man returned to his parents. A couple that wished to continue living together after the year would build their own separate dwelling. Marital separation was allowed, and after separation people could remarry. Men who could support more than one family might have more than one wife. Intermarriage was acceptable, and by 1900 most Ojibwe were of mixed heritage, typically French and Ojibwe.

Today Ojibwe people's courtships and weddings are reflective of contemporary U.S. culture. Couples may marry or not. Those who marry may have lengthy engagements or may elope or marry after short periods of time. Wedding services may take place in religious settings such as churches, or they may be civil ceremonies.

With the Ojibwe's greater financial stability in the twenty-first century, Ojibwe culture has been experiencing a renaissance as natives and non-natives are studying Ojibwe botany, crafts, traditional stories, and language. Wild ricing by canoe is still a valued, even sacred, part of the culture.

EMPLOYMENT AND ECONOMIC CONDITIONS

Modern Ojibwe live on reservations and in a variety of rural, suburban, and urban non-reservation areas. Like other Native peoples, the Ojibwe, particularly those on reservations, have high rates of unemployment. They may support themselves through seasonal work, including forestry, farming, tourism, trapping, and wild ricing. Since the 1970s many reservations have also supported small businesses: bait shops, campgrounds, clothing manufacturing, construction, fish hatcheries, hotels, lumber stores, marinas, restaurants, and service stations.

Treaty rights allow modern Ojibwe to hunt, fish, and harvest rice on lands once belonging to their ancestors. The Ojibwe right to use the natural resources of reservation lands ceded to the government was reaffirmed by the U.S. Court of Appeals for the Seventh Circuit in the 1983 Voigt Decision. In 1987 a federal court ruled that these rights extended to the use of traditional methods and that the Ojibwe had the right to use their natural resources to the extent that they could support a modest standard of living.

With the passage of the Indian Gaming Regulatory Act in 1988, reservations were accorded new employment venues related to gaming, including bingo halls, casinos, and spin-off businesses such as gas stations, hotels, golf courses, and restaurants. While there is some opposition to gaming, profits have contributed to higher employment levels and income for the Ojibwe. Tribes have invested gaming income in purchasing ancestral lands, in road and home construction, and in building new social service buildings or extending social services. Some reservations have passed employment-rights ordinances requiring employers on reservations to give preference to tribal members in hiring, training, and promotion.

American Indians, including the Ojibwe, have among the lowest per capita income within the United States. The Chippewa had a per capita income of $17,385, according to the American Community Survey (ACS) estimates for 2006–2010; the U.S. per capita income during the same period was an estimated $27,334. Features of the Ojibwe economy include seasonal employment in wild rice harvesting, fishing, and logging, as well as tribal social services such as education and health care. The ACS estimates for 2006–2010 indicated that the top three occupational areas among Chippewa were management, business, science, or art occupations (28 percent), service occupations (26 percent), and sales or office occupations (24 percent). The industry area with the largest percentage of Ojibwe employers was education, health, and social services (24 percent), followed by arts, entertainment, recreation, accommodation, and food services (17 percent). These rates do not distinguish between Ojibwe living on or off reservation lands. The results do support evidence that contemporary employment issues are impacted by tourism and hospitality.

POLITICS AND GOVERNMENT

Traditional Ojibwe governance followed a multitiered system of elders, civil chiefs, and, when necessary, war chiefs. Elders—older and respected tribe members—played vital roles in decision making and educating younger members of the band. Civil chiefs could inherit their position or be nominated. Elders met in councils to identify a potential civil chief who would manage day-to-day operations. The nominee, who could be female or male, could accept the invitation to serve as civil chief, though such acceptance was not mandatory. Chiefs had official assistants, including messengers and orators. Civil chiefs could also summon the council of elders to request assistance. Councils of chiefs and elders from a number of bands met to discuss major decisions that would affect more than one band. War chiefs were self-appointed; a war chief was any man who could convince others to join him in battle. Adult men and women were part of the general council, and while votes were not tallied, each individual could join in the discussion at tribal meetings.

Today reservation areas are striving for home rule—the right to set and follow laws of their own making. Ojibwe reservations in Minnesota, except for Red Lake, are each governed by an elected Reservation Business Council (RBC; also known as a Reservation Tribal Council) as well as a chairperson and a secretary-treasurer. The RBC discusses approval of loans, petitions requesting enrollment in the tribe, and issues relating to economic development. The six reservations of the Minnesota Chippewa Tribe also have a statewide Tribal Executive Committee (TEC), which meets every three months. While the RBC governs the reservation, the TEC governs the tribe, as constituted by its six member reservations. The Red Lake Reservation has an elected tribal council consisting of three officers (chairperson, secretary, and treasurer) and eight council members. Red Lake also maintains traditional governance through an advisory council of descendants of civil chiefs.

Each of the Ojibwe tribes in Michigan, Wisconsin, North Dakota, and Montana is also governed by a tribal council. Tribal constitutions will stipulate how the governing body of the tribe is elected, the number of board members, their terms of office, their roles, duties, and powers. Most boards are led by a chairperson who is assisted by a vice-chairperson, secretary/treasurer, and general board members.

During the Red Power movement of the late 1960s, some urban Ojibwe in Minneapolis formed an activist organization called the American Indian Movement (AIM). A modern proponent of the Native warrior ethic, AIM was involved in a number of civil rights protests that received national attention, including the occupation of Alcatraz Island in 1969–1971 and the occupation of the Bureau of Indian Affairs office in Washington, D.C., in 1972.

In 1971 members of Lac Courte Oreilles in Wisconsin protested the presence of a dam that flooded traditional rice beds by occupying the site, leading to tribal members gaining compensation for loss of the food supply and approval of the members to operate the dam. Two Lac Courte Oreilles challenged restrictions on off-reservation fishing on ceded lands in 1974, an action that led to years of court actions addressing Ojibwe hunting and fishing rights afforded by treaties. These actions culminated in a U.S. Supreme Court ruling in 1999 that affirmed that Ojibwe could gather food, including hunting and fishing, on their ceded lands in the states of Wisconsin, Michigan, and Minnesota.

Ojibwe tribal members continue to be involved in local and national political issues. Winona LaDuke, a member of the White Earth Reservation in northwestern Minnesota, was Ralph Nader's vice presidential candidate during his run for the U.S. presidency in 2000. In 2013 Ojibwe in Wisconsin coordinated protests against a proposed open-pit mine near tribal lands. The Saginaw Chippewa Tribe of Michigan has been involved in repatriation of human remains from locations such as the Michigan Department of Transportation and the University of Nebraska–Lincoln. The Saginaw also publicly supported Canada's Idle No More political protest movement, which calls on governments to acknowledge and negotiate with tribes. Ojibwe tribes, including the Saginaw, also released public announcements in support of the reauthorization of the U.S. Violence Against Women Act (VAWA) with revisions that would provide more protection to Native women living on reservations.

NOTABLE INDIVIDUALS

Academia White Earth enrollee Will Antell (1935–) served as an educational consultant on Native education for the state of Minnesota and founded the National Indian Education Association in 1969. Edward Benton-Banai (1934–), one of the founders of the activist organization the American Indian Movement (AIM), led the development of Ojibwe-based K-12 education. Duane Champagne (1951–) served as director of UCLA's American Indian Studies Center, where he was also the editor of the *American Indian Culture and Research Journal*. Patty Loew (1952–) is a journalism professor at the University of Wisconsin–Madison as well as an author, filmmaker, and television personality. Thomas Peacock (1951–), professor in the College of Education at the University of Minnesota at Duluth, has coauthored a number of books on Ojibwe culture. Loriene Roy (1954–) founded a national reading club for Native children and served as the first American Indian president of the American Library Association. Anton Treuer (1969–) has served as executive director of the American Indian Resource Center at Bemidji State University in Minnesota. He is known for his work on Ojibwe language revitalization, as is his brother, the writer and academic David Treuer (1970–).

Government and Politics Among those credited with founding AIM were Dennis Banks (1937–) and Clyde Howard Bellecourt (1936–). Both were instrumental in organizing events such as the 1972 Trail of Broken Treaties caravan to Washington, D.C., which resulted in the highly publicized takeover of the BIA offices. Leonard Peltier (1944–) took part in the 1973 occupation of Wounded Knee, South Dakota. Convicted of killing two FBI agents, he was imprisoned in Coleman, Florida. His controversial conviction is examined in the 1992 film *Incident at Oglala*. A number of foreign countries and organizations, including Amnesty International, have regarded Peltier as a prisoner of conscience. Economist Winona LaDuke (1959–) is an international spokesperson on environmental change and founder of the White Earth Land Recovery Project.

Literature Author and poet Louise Erdrich (1954–) is the best-known modern Ojibwe writer of fiction, nonfiction, and poetry and is also known for her bookstore, Birchbark Books, that serves as a central point for writers and for promoting Anishinabemowin publishing. The characters in Erdrich's fiction follow a rich genealogy of Pillager band Ojibwe and non-Native characters from the nineteenth century to the modern reservation milieu of gaming and competition dancing. Her novels include: *Love Medicine* (1984), *The Antelope Wife* (1998), *The Crown of Columbus* (1999), *The Plague of Doves* (2008), *The Round House* (2012), and The Birchbark House series for young readers. Her sister, the author, playwright, and poet Heid E. Erdrich (1963–), has taught writing workshops and, along with Louise, has been active in Ojibwe language publishing efforts.

Poet, novelist, and journalist Jim Northrup Jr. (1943–) has written about modern Anishinabe life on the Fond du Lac Reservation in northeastern Minnesota. His books include *Walking the Rez Road* (1993), a collection of his poems and short stories; *The Rez Road Follies: Canoes, Casinos, Computers and Birch Bark Baskets* (1997); and *Anishinaabe Syndicated: A View from the Rez* (2011). His humorous and often biting commentary appears in a column titled "Fond du Lac Follies," published in the *Circle* and *News from Indian Country*.

David Treuer (1970–) is a writer whose novels include *Little* (1995) and *The Hiawatha* (1999); in 2012 he published a nonfiction book titled *Rez Life: An Indian's Journey through Reservation Life*.

Gerald Vizenor (1934–), a member of the Minnesota Chippewa Tribe, is a professor of American studies at the University of New Mexico. A poet and novelist, his writing centers on traditional culture and includes such works as *Interior Landscapes: Autobiographical Myths and Metaphors* (1990); *The Heirs of Columbus* (1992); *Fugitive Poses: Native American Indian Scenes of Absence and Presence* (1998); and *Shrouds of White Earth* (2010), which won an American Book Award.

MEDIA

PERIODICALS

The Circle

Published by the Minneapolis American Indian Center, this monthly publication provides international, national, and local news relevant to Indian concerns and tracks issues of importance to the Ojibwe.

Catherine Whipple, Managing Editor
P.O. Box 6026
Minneapolis, Minnesota 55406
Phone: (612) 722-3686
Fax: (612) 722-3773
Email: thecirclenews@gmail.com
URL: http://thecirclenews.org/

Mazina'igan

Published by the Great Lakes Indian Fish and Wildlife Commission (GLIFWC), this quarterly publication (whose name means "Talking Paper") reports on GLIFWC activities and on a broader range of issues of importance to the Ojibwe, including antitreaty activity, treaty support, Indian education, Native culture, Native rights, and major federal legislation.

Susan Erickson, Editor
P.O. Box 9
72682 Maple Street
Odanah, Wisconsin 54861
Phone: (715) 682-6619
Email: pio@glifwc.org
URL: www.glifwc.org/publications/mazinaigan/Mazinaigan.html

Oshkaabewis Native Journal

Published at Bemidji State University, this is the only scholarly journal on Ojibwe culture. Many articles are written in Anishinabemowin, the Ojibwe language.

Anton Treuer, Editor
Bemidji State University
114 American Indian Resource Center #21
1500 Birchmont Drive Northeast
Bemidji, Minnesota 56601
Phone: (218) 755-2032
Fax: (218) 755-2138
Email: atreuer@bemidjistate.edu.
URL: www.bemidjistate.edu/airc/oshkaabewis/

ORGANIZATIONS AND ASSOCIATIONS

Great Lakes Indian Fish and Wildlife Commission (GLIFWC)

Founded in 1983, the GLIFWC's mission is to assist eleven Ojibwe tribes in Michigan, Minnesota, and Wisconsin to better manage their natural resources in off-reservation areas. It publishes a free quarterly newsletter, *Mazina'igin* (Talking Paper).

James Zorn, Executive Administrator
P.O. Box 9
72682 Maple Street
Odanah, Wisconsin 54861
Phone: (715) 682-6619

Fax: (715) 682-9294
Email: pio@pio@glifwc.org
URL: www.glifwc.org

MUSEUMS AND RESEARCH CENTERS

D'Arcy McNickle Center for American Indian and Indigenous Studies

Located within the Newberry Library, the McNickle Center provides access to scholarly material in the E. E. Ayer Collection. It also sponsors seminars, exhibits, summer institutes, and fellowships and publishes occasional papers, bibliographies, and monographs.

Scott Manning Stevens, Director
60 West Walton Street
Chicago, Illinois 60610-3394
Phone: (312) 255-3563
Email: stevenss@newberry.org,
URL: www.newberry.org/darcy-mcnickle-center-american-indian-and-indigenous-studies

Mille Lacs Indian Museum / Minnesota Historical Society

This tribal museum operates under the Minnesota Historical Society. It tells about the history and present-day life of the Mille Lacs Band of Ojibwe and hosts cultural events such as maple sugaring, birch-bark harvesting, and powwows.

Travis Zimmerman, Site Manager
43411 Oodena Drive
Onamia, Minnesota 56359
Phone: (320) 532-3632
Fax: (320) 532-4625
Email: millelacs@mnhs.org
URL: http://sites.mnhs.org/historic-sites/historic-sites/mille-lacs-indian-museum

Minnesota History Center

The center houses the Minnesota Historical Society's collection of artifacts. It includes an extensive research and archival collection on the Native peoples of the state. Among its vast and varied exhibits on the Ojibwe is a detailed exhibit on wild ricing.

D. Stephen Elliott, Director
345 Kellogg Boulevard West
Saint Paul, Minnesota 55102
Phone: (651) 259-3000
Fax: (651) 296-1004
Email: Director@mnhs.org
URL: www.minnesotahistorycenter.org

Ziibiwing Center of Anishinabe Culture & Lifeways

The Ziibiwing Center's collections and archives represent the cultural history of the Saginaw Chippewa Tribe of Michigan. The museum space includes exhibits, an archive, a library, a gift shop, and space for community events such as performances and community craft groups.

Shannon Martin, Director
6650 East Broadway
Mount Pleasant, Michigan 48858
Phone: (989) 775-4750
Fax: (989) 775-4770
Email: SMartin@sagchip.org
URL: www.sagchip.org/ziibiwing/

SOURCES FOR ADDITIONAL STUDY

Densmore, Frances. *How Indians Use Wild Rice Plants for Food, Medicine and Crafts*. New York: Dover, 1974. Originally published as *Uses of Plants by the Chippewa Indians*, 1928.

Hilger, M. Indez. *Chippewa Child Life and Its Cultural Background*. St. Paul: Minnesota Historical Society Press, 1992. First published 1951 by the Smithsonian Institution Bureau of American Ethnology.

Johnston, Basil. *Ojibway Ceremonies*. Lincoln: University of Nebraska Press, 1990.

Loew, Patty. *Indian Nations of Wisconsin: Histories of Endurance and Renewal*. Madison: Wisconsin Historical Society Press, 2001.

Peacock, Thomas, and Marlene Wisuri. *The Four Hills of Life: Ojibwe Wisdom*. Afton, MN: Afton Historical Society Press, 2006.

———. *Ojibwe Waasa Inaabidaa: We Look in All Directions*. Afton, MN: Afton Historical Society Press, 2002.

Treuer, Anton, ed. *Living Our Language: Ojibwe Tales and Oral Histories: A Bilingual Anthology*. St. Paul: Minnesota Historical Society Press, 2001.

Vennum, Thomas, Jr. *The Ojibwa Dance Drum: Its History and Construction*. St. Paul: Minnesota Historical Society Press, 2009.

———*Wild Rice and the Ojibway People*. St. Paul: Minnesota Historical Press, 1988.

Warren, William Whipple. *History of the Ojibway People*. 2nd ed. St. Paul: Minnesota Historical Society Press, 2009. First published 1885.

ONEIDAS

Angela Washburn Heisey and Richard C. Hanes

OVERVIEW

The Oneidas are a Native American people who traditionally lived in what is now modern-day central New York State. Their territory stretched from the St. Lawrence River in the north southward to the border of what is now Pennsylvania. The Oneidas, who were an Iroquois-speaking nation, primarily inhabited the lands south of Oneida Lake, a freshwater lake they called *Tsioqui* ("white water"). The largest lake in New York, it was part of a waterway system that connected the Atlantic coast of North America to the continental interior. English settlers coined the word *Oneida* from the French *Onneiouts* (a Huron name for the Oneida people) and the word *Onyota'a:ka*, which the Oneida called themselves. *Onyota'a:ka* translates as "People of the Standing Stone." Each village had a large stone around which the Oneidas would gather to conduct important ceremonies, such as telling of their Creation Narrative. The stone symbolized permanence and strength in a world full of change.

Europeans made first contact with the Oneida people in the early 1600s. Population statistics prior to contact are debatable. Archaeological evidence provides the best insights into demography, and scholars vary in their estimates, citing anywhere between 1,000 and 5,000 Oneida before contact. Around 1100 CE, the five Iroquois nations in what is today upstate New York—the Oneida, Maqua (Mohawk), Onondaga, Cayuga, and Seneca—began to band together, and in the late fifteenth century the tribes formed a confederacy known as the Five Nations. The Five Nations became the most powerful indigenous force in the region. They took on the name *Hodinonhsyo:ni*, which translates as "People of the Long House." Of the Five Nations, the Oneida had the smallest population, but they contributed greatly to the confederacy. They were considered by many to be the fiercest warriors. From 1000 CE on, the Oneida lived in comfort in semi-permanent settlements. They developed agricultural techniques, and their most important crops were corn, beans, and squash, known as the "Three Sisters."

In the nineteenth century the Oneida lost the majority of their land to the state of New York by multiple treaties, and many of them relocated, settling in Wisconsin and Ontario. Only about 200 Oneida remained in New York State. Today, the majority of Oneidas live on or near three independent and federally recognized reservations in New York, Wisconsin, and Ontario. These are the Oneida Nation of Wisconsin (west of Green Bay), the Oneida Indian Nation in New York, and the Oneida Nation of the Thames in Ontario, Canada. Additionally, nearly 2,000 Oneidas live on the Six Nations of the Grand River reserve in Ontario.

According to the 2012 *New World Encyclopedia*, there are more than 100,000 Oneidas living in North America. Oneida Tribe vice chair Kathy Hughes claims this number is too high, and that the Oneida population is closer to 26,000 (which is roughly equal to the number of undergraduate students at the University of California–Los Angeles). According to Hughes, there are 4,162 tribal members living on the Oneida Nation in Wisconsin and just over 12,000 tribal members living in the vicinity of the reservation. The other reservations combined have reported about 10,000 tribal members. While Wisconsin is the state with the largest number of Oneida, other states with small, but significant, Oneida populations include Arizona, California, Florida, Illinois, Michigan, Minnesota, New York, and Texas. Both the Oneida Nation of Wisconsin and the Oneida Indian Nation in New York own and operate their own casinos. The Turning Stone Resort Casino of the Oneida Indian Nation in New York has hotel accommodations, a PGA golf course, and a restaurant, all of which earn huge revenues annually. The Turning Stone Resort Casino is one of the top five tourist destinations in New York, with more than four million visitors a year.

HISTORY OF THE PEOPLE

Early History European contact with the Oneida people, who traditionally lived in a single principal village, occurred early in the seventeenth century, possibly as early as 1616. The Oneidas became fur traders to obtain European goods such as iron axes, brass ornaments, and glass beads. Jack Campisi in *Handbook of North American Indians* reported that by 1640 two trade networks competed, one made up of the Algonquin and Huron tribes and French traders, and the other consisting of the Oneidas and the Dutch and English. These two trade networks warred until the beginning of the eighteenth century.

During the American Revolutionary War, the Oneidas fought with the Continental Army against the British and supplied George Washington's starving army with hundreds of bushels of corn in the winter of 1777–1778 at Valley Forge. Their alliance with the Americans did not bode well for their relationships with other Iroquois tribes who were sympathetic to the British. Many of the other Iroquois moved to Canada after the war. However, in payment for their assistance, the U.S. Continental Congress offered the Oneidas the Treaty of Fort Stanwix (1784), which guaranteed their claim to their traditional lands. The treaty provided that the Oneidas "shall be secure in the possession of the lands on which they are settled."

However, many state officials and entrepreneurs viewed the Oneida land as valuable and strategic, and despite this treaty with the federal government, the New York State Legislature aided white settlement in these lands by means of their own treaties, dispossessing the Oneida of most of their land in New York. The Oneidas, at this time, were not unified. The various factions could not agree on political and religious issues and, therefore, could not fight against these pressures effectively. As a result of the 1785 Treaty at Fort Herkimer and the 1788 Treaty of Fort Schuyler, the Oneidas were stripped of most of their ancestral lands. Their territory was reduced from more than 6 million acres to about 300,000 acres.

In 1790 the U.S. Congress passed the Indian Trade and Non-Intercourse Act, forbidding anyone to purchase Indian land without prior federal consent, and in 1794 the Treaty of Canandaigua and the Veterans' Treaty were signed to protect the boundaries of the occupied Oneida lands. However, the state of New York continued to ignore federal efforts to protect the Indian lands. State and local governments imposed a total of twenty-six treaties (all later ruled illegal), and the Oneida territory was further reduced—to a mere 300 acres. In 1810 the Ogden Land Company acquired preemptive rights to native lands in New York, giving the company the right to purchase acreage before others.

Between 1821 and 1822 Chief Shenandoah of the Oneida established treaties with the Menominee in order to settle their lands in the Wisconsin Territory. After many disputes, the treaties were ratified in 1831 and 1832, thereby resolving the Menominee land cession to the Oneida. Between 1823 and 1838, close to seven hundred of the 1,500 Oneidas in New York relocated to a 4-million-acre tract in Wisconsin, which President James Monroe soon reduced to 500,000 acres. Then, in 1838, according to Campisi, the Treaty of Buffalo Creek directed the removal of all Iroquois from New York State while the Wisconsin land base was further decreased to only 65,000 acres. In reaction, more than two hundred Oneidas sold their New York land in 1839 and jointly purchased 5,200 acres near London, Ontario. During the early 1840s, more than four hundred Oneidas moved north into Ontario, reuniting with members of the Iroquois League who earlier had fled their traditional New York lands. Only about two hundred Oneidas were left in New York. Some settled around the town of Oneida, while many moved onto the Onondaga reservation near Syracuse.

Modern Era Throughout the late nineteenth and early twentieth centuries, the Oneidas of New York and Wisconsin lobbied the federal government and fought legal battles to regain land lost in previous centuries and to prevent further loss of land through land allotment and assimilationist policies. A significant blow to long-term tribal prosperity in Wisconsin was the allotment of reservation lands under authority of the General Allotment Act of 1887. By 1908 the entire reservation had been divided up among individual tribal members. Those eighteen years and older received about 40 acres of land each, and minors obtained a smaller land allotment of about 8 acres. Often the parcels allotted to members of the same tribal families were not adjoining, thus hampering farming efforts. The new tax burdens proved to be too heavy, and by the mid-1920s most lands had passed out of tribal ownership through foreclosures, and only a few hundred acres remained in the possession of the Oneida. The tribal government ceased operation, and many Oneidas moved to urban areas for wage employment in factories. The federal government repurchased some of the foreclosed lands after the tribe formed a new government in the 1930s.

Following World War II, the United States adopted an Indian "termination," or assimilationist, policy. Proponents of the policy rationalized this scheme of taking tribal lands and eliminating government services as a way to forcibly assimilate Oneidas into mainstream American society. Despite prior internal political divisions, the Oneidas of Wisconsin united in the effort to resist the federal government's attempts to sell off what tribal lands they still held. Wisconsin Oneida leaders such as Dennison Hill, Irene Moore, Charles A. Hill, Mamie Smith, Oscar Archiquette, and Morris Wheelock united to battle against termination legislation of the late 1940s and early 1950s. The Oneidas also struggled to preserve the terms of the 1794 Canandaigua Treaty, which, among other things, called for a government annuity to the Oneidas. The U.S. government paid it off in a lump sum. By 1956, federal government pressures began to lessen, and the threat passed. Two buildings in Oneida, Wisconsin, are named for key figures of this period in Oneida land claims history: Irene Moore and Oscar Archiquette.

By the 1970s the Wisconsin Oneidas owned just 2,200 acres in scattered panels interspersed with land of non-Indian ownership. In 1974 the U.S. Supreme Court ruled in favor of the Oneida Indian Nation, agreeing with its claim against New York's Madison and Oneida counties that native land had been taken without congressional approval, but the counties appealed this decision. In 1985 the Oneidas scored another major victory when the U.S. Supreme Court ruled that the 1790 Non-Intercourse Act negated the earlier treaties between the Oneidas and New York State. The 1985 decision, known as *County of Oneida v. Oneida Indian Nation* ruled that the 270,000 acres of Oneida lands that were transferred more than 175 years earlier had violated the Indian Non-Intercourse Act. In this landmark decision in American Indian law, the court found no applicable statute of limitations and no legal basis to deny the Oneidas' land claim, ruling that the Oneidas held a right to a large amount of land in central New York State in Oneida and Madison counties.

Taking their case before the federal courts brought together the three separate groups of Oneidas—the Oneida Indian Nation in New York, the Oneida Nation of Wisconsin, and the Oneida Nation of the Thames in Ontario. Beginning in 1987, the Oneidas began a decade-long attempt to negotiate a settlement with the state of New York, but with no success. Finally, in 1998, the Oneidas filed a lawsuit against the state in an effort to end the case. To assert their right to repossess the lands that had been illegally taken from them two centuries before, the suit named the thousands of landowners in the contested region as defendants. In late 1998 the U.S. government joined the suit on behalf of the tribes, but New York State declared immunity from the suit under the Eleventh Amendment. Finally, in October 2011 the case that had begun in 1974 with the Oneidas seeking 270,000 acres of former tribal land in New York came to an end when the U.S. Supreme Court announced that it would not hear the case.

Despite the ongoing court cases and litigation, since 1995 Colgate University and the Oneida Indian Nation have collaborated in summer archaeological workshops and fieldwork. The goal is to strengthen the relationship between the university and the Oneida Indian Nation and to provide hands-on opportunities to Oneida youth while keeping them in touch with their heritage. Much has been unearthed, such as skeletal remains and funerary objects. There has been positive local and national media coverage. Collaborative archaeology has helped bring together native and non-native communities.

In the twentieth century the Oneida Nation of the Thames in Ontario established its own community center, businesses, health clinic, radio station, rest home, and police station. Two main factions coexist in the reservation: those who continue to follow the teachings of Handsome Lake (an Iroquoian prophet living in the early nineteenth century), and those who reject his teachings. The Code of Handsome Lake is called the "Good Message" because it reconciles people with their Creator. The Code emphasizes the evils of alcohol, witchcraft, abortion, and promiscuity, and it promotes caring for the elderly, orphans, and the poor. Many of the social projects on the Oneida Nation of the Thames, such as the health clinic and community center, reflect the Code of Handsome Lake.

SETTLEMENT IN THE UNITED STATES

Game such as deer, elk, and turkeys were abundant in Iroquoia, and wild berries, fruit, and fishing helped the indigenous peoples flourish. Because of this natural food supply, semipermanent settlements began as early as 1000 CE. At times, soil depletion, sanitation problems, and insect infestations forced relocation. With more permanent villages, agriculture became increasingly important, and villages expanded. Individual tribes began to form around 1100 CE. The various tribes shared the same Iroquois language, with subtle differences becoming more pronounced over time. These tribes were the Oneida, Maqua (Mohawk), Onondaga, Cayuga, and Seneca. For the purpose of peace, the tribes banded together to form a league in the late fifteenth century, known at the Five Nations. They called themselves *Hodinonhsyo:ni*, or "People of the Long House." This term emphasized the importance placed on the extended family structure, or *ohwachira*, of the Iroquois. The Five Nations became a powerful indigenous force and expanded its territory by means of warfare.

The Oneidas primarily settled in the lands south of Oneida Lake. Like the other Iroquois tribes, they had a profound attachment to the land. The land held the spirits of their ancestors and deities. Corn, beans, and squash (the "Three Sisters") were the most important crops, and great value was placed on hunting and fishing. Warfare was central to Oneida culture. Warriors not only defended their land, but also expanded it and seized booty, such as furs. The Oneidas were highly respected among the other Iroquois, and they contributed greatly to the Five Nations. Not only were they considered by many to be the fiercest warriors, but they were also fine mediators who acted with good judgment.

The first migration of the Oneida people to Wisconsin happened between 1820 and 1838. Traveling primarily by lake steamers, the majority of the community followed the Indian missionary Eleazar Williams to Wisconsin (west of Green Bay) in 1821. The settlement pattern of the Oneidas in Wisconsin was largely based on religion. In eight small communities, the Anglicans settled on the northern portion of the reserve and the Methodists to the south. Today, this remains the largest Oneida community. The conditions for the Oneidas who remained in New York worsened, and many early accounts describe the squalor in which they lived. Because of this decline, most of the remaining Oneida moved to Wisconsin and Ontario in three separate groups between 1839 and 1845. By 1845, only about two hundred Oneidas lived in New York State.

The Oneidas today comprise three separately recognized groups: the Oneida Indian Nation in New York, the Oneida Nation of Wisconsin, and the Oneida Nation of the Thames in Ontario. Additionally, the Six Nations of the Grand River in Ontario is home to

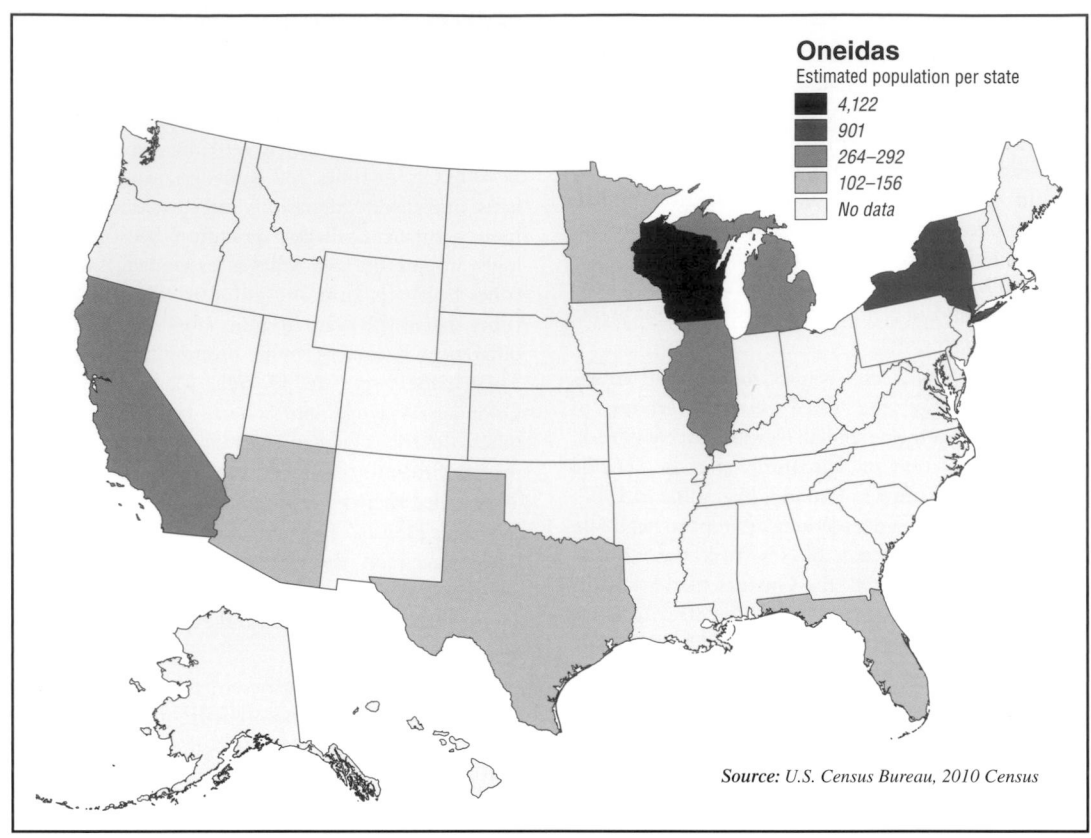

Oneidas
Estimated population per state

- 4,122
- 901
- 264–292
- 102–156
- No data

Source: U.S. Census Bureau, 2010 Census

members of all Iroquois tribes, including nearly two thousand Oneidas. Each group has its own government independent of the others.

As of 2010, there were more than one thousand Oneidas living on the reservation in central New York and about two thousand tribal members living in the vicinity. The tribe runs the successful Turning Stone Resort Casino, a top tourist destination in New York. They host a PGA tournament annually in the fall. The Oneida Indian Nation is the largest employer in the area, providing about five thousand jobs. Less well known is that the Oneida Indian Nation in New York offers classes on Oneida culture, such as learning how to make traditional Oneida dolls, beadwork, and baskets. Oneida youth have participated in collaborative archaeology workshops and fieldwork with Colgate University since 1995. It has been a keen interest of the tribe to educate its youth about Oneida culture and heritage.

As of 2010, 4,162 Oneidas lived on the reservation in Wisconsin, and overall tribal enrollment in the Oneida Nation of Wisconsin was more than 16,000. The successful Oneida Casino has five locations in and near Green Bay with hotel accommodations. The Oneida Nation of the Thames has about 5,500 tribal members, with more than 2,000 living on the reserve. The community center is popular because of weekly bingo and Oneida language lessons for children.

There is a health care facility that employs about eighty workers. Arizona, Texas, New York, California, Florida, Minnesota, Michigan, and Illinois are other states with significant numbers of Oneida.

The Six Nations of the Grand River in Brantford, Ontario, is the only reservation with all Iroquois tribes living together: Oneida, Mohawk, Onondaga, Cayuga, and Seneca, plus the Tuscarora. (The Tuscarora people were admitted to the Five Nations in the eighteenth century and are culturally and linguistically related to the Iroquois. The Five Nations thus became the Six Nations.) The Oneida population of the Six Nations of the Grand River is nearly two thousand, with about half living on the reserve. Great emphasis is placed on educating youth, with many students graduating from Assumption College School and Brantford Collegiate Institute and Vocational School.

LANGUAGE

Oneida is a Native American language of the Iroquoian family, related most closely to Mohawk. It is also distantly related to Cherokee and Huron. Oneida is considered an "endangered language" because so few people know and learn it. Most Oneidas today speak English and know only a handful of Oneida expressions. According to the Summer Institute of Linguistics, a linguistics forum of Wycliff Translators, in 1977 only 250 speakers of Oneida remained out of a total population of 7,000. In 1996 a survey by the Oneida Nation of Wisconsin and the University of Wisconsin indicated there were only twenty-five to thirty elders who spoke Oneida as a first language. More recent studies from the University of Wisconsin estimate there are about fifty native speakers, and only about three to ten of them are fluent. This small number of speakers included members of all three branches: the Oneidas of central New York, eastern Wisconsin, and Ontario. Dialect differences are very minor.

Oneida differs greatly from English. It has fewer sounds; for example, there are no labial phonemes (sounds produced from the lips) and there are many whispered syllables. Most words are structurally verbs, even if functioning as nouns. There are far fewer nouns and participles than English. Single verbs can equal entire English clauses. The traditional Oneida language connects the Oneida people to their ancestors and rich heritage, primarily through storytelling. The Oneida Creation Story—an explanation for the presence of good and evil in the world—provides a fine example of this.

Oneida people consider their language one of their most precious traditions. Language programs have been established in Oneida communities to foster the passing of the language to young people by older members. The Oneida Language Revitalization Program began in 1996 to help educate Oneida youth in Wisconsin, and the Wisconsin Oneida Language Preservation Project teaches stories and songs in the Oneida language to elementary students. The community center at the Oneida Nation of the Thames also teaches children the Oneida language. The Oneidas have produced audiotapes, CD-ROMs, online flashcards, and booklets to teach the traditional language. The dream of many Oneidas is that one day most members will be able to speak the language fluently.

Greetings and Popular Expressions Common Oneida greetings and expressions include the following: *shekoli* (hello); *wastehtsisliyo* (good morning); *sahsutiyohak* (good night); *i-kê* (I am walking); *ikkehe* (I see it); *o-nyohsa* (squash); *oga-oh* (it tastes good); *kalo-ya* (sky, or heaven); *ganoonyok* (a thanksgiving speech); *onéo* (corn); *o'gyo-dyo-h* (it is snowing); *agatho-de* (I hear it); and, *o-ge-k* (I ate it).

RELIGION

Before European contact, the Oneidas had many spiritual practices and beliefs. Sacred stories such as the Oneida Creation Narrative told of the struggle between good and evil. The Sky Woman's twins—Good Spirit and Bad Spirit—influenced both good and bad actions in this world. Animism, or the worldview in which animate and inanimate objects possess spiritual essence, best describes early Oneida belief. Animism is a type of spirituality in which trees, rivers, animals, and the sky were thought to have a spiritual essence. Deities and ancestor spirits filled the land.

After European contact, Christianity became predominant among the Oneidas. At the dawn of the nineteenth century an Iroquoian prophet known as Handsome Lake experienced visions that formed the basis of what became the Longhouse religion. This monotheistic Native American religion was strongly based on a Christian model, with some ancestral ceremonies included. The Christian influence in the Longhouse religion came from years of contact with neighboring Quakers, Catholics, and Protestants. According to Anthony F. C. Wallace in *Handbook of North American Indians*, Handsome Lake's visions were put into a moral code that outlawed drunkenness, gambling, quarreling, sexual promiscuity, wife-beating, and witchcraft. Although Handsome Lake belonged to the Seneca tribe and did not directly come to the Oneidas, some Wisconsin and Canadian Oneidas became believers. The prophet had more visions and kept advising the Iroquois, including on the continuation of celebrating the traditional Oneida religious ceremonies.

The Oneidas were also influenced strongly by Presbyterian minister Samuel Kirkland. The minister established a church among the Oneidas in 1766 and lived with the tribe for more than forty years, until his death in 1808. In the 1770s French entrepreneur Pierre Penet established a Catholic mission among the Oneidas. However, the governor of New York removed Penet and the Catholic mission shortly after.

When the Oneidas relocated from New York to Wisconsin, the majority of tribal members were Protestant Christians. Although many Wisconsin Oneidas have been members of Episcopal and Methodist churches throughout the twentieth century, others continue to adhere to the Longhouse Religion of Handsome Lake.

CULTURE AND ASSIMILATION

Despite all of their moves and changes, the Oneida have preserved many traditions by means of community centers, educational outreach, and their elders. Oneida traditions and customs can still be seen at festivals such as Oneida Day celebrations in New York, Wisconsin, and Ontario.

Traditions and Customs The gift of a *wampum* belt—a belt made of mollusk shells—traditionally accompanied a message of truth and great significance. A wampum of dark color signaled a serious purpose, sadness, or perhaps great political importance. The two-row wampum symbolized the agreement and conditions under which the Iroquois welcomed the Europeans to this land. Its message was, "You say that you are our father and I am your son. We say, we will not be like father and son, but like brothers. This wampum belt confirms our words. These two rows will symbolize two paths or two vessels, traveling down the same river side-by-side. One, a birch bark canoe, for the Indian People, their laws, their customs, and their ways. We shall each travel the river together, side-by-side, but each foot in our own boat. Neither of us will make compulsory laws or interfere in the internal affairs of the other. Neither of us will try to steer the other's vessel."

In 1975 Northeast Wisconsin In-school Telecommunications at the University of Wisconsin at Green Bay produced *Forest Spirits*, a series of seven half-hour shows concerning various aspects of Oneida and Menominee cultural heritage.

Cuisine Before European contact, the Iroquoian diet varied enormously. It consisted of many kinds of mammals, fish, birds, and reptiles, with deer, elk, and fish of particular importance in their diet. The interplanting of corn, pole beans, and squash, referred to as the "Three Sisters," was a key characteristic of Oneida and other Iroquois horticultural practices. The pole beans grew up the cornstalks, providing cover for the squash, and bacteria colonies on the bean roots captured nitrogen for the special needs of the corn. The Three Sisters were central to the spiritual well-being of the Oneidas, protected by Three Sister spirits. Considered special gifts, the three were grown and eaten together and were celebrated in thanksgiving traditions.

Traditional recipes include cornbread, soups, and stews cooked on stone hearths. Women gathered strawberries, huckleberries, blackberries, raspberries, greens, hickory nuts, walnuts, beechnuts, chestnuts, acorns, roots, skunk cabbage, poke, milkweed, and other edibles. Many berries were dried and packed for winter, and several of the nuts were used for their oils as well as for food. Today, traditional foods such as cornbread and stews are still very popular, but most Oneida eat what is accessible and affordable at local grocery stores.

Traditional Dress In the early days buckskin clothing, simple in design, was the traditional dress. Women wore a skirt and jacket; men, a loincloth, with leggings and shirts for cooler weather. Men and women wore moccasins, sometimes made from cornhusks. Clothing was at times decorated with paint or porcupine-quill embroidery. By the eighteenth century many Iroquois had adapted European fabrics to their dress. The most common traditional dress of the Iroquois was the women's ribbon dress, which was stitched out of printed fabrics and decorated with ribbons across the upper chest and back, hanging loosely down the front. Shorter ribbon shirts were worn by men. The Oneida ribbon shirt has become a Pan-Indian garment, worn particularly at powwows and other gatherings. The *kostoweh* is the traditional Iroquois headdress. Made from an ash splint frame, it is decorated with turkey feathers. Deer horns are mounted on top of a kostoweh worn by a leader. Today, some Oneida wear moccasins and beaded shirts, but most primarily wear contemporary clothing similar to that of the larger U.S. population.

Traditional Arts and Crafts Beadwork and porcupine quillwork were popular Oneida crafts. Before European contact, the Oneidas made beads from natural materials such as bone and shells. Glass beads obtained from the Europeans became popular ornamentation on Oneida clothing during the eighteenth century. In the late nineteenth and early twentieth centuries, Oneida women earned a good income by selling beadwork to non-natives at tourist centers. They began to make floral designs with their glass beads and applied these new shapes to many useful things, including pincushions, handbags, sewing cases, and clothing. Oneidas traditionally consider beadworking a special gift to share and use often. It is commonly believed that beadworking came from the Creator to teach patience and humility.

Wampum belts are made with purple and white mollusk shell beads and are designed to tell family stories and tribal history. These belts are complex and beautiful. The designs on belts aided memory about Oneida history, traditions, and laws. *Wampum* comes from the word *wampumpeag*, which means "white strings of shell beads." The Iroquois tribes, including the Oneida, used wampum as a trade item before European contact. With European contact, wampum became a type of currency.

From the eighteenth century to the present, basket making has been a popular Oneida craft. It was also an important element in their economy. Baskets were frequently traded for other goods. Splints of black ash were initially used, but by 1830 bright colors and painted motifs such as circular flowers were seen on the baskets. In the 1870s baskets became smaller and more intricate, meeting the demands of Victorian-era tourists. Today, basket-weaving classes and workshops are often held on the Oneida Indian reservations.

The Oneida produced and used cornhusk dolls for sacred healing ceremonies and as children's toys. Dry cornhusks were soaked in water to become pliable and then used for the doll's body. Corn silk was used for hair. The body was stuffed with leaves, and limbs were made from rolled or braided husks. The face was usually left featureless. The dolls, on average, measure between four and ten inches. Sometimes dolls have clothing made from animal hide or cornhusks; boy dolls often sport bows and arrows, and girl dolls hold sewing kits or hoes.

Mask carving is considered a sacred art. Outsiders are still not allowed to view many of the Oneidas' masks, some of which are used ceremonially. They are made of various types of wood and cornhusks. Facial features vary. Eyes are often deep-set, and noses are hooked. The masks are sometimes painted red and black. Horsetail, buffalo hair, and cornhusks are used for hair on the masks.

Dances and Songs Percussion instruments are predominant in traditional music, which involves narrow melodic lines. Rattles were commonly used in traditional ceremonies. The Oneida used the rattles for the Feather Dance—a dance that recognizes the importance of all creation. Rattles were made from turtle shells or hickory bark, but, more commonly, cow horn rattles with wooden handles and water drums were used. Rasps, or hand percussion instruments with scrapers, were another commonly used traditional instrument in dances.

The Oneida believed that ceremonial singing and dancing increased an individual's power. Medicine societies related to healing are prominent in the culture. A medicine man frequently led dances and songs that were believed to contribute to greater health and longevity. Traditional dances include the ceremonial Green Corn Dance, which celebrates the annual harvest, and the Fish Dance, a fun and social dance. A Personal Chant form of song, used in the twentieth century to express thanksgiving, is reminiscent of warrior death songs of the past. The Condolence ceremony, for installing new leaders or for mourning, is also maintained. The Wisconsin Oneida hold the Oneida Powwow annually in July.

Holidays The Oneidas observe many American holidays, including New Year's Day, Independence Day, Labor Day, Thanksgiving Day, and Christmas. The Oneidas in Wisconsin and New York observe Oneida Day on the fourth Friday in May and American Indian Heritage Day on the day after Thanksgiving. Oneida Day is a one-day celebration with traditional dancing and music. Words and songs of thanks are delivered in the Oneida language, and a brief history is often told. Traditional foods and crafts are abundant. Oneida Day was first observed in 1912. American Indian Heritage Day is a celebration of the history and heritage of all Native Americans, with a particular emphasis on contributions by Native American individuals.

Health Care Issues and Practices Jack Campisi reported two Oneida medicine societies: the False Face and Little Water. To become part of one of these societies an individual either had to be cured and purified by one of the societies or had to have dreamed of becoming a part of it. Dreaming was a large part of healing for the Oneidas; an ability to dream and know the future commanded respect. Dreamers were often asked about and consulted on different cures for specific ailments. There was also some belief in different types of witchcraft and magic potions for healing.

The Wisconsin Oneida are now served by the Oneida Community Health Center. With revenues from the Turning Stone Resort Casino, the New York Oneidas have established a Health Services Department that treats all Native Americans from a six-county region in central New York State. A wide range of services and preventive care programs are offered.

Death and Burial Rituals Before European contact and through the seventeenth century, the Condolence ceremony for mourning was an important

Marilyn Blacksmith (Crow) performs the Fancy Shawl Dance in "The World of American Indian Dance," a documentary produced by Four Directions Entertainment. Four Directions Entertainment, an enterprise of the Oneida Indian Nation, is the only film and television production company owned and operated by Native Americans. AP IMAGES / PRNEWSFOTO

event in Iroquois society and was influenced by the Hurons' Feast of the Dead. At its height, the Feast of the Dead was held once a decade and involved a ten-day feast. Traditionally, the dead were removed from individual graves and reburied at a common location. Much of the time was spent preparing the corpses for their final placement. Presents brought by friends of the deceased were distributed among those in attendance.

The Condolence ceremony focuses on deceased leaders and raising up their successors. The ceremony is still practiced where hereditary leaders exist, such as the Oneidas of the Thames. The ceremony lasts from early afternoon into the evening. A set of rites is performed, including the Condoling Song, which consists of a hymn of farewell composed of six or more verses. The song is often followed by the Requickening Address, symbolic for restoring life.

Recreational Activities The Oneida place tremendous value on recreation time. Many Europeans with first contact observed that the Oneida males enjoyed sports—lacrosse was a popular sport—and would discuss issues around a fire while smoking pipes. Women socialized and attending the athletic events as spectators. Today, Oneidas are members of community centers, where they play games such as bingo.

ONEIDA PROVERBS

Oneida myths and stories such as the Oneida Creation Narrative, "Thunder's Child," "Bear and Fox," and "The Cold Weather Man" are frequently told. Oneida proverbs, in contrast, are quite rare. "See your sons and daughters: they are your future" is a popular Oneida proverb. In 2012 Ray Halbritter—a member of the Oneida Indian Nation's wolf clan and CEO of Oneida Nation Enterprises—announced a ten million dollar gift from the Oneida Indian Nation of New York toward the construction of a new Revolutionary War Center in Philadelphia. He shared a popular American Indian proverb with the audience assembled on the lawn of the U.S. Capitol: "Tell me a fact and I'll learn; tell me a truth and I'll believe; but tell me a story, and it will live in my heart forever." According to Halbritter, the American Revolutionary War Center in Philadelphia will help tell the story of the Oneida people to the world.

FAMILY AND COMMUNITY LIFE

The Oneida are a matrilineal society, with clan membership following the mother's family line; however, the Wisconsin Oneida also trace patrilineal descent. The Iroquois traditionally lived in longhouses. Each longhouse family was headed by the oldest woman, and the members of that family were this woman's descendants and blood relatives. Each longhouse typically held between six and ten nuclear families, each of about five or six people, with one hearth for every two families. The size of the longhouse depended on the number of families it sheltered. They were typically about 25 feet wide, with an average length of about 80 feet. For each hearth, a two-apartment section added about 25 feet to the length of the longhouse. These apartment sections had low, flat platforms walled off at both ends by a partition and were open in the center, where the hearth was shared with the opposite apartment. Food and personal items were stored on long shelves above the platforms, dried food and corn were stored in large bark bins between apartments, and firewood was stacked near the end doors. Children generally did chores around the house but had some spare time for play. Lacrosse was popular with boys, and cornhusk dolls were favorite toys of girls.

Longhouses are now used for ceremonial purposes only, and the Oneidas today live in houses and apartments. The Oneida Nation of New York manages a housing program that provides single-family homes on aboriginal lands for all the members who want them. Since September 1994, single-family houses have been built ranging in size from two to four bedrooms, in addition to duplexes for tribal elders at the Village of the White Pines.

Gender Roles Before European contact, Oneida men and women worked together in order to prosper, but there was a distinct division of labor. Oneida men cleared forests, constructed houses, hunted, fished, attended councils, and fought wars. Oneida women were clan mothers with important political roles, cultivated crops, foraged for nuts and fruits, cooked, and raised children. Women also gathered firewood; prepared skins; made clothing; sowed bean, squash, and pumpkin in their cornfields; harvested apples; and tended tobacco plants.

Today, Oneida men and women live and work on and around the Indian reservations. Both participate in the struggle for land rights, the preservation of their traditional language and culture, and indigenous rights. Women's involvement in contemporary Oneida struggles is documented in Lina Sunseri's *Being of One Mind: Oneida Women and the Struggle for Decolonization*. An Oneida woman named Lisa states: "Colonialism has tried to make us forget the teachings of the Longhouse, which were ways to make sure we lived in a good way, and that needs to come back. We need the elders to tell us how to do that again, and we need us, the women, to be involved in all of that. We have much to lose if we don't get involved. Our role as mothers of the nation demands that we do, and it is better for us that we do, that way we make sure we help our nation to be good again. We leave a good legacy for the next generation."

Education Like many Native American groups in the early twenty-first century, the Oneidas use educational programs as a primary means of maintaining or restoring traditional tribal customs. Gaming revenues from the casinos in Wisconsin and New York provide substantial funding to support educational initiatives. In the late 1990s the New York Oneidas established the goal of lifelong learning as a key to continued economic prosperity. Beginning with the Early Learning Center for young children (located on the reservation in Oneida, New York), programs are available for tribal members throughout their lives, including educational programs as part of elders' services. Oneida culture and language are key aspects of the education offered, particularly for the youth programs. The Oneida Education Department sponsors programs for students and adults, including college and career counseling. In a unique partnership with the State University of New York at Morrisville, a degree program in casino management is offered to train future leaders of the Oneida resort. The old tribal bingo hall, replaced by Turning Stone Resort Casino, has been converted into an Educational Resource Center housing a tribal library, language facility, career resource center, and adult learning center. In

Wisconsin, the Oneida Tribal School (for kindergarten through eighth grade), located in the town of Oneida, is operated under the direction of the U.S. Bureau of Indian Affairs (BIA).

Valuing the education of their children, the Oneidas of Wisconsin built a daycare facility and an elementary school in the shape of a turtle—namesake of an Oneida clan and a familiar character of Oneida oral literature. The tribe has also invested heavily in reviving its culture and language among its youth through activities such as the creation of a new written form of the Oneida language and the production of a CD-ROM featuring oral literature told by Oneida elders. Interactive online learning, including online vocabulary flashcards, is utilized extensively.

Courtship and Weddings Like many Native Americans, Oneidas frequently plan weddings that incorporate their traditions. Traditional attire and music are common at Oneida weddings as well as blessings in the native language.

Surnames European surnames are common, as well as translated names. Some surnames—as with European names—describe a geographical place, ethnic background, or job. Some common surnames among the Oneida are Blue, Brant, Deer, Goodleaf, Green, Hill, Johnson, Longboat, Maracle, Martin, and Newhouse.

EMPLOYMENT AND ECONOMIC CONDITIONS

The traditional economy of the Oneidas relied on the cultivation of corn, beans, and squash; an extensive hunting territory; fishing stations on Oneida Lake; and the collection of various wild plants such as berries. Seizing territory and booty in warfare was central to the Oneida culture and economy. The American Revolutionary War disrupted the Oneidas' existing economy significantly. Afterward, communities and fields needed restoration. A massive influx of non-Indians onto Oneida lands also followed the war. During the nineteenth and early twentieth centuries, the sales of crafts such as baskets and beadwork to tourists provided substantial income. Subsistence farming and limited cash crops were vital to the local economies.

After the passage of the Indian Gaming Act of 1988, the Oneidas of Wisconsin opened a gambling complex with two thousand slot machines outside Green Bay. This was the first Oneida casino in operation. Because Indian reservations have tribal sovereignty, state law cannot interfere in tribal gambling. Today, there are more than 460 gambling operations run by over 240 tribes. Total annual revenue is about 27 billion dollars per year. Because of the huge revenues, gambling operations have radically transformed the Oneida and other tribal economies. The Oneidas of Wisconsin also established the Oneida Nation Electronics (ONE) Corporation to manage

THE THREE ONEIDA CLANS

Three clans compose Oneida society: the Turtle Clan, the Wolf Clan, and the Bear Clan. The turtle teaches patience and endurance and represents strength and solidarity; he is old, wise, and well-respected. The wolf demonstrates keen observation skills in listening and watching and illustrates a strong sense of family. The bear exemplifies gentleness and strength, displaying discipline and control. The Oneida culture also views the eagle as a protector, possessing great vision to watch over all the nations and warn them of danger. The Tree of Peace, a great white pine, is believed by the Iroquois to have been planted by the Peacemaker—a legendary lawmaker who can be compared to mythological and historical figures such as Solon, Lycurgas, and Moses—who originally inspired the formation of the Iroquois confederacy centuries before. The roots of this great tree spread out in all four directions, and the weapons of the Iroquois nations were buried there to create an everlasting peace.

the facility's electronics systems. The gaming income provided capital for other long-term business ventures. In 1997 the tribe, using income from ONE, signed an agreement with the electronics manufacturing company Plexus to build a $22 million plant on reservation lands. The plant was to be owned and financed by the Oneidas but operated by Plexus, with the profits shared. The Wisconsin Oneidas have already invested in and manage an industrial park, a printing company, a bank, a hotel, and convenience stores on the reservation. The tribal government uses casino revenues to provide services to Oneida members, including subsidized housing, health care, and student counseling.

In July 1993 the Oneida Indian Nation of New York opened the Turning Stone Resort Casino, which employed five thousand people as of 2012. The casino and resort is billed as a world-class tourist destination. It is the only legal casino in New York State. The resort includes a 285-room luxury hotel, five restaurants, a PGA golf course, several retail establishments known as the Shoppes at Turning Stone, and a recreational park. The resort has been credited with the stimulation of substantial economic growth in central New York. As of 2012, it was a top five destination for tourists in New York, with more than four million visitors a year.

The pace of economic recovery for the New York Oneidas was staggering. Through the 1990s the Oneida Indian Nation of New York progressed from employing only a handful of people in two businesses to becoming the largest employer in Oneida and Madison counties of central New York. The Oneidas became a major tourism promoter for the region. In fact, the economic picture for the Oneidas in New York improved so significantly that in 1998 and 1999 the tribe requested that the BIA allocate certain funds that had been earmarked for services for their tribe to more needy tribes. In the twenty-first century, the tribe offers more than sixty programs and services for tribal members, including a housing program, a child learning center, elder-care programs, community and development centers, and educational scholarship programs.

Through the years the Oneidas of New York have maintained a tenuous relationship with the U.S. government. One issue of continued conflict has been the obligation of the federal government through its trust and treaty relationships to provide social services to the Oneidas, despite their very small land base. The revenue from the resort enabled the Oneidas to provide better social programs for their people. The Elders' Program provides rides for elders to the Oneida Nation cookhouse for a luncheon three days a week as well as for museum visits, shopping excursions, and places to visit overnight. Seeking diversity in their business interests as a means to maintain a healthy economy on the reservation even if casino benefits were to wane, Oneida leaders acquired several businesses for the Oneida Nation in the 1990s, including a textile factory, a recreational vehicle park with a convenience and gift store, a newly built gas station, and a smoke shop. The Nation created almost three thousand jobs directly and claims to have stimulated the creation of another two thousand jobs in the region. In lieu of paying local taxes due to their sovereign status, the Oneidas provide hundreds of thousands of dollars in grants to local school districts and municipalities.

When the Oneidas of the Thames moved to Canada in the 1840s to the newly purchased reserve, they were allowed to claim as many acres as they could feasibly clear and farm. Several small communities grew up on the reserve. Through the nineteenth century, subsistence farming was the primary economic pursuit of the tribe, augmented by seasonal lumbering employment. By the twentieth century, however, farming had waned, and members sought wage-labor jobs in white communities. Less fortunate economically than the Oneidas in New York and Wisconsin, the Ontario group still relies on governmental support for basic services.

POLITICS AND GOVERNMENT

Forms of government vary considerably between the three Oneida branches. The Oneidas in Ontario instituted a traditional form of government upon their arrival in the 1840s. A tribal council was established on the basis of the three traditional Oneida clans: Wolf, Bear, and Turtle. Each appointed a *sachem* (chief) and deputy to the tribal council, which was coordinated with the Iroquois council at Six Nations of the Grand River. The Ontario Oneidas maintained this traditional system of hereditary leadership until 1934, when considerable internal tribal factionalism consumed the tribe, and the Canadian government imposed an elective form of government to resolve ongoing internal tribal conflict. The Ontario group

became governed by a tribal leader and twelve council members elected at-large for two-year terms. The government manages tribal business, housing, road maintenance, education, and welfare. The Handsome Lake Longhouse religion continues to be a strong influence for the Ontario group among the minority not accepting the elected form of government.

The Wisconsin Oneidas essentially dissolved their local tribal government following the loss of lands in the early twentieth century. With prospects of some lands being restored, the tribe organized an elected form of government in 1937 under the Indian Reorganization Act (IRA) of 1934. They adopted an IRA constitution and established a Business Council to govern themselves. The tribe became eligible for certain federal grants and loans, setting the basis for future economic growth. The Business Council is composed of nine members elected every three years.

The New York Oneidas, based on the remaining small land base, have experienced some political strife in the late twentieth century and early twenty-first century between one faction favoring an elective form of government and the other favoring a more traditional form based on hereditary clans.

NOTABLE INDIVIDUALS

Activism Laura Cornelius Kellogg (1880–1947), known as Minnie, was a descendent of two influential Oneida leaders and became noted for her own oratory skills. She attended finishing school, traveled in Europe, and attended several well-known institutions such as Stanford, Columbia, Cornell, and the University of Wisconsin. Minnie was a founder of the Society of American Indians in 1911 and became a national advocate for tribal self-sufficiency. Late in her life, Minnie focused on preservation of the Oneida language and the reacquisition of lost tribal lands.

Mary Cornelius Winder (1898–1954) was an activist for Oneida rights to lands lost in the nineteenth century. While living on the Onondaga Reservation with many other displaced Oneida families, Winder operated a small grocery store. She relentlessly lobbied the U.S. government to honor its 1794 treaty with the Oneidas and to grant full federal recognition to the Oneida Nation. Beginning in the 1940s, she initiated what became a thirty-year successful effort before the U.S. Land Claims Commission. She and other tribal members sought recognition that the lands were inappropriately taken. However, upon victory they discovered that only monetary awards were being offered, not return of the land itself. The Oneidas won a $3.3 million settlement to be split between the three groups.

Education Educator Norbert S. Hill Jr. (1946–) was born in Warren, Michigan, near Detroit. His father was an Oneida/Mohawk and his mother a Canadian Cree. Hill earned a B.A. from the University of Wisconsin–Oshkosh in 1969 and later an M.A. in guidance and counseling from the same institution. After serving as assistant to the dean of students at University of Wisconsin–Green Bay, Hill became director of the American Indian Education Opportunity Program at the University of Colorado, where he continued his graduate studies. Hill became chair of the Oneida education committee in the early 1970s, which led to a career of community service stressing the role of education in the improvement of tribal well-being. Hill started the noted magazine *Winds of Change* in 1986 and edited a book of historical and contemporary Indian quotes titled *Words of Power*. In the 1990s Hill became board chairman for the proposed Smithsonian National Museum of the American Indian, overseeing its development. He also served as executive director of the American Indian Science and Engineering Society (AISES) from 1983 into the 1990s. Hill received the Chancellor's Award at the University of Wisconsin–Oshkosh in 1988 and in 1994 was awarded a Rockefeller fellowship and an honorary doctor of laws degree from Cumberland College in Kentucky.

Government Robert LaFollette Bennett (1912–2002), Oneida lawyer and administrator, was born on the Oneida Reservation near Green Bay, Wisconsin, and attended the BIA's boarding school at the Haskell Institute in Lawrence, Kansas. He studied law at Southeastern University School of Law in Washington, D.C., earning his law degree in 1941. Bennett served in the U.S. Marine Corps during World War II. For his legal work supporting native land claims, he received the Indian Achievement Award in 1962 and Outstanding American Indian Citizen Award in 1966. In 1966 President Lyndon B. Johnson appointed Bennett head of the BIA. He served until 1969, when he moved to Albuquerque, New Mexico, and founded the American Indian Athletic Hall of Fame. Bennett was director of the American Indian Law Center at the University of New Mexico Law School from 1970 to 1975. He was recognized as Outstanding Member of the Oneida tribe of Wisconsin in 1988.

Literature Roberta Hill Whiteman (1947–), noted poet, is a member of the Oneida tribe of Wisconsin. She earned a BA from the University of Wisconsin, an MFA from University of Montana, and a PhD from the University of Minnesota. Her work has been included in *Carriers of the Dream Wheel: Contemporary Native American Poetry* (1975) and *The Third Woman: Minority Women Writers of the United States* (1980). She published her own collections *Star Quilt* in 1984 and *Philadelphia Flowers* in 1996. Her work was also included in *Harper's Anthology of Twentieth-Century Native American Poetry* (1988). Whiteman is noted for her very humanistic style, addressing personal and family relationships and the relation of humans to recurrent patterns of nature. She is an associate professor of English and American Indian Studies at the University of Wisconsin at Madison.

Music Aaliyah Dana Haughton (1979–2001), African American/Oneida singer, dancer, actress, and model, had a major influence in R&B and hip-hop, being recognized by MTV, *Billboard*, VH1, *Maxim*, the *New York Times*, and *Rolling Stone* as one of the greatest R&B artists of her time. Her album *One in a Million* has sold more than eight million copies worldwide. She died in a plane crash in 2001.

Joanne Shenandoah, a member of the Wolf clan of the Oneida Nation, is an internationally respected recording artist and songwriter whose material often reflects her Oneida heritage. Her releases include *Loving Ways* on Canyon Records in 1991 and contributions to *In the Spirit of Crazy Horse* (2001), dedicated to imprisoned Indian activist Leonard Peltier. Shenandoah, whose father was an Onondaga tribal leader and jazz guitarist, has performed in Europe as well as North America, including the 1991 American Music Festival in San Francisco. She is a Grammy Award winner and has more than forty music awards. Shenandoah founded Round Dance Productions, a nonprofit organization dedicated to native cultural preservation. Shenandoah has also pursued an acting career and has written musical scores and soundtracks.

Sports Wilson "Buster" Charles (1908–2006) participated in track, football, and basketball at the BIA's Haskell Institute in Lawrence, Kansas, where he was a star fullback. He attended the University of New Mexico from 1927 to 1931, where he won the 1930 AAU and Kansas Relays decathlon title, He joined the U.S. Olympic decathlon team in 1932. Charles was part of the inaugural class of inductees to the American Indian Athletic Hall of Fame in 1972.

Gordon House (1925–1950) was a boxer of Oneida and Navajo ancestry. House was the All-Armed Forces lightweight boxing champion in 1945 and became the state lightweight boxing champion in Arizona, Nevada, and Texas in 1948. He fought professionally from 1946 to 1949 and was inducted into the American Indian Athletic Hall of Fame in 1985.

Stage and Screen Film actor Graham Greene (1952–) has found success in both Canada and the United States. Greene, a full-blooded Oneida, was born on the Iroquois Six Nations of the Grand River Reserve in southwestern Ontario. He began his career in television, film, and radio in 1976. In the early 1980s Greene lived for a short time in Britain, where he performed on stage. Upon his return to Canada, Greene was cast in the British film *Revolution* (1985), starring Al Pacino and directed by Hugh Hudson. Greene is perhaps best known for his performance in *Dances with Wolves*, the 1991 Academy Award–winning movie. Greene portrayed Kicking Bird, an elder who strove to protect his people from attacks by American authorities. Greene has acted in many other films, including *The Green Mile* and *The Twilight Saga: New Moon* (2009). In addition, Greene has appeared in a number of television series.

MEDIA

PRINT

Indian Country Today Media Network

A prominent weekly magazine and online newspaper reporting on national news of relevance to Indian nations throughout the United States.

590 Madison Avenue
New York, New York 10022
Phone: (212) 600-2086
Email: customerservice@ictmn.com
URL: www.indiancountrytodaymedianetwork.com

Kalihwisaks

Official newspaper, in print and online, of the Oneida Tribe of Indians of Wisconsin.

URL: www.oneida-nsn.gov
or

P.O. Box 365
Oneida, Wisconsin 54155
URL: www.oneidanation.org/newspaper

RADIO

Onedia Radio 89.5–The Eagle

Unlicensed radio station at Oneida Nation of the Thames. Programs include music and news of the Oneidas.

2212 Elm Avenue
Southwold, Ontario NOL 2GO Canada
URL: www.oneida.on.ca

ORGANIZATIONS AND ASSOCIATIONS

Assembly of First Nations Resource Center

Extensive collection of materials on Ontario Indian tribes, including tribal histories and legal histories.

Kelly Whiteduck, Coordinator
1 Nicholas Street
Ottawa, Ontario K1N 7B7Canada
Phone: (613) 241-6789
Email: kwhiteduck@afn.ca
URL: www.library.usask.ca

Oneida Indian Nation

Official website of the Oneida Indian Nation in New York.

577 Main Street
Oneida, New York 13421
Phone: (315) 829-8335
Email: bstagnitti@oneida-nation.org
URL: www.oneidaindiannation.com

Oneida Nation of the Thames

Official website of the Oneida Nation of the Thames.

2212 Elm Avenue
Southwold, Ontario NOL 2GO Canada
URL: www.oneida.on.ca

Oneida Tribe of Indians of Wisconsin

Official website of the Oneida Nation of Wisconsin.

P.O. Box 365
Oneida, Wisconsin 54155
Phone: (920) 869-2214
URL: www.oneida-nsn.gov

Six Nations of the Grand River

Official website of the Six Nations of the Grand River.

1659 Chiefswood Road
Ohsweken, Ontario NOA 1MOCanada
Phone: (519) 445-2201
URL: www.sixnations.ca

MUSEUMS AND RESEARCH CENTERS

Iroquois Indian Museum

Houses and exhibits the material culture of the Oneidas and other Iroquois confederacy tribes, exhibits modern craftwork, and offers an educational trail highlighting the ethnobotany of the region.

Christina B. Johannsen
or

Stephanie E. Shultes
Box 7, Caverns Road
Howes Cave, New York 12092
Phone: (518) 296-8949
Email: info@irquoismuseum.org
URL: www.iroquoismuseum.org

Oneida County Historical Society

Houses primary historical sources and documents about Oneida County, including detailed documents on the Oneida Indians.

1608 Genesee Street
Utica, New York 13502
Phone: (315) 735-3642
Email: ochs@oneidacountyhistory.org
URL: www.oneidacountyhistory.org

Oneida Nation Museum

The museum is dedicated to the cultural heritage of the Oneidas, with exhibits and educational programming. Tours are offered, and a gift shop is on-site.

W892 Country Road EE
DePere, Wisconsin 54115
Phone: (920) 869-2768
URL: www.oneidanation.org/museum

Shako:wi Cultural Center

Located on tribal lands east of Syracuse, the white pine log building houses Oneida arts and crafts and stories of the tribe's past. The Oneidas use the facility for community gatherings and public presentations.

5 Territory Road
Oneida, New York 13421
Phone: (315) 829-8801
URL: www.oneidaindiannation.com

Six Nations Indian Museum

Houses collections of the material culture of the Oneidas and other tribes of the Six Nations. Also houses research materials on their history.

Ray Fadden
1462 Country Road 60, Onchiota
New York 12989
Phone: (518) 891-2299
Email: info@sixnationsindianmuseum.com
URL: www.sixnationsindianmuseum.com

SOURCES FOR ADDITIONAL STUDY

Campisi, Jack. "Oneida." In *Handbook of the North American Indians. Vol. 15: Northeast*, edited by Bruce G. Trigger. Washington, D.C.: Smithsonian Institution, 1978.

Campisi, Jack, and Laurence M. Hauptman, eds. *The Oneida Indian Experience: Two Perspectives*. Syracuse: Syracuse University Press, 1988.

Glatthaar, Joseph, and James Kirby Martin. *Forgotten Allies: The Oneida Indians and the American Revolution*. New York: Hill and Wang, 2006.

Halbritter, Ray. "The Truth about Land Claims." *Oneida* 7, no. 6 (1996).

Hauptman, Laurence, and L. Gordon McLester III. *The Oneida Indian Journey: From New York to Wisconsin, 1784–1860*. Madison: University of Wisconsin Press, 1999.

Kerber, Jordan. *Cross-Cultural Collaboration: Native Peoples and Archaeology in the Northeastern United States*. Lincoln: University of Nebraska Press, 2006.

Richter, Daniel K., and James H. Merrell, eds. *Beyond the Covenant Chain: The Iroquois and Their Neighbors in Indian North America, 1600–1800*. Syracuse: Syracuse University Press, 1987.

Shattuck, George C. *The Oneida Land Claims: A Legal History*. Syracuse: Syracuse University Press, 1991.

Sunseri, Lina. *Becoming Again of One Mind: Oneida Women and the Struggle for Decolonization*. Vancouver: University of British Columbia Press, 2011.

Wonderley, Anthony. *Oneida Iroquois Folklore, Myth, and History*. Syracuse: Syracuse University Press, 2004.

OSAGES

Katrina Oko-Odoi

OVERVIEW

The Osage are a Native American people who traditionally lived in the lower Midwest region of what is now the United States, spanning across parts of Missouri, Oklahoma, Kansas, and Arkansas. The Osage are considered a Northern Plains tribe; their traditional territory was bound by the Missouri River to the north, the Mississippi River to the east, the Arkansas River and the Ozarks to the south, and partially by the Cimarron River to the west. The tribe's location along the Ozark Uplift offered them rugged terrain that helped protect them from the invasion of enemies. In modern times, the Osage people refer to themselves as *Wah-Zha-Zhi*, which French explorers originally translated as "Ouazhigi," and the term was incorporated into the English language as *Osage*. The Osage's original name for themselves, however, was *Ni-u-ko'n-ska*, meaning "people of the middle waters."

The Osage people's first documented contact with Europeans was with French explorers in 1673, but the first population estimate was not until 1802, when there were approximately 5,500 Osage tribal members, according to the Osage Nation Historic Preservation Office. The lack of earlier population estimates is most likely due to the relatively small size of the tribe. Osage leaders performed certain seasonal rituals related to the harvest as well as rituals related to significant life moments, including child-naming ceremonies, death rituals, and rites associated with initiating war and bringing about peace. Prior to European contact, the Osage subsisted on a combination of hunting and agriculture. The Osage tribe had a relatively stable economy and ranked high among the established hunting tribes in the Great Plains region. Tribal members would go on semiannual buffalo hunts from their settlements in present-day Missouri and Arkansas into the Great Plains, which provided them with much of the meat they would consume during the six-month period between hunts.

The largest group of Osage today resides on tribal lands in Osage County, Oklahoma, located in the north-central area of the state. This was the result of a series of government actions that entailed the forced removal of the Osage from their remaining tribal lands in Missouri, Kansas, and Arkansas. The tribal nation continues to host several different gatherings each year, including the I'n-Lon-Schka—which translates literally to "playground of the eldest son"—a four-day series of rituals and dances held every June. At the ceremony a drum keeper is chosen from among the Osage families' eldest sons.

According to the U.S. Census Bureau's American Community Survey estimates for 2006–2010, there were over 18,000 individuals of Osage descent living in the United States (as a basis for comparison, this is more than half the population of Fairbanks, Alaska). The states with the largest numbers of Osage include Oklahoma, California, Texas, Missouri, Kansas, and Oregon.

HISTORY OF THE PEOPLE

Early History Although the first documented contact between the Osage and Europeans was in 1673, some historians suggest that they may have encountered the expeditions of Spanish explorers Hernando de Soto and Francisco Vásquez de Coronado in the 1540s, based upon descriptions that the explorers described of their contact with Native peoples. In 1673 Jesuit missionary Jacques Marquette and trader Louis Jolliet set out to explore the Mississippi, Missouri, Marmaton, and Osage rivers, mapping the location of the Osage villages along their journey. By 1680 French traders had established relationships with the Osage, trading weapons and other metal objects for pelts, textiles, and even slaves from neighboring tribes. The acquisition of French guns gave the Osage a distinct advantage over other tribes in the region, including the Pawnee, Wichita, and Caddoan people, who did not establish such relations with the French until the 1720s.

Despite certain moments of animosity between the Osage and the French, they maintained relatively amicable relations for the duration of the French crown's control of the area surrounding Osage territory into the 1760s. When France ceded control of the Louisiana Territory to Spain at the end of the Seven Years' War in 1763, it became clear how fiercely loyal the Osage people were to the French. Throughout Spain's control of the Louisiana Territory from approximately 1769 to 1803, tensions between the Osage and the Spanish remained high. The Osage carried out attacks against Spanish subjects and generally refused to trade with the Spanish, limiting their transactions to the French colonists who remained in the area.

During this period, the Osage Indians were the most powerful and influential Native American group in the Louisiana region, being the main suppliers of valuable pelts and hides and maintaining strategic blockades against European trade with other tribes between the Mississippi and Missouri rivers.

Following the United States' takeover of the Louisiana Territory through the 1803 Louisiana Purchase, relations between Osage and the new American settlers were tenuous. The Osage's frequent warfare against other Indian tribes instilled fear in American settlers who wished to travel west, and as a result, what was initially supposed to be a voluntary removal of the Osage people turned into an enforced removal by the U.S. military under the leadership of Andrew Jackson. Some Osage chose to move west to the Three Forks region (in what would later become Oklahoma). Those who remained in their traditional homeland first entered into treaty negotiations with the United States in 1808. At the time, U.S. policy toward native peoples was to encourage—by use of force if necessary—the relocation of Native Americans to lands farther west, and the Osage ceded their first plots of land in Missouri with this initial treaty. As a result, the remaining Osage who still resided along the Osage River moved to western Missouri.

Between 1808 and 1839, the Osage signed six other treaties ceding additional land holdings to the U.S. government. By 1830 the Osage had ceded all of their traditional lands across Missouri, Oklahoma, and Arkansas. The Osage residing on these lands were initially moved onto a reservation in southeastern Kansas. Later treaties and laws enacted through the 1860s reduced the lands of the Osage even further. Their final relocation was to Oklahoma in 1870.

The hardship suffered by the Osage people during the years of their enforced removal from tribal lands had a crippling effect on the nation. According to the Osage Nation Historic Preservation project, there was an almost 50 percent decline in the Osage population during the initial years of resettlement, largely resulting from the lack of access to medical care and the scarcity of clothing and food. Nevertheless, the Osage sought to assert their autonomy and maintain unity by issuing two constitutions, in 1861 and 1881. The 1861 constitution established a governorship and gave legislative powers to a council, both elected by popular vote. The 1881 constitution established a principal chief in place of a governor and a supreme court that became the ultimate legal authority for the Osage people. The Osage also adapted economically to their changing situation. Because of the poor soil quality of their new land, the Osage could only farm on a small scale, but the rich grazing pastures in their territory facilitated their success in cattle raising.

Modern Era Possibly the most pivotal decision in Osage history was the tribe's effort to maintain mineral rights to their new reservation lands, a negotiation that was headed by Principal Chief James Bigheart and finalized with the Osage Agreement of 1905. The Osage had known of the presence of petroleum on their lands in southeastern Kansas and northeastern Oklahoma prior to the nineteenth century (there were surface seeps of petroleum at several springs in the area). The first successful commercial oil well in the Osage reserve was on Butler Creek on the Foster Reserve in modern-day Oklahoma. This well prompted the Osage to reserve all mineral rights within the reservation lands as a condition of their agreement to allotment of the surface tribal lands. Written by the Osage themselves, the agreement ensured the protection of the future income that the Osage would derive from their mineral reserves. The great amounts of crude oil under their lands began to be tapped on a large scale in the early 1900s because of the growth of the automobile industry, causing the Osage to quickly become known as the "wealthiest people on Earth." With the passage of the Osage Allotment Act of 1906, every Osage member listed on tribe rolls prior to January 1, 1906, or who was born before July 1907 had a headright to royalties from the Osage mineral reserve. According to the Osage Nation records, when oil royalties peaked in 1925, a family of four who were all on the allotment list would earn approximately $52,800 annually, which is the equivalent of about $600,000 in the early 2000s.

Unfortunately, along with the Osage's newfound wealth came corruption, manipulation, and murder. In 1921 Congress passed a law requiring most Osage to have court-appointed guardians until they proved themselves "competent." White businessmen and lawyers went to great lengths to get their hands on the money that was pouring in from Osage oil reserves. Many non-Indian men (and possibly women also) married into an Osage family that had oil headrights for the specific purpose of profiting from their wealth (the headrights could be inherited by legal heirs, even if they were not Osage). In the 1920s this greed for the Osage's riches erupted in a series of cruel murders that gained national attention and became known as the Osage Indian Murders. Over the course of four years (1921 to 1925), at least two dozen wealthy Osages were murdered, and many others died under suspicious circumstances. The circumstances surrounding the Osage Indian Murders have been the subject of much investigation, and several books address the subject, including Dennis McAuliffe Jr.'s book *Bloodland: A Family Story of Oil, Greed and Murder on the Osage Reservation* (1994), which investigates the suspicious circumstances of his grandmother's murder in 1925; as well as John Joseph Mathews's semiautobiographical novel *Sundown* (1934) and Terry P. Wilson's historiography *The Underground Reservation: Osage Oil* (1985). As a result of the increasing violence against

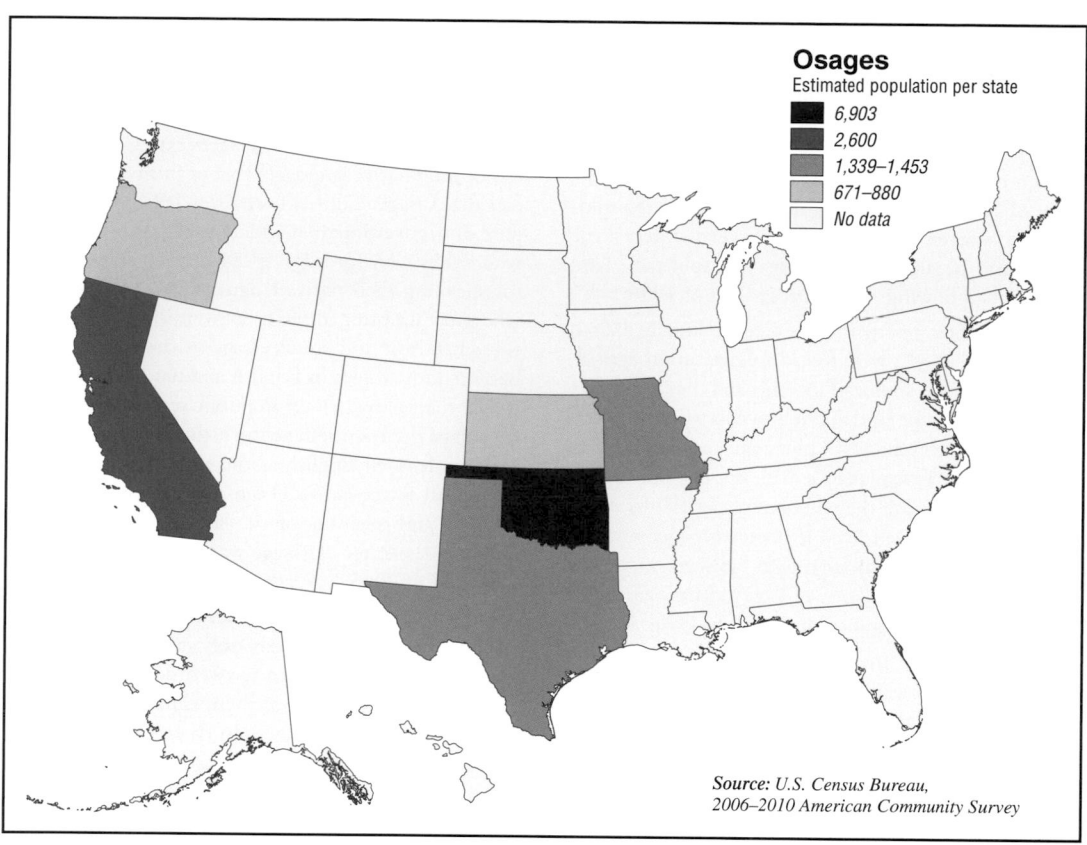

Osages

Estimated population per state

- 6,903
- 2,600
- 1,339–1,453
- 671–880
- No data

Source: U.S. Census Bureau, 2006–2010 American Community Survey

Osage allottees, Congress passed legislation in 1925 that limited the inheritance of headrights to those with Osage Indian blood.

By the beginning of the twenty-first century, Osage headrights had been distributed to the descendants of the original allottees, although the Osage Nation estimated that at least 25 percent of the headrights were still owned by non-Osage individuals and around 75 percent of all Osage did not possess a headright, placing their Osage citizenship in question. The passage of federal law PL 108-431 in 2004 ensured that the Osage tribe was able to determine their own definition of citizenship, which they then defined as anyone descending from a person named on the 1906 roll, regardless of whether they held a headright. Since this new citizenship was included in their 2006 constitution, today any person who can prove lineal descent of someone on the 1906 roll is considered Osage.

SETTLEMENT IN THE UNITED STATES

The Osage traditional territory prior to contact with Euro-Americans was most likely located in a region that spans the modern-day states of Oklahoma, Missouri, Kansas, and Arkansas. Traditional Osage villages lined the banks of the Osage River in the present-day state of Missouri. There were three main groups of Osage: the Little Osages, who were the northernmost group and resided between Malta Bend and Glasgow in Missouri; the supposed mother group

of the Osages, known as the Great Osages, who lived along the Osage River; and random bands of Osages that lived on the headwaters of several rivers, including the Niangua, Sac, and White rivers in Missouri and Arkansas. The Osage expanded their territory into the south and west between 1700 and 1800, claiming the portion of Kansas located in the Neosho-Grand Valley as their own. Throughout the eighteenth century, the Osage continued to expand their territory through several wars of expansion with neighboring tribes.

The Osage tribe had at least intermittent contact with French traders and explorers beginning in 1673, and by the early 1800s, when Jean Pierre Chouteau and his son traded furs with the Osage and lived among them, the western part of their territory had expanded into parts of Oklahoma, including present-day Salina, Oklahoma. Forced relocation of the Osage people began around this period, upon the tribe's signing of their first treaty with the U.S. government in 1808. While some groups of Osage had already resettled voluntarily in present-day Oklahoma, the band that still resided along the river in central Missouri was first relocated to western Missouri. Further mandatory relocations followed, from western Missouri to southeastern Kansas in 1828, and finally from Kansas to Indian Territory in the Cherokee Outlet, now north-central Oklahoma, in 1870.

The Osage people suffered terribly following their final relocation to Oklahoma in 1870; they endured severe poverty and were given inadequate rations supplied by the U.S. government. Many Osage starved, and others died due to a lack of necessary medical supplies and clothing needed to endure the harsh winters. After relocation to the Cherokee Outlet, the Osage established three towns that functioned as the center of the tribe's three core bands. These are the cities of Pawhuska, Hominy, and Fairfax. By the mid-1900s, however, the Osage people owned very little of the land because many Osages had sold their land allotments following the Allotment Act of 1906.

After their resettlement on agriculturally barren lands, Osage people were forced to give up on agriculture as their main source of income, and they eventually turned to leasing the land to cattle owners whose livestock grazed in the rich pastures of bluestem grass. Leasing fees provided most Osage people with enough money on which to subsist until the oil boom of the 1920s, which provided most Osage tribal members with large royalties that made them wealthy overnight. However, as a result of the Great Depression, many Osage Indians were forced to pursue job opportunities outside of the Osage lands.

According to the 2010 American Community Survey, the largest population of Osage still reside in Oklahoma. There are also significant numbers of Osage people living in California, Missouri, Texas, Oregon, and Kansas.

LANGUAGE

The Osage language belongs to the Dhegiha branch of the Siouan language family and is similar to Omaha, Ponca, Quapaw, and Kansa. Osage has similar sounds to Dakota, and the two dialects also share similar vowel length. According to Louis F. Burns's *A History of the Osage People*, the Osage language has approximately 2,000 root words, which are then compounded to expand meaning. The language relies heavily on context, and many words and phrases have multiple meanings depending on the circumstances in which they are spoken. As such, it is very difficult to translate Osage adequately into a standardized Latin-based language like English. In addition, Osage language reveals the regional origins of the tribe as well as their hunting-based society, with rich vocabulary related to prairie, woodland, plateau, and inland water words, as well as many words for animals.

Unlike many other American Indian tribes who acquiesced to the persistence of Christian missionaries during the eighteenth and nineteenth centuries, for almost two centuries the Osage people remained adamant in their refusal to abandon their traditional beliefs and accept Christianity.

The history of Osage language maintenance is closely intertwined with the history of tribal contact with Euro-Americans. Many historians claim that the traditional Osage language that existed prior to initial contact with Europeans was diluted and altered by the influence of Western culture. Osage who were born and raised after the forced relocation of their people to Indian Territory in Oklahoma were exposed to less and less of their native language. Part of this was due to the fact that Osage children born after 1905 were sent, as part of a government mandate, to boarding schools, where they were forced to speak English and punished for speaking their native language. Also, while Osage who grew up prior to the mid-twentieth century continued to hear and speak Osage in their homes, they became more fluent in English and tended to privilege it over their native Osage in public settings. By the latter half of the twentieth century, the majority of Osage children learned English as their first language. With fewer and fewer native Osage speakers, much of the richness and meaning of the language was lost. The last native speaker of Osage was Lucille Roubedeaux, who died in 2005.

Since the late twentieth century, the vast majority of Osage speak English only, and in 2013 there were approximately fifteen to twenty second-language speakers of Osage, most of them elderly. These Osage speakers often speak or pray in their native tongue as part of Osage meetings or ceremonies. In response to the threatened extinction of their language, the Osage Nation founded the Osage Language Program in 2003 with the goal of revitalizing and preserving the Osage language. The program provides audio and video learning materials on its website and holds Osage language classes at several different language centers in Osage territory. By 2006 there were approximately 300 students enrolled in language program classes, and 5 advanced students who were nearing fluency. In 2011 the Osage Language Program initiated an Annual Dhegiha Gathering to promote revitalization of the Dhegiha branch of the Siouan language family by bringing together Osage, Kaw, Quapaw, Ponca, and Omaha speakers. Each year Dhegiha speakers from these tribes gather to share practices and insights regarding language preservation.

Greetings and Popular Expressions *Howa* (hoh-wah) is a friendly greeting, often translated into English as "Hello." One greeting traditionally offered by the host upon the arrival of visitors is *òóali óachi che*, (ooh-ah-lee ya-chee cheh), meaning "it is good that you came." A greeting often made by an elder to welcome the public to an Osage dance or ceremony is *òóali huukói òalípe* (ooh-ah-lee whoo-koh-ah oh-ah-lee ah-peeh-ooh-eh), meaning "it's good a lot of you came back."

RELIGION

Traditional Osage religious beliefs were based on their faith in Wah-kon-tah, the great mystery spirit or power. According to one Osage creation myth, the People of the Sky (Tzi-sho) joined with the People of the Land (Hun-Kah) to form one tribe, the Children of the Middle Waters (Ni-u-ko'n-ska). The Osage prayed at sunrise, noon, and sunset, following the symbolism of the three eagles who indicated prayer time: the Red Eagle, which represented the red of sunrise; the White Eagle, which represented the shimmer of eagle's wings in the sun at noon; and the Black or Dark Eagle, which represented the darkened color of the eagle's wings in the shadows of dusk. For the Osage, sunrise was the most sacred time of day because it symbolized the beginning of life.

Osage religion is often associated with the act of mourning at sunrise, which references the cyclical worldview of life and death as intimately related to each other. Thus, the coming of the sun not only reminded them of new life, but of the end of life, leading many Osage people to mourn the loss of loved ones during the sunrise prayer. The act of mourning also played a central role in maintaining the harmony of the world, on which the Osage placed great importance. Whenever the harmony of the world was disturbed by a destructive or immoral act like robbery or taking the life of a human or animal, the individual needed to express regret and sadness at upsetting the balance and unity of nature. This meant that even Osage warriors who killed their enemies in battle were expected to mourn their enemy's death.

Unlike many other American Indian tribes who acquiesced to the persistence of Christian missionaries during the eighteenth and nineteenth centuries, for almost two centuries the Osage people remained adamant in their refusal to abandon their traditional beliefs and accept Christianity. It was not until the mid-nineteenth century that some Osage began to convert to Christianity, and even then many others still resisted. Because of the Osage's great religious tolerance, however, they would often unintentionally mislead missionaries by listening with respect and patience as the missionaries explained their Western faith for hours on end.

Of all of the Christian churches, the Catholic Church appealed most to Osage Indians because of the religion's symbolism and devout ceremonies, which shared similarities to traditional Osage religion. Over time, the Catholic Church has demonstrated an understanding of the Osage culture and traditions and has incorporated many Osage practices into the services at local parishes near Osage lands. Osage tribal members have responded positively to the church's tolerance, and in the early twenty-first century, many of the Catholic parishes in Osage County, Oklahoma, especially the Pawhuska parish, had a majority Osage Indian population.

CULTURE AND ASSIMILATION

Osage people in the twenty-first century continue to practice certain tribal traditions and ceremonies, but as a result of forced relocation and tribal

RIBBONWORK: A SYMBOL OF OSAGE PRIDE

The Osage have a history of making something distinctive out of ideas and concepts that are introduced to them by outside groups. They adapted elements of the I'n-Lon-Schka ceremonial dance from neighboring Ponca and Kaw tribes, and when writing their first constitution in 1861 they incorporated the idea of a constitutional government introduced by European settlers. One of the best-known cultural adaptations by the Osage is the art of ribbonwork, in which pieces of ribbon are cut into shapes and then woven or sewn together to form complex decorative designs.

The Osage were introduced to colorful textiles from Europe upon their first contact with French traders in 1673, but the first documented example of ribbonwork dates to 1804, suggesting that it was the introduction of household tools such as scissors at the beginning of the nineteenth century that set this art form in motion. The design of ribbonwork carries with it a great deal of significance: the colors and patterns used represented various elements of communal or spiritual importance, such as balance, prosperity, bravery, and protection. Changes in the style of ribbonwork over the years also tell the story of changing Osage fortunes: with the oil boom of the 1920s, for example, came a more intricate, eye-catching design style meant to indicate the wealth of one who wore it. Today, ribbonwork is commonly worn and displayed at tribal ceremonies, and it remains a popular form of self-expression and tribal affiliation among the Osage.

dispersal across the country, the majority of Osage have largely assimilated into dominant U.S. culture. Because they were located between the Mississippi and Missouri rivers—two major transportation thoroughfares in the nineteenth century—the Osage were exposed to diverse cultures and practices that inevitably brought about a dilution and transformation of Osage culture.

Most Osage who were born in the late twentieth century are likely to identify with mainstream U.S. culture and to feel disconnected from their Osage elders and their culture. In the late 1990s, however, the Osage Nation experienced a revitalization that has continued into the twenty-first century, and many Osage Indians have recommitted themselves to preserving their culture and language and passing on their traditions to future generations.

Cuisine Osage cuisine developed out of a hunting-and-gathering lifestyle, and early Osages were adept at making meals out of the foods available in their immediate surroundings. Few dishes from early Osage days are still cooked today. Some typical foods eaten by Osage people in the past were stanica, a dried-fruit leather made out of the pulp of wild persimmons, and sausages stuffed with buffalo meat and encased in deer skin or the lining of buffalo intestines.

OSAGE PROVERBS

Due to the fact that the Osage language came close to extinction at the end of the twentieth century, there are not many Osage sayings that are normally spoken in the native tribal language. The most popular proverbs are spoken in English. These include "Where I am, I build my house; and where I build my house, all things come to it;" "Strive to be a person who is never absent from an important act;" and "We are friends; we must assist each other to bear our burdens." One saying spoken in the Osage language is *"Háako skóstapi ta, oòípse hta akxai"* (hah-koh Ya-koh-Ya-oh-ah-apeeh tah oh-ohee-p-seh tah ah-k-cha-oh-eh), meaning "However you all want it to be, they're going to listen to you." A saying similar to an American English expression is *"Háazq ta iidáde hkóbra"* (hah-Yah-que tah eeh-Wah-ooh-eh Wah-koh-wh-ooh-ah), which roughly translates as "When you do something, I want to see it" (basically meaning, "I'll believe it when I see it"). Another common saying is *"Weh we naw,"* which means "Do your best."

Traditional Dress In earlier times, Osage men wore breechcloths and occasionally, during the cold winter months, hip-length buckskin leggings. Both men and women wore moccasins made of deer, buffalo, or elk skin. Women would traditionally wear wraparound skirts made of deerskin, which were always fastened on the right side, as well as a deerskin cloth that wrapped around one shoulder and fell below the left arm. Women also wore leggings, especially during winter months. Both men and women wore jewelry, including earrings, pendants, and necklaces, often made from bone, seeds, stone, or wood. Body painting was a common form of adornment.

Once the Osage began to trade with Europeans, their clothing and jewelry changed, adapting to Western styles of dress. Osage Indians in the early twenty-first century dressed in Western fashion, yet Louis F. Burns (in *A History of the Osage People*) asserts that they continued to dress in a more somber and muted manner than other Indians. Bright colors in clothing were usually toned down with more neutral colors, and designs were less colorful.

One prominent result of Osage interaction with European traders is the practice of cutting, folding, and weaving ribbons into complex geometric patterns that are then used in clothing and other textile products. This "ribbonwork" has come to be known as a distinctive feature of many Plains Indians tribes, particularly the Osage, and is an example of the Osage's ability to create unique products from the materials introduced by Europeans.

Dances and Songs A few Osage dances continued to be performed annually by members of the Osage Nation in the early twenty-first century. One of these is the I'n-Lon-Schka ("Playground of the Eldest Son"), which is danced each June. The Osage dancers stand erect, moving in a counterclockwise direction to simulate the rotation of the earth and keeping time with the rhythm of the ancient drum, referred to as the "voice of thunder." This dance was inherited from the Kaw, or Kansas, nation who taught it to the Osage in order for it to live on in their culture. The dance serves as part of a coming-of-age ritual for the eldest son of Osage families, and it also functions to choose a new keeper of the ancient Kaw drum, a young Osage man who is selected from among the eldest sons. A drum keeper will often remain in this role for several years before a new one is appointed. As Alice Anne Callahan notes in *The Osage Ceremonial Dance I'n-Lon-Schka* (1993), while not every Osage son has the chance of serving as drum keeper, any Osage boy can be brought into the dance ceremony as a rite of passage, officially presenting him to the tribe.

Health Care Issues and Practices Like other Indian tribes, the Osage people used different natural plants for their curative or medicinal functions. Osage tribal members in contemporary times generally go to practitioners of Western medicine. While it is difficult to find studies specifically on the health of Osage Indians, the Center for Disease Control reported on the health of the general Native American population between 2009 and 2011, finding that 13.6 percent had fair or poor health, and that the leading causes of death within the community were heart disease, cancer, and accidents.

Because health care and health education are less accessible on the tribe's reservation, Osages living on the reservation tend to have more health problems than those living in other parts of the country. Obesity, diabetes, and respiratory illnesses related to smoking are all particularly prominent among Osage living on the reservation. In 2013 the Osage Nation Health Division began sponsoring an annual 5k run to raise awareness of the dangers posed by these illnesses.

FAMILY AND COMMUNITY LIFE

As is the case with many Native American cultures, family and community were and continue to be, at the heart of Osage culture. Part of maintaining the harmony of the world was maintaining unity within Osage families, bands, and the nation as a whole. Ceremonies including dances, baptisms, and mourning rituals were collective actions that functioned to forge and strengthen bonds within the community. Families were seen as the vehicle through which to maintain Osage cultural traditions and clan lineage. In contemporary times, family and community continue to play an important role in the lives of Osage people.

Gender Roles Unlike certain Native American tribes where clan membership is passed through the mother, traditional Osage social organization was patrilineal, with the tribe being divided into twenty-four clans. Osage men were hunters and warriors and played a more assertive and prominent role in the public sphere than women did. Osage women worked in the fields farming, cared for the children, and did the cooking. During earlier centuries, only men could become Osage chiefs, but both genders took part in Osage traditions such as storytelling, artwork, music, and traditional medicine. As the Osage traditional marriage practices suggest, a girl had very little control over her life, decisions being made for her first by her father and then by her husband. Part of a husband's role was to control his wife, and he was allowed to kill her if she was unfaithful. Divorce, however, could only take place if both individuals agreed. If a woman's husband died, it was common practice for her to marry his brother.

Osage children were traditionally ranked by gender and birth order. The sons ranked higher than daughters, with the eldest son holding rank over his other siblings, and the oldest daughter ranked higher than her younger sisters. Male and female roles were clearly differentiated from an early age, with boys being raised to hunt and defend their families from enemy tribes, and girls being raised as caretakers, cooks, and farmers.

After contact with Europeans, Osage gender roles slowly became less rigid, and there was less differentiation between men and women's position or status in society. Osage women now serve on the Minerals Council, participate in the tribal police force, and own businesses. Nevertheless, some of the patriarchal gender divisions still persist, including the patrilineal clan membership and the privileging of elder sons within a family.

Education The Osage people's initiation into Western-style education was through the Christian missionary schools in the early nineteenth century. These schools' first goal was to convert them to Christianity, with actual knowledge acquisition coming second. Under the Treaty of 1865, the Bureau of Indian Affairs (BIA) established a "Civilization Fund," which was used to finance the creation and maintenance of "Indian schools." Most Osage Indians did not have access to these schools, however. Many decades later, the Osage Nation was compensated for the unjust allocation of their funds, but the compensation did little to fix the countless years of inadequate educational opportunities for tribal members.

As with most Native American tribes, the Osage people received inadequate education and often faced discriminatory treatment from teachers and students during the nineteenth and early twentieth centuries. The schools run by the Bureau of Indian Affairs were not at the same level of rigor as mainstream American schools, and Osage children were often shamed for speaking their native language in class. By the early twentieth century, most Osage children were sent away to boarding schools, but they faced many difficulties due to language and cultural barriers and the lack of any programs attempting to ease Native American children into the Western school system.

In the late twentieth and early twenty-first centuries, Osage education had improved substantially, due in part to the renewed efforts of the Osage Nation to promote higher education through scholarships and community programming. In general, the Osage are more educated than their rural Oklahoman counterparts. According to American Community Survey estimates for 2006–2010, over 93 percent of adult Osage have graduated from high school, and over 26 percent have attained a college degree.

Courtship and Weddings Prior to contact with Europeans, Osage marriage was traditionally arranged by the boy's family without his consent, and often without him even knowing about it. Marriages were required to take place between individuals outside of their tribal subgroup, or moiety, and individuals were not allowed to marry into any clans to which their grandparents belonged. Thus, a family's selection of their son's spouse was based both on clan affiliation and on the girl's family, work ethic, and physical strength. Boys were not eligible for marriage until their late teens or early twenties, but girls became eligible at a much earlier age, usually shortly after puberty. Many betrothed couples did not know each other prior to the ceremony. After selecting their son's intended wife, the boy's parents would send gifts to the parents of the girl. If the girl's family consented to the union, they accepted the gifts; if not, they sent the gifts back. While polygamy was practiced by the Osage in earlier periods, it was not widespread. In the most common form of polygamy, a husband would take his spouse's younger sisters as wives. Polygamy had mostly disappeared by the nineteenth century.

Contemporary Osage Indians no longer practice the traditional marriage arrangements. Osage youth are afforded much more agency than in earlier centuries, and men and women are free to choose their own spouses. Because the tribe is so small, marriage between Osages and non-Osages is common and is generally accepted by tribal members. This was not always the case. Mixed marriage was a source of great conflict in the early twentieth century due to laws stipulating who could and could not inherit Osage oil profits, and the manipulation of these laws by non-Osage individuals who married into the tribe.

Osage ballerina Maria Tallchief danced for the Ballet Russe De Monte Carlo and also for the New York City Ballet. She is considered to be America's first prima ballerina. COURTESY: CSU ARCHIVE / AGE FOTOSTOCK

EMPLOYMENT AND ECONOMIC CONDITIONS

In a 1996 U.S. Census Bureau review of income levels among Native Americans, the Osage was listed as the tribe with the highest average income at $29,211. That number declined to $24,475 in 2010 (but it was around $37,500 when counting only those who were employed full-time). Unemployment rates within the Native American population tend to be dramatically higher than the rates for the United States in general, partially due to the lack of employment opportunities in tribal areas and their isolation. Osage unemployment rates in the twenty-first century, however, have hovered around 6.8 percent, roughly equal to the national unemployment rate after the financial collapse of the early 2000s.

According to the American Community Survey estimates for 2006–2010, the most prominent industries for the Osage are health care, education, and social services, with nearly 30 percent of the employed population finding jobs in these areas. Other prominent industries include retail (10.3 percent), construction (9.5 percent), arts and entertainment (8.8 percent), and public administration (8.4 percent). The Osage Nation employs some 1,000 tribal members,

and many Osage people are also employed in Osage casinos. For Osage with headrights, the mineral royalties continue to supplement their income.

POLITICS AND GOVERNMENT

The Osage governing body, which is headquartered in Pawhuska, Oklahoma, contains executive, legislative, and judicial branches. The executive branch consists of a principal chief and an assistant principal chief. The Osage legislative branch is a Congress made up of twelve individuals, elected by Osage tribal members, that creates and maintains Osage legislation. The structure of the judicial branch is similar to the U.S. federal judicial structure, with a Supreme Court as well as a Trial Court and other inferior courts.

Osage participation in mainstream U.S. politics was not even possible until the twentieth century because they were not U.S. citizens. While some Indians of the United States were granted citizenship through treaty agreements with their tribes, the Osage were not. As such, most Osage did not become legal U.S. citizens until 1924, when Vice President Charles Curtis, who was himself of Osage descent, ushered the Indian Citizenship Act through Congress, thus granting all Native peoples U.S. citizenship.

Since obtaining citizenship, Osage have become active in regional and state politics and have served as soldiers in every major war. In World War II, for example, nearly 500 Osages served in all branches of the military. In the early 2000s the Osage Nation was represented by several tribal members in the Oklahoma Legislature, including Scott BigHorse and David Holt. The presence of Osage Indians in state politics provides tribal members with a greater voice in U.S. mainstream politics and governance outside of the tribal governing body. Although the Osage are generally divided along the same political lines as other Americans, they do manage to find consensus when it comes to protecting their rights to mineral resources. In 1999 the Osage Nation sued the U.S. government for 140 years of mismanaging the Osage Minerals Trust, and in 2011 the two sides reached a settlement of $380 million.

NOTABLE INDIVIDUALS

Dance Maria Tallchief (1925–2013) was the first Native American to become a prima ballerina. She danced with the Ballet Russe de Monte Carlo from 1942 to 1947, but Tallchief is best known for her time with the New York City Ballet from 1947 until her retirement in 1965. She is the subject of several books and films, including the 1989 documentary *Dancing for Mr. B.* She founded the Chicago City Ballet with her sister Marjorie in 1981. Marjorie Louise Tallchief (1927–), Maria's sister, was also a prominent ballerina. She danced with several ballet companies during her career, including the Paris Opera Ballet and the Grand Ballet du Marquis de Cuevas.

Education Louis F. Burns (1920–2012) was a respected historian and author, regarded as an expert on the history, culture, and mythology of the Osage people. Burns worked as a high school and college instructor, teaching at his alma mater, Emporia State University, among other institutions. He wrote thirteen books, including *A History of the Osage People* (1989) and *Symbolic and Decorative Art of the Osage People* (1994).

Government Clarence Leonard Tinker (1887–1942) was a U.S. major general and airman who was killed in action during World War II. Tinker Air Force Base in Oklahoma City, Oklahoma, is named in his honor. Tinker was the highest-ranking Native American in the U.S. Army during his lifetime. Scott BigHorse (1956–), assistant principal chief of the Osage Nation, served as a member of the Oklahoma House of Representatives from 2006 to 2008. David Holt (1979–) served as Oklahoma State Senator from the 30th district beginning in 2010 and was also the majority whip. Holt also wrote *Big League City: Oklahoma City's Rise to the NBA* (2012).

Journalism Dennis "Denny" McAuliffe Jr., a journalist and writer, worked as assistant foreign editor of the *Washington Post*. He joined the Post in 1983 and won two Front Page Awards for his work on the newspaper's National Weekly Edition. McAuliffe published two books about the suspicious 1925 death of his Osage grandmother, including *The Deaths of Sybil Bolton: An American History* (1994) and *Bloodland: A Family Story of Oil, Greed and Murder on the Osage Reservation* (1999). He also founded the Native American news website *Reznet* (www.reznetnews.org).

Literature John Joseph Mathews (1894–1979) was an author and historian who served in World War I. He was considered one of the most important spokesmen for the Osage people. He wrote several books on Osage history, including *Life and Death of an Oilman: The Career of E. W. Marland* (1951) and *The Osages: Children of the Middle Waters* (1961). Mathews received a posthumous induction into the Oklahoma Historians Hall of Fame in 1996.

Willard Hughes Rollings (1948–2008) was a historian and the author of *Unaffected by the Gospel: Osage Resistance to the Christian Invasion, 1673–1906; A Cultural Victory* (2004), a study of Christian missionaries and the Osage, who resisted Christianization to retain their own religion and practices.

MEDIA

Bigheart Times

This weekly newspaper covers news and events throughout Osage County, including the Osage Reservation.

Louise Red Corn, Publisher
116 North 5th Street
P.O. Box 469

Barnsdall, Oklahoma 74002
Phone: (918) 847-2916
Fax: (918) 847-2654
Email: louise@bighearttimes.com
URL: http://barnsdalltimes.com/

Indian Country Today Media Network

A media network that covers news across the Native American community, including the Osage nation. It publishes the weekly magazine *Indian Country Today* and maintains an online multimedia news platform that covers news as it breaks.

Raymond Wahnihtiio Cook, Op-Ed Editor
590 Madison Avenue
New York, New York 10022
Phone: (212) 600-2086
Email: customerservice@ictmn.com
URL: www.indiancountrytodaymedianetwork.com

Osage News

The tribal newspaper of the Osage Nation in Pawhuska, Oklahoma.

Shannon Shaw Duty, Editor
619 Kihekah Avenue
Pawhuska, Oklahoma 74056
Phone: (918) 287-5668
Fax: (918) 699-5282
Email: osagenews@osagetribe.org
URL: www.osagenews.org

Reznet News

A Native American news, information and entertainment website. *Reznet* also trains and mentors American Indian college students across the country to prepare for journalism careers. It was founded by Osage tribal member Denny McAuliffe, although it reports news related to all Native American tribes.

Jason Begay, Director
School of Journalism
The University of Montana
Missoula, Montana 59812
Phone: (406) 243-2191
Email: jason.begay@umontana.edu
URL: www.reznetnews.org

ORGANIZATIONS AND ASSOCIATIONS

Northern California Osage

Formed by Osages living in Northern California, this group meets for fellowship, to learn about Osage culture, and to discuss issues of concern to the Osage tribe.

Karen Elliot, Chairwoman
Address: 82 Jess Avenue
Petaluma, California 94952
Phone: (925) 351-8585
Email: osages@northerncaliforniaosage.org
URL: http://northerncaliforniaosage.org

Osage Nation Cultural Center

Preserves and celebrates Osage teachings, values, and traditions. The center also houses the Annette Gore Library.

Vann Bighorse, Director
1449 West Main Street
Pawhuska, Oklahoma 74056
Phone: (918) 287-5537
Email: vbighorse@osagetribe.org
URL: www.osagetribe.com/cultural/index.aspx

Osage Shareholders Association

Aims to ensure the efficient and honest administration of
the Osage Mineral Estates and to preserve the federal
trust status of that estate.

Roy St. John, Chairman
P.O. Box 418
Pawhuska, Oklahoma 74056
Phone: (918) 349-2326
Email: rstjohn1@totalesi.net
URL: www.osageshareholders.org

United Osages of Southern California (UOSC)

A regional organization of Osage tribal members
residing in Southern California. The UOSC meets
about four times a year with an average of fifty
members in attendance. The meetings focus on
topics related to the Osage tribe, ranging from
politics to culture. In the past UOSC has hosted
Osage language lessons.

Bill Meyers, Chairman
Phone: (760) 500-2266
Email: william.r.myers@us.army.mil

MUSEUMS AND RESEARCH CENTERS

Osage Nation Language Department

A division of the Osage Nation, the language department
works to promote language maintenance through
Osage language lessons and conferences and
events that bring together speakers of the Dhegiha
languages. There are several language centers,
including one in Fairfax and one in Edmond,
Oklahoma, but the headquarters are in Pawhuska.

Herman M. Lookout, Director
222 West Main
Pawhuska, Oklahoma 74056
Phone: (918) 287-5505
Fax: (918) 287-5535
Email: hlookout@osagetribe.org
URL: www.osagetribe.com/language/index.aspx

Osage Tribal Museum

Offers exhibits that educate the public about the history,
customs and traditions of the Osage people.

Kathryn Red Corn, Director
819 Grandview
Pawhuska, Oklahoma 74056
Phone: (918) 287-5441
Email: otm@osagetribe.org
URL: www.osagetribe.com/museum/

Osage Village State Historic Site

A former principal village site of the Osage Indians, the
area now has a walking trail and outdoor exhibits to
educate visitors about Osage culture and traditions.

The site was listed in the National Register of Historic
Places in 1971.

1009 Truman Street
Lamar, Missouri 64759-1543
Phone: (417) 682-2279
Email: moparks@dnr.mo.gov
URL: http://mostateparks.com/park/
osage-village-state-historic-site

Thomas Gilcrease Museum

Home to the largest collection of American and Native
American art in the world, including many examples
of Osage art.

Duane King, Director
1400 North Gilcrease Museum Road
Tulsa, Oklahoma 74127-2100
Phone: (918) 596-2700
Email: duane-king@utulsa.edu
URL: http://gilcrease.utulsa.edu

University of Oklahoma Libraries

The library's Western History Collection contains many
documents related to the Osage Indians. Most
notable among these include the Indian Pioneer
Papers and the Native American Manuscripts
Collection.

John Lovett, Curator of Western History Collections
401 West Brooks Street
Norman, Oklahoma 73019
Phone: (405) 325-3641
Fax: (405) 325-6069
Email: jlovett@ou.edu
URL: http://digital.libraries.ou.edu/homehistory.php

University of Tulsa Library Special Collections Department

Contains many rare and historic manuscripts and
documents related to Native American history.

Marc Carlson, Librarian of Special Collections and
University Archives
McFarlin Library
2933 East 6th Street
Tulsa, Oklahoma 74104
Phone: (918) 631-2496
Fax: (918) 631-5022
Email: marc-carlson@utulsa.edu
URL: www.utulsa.edu/libraries/mcfarlin/
special-collections/

White Hair Memorial and Osage Learning Resource Center

Located in the home of a descendent of Osage Chief
Pawhuska (White Hair), this memorial houses
historical documents, artifacts, and photographs
related to the Osage people.

Renae Brumley, Site Manager
White Hair Memorial
P.O. Box 353
Fairfax, Oklahoma 74637
Phone: (918) 538-2417
Email: whitehair@okhistory.org
URL: www.okhistory.org/sites/whitehair

SOURCES FOR ADDITIONAL STUDY

Bailey, Garrick, ed. *Traditions of the Osage*. Translated by Francis La Flesche. Albuquerque: University of New Mexico Press, 2010.

Bailey, Garick, et al. *Art of the Osage*. Seattle: University of Washington Press, 2004.

Burns, Louis F. *A History of the Osage People*. New Edition. Tuscaloosa: U. of Alabama Press, 2004.

———. *Osage Indian Bands and Clans*. New edition. Baltimore: Clearfield Company, 2001.

Dennison, Jean. *Colonial Entanglement: Constituting a Twenty-First-Century Osage Nation*. Chapel Hill: University of North Carolina Press, 2012.

McAuliffe, Dennis, Jr. *Bloodland: A Family Story of Oil, Greed and Murder on the Osage Reservation*. Tulsa: Council Oak Books, 1994.

Rollings, Willard Hughes. *Unaffected by the Gospel: Osage Resistance to the Christian Invasion (1673–1906); A Cultural Victory*. Albuquerque: University of New Mexico Press, 2004.

Tallchief, Maria, and Larry Kaplan. *Maria Tallchief: America's Prima Ballerina*. New York: Henry Holt, 1997.

Warrior, Robert A. *The People and the Word: Reading Native Nonfiction*. Minneapolis: University of Minnesota Press, 2005.

Wilson, Terry P. *The Underground Reservation: Osage Oil*. Lincoln: University of Nebraska Press, 1985.

PACIFIC ISLANDER AMERICANS

Liz Swain

OVERVIEW

Pacific Islander Americans are immigrants or descendants of people from the Pacific Islands region of the Pacific Ocean. The Pacific Islands, which lie east of the Philippines and north and east of Australia, consist of 25,000 islands, crescent-shaped atolls, coral reefs, and tiny islets in about 11 million square miles (28.5 million square kilometers) of ocean. The entire region is called Oceania and includes Australia and the large island nation of New Zealand. Six to ten thousand of the islands are inhabited, and there are twenty-two countries and territories in the region, each consisting of one or more clusters of islands or archipelagos. The countries of the Pacific Islands are divided into three cultural/geographic subregions: Melanesia, the area geographically closest to Australia; Micronesia, which is north of Melanesia and east of the Philippines; and Polynesia, a triangle that lies to the east of these. Most of the islands in the region are between 4 and 4,000 square miles in land surface area. The entire region's area of 11 million square miles is twenty times the size of Alaska.

The population of the Pacific Islands, not including Hawaii, was estimated to be just over 10 million in 2011, according to Secretariat of the Pacific Community. The U.S. Census estimated Hawaii's population in 2012 to be 1.39 million, about 10 percent of whom were Native Hawaiian or other Pacific Islander. The subregion with the largest population in 2010 was Melanesia, with 8.8 million, 70 percent of whom lived in Papua New Guinea. The population of Micronesia in 2010 was approximately 546,000, with 106,000 living in the Federated States of Micronesia (FSM), 187,140 living on Guam, 54,439 in the Marshall Islands, about 63,000 in the Northern Mariana Islands, and 20,518 in the Palau Islands. Polynesia, not including Hawaii, had a population of 668,000 in 2010, with the most populated island groups being French Polynesia (268,767), Tonga (103,365), Samoa (183,123), and American Samoa (65,896). The Pacific Islands are ethnically and religiously diverse, and religious affiliation there depends in large part on the extent of the islanders' contact with foreign cultures. For example, in Micronesia, many people living on Guam and the other Marianas Islands are Catholic, due to contact with the Spanish. In Fiji, which is part of Melanesia, there are significant numbers of Hindus and Muslims because the British sent Asian Indians there as contract laborers. In Polynesia, Tonga has significant Mormon population, and many Samoans belong to the Congregational Christian Church. For the most part, Pacific Islanders live in subsistence economies that offer little potential for economic mobility.

The first Pacific Islanders in the Americas were most likely seafaring Polynesian explorers who arrived in various places along the North and South American Pacific coast hundreds of years before the first Europeans came to the New World, as well as hundreds of years before Europeans invaded the Pacific Islands. Large groups of Pacific Islanders came under U.S. authority through the process of colonization. By the end of the eighteenth century, all of the South Pacific Islands—except for Tonga, which was never formally colonized—had come under the control either of Japan or one of the European powers, and by the latter 1800s, U.S. interests in the South Pacific had increased, partly due to conflict with Spain. When the United States won the Spanish American War in 1898, Spain ceded Guam and the Philippines to the United States, and the United States annexed the independent nation of Hawaii. At the time of annexation, there were some 40,000 indigenous Hawaiians and another 7,500 non-Hawaiians living in the Hawaiian Islands, according to a census taken in the islands in 1890. Apart from the early explorers, the first individual Pacific Islanders known to have come to the mainland United States arrived in California and New England aboard whaling ships in the 1800s. Missionary activity also brought individual Pacific Islanders to the United States, beginning in 1924 when the Mormons set up missions in Tonga. Despite U.S. involvement in the region, significant immigration to the United States did not begin until after World War II. One of the first significant migrations was of Samoans who had been employed at the naval base on American Samoa, which closed in 1951, destabilizing the territory's economy. The people of

Guam were also made U.S. citizens in 1950, which included unrestricted entry to the United States.

According to the 2010 U.S. Census, there were 1.2 million Native Hawaiian and other Pacific Islanders in the United States. The six-largest Pacific Islander American ethnicities were, in order: Native Hawaiian (527,077), Samoan (184,440), Guamanian or Chamorro (147,798), Tongan (57,183), Fijian (32,304), and Marshallese (22,434). Native Hawaiians are an indigenous minority group that has a "special trust relationship" with the United States, similar to other Native Americans and Native Alaskans. As the census methodology changed to account for multiracial identity, the count of Pacific Islanders greatly increased. For instance, from 1990 to 2000, the number of Pacific Islanders who reported being "Pacific Islander alone" decreased by 6 percent; however, when Pacific Islander alone or in combination with any other race or ethnicity is counted, the number of Pacific Islanders increased 71 percent. In the 2000 U.S. Census, nearly half of Pacific Islander Americans reported being multiracial, the highest percentage of any racial/ethnic group. Over half (52 percent) of the Native Hawaiian and Other Pacific Islander alone-or-in-combination population lived in the states of Hawaii (356,000) and California (286,000). Together with Hawaii and California, the states of Washington (70,000), Texas (48,000), Florida (40,000), Utah (37,000), New York (36,000), Nevada (33,000), Oregon (26,000), and Arizona (25,000) accounted for over three-fourths of the Pacific Islander American community.

HISTORY OF THE PEOPLE

Early History Archeological evidence suggests that the Papuan-speaking people of the island of New Guinea are descendants of travelers who settled there over 40,000 years ago. Additional evidence compiled by scholars working in various fields including linguistics, ethnography, and anthropology indicates that as far back as 3,500 years ago, the early inhabitants of New Guinea had established a complex set of relationships with Austronesian-speaking people (travelers from Taiwan, Malay, Indonesia, and other points in Southeast Asia) who visited the island. Findings from 1950 at Lapita Beach on the island of New Caledonia (in the eastern part of Melanesia) have led scholars to believe that the Austronesian-speaking people mixed with the Papuans, and this racially mixed group is believed to have migrated as far east as Fiji and the outer islands of Melanesia. The people who traveled through New Guinea and to points east have been called Lapita. Their descendants are what we now call Polynesians. According to archaeologists, Lapita from Tonga and Samoa settled the Marquesas Islands 2,000 years ago. Artifacts found on the Society Islands indicate that Polynesians settled in Tahiti around 850 CE.

The Lapita sailed in massive double-hulled canoes that held up to two hundred people. With no navigation instruments, these ancestors of modern Polynesians relied on *wayfinding*, the use of nature to navigate. The navigational course was determined by observing the stars, the sun, the wave currents, and the flight pattern of birds. The Lapita/Polynesians lived on the coasts of small islands, and when they traveled to settle a new island they brought with them everything they would need, including seed plants, domesticated animals, and tools for fishing and hunting. Polynesians established a hierarchical social structure in which children inherited their father's power and social status. A chief and his descendants ruled a territory that ranged in size from a village to a region. Within the hierarchical governing system were power struggles. These struggles sometimes resulted in war, forcing islanders to flee and settle other islands.

Spain and Portugal, vying for control of sea routes to Asia, were the first European countries to send explorers through the Pacific Islands. Spain became the first European country to colonize islands in what became known as Micronesia when, in 1565, it claimed Guam, the Mariana Islands, the Carolines, and the Philippines. A century later, Spanish Jesuits forced the conversion of the population, whose resistance was quelled by Spanish soldiers. Over the next centuries, Britain, Holland, France, Japan, Germany, and the United States would compete for control of the Pacific Islands region.

Dutch navigators Jakob LeMaire and Abel Tasman were the first Europeans to report seeing Tongan and Fijian islands in the first half of the seventeenth century. European exploration of the islands continued through the eighteenth century. English captain Samuel Wallis reached Tahiti in 1767 and claimed it for England. A year later, French explorer Louis de Bougainville landed in Tahiti. He did not realize Wallis had been there and claimed the land for his country. In 1774 British captain James Cook sailed through the islands. Cook first encountered what he named the "Sandwich Islands" (now the Hawaiian islands) in 1778. It is estimated that at that time, there were 400,000 to 800,000 indigenous people on the islands; due to diseases introduced by Europeans, less than 40,000 were there one hundred years later. Cook was followed by many explorers and traders, including British Captain William Bligh, whose failed attempt in 1789 to attain breadfruits led to the infamous mutiny on his ship, *The Bounty*.

The Pacific Islands region is a breeding ground for many species of whales, and whales have been both an important part of Pacific Island culture as well as a draw for European and American whale hunters. Thousands of sperm and humpback whales were killed by sail whalers beginning in the late 1700s. Commercial whaling greatly expanded in the 1800s, due in part to industrial ship building and advances in processing. New England, particularly Massachusetts, was a center of the whaling industry, with hundreds of whaling ships embarking each year to the Pacific Islands region. The ships often stopped in the islands to stock provisions and gather new crew members. In 1824, for instance, more than 100 ships stopped in Polynesian ports; by the peak year, 1846, more than 700 whalers stopped in Hawaii. The impact on the people and economy of the Pacific Islands was profound. The Native Hawaiians began to produce food the American sailors wanted (potatoes and beef) and were exposed to foreign cultures and diseases.

Christian missionaries brought more change to the islands. In 1797, members of the London Missionary Society settled in Tonga and Tahiti. The missionaries eventually succeeded in converting Tahitians, but they left Tonga in 1799. Catholic and Wesleyan missionaries also attempted to convert the Pacific Islanders. Wesleyan ministers succeeded in converting Tonga to Christianity. In the nineteenth century members of the islands' royalty converted. Fijian king Cokobau, for instance, converted to Christianity in 1854.

Modern Era France gained control of Tahiti in 1842 and made it a French colony in 1880. Fiji was colonized by England in 1874, while Tonga remained an independent kingdom. The colonization of the South Pacific devastated the region's peoples. Populations were killed by conquest, disease, and ignorance. The islands were used as penal colonies and to test nuclear weapons, and they were also the sites of battles between foreign nations. The three years of fighting between the United States and Japan, beginning with Japan's attack on Pearl Harbor on December 7, 1941, took place largely in the Pacific Islands region, on Papua New Guinea, the Solomon Islands, the Gilbert Islands (now Kiribati), the Marianas, the Carolines and many other islands and atolls. Between 1946 and 1962 the United States conducted nuclear weapons tests in the Marshall Islands and other locations in the South Pacific, as did the French, who conducted at least forty-one nuclear weapons tests on atolls in French Polynesia between 1966 and 1974.

Yet the story of the Pacific Islands since World War II is one of growing political independence. In 1962 Samoa became the first Pacific Island to attain independence in the twentieth century. Tonga and Fiji gained independence (from Britain) in 1970. Later in the 1970s, Papua New Guinea, the Solomon Islands, Tuvalu, and Kiribati attained independence. In the 1980s and 1990s, three independent countries entered into a Compact of Free Association with the United States, the Marshall Islands, the Federated States of Micronesia, and in 1994, Palau.

In 1995–1996, the French conducted more nuclear tests on the Mururoa atoll in French Polynesia, but abandoned them amid widespread protests. At the end of the twentieth century, the U.S. military bases in the Pacific Islands, in the Marshall Islands, Guam, American Samoa, and Hawaii were still major factors in the islands' economies. Widespread unemployment, overfishing, and dependence on U.S. aid were major issues. During the early part of the twenty-first century, the effects of climate change, particularly the warming of the oceans and intensifying weather patterns, were beginning to be felt and anticipated in the Pacific Island region. Scientists confirmed that equatorial fish were migrating to cooler waters, and they predicted that higher levels of rainfall may create increased habitat for freshwater fish. In countries such as Kiribati, where 40 percent of gross national product in 2010 was related to the fishing industry, preparing for these changes was a profound challenge.

SETTLEMENT IN THE UNITED STATES

The U.S. Census category "Native Hawaiian and Other Pacific Islander" was added in 2000. However, historical accounts and church records provide some description of migration and settlement patterns up until the government began documenting Pacific Islander immigration to the United States.

There is good evidence based on sweet potato and chicken bone DNA, linguistic analysis, and sewn plank boat findings that the first Pacific Islanders to come to the American continents were seafaring Polynesians who made multiple landfalls, some in southern California, well before Columbus. There is also abundant evidence of Pacific Islanders on the mainland in California during the gold mining era, and New England during the height of the whaling industry. As early as the 1830s, Polynesians, referred to as "Kanaka" (the Hawaiian word for "man") who boarded whaling and other trade ships as crew members disembarked and remained in California. At least six different mining towns in California were named "Kanaka Bar" after the Hawaiians. Due to discrimination, most did not stay past the 1880s; however, some moved up to Oregon and Washington, married Native American women, and worked primarily in the salmon fishing industry. It was unlawful for Pacific Islanders to marry white women in Washington and Oregon, but Native Americans did not have the same prejudice and some of the Hawaiians and their descendants became leaders of various tribes. Statistics indicate that Hawaiians were among the top three contributors to the Northwest Coast Indian gene pool, and it was estimated by a French priest that there were 500 Hawaiians living on the Northwest coast in 1842.

In 1809, twenty-year-old Henry Ōpūkaha'ia arrived in Massachusetts from Hawaii aboard a seal-trading ship. He was one of the early converts to Christianity and began the work of giving his native language an orthography. Ōpūkaha'ia wanted to travel back to Hawaii with other missionaries but died before he was able to. He and other Pacific Islanders and Native Americans were instrumental in the founding of the Foreign Mission School in 1816, administered from Boston by the American Board of Commissioners for Foreign Missions (ABCFM). During its ten years, about 100 students attended: "43 Native Americans, 13 Americans (white), and 20 Hawaiians, and other natives of the Pacific, including 2 Chinese" (Sydney K. Mitchell, *Phases of the History of Cornwall*, 1939).

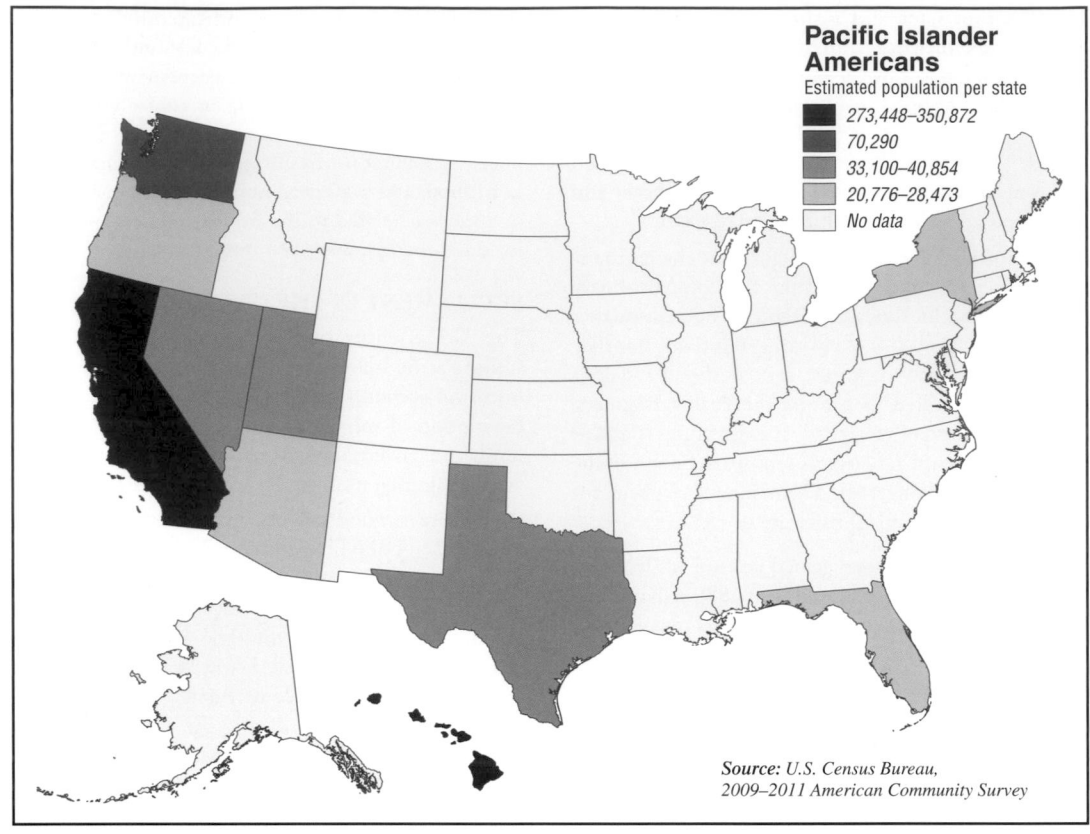

Pacific Islander Americans
Estimated population per state
- 273,448–350,872
- 70,290
- 33,100–40,854
- 20,776–28,473
- No data

*Source: U.S. Census Bureau,
2009–2011 American Community Survey*

According to the U.S. Department of Homeland Security, the first Pacific Islanders granted legal permanent resident status were French Polynesians in 1843 and Fijians in 1874. The next small wave of immigration was from Micronesia and Melanesia immediately after World War II, followed by larger numbers of Polynesians from Samoa and Tonga in the later 1940s and early 1950s. Many Samoans had been recruited into the U.S. military and later immigrated to the United States seeking jobs and education. They largely settled in the urban areas of California. By 2000 there were 50,000 Samoans in Los Angeles County alone.

A number of Pacific Islanders began to migrate when the Mormon Church sent students to Hawaii for higher education, and then to the United States, particularly to Utah. From 1889 to 1917, hundreds of Pacific Islander converts to Mormonism were brought to Utah, where they founded the tiny village of Iosepa in the remote Skull Valley, about 75 miles southwest of the church's headquarters in Salt Lake City. Although almost all of the Iosepa immigrants returned to the islands by 1917, Pacific Islanders continued to come to Utah to be close to the Mormon church, and non-Mormons came to be near relatives who had already made the move. Pacific Islanders were also attracted to Utah by the promises of economic opportunities and better educations for their children. By 1990 there were 7,700 Pacific Islanders living in Utah, according to a state report. Life in dry, cold, landlocked Utah

was a struggle. About half of Utah's Polynesian families were living below the poverty line in 2000, with many parents working long hours at menial, low-paying jobs. The immigrants' children, caught between two cultures, were overrepresented in gangs and dropped out of high school at twice the rate of Utah's white students. Still, Pacific Islanders continued to come to Utah. By 2010 there were 37,000 Pacific Islander Americans in Utah.

Waves of Pacific Islanders continued to arrive in other areas of the United States as well. During the 1970s, Fijian immigration to the United States ranged from 132 admissions in 1976 to 1,000 in 1979. The record year for French Polynesian migration was 1975, when 47 people were admitted. Tongan immigration ranged from 133 admissions in 1976 to 809 in 1979. Fijian migration jumped during the 1980s, when admission ranged from 712 people in 1983 to 1,205 in 1987. French Polynesian immigration ranged from 19 admissions in 1986 to 59 in 1984.

In 1996 a record 1,847 Fijians immigrated to the United States. The record year for the other groups was 1991, when 1,685 Tongans and 31 French Polynesians entered. During 1997, admission was granted to 1,549 Fijians, 21 French Polynesians, and 303 Tongans. Also during the 1990s, the cost of living in Hawaii increased due to the growing tourism, and many Native Hawaiians moved to the mainland. By 2010 there were more Native Hawaiians living in the mainland United States, mostly California, than in Hawaii. Other states in which significant numbers of Pacific Islanders live are Arizona, Florida, Nevada, New York, Oregon, Texas, Utah, and Washington.

LANGUAGE

With over one thousand distinct indigenous languages, the Pacific Island region hosts the highest ratio of languages per population of any region in the world. French and English are also widely used, with English often the language of school instruction. It is not unusual for people to speak several languages. The indigenous languages spoken by Pacific Islanders are descendants of two language groups, the Austronesian and Papuan, although there are so many Papuan languages that cannot be shown to be linguistically connected that they may best be referred to as "Non-Austonesian." For instance, 500 different languages are spoken in the interior of Papua New Guinea. On the coastal areas of Papua New Guinea and near islands offshore, there are 220 different Austronesian languages spoken. The 30 different Polynesian languages are all part of the Austronesian family, about half of these are spoken outside of Polynesia on small islands in Micronesia and Melanesia. Polynesian, American, and European missionaries developed written forms of Pacific Islander languages that were previously nonexistent in the predominantly oral culture.

In 1990, 25 percent of Pacific Islander Americans spoke their native language at home, and 11 percent were linguistically isolated, meaning no one in the family over fourteen years old spoke only English or spoke English very well. Among these, Tongans were by far the most likely, 72 percent, to speak their native language at home, and 21 percent were linguistically isolated. Only 8 percent of Native Hawaiians spoke Hawaiian at home. In 1990, 33 percent of Pacific Islander Americans judged themselves as not speaking English very well. As might be expected, people over the age of sixty-five had the least English proficiency. In 2000 nearly 30 percent of elder Native Hawaiians and Pacific Islanders did not speak English as their first language, and 28 percent reported not speaking English at all or not proficiently. By 2010 less than 9 percent of Pacific Islander Americans said they did not speak English very well, though about the same percentage spoke their native language at home. In 2010 there were at least 39 different Pacific Islander languages spoken in homes in the United States.

RELIGION

The religious practices of Pacific Islander Americans reflect blends of the missionary activity on their home islands with indigenous cultural beliefs and practices. Polynesian indigenous religion was not separate from culture, and even when Christianity was accepted, Polynesian culture was retained and incorporated into religious practice. Polynesian religious culture emphasizes beauty, reciprocity with the material universe,

the basic goodness of humans, and the fundamental importance of family, clan, and community. Christian missionaries to the Pacific Islands preceded political colonization, cooperated with colonization, and sometimes supported the post–World War II independence movements. The Protestant churches trained indigenous leaders for self-sustaining island ministries, and many of Pacific Islander American religious leaders were trained in their home countries. Each of the twenty-two countries of the Pacific Islands has its own particular religious history and tradition. Among the Christian missionaries who worked in the Pacific Islands were Anglicans, Methodists, Roman Catholics, Presbyterians, French Reformed, Lutherans, and Seventh-day Adventists. For instance, Guam and the Federated States of Micronesia are predominately Roman Catholic, while the Marshall Islands, also in Micronesia, are predominately Protestant, with only 8.9 percent Roman Catholic.

Polynesian indigenous religion was not separate from culture, and even when Christianity was accepted, Polynesian culture was retained and incorporated into religious practice. Polynesian religious culture emphasizes beauty, reciprocity with the material universe, the basic goodness of humans, and the fundamental importance of family, clan, and community.

In 2012 the San Francisco Bay Area had over a hundred Christian congregations of Tongans, Samoans, and Fijians. The denominations include Assemblies of God, Congregationalist, Methodist, Adventist, and Roman Catholic. In 2012 the United Methodists adopted a comprehensive plan for Pacific Islander ministries in the United States.

Roman Catholic Samoans in the Los Angeles area also combined their island traditions with Catholicism. Because of their sense of community, different parishes come together to celebrate in the Samoan language. Christmas, Easter, and patron feast days are celebrated in uniquely Samoan ways: people wear native costumes, and a lei may be draped around the Bible when it is placed on the pulpit.

CULTURE AND ASSIMILATION

With all their diverse ethnic, religious, and political backgrounds, most Pacific Islander Americans from the Austronesian/Polynesian cultures share values that include deference to the authority of elders, appreciation for reciprocal labor and time, and appreciation of communal and family connection and responsibility. The family extends to grandparents, aunts, uncles, and other relatives, as well as the community. Family members looked after one another, respected their elders, and shared with the community. Their history and traditions were relayed through songs, dance, poems, and stories.

For Pacific Islanders, language is both a cultural heritage in which history and tradition are relayed and also a barrier to adjusting to life in the United States. A limited knowledge of English has caused difficulties for islanders seeking housing, employment, health care, and legal representation. Although Pacific Islanders sometimes face intimidating challenges to assimilation, their cultural concept of community provides valuable support. For instance, family members can be relied upon to help find housing and work, and, just as their home villages were organized to support the community members, Pacific Islanders in the United States formed organizations such as the Utah Office of Polynesian Affairs and other religious and self-help groups to give assistance.

Dances and Songs One of the shared cultural aspects of Pacific Islanders is the expression through songs and dance of origins, journeys, connection to the spiritual world, and major life events. New songs and chants may be created for occasions such as the birth of a child. For Pacific Islander American religious congregations and other cultural organizations, the performance of songs and dances is a central activity. Musicians play the guitar and traditional Polynesian instruments like the *pahu* (a wood drum), ukulele, *uli uli* (small gourds), *ipu* (larger gourds), *puili* (split bamboo). In traditional Polynesian culture, drums hold sacred power and have important cultural/religious

A Pacific Islander woman stands in the doorway of a traditional grass hut in a tourism photo. KEVIN FLEMING / CORBIS

uses. In Tahiti and Melanesia, drums made out of hollowed logs are used. Drums in the Pacific Islands tend to have only one playing head, often made from fish, shark, or lizard skin. Hourglass shapes are common in Melanesia, and cylindrical types are widespread in Polynesia. The Hawaiian ceremonial Mele Hula dances utilize two drums: the larger *pahu hula* of wood, played with the hands, and the smaller *pūniu* made from a coconut shell, played with a braided fiber "stick." Although other instruments are also used, the drums are reserved for the most important dances.

Traditional Dress Like song and dance, Pacific Islander dress carries a lot of cultural tradition and is particular to each island's heritage. In Tahiti, people wear a *tiare* (a hibiscus blossom) behind one ear. A flower worn behind the right ear means the man or woman is available. When placed behind the left ear, the wearer is spoken for. The tiare is also added to a crown of braided palm fronds and greenery. Fijian dancers wear skirts of shredded leaves and paint their faces for war dances.

Cuisine While language and traditions changed as Polynesians migrated to other islands, many Pacific Islanders still hold communal feasts. In an outdoor pit that Tongans and Hawaiians call an *umu* ("oo-moo"), food is roasted/steamed wrapped in taro or banana leaves or in aluminum foil. Chicken, fish, pork, sweet potatoes, and *taro* (a starchy tuber) may all be cooked in the umu.

Pacific Islander cuisine includes numerous types of fish, breadfruit, *cassava* (a starchy plant), sweet potatoes, and fresh fruit such as bananas and coconut. Corned beef is also popular, and in Tonga it is cooked with taro leaves. Tongans also combine taro with other meats or serve it with onions or coconut milk. A favorite Tahitian dessert is *gateau a la banane* ("ga-tow a la bah-nan"), which is French for banana cake.

Kava (pronounced "kah-vah"), a nonalcoholic drink made from the ground root of the pepper shrub, is a ceremonial beverage throughout the Pacific Islands, and particularly among Tongans, Samoans, and Fijians. Called *yaqona* ("yanggona") in Fiji, the mildly intoxicating beverage is consumed during important occasions such as births, weddings, deaths, and the arrival of a dignitary. Kava is also drunk socially. Etiquette requires visitors to Fijian villages to bring it to the chief.

Holidays Most Pacific Islander Americans celebrate Christian holidays, including Christmas and Easter. Tahitian Americans in the United States may also observe the French Polynesian celebration of Bastille Day on July 14. This date is known as France's independence day in French-speaking countries. July 4 is celebrated by Tongan Americans as King Taufa 'ahau Tupou IV's birthday and a national holiday.

Health Issues For centuries, Pacific Islanders regarded obesity as a sign of wealth or nobility. Such excess weight can lead to diabetes. Hypertension is another concern for Pacific Islanders. A 1998 California Department of Health Services report indicated that Pacific Islanders living in the state were "less likely to be aware of their hypertension [or] to be under treatment with medication" than people from other ethnic groups. The report concluded that Asians and Pacific Islanders were likely to rely on traditional remedies, perhaps because of the lack of health care providers of from their ethnic background.

Pacific Islanders face other health issues. Pacific Islander Americans have the highest mortality rates for most cancers and incidences of chronic diseases, smoking, and binge and chronic drinking. In addition, they have the lowest rates for prenatal care and immunization of children.

FAMILY AND COMMUNITY LIFE

Among Pacific Islanders, ancestry determines a large part of an individual's identity. Pacific Islanders trace their genealogical roots and relationships with others as a way of developing personal and community identity. The *Kumulipo*, the Hawaiian creation chant, tells the story of the world's creation and also the genealogy of the Hawaiian royal families. Through such chants, Hawaiians and other Pacific Islander ethnic groups establish the importance of ancestry to present identity. However, genealogy and ancestry are much more than genetic relationships; people who come into a Pacific Islander community through adoption or marriage take on the cultural characteristics of the adopting family and are recognized as kin.

Pacific Islander children are taught they are part of an extended family, one that works together for the good of the community. Tongans call this *nofo a'kainga*, which means "everyone counts on one another." The Samoan word for extended family is *aiga*. Immigrants may rely on their extended family for social and economic support. Events such as marriages, funerals, and births call for the extended family's participation. Among Pacific Islanders, it is common to make long visits to family members, during which the visitors are expected to consider themselves at home.

Gender Roles Gender roles and relations vary widely in Pacific Islander communities; however, all have been affected by the disruption of traditional societies by colonization and by increasing urbanization in the late twentieth and early twenty-first centuries. Colonial governments and the effects of some Christian missionaries exacerbated inequalities between women and men, particularly in relation to land ownership, decision-making, and governance. In some areas of the Pacific Islands, land ownership, decision-making, and governance were traditionally matrilineal. In Guam, even though matrilineage was abolished by American rule, Chamorro women have continued to hold positions of authority as

PACIFIC ISLANDERS IN NANTUCKET

The whaling community of Nantucket Island, Massachusetts, has a history of Pacific Islander crewmen who settled in their community. The 1840 and 1850 U.S. Census counted, respectively, 793 and 593 "non-resident mariners or seamen," many of whom were Pacific Islander. A boardinghouse in those years in Nantucket's New Guinea section (the African American neighborhood), had a sign reading "WILLIAM WHIPPY CANACKA BOARDING-HOUSE," *Canacka* being a variation of *kanaka*, the Hawaiian word for "man." The character of the harpooner Queequeg in Herman Melville's renowned 1851 novel *Moby-Dick* is based on such Pacific Islander mariners. A native of a fictional South Pacific island, Queequeg meets the narrator in Nantucket before they set out to sea on a whaling ship.

guardians of kinship knowledge. In the United States, Pacific Islander American women are more likely than other American women to work outside the home and also to have unusually high risk factors for cardiovascular disease and cancer. Among Native Hawaiian women, there are multiple stress factors, such as high divorce rates, single-parenting, low income, and high mortality. At the same time, Native Hawaiian women are inheritors of a culture with female cosmic forces and with chiefly women claimed as genealogical ancestors.

Education There is almost universal literacy in the Pacific Islands (except in Papua New Guinea, where the literacy rate is about 57 percent), and a higher percentage of Pacific Islander Americans graduate from high school (88 percent) than Americans overall (85 percent). Yet, at the beginning of the twenty-first century, significantly lower percentages of Pacific Islander Americans completed a bachelor's degree or higher. In 2010, 5 percent of Pacific Islander Americans had a graduate or professional degree, compared with 10 percent of Americans overall. In 2008 Washington State, where Pacific Islanders made up 0.4 percent of the population, published an impressive report on Pacific Islander student achievement. The researchers found that, even though students and their parents expected the students to attend college, a high percentage of students did not graduate with the degrees they hoped for.

EMPLOYMENT AND ECONOMIC CONDITIONS

Pacific Islanders have the highest percentages of population in the workforce of any ethnic group in the United States, with about 70 percent of those aged sixteen or older in the workforce. Pacific Islander women, are also more likely to be in the workforce (66 percent) than all American women (59 percent).

However, in 2010, Pacific Islander Americans were also more likely to be unemployed (10.4 percent) than Americans overall (7.9 percent). Pacific Islander Americans are almost three times more likely to serve in the military (1.5 percent) than other Americans (0.5 percent); they were somewhat more likely to be in service occupations; and they were less likely to be in management jobs than other Americans. Although compared to other Americans, there were lower percentages of individual Pacific Islander Americans at the lowest earnings levels, Pacific American families were not as well off. Analysis showed that Pacific Islanders lived in larger households than the American average, with wage earners supporting more people.

POLITICS AND GOVERNMENT

In 2010 over 25 percent of Pacific Islander Americans were foreign-born or born in an island territory of the United States. As with other communities with large numbers of new immigrants, politics in the home country are typically more engaging than politics in the United States. The *Los Angeles Times* noted in a 2000 article, "Samoan Americans at Crossroads," that "Many older people born on the islands remain registered to vote there, often by absentee ballot, which has stymied efforts to win political power in Carson. Candidates for the governorship of American Samoa regularly campaign in Carson, but no person of Samoan ancestry has ever served on the Carson City Council." In the early twenty-first century, the U.S. government's practice of categorizing Asian Americans along with Pacific Islander Americans was beginning to be challenged. Pacific Islanders' unique contributions and strength, as well as their challenges, were obscured by this practice.

NOTABLE INDIVIDUALS

Academics Jonathan Kay Kamakawiwo'ole Osorio is professor of Hawaiian studies at the University of Hawaii at Manoa, a historian of the Hawaiian Kingdom, and a practicing musician and composer. He writes about the sovereignty movement in Hawaii.

Haunani-Kay Trask (1949–), born in the San Francisco Bay Area, is a Native Hawaiian academic, activist, and writer. Trask is a professor of Hawaiian studies with the Kamakakuokalani Center for Hawaiian Studies at the University of Hawaii at Manoa and has represented Native Hawaiians in the United Nations and various other global forums. She is the author of several books of poetry and nonfiction.

Activism William P. Afeaki is a Tongan American lawyer and director of the Utah Office of Pacific Islander Affairs. In 2004 he was appointed to the President's Advisory Commission on Asian Americans and Pacific Islanders by President George W. Bush.

Politicians Daniel Kahikina Akaka (1924–), born in Honolulu, was the first Native Hawaiian United States senator; he served in the U.S. Senate from 1990 to 2013.

Eni Fa'aua'a Hunkin Faleomavaega Jr. (1943–) was born in American Samoa and educated at the University of Houston and the University of Hawaii.

Pacific Islander Americans Sione Pouha, New York Jets; Chris Kemoeatu, Pittsburgh Steelers; Faleomavaega Eni Hunkin, American Samoa Congressman; Paul Soliai, Miami Dolphins; Maake Kemoeatu, Washington Redskins at a public appearance for the 2011 USA Seven. EVERETT / PHOTOSHOT

He is the non-voting delegate to the United States House of Representatives from American Samoa's at-large congressional district.

A. P. Lutali (Aifili Paulo Lauvao; 1919–2002) was twice elected governor of American Samoa, in 1984 and 1992. He was a founder of the American Samoa Bar Association and the U.S. commonwealth's Democratic Party.

Stage and Screen Dwayne Johnson (1972–), better known as "The Rock," is a former football player and wrestler turned actor. He was born in California to Samoan and Canadian parents and grew up partly in New Zealand and Hawaii. After a long wrestling career, Johnson began acting on television and in films, starring in Hollywood action blockbusters such as *The Scorpion King* (2002) and *Faster* (2010).

Joseph Jason Namakaeha Momoa (1979–), an actor born in Honolulu and raised in Iowa, starred first in the TV show *Baywatch* and then broke out as the star of the remake of *Conan the Barbarian* (2011) and as a key character in the hit television show *Game of Thrones*. He and actress Lisa Bonet are the parents of two children.

MEDIA

PRINT

Asian Pacific American Law Journal

Run by students at the UCLA School of Law, the journal seeks to facilitate discourse on issues affecting South Asian, Southeast Asian, East Asian, and Pacific Islander communities in the United States.

Box 951476
UCLA School of Law
Room 2416
Los Angeles, California 90095-1476
Phone: (310) 206-2201
Fax: (310) 206-6489
Email: apalj@lawnet.ucla.edu
URL: http://gsa.asucla.ucla.edu/services/publications/asian-pacific-american-law-journal

Hardboiled

This news magazine, published by the University of California–Berkeley, is created by students and focuses on Asian Pacific American issues.

University of California
112 Hearst Gym
MC 4520
Berkeley, California 94720-4500
Email: hardboiledmagazine@gmail.com
URL: http://hardboiled.berkeley.edu/

RADIO

KPOP-AM (1360)

"Ports of Paradise" is a weekly syndicated one-hour radio program featuring South Seas music from the 1920s to the present. Syndicated broadcasts are heard in:

Albany, New York, on WLAL-AM (1190); Las Vegas, Nevada, on KLAV-AM (1230); and Anchorage, Alaska, on KKHAR-AM (590).

J. Hal Hodgson, Executive Producer
P.O. Box 33648
San Diego, California 92163
Phone: (619) 275-7357
Email: aloharn@portparadise.com
URL: www.portparadise.com

ORGANIZATIONS AND ASSOCIATIONS

The Pacific American Foundation

The foundation was established in 1993 as a national organization dedicated to improving Pacific Islanders' lives by helping them to help themselves. The foundation educates and provides information to decision-makers and leaders about areas of public concern and policies that affect Americans who trace their ancestry to the Pacific Islands.

45-285 Kaneohe Bay Drive, #102
Kaneohe, Hawaii 96744-2366
Phone: (808) 664-3027
Fax: (808) 212-9509
Email: ohana@thepaf.org
URL: www.thepaf.org

Pacific Islanders' Cultural Association

Supports Pacific Islanders in Northern California. Includes information on all Pacific Islands, links, the Northern California Outrigger Canoe Association, and Pacific Island News sources.

1016 Lincoln Boulevard #5
San Francisco, California 94129-1721
Phone: (415) 281-0221
Email: webmaster@pica-org.org
URL: www.pica-org.org

MUSEUMS AND RESEARCH CENTERS

Center for Pacific Islands Studies

Part of the University of Hawai'i at Mānoa's School of Pacific and Asian Studies, the center's goal is to "promote an understanding of the Pacific Islands and issues of concern to Pacific Islanders."

University of Hawai'i at Mānoa
1890 East-West Road
Moore 215
Honolulu, Hawai'i 96822
Phone: (808) 956-7700
Fax: (808) 956-7053
Email: cpis@hawaii.edu
URL: www.hawaii.edu/cpis/

Polynesian Cultural Center

This organization, founded in 1963, seeks to preserve Polynesian cultures, and it provides information and education about arts, crafts, and lore. It also sponsors several recognition awards and funds the Institute for Polynesian Studies at the Brigham Young University—Hawaii campus. The 43-acre site has re-creations of the villages of Tonga, Tahiti, Fiji, and four other

Polynesian islands. An open-air shopping village features arts and crafts. Cultural demonstrations include dance performances.

55-370 Kamehameha Highway
Laie, Hawaii 96762
Phone: (808) 293-3333
Email: culturalexpert@polynesia.com
URL: www.polynesia.com

SOURCES FOR ADDITIONAL STUDY

Charlot, John. "Towards a Dialogue Between Christianity and Polynesian Religions." *Studies in Religion/Sciences Religieuses* 15, no. 4 (1986): 443–50.

Kirk, Robert W. *Paradise Past: The Transformation of the South Pacific, 1520–1920*. Jefferson, NC: McFarland & Company, 2012.

Lai, Eric Yo Ping, and Dennis Arguelles. *The New Face of Asian Pacific America: Numbers, Diversity and Change in the 21ˢᵗ Century*. San Francisco: AsianWeek, 2003.

Lal, Brij V., and Kate Fortune. *The Pacific Islands: An Encyclopedia*. Honolulu: University of Hawai'i Press, 2000.

Lebo, Susan. "Native Hawaiian Whalers in Nantucket, 1820–60." *Historic Nantucket* 56, no. 1 (2007): 14–16.

Miley, Sarah. "Remembering Iosepa." *Honolulu Magazine*, November 2008.

Osorio, Jonathan Kay Kamakawiwo'ole. "All Things Depending: Renewing Interdependence in Oceania: Association for Social Anthropology in Oceania 2011 Distinguished Lecture." *Oceania* 81, no. 3 (2011): 297+.

Small, C. A. "Pacific: Fiji, Tonga, Samoa." In *The New Americans: A Guide to Immigration since 1965*, edited by M.C. Waters, et al., 534–41. Cambridge, MA: Harvard University Press, 2007.

Takeuchi, D., and S. Hune. *Growing Presence, Emerging Voices: Pacific Islanders and Academic Achievement in Washington. A Report Submitted to the Washington State Commission on Asian Pacific American Affairs*. Seattle: University of Washington, 2008.

Trask, H. *From a Native Daughter: Colonialism and Sovereignty in Hawaii*. Honolulu: University of Hawaii Press, 1999.

PAIUTES

Richard C. Hanes and Laurie Collier Hillstrom

OVERVIEW

The Paiutes (PY-yoots) are a confederation of closely related groups of indigenous people who traditionally inhabited large portions of the Great Basin region in what is now the western United States. The vast desert area used by the Paiutes extended from central Oregon eastward to southwestern Idaho, south from there through the Las Vegas Valley and along the Colorado River on both the Arizona and Southern California sides, and southeastward into southern Utah. The Paiutes call themselves Numa (sometimes written Numu) or Nuwuvi, meaning "people," and were called many different names by whites, including the Snake and the Bannock. Some scholars group the Paiutes with other indigenous people of the Great Basin, including the Shoshone, Utes, and Washoe, who share many similar cultural traits as well as overlapping traditional territories. Although the exact origin of the word *Paiute* is unknown, today it is interpreted by many anthropologists to mean "true Ute" or "water Ute."

Estimates of the Paiute population prior to contact with Europeans differ, though it is widely accepted that despite relatively small numbers they were always a culturally influential and diverse group. The numerous Paiute bands are often recognized in three main tribes: the Northern Paiutes of northwestern Nevada, northeastern California, southeastern Oregon, and southwestern Idaho; the Owens Valley Paiutes, who traditionally inhabited the Owens River watershed of southeastern California; and the Southern Paiutes of southeastern California, southern Nevada, northwestern Arizona, and western Utah. These three main Paiute groups spoke mutually unintelligible languages of the Numic branch of the Uto-Aztecan language family. Prior to substantial contact with nonnative peoples, the Paiutes led a highly mobile nomadic lifestyle, subsisting by hunting small game and gathering roots, seeds, and berries. Some Southern and Owens Valley Paiute bands used irrigation techniques to grow corn, while some Northern Paiute bands were fishermen.

Today, the Paiute people have numerous federally allocated Indian reservations throughout the West, including the ten separate land parcels of the Paiute Indian Tribe of Utah (PITU) Reservation; the Pyramid Lake Indian Reservation in Nevada; the Kaibab Indian Reservation in Arizona; the Burns Paiute Reservation in Oregon; the Duck Valley Indian Reservation in Idaho; and California's Chemehuevi and Colorado River Indian Reservations. Many Paiutes were relocated to these and other reservations amid escalating hostilities between indigenous people of the West and white settlers during the mid- to late 1800s. At the start of the twenty-first century, nearly half of all Paiutes lived outside of reservations, often in small, federally recognized "colonies" that blend into surrounding urban areas. During modern times the Paiute people have suffered from shifting governmental policies and have struggled to resurrect their economies in the wake of the discrimination and upheaval of the previous 150 years.

Because Paiutes are a group of affiliated tribes, overall population numbers are difficult to determine. According to an estimate by the Four Directions Institute of Native American Studies, the Northern Paiute numbered around 13,250 in 2000. Around the same time, numbers sited by the Bureau of Land Management put the Southern Paiute population at 1,880, while a website for the Owens Valley Paiute recorded that that tribe had about 2,000 members. Paiute tribal members have largely been assimilated into the mainstream culture of the United States, though efforts are underway by individual groups to secure and support the traditional culture of the many affiliated tribes. According to the U.S. Census Bureau's American Community Survey estimates for 2006–2010, the states with significant numbers of Paiutes included Arizona, California, Colorado, Idaho, Nevada, New Mexico, Oregon, Texas, Utah, and Washington.

HISTORY OF THE PEOPLE

Early History Human population numbers in the Great Basin have always been comparatively small because of the scarce and widely distributed food and water sources of the desert steppe environment. Although there remains some debate regarding the initial settlement of the region, most scholars believe that it has been inhabited for around 14,000 years. Archeological discoveries in the area include some of the oldest fossils, skeletons, and textiles found in North America. The earliest arrivals were likely big game hunters and gatherers who either brought knowledge of agriculture with them from other areas or developed the techniques while living in the region. The exact connections between these ancient settlers and modern groups such as the Paiutes, Shoshone, Utes, and Washoe are unknown, and there remains some controversy over the date and circumstances under which the modern tribes arrived. Many indigenous histories contend that these peoples were always present in the Great Basin, but other theories say they immigrated from areas further to the southwest as recently as 2,000 years ago.

As part of their largely nomadic lifestyle, Great Basin Indians ranged from the forested highlands of the Rocky Mountains westward to the Sierra Nevada Range and throughout the desert lowlands in between. The lifestyles of the various bands across this expansive region were largely determined by the particular foods available in the area where they predominantly lived. The extended family was the main traditional unit of social organization. Bands were composed of loose affiliations of families led by a headman selected for his abilities.

The 400,000 square miles of the Great Basin constituted the last major "frontier" to be "explored" by Euro-American settlers. The earliest were Spanish explorers seeking waterways that might provide easy transit between their holdings on the southern rim of the Great Basin and those in California. By the 1820s European hunters and fur trappers began to arrive and found that many of the indigenous cultures had already been victimized by the Spanish slave trade. This situation led to some of the earliest accounts of the area by white writers (such as those by Mark Twain) belittling Great Basin Indians and stereotyping them as little more than "Digger Indians."

Although the Paiutes' early interaction with hunters and trappers was friendly, hostilities between the Paiute and non-Indian intruders grew over time. Epidemics of smallpox, cholera, and other diseases swept through Paiute communities in the 1830s and 1840s. The limited exposure to Euro-American explorers, fur trappers, and settlers changed abruptly when large-scale migration over the Oregon Trail began in the mid-1840s. Conflicts increased as more and more Paiute territory was claimed by whites. Mormons arriving from northern Utah began settling the most valuable lands of the Southern Paiutes, including the Las Vegas Valley. Also by the 1840s the Paiutes had acquired horses and guns and began raiding white camps and settlements. The majority of conflicts with whites took place after 1848, when the discovery of gold in California brought a flood of settlers through the center of the tribe's territory.

In 1859 a major silver strike occurred at Virginia City in western Nevada. The rapid influx of miners and ranchers into the region led to hostilities with Northern Paiutes, which escalated into the Pyramid Lake War, which ended in a cease-fire agreement in 1860. In an attempt to maintain distance and peace between the Paiutes and the newcomers, the U.S. government established relatively large reservations for the Northern Paiutes at Pyramid Lake and Walker River. Nevertheless, in 1860 traders at a Pony Express station on the California Trail kidnapped and raped two Paiute girls. Tribal members responded by attacking the Pony Express station, killing five whites in the process of rescuing the girls. The Paiutes then killed forty-three volunteers sent to avenge the killings. After several minor battles involving an 800-man volunteer army from California led by Colonel Jack Hays, peace with the Paiutes was restored. Most Paiutes returned to the Pyramid Lake Reservation, while others withdrew further north to southeastern Oregon. The military established Fort Churchill in 1860 in western Nevada to maintain peace.

During the U.S. Civil War years, when government troops were busy fighting in the East, the Paiutes continued numerous raids on ranches, farms, mining camps, and wagon trains. Following the Civil War U.S. Army troops returned in force to the West. In Oregon the United States established military posts in 1864 at Camp Alvord and in 1867 at Fort Harney. By 1866 the military had taken the offensive to end Paiute resistance to white incursions. The escalating conflict became known as the Snake Indian War, since Northern Paiutes were often called Snake Indians by settlers. Two war leaders, Paulina and Old Weawa, led the Paiutes in forty skirmishes with the federal forces over a two-year period before finally being forced to surrender in 1868. A treaty promising a reservation in Oregon was signed at Fort Harney with three Paiute bands, but it was never ratified by Congress. The Northern Paiutes were forced to relocate to other reservations located elsewhere in the region.

To the south the United States and Southern Paiutes had signed the 1865 Treaty of Spanish Forks. Also never ratified by Congress, the treaty was designed to place six Southern Paiute bands on the Uintah Reservation in northern Utah. The first reservation for Southern Paiutes, the Moapa Reservation, was finally created in 1872. That year in the north, the almost-2 million-acre Malheur Reservation was established in central Oregon by presidential executive order for the "free-roaming" Northern Paiutes of southeastern Oregon. This strategy proved unsuccessful, however, as some Paiutes refused to go, and many that did left the reservation shortly after arriving, citing poor living conditions there. The Malheur Reservation was returned to public ownership in its entirety following renewed, though brief, conflicts that made up the Bannock War in 1878. The Northern Paiute population scattered to other reservations or small communities; many Paiute bands refused to move to the reservations already occupied by other bands and instead established settlements on the outskirts of towns, where they worked as wage laborers. Two Paiute communities grew on Oregon military posts abandoned in the 1890s: Fort Bidwell and Fort McDermitt. Between 1910 and 1930 the government extended formal federal recognition to many of the nonreservation Paiute bands and set aside modest acreage for them, usually 10 to 40 acres.

Although several large reservations (Moapa River in Nevada, Pyramid Lake, Walker River, Duck Valley, and Malheur) had been established for the Paiutes in Oregon, Idaho, and Nevada between 1859 and 1891, by the turn of the twentieth century, tribal lands had been reduced to less than 5 percent of their original territory. The General Allotment Act of 1887 carved up tribal lands on many reservations throughout the nation, including the larger Paiute reservations, into small allotments allocated to individual tribal members and then sold the "excess" to non-Indians. The Walker River Reservation alone lost almost 290,000 acres of its best land in 1906.

During the winter of 1862 to 1863, the Owens Valley Paiutes and their Shoshone allies had been defeated in a series of skirmishes with the California Volunteers militia and local settlers. These conflicts, which became known as the Owens Valley Indian War, led to a large number of Owens Valley Paiutes being removed to nearby Fort Teton. Around the turn of the century, as the city of Los Angeles increasingly acquired former tribal lands so that they could control water rights to the Owens River, many of the Owens Valley Paiutes were restricted to areas far too small to support their former way of life.

Modern Era The Paiutes had suffered population loss from these violent conflicts and from disease. They were impoverished through the loss of their traditional economies and existed at a remove from the emerging market economies of non-Indian communities. During the first three decades of the twentieth century, they were largely ignored by the U.S. government. In 1934 U.S. policy toward Native Americans changed dramatically when Congress passed the Indian Reorganization Act, which allowed tribes to hold lands communally again, to manage their own land, and to self-govern; native groups were able to achieve federal recognition and gained access to grants and federal services. Relations with the U.S. government declined again after World War II, however, and in 1954 federal recognition was terminated for four of the Southern Paiute bands. This change in status led to discontinued health and education services vital to their well-being, in addition to the collective loss of more than 43,000 acres from their land base. In yet another swing in U.S. policy, federal recognition status and services were restored in 1980. Economic and cultural recovery for the Paiutes was difficult under such vacillating federal Indian policies.

Because of their location in the arid West, many Paiute bands were involved in water rights disputes throughout the twentieth century. For example, the Owens Valley Paiutes struggled to obtain enough

A Paiute woman grinds seeds in doorway of a thatched hut, 1872. NATIONAL ARCHIVES AND RECORDS ADMINISTRATION

water to operate a fishery from the Owens River, a primary water source for the downriver city of Los Angeles. The Paiutes of the Pyramid Lake region suffered when the United States built Derby Dam on the Truckee River, the primary water source for Pyramid Lake, as part of the Newlands Project in 1905. The dam diverted almost half the river flow to a separate valley, the Carson Basin. As a result the Pyramid Lake water level had dropped 78 feet by 1967, depriving the cui-ui trout of access to upstream spawning beds and significantly impacting tribal fisheries and waterfowl habitat on the Pyramid Lake Reservation. The cui-ui, which are central to Pyramid Lake Paiute identity, were listed under the Endangered Species Act in 1967. This helped the Paiutes regain control over their lake and fisheries. Similar water diversion plans by upstream non-Indian users severely degraded Walker River Reservation resources as well. Litigation over water rights persisted throughout much of the twentieth century, with frequently unsuccessful results for the Paiutes.

SETTLEMENT IN THE UNITED STATES

Prior to contact with non-Indians, the Paiutes lived a largely nomadic lifestyle supplemented by agricultural techniques they may have adopted through early interactions with the Pueblo peoples of the Southwest. They gathered food from their various natural sources through the year in an annual cycle necessitating a good deal of mobility. Groups separated into families then rejoined again seasonally. Consequently, Paiute society consisted of economically self-sufficient and politically independent families who occupied different "home" tracts at different times of the year. The families united semiannually with other families, forming a camp group of two or three families. The core family unit would continually expand or contract, and the camp group also changed size and composition seasonally and through the years, often foraging together and pooling resources.

Before the arrival of European settlers, the Paiutes' nomadic economy consisted of hunting, fishing, and gathering. Men hunted deer, mountain sheep, and antelope. Teams captured smaller mammals, particularly jackrabbits, using large nets. The bands also hunted waterfowl, such as American coots, at the various large lakes near their camps. Fish were netted or speared. Women gathered plants extensively, including a wide variety of roots (tubers), berries, and seeds. Camas bulbs were particularly important in the northern range, as were pine nuts in the south. To the furthest extent south, in the Las Vegas region, agave was a key food source. The southern Paiutes used irrigation to grow corn, squash, melons, sunflowers, gourds, and beans.

The Northern Paiutes often built settlements near lakes or wetlands that provided adequate fishing and water supply. Bands were typically named after a characteristic food source in their region, including the *Tibadika'a* (meaning "pine nut eaters") and the *Kucutikadi* (meaning "bison eaters"). Although they occupied specific territories, they gathered for communal big game hunts. Relations with their Shoshone neighbors were mostly peaceful. Similarly, bands of Southern Paiutes controlled their own separate territories but often traded with other communities and tribes in order to acquire such necessities as food, clothing, and tools. Southern Paiutes migrated with the seasons, subsisting as hunters, gatherers, and farmers.

A Paiute draws his bow and arrow, with two others in festive costume, 1872. NATIONAL ARCHIVES AND RECORDS ADMINISTRATION

Southern Paiutes were often the targets of slave raids by Navajo and Ute tribes, and their security became even more tenuous after they made contact with European explorers in the early 1800s. Northern Paiutes likely first encountered nonnatives sometime during the 1820s, and as the tide of white settlers into the region continued to rise throughout the nineteenth century, both Northern and Southern Paiutes experienced significant hardships. Relations between the Paiutes and Europeans varied from band to band, running the gamut between friendly and cooperative to openly hostile. Several significant armed conflicts in the late 1800s (the Pyramid Lake War of 1860 and the Bannock War of 1878, among others) hastened U.S. government efforts to confine the Paiutes to reservation lands. Many resisted, maintaining their traditional lifestyles as long as possible, some of them joining other nearby tribes when the government began relocating Paiutes to reservations in Oregon, Nevada, California, and Utah. By the late 1800s many Paiutes were living on small de facto reservations in communities near cities or farms, often comingling with Shoshone populations. After the turn of the century, the U.S. government began granting land to these colonies, though its policy regarding the Paiutes continued to shift throughout the next one hundred years.

Today, the Paiute population remains broadly scattered, living in numerous small communities and on a few large reservations. Significant Northern Paiute communities exist in Nevada (Pyramid Lake, Walker River, Fort McDermitt, Fallon, the Reno-Sparks area, Yerington, Lovelock, Summit Lake, and Winnemucca); Oregon (Burns and Warm Springs); and, California (Bridgeport, Cedarville, and Fort Bidwell). Notable Southern Paiute populations exist in and around Las Vegas, Nevada; Moapa, Nevada; Cedar City, Utah; Tuba City, Arizona; and the Kaibab Indian Reservation in Arizona. According to the 2010 American Community Survey estimates, California, Utah, Nevada, and Oregon are the states with the largest numbers of Paiutes. Other states with significant numbers include Colorado, Idaho, Arizona, New Mexico, Texas, and Washington.

LANGUAGE

The three main Paiute tribes speak distinct languages of the Numic group, the northernmost branch of the Uto-Aztecan language family. The languages spoken by Northern Paiutes and Owens Valley Paiutes are related to the language of the Mono (or Monache) peoples of California. Southern Paiute is similar to the language spoken by the Utes. Many Paiute groups have actively taken steps to preserve their language. In the 1980s the Yerington Paiutes of Nevada developed a dictionary and produced a series of storybooks and workbooks.

In 2008 the University of California, Berkeley Linguistics Department began the Northern Paiute Language Project, which seeks to "create comprehensive documentation of this language, involving a

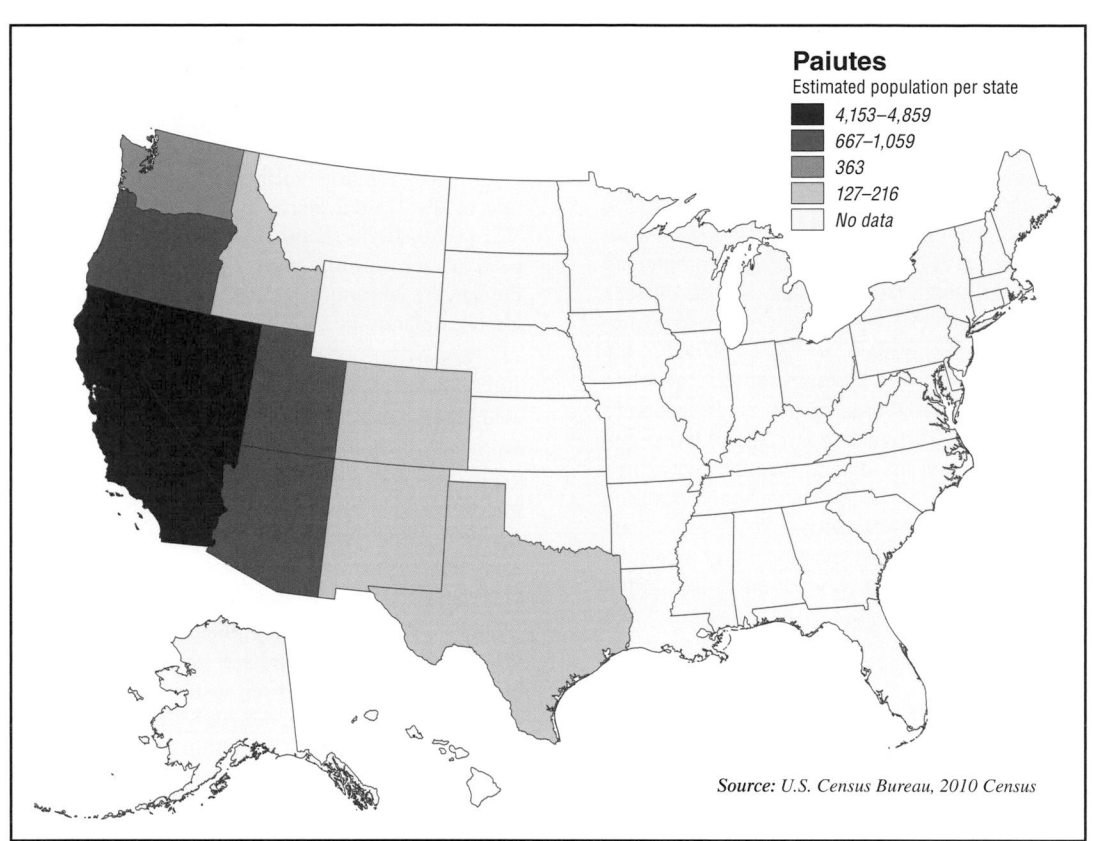

Paiutes
Estimated population per state

- 4,153–4,859
- 667–1,059
- 363
- 127–216
- No data

Source: U.S. Census Bureau, 2010 Census

dictionary and texts, and to develop [teaching] materials from this documentation" (http://linguistics.berkeley. edu/~paiute). The project has published numerous scholarly articles concerning the languages spoken by bands of Northern Paiutes and have presented their research at more than a dozen academic conferences. Efforts to save the languages of Southern Paiutes are also underway as part of a larger effort to preserve Ute language groups. Founded by tribal member Venita Taveapont in 2000, the Ute Language Revitalization Project works to ensure that the Ute language will not disappear.

Greetings and Popular Expressions Examples of common Numa words and expressions include: *ku'-na O-ho'-i-gi*—"around the fire"; *mu-a Tva'-i-to-a*—"moonlight"; *ta-shin'-ti-ai*—"cold feet"; *au*—"yes"; *To-a-Mi-yok*—"Give me the pipe"; *Pa-ha-vwuk-i-num Tik-er-ru*—"I am hungry"; *Ta'-kavw-yu'-mu-kim*—"The snow falls"; *ku-na Ma-ko-to*—"to light a fire"; *Ni-Tik-er'-ro-wa*—"I will eat"; *ya'-ni-kin*— "to laugh"; *to-ya'-pi*—"mountain"; *pi'-av*—"female"; *wan'-sits*—"antelope"; *ta'-mun*—"spring"; *to-namp*— "chokecherries"; *pan-so-wa'-bits*—"duck"; and *Pun-ko-U-nish Mi-er'-ro*—"The horse goes fast."

RELIGION

The Paiutes traditionally believed in many supernatural beings that manifested themselves in elements of the natural world, such as water, thunder, and animals.

A fundamental aspect of Northern Paiute religion is acquisition of "power," or *buha*. *Buha* could be acquired in dreams or at caves or grave sites. It could heal, help control weather, enhance sexual prowess, limit vulnerability in warfare, and invite gambling success. One powerful spirit was Thuwipu Unipugant, or "the One Who Made the Earth," who was represented by the sun. The Paiutes prayed to the spirits in order to influence them in providing human success and also to show their respect.

According to Bertha Dutton in *American Indians of the Southwest* (1983), early efforts to convert the Paiutes to Christianity were relatively successful, particularly in the case of those Paiutes who lived among the Mormons in Utah. As Fowler noted in *Native America in the Twentieth Century*, most contemporary Paiutes attend religious services in some Christian denomination, though some also participate in Indian religious movements such as the Native American Church, the Sweat Lodge movement, and the Sun Dance.

CULTURE AND ASSIMILATION

The diverse and far-flung Paiutes have long shared cultural similarities with other nearby indigenous groups, though sometimes relations with these other tribes were adversarial. Paiutes were closely related to the Shoshone peoples of the Northwest, and both

THE GHOST DANCE

The Paiutes made a direct contribution to one of the major nineteenth-century Native American religious movements. In 1889, when most Paiutes had been pushed off of their ancestral lands and forced to live in hiding or on reservations, a spiritual leader of the Northern Paiute named Wovoka founded the Ghost Dance religion, which prophesied a peaceful end to white domination. During a solar eclipse Wovoka experienced a powerful vision in which the earth was reborn in a natural state, with unfenced plains full of buffalo, and was returned to the Indians and their ancestors, who lived in harmony, free of the white man's control. Wovoka preached that in order to achieve this vision of the future, the Indians needed to eschew the artifacts of white culture, particularly the use of alcohol. In addition, Wovoka advocated peace with whites, universal love, not harming anyone, and not lying or stealing. He especially called upon the Native peoples to pray, meditate, chant, and dance. Within a few years the Ghost Dance religion had spread to angry and frustrated tribes all over the West. Some influential leaders, such as the Sioux chief and holy man Sitting Bull, interpreted the Ghost Dance as a call for renewed violence against whites. Although the Paiutes largely refrained from resorting to violence, they embraced the Ghost Dance for many years as a form of resistance to white culture. On some reservations the Bureau of Indian Affairs requested military protection for white settlers against practitioners of the Ghost Dance, and in some instances the religion was outlawed.

the Northern Paiutes and the Owens Valley Paiutes spoke languages similar to that of the Mono people, who lived in California west of the Sierra Nevada. That *Paiute* is interpreted to mean "true Ute" or "water Ute" reflects the group's relationship to the Ute Indians of Utah. The Chemehuevi (who lived along the lower Colorado River on the Arizona and California border, south of the Las Vegas Valley) are generally considered Southern Paiutes, but they actually shared more traits with Southern California tribes than with other Paiutes, such as floodplain farming and the earthen house construction of the Mohave culture.

Although relations were generally good between the Paiutes and the Utes, the Utes were once active in raids on their neighbors, trading abducted Southern Paiutes to other tribes and to Spanish colonists in the Southwest as slaves. Despite being fearful of the Navajo to the east, who also dealt in the slave trade, the San Juan Paiutes actually assimilated some Navajo customs regarding dress, housing, and linguistic traits.

During the early stages of their interactions with Euro-Americans, many Paiute leaders were hospitable toward the new settlers and explorers. According to her firsthand account *Life Among the Piutes: Their Wrongs and Claims*, published in 1883, Paiute writer and lecturer Sarah Winnemucca described Paiute elders enthusiastically welcoming the first whites to the region. Although historians question parts of her work, Winnemucca contends that her grandfather guided the American military officer and explorer John C. Fremont during his two-year survey and map-making expedition across the Great Basin region from 1843 to 1845. Some Northern Paiutes fought on the side of the United States in the Mexican-American War (1846–1848). Southern Paiutes forged a mostly peaceful relationship with Mormon settlers, even though the Mormons had laid claim to strategically important lands around Paiute water sources.

When the influx of whites increased, however, and violent conflicts arose and reservations were established, many Paiutes resisted relocation and assimilation, choosing to stay in their own, independently founded settlements and remain true to their traditional ways. Once it became clear they would be unable to avoid contact with whites, some sought paid work among them.

Today, most members of the three primary groups of Paiutes consider themselves part of the same tribe, despite cultural and linguistic differences. Nearly all Paiutes have been assimilated into mainstream American culture, though by the late twentieth century many tribes had begun an effort to preserve and celebrate Paiute culture, including traditional dress, languages, and customs.

Traditions and Customs Traditional Paiute customs and beliefs relied largely on oral histories passed down from generation to generation. Techniques for hunting, fishing, and farming were also transmitted. While much of the land occupied by Paiutes was arid and unforgiving, the oral tradition allowed each generation to build on the knowledge of the previous generation, and over centuries the Paiute lifestyle became efficient and highly advanced. Families and individuals often moved freely among several peaceful tribes, and a rich storytelling tradition allowed for easy exchange of new information as well as providing an important link to the past.

Because of their nomadic existence, Paiutes traditionally lived in small, temporary huts. Building materials often consisted of wood or other available plant material and differed from tribe to tribe, usually depending on environmental factors and the availability of resources. The homes were frequently constructed near streams, where the Paiutes could fish or draw water for sustenance and irrigation.

The Paiutes observed two unique rituals: one for young women at the time of their first menstrual period and the other for young couples expecting their first child. In the menarche rites the young woman was isolated for four days. During this time she observed taboos against touching her face or hair with her hands, eating animal-based foods, and drinking cold liquids. She ran east at sunrise and west at sunset and sat with older women of the tribe to learn about her responsibilities as a woman. After the four days of isolation had passed, a series of rituals brought the menarche ceremony to a close: the young woman was bathed in cold water, her face was painted, the ends of her hair were singed or cut, and she ate animal foods and bitter herbs and spat into a fire. The custom for couples expecting their first child also included isolation and traditionally lasted thirty days. The pregnant woman observed the same taboos and received advice from older women, while the expectant father ran east at sunrise and west at sunset. The marriage itself had few important traditional ceremonies associated with it.

Cuisine The Paiutes were a nomadic people, moving about the region to take advantage of various food sources. The means of subsistence for specific Paiute bands depended to a large extent on their particular location. In general the Paiutes ate vegetables such as roots and rice grass, as well as berries and nuts. Many used stones to grind seeds and nuts into flour for making bread. The Paiutes also hunted ducks, rabbits, and mountain sheep using bows and arrows or long nets. Some bands in mountainous regions fished, while others in arid desert regions dug for lizards, grubs, and insects, which were valuable protein sources. The Southern Paiutes may have adopted corn agriculture from the Pueblo peoples, and the Owens Valley Paiutes developed irrigation techniques, enabling them to grow various crops.

Today, the diets of most Paiutes reflect the modern mainstream culture of their regions, though many traditional foods are still key elements in tribal ceremonies and other community events. Pinyon pine nuts, a traditional dietary staple of some Paiute tribes, were harvested in fall and provided important sustenance throughout difficult winters. Traditional harvesting methods and recipes involving pine nuts are still passed from generation to generation in some Paiute families.

Dances and Songs While singing was common among the Paiutes, their use of musical instruments was notably limited. They did not play drums until after contact with whites. The primary traditional instruments were shamans' rattles and the sticks beaten during hand games. For some curing practices, healers played a small flute made of elderberry stems.

The oldest and most common musical event in Paiute tradition was the Round (or Circle) Dance. Participants formed a circle and danced in a clockwise direction to music made by a singer situated in the center. Tribal variations included the Northern Paiute Hump Dance. The dance was commonly held three times a year: during the spring fishing season, just before the fall pine nut harvest, and during the November rabbit drives. Such dances served to periodically affirm social unity and focus participants on the particular subsistence tasks at hand. The Ghost Dance incorporated the earlier Round Dance elements, including the lack of percussion accompaniment.

Today, traditional Paiute music and dancing is often performed at important cultural gatherings, festivals, and powwows. Like indigenous Paiute languages, the tribes' music has been a primary area of study, and many examples of Paiute music and dance can be found online at popular video- and music-sharing websites.

Revival of the Ghost Dance being performed by Paiute women. MIKE STOTTS / ZUMA PRESS / CORBIS

Paiute men don headdresses and buckskins for a festival. W. ROBERT MOORE / NATIONAL GEOGRAPHIC SOCIETY / CORBIS

Traditional Dress Paiute men traditionally wore a skin breechcloth and women wore a double apron of animal skin or vegetable fiber such as sagebrush bark or rushes. The cloth was suspended from a belt made from cliff rose bark or antelope skin. Men and women also typically wore animal skin moccasins, sometimes ankle high, or woven yucca or sagebrush bark sandals. In the winter they used skin capes or robes made of rabbit fur strips. Southern Paiute men and women wore twined-bark leggings, and Northern Paiute men wore simple buckskin shirts. Members of some Paiute bands wore hats decorated with bird feathers (often quail). Except in Oregon, women wore basketry hats. Throughout Paiute country men wore tanned-hide hats. By the mid-nineteenth century, men's shirts and leggings and women's full-length dresses were made from fringed hide, a custom most likely adopted from the Utes. Today, traditional dress is still often worn during Paiute cultural events, to dances, and during musical performances.

Arts and Crafts Paiute women have long been noted for their skilled basketry. Paiute baskets were typically made from light and resilient material and were sometimes covered with clay or pitch and used to carry water and other precious resources in the arid Great Basin region. Basketry and weaving were also utilized to make many other necessary items, including clothing, cradles, mats, and fish traps. Archeologists have discovered Northern Paiute baskets in areas of Southern Oregon believed to date from 9,000 years ago.

Paiute weavers and basket makers continue to practice the craft, both for economic reasons and to maintain a link to traditional culture. Numerous Paiute craftspeople have become renowned as basket makers; examples of their basketry are part of displays and collections curated by the Oregon Historical Society. A page on the website *Online Nevada Encyclopedia* (www.onlinenevada.org/contemporary_great_basin_basketmakers) lists such influential contemporary Paiute weavers and basket makers as Norman Delorme, Rebecca and Sandra Eagle, Larena Burns, and Everett Pikyavit.

Holidays In addition to the popular mainstream American holidays, Paiute tribes recognize special days important to their particular communities. For example, the Burns Paiute Tribe celebrates Reservation Day on October 13 in honor of the date the tribe officially received reservation lands in 1972.

From spring through late fall, powwows are held around the region inhabited by the Paiutes. These intertribal festivals include the Shoshoni-Paiute Annual Powwow in July and the Veteran's Day Powwow in November at Owyhee, Nevada; the Snow Mountain Powwow in May in Las Vegas; the Mother's Day Powwow in May at Burns, Oregon; and powwows at Bishop and Big Pine in California. Such festivals include arts and crafts shows, hand-game tournaments, dancing, and traditional foods. The Paiutes commonly attend similar events hosted by tribes in surrounding regions as well, largely motivated by kinship ties.

Health Care Issues and Practices Until the 1930s most Paiutes sought cures for illnesses from male or female tribal healers known as *puagants*, believed to possess supernatural powers. Puagants formed a magical relationship with one or more animal spirits and used the fur or feathers of the animal to call upon the spirits to assist in their work. Today, modern health care facilities are available to most Paiutes, often through the U.S. Department of Health and Human Services' Indian Health Services (IHS). Examples of such facilities include the McDermitt Tribal Health Center in Humboldt, Nevada; the Fallon and Schurz Indian Health Centers in western Nevada; the Pyramid Lake Health Department in northwestern Nevada; and the Owyhee Indian Health Service Hospital in southeastern Oregon.

Projects addressing health care were a top priority among Paiute bands during the late twentieth century, as were economic development programs; poverty compounded the high rates of certain diseases, dysfunctional family relations, and substance abuse in the communities. Health screening programs were instituted where feasible. Care programs for the elderly were also implemented, including regular health monitoring, in-home care, hot lunches, craft workshops, firewood supplies, and special housing.

FAMILY AND COMMUNITY LIFE

Maintaining extended families as the basic social unit has been the most enduring Paiute tradition through all the dramatic changes of the past two centuries.

Gender Roles As in most Native societies in North America, women played a crucial role in traditional Paiute culture, raising children, managing home life, and gathering traditional plant foods. Today, these foods continue to provide a spiritual focal point in traditional ceremonies and feasts, and women continue to be primarily responsible for collecting them.

Education The educational services available to Paiutes on their various reservations and colonies during the 1800s and early 1900s were inconsistent and often substandard. In some states, such as Nevada,

children of indigenous families were not allowed to attend the same schools as whites, which meant that native children were often separated from their parents and sent to boarding schools in other towns or other states, occasionally as far away as California.

Schools were established at the Pyramid Lake and Walker River reservations in the late 1870s and early 1880s. In 1897 Indian schools were opened in California at the Bishop and Big Pine Paiute communities and shortly afterwards at Independence. Not until after the turn of the century did other Paiute communities establish schools, including those for the Lovelock Paiutes in 1907 and the Burns Paiutes in 1931, among the Northern Paiute tribes; Southern Paiutes built schools at the Las Vegas, Shivwits, Moapa, and Kaibab reservations between 1900 and 1940. The success of these schools varied: some lasted only a year while others carried on for decades. The Stewart Institute, a boarding school for Nevada Indians, was established in western Nevada in 1890, and Paiute children attended until the 1970s. Today, most Paiute children are educated in local public schools (some on reservations), though some tribes continue to operate their own educational services with outreach programs designed to aid Paiutes in their efforts to acquire skills.

Although Paiute populations have traditionally been small compared to other Native North American groups, several Paiutes have made key contributions to education and the arts.

Funerals Funerals historically received considerable emphasis among Paiutes. A traditional funeral observance known as the cry ceremony was introduced to the Paiutes by nearby Mojave tribes in the 1870s. Within the next twenty years, it became pervasive within the cultures of the Owens Valley Paiutes and Southern Paiutes. The cry took place over one or two nights after a person's death and before the funeral and then was repeated a year or two later as a memorial. During the cry ceremony two groups of singers perform song cycles known as Salt Songs and Bird Songs. Today, though nearly all Paiutes are buried according to the laws and traditions of the United States, cry ceremonies remain a significant and fairly common part of the grieving process. Between songs people close to the deceased offer emotional speeches and sometimes give away the deceased person's valuables to guests.

EMPLOYMENT AND ECONOMIC CONDITIONS

Like other Native American groups who could no longer pursue their traditional economies after being supplanted from their lands by whites, the Paiutes experienced difficulties in securing sources of food and income for tribal members, as well as revenue for the tribes to provide services formerly integrated into tribal life. After relocation to reservations the Paiutes increasingly made a living by working for wages in nearby towns or ranches. In the Owens Valley after the 1870s, Paiutes worked as wage laborers in the local farming and ranching economy and later became involved in tourism and mining operations. Elsewhere, some Paiutes raised cattle. Pyramid Lake and Walker River Paiutes were able to keep fishing and to sell their catch in local town markets until the 1920s, when river diversions reduced the lake levels and disrupted fish runs upstream from the lakes.

The federal Indian allotment policies from the 1890s through 1910 hit some Paiutes particularly hard, carving up reservations and giving the more economically productive lands within reservation boundaries to non-Indians. For example, the Fallon Paiutes on the original Nevada Stillwater Reservation lost 90 percent of their land base, and the Pyramid Lake Paiutes lost a 20,000-acre timber reserve. Much of the remaining Paiute lands suffered from cattle trespassing and from poaching of big game and fish resources.

In 1965 the Southern Paiutes sued the U.S. government for almost 30 million acres of tribal lands wrongfully taken and received approximately $7.2 million in compensation. Many bands, such as the Moapa and Kaibab, used the money as capital to improve living conditions and develop educational and employment opportunities. Also during the 1970s five bands of Utah Paiutes formed a legal corporation, the Paiute Indian Tribe of Utah, and received a government grant to build an industrial complex.

Passage of the Indian Self-Determination and Education Act in 1974 stimulated economic development from the late 1970s into the 1990s. The act promoted Indian economic self-sufficiency through loan and grant programs. Monies from land claim settlements and federal loans led to various forms of development. The Pyramid Lake, Walker River, Reno-Sparks, Las Vegas, and Fallon communities opened smoke-shops and minimarts. At smoke-shops on tribal lands, tribes could

Paiute salt miners at work in Nevada. HISTORICAL / CORBIS

sell cigarettes to the public without federal taxes added, making them lucrative businesses, especially when they were located near well-used travel routes. The Pyramid Lake Paiutes also built two commercial fish hatcheries, received revenue from issuing recreational fishing permits for the lake, and, like the Walker River, Fort McDermitt, and Utah Paiute groups, grazed livestock or issued grazing leases. Attempts at developments such as business parks, as at Big Pine, had limited success because of the isolation of tribal lands. Traditional crafts continued, and a few artisans became commercially profitable.

Many of the Paiute populations, however, among them Fort Bidwell, Summit Lake, Burns, and Lovelock, have enjoyed few successes in establishing employment opportunities and revenue sources. Still, by the latter twentieth century, most Paiute communities had successfully installed electrical and telephone services and plumbing, had paved streets, and had built better housing. Economic hardship led two Paiute bands to consider controversial projects in the 1990s. The Northern Paiute of the Fort McDermitt Reservation in Nevada discussed the possibility of building a storage facility for high-level nuclear waste on their lands, while the Southern Paiute of the Kaibab Reservation in Arizona debated whether to construct a hazardous waste incinerator. The financial rewards these projects offered the bands made them appealing, but both projects were ultimately defeated because of environmental concerns.

Today, many Paiute bands depend largely on tourism. The Owens Valley Lake and Mono Lake areas are popular camping destinations. Some tribes have turned to establishing large gambling houses in order to produce revenue. In California the Bishop Paiute Tribe operates the Paiute Palace Casino, which, in addition to offering gaming activities, advertises its close proximity to popular rock climbing and skiing destinations. The Pyramid Lake Paiutes are studying the feasibility of constructing a geothermal power plant. In Utah Paiute tribes are considering a number of economic growth initiatives, including continued agricultural efforts and more tourist amenities.

POLITICS AND GOVERNMENT

Traditional Paiute leadership roles recognized leaders as spokespersons rather than as autonomous decision makers or authority figures. Decisions were frequently made in a consensus-seeking manner among all adult band members. When the tribe was displaced onto remote reservations and lost its traditional structure, a whole host of issues arose regarding health care, schools, law enforcement, sanitation, housing, and utilities. In order to qualify for federal assistance and establish relations with the U.S. government, most Paiute bands formally organized under the 1934 Indian Reorganization Act. The act encouraged the tribes to form governments based on Western social models rather than on traditional tribal arrangements. The model included tribal councils composed of elected individuals, headed by a chairperson, and written constitutions with by-laws.

Although these local governments became the focal point of intergovernmental relations with the United States, with state governments, and with other non-Indian organizations, traditional leaders frequently influenced policy directions internally. In some cases the Indian Reorganization Act stimulated factionalism within tribal politics by aligning traditional elements of the membership against "progressive" ones. The contemporary Paiute councils commonly serve as business corporations, overseeing use of tribal funds and promoting economic self-sufficiency. Elections are held every two or three years. The guidance of committees of traditional leaders, including elders, is usually respected by the elected tribal council.

Four of the Southern Paiute governments in Utah (the Shivwits, Indian Peaks, Koosharem, and Kanosh) were targeted by the federal termination policies of the 1950s and lost their federal recognition and services. The Utah bands later reorganized under the Paiute Restoration Act of 1980, and their official status was reinstated. The San Juan Paiutes were not able to organize in such a manner and did not regain federal recognition until 1990.

Most Paiute tribes continue to operate local, democratic systems of government, though the specific format varies from tribe to tribe. For example, the Paiute Indian Tribe of Utah consists of five separate constituent bands, each of which elects a chairperson to serve on an umbrella tribal council. Headed by an elected tribal chairperson, the council is responsible for all executive and legislative decisions regarding the tribe. Meanwhile, the Bishop Paiute Tribe in California operates under a five-person tribal council that includes a chair, vice chair, and treasurer, while Nevada's Pyramid Lake Paiutes are governed by a ten-member council, which includes members chosen in biannual elections serving staggered terms.

NOTABLE INDIVIDUALS

Art Lucy Parker Telles (1870–1956), a woman of Yosemite Miwok and Mono Lake Paiute ancestry, is regarded as an influential and innovative contributor to Paiute basket culture. Telles augmented customary designs by incorporating multiple colors, changing the traditional shape of her baskets, and adding influences from outside groups, such as the showy beadwork of Plains tribes.

Education Nellie Shaw Harner (1905–1985), linguist and historian, was born in Wadsworth, Nevada, on the Pyramid Lake Reservation. After attending the Carson Indian School in Stewart, Nevada, and the Haskell Institute in Lawrence, Kansas, Harner received a BA in elementary education from Northern Arizona University and an MA from the University of Nevada. Fluent in the Paiute language and keenly interested in traditional stories, histories, and lifestyles of Native Americans, Harner taught and counseled in Bureau of Indian Affairs schools in Arizona, Kansas, Nevada, New Mexico, and Wyoming. Her master's thesis, *The History of the Pyramid Lake Indians, 1842–1959*, contributed greatly to Paiute written history. Harner was named Nevada's Outstanding Woman of the Year in 1975 and spent her retirement years on the Pyramid Lake Reservation.

Literature Author Adrian C. Louis (1945–), a member of the Lovelock Paiute Tribe, was born and raised in northern Nevada. He has published a number of poetry collections, including *Fire Water World* (1989), *Among the Dog Eaters* (1992), *Blood Thirsty Savages* (1994), *Vortex of Indian Fevers* (1995), and *Ceremonies of the Damned* (1997). His other work includes the novel *Skins* (1995) and the story collection *Wild Indians and Other Creatures* (1996). Louis received an MA from Brown University and has been an instructor at the Oglala Lakota College on the Pine Ridge Reservation in South Dakota. His literary focus has been on the forced assimilation of Native culture into the dominant Western society and its ramifications, including poverty, alcohol and drug abuse, humiliation, and demoralization. For the last decade he's taught literature in the Minnesota University system.

Annie Lowry (1866–1943) was born in Lovelock, Nevada, to a Paiute mother. She became the subject of a book by Lalla Scott as part of the 1930 Writer's Project of the Works Progress Administration. Through the project, published in 1966 as *Karnee: A Paiute Narrative*, Lowry related many Paiute traditions and events of the late nineteenth century.

One of the better-known Paiutes is Sarah Winnemucca (1844–1891), who published *Life Among the Piutes: Their Wrongs and Claims* in 1883. The book is considered the first autobiography by a Native American woman and one of the few Indian autobiographies from the later part of the nineteenth century. Born near Humboldt Lake in northern Nevada, Winnemucca was the daughter of Paiute leader Old Winnemucca. She served as an interpreter for Paiute raiding groups and the U.S. military in 1866 and again in 1878. She was a school teacher at the Malheur and Yakima reservations in the 1870s. Following the period of armed conflict, Winnemucca began touring first the West Coast in 1879 and then the East Coast through the early 1880s, giving numerous eloquent lectures on the plight of Native Americans in the Great Basin region. In 1884 she testified before a U.S. Senate subcommittee on the state of the reservation system. Elizabeth Palmer Peabody, a noted education proponent in the East, met Winnemucca and encouraged her to publish her story to educate the public about governmental injustice against the Native population. The book is a blend of autobiography, ethnography, and history of the Paiute peoples between 1844 and 1883. Winnemucca also published an 1882 article on Paiute ethnography in *The Californian* journal. She founded the Peabody Indian School in Nevada in 1884 and operated it until 1887. She was the first woman honored in Nevada with a historical marker. Her book was reprinted in 1994 by the University of Nevada Press.

Religion A Northern Paiute of the Walker River band, Wovoka (ca. 1856–1932) founded the Ghost Dance religion in 1889. He grew up in Mason Valley, Nevada, near the present Walker Lake Reservation. His proper name means "the cutter" in Paiute. At the time of his father's death, Wovoka was taken into the family of a white farmer named David Wilson and was given the name Jack Wilson, by which he was known among local American settlers.

MEDIA

Bishop Paiute Tribal Newsletter

This monthly newsletter features current events, announcements, profiles of community members, and local history and folklore for the Bishop Paiute Tribe in Bishop, California. An archive of issues dating to 2009 is available online. Many other Paiute tribal newsletters can also be found online.

Paiute Professional Building
50 Tu Su Lane
Bishop, California 93514
Phone: (760) 873-3584
Fax: (760) 873-4143
Email: chad.delgado@bishoppaiute.org
URL: www.bishoppaiutetribe.com/tribal-newsletters.html

Pyramid Lake Paiute Tribal Newspaper

Founded in 2008, this quarterly newspaper covers news and events relevant to the Pyramid Lake Paiute tribe in western Nevada. Current and archived issues are available online.

PLPT Tribal Offices
P.O. Box 256
Nixon, Nevada 89424
Phone: (775) 574-1000
Fax: (775) 574-1008
Email: newspaperweb@plpt.nsn.us
URL: http://plpt.nsn.us/newspaper/index.html

Indian Country Today Media Network

This media network includes a weekly newsmagazine, *This Week from Indian Country Today*. The website focuses on news related to Native people throughout North America and often features articles on the Paiute Tribe.

590 Madison Avenue
New York, New York 10022
Phone: (212) 600-2086
Email: editor@ictmn.com
URL: http://indiancountrytodaymedianetwork.co

ORGANIZATIONS AND ASSOCIATIONS

Big Pine Reservation

A 279-acre reservation located in Owens Valley of eastern California.

P.O. Box 700
Big Pine, California 93513
Phone: (760) 938-2003
Fax: (760) 938-2942
Email: info@BigPinePaiute.org
URL: www.bigpinepaiute.org

Bishop Paiute Tribe

A reservation of nearly 900 acres located in Owens Valley of eastern California.

50 Tu Su Lane
Bishop, California 93514
Phone: (760) 873-3584
Fax: (760) 873-4143
URL: www.bishoppaiutetribe.com

Burns Paiute Tribe

In 1897 homeless Northern Paiutes who had gathered around Burns, Oregon, were provided 115 allotments of land. In 1972 Congress created a 750-acre reservation. The band gained federal recognition in 1968.

100 Pasigo Street
Burns, Oregon 97720
Phone: (541) 573-1910
Email: bpt.council@gmail.com
URL: www.burnspaiute-nsn.gov

Kaibab Paiute Tribe

The tribe holds a 120,000-acre reservation in the "Arizona Strip" area of Arizona north of Grand Canyon National Park.

Tribal Admin Building
1 North Pipe Spring Road
Fredonia, Arizona 86022
Phone: (520) 643-7245
Fax: (888) 939-3777
Email: info@kaibabpaiute-nsn.gov
URL: http://www.kaibabpaiute-nsn.gov

Moapa Paiute Band of the Moapa Indian Reservation

Shortly after an 1873 Presidential Executive Order established a 2-million-acre reservation, Congress severely reduced it to 1,000 acres in 1875. Since 1980 Congress has added back slightly more than 70,000 acres. The reserve is located approximately 55 miles northeast of Las Vegas, Nevada.

1 Lincoln Street
P.O. Box 340
Moapa, Nevada 89025
Phone: (702) 865-2787
Email: sherryl@mvdsl.com
URL: www.moapapaiutes.com

Paiute Indian Tribe of Utah

Composed of five separate Paiute bands, the alliance holds, in total, more than 32,400 acres of land scattered in five parcels in southern Utah.

440 North Paiute Drive
Cedar City, Utah 84720
Phone: (435) 586-1112
Fax: (435) 867-2659
Email: webmaster@utahpaiutes.org
URL: http://www.utahpaiutes.org

Pyramid Lake Paiute Tribe.

The 475,000-acre reservation fully contains a 112,000-acre desert lake, Pyramid Lake.

208 Capitol Hill
Nixon, Nevada 89424
Phone: (775) 574-1032
Email: webmaster@plpt.nsn.us
URL: http://plpt.nsn.us

MUSEUMS AND RESEARCH CENTERS

Eastern California Museum

Offers extensive collections of the Owens Valley Paiute.

Jon Klusmire
155 Grant Street
Box 206
Independence, California 93526
Phone: (760) 878-0364
Fax: (760) 878-0412
Email: ecmuseum@inyocounty.us
URL: www.inyocounty.us

Nevada State Museum, Carson City

The museum houses extensive archaeological collections from traditional Paiute territory and routinely offers exhibits for the public on traditional Paiute life.

Jim Barmore
600 North Carson Street
Capitol Complex
Carson, Nevada 89710
Phone: (775) 687-4810
Fax: (775) 687-4168
Email: jbarmore@nevadaculture.org
URL: http://museums.nevadaculture.org

Stewart Indian School Museum

Established in 1982 after the closure of the Stewart Indian Boarding School. Operative for ninety years, the boarding school opened on December 17, 1890, with thirty-seven students from local Washoe, Paiute, and Shoshone tribes and three teachers. The museum assists research efforts of tribes and individuals and sponsors the Dat-So-La-Lee Basket Maker's Guild.

5500 Snyder Avenue
Carson, Nevada 89701
Phone: (775) 687-8333
Email: info@stewartindianschool.com
URL: www.stewartindianschool.com

SOURCES FOR ADDITIONAL STUDY

Bunte, Pamela A., and Robert J. Franklin. *From the Sands to the Mountain: Change and Persistence in a Southern Paiute Community*. Lincoln: University of Nebraska Press, 1987.

———. *The Paiute*. New York: Chelsea House, 1990.

———. "Southern Paiute." *Native America in the Twentieth Century: An Encyclopedia*. Edited by Mary B. Davis. New York: Garland Publishing, 1994.

Dutton, Bertha P. *American Indians of the Southwest*. Albuquerque: University of New Mexico Press, 1983.

Fowler, Catherine S. "Northern Paiute" and "Owens Valley Paiute." *Native America in the Twentieth Century: An Encyclopedia*. Edited by Mary B. Davis. New York: Garland Publishing, 1994.

Fowler, Don D., and John F. Matley. *Material Culture of the Numa: The John Wesley Powell Collection, 1867–1880.* Smithsonian Contributions to Anthropology, no. 26. Washington, D.C.: Smithsonian Institution Press, 1979.

Johnston, Charlie. "Cultural Guardians: A Dedicated Few Who Keep Nevada's Native Traditions Alive." *Nevada Magazine,* July/August 2011.

Mims, Bob. "Ute Language in Danger of Withering Away." *Salt Lake Tribune,* 17 June 2000.

Steward, Julian H. *Basin-Plateau Aboriginal Sociopolitical Groups.* Smithsonian Institution Bureau of American Ethnology Bulletin, no. 120; 1938. Reprint, Salt Lake City: University of Utah Press, 1970.

Wheat, Margaret M. *Survival Arts of the Primitive Paiutes.* Reno: University of Nevada Press, 1967.

Winnemucca, Sarah. *Life Among the Piutes: Their Wrongs and Claims.* Boston: Cupples, Upham, and Co., 1883. Reprint, Reno: University of Nevada Press, 1994.

PAKISTANI AMERICANS

Tinaz Pavri

OVERVIEW

Pakistani Americans are immigrants or descendants of people from Pakistan, a country in South Asia bordered by India on the east, Iran and Afghanistan on the west, the great Karakoram mountain range and China on the north, and the Arabian Sea on the south. Pakistan received its independence from British India in 1947. It was created on the basis of religious identity, so that Muslims from British-ruled India, which had an overwhelming majority of followers of the Hindu religion, would have a nation to call their own. Modern-day Pakistan is divided into four major geographic divisions known as the Khyber Pakhtunkhwa (KP), Punjab, Sind, and Baluchistan. Each of these regions has its own language and ethnic groups. The capital of Pakistan is the modern city of Islamabad, though the country's cultural and economic centers continue to be Lahore and Karachi. The area of the country is 307,373 square miles (796,095 square kilometers), approximately the size of the states of Texas and Kentucky combined.

The population of Pakistan was 176.7 million in 2011, according to World Bank figures. An overwhelming 98 percent of the Pakistani population are Muslim; small communities of Hindus, Christians, and Zoroastrians account for the rest. Pakistan was designed to be a state for Muslims, and this fact influences many aspects of Pakistani political and social life. Ethnic and linguistic groups in Pakistan include Pathans, Punjabis, Sindhis, and Baluchs. The Pathans, also known as the Pushtoons, Pashtuns, or Pakhtoons, come from the region of the KP and include tribes on the border of Pakistan and Afghanistan. The Punjabi community dominates education and industry in Pakistan. The Baluchs (or Balochs) are largely from Baluchistan (they also live in neighboring Iran and Afghanistan). They were originally a seminomadic people; today, while many continue to follow ancient traditions, others have moved to the city of Karachi. The Sindhi come from Sind and are a mixture of several different ethnic groups that all share a common language, Sindhi. Years of political instability have taken their toll on economic growth in the country. According to the *CIA World Factbook*, both unemployment and inflation are high and growth has remained low, making life hard for the average citizen. One significant source of revenue for the economy is the remittances of foreign workers to Pakistan. Since 2011 this has averaged about $1 billion a month. Pakistan's key industries include textiles and apparel, food processing, and pharmaceuticals; about 45 percent of the population is engaged in the agricultural sector.

The first notable wave of Pakistanis immigrated to the United States after 1965, when the U.S. government first eased immigration restrictions. That wave brought many students who came for higher education and professionals who came for career and economic opportunities. More recent Pakistani immigrants have not always had the same educational qualifications and socioeconomic profile of the post-1965 wave of immigrants. Many have immigrated as dependents of Pakistani American citizens, and others have left Pakistan because of the country's economic hardship and political turmoil. According to a 2008 report in Migration Information Source, of all Pakistani-born immigrants in the United States, more than a quarter came to the country during or after 2000. Of these, more than 90 percent continue to speak a native language in their homes. A 2011 Pew Center report states that Pakistan is the country of origin of the greatest number of first-generation Muslim immigrants to the United States.

The 2010 U.S. Census indicated that there were about 409,163 Pakistani Americans in the United States; however, community organizations put the figure higher, at about twice that number. The largest percentage, around 32 percent, live in the Northeast; around 27 percent live in the South, 21 percent in the West, and 20 percent in the Midwest. States with the largest concentrations of Pakistani Americans are New York, California, and Texas. Illinois, New Jersey, and Virginia are home to smaller numbers of Americans of Pakistani descent. Cities with significant Pakistani American communities include New York, Chicago, Philadelphia, and Los Angeles. Pakistani Americans tend to settle in large cities, reflecting the fact that most of the post-1965 immigrants were from the cities of Lahore, Karachi, and Rawalpindi. Their settlement patterns also reflect employment opportunities.

HISTORY OF THE PEOPLE

Early History Pakistan contains the site of the famed Indus Valley civilization (2500 BCE to 1700 BCE), including prehistoric remains at Mohenjo-Daro, near the modern Pakistani city of Larkana, and at Harappa, near the city of Lahore. The Indus Valley civilization has remained an interest for archaeologists because of the society's high level of sophistication and stability over several centuries.

Pakistan's ethnic and cultural diversity was formed through the mingling of Persians, Turks, Arabs, Huns, Greeks, and Mongols, most of whom practiced Islam. From about the eighth century CE until British dominance increased in the eighteenth century, Muslim rulers established kingdoms in northern India. As a result, many Pakistanis and others in British India converted to the religion of the new people.

When the struggle for independence from the British colonizers started in India at the beginning of the twentieth century, Hindus—followers of India's majority religion—and Muslims fought side by side for their freedom. The Indian National Congress, the political party that eventually led India to its independence, had many devoted Muslim members who were willing to give up their lives for the cause of India's freedom.

Great Britain formally relinquished its control over the subcontinent in 1947. As the goal of India's independence appeared more likely to be achieved, a section of the Muslim leadership led by Mohammed Ali Jinnah (1876–1948), who later became independent Pakistan's founder and first governor general, felt that Muslims would never be accorded equal treatment in a largely Hindu India. Because Jinnah feared political, social, and cultural subordination to the Hindu majority, he started a movement to establish a separate state based on Islam for the Indian Muslims. This group felt that in order to be truly free, Indian Muslims needed their own homeland. The independence leaders, both Hindus like Jawaharlal Nehru (1889–1964) and Mohandas Gandhi (1869–1948), and Muslims like Jinnah and Liaquat Ali Khan (1895–1951), who later became Pakistan's first prime minister, worked together with the British to make the transition from British India into independent India and Pakistan a reality.

Modern Era Following India's independence and Pakistan's inception, the two countries suffered riots and violence stemming from the migration of millions of Muslims to Pakistan from India and millions of Hindus from Pakistan to India. Refugee camps were created on both sides of the border between the two countries to deal with these mass migrations in which whole communities were uprooted from their homes.

Since then, India and Pakistan have fought three wars and have been involved in many other confrontations, particularly over the disputed Kashmir region that lies between the two countries, which remains the scene of a protracted, three-way conflict among the Indians, Pakistanis, and Kashmiris, who are seeking independence from both India and Pakistan. However,

the two countries share a history and culture that creates some ties between them. Many Muslims who chose to remain in India have close family members who moved to Pakistan, and some Hindus remained behind in Pakistan.

After the death of Jinnah, Pakistan was ruled by a series of army chiefs under martial law regimes. In 1971 Pakistan was divided again as a result of a violent ethnic insurgency in its eastern wing, which was populated mainly by Bengali-speaking Muslims, and the subsequent war with neighboring India. As a result of this division, a new sovereign country—Bangladesh—was created; Pakistan has since recognized Bangladesh and has established diplomatic and trading relations with the new nation.

Pakistan has had four constitutions since 1947. Zulfikar Ali Bhutto (1928–1979), served as Pakistan's prime minister from 1971 to 1977. His daughter Benazir Bhutto (1953–2007) was voted into power in 1988, in the country's first largely free national elections. She led her father's political party, the Pakistan People's Party (PPP), to victory. Under Benazir Bhutto, Pakistan made significant strides toward democracy. Another bout of military rule under General Pervez Musharraf (1943–) followed from 2001 to 2008, and now Pakistan is a parliamentary democracy, albeit one facing many severe challenges. Since the 1990s, the country has faced ethnic strife and religious fundamentalism. Terrorist and radical groups with bases within Pakistan have repeatedly threatened citizens of the country itself as well as the larger region, and Al-Qaeda leader Osama Bin Laden was finally killed there in 2011 after a decade in hiding. In the last decade, a handful of Pakistani Americans have been convicted for terrorist acts, including the 2010 Times Square car bombing, and many Pakistani Americans say that have felt increased scrutiny since the "War on Terror" began.

SETTLEMENT IN THE UNITED STATES

Even though Pakistan came into existence recently, Muslim immigrants from India and the region that is now Pakistan entered the United States as early as the nineteenth century, working alongside their Hindu or Sikh brethren in agriculture, logging, and mining in the states of California, Oregon, and Washington.

In 1907 around 2,000 Indians, including Hindus and Muslims, worked alongside other immigrants from China, Japan, Korea, and Italy on the building of the Western Pacific railway in California. Other Indians worked on building bridges and tunnels for California's other railroad projects. As the demand for agricultural labor increased in California, Indians turned to the fields and orchards for employment. Muslim agricultural workers in California sometimes brought with them to the fields an imam or learned man, who would pray several times a day when the men took their breaks.

In the early twentieth century, Muslims from the Indian subcontinent found success as farmers, leasing or owning land in many California counties in order to grow rice. Many Indian Americans, Hindu and Muslim, prospered financially as they increased their acreage and even bought small farms and orchards. However, heavy rains in 1920 devastated some rice crops and drove some of these farmers into bankruptcy.

L ike early Hindu and Sikh Indian immigrants, some Muslim immigrants chose to return to India after they had achieved some financial success in the United States. Many others, however, sowed firm roots in California and the adjoining Western states, sometimes by marrying Mexican women, because the immigration of Muslim women from the subcontinent was nonexistent.

While all Indian immigrants faced racial prejudice, Muslims from the subcontinent were also subject to added discrimination due to their religion. Some erroneously viewed Muslims as polygamists and called for them to be deported. The Asiatic Exclusion League (AEL) was organized in 1907 to encourage the expulsion of Asian workers, including Indian Hindus and Muslims.

The immigration of all Hindu and Muslim Indians was tightly controlled by the U.S. government during this time, and those applying for visas to travel to the United States were often rejected. In addition, legislation was introduced in the United States that attempted to legally restrict the entry of Indians and other Asians into the country as well as to deny them residency and citizenship rights. Some of this legislation was defeated and some was adopted. For instance, a number of bills required immigrants to pass a literacy test to be considered eligible for citizenship. This effectively ensured that most Indians would not be able to meet the requirements. Only in 1947 did Congress pass a bill allowing naturalization for Indian immigrants. Between 1947 and 1965, according to the Immigration and Naturalization Service, only around 2,500 Pakistani immigrants lived in the United States.

Pakistani immigration to the United States increased in 1965, when the U.S. government repealed quotas and lifted immigration restrictions. Numbers of Pakistani immigrants swelled after 1970, and thousands of Pakistanis have entered the United States each year since then. Since the 1990s, members of Pakistan's religious minorities, including the Ahmadis (or Ahmedis) and Hazaras, have made the United States their home in order to escape religious persecution in Pakistan. The Ahmadis, adherents of the Ahmadiyya sect of Islam, originate from the Punjab region. They share many beliefs with Islam, except for the fact that they believe that their founder, Hadhrat Mirza Gulam Ahmad, is the messiah, a view that is

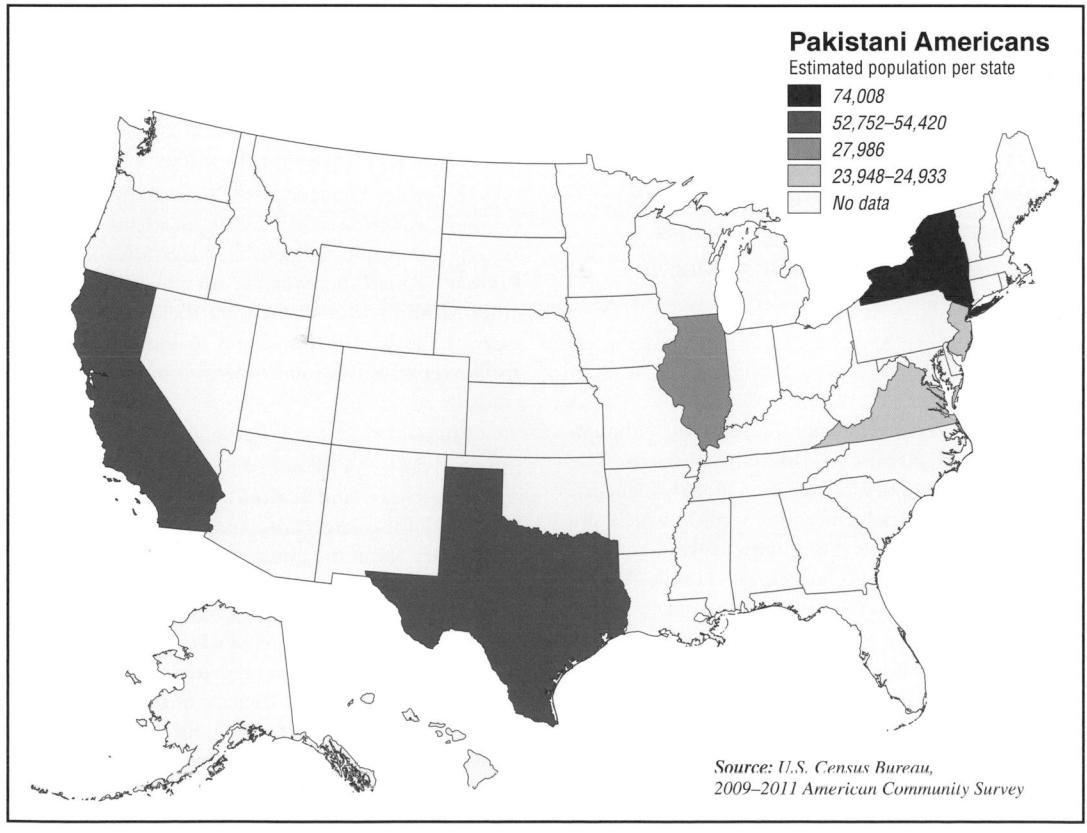

Pakistani Americans
Estimated population per state

- 74,008
- 52,752–54,420
- 27,986
- 23,948–24,933
- No data

Source: U.S. Census Bureau, 2009–2011 American Community Survey

considered heretical by mainstream Islam. Thus, in 1974, Pakistani officials declared them to be non-Muslims. They are forbidden from calling themselves Muslim or worshipping in mainstream mosques; such practices have become punishable offences under Pakistani law, creating precarious conditions for the community. The Hazaras, a Shiite ethnic minority in Pakistan with roots in Afghanistan, have also faced persecution because of their distinctive ethnicity, their political alliances during the U.S. involvement in Afghanistan, and the Sunni-Shia tensions within Pakistan. Since 2001, over a thousand Hazaras have been killed, most of them in their stronghold in Quetta, Baluchistan.

Like their Asian Indian counterparts, many of the first-wave Pakistani immigrants were urban, well-educated, and professional. Those who came from Karachi and Lahore were familiar with Western culture. However, many of the dependents and relatives these immigrants later sponsored for permanent residence in and citizenship of the United States tended to have less education. Since 2000, the experiences of these less-educated Pakistani immigrants have differed considerably from that of their professional counterparts in that they do not necessarily share their comfortable middle-class experiences and upward mobility.

According to the 2010 U.S. Census American Community Survey estimates for 2006–2010, New York, Texas, California, Illinois, New Jersey, and Virginia were the states with the largest numbers of Pakistani Americans.

After 9/11, some Pakistani Americans reported feeling as if their loyalties to the United States were in question. Many have reached out under umbrella Muslim organizations to educate American citizens about who they are and what their values are, and to demonstrate the peaceful foundations of Islam.

LANGUAGE

Urdu is the official language of Pakistan, although only about 10 percent of Pakistanis speak it. The majority of the population speaks regional languages, such as Punjabi, Baluchi, and Sindhi, which are taught in some schools along with Urdu. Urdu is a blend of four different languages—Hindi, Arabic, Persian, and Turkish. English is also spoken extensively in Pakistan.

About 30 percent of Pakistani Americans speak Urdu. A larger percentage, perhaps 50 percent, speak Punjabi (most of whom also speak Urdu). Others might speak Sindhi or Gujrati, reflecting the regions from which they trace their ancestry. As a result of the legacy of British colonization, many Pakistani

Americans are also fluent in English. While a majority of first-generation Pakistani Americans continue to speak their native languages at home, offspring generally speak English but understand their parents' native tongue.

Greetings and Popular Expressions Pakistani Americans often salute each other with the traditional Islamic greeting *Salaam Aleikum* ("sahlaam alaykoom")—Peace be with you. The response to that greeting, conveying the same meaning, is *Waleikum Salam*. Another common phrase is *Inshallah* ("insha-allah")—God willing.

RELIGION

Many Pakistani Americans are devout Muslims, and the Holy Quran and the teachings of the Holy Prophet serve as their guiding principles. Families often visit the mosque once a week, usually on Friday afternoons. Children are encouraged to attend religious education classes held on weekends and during the summer vacation. Both men and women must dress modestly while in the mosque, and covering the head is also encouraged. Men and women must sit either in separate rooms or in separate groups within the same room for the duration of the prayers.

The majority of Pakistanis belong to the Sunni sect of Islam, although there are smaller Shi'ite sects, such as an Ismaili sect, which follows the Aga Khan as its spiritual leader, and the previously mentioned Hazaras. Sunnis believe that the community is responsible for maintaining Islamic law. This law, *shari'a*, is based on four sources, which in descending order of importance are: the Quran; the examples and teachings of the Prophet; communal consensus (later the consensus of religious scholars) on Islamic principles and practices; and reasoning by analogy.

In smaller U.S. towns without nearby mosques, Pakistani Americans will travel to attend the nearest one on major religious holidays and occasions. Pakistani Americans worship at mosques alongside other Muslims who might trace their ancestry to all parts of the Islamic world and to India. There may also be separate Pakistani American mosques in large cities.

Pakistani Americans also participate in and contribute to the larger Islamic community, which includes Arab Americans and African Americans. They have been part of this larger community's efforts to educate the country about the ideals of Islam in the years since the terrorist attacks in the United States on September 11, 2001. This education has taken the form of participation in conferences about Muslim life in the United States and through student organizations on campuses. Ameena Ghaffer-Kucher, director of the International Educational Development program at University of Pennsylvania, has undertaken studies that document the voices of young Pakistani Americans, the prejudice they faced after 9/11, and their reactions to it.

Although the overwhelming majority of Pakistani Americans are Muslims, some are Hindu, Christian, or Zoroastrian. The Hindu community today has access to over a thousand temples all over the United States, but many Pakistani American Hindus prefer to visit North Indian or Sikh temples rather than South Indian temples. It is also common for Hindus in the United States to worship at home, in a small room or portion of a room set aside for worship and meditation.

Pakistani Christians worship and participate at churches throughout the country. Zoroastrians in Pakistan, or Parsis, trace their roots to ninth-century Persia when they migrated into the Indian sub-continent to escape religious persecution under Muslim rule., The Parsis form a minuscule religious minority in both India and Pakistan. They have prospered in both these countries, as well as in the United States. The earliest Zoroastrians came to the country at the turn of the twentieth century. In recent times, Pakistani Zoroastrians have come to the United States mainly from the Pakistani cities of Lahore and Karachi.

CULTURE AND ASSIMILATION

Previously, many scholars tended to lump the Pakistani American community together with the larger Asian Indian community, thereby glossing over its distinctiveness. For instance, in *Arab, Armenian, Syrian, Lebanese, East Indian, Pakistani and Bangladeshi Americans: A Study and Source Book* (1977), Kananur Chandras offers little distinction between the Asian Indian, Pakistani American, and Bangladeshi American communities. Others tended to assume, incorrectly, that Pakistani Americans, because they are overwhelmingly Muslim, could be described as a part of America's Arab Muslim community. This has changed in recent decades, as Pakistani Americans have become more visible and have established social and religious organizations that distinguish themselves from other communities and celebrate their particular religious and social traditions.

Traditions and Customs One of the most popular traditions for the Pakistani American community has been the celebration of Pakistan Day in different cities. The Pakistan Day parade in New York City has been held for over twenty-five years on or around August 14, Pakistan's independence day, and is attended by thousands. Cricket games that sometimes involve Pakistani cricketers are held in cities like New York and are well attended by the community. Rituals surrounding the breaking of the fast with family and friends during Ramadan and especially celebrations of Eid-al-Fitr at the end of Ramadan involve a large part of the community.

Cuisine The cuisine of northern India and that of Pakistan is similar. Hence, it is common to see restaurants featuring both Indian and Pakistani cuisine, although Pakistani-only restaurants are also popular. However, Pakistani cuisine has many traditional dishes that are not necessarily shared with Asian Indians.

Despite regional variations, Pakistani cuisine in general uses many spices. Cumin, turmeric, and chili powder are common in Asian Indian cuisine, and Pakistani American cuisine also includes such spices as cloves, cinnamon, saffron, and cardamom.

Pakistani Americans gather in Madison Square Park in NYC to celebrate India's and Pakistan's independence from the British Empire. RICHARD LEVINE / ALAMY

THE FAMILY MEAL

Most Pakistani American families eat at least one traditional meal a day, usually prepared with fresh ingredients by the woman of the house. Although Western-style shortcuts to food preparation, such as the use of canned substitutes, are increasingly being used, cooking the main meal still remains a laborious chore. The woman, often with the help of daughters, usually cooks for the family. Male family members, once rarely engaged in domestic chores like cooking and household cleaning, now find themselves willingly participating in such endeavors. Pakistani Americans regard the family meal as an important event in their daily lives. It is a time for the family to talk to each other about what events have transpired during the day and a time to be together and maintain contact in the face of busy individual schedules.

Meat dishes—lamb, goat, and beef—are common. Meat must be *halal*, that is, cut in a way that ensures the slow draining of blood from the animal in accordance with Islamic law. Many large American cities have halal butcher shops where such meat is sold. Also in accordance with halal customs, Muslims do not eat pork. Pakistani food tends to be more meat-based than Indian food. Kebabs of chicken, beef, and lamb are very popular. Rice dishes include *pulao*, a fragrant dish of mildly spiced rice with peas or dried fruits, and *biryani*, which consists of rice and meat marinated in yogurt and spices. *Dals*, or lentils and split peas prepared in spicy sauces, are common. Whole chickpeas are prepared in a flavorful sauce called *cholle* ("chollay"). Vegetable dishes include *saag* ("sahg") or spinach and *aloo-mattur*—potatoes and peas. Unleavened breads made with white and wheat flour are eaten with many meals; these include the robust *naan*, clay-baked *roti*, and *paratha*.

Traditional Pakistani sweets include *zarda* ("zahrdah"), a sweet, yellow, rice dish; *jalebi* ("jahlaybee"), an orange-colored, fried pastry made of a sugary syrup and flour; and *ladoo* ("lahdoo"), a round ball of sweetened chick-pea flour embellished with pistachios or cashews. *Burfi*, a sweet made of scalded milk, and *kheer*, a dessert of milk and rice or vermicelli, are also popular. Tea flavored with cinnamon and cardamom is a favorite drink. Another way to round off a meal is to chew *paan*, which is the broad leaf of the betel plant sprinkled with a lime powder.

Traditional Dress Pakistani American men and women wear the traditional *salwar kameez* on festive occasions. The outfit, consisting of a long tunic and tight or loose-fitting leggings or trousers and often including a diaphanous shawl or veil called the *dupatta* ("dooputtah") for women, is commonly made of cotton or silk. Women's clothing tends to be more colorful and intricate, often including exquisite embroidery or *zari*, a technique that involves the weaving of gold or silver thread into the cloth. It is more rare, but not

unheard of, for some Pakistani American women to wear the sari, the traditional costume of Asian Indian women. Some women wear the Islamic burqa that encases them from head to toe. However, others wear only a colorful head scarf, and many do not use any form of head covering at all.

Like their Asian Indian counterparts, Pakistani American women enjoy wearing gold jewelry, including bangles, bracelets, rings, and necklaces. Simple jewelry is worn daily, while more opulent pieces with precious stones are worn at weddings and other celebrations. Pieces of jewelry are often passed down through the generations as family heirlooms.

Traditional Arts and Crafts On festive occasions and weddings, *mehndi*, or the application of a paste made with henna that dries in delicate, intricate designs on the palms of the hands, is sported by some women and girls in the community. The wearing of gold jewelry including bangles, necklaces, rings, and earrings in traditional and modern settings with precious or semiprecious stones is popular, and traditional wedding designs are available. Woodcarving of furniture, chests, and other objects has a long history within Pakistan. Embroidered shawls of wool, silk, and cotton as well as fabrics stitched in geometric patterns with small mirrors (*sheesha*) are common. Along with other countries in the region, such as Afghanistan and Iran, Pakistan is home to a centuries-long carpet and rug-making tradition and is well known for the handmade Bokhara rug. The Peshawar region of Pakistan is known for its hand-hammered copperware and copper utensils and Multan is known for terracotta tiles. Many Pakistani American homes have native rugs and other crafts displayed in them. Although the majority of these crafts are brought back from Pakistan, Pakistani American grocery stores sometimes sell crafts as well in addition to online outlets.

Dances and Songs A common dance performed by Pakistani American women on festive occasions like weddings and other celebrations is the *giddha*, in which women dance in a circle while rhythmically clapping their hands. *Qawaali* ("kawalee"), a genre of music that traces its roots to Sufi Muslim devotional and mystical music and that is meant to encourage religious ecstasy among its listeners, has many adherents within the Pakistani American community and is also drawing increasing numbers of other Americans into its fold of admirers. It encourages intense listener involvement and response. The best-known group performing this music that has toured the United States is the Pakistani group Nusrat Fateh Ali Khan and Party. Groups performing the Qawaali generally include several singers and such instruments as the harmonium and the *tabla* ("tublah"), a type of drum. The *ghazal*, a mellow, emotional style of ancient Persian lyric verse set to music and sung by both men and women, is also popular among members of the community. Film music, from both popular Pakistani films and Indian Bollywood films in Hindi, also has many adherents within the community, particularly first-generation and recent immigrants. Pakistani bands that combine Western rock and pop tunes with Urdu lyrics are popular at celebrations.

Holidays The New Year is widely celebrated among members of the community. In addition, Pakistani Americans celebrate the creation of Pakistan on August 14 as Independence Day. The birthday of Jinnah, the founder of the Pakistani nation, is celebrated on December 25, and Pakistan Day is on March 23. Religious celebrations include *Eid-al-Fitr*, festivities that signify the end of the month of fasting during *Ramadan*, and *Eid-al-Adha*, a joyous

observance of the pilgrimage to Mecca. Pakistani Hindus celebrate *Diwali* ("deevalee"), the festival of lights, and *Holi* ("hoelee"), the festival of color that traditionally welcomes the spring.

Celebrations on such days typically include visits to friends and family, the exchange of gifts and sweets, and invitations to feasts. Many people wear traditional outfits. Celebratory parades in cities and towns where there are large Pakistani American communities are increasingly popular. Celebrations at local community centers often include *mushaira* ("mooshaeera"), or Urdu poetry readings, and showings of Pakistani and Hindi films. Less common, but no less enjoyed in large cities with great ethnic diversity like New York, is the occasional cricket match that will be organized

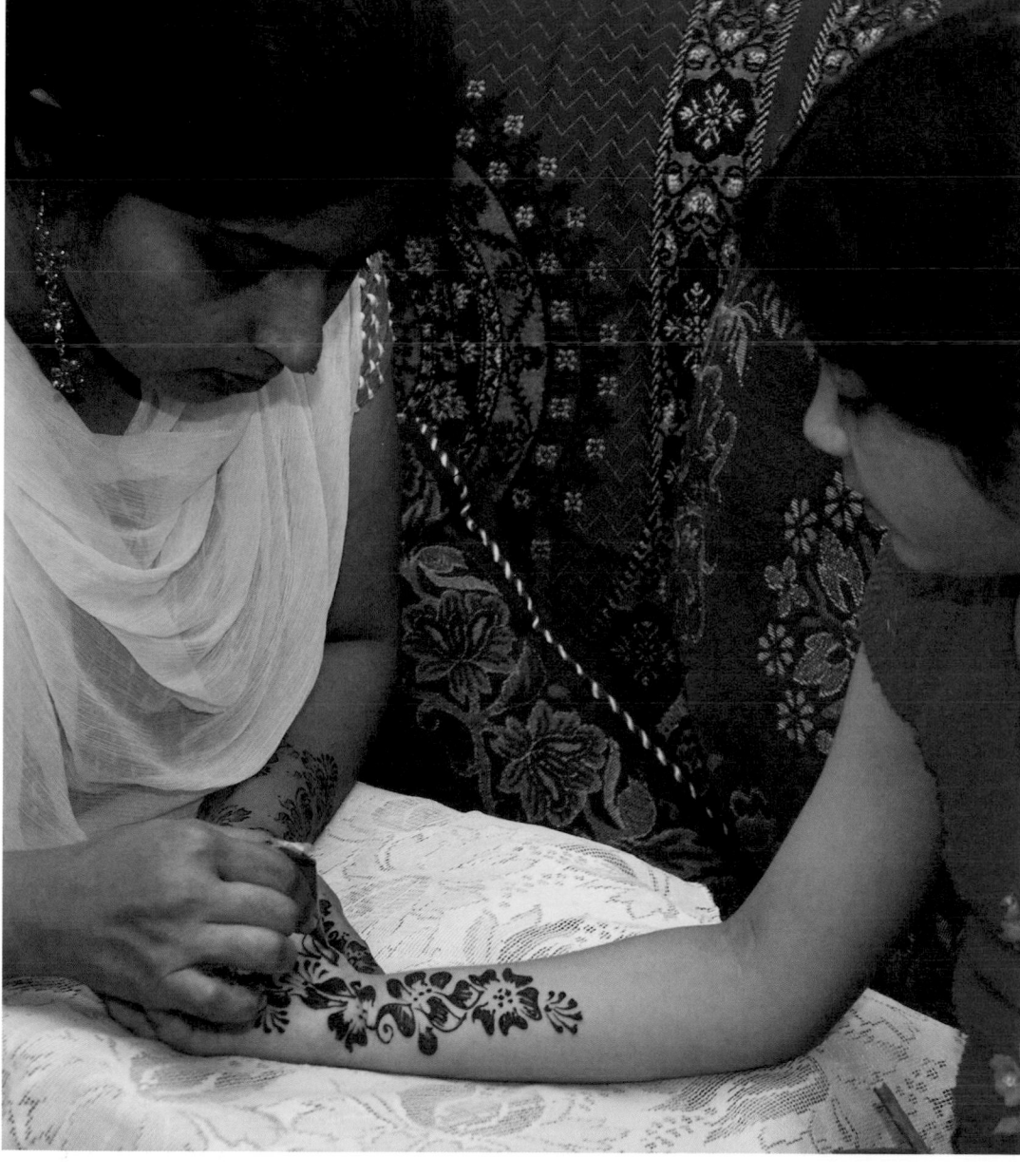

Pakistani American young women decorate their hands with Mehandi on the eve of Eid-ul-Fitr. AP PHOTO / MAHESH KUMAR A

PAKISTANI PROVERBS

Common Pakistani proverbs include the following:

■ If you and I agree, what is a lawyer needed for?

■ Turn your face to virtue and your back to vice

■ A friend appears during hard times, not during dinners.

within the community or a larger cricket-playing community that includes Asian Indians and West Indians.

Health Care Issues and Practices Pakistani Americans take health issues seriously and consult health-care providers regularly. Family physicians are often chosen from within the community. Traditional herbal remedies might be used to battle minor illnesses. Ayurveda and homeopathy are also employed. Ayurveda focuses on spiritual healing as an essential part of physical healing and bases its cures on herbs and other natural ingredients such as raw ginger and garlic. Homeopathy attempts to cure by stimulating the body's own defenses against the illness.

Members of the community are less likely, however, to seek help for mental health issues, a reflection of the traditionally low levels of awareness of the subject in Pakistan and on the Indian subcontinent in general. Pakistani Americans generally believe that families rather than institutional settings are best suited to take care of the mentally ill.

Death and Burial Rituals Muslim Pakistani Americans follow Islamic rites in burying the deceased. According to the Islamic Society of North America, the body is washed, usually by persons of the same gender. It is then wrapped in pieces of white cotton cloth and tied at the head and feet. This ritual wrapping is called *kafan*. Prayers are led by the imam. The body is placed without a casket into the grave, lying on the right side and facing Mecca. Islamic law stresses that the burial should happen as soon as possible after death. No separate cemeteries exist for the Pakistani community in the United States; rather, they may use cemeteries that are designated for Muslims and operated by Islamic centers in U.S. cities in states like Florida, Texas, California, and New Jersey. In rare cases, the body might be flown to Pakistan for burial. Generally, only males participate in the actual burial ceremony. Pakistani Hindus are cremated according to Hindu religious tradition. In this ceremony, males are given greater prominence. Death is a time for the Pakistani community to come

together to provide emotional and sometimes financial support for the bereaved family.

Recreational Activities Pakistani American culture centers are popular meeting places for the community and hold such activities as kite-flying contests, picnics, film and karaoke nights, and performances by artists and musicians from Pakistan or within the community. Exploring restaurants is popular, but in keeping with Islamic values that forbid drinking, frequenting bars is not. Many avidly watch television serials and movies from Pakistan. While second-generation Pakistani Americans play all the American popular sports, first-generation Pakistani Americans might start a cricket league when possible.

FAMILY AND COMMUNITY LIFE

Pakistani American families tend to be tightly knit and patriarchal. In the case of the early immigrants, often only men had formal educations, and they became the sole breadwinners. The nuclear family is most common, but members of the extended family, including grandparents, aunts, and uncles, visit frequently and for long periods of time. Siblings and close relatives are encouraged to visit the United States and are provided with financial and emotional support should they decide to eventually immigrate. Many leisure activities for Pakistani Americans tend to be family and community oriented. Pakistani Americans often prefer to live near other Pakistani Americans in order to feel a sense of community. Because family ties are so strong, they also try to live close to relatives.

Gender Roles Most first-generation Pakistani American women continue to fulfill traditional female roles, choosing to take care of the home and family rather than pursuing demanding careers. Second-generation Pakistani American women tend to be more resistant to traditional roles, and many have launched professional careers across the spectrum, in fields including law, academia, and medicine. Like many South Asians in general, Pakistani Americans place a high value on careers in the sciences, including information technology, medicine, and pharmacy, and young women are encouraged to enter these careers. Young women and girls generally have less freedom to date or socialize than their male counterparts.

Education On the whole, education is highly valued among Pakistani Americans. Many first-generation males came to the United States in the post-1965 period with high levels of education and obtained advanced degrees in the United States. This generation imparted the value of education to their children. Both girls and boys are encouraged to study hard and pursue careers of which the family can be proud. A particular bias within the South Asian community is toward careers in the sciences, information technology, and engineering, and there are some biases against young people choosing careers in the arts or humanities. Science careers are perhaps viewed as allowing the next generation a better chance for upward mobility. According to a 2011 Pew Research Report, 55 percent of Pakistani Americans hold a bachelor's or master's degree. This is higher than the general U.S. population, around 30 percent of which holds a bachelor's degree, with an additional 10 percent holding a master's degree, according to a 2011 Census Bureau report.

Courtship and Weddings In the Pakistani American community, dating is discouraged for girls. Young men and women are expected to marry within their ethnicity and with parental approval. Formerly, family and community members were widely consulted in selecting prospective marriage partners for young adults, but now many young people make their own decisions, and "love" marriages are more common and acceptable. Pakistani Sindhi Hindus prefer to marry within the Sindhi Hindu community rather than marrying a Hindu from India.

Most Pakistani weddings observe Muslims rites. Friends and relatives are invited to join festivities that might stretch over several days. The legal portion of the ceremony is accomplished with the signing of the *nikaah*, or marital agreement, by the bride and groom. A *moulvi* ("moolvee"), or knowledgeable one, is present at all ceremonies and formally asks the bride and groom whether they accept each other in matrimony. Weddings are generally held in large halls, not in mosques, and traditional Pakistani music is played before and after the ceremony. The application of henna, or mehndi, in intricate patterns on the hands of the bride and other guests is very common across South Asian communities, and it is also true of Pakistani Americans, where the ceremony is also referred to as Rasm-e-Henna. It occurs a day or two before the actual wedding and could involve henna being applied to the groom's head in a separate ceremony. It may be designed around a theme, or a particular shade of the henna that will be used. While gifts of money and jewelry are traditionally given at weddings in Pakistan, in the United States gifts may also include appliances or other household items. Jewelry is still frequently passed down from mother to daughter or daughters-in-law at weddings. Pakistani Hindus, on the other hand, follow the traditional Hindu ceremony, with the bride and groom circling a holy fire from three to seven times, and the priest chanting prayers.

Relations with Other Americans Pakistani Americans mingle with their American counterparts or with members of other immigrant ethnic groups in work and school, but they often choose to spend their leisure time with members of their own community. Many Pakistani Americans report conflicting feelings about American culture and ways of life. While they may admire the American approach to personal and political freedom, individualism, the country's achievements in science and technology, and American economic efficiency, other aspects—such as premarital relations, dating, and divorce—are frowned upon. Regional differences prevail, with the more urban immigrants in big cities tending to be more receptive of American culture and values than the more traditional immigrants who trace their roots to the provinces and rural areas of Pakistan.

Members of the larger Pakistani community hold distinct perceptions of the different subgroups within the community. For instance, Pakistanis tracing their roots to Lahore are generally considered to be traditional compared with the more cosmopolitan and Westernized immigrants from Karachi. The Sindhi and Baluch are also considered traditional and conservative.

There is some overlap between members of the Asian Indian and Pakistani American communities. This is particularly the case for those who share the bond of Islam. After 9/11, some Pakistani Americans reported feeling as if their loyalties to the United States were in question. Many have reached out under umbrella Muslim organizations to educate American citizens about who they are and what their values are, and to demonstrate the peaceful foundations of Islam. Organizations such as Muslims for a Safe America engage the American public about Muslim stereotypes. The Islamic Networks group based in San Jose, California, lends speakers on Islam to schools, colleges, corporations and law-enforcement agencies. The Islamic Circle of North America, based in Queens in New York City, runs a hotline to answer questions about Muslims and Islam that the general public might have.

Philanthropy The American Pakistan Foundation was founded in 2009 to channel the philanthropy of the Pakistani American community. One Pakistani American Ismaili sect follows the Aga Khan as its spiritual leader, and the Aga Khan Development Network (AKDN) funds numerous charitable causes throughout the world. According to professor Adil Najam, author of *Portrait of a Giving Community: Philanthropy by the Pakistani-American Diaspora* (2006), the community gives 40 percent of its philanthropic monies to charities in Pakistan, 20 percent to Pakistan-related causes, and the remainder to non-Pakistani causes like disaster relief for Haiti or Hurricane Sandy, to name two recent disasters that the Pakistani American community galvanized support around. Their total giving is 3.5 percent of their household income, about the same as the average American household.

Surnames Common Pashtun surnames include Agha, Babar, and Khan. Kashmiri last names include Mir and Mian; and Punjabi surnames of Chaudhry, Bajwa, and Malik are quite common. Sindhi last names include Junejo, Lakhani, and Qureshi.

EMPLOYMENT AND ECONOMIC CONDITIONS

Many Pakistani American males who entered the United States after 1965 were highly educated and soon found employment in a variety of professions such as law, medicine, and academia. In the post-1965 wave of immigration, many Pakistanis also came to the United States as students who earned graduate and professional degrees that enabled them to pursue successful careers in a variety of fields. They are particularly well represented in the field of medicine. Some members of the community immigrated to the United States with specific educational backgrounds in fields like the law but failed to find positions because their qualifications and experience did not transfer to the United States. They either retrained themselves in another professions or fields or accepted a position that was beneath their education level.

Many Pakistani Americans lead a comfortable, middle-class existence, although poverty is more prevalent among newer, undereducated immigrants. The poverty rate in the community is around 15 percent, according to the 2011 Pew Research Center report, which also states that the per capita income in the community from 2007 to 2009 was $24,663. Many Pakistani Americans also own their own businesses, including restaurants, gas stations, groceries, clothing and appliance stores, newspaper booths, and travel agencies. It is common to include members of the extended and immediate family in the business.

Pakistani Americans tend to follow the residence pattern set by other Americans, in that they move from cities to more affluent suburbs as their prosperity increases. Members of the community believe in the symbolic importance of owning homes; accordingly, Pakistani Americans tend to save and make other monetary sacrifices earlier on in order to purchase their own homes as soon as possible.

Members of the family and the larger community tend to take care of each other, and to assist in times of economic need. Hence, it would be more common to turn to a community member for economic assistance rather than to a government agency. Relatively low levels of the community are therefore on welfare and public assistance.

POLITICS AND GOVERNMENT

In the early part of the twentieth century, Muslim and Hindu immigrants were actively involved in the struggle for residence and citizenship rights in the United States. The second wave of immigrants, beginning in 1965, were not especially politically inclined. In the twenty-first century this has been changing. Pakistani Americans now contribute funds to candidates in both major political parties, and some are running for elected office in districts with large Pakistani American populations. Pakistani American candidates have, for instance, run for the state senate in New York City

and other urban areas. Because the community is geographically dispersed, the formation of influential voting blocs has not generally been possible, making it difficult to for the community to impact the political system as a whole. However, there are increasing efforts on the part of community leaders to ensure voter registration and involvement. Like Asian Indian Americans, Pakistani Americans have tended to vote Democratic in much larger numbers than Republican since the 2004 elections.

Relations with Pakistan Most Pakistani Americans maintain close links with relatives and friends in Pakistan. First-generation Pakistani Americans travel to their native land at least once every few years if they are able. They often take with them gifts of money, food, and clothing for friends and family. Second-generation Pakistani Americans tend to travel to Pakistan less frequently, as their family ties become attenuated. Prior to the "War on Terror," the relationship of the U.S. and Pakistani governments had been very close, and the Pakistani American community benefitted from this. This relationship has been strained in recent years, particularly when the U.S. military carried out a top secret mission to kill Osama bin Laden inside Pakistan, without the knowledge of the Pakistani government.

Pakistani Americans maintain a deep interest in the society and politics of Pakistan. They raise funds for the different political parties and groups in Pakistan. Long-standing tensions between India and Pakistan also tend to be reflected in the relationships between Asian Indians and Pakistani Americans, but by and large, relations are very amicable.

NOTABLE INDIVIDUALS

Academia Mazhar Ali Khan Malik is a professor of economics and engineering and founder of the Pakistan League of America (PLA). Samuel Iftikhar (1923–1991) was an Asian scholar and reference librarian at the Library of Congress for more than twenty-five years. Ayesha Jalal is a historian at Tufts University and a 1998 MacArthur Fellow. Bashir Syed is a solar physicist with NASA and a member of the New York Academy of Sciences. Sara Suleri, a Pakistani author and professor of English at Yale University, is a long-time resident of the United States.

Art Samina Quraeshi (1946–), artist, designer, and author, has served as director of design arts at the National Endowment for the Arts (NEA) in Washington, D.C. Shahzia Sikander (1969–) has had her work exhibited at the Museum of Modern Art and the Guggenheim Museum. She received the U.S. State Department's Medal of Arts in 2013. Fazlur Rahman Khan (1929–1982) was the structural engineer who designed the Sears Tower (now the Willis Tower) in Chicago.

Business Tariq Farid (1969–) is the founder and CEO of Edible Arrangements International, Inc. Michael Chowdry (1955–2001) founded the air cargo company Atlas Air. Fred Hasan (1946–) served as CEO of Schering-Plough, the pharmaceutical company, from 2003 to 2009.

Government Saghir Tahir served as a Republican member of the New Hampshire House of Representatives from 2000 to 2010. He was the first Pakistani American state legislator. Huma Abedin (1976–) is an American deputy chief of staff who served as the top aide to Secretary of State Hillary Clinton.

Journalism Tashbih Sayyed (1941–2007) was editor of *Pakistan Today* and *Muslim World Today* and wrote several books focused on Pakistani foreign policy and a secularist interpretation of Islam.

Literature Ayad Aktar (1970–) is a playwright and actor whose 2012 debut novel, *American Dervish*, deals with identity, religion and adjustment issues of Pakistani American immigrants in the American Midwest. Bapsi Sidhwa (1938–) is a Pakistani American novelist of Parsi origin. Her books include *Cracking India*, about the partition of India and Pakistan. Asma Gul Hasan (1974–) is a Pakistani American author whose books include *Why I Am a Muslim* (2004) and *Red, White and Muslim* (2008). Daniyal Mueenuddin (1963–) won the Commonwealth Writers' Prize for his book of short stories, *In Other Rooms, Other Wonders* (2009).

Music Nadia Ali (1980–) is a successful singer-songwriter who rose to prominence as a member of the dance-music duo iiO. Roger David (1979–) is a rapper with stage name Bohemia who raps in Punjabi.

Science and Medicine Salam Shahidi (1933–1992) was a leading medical researcher in New York City's Department of Health. He was also vice-chairman of the Pakistan League of America (PLA) and president of the cultural organization the National Association of Pakistani Americans.

Mohammad Akhter, physician, has had many leadership positions in the field of public health, including commissioner of Public Health for Washington, D.C. (1991–1994) and executive director of the American Public Health Association (1997–2001).

Mohammed Sayeed Quraishi (1924–) served at the National Institutes of Health in Bethesda, Maryland and the National Institute of Allergy and Infectious Diseases. He is the author of many books and received the Recognition and Appreciation of Special Achievement Award by the National Institute of Health in 1988.

Sports Nur Ali (1974–) is a prize-winning professional race car driver. Shahid Khan (1952–) is one of the wealthiest people in the United States. He owns the NFL Jacksonville Jaguars as well as the auto parts business Flex-N-Gate.

Stage and Screen Faran Tahir (1964–), actor, has appeared in several films and televisions shows, including *Monk* and *24*.

Shahzia Sikander is a Pakistani American artist known for Persian and Mughal miniature painting, performance art, and digital animation. KRIS CONNOR / GETTY IMAGES

MEDIA

PRINT

Pakistan Link

Provides news about Pakistan for the Pakistani American community.

Akhtar M. Faruqul, Editor
P.O. Box 1238
Anaheim, California 92815
Phone: (714) 400-3400
Fax: (714) 400-3404
Email: editor@pakistanlink.com
URL: www.pakistanlink.org

Pakistan Post

An Urdu-English newspaper for Pakistani Americans.

Mohammad Afaq Khaili, Editor in Chief
78-26 Parsons Boulevard
Fresh Meadows, New York 11366
Phone: (718) 739-3262
Fax: (718) 739-3249
Email: thepakistanpost@gmail.com
URL: www.pakistanpost.net

TELEVISION

TV Asia

A program often shown on international cable channels all over the United States; it includes Pakistani soap operas, films, and plays. Cities like New York and Los Angeles with relatively large Pakistani American settlements have weekly Pakistani feature and news programs.

TV Asia
c/o International Channel
12401 West Olympic Boulevard
Bethesda, Maryland 20814
Phone: (310) 826-2429
URL: www.tvasiausa.com

ORGANIZATIONS AND ASSOCIATIONS

Association of Physicians of Pakistani Descent (APPNA)

An organization of Pakistani American physicians and dentists that focuses on how to better serve the health needs of the Pakistani American community and of all Americans. Formerly known as Association of Pakistani Physicians.

Dr. Javed Suleman, President
6414 South Cast Avenue
Suite L2
Westmont, Illinois 60559
Phone: (630) 968-8585
Fax: (630) 968-8677
URL: www.appna.org

Pakistan League of USA (PLUS)

Advocates for the Pakistani American community and promotes Pakistani culture in the United States.

URL: www.pakleagueusa.org

Pakistan American Leadership Center

Political advocacy organization for the interests of Pakistani Americans.

236 Massachusetts Avenue NE
Suite 207
Washington, D.C. 20002
Phone: (202) 675-2004
Fax: (202) 675-2006
Email: taha@pal-c.org
URL: www.pal-c.org

U.S.-Pakistan Business Council (USPBC)

Promotes trade between the United States and Pakistan. Offers information on economic and social conditions in Pakistan.

U.S. Chamber of Commerce
1615 H Street NW
Washington, D.C. 20062
Phone: (202) 463-5732
Fax: (202) 822-2491
Email: uspbc@uschamber.com
URL: www.uspakistan.org

MUSEUMS AND RESEARCH CENTERS

American Institute of Pakistan Studies (AIPS)

Founded in 1973 for the study of Pakistan and exchanges between the United States and Pakistan.

Dr. Kamran Ali, President
University of Texas
1 University Station G-9300
Austin, Texas 78712
Phone: (512) 475-6039
Email: asdar@mail.utexas.edu
URL: www.pakistanstudies-aips.org

Center for Pakistan Studies, Middle East Institute

Provides research on different aspects of Pakistan.

Marvin Weinbaum, Scholar in Residence
1761 North Street NW
Washington, D.C. 20036
Phone: (202) 785-1141
Fax: (202) 331-8861
Email: information@mei.edu
URL: www.mei.edu/center-pakistan-studies

South Asian Digital Archive

Founded by Samip Mallick to codify and document the rich history of South Asians in the United States from the earliest times.

Samip Mallick, Executive Director
South Asian American Digital Archive
1219 Vine Street
Studio G
Philadelphia, Pennsylvania 19107-1111
Phone: (215) 259-8055
Email: info@saadigitalarchive.org

or

Email: samip@saadigitalarchive.org
URL: www.saadigitalarchive.org

SOURCES FOR ADDITIONAL STUDY

Asghar, Rob. *Lessons from the Holy Wars: A Pakistani-American Odyssey*. Tucson, AZ: Wheatmark, 2010.

Balagopal, Padmini, et al. *Indian and Pakistani Food Practices, Customs, and Holidays*. Chicago: The American Dietetic Association, 1996.

Helwig, Arthur, and Usha M. Helwig. *An Immigrant Success Story: East Indians in America*. Philadelphia: University of Pennsylvania Press, 1990.

Jensen, Joan. *Passage from India: Asian Indian Immigrants in North America*. New Haven: Yale University Press, 1988.

Malik, Iftikhar Haider. *Pakistanis in Michigan: A Study of Third Culture and Acculturation*. New York: AMS Press, 1989.

Najam, Adil. *Portrait of a Giving Community: Philanthropy by the Pakistani American Diaspora*. Harvard University: Global Equity Initiative, 2007.

Taus-Bolstad, Stacy. *Pakistanis in America*. Minneapolis: Lerner Publications, 2006.

Williams, Raymond Brady. *Religions of Immigrants from India and Pakistan: New Threads in the American Tapestry*. New York: Cambridge University Press, 1988.

PALESTINIAN AMERICANS

Ken Kurson

OVERVIEW

Palestinian Americans are immigrants or descendants of immigrants from the region inhabited by historical Palestine. This area stretched from the eastern shore of the Mediterranean Sea to lands east of the Jordan River and was bordered by Syria on the north and Egypt on the south. In 1923, after the conclusion of World War I, the British government divided historical Palestine into two distinct regions under the auspices of the League of Nations: Mandate Palestine, which was bordered by Syria and the newly defined Lebanon to the north, the Jordan River to the east, and Egypt to the south; and Transjordan, which spread across the area east of the Jordan River and later became part of the Hashemite Kingdom of Jordan. With the establishment of the State of Israel within the borders of Mandate Palestine on May 14, 1948, the Palestinian region was again divided into two disconnected territories: the West Bank of the Jordan River (including east Jerusalem), which includes around 2149 square miles (5565 square kilometers); and the Gaza Strip, a small area on the eastern coast of the Mediterranean Sea, which includes around 141 square miles (365 square kilometers). Because the Jordan Valley in Palestine is below sea level, it contains very rich soil, but water resources remain limited. The Gaza Strip is generally arid and subject to drought. The West Bank region is slightly smaller than the state of Delaware, and the Gaza Strip is about twice the size of Washington, D.C.

According to the World Bank, the combined population of the West Bank and the Gaza Strip was 4,019,433 in 2011, but this total does not account for Palestinians who have been displaced by geopolitical violence since 1948. The Palestinian Central Bureau of Statistics (PCBS) estimated the total number of Palestinians worldwide to be 11.6 million in 2012. Both the West Bank and the Gaza Strip are predominantly Muslim (around 99 percent of the population of Gaza and 94 percent of the West Bank). As a result of foreign aid and government spending, the West Bank has experienced strong economic growth since the mid-1990s, and the overall standard of living has improved. The PCBS reported that the West Bank's gross domestic product (GDP) increased by 124 percent between 1994 and 2010. The area will remain largely dependent on donor aid to sustain its economy, however, and it experienced an excessive unemployment rate of 23 percent in 2012, as well as a high number of residents who live below the poverty line—18.3 percent in 2010. The economic situation in the Gaza Strip is markedly worse, in large part because of trade embargoes and economic sanctions levied on the region by Israel, Egypt, and the United States (among others), with unemployment reaching as high as 60 percent since the mid-2000s.

Palestinian American immigrants first began settling in the United States in the 1870s but were identified as Ottoman subjects or Turks and Syrians by U.S. immigration officials. Most of these initial Palestinian immigrants were Christians who came to the United States in search of opportunity on the advice of American missionaries. The majority settled in New York City, though many found work as peddlers and quickly dispersed throughout the country, particularly to Chicago. In 1948 around 700,000 Palestinians fled their homeland during the first of several Arab-Israeli wars—a series of conflicts between Arab and Jewish forces over the creation of the Jewish state of Israel. While most Palestinian refugees settled in the West Bank and the Gaza Strip or in neighboring Arab countries, Palestinian immigration to the United States began to increase during this period, as the mostly male population of refugees started to bring their families to the West. Toward the end of the twentieth century, the majority of Palestinian immigrants to the United States were students seeking advanced degrees who considered their stay temporary. After the terrorist attacks in the United States in September 2001, however, student visas from Arab countries became more difficult to obtain. By the mid-2000s the majority of Palestinian immigrants were refugees from war-torn countries such as Iraq and Syria.

According to the U.S. Census Bureau's American Community Survey estimates for 2011, there were 97,345 Palestinian Americans residing in the United States. Actual numbers may have been significantly higher (as high as around 200,000), however, because of the number of Palestinians self-identifying only as Arab or as having another nationality, such as Syrian. By the early twenty-first century, Palestinian Americans lived across the United States, with the largest groups residing on the East Coast and many others inhabiting major metropolitan centers in other regions, including Los Angeles and San Francisco in California; Detroit and Chicago in the Midwest; and Atlanta and Jacksonville, Florida, in the South. Besides in Illinois, Florida, California, and Michigan, Palestinian Americans also reside in significant numbers in Texas, Ohio, New York, and New Jersey.

HISTORY OF THE PEOPLE

Early History The Middle East has long been the crossroads of major trade routes between East and West. The economic and political significance of these lands has made them the object of continual conquest by various armies since biblical times. This is especially true for Palestine, because ancient Palestine was also the birthplace of two major world religions—Judaism and Christianity. It later became very significant for Islam as well, surpassed only by Mecca and Medina in Saudi Arabia, because Jerusalem contains Baitul-Maqdis, or Al-Aqsa mosque, the second Islamic mosque ever built and one of the holiest; and the Dome of the Rock, the site from which Muhammad ascended to heaven, according to the Quran. It also serves as the first *Qibla*, or direction, that Muslims point during prayer. Thus, Palestine has played a tremendous role in the world's religious and cultural history.

The ancient name for Palestine was Canaan, and the people living there were known as Canaanites. By 1500 BCE their culture had given birth to the first known alphabetic writing system. During the late Bronze Age (1500–1200 BCE), Canaan was controlled by Egypt. A period of great religious activity, these centuries saw many temples built and the mythology of the Canaanite gods and goddesses inscribed in tablets.

The name Palestine resulted from the influx of the Philistines, who migrated to the region after Ramses III refused them entrance into Egypt. By the eleventh century BCE, the Philistines dominated Palestine's Mediterranean coast. Also during this period, the Israelites, who were nomads and farmers from Egypt, moved to the more remote highlands of the central hilly region of Palestine. They eventually wrested control from the Philistines and established a kingdom led by Saul and his successors, kings David and Solomon, who reigned from approximately 1020 BCE to 920 BCE. Historians claim that most of the Hebrew scriptures, which form the Old Testament of the Bible, were composed during this time in what had become ancient Israel.

After Solomon's death in 921 BCE, the kingdom was divided into two Hebrew states—Israel in the north and Judah (from which the name "Jew" derives) in the south—that were at war with each other for much of the next four hundred years. Israel was conquered from the south by the neo-Assyrian empire in 722 BCE, and Judah was defeated by the Babylonians, who lived to the east in present-day Iraq, in 586 BCE. This period saw the ascendancy of the kings Hezekiah and Josiah and the Hebrew prophets Isaiah, Jeremiah, and Micah. The Babylonians were soon conquered by the Persians, however, and the whole of Palestine came under the purview of the Persian Empire.

The conquest of the Persian Empire by Alexander the Great in 332 BCE ushered in the Hellenistic, or Greek, period, in which Hebrew was supplanted by Greek and Aramaic as the dominant languages. This influence remained after Alexander's death in 323 BCE, when the Alexandrian Empire was divided into the Ptolemaic Empire in the west and the Seleucid Empire in the east, and the Seleucid kings enforced the worship of Greek gods in Palestine. Under the leadership of the Maccabees, a Jewish rebel army, the Jews revolted in 167 BCE and established a Jewish state, which, by the time of the Roman conquest in 63 BCE, controlled much of Palestine. By 132 CE, however, another rebellion led the Romans to evict the Jews from Jerusalem and to establish the city of Aelia Capitolina on its ruins.

In 638 Muslim invaders built a mosque on the site of the ruins of the Jewish Temple in Jerusalem. Some Christians remained in isolated towns on the Mediterranean coast (such as Ramla, Jaffa, and Lydda). In 1099 Christian Crusaders from Western Europe took Jerusalem and imposed their own kingdom for nearly a century. For the most part, however, the inhabitants of Palestine became Arabized, converting to Islam and speaking Arabic.

In 1516 Palestine was conquered by the Ottoman Turks, whose empire dominated the region for most of a 400-year period until its demise during World War I. Egyptian ruler Muhammad Ali gained control of Palestine in 1832, and his son, Ibrahim Pasha, instituted a period of modernization there by establishing secular schooling and civil rights, so that Christians and Jews could exist somewhat on par with the Muslims. When the rural people rebelled against this secularism, the European powers forced Ibrahim out in 1840, and the Ottoman Empire regained control until British troops took power in 1918. In 1923 the British issued the Mandate for Palestine claiming administrative jurisdiction over the region west of the Jordan River for the next twenty-five years.

Modern Era In 1919 Jews represented 10 percent of Palestine's population; by 1944 they made up 32 percent of the population and owned 6 percent of Palestine's total land area. Many of the Jews immigrating to the area arrived during a period of increased anti-Semitism in Europe that culminated with Hitler's rise to power in 1933. The legality of the Jewish settlers' methods of land acquisition during the 1923 to 1948 British Mandate have been highly contested among historians and scholars, but ultimately Palestinian farmers and peasants who had worked the land for decades were suddenly dispossessed and forced to seek a living in the cities.

This event spurred an Arab revolt lasting from 1936 to 1939. Fears that the Arabs would side with the Germans in the incipient war led the British colonial government to issue a "white paper" in 1939 that limited Jewish immigration to 75,000 people over the next five years and guaranteeing an "independent Palestine state" within ten years. The Arabs rejected the delayed independence, and the Jews found the immigration quota unconscionable owing to the plight of the Jews in Europe.

In 1947 the United Nations General Assembly overwhelmingly passed a resolution calling for the partition of Palestine into separate Jewish and Arab states, with Jerusalem to exist under international administration. Jewish leaders accepted the plan, but the Arabs rejected it on the grounds that the Jewish minority presence did not justify creating a state at the expense of the Palestinians, regardless of the atrocities committed in Europe, and launched a guerilla war against Jewish forces in the region.

Jewish leaders declared the establishment of the state of Israel on May 14, 1948, the same day that the British Mandate expired. While Palestinian Arabs continued their guerilla war, the Arab countries of Egypt, Syria, Jordan, and Iraq launched the Arab-Israeli War, attempting an invasion of Israel on May 15 with disastrous consequences. Although the Arab forces vastly outnumbered the Israelis, they were fragmented along national, religious, and clan lines, whereas the Israeli forces were unified, regimented, and better armed. By mid-July, 1948, the Israeli armies were on the offensive, claiming territory beyond the area defined by the U.N. partition plan and inflicting casualties on Arab forces at a rate of two to one.

When armistices were signed between Israel and the surrounding Arab countries of Egypt, Jordan, Lebanon, and Syria in early 1949, Israelis accounted for less than a third of the population of Palestine but controlled three-quarters of its territory. More than half of the 1,300,000 Palestinian Arabs were living in refugee camps at the end of the war, including about 400,000 from lands designated for the Jewish state by the U.N. partition plan. The terms of Israel's armistice agreements with its Arab neighbors stipulated that the West Bank would remain under Jordanian control, while the Gaza Strip would be occupied by Egyptian forces until a permanent resolution could be reached.

In 1964 leaders from thirteen Arab countries formed the Palestine Liberation Organization (PLO) to establish an independent Palestinian state within the borders originally defined by the British Mandate. Tensions between the PLO and Israel escalated to another of the Arab-Israeli wars, this one better known as the Six-Day War, in 1967. Within six days Israel had captured the Gaza Strip and the Sinai Peninsula from Egypt; East Jerusalem and the West Bank from Jordan; and the Golan Heights from Syria. Despite calls from the United Nations for Israel to withdraw from all of these territories, Israel continued to occupy the West Bank and the Gaza strip.

In December 1987 Palestinian resistance to the Israeli occupation of the West Bank and Gaza Strip coalesced into a popular uprising known as the *intifada*, which literally means "shaking off" in Arabic. Although it was met with a brutal response from Israel, the intifada strengthened Palestinian self-reliance, as groups formed in each locality to organize resistance activities and provide medical services, food, and education to those who were in need. It also brought international attention to the plight of Palestinians. The major developments of this period include the rise of the militant Islamic fundamentalist group Hamas, as well as the official declaration of the State of Palestine, proclaimed on November 15, 1988, by the political wing of the PLO.

After much diplomacy and pressure from the United States, Prime Minister Yitzhak Rabin of Israel and Chairman Yasser Arafat of the PLO signed a peace agreement in September 1993 known as the Oslo Accords, which called for a five-year period of limited autonomy for the occupied Palestinian territories (the West Bank and the Gaza Strip) and further negotiations to develop a permanent solution after three years.

In July 1994 Arafat began his administration of Gaza and the West Bank town of Jericho, forming the Palestinian National Authority (PNA) as the governing body. In 2000 Arafat and the Israeli prime minister, Ehud Barak, convened at Camp David in the United States with President Bill Clinton to conclude the 1993 Oslo Peace Accords. The PLO refused to accept any terms that would not give the PNA control over the West Bank and East Jerusalem. After the talks failed, the Palestinians launched the second intifada, or the Al-Aqsa Intifada, and the Israeli Defense Force responded with force and strict civilian policing methods.

Before the end of President Clinton's second term, he offered a proposal by which the Palestinians would maintain control over the Gaza Strip and 97 percent of the West Bank, as well as jurisdiction of Arab areas in Jerusalem. Both sides claimed to accept this solution with caveats, but no conclusion was reached. In 2002 the United States formed an organization called the Quartet on the Middle East with the European Union, the United Nations, and Russia; the group mapped out a potential solution that would establish a Palestinian state in 2005. In 2005 a summit was held in Egypt to try to conclude the conflict. Despite a seemingly successful agreement, the announced cease-fire was broken days later.

In 2006 Hamas, labeled a Foreign Terrorist Organization by the U.S. Department of State in 1997, won elections in Palestine. By mid-2007 Hamas had seized control of the Gaza Strip. In response Israel stepped up its military control of borders. Also around this time Israel began deploying more powerful weaponry and technology, receiving international censure for the use of cluster bombs. In 2009 Israel initiated air strikes and sent ground forces to attack Hamas forces within Gaza. Around 1400 Palestinians died in this skirmish, and again Israel received international condemnation. This criticism continued through 2010, because of Israel's blockade of humanitarian aid destined for the Gaza Strip.

The United Nations granted Palestine nonmember observer status in 2011, and at the end of 2012, the General Assembly upgraded Palestine's status to that of a nonmember state, with 138 of 193 nations in favor of the proposal. The United States and Israel objected to the decision because it allows Palestine to appeal to the United Nations for consequences against Israel should that country commit war crimes.

SETTLEMENT IN THE UNITED STATES

Because no universally recognized Palestinian state exists for immigrants to claim as their country of origin, estimates of how many Palestinian settlers have arrived in the United States are often conflated with figures from other Arab populations. The numbers are also difficult to establish because until 1920, all Arabs, Turks, Armenians, and other Middle Easterners were classified as arriving from "Turkey in Asia." Only in the last few decades of the twentieth century did the Immigration and Naturalization Service recognize "Palestinian" as a nationality. Furthermore, Palestinian immigrants frequently arrive by way of a secondary nation, such as Israel; one of the Arab countries that received refugees from the Arab-Israeli wars, especially Egypt, Jordan, Lebanon, and Syria; or a country to which Palestinians immigrated in search of economic opportunity.

Palestinian immigration to the United States occurred in three waves, the first extending from the late nineteenth century through the early twentieth. The earliest group consisted of predominantly Christian people from the town of Ramallah who were enticed to seek opportunity in the United States by American missionaries stationed there. Their numbers increased after 1908, the year the Ottoman Empire began requiring military service of its subjects in certain regions. During the early years of the British Mandate (from 1923 on), Muslim Palestinians began to immigrate to the United States. They were primarily young men, although married men and some families followed when positive reports were sent back or when individuals returned home and displayed their success. Unlike the Christian Palestinians who preceded them, many of these immigrants sought to make money in the United States in order to return and live a more comfortable life, and often a family pooled its resources to send a member over in search of opportunity. Although they had not been peddlers in their homeland, the vast majority in the early waves of immigrants (both Christian and Muslim) took up the occupation, with some traveling across the country selling jewelry and other small items. As their numbers grew, a network of services developed—helping to bring new immigrants over and organizing and supplying the peddlers already here—adding a new level of jobs for the more experienced.

The particularly restrictive Immigration Act of 1924 reflected the isolationism prevalent in the United States between the World Wars. This, in addition to the Great Depression in the 1930s and World War II, served to reduce immigration greatly during the second quarter of the century. In the aftermath of World War II, the 1948 establishment of the State of Israel, and the 1948 to 1949 Arab-Israeli War, a second major wave of Palestinians immigrated to the United States, the majority of whom were highly educated Muslims hoping to return someday to their homeland.

The third and greatest wave of Palestinian immigration began after the 1967 Six-Day War and has continued to the present, peaking in the 1980s. In 1985 the Palestinian American community was estimated at approximately 90,000; by the end of the decade, its size had nearly doubled. While some Palestinian immigrants came to the United States for political reasons, the vast majority immigrated for economic and educational opportunity. Unlike early immigrants from Palestine, those who came after 1967 were highly educated. This change resulted from the efforts of the United Nations Relief and Works Agency for Palestine Refugees in the Near East (UNRWA), which established 700 schools in Jordan, Syria, the West Bank, and Gaza in 1950; this, in turn, increased attendance at universities in the Middle East and abroad. Thus, many in this third wave were professionals who met the preference for skilled and educated immigrants stipulated in the Immigration and Nationality Act of 1965. Immigration to the United States contributed to a "brain drain" of many of the most educated in Palestine specifically and in the Middle East in general.

With the failure of the peace talks between Palestine and Israel at the end of the twentieth century, many Palestinians have immigrated to the United States to avoid the considerable violence that has occurred almost continuously since then. Palestinian arrivals continue to be well educated, especially because the unemployment rates for the most highly accomplished professionals in Palestine increased after the second intifada, reaching 27.2 percent in 2008. Although the United States has encouraged Arab countries such as Syria to find homes for Palestinian refugees displaced by Arab-Israeli violence, the United States has also accepted a limited number of Palestinian refugees. Most recently, in 2009 1,350 Palestinians from Iraq were granted refugee status in the United States. This group settled primarily in southern California.

According to the American Community Survey administered by the U.S. Census Bureau, in 2010 the largest numbers of Palestinian Americans lived in California (18,442), Illinois (9,810), Texas (6,557), Florida (5,557), and New York (5,501). Other states with significant Palestinian populations included Ohio

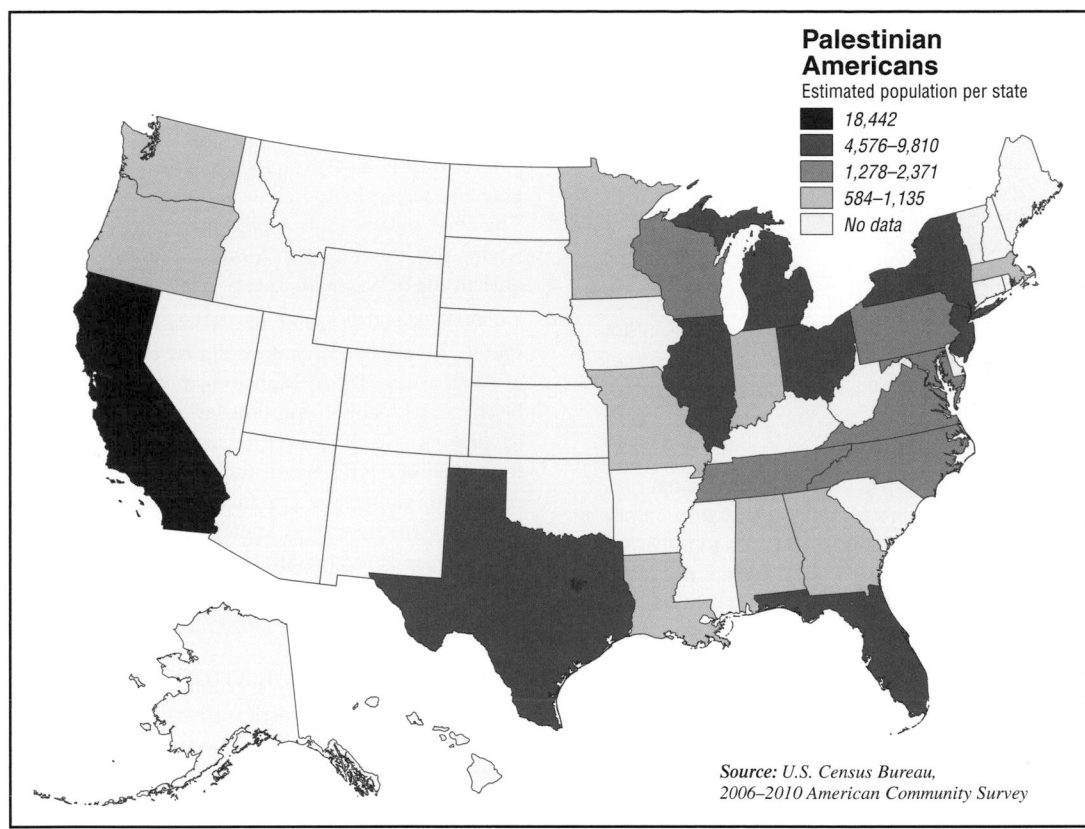

Palestinian Americans
Estimated population per state

- 18,442
- 4,576–9,810
- 1,278–2,371
- 584–1,135
- No data

Source: U.S. Census Bureau, 2006–2010 American Community Survey

(4,705), New Jersey (4,613), and Michigan (4,576). Patterson, New Jersey, has earned the nickname "Little Ramallah" for the large number of Palestinian Americans who live there.

LANGUAGE

Although many Palestinians living or working in Israel speak Hebrew as a necessary second language, Arabic has been the language of the Palestinians since the seventh century. Arabic is the youngest of the Semitic languages. It developed a sophisticated oral tradition through the poetry of the nomadic Bedouin tribes before it became the language of the Islamic religion and its holy text, the Quran, in the seventh century. As the Arab Empire grew, Arabic replaced Aramaic, Coptic, Greek, and Latin and became the main instrument of Arab culture. *One Thousand and One Nights* (known in English as *Arabian Nights*), a collection of folk tales recorded in Arabic in around the twelfth century, and the *Muqaddama*, a fourteenth-century history of the rise and fall of civilizations, are the great masterpieces of Arabic literature.

Arabic is the native language of virtually all Arabs, from northern Africa to the Arabian Peninsula. The dialects vary widely, though a common form called Modern Standard Arabic, a simplified version of the Classical Arabic of the Quran, facilitates pan-Arab communication. Modern Standard Arabic is the main

form of written Arabic throughout the Arab world, as well as the language used in radio and television broadcasts and in most schools. The Arabic alphabet has twenty-eight letters.

In Palestinian culture knowledge of languages is strongly emphasized, and many Palestinians arrive in the United States speaking more than one language, including English—some have learned English in school or through exposure to American media. According to the American Community Survey, in 2010 more than 70 percent of Palestinian Americans spoke languages other than English at home (presumably Arabic, though the survey does not explicitly state this). Of those who primarily spoke a language other than English, however, at least 70 percent also spoke English at least at a proficient level. Almost one-third of Palestinian Americans spoke English exclusively, though there were dramatic differences between those who were born in the United States and those were born elsewhere. Among U.S.-born Palestinian Americans, those who spoke only English constituted around 45 percent of the population, while 55 percent spoke both English and another language. Among foreign-born Palestinian Americans, only 10 percent spoke English exclusively, whereas up to 80 percent spoke both English and another language.

Greetings and Popular Expressions Common Arabic greetings include the following (in

DEAN OBEIDALLAH: THE MUSLIMS ARE COMING!

In the aftermath of the 2001 terrorist attacks on the United States, Arab Americans faced extreme scrutiny and even suffered violence at the hands of other Americans, who often viewed people of Arab descent as potential terrorists, no matter how long they and their families had been proud American citizens. In a matter of moments, they had become second-class citizens. For many Arab and Muslim Americans, such persecution led to feelings of isolation and exclusion. As Palestinian American comedian Dean Obeidallah put it, "September 10th, 2001, I went to bed a white American. On September 11th I woke up an Arab. I woke up an outsider."

Some Arab Americans responded by retreating to the margins of society and limiting their interactions to members of their family and to other Arabs in their community, Obeidallah chose to publically confront the stereotypes, using comedy as way of underscoring the things that Arab and Muslim Americans have in common with the rest of the country. In 2011 Obeidallah and three other Arab American comedians embarked on a tour of the Southern United States called "The Muslims are Coming!," offering free performances that touched on widespread fears about Muslim extremism and pointed out the absurdity of labeling all Arab or Muslim Americans terrorists. The performance was made into a successful documentary in 2012, and while racism and Islamophobia continue to plague American society, Obeidallah has used his newfound celebrity to pursue a singular goal: "It is my hope that in time, Muslims will not be defined to my fellow Americans by the handful of terrorists, but by the millions of others who are involved in all aspects of American life."

transliteration): *Issálamu alékum*—"Peace be upon you"; *Wi alékuma salám*—"And upon you"; *nahárik saíd*—"good day"; *saíd mubárak*—"may your day be pleasant"; *sabáh ilxér*—"good morning"; *misá ilxér*—"good evening"; *saída*—"good-bye"; *Maássalama*—"(Go) with safety"; *Izzáy issíha?*—"How are you?" ("How is the health?"); *Alláh yisallímak*—"May God keep you."

RELIGION

Although most Arab Americans are Christian—representing Eastern Orthodox, Roman Catholic, and Protestant churches—the vast majority of Palestinian Americans are Muslim. Islam is based on the teachings of Muhammad (ca. 570–632), who called on Arabs to surrender to the will of God (Allah) and to commit themselves anew each day. Muslims have five basic religious duties, which are known as the five pillars of Islam.

First, Muslims must repeat their creed, the *shahada*: "There is no God but the one God, and Muhammad is his prophet." The second pillar, *salat*, consists of ritual prayers said five times each day while facing toward Mecca, Muhammad's birthplace; also,

on Fridays Muslims attend a service at a mosque in which an imam leads the prayer and usually gives a sermon. *Zakat*, the giving of alms, is the third pillar. The fourth pillar requires the adherent to fast during the month of Ramadan, refraining from food, drink, and sex during daylight hours. It is also customary to pray and recite the Quran at night during Ramadan. The final pillar entails a pilgrimage, or *hajj*, to the Kaaba, the holy shrine in Mecca, to be made at least once in the believer's lifetime.

The sacred book of the Islamic religion is the Quran. It contains what are believed to be the words of Allah as revealed to Muhammad at different times by the angel Gabriel. Muslims believe that the words of previous, lesser prophets, including Moses and Jesus, were also given by Allah, but their messages were corrupted, and so the Quran was sent to purify the message. This message is known as the *sharia*, which provides guidance for all specific situations in life. Included are proscriptions against drinking wine, eating pork, usury, and gambling.

CULTURE AND ASSIMILATION

Although Palestinian Americans have generally managed a smooth transition to American life, many feel unsettled by the almost constant violence in their homeland and by the continuing lack of a sovereign Palestinian state. In addition, in the aftermath of the terrorist attacks on the United States in 2001, many Arab Americans, including Palestinian Americans, have experienced strong prejudice from other Americans, prompting them to feel that they have not been allowed to assimilate. Some find that although they are accepted personally, a distinction is drawn between them and their people in the Middle East, who are associated with the few extremists who commit terrorist acts to publicize the plight of Palestine. Palestinians Americans resent this characterization, and they often fault the U.S. media coverage of the Arab-Israeli conflict, which, in their view, does not do enough to educate the public about their history and the injustices they continue to suffer. Some feel, however, that the ongoing violence and the Israeli reaction to it has done a lot to dramatize the Palestinians' plight and turn public opinion towards a solution that benefits Palestine alongside Israel.

In efforts to reverse or revise the existing stereotypes of Arab Americans, many Palestinian Americans specifically have made great efforts to counter negative conceptualizations of them. They have highlighted the ways that they participate in American culture, including their contributions in comedy, music, and other arts; this serves as a way for them to present and circulate a stronger and more positive image that can transcend negative stereotypes. The prominent Palestinian American comedians Masoon Zayid and Dean Obeidallah have helped inaugurate and strengthen this practice.

Traditional Dress Because they did far more traveling than the women, men throughout the Middle East conformed to a fairly uniform style of traditional clothing: pants, a tunic, an over-garment secured with a belt, and sometimes a vest. Various styles characterized the clothing of Palestinian villagers, townspeople, and Bedouins, but within each group, the rich and poor were distinguished primarily by the quality of their garments' fabric. Both sexes covered the head as a sign of modesty and respect. Men wore a skullcap wrapped by a simple cloth, a more elaborate turban, or a *kafiyyeh*, a scarf secured by a cord. In the United States most Palestinian men wear Western dress, although they may wear the traditional *kafiyyeh* for special occasions.

In Palestine women traditionally wore an outfit comprised of pants, a dress, an over-garment, a jacket or vest, and a shoulder mantle. They often wore a bonnetlike hat trimmed with coins. In certain areas this was replaced by a *kafiyyeh* held in place by a folded scarf. Their dresses were very elaborate, at times sewn of as many as twenty-one individual pieces of fabric. The colors and embroidered patterns differed from one locality to the next and evolved over time. Fine embroidered dress panels were considered works of art and as such were handed down from mother to daughter. Jewelry was also a very important part of costume in traditional Palestine, and its function went beyond adornment and display of wealth. Amulets were worn to ward off the dangers of the Evil Eye, which was believed to take the lives of half of the population. Usually, what the upper classes wore in gold, the lower classes reproduced with baser metals or with less elaboration, such as necklaces that did not completely encircle the neck.

Most Palestinian Americans wear mainstream Western clothing; however, sometimes more ornate traditional garments are worn for festivals and holidays or on special occasions.

Cuisine As in most Arab cultures, Palestinian dishes feature beans, chickpeas, lentils, and rice as their staple ingredients. Water, oil, vegetables, and seasonings are added to produce different kinds of pastes, which are usually scooped up with pita bread—a round, flat bread with a pocket in it. Sesame seed paste or oil may be used to embellish a meal. Stews are very popular and may be made with a variety of different meats, especially lamb. Fish dishes are also common. Various kinds of salads and cooked vegetables complement these dishes, and one of a number of different kinds of yogurt often accompanies a meal. Desserts include sweet pastries such as *baklawa*, which is made with honey and chopped nuts, as well as fresh and dried fruits. Coffee and tea are the most common beverages.

Palestinian Americans often serve typical Palestinian dishes at festivals and holiday celebrations. In addition, many restaurants across the United States

PALESTINIAN PROVERBS

Koll 'ein o elha naTHrah.

Every eye has its look.

El-maktoob 'ala el-jabeen laazem etshoofol 'ein.

Whatever is written on the forehead is always seen.

El-wejh elly betSabHoh, keef elak 'ein etqabHoh.

You will not dare mistreating the face you see in the morning.

El-'ein elly btoakel.

The eye is the one that eats.

ET'am eththim, testHyl 'ein.

If you feed the mouth, the eye becomes shy.

El-'ein baSeerah wel-eid qaSeerah.

The eye sees, but the hand can't reach.

Gheeb 'an el-'ein, betgheeb 'an eThThehen.

Away from the eye, away from the mind.

feature Palestinian cuisine. One of these is *Mirage Mediterranean Restaurant* in Louisville, Kentucky. Restaurants in almost every major city in the United States focus on Middle Eastern cuisine in general but offer specifically Palestinian dishes as part of their menu.

FAMILY AND COMMUNITY LIFE

As with many other immigrant groups who came from a more traditional society to a modern Western one, the Palestinian immigrants in the first half of the twentieth century experienced a breakdown in the hierarchical and patriarchal nature of the extended family. Whether the father was away from home as an itinerant peddler or just working long hours, his authority decreased, especially when the mother was also involved with the family business. The influence of education, economic opportunities, and American culture generally led to the existence of more nuclear families with fewer children, though many Palestinian Americans maintain a strong connection to their extended family. Women's participation in the economic maintenance of the family reduced the number of restrictive customs over time. Aside from in some families that remained highly traditional, most Muslim women shed their veils when they emigrated, and Palestinian Christian and Muslim women generally ceased to cover their heads as they had been required to do in their former culture.

By World War II, women had become increasingly independent. They were more often allowed to remain single, and the family exercised much less control over their choices. The segregation of the sexes was mostly limited to mosques, and marriages occurred later in life and were not typically arranged. Many second-generation immigrants saw marriage as the opportunity to liberate themselves from parental control and to establish their own identity—one that was more in line with the mainstream culture that they had grown up with through school and the media.

Evidence suggests that in the 1990s, many families encouraged marriage to other Palestinians either through participating in community organizations that fostered social contacts with others in the group or even through traveling to hometowns in the Middle East to find potential spouses. Despite these efforts some interethnic and interreligious marriages took place, and in most cases this did not put insurmountable strain on relations between the generations. In the families that remained the most traditional, however, prohibitions on dating, limits on friendships with non-Palestinians, and even extensive restrictions on the style of dress were all used to limit the influence of American culture. When they existed, though, these conditions were much more likely to be applied, or more severely applied, to girls than to boys.

Although Palestinian Americans have generally managed a smooth transition to American life, many feel unsettled by the almost constant violence in their homeland and by the continuing lack of a sovereign Palestinian state. In addition, in the aftermath of the terrorist attacks on the United States in 2001, many Arab Americans, including Palestinian Americans, have experienced strong prejudice from other Americans, prompting them to feel that they have not been allowed to assimilate.

In the twenty-first century, Palestinian Americans of both sexes experienced greater freedoms than they had in the past. They engaged in Western dating practices, and they used social media as a way to socialize and get to know members of the opposite sex. More traditional households still arranged marriages or encouraged young adults to mingle at weddings and other community events in the hopes that they would meet a Palestinian potential spouse.

Courtship and Weddings In Palestine traditional marriages required a gift to the bride's family, usually money but sometimes real estate. Weddings lasted from three days to a week, beginning with celebrations on Tuesday followed on Thursday by a procession to the groom's house accompanied by singing, drums, and the firing of guns. Islamic law permitted a man to have as many as four wives, but a second wife was usually only taken when the first wife was ill or could not produce male children. In the United States many Palestinian marriage traditions have changed in order to conform to American law. Palestinians are encouraged to marry within their ethnic community and are expected to respect their parents' wishes when choosing a spouse. Many young adult Palestinian Americans marry spouses of their own choosing, however. The ceremony itself remains a festive event and celebrations may last several days.

Education Along with the Lebanese, Palestinians have the highest education rate in the Middle East. In the United States approximately 18 percent of Palestinian American men have earned a graduate degree of some sort, and 42 percent have earned at least a bachelor's degree. Of Palestinian American women, 13 percent have earned a graduate degree and 35 percent possess a four-year college degree or higher. Although they have always been aware of the politics and history of their homeland, Palestinian American students are increasingly taking an interest in studying Arabic and Arab culture more formally in college and graduate school. A number of Palestinian or Arab organizations are making an effort to monitor and improve the teaching of Arab history and culture in American schools.

Gender Roles Palestinian Americans have experienced notable shifts in gender roles during the last decades of the twentieth century and the early decades of the twenty-first century. Women are pursuing college degrees—including graduate degrees—at a much higher rate than ever before; 20 percent more women had a college degree in 2010 than in the mid-1990s. Women are also pursuing employment outside the home to a greater degree. Although, depending on their age, Palestinian Americans still hold to somewhat conventional gender-determined role responsibilities, this situation has altered as general practice has changed in mainstream U.S. culture. The number of women who participate in Palestinian American activist organizations also skyrocketed since the beginning of the twenty-first century, perhaps as a result of their community's response to the continuous, severe violence between Israel and Palestine during that period.

EMPLOYMENT AND ECONOMIC CONDITIONS

Many early Palestinian immigrants became itinerant peddlers in the United States, selling jewelry and trinkets that could be carried easily in a suitcase. They quickly learned enough English to emphasize that their wares were authentic items from the Holy Land. As this population grew, new opportunities arose for the more experienced to provide services related to bringing immigrants to the United States and setting them up in business as peddlers.

The large percentage of Palestinian immigrants arriving after the 1967 Six-Day War who were educated was reflected in the increased number of professionals among the community's ranks. This trend was even more prominent in the results of the American Community Survey for 2010: 38 percent of Palestinian American males were employed in management, business, science, and arts occupations and another 38 percent were employed in sales and office positions; the remaining males worked in service occupations (8 percent), the natural resources and construction industries (6 percent), and production and transportation (10 percent). Forty-five percent of Palestinian American women worked in management, business, or the arts; 17 percent worked in service occupations; 35 percent worked in sales; and 3 percent worked in production and transportation.

POLITICS AND GOVERNMENT

Although, historically, Palestinian Americans were not more politically active than the U.S. population at large, they have always remained highly aware of their history and the issues facing their homeland. They have traditionally been more active in social organizations, such as mosques, churches, and local associations, than in political ones, though the former have strong political implications. Until the recognition of Palestine as a nonmember state by the U.N. in late 2012, the unity and preservation of communities in the diaspora served to maintain Palestinian identity.

One example of this unity occurred in Jacksonville, Florida, where a large contingent of immigrants from the Christian town of Ramallah in the West Bank just north of Jerusalem formed a strong community. This population was long a close-knit Palestinian social unit, and it was strengthened by the formation in 1958 of the American Federation of Ramallah, Palestine, which now has more than 25,000 members nationwide. Until the mid-1960s the community identified primarily as having its roots in Ramallah rather in than Palestine. George Salem, a member of the Reagan administration who grew up in the community, said that in the 1950s and early 1960s, "We knew we were from Ramallah; we didn't really know whether it was Jordan or Palestine or what." But this perception changed after the PLO was formed and especially after the Israeli occupation of the West Bank. These events, culminating in the first intifada, heightened Palestinian American solidarity with those in their homeland and added a sense of urgency to finding a lasting solution to the Arab-Israeli conflict.

After violence and high unemployment rates in Palestine brought a more highly educated and vocal group of immigrants to the United States, many Palestinian Americans adopted a much stronger stance on the politics of Palestine; these individuals and others have been instrumental in founding notable activist groups, and their influence has been considerable, especially in relation to their emphasis on the formation of a Palestinian state. They view such a state as a potential means of diminishing the violence and bloodshed, particularly in the Gaza Strip.

Groups that supported the formation of a Palestinian state prior to the UN upgrading of Palestine from observer status were located mostly on university campuses; they subsequently spread to other sectors

Concern for the Palestinian people has inspired many to march in Washington, D.C. over the years. WASHINGTON STOCK PHOTO / ALAMY

of society. Membership in the United Nations allows Palestine to object to Israeli measures in a more robust manner. In addition, many Palestinian Americans wished to see the United Nations enact more effective resolutions, including one that would end Israel's blockade of persons and goods from entering or leaving the Gaza Strip that began in 2007.

Finally, because of the rise of prejudice against Arab-Americans in general, including Palestinian Americans, in the wake of the 2001 terrorist attacks on the United States, many young adult Palestinian Americans have taken it upon themselves to cultivate a more positive cultural and ethnic identity to combat the damaging influences of negative stereotypes. Persons involved in this type of activism have highlighted the artistic contributions that Palestinian Americans have made to the music, arts, and comedy industries.

NOTABLE INDIVIDUALS

Academia Edward Said (1935–2003) was a professor of English and comparative literature at Columbia University in New York City and the author of numerous scholarly and general interest books, including *The Question of Palestine* (1979). Born in Jerusalem in 1935, the son of Arab Anglicans (Christians), he was educated in Cairo after the family fled to that city in 1947. He served as a member of the Palestine National Council from 1977 to 1991.

Mohamed Rabie (1940–) is another of many Palestinian Americans in academia. He has a PhD from the University of Houston in economics and is professor of international political economy at the School of Governance and Economics in Rabat, Morocco. He has taught at many Arab and American universities, including Kuwait University and Georgetown. Among the many books on Middle East affairs he has authored are *U.S.-PLO Dialogue: Secret Diplomacy and Conflict Resolution* (1995) and *Global Economic and Cultural Transformation: The Making of History* (2013). He has also published fiction and poetry.

Business Tom Gores (1964–), is an American billionaire with ethnic origins in Palestine.

Film Cherien Dabis (1976–) is a Palestinian American director, producer, and writer named as an up-and-coming director by *Variety* magazine in 2009.

Government Justin Amash (1980–), a second-generation Palestinian and Syrian American, is a lawyer who was elected to represent Michigan in the U.S. House of Representatives in 2011.

George Salem served as chief legal officer for the U.S. Department of Labor during the Reagan administration. He grew up in the Jacksonville, Florida, Ramallah community. Even though the community had a strong identity and there were thirteen Ramallah families within a three-block radius of his

house, his parents discouraged him, unsuccessfully, from running for president of the student council at his high school because they feared his becoming too Americanized. He credits youth clubs and other social organizations with upholding a distinct Ramallan identity long before the turbulent events of the 1960s forged a larger Palestinian one.

John Edward Sununu (1964–) is a politician from New Hampshire whose paternal ancestors were Greek Orthodox Palestinians. He served in the U.S. House of Representatives from 1997 to 2003 and in the U.S. Senate from 2003 to 2009.

John Henry Sununu (1939–), John Edward Sununu's father and a career politician, has served as the governor of New Hampshire and the White House chief of staff for the George H. W. Bush administration.

Literature Susan Abulhawa (1957–), author of the novel *Mornings in Jenin* (2010), is the daughter of Palestinian refugees. She completed her graduate studies at the University of South Carolina and had a professional career in medicine before becoming involved in journalism and fiction writing.

Politics Alex Odeh (1944–1985), born into a Palestinian Christian family on the West Bank, was an Arab-American antidiscrimination activist. Odeh helped found the American-Arab Anti-Discrimination Committee, which provides legal counseling and general assistance to victims of anti-Arab discrimination and works to fight stereotypes of Arab Americans by educating the public, particularly through schools. Odeh was killed by a bomb in California.

Sports Oday Aboushi (1991–), a professional football player, was drafted in 2013 as an offensive lineman for the New York Jets. He was born in Brooklyn, New York, to Palestinian parents from the West Bank.

MEDIA

PRINT

American-Arab Message.

A weekly Arabic and English language paper published on Friday with a circulation of 8,700. Founded in 1937.

Rev. Imam M. A. Hussein, Publisher
17514 Woodward Avenue
Detroit, Michigan 48203
Phone: (313) 868-2266
Fax: (313) 868-2267
Email: imam4@juno.com

Journal of Palestine Studies

A publication of the Institute for Palestine Studies and the University of California Press, the journal was founded in 1971 and appears quarterly with information exclusively devoted to Palestinian affairs and the Arab-Israeli conflict.

University of California Press
Journals and Digital Publishing
2000 Center Street
Suite 303
Berkeley, California 94704-1223
Phone: (510) 643-7154
Fax: (510) 642-9917
Email: jps@palestine-studies.org
URL: www.palestine-studies.org/journals.
aspx?href=current&jid=1

Other Israel

Founded in 1983 and published four or five times per
year, the journal seeks to promote peace between
Israelis and Palestinians.

Adam Keller, Editor
405 Davis Court
Apartment 2106
San Francisco, California 94111
Phone: (415) 956-6377
Email: aicipp@mcimail.com

ORGANIZATIONS AND ASSOCIATIONS

American Arabic Association (AMARA)

Individuals interested in promoting a better understanding
among Americans and Arabs through involvement
in charitable and humanitarian causes; supports
Palestinian and Lebanese charities that aid orphans,
hospitals, and schools.

Dr. Said Abu Zahra, President
29 Mackenzie Lane
Wakefield, Massachusetts 01880

Bethlehem Association

Promotes understanding by the American public of the
Arab people and especially of Palestinian culture.

6161 El Cajon Boulevard #249
San Diego, California 92115
Phone: (619) 448-2200
Fax: (619) 448-2238
Email: info@bethlehemassociation.org
URL: www.bethlehemassoc.org

Institute for Palestine Studies

The institute produces the quarterly *Journal of Palestine
Studies*. It also develops outreach and information
about Palestine for the United States.

3501 M Street NW
Washington, D.C. 20007
Phone: (202) 342-3990
Fax: (202) 342-3927
Email: ipsdc@palestine-studies.org
URL: www.palestine-studies.org

Palestine Aid Society of America (PAS)

Founded in 1978, the PAS works to raise American
awareness of the Palestinian point of view of issues
regarding the Middle East. It also provides financial
aid to educational and community empowerment
projects in the occupied territories.

3325 Bluett Road
Ann Arbor, Michigan 48105
Phone: (734) 668-6430
URL: www.palestineaidsociety.org

Palestine Arab Delegation (PAD)

Presents the views of Palestinian Arabs on the special
political committee of the United Nations during
meetings of the U.N. General Assembly.

Issa Nakhleh, Chair
P.O. Box 608
New York, New York 10163
Phone: (212) 758-7411
Fax: (212) 319-7663

Union of Palestinian Women's Associations in North America (UPWA)

Promotes national and social self-determination
and independence for Palestine; strives toward
emancipation and empowerment of Palestinian and
Arab women.

Maha Jarad
3148 West 63rd Street
Chicago, Illinois 60629-2750
Phone: (312) 436-6060

MUSEUMS AND RESEARCH CENTERS

Institute for Palestine Studies

The institute was founded in 1963 to study the Arab-
Israeli conflict, as well as Palestinian cultural and
economic life in the occupied territories, particularly
in Gaza.

Dr. Philip Mattar, Executive Director
3501 M Street
NW
Washington, D.C. 20007
Phone: (202) 342-3990
Fax: (202) 342-3927
Email: ips-dc@ipsjps.org
URL: www.ipsjps.org

Oriental Institute Museum, University of Chicago

Founded in 1919 in conjunction with university
archaeological work in the ancient Near East, the
institute's collection contains art from Palestine.

1155 East 58th Street
Chicago, Illinois 60637
Phone: (773) 702-9521
Fax: (773) 702-9853
Email: oi-museum@uchicago.edu

University of Pennsylvania Museum

Founded in 1889, this museum contains materials
regarding Syro-Palestinian anthropology and
ethnology.

33rd and Spruce Streets
Philadelphia, Pennsylvania 19104
Phone: (215) 898-4001
Fax: (215) 898-0657
URL: www.upenn.edu/museum

SOURCES FOR ADDITIONAL STUDY

Abrams, Elliott. *Tested by Zion: The Bush Administration and the Israeli-Palestinian Conflict*. Cambridge, England: Cambridge University Press, 2013.

Abu-Ghazaleh, Faida N. *Ethnic Identity of Palestinian Immigrants in the United States: The Role of Cultural Material Artifacts*. El Paso, TX: LFB Scholarly Publishing, 2011.

Christison, Kathleen. "The American Experience: Palestinians in the U.S." *Journal of Palestine Studies* 18, no. 4 (1989): 18–36.

Cohen, Yinon, and Andrea Tyree. "Palestinian and Jewish Israeli-born Immigrants in the United States." *International Migration Review*, 28, no. 2 (1994): 243–54.

Hammad, Suheri. *Born Palestinian, Born Black*. New York: UpSet Press, 2010.

Kanj, Jamal K. *Children of Catastrophe: Journey from a Palestinian Refugee Camp to America*. Reading, England: Garnet, 2010. Print.

Kushner, Tony, and Alisa Solomon. *Wrestling with Zion: Progressive Jewish-American Responses to the Israeli-Palestinian Conflict*. New York: Grove Press, 2003.

Obenzinger, Hilton. *American Palestine*. Princeton, NJ: Princeton University Press, 1999.

Marshood, Nabil, comp. *Palestinian Teenage Refugees and Immigrants Speak Out*. New York: Rosen Publishing Group, 1997.

Shamir, Shimon, and Bruce Maddy-Weitzman. *The Camp David Summit—What Went Wrong?: Americans, Israelis, and Palestinians Analyze the Failure of the Boldest Attempt Ever to Resolve the Palestinian-Israeli Conflict*. East Sussex, England: Sussex Academy Press, 2005.

PANAMANIAN AMERICANS

Rosetta Sharp Dean

OVERVIEW

Panamanian Americans are immigrants or descendants of people from Panama, a country in Central America. Panama is bounded by the Caribbean Sea to the north, Colombia to the east, the Pacific Ocean to the south, and Costa Rica to the west. The country has a tropical climate with a dry season that extends from January to May and a rainy season that goes from May to December. Panama's land mass measures 29,762 square miles (77,381 square kilometers), which makes it slightly smaller than the state of South Carolina.

Panama has a population of 3,405,813 (U.S. State Department, March 2012), which is comparable to that of Los Angeles, California. The majority of Panamanians are Roman Catholic (84 percent), while the rest are Protestant (15 percent) or are Jewish or Muslim (1 percent). The majority of Panamanians, 67 percent, are of mestizo origin (mixed Spanish and Native American, or mixed Spanish, Native American, Chinese, and West Indian). The rest of the population is composed of various ethnic minorities, including indigenous peoples (12.3 percent), persons of African descent (9.2 percent), and Caucasians and Asians (11.5 percent). Many Panamanians have ancestors who arrived in the country from Africa (primarily through the African slave trade); others have ancestors who migrated from the West Indies, perhaps largely to gain employment, including working on the Panama Canal. Most of Panama's economy remains under the control of a small, elite segment of the population descended from Europeans, while 28 percent of the population lives below the poverty line, with 11.4 percent living in extreme poverty.

Panamanians have settled in the United States since 1820. Throughout the nineteenth and twentieth centuries Panamanians congregated in urban areas, especially in very large cities. In 1920, for example, when 49 percent of the U.S. population lived in rural areas, 87 percent of Panamanian Americans resided in cities. They gravitated to cities because their education, occupational skills, and lifestyles were suited to urban society and because these areas were more receptive to new immigrant populations. Most recently, one of the largest Panamanian American communities is in the borough of Brooklyn in New York City; in addition, large numbers of Panamanian Americans can also be found in Miami, Florida, and San Diego, California.

The U.S. Census Bureau's American Community Survey estimated that in 2009–2011 there were 176,287 Panamanian Americans; this is about the size of the population of Huntsville, Alabama. Panamanian Americans congregate in several regions across the country, including New England, the Pacific Coast, the Gulf Coast, the middle Atlantic, and the Great Lakes area. New York City contains by far the largest urban population of Panamanian Americans; mestizo, black, and native Panamanians living in New York numbered more than 30,000 in 2008.

HISTORY OF THE PEOPLE

Early History *Panama* was the native name of a village on the Pacific Coast of the Isthmus of Panama. Before contact with the Spanish, Panama was inhabited by a large number of Native Americans who lived in chiefdoms. They depended on the area's fish, birds, and sea turtles for food, as well as on starchy root crops. Numbering nearly one million when the Spanish arrived in 1501, the largest group was the Cuna. The country's name, which means "land of plenty of fish," may also come from the Cuna words *panna mai*, or "far away," a reply to Spaniards who asked where to find gold. The name *Panama* is also believed to be a Guarani Indian word meaning "butterfly," but also signifying a mud fish, perhaps because the flaps of the mudfish resembled the wings of a butterfly.

Since the 1500s the area that is now Panama has been controlled by foreign powers. In 1513 the Spanish explorer Vasco Nuñez de Balboa landed in Panama; crossed its narrow strip of land, or its isthmus; and reached the Pacific Ocean. From that time forward, the Isthmus of Panama has been a major crossroad of the world, linking the two American continents and separating the Pacific and Atlantic Oceans. Balboa's discovery opened up a shorter route to Peru and the silver of the Incan Empire. Fortune seekers from Europe could land at Colón, cross the narrow isthmus, and set sail on the Pacific for Peru. Shortly after his discovery, Balboa was condemned for treason and put to death with the help of a former aide, Juan Pizarro, who then used the route to conquer the Incas. Afterward, Panama became an important thoroughfare and supply post for Spanish conquistadors and later government troops, officials, and traders.

By 1519 Spanish settlements had been established, and the Spanish king's appointed governor, Pedro Arias de Avila, had settled in the village of Panama. Under his rule, Balboa's native allies were killed and other natives enslaved. Many fled to the jungle or to the swampland and isolated islands on the northeast coast. A priest, Bartolomé de las Casas, was outraged by the natives' enslavement throughout Spain's New World Empire and persuaded the Crown to end this practice. By this time, many natives had died from disease and mistreatment, while those who escaped had become isolated in the forests and swamps. The separation of native groups from European descended Panamanians remains today. African slaves became so important to the Spanish that the British were given a contract to deliver 4,800 slaves per year for thirty years despite actual and feared slave revolts.

From the beginning of the colonial era, the narrowness of the land had inspired the idea of building a canal through Panama. The Spanish, however, were disinclined to build one, as they wanted to keep rival fortune seekers away from the Pacific Ocean. For the next three hundred years, the only route from the Atlantic Ocean to the Pacific Ocean other than sailing around the tip of South America was a muddy jungle road through Panama, and travelers were frequently attacked. The area became hotly contested by European powers. British forces captured a fortress on the Atlantic side, Portobello, several times, and buccaneers troubled the area in the 1600s. The Scots attempted to begin a colony in Panama and open the land to trade in 1698, but they failed due to disease and Spanish resistance. Spain held on to the land and controlled its markets. From 1718 to 1722, the Spanish government in Peru held authority over Panama. Spain's viceroy of Granada (who ruled Panama, Colombia, and Venezuela) assumed control in 1739. When this government fell in 1819, the viceroy moved to Panama and ruled there for two more years.

Although Panama obtained its independence from Spain in 1821, close relations between the two continued. From the very beginning of Spain's relationship with Panama, natives of both groups had interacted and intermarried. These practices continued after Panama's independence, and the mestizo heritage—or Panamanians of both Spanish and native Panamanian heritage—continued to flourish. The ancestors of the modern Panamanian people managed to preserve their Spanish heritage despite governance by various European and Colombian conquests. At independence, Panama joined the new republic of Greater Colombia. This body was formed from a large majority of South America and sections of Central America between 1819 and 1830, and it included the present-day nations of Panama, Colombia, Venezuela, and Ecuador. The president of the country was Simón Bolívar, who assumed control in 1819 at the Congress of Angostura. Because of conflicts that arose between the various regions, the body was dissolved in 1830. Panama and Colombia remained joined until 1903.

The California gold rush in the late 1840s renewed interest in travel between the oceans, so in 1845 the United States helped to build the first transcontinental railroad across Panama. Meanwhile, France, Britain, and the United States explored the possibility of building a canal to join the two oceans by way of either Panama or Nicaragua. In 1879 Ferdinand de Lesseps of France, the builder of the Suez Canal in Egypt, began construction of a canal through Panama under a license from Colombia. After years of struggle with finances, the jungle, and especially disease (yellow fever and malaria), he abandoned the project. All told, 16,000 to 22,000 workers had died.

Modern Era In the early 1900s the Colombians fought a civil war—the War of a Thousand Days. Colombian rebels operated from bases in Nicaragua, passing through Panama on their way to fight in Colombia. Because the United States had a continued interest in building a canal in Panama, it intervened in the war and established a truce in 1902. In 1903–1904, with U.S. support, Panama declared its independence from Colombia, drew up its first constitution, and elected its first president. In 1903 the United States signed the Hay–Bunau-Varilla Treaty with Panama, in which a concession for a public maritime transportation service (or the building of a canal) across the isthmus was granted. The treaty also gave the United States control over strips of land five miles (eight kilometers) wide on either side of the canal. The United States did not own what would become known as the Canal Zone, but the treaty allowed it to lease the area "in perpetuity." In return the United States agreed to pay Panama $10 million plus an annual rent of $250,000, which was later increased to $1.93 million.

In 1904 the United States purchased France's rights to the unfinished canal for $40 million and began the herculean task of carving a canal through the isthmus. Many able and dedicated people were involved in this venture, including Americans and a considerable number of local workers. Among them were Colonel William C. Gorges, an army doctor who achieved a major triumph in wiping out yellow fever and reducing malaria, the mosquito-borne diseases that had decimated workers in previous attempts to build a canal, and Colonel George W. Goethals, an army engineer who was put in charge of the operation in 1907 and who later became the first governor of the Canal Zone. The giant excavation through the mountains of the Continental Divide at Culebra Cut, later renamed Gaillard Cut, was directed by engineer David Gaillard. After seven years of digging and construction, and the expenditure of $380 million, the Panama Canal was officially opened on August 15, 1914, and the U.S. cargo ship *Ancon* made the first transit.

After World War II, Panamanians opposed to the U.S. presence in the Canal Zone demanded renegotiation of the 1903 treaty, but it nonetheless remained in effect until the 1960s, when disputes again arose over U.S. control of the zone. The United States agreed to reopen negotiations concerning the Canal Zone, and in 1977 General Omar Torrijos Herrera, head of the Panamanian government, and U.S. president Jimmy Carter stipulated joint administration of the canal starting in 1979 and the complete return of the zone to Panama on December 31, 1999. The new agreements replaced the treaty of 1903 and turned over to Panama the governance of the Canal Zone and the territory of the Canal Zone itself, except for areas needed to operate and defend the actual canal. The United States remained responsible for the operation and military defense of the canal until December 31, 1999, after which it came under complete Panamanian control.

The presence of the canal changed lifestyles in the country. A people that had primarily earned their living as subsistence farmers now gained most of their income from the canal. The canal employs about 3,500 U.S. citizens and some 10,000 Panamanians.

The canal has resulted in sustained relations between the United States and Panama, and the U.S. federal government has had a large influence on Panamanian affairs. In 1988 General Manuel Noriega used his military prominence to seize control of the Panamanian government, establishing a dictatorship, which brought him great personal wealth. Previously supported by the United States, Noriega became the object of condemnation, based on evidence linking him to drug trafficking, murder, and election fraud. In an attempt to quash Noriega, the United States imposed severe economic sanctions on Panama. Although the Panamanian working class suffered from these actions, Noriega himself was virtually unaffected. In December 1989 a U.S. invasion of Panama led to the ousting of Noriega, who officially surrendered in January 1990. He was taken to the United States and convicted on drug charges in 1992. Since then, Panama has enjoyed a more democratic form of government.

SETTLEMENT IN THE UNITED STATES

Panamanians began immigrating to the United States in 1820 in numbers that have steadily increased. Overall, more than a million Panamanians have relocated to the United States over the past 175 years. However, the U.S. Census Bureau did not tabulate separate statistics for Panama and other Central and South American nations until 1960. In the 1830s only 44 arrivals were recorded, but by the early twentieth century, more than 1,000 came annually. After World War I, immigration numbers decreased, partially because of the Organic Act and other immigration legislation put in place during the early 1920s. The 1940 Census listed only 7,000 Central Americans; many apparently had died or returned home. A substantial number of Panamanians settled in Florida and California. An investigation of legal permanent residents, though, reveals high immigration rates during the 1940s and upon the conclusion of World War II, likely because of the influx of female Panamanians as brides. Over 15,000 Panamanians lived in New York in 1970, with fewer than 600 in San Francisco. After World War II, the number of immigrants increased rapidly, and by 1970, Central Americans numbered 174,000. In addition, it is believed that Panamanian Americans, in general, experienced a relatively warm reception from the United States, in light of the U.S. relationship with Panama itself (the country was designated a protectorate of the United States).

Paradoxically, the flow of emigrants from Panama was small for nearly the entire period in which there were no immigration restrictions on applicants from the Western Hemisphere, but increased dramatically after the 1965 Immigration Act, which imposed a ceiling of 120,000 admissions from that hemisphere. By 1970 Panamanians constituted one of the largest of the Central American groups in the United States.

Women outnumbered men among Panamanian immigrants by about one-third, in contrast to other Latin American immigrant groups, who typically had more men than women. The number of immigrant males per hundred females was very low in the 1960s, falling to 51 for Panama. The percentage of immigrants under twenty years of age was higher for males than for females; most female immigrants were between the ages of twenty and fifty, many of them service, domestic, or clerical workers who immigrated to earn money to send home, like many others from Central and South America.

Since 1962 the percentage of employed newcomers who are domestic workers has remained high, ranging from 15 to 28 percent. The entry of domestic workers and children after 1968 was eased by a new immigration policy with a preference system that established family reunification as the foundation for admission. As of 1990 there were approximately 86,000 people of Panamanian descent living in the United States. Twenty years later the population had risen to 176,287, according to the American Community Survey (ACS) estimates for 2009–2011.

Over the past few decades, more Panamanians have entered the United States through marriage and to pursue higher educational opportunities or to cultivate professional relationships. These trends have led to an increasing number of Panamanians becoming naturalized U.S. citizens and entering the U.S. military during the War on Terror. The 2009–2011 ACS reported that 65 percent of foreign-born Panamanian Americans had gained U.S. citizenship.

LANGUAGE

The Panamanian dialect is distinctive. For the first generation of immigrants, regardless of the period of arrival in the United States, Spanish was the primary language—Caribbean Spanish in particular. Subsequent generations spoke Spanish less often, eventually switching to English as their principal language. Among Central American ethnic groups,

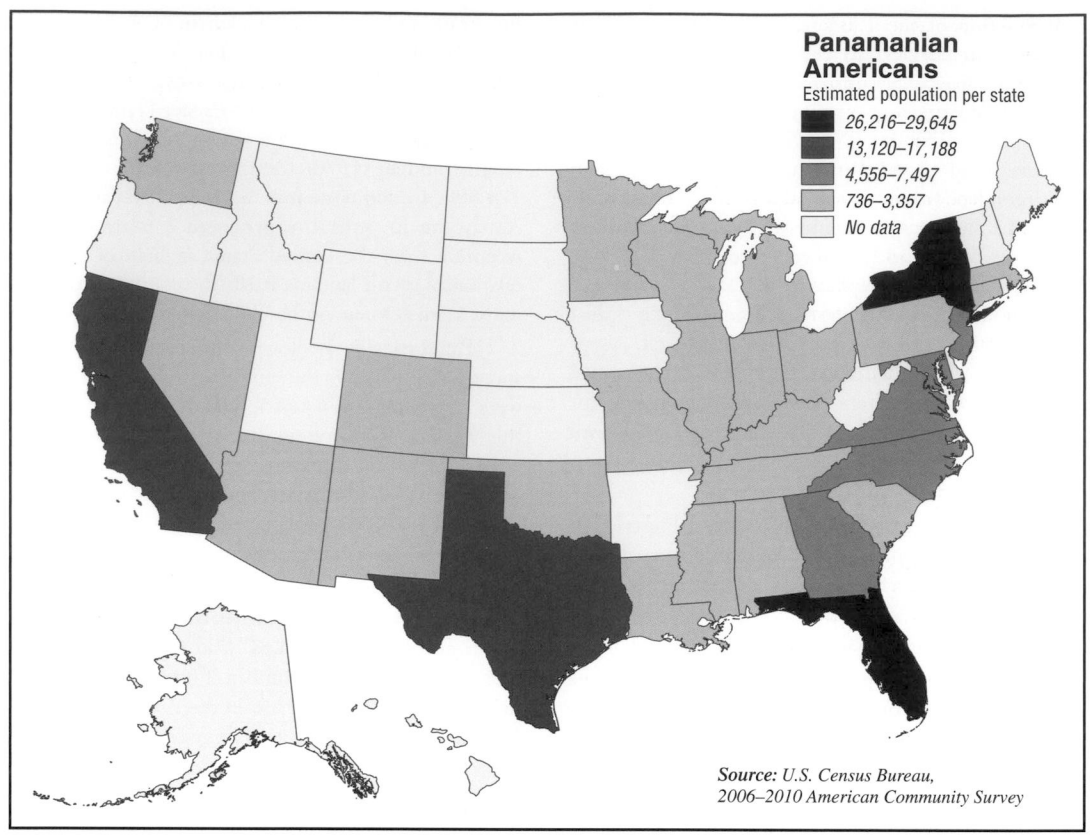

**Panamanian
Americans**
Estimated population per state

- 26,216–29,645
- 13,120–17,188
- 4,556–7,497
- 736–3,357
- No data

*Source: U.S. Census Bureau,
2006–2010 American Community Survey*

Panamanians are the most likely to speak English as their primary language in the home; 71 percent of them do so. This practice most likely results from the high levels of English instruction available in Panama due to the presence of U.S. citizens, military, and workers. Similarly, Panamanian Americans tend to intermix with other ethnic groups, including through marriage, which means that they have not stayed in isolated communities.

RELIGION

Approximately 84 percent of Panamanians nominally belong to the Roman Catholic Church, and 15 percent are Protestant. Most of these are Evangelicals, although other Christian denominations in Panama include Seventh-Day Adventists, Baptists, Lutherans, Presbyterians, and Unitarians. A small minority of Jews and Muslims are also found there. In Panamanian Catholicism, as in the Catholic tradition worldwide, much emphasis is given to the mother of Jesus, Mary, who is held up as an example for the women.

Although most Panamanians are Roman Catholic, church and state are separate, and religious freedom is guaranteed by the constitution. The religious sensibility of the Panamanians is reflected in their frequent celebration of religious holidays. Perhaps because of the diversity of their home country, Panamanian Americans practice a variety of religious faiths.

CULTURE AND ASSIMILATION

Little is known about the early Panamanians in the United States. Because the U.S. Census Bureau did not tabulate separate statistics for individual Central and South American nations until 1960, the characteristics of the individual national groups were buried in aggregated immigration and census statistics. It is often assumed that the Panamanians share a common culture with other Latin Americans. Although the majority of Latin Americans do share a Spanish or Portuguese heritage, they represent diverse peoples. In the past, insufficient knowledge of Panamanian ethnic characteristics generated misconceptions among Americans. This lack of clarity has been exacerbated by the fact that Panamanian Americans—like many peoples from Central and South America—identify with different ethnic groups. For example, some Panamanian Americans view themselves as African American, whereas others see themselves as Hispanic.

In general, Panamanian Americans have found ways to retain connections with Panama, one of which involves the numerous social organizations associated with Panama that exist across the United States. Some organizations arrange celebrations of festivals and holidays. Other Panamanian Americans have found new ways to conduct celebrations native to the United States, but which exalt Panamanian foods and traditions: the elaborate parade held in Brooklyn every year (in "Little Panama") in celebration of "Panama Day" is one example. The increased sophistication of communications technology has also assisted in this purpose. The fact that many Panamanians moved to the United States to obtain employment and sent funds home for support is another indicator of the sustained ties between Panama and Panamanian Americans. Despite these connections, however, Panamanian Americans in general do not seem to maintain as strong a tie to their home country as some of their Latin American counterparts. This may be because their culture in general is less homogenous than that of other Latin American countries. In addition, Panamanians became accustomed to U.S. workers living in their country to work to construct the Panama Canal, so Panama's interactions with the United States and other nations has been more fluid.

Traditions and Customs Urban and rural Panamanians share a certain set of common values. One of these values can be found in the idea of *personalismo* ("formal friendliness"). This term represents a belief in interpersonal trust and in individual honor and is accompanied by a distrust of organizations and a high sensitivity to praise or insult. Family is extremely important to Panamanians, and they value most highly members of their extended family. Within families a personal characteristic that is universally valued is *machismo*, the image of men as strong, daring, and dominant. Perhaps in contrast to this popular persona for males, is the expectation of women to be gentle, forgiving, and dedicated to their children. Other traits that are highly valued include *respeto* ("respect"), *confianza* ("trust"), and *familismo* ("closeness of the extended family"). Since Panamanian Americans are influenced by the customs of the United States, some of their practices have shifted these roles slightly. For example, women are now sometimes the heads of households in Panamanian American families. For Panamanian Americans, family continues to be a crucial and high priority, even if the distinctive roles and characteristics associated with gender and familial responsibility shift because of their experiences in the United States.

Besides Christian and Catholic holidays, Panamanian Americans also celebrate the Independence Day of Panama on November 3, the date on which Panama separated from Colombia. Panamanian Americans in New York have set up a practice of organizing a pre–Independence Day Parade (frequently in October). In other areas of the country, Panamanian organizations congregate for Independence Day parades as well, especially in Los Angeles and other cities in Southern California. Other holidays are also celebrated, though Mother's Day might be observed by some on December 8, as it is in Panama. Because of the strong Catholic tradition in Panama, Carnival might also be celebrated on the four days before Ash Wednesday, which begins the Catholic Lenten fast. In addition, the Festival of the Black Christ on October 21 inspires a lively celebration.

Dances and Songs Panamanian Americans most frequently demonstrate the traditions and customs of their heritage in celebrations like Brooklyn's Panama Day, held in "Little Panama". During such celebrations, Panamanian Americans don costumes, engage in their traditional dances, and sing songs that have been famous in Panama for generations. Other similar but perhaps smaller festivals are held around the United States. In general, Panamanians love festivity, and during their celebrations, one can see in their traditional costumes and folk dances some of the more colorful aspects of life in Panama.

It is often assumed that the Panamanians share a common culture with other Latin Americans. Although the majority of Latin Americans do share a Spanish or Portuguese heritage, they represent diverse peoples.

The tradition of Panamanian song and dance dates back to the seventeenth century. The national dance is the *tamborito*. It is of African origin and involves a man and a woman dancing and pretending to flirt with each other while surrounded by a circle of other dancers. Other couples take turns dancing at the center of the circle. The dance is performed to the beat of the *caja* and *pujador*, drums that were originally used by slaves brought to Panama from Africa and the West Indies during the colonial period. During the dance the woman wears the *pollera* (a full, long, white dress decorated with embroidery) or the *montuna* (a long skirt with bright floral patterns worn with a white, embroidered, off-the-shoulder blouse). The man's costume, the *montuno*, consists of a long white cotton shirt with fringe or embroidered decorations and knee-length trousers. The *tamborito* is especially popular during Carnival. Lively salsa—a mixture of Latin American popular music, rhythm and blues, jazz, and rock—is a Panamanian specialty. In addition to these genres, Panamanian music preferences also include jazz and calypso. More recently, reggae, especially Spanish reggae, has gained a strong following.

Panama's two traditional song forms are both derived from Spanish influences. The *copla* is performed by women, whereas men sing the *mejorana* to the accompaniment of a guitar, also called a *mejorana*. Another popular song form is the *saloma*, which is also performed by men using yodeling and falsetto tones. Los Angeles based Viva Panama has popularized Panamanian music in the United States and offers instruction in traditional dances and songs.

FAMILY AND COMMUNITY LIFE
During the first three decades of the twentieth century, the Panamanian American family underwent profound changes. The first immigrants were typically

single males who had left their families behind temporarily to save enough money to send for them later. In most early discussions of immigration, Panamanians were not considered separately from other Latin American groups. The number of African Panamanian Americans, for example, can be inferred only from the count of nonwhites in the 1960 and the 1970 censuses.

Demographics show that Panamanian families usually have two or three children. Panamanian Americans have a higher rate of divorce than their Latin American counterparts, which means that single mothers often serve as the heads of households. Grandparents often play a major role in childrearing, too. At the time of the 2000 U.S Census, nearly 50 percent of Panamanian Americans are married. The 2009–2011 ACS estimates indicated that that figure had dropped to 40 percent. Since many Panamanian American women work outside the home (65.6 percent were in the labor force, according to the 2009–2011 ACS), economic conditions have gradually improved, and immigrants have been able to purchase homes, cars, and modern appliances or to rent larger apartments in more prosperous neighborhoods.

Courtship and Weddings Most wedding ceremonies, as they have been traditionally practiced in Panama, involve two requirements: (1) the man and woman must say that they want to become husband and wife, and (2) the ceremony must have witnesses, including the official who marries the couple. If the couple has a religious ceremony, it is conducted by a member of the clergy, such as a minister or priest. If a couple is marrying in a civil (nonreligious) ceremony, a judge or other authorized official performs it. Panamanian American weddings are not all that different than standard American weddings, particularly Latino ones. Many couples prefer a traditional religious ceremony, though some Panamanians depart from this custom. Some even write their own wedding service.

Baptisms When a child is ready for baptism, the parents first select the godparents. The godfather—the *padrino*—and godmother—the *madrina*—are often the same couple who served as best man and matron of honor at the parents' wedding. The parents bring the child to the church, where the priest confers the sacrament by putting his hand on the child and then anoints the child on the forehead with holy oil. The baptism is completed by sprinkling the child with holy water. It is customary to have a banquet after the baptism.

Funerals A death in the family is followed by a funeral. The funerary practices include public announcement of the death, preparation of the body, religious ceremonies or other services, a procession, a burial, and mourning. The body typically is washed, embalmed, and then dressed in special garments before being placed into a coffin. Many people hold an all-night watch called a *velorio*. The funeral may include prayers, hymns and other music, and speeches called *elogio* that recall and praise the dead person. Many funeral services take place at a funeral home with the embalmed body on display. After the funeral, the mourners return home with the bereaved family and share food.

EMPLOYMENT AND ECONOMIC CONDITIONS

Panamanian American households have achieved relative financial success, as their median incomes exceed those of Latin American immigrants as a whole. However, as of 1999, about 13 percent of Panamanian American families lived below the poverty line. Ten years later, according to the American Community Survey (ACS) estimates (2009–2011), that number had not changed. Nevertheless, the ACS also showed that the median household income for Panamanian Americans was $48,365 (compared with $51,484 for the general U.S. population). Panamanian Americans have experienced an increase in the number of businesses they own; this trend has increased especially in the past few decades. In 2000 Census statistics indicated that 3.6 percent of Panamanians were self-employed in their own business; by 2011 the figure had increased to 4.8 percent. An upward surge continuing this type of economic growth is expected to continue.

Panamanian Americans are active members in the nation's workforce. The ACS (2009–2011) reported that 35 percent of employed Panamanian Americans were in management, business, science and arts occupations, 23 percent were in service occupations, and 28 percent were in sales and office occupations.

A Panamanian presence is evident throughout all departments and agencies of the federal government, including the departments of Education, Health and Human Services, Housing and Urban Development, and Commerce and Labor, Panamanian Americans are also represented in the Interior, Defense, and State departments, as well as the White House. During the past two decades, Panamanian Americans and other Hispanics have been ambassadors to numerous Central and South American countries.

POLITICS AND GOVERNMENT

Panamanian Americans are quite aware that their increasing numbers translate to increased political influence, and they are exerting political power that reflects their growing numbers and economic influence. In addition, they are carefully identifying issues that bring a measure of political unity to their diverse population.

Each Hispanic group has its own identity; nevertheless, they are finding that their commonalities provide them with a more effective political voice. In recent years Hispanic politicians have been rallying around points of commonality as their political involvement increases. Panamanian Americans have also made significant political contributions to U.S. foreign policy in Latin America. Domestic issues such as civil rights, affirmative action, and bilingual education have often brought them together in a unified front.

Three million Panamanian and other Hispanic voters are concentrated in six states, which, when combined, account for 173 of the 270 electoral votes needed to win a presidential election. This underscores the importance of Hispanics as a voting bloc, particularly in the Southwest. There has been a significant increase in registered Hispanic voters in recent years, and as more young Hispanics reach voting age, Hispanic strength as a political force will increase even more significantly. Hispanic political influence is directed by such organizations as the National Council of La Raza, the League of United Latin American Citizens (LULAC), National Image, and many others.

Panamanian Americans have even employed their power as U.S. citizens to influence political events in their home country. Specifically, the National Conference of Panamanians in New York influenced the creation of the Carter-Torrijos Treaties (1977) that guaranteed that control of the canal would return to Panamanian jurisdiction.

Cultural ties between the two countries are strong, and many Panamanians come to the United States for higher education and advanced training. In cooperation with the U.S. government, many Panamanian Americans provide needed resources, training, and cooperation with the U.S. Drug Enforcement Administration to fight illegal narcotics trafficking. In addition, Panamanian Americans have supported the renewal of democracy and stability in Panama and a fundamentally strong relationship with the United States, which had become severely strained by the Noriega regime during the late 1980s. Some Panamanian Americans are involved in developing business ventures in Panama. The practice of granting dual citizenship has also contributed to the political connections that Panamanians have sustained with their home country, even when they obtain U.S. citizenship. This practice has been in place since 1972, when the Republic of Panama adopted it.

NOTABLE INDIVIDUALS

Academia Kenneth Clark (1914–2005) moved to New York from Panama as a child and later became the first African American to earn a PhD from Columbia University. He was the first established

U.S. Army Specialist and Panamanian American Shoshana Johnson became the first female black American prisoner of war when she was taken prisoner during the war with Iraq. She was found by U.S. troops after the fall of Baghdad. Here she is being honored. STEFAN ZAKLIN / GETTY IMAGES

African American professor at the City College of New York and, with his wife, conducted numerous studies in racism, prejudice, and child development. Their now famous doll study provided empirical evidence for attorney Thurgood Marshall to successfully argue before the U.S. Supreme Court in *Brown v. the Board of Education* (1954), which decision outlawed racial segregation in education.

Government Shoshana Johnson (1973–) moved to the United States as a child and served in the Army after her graduation from college. She became the first African American female prisoner of war (POW) on April 6, 2003, in Operation Iraqi Freedom. Because of her Panamanian ancestry, she is considered the first Latina POW as well.

Music Danilo Perez (1965–) came to the United States from Panama as a young adult. He is a renowned jazz musician and has founded and organized the Panama Jazz Festival. His accomplishments include numerous Grammys for his piano, composing, and conducting abilities.

Sports Famous Panamanian American jockeys include Braulio Baeza (1940–), Lafitte Pincay (1946–), Heliodoro Gustines (1940–), Jorge Velásquez (1946–), and Jacinto Vásquez (1944–). These jockeys have

Panamanian American Rod Carew of the Milwaukee Brewers during Spring Training at Maryvale Baseball Park in Phoenix, Arizona, 2001. BRIAN BAHR / ALLSPORT / GETTY IMAGES

ridden at race tracks in Panama and at Belmont and Aqueduct in the United States.

Rod Carew (1945–) immigrated to the United States from Panama as a teenager and received a contract from Major League Baseball's Minnesota Twins upon graduating from high school. After twelve years with that team and seven years with the California Angels, he retired and was voted into the Hall of Fame in 1991.

MEDIA

El Diario/La Prensa

Appearing Monday through Friday since 1913, this publication focuses on general news in Spanish.

Rossana Rosado, Publisher
1 Metrotech Center
18th Floor
Brooklyn, New York 11201
Phone: (212) 807-4600
Fax: (212) 807-4617
URL: www.eldiariony.com

Mundo Hispanico

Founded in 1979 and published twice a month in Spanish with some English and distributed free or by subscription.

6455 Best Friend Road
Norcross, Georgia 30071
Phone: (404) 881-0441
Fax: (404) 881-6085
Email: mundohispanico@mundohispanico.com
URL: www.mundohispanico.com

ORGANIZATIONS AND ASSOCIATIONS

ASPIRA Association

A grassroots organization that works to provide leadership development and educational assistance to Latino persons, thus advancing the Hispanic community.

Ronald Blackburn-Moreno, National Executive Director
1444 Eye Street NW
Suite 800
Washington, D.C. 20005-2210
Phone: (202) 835-3600
Fax: (202) 835-3613

Hispanic Institute at Columbia University

Hernán Díaz, Associate Director
612 West 116th Street
New York, New York 10027
Phone: (212) 854-8787
Fax: (212) 854-7509
Email: hdiaz@columbia.edu
URL: www.columbia.edu/cu/spanish/hispanicinstitute/hispinstintro.html

Las Molas Association

Organizes events such as Panamanian holiday celebrations and contracts with local performers to present cultural dances.

P.O. Box 8295
Lacey, Washington 98509
Phone: (425) 264-6529
Email: lasmolas2006@yahoo.com
URL: http://lasmolasassociation.com

National Council of La Raza

A Pan-Hispanic organization founded in 1968 that provides assistance to local Hispanic groups, serves as an advocate for all Hispanic Americans, and is a national umbrella organization for eighty formal affiliates throughout the United States.

1126 16th Street NW
Washington, D.C. 20002
Phone: (202) 785-1670
URL: www.nclr.org

National Panamanian Friendship Reunion, Inc.

Organizes a gathering every July at various locations around the United States. It attracts Panamanians from across the United States and Panama.

P.O. Box 35873
Fayetteville, North Carolina 28303
Phone: (910) 904-0306
URL: www.panamanianreunion.org/index.htm

SOURCES FOR ADDITIONAL STUDY

Chambers, Veronica. *Mama's Girl*. New York: Riverhead Books, 1996.

Dolan, Edward F. *Panama and the United States: Their Canal, Their Stormy Years*. New York: Franklin Watts, 1990.

Harding, R. C. *The History of Panama*. Westport, CT: Greenwood Press, 2006.

Hartson, W. "Ten Things You Never Knew about Panama." *Express*, December 12, 2007.

Jones, K. J., ed. *Focus on Panama*. Vol. 10. Panama: Focus, 1981.

Labrut, M. *Getting to Know Panama*. 2nd ed. El Dorado, Panama: Focus Publications, 1997.

Soley, L. Seales. *The Culture and Customs of Panama*. Westport, CT: Greenwood Press, 2009.

Webb, S. C., et al. *A Mosaic: Hispanic People in the United States*. New Orleans: Defense Equal Opportunity Management Institute, Topical Research Intern Program, 1991.

Wright, Almon R. *Panama: Tension's Child, 1502–1989*. New York: Vantage Press, 1990.

PARAGUAYAN AMERICANS

Olivia Miller

OVERVIEW

Paraguayan Americans are immigrants or descendants of people from Paraguay, a landlocked country located in South America. Paraguay is bordered by the countries of Brazil, Argentina, and Bolivia, and it is sometimes called *Corazón de América* (Heart of America) because of its central location. The country is named after the Río Paraguay, which is the third largest river in the Western Hemisphere and flows from north to south across the country. Eastern Paraguay's geography is typified by grasslands and wooded hills. The western part of the country is dominated by an infertile and sparsely populated region of low wetland plains known as the Gran Chaco or simply "the Chaco." With a total area of 157,048 square miles (406,752 square kilometers), Paraguay is slightly smaller than the state of California.

According to a 2012 estimate by the *CIA World Factbook*, Paraguay has a population of 6.54 million. More than 98 percent of the population lives in the eastern part of the country in and around major cities such as Asunción (the capital and a large commercial port), Encarnación, Concepción, Coronel Oviedo, and Caaguazú. The majority of Paraguayans are *mestizos*, descendants of the country's indigenous Guarani people and Spanish colonists. Nearly 90 percent of Paraguayan citizens are Roman Catholic, though the Gran Chaco population also includes some Mennonites, a German-speaking religious group that came to Paraguay mostly from western Russia, Canada, and Mexico. Paraguay remains one of South America's poorest and least-developed countries, with an economy based largely on agriculture and some limited manufacturing for local consumption. Its large untaxed informal sector makes specific numbers difficult to ascertain, but the *CIA World Factbook* reports that the near 15 percent growth of the Paraguayan economy during 2010 was the highest in South America.

Paraguayans began immigrating to the United States in notable numbers during the country's civil war in 1947, and many of them settled in major metropolitan areas such New York, Miami, Los Angeles, Dallas, and Atlanta. Although some Paraguayans immigrated for political reasons or to escape civil disturbance, many were young people seeking educational opportunities to develop professional knowledge and skills and to find better jobs. For similar reasons, Paraguayans also immigrated in even larger numbers to neighboring countries such as Brazil and Argentina. Since the late 1940s, Paraguayans have continued to immigrate to the United States, but in fairly small numbers compared with immigration from many other Latin American countries.

The U.S. Census Bureau's American Community Survey estimates for 2009–2011 listed the population of Paraguayan Americans at 22,000 though a large number of undocumented Paraguayan immigrants likely makes the actual population much higher. This number is more than double the 8,769 population in the 2000 U.S. Census but still makes Paraguayan Americans the smallest Hispanic immigrant group specifically identified by the census. The highest concentration of Paraguayans in the United States is in Somerset County (New Jersey), while Queens County (New York), Westchester County (New York), Los Angeles County (California), Miami-Dade County (Florida), and Montgomery County (Maryland) also boast a significant population of Paraguayans. In addition, the state of Kansas, which has partnered with Paraguay in an exchange program through a nonprofit volunteer organization called Partners of the Americas, is home to many Paraguayans.

HISTORY OF THE PEOPLE

Early History Before the arrival of Europeans, Paraguay's indigenous Guarani lived as a group of semi-nomadic tribes in the southeastern part of the country, subsisting on fish, wild game, and a shifting crop of maize (corn) and manioc (cassava). Early Paraguayans developed five distinct language families, and today seventeen different ethno-linguistic groups remain in the country. In 1524, with the aid of Guarani guides, Aleixo García became the first European to cross the region of Paraguay. Thirteen years later, Spanish explorer Juan de Salazar founded Asunción, which would become the capital city of present-day Paraguay. By the mid-sixteenth century, the Roman Catholic church of Spain dispatched missionaries to subdue and "civilize" the indigenous people, who were known for their fierce warrior tradition.

In 1609 Jesuit missionaries organized about 100,000 Guarani into communal settlements called *reducciones* and for 150 years protected the native population from exploitation attempts by incoming colonial settlers. Conflicts with Spanish rulers, however, resulted in a royal decree that banished the Jesuits from all of Spain's colonies in 1767.

From the middle of the **sixteenth** century to the beginning of the nineteenth century, Paraguay was ruled by a succession of European governors. The native population gradually absorbed the Spaniards, who in turn adopted Guarani food, language, and customs. Over time, a Spanish Guarani society emerged, with Spaniards dominating politically and the mestizo offspring adopting Spanish cultural values.

Modern Era Paraguay declared its independence from Spain in 1811 and fell under the rule of dictator José Gaspar Rodríguez de Francia (known as "El Supremo"), who closed the country's borders and kept it isolated from the rest of the region. Upon Francia's death in 1840, successor Carlos Antonio López ended Paraguay's isolation and began the process of modernization. The first official U.S. notice of Paraguay occurred in 1845 when President James K. Polk appointed Edward Augustus Hopkins as special agent to the nation. In 1854 the two countries engaged in a brief military skirmish after Paraguayan gunners fired on an American ship sent to conduct scientific research on local rivers. The United States responded by sending 19 ships and 2,500 men to force Paraguay to pay damages for the incident. The expedition ultimately failed however, as ships from the United States were unable to reach Asunción because the river was too shallow during that season. Polk's administration was unable to force Paraguay to give in to its demands for reparations and both nations eventually accepted mediation.

Paraguay suffered disastrous consequences from the War of the Triple Alliance (1864-1870), a conflict between Paraguay, Argentina, Uruguay, and Brazil in which Paraguay lost more than one-half its population and territory. After the war, the United States sided with Paraguay in a land dispute with Argentina. The land won by Paraguay as a result of U.S. mediation was dubbed "Presidente Hayes" in honor of U.S. President Rutherford B. Hayes and his role in the mediation. In the wake of the War of the Triple Alliance, Paraguay's agricultural sector was resuscitated by a new wave of European and Argentine immigrants, but political instability persisted.

A succession of presidents governed under the banner of the Colorado Party from 1880 to 1904, when the Liberal Party seized control and ruled with only a brief interruption until 1940. In the 1930s and 1940s, Paraguayan politics were defined by periods of extreme uncertainty brought on by the Chaco War with Bolivia, its own civil war in 1947, and the rise and fall of several dictatorships. In 1945 Paraguay became a charter member of the United Nations.

For much of the latter half of the twentieth century, Paraguay was ruled by General Alfredo Stroessner, who took power in May 1954 and began a thirty-four-year reign of oppression, persecution, and harassment in the name of national security and anticommunism.

On May 9, 1993, Juan Carlos Wasmosy of the Colorado Party was elected as Paraguay's first civilian president in almost forty years. International observers deemed the election fair and free, but political unrest continued to plague Paraguay throughout the 1990s and early 2000s, as the country suffered through an attempted military coup and the assassination of a vice president. In 2008 the election of leftist former Roman Catholic bishop Fernando Lugo was hailed by supporters as a historic victory after six decades of conservative rule. Lugo served as president for four years but was impeached and removed from power in June 2012.

SETTLEMENT IN THE UNITED STATES

The first Paraguayans probably arrived in the United States between 1841 and 1850, though early records merely classify them as "other" South Americans entering the United States from origins outside of Brazil, Argentina, and Peru. Numbers of Paraguayans immigrating to the United States began to increase during Paraguay's civil war in 1947 and continued in fairly steady, if comparatively small, numbers through the second half of the twentieth century. The high watermark may have been the late 1970s, when about 11,000 Paraguayans immigrated to the United States in 1979. In the years immediately following, the numbers began to steadily decline, and according to the Office of Homeland Security, fewer than 1,500 Paraguayans entered the United States during a three-year period from 2009 to 2011. Today, Somerset County (New Jersey), Queens County (New York), Westchester County (New York), Atlanta, Los Angeles, Miami, and Montgomery County (Maryland) all have notable Paraguayan American communities.

Some immigrants from Paraguay were also infants adopted by American families. In 1989, 254 adoptions were completed in Paraguay. In 1993 U.S. citizens adopted 405 Paraguayan infants, and in 1995 they adopted 351. However, according to the U.S. State Department, international adoption is no longer allowed in Paraguay. From 1999 to 2011 only 11 Paraguayan children were adopted by families in the United States.

A significant percentage of unskilled Paraguayan Americans have taken jobs in the service industry in urban areas such as New York, Chicago, New Jersey, and Minneapolis. Some Paraguayan American women have also accepted jobs in hotel housekeeping, an employment opportunity that other Americans felt was unattractive. Although some Paraguayan Americans are professionals who immigrated in search of better pay and more stable social conditions, others have found agricultural employment in California and in Kansas. Kansas, in particular, has become a magnet for

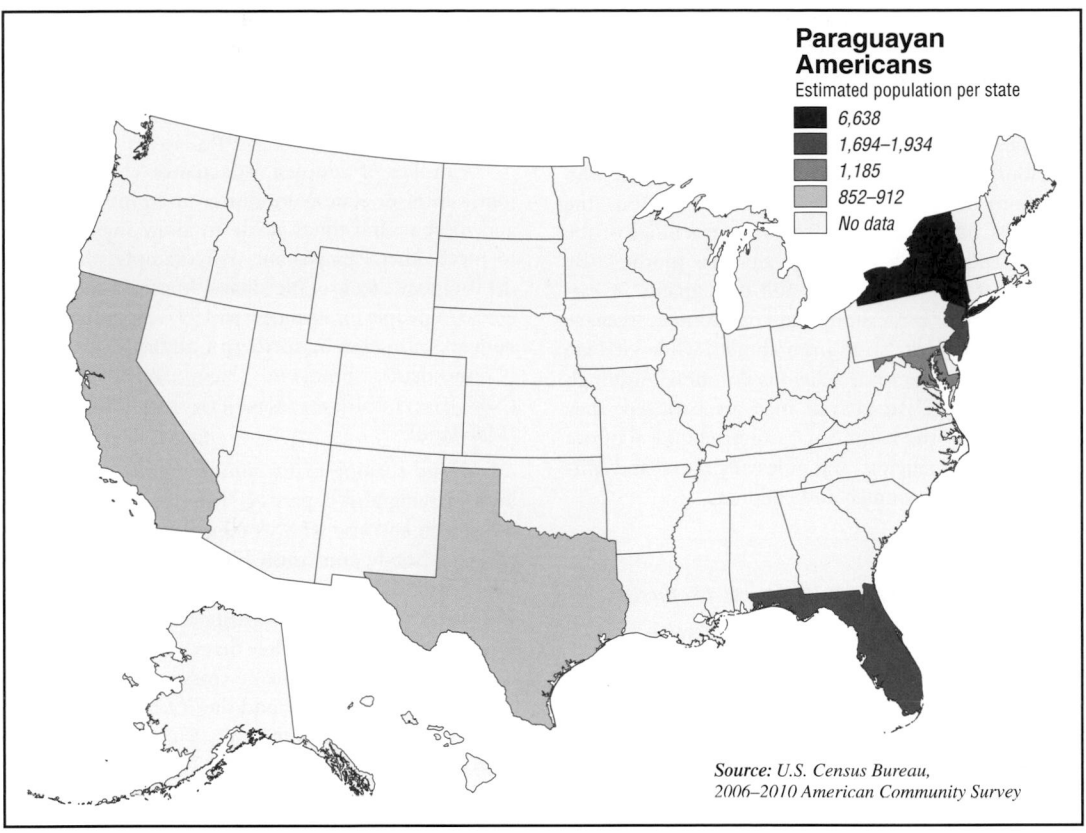

Paraguayan Americans
Estimated population per state

- 6,638
- 1,694–1,934
- 1,185
- 852–912
- No data

Source: U.S. Census Bureau,
2006–2010 American Community Survey

Paraguayan Americans. The state's popularity among Paraguayans is largely a result of the efforts of Kansas Paraguay Partners and its Paraguayan counterpart, the Comité Paraguay Kansas. Both of these volunteer organizations work to promote reciprocal exchange programs between Paraguay and Kansas. Together, the groups have facilitated a popular program that allows both Kansan and Paraguayan college students to study abroad in their counterpart countries. Kansas Paraguay Partners and Comité Paraguay Kansas also facilitate high school exchanges, medical exchanges, and cultural exchanges to promote the link between Kansas and Paraguay.

LANGUAGE

The two official languages of Paraguay are Spanish and its indigenous Guarani, with about 70 percent of the population speaking and understanding Spanish and about 90 percent of Paraguayans speaking and understand Guarani. With such a high percentage of the population speaking both languages, the country boasts that it is truly bilingual. Continuing to speak Guarani is one way many Paraguayans distinguish themselves from other South American peoples.

Guarani is an oral language first recorded in written form by the Jesuit missionaries who arrived in Paraguay in the sixteenth century. The Guarani alphabet contains 33 signs, including 12 vowels and 21 consonants written as either single letters or digraphs. Vowel sounds are classified as either oral or nasal and are generated by a continuous, unrestricted flow of air through the nose and mouth. In modern Paraguayan orthography, the nasal vowels of Guarani are represented with the nasal tilde (~) over the oral version of the vowel. Consonants are produced by restricting or stopping the flow of air through the nose or mouth by putting both lips together or touching the tongue to the teeth.

Guarani-speaking native Paraguayans express greetings with the word "*Maitei.*" For example, "Send my greeting to your mother" is "*Maitei nde sipe.*" Other forms of courtesy include "*Mba eichapa neko'e?*" which means "good morning, how are you?" The language of the Guarani is oral and onomatopoeic as well as being adaptive and modern. For example, it has incorporated words for "television" and "representative democracy."

Many Paraguayan Americans use Spanish to navigate American culture, but first-generation Paraguayan immigrants typically learn English.

RELIGION

Roman Catholicism was established as Paraguay's state religion in 1547, and Jesuit missionaries continued to propagate the faith among the Guarani people for 100 years afterward. Today, it is estimated that nearly 90 percent of the population identify themselves as Roman Catholic, though there are increasing numbers of evangelical Protestants and Mormons in the country. Paraguay's 1967 constitution guarantees freedom of religion, but law still requires that the president be Roman Catholic.

For Paraguayan American families, the role of religious instruction usually falls to the mother, who functions as the family representative before the church. Children are exposed to the teachings of the church and are taken to mass by their mothers. By the age of ten, children are full participants in catechism classes, confession, and communion. Teenage boys typically drift away from church, while girls are encouraged to continue religious devotion. Although the majority of Paraguayan men are baptized, they tend to follow the Latin American macho ideal of not being strongly religious and of leaving moral and spiritual concepts to women and children.

The Spanish influence on Paraguayan culture has prepared Paraguayan Americans to be at home in American culture. Because most Paraguayans speak Spanish, and because of the growth of the Hispanic ethnic group in the United States, many Paraguayan Americans are able to communicate in American society with less difficulty than before.

CULTURE AND ASSIMILATION

Because about 4,000 South Americans immigrated to the United States each year from 1910 to 1930, the population of the United States now includes third- and fourth-generation Paraguayan Americans. U.S. Census statistics indicate that by 2010 there were more than 2.7 million people of South American descent living in the United States, with major settlements concentrated in cities such as New York and Chicago. Paraguayan Americans gravitated toward urban areas because their education, occupation skills, and lifestyles matched urban life.

The Spanish influence on Paraguayan culture has prepared Paraguayan Americans to be at home in American culture. Because most Paraguayans speak Spanish, and because of the growth of the Hispanic ethnic group in the United States, many Paraguayan Americans are able to communicate in American society with less difficulty than before. Newsstands offer publications in Spanish, banks provide automated tellers in Spanish, and many retail stores have Spanish-speaking salespeople. Many product labels and instructions include a Spanish version and grocers offer products known and consumed by the Hispanic community.

Traditions and Customs Because most Paraguayan Americans have a Roman Catholic heritage, their customs and traditions are similar to those of all Latin American groups. In general, attitudes toward community and family follow the traditional Hispanic heritage of emphasis on bonds of family loyalty. Paraguayan Americans establish kin-based mutual support by settling in communities where other Paraguayan Americans live.

Families of adopted Paraguayan children often join a local or state community of adoptive families and meet several times yearly to allow their children to meet other Paraguayans. For example, the Niños del Paraguay Picnic of Needham, Massachusetts, gathered 625 people for its picnic in 1997. Adoptive family networks also exist in northern California, Unionville (Connecticut), Brooklyn (New York), Princeton (New Jersey), Fairlawn (New Jersey) and Silver Spring (Maryland).

Hand shaking is the common greeting done on both arriving and departing. Men shake hands with other men and also with women. Women friends will embrace briefly and brush both cheeks in a pretend kiss. This is different from most other South American countries, where women brush cheeks only on one side. Two American gestures that can cause offense are the "good luck" sign made by crossing the middle finger over the index finger, and the "O.K." gesture, with thumb and forefinger forming a circle. Tilting the head backward signifies "I forgot." Winking is usually done only for romantic or sexual connotations.

Cuisine Paraguayan foods are simple but tasty. The most popular dishes consist of maize (corn), meat, milk, and cheese. In general, Paraguayan cuisine is very similar to that of Argentina. For example, *milanesa*, a breaded fillet of meat typically served with potatoes, is a common dish among both Argentine and Paraguayan Americans. The same is true of *empanadas*, which are pastries with savory filling, and *asado*, which refers to grilled beef and other meats. However, Paraguay has a number of unique traditional foods that are consumed by Paraguayan Americans.

Two of the most common traditional foods among Paraguayan Americans are *chipa guazu*, a maize casserole eaten as a side dish, and *mbeyu*, a bread made of manioc (cassava) flour and cheese. Manioc, a starchy tuber, is the main source of carbohydrates in many Paraguayan dishes and is added to just about everything. Meat dishes as well as tropical and subtropical foodstuffs play an important role in the Paraguayan diet. Along with *asado*, another favorite meat dish is *guiso*, made with sausage or organ meat with rice browned in oil and flavored with tomato paste and onion. Main dishes are often accompanied by toasted *chipa*—small, baked, cheese-flavored rolls.

Puchero, a meat stew, is made of boiled hominy and chopped parsley, pepper, squash, carrots, or tomatoes. It is flavored with garlic or onion, and thickened with rice or maize-meal dumplings. Bori-Bori is a Paraguayan dumpling soup similar to other dumpling-style soups common in South America.

Grains, particularly maize, and manioc are incorporated into almost all Paraguayan meals. A typical meal includes *locro* (a maize stew), *mazamorra* (maize-meal mush), *mbaipy so ó* (a hot maize pudding with meat chunks), and *so'o yosopy* (a thick soup made of ground meat and served with rice or noodles). Desserts include *mbaipy he é* (a mix of maize, milk, and molasses).

For ceremonial occasions and traditional Paraguayan holidays, Paraguayan Americans often smoke pork in brick ovens and serve it with *pastel mandio* (an empanada made with manioc), *chipa gauzu*, chicken *milanesa*, *asado*, turkey, and generous portions of *sopa paraguaya*, which is prepared using maize meal cooked in oil with milk, eggs, cheese, onion, and other ingredients. *Clerico*, a drink similar to sangria, is also typically served.

Traditional drinks preferred by Paraguayan Americans include a locally produced dark rum made from sugar cane called *caña*, *mate* (green tea), *mosto* (sugar-cane juice) and *terere* (an infusion of *yerba mate* as well as cold water sometimes flavored with medicinal herbs).

Traditional Dress Traditional clothing worn by Paraguayans is similar to that worn by other Latin American countries, though Paraguayan women favor particularly bright colors. It is uncommon among Paraguayan Americans to dress traditionally, but they do often incorporate *ao' poi*, a kind of fine linen cloth embroidered with threads of the same color, generally white. In addition to being popular among Paraguayans in the United States, *ao' poi* shirts, blouses, tablecloths, and napkins are in great demand around the world.

Traditional Arts and Crafts Like many South American countries that fell under European rule, Paraguay's artisan culture has been partially influenced by Spanish colonialism. This can be seen in the arts and crafts produced there today, including folk art and handmade products such as guitars, pottery, and jewelry that are sold in markets (largely to tourists) in Paraguayan cities such as Luque and Itaugua. The country is renowned also for its handmade harps, made from tropical wood, pine, and cedar and characterized by a rounded base, large sound box, and very light weight.

In addition, embroidery and lacework are common in Paraguay. For example, the Guarani are famous for their *Ñandutí*, a kind of lace characterized by distinctive roundels. In Guarani, *Ñandutí* means "spider web."

Dances and Songs Fiestas always include dancing. In Paraguay, town halls and affluent homes usually include outdoor dance floors made from tile or clay. Among Paraguayan Americans, traditional dancing is performed mostly during celebrations. Many Paraguayan dances resemble the polka, the waltz, or the tango. Other dances, such as *el baile de la botella*

The Paraguayan "Bottle Dance" is always performed by a woman, who adds bottles to her head one at a time. The number of bottles depends on the skill of the dancer, but ten bottles is not uncommon. EDUARDO MUNOZ / REUTERS / LANDOV

(the "bottle dance") are much livelier. In the bottle dance, which is performed mainly as a folkloric show, one dancer performs with a bottle on her head while several others dance around her. During the dance, several bottles are stacked on top of each other. Music is usually provided by a pair of guitars accompanied by the small native harp, the *arpa*.

Among Paraguayan Americans, the *guarania* is perhaps the most popular musical style. A distinctly Paraguayan form that was invented in the early twentieth century by José Asunción Flores, the *guarania* features the *arpa* and typically includes melancholy lyrics. Though popular throughout Paraguay and within much of the Paraguayan American population, the *guarania* resonates especially among urbanites, whereas traditional folk forms such as waltzes are more common in rural populations.

Holidays Paraguayan Americans typically observe and celebrate a number of traditional national and religious holidays. Paraguayan Independence Day is celebrated on May 14 and 15. The Fiesta de San Juan, which is the largest national celebration, takes place on June 24. Rather than only observing Easter, many Paraguayan Americans, in keeping with other Hispanic Catholics, observe Semana Santa from Palm Sunday to Easter Sunday. The Virgin of Caacupe celebration, which takes place on December 8, honors the Virgin Mary and is an important event among many Catholic Paraguayan Americans.

In addition to Christmas and New Year's Day, other prominent celebrations include *Día de San Blas* (Patron Saint of Paraguay) in February; *Paz del Chaco* (End of the Chaco War) on June 12; and Friendship Day, the Day of the Child, and the *Fundación de Asunción* (Founding of Asunción) in August.

FAMILY AND COMMUNITY LIFE

Paraguayan Americans continue the ancient Guarani custom of *minga*, which is the provision of mutual assistance in household and occupational needs. Family and kin are the primary focus of an individual's loyalties and identity. The family unit includes godchildren, godparents, and many other members of the extended family. Political alliances are reflected in families, while the community is of secondary importance to the family unit. Most Paraguayan Americans live in nuclear families consisting of spouses and children. These family units are smaller than those in Paraguay, where grandparents and other relatives may also live with the nuclear family.

Gender Roles Paraguayan women have not traditionally occupied significant positions in society outside of their family and household roles. Traditionally, women have been cast in the role of caretaker. If a marriage dissolves, the mother typically keeps the children. In Paraguay abortion is illegal in all circumstances, even to save the life of the mother. Paraguayan women begin childbearing on average at the age of twenty years, and they average 4.4 children per household. Among Latin American nations, Paraguay's fertility rate is second only to that of Bolivia. According to a survey conducted by the National Demographic and Reproductive Health survey of Paraguay, Paraguayan women on average consider 3.6 children ideal. Paraguayan Americans tend to have fewer children than Paraguayans, in part because of the greater availability of contraceptives in the United States.

In accordance with Latin American customs, males are often seen as the primary breadwinners and authority figures in traditional Paraguayan families. Today, however, changing societal norms and economic pressure have begun to alter this relationship in some instances. Women who seek employment outside the home do so in order to give their children a better life. Many Paraguayan American women work in service-related jobs such as hotel housekeeping and restaurant staff (the American Community Survey estimates for 2009–2011 indicated that 47 percent of employed Paraguayan American females worked in service occupations, compared with 16 percent of their male counterparts), though some have joined the entrepreneurial ranks as restaurant owners. Some women have also pursued educational and employment opportunities.

Education Paraguayan Americans find schools in the United States to be superior to those in Paraguay, where only six years of attendance is required. The number of schools in Paraguay is also inadequate, and about 20 percent of the adult population is illiterate. Many immigrants are students seeking educational opportunities or young professionals seeking professional knowledge and skill development.

Courtship and Weddings Latin American and Roman Catholic traditions of courtship include the close supervision of young unmarried women, but such chaperonage does not take place for Paraguayan Americans, who often meet at community Catholic Church activities or through educational pursuits.

In Paraguay a formal church wedding represents a major expense for families. A fiesta is an essential part of the ceremony, and it is customarily as large and expensive as the two families can possibly afford. For the civil wedding, the families meet for a much less expensive party and barbecue. In the rural areas of Paraguay, common-law marriages are more prevalent than formal marriages. Among Paraguayan Americans, a formal church wedding in the traditional Roman Catholic practice or a civil wedding is the norm, and wedding receptions are usually conducted much like typical American receptions. Because in the United States many Paraguayans have intermarried with Americans and other Latin Americans, there is some concern that the next generation of Paraguayan Americans may not feel as close a kinship to Paraguay's distinctive cultural practices. This may manifest itself in many ways, such as the continued Americanization of courtship and wedding rituals and a decline in the understanding of Guarani among future generations of Paraguayan Americans.

EMPLOYMENT AND ECONOMIC CONDITIONS

Paraguayan American attitudes toward work are fundamentally different from those of the typical American. Paraguayans regard employment as a way of establishing a personal relationship more than as a source of income. The individualistic, capitalist work ethic is considered antisocial.

According to the U.S. Census Beaureau's American Community Survey estimates for 2009–2011, 72 percent of Paraguayan Americans ages sixteen and older were in the labor force (by comparison, among the general U.S. population, the figure was 64 percent). Employment was highest in service occupations (33 percent) and in management, busines, science and arts occupations (31 percent), followed by sales and office occupations (15 percent). Around 18 percent of Paraguayan Americans were self-employed. (compared with just 6 percent of the total U.S. population).

In Paraguay the economy is predominantly agricultural and commercial. The principal industries are those related to cattle, such as cold-storage plants, tanneries, leather goods, and manufacturing. Other important industries include textiles, cotton oil, tung, soy bean, construction materials, cement and lime, tobacco, and sugar. Paraguay's labor laws forbid work by children under twelve and state that children from ages fifteen to eighteen can be employed only with parental authorization. In reality, however, several thousands of children—many under the age of twelve—work in urban areas as part of the informal economy.

Paraguayan law provides for a minimum wage of $240 per month, an annual bonus of one month's salary, and a minimum of six vacation days a year. However, enforcement of this law is lax. U.S. investors in Paraguay provide better working and pay conditions than their national counterparts, and Paraguayan Americans in the United States are more affluent than other Paraguayans.

POLITICS AND GOVERNMENT

In Paraguay, politics are far more turbulent and divisive than in the United States. For Paraguayans, political parties are generally not a matter of personal conviction. Instead, citizens typically become a member of a major political party—Liberal or Colorado—at birth, and allegiance is lifelong. A person claiming political neutrality is suspected of hiding true motivations. By contrast, American political party affiliation by personal conviction is a very different experience for Paraguayan Americans. There is no record of Paraguayan American political activity on a national scale.

NOTABLE INDIVIDUALS

Academia Former Paraguayan foreign minister Pablo Max Ynsfrán (1894-1972) served for many years as a professor at the University of Texas, where he was a member of the history department and also taught courses on economics and government.

Poet, essayist, and literary critic Hugo Rodríguez Alcalá (1917-2007) authored numerous books of poetry, prose, and criticism and worked as a professor of Spanish literature at the University of California–Riverside from the 1960s until the mid-1980s.

Art In 1961 the artist Faith Wilding (1943–) immigrated to the United States from Paraguay. In the five decades since, she has established herself as an important feminist artist and art educator whose influence has spread internationally. Working in a variety of media, she has explored the somatic, psychic, and sociopolitical history of the body in sculpture, painting, performance, and writing, among other disciplines. Her recent work has focused especially on the relationship between women and biotechnology. From early work as a founding member of the Feminist Art Program at the California Institute of the Arts, Wilding has gone on to teach at the School of the Art Institute of Chicago, and she has been the recipient of grants from the National Endowment for the Arts among other organizations.

Fashion Cindy Taylor (1977–) was eighteen years old when she moved from her home country of Paraguay to Miami. Upon her arrival in Florida, Taylor began a modeling a career that quickly took off. After appearing in advertising campaigns for Guess?, Pantene, Perry Ellis, and Rampage, she was featured on the cover of various magazines, including *Glamour*, *Shape*, and *Men's Journal*. From there, she moved to television, where she appeared on several E! Entertainment Channel shows and specials, including Wild On!, which she hosted. After appearing in magazines, on television, and in film, Taylor took a three-year hiatus from her career to return to Paraguay and help care for her mother,

Berta Rojas, originally of Paraguay, talks before she performs a guitar and requinto duet with Juan Cancio Barreto at Lincoln Center in New York, 2005. JEFF CHRISTENSEN / REUTERS

who had been diagnosed with Lou Gehrig's disease. That experience led to work on a documentary about homeless children in Latin America as well as to Taylor's founding a charity to fight Lou Gehrig's disease.

Music Berta Rojas (1966–), a native of Paraguay and a professor of guitar at George Washington University in Washington, D.C., is one of the world's most renowned classical guitarists. Rojas first left Paraguay for Uruguay, where she completed her undergraduate studies at the Escuela Universitaria de Música. She then came to the United States to study at the Peabody Conservatory in Baltimore, Maryland. Rojas has performed at New York's Lincoln Center and Carnegie Hall as well as London's South Bank Centre, among many other venues, and she has been praised by critics in the *Washington Post* and *Classical Guitar*. In addition to teaching in Washington, D.C., Rojas has served as Paraguay's Ambassador of Tourism.

ORGANIZATIONS AND ASSOCIATIONS

Friends of Paraguay

Nonprofit organization created in 1987 that has established a network of returned Peace Corps volunteers and others interested in improving communication and information exchange in support of social, cultural, and economic development in Paraguay.

P.O. Box 27028
Washington, D.C. 20038-7028
URL: www.friendsofparaguay.org

Minga

Organization working for human rights and grassroots development in the Alto Paraná region in eastern Paraguay. Provides small grants to assist communities, emergency relief for displaced people, and seed grants for community-based sustainable development projects to fight poverty.

705 East Woodley Street
Northfield, Minnesota 55057
Phone: (507) 645-6435

Paraguay Hecho a Mano USA, Inc.

Nonprofit organization, whose name means "Paraguay Made by Hand," focusing on the preservation of the native Paraguayan culture through education and the sale and exhibition of Paraguayan crafts in the United States.

Carol Vollmer Pope
P.O. Box 94
Brookfield, Wisconsin 53008
URL: www.paraguayhechoamano.org

Partners of the Americas: Kansas and Paraguay

Nonprofit, volunteer organization, with headquarters in Washington, D.C., has developed exchanges between Paraguay and the state of Kansas in areas such as agriculture, citizen participation, cultural arts, international trade, emergency preparedness, health, natural resources, university relationships, and women in development and youth.

1424 K Street NW, #700
Washington, D.C. 20005
Phone: (202) 628-3300

Project for the People of Paraguay

Operates several programs for helping the poor in Paraguay, including sponsorships of children living in Paraguay.

P.O. Box 251
Avon, Minnesota 56310

Email: sbitzan@albanytel.com
URL: www.projectpy.org

MUSEUMS AND RESEARCH CENTERS

Denver Art Museum

Houses a collection of Paraguayan native art that includes textiles, jewelry, paintings, sculpture, furniture, and silver.

100 West 14th Avenue
Denver, Colorado 80204
Phone: (303) 640-4433

Indiana University Main Library

Holds an outstanding collection of sound recordings of various Guarani groups.

1320 East Tenth Street
Bloomington, Indiana 47405
Phone: (812) 855-0100

I Tomás Rivera Library at the University of California

Possesses the best collection of Paraguayan primary materials on the West Coast.

900 University Avenue
Riverside, California 92521
Phone: (951) 827-3220

SOURCES FOR ADDITIONAL STUDY

Cooney, Jerry W. *Paraguay: A Bibliography of Immigration and Emigration*. Longview, WA: J. W. Cooney, 1996.

Hanratty, Dennis M., and Sandra Meditz. *Paraguay: A County Study*. Washington, D.C.: U.S. Government Printing Office, 1990.

Kelly, Robert, Debra Ewing, and Stanton Doyle. *Country Review, Paraguay 1998/1999*. Houston, TX: Commercial Data International, Inc., 1998.

Roett, Riordan, and Richard Scott Sacks. *Paraguay: The Personalist Legacy*. Boulder, CO: Westview Press, 1991.

Whigham, Thomas, and Jerry W. Cooney. *A Guide to Collections on Paraguay in the United States*. Westport, CT: Greenwood Press, 1995.

PERUVIAN AMERICANS

John Packel

OVERVIEW

Peruvian Americans are immigrants or descendants of people from the country of Peru, the third-largest nation in South America. Peru is bounded by Ecuador and Colombia to the north, Brazil and Bolivia to the east, Chile to the south, and the Pacific Ocean to the west. This picturesque land is divided into three main geographic regions: the *costa*, or sea coast, along the South Pacific; the *sierra*, or highlands, of the Andes mountains; and the *selva*, or the Amazon jungle, in the east. At 496,222 square miles (1,285,210 square kilometers), Peru is roughly the size of Kansas, Nebraska, North Dakota, and South Dakota combined.

According to the 2010 *World Population Prospects*, prepared by the United Nations, Peru has a population of about 29 million. Approximately 95 percent of Peru's population is at least nominally Roman Catholic, a legacy of the church's deep-rooted involvement in the country's affairs since the Spanish conquest. There are also small numbers of Protestants, Jews, and Buddhists; they make up about 1 percent of the population. About 45 percent of Peruvians today are of unmixed indigenous (Amerindian) ancestry, about 43 percent are mestizos (people of mixed indigenous and Spanish heritage), and about 10 percent are of unmixed European ancestry (primarily Spanish). Blacks, who are descendants of the slaves from Africa, and people whose ancestors were immigrant Chinese and Japanese laborers make up less than 1 percent of the population. Spanish colonization left a legacy of social stratification that is, for the most part, unbroken today. Traditionally, the small Spanish upper class ruled the native and mestizo underclass. In the twentieth century, a middle class of whites and some mestizos developed, but most mestizos and almost all of the indigenous population belong to the underclass. Like most other South American countries, Peru is poor, its economy hampered by the inefficiency and obsolescence of many of its social structures. Much of its food must be imported because domestic production is inadequate and because transportation is severely limited by the small percentage of roads that are paved.

Peruvians began immigrating to the United States in small numbers during the California gold rush in the mid-1800s and again early in the twentieth century, due largely to the burgeoning textile industry in New York and New Jersey. Beginning in the 1970s another wave of Peruvians arrived in the United States, most of whom were fleeing Peru's militaristic government. The 1980s and 1990s saw the most significant influx of Peruvians to U.S. shores, this time in response to political instability and to a collapsing economy in Peru.

The 2010 U.S. Census indicated that the Peruvian American population was about 531,400, although other estimates are much higher due to the large number of undocumented Peruvians in the United States. Immigrants often come from urban areas of Peru, especially Lima, and the majority settle in the New York City metropolitan area—particularly in Paterson and Passaic in New Jersey and the New York City borough of Queens. Peruvian Americans are also clustered in the metropolitan areas of Miami, Florida; Los Angeles; Houston, Texas; Washington, D.C.; and Virginia.

HISTORY OF THE PEOPLE

Early History Most anthropologists believe that the first inhabitants of the Americas came from Asia about 30,000 years ago, during the last ice age, by crossing over a land bridge where the Bering Strait is now. Some of these people migrated from the area of present-day Alaska down the Pacific coast and arrived in the region of the Andes about 20,000 years ago. Little is known about this time, but the first settlements, such as Chivateros and Toquepala, were along the coast and their inhabitants relied on a diet consisting mainly of fish and wild plants and animals. Agriculture probably began around 4000 BCE, and by 2000 BCE civilization had advanced to the point where ceremonial centers were being built in coastal areas and the skill of making pottery had developed.

Until approximately 900 BCE, a number of small states in the Andean region existed relatively independently. However, advances in agriculture led to population growth and the first truly urban societies in Peru. These urban environments provided the structure and personnel required for a more specialized society. A measure of communication between neighbor societies helped provide the right conditions for expansion to full-fledged empires, and a number of these, such as the Caral and Chavin, rose and fell prior to the Inca empire.

This tribal period ended around 1000 CE with the ascendance of the Chimú kingdom, which had grown out of the Mochica empire and spanned nearly 600 miles of coast from present-day Lima to Ecuador. The Incas of Peru were one of the most advanced civilizations in pre-Columbian America, rivaled only by the Mayans and the Aztecs of Mesoamerica. More is known about the Incas than their Andean predecessors because of their contact with the Spanish conquistadors in the sixteenth century. Though the Incas never developed a written language, a number of Spaniards chronicled the Incan oral history and legends, including Garcilaso de la Vega, who was born in Cuzco in 1540 to an Inca princess and a Spanish conquistador.

Manco Capac was the first of eight Incan rulers from approximately 1200 to 1400 CE who built a small state centered in Cuzco. The expansion to a mighty empire began after 1430, when the powerful Chanca nation to the west of Cuzco attacked the Incas. Prince Yupanqui, who had been exiled to a distant llama ranch by his father, returned and defeated the Chancas. He became the ninth Incan ruler in 1438, renamed himself Pachacuti—"he who transforms the earth"—and set about unifying the Andean tribes into a powerful empire. He expanded the empire to the point where it reached from Lake Titicaca in the southeast to Lake Junín in the northwest. Pachacuti's son, Topa Inca, expanded it northward almost to what is now Quito, Ecuador, and then turned west toward the coast. He persuaded the Chimú people to join in the empire and then continued southward along the coast beyond Lima into the northern territories of present-day Chile, Bolivia, and Argentina. His son, Huayna Capac, became the eleventh Lord Inca in 1493 and pushed the boundaries of Inca control into the highlands of Ecuador. At this point, the Inca empire was at its peak, extending 2,500 miles north to south and covering 380,000 square miles. Close to twelve million people speaking twenty languages and making up at least 100 distinct Indian nations, had been unified under the all-important Inca ruler.

In 1525 Huayna Capac died in an epidemic that may have been smallpox or the measles, diseases introduced by the Spanish for which the native population had no immunity. Because the ruler had failed to designate his successor, two of his sons shared the role for a time—Atahualpa ruling the north from Quito and Huáscar ruling the south from Cuzco. Soon, however, tensions broke out between the two, and Atahualpa sent his father's army against Huáscar, who was defeated and later killed. This civil war lasted a number of years and severely weakened the empire at an inopportune time, for reports of strange white-faced, bearded men in "sea houses" were brought to the Inca, who thought it best to ignore such stories.

In May 1532 Francisco Pizarro, a Spaniard seeking to conquer land and plunder gold for himself and his king, landed near the coastal city of Tumbes with a force of 180 cavalrymen and foot soldiers. He was aware of the civil war and set out toward the mountain city of Cajamarca, where Atahualpa and 30,000 Incas waited. Apparently, the Inca thought that the foreigners were there to surrender. However, a massacre ensued in which the Spaniards used crossbows, cannons, and muskets to slaughter 2,000 Incas and take their leader, Atahualpa, prisoner. Atahualpa tried to ransom himself with the promise of enough gold and silver to fill his cell. This did not help Atahualpa or the Incas, however, because the invaders feared a rebellion and thought it safer to have the ruler burned at the stake. Atahualpa objected that this would deprive him of proper burial and an afterlife, and so he was given the option of being baptized a Christian and then strangled. The last king of the majestic Incan empire was killed in this manner on August 29, 1533. For a number of years, Huáscar's half-brother and his sons battled the Spanish fruitlessly; the last resistor, Túpac Amaru, was executed in Cuzco in 1572.

Modern Era Spain ruled Peru as a viceroyalty for nearly 300 years after the conquest, regarding it more or less as a huge mine that existed to fill the crown's coffers. The Spaniards felt that they formed a superior culture and that their customs and particularly the church brought civilized society to the natives. The political and economic system they instituted to carry out their aims, called *encomienda*, granted soldiers and colonists land and mining permits, as well as the slave labor of the natives. Living and working conditions for the native Peruvians on the farms and especially in the mines were horrendous. Hard labor, malnutrition (exacerbated by the Spaniards' introduction of European crops and the elimination of many native ones), and disease wiped out an estimated 90 percent of the pre-conquest native population within a century.

During this colonial period, Spain passed legislation attempting to protect the native population, but it was ineffectual. Practices that were supposed to be outlawed—such as debt peonage, in which subjects were trapped in a cycle of indebtedness that could not be overcome through their labor—were, in reality, widespread. The influx of Spaniards taking advantage of these opportunities, as well as 100,000 African slaves, became part of a highly stratified society in which European-born Spaniards were at the top, followed respectively by Peruvian-born Spaniards (Creoles), the urban working poor, black slaves, and the indigenous population.

In 1780 a descendant of the last Inca took the name Túpac Amaru II and led a rebellion by the indigenous population. The rebellion began to gain wider support by condemning the corruption of colonial officials, but indiscriminate attacks on Spaniards and Creoles promptly caused the movement to lose its backing. Ultimately, the campaign for independence resulted from conditions outside Peru and was led by outsiders. When Napoleon invaded Spain and imprisoned the king in 1808, the vacuum of authority allowed the Creoles in the colonial capitals to set up autonomous regimes. Then between 1820 and 1824, José de San Martín and Simón de Bolívar, two generals who had liberated Argentina, Chile, Venezuela, Colombia, and Ecuador from Spanish rule, completed the process by adding Peru to the list. Bolívar, elected for life as president, attempted to modernize the country by cutting taxes, funding schools, and lifting many of the worst abuses against the indigenous population, but conservative Creole opposition forced him to leave after only two years.

Peru's humiliating defeat by Chile in the War of the Pacific (1879–1883), fought over lands with rich nitrate deposits, led many to call for an improvement in the lot of indigenous Peruvians so that they might contribute more fully to the society. The late nineteenth and early twentieth centuries showed evidence of efforts to modernize the society and economy. Public administration was improved, the armed forces were professionalized, public education was fostered, and modern labor legislation was enacted. These reforms contributed to the conditions that encouraged foreign investment capital in the burgeoning sugar, cotton, copper, and rubber industries. In turn, the middle class grew stronger.

In the 1930s the Great Depression had a crippling effect on the Peruvian economy, as export markets collapsed and foreign loans dried up. This situation seems to have contributed to the rise of a political movement known as the American Popular Revolutionary Alliance (APRA), which was anticommunist but borrowed from the ideologies of Marxism and Italian fascism and advocated agrarian reform, the nationalization of industry, and opposition to U.S. imperialism. APRA's leader, formerly exiled student organizer Víctor Raúl Haya de la Torre, never won the presidency, but the party maintained a major presence on the political scene for more than forty years, both through bloody conflicts with the armed forces and congressional coalitions.

The Peruvian military had long played a large role in the state, either through generals assuming the presidency or by influencing elections. In 1962, for example, a slight plurality by the APRA brought a nullification of the results and the election of Fernando Belaúnde Terry a year later. From 1968 to 1975, General Juan Velasco Alvarado and the Revolutionary Government of the Armed Forces ruled in an attempt to create a new and prosperous Peru. The general forged ties with socialist countries and made Peru a voice for third-world interests. He nationalized most of the country's banks, railroads, and utilities, as well as many foreign corporations.

Central to this effort to control the economy and increase social justice was Velasco's land reform, which was among the most extensive in Latin America. Ninety percent of Peru's farmland had been owned by a landed aristocracy that made up just 2 percent of the population, so the administration appropriated twenty-five million acres of this land and distributed it to worker-owned cooperatives and individual families. This failed to achieve the far-ranging effects hoped, however, in part because of the insufficient amount of arable land relative to the large number of people and also because of the absence of policies giving the poor a greater share of the benefits.

Civilian rule returned with the reelection of Belaúnde Terry in 1980 after a constituent assembly had drawn up a new constitution. The presidency was transferred peacefully in 1985 to Alan García Perez of APRA and again in 1990 to Alberto Fujimori, a Peruvian university professor of Japanese descent who won in a run-off against the novelist Mario Vargas Llosa. Peru's poor economic performance, including inflation that soared as high as 2,800 percent annually, continued to wreak social havoc. After a period of accepting austerity measures as conditions for aid from the International Monetary Fund, Peru declared a severe reduction in the debt payments it would make to foreign investors and nationalized an American oil company, which resulted in a cut-off of needed credit and U.S. aid.

In addition to these economic woes, Peru suffered from social disruption caused by leftist terrorist groups and the governmental response to them. A guerrilla organization founded by university professor Abimael Guzmán Reynoso and guided by the principles of the Chinese dictator Mao Zedong, the *Sendero Luminoso* (Shining Path) specialized in assassination and the use of violent intimidation against the peasants, such as cutting off their fingers to prevent them from voting. In a period of fewer than twenty years, 30,000 people were killed. The Revolutionary Túpac Amaru Movement was another group carrying out equally vicious attacks in Peru's urban areas. The coca harvests, which supplied much of the huge cocaine market in the United States, also brought violence as U.S. pressure to destroy crops led to terrorist attacks on local officials by those profiting from the drug trade. In the midst of these social woes, the country's pride received a boost in 1981 when the United Nations elected a Peruvian, Javier Pérez de Cuéllar, to a five-year term as Secretary General.

In 1992 President Fujimori responded to these economic and social crises by dissolving the congress and judiciary and consolidating power in a Government of Emergency and National Reconstruction while also promising to submit a revised constitution to a referendum and hold elections at some point in the future. Referred to as an *autogolpe*, or self-coup, Fujimori's takeover also involved a suspension of civil liberties. These bold moves were well-received by the public, however, and his popularity increased further when *Sendero Luminoso* leader Guzmán was captured and the movement's stronghold on certain rural areas, such as Ayacucho, was broken.

After seeking a contested third term in 2000, Fujimori resigned from office in 2001, fleeing to Japan to avoid prosecution for human rights violations and corruption charges. He was arrested in Chile in 2005 and extradited to Peru, where he was convicted on various charges and sentenced to prison. Fujimori was followed in office by Alejandro Toledo, who was elected to the presidency in 2001, and by former president Alan García, who was re-elected in 2006. In 2011 Ollanta Humala became the first leftist president in several decades. While Peru has stabilized to a degree following Fujimori's departure, Peruvians continue to leave the country for both political and economic reasons.

SETTLEMENT IN THE UNITED STATES

Peru's social and economic crises are at the root of internal migration from rural areas to the cities, as well as immigration to the United States. Unemployment rates of over 50 percent have left many without a means to earn the basic necessities of life, and others are chronically underemployed. An unstable political climate and especially political violence by terrorist groups have caused many to flee. Peruvians are attracted to the political and economic stability of the United States, the work opportunities, and the chance for their children to go to school and have a better future. A majority of these immigrants have family or acquaintances established in the United States who serve as intermediaries in their transition to a new culture.

Little is known about the earliest Peruvian immigrants who came to the United States during the California gold rush. Later Peruvian immigrants began arriving in the early twentieth century to work in textile mills in Paterson, New Jersey, which is now home to one of the largest Peruvian communities in the United States. Paterson has a significant number of businesses run by Peruvian Americans, as well as social and political organizations, and remains a destination for Peruvian immigrants of all social classes.

Peruvians from the upper class have benefited economically from their immigration to the United States because they generally have been able to transfer their capital and business expertise. They range from owners of factories and large stores to accountants for major banks and corporations to agro-industrial managers. However, these Peruvians have faced major obstacles to their assimilation. Although they are well off financially, they do not have the economic or political power in the United States that they had in Peru. Yet because of their background, they tend not to identify with the middle-class Americans whose status they share. Many try to compensate by joining relatively exclusive associations that have social gatherings for holidays and weddings. Peruvians from this group tend to settle in urban areas with a strong Peruvian presence or established Latino communities.

Middle-class Peruvian immigrants did not arrive in large numbers until the 1970s, when the exodus was led by doctors and engineers. Assimilation has been relatively easy for this group, and consequently it has been labeled the "children of success." Like those from the upper class, these immigrants had been familiar with American cultural practices before their arrival. The difference is that they did not lose any

A Peruvian American shepherd prepares an innoculation for his sheep in, Bridgeport, California, 1995. PHOTOGRAPH BY PHIL SCHERMEISTER. CORBIS. REPRODUCED BY PERMISSION.

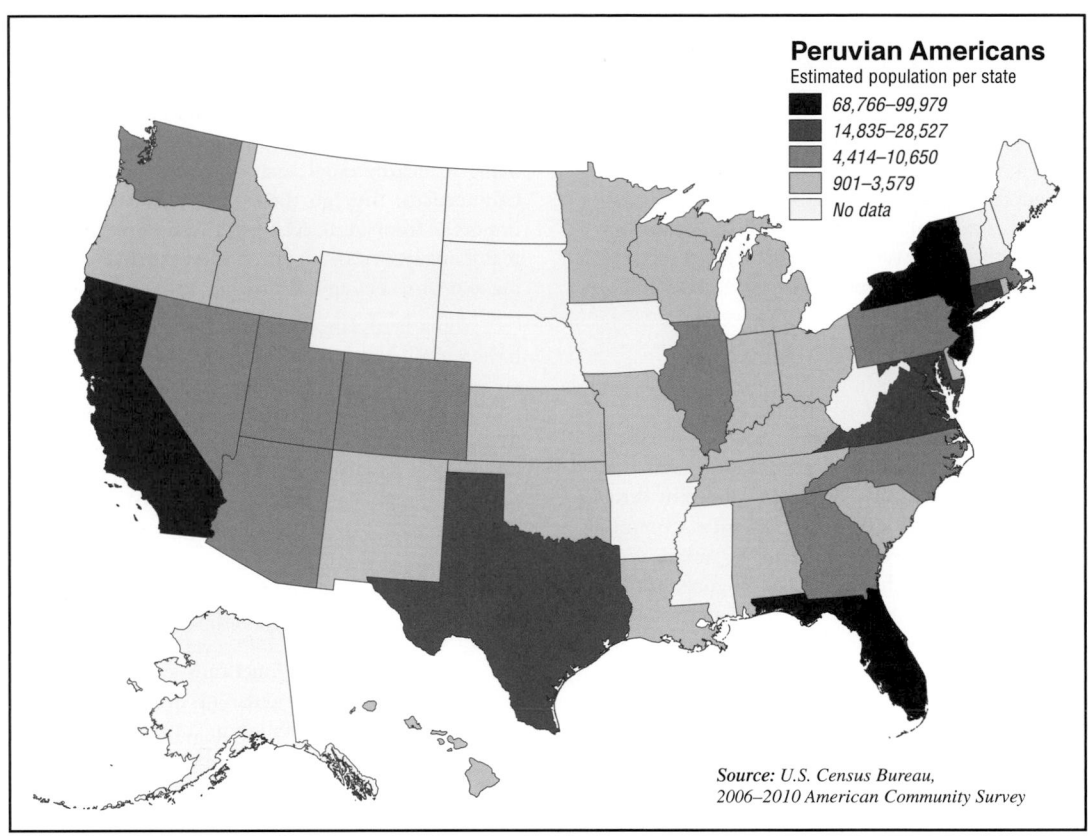

Peruvian Americans
Estimated population per state

- 68,766–99,979
- 14,835–28,527
- 4,414–10,650
- 901–3,579
- No data

Source: U.S. Census Bureau,
2006–2010 American Community Survey

prerogatives or privileges. This group tends to maintain a stronger cultural and religious identity through participation in church and other social activities.

With the exception of those brought to work as sheep herders on ranches in the western United States, Peru's lower classes were the last to take advantage of the opportunities in the United States. Since the mid-1980s, their immigration numbers have increased. These immigrants have come from positions ranging from low-level bureaucrats to manual laborers, and they have had the most difficulty assimilating because of their lack of formal education, which has made it difficult for them to learn English. They cling more tightly to their home culture and generally live in areas of urban poverty. Many had only recently made the transition from rural to urban life in Peru prior to immigrating, and they feel great pressure to send money back to their families in their native country upon settling in the United States.

Undocumented immigrants of all but the highest social classes face obstacles in finding employment in the United States; many are forced into service and labor occupations that do not represent their educational degrees or previous career achievements in Peru. For professionals from the middle classes, this can be disruptive to concepts of personal identity.

The states with the largest number of Peruvian Americans are Florida, California, New Jersey, and New York. Texas and Virginia are also home to significant communities of people of Peruvian descent.

LANGUAGE

Spanish (commonly called *Castellano* in Peru) has been Peru's official language since the Spanish conquest. Approximately 80 percent of all Peruvians speak Spanish today, including some who also speak one of the indigenous languages, Quechua ("KECH-wah") or Aymara. A language that grew out of the Latin brought to Spain by conquering Romans, Spanish has a vocabulary and structure similar to those of other Romance languages, such as French and especially Italian. Its alphabet generally overlaps with that of English and contains twenty-eight letters. "K" and "w" occur only in words of foreign origin, and additional letters are "ch" (as in "chest"), "ll" (generally pronounced like the English "y"), "ñ" (like the "ny" in "canyon," which comes from the Spanish *cañón*), and "rr" (a rolled "r" sound). The "b" and "v" are interchangeable in Spanish and are a bit softer than an English "b." The "h" is silent, and the "d" can have a soft "th" sound within a word. Spanish vowels have one primary sound, making spelling and pronunciation on sight much easier than in English: "i" (as in "feet"), "e" (as in "they"), "a" (as in "hot"), "o" (as in "low"), "u" (as in "rude"). Words ending in a vowel, "n," or "s" are accented on the next-to-last syllable, those ending in

LUNCH: THE MAIN MEAL IN PERU

Peruvian Americans have adapted to eating patterns in the United States, where dinner is the main meal and lunches are lighter. But for Peruvians the biggest meal of the day is traditionally lunch (*almuerzo*). On weekends Peruvian Americans often use lunch as an excuse for family gatherings and have long meals with *parrilladas* (grilled food) or even the more traditional *pachamanca* (food cooked in an open pit).

other consonants have stress on the last syllable, and any exceptions require an accent mark.

Both Spanish and English are spoken by Peruvian Americans. In the 2011 U.S. Census Community Survey, only 14 percent of Peruvian American families reported English as the sole language spoken at home, but 60 percent of the respondents indicated that they spoke English very well. Most second- and third-generation Peruvian Americans are bilingual, especially those who live with older relatives.

RELIGION

The Catholic Church is one of the main social institutions that has aided the assimilation of Peruvians to American culture. The church is important to newly arrived Peruvians because of its familiarity, the services it often extends in terms of finding work and applying for citizenship, and the opportunity it affords for meeting other Peruvians, including those of higher social classes.

As in Peru, a wide range of religious commitment exists among Peruvian Americans, and women tend to be more devout than men. While middle-class Peruvians tend to be strict in their Catholic beliefs and adherence to rituals, people further down the social scale might blend elements of superstition and folk religion with formal Catholicism. *Fiestas*, or parties, corresponding to church holidays are among the most important social events in Peruvian American communities, with the processions associated with St. Rose of Lima (August 30), El Señor de los Milagros (October 18), and St. Martin of Porras (November 3) acting as prominent expressions of the Peruvian cultural and religious identity. Second-generation immigrants who have more contact with the larger, more secular society may be less immersed in religious life, which can be a source of conflict in families.

CULTURE AND ASSIMILATION

Peruvian immigrants generally settle in urban areas with either a strong Peruvian American or Latino presence. Many Peruvian immigrants initially stay with family or friends and may also find employment through these networks, particularly if they are undocumented. Cities such as Paterson have a Peruvian business district with restaurants and bakeries that serve as places to meet and socialize, especially for men who have come ahead of their families in order to earn money and establish homes. Paterson's business district is also a destination for Peruvian Americans living in nearby cities such as Boston and Hartford, Connecticut; they go there to stock up on supplies imported from Peru. Many Peruvian Americans also maintain close ties with family members in Peru, sending and/or receiving information, money, and goods.

Some Peruvian Americans from the middle class have appropriated elements of indigenous culture in an attempt to create a national identity distinct from that of the broader Latino community. Such appropriation has led to conflict between members of various immigrant classes about the appropriateness of middle-class Peruvian Americans self-identifying with Andean cultural symbols and, to a lesser degree, representations of the Incan tradition, both of which are more commonly associated with an ethnically and culturally distinct peasantry in Peru.

Cuisine Peruvian Americans eat many of the same dishes that are popular in their native country. Some of the most common include *ceviche* (raw fish seasoned with citrus), *mondonguito* (tripe stewed with potatoes, cilantro, and vegetables), and *papa a la Huancaína* (sliced potatoes layered with cheese, sliced boiled eggs, cilantro, and mild peppers). On holidays and for other celebrations, large meals are often prepared by women for extended family and friends.

Holidays Peruvian Americans celebrate major U.S. holidays, especially those associated with Christianity, such as Christmas and Easter. In addition, most celebrate *Fiestas Patrias* on July 28, a national holiday in Peru celebrating the country's independence from Spanish rule in 1824. This holiday is marked by Peruvian Americans with barbeques and parades, the most notable of which, the Peruvian Parade, travels a six-mile route between Passaic and Paterson in New Jersey.

Dances and Songs The *marinera* is a dance originating in Peru during colonial times; it was originally called *zamacueca* and took its current name in the late nineteenth century as a tribute to the Peruvian navy. The dance enacts a courtship ritual between a wealthy landowner and a peasant woman, and the unacceptability of the relationship is represented by the wide distance between the dancers. After falling out of fashion during the early twentieth century, the dance became popular again in Peru in the 1950s and 1960s, with the National Marinera Tournament and other contests that attracted many entrants. Tournaments have also been started in the United States. In Paterson, for example, the first tournament was staged in 1995 as part of the Peruvian Independence Day. In addition, a number of schools have opened in Paterson to teach the dance to new generations of Peruvian Americans, many of whom perform it during religious celebrations such as the procession of the Lord of Miracles as well as during Peruvian Independence Day festivities.

Recreational Activities Soccer is a popular recreational activity among Peruvian Americans, and in large urban areas such as New York and Los Angeles, Peruvian American teams play against other "nations" in World Cup-style tournaments. In this sense, soccer instills Peruvian Americans with a sense of national identity, many of whom organize soccer clubs with the same names as Peruvian professional teams, such as Alianza Lima, Universitario de Deportes, and Sporting Cristal.

Among women, the main sport is volleyball, and with good reason: Peru has won many world and Latin American tournaments. Volleyball also serves as a form of entertainment at family gatherings.

FAMILY AND COMMUNITY LIFE

All social classes and ethnicities in Peru place a great deal of emphasis on family, including distant relatives and godparents. Peruvian social life revolves around the extended family, especially among the indigenous Peruvians, who may have few important social ties beyond this unit. The extended family commonly serves an economic function, too, with members working together and pooling their resources. The nuclear family tends to be male-dominated, and fathers have great authority over their children, even into adulthood. These attitudes and practices persist in Peruvian American families as much as circumstances allow. New immigrants may temporarily live with extended family already established in the United States, and in expensive urban centers, such arrangements sometimes are permanent.

Gender Roles Conceptions of gender roles in the Peruvian American community vary between generations, much as they do in American culture in general. Older, first-generation immigrants tend to hold more traditional views of the division between male and female roles: men are expected to be the breadwinners, while women are charged with the care of the home and children. Although Peruvian American women have entered the workforce out of economic necessity, many still bear the brunt of the responsibility for childcare and the household. However, younger generations, particularly those born and raised in the United States, are likely to hold more egalitarian views. During childhood, Peruvian American females are typically more sheltered than males, and conflict is common when the girls attempt to emulate their non-Peruvian peers, who have more freedom.

Education Peruvian American families tend to emphasize education as a way to achieve a higher status in society. This, however, is not always the case among recently arrived immigrants who lack a legal status. For these people, working (often in low-paying

CEVICHE

Ingredients

1¾ pounds of white fish (corvina or sole)

1 red onion, thinly sliced

½ red chile pepper, diced

½ orange or yellow chile pepper, diced

juice of 16 key limes

salt

Preparation

Cut the white fish into small squares and mix with the red onion in a bowl. Season the ingredients with salt and the two types of chile peppers. Mix this mixture with the lime juice and let it rest for 5 minutes. If it's too acidic, add ice cubes, mixing well and removing immediately before they start to melt. Serve the ceviche in a deep dish accompanied by cooked sweet potato, corn and lettuce.

jobs) and sending money to their families back home are higher priorities. Recent statistics, however, show that a greater majority of Peruvian Americans would rather seek an education: according to the U.S. Census Bureau's 2010 American Community Survey, 85 percent of Peruvian Americans were high school graduates or had achieved further education, and 30 percent had college degrees or higher.

Relations with Other Americans The broader Latino community in the United States is important to many Peruvian Americans, who benefit from a shared language and similar cultural traits. The travel, legal, and labor services that already exist in these communities assist newer immigrants. State social service programs are also available to the most indigent. Some, especially second-generation Peruvian Americans, self-identify as Latino rather than Peruvian American and express feelings of closer affiliation with the broader Latino community rather than with people who came from Peru specifically.

EMPLOYMENT AND ECONOMIC CONDITIONS

Beginning in the second half of the twentieth century, many Peruvian Americans came to the United States to work in textile factories. They were relatively well-paying jobs, and workers settled in nearby communities, prompting a demand for small businesses such as Peruvian restaurants. Later waves of immigrants, especially those without documentation, were often forced into lower-wage jobs, with men typically pursuing manual labor and women taking work cleaning or in food preparation. Later generations of well-educated immigrants who have entered the country through

PERUVIAN PROVERBS

Peruvian proverbs include the following:

Poco a poco, uno camina lejos.

Little by little, one walks far.

De tu casa a la ajena sal con la barriga llena.

From your own to a stranger's house, go forth with a well-filled belly.

El amor mira con unos anteojos que hacen parecer oro al cobre, a la pobreza riqueza, y a las legañas perlas.

Love looks through spectacles which make copper look like gold, poverty like riches, and foul tears like pearls.

official channels have wider prospects. In the twenty-first century, Peruvian Americans hold a wide variety of positions in business, the sciences, education, and service industries.

POLITICS AND GOVERNMENT

Peruvian Americans can attain dual citizenship, which affects the political process in Peru. If born in Peru and naturalized in the United States, they still can vote in Peruvian national elections, unless, of course, they renounce their Peruvian citizenship. If born in the United States, they can become naturalized Peruvian citizens if they follow an administrative procedure at a Peruvian consulate and show that at least one of their parents is a Peruvian citizen. This is the result of Peruvian laws passed from 1990 to 2001 by former president Alberto Fujimori, who wanted to gain the Peruvian vote from abroad.

Peruvian Americans, then, tend to participate in the Peruvian political process, particularly in cases of distress or natural disasters. For example, several action committees were formed to provide humanitarian relief during the 1988 El Niño catastrophe, when pouring rains in normally dry areas caused devastation in Peru. Other cases include the recent earthquakes in Pisco and Ica.

NOTABLE INDIVIDUALS

Academia José R. Deustua (1954–), a Peruvian American historian and sociologist, received bachelor's and master's degrees in Peru at the Catholic University of Lima and then a doctorate at the École des Hautes Études en Sciences Sociales in Paris in 1989. In the 1990s he moved to the United States, where he was a professor at Stanford University, the University of Miami, the University of Illinois at Chicago, and Eastern Illinois University. He is the author of several books, including *The Bewitchment of Silver: A Social and Economic History of Mining in 19th-Century Peru* (2000).

José Luis Rénique (1952–), historian and social scientist, was born in Lima, Peru. He studied at the Catholic University and then pursued a master's degree and a PhD at the University of Columbia in New York, where he graduated with a dissertation on the rural changes and the *indigenista* movement in the region of Puno in southern Peru. His books include *La Voluntad Encarcelada: Las Luminosas Trincheras de Combate de Sendero Luminoso del Perú* (2003), *La Batalla por Puno: Conflicto Agrario y Nación en los Andes Peruanos* (2004), and, in collaboration with Carmen Mc Evoy, *Soldados de la República: Guerra, Correspondencia y Memoria en el Perú, 1830–1844* (2010).

Art Carlos Llerena Aguirre (1952–) is an artist and educator born in Arequipa, Peru. He received a bachelor's degree from the School of Visual Arts in New York City in 1979, a master's from Hunter College in 1982, and a master's from the University of Illinois in 1994. He taught at the School of Visual Arts, Philadelphia University of the Arts, Syracuse University, California College of Arts and Crafts, the University of California at Berkeley, Ringling School of Art and Design, the University of Illinois, Poynter Institute for Media Studies, and the University of Miami. A member of the Society of Newspaper Designers, he has had exhibitions of his woodcuts and engravings in Urbana, Illinois; Lima; and London.

Government and Politics Ian Vásquez was the director of the Cato Institute's Center for Global Liberty and Prosperity and previously worked on inter-American issues at the Center for Strategic and International Studies and Caribbean/Latin American Action. He earned his bachelor's degree from Northwestern University and a master's from the School of Advanced International Studies at Johns Hopkins University.

Journalism Marie Arana (1949–) is a writer at large for the *Washington Post* and a senior consultant to the U.S. Librarian of Congress, as well as a novelist, essayist, and biographer. An active spokesperson on Latin America and biculturalism, she earned a bachelor's degree in Russian language and literature at Northwestern University, a master's in linguistics and sociolinguistics at Hong Kong University, and a certificate of scholarship (Mandarin language) at Yale University in China.

Pedro M. Valdivieso (1932–) was the editor of the paper *Actualidad* in Los Angeles. He was born in Piura, Peru, and studied journalism and public relations at San Marcos University and Lima University, respectively. He edited newspapers in Lima before moving to the United States and editing *Noticias del Mundo* (Los Angeles) and *El Diario de Los Angeles*. Valdivieso also reported for channel 34-TV in Los Angeles and was a member of the Association of Journalists in the Spanish Language and the Federation of Journalists from Peru.

Literature Daniel Alarcón (1977–) is a fiction writer whose short story collection *War by Candlelight* was a finalist for the 2005 PEN-Hemingway Award. He also was an associate editor of *Etiqueta Negra*, a quarterly literary publication in his native Peru, and a contributing editor to *Granta*, another literary journal.

Isaac Goldemberg (1945–), poet and novelist, was born in Peru. He became a distinguished professor of humanities at Eugenio María de Hostos Community College of the City University of New York, where he was also the director of the Latin American Writers Institute and the editor of the *Hostos Review*, an international journal of culture. His novels include *La Vida Contado* (1992), *Tiempo al Tiempo* (1984), and *La Vida a Plazos de Jacobo Lerner* (1980). In addition, he published books of short stories and poetry, as well as plays. He was the recipient of the Orden de Don Quijote (2005), the Lluvia Editores Short Story Award (2000), the Nathaniel Judah Jacobson Award (1996), and the Nuestro Award in Fiction (1977).

Medicine and Health Graciela Solís Alarcón (1942–) is a physician and educator who was originally from Chachapoyas, Peru. She earned her MD in Peru in 1967 and an MPH from Johns Hopkins University in 1972. She then did her residency in Baltimore and in Peru and became a professor at the University of Alabama at Birmingham (UAB) in 1980. A member of the American College of Rheumatology and the American College of Physicians, she authored a number of articles in her field. In 2009 she was named professor emerita of medicine at the UAB School of Medicine.

Carlos Castaneda (sometimes spelled Castañeda) (1925–1998) is perhaps the best-known Peruvian American. While attempting a thesis on medicinal plants for the University of California, Los Angeles, in the late 1960s, he met a Yaqui (Mexican) *brujo*, or medicine man, living in Arizona and became heavily influenced by his way of life. Castaneda wrote a series of best-selling books based on these experiences, beginning with *The Teachings of Don Juan: A Yaqui Way of Knowledge* in 1976. The books relate a hallucinogen-induced search for a nonrational reality and an attempt to become a Yaqui warrior. The author considered them anthropological field studies, and indeed they served as his master's and doctoral theses, though critics within the field of anthropology say they are more properly regarded as fiction. While Castaneda seemed to have been purposely elusive regarding his biographical details, he is thought to have been born in Cajamarca, Peru.

Science Jaime A. Fernandez-Baca (1954–) is a physicist at the Oak Ridge National Laboratory. He earned his BS degree in Lima in 1977 before coming to the United States for an MS (1982) and a PhD (1986) at the University of Maryland. Fernandez-Baca did his research at the Instituto de Energía Nuclear in Peru and at the University of Maryland. He was awarded a fellowship by the International Atomic Energy Agency in 1977 and published numerous technical articles.

Fiestas, or parties, corresponding to church holidays are among the most important social events in Peruvian American communities, with the processions associated with St. Rose of Lima (August 30), El Señor de los Milagros (October 18), and St. Martin of Porras (November 3) acting as prominent expressions of the Peruvian cultural and religious identity.

MEDIA

PRINT

Chasqui

A scholarly journal covering Latin American literature.

David William Foster, Editor
Arizona State University School of International Letters and Cultures
Tempe, Arizona 85287-0202
Phone: (480) 965-3752
Email: david.foster@asu.edu

El Diario La Prensa

Founded in 1913, *El Diario La Prensa* is the oldest Spanish-language daily in the United States. It has coverage of Peru in its international pages.

Erica Gonzalez, Executive Editor
1 MetroTech Center
18th Floor
Brooklyn, New York 11201
Phone: (212) 807-4785
URL: www.eldiariony.com

El Nuevo Herald

Spanish-language daily that includes Peru in its coverage of South America. It was founded in 1976 and has a circulation of 98,000.

Manny Garcia, Director
1 Herald Plaza
Miami, Florida 33132
Phone: (305) 376-3445
Email: magarcia@elnuevoherald.com
URL: www.elnuevoherald.com

ORGANIZATIONS AND ASSOCIATIONS

Association of Peruvian American Professionals

Works to promote education, professional development, and cultural awareness in the Peruvian American and broader Latino communities.

593 Farmington Avenue
Hartford, Connecticut 06105
Email: info@apapro.org
URL: www.apapro.org

Peruvian American Dental Association

Nonprofit organization founded in 2006 and dedicated
to promoting oral health throughout the Latino
community.

1744 University Avenue
#102
Riverside, California 92507
Phone: (951) 742-8112
Fax: (951) 782-9808
URL: www.padausa.org

The Peruvian-American Medical Society

Professional organization of Peruvian American doctors
that raises money for equipment needed by Peruvian
hospitals.

Ana May Salgado
6488 Tamerlane Drive
West Bloomfield, Michigan 48322
Phone: (248) 851-2709
Email: pamsusa@comcast.net
URL: www.pamsweb.org

MUSEUMS AND RESEARCH CENTERS

American Museum of Natural History

Landmark museum in New York City with a wing
dedicated to South American peoples that features
Peruvian civilizations, especially the Incas.

Central Park West at 79th Street
New York, New York 10024
Phone: (212) 769-5100
URL: www.amnh.org

Center for Latin American Studies

Founded in 1956 at the University of California, Berkeley.
Incorporates social sciences and the humanities in
its scope and gives particular emphasis to the native
populations of South America.

Harley Shaiken, Director
2334 Bowditch
Berkeley, California 94720-2312
Phone: (510) 642-2088
Fax: (510) 642-3260
Email: hshaiken@socrates.berkeley.edu
URL: www.clas.berkeley.edu

Institute for Latin American Studies

Located at the University of Florida in Gainesville and
founded in 1931, the institute features studies in the

humanities and social sciences and has a project on
Aymara language and culture.

Philip J. Williams, Director
319 Grintner Hall
P.O. Box 115530
Gainesville, Florida 32611-5531
Phone: (352) 392-0375
Fax: (352) 392-7682
Email: info@latam.ufl.edu
URL: www.latam.ufl.edu

Latin American Institute

Located at the University of California, Los Angeles, the
institute coordinates research on the region's socio-
politics, environment, technology, literature, and arts.

Kevin Terraciano, Interim Director
10343 Bunche Hall
Box 951447
405 Hilgard Avenue
Los Angeles, California 90095-1447
Phone: (310) 825-4571
Fax: (310) 206-6859
Email: lainamctr@international.ucla.edu
URL: www.international.ucla.edu/lai

SOURCES FOR ADDITIONAL STUDY

Cameron, Maxwell, and Philip Mauceri. *The Peruvian
Labyrinth: Polity, Society, Economy*. University Park:
Pennsylvania State University Press, 1997.

De Ferrari, Gabriella. *Gringa Latina: A Woman of Two
Worlds*. Boston: Houghton Mifflin, 1996.

Degregori, Ivan Carlos. *How Difficult It Is to Be God:
Shining Path's Politics of War in Peru, 1980–1999*. Ed.
Steven Stern. Trans. Nancy Appelbaum. Madison:
University of Wisconsin Press, 2012.

Dostert, Pierre Etienne. *Latin America 1994*. Washington,
D.C.: Stryker-Post Publications, 1994.

Monaghan, Jay. *Chile, Peru, and the California Gold Rush
of 1849*. Berkeley: University of California Press,
1973.

Paerregaard, Karsten. "Inside the Hispanic Melting Pot:
Negotiating National and Multicultural Identities
among Peruvians in the United States." *Latino Studies*
3 (2005): 76–96.

The Peru Reader: History, Culture, Politics. 2nd ed. Ed.
Orin Starn, Carlos Iván Degregori, and Robin Kirk.
Durham, NC: Duke University Press, 2005.

Takenaka, Ayumi, and Karen Pren. "Leaving to Get
Ahead: Assessing the Relationship between Mobility
and Inequality in Peruvian Migration." *Latin American
Perspectives* 137, no. 5 (2010): 29–49.

Wright, Ronald. *Cut Stones and Crossroads: A Journey
in the Two Worlds of Peru*. New York: Viking Press,
1984.

POLISH AMERICANS

J. Sydney Jones

OVERVIEW

Polish Americans are immigrants or descendants of people from Poland, the seventh largest country in Europe. Located in east-central Europe, Poland is bordered to the east by Russia and the Ukraine, to the south by the Czech Republic and Slovakia, to the west by Germany, and to the north by the Baltic Sea. Poland's landscape is varied, distinguished by the central lowlands, the sand dunes and swamps of the Baltic coast, and the mountains of the Carpathians to the south. Poland's total land area is 120,727 square miles (312,685 square kilometers), somewhat smaller than the state of New Mexico.

According to the *CIA World Factbook*, the population of Poland was an estimated 38,415,284 in July 2012, making it the thirty-third most populated country in the world. Some 97 percent of the people identified themselves as Polish, but there were also small groups of Germans (0.4 percent), Belarusians (0.1 percent), and Ukrainians (0.1 percent). The overwhelming majority of the population, 98 percent, speak Polish, the official language. Roman Catholics make up 90 percent of the Polish population, but only 75 percent actively follow the Catholic faith. There are also small groups of Eastern Orthodox and Protestants. Poland is considered a major economic success when compared to the transitional economies in Eastern Europe that began to redefine themselves after the fall of the Soviet Union and the subsequent end of the Cold War. The per capita income of $20,200 (2011) is the sixty-first highest in the world. However, since the onset of the global economic crisis in 2007, Poland has endured some economic challenges. In 2010, unemployment was 12.4 percent, and it was even higher, 21 percent, among Polish youths age fifteen to twenty-four.

The first Poles arrived in what would become the United States in 1608, and more came between 1800 and 1860. However, industrialization was the draw for the first significant wave of Polish immigrants. Between 1880 and 1924, they were lured by the factories, mills, mines, and slaughterhouses that fueled American industrialization. Polish immigrants settled in New York, Illinois, Michigan, Pennsylvania, and New Jersey. Chiefly from the working class, they tended to be young males who were either unmarried or recently married. Upon arriving in the United States, they began producing large families and became enthusiastic Americans. Chicago soon had more Poles living within its borders than any other city in the world except Warsaw. A new wave of Polish immigrants began arriving during and immediately after World War II in response to communist displacement, with 179,000 arriving between 1940 and 1953. Between 1980 and 1990, the number of Polish Americans climbed from 3,805,740 to 6,542,844. By the early twenty-first century, new Polish immigrants were continuing to settle in Chicago and New York, but they also began making their homes in cities throughout the United States. Because of the high rate of assimilation among earlier Polish immigrants, the group reflected the trend among modern Americans to move away from cities and into the suburbs. However, many Polish American suburbanites continued to commute into cities to attend large Catholic churches.

In 2011, data gathered for the Census Bureau's American Community Survey reported that the size of the Polish American population was 9,530,571, and Poles continued to concentrate in New York, Illinois, Pennsylvania, and Michigan. Other states with large populations of people of Polish descent include California, New Jersey, Florida, Ohio, and Wisconsin.

HISTORY OF THE PEOPLE

Early History The very name of Poland harkens back to its origins in the Slavic tribes that inhabited the Vistula valley as early as the second millennium BCE. Migrations of these tribes resulted in three distinct subgroups: the West, East, and South Slavs. It was the West Slavs who became the ancestors of modern Poles, settling in and around the Oder and Vistula valleys. Highly clannish, these tribes were organized in tight kinship groups with commonly held property and a rough-and-ready sort of representative government regarding matters other than military. These West Slavs slowly joined in ever-larger units under the pressure of incursions by Avars and early Germans, ultimately being led by a tribe known as the Polanie. From that point on, these West Slavs, and increasingly the entire region, were referred to as Polania or later, Poland. Under the Polanian duke Mieszko and his Piast dynasty, further consolidation around what is modern Poznan created a true state; and in 966, Mieszko was converted to Christianity. It is this event that is commonly accepted as the founding date of Poland. It is doubly important because Mieszko's conversion to Christianity—Roman Catholicism—ultimately linked Poland's fortunes to those of Western Europe. The East Slavs, centered at Kiev, were converted by missionaries from the Greek church, which in turn linked them to the Orthodox east.

Meanwhile, the South Slavs had been coalescing into larger units, forming what is known as Little Poland, as opposed to Great Poland of the Piasts. These South Slavs joined Great Poland under Casimir I, and for several generations the new state thrived, checking the tide of German expansionism. But from the twelfth to thirteenth centuries, the new kingdom became fragmented by a duchy system that created political chaos and civil war among rival princes of the Piast lineage. Following devastations caused by Tatar invasions in the early thirteenth century, Poland was defenseless against a further tide of German settlement. One of the last Piasts, Casimir III, succeeded in reunifying the kingdom in 1338, and in 1386 it came under the rule of the Jagiellonian dynasty when the grand duke of Lithuania married the crown princess of the Piasts, Jadwiga. Known as Poland's Golden Age, the next two centuries of Jagiellonian rule enabled Poland-Lithuania to become the dominant power in central Europe, encompassing Hungary and Bohemia in its sphere of influence and producing a rich cultural heritage for the nation, including the achievements of such individuals as Copernicus (Mikołaj Kopernik, 1473–1543). At the same time, Poland enjoyed one of the most representative governments of its day as well as the most tolerant religious climate in Europe.

But with the end of the Jagiellonian dynasty in 1572, the kingdom once again fell apart as the landed gentry increasingly assumed local control, sapping the strength of the central government in Krakow. This state of affairs continued for two centuries until Poland was so weakened that it suffered three partitions: Austria took Galicia in 1772; Prussia acquired the northwestern section in 1793; and Tsarist Russia possessed the northeastern section in 1795. By the end of the three partitions, Poland had been completely wiped off the map of Europe. Poland as an independent nation did not exist again for a century and a half, though a nominal Kingdom of Poland was established within the Russian Empire by the Congress of Vienna in 1815. In both Russia and Germany a strict policy of suppression of the Polish language and autonomous education was enforced.

Modern Era After World War I, an independent Poland was once again reestablished. With Josef Pilsudski (1867–1935) as its president and dictator from 1926 to 1935, Poland maintained an uneasy peace with the Soviet Union and Nazi Germany. Poland became the site of the first aggression of World War II when Germany invaded on September 1, 1939. This invasion triggered declarations of war from France, Great Britain, and the Commonwealth, though Poland was quickly defeated and was once again subsumed into other countries: Germany and the Soviet Union initially and then Germany alone. The Nazis attempted to subdue and eradicate Polish culture by executing its intellectuals and nobles, and by "settling" the Jewish question once and for all through the extermination of the Jews of Poland and Europe. In concentration camps such as Auschwitz-Birkenau this gruesome strategy was put into effect, and by the end of the war in 1945, Poland had lost a fifth of its population, half of which—more than 3 million—were Jews.

Liberation, however, did not mean freedom, for after the war Poland fell under the Soviet sphere; a communist state was set up, and Poland once again became a fiefdom to a foreign power. In 1956 Poland's workers went on a general strike to protest Moscow's heavy-handed domination. Though brutally suppressed, the strike did force Poland's new leader Władysław Gomułka to relax some of the totalitarian controls imposed by Warsaw and Moscow, and farms were decollectivized. Through successive leadership of Edward Gierek and General Wojciech Jaruzelski, however, economic conditions worsened, and the Poles struggled increasingly for more autonomy from Moscow. By 1980 three events had coincided that became decisive for Poland's future: the Soviet Union was going bankrupt; Karol Cardinal Wojtyła became Pope John Paul II; and a new and illegal union, Solidarity, had been formed under Lech Wałesa. These last two especially brought Poland into international focus. By 1989, Solidarity won concessions from the government that included participation in free elections. After an overwhelming victory, which installed Lech Wałesa as president, Solidarity set up a coalition government with the communists; and with the fall of the Soviet Union, Poland, along with all of central Europe, regained new breathing room in its heartland.

Under the guidance of Solidarity, the country faced the difficult task of transforming from a centrally planned economy to a market economy, a change that caused enormous dislocations including inflation rates as high as 600 percent. To combat this, Poland's minister of finance, Leszek Balcerowicz, along with several other leading economists including George Soros and Jeffrey Sachs, drafted the Balcerowicz Plan, a program of what Sachs called "shock therapy," which included such measures as privatizing public assets, eliminating state subsidies, and withdrawing state-imposed price controls. Most economists agree that these policies, designed to protect free trade, raised the standard of living in Poland, even though the plan may have been responsible for a new set of problems, including rising crime and unemployment rates. Economic growth continued into the early twenty-first century, and Poland became the only country in the European Union to escape major recession between 2008 and

2009. However, the government continues to struggle with rebuilding infrastructures and with attracting businesses capable of boosting the economy.

SETTLEMENT IN THE UNITED STATES

Poles were among the earliest colonists in the New World, and as of 2010, when their numbers approached 10 million, they represented the largest of the Slavic groups in the United States. Claims have been made that Poles sailed with Viking ships exploring the New World before 1600, but there is no hard evidence to support this. By 1609, however, Polish immigrants began to appear in the annals of Jamestown, having been recruited by the colony as skilled craftsmen to create products for export. These immigrants were integral to the establishment of both the glassmaking and woodworking industries in the new colonies. In 1719, Anthony Sadowski, a Polish explorer, founded the Amity Township in Berks County, Pennsylvania, which developed into a stable middle-class American community with a population of more than 12,000 as of 2010. Two other names of note occur in the early history of what became the American republic: the noblemen Tadeusz Kościuszko (1746–1817) and Casimir Pulaski (1747–1779) both fought for the Patriots in the Revolutionary War. Pułaski, killed in the battle of Savannah, is still honored by Polish Americans by annual marches on Pulaski Day, which is celebrated on October 11.

Since the times of those earliest Polish settlers—romantics, adventurers, and men simply seeking a better economic life—there have been four distinct waves of immigration to the United States from Poland. The first and smallest, occasioned by the partitioning of Poland, lasted from roughly 1800 to 1860 and was largely made up of political dissidents and those who fled after the dissolution of their national homeland. The second wave was far more significant and took place between 1860 and World War I. Immigrants during this time were in search of a better economic life and tended to be of the rural class, so-called *za chleben* (for bread) emigrants. A third wave lasted from the end of World War I through the end of the Cold War and again comprised dissidents and political refugees. Since the fall of the Soviet Union and Poland's democratic reforms, there has been yet a fourth wave of a seemingly more temporary immigrant group, the *wakacjusze*, or those who come on tourist visas but find work and stay either legally or illegally. These economic immigrants generally plan to earn money and return to Poland.

The first wave of immigrants, from approximately 1800 to 1860, was largely made up of intellectuals and lesser nobility. The partitioning of Poland and insurrections in 1830 and 1863 also forced political dissidents from their Polish homeland. Many fled to London, Paris, and Geneva, but New York and Chicago also received their share of such refugees from political oppression. Immigration figures are always a problematic issue, and those for Polish immigrants to the United States are no different. For much of the modern era there was no political entity of Poland, so immigrants coming to the United States had an initial difficulty describing their country of origin. Also, with Poles, there was more back-and-forth travel between host country and home country. This group tended to save money and return to their native country in higher numbers than many other ethnic groups. Additionally, minorities within Poland who immigrated to the United States confuse the picture. Nonetheless, numbers that exist from U.S. Immigration and Naturalization Service records indicate that fewer than 2,000 Poles immigrated to the United States between 1800 and 1860.

The second wave of immigration began in 1854 when some 800 Polish Catholics from Silesia founded Panna Maria, a farming colony in Texas. Dedicated to the Virgin Mary, the community still exists and is the oldest permanent Polish settlement in the United States. In the 1860s Poles began arriving in large numbers due to harsh economic conditions in Poland. Known as *za chlebem*, or "for bread" immigrants, these new arrivals tended to cluster in industrial cities and towns of the Midwest and Mid-Atlantic states—New York, Buffalo, Pittsburgh, Cleveland, Detroit, Milwaukee, Minneapolis, Chicago, and St. Louis—where they became steelworkers, meatpackers, miners, and, later, autoworkers. These cities still retain their large contingents of Polish Americans.

Confusion over exact numbers of Polish immigrants continued, with large underreporting, especially during the 1890s when immigration was highest. Most scholars agree, however, that between the mid-nineteenth century and World War I, some 2.5 million Poles immigrated to the United States. This wave of immigration can be further broken down into two successive movements of Poles from different regions of their partitioned country. The first to come were the German Poles, who tended to be better educated and more skilled at crafts than the Russian

A Polish woman and her three sons arrive in the U.S. UPI / CORBIS-BETTMANN. REPRODUCED BY PERMISSION.

and Austrian Poles. High birthrates, overpopulation, and large-scale farming methods in Prussia, which forced small farmers off the land, all combined to send German Poles into emigration in the second half of the nineteenth century. German policy vis-à-vis restricting the power of the Catholic Church also played a part in this exodus. Those arriving in the United States totaled roughly a half million during this period, with numbers dwindling by the end of the nineteenth century.

However, just as German Polish immigration to the United States was diminishing, that of Russian and Austrian Poles was getting under way. Again, overpopulation and land hunger drove this emigration, as well as the enthusiastic letters home that new arrivals in the United States sent to their relatives and loved ones. Many young men also fled from military conscription, especially in the years of military buildup just prior to and including the onset of World War I. Moreover, the journey to the United States itself had become less arduous, with shipping lines such as the North German Line and the Hamburg American Line now booking passage from point to point, combining overland as well as transatlantic passage and thereby simplifying border crossings. Numbers of Galician or Austrian Poles totaled approximately 800,000. Another group of 800,000 was comprised of Russian Poles, the last large immigration contingent from Poland. It has been estimated that 30 percent of Galician and Russian Poles arriving between 1906 and 1914 ultimately returned to their homelands.

During the last half of the nineteenth century, immigrants from Poland, like those from other parts of Europe, experienced racial intolerance. As was typical for immigrant groups, Polish Americans sought support from members of their community and from the local organizations that developed within those communities. Polish fraternal, national, and religious organizations such as the Polish National Alliance, the Polish Union, the Polish American Congress, and the Polish Roman Catholic Union were instrumental not only in maintaining a Polish identity for immigrants, but also in obtaining insurance and home loans that provided opportunities within the United States. Friction abated as Poles assimilated in their host country, only to be supplanted by new waves of immigrants from other countries. Polish Americans continued to maintain a strong ethnic identity into the late twentieth century, and efforts to reclaim that identity and pass it down to children and grandchildren who had never even seen Poland continued into the twenty-first century.

With the end of World War I and the reestablishment of an independent Polish state, it was believed that there would be a huge exodus of Polish immigrants returning to their homeland. Such an exodus did not materialize, though there was a general decline in immigration to the United States among all Europeans due to a number of factors including immigration quotas imposed in the United States during the 1920s as well as the Great Depression. But political oppression in Europe between the wars, displaced persons brought on by World War II, and the flight of dissidents from the communist regime did account for an additional half million immigrants—many of them refugees—from Poland between 1918 and the late 1980s and the fall of communism. Large numbers of Polish American families sponsored displaced Poles and facilitated their entry into the United States. However, almost immediately, dissension broke out between the new immigrants and those highly acclimatized Poles already living in the United States. The new immigrants frequently opted to build their own more radical organizations rather than joining those already in existence. Despite disagreements, most Polish Americans were united against communism.

The fourth wave of Polish immigration was comprised mostly of younger people who immigrated to the United States to escape difficult transition times brought on by the decline of Soviet communism and the rise of free-market capitalism in Poland. Though not significant in numbers because of immigration quotas, this newest wave of post-Cold War immigrants, whether they were short-term workers, *wakacjusze*, or long-term residents, continued to swell the number of Polonians living in the United States. Estimates from the 1970 U.S. Census placed the number of either foreign-born Poles or native born with at least one Polish parent at nearly 3 million. More than 8 million claimed Polish ancestry in their background in the 1980 Census, and 9.5 million did so in the 1990 Census, 90 percent of whom were concentrated in urban areas. A large part of such identity and cohesiveness was the result of outside conditions. It has been noted that initial friction between Polish immigrants and "established" Americans played some part in this inward-looking stance. Additionally, such commonly held beliefs as folk culture and Catholicism provided further incentives for communalism. Newly arrived Poles generally had their closest contacts outside Polish Americans with their former European neighbors: Czechs, Germans, and Lithuanians. Over the years there has been a degree of friction specifically between the Polish American community and Jews and African Americans. However, during the years of partition, Polish Americans kept alive the belief in a free Poland. Such cohesiveness was further heightened in the Polish American community during the Cold War, when Poland was a satellite of the Soviet Union. But since the fall of the Soviet empire, which was followed by free elections in Poland and the revitalization of the Polish economy, Polish Americans have had fewer reasons to worry about affairs in their native Poland and the well-being of members of the extended family still living there. Poland's prosperity has, to some degree, led to a decrease in cohesiveness among Polish Americans.

In 2000 the U.S. Census Bureau reported that there were almost 9 million people of Polish descent living in the United States. Approximately 500,000 had been born outside the United States, and many of the rest were second- and third-generation Americans. Almost one-third of the Polish American population lived in the Chicago area. In 2008, census data indicated that the number of Polish immigrants was declining in conjunction with that of other European immigrants. New York (55,000) displaced Chicago (46,000) as the city with the largest Polonian population. However, Chicago continued to have the largest concentration of Polish Americans because those who lived in New York were dispersed among various communities. According to the Modern Polonia Survey conducted by the Piast Institute in 2009, Polish Americans continued to cluster in major urban areas (41.2 percent) and the suburbs of those urban areas (41 percent). In 2011 the U.S. Census Bureau reported that there were over 9.6 million people of Polish descent living in the United States. Five states continued to claim the largest numbers: New York (985,593), Illinois (957,355), Michigan (881,668), and Pennsylvania (861,914). Other states with populations over 400,000 included Wisconsin, California, New Jersey, Ohio, and Florida.

LANGUAGE

Polish is a West Slavic language, part of the Lekhite subgroup, and is similar to Czech and Slovak. Modern Polish, written in the Roman alphabet, stems from the sixteenth century. It is still taught in Sunday schools and parochial schools for children. It is also taught in dozens of American universities and colleges. The first written example of Polish is a list of names in an 1136 Papal Bull. Manuscripts in Polish exist from the fourteenth century. The Polish vocabulary is in part borrowed from Latin, German, Czech, Ukrainian, Belarusian, and English. Dialects include Great Polish, Pomeranian, Silesian, and Mazovian. Spelling is phonetic with every letter pronounced. Consonants in particular have different pronunciation than in English. *Ch*, for example, is pronounced like the "h" in horse; *j* is pronounced like the "y" at the beginning of a word; *cz* is pronounced "ch" as in chair; *sz* is pronounced like "sh" as in shoe; *rz* and *z* are pronounced alike as the English "j" in jar; and *w* is pronounced like the English "v" in victory. Various diacriticals are also used in Polish: ż, ź, ń, ć, ś, ą, ę, and ł.

According to the American Community Survey's 2011 estimates, 92 percent of Polish Americans over the age of five spoke only English at home, and 97 percent reported that they spoke English fluently.

Greetings and Popular Expressions Typical Polish greetings and other expressions include: *Dzien dobry* ("gyen dobry")—Good morning; *Dobry wieczor* ("dobry viechoor")—Good evening; *Dowidzenia* ("dovidzenyah")—Good-bye;

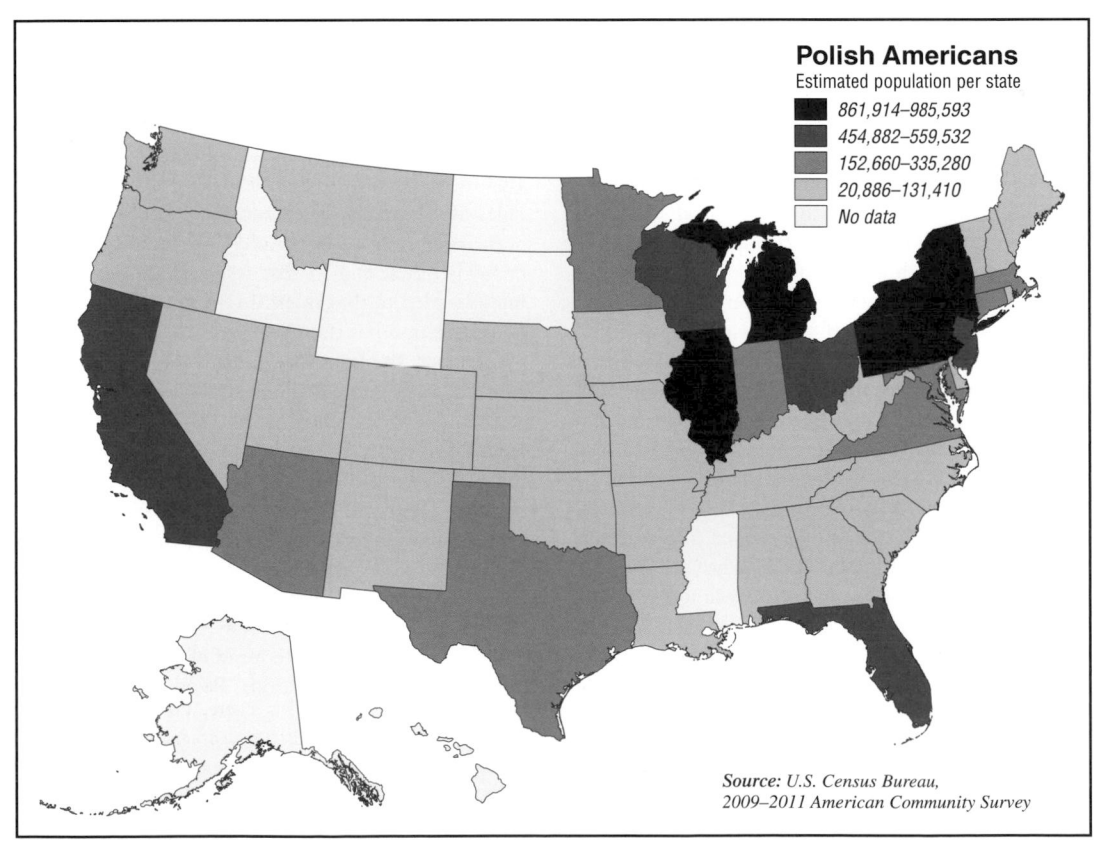

Polish Americans
Estimated population per state
- 861,914–985,593
- 454,882–559,532
- 152,660–335,280
- 20,886–131,410
- No data

Source: U.S. Census Bureau, 2009–2011 American Community Survey

Dozobaczenia ("dozobahchainya")—Till we meet again; *Dziekuje* ("gyen-kuyeh")—Thank you; *Przepraszam* ("psheprasham")—I beg your pardon; *Nie* ("nyeh")—No; *Tak* ("tahk")—Yes.

> "We wanted to be Americans so quickly that we were embarrassed if our parents couldn't speak English. My father was reading a Polish paper. And somebody was supposed to come to the house. I remember sticking it under something. We were that ashamed of being foreign."
>
> Louise Nagy in 1913, cited in *Ellis Island: An Illustrated History of the Immigrant Experience*, edited by Ivan Chermayeff et al. (New York: Macmillan, 1991).

RELIGION

The major religion of Poland is Catholicism, which survived even under the anticlerical reign of the communists. Religion is a deeply ingrained part of Polish life, and immigrants to the United States brought their religion with them. Initially, Polish American parishes were established from simple meetings of the local religious in stores or hotels. These meetings soon became societies, taking on the name of a saint, and later developing into the parish itself, with priests arriving from various areas of Poland. The members of the parish were responsible for financial support of their clergy as well as for construction of a church and any other buildings needed by the priest. Polish American Catholics were responsible for the creation of seven religious orders, including the Resurrectionists and the Felicians, who in turn created schools and seminaries and brought nuns from Poland to help with orphanages and other social services.

The new arrivals quickly turned their religious institution into both a parish and an *okolica*, a local area or neighborhood. There was rapid growth in the number of such ethnic parishes: from 17 in 1870 to 512 only forty years later. The number peaked in 1935 at 800 and has tapered off since, with 760 in 1960. The close of Vatican II (an ecumenical council that sought to strengthen the church's relationship with the modern world) in 1965 led to a declaration that Mass could be said in any language, not just in Latin. Consequently, in many Polish parishes throughout the East and Midwest, Mass was said in Polish. However, in the 1970s as churchgoing declined and as fewer young Poles spoke their native language, the number of churches offering Mass in Polish declined as well.

Many Polish American Catholics have endured some measure of hardship since their arrival in the United States. A largely Protestant nation in the nineteenth century, the United States proved somewhat intolerant of Catholics, a fact that only served to separate immigrant Poles from the mainstream even more. Also, within the church, there was dissension. Footing all the bills for the parish, Polish American Catholics

often had little representation in the church hierarchy, which was largely controlled by Irish Americans. There were also differences in the ways in which rituals were conducted in Polish Catholic and Irish Catholic churches within the United States. In areas where Irish Catholics dominated, Polish Catholics were often forced to adopt Irish Catholic rituals. However, in areas where Polish Americans made up the majority, they were able to worship in their own way. Disputes among Polish and Irish Catholics ultimately led to the establishment of the Polish National Church in 1904. The founding bishop, Reverend Francis Hodur, built the institution to thirty-four churches and more than 28,000 communicants in a dozen years' time. In the 1980s, Polish Americans that had been living in cities such as Detroit, Chicago, Hartford, and Philadelphia began to move to the suburbs, and the number of parishes that held Polish American majorities declined significantly. However, by the early twenty-first century, Polish American Catholics had influenced American Catholicism to such an extent that rituals such as celebrating with the *oplatek* wafer on Christmas Eve had become common in many Catholic parishes, including those without large numbers of Polish American members.

CULTURE AND ASSIMILATION

As part of the European emigration, Polish immigrants have had an easier time racially than many other non-European groups in assimilating or blending into the American scene. However, Polish immigrants were not treated as equals by the various white-skinned peoples who had arrived in the United States before them. Culturally, the Polish contingent has held tightly to its folk and national roots, making Polonia more than simply a name. It has been at times a country within a country, Poland in the New World. By and large, Poles have competed well and succeeded in their new homeland; they have thrived and built homes and raised families, and in that respect have participated in and added to the American dream. Yet this process of assimilation has been far from smooth as witnessed by one fact: the Polish joke. Such jokes have at their core a negative representation of the Poles as backward and uneducated simpletons. This stereotype—perhaps hardest for Polish Americans to combat—is a legacy of the second wave of immigrants, the largest contingent between 1860 and 1914, which consisted mostly of people from Galicia and Russia. Though recent studies have shown Polish Americans to have high income levels as compared to British, German, Italian, and Irish immigrant groups, the same studies demonstrate that they come in last in terms of occupation and education. For many generations, Polish Americans, like many immigrants in the United States who held wage-earning jobs, had limited opportunities to pursue college degrees. However, this trend changed significantly in the late twentieth century and early twenty-first century. Polish Americans are now heavily represented in the professions as well as in the blue-collar world. Yet the Polish joke persists, and since the 1970s, Polish Americans have been actively fighting the stereotype through educational programs. In addition, groups such as the Polish American Guardian Society have lobbied to eliminate the propagation of anti-Polish stereotypes on national television.

The days of Polish Americans anglicizing their names seem to be over; Polish Americans now talk of ethnic pride. They keep their culture alive both within the Polonian community and among the general public through annual observances such as cultural festivals and parades. Since 1981, Chicago has held a parade on May 3 to celebrate the Polish Constitution of 1791. New York has been hosting the Pulaski Day Parade each March since 1937. Milwaukee holds an annual Polish Fest.

Traditions and Customs It had been noted that clans and kinship communities were extremely important in the early formation of Slavic tribes. This early form of communalism has been translated into today's world by the plethora of Polish American fraternal organizations. By the same token, other traditions out of the Polish rural and agrarian past still hold today.

Gospodarz may well be one of the prettiest sounding words in the Polish language—to a Pole. It means landowner, and it is the land that has always been important in Poland. Ownership of land was one of the things that brought the huge influx of Poles to the United States, but less than 10 percent achieved that dream, and these were mainly the German Poles who arrived first—when there was still a frontier to carve out. The remaining Poles were stuck in urban areas as wage earners, though many managed to save the money to buy a small plot of land in the suburbs. Contrasted to this is the *Górale*, or mountaineer. To the lowlanders of Greater Poland, the stateless peoples of the southern Carpathians represented free human spirit, unbridled by convention and laws. Both of these impulses run through the Polish people and inform their customs.

Cuisine The diet of Polish Americans has changed over the years. One marked change from Poland is the increased consumption of meat. Polish sausages, especially the *kielbasa*—garlic-flavored pork sausage—have become all but synonymous with Polish cuisine. Other staples include *barszcz*, or beet soup, cabbage in the form of sauerkraut or cabbage rolls, dark bread, potatoes, beets, barley, and oatmeal. Of course this traditional diet has been added to by usual American fare, but Polish Americans still serve their traditional food, especially at festivities and celebrations such as Christmas and Easter. In addition to *kielbasa*, Polish Americans have also contributed staples to American cuisine, including the breakfast roll, *bialys*, the *babka* coffeecake, and pierogi, dumplings stuffed with potato, sauerkraut, meat, or cheese.

A Polish American woman prepares homemade perogi with a friend in Brooklyn, New York. DAVID GROSSMAN / ALAMY

Traditional Dress Traditional clothing is worn less and less by Polish Americans but may still be seen during certain ethnic celebrations. An example is Pulaski Day, when upward of 100,000 Polish Americans parade between 26th Street and 52nd Street in New York, many of them wearing traditional dress. For women this means a combination blouse and petticoat covered by a full, brightly colored or embroidered skirt, an apron, and a jacket or bodice, also gaily decorated. Headdress ranges from a simple kerchief to more elaborate affairs made of feathers, flowers, beads, and ribbons decorating stiffened linen. Men also wear headdresses of felt or straw that are significantly less elaborate than those worn by females. Trousers are often white with red stripes, tucked into the boots or worn with mountaineering moccasins typical to the Carpathians. Vests or jackets cover white embroidered shirts, and the favorite colors—red and white—replicate the flag.

Holidays In addition to Pulaski Day, which President Harry Truman decreed an official remembrance day in 1946, Polish American celebrations consist mainly of the prominent liturgical holidays such as Christmas and Easter, as most Polish Americans follow the Catholic calendar of feast days. The traditional Christmas Eve dinner, called *wigilia*, begins when the first star of the evening appears. The dinner, which is served upon a white tablecloth under which some straw has been placed, consists of twelve meatless courses— one for each of the apostles. An empty chair is also kept at the table for a stranger who might happen by. This vigil supper begins with the breaking of a wafer, the *oplatek*, and the exchange of good wishes; it moves on to such traditional fare as apple pancakes, fish, *pierogi* or a type of filled dumpling, potato salad, sauerkraut, and nut or poppy seed torte for dessert. To ensure good luck in the coming year one must taste all courses, and there must also be an even number of people at the table to ensure good health. The singing of carols follows the supper. In Poland, between Christmas Eve and the Epiphany (January 6, or "Three Kings") "caroling with the manger" takes place: carolers bearing a manger visit neighbors and are rewarded with money or treats. The Christmas season comes to a close with Candelmas day on February 2, when the candles are taken to church to be blessed. It is believed that these blessed candles will protect the home from sickness or bad fortune.

The Tuesday before Ash Wednesday is celebrated by much feasting. Poles traditionally make fried *pączki* (fruit-filled doughnuts) in order to use the sugar and fat in the house before the long fast of Lent. In the United States, especially in Polish communities, the day before Ash Wednesday has become popularized as Pączki Day; Poles and non-Poles alike wait in line at Polish bakeries for this pastry. Easter is an especially important holiday for Polish Americans. Originally an agrarian people, the Poles focused on Easter as the time of rebirth and regeneration not only religiously, but for their fields as well. It marked the beginning of a farmer's year. Consequently, it is still celebrated with feasts that include meats and traditional cakes, butter molded into the shape of a lamb, and elaborately decorated eggs (*pisanki*), along with a good deal of drinking and dancing.

In the first half of the twentieth century these holiday traditions were kept alive in most Polish American parishes. Over the course of the latter half of the twentieth century and into the twenty-first century, churchgoing on holidays such as Epiphany and Candelmas declined substantially. However, many contemporary Polish Americans honor these traditions by remembering them, if not by practicing them. The website for the Polish American Journal, for example, contains a series of articles on how native Polish people celebrated the various days of the Easter and Christmas seasons and how they conducted all of the rituals associated with these holidays. Although most of the writers note that contemporary Polish Americans no longer celebrate Catholic holidays in

POLISH PROVERBS

Polish proverbs emphasize the undercurrents of Polish nature, highlighting hospitality, belief in simple pragmatism and honesty, and cynical distrust of human nature. Some examples include the following:

Gose w dorn, Bog w dorn.

When a guest enters the house, God enters the home.

Czym chata bogata, tym rada.

What's ours is yours.

Ani kura darmo nie gdacze.

You cannot get something for nothing. (Literal translation: The only free cheese is in the mousetrap.)

Czasowi ludzie slusa.

Gnaw the bone that falls to your lot.

I cyprysy majaswoje kaprysy.

Every fool is pleased with his own folly.

Tonacy brzytuy sie chwyta.

A drowning man plucks at a straw.

Anielskie usta a szatanskie serce.

A honey tongue, a heart of gall.

Biada bez dzieci, biada i z dziećmi.

Children are uncertain comforts but certain cares.

Broda nie czyni filozofa.

If the beard were all, the goat might preach.

Dar za dar, słowa za słowa.

He who works for nothing shall receive nothing from others except complaint.

Domowe psy, choć się kąsają, wilka ujrzawszy naź się rzucają.

Don't go between the tree and the bark.

traditional ways, they write fondly of traditional celebrations held in their childhoods in places such as Detroit and New York City.

Health Care Issues and Practices Health problems among Polish immigrants during the American Industrial Revolution were often connected to living conditions such as overcrowding and inadequate sanitation. The creation of fraternal and insurance societies such as the Polish National Alliance in 1880, the Polish Roman Catholic Union in 1873, and the Polish Women's Alliance in 1898 helped to bring life insurance to a larger segment of Polonia. By the late twentieth century, health problems being diagnosed among recent Polish immigrants were generally related to lifestyle and to workplace conditions common in Poland. Such immigrants were especially susceptible to obesity because of inadequate exercise and to respiratory illnesses and cancers, particularly leukemia, because of the lack of safety measures used in Polish mills and mines.

Death and Burial Rituals Polish Americans retain some of the traditional funeral practices of their home country. The word "death" in Polish (śmierć) is a feminine noun and is characterized as a tall woman draped in white. Once again, Catholic rites take over for the dead. Often the dead are accompanied in their coffins by strong shoes for the arduous journey ahead or by money as an entrance fee to heaven. The funeral itself is followed by a feast or *stypa*, which may also include music and dancing.

FAMILY AND COMMUNITY LIFE

Typically, the Polish family structure is strongly nuclear and patriarchal. However, as with other ethnic groups coming to the United States, Poles have adapted to the American way of life, which means a stronger role for the woman in some Polish American families and in the working world. Initially, single or married men were likely to immigrate alone, living in crowded quarters or rooming houses, saving their money and sending large amounts back to Poland. That immigration trend changed over the years, to be replaced by family units immigrating together. By the 1990s, however, the immigration pattern had come full circle, with many single men and women moving to the United States in search of work.

Gender Roles Before the fall of the Soviet Union and the subsequent transition in the early 1990s to a free market economy in Poland, all adults there, even married women with children, were expected to hold full-time jobs. Despite this demand, it was still assumed that women would look after most of the domestic chores, with men helping only occasionally. During the 1990s, the expectation that women, no matter what their circumstances, would stay gainfully employed, diminished, but the new set of economic challenges frequently required women to continue earning money for their families. Economists such as George Soros and Jeffrey Sachs have recognized that the most pressing challenge for many adults throughout Eastern Europe at the time was coping with unusually high levels of anxiety. In Poland, as in other countries, prices were changing rapidly, and there was the persistent threat of widespread unemployment. Though the threat never materialized in Poland, most people thought it unwise to leave work during such stressful times. In other words, though democracy and free market capitalism presented women with more choices, the reality was that most women needed to stay employed to make ends meet.

Moreover, as tempestuous as the economic and social climate was at the time, the massive changes also granted new opportunities for women in the working world and in education. Women could choose not to work, but they could also pursue loftier career goals and obtain more clout in the workplace. These radically different options caused a sense of role conflict in many Polish women who had been raised to accept their place in the traditional Polish family. In homes in which both spouses have obtained advanced degrees, this sense of role conflict has been diminished as the men have been more likely to take on domestic duties normally reserved for women. Also, most Polish parents want their daughters to achieve some level of economic independence so they push them to graduate from college and pursue jobs. Even so, unemployment rates in Poland are still higher among women, and average wages remain lower.

A woman shares photos stored on her digital camera with her aunt. Both emigrated from Poland to the U.S. DAVID GROSSMAN / ALAMY

Polish American families tend to be more traditional than Polish families. For example, second- and third-generation Polish Americans, especially those born in the Rust Belt (specifically western New York, western Pennsylvania, and eastern Ohio), are likely to live close to their birth homes as adults and to marry within the Polish American community. Such families, many of which practice Roman Catholicism, tend to adhere to traditional values, with men earning most of the family's wages and women overseeing the children and the domestic chores. Polish American communities in the Midwest and other parts of the United States adhere less closely to these traditional values, but even in these communities Polish American women may be less progressive than their Polish counterparts. One example that illustrates this point is the fact that most Polish women celebrate International Women's Day (held annually on March 8), whereas most Polish American women do not.

Education Education took on additional importance throughout the twentieth century. Where a primary education was deemed sufficient for males in the early years of the twentieth century—much of it done in Catholic schools—the value of a university education for children of both sexes now mirrors the trend for American society as a whole. A 1972 study from U.S. Census statistics showed that almost 90 percent of Polish Americans between the ages of twenty-five and thirty-four had graduated from high school, as compared to only 45 percent of those over age thirty-five. Additionally, a full quarter of the younger generation, those between the ages of twenty-five and thirty-four, had completed at least a four-year university education. In general, as is the case in many immigrant groups, it appears that the higher the socio-economic class of the Polish American, the more rapid the transition from Polish identity to that of the dominant culture.

In the twenty-first century, Poland has a literacy rate of 99.5 percent. Among Polish Americans, the literacy rate reflects that of the United States as a whole (99 percent). A similar pattern also holds true for educational attainment. In Poland, most females attend school for an average of sixteen years and males for an average of fifteen years. In the United States, females attend school for seventeen years and males for fifteen years. Heightened emphasis on education continues to lead to increases in the number of Polish Americans pursuing education beyond the secondary level. In 2008 the Piast Institute's Modern Polonia Survey revealed that 13.9 percent of Polonians had either a graduate or professional degree. The number with a bachelor's degree was 21.4 percent; 28.9 percent had attended college without graduating or had obtained a technical certification.

Courtship and Weddings Until the latter part of the twentieth century, Polish Americans tended to marry within the community of Poles, but this too has changed over the years, and 80 percent of Polish Americans now marry outside the Polish American community. A strong ethnic identity is maintained now not so much through shared traditions or folk culture, but through national pride. As with many European immigrant groups, male children were looked upon as the breadwinners whereas females were seen as future wives and mothers. This held true through the second wave of immigrants, but with the third wave and with second- and third-generation families, women in general took on a more important role in extra-familial life.

The Poles maintain traditions most closely in those ceremonies for which the community holds great value: weddings, christenings, and funerals. Weddings are no longer the hugely staged events of Polish heritage, but they are often long and heavy-drinking affairs, involving several of the customary seven steps: inquiry and proposal; betrothal; maiden evening and the symbolic unbraiding of the virgin's hair; baking the wedding cake; marriage ceremony; putting to bed; and removal to the groom's house. Traditional dances such as the *krakowiak*, *oberek*, *mazur*, and the *zbo'jnicki* are performed on such occasions. Almost all Polish American weddings include the polka. Although the polka originated in Bohemia, not Poland, Polonians have adopted the lively dance as their own, and the Polish American form of the polka, which was a product of the early twentieth century, was heavily influenced by American jazz. Also to be enjoyed at such gatherings are the national drink, vodka, and such traditional fare as roast pork, sausages, *barszcs* or beet soup, cabbage rolls, and poppy seed cakes.

Christenings generally take place within two weeks of the birth on a Sunday or holiday, and for devoutly Catholic Poles, it is a vital ceremony. The selected godparents present the baby with gifts, more commonly money now than the traditional linens or caps of rural Poland. The christening feast, once a multiday affair, has been toned down in modern times, but still involves a panoply of holiday foods. The ceremony itself may include a purification rite for the mother as well as baby, a tradition that goes back to the pre-Christian past.

EMPLOYMENT AND ECONOMIC CONDITIONS

Early Polish immigrants were largely agrarian except for those intellectuals who fled political persecution. By and large they came to the United States hoping to find a plot of land, but instead found the frontier closed. Thus, they were forced into urban areas of the Midwest and Mid-Atlantic states where they worked in steel mills, coal mines, meatpacking plants, oil refineries, and the garment industry. Subsequent groups of Polish immigrants went directly to urban centers where Polish communities had been established and where factory jobs were available. The pay was low for such work: the average annual income for Polish immigrants in 1910 was only $325. The working day was long, averaging about ten hours a day, as was typical throughout the United States at the time. But still Polish Americans managed to save their money; and by 1910, it is estimated that these immigrants had been able to send $40 million back to their relatives and loved ones in Russian and Austrian Poland. The amount was so large, in fact, that a federal commission was set up to investigate potential damages to the U.S. economy from such a large outflow of funds.

Polonian families pulled together, with education coming second to the need for young boys to contribute to the annual income. The need for such economies began to decline after World War I, however, and by 1920 only 10 percent of Polish American families derived income from the labor of children, and two-thirds were supported by the head of family.

Over the years of the twentieth century—except for the years of the Great Depression—the economic situation of Polish Americans steadily improved, with education taking on increasing importance, creating a parallel rise in Polish Americans in the white-collar labor market. By 1970 only 4 percent were laborers, and 23 percent were craftsmen. This trend has continued over the latter part of the twentieth century and beginning of the twenty-first. According to the 2011 American Community Survey, almost half (42.9 percent) of the 9.5 million Polish Americans living in the United States at the time were employed in the management, business, science, or arts fields. Just over 25 percent held sales or clerk positions. Overall, Polish Americans have tended to prosper economically. In 1999, for instance, the median income of Polonians was $50,887. By 2011, the median household family income had climbed to $61,846.

POLITICS AND GOVERNMENT

Though heavily concentrated in nine industrial states, Polish Americans did not, until the 1930s, begin to flex their political muscle. Language barriers played a part in this, but more important was the fact that earlier immigrants were too concerned with family and community issues to pay attention to the national political scene. Even in Chicago, where Polish Americans made up 12 percent of the population, they did not elect one of their own to the U.S. Congress until 1920. The first Polish American congressional representative was elected from Milwaukee in 1918.

Increasingly, however, Polish Americans began playing a more active role in domestic politics and have tended to vote in large numbers for the Democrats. Al Smith, a Democrat and Roman Catholic who was opposed to Prohibition, was one of the first beneficiaries of the Polish American block vote. Though he lost the election, Smith received an overwhelming majority of the Polish American vote. The Great Depression mobilized Polish Americans even more; they organized the Polish American Democratic Organization and supported the New Deal policies of Franklin D.

JOSEPH YABLONSKI AND UNION REFORM

Polish Americans played a significant role in the U.S. labor movement during the twentieth century. One of the most important figures in the history of the movement was Joseph Yablonski, a union activist in the United Mine Workers of America (UMWA). Born in 1910 to Polish immigrants in Pittsburgh, Yablonski began working in the coal mines as a teenager. After unsuccessfully running against incumbent union president W. A. Boyle in 1969, Yablonski called for the Department of Labor to investigate the union for election fraud. Three weeks later he was murdered, along with his wife and daughter, by assassins contracted by Boyle. Yablonski's death initiated a number of reforms in the conduct of internal union affairs throughout the country, including legislation requiring that union elections be conducted by secret ballot.

Roosevelt. By 1944 this organization could throw large numbers of Polish American votes Roosevelt's way and was correspondingly compensated by federal patronage.

James S. Pula, one of the most noted of Polonian scholars, asserts in an October 1, 2012, interview with the *Polish American Journal* that the high level of assimilation among modern Polish Americans has led to a loss of interest in Polish politics beyond the establishment of the country's independence. A 2008 study of Polish American voting behavior conducted by the Piast Institute noted continued "intense involvement" with the issue of Polish independence. That same study revealed that 36.5 percent of Polonians identified themselves as Democrats, 33.2 percent as Independents, and 26.1 percent as Republicans. Somewhat surprisingly, however, 43.6 percent of Polonians identified themselves as conservative as compared to 33.2 percent, who considered themselves liberal. Some 23 percent identified themselves as moderate. The conservative orientation of Polish Americans is due in part to strong religious beliefs and alignment with the Catholic stance on abortion.

Polish Americans continue to be active participants in the American political process: 92 percent were registered to vote in 2008, and 52.3 percent voted for Barack Obama, the Democratic candidate. In 2012, however, some Polonians grew disenchanted with President Obama, who had represented the Chicago area in Congress before becoming president, because of what they considered neglect of Polish and Polish American issues. Republican candidate Mitt Romney, on the other hand, actively courted the Polish American vote because of its importance in several key states. Despite Romney's courting of

Polonians, Polish Americans continue to identify with the Democratic Party, and the Polish American labor movement insisted that it had not been enticed by Romney's actions.

Relations with Poland Internationally, Polish Americans have been more active politically than domestically. The Polish National Alliance, founded in 1880, was—in addition to being a mutual aid society—a fervent proponent of a free Poland. Such a goal manifested itself in very pragmatic terms: during World War I, Polish Americans not only sent their young to fight, but also sent the $250 million they subscribed in liberty bonds. Polish Americans also lobbied Washington with the objective of a free Poland in mind. The Polish American Congress (PAC) was created in 1944 to help secure independence for Poland, opposing the Yalta and Potsdam agreements, which established Soviet hegemony in Eastern Europe. During this same time, Polish American socialists formed the pro-Soviet Polish American Council, but its power waned in the early years of the Cold War. PAC, however, fought on into the 1980s, supporting Solidarity, the union movement in Poland largely responsible for the downfall of the communist government. Gifts of food, clothing, and lobbying in Washington were all part of the PAC campaign for an independent Poland, and the organization has been very active in the establishment of a free market system in Poland since the fall of the communist government. Polish Americans continue to lobby for Poland's inclusion in the American Visa Waiver Program, a move that would allow Poles to spend up to ninety days in the United States without obtaining a visa.

NOTABLE INDIVIDUALS

Throughout their history, Polish Americans have influenced the nation's arts and sciences and popular culture in greater proportion than is suggested by their numbers, a reported 3.2 percent of the American population in 2008.

Academia Bronislaw Malinowski (1884–1942), a pioneer of cultural anthropology, emphasized the concept of culture in meeting humankind's basic needs; he taught at Yale University late in his life, after writing such influential books as *The Sexual Life of Savages in North-Western Melanesia* (1929) and *Argonauts of the Western Pacific* (1932). Linguist Alfred Korzybski (1879–1950), born in Warsaw, came to the United States in 1918; his work in linguistics focused on the power of the different value and meaning of words in different languages in an effort to reduce misunderstanding; he founded the Institute of General Semantics in 1938 in Chicago, and his research and books—including *Manhood and Humanity* (1921) and *Science and Sanity*(1933)—have been incorporated in modern psychology and philosophy curricula as well as linguistics. The work of these earlier Polish American scholars is being carried on by contemporary academicians such as James S. Pula (1946–) and John Kromkowski (1939–). In addition to authoring such works as *The Polish American Encyclopedia*, Pula was a professor of history at Perdue University and edited *Polish American Studies*. Kromkowski was a professor at Catholic University of America, where he also served as the president of the National Center for Urban and Ethnic Affairs.

Arts Korczak Ziolkowski (1909–1982), an assistant to sculptor Gutzon Borglum in the monumental Mount Rushmore project in South Dakota, continued that style with a 500-foot by 640-foot statue of Chief Crazy Horse. After his death, his family continued his work, blasting the piece out of solid rock in the Black Hills.

Broadcasting Television entertainer Martha Stewart (1941–), who is best known for her home decorating expertise and line of home furnishings as well as her various business endeavors, is the child of Polish Americans. Versatile ventriloquist and voice actor Paul Winchell (1922–2005) was the son of Jewish immigrants who came to the United States from Poland and Austria-Hungary. Pat Sajak (1946–), the host of the long-running game show *Wheel of Fortune*, is the son of a Polish American. Comedian Bonnie Hunt (1961–) and actress Jane Kaczmarek (1955–) are both of Polish American ancestry.

Commerce and Industry Ruth Handler (1917–), cofounder of the Mattel toy company and creator of the Barbie doll, was born to Polish immigrant parents in Colorado. William Filene (1830–1901) was born in Posen and founded Boston's Filene's department store. Iowa's largest department store, Younker's, was founded by three Polish immigrant brothers—Samuel, Marcus, and Lipma Younker—in 1850. Polish-born Helena Rubinstein (1870–1965) was one of the giants of the cosmetic industry. The food industry in the United States has also had prominent Polish Americans among its ranks. Mrs. Paul's Fish was the creation of Polish American Edward J. Piszek (1917–). A Polish-Jewish couple, Reuben (1912–1994) and Rose (1916–2006) Mathus, established Häagen Dazs ice cream. Leo Gerstenzang (1923–), a Polish immigrant from Warsaw, invented the Q-Tip cotton swab.

Although less well known than his visionary friend Steve Jobs, Steve Wozniak (1950–) was the cofounder of Apple and was involved in Apple's rise to the top of the technology industry. Since leaving Apple, Wozniak has devoted his time to developing GPS technology and to philanthropies such as the Tech Museum of Innovation and the Children's Discovery Museum, both of which are located in San Jose, California.

Literature and Journalism Jerzy Kosinski (1933–1991), the Polish-born novelist, came to the United States after World War II; his *The Painted Bird* (1965) relates the experiences of a small boy in

Nazi-occupied Poland and is one of the most stirring and troubling novels to come out of that time. The poet Czesław Miłosz (1911–2004), naturalized in 1970, won the Nobel Prize for Literature in 1980. Born in Lithuania of Polish parents, Miłosz studied law and served in the diplomatic corps as well as establishing a name for himself as a poet before immigrating in 1960. His poetry collections include *The Light of Day* (1954), *City Without a Name* (1969), and *In Search of Homeland* (1992). His best-known works in other genres are *The Captive Mind* (1953), a prose account of life under totalitarian rule, and *The Issa Valley* (1955), a novel about a boy growing up in a rural parish haunted by the ghost of a dead woman. The cartoonist Jules Feiffer (1929–), known for his offbeat and biting wit, was born to Polish immigrant parents in the United States. One of the most respected playwrights of the twentieth century, Arthur Miller (1915–2005) was the son of Polish Jewish immigrants. He is best remembered for his haunting *Death of a Salesman* (1948) and for his brief marriage to Hollywood legend Marilyn Monroe.

Music Leopold Stokowski (1882–1977); who was born in London of Polish and Irish parents and became a naturalized US citizen in 1915, was a renowned conductor. He was best known for his work leading the Philadelphia Orchestra for many years and for popularizing classical music in the United States. His appearance in the 1940 Disney film *Fantasia* is an example of such popularizing efforts. The jazz drummer Gene Krupa (1909–1973), the measure for drummers long after, was also of Polish heritage; Krupa was born in Chicago and played with Benny Goodman's orchestra before forming his own band in 1943. He revolutionized the role of the drummer in a jazz band.

Contemporary Polish American musicians include rock star Pat Benatar (1953–), the winner of four Grammy Awards, who is the daughter of a Polish father and an Irish mother. Other Polish American musicians run the gamut from 1960s heartthrobs Bobby Vinton (1935–) and Gene Pitney (1940–2006) to rap artist Eminem (1972–) and shock rocker Marilyn Manson (1969–). Falling somewhere in between are rocker Steven Tyler (1943–) and adult contemporary artist Neil Diamond (1941–).

Politics and Government A number of Polish Americans have made names for themselves in the field of politics and government. Leon Jaworski (1905–1982) was the prosecutor in the 1973 Watergate investigation of then President Richard Nixon, and Zbigniew Brzezinski, born in Warsaw in 1928 and naturalized in 1958, was an important adviser on the National Security Council to President Carter from 1977 to 1980. Democrat Barbara Mikulski (1936–) has represented Maryland in the U.S. Senate since 1986. She previously represented Maryland's Third District in the House of Representatives. John M. Shalikashvili (1936–) headed the Joint Chiefs of Staff from 1993 to 1996. Alan Greenspan (1926–) is one of the most respected economists in American history. He was chair of the Federal Reserve Board from 1987 to 2006, serving under both Democratic and Republican presidents. Illinois Democrats Dan Rostenkowski (1928–2010) and Roman Pucinski (1919–2002) as well as Maine Democrat Edmund Muskie (1914–1996) also came from Polish American heritage.

Science The biochemist Casimir Funk (1884–1967) was, in 1912, the first to discover and use the term "vitamin"; his so-called vitamin hypothesis postulated that certain diseases such as scurvy and pellagra resulted from lack of crucial substances in the body; Funk also went on to do research in sex hormones and cancer. He lived in the United States from 1939 until his death. Stanley Dudrick developed the important new method of vein feeding, termed IHV—intravenous hyperalimentation. Stephanie Kwolek (1923–) invented Kevlar, the material that is used in making bulletproof vests.

Sports Many notable Polish Americans have made their names household words in baseball as well as in other sports. Included among baseball's most noted names are pitcher Stan Coveleski (1888–1984), whose seventeen-year career from 1912 to 1928 earned him a place in the Hall of Fame in 1969; Stan Musial (1920–2013), right field, another member of the Baseball Hall of Fame, who played for St. Louis from 1941 to 1963; Carl Yastrzemski (1939–), left fielder for the Boston Red Sox, who was voted to the Hall of Fame in 1989; and Al Simmons (1902–1956), born Aloysius Harry Szymanski, who played center field for the Philadelphia Athletics from 1924 to 1944. Both Phil (1939–) and Joe Niekro (1944–2006), brothers known for their prodigious skill with knuckle balls, became legends in American baseball history.

In football there have been numerous outstanding Polish American players and coaches. Among them Chicago's Mike Ditka (1939–) was a standout, playing as a tight end for the Bears from 1961 to 1972 and later coaching the team to a Super Bowl championship in 1985. A Hall of Fame player, Ditka also worked as a television sports commentator. Dan Marino (1961–) had an illustrious career as quarterback for the Miami Dolphins, and Tony Romo (1980–) played in that position with the Dallas Cowboys.

Female athletes of Polish American descent have also played a major role in American sports. Tara Lipinski (1982–) became the youngest gold medal winner for individual performance by an ice-skater during the 1998 Olympics. Janet Lynn, another figure skater, carried home a bronze medal at the 1972 Olympics. Other Polish American female athletes include basketball player Carol Blazejowski (1956–), golfer Betsy King (1955–), and tennis player Jane Bartkowicz (1949–).

Stage and Screen Hollywood has had its fair share of Polish-born men and women who have helped to shape that industry, including Harry Warner (1881–1958) and Jack Warner (1892–1978) of Warner Bros. Entertainers and actors such as Sophie Tucker and Pola Negri also managed to hide their ethnic roots by changing their names. The pianist and performer Liberace (1919–1987), half-Polish and half-Italian, was born Władziu Valentino Liberace. More recently, the Polish-born Hollywood and international cinematographer Hubert Taczanowski (1960–) made outstanding contributions. David Geffen (1943–) was a well-known film producer and music industry executive. Actress Christine Baranski (1952–) was a triple threat, making her mark on television as a sidekick to Cybill Shepherd on *Cybill* in the 1990s, in movies such as *Mamma Mia!* (2008), and on Broadway in such productions as *The Real Thing* (1984), for which she won a Tony Award as the Best Featured Actress.

MEDIA

PRINT

Glos Polek/Polish Women's Voice

Published four times a year by the Polish Women's Alliance of America.

Virginia Sikora, Managing Editor
6643 North Northwest Highway
2nd Floor
Chicago, Illinois 60631
Phone: (847) 384-1200
Fax: (847) 384-1494
Email: editor@pwaa.org
URL: www.pwaa.org

Gwiazda Polarna (Northern Star)

Published weekly in Polish, it provides national and international news for the Polish American community as well as information about Polish activities and organizations domestically.

Jacek Milgier, Publisher and Editor in Chief
2804 Post Road
Stevens Point, Wisconsin 54481-6452
Phone: (715) 345-0744
Fax: (715) 345-1913
Email: pointpub@sbcglobal.net

Polish American Journal

Published monthly since 1911, this newspaper covers national, international, and regional news of interest to Polish Americans.

Mark Kohan, Editor in Chief
P.O. Box 328
1275 Harlem Road
Buffalo, New York 14025-0328
Phone: (716) 312-8088
Email: info@polamjournal.com
URL: www.polamjournal.com

Polish American Studies

A journal of the Polish American Historical Association devoted to Polish American history and culture.

James S. Pula, Editor
Purdue University North Central
1401 South U.S. Highway 421
Westville, Indiana 46391-9542
Email: jpula@pnc.edu
URL: www.polishamericanstudies.org

Polish Heritage

A biannual review of the American Council for Polish Culture.

David Motak, Editor
381 Mansfield Avenue
Pittsburgh, Pennsylvania 15220-2751
Email: dmotak@polishfalcons.org

Polonia Today

Established in 2011, this monthly newsmagazine is the most widely read Polish American publication in the world.

T. Ron Jisinski-Herbert, Editor
6348 West Milwaukee Avenue
#360
Chicago, Illinois 60646
Email: editor@poloniatoday.com
URL: www.poloniatoday.com

Super Express USA

Founded in 1996, this is the most widely circulated Polish American newspaper in the United States.

Adam Michejda, Editor
11 John Street, Floor 28
New York, New York 10038
Phone: (212) 227-5800
URL: www.seusa.info

RADIO

Since Polish Americans have 24/7 access to online radio stations, the number of traditional radio stations serving the community has declined significantly.

WBRK-AM (1340 AM) and Star 101.7

Offers Polish American programming.

Willard "Chip" Hodgkins, President
100 North Street
Pittsfield, Massachusetts 01201
Phone: (413) 442-1553
Fax: (413) 445-5294
Email: chip@wbrc.com
URL: www.wbrc.com

TELEVISION

Just as with radio, most Polish American television stations are now available online 24/7 through stations such as Polvision and TV4U. However, access to more traditional broadcasts continues via cable and satellite. That access includes such Polish channels as Polsat 2 International and TVP Polonia, which target Polonians around the world, and TVN International, which offers programming ranging from documentaries to Polish soap operas.

ORGANIZATIONS AND ASSOCIATIONS

American Council for Polish Culture (ACPC)

National federation of groups devoted to fostering and preserving Polish ethnic heritage in the United States.

Richard M. Wiermanski, President
35 Fernridge Road
West Hartford, Connecticut 06107
Phone: (410) 798-7512
Email: Rwierman@aol.com
URL: www.polishcultureacpc.org

American Institute of Polish Culture

Established in 1972 to promote Polish culture through publications, films, lectures, exhibitions, and events.

Blanka Rosenstiel, Founder and President
1440 79th Street Causeway
Suite 117
Miami, Florida 33141
Phone: (305) 864-2349
Fax: (305) 865-5150
Email: info@ampolinstitute.org
URL: www.ampolinstitute.org

Polish American Congress (PAC)

Umbrella organization for local and national Polish organizations in the United States with more than 3 million combined members. Promotes improved quality of life for Poles and Polish Americans.

Frank J. Spula, President
5711 North Milwaukee Avenue
Chicago, Illinois 60646-6215
Phone: (773) 763-9944
Fax: (773) 763-7114
Email: pacchgo@pac1944.org
URL: www.pac1944.org/index.html

Polish Falcons of America

Founded in 1887, the Polish Falcons have a membership of 31,000 in 143 groups or "nests." Established as a fraternal benefit insurance society for people of Polish or Slavic descent, the Falcons also took on a strong nationalist sentiment, demanding a free Poland. The society promotes athletic and educational events and provides a scholarship fund for those majoring in physical education. The Falcons also publish a bimonthly publication in Polish, *Sokol Polski*.

Timothy L. Kuzma, President and CEO
381 Mansfield Avenue
Suite 200
Pittsburgh, Pennsylvania 15220
Phone: (412) 922-2244 or (800) 535-2071
Fax: (412) 922-5029
Email: info@polishfalcons.org
URL: www.polishfalcons.org

Polish National Alliance of the United States (PNA)

Founded in 1880, the PNA has a membership of 286,000 made up of nearly 1,000 regional groups. Originally founded as a fraternal life insurance society, PNA continues this original role while also sponsoring education and cultural affairs. It maintains a library of 14,000 volumes.

6100 North Cicero
Chicago, Illinois 60646-4385
Phone: (773) 286-0500 or (800) 621-3723
Fax: (773) 286-0842
Email: pna-znp.org
URL: www.pna-znp.org/

Polish Roman Catholic Union of America

Founded in 1873, the Roman Catholic Union has a membership of 90,000 in 529 groups. Founded as a fraternal benefit life insurance society, the union sponsors sports and youth activities, and conducts language school as well as dance and children's programs. It also has a library of 25,000 volumes.

Wallace Michael Ozog, President
984 North Milwaukee Avenue
Chicago, Illinois 60642-4101
Phone: (773) 782-2600 or (800) 772-8632
Email: info@prcua.org
URL: www.prcua.org

Polish Women's Alliance of America

Founded in 1898, the Polish Women's Alliance has a membership of 65,000 in 775 groups or chapters. It is a fraternal benefit life insurance society administered by women and maintains a library of 7,500 volumes on Polish and American culture and history.

Delphine Huneycutt, National President
6643 North Northwest Highway
Chicago, Illinois 60631
Phone: (847) 384-1200 or (888) 522-1898
Email: padowski@pwaa.org
URL: www.pwaa.org

MUSEUMS AND RESEARCH CENTERS

American Institute for Polish Culture

Founded in 1972 to promote the appreciation for history, culture, science, and art of Poland, the American Institute for Polish Culture sponsors exhibits, lectures, and research; maintains a 1,200-volume library; and publishes books on history and biography.

Blanka A. Rosenstiel, President
1440 79th Street
Causeway
Suite 117
Miami, Florida 33141
Phone: (305) 864-2349
Fax: (305) 865-5150
Email: info@ampolinstitute.org
URL: www.ampolinstitute.org

Kosciuszko Foundation

Founded in 1925, the Kosciuszko Foundation is named after the Polish nobleman who fought in the American revolution. The foundation is a clearinghouse for information on Polish and American cultural affairs. Also known as the American Center for Polish Culture, the foundation has a reference library and arranges educational exchanges as well as administers scholarships and stipends.

Alex Storozynski, President and Executive Director
15 East 65th Street
New York, New York 10065
Phone: (212) 734-2130
Fax: (212) 628-4552
Email: alex@thekf.org
URL: www.thekg.org

Polish American Historical Association (PAHA)

Concerned with Polish Americana and the history of Poles in the United States.

Neal Pease, President
984 North Milwaukee Avenue
Chicago, Illinois 60622
Phone: (773) 384-3352
Fax: (773) 384-3799
Email: pease@uwm.edu
URL: www.polishamericanstudies.org

Polish Museum of America

Founded in 1937 and sponsored by the Polish Roman Catholic Union of America, the Polish Museum preserves artifacts of the Polish American experience and mounts displays of costumes, religious artifacts, and Polish art. It also maintains a 25,000-volume library for researchers and the Polish American Historical Association, which is concerned with the history of Poles in America.

Maria Ciesla, President
984 North Milwaukee Avenue
Chicago, Illinois 60622-4101
Phone: (773) 384-3352
Fax: (773) 384-3799
Email: PMA@PolishMuseumofAmerica.org
URL: www.polishmuseumofamerica.org

Polish Museum of Winona in Minnesota

Founded in 1890 by the Laird-Norton Lumber Company, the museum operates in association with the Polish Cultural Institute.

Lorraine Walski, President
102 Liberty Street
Winona, Minnesota 55987
Phone: (507) 454-3431
Fax: (507) 452-5570
URL: www.polishmuseumwinona.org

SOURCES FOR ADDITIONAL STUDY

Biskupski, Mieczyslaw B. *Hollywood's War with Poland, 1939–1945*. Lexington: University Press of Kentucky, 2010.

Bukowczyk, John. *And My Children Did Not Know Me: A History of the Polish-Americans*. Bloomington: Indiana University Press, 1987.

Bukowczyk, John J., ed. *Polish Americans and Their History: Community, Culture, and Politics*. Pittsburgh: University of Pittsburgh Press, 1996.

Jaroszyńska-Kirchmann, Anna D. *The Exile Mission: The Polish Political Diaspora and Political America, 1939–1956*. Athens: Ohio University Press, 2004.

Johannsen, Lars, and Karin Hilmer Pedersen, eds. *Pathways: A Study of Six-Post Communist Countries*. Oakville, CT: Oxbow Books, 2009.

Majewski, Karen. *Traitors and True Poles: Narrating a Polish-American Identity, 1880–1939*. Athens: Ohio University Press, 2003.

Pula, James S. *Polish America: American Ethnic Community*. New York: Twayne, 1995.

Pula, James S. *Polish American Encyclopedia*. Jefferson, NC: McFarland, 2011.

Renkiewicz, Frank. *The Poles in America, 1608–1972: A Chronology and Fact Book*. Dobbs Ferry, NY: Oceana Publications, Inc., 1973.

PORTUGUESE AMERICANS

Ernest E. Norden

OVERVIEW

Portuguese Americans are immigrants or descendants of people from Portugal, officially called the Portuguese Republic, which is the westernmost country of continental Europe. It is bordered on the east and north by Spain, with which it shares the Iberian Peninsula, and on the west and south by the Atlantic Ocean. Portugal also includes the Azores (Açores) and the Madeira Islands in the North Atlantic Ocean. Torre, in the Serra da Estrela (Mountain Range of the Star), marks mainland Portugal's highest elevation. The peak stands at 6,539 feet (1,993 meters) and is accessible by a paved road much like Colorado's Pike's Peak. Ponta do Pico, located on the Portuguese island of Pico in the Azores, is more than 1,000 feet taller at 7,713 feet (2,351 meters). It is a dormant volcano, although some minor activity has been noted as recently as September 2009. Portugal is about the size of Ohio, having an area of 35,556 square miles (92,090 square kilometers) and measuring 360 miles at its longest point and 140 miles at its widest.

According to the *CIA World Factbook*, Portugal's population as of July 2012 was 10,781,459. Although there is no official religion in Portugal, more than 90 percent of the people are Roman Catholic. Other Christian groups include Protestants, Apostolic Catholics, and Jehovah's Witnesses. There also are small minorities of Jews and Muslims. Nearly 99 percent of the population is of Portuguese origin; the largest ethnic minorities include Cape Verdeans, Brazilians, Spanish, British, Angolans, Mozambicans, and Americans. The unemployment rate in Portugal was 12.7 percent as of 2011, with 18 percent living below the poverty level. Portugal's chief products are grapes, wine, potatoes, hogs, beef cattle, fish, paper products, electrical machinery, wood and cork products, ceramics and glassware, and textiles.

Due to their traditional maritime heritage, the Portuguese were some of the earliest immigrants to the United States, possibly dating back to the pre-Columbian era. The earliest recorded Portuguese American was Mathias de Sousa, a Portuguese Jew, who immigrated to present-day Maryland in 1634. Significant immigration did not occur until nearly two centuries later when Portuguese sailors in the mid-1800s moved to the northeastern coastal communities of Massachusetts, New York, and Rhode Island, working as fishermen and whalers. Portuguese immigrants settled the West Coast during this time as well, following the California Gold Rush and joining coastal communities as fishermen and sailors. Immigration quotas put in place after World War I were raised in the mid-1940s, and roughly 100,000 Portuguese entered the United States in the quarter century following World War II. In the twenty-first century, Portuguese Americans have maintained their cultural identity by remaining active with civic associations, educational foundations, university programs, historical societies, local news outlets, and countless other regional and national cultural resources.

According to the U.S. Census, by the turn of the twenty-first century there were roughly one million people of Portuguese descent living in the United States, with the largest populations living in California, Hawaii, Massachusetts, New Jersey, Florida, and Rhode Island. In 2009 the U.S. Census website cited more than 1,477,000 Portuguese Americans living in the United States, which is comparable to the population of Manhattan. The rough population breakdown for major settlement areas was as follows: California (381,000), Hawaii (58,000), Massachusetts (320,000), New Jersey (54,000), New York (54,000), and Rhode Island (102,000). While there are still isolated Portuguese communities in these areas, Portuguese Americans have generally assimilated with the broader population of the United States. Significant numbers of Portuguese Americans can also be found in New York, Connecticut, Texas, Washington, and Oregon.

HISTORY OF THE PEOPLE

Early History Portugal's early history saw occupation by North African Iberians, French Celts, Phoenicians, and Carthaginians. After the Second Punic War (218–201 BCE), the Roman conquest of Portugal began. Lusitania was a Roman province that comprised most of modern-day Portugal and part of Spain. The murder of Celtic Lusitanian rebel leader Viriathus in 139 BCE brought a rapid end to Lusitanian resistance, and Portugal was occupied by Roman forces. Despite his defeat, Viriathus is still lauded as a Portuguese hero of independence. Roman contributions to Portugal included roads, buildings, and the Latin language, from which Portuguese developed. Portugal's name derives from Portus Cale, a pre-Roman or Roman settlement near the mouth of the Douro River, where Porto is now located. In the fifth century CE, as Roman control of the peninsula weakened, the land was overrun by Suevi, followed by the Visigoths. In 711 the Muslims invaded the peninsula, and Christian forces spent the next 500 years trying to expel them. To fight off the African Almoravids, King Alfonso VI of León and Castile enlisted the aid of Henry of Burgundy, whom he rewarded with the title of Count of Portucale and the hand in marriage of his illegitimate daughter, Teresa. Henry's son, Alfonso Henriques, claimed the title Alfonso I, King of Portugal, in 1139. By 1179 his kingdom, occupying the northern third of present-day Portugal, was recognized as autonomous and separate from Castile.

Alfonso I and his son Sancho I reconquered the remaining Portuguese territory from the Muslims. When Sancho II died in 1248 without leaving an heir to the throne, the Count of Boulogne declared himself King Alfonso III. He was responsible for moving the capital from Coimbra to Lisbon, for lessening the power of the church in his land, and for convoking the Cortes at Leiria, an assembly consisting of clergy, nobility, and bourgeoisie representatives to address issues important to all three groups. This Cortes in 1254 was the first assembly to address the concerns of commoners alongside those of the upper class.

Alfonso III's son Diniz, who ruled Portugal from 1279 to 1325, built a navy; founded the University of Coimbra (1290), which was first located in Lisbon; and showed interest in literature, shipbuilding, and agriculture, for which he came to be called the *rei lavradór* (farmer king). His wife, Elizabeth, who worked to maintain peace in Portugal, was known as the Holy Queen (*rainha santa*) and was later canonized as St. Elizabeth of Portugal. After the death of Ferdinand I in 1383, his wife, Leonor Telles, married their daughter Beatriz to the King of Castile. There was disagreement as to whether Beatriz should be heir to the throne, and in 1385 the Cortes chose John, an illegitimate son of Peter I (the Cruel), a former king of Portugal, to rule as John I. John was master of a religious-military order, the Order of Aviz.

John's son, known as Prince Henry the Navigator, utilized the resources of geographers and navigators to launch a series of explorations beyond the frontiers of Portugal. The Portuguese drive for expansion continued out of a desire to explore unknown lands, to seek a trade route for transporting spices from India, and to spread the Christian religion. Henry financed the expeditions that discovered Madeira and the Azores; these islands were uninhabited but were quickly colonized by the Portuguese. Portugal was also the first maritime power to explore the coast of Africa and set up detailed trading relationships with Africans.

Under Manuel I (1495–1521), Vasco da Gama reached India and Pedro Àlvares Cabral discovered Brazil. Manuel, who married Isabella, the eldest daughter of Spain's Ferdinand and Isabella, never realized his dream of uniting Spain and Portugal under his power. As part of his marriage contract with Isabella, he was required to rid Portugal of the Jews who had taken refuge there after being expelled from Spain. A few were allowed to emigrate, but most were forcibly converted to Christianity. Manuel's son, John III (1521–1557), established the Inquisition in Portugal. In 1580, when Portugal again found itself with no heir to the throne upon the death of Cardinal Henry, last of the House of Aviz, Philip II of Spain seized control as Philip I of Portugal (1580–1598). Portugal remained under Spain's control for sixty years until John, Duke of Bragança, defeated the Spanish and founded his own dynasty as John IV in 1640. The Portuguese had increasingly resented Spanish rule because of taxation and because Philip had soon broken the promises he had made to maintain Portugal's autonomy and to name only Portuguese to government posts. Spain finally recognized Portuguese independence in 1668.

Modern Era During the eighteenth century, wealth from the Portuguese colony in Brazil began to pour into the country. Gold was discovered in Minas Gerais in 1693, and Brazil became a source of diamonds beginning in 1728. Great wealth was extracted from their new world colonies by the Portuguese, and a 20 percent tax on it maintained their monarchs. John V (1706–1750) sought to establish an absolute monarchy. His son Joseph (1750–1777) was weak and allowed his minister Sebastião José de Carvalho e Melo, the Marquis of Pombal, to run the government in a more enlightened fashion. The latter is credited with the competent governmental response to the earthquake that leveled Lisbon in 1755. Pombal also ordered the expulsion of the Jesuits in 1759 and the consequent reform of the educational system. In 1762 Spain invaded Portugal, and peace was not achieved until 1777 through the Treaty of San Ildefonso.

When Napoleon declared war on England, Portugal, allied by treaties, was drawn into the struggle. In 1806 Napoleon issued a decree intended to close all continental ports to British ships, and he later invaded Portugal to ensure that his decree was carried out there. As the French army neared Lisbon, the royal family boarded British ships, which carried them to Rio de Janeiro, Brazil, where they remained for fourteen years. Meanwhile, the Portuguese and British armies, under the Duke of Wellington, drove the French from the country. Portugal made peace with France in 1814. In 1815 Brazil's status was elevated to that of a kingdom united with Portugal. The royal family did not seem anxious to return to Portugal, and when William Carr Beresford, the British commander in charge in Portugal, traveled to Brazil to convince John VI to return, the Portuguese drew up a national constitution and would not allow Beresford back into the country. John VI returned in 1821 and swore to uphold the constitution. His eldest son, Peter, declared Brazil independent from Portugal in 1822 and became its emperor. John VI recognized Brazil's independence in 1825. John's death in 1826 marked the beginning of a period of political strife that lasted until after mid-century, when party government was established. The main parties were the Historicals and the more moderate Regenerators. Although Portugal claimed and successfully colonized Angola, Mozambique, and several smaller colonies in Africa, the latter part of the century was occupied with disputes over Portugal's claims to other territories in Africa.

In the early twentieth century the republican movement grew in strength. In 1908 King Charles I and his heir, Louis Philip, were assassinated. King Manuel II (1908–1910) was the last monarch, because the republican revolution that began on October 4, 1910, forced Manuel to seek refuge in England until his death in 1932. The revolutionary government gave the vote to adult males and drew up a constitution. It expelled religious orders from the country and disestablished the Roman Catholic Church. It founded new universities in Lisbon and Porto. But the republicans were divided into many factions, and there was great political instability. Within fifteen years, forty-five different regimes held the reins of government. Portugal's bad economic situation became even worse when the country joined the Allies in World War I (1914–1918). In 1926 the army overthrew the government and set up a dictatorship under General António Oscar de Fragoso Carmona, who named António de Oliveira Salazar, an economics professor at the University of Coimbra, as his minister of finance. After his successful handling of the budget, Salazar was named prime minister in 1932. As dictator he kept Portugal neutral during World War II yet allowed British and American planes to refuel in the Azores; he improved the country's roads and its means of transportation and promoted new industries and other development.

After World War II Portugal had a very small upper and middle class; the country was mostly inhabited by an urban working class and rural peasant population. Portugal became a charter member of the North Atlantic Treaty Organization (NATO) in 1949 and a member of the United Nations in 1955. Nonetheless, Salazar's government was extremely conservative; people enjoyed few rights and were under surveillance by the secret police. The wealthy enjoyed economic advantages under his regime, but the poor became poorer. Salazar suffered a stroke in mid-1968 and died two years later. Marcelo Caetano then became head of the government and liberalized many governmental policies, but he did not go far enough or fast enough for many Portuguese. Emigration increased, inflation grew, and the country faced a grave economic crisis.

On April 25, 1974, a group of military officers became dissatisfied with Portugal's long wars to retain possession of its African colonies such as Angola.

Under the leadership of Otelo Saraiva de Carvalho, they overthrew Caetano's dictatorship. This is often referred to as the "Carnation Revolution" as no shots were fired and carnations were placed in the soldiers' rifles. The new democratic government, called the Movimento das Forças Armadas (Armed Forces Movement), granted independence to the Portuguese colonies in Africa, drafted a constitution, and held general elections in 1976. Although the country became more stable, it also faced the new problems of rapid inflation and high unemployment with the return of more than half a million Portuguese citizens from its newly liberated colonies. The new government continued to evolve over the next quarter century, revising the constitution in 1982 to limit presidential powers, joining the European Economic Community (Common Market) in 1986, hosting the 1998 World's Fair Expo, and adopting the euro in 1999. Portugal officially relinquished all of its colonial holdings on December 20, 1999, by signing control over Macau to the People's Republic of China, although many Portuguese citizens still live on the island.

Wherever they settled, Portuguese immigrants had to face many disconcerting changes in their new environment. Rather than living in the same town or even the same neighborhood as the rest of their family—grandparents, aunts, uncles, cousins—upon whom they could depend for help when they needed it, they found themselves alone and without the support system that the extended family could provide.

The earlier class/caste system in Portugal is less noticeable in the twenty-first century, as widespread education and social reforms allow for more opportunity and a growing middle class. In 2004 Portugal hosted the European Football Association EURO Championships. The country took over control of the European Union presidency in July 2007, and later that year EU member countries signed the Treaty of Lisbon to address globalization, climatic, and demographic issues. Portugal became a nonpermanent member of the UN Security Council in 2011. Anibal Cavaco Silva of the Social Democratic Party was elected president of Portugal in 2006.

SETTLEMENT IN THE UNITED STATES

There were three significant waves of Portuguese immigration to the United States: the first beginning after the Civil War, the second prior to and during World War I, and the third occurring from the mid-1960s to the present day. At first the Portuguese who came to the United States tended to settle near their ports of entry. The greatest number made their homes in New England (especially in Massachusetts and Rhode Island), New York, central California, and Hawaii. A small group settled in central Illinois. The Homestead Act of 1862 encouraged some Portuguese to go west to obtain ownership of land. Those who settled on the East Coast also spread into Connecticut and New Jersey, and most recent immigrants cluster in the greater New York area. The number of Portuguese immigrants settling in California or Hawaii has slowed greatly. Many Portuguese immigrated to America in search of higher living standards and employment and in an attempt to avoid mandatory military conscription. Many of these Portuguese immigrants lacked formal education, so they tended to remain for a long time in the lower middle class or middle class unless they attained the background necessary for advancement.

Early mariners explored Brazil on the eastern coast of South America in the earliest years of the 1500s. João Rodrigues Cabrillo arrived in San Diego Bay on September 9, 1542, and was the first European to explore the land that is now California. Portuguese Jews immigrated early to North America as well as to other countries to escape persecution in their native land. Since the late sixteenth century, there have been reports of olive-skinned, dark-haired people residing in the Appalachian mountains of Tennessee, North Carolina, and Virginia known as Melungeons who claim to be of Portuguese ancestry, or "Portyghee." The term Melungeon bears a striking resemblance to the Afro-Portuguese word melungo, meaning "shipmate" or "comrade." Manuel Mira's 2001 book, The Portuguese Making of America: Melungeons and Early Settlers of America, discusses this isolated group of early settlers and their history in the United States.

Mathias de Sousa is the first known Portuguese immigrant on record to what would become the United States; he arrived in Maryland in 1634. Aaron Lopez, another Portuguese Jew, played an important role in bringing the sperm-oil industry to the Newport, Rhode Island, area in the eighteenth century, and Abraham de Lyon introduced the cultivation of grapes to Georgia in 1737. Portuguese Sephardic Jews settled in precolonial New York and Rhode Island communities in the mid-1700s. Portuguese from the Azores and the Cape Verde Islands worked on New England's whaling ships in the mid-1800s. Many of them settled in New England, especially around New Bedford, Massachusetts.

Portugal has one of the highest rates of emigration in Europe. Until the middle of the twentieth century, most Portuguese emigrants (about 80 percent of them) went to Brazil. The Portuguese began to arrive in the United States in relatively large numbers around 1870. The majority of early Portuguese immigrants were men from the Azores, a group of islands and islets in the North Atlantic Ocean. There was also immigration to the Sandwich Islands (now the state of Hawaii), where the Portuguese went originally to labor on sugar plantations. The majority of the immigrants came to the United States seeking a higher standard of living; they were not drawn by educational opportunity or political or religious freedom. Besides wanting to escape poverty, high taxes, and the lack of economic advancement at home, many men emigrated to avoid mandatory conscription into Portugal's army. Natural disasters also stimulated many to seek opportunities to live and work elsewhere. The drought in the Cape Verde Islands in 1904 and the volcanic eruptions and earthquakes in the Azores in 1958 sent waves of people abroad.

Once substantial immigration to the United States had started, it increased steadily, peaking between 1910 and 1920. In 1917 the U.S. government instituted a literacy test requiring that people over the age of sixteen had to be able to read and write some language at a basic level in order to settle in the United States. Since the literacy rate in Portugal was extremely low, this test effectively barred many Portuguese from entry; of the Portuguese immigrants admitted shortly before the literacy test was instituted, nearly 70 percent were illiterate. In addition, the U.S. Immigration Act of 1924 established a quota system that allowed only a small number of Portuguese immigrants to enter per year. The Great Depression further discouraged immigration to the United States.

The third distinct wave of immigration began in 1958 in reaction to the immense displacement of more than 25,000 refugees in the wake of the 1957–1958 Capelhinos volcanic eruptions on the Azorean island of Faial. The U.S. Congress passed the Azorean Refugee Act in September 1958, allowing 1,500 Azorean Portuguese to emigrate after the volcanic destruction that took place there. Many of these Azoreans settled in California as manual laborers, although some later returned to Portugal either because they preferred living there or because they were unable to adjust to their new environment. Of those who returned to live in the Azores, at least, the impressions of their life in the United States, which they related to their friends and families, created a favorable attitude toward the United States. The many Portuguese immigrants who stayed have contributed substantially to American society through academia, politics, literature, the arts, and a variety of other fields.

Later, the Immigration and Nationality Act of 1965 abolished the quota system and consequently spurred a sharp increase in Portuguese immigration. At that time the Portuguese began to enter the United States at the rate of 11,000 to 12,000 per year. This rate started to decline in the early 1980s and stabilized at 3,000 to 4,000 per year over the next two decades. By 1990 the U.S. Census reported 1,148,857 Portuguese Americans living in the United States. The 2009 Census recorded 1,477,000 Portuguese immigrants in the country living mostly in the Northeast (47 percent) and West Coast (37 percent) regions, with 12 percent in the South and 4 percent in the Midwest. Many of these more recent immigrants to the United

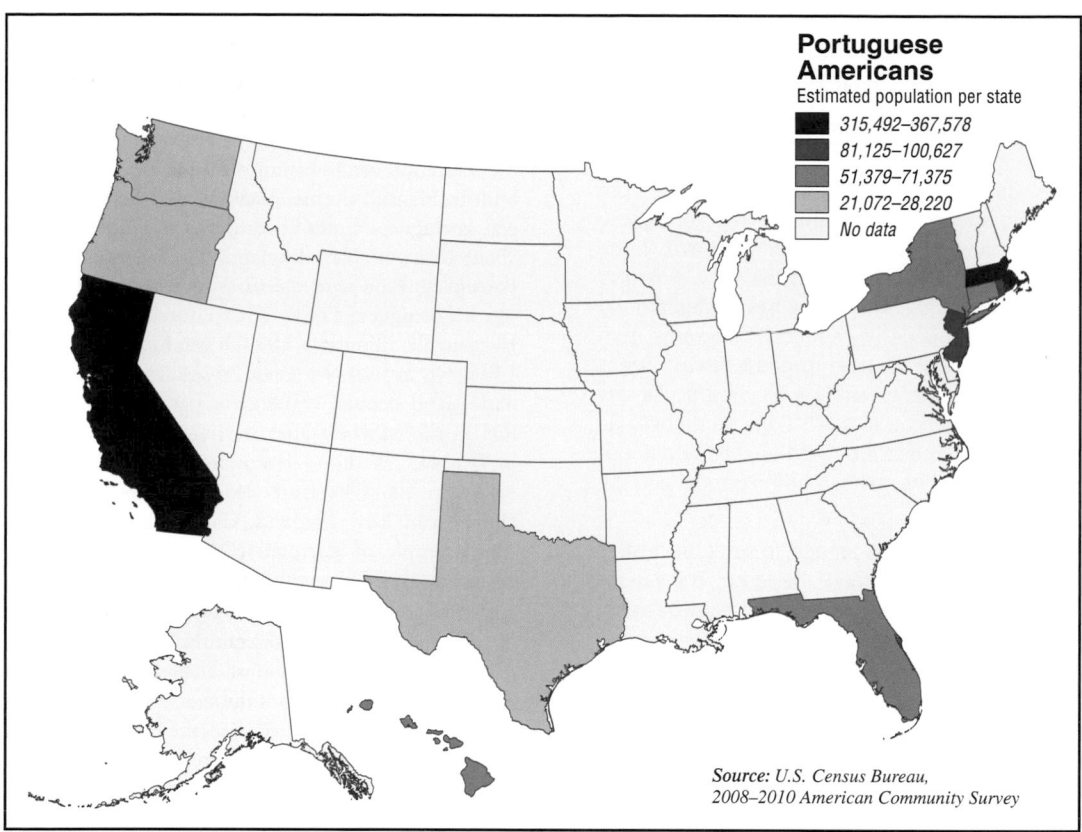

Portuguese Americans

Estimated population per state

- 315,492–367,578
- 81,125–100,627
- 51,379–71,375
- 21,072–28,220
- No data

Source: U.S. Census Bureau, 2008–2010 American Community Survey

States sought greater opportunity for education and jobs not available to them in their home country. Some worked traditional jobs as fishermen, farmers, and factory workers; others sought an American education to work more professional jobs in academia, law, business, and politics. Many Portuguese immigrants return home after receiving their education, while others seek jobs in the United States, choosing to remain as American citizens or permanent residents.

According to the 2010 U.S. Census, the state with the highest total population of Portuguese Americans is California. There are also many Portuguese Americans living in the Northeastern states of Massachusetts, Rhode Island, New Jersey, New York, and Connecticut, as well as in Florida and Hawaii. People of Portuguese descent have also settled in smaller numbers in Texas, Washington, and Oregon.

LANGUAGE

Portuguese is a Romance language derived from Latin. Today it is spoken by people on five continents, including about 300,000 in the United States. Linguists see its development as consisting of two main periods. The language of the twelfth century to the sixteenth is called Galician-Portuguese; it was essentially the same as that spoken in northwestern Spain. The language of central Portugal, between Coimbra and Lisbon, came to be considered the standard dialect, and this language, from the sixteenth century on, is called modern Portuguese.

Modern Portuguese is characterized by an abundance of sibilant and palatal consonants and a broad spectrum of vowel sounds (five nasal phonemes and eight to ten oral ones). Portuguese has an uvular "r" similar to the French "r." On occasion, unstressed vowels tend not to be pronounced, for example, *professor* is pronounced "prufsor." Portuguese has a northern and a southern dialect. The northern dialect is more conservative and has retained more traits of Galician-Portuguese; the southern one has evolved further. The Portuguese spoken in the Azores and in Madeira might be considered a third dialect. Brazilian Portuguese differs from continental Portuguese in sound (diphthongs in final positions are not nasalized, and unstressed vowels are not omitted in pronunciation), in vocabulary (words from indigenous languages have been incorporated), and in syntax. As of 2009, the U.S. Census recorded 731,282 individuals as speaking Portuguese or Portuguese Creole in their households, although many of these immigrants are presumably Brazilian or Native Islanders. While many Portuguese Americans speak their native tongue at home or among other Portuguese Americans, they tend to adopt English as a primary language in their daily lives. In the twenty-first century, the number of students taking Portuguese-language classes in colleges across the United States has risen as well. According to Dartmouth Portuguese-language professor Rodolfo Franconi, this increased interest is related to two distinct factors: "One, knowing just Spanish limits them to working in only

RIVALRY AMONG PORTUGUESE-SPEAKING IMMIGRANTS

Portuguese immigrants tend to differentiate themselves from Portuguese-speaking immigrants of other countries. The Portuguese from Portugal, the Cape Verde Islanders, those from Madeira, immigrants from the Eastern Azores, and those from the Central Azores often feel little affinity for each other, and rivalry has existed among them despite their common language. Except for immigrants from Portugal, they do not think of themselves as Portuguese but as citizens of a particular island. Azoreans often identify with a particular city rather than with the island as a whole. In 1975 Cape Verde became independent from Portugal, which exacerbated the already tenuous relations between mainlanders and islanders in both Portugal and the United States.

In the United States each group has tended to settle in clusters near others with whom they feel kinship and allegiance. The various groups do not know one another well, and prejudices exist between them. They even ridicule each other's dialects. The groups with lighter skin have looked down upon those with darker skin, and fraternal organizations founded by one group have not admitted members of the other groups. The well-educated Portuguese who belonged to a higher social class often feel little in common with those of the lower classes. This internal fragmentation has lessened with time but has inhibited Portuguese immigrants from presenting a united front for their own betterment in the United States.

one side of Latin America, and right now the Brazilian side is becoming more appealing, and, two, the growing interest in emerging countries on the part of the richest nations, especially U.S. interest in Brazil."

Greetings and Popular Expressions Common Portuguese greetings and expressions include: *Bom dia* ("bong DEE-uh")—Good morning; *Boa tarde* ("BOH-uh tard")—Good afternoon; *Boa noite* ("BOH-uh noyt")—Good night; *Por favor* ("poor fuh-VOR")—Please; *Obrigado* ("o-bree-GAH-doo")— Thank you; *Adeus* ("a-DEH-oosh")—Good-bye; *Desculpe!* ("dush-KOOLP")—Excuse me!; *Como esta?* ("KOH-moo shta")—How are you?; *Saúde!* ("sa-OOD")—Cheers!; *Feliz Natal* ("Fe-LEEZ na-TA-o")— Merry Christmas; and *Próspero Ano Novo* ("PRAHS-pe-roo UN-new NO-voo")—Happy New Year.

RELIGION

Portuguese Sephardic Jews migrated to the United States in the first wave of immigration (seventeenth and eighteenth centuries), forming the Sephardim Touro Congregation and dedicating the first Jewish synagogue in Newport, Rhode Island, in 1663. Nearly all subsequent waves of Portuguese immigrants to the United States were Roman Catholic. Immigrants came into conflict with the Catholic Church because its laws made it difficult and frustrating to try to establish a Portuguese Catholic church in a community. A church, which had to be built with money contributed by the Portuguese immigrants, could be stripped of its Portuguese identity at the discretion of the bishop. Although none was ever built in Hawaii, the mainland United States has several Portuguese Catholic churches in California and about thirty in New England. There are also a few Portuguese Protestant churches in existence. The first was a Portuguese Presbyterian church established in Jacksonville, Illinois, in 1850. It was founded by about 130 newly arrived Madeiran Protestants who left their native land because of religious persecution and settled in the Midwest after having spent several years in Trinidad. Within a few years, their numbers had grown to 400. There are also Portuguese Protestant churches in New England, California, and Hawaii. Many people of Portuguese descent have found a church home in non-ethnic Roman Catholic churches and in mainstream American Protestant churches.

Early in the twentieth century, Portuguese immigrants revived three religious celebrations from their homelands—the Festival of the Blessed Sacrament, the Festival of the Holy Ghost, and the Senhor da Pedra Festival. While some traditional religious festivals have been adapted to fit life in their new homeland, these three are still observed in the United States through large celebrations in cities across the country.

The Festival of the Blessed Sacrament, which originated on the island of Madeira, was initiated in 1915 in New Bedford, Massachusetts. This four-day festival, which takes place over the first weekend of August, has grown to be the largest Portuguese American celebration, attracting more than 150,000 visitors to New Bedford each year. Throughout the festival there is entertainment, including Portuguese and American music, singing, dancing, and famous entertainers. Decorative arches are erected in the festival area and are covered with bundles of bayberry branches. Colored lights and banners are also used for decoration. Vendors sell American and Madeiran foods including *carne de espeto* (roasted meat on a skewer), *linguiça* (sausage), *cabra* (goat), *bacalhau* (codfish) in spicy Portuguese sauces, *favas* (beans), and Madeiran wine. Local groups perform Portuguese folk music and dances; fireworks and raffles add to the festivities. On Sunday, the final day of the festival, organizers march with a band to the church for the 11 a.m. mass. At 2 p.m. there is a colorful parade that includes children in native costumes, bands, floats, and beauty queens. Although this festival includes a mass and a procession, it is basically a secular celebration meant for socializing and having fun.

The Festival of the Holy Ghost, modeled after an Azorean island festival, is celebrated in California and in New England each year. The first Hawaiian festival was held in 1901 at the Holy Ghost Chapel at Punchbowl. Depending on the location, it is celebrated during the two months between Easter through Trinity

"They Also Faced the Sea" is an art installation in Provincetown, MA by Ewa Nogiec and Norma Holt. It features five women (one unshown) of Portuguese descent and is meant to pay tribute to the generations of Portuguese American women who have supported the fishing community in Provincetown. © EWA NOGIEC / IAMPROVINCETOWN.COM

Sunday and Pentecost. The celebration originated with Queen Saint Isabel of Portugal in the fourteenth century. As an act of humility, she gave the royal scepter to the poorest man in town and had the royal crown placed on his head. After the mass, the queen and other nobles served a sumptuous meal to the poor.

The tradition was passed from royalty to the middle class, with silver crowns replacing the gold one. Details of the celebration vary from place to place, but sometimes a drawing is held to determine which families will have the honor of keeping the Holy Ghost crown and flags at their house for one of seven weeks leading up to the festival. The child of the first winner is crowned as the child-emperor/empress. Amid a week of feasting and celebration, the child keeps the crown in a place of honor in his or her house, surrounded by candles and flowers. At the end of the week, the child walks in a procession to the house of the second winner, where the second child-emperor/empress is then crowned. The crown passes through seven successive households. A few days before the final Sunday of the festival, the priest blesses the food that has been collected for the poor, although today this food is more commonly used for a community banquet. On the final weekend there may be a special

mass, procession, and carnival or fair that includes fireworks, charity auctions, music, ethnic food, and dancing the *chamarrita*, an Azorean folk square dance. Although the festival is no longer officially celebrated in Portugal, it is still a popular tradition in the Azores and among Azorean Portuguese in Brazil, Canada, and the United States. In August 2012 approximately 150,000 people attended the Twenty-Sixth Holy Ghost Festival of New England in Fall River, Massachusetts (population 95,000), a town that boasts the highest population of Portuguese Americans (43 percent).

The Senhor da Pedra Festival, begun in New Bedford, Massachusetts, in 1924, is celebrated on the last Sunday in August. It is also based on an Azorean festival. Its promoters emphasize the religious aspect of this celebration. After mass the image of Senhor da Pedra and those of nine other church figures are carried in procession on floats through the streets on the shoulders of the faithful. They are accompanied by a band, other church members carrying crucifixes and banners, and children wearing their first communion outfits or dressed as angels; children also carry six smaller floats topped by the images of saints. The priest marches in the procession carrying the sacrament. As the figure of

A Portuguese festival in New York City. © ROBERT BRENNER/ PHOTO EDIT. REPRODUCED BY PERMISSION.

Senhor da Pedra passes, onlookers attach money to his float. One neighborhood decorates its street with sand paintings and flower petals over which the procession will pass. A carnival with public entertainment, ethnic foods—*caçoila* (marinated pork), *bacalhau*, and *linguiça*—and raffles are also part of the festival.

Other regional celebrations include the Santo Cristo festival in Fall River, Massachusetts; the Festival of Our Lady of Fatima, which commemorates the reported appearance of the Virgin Mary in Fatima, Portugal, in 1917; and the Festival of Our Lady of Good Voyage in Gloucester, Massachusetts, during which the fishing fleet is blessed.

CULTURE AND ASSIMILATION

The Portuguese who settled in Hawaii in the late nineteenth and early twentieth centuries tended to lose their ethnic identity most rapidly. The majority of Portuguese who immigrated to the islands came for work, initially farming and working on sugar plantations. From these plantations, many moved on to the state's large cities, where they became involved in trades and service industries, while others went into farming for themselves. These new jobs were a major factor forcing Portuguese immigrants to adapt to their new surroundings in both language and culture. While many of the early immigrants came with their families, future generations of these immigrants tended to intermarry with other ethnic groups and assimilate into the native culture, quickly losing their Portuguese identity.

In California, Portuguese immigrants generally settled in rural areas, operating farms or dairies. They maintained a strong sense of ethnicity, hiring other Portuguese as farmhands. Under these semi-isolated conditions, it was easier to preserve their old customs. Fathers were the decision makers of the household. They allowed their daughters to attend school only as long as the law required; after that they kept them at home. Boys enjoyed more freedom than girls, but they also tended to quit school as soon as possible to work

on the farm or dairy, and they were expected to marry Portuguese girls. Later in the twentieth century, when the rate of arrival of new immigrants slowed and American-born descendants far outnumbered the foreign-born Portuguese, assimilation began. Organizations such as the Cabrillo Civic Clubs, however, were formed to preserve pride in the Portuguese heritage.

The situation on the east coast was different. There the Portuguese, mainly of rural origin, settled in urban areas. This change in environment forced family life and attitudes to change, and assimilation occurred more rapidly. When times were bad, women worked in factories, mills, and other businesses to help support the family. In general, children were expected to leave school at the first opportunity to go to work to contribute to the family's maintenance as well. This tended to keep the Portuguese in the lower middle class, but it freed the women from their traditionally subordinate roles and granted them more independence. While other immigrant groups sought to keep women out of the workforce, Portuguese American women had the opportunity to provide for their families in the workforce alongside their male counterparts.

Wherever they settled, Portuguese immigrants had to face many disconcerting changes in their new environment. Rather than living in the same town or even the same neighborhood as the rest of their family—grandparents, aunts, uncles, cousins—upon whom they could depend for help when they needed it, they found themselves alone and without the support system that the extended family could provide. Unlike the milieu to which they were accustomed, in the United States education was compulsory for children, women were more emancipated, young people were freer to select the mates of their choice, and families were more democratic rather than being dominated by the father. A generation gap often existed within families because the young had developed better language proficiency and had attended public schools where they were exposed to the attitudes of their American peers.

Traditions and Customs The Portuguese have a variety of folk beliefs, many of which coincide with those of other cultures. Some believe that certain people have the power of the evil eye, which endows them with the ability to cast evil spells on others. One may ward off the evil eye by making a gesture called "the fig," in which one closes the fist and sticks the thumb between the first and second fingers. Many believe the devil is real and has the power to work evil. The word devil (*diabo*) is avoided for fear of evoking him; he may also be kept away by making the sign of the cross. Fridays and the number thirteen are considered bad luck. Some people trust their health to witch doctors called *curandeiros*, who attempt to cure illnesses with herbal medicines or magic. Many of these beliefs are now looked upon as superstitions by Portuguese Americans, although some still practice these traditional arts.

Cuisine Portugal's cuisine shows great variety because each of its provinces has its own specialties. Along the coast a shellfish *açorda* is popular. This is a type of soup made from soaking country bread in a broth used to boil shellfish. Just before serving, hot shellfish and chopped coriander are added, and the dish is topped with raw eggs that poach in the hot liquid. The city of Porto is famous for its tripe recipes. Tripe stew, for example, contains tripe, beans, veal, *chouriço* or *linguiça*, *presunto* (mountain-cured ham similar to prosciutto), chicken, onion, carrots, and parsley. The city of Aveiro is known for its *caldeirada*, a fish and shellfish stew seasoned with cumin, parsley, and coriander. Around the city of Coimbra one might find *bife à portuguésa* (steak prepared in a seasoned wine sauce and covered with thin slices of *presunto* ham) and *sopa à portuguésa* (soup made of pork, veal, cabbage, white beans, carrots, and macaroni).

Cod is the most commonly served fish, perhaps as *bolinhos de bacalhau* (codfish cakes) or *bacalhau à Gomes de Sá* (fried with boiled potatoes, onions, eggs, and olives). Indeed, since Portugal is bordered on two sides by the ocean, seafood is fresh and plentiful throughout the country. *Escabeche* consists of fish pickled with carrots and onions and stored in the refrigerator for several days before serving.

The Portuguese, like the Spanish, use olive oil and garlic generously in their cuisine, but they cook with herbs and spices more widely, especially cumin, coriander, and paprika. *Caldo verde* (green soup) is made of fresh kale, potatoes, garlic-seasoned smoked pork sausage (either *linguiça* or *chouriço*), olive oil, and seasonings. It is served with *pão de broa* (rye bread) and red wine. Tender slices of lamprey eel prepared in a spicy curry sauce is also a typical dish.

Cozido à portuguésa is a stew made of beef, chicken, and sausage boiled with chickpeas, potatoes, turnips, carrots, cabbage, turnip greens, and rice. Chicken, roasted suckling pig, lamb, and goat are also important in Portuguese cuisine. *Massa sovada*, a delicious Portuguese sweet bread, is even commercially available in parts of the United States.

Typical desserts and confections include *pudim flan* (a baked custard topped with a caramelized sugar sauce), *toucinho do céu* ("bacon of heaven" almond cake), and *ovos moles* (a sweet mixture of egg yolks and sugar syrup), which may be served as dessert or used as icing on a cake. *Figos recheados* (dried figs stuffed with almonds and chocolate) are often served after dinner accompanied by a glass of port wine.

In 2012 the Emmy-nominated public-television cooking show *Simply Ming* presented a five-episode series on Portuguese/Azorean cuisine. The official website of the show's host, chef Ming Tsai, describes the experience: "The Azores is home to a wide variety of culinary influences, and Ming travels from island to island uncovering each location's unique cuisine— from Portuguese-inspired stews to local fish and clams

only found in the waters off the islands." Amaral's Market of New Bedford, Massachusetts, is a store and online market that sells traditional Portuguese ingredients. While many standard items can be found at most grocery stores or ethnic markets in larger metropolitan areas, specialty items such as oils, spices, dried fish, cheeses, and spicy homemade sausages like chourico and linguica are harder to find.

Portuguese wines have a good reputation. Some of the best red wine comes from Colares, the only region that still produces grapes from native European rootstock. The best white wines come from Carcavelos and Buçelas. Although they are really either red or white, the so-called green wines (*vinhos verdes*), made from grapes picked before they are fully ripe, are produced in the north. They are crackling wines and have an alcohol content of 8 to 11 percent. Portugal is famous for its port wine (named for the city of Oporto); it is a fortified wine with an alcohol content of 20 percent. The best ports are aged for a minimum of ten years, but some are aged for as many as fifty. Madeira wine, coming from the Madeira Islands, is similar to port. Portuguese food and wines have become popular in the United States over the past few decades. Many major cities in New Jersey, New York, and California have a variety of Portuguese restaurants, especially in coastal communities.

Traditional Dress The clothing worn in modern-day Portugal is similar to that worn in the United States and other Western countries. However, for certain festivals, traditional costumes are worn. These vary from region to region, but men often wear black, close-fitting trousers with a white shirt and sometimes a bright-colored sash or vest. On their heads they might wear a long green and red stocking cap with a tassel on the end that hangs down to one side. Women wear colorful gathered skirts with aprons and shawls over their shoulders. During the festival of *tabuleiros* in the region around Tomar, the harvest is celebrated by girls clad in ankle-length, long-sleeved white cotton dresses adorned by a wide colored ribbon that goes around the waist and over one shoulder. On their heads they wear a tall crown made of bread and weighing more than thirty pounds. The crown, which is at least as tall as the girl herself, is decorated with paper flowers and sprigs of wheat and is topped by a white dove or a Maltese cross. In general, Portuguese Americans have assimilated into modern culture, donning traditional dress only for celebrating the aforementioned cultural festivals or religious events.

Dances and Songs The *fado* is a melancholy type of song from Portugal. It is performed in certain Lisbon bars late at night and in the early hours of the morning. These songs are believed to have originated among Portuguese sailors who had to spend months or even years at sea, away from their beloved homeland. The fado, meaning "fate," praises the beauties of the country for which the singer is homesick or

PORTUGUESE PROVERBS

Não ha rosas sem espinhos.

You can't have roses without having thorns too.

Amar e saber não póde ser.

Love and prudence do not go together.

Mais quero asno que me leve, que caballo que me derrube.

I'd rather have an ass that carried me than a horse that threw me off.

A caridade bem entendida principia por casa.

Charity begins at home.

A Deus poderás mentir, mas não pódes enganar a Deus.

You may lie to God, but you cannot deceive him.

Da ma mulher te guarda, e da boa não fies nada.

Beware of a bad woman, and don't trust a good one.

Aonde o ouro falla, tudo calla.

When money speaks, all else is silent.

Do mal o menos.

Of evils, choose the least.

---

of the love that he left behind. Regional folk dances include the *chula*, the *corridinho* (a polka-like dance from southern Portugal), the *fandango*, the *tirana*, and the *vira*. Portuguese Americans are also attributed with introducing the ukelele, a four-stringed guitar-like instrument related to the Portuguese cavaquinho as well as the steel guitar used in the music of Hawaiian islanders.

Holidays Portuguese Americans celebrate the traditional Christian/Catholic holidays. Their celebration of Christmas (*Dia do Natal*) includes attending midnight mass on Christmas Eve (*missa do galo*), getting together with the extended family to share a meal and converse, singing carols outside friends' homes, and displaying a manger scene. New Year's Eve is celebrated by picking and eating twelve grapes as the clock is striking midnight in order to ensure twelve months of happiness in the New Year.

On January 6, *Dia de Reis* (Day of the Kings), gifts are exchanged. Families share a ring-shaped cake called a *bolo Rei*, which contains toy figures that bring good luck to the person who discovers one in his or her portion. During Holy Week there are processions through the streets carrying portrayals of the Passion of Jesus. The most famous processions are in the cities of Covilhã and Vila do Conde. On Easter, after attending mass, the family enjoys a special meal. This may include *folar*, a cake made of sweet dough and topped with hard-boiled eggs. On Pentecost (fifty days after Easter), Holy Ghost societies in the Azores provide food for the poor in the community. *Véspera de São João* (Saint John's Eve), on June 23, is a celebration in honor of St. John the Baptist. The traditions associated with this festival have to do with fire and water. People build bonfires, dance around them, and leap over their flames. It is said that water possesses a miraculous quality that night and that contact with it or dew can bring health, good fortune, protection to livestock, marriage, or good luck. On May 13 and October 13, people throng to the sanctuary of Our Lady of Fatima in search of miraculous cures or the granting of a prayer.

In the United States, all of these celebrations have become Americanized or have been abandoned for American equivalents (for example, *Dia das Almas* has been replaced by Memorial Day). Many are still celebrated by some Portuguese American families out of ethnic pride, but they are not recognized as public holidays in the greater community.

FAMILY AND COMMUNITY LIFE

In the earliest years of Portuguese immigration to the United States, most of the new arrivals were young, single men or married men hoping to bring their families over when their financial condition allowed. Most Portuguese immigrants came from rural villages and were illiterate; those who settled in urban areas had great adjustments to make. Their poor educational background and their lack of marketable skills condemned them to unskilled labor. They brought with them an anti-intellectual attitude derived from their belief that the father ruled the household and the children worked under his supervision to contribute to the common good by working on the land that their family was farming. In their new environment they resisted compulsory education for the young. When they were required to send their children to school, they sent them to public schools rather than to parochial ones. After a generation or two, however, families were more financially able to allow their children to continue their education. As a result, Portuguese American families have produced many physicians, lawyers, and university professors.

Immigrants also had to make adjustments to their diets. Since many of the early arrivals lived in boarding houses, they had to acclimate quickly to American food, which generally represented an improvement over the bread, codfish, beans, and wine that were staples in Portugal. On the negative side, it was more difficult and more expensive to obtain fresh fruit, vegetables, and fish in the United States than it had been in Portugal. Children had to adjust to drinking cow's milk after being used to goat's milk. Immigrants who settled in rural areas, however, were not subject to such sudden changes in diet and could preserve their traditional eating habits more easily.

Because they could no longer depend upon their extended family for support, Portuguese immigrants formed mutual aid societies in the United States. The first was founded around 1847. The early societies were established for men only. Each member would pay a monthly amount into the treasury of the society or periodically would be assessed; in turn he would receive benefits if he lost his job or was unable to work because of illness or disability. These societies sometimes afforded the opportunity to socialize with other Portuguese. Similar organizations for women began to appear about twenty years later.

Gender Roles Under Salazar's rule of Portugal before the 1974 revolution, women traditionally held a subordinate position both in the family and in society. After the 1976 drafting of Portugal's constitution, which made it illegal to discriminate by sex, women gained the right to carry passports, vote, and hold jobs. Portuguese American women gained even more rights and equality with men in the United States. Many of them had to leave the home to work in factories in order to help support the family. Their progress is reflected in their participation in organizations founded by Portuguese Americans. At first they did not participate at all; then they established organizations for themselves. Later they served as auxiliaries for men's organizations, and now they enjoy equal membership with men in most of these clubs and organizations.

EMPLOYMENT AND ECONOMIC CONDITIONS

Portuguese immigrants who settled on the East Coast tended to find work in factories, especially in textile mills, as well as in whaling and fishing and in truck farming. Some found jobs as itinerant farm workers, picking cranberries and strawberries. Women worked as seamstresses in garment shops. In California, early Portuguese immigrants participated in gold mining as well as migrant work, whaling, and fishing. Many went into various types of farming. The first Portuguese in Hawaii worked on sugar plantations but soon moved to the urban centers to work in more skilled jobs. As new arrivals, the first Portuguese immigrants were assigned some of the most undesirable jobs, but as their proficiency in English and their work skills and educational levels improved, they rose to higher, more responsible positions. Their success in farming is demonstrated by the fact that, by 1974, 34 percent of all market milk produced in California came from Portuguese American dairies. Many Portuguese Americans went into business for themselves and opened restaurants, hotels, and banks. Others took advantage of educational opportunities in the United States and went on to become some of America's greatest leaders in business, politics, arts, and entertainment. They now occupy a broad spectrum of jobs and careers and are found at all socioeconomic levels of society. While many still hold traditional working-class jobs in construction, farming, migrant labor, and commercial fishing, others hold professional jobs in business, education, law, politics, and health care.

POLITICS AND GOVERNMENT

Portuguese Americans have mostly assimilated into American society. Newly arrived Portuguese immigrants therefore find it easier to adjust to life in the United States, availing themselves of welfare programs only as a last resort. They have organized themselves, however, through mutual aid societies as well as civic, educational, social, and fraternal organizations. Over the years, some of these organizations have included the Portuguese Union of the State of California, the Portuguese American Civic League of Massachusetts, the Portuguese Civic League of Rhode Island, the Portuguese Educational Society of New Bedford, Massachusetts, the Luso-American Education Foundation, the Luso-American Federation, the League of Portuguese Fraternal Societies of California, and the Cabrillo Civic Clubs of California.

Since the nineteenth century, Portuguese Americans have asserted political influence, beginning early in Hawaii; in 1894 three of the eighteen elected delegates to the Constitutional Convention were Portuguese. In California the first Portuguese American was elected to the state legislature in 1900. This did not happen in Massachusetts until the early 1940s. State governments have formally recognized the contributions that some Portuguese have made to the United States. Since 1935 California has celebrated Cabrillo Day on September 28, honoring the discoverer of that state. In 1967 the state of California further proclaimed the second week in March of each year Portuguese Immigrant Week. In 1974 Massachusetts set aside March 15 as Peter Francisco Day. Peter Francisco was a boy of Portuguese origin who, during the Revolutionary War, enlisted in the Continental Army at the age of sixteen; his courage and patriotism earned the respect of General George Washington. There is a Peter Francisco Park in the Ironbound district of Newark, New Jersey, a predominately Portuguese neighborhood. Portuguese Americans have served with distinction in the U.S. armed services since the Revolution. Several Portuguese Americans have served in high political positions including lieutenant governors, mayors, state assembly members, and senators.

NOTABLE INDIVIDUALS

Although most of the early first and second waves of Portuguese immigrants who arrived on North American shores lacked education and skills, and therefore found it harder to break away from blue-collar jobs and a middle-class existence, descendants of these early Portuguese immigrants, having had greater educational opportunity in the United States, have gone on to make their mark on American society. Portuguese Americans constitute only a fraction of a percent of the population of the United States, yet they have achieved success in academics, literature, business, politics, the arts, music, farming, fishing, and many areas besides those listed below.

Academia Joaquim de Siqueira Coutinho (1885–1978) was a professor at George Washington University and at the Catholic University of America. From 1910 to 1920 he headed the Brazilian section of the Pan-American Union. Francis Millet Rogers (1914–1989) was professor of Portuguese at Harvard University, where he chaired the Department of Romance Languages and Literatures. He also served as a colonel in the U.S. Navy during World War II. Upon his return, he became the dean of the School of Arts and Sciences at Harvard and authored a number of books.

Architecture William L. Pereira (1909–1985) was an internationally known architect and city planner. He designed or planned such complexes as Cape Canaveral, CBS Television City, the Los Angeles Museum of Art, the Crocker Citizens Bank in Los Angeles, the Central Library at the University of California–San Diego, and the Union Oil Center.

Art Henrique Medina and Palmira Pimental were painters in the 1930s. Peter Souza (1954–), chief White House photographer for the Obama administration, is of Portuguese descent.

Commerce and Industry Abilio de Silva Greaves invented a fire-alarm system and several devices used in aviation. In the field of textiles, Steve Abrantes invented a wool-carding device, and José Pacheco Correia invented one for combing cotton. Sebastião Luiz Dias patented an irrigation control system. John C. Lobato developed a new type of army tank.

Government Francis Barretto Spinola (1821–1891) served as a Union general in the Civil War, and he was the first American of Portuguese descent to be elected to the House of Representatives (New York), in 1887. Joseph F. Francis and Mary L. Fonseca (1915–2005) were senators in the Massachusetts state legislature. João G. Mattos served in the state legislature of California. Helen L. C. Lawrence became chair of the city council of San Leandro, California, in 1941. In that position she exercised the power of mayor. Clarence Azevedo (1909–2001) was mayor of Sacramento, California. In 1979 Peter "Tony" Coelho of California was elected to the U.S. House of Representatives; he was the first recorded Portuguese American to serve in the U.S. Congress. Ernest Ladeira served as President Richard M. Nixon's advisor on social welfare. He was also an assistant to John Volpe, Secretary of Transportation. John M. Arruda

(1920–2010) was mayor of Fall River, Massachusetts, for six years. In 1992 Kathleen Honeycutt became the first female California state assembly member of Portuguese descent. More recently, James R. Aiona Jr. (1955–) was the Hawaiian lieutenant governor from 2002 to 2010, and Jack M. Martins (1967–) served as mayor of Mineola, New York, before becoming a New York State Senate representative in 2011.

Literature Some Portuguese immigrants recorded their experiences in their adopted country: Laurinda C. Andrade (1899–1980) immigrated to Massachusetts from the Azores in 1917. She worked as editor of the Newark, New Jersey, newspaper *Tribuna*, served as secretary to the Portuguese envoy in Washington, D.C., and later founded the Portuguese Educational Society of New Bedford, Massachusetts. Her 1968 autobiography, *The Open Door*, describes her impressions of growing up as a young Portuguese American girl in the northeastern United States. Lawrence Oliver (1887–1977) wrote an autobiography titled *Never Backward*, and Alfred Lewis (1902–1977) composed the autobiographical novel *Home Is an Island* as well as poetry. Onésimo Almeida (1946–), who completed his university training in Portugal and then earned a PhD at Brown University, where he later served as professor, wrote *Da vida quotidiana na Lusalândia* (1975), *Ah! Mònim dum Corisco* (1978), and *(Sapa)teia Americana* (1983). Immigrants who tell of their experiences in poetry include Artur Ávila in his *Rimas de um imigrante* (1961) and José Brites in his *Poemas sem poesia* (1975). John Roderigo Dos Passos (1896–1970) is the only American novelist of Portuguese descent who gained an international reputation. His works include *Manhattan Transfer* (1925) and the trilogy *U.S.A.* (1937), for which he is best known. It comprises the novels *The 42nd Parallel* (1930), *1919* (1932), and *The Big Money* (1936). He published a second trilogy titled *District of Columbia* in 1952. Jorge de Sena (1919–1978) came to the United States from Portugal via Brazil. He was a professor at the University of Wisconsin—Madison. At the University of California—Santa Barbara, he was chair of the comparative literature program. He was a well-known literary critic, poet, playwright, novelist, and short-story writer. His works include the novels *O físico prodigioso* (*The Wondrous Physician*) and *Sinais de fogo* as well as the short story collections *Génesis* and *Os grao-capitaes*. English readers can obtain his work *By the Rivers of Babylon and Other Stories*. The novelist and short-story writer José Rodrigues Miguéis (1901–1980) wrote fiction such as *Saudades para Dena Genciana* and *Gente da terceira classe*. Famed fiction writer Danielle Steel (1947–), many of whose novels have been made into TV movies, is second-generation Portuguese American on her mother's side.

Music John Philip Sousa (1854–1932) was director of the U.S. Marine Band from 1880 to 1892. He then founded his own Sousa Band in 1892; it became the world's most famous concert band in its more than forty years of existence. At the outbreak of World War I, Sousa, at the age of sixty-two, joined the navy to train bands at the Great Lakes Naval Training Center. He was famous as the composer of such marches as "Stars and Stripes Forever," "Semper Fidelis," "The Washington Post March," and "Hands Across the Sea." He also composed several operettas, including *The Captain*, *The Charlatan*, and *The Queen of Hearts*, as well as several suites for piano. Ilda Stichini and Maria Silveira were opera divas in the 1930s. Raul da Silva Pereira was a composer and conductor. Violinist Elmar de Oliveira (1950–) is a second-generation Portuguese American who began studying music at the age of nine. He played with some of the world's most renowned orchestras, including the New York Philharmonic, the Boston Symphony, the London Philharmonic, and the Seattle Symphony. He taught at New York's Manhattan School of Music and was an artist in residence at the Lynn University Conservatory of Music in Boca Raton, Florida. He is the only American to win the gold medal in Moscow's Tchaikovsky competition. In the field of popular music, vocalist Tony Martin (1913–2012) produced many hit records between 1938 and 1967. He had his own radio show and also appeared in more than twenty films. His most memorable role was that of a jewel thief in *Casbah* (1948) alongside Yvonne De Carlo and Peter Lorre. He appeared in nightclubs in the 1970s. A general contribution the Portuguese people have made to American music is the ukulele, which originated in Madeira and is now popular in Hawaii. Another Portuguese Hawaiian, Don Ho (1930–2007), continued to popularize the ukelele through the millennium. Contemporary musicians Katy Perry (1984–), Nelly Furtado (1978–), and Van Halen's David Lee Roth (1954–) all hail from Azorean/Portuguese descent.

Religion The charismatic religious leader Marcelino Manoel de Graça (1882–1960), also known as "Sweet Daddy Grace," founded the United House of Prayer for All People in the Harlem area of New York. His congregation, made up mainly of African Americans, included more than three million people. Humberto Sousa Medeiros (1915–1983), who had been bishop of Brownsville, Texas, was named to succeed Cardinal Cushing as Archbishop of Boston in 1970. He was the first non-Irish American to fill that position in 124 years. He was elevated to the College of Cardinals in 1973. Clarence Richard Silva (1949–) was appointed the fifth Roman Catholic bishop of Honolulu by Pope Benedict XVI in 2005.

Science and Medicine José de Sousa Bettencourt (1851–1931) earned degrees in both law and medicine. He practiced medicine and taught at the San Francisco Medical School. João Sérgio Alvares Cabral (d. 1909) practiced medicine in Oakland, California. He gave free consultations to the poor and ones at reduced rate

to Portuguese. He also served as editor-in-chief of *A Pátria*, a Portuguese newspaper published in Oakland. Mathias Figueira (1853–1930) founded the American College of Surgeons. M. M. Enos (1875–1951) was head of the Portuguese Association of the Portuguese Hospital of Saint Anthony in Oakland, California. He was also director of the Portuguese American Bank and taught at the National Medical School of Chicago. Carlos Fernandes (d. 1977) was director of St. John's Hospital in San Francisco. University of Massachusetts professor and biologist Craig Mello (1960–), of Portuguese descent, was corecipient of the 2006 Nobel Prize for Physiology or Medicine for his RNA research.

Sports Bernie de Viveiros (1901–1994) played baseball with the Detroit Tigers and the Oakland Oaks. Manuel Gomes also was a baseball player, as was Lew Fonseca (1899–1989), who played for the Cincinnati Reds, the Philadelphia Phillies, and the Cleveland Indians and coached the Chicago White Sox; Fonseca was a pioneer in the use of film to analyze players' performance during a game. In boxing, Al Melo (1906–1993) participated as a welterweight in the Olympics in 1924. George Araujo (1931–1997), Johnny Gonsalves (1930–2007), and Babe Herman (1902–1966) were contenders for the world boxing championships. Justiano Silva was a professional wrestler. Henrique Santos won the U.S. fencing championship in 1942. Tony Lema (1934–1966), "Champagne Tony," was the winner of numerous professional golf tournaments. At the time of his death, he ranked tenth in all-time earnings in the PGA. Tennis star Vic (E. Victor) Seixas Jr. (1923–) won the U.S. Open Championship in 1954. Billy Martin (1928–1989), famed major-league baseball player and manager, was a second-generation Portuguese American whose father emigrated from the Azores.

Stage and Screen Harold José Pereira de Faria (Hal Peary) (1908–1985) achieved fame in the title role of the series "The Great Gildersleeve," which he played for sixteen years on radio and television. He also appeared in motion pictures. John Mendes (1919–1955) performed as a magician under the name Prince Mendes. He was also a stage, screen, and television actor. Other Portuguese American motion picture actors include Rod de Medicis (1901–1998) and Nestor Paiva (1905–1966). Carmen Miranda (1914–1955), although known as the Brazilian bombshell, actually was born in Portugal. She was a popular film star of the 1940s known for her humor, her singing, and her extravagant hats piled high with fruit. She popularized Latin American dance music in the United States. Academy Award-winning actor Tom Hanks (1956–) of *Forest Gump* and *Saving Private Ryan* fame, *Pineapple Express*/*Spiderman* actor James Franco (1978–), and *The Matrix*'s Keanu Reeves (1964–) are all second- or third-generation Portuguese Americans.

An early 20th century farmer sits in his kitchen in Massachusetts. DELANO, JACK / LIBRARY OF CONGRESS PRINTS & PHOTOGRAPHS DIVISION [LC-USF34-042788-D]

MEDIA

PRINT

Luso-Americano

This newspaper, established in 1928, serves as a communication and media outlet for Portuguese communities worldwide, addressing news both in the United States and abroad.

Antonio Matinho, Editor and Publisher
88 Ferry Street
Newark, New Jersey 07105
Phone: (973) 589-4600
Fax: (973) 589-3848
Email: amatinho@lusoamericano.com
URL: www.lusoamericano.com

Nossa Gente (Our People)

This Portuguese-language newspaper focuses on news, economics, interviews, tourism, business, and other issues related to Brazilians and Portuguese-speaking peoples in the United States and abroad.

Paulo Sergio de Souza, Editor
7031 Grand National Drive
Orlando, Florida 32819
Phone: (407) 276-6108
Fax: (866) 659-9817
Email: info@nossagente.net
URL: www.nossagente.net

OJornal

The *OJornal* newspaper was founded in 1975 by Azorean community leaders seeking information about the turbulent Portuguese revolution.

10 Purchase Street
Fall River, Massachusetts 02720
Phone: (508) 678-3844
URL: ojornal.com

Portuguese American Journal (PAJ)

An interactive news blog, PAJ provides insight into the Portuguese American experience through articles on business, politics, sports, lifestyle, and other news.

Carolina Matos, Editor
Phone: (516) 668-9418
Email: editor@portuguese-american-journal.com
URL: portuguese-american-journal.com

Portuguese Times

Portuguese-language newspaper based out of Rhode Island addressing local and world news, the arts, entertainment, and other issues of interest to Portuguese Americans. Published every Thursday; circulation 15,000.

Francisco Resendes, Director
1501 Acushnet Avenue
New Bedford, Massachusetts 02740
Phone: (508) 997-3118
Fax: (508) 990-1231
Email: ptimes@aol.com
URL: www.portuguesetimes.com

Portuguese Tribune

Founded in 1979 in San Jose, California, and published biweekly.

José B. Ávila, Publisher and Editor in Chief
P.O. Box 57986
Modesto, California 95357-5866
Phone: (209) 576-1951
Fax: (408) 971-1966
Email: portuguesetribune@sbcglobal.net
URL: www.tribuneaportuguesa.com

24 Horas

The only Portuguese-language newspaper published and distributed daily in New Jersey, New York, and Connecticut.

68 Madison Street
Newark, New Jersey 07105
Phone: (973) 817-7400
Fax: (973) 817-8383
Email: subscribe@24horasnewspaper.com
URL: www.24horasnewpaper.com

RADIO

Radio Globo, WJFD 97.3

Radio Globo broadcasts news and sports for a Portuguese-speaking audience.

651 Orchard Street, Suite 300
New Bedford, Massachusetts 02744
Phone: (508) 997-2929
Email: jorge@wjfd.com
URL: www.wjfd.com

Radio Portugal, WFAR 93.3

Radio Portugal is available online and via radio, with entertainment, music, and news related to Portugal, Brazil, and Portuguese-speaking Americans.

25 Chestnut Street
Danbury, Connecticut 06810
Phone: (203) 748-0001
Fax: (203) 746-4262
URL: www.radioportugal.com

ORGANIZATIONS AND ASSOCIATIONS

American Portuguese Studies Association

"The association strives to foster the expansion and spreading of knowledge about the languages, peoples and cultures of Portuguese-speaking countries and to increase awareness of the Portuguese-speaking world among academic programs and communities; and to promote the development of Portuguese language programs in North America."

Leila Lehnen, Secretary
Department of Spanish and Portuguese
University of New Mexico
MSC03-2100
Albuquerque, New Mexico 87131-0001
Phone: (505) 277-5907
Fax: (505) 277-3885
Email: llehnen@unm.edu
URL: www.portuguese-apsa.com

Luso-American Education Foundation

Seeks to perpetuate the ethnic and national culture brought to the United States by immigrants from Portugal; assists qualified students and others in studying and understanding Portuguese culture. Develops high school and college courses for the teaching of Portuguese language, history, and culture.

Bela Ferreira-Goncalves, Administrative Director
7080 Donlon Way
Suite 200
Dublin, California 94568
Phone: (925) 828-3883
Email: education@luso-american.org
URL: www.luso-american.org/laef

Luso-American Life Insurance Society

Originally founded by Portuguese immigrants in 1868 as the Portuguese Protective and Benevolent Association. Mission statement: "To be the premier provider of life insurance, financial and fraternal services to individuals and families in the Luso-American Communities." Associated with the Luso-American Fraternal Federation, the Portuguese Continental Union, the Sociedade Portuguesa Rainha Santa Isabel, and the Luso-American Education Foundation.

Lino Amaral, Vice President/CEO
7080 Donlon Way
Suite 200
Dublin, California 94568
Phone: (925) 828-4884 or (877) 525-5876
Fax: (925) 828-4554
Email: lino.amaral@luso-american.org
URL: www.luso-american.org

National Organization for Portuguese Americans

Established in 2009. Supports communities and organizations to advocate for and empower Portuguese Americans.

Francisco Semião, Executive Director
P.O. Box 2652
Falls Church, Virginia 22042
Email: info@nopa-us.org
URL: www.nopa-us.org

Portuguese Fraternal Society of America/União Portuguesa do Estado da California/J. A. Freitas Library (UPEC)

Fraternal insurance society founded in 1880. Maintains the J. A. Freitas Library with more than 11,900 works dealing with Portugal and Portuguese Americans.

1120 East 14th Street
San Leandro, California 94577
Phone: (510) 483-7676
Fax: (510) 483-5015
Email: mypfsa@mypfsa.org
URL: portfsa.org

Portuguese Historical and Cultural Society

Works to promote Portuguese history and culture.

Mary Ann Marshall, President
P.O. Box 161990
Sacramento, California 95816
Phone: (916) 421-7161
Fax: (916) 427-3903
Email: cakemom102@aol.com
URL: www.sacramentophcs.com

MUSEUMS AND RESEARCH CENTERS

Association for Spanish and Portuguese Historical Studies

A. Katie Harris
Department of History
University of California, Davis
2216 Social Science & Humanities
1 Shields Avenue
Davis, California 95616-8611
Email: akharris@ucdavis.edu
URL: asphs.net

The Oliveira Lima Library

Located on the campus of the Catholic University of America in Washington, D.C., this is the oldest and most extensive library of materials specializing in Luso-Brazilian history and culture.

Maria Leal, Librarian

or

Thomas Cohen, Curator
Mullen Library
Room 22
Catholic University of America
620 Michigan Avenue NE
Washington, D.C. 20064
Phone: (202) 319-5059
Fax: (202) 319-4735
Email: leal@cua.edu or cohent@cua.edu

Portuguese American Historical and Research Foundation

Established in 1996. Has important links to Portuguese American immigrants in the United States, including Melungeons, and an extensive database of famous people of Portuguese descent.

Susan Deetz, Executive Secretary
277 Industrial Park Road
Franklin, North Carolina 28734
Fax: (828) 369-3751
Email: portugal@portuguesefoundation.org
URL: www.portuguesefoundation.org

Portuguese Historical Museum and History San Jose

Established in 1997, this replica of the first Portuguese Chapel of the Holy Spirit, which was built in San Jose in 1915, hosts revolving exhibits on the history of local Portuguese immigrants.

1650 Senter Road
San Jose, California 95112
Phone: (408) 287-2290
URL: historysanjose.org or www.
portuguesemuseum.org

SOURCES FOR ADDITIONAL STUDY

Almeida, Carlos. *Portuguese Immigrants: The Centennial Story of the Portuguese Union of the State of California.* San Leandro, CA: Supreme Council of U.P.E.C., 1992.

Anderson, James Maxwell. *The History of Portugal.* Westport, CT: Greenwood Press, 2000.

Barrow, Clyde W., ed. Portuguese-Americans and Contemporary Civic Culture in Massachusetts. Dartmouth: Center for Portuguese Studies and Culture, University of Massachusetts, 2002.

Cabral, Stephen L. *Tradition and Transformation: Portuguese Feasting in New Bedford.* New York: AMS Press, 1989.

Cardozo, Manoel da Silveira. *The Portuguese in America: 590 BC-1974: A Chronology & Fact Book.* Dobbs Ferry, NY: Oceana Publications, 1976.

Gilbert, Dorothy Ann. *Recent Portuguese Immigrants to Fall River, Massachusetts: An Analysis of Relative Economic Success.* New York: AMS Press, 1989.

Mira, Manuel. *The Portuguese Making of America: Melungeons and Early Settlers of America.* Franklin, NC: P.A.H.R. Foundation, 2001.

Moser, Robert, and Luciano de Andrade Tosta, Antonio, eds. *Luso-American Literature: Writings by Portuguese-Speaking Authors in North America.* New Brunswick, NJ: Rutgers University Press, 2011.

Pap, Leo. *The Portuguese-Americans.* Boston: Twayne Publishers, 1981.

Ribeiro, José Luís. *Portuguese Immigrants and Education.* Bristol, RI: Portuguese American Federation, 1982.

Wolforth, Sandra. *The Portuguese in America.* San Francisco: R&E Research Associates, 1978.

PUEBLOS

D. L. Birchfield

OVERVIEW

The Pueblo peoples are a vast confederation of diverse indigenous tribes who have lived in the region of the Southwest United States for thousands of years. Some archeologists believe they were occupying their lands in what would become Arizona, Colorado, Utah, and New Mexico as early as 1200 BCE, and the traditional origin stories of many Pueblo peoples assert that they have always resided on this land, where the first humans were created. Archeological evidence suggests that by end of the fourteenth century, Pueblo peoples had begun to settle primarily within the watersheds of the upper Rio Grande River Valley in New Mexico and the Little Colorado River in Arizona. Upon first contact with Spanish explorers during the 1500s this eclectic coalition of as many as thirty separate tribes were dubbed "Pueblos" (the Spanish word for "town") by European explorers because of the distinctive stone or adobe architecture prominent in many of their villages.

The total population of the numerous independent Pueblo towns was likely between forty and eighty thousand when sixteenth-century Spanish explorers arrived, according to an estimate made by University of California, San Diego, Professor Ross Frank in 1998. The diverse cultures within the Pueblo civilization are sometimes subdivided into two groups: Western Pueblos (which include the Hopi tribes of northern Arizona as well as the Zuni, Acoma, and Laguna villages of western New Mexico) and Eastern Pueblos (including the easternmost Pueblo villages of New Mexico along the Rio Grande). While these groups share some similarities, many are linguistically and culturally distinct. Prior to the arrival of the Spanish, Pueblo tribes were among the dominant indigenous groups of the Southwest, practicing a relatively stable and sedentary lifestyle founded on an agricultural and trade-based economy.

Today, the majority of Pueblo peoples continue to reside in communities throughout the Southwest, with the largest populations existing in New Mexico and smaller numbers living in Arizona and Texas. Although by and large the Pueblos remained in their ancestral homelands, during the political upheaval of the nineteenth and twentieth centuries many Pueblo tribes lost the bulk of these lands to the incursion of

white settlers—through sales they arranged themselves as well as through treaties with and seizures by the U.S. government. Throughout these changes, tribes within the Pueblo civilization worked diligently to maintain their traditional languages, unique customs, and forms of government. Today, the pueblos (the lowercase *p* indicating a village as opposed to a tribe) operate alongside the Southwest's larger Navajo, Jicarilla Apache, and Mescalero Apache reservations as semisovereign entities, each with its own governmental and religious leaders, but their title is different because the history of their relations with the U.S. government is anomalous.

The 2010 U.S. Census listed the population of Pueblo Indians in the United States at 62,540. Many people of Pueblo descent have assimilated into the mainstream culture of the United States, moving to the major population centers and small towns of the Southwest region, although some still live in traditional pueblo communities. According to the U.S. Census Bureau's American Community Survey estimates for 2006–2010, the states with the largest populations of Pueblo people were Arizona, California, Colorado, New Mexico, Oklahoma, and Texas. In 2013 twenty-one federally recognized pueblos—nineteen in New Mexico, one in Arizona, and one in Texas—were home to Pueblo tribal populations.

HISTORY OF THE PEOPLE

Early History Traditional Native American oral history states that Pueblo peoples have lived in the American Southwest since human creation. Archaeologists understand and classify this history through patterns seen in the material remains of ancestral sites across the region. As a result the history of the many distinct Puebloan peoples has been divided into eight clearly defined periods called Basketmaker I through III and Pueblo I through V.

Basketmaker I spans the period from 1200 BCE to 1 CE and is sometimes also referred to as the "late Archaic" phase in Pueblo history. During this period people of Pueblo tribes began using caves as seasonal shelters, creating primitive rock art, and developing rudimentary agricultural systems for the production of the first corn and squash plants. The transition into the Basketmaker II period (1–500 CE) is noted by some archeologists as being more subtle than those between other subdivisions of Pueblo history. This period featured the advent of beautifully woven baskets, the further cultivation of corn and pumpkins, and the production of rare, crude gray pottery. In the Basketmaker III period (500–700), the first beans were cultivated and the first wild turkeys domesticated; also, the short spear and *atlatl* (a spear-throwing implement) were replaced with the bow and arrow. The use of pottery (either gray or with a black pattern on a white base) increased, and the people began establishing villages featuring deep-pit or slab houses.

The Pueblo I or "Proto-Pueblo" period (700–900) brought the cultivation of cotton. Pit houses, sometimes made of the wood of pinyon pine trees, became ceremonial spaces called kivas, while habitations were built above ground from stone and were set directly against one another. Cradle boards were introduced for infants and white, red, and orange ceremonial pottery was made with black or red decorations. The Pueblo II period (900–1100) featured the rise of the cultures described as "Ancestral Puebloan." This stage in the people's history is typified by multistoried stone masonry apartments and an elaborate system of roads. The Pueblo III period (1100–1300) saw the Ancestral Puebloan culture reach its greatest height in communities on the Colorado Plateau such as Chaco Canyon and Mesa Verde. The period featured extensive trade and the development of polychrome pottery and pots of diverse shapes. During the Pueblo IV period (1300–1540), pottery was glazed for the first time, but only for ornamentation, and the people painted the walls of their kivas. The population centers shifted from the Colorado Plateau to the Little Colorado River and the upper Rio Grande River. The Pueblo V period (1540–present) is characterized by the adjustments Pueblo peoples made after the arrival of Europeans in the region. By 1700 only the Zuni, Acoma, Taos, Picuris, and Hopi groups had not been forced to move to new locations by the arrival of the Spanish.

Pueblo peoples were visited by a number of large Spanish exploratory expeditions during the sixteenth century, beginning with that of Francisco Coronado in 1540. These groups brought diseases to which the Pueblos had no resistance, and the result was a large decrease in the Pueblo population. The 1598 expedition of Juan de Oñate cemented the Spanish colonization of New Mexico. During this nearly sixty-year period, the Pueblo people suffered severe disruptions of their lives and cultures, and the number of Pueblo villages in New Mexico was reduced from between seventy and one hundred to nineteen.

In similar events to those that occurred between other Native American tribes and the European settlers who encountered them, the Spanish tried to impose Christianity on the Pueblo peoples and exacted forced labor from them. Many pueblos were moved or consolidated to benefit Spanish labor demands. In the mid-seventeenth century, serious disputes developed between the civil and religious authorities in New Mexico; the Pueblos were caught in the middle. In 1680 the Pueblos revolted and successfully drove the Spanish out of New Mexico for more than a decade, but the Spanish returned in force and had reconquered the region by 1694.

The historic southward migration of Comanche Indians onto the Southern Plains, which began in about 1700, pushed the Eastern Apaches from the plains southward, greatly altering Spanish-Indian relations in New Mexico for the remainder of the Spanish colonial era. Depending on what the Spanish Indian policies and alliances were at any given time, Pueblo auxiliary troops were often coerced into fighting alongside Spanish troops against tribes of Apache, Navajo, Ute, and Comanche. In the early 1820s, after the Mexican War of Independence freed the area from Spanish domination, Mexican law conferred citizenship on the Pueblo peoples. When the Mexican-American War ended in 1848, the resultant Treaty of Guadalupe-Hidalgo required that Mexico cede the region to the United States and that the Pueblos (like the Mexican residents of New Mexico) become owners of their remaining lands and receive U.S. citizenship. They were the only Indians in the Southwest to gain American citizenship in this manner; other indigenous groups in the region did not become U.S. citizens until Congress passed the Indian Citizenship Act of 1924. They were also the only Native Americans to gain possession of their lands through a means other than U.S. government-Indian treaty, so that the pueblos are not technically reservations, though they operate in the same manner.

Their early land ownership had both positive and negative consequences for the Pueblo. Whereas federal law prohibited other Indian groups from selling their land without congressional approval, the Pueblo tribes could conduct land transactions with non-Indians with no federal intervention. During the next sixty years, the U.S. Supreme Court and lower territorial courts of New Mexico repeatedly reaffirmed this right. This unique position opened the door for the unchecked sale of Pueblo lands to white settlers and speculators. In 1916 the U.S. government granted Pueblo groups federal recognition as Indian tribes, which curtailed their ability to sell land, and in 1924 Congress passed the Pueblo Lands Act, which created a Pueblo Land Board to investigate the claims of some three thousand non-Indians to lands historically held by Pueblos. The land board largely affirmed the rights of white settlers to remain in possession of disputed lands.

Modern Era The experience of Pueblo peoples in the United States during much of the twentieth century was typified by hardship and the quest to find a balance between assimilating into mainstream culture and preserving traditional lifeways. In the early 1900s

For the first time since the Lincoln Administration, the Pueblo Indians sent a delegation to Washington, D.C. in 1923. LIBRARY OF CONGRESS PRINTS AND PHOTOGRAPHS DIVISION [LC-DIG-PPMSCA-05084]

Pueblo groups faced a surfeit of discriminatory policies at the hands of the U.S. government and a white society they felt either viewed them with hostility or ignored them entirely. The attitudes of early-twentieth-century administrators toward Pueblo culture is typified by the actions of Indian Affairs Commissioner Charles H. Burke in 1927. Burke waged a public campaign among whites, claiming that traditional Indian religions were "sadistic and obscene." His crusade brought him to declare to the Taos Pueblo Council that Pueblo people were "half-animals" who practiced a pagan religion.

Throughout the century Pueblo groups continued to lose control of their traditional land, piece by piece; they faced harsh economic and living conditions and substandard educational opportunities. The increased availability of jobs in larger towns and cities led many Pueblo to move out of their traditional communities, though most maintained ties to their original clans and homelands. Even though the Pueblo (and other New Mexican Native Americans) were not granted the right to vote until 1948, some joined the military and fought for the United States in World War II.

During the second half of the century, Pueblo tribes redoubled their efforts to keep their traditional indigenous customs, including languages, alive and their lands sovereign. They found ways to record their languages, improved schools on pueblo lands, and took legal action against federal and state authorities over lost land and water rights. Relations with United States during this period were largely characterized by the tribes' struggle for water rights. For example, Taos Pueblo had lost Blue Lake and its watershed in the Sangre de Cristo Mountains above the pueblo by executive order of President Theodore Roosevelt in 1906. The watershed became federal property and was later administered by the U.S. Forest Service as a national forest. The tribe had always considered the lake their place of origin and thus a sacred site. In 1975, after a thirty-year fight, Taos Pueblo succeeded in regaining its sacred lake and 55,000 acres of surrounding land. This marked one of the few times that the United States has returned a major sacred site to Indian control.

The Pueblo peoples achieved many improvements in their standard of living during this time, but Pueblo historian Joe S. Sando noted in his 1992 book *Pueblo Nations* that there was still much work to be done. During the twentieth century, Sando wrote, the federal government "made many pious gestures and floated much rhetoric" aimed at conciliation while simultaneously allowing Pueblo lands and water sources to fall into disrepair.

In the twenty-first century, historic events have taken the form of economic struggles and gains.

All the tribes were hit hard by the financial crisis of 2008, though government appropriations expanded health care options for the pueblos that year, too. Across the board government spending cuts—or budget sequestration—in 2013 reversed these advances, deeply affecting all government social services on reservations.

Several Pueblo tribal governments, such as those in Sandia, Santa Clara, and Isleta pueblos, began operating gaming casinos on tribal land. Others looked for different sources of revenue. In 2011 Jemez pueblo began construction of a large-scale commercial solar power plant that, when completed, will be the first of its kind on tribal land. The government of Jemez is also exploring geothermal and biomass energy solutions as ways to increase the pueblo's revenue and solve local energy concerns.

Today, many Pueblo peoples still live in their traditional villages. They and their compatriots around the country persist in working to carry their language and culture into the future, an effort that includes caring for—and demanding that the government help them care for—their historic archeological sites and natural resources.

SETTLEMENT IN THE UNITED STATES

Historical and archaeological evidence corroborates Native tradition in the understanding that nomadic hunters and gatherers were already roaming the areas that would become Arizona, Colorado, New Mexico, and Utah more than 2,000 years ago. As the Native peoples began to develop agricultural systems that allowed for more sedentary lifestyles, they built complex permanent settlements. The best known of the Ancestral Puebloan communities are the Chaco, Mesa Verde, Kiet Siel, Bandelier, and Aztec sites. By the end of severe, prolonged droughts that occurred in the late 1300s, the ancestors of the contemporary Pueblo peoples began migrating south toward the Little Colorado River and Rio Grande Valley.

Following the arrival of Europeans, Pueblo groups lost much of their sovereignty and traditional landholdings to white intruders. They did not, however, face the kind of long-distance relocations suffered by southeastern tribes such as the Muscogee (or Creek), Cherokee, and Seminole, all of whom followed the Trail of Tears to "Indian Territory" in Oklahoma. Rather, the Pueblo peoples of the American Southwest mostly remained on tracts of land near their ancestral homes. Throughout their interactions with white settlers and continuing into the twentieth century, Pueblo peoples suffered many of the same hardships as other indigenous groups in the United States, including low incomes, poor health care, substandard educational opportunities, unemployment, and an overall clash with the dominant mainstream culture.

Today, most Pueblo peoples still live in the American Southwest, primarily in the upper Rio Grande River Valley in northern New Mexico and in multiple locations in west-central New Mexico. These settlements include the Acoma, Cochiti, Isleta, Jemez, Laguna, Nambe, Ohkay Owingeh (also called San Juan), Picuris, Pojoaque, Sandia, San Felipe, San Ildefonso, Santa Ana, Santa Clara, Santo Domingo, Taos, Tesuque, Zia, and Zuni. The Hopi Tribe is based in northeastern Arizona and in the small community of Ysleta del Sur near El Paso, Texas. The 2010 American Community Survey also reports significant numbers of Pueblo people living in California, Arizona, Colorado, and Oklahoma.

LANGUAGE

Languages spoken by Pueblo tribes are organized into four families: Keresan, Kiowa-Tanoan, Uto-Aztecan, and Zuni. Among these families Zuni is the only linguistic isolate (not related to any other languages); it is classified as part of the larger Penutian Phylum. All other Pueblo languages are classified within the Aztec-Tanoan Phylum and are further differentiated into multiple distinct dialects spoken by various subdivisions within the Pueblo tribes.

Dialects of the Keresan family are spoken by Pueblo tribes including the Acoma, Cochiti, Laguna, San Felipe, Santa Ana, Santo Domingo, and Zia. The 2010 U.S. Census identified 12,945 native speakers of Keresan languages, making them the most prevalent of all living Pueblo languages. Nearly all of these native speakers live in New Mexico.

Within the Kiowa-Tanoan family are three Tanoan languages: Tiwa, Tewa, and Towa. Tiwa is spoken by the Taos, Picuris, Sandia, and Isleta Pueblo peoples. Tewa is spoken by the San Juan, Santa Clara, San Ildefonso, Nambe, Tesuque, and Pojoaque. Towa is spoken only by the Jemez. The language group is thought to be related to the languages of the nomadic Kiowa people of the Great Plains. Although the Kiowa and Pueblo peoples lived radically different lifestyles and no historic link can be found between the two, the similarity of language leads some anthropologists to conclude that they must possess shared or similar ancestors.

The Hopi language is considered part of the Pueblo language group and is among the thirty indigenous languages throughout the West included in the Uto-Aztecan family. The 2010 U.S. Census listed the number of people speaking the Hopi language as 6,780 and noted just 40 monolinguals (people who spoke only Hopi) among that population. While Hopi is considered to be declining, efforts are underway to preserve the language. A Hopi-English dictionary (*Hopiikwa Lavaytutuveni*) was published by the University of Arizona Press in 1998, and in 2007 the tribe founded the Hopi Language Project, a program produced by KUYI Hopi Radio and dedicated to preserving the traditional language.

Although it is unrelated to any other known language, the 7,000-year-old Zuni language remains the second most prevalent of all Pueblo languages.

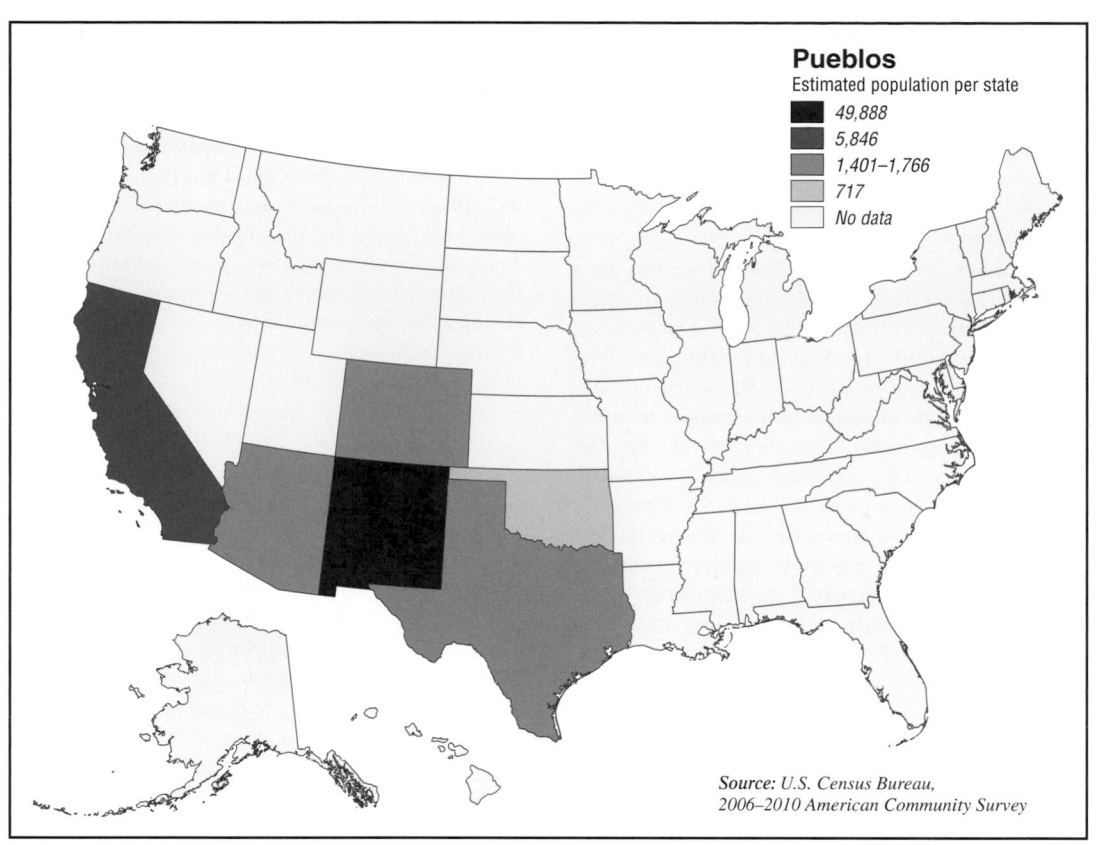

Pueblos
Estimated population per state
49,888
5,846
1,401–1,766
717
No data

Source: U.S. Census Bureau,
2006–2010 American Community Survey

It is spoken only by the Zuni people but is considered comparatively less threatened than other Native American languages. It is still the primary language in many homes near the Zuni pueblo in New Mexico. According to the 2010 U.S. Census, there were 9,686 native speakers of Zuni, most of them living in New Mexico. Native speakers also exist in Arizona, though in much smaller numbers.

RELIGION

For Pueblo peoples, culture and religion are inseparable. Religious beliefs are deeply interwoven in many aspects of Pueblo culture, including farming, storytelling, dance, art, and architecture. For the Hopi agriculture is especially symbolic; it carries a sacred significance and determines a great deal about their work cycles, ceremonies, and feasts. Much Hopi spirituality centers on the belief that when their ancestors emerged from the depths of the earth, they were confronted by a spiritual deity who asked them to select an ear of corn, which would thereby symbolize their life's path. The Hopi chose an ear of short blue corn, representing a life of hardship, humility, and hardiness, since the short blue corn is the most difficult to harvest successfully but is also the most durable. The planting and harvesting of corn is a tangible way that the Hopi people connect to their earliest ancestors and the creation of the world. Many Pueblo religious ceremonies and rituals are tied to the bringing of rain

and a successful harvest, and Pueblo groups across the region still practice many of these traditions today.

A central theme of Pueblo religions was the belief that a life force existed in all objects of the universe and that human beings must be respectful of this life force. Another common theme across Pueblo folklore and religion is represented in the Hopi story of the creation of the world, which is based on the concept of emergence. The Hopi believe that their ancestors—spirit beings—migrated through three underground worlds before emerging into the Fourth World, in which they currently exist. Upon emerging, they made a covenant with the spirit being Maasaw, who allowed them to remain on the land as long as they followed sacred rules that ensure harmony among people, maintenance of the land, and provision of enough water to grow their crops. The Hopi still work to honor this sacred covenant.

Not all Puebloan religious beliefs may be shared with outsiders, and some Pueblo groups such as the Taos (among the most traditional of the Eastern Pueblo) are noted for the secrecy surrounding their religious ceremonies. Historians believe, however, that beginning at least two centuries before the arrival of the Spanish, the most widespread religion among Pueblo groups was kachina worship. "Kachina" is a term denoting the spirit beings who figure heavily in the history and mythology of many Pueblo cultures and who serve as intermediaries between humans and gods; it also refers to masked dancers who dress as these spirits during festivals and religious ceremonies. More than four hundred different kachinas were recognized and worshipped by Pueblo peoples, and the concepts they were meant to represent could take many forms. Kachinas could symbolize part of the natural world, an animal, an ancestor, or an important historical event, and they could vary from one pueblo community to another.

In modern times many Pueblo groups have modified Christian (Catholic) teachings to make them compatible with traditional views. The result is a form of Christianity found nowhere else in the world. Pueblo Catholicism nevertheless has much in common with the experiences of Native peoples throughout Latin America who are nominally Catholics but whose practices and beliefs are greatly at odds with official canon. The church is tolerant of their manner of worship, having found after exerting great effort that it cannot uproot traditional indigenous religious beliefs. The church made its greatest effort in the 1660s and 1670s, with public hangings and whippings. In the Pueblo Revolt of 1680, twenty-one of the thirty-three Spanish Catholic priests in New Mexico were killed. The Catholic influence has resulted in the creation and observance of a number of Christian holidays and feast days that coincide with traditional celebrations and the performance of traditional dances. Some Pueblo groups observe feast days in honor of their patron saints.

CULTURE AND ASSIMILATION

For nearly five hundred years, Pueblo peoples have felt the effects of Euro-American incursion into the Southwest. The European settlers caused enormous loss of life and land holdings among the Pueblo; they subjugated traditional cultures and made efforts to undermine the Pueblo peoples' sense of self. Several twentieth-century Pueblo writers have chronicled the damage wrought by the influx of whites and the obstacles facing Pueblo peoples when determining how best to make their way in mainstream American society. In his 2003 essay "The Pueblo People and the Dominant Culture," Joseph H. Suina wrote: "At the time of [...] first contact, the native culture of my people was intact. It was viable in all ways. The Europeans subordinated it to their own culture, sometimes through brute force. The result was tremendous conflict, confusion, and astonishment, as well as heartbreak and tragedy."

Pueblo groups have fought successfully to maintain many of their traditional values, however, some of which they have shared with mainstream society and some of which they have kept secret, safe from outside impact. Puebloan influence is readily apparent in elements of modern Southwestern culture, including in its well-known styles of artwork, architecture, and pottery. Today, most Pueblo people are at home in both their native world and in the world of the dominant American culture.

Most Pueblo people who live in the large cities and small towns of the American Southwest have assimilated fully into mainstream society. They contribute to all strata of the Southwestern economy, working in blue-collar jobs and white-collar fields such as medicine, law, and teaching. Those who still live in traditional pueblo dwellings may be less assimilated, often living fairly traditional, albeit modernized lives. Their economies are largely based on tourism and the sale of crafts. Although they have adopted many elements of white culture, some continue to speak Spanish and indigenous Pueblo languages and to commemorate traditional religious and cultural practices.

During the late 1900s Pueblo peoples began spearheading an effort to record and revitalize their traditional cultures, including their indigenous languages and traditional beliefs. In 1976 the Indian Pueblo Cultural Center opened in Albuquerque with a mission to "preserve and perpetuate Pueblo culture and to advance understanding by presenting with dignity and respect the accomplishments and evolving history of the Pueblo people." In 1983 the center founded the Institute for Pueblo Indian Studies/Pueblo Archives, which seeks to provide educational programs that celebrate Pueblo culture through lectures, symposia, seminars, poetry readings, and multimedia events. Prior to his death in 2011, Joe Sando served as the director of the institute for many years.

Traditions and Customs Puebloan architecture is widely recognized for its distinctive styles and customary uses. Traditional Pueblo dwellings were often interconnected multilevel structures made of limestone and plaster or adobe bricks. They housed multiple families and sometimes reached five stories in height, with ladders leading through holes in the ceilings enabling inhabitants to move from one floor to the next. This structural design allowed for elements of communal living and also served as a safeguard against outside attacks. Some Pueblo people continue to live in historic pueblo dwellings, maintaining the structures while modernizing them as needed. The influences of Pueblo architecture can also be seen in modern buildings throughout the Southwest.

Pueblo communities often held religious gatherings in kivas, subterranean structures usually situated in a central location in the pueblo. Many such kivas are associated with the traditional Puebloan kachina religion, though the existence of similar subterranean ritual sites in early pueblos suggests that they predate the development of kachina. Family members, usually men, meet and hold ceremonies or social events inside the kiva.

Cuisine Corn was a mainstay of early Pueblo peoples' diets. The development of the agricultural techniques necessary to cultivate corn and other crops such as squash and beans is considered a major landmark in ancient Pueblo history, because it allowed Pueblos to move away from a nomadic lifestyle in favor of permanent settlements. Corn was used not only for sustenance but also for trade with nearby tribes as part of the region's early economy. Pinyon nuts were another common source of nourishment, called by Tewa Pueblos "the oldest food of the people of past days." By the thirteenth century Pueblos were also domesticating turkeys, both for food and for the production of warm blankets made from their feathers. Varieties of sweet and hot chilies, now a common part of Southwestern cuisine, are believed to have entered the Pueblo diet as a result of later contact with settlers from Mexico. These immigrants from the south also brought wheat to make bread and the adobe *horno*, a mud oven, in which to bake it. *Hornos* still sit outside many traditional pueblo homes.

Most traditional pueblo communities cultivate both communal and individual gardens, and corn, chili peppers, beans, squash, and pinyon nuts remain common ingredients in traditional Pueblo foods. They can be combined and prepared in many different ways. Often they are eaten on tortillas made of cornmeal or wheat or are paired with meats and cheeses in stews and soups. Common Pueblo dishes still prepared today include: menudo, a dish of green chilis baked with potatoes and tripe; pozole, a stew of red chiliflavored hominy and pork; and tamales made from cornmeal masa stuffed with spiced beans and meat and wrapped in corn husks to be steamed or baked. Some pueblos have established groups composed of elders and youths who work together to preserve and transmit traditional methods of food preparation from one generation to the next.

Pueblo communities hold feasts to accompany various days of religious significance. Some of these festivals are open to the public and may feature the finest traditional foods prepared by the best cooks in the community. For these large gatherings, foods are sometimes prepared on wood-fired cookstoves, and simple, traditional meals are "dressed up" to include more meat or spices.

Traditional Dress Although historical methods of dress varied among different Pueblo tribes, men generally wore breechcloths or short kilts, while women wore knee-length cotton dresses called mantas that fastened at the shoulders. Later, European missionaries of the 1800s and 1900s influenced Pueblo women to wear blouses or shifts beneath their traditional dresses to render them less revealing. Both men and women often wore animal skin moccasins. Religious or ceremonial garb often differed from everyday dress. Pueblo peoples' costumes for dances and festivals are among the most striking of any Native peoples. Masks and textiles are important aspects of Pueblo ritual, as are ornamental silver and turquoise in such forms as elaborate necklaces.

Dances and Songs Ceremonial dances are at the heart of Puebloan tradition. They are unique to each tribe, and the roles for the leaders, singers, dancers, and spectators are prescribed. They are often

NOTABLE PUEBLOS

The Acoma Pueblo, west of Albuquerque, is the oldest continuously inhabited settlement within the United States, dating from the twelfth century. Called the Sky City, it sits atop a 350-foot mesa. In 2011 about thirty people inhabited the ancient town year-round. It has no electricity or running water. Most of the Acoma people live in the nearby communities of Acomita, Anzac, and McCartys.

Isleta Pueblo is the largest Tiwa-speaking pueblo. San Juan (site of the first Spanish capitol of New Mexico) is the largest Tewa-speaking pueblo, and Jemez is the last remaining Towa-speaking pueblo. It absorbed the Towa-speaking survivors of Pecos Pueblo when Pecos was abandoned in the 1830s. On the outskirts of El Paso, Texas, just across the border with New Mexico, is Ysleta del Sur Pueblo, which was founded by Pueblo people who fled Isleta Pueblo (near Albuquerque, New Mexico) with the Spanish during the Pueblo Revolt of 1680.

performed by masked male dancers dressed as kachinas, who are said to actually become the personages they portray. The dancers perform ceremonial rituals in the plazas on feast days and other important occasions. Some ceremonials, such as the Zuni Shalakos, feature kachinas in ten-foot-high costumes. Among the Hopi the kachinas are said to live in the San Francisco Peaks near Flagstaff, Arizona. They come to the Hopi for six months each year, arriving during the February Bean Dance. Although men are usually the performers, singing and dancing in line formations or in procession, women also have important roles in religious ceremonies and activities; they are responsible for preparing feasts and helping to organize and maintain communal gatherings. There are also certain sacred dances and rituals in which women play a central role.

The Pueblos use gourd rattles and wood and rawhide drums as musical instruments for their ceremonies and dances. Many dances are held in honor of seasonal change and their related duties, such as winter hunting and autumn harvest. Numerous dances relate to the bringing of rain. Most of the Pueblo groups perform versions of the Corn Dance and the Matachines Dance—a dance with Spanish and Mexican roots—and many perform dances in honor of buffalo or deer.

Holidays On January 6 most Pueblo communities celebrate the Day of the Three Kings, a religious tradition with Christian roots that commemorates Pueblo self-government; on this day new governors and officials are installed in office. The Governor's Feast is observed at Acoma Pueblo in the first week in February. May 3 is Santa Cruz Feast Day at Cochiti and Taos Pueblos. Grab Day provides a chance to give thanks for abundance and to celebrate renewal at several of the pueblos in June and at others in August. At Laguna people throw water, food, and household articles from a roof to crowds below; Laguna writer, director, and producer Billy Luther documented the tradition in a film titled *Grab*. The Eight Northern Indian Pueblos Spring Artist and Craftsman Show, one of the largest Native-operated outdoor exhibitions and markets in the West, usually takes place in July. The Nambe Pueblo commemorate July 4 with the Falls Ceremonial, which includes dances above the village at Nambe Falls. Pueblo groups participate in the Gallup Inter-Tribal Indian Ceremonial, with dances, a rodeo, parades, and powwows, each August. In late November or early December, the Zuni celebrate the harvest with the Shalako Ceremonial, their most important event of the year. Numerous other ceremonial events occur at Pueblo communities through the year in celebration of traditional history, religion, and the agricultural cycle.

FAMILY AND COMMUNITY LIFE

Western Pueblo families were matrilineal, meaning surnames and lineages were passed down through the mother's family. Related families grouped to form larger clans, which did not allow members to intermarry. Families were also matrilocal, meaning married couples lived with the mother's family. All families cohabitated in clusters of apartments within a larger pueblo structure. Eastern Pueblos typically organized patrilineally into moieties sometimes known as the Summer People and the Winter People or the Turquoise People and the Squash People, depending on the individual tribe. These clans exchanged household and social responsibilities throughout the year.

Kinship continues to play an important role in contemporary Pueblo communities. Clans remain significant social units that influence marriage partnerships, delineate membership in religious societies, and determine a variety of social and economic duties.

Gender Roles Women are held in high regard in traditional Pueblo families. Historically, the matrilocal organization of Western Pueblo families gave women ownership of the family home. In most Western and Eastern Pueblo tribes, women were also largely responsible for tending family gardens and producing pottery. Men were accountable for hunting efforts, and in some Pueblo societies, they were responsible

The Pueblo Comanche Dance is performed in San Ildefonso, New Mexico. EDUCATION IMAGES / UNIVERSAL IMAGES GROUP / GETTY IMAGES

for the weaving of textiles. Men also held exclusive religious ceremonies in kivas. In matrilocal societies related men did not live together, and they sometimes gathered in kivas for purely social reasons.

In many Pueblo families today, such as in the Taos pueblo community, descent on both male and female sides is equally regarded. Men and women live in separate houses until marriage, after which they are allowed to cohabitate. Caring for children may be a communal affair within the family unit.

Courtship and Weddings Traditions accompanying courtship and marriage can vary greatly among Puebloan peoples, depending on the practices of individual tribal groups. Most Pueblo tribes historically encouraged monogamous relationships, and many afforded women considerable status within their social structures. Among groups that traced their ancestry through the mother's family, women often took an active role in courtship and in choosing their mates. Upon marriage a new husband moved into the residence of his bride's family, and the women typically maintained ownership of the home. Women could demand a divorce; in instances of official separation, men would return to their own families or leave the area entirely. By contrast, in more patriarchal Pueblo groups, men dictated the circumstances regarding courtship, marriage and divorce.

The Catholicism of early Spanish explorers greatly affected the religious practices—including the marriage rituals—of nearly all Pueblo tribes. European interlopers and missionaries often enforced the use of Western marriage rites. In modern times many Pueblo couples choose to acknowledge both their own indigenous traditions and the Western practices that have influenced the history of their tribes. One traditional Pueblo marriage practice that has been reinstated involves a wedding vase. Featuring two spouts to represent the two partners, the vases are often built and fired by the groom's family using clay from area riverbeds. Historically, the vase was filled with a special nectar made by a spiritual leader, but today's couples often use water or tea. During the wedding the bride and groom take turns drinking from opposite sides of the vase, and at the culmination of the ceremony, both drink from the vessel simultaneously. Tradition dictates that if they can accomplish this act without spilling any of the contents, they will have a long and happy partnership. After the ceremony is complete, the wedding vase typically becomes an important and prized possession in the couple's home.

Education Pueblo children historically encountered many of the hardships common to Native people when entering a Westernized education system: their cultures were ignored by European teachers and administrators who sought to "civilize" them by forcibly indoctrinating them into white culture. This often included isolating Native children from their cultures by sending them to boarding schools, and New Mexico's Santa Fe

SACRED CLOWNS

Many Native American stories feature a trickster, often Coyote or Raven. For the Pueblo this character is supplanted by the clown, a revered figure of the kachina religion whose role goes beyond humor to the subversion of reality. Commonly called *koshares* (the name varies from village to village), ritual clowns were traditionally an essential part of Pueblo ceremonies. They wore white face paint with the eyes and mouth encircled in black; their bodies were painted in horizontal black and white stripes; and horns sprouting corn husks protruded from a black and white skullcap. The clowns engaged in funny, sexual, and absurd behavior. Despite their antics, which are often interpreted as a reminder of foolish human behavior, clowns are sacred figures whose actions possess more profound reasons and motivations. As part of their suppression of Pueblo culture, European Americans particularly targeted the *koshares* for their seeming irreverence, and tribes learned to hide the sacred function of them. *Kosheares* today rarely do more than entertain.

Indian School was among the first wave of such institutions established in the United States. From 1890 to 1962, the Santa Fe Indian School taught Pueblo, Apache, and Navajo students a Western curriculum of arithmetic, writing, history, and geography.

Consistent with other early Indian boarding schools, Santa Fe Indian School organized children into military-style battalions; they wore military dress, had their hair cut short, and were punished for attempting to speak Native languages. In addition to some industrial vocational training, boys were taught to drill with rifles, and girls often studied sewing, cooking, and housekeeping. Within a few decades, however, the militaristic bent of the Santa Fe School softened, and it came to be regarded as an Indian art school. Renowned Pueblo artists such as Geronima Cruz Montoya from San Juan and Pablita Velarde from Santa Clara studied there before the school was closed in the early 1960s. In 1981 it was reopened under the control of New Mexico's nineteen pueblos, and it continues to operate as a boarding school, educating children from pueblos around the state in a curriculum emphasizing both European and Native cultures.

After the closure of many Indian boarding schools in New Mexico and Arizona during the mid-twentieth century, Native students were largely shuffled into public schools. Again, their traditional lifeways and cultures were disregarded, until states such as New Mexico began to implement bilingual education programs during the 1960s and 1970s. Nonetheless, inadequate instruction and high dropout rates plagued Pueblo students throughout 1980s.

Efforts are underway to improve the educational experience of Pueblo students. According to a 2009 study by the New Mexico Education Department, sixteen of the state's twenty-three school districts reported efforts to incorporate study of indigenous cultures into the curricula. Graduation rates among Native students, however, remained low at 49.8 percent, compared to 70.1 percent for Caucasian students, 60.9 percent for African Americans, and 56.2 percent for Hispanics. Numerous pueblos have enacted programs such as the Eight Northern Pueblos Talent Search that are designed to boost the number of Pueblo students who attend college.

EMPLOYMENT AND ECONOMIC CONDITIONS

Although the traditional agro-pastoralist economy of Puebloan peoples has diminished during modern times, some people continue to cultivate crops and raise cattle in order to subsist. The Pueblo people are among the most successful dryland farmers in the world and are also skilled at irrigation farming. Many Pueblos continue the agricultural traditions of their ancestors, cultivating the land in the same time-honored manner.

Private enterprise has provided some jobs for Pueblo peoples over the years. In 1953, for example, the Anaconda Copper Mining Company (a subsidiary of Atlantic Richfield Company) built a uranium mine on Laguna land and employed local Pueblos. After the mine closed in 1982, the company rehired them to work on the reclamation project from 1986 to 1995 that attempted to restore the mined land.

Traditional Pueblo craft economies have flourished during the modern era; locally produced pottery, weavings, jewelry, drums, and other items are important sources of income in many pueblos. For example,

A Pueblo mother takes her three children for a walk, in Taos, New Mexico. CORBIS-BETTMANN. REPRODUCED BY PERMISSION.

the inhabitants of Jemez, known historically for making baskets of yucca fronds (a lost art), now include well-known jewelers, potters, and storyteller doll makers; Taos Pueblo is famous for its drums; and San Juan is home to the Oke Oweenge Crafts Cooperative. Many of the pueblos are also open to tourists for visitation, and numerous pueblo communities sponsor festivals and celebrations that are open to the public.

Pueblo people are often employed in the urban areas near their homes, and many return to their pueblo frequently. Many of Nambe's residents work in Santa Fe, in Española, or at Los Alamos National Laboratory. Tribal enterprises also provide jobs. The Hopi Cultural Center, with its restaurant and inn, in Kykotsmovi Village, Arizona, offers employment opportunities. Cochiti provides services for Cochiti Lake, which leases its land from Cochiti Pueblo and has a commercial center, a marina, and an eighteen-hole golf course. The majority of Isleta's residents work in Albuquerque, but others operate the bingo hall, the town's grocery stores, and the campgrounds at Isleta Lakes. Laguna Industries designs, manufactures, integrates, and supports electromechanical systems for the U.S. Army and commercial groups and is only one of a number of Laguna tribal industries.

Gaming casinos have become important for many Native American tribal economies. Some pueblo communities, such as Taos and Acoma, have enthusiastically embraced casinos as a source of economic opportunity. Other Pueblos, such as the Nambe, resist gaming on traditional views that forbid the practice. The Sandia Indian Bingo Parlor is one of the largest in New Mexico. Sandia also operates Bien Mur Indian Market Center and Sandia Lakes Recreation Area. Zuni has been a model for tribal enterprise, taking advantage of direct federal grants through the Community Action Programs to gain administrative control of almost all of the Bureau of Indian Affairs contract services on the reservation, which now run more efficiently and with much greater community commitment and participation.

POLITICS AND GOVERNMENT

Despite the Indian Reorganization Act of 1934, which returned a degree of self-government to recognized tribes but demanded a certain amount of conformity to U.S. governmental structures, many Pueblos refused to allow their traditional form of government to be fully replaced by a Westernized system. Traditional Pueblo government features leadership from different sources of strength within the community. Clans are eminent in governing bodies, and among some Pueblo communities, specific clans have traditional obligations to provide leaders. This is true of the Bear Clan among the Hopi, the Antelope Clan at Acoma, and the Bow Clan at Zuni. The Tewa pueblos have dual village leaders: the heads of the Winter and Summer moieties each exercise responsibility for half of the year. In matters of traditional religion, spiritual leaders have serious responsibilities to the people. Along with their assistants they not only perform ceremonies but also organize hunts and the planting of crops.

Today all tribal governments elect their own governors and councils. In New Mexico the All Indian Pueblo Council (AIPC) had its first recorded meeting in 1598, when Juan de Oñate met with thirty-eight Pueblo leaders at Santo Domingo. Pueblo oral history recounts that the various pueblos had been working together long before the arrival of the Spanish and that secret meetings of the council were a major factor in the successful planning of the Pueblo Revolt of 1680. The AIPC's modern phase began on November 5, 1922, when Pueblo leaders assembled at Santo Domingo to meet with the U.S. commissioner of Indian affairs under Franklin Delano Roosevelt, John Collier, who warned them of a Congressional bill that heavily disadvantaged them. The council sent testimony and a protest to Congress. The AIPC's present constitution was adopted in 1965. The body is a confederation of New Mexico Pueblo communities that today administers social services, addresses governmental policy, and promotes the common welfare. Its mission statement also articulates a commitment to the preservation and revitalization of Pueblo culture and language.

During the latter half of the twentieth century and into the early twenty-first, some pueblo governments became more active in addressing economic, environmental, and energy issues. This was particularly true in Laguna Pueblo, where the Anaconda Mining Company leased nearly 8,000 acres from the tribal government from 1953 to 1982 to operate the largest open pit uranium mine in the world. The mine employed a large percentage of Laguna's population and made the pueblo among the richest in New Mexico, but when it closed, it left behind open pits, waste dumps and ore stockpiles. Even after a five-year reclamation effort and fifteen-year monitoring period spearheaded by the tribe, a 2007 study by the Environmental Protection Agency found the site still showed signs of contamination. In 2012, after a lobbying effort by Laguna Pueblo leaders the site was added to the National Priorities List of Superfund sites.

NOTABLE INDIVIDUALS

Academia Laguna Pueblo educator Lee Francis (1945–2004) was the director of the American Indian Internship program at American University in Silver Springs, Maryland, and the national director of Wordcraft Circle of Native American Mentor and Apprentice Writers. In 1994 Francis led a team of Native writers in guest editing a special Native American Literatures issue of the journal *Callaloo* for the University of Virginia and Johns Hopkins University Press.

Ted Jojola (1951–), an educator and administrator of Isleta Pueblo descent, is known for his research on Native American culture. His numerous publications have dealt with subjects ranging from urban planning to teaching, architecture,

and ethnography. He is currently a professor at the University of New Mexico, where in 2011 he became the first faculty member of the School of Architecture and Planning to be designated a distinguished professor by the school.

Alfonso Ortiz (1939–1998) was a well-known Pueblo anthropologist, scholar, and activist whose books on Southwest Indian tribes, including *The Tewa World: Space, Time, Being, and Becoming in a Pueblo Society* (1969) and *American Indian Myths and Legends* (1984), are considered classics in anthropological scholarship. In addition to his academic work, Ortiz was president of the Association of American Indian Affairs (AAIA) in the 1970s. During his term the organization played a central role in the return of the sacred Blue Lake to the Taos Pueblo people in 1970 and the 1978 passage of the Indian Child Welfare Act, which ensured that Indian orphans are placed in Indian foster homes. Ortiz was a professor in the University of New Mexico's Anthropology Department from 1974 until his death.

The Hopi believe that their ancestors—spirit beings—migrated through three underground worlds before emerging into the Fourth World, in which they currently exist. Upon emerging, they made a covenant with the spirit being Maasaw, who allowed them to remain on the land as long as they followed sacred rules that ensure harmony among people, maintenance of the land, and provision of enough water to grow their crops.

Noted historian, author, and lecturer Joe Sando (1923–2011), a member of Jemez Pueblo, served for two decades as the director for the Institute for Pueblo Indian Studies/Pueblo Archives at the Indian Pueblo Cultural Center in Albuquerque. His books *Nee Hemish, a History of Jemez Pueblo* (1982), *Pueblo Nations: Eight Centuries of Pueblo Indian History* (1992), and *Pueblo Profiles: Cultural Identity through Centuries of Change* (1998), have been honored with multiple awards, including the Bravo Award for Literary Achievement, the New Mexico State Heritage Preservation Award, and the Excellence in the Humanities Award. Sando was regarded as the first academic author to address the Pueblo experience from a Pueblo point of view. His work changed the modern view of Po'Pay, a leader of the Pueblo Revolt of 1680, and may have been instrumental in the addition of a statue of Po'Pay to the National Statuary Hall in the rotunda of the U.S. Congress building in Washington, D.C., in 2005. Sando received the Lifetime Achievement Award of Indian Librarians and was named an outstanding alumnus of Eastern New Mexico University.

Art Pueblo communities have produced a number of renowned artists, including Maria Montoya Martinez (1887–1980), who has been called perhaps the most famous Native American artist of all time. In her award-winning pottery, she revived and transformed indigenous pottery into high art. Martinez was a San Ildefonso Pueblo resident who spent much of her career producing pottery with her husband and other family members, including their son Popovi Da, who became a well-known artist in his own right. Martinez and her husband displayed and demonstrated their craft at the 1904 World's Fair in St. Louis, Missouri, and it was exhibited in museums and art shows. Martinez was particularly respected for her black-on-black pottery designs, which came to be known as blackware pottery.

Helen Quintana Cordero (1915–1994) was a Cochiti Pueblo woman responsible for reviving the nearly lost art of clay doll-making among her people. Clay dolls, typically embodying women singing to children, had been used by Southwest Indians for centuries for religious purposes and during harvest ceremonies, but this custom had declined with the arrival of white settlers in the region. Cordero specialized in what has come to be known as the "storyteller doll," drawn from her memories of her grandfather, who would gather the Pueblo children around him and tell them traditional Indian tales of the past. She was the first to use the male figure in her pioneering clay doll arrangements, which include the storyteller with as many as thirty clay children dolls sitting in various positions around him.

Pablita Velarde (1918–2006) was a Tewa writer and artist from Santa Clara Pueblo who was best known for her paintings depicting numerous aspects of daily Pueblo life, including religious ceremonies, tribal government, arts and crafts, costumes, and farming. She painted murals at Bandelier National Park in New Mexico and at the 1934 Chicago World's Fair in an authentic and detailed style that drew on her knowledge and study of her ancestry. Her works are sometimes used as secondary source materials for scholars researching the life of ancient Indians. The New Mexico Department of Agriculture honored Velarde in 1996 with its Rounders Award, which is given to "those who live, promote, or articulate the western way of life."

Film Victor Masayesva Jr. (1951–) is a photographer and filmmaker of Hopi descent whose work has been noted for honoring the culture and tradition of indigenous peoples in the Southwest. Among his nine films is the documentary *Imagining Indians*, which explores many facets of what happens when Native stories, rituals, and objects become commercial commodities. Masayesva is from Hotevilla, Arizona, a village of about five hundred people on Third Mesa, but he moved to New York City at the age of fifteen. After receiving a degree from Princeton University,

Masayesva served as an artist-in-residence there and at schools in Chicago and Montana. He has been awarded fellowships from the National Endowment for the Arts, the Ford Foundation, the Rockefeller Foundation, and the Arizona Commission on the Arts.

Literature The various Pueblo communities have produced some of the most outstanding contemporary Native literary writers. Two of the first three Lifetime Achievement Award honorees of the Native Writers' Circle of the Americas have been Pueblos: Simon J. Ortiz (1941–) from Acoma pueblo and Laguna pueblo's Leslie Marmon Silko (1948–). In the early 1970s Ortiz was editor of *Americans before Columbus*, the newspaper of the Indian Youth Council in Gallup, New Mexico. In the 1980s he held official tribal positions as interpreter and first lieutenant governor of Acoma. He has taught at the Institute of American Indian Arts, the University of New Mexico, Navajo Community College, Sinte Gleska College, San Diego State University, the College of Marin, Lewis and Clark College, and Colorado College. He edited one of the most important collections of Native literature, the short-story anthology *Earth Power Coming* (1988), published by Navajo Community College Press. He has also written many books of poetry, short fiction, and children's literature, among them *From Sand Creek* (1941); *Going for the Rain* (1976); *A Good Journey* (1977); *The People Shall Continue* (1977); *Fightin': New and Collected Stories* (1983); *Woven Stone* (1992); *Out There Somewhere* (2002); and *The Good Rainbow Road: Rawa Kashtyaa'tsi Hiyaani (A Native American Tale in Keres and English, Followed by a Translation into Spanish)* (2004).

Silko has also taught at a number of universities, including the University of Arizona and the University of New Mexico. In 1981 she was one of the original recipients of a MacArthur Foundation Grant (also called the "Genius Grant"), and her work has had a profound influence on the Native literary community. Her best known books are the short story collections *Ceremony* (1977) and *Storyteller* (1981) and the novel *Almanac of the Dead* (1991). Silko delivered a plenary session speech at the historic Returning the Gift Conference of North American Native writers at the University of Oklahoma in 1992, a conference that drew nearly four hundred Native literary writers from throughout the northern Western hemisphere. Silko's recent works include a 2010 memoir titled *The Turquoise Ledge* and the novella *Oceanstory*, published in 2011.

Paula Gunn Allen (1939–2008), who grew up in Laguna Pueblo, was a noted literary critic, lesbian activist, and author of fiction, poetry, biography, and academic nonfiction. She won a 1990 American Book Award for her work on the anthology *Spider Woman's Granddaughters* (1989) and in 2001 was honored with the Native Writers' Circle of the Americas' Lifetime Achievement Award. Her works include *Shadow*

Country (1982); *The Woman Who Owned the Shadows* (1983); *Studies in American Indian Literatures: Critical Essays and Course Designs* (1983); *The Sacred Hoop: Recovering the Feminine in American Indian Traditions* (1986); *Skin and Bones: Poems, 1979–1987* (1988); and *Pocahontas: Medicine Woman, Spy, Entrepreneur, Diplomat* (2004).

Laguna poet Carol Lee Sanchez (1934–2011) published numerous collections, including *Conversations From the Nightmare* (1975), *Time Warps* (1976), *Excerpt From a Mountain Climber's Handbook: Selected Poems, 1971–1984* (1985), *Message Bringer Woman* (1977), *From Spirit to Matter: New and Selected Poems, 1969–1996* (1997), and *Rainbow Visions & Earth Ways* (1998).

Hopi/Miwok writer Wendy Rose (1948–) is a poet, anthropologist, and artist. She has held positions as the coordinator of American Indian Studies at Fresno City College and with the Women's Literature Project of Oxford University Press, the Smithsonian Native Writers' Series, the Modern Language Association Commission on Languages and Literature of the Americas, and the Coordinating Council of Literary Magazines. Her books include *Hopi Roadrunner Dancing* (1973); *Academic Squaw: Reports to the World from the Ivory Tower* (1977); *The Halfbreed Chronicles* (1980); *Long Division: A Tribal History* (1981); *What Happened When the Hopi Hit New York* (1982); *Lost Copper* (1985; a Pulitzer Prize nominee); *Going to War with All My Relations* (1993); *Bone Dance* (1994); and *Itch Like Crazy* (2002).

Science Frank C. Dukepoo (1943–1999), a Hopi-Laguna geneticist, was the first Hopi to earn a doctoral degree. Born in Arizona, he earned a PhD from Arizona State University in 1973 and held teaching or research positions there and at San Diego State University, Palomar Junior College, and Northern State University. Dukepoo also served as director of Indian education at Northern Arizona University and held administrative positions with the National Science Foundation and the National Cancer Institute. In addition to founding and coordinating the National Native American Honor Society, which assists Native American students, Dukepoo conducted extensive research on birth defects in Indians.

MEDIA

NEWSPAPER AND PERIODICALS

Isleta Pueblo News

The monthly newsletter of Isleta Pueblo, available in print and online.

Ulysses Abeita, Editor
P.O. Box 1270
Isleta, New Mexico 87022
Phone: (505) 307-1582
Email: uabeita@yahoo.com
URL: www.isletapueblo.com

The Navajo-Hopi Observer

A newspaper serving the Navajo and Hopi Nations and area communities of Flagstaff, Arizona.

Ryan Williams, Managing Editor
2717 North Fourth Street
Suite 110
Flagstaff, Arizona 86001
Phone: (800) 408-4726
Email: rwilliams@williamsnews.com
URL: http://navajohopiobserver.com

RADIO

KSHI-FM (90.9)

A tribe-owned variety radio station broadcasting from Zuni, New Mexico.

P.O. Box 339
Zuni, New Mexico 87327
Phone: (505) 782-4811

KUYI-FM (88.1) Hopi Radio

Serving the Hopi Reservation, Flagstaff, Tuba City, Winslow, and the I-40 corridor, KUYI strives to appeal to a broad-based audience and broadcasts Native Voice One and NPR programs.

Richard Alun Davis, Station Manager
P.O. Box 1500
Keams Canyon, Arizona 86034
Phone: (928) 738-5505
Email: info@kuyi.net
URL: www.kuyi.net

ORGANIZATIONS AND ASSOCIATIONS

All Indian Pueblo Council (AIPC)

Advocates on behalf of New Mexico's nineteen Pueblo Indian tribes regarding educational, health, social, and economic issues and lobbies before state and national legislatures.

Chandler Sanchez, Chair
2401 12th Street NW
Albuquerque, New Mexico 87104
Phone: (505) 881-1992
Email: chairmansanchez@aipcnm.org
URL: www.aipcnm.org

Arizona Commission of Indian Affairs

A governmental organization working to "enhance communication and build sustainable relationships between tribal entities and the State of Arizona."

Nathan Pryor, Chair
1700 West Washington Street
Suite 430
Phoenix, Arizona 85007
Phone: (602) 542-3123
Email: iainfo@az.gov
URL: http://azcia.gov

Eight Northern Indian Pueblos Council (ENIPC)

Founded during the 1960s, this nonprofit organization helps secure funding for projects aiding the eight northern New Mexico pueblos of Tesuque, Pojoaque, Nambe, San Ildefonso, Santa Clara, Ohkay Owingeh, Picuris, and Taos as well as surrounding communities.

Michael Miller, Executive Director
327 Eagle Drive
P.O. Box 969
San Juan Pueblo, New Mexico 87566
Phone: (505) 747-1593
URL: www.enipc.org

New Mexico Commission on Indian Affairs

A governmental service that refers to itself as "the lead coordinating agency in New Mexico state government for ensuring effective interagency and state-tribal government-to-government relations."

Angela Crespin, Executive Assistant
Wendell Chino Building
Second Floor
1220 South Saint Francis Drive
Santa Fe, New Mexico 87505
Phone: (505) 476-1600
Email: angela.crespin@state.nm.us
URL: www.iad.state.nm.us

MUSEUMS AND RESEARCH CENTERS

Albuquerque Museum

Since 1967 this museum has celebrated culture, history, and art through regional, national, and international exhibitions. It offers information and frequent exhibits featuring Pueblo culture.

Cathy Wright, Museum Director
2000 Mountain Road NW
Albuquerque, New Mexico 87104
Phone: (505) 243-7255
Fax: (505) 764-6546
Email: clwright@cabq.gov
URL: http://albuquerquemuseum.org

Center for Indian Education

An organization at Arizona State University that emphasizes "world-class research and the preparation of a new generation of Indigenous scholars" pursuing information and study regarding Hopi culture. In 2012 the center announced the creation of a Pueblo Indian doctoral project to train scholars and researchers "committed to developing Pueblo peoples and communities in the U.S. Southwest and beyond."

Bryan Brayboy, Director
Arizona State University
Payne Hall
Suite 302
P.O. Box 876403
Tempe, Arizona 85287-6403
Phone: (480) 965-6292
Email: CIEhelp@asu.edu
URL: http://center-for-indian-education.asu.edu

Heard Museum of Anthropology

The Heard Museum is "dedicated to the sensitive and accurate portrayal of Native arts and cultures,"

including those of both Hopi and Pueblo traditions. It offers programs, exhibits, and festivals.

Debra Krol, Media Contact
2301 North Central Avenue
Phoenix, Arizona 85004
Phone: (602) 252-8848
Fax: (602) 252-9757
Email: contact@heard.org
URL: http://heard.org

The Hopi Cultural Center

A cultural center dedicated to Hopi traditions. Includes a small gallery museum, restaurant, and an inn.

Darren Tungovia, General Manager
P.O. Box 67
Second Mesa, Arizona 86043
Phone: (928) 734-2401
Fax: (928) 734-6651
Email: info@hopiculturalcenter.com
URL: www.hopiculturalcenter.com

Indian Pueblo Cultural Center

An Albuquerque-based organization owned by the nineteen pueblos of New Mexico, the center has a mission to "preserve and perpetuate Pueblo culture and to advance understanding by presenting, with dignity and respect, the accomplishments and evolving history of the Pueblo people of New Mexico."

Travis Suazo, Executive Director
2401 12th Street NW
Albuquerque, New Mexico 87104
Phone: (866) 855-7902
URL: www.indianpueblo.org

Maxwell Museum of Anthropology

Located at the University of New Mexico, the museum offers exhibits on cultures around the world with an emphasis on the heritage of the Southwest and includes permanent exhibits of prehistoric indigenous pottery and frequent exhibits on Pueblo culture.

E. James Dixon, Director
MSC01 1050
1 University of New Mexico
Albuquerque, New Mexico 87131-0001
Phone: (505) 277-4405
Email: maxwell@unm.edu
URL: www.unm.edu/~maxwell

Sky City Cultural Center and Haaku Museum

Located in Acoma Pueblo, this cultural center and museum strive to preserve the indigenous traditions of the pueblo and offer guided tours, exhibits, and crafts available for sale.

Emerson Vallo, Director
P.O. Box 310
Pueblo of Acoma, New Mexico 87034
Phone: (800) 747-0181
Email: ervallo@skycity.com
URL: http://sccc.acomaskycity.org

SOURCES FOR ADDITIONAL STUDY

Bruggmann, Maximilien, and Sylvio Acatos. *Pueblos: Prehistoric Indian Cultures of the Southwest.* Translated by Barbara Fritzemeier. New York: Facts on File, 1990.

Department of the Interior, Bureau of Indian Affairs. *Corn Dancers: United Pueblo Agency and Indian Irrigation Service.* DVD. Washington, D.C.: National Archive and Records Administration, 2006.

Gutiérrez, Ramón A. *When Jesus Came, the Corn Mothers Went Away: Marriage, Sexuality, and Power in New Mexico, 1500–1846.* Stanford, CA: Stanford University Press, 1991.

Keegan, Marcia. *Pueblo People: Ancient Traditions, Modern Lives.* Santa Fe, NM: Clear Light Publishers, 1999.

Nickens, Kathleen and Paul. *Pueblo Indians of New Mexico.* Mount Pleasant, SC: Arcadia Publishing, 2008.

Ortiz, Alfonso. *The Pueblo.* New York: Chelsea House, 1994.

The Pueblo Today and Yesterday: The History and Culture of the Anasazi and Hopi. NP: Charles River Editors, 2013. Kindle Edition.

Sando, Joe S. *Pueblo Nations: Eight Centuries of Pueblo Indian History.* Santa Fe, NM: Clear Light Publishers, 1992.

Suina, Joseph H. "The Pueblo People and the Dominant Culture: Conflict, Confusion and Astonishment." *Encounter* 16, no. 1 (spring 2003): 5–10.

Trimble, Stephen. *The People: Indians of the American Southwest.* Santa Fe, NM: Sar Press, 1993.

PUERTO RICAN AMERICANS

Derek Green

OVERVIEW

Puerto Rican Americans are people from the island of Puerto Rico (a commonwealth of the United States); they include people who have migrated from the island to the mainland United States and their descendants. The name *Puerto Rico*, meaning "rich port," was given to the island by its Spanish *conquistadors* (conquerors); according to lore, the name comes from Ponce de León himself, who upon first seeing the port of San Juan is said to have exclaimed, "¡Ay que puerto rico!" ("What a rich port!"). The island is the most easterly of the Greater Antilles group of the West Indies island chain. Located more than a thousand miles southeast of Miami, the American commonwealth of Puerto Rico is bounded on the north by the Atlantic Ocean, on the east by the Virgin Passage (which separates it from the Virgin Islands), on the south by the Caribbean Sea, and on the west by the Mona Passage (which separates it from the Dominican Republic). Puerto Rico is 35 miles wide (from north to south) and 95 miles long (from east to west) and has 311 miles of coastline. Its land mass measures 3,423 square miles (8,865.5 square kilometers)—about two-thirds the area of the state of Connecticut.

According to a 1990 U.S. Census Bureau report, the island of Puerto Rico had a population of 3,522,037. This represented a threefold increase since 1899. 810,000 of those new births occurred between the years of 1970 and 1990 alone. In 2012 the island population was 3.7 million. Most Puerto Ricans are of Spanish ancestry. Approximately 99 percent of the population is Hispanic, .7 percent is white, and about 0.8 percent is of African or mixed descent. As in many Latin American cultures, Roman Catholicism is the dominant religion, but Protestant faiths of various denominations have some Puerto Rican adherents as well. Until the 1940s, agriculture (coffee and, later, sugar) was the island's major source of revenue, but that has been replaced by manufacturing and tourism. According to the *CIA Factbook*, the gross domestic product in 2010 was composed of 47.8 percent industry and 51.6 percent services. In 2005, 79 percent of the labor force was employed in the services industry, which includes tourism. The *CIA Factbook* also estimated the number of tourists who visited the island in 2008 at 3.6 million. Beginning in 2006, Puerto Rico experienced a recession greater than the one on

the U.S. mainland. As of 2013, the recession had not abated.

Puerto Rico became a U.S. territory after the Spanish-American War in 1898. The U.S. granted citizenship to Puerto Ricans in 1917, but islanders did not begin coming to the mainland in large numbers until after World War II. This first major wave began around 1945, when Puerto Rico experienced an economic downturn and net jobs loss. These Puerto Ricans were mainly urban and educated. In the late 1950s, farmers and unskilled laborers began to migrate as well. The majority of Puerto Ricans who moved to the United States settled in big cities such as New York City; Newark, New Jersey; Philadelphia; and Chicago, as well as in New England mill towns. Though many had been farmers in Puerto Rico, they found themselves working in a variety of occupations in their new home, including factory work, the service industry, and police departments. Others moved to agricultural areas in the mid-Atlantic region, where they continued to farm. During those years, New York City served as the cultural hub for stateside Puerto Ricans. U.S. citizenship makes migration relatively easy for Puerto Ricans, with the result that many have moved back and forth between the two places. The number of Puerto Ricans moving to the U.S. mainland dropped significantly after 1960, when an economic slowdown in the urban centers led many to return home. Those who stayed became more politically and civically engaged in their new home, advocating for their rights as citizens, running for office, forming organizations, and setting down roots for their children. Another wave of migration from the island started in the first decade of the twenty-first century, consisting primarily of professionals and tech workers in search of better pay and increased career opportunities. The hub for the latest arrivals is no longer New York but Orlando, Florida.

As of the year 2000, there were more Puerto Ricans living on the mainland (58 percent) than on the island. According to the 2010 U.S. Census, 4.7 million Puerto Ricans lived on the mainland, roughly the same number as the population of the state of South Carolina, making up the second-largest Hispanic population in the United States, after Mexican Americans. New York and the Northeast were prime destinations for Puerto Ricans through much of the twentieth century. The second wave of migration has chosen to settle in the more temperate climes of central Florida, Texas, North Carolina, and Georgia.

HISTORY OF THE PEOPLE

Early History Fifteenth-century Italian explorer and navigator Christopher Columbus, known in Spanish as Cristobál Colón, "discovered" Puerto Rico for Spain on November 19, 1493. The island was conquered for Spain in 1509 by Spanish nobleman Juan Ponce de León (1460–1521), who became Puerto Rico's first colonial governor.

Puerto Rico's indigenous name is *Borinquen* ("bo REEN ken"), a name chosen by its original inhabitants, members of a native Caribbean and South American people called the Arawaks. A peaceful agricultural people, the Arawaks on the island of Puerto Rico were enslaved and virtually exterminated at the hands of their Spanish colonizers. Although Spanish heritage has been a matter of pride among islander and mainlander Puerto Ricans for hundreds of years—Columbus Day is a traditional Puerto Rican holiday—recent historical revisions have placed the *conquistadors* in a darker light. As is the case in many Latin American cultures, Puerto Ricans, especially younger generations living in the mainland United States, have become increasingly interested in their indigenous as well as their European ancestry. In fact, many Puerto Ricans use the terms *Boricua* ("bo REE qua") or *Borrinqueño* ("bo reen KEN yo") when referring to each other.

Because of its location, Puerto Rico was a popular target of pirates and privateers during its early colonial period. For protection, the Spanish constructed forts along the shoreline, one of which, El Morro in Old San Juan, still survives. These fortifications also proved effective in repelling the attacks of other European imperial powers, including a 1595 assault from British general Sir Francis Drake. In the mid-1700s, the Spanish brought African slaves to Puerto Rico in great numbers. Slaves and native Puerto Ricans mounted rebellions against Spain throughout the early and mid-1800s, but the Spanish were successful in resisting these rebellions.

In 1873 Spain abolished slavery on the island of Puerto Rico. The Spanish National Assembly freed African slaves by agreeing to compensate slave owners at the rate of 35 million pesetas per slave and requiring the former slaves to work for their ex-masters for another three years. By that time, West African cultural traditions had been deeply intertwined with those of the native Puerto Ricans and the Spanish conquerors, and intermarriage had become a common practice among the three ethnic groups.

Modern Era As a result of the Spanish-American War of 1898, Puerto Rico was ceded by Spain to the United States in the Treaty of Paris on December 19, 1898. In 1900 the U.S. Congress established a civil government on the island. In 1917, in response to pressure from Puerto Rican activists, President Woodrow Wilson signed the Jones Act, which granted American citizenship to all Puerto Ricans born on the island. Those born on the mainland already had citizenship under the Fourteenth Amendment, passed in 1868. Following the Jones Act, the U.S. government instituted measures to resolve the various economic and social problems of the island, which even then was suffering from overpopulation. Those measures included the introduction of American currency, health programs, hydroelectric power and irrigation programs, and economic policies designed to attract U.S. industry and provide more employment opportunities for native Puerto Ricans.

Puerto Rico is unique in that it is an autonomous commonwealth of the United States, and its people think of the island as *un estado libre asociado*, or a "free associate state" of the United States—a closer relationship than the territorial possessions of Guam and the Virgin Islands have to the United States. The question of whether to continue the commonwealth relationship with the United States, to push for U.S. statehood, or to rally for total independence has dominated Puerto Rican politics throughout the twentieth century. Puerto Ricans have their own constitution and elect their own bicameral legislature and governor but are subject to U.S executive authority, federal laws, and some federal taxes. The island is represented in the U.S House of Representatives by a resident commissioner, who may vote on legislation in committees but does not have a vote on the House floor.

In the years following World War II, Puerto Rico became a critical strategic location for the U.S. military. Naval bases were built in San Juan Harbor and on the nearby island of Culebra. In 1948 Puerto Ricans elected Luis Muñoz Marín governor of the island, the first native *puertorriqueño* to hold such a post. Marín favored commonwealth status for Puerto Rico. Following the 1948 election of Governor Muñoz, there was an uprising of the Nationalist Party, or *independetistas*, whose official party platform included agitation for independence. On November 1, 1950, as part of the uprising, two Puerto Rican nationalists carried out an armed attack on Blair House in Washington, D.C., which was being used as a temporary residence by President Harry Truman. The president was unharmed in the melee, but one of the assailants and one Secret Service presidential guard were killed by gunfire.

Puerto Rico's status as a semiautonomous commonwealth of the United States has sparked considerable political debate. Historically, the main conflict has been between the nationalists, who support full Puerto Rican independence, and the statists, who advocate U.S. statehood for Puerto Rico. The first nonbinding referendum on the question of statehood was held in 1967, with 60 percent voting to become a commonwealth, 39 percent for statehood, and 1 percent for independence. In 1968, the first pro-statehood leader was elected governor. Ongoing nationalist activity was suppressed by both the United States and Puerto Rican territorial governments. However, in 1979, President Jimmy Carter granted clemency, freeing four Puerto Rican nationalists who had been in prison since 1954. An island-wide vote was held in 1991, in which the majority rejected an amendment to review their commonwealth status..The results of Puerto Rico's next nonbinding referendum, held in 1993, were very close. A slim majority voted to remain a commonwealth, with 48.6 percent in favor of remaining a commonwealth, 46.3 percent in favor of statehood, and 4.4 percent in favor of independence. A referendum held in 1998 offered five choices for governance, and the results were inconclusive, with the majority voting for the option "none of the above." During the 2012 U.S. presidential election, Puerto Rico held its most recent nonbinding referendum on statehood in which it was reported that 61 percent of the voters supported statehood. However, experts do not agree on the outcome, with some arguing that the two-part plebiscite was not clearly worded and therefore not determinative. Currently, the decision of whether or not Puerto Rico will become the fifty-first state is not in the hands of the Puerto Rican people. U.S. law dictates that the decision must be made by Congress.

SETTLEMENT IN THE UNITED STATES

Because Puerto Ricans are American citizens, they are considered U.S. migrants as opposed to foreign immigrants. The 2010 U.S. Census reported that of the 4.7 million Puerto Ricans living on the mainland, only 1.4 million were born on the island. The rest were born stateside. Early Puerto Rican residents on the mainland included Eugenio María de Hostos (1839–1903), a journalist, philosopher, and freedom fighter who arrived in New York in 1874 after being exiled from Spain (where he had studied law) because of his outspoken views on Puerto Rican independence. Among other pro-Puerto Rican activities, María de Hostos founded the League of Patriots to help set up the Puerto Rican civil government in 1900. He was aided by Julio J. Henna (1848–1924), a Puerto Rican physician and expatriate. Nineteenth-century Puerto Rican statesman Luis Muñoz Rivera Sr. (1859–1916)—the father of Governor Luis Muñoz Marín—lived in Washington, D.C., and served as Puerto Rico's ambassador to the United States.

Although Puerto Ricans began migrating to the United States almost immediately after the island became a U.S. protectorate, the scope of early migration was limited because of the severe poverty of average Puerto Ricans. As conditions on the island improved and the relationship between Puerto Rico and the United States grew closer, more Puerto Ricans moved to the U.S. mainland. According to the Center for Puerto Rican Studies at the City University of New York, 11,811 Puerto Ricans lived in the continental United States in 1920. By 1930, the number had reached 52,000. Still, by 1920, less than five thousand Puerto Ricans were living in New York City. During World War I, as many as one thousand Puerto Ricans—all newly naturalized American citizens—served in the U.S. Army. By World War II that number had soared to more than 100,000 soldiers. The hundredfold increase reflected the deepening cooperation between Puerto Rico and the mainland. World War II set the stage for the first major migration wave of Puerto Ricans to the mainland.

That wave, which spanned the decade between 1947 and 1957, was brought on largely by economic factors: Puerto Rico's population had risen to nearly two million people by mid-century, but the standard of living had not followed suit. Unemployment was high on the island, and opportunity was dwindling. The economy went from being agriculture-based, with sugarcane as the main export, to manufacture-based. On the mainland, however, the economy was experiencing a postwar boom. Jobs were widely available. According to Ronald Larsen, author of *The Puerto Ricans in America*, many of those jobs were in New York City's garment district. Hard-working Puerto Rican women were especially welcome in the garment district shops. The city also provided the sort of low-skilled service-industry jobs that non-English speakers needed to make a living on the mainland.

New York City became a major focal point for Puerto Rican migration. Between 1951 and 1957 the average annual migration from Puerto Rico to New York was more than 48,000. Many settled in East Harlem, located in upper Manhattan between 116th and 145th streets, east of Central Park. Because of its high Latino population, the district soon came to be known as Spanish Harlem. Among New York City *puertorriqueños*, the Latino-populated area was referred to as *el barrio*, or "the neighborhood." Most first-generation Puerto Ricans to the area were young men who later sent for their wives and children when finances allowed.

By the early 1960s the Puerto Rican migration rate had slowed, and a "revolving door" migratory pattern—a back-and-forth flow of people between the island and the mainland—developed. Since then, there have been occasional bursts of increased migration from the island, especially during the recession of the late 1970s. In the late 1980s Puerto Rico became increasingly plagued by a number of social problems, including rising violent crime (especially drug-associated crime), increased overcrowding, and worsening unemployment. These conditions kept the flow of migration into the United States steady, even among professional classes, and caused many Puerto Ricans to remain on the mainland permanently. According to U.S. Census Bureau statistics, more than 2.7 million Puerto Ricans were living in the mainland Unites States by 1990. A new wave of migration started in the early twenty-first century with the onset of another recession. As the U.S. economy suffered, the Puerto Rican economy suffered even more. Unemployment on the mainland hovered between 8 percent and 9 percent, while island unemployment reached 14 percent. Many Puerto Ricans who moved to the mainland during this period were college-educated professionals who were either recruited for or sought out professional jobs. As of 2010, the number of Puerto Ricans living in the mainland had risen to 4.7 million.

Most early Puerto Ricans who moved to the mainland settled in New York City and, to a lesser degree, in other urban areas in the northeastern United States. This migration pattern was influenced by the wide availability of industrial and service-industry jobs in the eastern cities. New York remained the chief residence of Puerto Ricans living outside of the island for most of the twentieth century: of the 2.7 million Puerto Ricans living on the mainland in the 1990s, more than 900,000 resided in New York City and another 200,000 lived elsewhere in the state of New York.

That pattern has been changing, however. A new group of Puerto Ricans—most of them younger, wealthier, and more highly educated than the urban settlers—have increasingly begun settling in other states. The more recent group of Puerto Ricans have settled in places with warmer climates and growing economies, such as central Florida, Texas, North Carolina, and Georgia. The 2010 Census reported that one million Puerto Ricans were living in New York, and 847,000 were living in Florida.

LANGUAGE

Puerto Ricans speak proper Castillian Spanish, which is derived from ancient Latin. Among Puerto Ricans over the age of five, more than eight in ten speak English proficiently. Although Spanish uses the same Latin alphabet as English, the letters "k" and "w" occur only in foreign words. However, Spanish has three letters not found in English: "ch" ("chay"), "ll" ("EL-yay"), and "ñ" ("AYN-nyay"). Spanish uses word order, rather than noun and pronoun inflection, to encode meaning. In addition, the Spanish language tends to rely on diacritical markings such as the *tilde* (˜) and the *accento* (´) much more than English does.

The main difference between the Spanish spoken in Spain and the Spanish spoken in Puerto Rico (and other Latin American locales) is pronunciation. Differences in pronunciation are similar to the regional variations between American English in the Southern United States and New England. Many Puerto Ricans have a unique tendency among Latin Americans to drop the "s" sound in casual conversation. The word *ustéd* (the proper form of the pronoun "you"), for instance, may be pronounced as "oo-TED" rather than "oo-STED." Likewise, Puerto Ricans often change the participial suffix "*-ado*"; the word *cemado* (meaning "burned") is thus pronounced "ke-MOW" rather than "ke-MA-do."

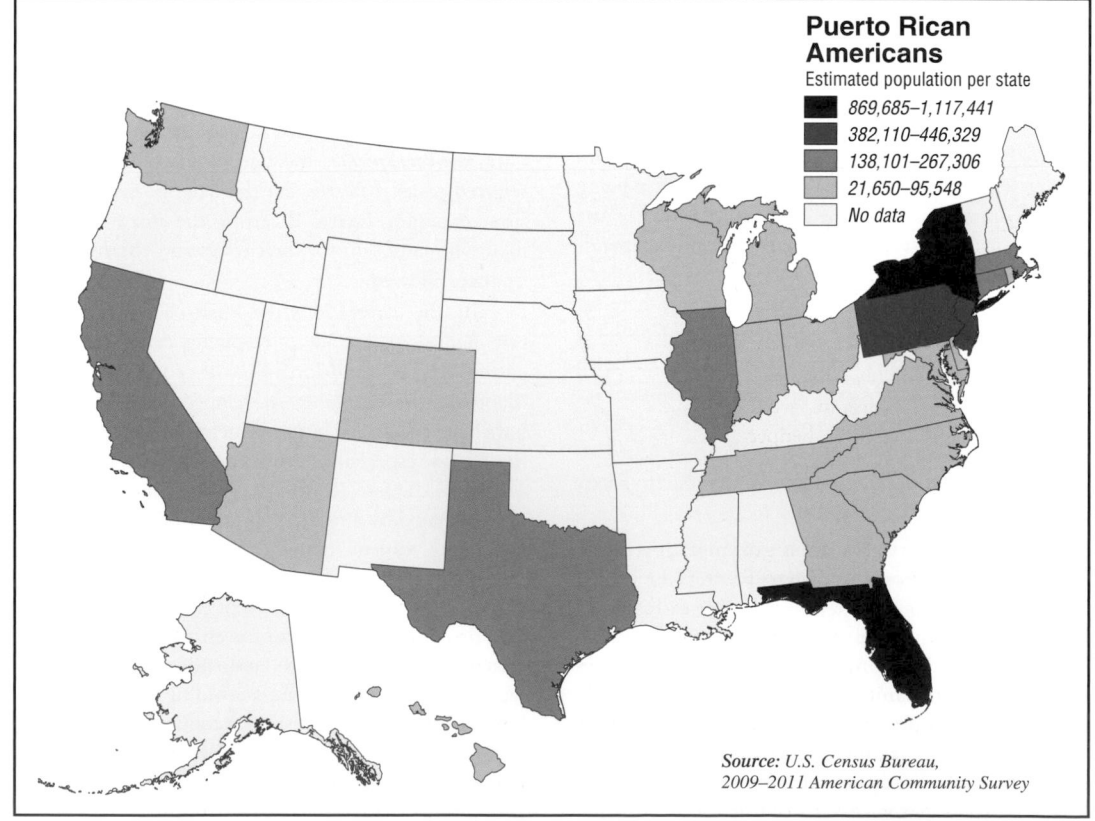

Puerto Rican Americans
Estimated population per state

- 869,685–1,117,441
- 382,110–446,329
- 138,101–267,306
- 21,650–95,548
- No data

Source: U.S. Census Bureau, 2009–2011 American Community Survey

Although English is taught to most elementary school children in Puerto Rican public schools, Spanish remains the primary language on the island. On the mainland, many first-generation Puerto Ricans are less than fluent in English. According to the 2011 American Community Survey, 18.4 percent of the population over the age of five report speaking English "less than well." Subsequent generations are often fluently bilingual, speaking English outside of the home and Spanish in the home. The 2011 survey also reports that 63.3 percent speak a language other than English at home. Bilingualism is especially common among young, urbanized, professional Puerto Ricans.

Long exposure of Puerto Ricans to American society, culture, and language has also spawned a unique slang known as "Spanglish." Other Latino groups have their own versions of Spanglish. It is a dialect that does not yet have formal structure, but its use in popular songs has helped spread terms as they are adopted. In New York itself the unique blend of languages is called *Nuyorican*, a term coined by Miguel Algarin, founder of the Nuyorican Poet's Café in New York, for the unique blend of Spanish and English used among young Puerto Ricans living in New York City. In this form of Spanglish, "New York" becomes *Nuevayork*, and many Puerto Ricans refer to themselves as *Nuevarriqueños*. Puerto Rican teenagers are as likely to attend *un pahry* (a party) as to attend a *fiesta*; children look forward to a visit from *Sahnta Close* on Christmas; and workers often have *un Beeg Mahk y una Coca-Cola* on their lunch breaks.

Greetings and Popular Expressions For the most part, Puerto Rican greetings are standard Spanish greetings: *Hola* ("OH-lah")—Hello; *¿Como está?* ("como eh-STAH")—How are you?; *¿Que tal?* ("kay TAHL")—What's up?; *Adiós* ("ah-DYOSE")—Goodbye; *Por favór* ("pore fah-FORE")—Please; *Grácias* ("GRAH-syahs")—Thank you; *Buena suerte* ("BWE-na SWAYR-tay")—Good luck; *Feliz Cumpleaños* ("feh-LEEZ coom-plee-AHN-nyos")—Happy New Year.

Some expressions, however, appear to be unique to Puerto Ricans. These include: *mas enamorado que el cabro cupido* (more in love than a goat shot by Cupid's arrow; or, head over heels in love); *sentado an el baúl* (seated in a trunk; or, to be henpecked); and *sacar el ratón* (let the rat out of the bag; or, to get drunk).

RELIGION

The Puerto Rican Constitution guarantees the right to religious freedom. Most Puerto Ricans are Roman Catholics. Catholicism on the island dates back to the earliest presence of the Spanish *conquistadors*, who brought Catholic missionaries to convert native Arawaks to Christianity and train them in Spanish customs and culture. For more than four hundred years Catholicism was the island's dominant religion, with a negligible presence of Protestant Christians. That has changed over the last century. As recently as

1960, more than 80 percent of Puerto Ricans identified themselves as Catholics, but by the mid-1990s, according to U.S. Census Bureau statistics, that number had decreased to 70 percent. Of the rest of the population, nearly 30 percent of Puerto Ricans identified themselves as Protestants of various denominations, including Lutheran, Presbyterian, Methodist, Baptist, and Christian Scientist. The Protestant shift is about the same among mainlander Puerto Ricans. Although this trend may be attributable to the overwhelming influence of American culture on the island and among mainland Puerto Ricans, similar changes have been observed throughout the Caribbean and into the rest of Latin America.

Puerto Ricans who practice Catholicism observe traditional church liturgy, rituals, and traditions. These include belief in the Creed of the Apostles and adherence to the doctrine of papal infallibility. Puerto Rican Catholics observe the seven Catholic sacraments: Baptism, Eucharist, Confirmation, Penance, Matrimony, Holy Orders, and Anointing of the Sick. According to the dispensations of Vatican II, Puerto Ricans celebrate mass in vernacular Spanish as opposed to ancient Latin. Catholic churches in Puerto Rico are ornate, rich with candles, paintings, and graphic imagery; like other Latin Americans, Puerto Ricans seem especially moved by the Passion of Christ and place particular emphasis on representations of the crucifixion.

Among Puerto Rican Catholics, a small minority actively practice some version of *santería* ("sahn-teh-REE-ah"), an African religion with roots in the Yoruba religion of western Africa. (A *santo* is a saint of the Catholic Church who also corresponds to a Yoruban deity.) *Santería* is prominent throughout the Caribbean and in many places in the southern United States and has had a strong influence on Catholic practices on the island.

Although awareness of Puerto Rican culture has increased within mainstream America, many common misconceptions still exist. For instance, many Americans fail to realize that Puerto Ricans are natural-born American citizens or wrongly view Puerto Rico as a primitive tropical land. Puerto Rican culture is often confused with other Latino cultures, especially that of Mexican Americans.

CULTURE AND ASSIMILATION

The history of Puerto Rican American assimilation has been one of great success mixed with serious problems. Many Puerto Rican mainlanders hold high-paying white-collar jobs. Outside of New York City, Puerto Ricans often boast higher college graduation rates and higher per capita incomes than their counterparts in other Latino groups, even when those groups represent a much higher proportion of the local population. President Obama's 2011 visit to Puerto Rico signaled a change in the federal government's attitude toward the island commonwealth and toward stateside Puerto Ricans as well, acknowledging their importance as a political voting bloc.

However, U.S. Census Bureau reports indicate that poverty is a serious problem for at least 25 percent of all Puerto Ricans living on the mainland. For Puerto Ricans living on the island, the number is closer to 85 percent. Despite the presumed advantages of American citizenship, Puerto Ricans are—overall—the most economically disadvantaged Latino group in the United States. Some of this has been attributed to residential segregation due to housing discrimination. Puerto Rican communities in urban areas are plagued by problems such as crime, drug use, poor educational opportunity, unemployment, and the breakdown of the traditionally strong Puerto Rican family structure. A great many Puerto Ricans of mixed Spanish and African descent have had to endure the same sort of racial discrimination often experienced by African Americans in addition to discrimination attributed to their Latino status. And some Puerto Ricans are further handicapped by the Spanish-to-English language barrier in American cities.

Although awareness of Puerto Rican culture has increased within mainstream America, many common misconceptions still exist. For instance, many Americans fail to realize that Puerto Ricans are natural-born American citizens or wrongly view Puerto Rico as a primitive tropical land. Puerto Rican culture is often confused with other Latino cultures, especially that of Mexican Americans.

Despite these problems, Puerto Ricans, like other Latino groups, are beginning to exert more political power and cultural influence on the mainstream population. The growth in influence is especially true in cities like New York, where the significant Puerto Rican population represents a major political force when properly organized. In the 2000 and 2004 national elections, Puerto Ricans have found themselves in the position of holding the all-important "swing vote"—often occupying the sociopolitical ground between African Americans and other minorities on the one hand and white Americans on the other. Puerto Rican voters played an even more significant role in the 2008 and 2012 presidential elections and were heavily courted by both parties. In 2009, President Obama appointed the first Puerto Rican to the U.S. Supreme Court, Justice Sonya Sotomayor. The pan-Latin sounds of Puerto Rican singers Ricky Martin, Jennifer Lopez, and Marc Anthony, and jazz musicians such as saxophonist David Sanchez, have not only brought a cultural revival, they have also sparked an increased interest in Latin music. Their popularity has also had a legitimizing effect on *Nuyorican* dialect.

Because of the long history of intermarriage among Spanish, Indian, and African ancestry groups, Puerto Ricans are among the most ethnically and racially diverse people in Latin America. As a result,

Residents look on during the 116th Street Festival in Spanish Harlem in 2009 in New York City. The 28-block Puerto Rican-Pride festival draws around 100,000 Latinos and always occurs a day before the annual Puerto Rican Day Parade. MARIO TAMA / GETTY IMAGES

relations between whites, blacks, and ethnic groups on the island—and to a somewhat lesser extent on the mainland—tend to be cordial. This is not to say that Puerto Ricans fail to recognize racial variance. Skin color on the island ranges from black to fair, and there are many ways of describing a person's color. People with light skin are usually referred to as *blanco* (white) or *rúbio* (blond). Those with darker skin who have Native American features are referred to as *indio* (Indian). People with dark skin, hair, and eyes—like the majority of the islanders—are referred to as *trigeño* (swarthy). Blacks have two designations: African Puerto Ricans are called people *de colór*, or people "of color," and African Americans are referred to as *moreno*. The word *negro*, meaning "black," is quite common among Puerto Ricans and is used today as a term of endearment for people of any color.

Traditions and Customs The traditions and beliefs of Puerto Rican islanders are heavily influenced by Puerto Rico's Afro-Spanish history. Many Puerto Rican customs and superstitions blend the Catholic religious traditions of Spaniards and the pagan religious beliefs of the West African slaves who were brought to the island beginning in the sixteenth century. Among these are weddings, baptisms, and funerals. And like other Caribbean islanders and Latin Americans, Puerto Ricans traditionally believe in *espiritismo*, the notion that the world is populated by spirits who can communicate with the living through dreams.

In addition to the holy days observed by the Catholic Church, Puerto Ricans celebrate several other days that hold particular significance for them as a people. For instance, *El Dia de las Candelarias*, or "Candlemas," is observed annually on the evening of February 2; people build a massive bonfire, around which they drink and dance and chant "*¡Viva las candelarias!*" ("Long live the flames!") And each December 27 is *El Dia de los Innocentes*, or the "Day of the Children." On that day Puerto Rican men dress as women and women dress as men, and the community celebrates together as one large group.

Many Puerto Rican customs revolve around the ritual significance of food and drink. As in other Latino cultures, it is considered an insult to turn down a drink offered by a friend or stranger. It is also customary for Puerto Ricans to offer food to any guest, whether invited or not, who might enter the household; failure to do so is said to bring hunger upon one's own children. Puerto Ricans traditionally warn against eating in the presence of a pregnant woman without offering her food, for fear she might miscarry. Many Puerto Ricans also believe that marrying or starting a journey on a Tuesday is bad luck, and that dreams of water or tears are a sign of impending heartache or tragedy. Common centuries-old folk remedies include the avoidance of acidic food during menstruation and the consumption of *asopao* ("ah-so-POW"), or chicken stew, for minor ailments.

Cuisine Puerto Rican cuisine consists mainly of seafood and tropical island vegetables, fruits, and meats. Although herbs and spices are used in great abundance, Puerto Rican cuisine is not spicy in the sense of peppery Mexican cuisine. Native dishes are often inexpensive, though they require some skill in preparation. Puerto Rican women are traditionally responsible for the cooking and take great pride in their role. Toward the end of the twentieth century a substantial percentage of the food eaten on the island began to be imported from the U.S. mainland. This impacted the local diet, with convenience items like pizza, hot dogs, cold cereal, and canned soups and spaghetti becoming popular, along with fast food. For Puerto Ricans living on the mainland, diet is a matter of family preference. Some continue to cook and eat traditional Puerto Rican food even after generations of living stateside, and others have adopted a more mainstream "American" diet.

Many Puerto Rican dishes are seasoned with a savory mixture of spices known as *sofrito* ("so-FREE-toe"). This is made by grinding fresh garlic, seasoned salt, green peppers, and onions in a *pilón* ("pee-LONE"), a wooden bowl similar to a mortar and pestle, and then sautéing the mixture in hot oil. This serves as the spice base for many soups and dishes. Meat is often marinated in a seasoning mixture known as *adobo* ("ah-DOE-boe"), which is made from lemon, garlic, pepper, salt, and other spices. *Achiote* ("ah-chi-OE-tay") seeds are sautéed as the base for an oily sauce used in many dishes.

Bacalodo ("bah-kah-LAH-doe"), a staple of the Puerto Rican diet, is a flaky, salt-marinated codfish. It is often eaten boiled with vegetables and rice or on bread with olive oil for breakfast. *Arroz con pollo* ("ah-ROES cone POY-oe"), or rice and chicken, another staple dish, is served with *abichuelas guisada* ("ah-bee-CHWE-lahs gee-SAH-dah"), marinated beans, or a native Puerto Rican pea known as *gandules* ("gahn-DOO-lays"). Other popular Puerto Rican foods include *asopao* ("ah-soe-POW"), a rice and chicken stew; *lechón asado* ("le-CHONE ah-SAH-doe"), slow-roasted pig; *pasteles* ("pah-STAY-lehs"), meat and vegetable patties rolled in dough made from crushed plantains (bananas); *empanadas dejueyes* ("em-pah-NAH-dahs deh-WHE-yehs"), Puerto Rican crab cakes; *rellenos* ("reh-YAY-nohs"), meat and potato fritters; *griffo* ("GREE-foe"), chicken and potato stew; and *tostones* ("toe-STOE-nehs"), battered and deep-fried plantains, served with salt and lemon juice. These dishes are often washed down with *cerveza rúbia* ("ser-VEH-sa ROO-bee-ah"), "blond" or light-colored American lager beer, or *ron* ("RONE"), the world-famous, dark Puerto Rican rum.

Clothing Traditional dress in Puerto Rico is similar to other Caribbean islanders. Men wore baggy

ARROZ CON POLLO (RICE AND CHICKEN)

Ingredients

3½ pounds chicken, cut into pieces

3 cups long-grain rice

3½ cups water

½ cup basic sofrito (¼ onion, green pepper, chopped, with 3 mashed garlic cloves)

½ teaspoon ground cumin

2 tablespoons alcaparrado (olives and capers)

1 teaspoon culantro and annatto seasoning

2 ounces tomato sauce

2 tablespoons oil

salt and black pepper to taste

Preparation

Season chicken ahead of time with salt and pepper; let stand in the refrigerator until you are ready to cook.

Heat the oil in a Dutch oven over medium heat. Brown chicken on each side for approximately 5 minutes, remove and store covered.

Stir in sofrito, olives, capers, seasoning, tomato sauce, and cumin into the Dutch oven and sautÉ for about 4 minutes at low heat. Stir in rice. Mix well with the sofrito. Add water and bring to boil. When rice mixture is boiling, lower heat to the lowest and cover. Continue cooking for about 20–25 more minutes, until rice is completely cooked.

Once cooked, stir and add the chicken. Cover and let cook for 20 more minutes.

Serves 6

pantalons (trousers) and loose cotton shirts known as a *guayaberras*. For certain celebrations, women wore colorful dresses, or *trajes*, that have African influence. Straw hats or Panama hats (*sombreros de jipijipa*) were often worn by men on Sundays or holidays. Spanish-influenced garb was worn by musicians and dancers during performances—often on holidays. Puerto Ricans on the mainland have adopted a more Western style of dress. Jeans and T-shirts are among some of the popular clothing worn.

The traditional image of the *jíbaro*, or peasant, has to some extent remained tied to Puerto Ricans. Often depicted as a wiry, swarthy man wearing a straw hat and holding a guitar in one hand and a *machete* (the long-bladed knife used for cutting sugarcane) in the other, the *jíbaro* to some symbolizes the island's culture and its people. To others, he is an object of derision, akin to the derogatory image of the American hillbilly. While Western-style clothes have been adopted by many Puerto Ricans in the late twentieth and early twenty-first centuries, fashions on the island still retain echoes of Caribbean and Spanish influences, such as loose, cotton shirts and lightweight baggy pants.

Dances and Songs Puerto Rican people are famous for throwing big, elaborate parties with music and dancing to celebrate special events. Puerto Rican music is polyrhythmic, blending intricate and complex African percussion with melodic Spanish beats. The traditional Puerto Rican group is a trio, made up of a *cuatro* (an eight-stringed native Puerto Rican instrument similar to a mandolin); a *guitarra*, or guitar; and a *basso*, or bass. Larger bands have trumpets and strings as well as extensive percussion sections in which maracas, guiros, and bongos are primary instruments.

Although Puerto Rico has a rich folk-music tradition, fast-tempo *salsa* is the most widely known indigenous Puerto Rican music. Also the name given to a two-step dance, *salsa* has gained popularity among non-Latin audiences. The *merengue*, another popular native Puerto Rican dance, is a fast step in which the dancers' hips are in close contact. Both *salsa* and *merengue* are favorites in American barrios. *Bombas* are native Puerto Rican songs sung *a cappella* to African drum rhythms.

Holidays Puerto Ricans celebrate most Christian holidays, including *Noche Buena* and *La Navidád* (Christmas Eve and Christmas Day) and *Pasquas* (Easter), as well as *El Año Nuevo* (New Year's Day). In addition, Puerto Ricans celebrate *El Dia de Los Tres Reyes*, or "Three King's Day," each January 6. It is on this day that Puerto Rican children expect gifts, which are said to be delivered by *los tres reyes magos* ("the three wise men"). On the days leading up to January 6, Puerto Ricans have continuous celebrations. *Parrandiendo* (stopping by) is a practice similar to American and English caroling, in which neighbors go visiting house to house. Other major celebration days are *El Día de Las Raza* (The Day of the Race—Columbus Day) and *El Fiesta del Apostal Santiago* (St. James's Day). Every June, Puerto Ricans in New York and other large cities celebrate Puerto Rican Day. The parades held on this day have come to rival St. Patrick's Day parades and celebrations in popularity.

Health Care Issues and Practices Because of the low economic status of many Puerto Ricans, especially in mainland inner-city settings, the incidence of poverty-related health problems is a very real concern. According to one study, Puerto Ricans living on the mainland tend to have higher rates of high blood pressure, heart disease, and diabetes (three to five times greater risk than the general population), as well as increased instances of cancer, gastrointestinal disorders, and obesity because of poor diet due to poverty.

AIDS, alcohol and drug dependency, and a lack of adequate health care coverage are the biggest health-related concerns facing the Puerto Rican community both on the mainland and on the island.

FAMILY AND COMMUNITY LIFE

Puerto Rican family structure is extensive; it is based on the Spanish system of *compadrazco* (literally "co-parenting") in which many members—not just parents and siblings—are considered to be part of the immediate family. Thus *los abuelos* (grandparents), and *los tios y las tias* (uncles and aunts) and even *los primos y las primas* (cousins) are considered extremely close relatives in the Puerto Rican family structure. Likewise, *los padrinos* (godparents) have a special role in the Puerto Rican conception of the family: godparents are friends of a child's parents and serve as "second parents" to the child. Close friends often refer to each other as *compadre y comadre* to reinforce the familial bond. Respect for family and family loyalty are central to the culture both on the island and on the mainland. Mothers and elders are revered. Also, religion plays an important role in the family structure. Religious ceremonies are often at the center of family gatherings.

It is not uncommon for three generations of a Puerto Rican family to live under one roof or in close proximity. On the island, adult children are expected to live at home until marriage. Although the extended family remains standard among many Puerto Rican mainlanders and islanders, the family structure has suffered a serious breakdown in recent decades, especially among urban mainlander Puerto Ricans. This breakdown seems to have been precipitated by economic hardships among Puerto Ricans as well as by the influence of America's social organization, which deemphasizes the extended family and accords greater autonomy to children and women.

For Puerto Ricans, the home has special significance, serving as the focal point for family life. Puerto Rican homes, even in the mainland United States, thus reflect Puerto Rican cultural heritage to a great extent. They tend to be ornate and colorful, with rugs and gilt-framed paintings that often reflect a religious theme. In addition, rosaries, busts of *La Virgin* (the Virgin Mary) and other religious icons have a prominent place in the household. For many Puerto Rican mothers and grandmothers, no home is complete without a representation of the suffering of Jesús Christo and the Last Supper. As young people increasingly move into mainstream American culture, these traditions and many others seem to be waning, but only slowly, over the last few decades.

Gender Roles Puerto Rican family and community dynamics have a strong Spanish influence and still tend to reflect the intensely patriarchal social organization of European Spanish culture. Traditionally, husbands and fathers are heads of households and serve as community leaders. Older male children are expected to be responsible for younger siblings, especially females. *Machismo* (the Spanish conception of manhood) is traditionally a highly regarded virtue among Puerto Rican men. Men are expected to earn their

Puerto Rican teens at Columbus Square, Old San Juan, Puerto Rico. ROBERT FRIED / ALAMY

family's respect by providing income; thus, if they are unemployed, it is difficult for them to feel valued as head of household. Women, in turn, are responsible for the day-to-day running of the household. Puerto Rican women living on the mainland have joined the workforce in substantial numbers. They enjoy greater income parity with Puerto Rican men than women in all other racial-ethnic groups.

Both Puerto Rican men and women care very much for their children and have strong roles in childrearing; children are expected to show *respeto* (respect) to parents and other elders, including older siblings. Traditionally, girls are raised to be quiet and diffident, and boys are raised to be more aggressive, though all children are expected to defer to elders and strangers.

Education The literacy rate on the island is approximately 94 percent. Puerto Ricans living on the mainland lag behind the overall average in terms of graduation rates, but the rates increased dramatically between 2000 and 2010, rising from 50 percent to 67 percent (high school graduation), and from 15 percent to 21 percent with a bachelor's degree or higher. According to the 2000 U.S. Census, 64.2 percent of Puerto Ricans over the age of twenty-five had high school degrees, and only 9.9 percent had college degrees or higher. By 2010, the percentage of high school graduates rose to 74.8 percent (compared with the U.S. average of 87.1 percent), and those with college degrees or higher reached 17.5 percent (compared with the U.S. average of 29.9 percent). Graduation rates on the mainland are slightly higher among Puerto Rican females than males.

Courtship and Marriage Young men initiate courtship, though dating rituals have for the most part become Americanized on the mainland. And like most Latino groups, Puerto Ricans are traditionally opposed to divorce and birth out of wedlock. However, economic difficulties have wrought changes in both locations. According to the 2011 American Community Survey, divorce rates among Puerto Ricans living on the mainland are not significantly higher than those living on the island. Once more common in the mainland, the number of female-headed households on the island appears to have caught up with the numbers in the United States.

EMPLOYMENT AND ECONOMIC CONDITIONS

Early Puerto Ricans on the mainland, especially those settling in New York City, found jobs in service and industry sectors. Among women, garment industry work was the leading form of employment. Men in urban areas most often worked in the service industry, often at restaurant jobs—busing tables, bartending, or washing dishes. Men also found work in steel manufacturing, auto assembly, shipping, meatpacking, and other related industries. In the early years of mainland

migration, a sense of ethnic cohesion, especially in New York City, was created by Puerto Rican men who held jobs of community significance: Puerto Rican barbers, grocers, barmen, and others provided focal points for the Puerto Rican community to gather in the city. Since the 1960s there has been a continual pattern of migration to the mainland for temporary contract work and then returning home. Hundreds of thousands of migrants have made the circuit over the last fifty years—working seasonally to harvest crop vegetables in various states and then returning to Puerto Rico after harvest.

As Puerto Ricans have assimilated into mainstream American culture, many of the younger generations have moved away from New York City and other eastern urban areas, taking high-paying white-collar and professional jobs. Still, in the 1990s less than 2 percent of Puerto Rican families had a median income above $75,000. That number has risen in the past two decades. In 1990, the income rate of Puerto Ricans living on the mainland was 66 percent of that of non-Hispanic whites. By 2008, that had risen to 69 percent. Poverty levels and unemployment rates also fell during this period. In 2002, the average household income for Puerto Ricans living on the mainland was $33,927. In 2010, that number grew to $36,558, well below the national average of $50,046. Scholars have proposed various hypotheses for this phenomenon. They cite discrimination, the shrinking economies of the places where they settled, or a connection between poverty on the island and Puerto Ricans on the mainland as possible explanations. There appears to be no consensus on this issue.

According to 1990 U.S. Census Bureau statistics, 31 percent of all Puerto Rican American men and 59 percent of all Puerto Rican American women were not considered part of the American labor force. One reason for these alarming statistics may be the changing face of American employment options. The sort of manufacturing sector jobs that were traditionally held by Puerto Ricans, especially in the garment industry, have become increasingly scarce. Institutionalized racism and the rise in single-parent households in urban areas may also be factors in the employment crisis. Urban Puerto Rican unemployment—whatever its cause—has emerged as one of the greatest economic challenges facing Puerto Rican community leaders in the Northeast and New York. An article in the *New York Times* in 2008 reported that this was still a significant concern for the urban, northeastern Puerto Rican population. The 2010 U.S. Census reported that the total rate of Puerto Rican men living in the mainland who were not considered part of the American labor force had risen to 38.1 percent, but the rate of women not considered part of the labor force had dropped to 42 percent. By contrast, Puerto Ricans who have settled in the Midwest and the South, particularly Florida, tend to be middle class or affluent and have a different set of political concerns.

POLITICS AND GOVERNMENT

Throughout the twentieth century, Puerto Rican political activity followed two distinct paths—one focusing on accepting the association with the United States and working within the American political system, the other pushing for full Puerto Rican independence, often through radical means. In the latter part of the nineteenth century, most Puerto Rican leaders living in New York City fought for Caribbean freedom from Spain in general and Puerto Rican freedom in particular. When Spain ceded control of Puerto Rico to the United States following the Spanish-American War, those freedom fighters turned their attention to working for Puerto Rican independence from the United States. Eugenio María de Hostos founded the League of Patriots to help smooth the transition from U.S. control to independence. Although full independence was never achieved, groups like the League paved the way for Puerto Rico's special relationship with the United States. Still, Puerto Ricans were for the most part blocked from wide participation in the American political system.

In 1913 New York Puerto Ricans helped establish *La Prensa*, a Spanish-language daily newspaper, and over the next two decades a number of Puerto Rican and Latino political organizations and groups—some more radical than others—began to form. By the 1920s, Puerto Ricans living in New York started seeking election to public office..In 1937 Puerto Ricans elected Oscar García Rivera (1900–1969) to a New York City Assembly seat, making him New York's first elected official of Puerto Rican descent. There was some Puerto Rican support in New York City for radical activist Pedro Albizu Campos (1891–1965), who staged a riot in the Puerto Rican city of Ponce on the issue of independence that same year; nineteen were killed in the riot, and Campos's movement died out.

The 1950s saw wide proliferation of community organizations, called *ausentes*. More than seventy-five such hometown societies were organized under the umbrella of *El Congresso de Pueblo* (the "Council of Hometowns"). These organizations provided services for Puerto Rican Americans and served as a springboard for activity in city politics. In 1959 the first New York City Puerto Rican Day parade was held. Many people viewed this as a major cultural and political "coming out" party for the New York Puerto Rican community.

Puerto Ricans living on the mainland have become politically active in a number of ways, such as voting, lobbying, engaging in protests, and making campaign contributions. Puerto Ricans living on the island have a long record of high voter participation, far higher than that in the United States. In the governor's race in Puerto Rico in 2000, 90.1 percent of eligible voters registered to vote, and 74.4 percent of eligible voters cast their ballots. By way of comparison, slightly less than half of all eligible voters in the

Supporters of the Puerto Rican New Progressive Party (NPP), in Guanica Puerto Rico, 1998. AP PHOTO / LYNNE SLADKY

United States registered in 2000, and just 42.3 percent of those registered actually voted. Until 2000, Puerto Ricans living stateside exercised their right to vote in far smaller numbers.

Recognizing that the increased political influence of stateside Puerto Ricans also benefits the island, the government of Puerto Rico has, since the late 1980s, launched two major voter registration campaigns to increase the level of stateside Puerto Rican voter participation and help ensure that stateside Puerto Rican interests are well represented in the electoral process. Until the early twenty-first century, Puerto Ricans had never been courted by either party in the American system. And still others suggest that the lack of opportunity and education for the immigrant population resulted in widespread political cynicism among Puerto Ricans. In the 2008 and 2012 national elections, however, the Puerto Rican population played a major political role. Puerto Rican Nelson Merced was the first Latino elected to the Massachusetts House of Representatives (serving from 1989 to 1993) as well as the first Latino to hold statewide office in that state. As of 2013 there were four Puerto Rican members of the U.S. House of Representatives: Democrats Luis Gutierrez of Illinois (serving since 1993), José Enrique Serrano of New York (also serving since 1993), and Nydia Velázquez of New York (elected in 2012), and Republican Raúl Labrador of Idaho (elected in 2010), in addition to the resident commissioner from Puerto Rico. Puerto Ricans have served as mayor of Miami, Florida; Hartford, Connecticut; and Camden, New Jersey. Puerto Rican politicians engaged in U.S. politics have been active on issues specific to their states or regions, but also in the fight to reform immigration laws.

Puerto Rican voters became a major force in the 2008 and 2012 presidential elections. Along with the population increase in the mainland Puerto Rican community, there has been an increase in Puerto Rican voter registration and turnout: In the crucial swing state of Florida, Latinos (primarily Cuban Americans and Puerto Ricans) comprised 14 percent of the voters in 2008. That number rose to 17 percent in 2012. The numbers in Florida represent a national trend. Presidential candidates and their teams worked hard to get Puerto Ricans to the polls. Along with the Spanish-language ads on TV and radio, the Obama campaign organized raucous caravans with decorated car windows and loud speakers on trucks, a tradition in Puerto Rico elections.

The issue of Puerto Rican statehood continues to be debated and discussed. During the November 2012 U.S. national elections, Puerto Rico held its own plebiscite on statehood. On the first part of the plebiscite, 54 percent of those who voted disagreed with the "present form of territorial status." On the second, 61 percent voted for statehood, 5 percent for independence, and 33 percent for a sovereign free associated state. The current commonwealth status was not listed as an option. Resident Commissioner Pedro Pierluisi (Puerto Rico's representative to the executive branch and in Congress) favors making Puerto Rico the fifty-first state. On November 14, 2012, he gave a speech on the House floor defending both the process and the results of the November 6 plebiscite. Mr. Pierluisi called the island's current status "colonial in nature" and made a forceful argument against those who would dismiss the election's outcome.

NOTABLE INDIVDUALS

Although Puerto Ricans have only had a major presence on the mainland since the mid-twentieth century, they have made significant contributions to American society. This is especially true in the areas of the arts, literature, and sports. The following is a select list of individual Puerto Ricans and some of their achievements.

Academia Joseph M. Acaba (1967–) was born in the United States. An educator, hydrogeologist, and NASA astronaut, Acaba flew his first space mission in 2008.

Frank Bonilla (1925–2010) was a Harvard-educated political scientist and a pioneer of Hispanic and Puerto Rican studies in the United States. He served as the director of the City University of New York's Centro de Estudios Puertorriqueños and was the author of numerous books and monographs.

Author and educator Maria Teresa Babín Cortes (1910–1989) was an educator, essayist, literary critic, poet, and playwright. She served as director of the University of Puerto Rico's Hispanic Studies Program. She also edited an English anthology of Puerto Rican literature. In the United States she taught at different times at Hunter College, Washington Square College, Lehman College, and the City University in New York. Later in her life she worked as a consultant for the Ford Foundation on issues surrounding minority student scholarships.

Art Olga Albizu (1924–2005), an abstract expressionist born and raised in Puerto Rico, became famous for painting Stan Getz's RCA record covers in the 1950s. She later became a leading figure in the New York City arts community.

Other well-known contemporary and avant-garde visual artists of Puerto Rican descent include Rafael Ferre (1933–), who received a Pew Fellowship in the Arts in 1993 and an Annalee and Barnett Newman Foundation Grant in 2011, and Ralph Ortíz (1934–), who received a BA and an MFA from Pratt Art Institute and founded El Museo del Barrio in East Harlem.

Business Deborah Aguiar-Veléz (1955–) was trained as a chemical engineer but became one of the most famous female entrepreneurs in the United States. After working for Exxon and the New Jersey Department of Commerce, Aguiar-Veléz founded Sistema Corp. In 1990 she was named the Outstanding Woman of the Year in Economic Development.

John Rodriguez (1958–) is the founder of AD-One, a Rochester, New York-based advertising and public relations firm whose clients include Eastman Kodak, Bausch and Lomb, and the Girl Scouts of America.

Stage and Screen José Ferrer (1912–1992), one of cinema's most distinguished leading men, earned an Academy Award for best actor in the 1950 film *Cyrano de Bergerac.*

Singer and dancer Rita Moreno (1935–), born Rosita Dolores Alverco in Puerto Rico, began working on Broadway at the age of thirteen and hit Hollywood at age fourteen. She earned numerous awards for her work in theater, film, and television.

San Juan-born actor Raúl Juliá (1940–1994), best known for his work in film, was also a highly regarded figure in the theater. Among his many film credits are *Kiss of the Spider Woman* (1985), based on South American writer Manuel Puig's novel of the same name, *Presumed Innocent* (1990), and the *Addams Family* movies (1991 and 1993).

Miriam Colón (1945–) was known as New York City's first lady of Hispanic theater. She also worked widely in film and television and may be best remembered for her longtime role on the PBS children's show *Electric Company.*

Puerto Rican-born Benicio del Torro (1967–) gained fame as an actor. Some of his best-known roles were in *The Usual Suspects* (1995), *Fear and Loathing in Las Vegas* (1998), *Traffic* (2000), and *Che* (2008). He won an Academy Award for best actor for his role in *Traffic.*

Daisy Martinez, the Brooklyn-born daughter of Puerto Rican parents, established a career as an actress, model, chef, and TV personality. She graduated from the prestigious French Culinary Institute in 1998. She launched her own PBS series, *Daisy Cooks!*, in 2005, and in 2009 she launched *Viva Daisy* on the Food Network.

Jennifer Lopez (1970–) was born in the Bronx. The dancer, actress, and singer began her career as a dancer in stage musicals and music videos and in the Fox network TV show *In Living Color*. After a string of supporting roles in Hollywood movies, she became the highest-paid Latina actress in films when she was selected for the title role in *Selena* in 1997. She went on to act in numerous other films. Her first solo album, *On the 6*, released in 1999, produced the hit single "If You Had My Love." In 2001 she released the album *J.Lo* and starred in *The Wedding Planner*. The success of both made her the first entertainer ever to have a number one movie and a number one song in the same week. Lopez was a judge on Fox's *American Idol* for two seasons.

Journalism Jesús Colón (1901–1974) was the first Puerto Rican journalist and short story writer to receive wide attention in English-language literary circles. Born in the small Puerto Rican town of Cayey, Colón stowed away on a boat to New York City at the age of sixteen. After working as an unskilled laborer, he began writing newspaper articles and short fiction. Colón eventually became a columnist for the *Daily Worker*; some of his works were later collected in *A Puerto Rican in New York and Other Sketches*

Geraldo Rivera (1943–) won ten Emmy Awards and a Peabody Award for his investigative journalism. A polarizing media figure and veteran war correspondent, he hosted his own talk show, *The Geraldo Rivera Show* (1987–1998), and Fox News Channel's newsmagazine *Geraldo at Large* (beginning in 2005).

Literature As of 2013, Nicholasa Mohr (1935–) was the only Hispanic American woman to write for major U.S. publishing houses, including Dell, Bantam, and Harper. Her books include *Nilda* (1973), *In Nueva York* (1977), and *Gone Home* (1986).

Victor Hernández Cruz (1949–) was the most widely acclaimed of the Nuyorican poets, a group of Puerto Rican poets whose work focuses on the Latino world in New York City. His collections include *Mainland* (1973) and *Rhythm, Content, and Flavor* (1989).

Tato Laviena (1950–), the best-selling Latino poet in the United States, gave a 1980 reading at the White House for President Jimmy Carter.

Music Ricky Martin (1971–), born Enrique Martin Morales in Puerto Rico, began his career as a member of the teen singing group Menudo. He gained international fame at the 1999 Grammy Awards ceremony. His music was a major influence in the growing interest in new Latin beat styles in the late 1990s.

Marc Anthony (1968–), born Marco Antonio Muniz, gained renown as an actor and as a top-selling salsa songwriter and performer. Anthony contributed hit songs to albums by other singers and recorded his first album, *The Night Is Over*, in 1991 in Latin hip-hop style.

Politics José Cabranes (1949–) was the first Puerto Rican to be named to a federal court on the U.S. mainland. He graduated from Yale Law School in 1965 and received his LLM from England's Cambridge University in 1967. He was first appointed to the federal bench by President Carter in 1979 and later to the Second U.S. Court of Appeals for the Second Circuit by President Clinton in 1994.

Antonia Novello (1944–) was the first Hispanic woman to be named U.S. surgeon general. She served in the Bush administration from 1990 until 1993. From 1999 to 2006, she served as health commissioner for the state of New York. In 2009, she pled guilty to a federal felony for misuse of a government employee. The charge accused her of using state workers to chauffer her around on personal business and to move furniture in her apartment. Her plea agreement ordered her to do 250 community service hours in a health clinic and pay restitution and fines amounting to approximately $27,000. As part of the plea agreement, Dr. Novello was allowed to keep her medical license

Sonya Sotomayor (1954–) was born in the Bronx. In 2009 she became the first Puerto Rican to be named to the U.S. Supreme Court. She graduated from Princeton University in 1976 and Yale Law School in 1979.

Sports Roberto Walker Clemente (1934–1972) was born in Carolina, Puerto Rico, and played center field for the Pittsburgh Pirates from 1955 until his death in 1972. Clemente appeared in two World Series contests, was a four-time National League batting champion, earned MVP honors for the Pirates in 1966, racked up twelve Gold Glove awards for fielding, and tallied 3,000 hits. After his untimely death in a plane crash en route to aid earthquake victims in Central America, the Baseball Hall of Fame waived the usual five-year waiting period and inducted Clemente immediately.

Orlando Cepeda (1937–) was born in Ponce, Puerto Rico, but grew up in New York City, where he played sandlot baseball. He joined the New York Giants in 1958 and was named Rookie of the Year. Nine years later he was voted league MVP with the St. Louis Cardinals. Cepeda was inducted into the National Baseball Hall of Fame in 1999.

Angel Tomas Cordero (1942–), a famous name in the world of horseracing, is the only Puerto Rican to win all three of the American Classic Races: the Kentucky Derby, the Preakness Stakes, and the Belmont Stakes. He was the first Puerto Rican inducted into the United States Racing Hall of Fame.

Sixto Escobar (1913–1979) was the first Puerto Rican boxer to win a world championship, knocking out Tony Matino in 1936.

Juan Antonio "Chi Chi" Rodriguez (1935–) was one of the best-known American golfers in the world. In a classic rags-to-riches story, he started out as a caddy in his hometown of Rio Piedras and went on to become a millionaire player. The winner of numerous national and world tournaments, Rodriguez is also known for his philanthropy, including his establishment of the Chi Chi Rodriguez Youth Foundation in Florida. He was the first Puerto Rican to be inducted into the World Golf Hall of Fame.

MEDIA

Despite the recession that began in the United States in 2008 and the shrinking media market, the number of Spanish-language media outlets continued to grow exponentially. Television and radio are the most popular, but Spanish-language and bilingual Internet sites are very popular, and even print newspapers have held their own. According to a report by the Pew Hispanic Center, demand for Spanish-language print media has remained stable, unlike their English-language counterparts. Latino Americans account for a significant share of the media market, and many major news outlets have responded accordingly. CNN, HBO, ESPN, and the Cartoon Network, to name a few, all have Spanish-language channels. The Discovery Channel has three Spanish-language channels. In 2000, Spanish radio stations numbered in the low hundreds. In its 2011 annual report on the American media, a group called stateofthemedia.org reported there were 1,323 Spanish-language radio stations in the United States. The No. 1 Spanish-language television corporation, Univision, reported $2 billion in revenue in 2010 alone.

PRINT

El Diario/La Prensa

Published Monday through Friday since 1913, this publication has focused on general news in Spanish. The paper merged with Los Angeles-based *La Opinion* in 1995. The group that owns *El Diario/La Prensa* was acquired by the Argentinian media corporation S.A. La Nacion in 2012.

Rosan Rossado, Publisher
1 MetroTech Center
Brooklyn, New York 10013
URL: www.eldiariony.com

Hispanic Business

Established in 1979, this monthly English-language business magazine caters to Hispanic professionals. The last print edition was published in April 2012, and *Hispanic Business* is now available only online.

Jesus Chavarria, Publisher
URL: www.hispanicbusiness.com/magazine

Hispanic Link Weekly Report

Established in 1980, this weekly bilingual community newspaper covers Hispanic interests.

Felix Perez, Editor
1420 N Street
NW
Washington, D.C. 20005
Phone: (202) 234-0280
URL: www.hispaniclink.org

RADIO

There are more than one thousand Spanish-language radio stations catering to Latinos. They offer music, news, talk, and more. Many stations are streamed live over the web. A couple of examples are La Kalle 105.9 New York City, which plays salsa and reggaeton, and AccuRadio: Sounds of Puerto Rico in Chicago.

Lotus Hispanic Radio Network

As of 2012, Lotus owned twenty-nine Spanish-language radio stations in the United States.

Howard Kalmenson, President
3301 Barham Blvd
Suite 200
Los Angeles, California 90068
Phone: (323) 512-2225
URL: www.lotuscorp.com/ourstations.asp?tpm=1_1

TELEVISION

Galavision

Hispanic television network headquartered in New York and owned by media giant Univision.

Tim Krass, Executive Vice President, Affiliate Relations
Phone: (310) 348-3865
URL: tv.univision.com/galavision

Telemundo Spanish Television Network

This television network was originally founded in Puerto Rico in 1954 but is now owned by an American parent company, NBCUniversal. It is the one of the largest providers of Spanish-language television in the United States and the world, second only to Univision. Telemundo is headquartered in Hialeah, Florida.

Steven Mandala, Senior Vice President
Phone: (212) 664-3599
URL: msnlatino.telemundo.com

Univision

Spanish-language television network headquartered in Los Angeles and offering news and entertainment programming.

Tim Krass, Executive Vice President, Affiliate Relations
Phone: (310) 348-3865
URL: www.univision.com

ORGANIZATIONS AND ASSOCIATIONS

Council for Puerto Rico-U.S. Affairs

Founded in 1987, the council was formed to help create a positive awareness of Puerto Rico in the United States and to forge new links between the mainland and the island.

Roberto Soto
14 East 60th Street
Suite 605
New York, New York 10022
Phone: (212) 832-0935

National Conference of Puerto Rican Women (NACOPRW)

Founded in 1972, the conference promotes the participation of Puerto Rican and other Hispanic women in social, political, and economic affairs in the United States and in Puerto Rico. Publishes the quarterly *Ecos Nationales*.

Vilma Colon, National President
1220 L Street
Washington, D.C. 20005
Phone: (773) 405-3535
Email: nationalpresident@nacoprw.org
URL: www.nacoprw.org

National Congress for Puerto Rican Rights (NCPRR)

The group was established in the Bronx in 1981. It addresses civil rights issues concerning Puerto Ricans in legislative, labor, police, and legal and housing matters, especially in New York City.

Ramon Gonzales, Communications Officer
PO Box 1307
Madison Square Post Office
New York, New York 10159
Phone: (212) 631-4263
Email: rmg36@columbia.edu or frescofua@boriucanet.org

National Council of La Raza

Founded in 1968, this Pan-Hispanic organization provides assistance to local Hispanic groups, serves as an advocate for all Hispanic Americans, and is a national umbrella organization for eighty formal affiliates throughout the United States.

Raul Yzaguirre Building
1126 16th Street
NW
Suite 600
Washington, D.C. 20036-4845
Phone: (202) 785-1670
Fax: (202) 776-1792
Email: comments@nclr.org
URL: www.nclr.org

National Puerto Rican Coalition (NPRC)

Founded in 1977, the NPRC advances the social, economic, and political well-being of Puerto Ricans. It evaluates the potential impact of legislative and government proposals and policies affecting the Puerto Rican community and provides technical assistance and training to start-up Puerto Rican organizations.

Rafael Fantauzzi, President
1444 I Street
NW
Suite 800
Washington, D.C. 20005
Phone: (202) 223-3915
Fax: (202) 429-2223
Email: nprc@nprcinc.org
URL: www.bateylink.org

Puerto Rican Family Institute (PRFI)

Established in 1960s by Puerto Rican social workers, this not-for-profit is committed to the preservation of the health, well-being, and integrity of Puerto Rican and Hispanic families in the United States.

Maria Elena Girone, Executive Director
145 West 15th Street
New York, New York 10011
Phone: (212) 924-6320
Fax: (212) 691-5635
Email: mgirone@prfi.org
URL: www.prfi.org

The United States Council for Puerto Rican Statehood

Founded in 1998, the council is a nonprofit organization that engages in advocacy and education about the need for Puerto Rican statehood. There are members in forty-seven states.

William J. Althaus, Member, Board of Directors
1620 Eye Street
NW
Suite 300
Washington, D.C. 20006
Phone: (202) 429-0160
Fax: (202) 293-3109
Email: info@prstatehood.org
URL: www.prstatehood.com

MUSEUMS AND RESEARCH CENTERS

Brooklyn College of the City University of New York Center for Latino Studies

This research institute is centered on the study of Puerto Ricans in New York and Puerto Rico. Focuses on history, politics, sociology, and anthropology.

Maria Perez y Gonzales
1205 Boylen Hall
Bedford Avenue at Avenue H
Brooklyn, New York 11210
Phone: (718) 951-5561
Fax: (718) 951-4183
Email: prls@brooklyn.cuny.edu
URL: www.brooklyn.cuny.edu

Hunter College of the City University of New York Centro de Estudios Puertorriqueños

Founded in 1973, this is the first university-based research center in New York City designed specifically to develop Puerto Rican perspectives on Puerto Rican problems and issues.

Edwin Melendez, Director
695 Park Avenue
New York, New York 10021
Phone: (212) 772-5688
Fax: (212) 650-3673
Email: hcordero@shiva.hunter.cuny.edu
URL: www.centropr.hunter.cuny.edu

PRLDEF Institute for Puerto Rican Policy

The Institute for Puerto Rican Policy merged with the Puerto Rican Legal Defense and Education Fund in 1999.

Juan Figueroa, Director
99 Hudson Street
14ᵗʰ Floor
New York, New York 10013-2815
Phone: (212) 219-3360, ext. 246
Fax: (212) 431-4276
Email: ipr@iprnet.org
URL: latinojustice.org

SOURCES FOR ADDITIONAL STUDY

Acosta-Belén, Edna, and Carlos E. Santiago, eds. *Puerto Ricans in the United States: A Contemporary Portrait.* Boulder, CO: Lynne Rienner, 2006.

Briggs, Laura. *Reproducing Empire.* Berkeley: University of California Press, 2002.

Camara-Fuertes, Luis Raúl. *The Phenomenon of Puerto Rican Voting.* Gainesville: University Press of Florida, 2004.

DeJesus, Joy L., ed. *Growing up Puerto Rican: An Anthology.* New York: Morrow, 1997.

Dietz, James L. *Economic History of Puerto Rico: Institutional Change and Capitalist Development.* Princeton: Princeton University Press, 1986.

Fitzpatrick, Joseph P. *Puerto Rican Americans: The Meaning of Migration to the Mainland.* Englewood Cliffs, NJ: Prentice Hall, 1987.

———. *The Stranger Is Our Own: Reflections on the Journey of Puerto Rican Migrants.* Kansas City, MO: Sheed & Ward, 1996.

Pérez, Gina M. *The Near Northwest Side Story: Migration, Displacement, & Puerto Rican Families.* Berkeley: University of California Press, 2004.

Perez y Mena, Andres Isidoro. *Speaking with the Dead: Development of Afro-Latin Religion Among Puerto Ricans in the United States: A Study into Interpenetration of Civilizations in the New World.* New York: AMS, 1991.

Urciuoli, Bonnie. *Exposing Prejudice: Puerto Rican Experiences of Language, Race, and Class.* Boulder, CO: Westview, 1996.

ANNOTATED BIBLIOGRAPHY

Acuña, Rodolfo, and Guadalupe Compean. *Voices of the U.S. Latino Experience.* Westport, CT: Greenwood Press, 2008. The history of Latinos in the United States derived from letters, memoirs, speeches, articles, essays, interviews, treaties, government reports, testimony, and more.

Aguirre, Adalberto. *Racial and Ethnic Diversity in America: A Reference Handbook.* Santa Barbara, CA: ABC-CLIO, 2003. Examines, through current and historical census data, the populations and social forces that contribute to the racial and ethnic diversity of the United States.

Alba, Richard D., and Victor Nee. *Remaking the American Mainstream: Assimilation and Contemporary Immigration.* Cambridge, MA: Harvard University Press, 2003. Demonstrates the importance of assimilation in American society by looking at language, socioeconomic attachments, residential patterns, and intermarriage.

Alba, Richard D., and Mary C. Waters. *Next Generation: Immigrant Youth in a Comparative Perspective.* New York: New York University, 2011. An examination of second-generation immigrant youth in the United States and Western Europe.

American Ethnic Writers. Rev. ed. Pasadena, CA: Salem Press, 2009. Compiles and describes the works of African American, Asian American, Jewish American, Hispanic/Latino, and Native American writers.

Anderson, Wanni W., and Robert G. Lee, eds. *Displacements and Diasporas: Asians in the Americas.* New Brunswick, NJ: Rutgers University Press, 2005. An interdisciplinary look at the experiences of Asians in North and South America and how they have been shaped by the social and political dynamics of the countries in which they have settled as well as by their countries of origin.

Angell, Carole S. *Celebrations around the World: A Multicultural Handbook.* Golden, CO: Fulcrum, 1996. A month-by-month look at festivals from around the world.

Anglim, Christopher. *Encyclopedia of Religion and the Law in America.* 2nd ed. Amenia, NY: Grey House, 2009. Covers topics from prayer in schools to holiday displays on public property; includes a description of major cases.

Atwood, Craig D., et al. *Handbook of Denominations in the United States.* 13th ed. Nashville: Abingdon Press, 2010. This frequently updated handbook serves as a guide to the many denominations that make up the American religious experience.

Axtell, Roger E. *Gestures: The Do's and Taboos of Body Language around the World.* Rev. ed. New York: Wiley, 1998. Lists, illustrates, and explains the meaning of gestures from eighty-two countries around the world.

Banks, James A., ed. *Encyclopedia of Diversity in Education.* Thousand Oaks, CA: SAGE, 2012. A guide to research and statistics, case studies, best practices, and policies.

———, ed. *Handbook of Research on Multicultural Education.* 2nd ed. San Francisco: Jossey-Bass, 2004. A guide to advances in the research of multicultural education.

———. *Teaching Strategies for Ethnic Studies.* 8th ed. Boston: Pearson/Allyn & Bacon, 2009. Examines the current and emerging theory, research, and scholarship in the fields of ethnic studies and multicultural education.

Barkan, Elliott Robert, ed. *Immigrants in American History: Arrival, Adaptation, and Integration.* Santa Barbara, CA: ABC-CLIO, 2013. Covers the arrival, adaptation, and integration of immigrants into American culture from the 1500s to 2010.

Barkley, Elizabeth F. *Crossroads: The Multicultural Roots of America's Popular Music.* 2nd ed. Upper Saddle River, NJ: Pearson Prentice Hall, 2007. A comparative exploration of the music of Native Americans, European Americans, African Americans, Latino Americans, and Asian Americans.

Bayor, Ronald H., ed. *The Columbia Documentary History of Race and Ethnicity in America*. New York: Columbia University Press, 2004. Seeks to shed light on the many ways in which immigration, racial histories, and ethnic histories have shaped contemporary American society.

——, ed. *Multicultural America: An Encyclopedia of the Newest Americans*. Santa Barbara. CA: Greenwood, 2011. Profiles fifty of the largest immigrant groups in the United States.

Benson, Sonia, ed. *The Hispanic American Almanac: A Reference Work on Hispanics in the United States*. 3rd ed. Detroit: Gale, 2003. Examines the history and culture of Hispanic Americans with coverage of events, biographies, and demographic information.

Berlin, Ira. *The Making of African America: The Four Great Migrations*. New York: Viking, 2010. Interprets the history of African Americans by examining the forced migration of slavery, the relocation of slaves to interior southern states, the migrations to the north, and the more recent arrival of immigrants from African and Caribbean nations.

Berzok, Linda Murray, ed. *Storied Dishes: What Our Family Recipes Tell Us about Who We Are and Where We've Been*. Santa Barbara, CA: Praeger, 2011. An exploration of family history through recipes.

Bird, Stephanie Rose. *Light, Bright, and Damned Near White: Biracial and Triracial Culture in America*. Westport, CT: Praeger, 2009. Explores the challenges for, and psychological issues of, people with ethnically mixed ancestry.

Blank, Carla. *Rediscovering America: The Making of Multicultural America, 1900–2000*. New York: Three Rivers Press, 2003. A retelling of American history through the contributions of women, African Americans, Asian Americans, Hispanic Americans, and Native Americans, immigrants, artists, "renegades, rebels, and rogues."

Bona, Mary Jo, and Irma Maini, eds. *Multiethnic Literature and Canon Debates*. Albany: State University of New York Press, 2006. Critiques the debate over the inclusion of multiethnic literature in the American literary canon.

Boosahda, Elizabeth. *Arab-American Faces and Voices: The Origins of an Immigrant Community*. Austin: University of Texas Press, 2003. Looking at the long history of Arab Americans in the United States, this book includes personal interviews, photographs, and historical documents.

Bowler, Shaun, and Gary M. Segura. *The Future Is Ours: Minority Politics, Political Behavior, and the Multiracial Era of American Politics*. Thousand Oaks, CA: SAGE, 2012. A data-based examination of whether and how minority citizens differ from members of the white majority in political participation.

Brettell, Caroline. *Constructing Borders/Crossing Boundaries: Race, Ethnicity, and Immigration*. Lanham, MD: Lexington Books, 2008. Essays on a diverse range of immigrant populations from past to present that look at the boundaries and borders created by the social construction of race and ethnicity.

Bronner, Simon J., ed. *Encyclopedia of American Folklife*. Armonk, NY: M. E. Sharpe, 2006. Looks at the oral and written literary traditions, songs, and stories that make up a community's identity.

Brooks, Christopher Antonio, ed. *The African American Almanac*. 11th ed. Farmington Hills, MI: Gale Cengage Learning, 2011. A continually updated work from Gale's series of multicultural reference sources. Provides chronology, biography, events, and demography.

Buenker, John D., and Lorman A. Ratner, eds. *Multiculturalism in the United States: A Comparative Guide to Acculturation and Ethnicity*. Rev. ed. Westport, CT: Greenwood Press, 2005. Discusses how American culture has affected immigrants as well as how it has been shaped by them.

Cannato, Vincent J. *American Passage: The History of Ellis Island*. New York: Harper, 2009. Tells the story of Ellis Island from 1892 to 1924 using a variety of primary sources.

Carlisle, Rodney P., general ed. *Multicultural America*. 7 vols. New York: Facts On File, 2011. Presents the social history, customs, and traditions of ethnic groups throughout American history.

Carter, Susan B., ed. *Historical Statistics of the United States: Earliest Times to the Present*. 5 vols. New York: Cambridge University Press, 2006. Provides a historical perspective on statistics about the U.S. population, economy, government, and international relations.

Cesari, Jocelyne, ed. *Encyclopedia of Islam in the United States*. Westport, CT: Greenwood Press, 2007. Based on primary documents, this encyclopedia provides historical context for the current state of the practice of Islam in the United States.

Chi, Sang, and Emily Moberg Robinson, eds. *Voices of the Asian American and Pacific Islander Experience*. Santa Barbara, CA: Greenwood, 2012. Explores the experiences, views, and politics of recent Asian immigrants, emphasizing the diversity of experiences and viewpoints of individuals within the different nationalities and generations. Based on primary documents.

Ciment, James, and John Radzilowski, eds. *American Immigration: An Encyclopedia of Political, Social, and Cultural Change*. 2nd ed. 4 vols. Armonk, NY: M. E. Sharpe, 2013. American immigration from historic and contemporary perspectives. Primary documents include laws and treaties, referenda, Supreme Court cases, historical articles, and letters from 1787 to 2013.

Cohen, Selma Jeanne, ed. *International Encyclopedia of Dance*. 6 vols. New York: Oxford University Press, 2004. The definitive reference book for dance, documenting all types and styles of dance from around the world and throughout history.

Condra, Jill, ed. *The Greenwood Encyclopedia of Clothing through World History*. 3 vols. Westport, CT: Greenwood Press, 2008. Examines the history of clothing from all corners of the globe from prehistory to modern times.

Coontz, Stephanie, ed. *American Families: A Multicultural Reader*. 2nd ed. New York: Routledge, 2008. Brings together articles that look at the ethnic and racial diversity within families.

Cullum, Linda, ed. *Contemporary American Ethnic Poets: Lives, Works, Sources*. Westport, CT: Greenwood Press, 2004. Presents the lives and works of seventy-five poets.

Cordry, Harold V. *The Multicultural Dictionary of Proverbs: Over 20,000 Adages from More than 120 Languages, Nationalities and Ethnic Groups*. Jefferson, NC: McFarland, 1997. Presents 1,300 headings arranged by nationality, with a focus on European cultures.

Daniels, Roger. *Coming to America: A History of Immigration and Ethnicity in American Life*. 2nd ed. New York: Perennial, 2002. An overview of immigration to the United States from the colonial era to the beginning of the twenty-first century.

Danilov, Victor J. *Ethnic Museums and Heritage Sites in the United States*. Jefferson, NC: McFarland, 2009. A directory of all ethnic heritage sites in the United States.

Danky, James P., and Wayne A. Wiegand, eds. *Print Culture in a Diverse America*. Urbana: University of Illinois Press, 1998. Examines the multicultural world of reading and readers in the United States.

Davis, Rocío G., ed. *The Transnationalism of American Culture: Literature, Film, and Music*. New York: Routledge, 2012. A study of the border-crossing aspects of literature, film, and music.

Dinnerstein, Leonard, and David M. Reimers. *Ethnic Americans: A History of Immigration*. 5th ed. New York: Columbia University Press, 2009. Chapters examine the history of immigration to the United States chronologically, from the fifteenth century to 2008.

Dinnerstein, Leonard, Roger L. Nichols, and David M. Reimers. *Natives and Strangers: A History of Ethnic Americans*. 5th ed. New York: Oxford University Press, 2010. Examines the history of American ethnic groups and their impact on the character and social fabric of the United States.

Dodge, Abigail Johnson. *Around the World Cookbook*. New York: DK Publishing, 2008. A children's cookbook with fifty step-by-step recipes for preparing ethnic cuisine.

Ellicott, Karen, ed. *Countries of the World and Their Leaders Yearbook 2014*. 2 vols. Detroit: Gale, 2014. U.S. Department of State reports looking at all social, political, legal, economic, and environmental aspects for selected countries of the world.

Fleegler, Robert L. *Ellis Island Nation: Immigration Policy and American Identity in the Twentieth Century*. Philadelphia: University of Pennsylvania Press, 2013. Uses World War II films, records of Senate subcommittee hearings, and anti-Communist propaganda to view the evolution in the debate over immigration in the United States.

Franco, Dean J. *Ethnic American Literature: Comparing Chicano, Jewish, and African American Writing*. Charlottesville: University of Virginia Press, 2006. Provides a comparative approach to American ethnic literature.

Frazier, John W., Eugene L. Tettey-Fio, and Norah F. Henry, eds. *Race, Ethnicity, and Place in a Changing America*. 2nd ed. Albany: State University of New York Press, 2011. Looks at how race and ethnicity affects all aspects of everyday life.

Fredrickson, George M. *Diverse Nations: Explorations in the History of Racial and Ethnic Pluralism*. Boulder, CO: Paradigm Publishers, 2008. A comparative exploration of slavery and race relations in the United States, Europe, South Africa, and Brazil.

Gillota, David. *Ethnic Humor in Multiethnic America*. New Brunswick, NJ: Rutgers University Press, 2013. Investigates the role of humor in the national conversation on race and ethnicity and the response of contemporary comedians to multiculturalism.

Gilton, Donna L. *Multicultural and Ethnic Children's Literature in the United States*. Lanham, MD: Scarecrow Press, 2007. The history of and contemporary trends in U.S. multicultural children's literature.

Glenn, Evelyn Nakano. *Unequal Freedom: How Race and Gender Shaped American Citizenship and Labor*. Cambridge, MA: Harvard University Press, 2002. A comparative look at the history of inequality and specifically how labor and citizenship have been defined, enforced, and challenged in the United States.

González, Alberto, et al., eds. *Our Voices: Essays in Culture, Ethnicity, and Communication*. 5th ed. New York: Oxford University Press, 2012. Short first-person accounts that examine the varieties of intercultural communication covering discourses of gender, race, and ethnicity.

Grant-Thomas, Andrew, and Gary Orfield, eds. *Twenty-First Century Color Lines: Multiracial Change in Contemporary America*. Philadelphia: Temple University Press, 2009. The result of work initiated by the Harvard Civil Rights Project, this book provides an overview of contemporary racial and ethnic conditions in the United States.

Graves, Joseph L., Jr. *The Race Myth: Why We Pretend Race Exists in America*. New York: Dutton, 2004. Writing from a scientific perspective, Graves posits that racial distinctions are in fact social inventions, not biological truths.

Greene, Victor R. *American Immigrant Leaders, 1800–1910: Marginality and Identity*. Baltimore: Johns Hopkins University Press, 1987. The history of immigration through the lives of those who led.

Handlin, Oscar. *The Uprooted: The Epic Story of the Great Migrations That Made the American People*. 2nd ed. Philadelphia: University of Pennsylvania Press, 2002. Looks specifically at European migration to the United States during the late nineteenth and early twentieth centuries.

Hoerder, Dirk, ed. *The Immigrant Labor Press in North America, 1840s–1970s: An Annotated Bibliography*. New York: Greenwood Press, 1987. A look at the European immigrant press in the United States.

Jackson, Kenneth T., ed. *The Encyclopedia of New York City*. New Haven, CT: Yale University Press; New York: New York Historical Society, 2010. Entries on every aspect of the life and culture of the population of New York City.

Johansen, Bruce E. *Native Americans Today: A Biographical Dictionary*. Santa Barbara, CA: Greenwood Press, 2010. Biographical profiles of Native Americans from the twentieth and twenty-first centuries.

Johnson, Michael. *Encyclopedia of Native Tribes of North America*. Richmond Hill, Ontario: Firefly Books, 2007. An illustrated encyclopedia that provides information on North America's Native American populations.

Koppelman, Kent L., ed. *Perspectives on Human Differences: Selected Readings on Diversity in America*. Boston: Allyn & Bacon, 2011. An anthology of essays and short stories that explores issues of human diversity from multiple perspectives.

Kukathas, Uma, ed. *Race and Ethnicity*. Farmington Hills, MI: Greenhaven Press, 2008. Reflections on racial and ethnic identity in the United States as represented through institutional classification and the media.

Kurian, George Thomas, and Barbara A. Chernow, eds. *Datapedia of the United States: American History in Numbers*. 4th ed. Lanham, MD: Bernan Press, 2007. Based on historical statistics of the United States and the annual Statistical Abstract of the United States, Datapedia provides statistics in twenty-three areas for the years 1790–2003 with demographic projections to 2050. Updated regularly.

Lee, Erika, and Judy Young. *Angel Island: Immigrant Gateway to America*. New York: Oxford University Press, 2010. A comprehensive history of the Angel Island Immigration Station in the San Francisco Bay.

Lippy, Charles H., and Peter W. Williams, eds. *Encyclopedia of Religion in America*. Washington, DC: CQ Press, 2010. Explores origins, development, influence, and interrelations of faiths practiced in North America.

Mason, Patrick L., ed. *Encyclopedia of Race and Racism*. 2nd ed. 4 vols. Detroit: Macmillan Reference USA, 2013. A survey of the anthropological, sociological, historical, economic, and scientific theories of race and racism in the modern era.

McDonald, Jason. *American Ethnic History: Themes and Perspectives*. New Brunswick, NJ: Rutgers University Press, 2007. Looks at the reasons different ethnic groups have come to the United States, their treatment and adaptations, and the aspects that together build a sense of ethnic identity.

Min, Pyong Gap, ed. *Encyclopedia of Racism in the United States*. 3 vols. Westport, CT: Greenwood Press, 2005. Seeks to provide an understanding of U.S. minority groups and their experiences with the dominant culture.

Morgan, George G. *How to Do Everything: Genealogy*. 3rd ed. New York: McGraw-Hill, 2012. A guide to genealogical research in the twenty-first century.

Morrison, Joan, and Charlotte Fox Zabusky. *American Mosaic: The Immigrant Experience in the Words of Those Who Lived It*. Pittsburgh, PA: University of Pittsburgh Press, 1993. First-person accounts of the experiences of immigrants from Europe, Asia, the Middle East, South America, and South Africa.

Nelson, Emmanuel S., ed. *The Greenwood Encyclopedia of Multiethnic American Literature*. 5 vols. Westport, CT: Greenwood Press, 2005. Entries on authors and literature from multiethnic America.

Nettl, Bruno, et al., eds. *Garland Encyclopedia of World Music*. 10 vols. with CDs. New York: Garland, 1998–2002. A comprehensive look at music around the world by region and country. Also available online through Alexander Street Press.

Neusner, Jacob, ed. *World Religions in America: An Introduction*. 4th ed. Louisville, KY: Westminster John Knox Press, 2009. Each chapter examines the religious beliefs and practices of a separate American immigrant group.

Nimer, Mohamed. *The North American Muslim Resource Guide: Muslim Community Life in the United States and Canada.* New York: Routledge, 2002. Presents the history and contemporary status of Muslim communities in the United States. Also provides a directory of organizations, schools, centers, publications, and more.

Norton, Donna E. *Multicultural Children's Literature: Through the Eyes of Many Children.* 2nd ed. Upper Saddle River, NJ: Pearson/Merrill Prentice Hall, 2005. Highlights outstanding multicultural literature for children and young adults.

Ochoa, George, and Carter Smith. *Atlas of Hispanic-American History.* Rev. ed. New York: Facts on File, 2009. Using text, maps, and illustrations, this volume looks at the history of Hispanic American cultures.

Olson, James Stuart, and Heather Olson Beal. *The Ethnic Dimension in American History.* 4th ed. Malden, MA: Wiley-Blackwell, 2010. A survey of the role that ethnicity has played in shaping the history of the United States.

Overmyer-Velázquez, Mark. *Latino America: A State-by-State Encyclopedia.* 2 vols. Westport, CT: Greenwood Press, 2008. A chronological account of the presence and contributions of Latinos in each state and the District of Columbia from the beginning of recorded American history to the present.

Parrillo, Vincent N. *Strangers to These Shores: Race and Ethnic Relations in the United States.* 10th ed. Boston: Allyn & Bacon, 2011. A frequently updated text on racial and ethnic relations in the United States that looks at the experiences of more than fifty racial, ethnic, and religious groups.

Pinder, Sherrow O., ed. *American Multicultural Studies: Diversity of Race, Ethnicity, Gender, and Sexuality.* Thousand Oaks, CA: SAGE, 2013. Provides an interdisciplinary view of multicultural studies in the United States that addresses current and continuing issues of race, gender, ethnicity, sexuality, cultural diversity, and education.

Queen, Edward L., et al., eds. *Encyclopedia of American Religious History.* 3rd ed. 3 vols. New York: Facts On File, 2009. Covers the social and cultural histories of religious practices in the United States.

Ramsey, Paul J., ed. *The Bilingual School in the United States: A Documentary History.* Charlotte, NC: Information Age Pub., 2012. A history of bilingual education in the United States from the nineteenth century forward.

Rappoport, Leon. *Punchlines: The Case for Racial, Ethnic, and Gender Humor.* Westport, CT: Praeger, 2005. Looks at ethnic, racial, and gender humor as an instrument of prejudice and as a defense against it.

Recinos, Harold J., ed. *Wading through Many Voices: Toward a Theology of Public Conversation.* Lanham, MD: Rowman & Littlefield, 2011. Examines Christian theology as expressed by different immigrant and minority groups in the United States as well as its impact and implications for public discourse.

Reimers, David M. *Other Immigrants: The Global Origins of the American People.* New York: New York University Press, 2005. Chronicles the history of black, Hispanic, and Asian immigrants to the American continent from the fifteenth century through World War II.

Rhodes, Leara. *The Ethnic Press: Shaping the American Dream.* New York: Peter Lang, 2010. Documents the history of immigrants in America through an examination of their newspapers and their impact on American culture.

Rose, Christine, and Kay Germain Ingalls. *The Complete Idiot's Guide to Genealogy.* 3rd ed. New York: Alpha, 2012. The how-tos of exploring personal heritage through genealogical practice.

Rudnick, Lois Palken, Judith E. Smith, and Rachel Lee Rubin, eds. *American Identities: An Introductory Textbook.* Malden, MA: Blackwell, 2006. A collection of critical essays and primary documents taken from American history, literature, memoir, and popular culture that focuses on American identities of ethnicity and gender from World War II to the present.

Rumbaut, Rubén G., and Alejandro Portes, eds. *Ethnicities: Children of Immigrants in America.* Berkeley: University of California Press, 2001. Draws on the Children of Immigrants Longitudinal Study to look at second-generation immigrant youth from families of Mexican, Cuban, Nicaraguan, Filipino, Vietnamese, Haitian, Jamaican, and West Indian origin.

Sadie, Stanley. *The New Grove Dictionary of Music and Musicians.* 29 vols. New York: Grove, 2001. A 29-volume encyclopedic look at music from all time periods and all countries covering folk music and folk instruments as well as the classical tradition. Updated by Oxford Music Online.

Shay, Anthony. *Choreographing Identities: Folk Dance, Ethnicity and Festival in the United States and Canada.* Jefferson, NC: McFarland, 2006. A look at the importance of dance in the representation of cultural identity.

Sherrow, Victoria. *Encyclopedia of Hair: A Cultural History*. Westport, CT: Greenwood Press, 2006. Everything about hair across cultures and throughout time.

Shinagawa, Larry Hijime, and Michael Jang. *Atlas of American Diversity*. Walnut Creek, CA: AltaMira Press, 1998. A visual exploration through maps and charts of the social, economic, and geographic state of an ethnically diverse United States.

Shorris, Earl. *Latinos: A Biography of the People*. New York: W. W. Norton, 1992. Looks at Latino history from the time of the Spanish conquest of North and South America.

Snodgrass, Mary Ellen. *World Clothing and Fashion: An Encyclopedia of History, Culture, and Social Influence*. Armonk, NY: M. E. Sharpe, 2013. Approaches fashion from a global, multicultural, social, and economic perspective, covering prehistory to the present time.

Spickard, Paul R., ed. *Race and Immigration in the United States: New Histories*. New York: Routledge, 2012. Each essay looks at a particular aspect of immigrant experience, drawing attention to the ways the experiences differ depending on country of origin.

Statistical Abstract of the United States. Washington, DC: U.S. Gov. Print. Off., 1878–2012. The *Statistical Abstract* was compiled and published annually by the U.S. Census Bureau through 2012; beginning in 2013 it was instead published digitally by ProQuest. Provides an annual update of statistics about the characteristics and conditions of most aspects of life in the United States. For the historical perspective see *Historical Statistics of the United States: Earliest Times to the Present*, edited by Susan B. Carter.

Stave, Bruce M. Salerno, John F. Sutherland, and Aldo Salerno. *From the Old Country: An Oral History of European Migration to America*. New York: Maxwell Macmillan International, 1994. A compilation of oral histories describing the experience of migration and all aspects of the transition to life in a new country.

Strobel, Christoph. *Daily Life of the New Americans: Immigration since 1965*. Santa Barbara, CA: Greenwood, 2010. A history of twentieth- and twenty-first-century American immigrants through first-person and biographical narratives.

Stuhr, Rebecca. *Autobiographies by Americans of Color 1980–1994: An Annotated Bibliography*. Troy, NY: Whitston, 1997.

Stuhr, Rebecca, and Deborah Stuhr Iwabuchi. *Autobiographies by Americans of Color, 1995–2000: An Annotated Bibliography*. Albany, NY: Whitston, 2003. These two works together provide a comprehensive bibliography with extensive annotations for autobiographical works and oral histories.

Takaki, Ronald T. *A Different Mirror: A History of Multicultural America*. Boston: Little, Brown, 1993.

———. *Double Victory: A Multicultural History of America in World War II*. Boston: Little, Brown, 2000.

———. *Strangers from a Different Shore: A History of Asian Americans*. Boston: Little, Brown, 1989. Ronald Takaki was a pioneer in the field of ethnic studies. His books were among the very first to carefully and comprehensively explore the history and contemporary experiences of immigrants who crossed the Pacific to North America.

Thernstrom, Abigail M., and Stephan Thernstrom, eds. *Beyond the Color Line: New Perspectives on Race and Ethnicity in America*. Stanford, CA: Hoover Institution Press, Stanford University, 2002. Examines social, political, and economic changes that have taken place within ethnic America and the persistence of attitudes that create conditions of inequality.

Thernstrom, Stephan, ed. *Harvard Encyclopedia of American Ethnic Groups*. Cambridge, MA: Belknap Press of Harvard University, 1980. Although this work has never been updated, it continues to serve as a foundational text on the history and makeup of the population of the United States.

Thompson, William N. *Native American Issues: A Reference Handbook*. 2nd ed. Santa Barbara, CA: ABC-CLIO, 2005. An assessment of the problems faced by Native Americans, both historically and in the twenty-first century.

Ueda, Reed, ed. *A Companion to American Immigration*. Malden, MA: Blackwell, 2006. Scholarly essays on a range of topics, including law, health, politics, prejudice and racism, housing, education, labor, internationalism, and transnationalism.

Upton, Dell, ed. *America's Architectural Roots: Ethnic Groups That Built America*. New York: Preservation Press, 1986. An illustrated overview of the ethnic derivations of American architecture.

U.S. Census Bureau. *2000 Census of Population and Housing: Population and Housing Unit Counts* and *Summary Social, Economic, and Housing Characteristics*. Washington, DC: U.S. Dept. of Commerce, Economics, and Statistics Administration, U.S. Census Bureau, 2003. Two separate publications from the United States decennial census providing demographic and economic statistics on all populations within the United States.

Verbrugge, Allen, ed. *Muslims in America*. Detroit: Greenhaven Press, 2005. Looks at different aspects of life for Muslims in the United States, including gender, family, college life, politics, and the repercussions of 9/11, with narratives of personal experiences.

Vigdor, Jacob L. *From Immigrants to Americans: The Rise and Fall of Fitting In*. Lanham, MD: Rowman & Littlefield, 2009. A view of the challenges of belonging in the United States, with chapters on economics, linguistics, citizenship, neighborhoods, and family.

Walch, Timothy, ed. *Immigrant America: European Ethnicity in the United States*. New York: Garland, 1994. Examines the experiences of European immigrants to specific regions of the United States.

Waldman, Carl. *Encyclopedia of Native American Tribes*. 3rd ed. New York: Facts On File, 2006. Covers more than 200 American Indian tribes of North America.

Walkowitz, Rebecca L., ed. *Immigrant Fictions: Contemporary Literature in an Age of Globalization*. Madison: University of Wisconsin Press, 2006. A look at contemporary literature by immigrant authors from China, Eastern Europe, and other countries. Includes interviews.

Webb, Lois Sinaiko, and Lindsay Grace Roten. *The Multicultural Cookbook for Students*. Rev. ed. Santa Barbara, CA: Greenwood Press, 2009. Recipes are arranged by region and country and are preceded by an account of the geography, history, and culinary traditions of their country of origin.

Weil, François. *Family Trees: A History of Genealogy in America*. Cambridge, MA: Harvard University Press, 2013. A history of the practice of genealogy from its early methodology to the use of the database Ancestry.com and DNA testing; from a preoccupation with social status to an acceptance and celebration of diverse ethnic heritage.

Welsch, Janice R., and J. Q. Adams. *Multicultural Films: A Reference Guide*. Westport, CT: Greenwood Press, 2005. Provides brief synopses and critiques of motion pictures that explore race and ethnicity.

Wertsman, Vladimir. *What's Cooking in Multicultural America: An Annotated Bibliographic Guide to Over Four Hundred Ethnic Cuisines*. Lanham, MD: Scarecrow Press, 1996. An annotated bibliography to cookbooks, covering the cuisines of more than four hundred ethnic groups from all continents.

Wills, Chuck. *Destination America*. New York: DK Pub., 2005. Through personal accounts, letters, diaries, photographs, statistics, maps, and charts, examines the reasons immigrants leave home to travel to the United States and the conditions of their lives once they arrive.

York, Sherry. *Ethnic Book Awards: A Directory of Multicultural Literature for Young Readers*. Worthington, OH: Linworth, 2005. Provides an alphabetical listing of titles winning various book awards, including the Coretta Scott King, Carter G. Woodson, and Tomás Rivera Mexican American Children's book awards.

PERIODICALS

African American Review (1992–). Terre Haute: Dept. of English, Indiana State University. Print and online. Continues *Black American Literature Forum* (1976–1991). History and criticism of African American literature.

Amerasia Journal (1971–). Los Angeles: University of California, Los Angeles; and Yale Asian American Students Association. Print and Online. An interdisciplinary journal studying all aspects of Asian American society, jointly published by the UCLA Asian American Studies Center and the Yale Asian American Students Association.

Callaloo (1976–). Baltimore, MD: Johns Hopkins University Press. Print and Online. An African diaspora literary journal founded at Southern University in Baton Rouge, Louisiana, and now sponsored by Texas A&M University and published by Johns Hopkins University Press.

Ethnic NewsWatch (1998–). ProQuest Information and Learning. Online. Newspaper articles from the ethnic American presses. Dates of coverage depend on arrangements with each particular newspaper. Searchable via keywords and broad ethnic group.

Ethnic Studies Review: The Journal of the National Association for Ethnic Studies (1996–). Tempe, AZ: National Association for Ethnic Studies. Print and Online. A multidisciplinary international journal devoted to the study of ethnicity, ethnic groups and their cultures, and intergroup relations. Preceded by *Explorations in Ethnic Studies*.

Hispanic American Historical Review (HAHR) (1918–). Durham, NC: Duke University Press. Print and Online. Covers Latin American history and culture.

International Migration Review: IMR (1966–). New York: Center for Migration Studies. Print and Online. A quarterly interdisciplinary, peer-reviewed journal created to encourage and facilitate the study of all aspects of international migration.

Journal of American Ethnic History (1981–). Champaign: University of Illinois Press. Print and Online. Addresses various aspects of American immigration and ethnic history, including history of emigration, ethnic and racial groups, Native Americans, immigration policies, and the processes of acculturation.

Journal of Intercultural Studies (1980–). Melbourne: River Seine Publications. Print and Online. Covers cultural studies, sociology, gender studies, political science, cultural geography, urban studies, race, and ethnic studies.

MELUS: Society for the Study of the Multi-Ethnic Literature of the United States (1974–). Storrs: University of Connecticut, Dept. of English. Provides interviews and reviews that explore and bring light to the multiethnic character of American literature.

Multicultural Education (1993–). San Francisco: Caddo Gap Press. An independent quarterly magazine featuring research on promising pedagogical practices in art, music, and literature.

Rebecca Stuhr